ALSO BY STOKELY CARMICHAEL (KWAME TURE)

Black Power: The Politics of Liberation
Stokely Speaks: Black Power Back to Pan-Africanism

ALSO BY EKWUEME MICHAEL THELWELL

The Harder They Come
Duties, Pleasures, and Conflicts: Essays in Struggle

READY FOR REVOLUTION

The Life and Struggles of
STOKELY CARMICHAEL
(KWAME TURE)

STOKELY CARMICHAEL

with Ekwueme Michael Thelwell

SCRIBNER

NEW YORK   LONDON   TORONTO   SYDNEY   SINGAPORE

SCRIBNER
1230 Avenue of the Americas
New York, NY 10020

Copyright © 2003 by Kwame Ture and Ekwueme Michael Thelwell

SCRIBNER and design are trademarks of Macmillan Library Reference USA, Inc.,
used under license by Simon & Schuster, the publisher of this work.

For information about special discounts for bulk purchases,
please contact Simon & Schuster Special Sales:
1-800-456-6798 or business@simonandschuster.com

DESIGNED BY ERICH HOBBING

Text set in Plantin

Manufactured in the United States of America

1   2   3   4   5   6   7   8   9   10

Library of Congress Cataloging-in-Publication Data is available.

ISBN 0-684-85003-6

Permissions acknowledgments appear on page 836.

THIS BOOK IS DEDICATED TO

My mother, May Charles, and Bocar Biro, my son.
My people who everywhere suffer, struggle, and endure.
Those brave and selfless sisters and brothers who,
without thought of personal gain or even survival,
continue the struggle to liberate and uplift humanity
with undying love and gratitude.

"When you have chosen your part, abide by it and do not weakly try to reconcile yourself to the world. The heroic cannot be the common, nor the common heroic. Congratulate yourself if you have done something strange and extravagant, and broken the monotony of a decorous age."

—Ralph Waldo Emerson, *On Heroism*

"Men make history, but only so much history as it is possible for them to make."

—C. L. R. James

"A man is worked on by what he works on. He may carve out his circumstances, but his circumstances will carve him out as well."

—Frederick Douglass

"Mask no difficulties, tell no lies. Claim no easy victories and hide nothing from the masses of the people."

—Amilcar Cabral, *Instructions to His Cadres*

CONTENTS

Contents

READY FOR REVOLUTION

COLLABORATOR'S NOTE

It does seem only reasonable that a few words may well be necessary to explain the genesis and provenance of any autobiography making its first appearance on the fifth anniversary of its author's death. So here goes.

Of course, such a work has to be the result of collaboration. But it is not a biography. It is Kwame Ture's (peace be unto him) account of his life and political career. It is his story. That portion of his personal, political and intellectual life which he wished to share with posterity. Hence an autobiography: a man's vision of the events, decisions, and meaning of his public life, by his account, in his language and in accordance with his wishes and instruction. All public figures are entitled to such an account. Indeed, in rare cases such as this one, history would even seem to demand it. After which, as was the case with Malcolm, the tribe of pedants, closet scholars, nitpickers, and hair splitters can come scratch around the life on their revisionist missions. But this is the man's account of his life and intentions.

The brother was particularly fond of the wisdom in a Yoruba proverb which says, "When an elephant dies, and the village comes to share the meat, you will see all sizes and shapes of cutting tools brought to the task." Each villager will carve out and carry off what they need, want, or whatever they are able to. We expect that. It was ever thus.

THE NATURE OF THE COLLABORATION

In the formal legalese of the collaboration agreement Kwame is referred to as "the Author" and I as "the Writer." Thoroughly serviceable, cut and dried language which, while convenient enough, is, at least in my case, not as accurate as it would appear. It misrepresents, perhaps even inflates, a role which, while more than editor, is somewhat less than writer in the usual sense of that term. The formulation which seems to me most accurate comes from music: Kwame being the composer and I the arranger.

1

GENESIS

In December of 1996, Kwame was diagnosed with terminal cancer. A few months later (Spring 1997), I agreed to work with him on this project and we began. Some eighteen months later (November 15, 1998), he died. Before our brother danced and went to join the ancestors, having read, edited, and approved only six chapters, he left me with a great many hours of taped narrative; clear, detailed, and complete instructions and the disingenuous observation, "Well, Thelwell, looks like you going have to finish the book."

That this book exists at all is due entirely to the uncommon discipline and single-minded determination which, over those very hectic eighteen months, our brother was able to devote to the task of leaving us the oral record out of which this book could be constructed. Give praise and thanks.

PROVENANCE

I take responsibility only for technical aspects: the literary presentation of Kwame's material. For the logic of the organization of the material into chapters. For the sequences of these chapters and their internal composition, i.e., the placement of various stories and events within the chapters, so to say, for the overall shape of the book. In these purely editorial matters I was greatly comforted by the professional advice of the excellent Sarah McGrath of Scribner, but the final responsibility is mine alone.

However, the version, which is to say the perspective: the politics, insights, emphases, values and judgements—whether of people or events—and, of course, the conclusions are entirely those of our brother. Also, I am confident that anyone privileged to have known the brother will readily recognize that the inimitable voice and personality informing this narrative, the pervasive, overarching spirit of the book, are Kwame's alone.

There were on the tapes a few places where he would say, "Thelwell, this part is very rough. You will have to fix the language here. That's your job." I've done that job, one hopes very judiciously. At times in our conversations, when pressed for greater detail, he'd explode somewhat impatiently, "Thelwell, I'm giving you the overall meaning here. That's my job. There's no time for details. If you need details, go talk to so-and-so." Or else, "go read such and such a document. I'm not doing your job for you." When it proved necessary to consult such sources, these interventions are marked in the text by a clear break in the narrative, set off in brackets with the source and speaker clearly identified.

Similarly, at other points where clarity, context, or continuity seemed to require it, I've intervened in my own editorial voice. These interventions are few in number, only when necessary, as brief as possible, and clearly identified.

The greatest regret is, of course, that the author is not with us to read over the completed text. To subject his words and thoughts, as represented here, to final review, in order to rethink, revise, refine, retract, expand, or fine-tune them as he felt necessary. Once, when we were doing precisely that to an early chapter, he questioned a passage. I pointed out that those were his exact words. He was unfazed. "I know. So, I changed my mind. We're going to change our minds many times in these pages before they're finished, you know that." Well, except for those early chapters and the final two, he never had the opportunity, as all writers do, to change his mind one last time. So what you are about to read is, in effect, his first draft.

Now as the process nears its end, I'm more than ever convinced that we—all of us—have excellent reason to be grateful for our brother's gritty, clenched-teeth tenacity over those terminal eighteen months. "Thelwell, I can't go to sleep now. I got to finish this work." Give praise and thanks. I am proud and deeply honored to have been associated with this work.

Ekwueme Michael Thelwell
Pelham, Massachusetts
April 2, 2003

P.S. The final word of explanation should be the brother's. The very first tape he handed me began with a caveat. Those are the words and the spirit in which he began this account. That is where you too should begin.

Caveat

What we are writing here is history. Or at least the personal account of an eyewitness to history. Our brother, Jimmy Baldwin (peace be unto him), used to constantly tell us in SNCC that "you all have to bear witness."

That is all we are doing here, bearing witness to what we have done and seen in the hope, God willing, that it will prove instructive to those who follow us. And it was President Ahmad Sékou Touré (peace be unto his fighting spirit) who unfailingly reminded us that "only the people make history. It is not individual heroes, not individual geniuses but only the people who make history."

I have never forgotten his teaching. So you should understand that, more than anything else, this is an account of my people. My remarkable, heroic, struggling people who have supported, inspired, and protected me in all my years of strife.

It is for this reason that I am embarrassed by the relentless repetitions of the first person singular, the omnipresent and egotistic I, I, I, which is so inappropriate to an account of this kind. But we are stuck with it. My literary friend and brother assures me it is merely a "convention of the form" which I am stuck with because when all is said and done that is what I am, an eyewitness to history. Hence the omnipresence of the dreary "first person confessional." It is purely formal not egotistic, but I fear we cannot escape it. You have been duly warned. Get used to it.

With undying love for our people,
Kwame Ture
Conakry, Guinea
December 1997

INTRODUCTION

A Meditation on a Life

They say that freedom . . .
is a constant sorrow
    —SNCC freedom song

To be alive. To arrive here and leave here. Why? What's it mean? Maybe it's about freedom. That place, that land we will never reach, only visit, but dream of, always. Where we would be at our best. A land that would treat us as if we are its children and it is our mother. Motherland birthing us into a vale of tears, then caring for us. Motherland humming and whispering into our ear while she rocks us on her bosom. Everything is possible. You are possible my daughter, my son, the best inside you is something you can achieve because you are loved and all things are possible—the song we hear when we hear freedom. Our bodies, our minds, cradled by the memory, the promise of what we might become, yes, and surely will become, if given half of a chance.

Freedom so much larger than we are. Enlarging us. Glimpse of a new day. A great getting-up morning when everything in creation finds its voice and we dance to the music, music alive in our hands and feet and minds, music teaching us to overcome enemies within and outside ourselves, not a morning when war's over and won but the peace of freedom declaring itself, declaring that after all is said and done, the race wars, religious wars, wars over things and who owns what, the deepest goal, surest reward for the self and the people equally, is to sing and dance in community, each of us, his or her way, a step at a time for a sweet time, celebrating, resting, gathering new strength for the next struggle that might be a better struggle than these conflicts that destroyed so many, so many lost and gone to bring us dancing through a victory gate.

So freedom embraces life. It's love. Dancing together to Bob Marley songs. Joyous songs or anthems of our troubles when we're wrong or wronged and wishing for better. Freedom is what Stokely Carmichael was talking about, hollering about, demanding. The goal for which he staked his life daily in Mississippi in the sixties, what he sought in newly decolonized Africa, what he preached returning to the States persona non grata, spokesperson for impossible dreams of the dispossessed, or rather, seemingly impossible because, like the Motherland, a place we've never been and probably won't get to, dreams are no less valuable, no less real, for that reason, driving us to push for the unattainable, the best of ourselves we may choose if we dare, if we commit ourselves to struggling for freedom.

A vexed and vexing idea, freedom, if you really think about it. Who's free? Who's not? Why? Who says so? For sure, no one can give you freedom. Mr. Lincoln with an Emancipation Proclamation changed the legal status of some slaves in America in 1863, but he didn't give freedom to one person unless, in his heart, Lincoln had seen the light and truly, truly freed himself from the error, the terror, the self-destructive burden of believing one human being could or should own another. And no one's been given freedom by America's bloody wars—from the Revolution and the Civil War to the present crusades in Afghanistan or Iraq. If you confer upon someone else the power to free you, you are also granting them the power to enslave. How can freedom reside in a piece of paper or in someone else's decision to define you as property or not, to feed and clothe you, provide shelter, allow you to live or die. And even if someone could give the gift of freedom, wouldn't such an enormous, overwhelming gift establish permanent inequality, a permanent sense of dependency, indebtedness, unfulfillable obligation?

The freedom that matters most is how we feel inside about ourselves. Prisons, ghettos, concentration camps, barrios, favelas, colonies, can restrict mind and body, kill both, but until the spirit is extinguished, the possibility of freedom lives. Freedom's about choice. The self-grounded, self-motivated decision to imagine (create) a range of choices and the resolve to choose among them. This internal work orients us to our surroundings not magically but with a force literally transcendent since it's nonmaterial, beyond any external measure of verification. Even in the most extreme circumstances, freedom exists—the African who jumped from a slave ship into the roiling Atlantic Ocean. The philosopher who defies torture, asking for more weight, rather than abjure his understanding of truth.

Freedom is an attitude, a principle that operates perhaps most visibly in spite of resistance. Without resistance, without the restraint of physical or metaphysical shackles, without the tyranny of our passions, without the necessity of unwavering discipline to negotiate difficult tasks, without the body's decay, the mind's fallibility, how would any of us discover our capacities, our freedom, in spite of those obstacles, in spite of slavery, colonialism, the social pressure to conform? Not that freedom springs only from adversity—consider the choice to love, for instance—but how would we understand the value of an internal landscape where each of us strives to be the final arbiter and arranger of meaning, the giver of meaning to a life, if we did not confront the forces always clamoring to seize this inner territory from our grasp? To be known and performed, the dance of freedom—as pleasure needs pain and light needs dark—depends on creative tension, reciprocity, dialectic. Performed because freedom's impermanent, mutable, embodied, and framed in rhythmic counterpoint with its opposite. Performed because each dancer must be responsive to shifting circumstances, must be prepared to spontaneously improvise. Chimerical as dreams, and bearing, like dreams, immense weight, responsibility, and emotional necessity. How you gon keep them down on the farm after they see Paree? Freedom's a bit like that, a fabled city, unforgettable once glimpsed, a myth, a destination no less real because it's unreachable. To experience freedom even citizens of Paree must dream a Paree.

An elusive concept, perhaps always more apparent in its absence than presence—who better to keep alive the idea of freedom than a prisoner. However, a clear danger follows from an either/or notion of freedom: the unfreedom of some defines the freedom of others. Certain social orders—capitalism, for example—are based on division, depend on a permanent underclass of have-nots. The prisoner's perspective on freedom emphasizes opposition, loses sight of process and the necessity of continuing negotiation. Workers are not slaves, but the logic and dynamics of the plantation condition the lives and choices of a laboring underclass. Rigid categories of free and not-free lead backward to shortsighted dependence on a Great Emancipator, put freedom in someone else's hands.

Art is a particular case of freedom as action. When asked what it means to be a writer, novelist Chester Himes replied, "A fighter fights, a writer writes." I amen his clarity, his emphasis on process, on doing. No matter how many books I publish, the day I stop writing, I'll no longer be a writer. Other people might call me a writer, but that won't transform my inactivity into writing. Stokely Carmichael understood this principle. In these pages he tells us what he learned early in Mississippi jails: We are not what we think or say we are, not what we hope, not what we pretend we are. We are simply what we do.

In America, the idea of being free has been rigidified, materialized, turned into a onetime, one-stop shopping affair. We're born free, aren't we, by virtue of being Americans. Freedom's protected, isn't it, by the checks and balances of our political system. As one state's license plates declare, we Americans are determined to "live free or die." Strangely, ominously, even the frontal assault on our civil rights after 9/11 hasn't disturbed our confidence (or should I say sleep?).

Leaving aside for the moment the question of whether we still possess them or not, leaving aside also the possibility our leaders have duped us into believing fear and conformity rather than eternal vigilance protect our civil liberties, ask instead a simpler question: How are we practicing freedom? Are we writing it?

Unfortunately, the exercise of freedom has become synonymous with the power to buy, the privilege to display and consume what we purchase. This materialized version of the rewards of freedom and democracy has supplanted the idealized American Dream, once so attractive to the rest of the world. Because of the *thingness* of our culture, because money first and last determines value, because everything's for sale, from the presidency to prisons, economic power is the only power, the sole incentive. Getting paid is the bottom line. And what's wrong with that? We all like nice things, don't we? And nice things cost money. But what's the cost of a paycheck? Aren't there other, more crucial forms of compensation? If we don't exercise our freedom to create and to demand a wide range of life-enhancing returns for our labor, we're captives of a system with no center—moral, ethical, aesthetic—except production of wealth.

In *Black Skin, White Masks,* Frantz Fanon explained that for marginalized black people the first step away from oppression must be obtaining basic necessities—food, shelter, work, health, security—but without the next step—an emergent critique of self and society—the old order of exploitation that breeds the "wretched of the earth" will remain in force. Even if a large number of Americans could liberate themselves from handicaps imposed by racial, gender, and class inequities, these inequities wouldn't disappear. Neither inside the minds of individuals who pull themselves up by their bootstraps nor in the material circumstances of other Americans who don't make it up the economic ladder nor in the global economy where marginalized people will be recruited to fill the underclass necessary to maintain luxury for a few, here and abroad. In the absence of the new vision Fanon calls for, oppression simply migrates or creates a class of perpetual migrants, stateless, without rights, doing every nation's dirty work. In this situation, the psychological and moral landscape of each of us, haves or have-nots, deteriorates. Greed, fear, hate, cynicism, desperation proliferate.

Enter Stokely Carmichael/Kwame Ture. Carmichael's call for Black Power was a dream, an enabling, positive call for change, as much a dream as the one enunciated by Martin Luther King in Washington, D.C., in 1963. A dream because a blueprint or blackprint-in-progress for a revolutionary, never-seen-before way of being in the world. Kwame beseeches us, compels us, to put our best foot forward, step out, step away from a stalled, yet hopelessly self-congratulatory society, a powerful, complacent society, full of contradictions and lies, that allows great evil to be perpetrated in its name, in the name of promoting worldwide democracy and freedom when neither democracy nor freedom rule at home.

Kwame Ture's dreaming was visionary, a countervision, counterreality, to the reigning myths. He shouted, *The emperor is naked.* Pointed at the emperor with a finger attached to a black hand, stepped forward, stepped away with a black foot. *Black* not because of their color, but because Stokely Carmichael was an African-descended man, and, yes, it's his voice, his finger-pointing, his foot, so they're *black* and thus negative in the eyes of lots of folks, then here comes Stokely challenging the obscene spectacle of Empire, uh-uh; and call his anger, his critique, his truth, black if you want to, in fact he's also calling it black, but with a difference—*black* equals pride, fierce militancy, a determination to pursue the dream of freedom on his terms, *black* terms if you please, but really a new dream replacing an old one, so try to wrap your mind and heart around that too, recognize the legitimacy of his vision not its color, acknowledge its applicability, the seeds of clarity, its promise to seek change, to move all willing Americans to a more equitable, fulfilling social order, more freedom for so-called *whites* and so-called *blacks* than Stokely found when he arrived here.

Black Power was more than a dream of course. It was a call to action, a call for organization, for consciousness raising. Its concreteness was expressed by dangerous, grassroots campaigns for voting rights in the South, countless meetings, memos, study groups, alliances erected and dismantled, its growth and change, the business of raising and spending money, jail time, street time, hospital time, friendships formed and shattered, press releases and world tours, its birthing of SNCC, the bodies and minds sacrificed, sanctified, the songs, poems, narratives, and fashions it generated, its failures and successes that radically transformed the lives of so many.

All that and much more is the story Michael Thelwell tells. A freedom story grounded in Kwame Ture's recorded words. A story timely beyond words. More than timely, absolutely urgent. How many lives like Ture's are available for young people to study? His career wasn't engineered to catapult him to Hollywood or the NBA nor Wall Street, nor convert him to a beige Great White Hope. His *career* was service. Preparing himself through study and activism to participate in humankind's progressive emancipation. Learning to look for trouble, to agitate for change and mandate solutions. For him success meant a life situated in conflict, in sync with people's aspirations to do better, free themselves from an outmoded social and political order. He aligned and identified himself with Africa, a continent, an idea, a people bearing a horrific heritage of exploitation. His work revealed to oppressed people everywhere the power within their supposed weakness, exposed the weakness of unjust power. Ture demanded payment for his labors far beyond the reductive notion of monetary wages and demonstrated till the end of his life a willingness to pay back, to squeeze down to the last precious drop, the gift of life given to him, sharing that vital energy, distilling it so it became supportive of other human beings.

The struggle never ends. Across the globe young people are standing up, shouting, demanding more from their societies, more from their lives.

Reading Michael Thelwell's scrupulous, engaged, respectful rendering of Stokely Carmichael's life will remind protesters and marchers and street fighters, guerrillas in the hills, voters at the ballot box, reformers in tenements or legislatures, revolutionaries young and old, they are not alone, never have been, never will be.

John Edgar Wideman
Spring 2003, New York

CHAPTER I

Oriki:
Ancestors and Roots

ORIKI

Among many of the West African peoples from among whom our ancestors were seized, whenever a child is born, a birth poem or praise song is composed in its honor. Among the Yoruba this birth poem is called oriki.

Some days later at the naming ceremony by which the infant is ushered formally into its place in human society, the child's oriki *is recited publicly, first into the ear of the child and then to the assembled community of family and neighbors. The first language a child will be required to commit to memory, the* oriki *imprints the child with its complex historical, spiritual, and social identities.*

I have called the oriki *a praise song and birth poem, and so it is, but its functions are many more than those terms might imply. It is at once prayer, thanksgiving, celebration, and prophecy. It is a meditation on the meaning and significance of the new human's name. It is an evocation of the strong deeds, character, and praise names of the infant's ancestors, and, perhaps most important, it is an optimistic attempt to project (and define) in desirable ways the child's future personality and life prospects.*

By evoking lineage, the oriki *is ultimately about spiritual inheritance: that eternal life force that has many names (Ase among the Yoruba, Magara among the Dogon, Ike among the Igbo), which we receive from our ancestors. A vital force of which we, in each generation, are only the contemporary incarnations. And which in turn we pass on to our children and they to theirs, so that the lineage never dies.*

So, as we have seen, oriki, *while memory and history, is also character, at once both individual and collective. Individual because each human being has his or her own particular and unique* oriki. *Collective because being anchored in lineage, it is fundamentally about group identity. We Africans know that each individual one of us is ultimately the sum of that long line of ancestors— spiritual forces and moral arbiters—who have gone before to produce us. The psychic forces out of which we all come.*

In this sense oriki *is a salute to family. It is also an inheritance one acquires*

at birth. No one composes his or her own. But although in the changed cir-
cumstance of our diaspora I have myself written this section, it is in its way a
kind of oriki, *a salute to roots, origins, and family.*

Kwame Ture
January 1998, Conakry

[We stumbled onto this earlier Makeba letter sometime after Kwame had
drafted his remarks on the oriki *concept. He had not known of Miriam's*
letter to Time *magazine, but felt it to be a charming description of the*
Xhosa version of the same concept and quite a coincidence. "That's def-
initely her. She loved her culture. Let's put it in." —EMT]

Feb. 29, 1960

There was a slight error, which I do not think you will mind my
calling attention to. It concerns my African name. I would like to
spell it correctly for you:

Zenzile Makeba Qgwashu Nguvama Yiketheli Nxgowa Bantana
Balomzi Xa Ufun Ubajabulisa Ubaphekeli, Mbiza Yotshwala Sithi
Xa Saku Qgiba Ukutja Sithathe Izitsha Sizi Khabe Singama Lawu
Singama Qgwashu Singama Nqamla Nqgithi.

The reason for its length is that every child takes the first name
of all his male ancestors. Often following the first name is a descriptive word or two, telling about the character of the person, making
a true African name somewhat like a story.

Miriam Makeba

ORIKI: ANCESTORS AND ROOTS

I was born in the house my father built for his family at 54 Oxford
Street at the bottom of the forty-two steps in the city of Port of Spain,
Trinidad. This is in the Belmont section of the city—at that time a centrally located, working-class African neighborhood where the land rose
sharply upward. To traverse this steep incline, the government built the
large concrete steps that became something of a popular landmark.
"Meet me at the top of the forty-two steps at nine o'clock, eh?"

At the bottom of those steps my father built his dream house, "for," as
my mother thought she understood clearly, "his new bride." Later, for me
and my cousin Austin, the location would prove ideal. It was in easy walking distance to the Savannah—a kind of Central Park–like open space—
and the Botanical Gardens, truly a place of spectacular, exotic, almost
magical natural beauty where small boys could explore and dream.

Among his varied talents, the late Adolphus Carmichael was by profession a master carpenter. As was his close friend Mr. Frank Wilson, while their other friend Mr. Serapio was a stone mason. So that the house my father lovingly designed and the trio painstakingly erected was much larger and more elegantly finished than any my father could have afforded to buy. After which the three friends pooled their labor to build Mr. Serapio's equally impressive home, and then a house for Mr. Wilson. But of the three, our house appeared to have been, by virtue of its unusual design, the real novelty.

So much so, in fact, that the consensus in the communities of Belmont and neighboring East Dry River was that "Mr. Carmichael had built his family a mighty grand house, *oui.*" Most astonishing to visitors was a system of movable walls that, when rolled back, created a single large room. The space thus created was greatly in demand as a venue for weddings, birthdays, and similar celebrations by friends, family, and neighbors. Consequently, music, dancing, and joyous gatherings of all kinds, good fellowship, and *fêtes*, as Trinidad's Africans called them, were common in the home where I was born. They were an integral part of the ambience of my early childhood. Which may be why, to this day, like any good African, "Ah jes' loves to party"—that is, when possible and appropriate.

Something else in the neighborhood almost certainly contributed strongly to that aspect of my personality. At the top of the forty-two steps was a "pan yard," which is the local term for the home base of a steel band. Our resident band was called Casa Blanca, traditional rivals at carnival of the crosstown power who called themselves Invaders.

In those days, and almost certainly true today, no African neighborhood in Port of Spain could even think of holding its head up without a steel band to call its own. Casa Blanca was ours. Win or lose, we supported them at carnival. Two of our cousins even "beat pan" with Casa Blanca. "Two *distant* cousins," Tante Elaine might sniff, not entirely sure she approved of the raffish, combative, not at all respectable elements— "the vagabonds and Bad-Johns"—who were attracted to the steel bands. These were the same urban youth, the Trinidad equivalent of the "rude *bwai* posses," who would later create reggae in Jamaica.

But nonetheless, the one year in my memory that Casa Blanca took first prize in the carnival "panorama," an annual battle of the steel bands, the entire neighborhood erupted in leaping, dancing paroxysms of pride and celebration. One "big *fête*" for true, boy! Even the most obdurate, grimly "respectable" elements of the community were drawn into the spontaneous exuberance. For the moment, the pan men were magically and instantly transformed from "bad-Johns and vagabonds" to local heroes. And their best musician, a brother called Patsy Haines, became a neighborhood celebrity even before the announcement that he had been elevated to the most elite possible level of panmanship: The news that he had been selected to "beat" first pan in the Trinidad All Steel Percussion Orchestra, or TASPO. Then, in the awestruck eyes of me and my cousin Austin, Patsy walked the world in seven-league boots.

"Oh, God, boy," we exulted, "Patsy gone clear, *oui*?"

Those pan men were serious musicians and driven by more than dreams of carnival glory; they practiced just about every night of the year except for Sundays and the forty days of Lent. So that almost any night of my life, from the day I was born until the age of twelve when I left the island, I drifted into sleep to the beat of steel band music on the night wind. Nightly, I floated off on a wave of distant rhythms from the top of the forty-two steps, Casa Blanca's booming base lines pounding in my head and throbbing in my blood. *"Oh, God, boy!"*

I cannot imagine that this constant, distant, almost subliminal music and the frequent communal festivity inside the house can have failed to imprint themselves on my developing consciousness in important ways.

The Igbo man Oloudah Equiano, the African who first addressed the world in written English, began his 1789 masterpiece talking about his Igbo homeland with the words, "We are mostly a nation of poets, musicians, and dancers." He could have been talking about the Trinidad of my youthful memories.

Diaspora means survival. Like most African families of the diaspora, my family is a collection of people who are ordinary in extraordinary ways. I claim no special distinction for us. Like all our neighbors and friends in the surrounding communities—whether in Trinidad, the Bronx, or Mississippi—we are simply the survivors of dispersal.

Although I was born in Trinidad, in a real sense it would be inaccurate—actually *incomplete* would be a better word—to call me Trinidadian. Ultimately our roots are in Africa, but in a more immediate and recent sense they truly are pan-Caribbean. Consider.

My mother's mother was born in Montserrat to an Irish planter and his wife, an African woman, said to have been his former slave. But my mother was born in the U.S. Canal Zone in Panama, from whence as a child she returned to the care of maternal relations in "the Emerald Isle," as Montserrat is known, while her parents and older siblings left for New York. (I think there was a problem with her birth certificate.)

Later, as a young woman, my mother went to the U.S. consulate in Trinidad seeking to reunite with her parents in America. Again, that fateful, missing birth certificate delayed her long enough for young Adolphus Carmichael to meet, court, and marry her. This naturally delayed the reunion with her parents in New York for some years.

My mother's father, Mr. Joshua Charles, was born in Antigua. A colonial policeman, he had been posted to Montserrat, where he met my grandmother. He was then posted to Nevis, where, like thousands of Caribbean black men, he was forced by economic conditions to work in the building of the Panama Canal. Unlike most though, Grandfather Charles brought along his young bride, which is how my mother and all her siblings came to be born in the Canal Zone. After which, as I've said, the couple with their older children emigrated to New York, sending my mom to her grandparents in Montserrat. This little island of my grandmother's birth has an interesting history. It is called the Emerald Isle for two reasons, the lush greenery of its forested mountains being only the obvious one. The real reason is that its European population was overwhelmingly Irish Catholics, in headlong flight before Oliver Cromwell's victorious Puritans. Anyone who watched television reports of the destruction wrought by the Soufrière volcano in 1997 will have noticed a succession of African faces answering to names like Houlihan, O'Reilly, and O'Connell. Another of the ironies of colonialism.

On the paternal side—the Carmichaels—the story constitutes no less of an odyssey. Cecilia Harris, my paternal grandmother, the first important influence on my life, was born in Tobago in 1877 and is believed to have had Carib★ blood. Her husband, Mr. Joseph Carmichael, was a tailor from Barbados, but I believe the couple met and married in Trinidad.

I never knew Grandpa Carmichael, according to family lore a stern, circumspect, and exacting man, very black, very dignified. He was said to be a man of few words with a well-developed High Victorian sense of propriety and rectitude. A typical "Bajun" of the old school in that regard.

Having established my own Barbadian connection, I think I can afford to "lime" on them a little bit. Among Caribbean people, the popular, slightly ironic name for Barbados is "Little Britain," a title that, however mocking in its inspiration, was accepted by the Bajans with no little pride.

It could be apocryphal, but the oft-told story is that upon the advent of World War II, the Barbadian legislature responded to news of Britain's entry into the war with a famous telegram to Whitehall (or was it to the monarch himself?): "Forward, Great Britain! Little Britain is fully behind you." The kind of loyal colonial action of which, I suspect, Grandpa Carmichael might have heartily approved.

Once you start the "ol' lime" it's hard to stop. I can't resist this one: I once encountered a local historical explanation of the Barbadian national character vis-à-vis the rest of the Caribbean that goes as follows.

Because Barbados is the easternmost of the Caribbean islands, it became the first landfall for slave ships from Africa. When they landed for freshwater and provisions, the Barbadian planters got first pick over the cargoes. Wisely, they selected the "calmer, more civilized, cerebral, and

★Carib—the original inhabitants for whom the Caribbean is named.

peaceable" of the Africans. (You must remember this is a "Bajan" version. The Jamaican adjectives are "meek, passive, and enslavable," but we shan't fan those particular nationalist fires here.)

As the story goes, the intellectuals, craftsmen, and skilled Africans collected in Barbados. Hence the relative courtliness, restraint, and civility of which the culture so pridefully boasts. Among the Africans, the most boisterous physical types—warriors, hunters, desperadoes of all kinds, the rough and rebellious elements—ended up in places like Jamaica, Haiti, and Cuba, which, according to my Bajan informant, is supposed to explain their histories of bloody insurrection and the relative "coarseness" of these cultures and societies even today. I still can't decide whether the brother was serious or merely "sending me wide," as they say in cricket. He cannot really have been entirely serious because this version is belied by history. The three major and bloody African insurrections Barbados experienced during slavery are eloquent testimony to the total failure of Barbadian slaveowners' carefully calculated selection process.

Once I teased a Jamaican-born African about this version of history. To my great surprise, he conceded at least a possibility. "Something much like that could well be true," he mused. "When I was a kid, I thought all Barbadians were stiff, close-cropped, very black men who always wore the classic colonial expatriate attire—khaki short pants, khaki knee socks, and sandals—taught Latin and Greek, and rarely smiled. Why? Because our classics masters at school seemed invariably to be Bajan and to fit that description.

"The first, Mr. Jackman, was such an exacting taskmaster and stern disciplinarian that we christened him Tarquinius Superbus—Tarquin the Tyrant—after the wicked Roman despot. The next Latin master, Mr. Crick, was worse—'Boy, are you laughing *with* me, *for* me, or *at* me?'—so we called him Tarquinius Superbus Secondem."

From all family accounts, Grandfather Carmichael was firmly in that tradition. The two youngest of his eight children—my father and his sister Olga—were serious dancers. They just loved to dance and, as they got older and bolder, apparently began to sneak out to dances sans parental permission. But Grandpa Carmichael nipped that in the bud. One night Tante Olga, then a young lady, was out dancing up a storm when the hooked end of a walking stick snaked out onto the dance floor, ensnared her neck, and escorted her captive out of the dance and all the way home, the old gentleman uttering nary a word.

So there you have it: Montserrat, Grenada, Barbados, Antigua, Nevis, Tobago, Panama, Trinidad, New York. We truly are African people of the diaspora, which, of course, means people of dispersal. Which is exactly the word for what went on in the eastern Caribbean. If you know the eastern

English-speaking Caribbean, you will understand why a family of such disparate origins as ours could come together in Trinidad and be in no way unusual.

The eastern Caribbean is an archipelago of small islands of mostly volcanic formation with limited natural resources except for its people, which today are mostly African. In those days, Trinidad, the largest, was a kind of commercial and administrative hub. Also, with its pitch lake, nascent petroleum industry, and the American military base at Chaguaramas, Trinidad was something of an economic magnet for people from the smaller territories. So much so that two of Trinidad's national heroes—Uriah Butler and Elnora Frances, militant leaders in the labor and independence movements, which were in full flood at the time of my birth—had both been born in Grenada.

Which is how in this small, bustling city of Port of Spain, across the Gulf of Paria from Venezuela on what was once called the Spanish Main, my family, a truly pan-Caribbean aggregation—in whose veins were mingled African, Irish, Carib, and so it is rumored, Sephardic blood—came together.

In this heritage I assert for my family no particular distinction. The story remains, even as I speak, a common one in the eastern Caribbean—displacement and dispersal. Poor African people in constant motion always in search of economic survival and a fair deal. Plucked out of Mother Africa and transplanted into alien territories where they controlled neither land, nor wealth, nor ruling institutions of government. A people of dispersal, of course. But dispersal only begins the process, it does not end it. There is another key word—*survival.* A people of dispersal and survival. *Let the church say "Ahmen."* Survivors—of the slave coffles and slave dungeons, of the unspeakable horrors of the Middle Passage; of slavery, whether of house or field, cotton or sugarcane; of colonialism; and in our time, of the unending struggle for independence and full civil and human rights. This journey is in itself no mean accomplishment. But more than that, we survived intact, or at least far, far more intact than is generally understood and conceded.

So . . . our people of diaspora and survival. Our people, whose only resource was themselves, their labor, and their intelligence: the skills of their hands and of the cunning of their minds. Carrying deep within themselves a dynamic inheritance from Africa—a deep reverence for the creator; an abiding, unshakable respect for self and kindred; a culture generous in spirit, rich in music, dance, the power of sacred poetry and eloquence; and the love of language for its own sake and beauty. Naked and chained we may have come, but we surely did not come defenseless. *We did not come defenseless!*

So, I claim no special distinction for my immediate family, for in these things we were neither different from nor better than the neighbors and friends in the surrounding communities in which my early years were passed.

In 1936, Mabel Florence Charles, an adventurous young woman of fifteen years, left Montserrat for Trinidad to pick up the U.S. visa that would reunite her with her parents in the Bronx. That fateful, lost birth certificate would once again intervene to interrupt the journey and delay the reunion for another eight years, a marriage, and three children.

One day in 1937 she dutifully accompanied a girlfriend on a church task, a visit to a respected church member, Ms. Cecilia, who had been unwell. There she met my grandmother's three daughters, Elaine, Olga, and Louise, and caught her first glimpse of the family's only surviving son. That was scarcely an auspicious beginning because my mother professes to have been exceedingly unimpressed by that initial sighting. Why?

She had caught the young man in what, in her eyes, was a profoundly unmanly activity. In fact, she could hardly credit her eyes. This was unheard of: not only was the young man *ironing* (a skill he had no doubt picked up in his late father's tailor shop—he of the hooked cane), but the garment being ironed was unmistakably a *woman's* dress!

(Quite obviously my father was a liberated male, evolved way beyond that time and culture.) But in my mother's experience, men *never* did women's work. They never ironed and only in the direst emergency ever cooked—that is, *if* they even *knew* how to do so.

"My Lord, did you see that?" she giggled to her friend. "He was *ironing* his sister's *dress,* the sissy."

"I like her," my father pointed her out to his friend Frank Wilson a few days later. The young men were on their way home from their work on a house. "That's the woman I'm gonna marry."

"Better you chose you a different one," Wilson counseled. "She well pretty but she look stuck-up, *oui*? You know how these light skin ones are. Best you choose you a darker one."

"You think so? Look, you see these dirty work clothes I got on? Well, one day, that same light-skin, stuck-up one going wash them and like it too." My father promised with the confidence that was always part of the personality I came to know.

The ill-started couple next met at a dance some weeks later, "and he was ever so nice," my mom discovered to her great surprise. It probably didn't hurt that he could really dance too. That night, my father walked her home "and we held hands all the way."

In a relatively short time, the "dream" house being completed, and the marriage celebrated, my parents set up housekeeping on October 8, 1939.

But the house at the forty-two steps—at least in the living arrangements—was proving less the honeymoon cottage of a young bride's dream than it was the compound of an extended family, and a rather close-knit extended family at that. The house came fully encumbered. For, when the young couple began married life it was with the groom's entire family in residence—my grandmother Cecilia; my father's three sisters, Elaine, Olga, and Louise; and Elaine's young son, my cousin Austin.

One can readily see how my moms might be forgiven if she felt somewhat outnumbered among all these formidable women of the Carmichael clan. And from my mother's perspective, my aunts were probably ill disposed to share their only brother with another woman. And certainly, they were not about to be replaced in his affections by any "small island girl" who clearly was not good enough (as only a veritable paragon of womanhood could possibly have been) for their only brother!

It was, from the get-go, an arrangement fraught with tension and the inevitability of competition and conflict. Especially since my diminutive mother has never been disposed to avoid confrontation, particularly when right was on her side. (And from her perspective, it invariably was.) And even though my father was indeed *their* brother, was he or was he not indeed *her* husband? There was an obvious need for clarification here.

The oldest of the sisters, Tante Elaine Letren, was a divorced schoolteacher, a firm disciplinarian, and the undisputed leader—or at least *primus inter pares**—among the Carmichael women. Tante Elaine had the proverbial will of iron and a strong sense of family prerogatives.

So, as I have come really to understand only after two marriages of my own, the lines were drawn, with my poor father torn between equally compelling loyalties and affections embodied by these two equally strong-willed women. I've always assumed that the presence of Grandma Cecilia, a gentle, devout lady, served to hold off the final confrontation, a crisis that, in hindsight, though clearly inevitable, was further postponed by the arrival, in fairly rapid succession, of the children. Three in number: first my sister Umilta, then in June of 1941 myself, like my father before me destined to be the family's lone boy child, and then my little sister Lynette.

As was our people's habit, the infant boy was elaborately, even portentously, named, in my case Stokely Standiford Churchill Carmichael. Help him, Jesus. The Churchill speaks for itself. It being the depths of the war, there must be literally thousands of African Caribbean men of my age who answer to one or the other of the names of the "indomitable British Bulldog." (Some poor devils even go through life encumbered with both, as in Winston Churchill Jones.)

*First among equals.

The Stokely is another matter. I've never met anyone else who shared the name by which I was known for the first half of my life. The christening at Trinity Anglican was unusual only in one important regard. The godfather and the presiding clergyman were one and the same—the Reverend Winston Lamont. He contributed the Stokely, the name of a legendary and dedicated teacher at Queens Royal College who had greatly influenced the reverend when he was a student there. I have no idea whether Stokely was his first or last name, or whether the schoolmaster was native or expatriate British. But it is not impossible, however ironic, that I could originally have been named for not one but two British gentlemen!

My cousin Austin keeps insisting—my aunts tend to corroborate—that as a small boy I found it necessary to further embellish what was already an overgenerous portion of names. But, claims Austin, whenever my name(s) were mentioned, I would invariably correct the speaker by chirping, "Stokely Standiford Churchill *Great Man* Carmichael." Of course, I have no recollection of this. But it seems obvious that the little boy was merely properly identifying the original owner of the name Churchill and not necessarily claiming "greatness" for his little self.

However, by the time Lynette was properly weaned, the domestic tension and rivalry had apparently again become insupportable. As if on cue, the errant birth certificate materialized. It had been hiding all along among official government records in the U.S. Canal Zone. All this time my mother had been a citizen of the United States. At the next confrontation—so to say, the straw that broke the camel's back—my mother felt newly empowered to lay down her ultimatum.

"It's me or them. Who you love? Make up your mind for you are going to have to choose."

"Hey, remember now, they are my sisters and my mother."

"So I have a mother and sister too. You know. They are in the Bronx. I can run to my family too, y'know."

"Then what about the children . . . and, what about me?"

"All of you are Carmichaels. I'm May *Charles*. You all can keep the children for the time being. I'll send for them . . . or *you* can bring them when you come."

"When I come? Where I going, eh? I told you that I want to leave Trinidad?"

"Well, you will have to choose . . . 'cause I'm going."

So in October of 1944, leaving husband, young children, and the ultimatum "You will have to choose," behind her, Mabel Florence Charles Carmichael, aged twenty-three and looking much younger, set out for God's Country. Not in search of a "better" life or the American Dream, but in impulsive flight and as a personal declaration of independence from domineering in-laws. This was no mean journey during wartime. Covering two days, it entailed first a seaplane to Puerto Rico, then another to Miami, and over much of the next day, a propeller-driven flight to La Guardia.

At a casual glance, the odds were not in her favor. In fact, the closer one looked, the more heavily weighted against her the wager appeared. My father, he who was enjoined "to choose," was an extremely family-oriented man, and his mother, sisters, and his children remained in Trinidad in the home he had built with his two hands. As did his two partners in the modest but growing house-building business, and also his church. This was important, for my father remains one of the most deeply and sincerely religious men I had ever met before I encountered the Reverend Martin Luther King Jr.

Then too my father was an inordinately social being. Although he never drank, he loved to dance, he lived for carnival and "*big fête.*" He loved his culture. His economic place in the society, if modest, was at least secure. It was, all in all, a great deal to walk away from . . . all for the love of *one* woman.

And if that were not enough, there were also the practical, not to say legal, difficulties involved. Then as now, U.S. consulates in the black world see their central mission as preventing too many working people of color from getting visas to the United States. If he were to follow his wife legally, a visa could easily mean a wait of some five years or more. Or, he would have to take uncharacteristic risks—evading the law and becoming in effect a criminal. He, up until then the most lawful and conventionally respectable of men? Small chance. But that was the gamble my impetuous mother made. And won.

My father toughed it out for over a year and a half. Then, like the Prince of Wales before him (a simile that came naturally to the lips of Carmichael family historians), he would abdicate and give it all up to follow his heart and "the woman I love." There, however, the comparison breaks down: of the two men, my father gave up much more of value but certainly got a far, far better return as wives go than did the feckless British nobleman, he of allegedly fascist sympathies. Not even close. Hands down, my mother was the better woman.

So in June of 1946, the otherwise utterly law-abiding Adolphus Carmichael signed on as an able seaman on a northbound freighter, jumped ship in New York harbor, and reunited with his wife. My sister was four, I almost five, and Lynette an infant. We were not to see either parent again until I was almost eleven.

CHAPTER II

The House
at the Forty-Two Steps

The house of my childhood memories was a lively, well-ordered place filled with women and children. In my memory, it is bright, airy, and spacious, its many rooms being cooled by sea breezes off the Gulf of Paria. I fully understand that an adult return to the places of childhood is often disappointing, the passage of time and adult perceptions rudely dissolving at once the scale, the wonder, and the magic of our childish remembrances. Mercifully, I have returned to that house only once and then briefly so the magic of childhood memory has remained with me unspoiled.

Although my father's labor of love was ostensibly built for his bride, neither he nor my mother, who left for America when I was three, is present in my earliest recollections of that household. It is my paternal grandmother, Mrs. Cecilia Harris Carmichael, who was the adult center and anchor of my early years. As were her three daughters, Tante Elaine, Tante Louise, and Mummy Olga, who was vivacious and pretty but unlucky with husbands, since she was twice widowed and childless. So the children of the household called her Mummy. And "Mummy Olga" she became to us children and "Mummy Olga" she remains to this day.

The interior was organized around a large, central dining and living room, off from which lay the bedrooms. How many, I'm not sure. But I have no recollection of our ever feeling crowded. I do remember that "the boys," Cousin Austin and I, had our own room. I imagine the little girls did also, or perhaps shared a large room with my grandmother.

From the outside, the approach from the front was the most imposing. In its unconventional design my father must clearly have intended it to make a statement, and he seems to have succeeded.

From the front, one entered the house by a wide flight of steps leading up to the *galerie*—a porchlike area that in other parts of the English-speaking Caribbean is called the veranda. In the American South it is the *porch*. The *galerie* itself, as well as the roof that sheltered it, was built on five levels. Why? That's how my father wanted it.

The *galerie* was a cool, fragrant place alternating between sun and shadow. This impression was created by the many potted palms, ferns drooping from tall clay stands, and hanging baskets of broad-leafed, flowering plants that must have been orchids of different kinds. These were the province of Tante Louise, the sister with the green thumb. She was also the force behind the beds of colorful tropical flowers and assorted herbs for bush medicines that adorned the front yard.

This, then, was the family of my childhood, my grandma, her three adult daughters, and the four children. George Lamming, the distinguished Barbadian novelist, has a celebrated line in his classic Caribbean coming-of-age novel, *In the Castle of My Skin*. The line speaks to the so-called matriarchal nature of Afro-Caribbean societies. In introducing his mother, Lamming had famously written, "My mother who fathered me." As young children we were "mothered" and "fathered" by these four women equally, as we thought, without differentiation. In retrospect, I can see a natural and unspoken division of roles and responsibilities among them according to personality and inclination. From each according to his ability . . . ?

Recently I listened to the report of a Caribbean brother's first trip to the continent. In Kenya he befriended a local youth who invited him home "because, my brother, I want you to meet my four mothers." The visitor was bemused by the quaint locution. "And the thing is," he exclaimed, "he said it so naturally, 'my four mothers.' " I merely smiled because that "African" formulation described with complete accuracy the emotional reality of the household of my early memories.

All the aunts worked while Grandma was responsible for the children during the day. Tante Elaine, Austin's mom, was a teacher at Mr. Young's private school. She brought to the household a rigorous attention to order, detail, and duty. She also brought home her reverence for education and the strict administration of discipline, which were projections of the classroom persona of all colonial schoolteachers of the time. Mummy Olga, more fun-loving and easygoing, worked in a department store, where dealing with the public was an occupation well suited to her outgoing, friendly nature.

Tante Louise also worked out of the house but I cannot remember where. Her presence in the house does not loom as large, perhaps because she at some point got married and moved to the country. But the weekend family excursions to visit Tante Louise at Point Fortin loom large in my memory. We passed through the unbroken green mass of sugarcane fields, caught glimpses of the bright blue Caribbean, its breakers foaming white against rocky shores, and drove over narrow mountain roads lined by lush tropical forests, where flocks of birds, an occasional band of monkeys, or a small deer could be glimpsed.

Richly colorful as that landscape was, it paled to insignificance beside the embellishments of my small boy's imagination. The twenty-mile trip became an adventure in African exploration, triggered by Austin's adventure books, which I had read. My eyes scanned the surrounding foliage for the bands of "natives" and the lions, tigers, great apes, and elephants that just had to be lurking there. That none of the above ever appeared did little to diminish the excitement of my searching eyes each time we took the trip.

During the days while the aunts worked, we were Grandma Carmichael's and she totally ours. Mine in particular. I got a great deal of care, a lot of attention, and also a lot of medicine from my grandmother. As a small child, indeed from birth, I had been so asthmatic that my very survival had been in doubt. My Grandma, along with my mother, as soon after delivery as she was able, had nursed, coaxed, prayed, and medicated me out of danger. Those two women watched me like hawks, noting every slightest change in my breathing, every sign of a weakening condition, literally forbidding by sheer force of personality, will, faith, and traditional medicine the early death that seemed to be stalking me. My mother vividly recalls to this day a succession of sleepless nights pacing the floor with me wheezing in her arms, laboring for every breath.

Despite her delicacy of feature and diminutive size, there was nothing *fragile* about Grandma Carmichael. She was a woman as strong and resolute in her faith as in her determination. As a child, most of my time, from my first awareness of things, was spent with her. From her nurturing spirit I took for granted unconditional love, protection, and care. She administered the constant and endless succession of bush medicines that in all likelihood saved my life. A great variety of medicinal herbs grew in Tante Louise's garden, all apparently for the purpose of making me strong. Some were bitter. Others vile-tasting in other ways. I believe Grandma, being of the old school, linked bitterness with potency. For her, the more bitter the medicine the better it was.

Thanks to her, I developed an early taste tolerance; thus I have always been able to eat almost anything and to swallow almost any medicine. My grandma's combination of love, attention, care, and medicine shored up my health, so that all my life since I've been exceedingly healthy until the recent advent of cancer, but more of that later.

Grandma Cecilia was the major influence on my young personality, the adult with whom I spent most of my time and with whom I was closest. She was a devout woman. A pillar of Trinity Anglican Church, close friend and adviser to the parish parson, she was entrusted with the baking of the communal wafers each week. My earliest and most enduring ethical instruction came from her.

"Don't ever lie, always speak the truth. Think of others always. Remem-

ber the less fortunate. Never waste food. Never waste anything that someone else might need. Waste not, want not." And so forth. And the "memory gems" so much a part of any respectable colonial child's training:

> If you in the morning throw minutes away,
> You can't pick them up the course of the day.

and

> Whatsoever you set your hand to do,
> do it with all your might.

My early encounter with the ethical and moral aspects of life, I trace
squarely to my paternal grandmother. And of course, it was her death in
January of 1952, and the child-care vacuum it created in the household,
that made it inevitable that my sisters and I would accompany my aunt to
New York.

If grandmother "mothered" me, then it was the strict and exacting
Tante Elaine who, first, in the patriarchal sense of that word, "fathered"
me. Like all colonial pedagogues, Tante Elaine believed in discipline, fully
convinced that sparing the rod meant certain ruination for the child. She
was also the "competent authority," the central force in deciding and
directing the affairs of the household, in making sure that everything was
properly maintained and that everyone met his or her responsibilities.
From a young age even the children had their appropriate responsibility.
I cannot remember exactly at what age it first fell to me, but my duty was
to clean the chicken coop each week. And those chickens were prolific in
more than eggs, which is why later, whenever I've heard anyone deroga-
tively described as a "chicken s—" so-and-so, I've fully understood precisely the severity and the grossness of that particular abuse.

Tante Elaine was the arbiter of order, not only the maintenance of
proper standards but of the *appearance* of the same. She also administered
whatever whippings Austin and I earned, and we earned ourselves quite
a few. While she was very, very strict with me, that was nothing compared
to her strictness with Austin, who was, after all, her son. Poor Austin. It
was unthinkable to her that a teacher's son, especially hers, could be anything less than brilliant in school and impeccable in behavior and deportment. Put that way, what chance did he have? I can remember thinking,
"Poor Austin, I sorry for he, *oui.*" Today Austin is a dedicated and effective teacher in the Miami schools. I see that as entirely due to his
mother's influence.

But Tante Elaine was fair. She was a hard woman, but fair. And I never
for a moment doubted that her punishments were anything other than an

expression of her love and her wanting only the best for and of us. On such occasions her method was unvarying. First came the summons. Once present, you would be secured and immobilized by her firm, pinching grip on your earlobe. Then the charge would be announced, telling you in explicit detail just what your offense had been. For Tante Elaine, justice had not only to be done, it had to be *seen* and *understood* to have been done. Then, after the indictment came the question, a kind of ritual incantation, really.

"How *could* you have done this? You have been taught better! What *on earth* could have possessed you to do it? Well, I don't know *what* got into you, I'm going to get it *out* today. I promise you that. I'll bet you, when I'm finished with you, you will not even *think* of doing it again. I bet you."

Not a bet to take 'cause that was one Tante Elaine would invariably win. But after the whipping, Tante Elaine was finished with it. With her "Now, let this be a lesson to you!" the matter was ended and the incident behind you both. The record was expunged. You didn't carry a juvenile record into the future.

Not so Mummy Olga, who never, ever beat us. But would she scold! *Lord ha' mercy.* And those scoldings were almost worse than a beating. They were very, very effective, being predicated on convincing you of your betrayal of confidence and trust. Of your causing *pain* and *shame* to someone who loved you, to wit, herself. By the time Mummy Olga got through telling you how ashamed you had made her and the entire Carmichael family, you really felt so bad that a beating from Tante Elaine seemed a bargain in comparison.

When you looked at the shame and sadness dramatically etched into her face, the hurt in her gentle eyes as she told you, "How ashamed you make she. And here she thinking she have such a big, lovely, responsible son, an' look you come shame she so? How could you? An' look she can't even hold up her face before people now," the intensity of the remorse that flooded over you was certainly more lasting than any whipping.

The blessed Tante Louise tended her garden and neither scolded nor whipped, as I recall. But she may well have moved to the country before I was old enough to have merited either from her.

So the formative presences for me in the beginning were women, and that has continued true. In my life, I've always been surrounded by women, educated and protected by them.

Just recently I even heard my mother on the telephone with a journalist who must have asked her something about the effect of my present illness on her. I'm not sure just what the question was or how intrusive it might have been, but I was proud of the clarity and grace of her answer. And the strength:

"No, it doesn't scare me. Why should it? Look, when he was born, they said he wouldn't live. We thought we might lose him then. And see, I've had my son with me for over fifty wonderful years. And he is here with me right now, so, my dear, what do I have to complain about?"

Even my first year at school was defined by a woman, though I could have been no more than three, for my mother was still at home. (And even had I not remembered this, my mother made certain that I and the rest of the family would never forget the story.) This was Ms. Stafford's infant school, a small private school that Ms. Stafford ran out of her house. We started school early—it probably was more like kindergarten—but we learned the alphabet, did simple sums, and played a lot. And by age four or so we could read simple children's books and write our names.

It's my first week of school. There I meet a little girl who evidently must have made quite an impression, big time. Because after school nothing would do but that she accompany me home to be presented to my mother. She was willing enough. But to "make assurance doubly sure," I found it prudent to grasp her firmly by the hand and off we went. Or perhaps she grasped mine. Or else it was mutual. There is always such ambiguity about matters of the heart, but what is certain is that we proceeded hand in hand. And this holding of hands must have distracted or occupied me fully. Because, when I proudly presented my new friend to my mother, she could scarcely suppress her mirth. There I was, holding her hand and announcing proudly, "I'm walking little Eva Walton home," with my pants, socks, and shoes sodden with pee. It has always come back to haunt me: "Boy, remember that before you could even hold your water, you were holding women's hands."

The next time I got myself in trouble over a woman—a fatally seductive "older woman"—I was nine. *Auntie Kaye's Children's Hour* was a popular radio program. Much to the pride of the aunts I was selected to recite a poem on the air. I think that I was one of the youngest to be selected, and this may have contributed a great deal to the aunts' pride. It was an event. Friends and family were duly alerted to listen for "Stokely on the radio, chile. Ah tell you." So much of an occasion in fact that the proud parents in the Bronx were duly informed. My parents went out and bought a shortwave radio, guaranteed, as they thought, "to pick up anywhere in the world," and spent an entire Saturday morning vainly trying to tune in Trinidad. Tante Elaine escorted me to the station and left me in a room with the other children. And of course, I was *clean*, bow tie, suit, mature and sophisticated. (More of that suit later.) The only vacant seat was next to a charming young lady. We looked each other over. She smiled, asked my name, then revealed, much to my distress, that she was ten. And how old was I? What could I do? I told her calmly that I was eleven. Her smile grew warmer.

When my turn at the microphone came, Auntie Kaye asked my name and age. The little girl was looking admiringly at me. So naturally I gave my age over the air as eleven.

A Rasta elder I know who is fond of commenting on the scandals of the day says, "Thus are the minds of men made foolish by the gleaming smiles of women." Let the church say "Ahmen." Talk about snatching defeat from the jaws of victory. I absolutely cannot remember what poem I recited that day. But I also know I shall never forget the look on Tante Elaine's face when she came to fetch me home. (Apart from lying I had foolishly blown the aunts' bragging rights of being the youngest to have been selected.)

"Young man, I *promise you*, you will *never* tell a lie again. And certainly not publicly over the radio!"

The offending orifice, my lying mouth, was thereupon thoroughly washed out with soap. A high price to pay for an older woman's smile. But it appears to have worked. Since then I can honestly say I've never wittingly told any kind of lie over the radio or any other public medium. Not even for a woman's favor.

I was born at a time of bustling change and a sudden if superficial wartime prosperity in Port of Spain. Numbers of folk were crowding into the city in search of the work that could not be found in the cane fields or the countryside.

The streets were filled with Yankee soldiers and airmen from the U.S. base at Chaguaramas. Also large numbers of Allied sailors from the British, Canadian, and American merchant ships that congested the harbor while they awaited destroyer escorts to convoy them across the Atlantic. I can remember dramatic blackouts when the entire city was kept completely dark as a precaution against Axis air raids, which mercifully never came.

A calypso, popular at the time, commented wryly on the easy-money, boomtown, wartime atmosphere that prevailed in the nightlife of the town. Calypsonians are the Trinidadian descendants of the African troubadours who enjoyed license to comment sharply in song on any political misdeeds by the rulers, or on any domestic scandals or gossip within the community.

This calypso was called "Rum & Coca-Cola" after the drink of choice of the foreign troops and the refrain lamented:

> Both mother and daughtah
> working for the Yankee dollar.

We children had no idea what the words meant, but the tune was catchy and we never quite understood why we were forbidden to sing the song.

Naturally all this bustle of displacement and transition stimulated the organization of the masses of the workers. And the undisputed leader of this resistance was a diminutive black man called Tubal Uriah "Rab" Butler, who seemed always to be organizing and making what I now understand to be incendiary speeches against economic exploitation and the "wickedness" of the colonial government and subsequently being jailed for these "seditious utterances."

Of course I could not then have *understood* any or all of this, and certainly not in the way I've just summarized it. But it certainly was in the air of the times. It was on the radio and it was the subject of the adult conversation at dinner. I have a strong impression that Tante Elaine was either involved with or supportive of the trades-union, worker's-rights movement.

Then, as now, economic conditions were harsh, especially for the growing numbers of unemployed or marginally employed who were flocking into the city. Many people around us *were* real poor, as I came to recognize early on. But our household was insulated from that grinding poverty for a number of reasons.

All the aunts were industrious and always fully employed. And all the aunts baked cakes and pastries for sale so the house was always full of baked delicacies. I am sure that the per capita income of the family would appear pathetic in the dollar terms of the economic calculus so dear to the U.S. media. In U.S. dollars, the income of a Trinidad teacher or salesclerk would undoubtedly seem puny indeed.

But *collectively* the household had three incomes and we owned our home, so the Carmichaels did quite well, thank you very much. Then too we had the added purchasing power in the local economy of the U.S. dollars remitted regularly from New York by our parents.

As children, therefore, we knew no material hardship. We ate regularly and well and, again courtesy of the parents, were probably the most elegantly dressed children in church or school. The periodic clothes packages—and once shipping resumed after the war they were as regular as clockwork—ensured that, attired in their Yankee finery, the Carmichaels turned heads en route to church. Which made me very fond of Sundays. In our family, Sunday meant church, and I was very taken by the passionate singing, eloquent preaching, and solemn ritual. No small part of my attraction was the elaborate dressing up, which was the first step in it all.

In the Caribbean, at least in our circles, the standard and accepted church uniform for adolescent boys was a white "dress" shirt, a tie, and short pants. For all my cousins and friends, that was formal Sunday attire.

The American extravagance—not to mention the outrageous precocity—of dressing a little kid in an *adult*-styled suit was unheard of. So on Sundays when the family set out, Austin and I were *clean*, Jack. I, in my little blue suit with *long* pants, bow tie, with a stylish handkerchief showing from the breast pocket. I am a little embarrassed now to confess how much I enjoyed the public sensation we created. (Austin was similarly outfitted, but being older and bigger, the effect was not so nearly startling as with my pint-size, six-year-old self.) It never failed. As soon as I appeared, someone was sure to do a double take, point, and exclaim with genuine surprise, *"Waai,* look at that little man!" This had nothing to do with my character being "mannish," though it could have been. But that is literally and exactly what I must have seemed in local eyes, a miniature man. The name took and for a while I was known as Little Man. It probably was the suit that got me in trouble with the "older woman" at the radio station too.

When the adults in our family said, "Sunday is the Lord's day," it was no hollow cliché. Talk about ecumenical, we covered all bases. A typical Sunday would find the Carmichaels at Hanover Methodist for morning service from nine to ten-thirty. Eleven o'clock would find us at Gray Friars Presbyterian, where the children had Sunday school till noon. Then a break for lunch, and while Grandma was alive, it was her beloved Trinity Anglican for evening worship.

Sometimes later on a Sunday, perhaps once a month, there would be spiritual activity of a more exotic sort at the home of a Ms. Baines. Then, as I seem to remember, Austin and I would hide ourselves behind thick curtains to secretly observe what I remember as a vaguely "African" religious observance. Austin, who is older, says it was "like but not quite a Shango ceremony since there was neither drumming nor sacrifice." But it had aspects of a secret society. It was quiet, private, almost secretive, which is why we hid to observe it. Spirits would be evoked and consulted. The participants were possessed by "saints," so clearly it was a derivative of the *orisha* worship, which to this day survives in Trinidad from ancestral Africa. It was all deliciously mysterious and exciting, a feeling no doubt highlighted by the secrecy of our concealment.

At about seven years of age I started school at Eastern Boys School, a public government school some distance from our home. One did not have to be very old to quickly see the real differences among the boys. No one there was rich, but some were obviously poor. They had poor clothes, usually no shoes, and inadequate food. Even a kid as young as I could see that. It puzzled me. I did not understand it and I remember only that it seemed unfair to me. It made me sad.

In June of 1996, I was invited to Trinidad by the Emancipation Committee and so returned to my native land for the first time in thirty years. The reception was really most extraordinary, especially for someone who had officially been banned from the country for most of his adult life. Moving as the public occasions were, the best part was the opportunity to visit with Tante Elaine and Mummy Olga on the childhood turf. One day, a visiting journalist got Tante Elaine to dig deep into her store of family history. The *Trinidad Guardian* reported the next day:

> "The boy Stokely was always different," Tante Elaine said. "He used to always hide food in a butter can to take to a classmate who only ate crackers at lunchtime. On another occasion," she recalled, "a friend of his grandmother's admonished him one Sunday after church for keeping company with some barefoot, scruffy little boys."
>
> As Tante Elaine tells it, little Stokely looked solemnly at the woman.
>
> "Miss Annie, I go to Sunday school. There we sing a hymn that God loves all the little children of the world. An' now you say I shouldn't play with them just because they poor and haven't got? I'm sorry, Ms. Annie, I can't listen to you. I have to do what the Bible say."

That one I did not remember. But a number of things struck me when I read it. I was touched that the aunt I remembered as so strict and unyielding had carried that story in her head for half a century. But I was even more struck by the kid's reply. Because in those days, it was absolutely unheard of for any kid to successfully contradict *any* adult. And if it were to be done, almost certainly the only way one could even hope to get away with it was to base your defiance on a higher morality, on specific and irrefutable biblical authority. But what I do not know is whether that was guileless, simple faith on the boy's part, or whether it was a clever strategic maneuver, using her professed Christianity to score points as I would deliberately do later in life, especially when organizing in the Bible Belt South. I think it was conscious. Another case of the child being father of the man?

I also wished there was some record of old Ms. Annie's response.

In that community, any adult could and would correct or discipline your public behavior whether he or she knew your family or not. And you expected no less and were expected to meekly accept the correction.

This next incident I do absolutely remember, but it would hardly have been cherished and preserved among Tante Elaine's repertoire of stories to be brought out before strangers on appropriate occasions.

I was coming home from school with two friends. Even if they were the proverbial "bad company," which is every parent's excuse for the misdeeds of his or her little darlings, they were certainly not "barefoot and scruffy." But we were singing some vulgar rhymes and singing them loud too. The kind universally irresistible to small boys wanting to be daring and "rude." This song not only had forbidden words, but the unnatural action being described was even worse. I don't even know that I fully understood the meaning. But it was "rude." There we were bellowing out at the top of our voices:

> I know a boy with a big, roun' head
> He [unmentionable] he mother on top the bed.

Out of nowhere, an elderly lady (Ms. Annie?) loomed. We certainly had had no idea she was around. She was glaring at us, but spoke only to me. My friends fled.

"Listen to you. And you are a Carmichael too. And this is what you out here doing? Well, young man, you will soon see . . ."

And mouth pursed ominously, she stalked off. I knew trouble was ahead. My friends asked, "You know she?"

"No, I don't know she."

"But, if you don't know she . . . t'ain't no problem," they said dismissively.

"No, but she knows me, *that's* the problem."

Actually, had I known the woman, she would probably have administered a serious whupping on the spot. All adults were automatically to be respected. And later that evening when Tante Elaine came home, it was immediately clear that she already knew. Let us just say swift and summary justice was administered.

But that would not have been the kind of story with which she would have entertained a visitor.

One that she did tell often is in that ambiguous category where you can't quite decide whether you remember the event or only the story. It reemerged from Tante Elaine's storehouse during the sixties after I had begun to work on voter registration in Mississippi. Mr. Butler was much in the news at the time of the story—demonstrations, marches, detention. Also, it must have been about that time that Tante Elaine left the classroom for a clerical position at Gwendolyn's Department Store. There she became deeply involved with the trade union struggle. She was first elected shop steward, then, for many years, a vice president of the Clerical Workers Union. I did not really understand it all then, beyond a vague conviction that Mr. Butler was "brave" and firmly on "our" side against "them," whoever they might be. I certainly had not made any conscious connection between Mr. Butler's mass demonstrations and my barefoot, hungry schoolmates.

[Tante Elaine:

"When he was seven, we had an election. The child started nagging and worrying me about going to vote. I kept telling him that I wasn't going to meddle in politics, what with all the noise and contention. But would he stop?

" 'Tante Elaine,' he asked, 'isn't it true that Mr. Butler went to jail for us?'

"I told him it was so.

" 'Well, then, you have to vote for him. If he went to jail for us, now he can do even more for us.' He pleaded and pleaded.

"On election day, what you suppose the boy did? He dressed himself up in the suit with the big lapels that his parents had sent him from New York. When he went to church in that suit with his bow tie and pocket handkerchief, people used to call him Little Man.

"Then, he marched his little self right down to the polling station. It wasn't far, right on the corner of Belmont Road and Observatory Street, and declared to the returning officer:

" 'I come to vote.'

" 'You have to wait until you are twenty-one,' the man told him.

"He raced home in tears. 'Oh, Tante Elaine, that's fourteen more years. Is so long.' And would he stop complaining and harassing me? Until finally I had to get dressed and he followed me while I went down to vote."]

Tante Elaine maintains that this made her the first voter I ever registered, for, as the paper reported, "she could get no rest from her nephew with the hooded, brooding eyes and concerns that seemed too weighty for a child of seven."

School was great fun actually. Especially the journey back and forth, as one could dawdle, explore, meander, or, as we have seen, sing vulgar verses. And if one had a few coppers, there was no end to the delicacies on which one could feast. The entire business of some adult vendors, people with families, was based on the passing-schoolchildren market. I shudder to think what their profit margin must have been.

But, depending on the season, one could buy fresh tamarind or sugared tamarind balls, mangoes or poncete, a fruit known elsewhere in the English-speaking Caribbean as the June plum. There were big, red, delicately fleshed pomerakes (Otaheite apples), tangy, succulent cashew fruits (not the nuts, which required roasting and extraction), and the boiled and salted seeds of the chatine, also called breadnuts. It was advisable to limit your consumption of these. Their popular name—if no censorious adult were present—was "farting pills," because of the flatulence they were certain to induce. Or one might have tolum, a confection of grated coconut stirred with sugar and spices, or perhaps a sugar cake washed down by the milk of a young coconut. Or you could chew on sugarcane, suck on the ubiquitous mango, the list is endless. . . .

Then too you could play in the Savannah's open green spaces or walk through the Botanical Gardens. There in the gardens I seem to remember steamy greenhouses filled with orchids and ornate lily ponds where exotic, brightly hued fish darted around the lily roots. I think these immaculately maintained botanical gardens, established by royal charter all over the British Caribbean, are perhaps the only completely unambiguous good produced by colonialism.

Within these enclaves, established under the direction of the Royal Botanical Society, were gathered just about every exotic species of tropical plant to be found within the far-flung borders of the "empire on which the sun never sets."

They started with the more picturesque of native species, then ranged through what must have been hundreds of spectacular "exotics." These all bore little identifying plaques: Latin name, common name, and provenance, i.e., native to equatorial Africa, the Kenyan highlands, Egypt, Polynesia, Madagascar, Malaysia, Australia, Central America, ad infinitum. The selection seemed to cover the known tropical world. Those sonorous names of faraway places would have stimulated great flights of the imagination in even the most pedestrian of minds. To a small, inquisitive boy, they were magic.

Traces of our specifically West African origins also surfaced, though they were not identified in that way. But I now realize that the stubby palms with massive clusters of orange-colored fruit were oil nut palms from West Africa, and the little trees called *bizi* were the kola nut, which is so central in traditional African cultural practice.

Let the record show that I've attributed at least one unconditional good result to colonialism. Speak the truth and shame the devil.

Eastern Boys was a government school and so charged no fees. The physical plant was not elaborate, so as many as four different classes could be meeting in the same large space, differentiated from each other only by their own blackboards and a narrow aisle. This was not ideal, but our teachers made "of necessity a virtue."

Upon our teacher's entrance, each class would rise.

"Good mornin', teacha."

"Good morning, pupils. Please be seated."

After which there was not—could not have been without serious disruption to other classes—the slightest sound or fidgeting. Order and discipline were paramount. In that enveloping silence in which you could neither whisper nor fidget, you had to pay attention. It was the path of least resistance. If the teacher's eloquence and skill were not sufficient incentive, then sheer boredom—the absence of anything else to do—would compel attention to the lesson at hand. So whether you wanted to or not, you learned, even if only in self-defense to have the time pass more quickly.

Once we'd meandered and munched our way home, we'd change out of our school clothes and play football, cricket, or some other game with the boys in the neighborhood. This was usually in the street outside my house's gate. One by one the aunts would return from their jobs. When Tante Louise came in, we greeted her and continued playing. When Mummy Olga came, the same thing. But, soon as Tante Elaine broached the corner, *whoosh,* we'd fly up to the porch and be bent over our homework before she reached the gate. That evening after supper she'd check our homework. Austin and I had no choice. We were regularly expected to place within the top three of our class, and for the most part, we did.

I'd give British colonialism a good mark for the educational system except for one thing. I can now see the extent to which it was colonial: the Eurocentricism, the cultural chauvinism, the undisguised, brazen "civi-lizing" mission of converting we heathen if not into English gentlemen, then at least into dutiful colonial subjects. To this end the reading books we were issued were a sho-nuff trip. Poems about *daffodils, skylarks, deserted villages, wintry landscapes,* flora and fauna never dreamt of in the tropics.

More blatant was the omnipresence of patriotic, heroic, vaguely mar-tial odes celebrating the glories of empire-building.

"The boy stood on the burning deck" or that curious celebration of military ineptitude and collective suicide, "The Charge of the Light Brigade," viz:

> Cannon to right of them,
> Cannon to left of them . . .
> Rode the six hundred.

Or "The Burial of Sir John Moore at Coronna":

> Slowly and sadly we laid him down,
> From the field of his fame fresh and gory.

Or, of course, that classic of colonial fidelity, "Gunga Din." Gimme an ever-loving break. But at least our histories did not begin like the one issued to young Africans in Guinea and Senegal: "Our ancestors, the Gauls . . ." At least we learned discipline and good study habits.

Actually, the colonialism was so all-enveloping and pervasive that as a child one did not notice it. At the lower levels of the civil service, the only ones we were likely to encounter, the functionaries—policemen, teachers, nurses, bus drivers, sanitary inspectors—were all local folk. The expatriate community—the governor, High Court magistrates, commanders of security forces, and various technical managers and executives—were quite remote. So too the relatively small population of local whites, the descendants of landed gentry, slaveowners, and their agents. So these people were not really a presence in our lives. One might say we moved in somewhat different circles. In fact, I can remember but three instances when the white presence made any impression on my conscious experience.

Once when I was very small, Mummy Olga took me to play in the Savannah. Under the protective eye of my gentle, kindhearted aunt I was playing on the lawn. A policeman ordered me rather roughly off the grass. I think I was just about setting my face to cry when my sweet-natured aunt turned tigress. She flew in the cop's face, arms akimbo.

"You don't see that li'l white boy over there on the grass? Why you don't go chase him? Or is it only black people's children you got strength for? Why ain't you go chase that one, eh?"

The cop quailed and beat as dignified a retreat as he was able. I hadn't even noticed the other little boy before my aunt's outburst. I never forgot that incident.

Later, when I went to Tranquillity Boys' Intermediate School, I found a scattering of expatriate boys. They kind of knew their place, though, because the school leaders, the best athletes and the best students, seemed always to be Trinidadian—African, East Indian, or Chinese.

One day, however, we were reading and there was a reference to snow. Our teacher, who was local African, began to explain and describe it when he was interrupted by an English boy, who stopped him and explained exactly what snow was. Interrupting *and* correcting a teacher was unheard of. After class there was an excited discussion among us. Some boys were saying that our teacher had been exposed in his stupidity. My position was that it was not a question of our teacher being stupid. He, never having been to England, should not be expected to know as much about snow as someone born there. What was so special about snow that our teacher should be expected to know it? What could we in Trinidad be expected to know about snow anyway? Why was it even in our book? Do English schoolbooks teach about Trinidad? I remember taking this position rather fiercely, largely because in some vague, unarticulated way I felt the humiliation of our teacher as an insult to us all.

Apart from those two incidents, the annual obligatory Empire Day observances, and one visit by a member of the "royal" family, Princess Margaret, colonialism in Trinidad was everywhere present but rarely obvious to a kid.

Empire Day was a head trip. This judgment is by no means retrospective; even then we found it a little odd, kind of *artificial*, and pointless.

Once annually, what seemed like all the schoolchildren of the city would be assembled on the Savannah, there to sing "Rule Britannia,"

"The British Grenadiers," "God Save the Queen," and other such uplifting compositions of Anglophiliac excess. After which we were addressed briefly and perfunctorily by the governor or some other British dignitary. An utter nonevent so far as I and my friends were concerned.

Now the visit of Her Royal Highness Princess Margaret was a different story. I was about ten, and for weeks that was all you could hear, in school, in church, on the radio, in the newspapers, and in the marketplace. "Princess Margaret is coming. Royal visit! A national honor. Historic event. The country must put its best foot forward."

So of course I was prepared, if I could figure out which one it was, to put my "best foot" forward too. And from all the hype one could not avoid a growing anticipation. We children—alas, the crimes against the young—were again enlisted. We were each given a tiny Union Jack and attired as though for church. We lined the route, where we were promised a good look at the "princess." So, of course, the noble wench is late. We children stood for some four hours in the hot sun. At first it was sun hot, but then came a tropical deluge that drenched us thoroughly. No princess. After which the sun pops out and dries us out again. No Princess. After about another hour, the long-awaited moment. A couple of police outriders with some kind of flags streaming above their motorbikes. A ripple of whispered excitement, "Princess coming, princess coming," moves along the line of kids. We start waving the small Union Jacks. We all perk up. At last a look at this royal paragon. Maybe she'll smile at us and wave. Finally this weird covered carriage with drawn curtains rolls on by. That was it.

The response was unanimous: "What were we standing there for if we didn't even get to see her?" And obviously *she* did not want even to look at *us*.

As I said, the European presence was, at least for me, distant and remote.

Not so the East Indian community though. They were very much a presence in my youth. After the abolition of slavery in the Empire in 1838, the sugar planters in the West Indies and South Africa were hardest hit. In both places the importation of labor from the Indian subcontinent to replace the Africans in the cane fields began in earnest.

In Trinidad, the recruitment of these indentured workers, whom the planters referred to as "coolie" labor (a term we were forbidden to use in our house), continued until the numbers of Africans and Indians reached parity. My impression is that, with the exception of a few demagogic bigots on both sides (V. S. and Shiva Naipaul come to mind), the relationship between these two very different peoples was reasonably civil and tolerant.

At about seven or eight I was playing with a group of boys in the street. An old, bearded, and turbaned Indian man passed by.

"Look at that ol' coolie man," someone shouted, and we laughed.

"Shame on you, boys." Glowering down on us was a large, disapproving African woman. "Don't call them coolies. You know they don't like that."

"Then what we to call them, ma'am?" someone asked, genuinely perplexed.

"They are East Indians. That is what they call themselves. And when you see an old man like him, say, '*Salaam babu.*' That's how his people call him." I could hardly wait to see another elderly Indian to test this novel salutation.

The Indians made a profound impression on me. At this time, being the more recent arrivals, they frequently wore their national dress, spoke their national languages, and maintained their religious faith and practice. Periodically, they would have colorful religious festivals and processions. I think in addition to the Hindus, some were Moslem, because one such festival seems to have been the Shiite festival of Hussein and Hassan.

I used to look at their colorful dress and say, "Wow. India must really be beautiful because all the people in India must be dressed like this." I thought we Africans suffered in comparison. Since we wore only Western clothes, were mostly Christian, and spoke only English, I for a long time considered slavery and the ruthlessness of oppression and imperialism to have seriously trampled on, even stamped out, our original culture. Indeed, I can remember once answering a question about African culture in Trinidad to the effect that the only element I'd experienced was those meetings at Ms. Baines's, which I thought "vaguely African."

Of course now I know better. I now understand how thoroughly "African" the base of Trinidadian popular culture is. And the extent to which, instead of dissipating away, African culture has informed, indeed to an extent colonized, the European and Indian cultures in Trinidad.

In the late sixties, on a visit to England, I can remember once meeting Sam Selvon (peace be unto him), the distinguished Trinidadian comic novelist of Indian descent. An African brother born in Jamaica greeted him:

"Aha, a writer, huh? So you must be one of that Naipaul gang, eh?"

"Oh, God, boy," he wailed. "I don' business with them boys, eh? I *creolize*, boy. I completely *creolize*. No, man, doan say that."

We just laughed and hugged him.

"We just yanking your chain, bro. We know your work and we know you."

"Yeah, man. But don't make them kina joke, *oui*? I don't know what wrong with those two, eh?"

Selvon's comic masterpiece, *The Lonely Londoners,* chronicles the mis-adventures of the Pan-African emigrant community in postwar London. It is a true classic of the Pan-African spirit. Its rich cast includes working-class characters from Trinidad, Jamaica, Guyana, all parts of the Caribbean, the countries of British colonial Africa, and the Indian sub-continent all thrown together in close alliance in the alien culture and cli-mate of London. Bro Selvon, ostensibly a "Trinidadian Indian," displays in his work not only comic genius but a remarkable spirit of Pan-African brotherhood.

Ironically enough, my experience of Africa and the American South has enabled me to recognize the extent to which the Trinidad of my youth was very much one of those deceptive creolized cultures in which "Europe rules but Africa governs." And certainly in the tonalities and styles of speech, our music, the cuisine, the style and sensibility of popular culture, and the rhythms of daily family and community life, it was Africa that gov-erned there. Or at least did when I was a child.

My mistake as a youth with regard to the culture is easy to understand. In school, we learned about snow, daffodils, and skylarks. I had no ref-erences by which to properly understand, identify, or analyze the culture that was all around me. So much all around us, in fact, that we never rec-ognized it as culture. (The distinctive Indian dress was *culture.*) What we were looking at all around us was simply what folks did naturally. We took it for granted. Carnival and the steel band phenomenon is an excellent case in point.

As I said, the Casa Blanca steel band was a natural and constant part of my earliest environment, like the moon or the sun. Some things are simply accepted and never really examined. And of course, it was not a fit subject for discussion in school.

It took me, therefore, a long time to realize just how unique an act of creative genius *and* what an aggressive and subversive act of African cul-tural resistance those steel bands actually represented.

It is quite a story. Sometime in the late 1930s, the government in another of its persistent and futile attempts to suppress African cultural survivals, decided that the colony would more easily be governable if drums and other traditional musical instruments were outlawed. The colonials must have sensed, and correctly, the importance of music in the cultural independence and political resistance of the African masses. I would, of course, encounter this phenomenon again in the American South. But at least the George Wallaces and Ross Barnetts of that world never tried to outlaw our spirituals and freedom songs. Though I'm sure they must often have wished that they could have.

So in Trinidad by legislative fiat an African could be jailed for posses-sion of drums and other musical instruments? Not a gun, not a grenade, or some dynamite, but a *drum*? I have often tried, and failed, to visualize the campaign to enforce that law. In implementation of this policy, did armed police and soldiers—the governor's minions—surround African communities and conduct house-to-house searches? And for what, those threats to public order, drums, tambourines, maracas, and marimbas? Did they kick down the doors to shacks with guns drawn: "Freeze. You're under arrest. Seize that drum!"

So, suddenly deprived of their traditional instruments of musical expression, Africans resorted to their creativity and whatever materials lay to hand. In this case, the fifty-five-gallon steel drums used to store oil at the refinery.

These they took and cut to varying depths. Say nine inches down for an alto pan, two feet deep for a tenor pan, and twice that for a bass. Then on the top they would heat and pound out a number of raised areas, each of which when struck would produce a precise musical note of a certain pitch. Over the years the brothers experimented with ways to refine the basic instruments and to create others. The result is what is today known the world over as the Trinidad steel band: an ensemble of musical instruments of great range and flexibility, capable of playing not only calypso and other forms of local popular music, but the most complex and demanding of jazz compositions or any form from the European classical tradition you care to name. A sound immediately recognizable in the distinctive, liquid purity of tones and the fluency of its melodic lines.

Hey, as you may have noticed, I can't pretend to be an ethnomusicologist. I'm a revolutionary. But that description should give you a fairly accurate sense of the accomplishment represented by the creation of the steel bands. And remember, this unique innovation and the musical tradition it evolved into came directly out of the determined and indomitable will of Trinidad's Africans to resist colonization and to maintain their culture.

The music of the steel bands became an integral part of carnival and Trinidad's popular music. Carnival proper takes place over the four days immediately preceding Ash Wednesday, which begins the forty austere days of Lent. This explosion of music, spectacle, and fervent celebration before the dour solemnity of Lent is common to many Catholic cultures, especially the Latin ones.

It comes the Saturday, Sunday, Monday, and Tuesday before Lent, but the bands will have been rehearsing and composing all year. The masquerade troupes will have started constructing their elaborate and fantastical costumes from the day after Christmas. But many a poor worker will have been saving pennies all year for carnival costume in which to "play Mas'."

The origins of this giant communal *fête* are interesting. It followed pretty much the same pattern in those "creolized" societies where powerful currents from Europe and Africa mingled and combined—New Orleans, Brazil, and Trinidad. In all these places during slavery, elements of European Catholic ritual and spectacle merged with similar aspects of African religious cultures. Specifically, these were the colorful and spectacular rituals of the saint's day parades of Latin Catholic culture, the frenzied pre-Lenten or spring festivals of pagan Europe merging with the masked ancestral dances or masquerades of West African cultures, to evolve into carnival in Rio or in the New Orleans Mardi Gras. The quality of the music, the dance, and the elaborate, colorful masked dancers are clearly African in origin: "Europe ruled but Africa governed."

As I recall, the excitement and anticipation began to build in January with the launching of the Mas' camps. In these camps the construction of the floats and costumes for the Grande Marche took place. As the time approached, people—our family included—would stroll from camp to camp previewing the models and drawings of the costumes under construction. We would argue over our favorites to win the grand prize. Then the bands would begin to refine and rehearse their musical routines composed for the contest called Panorama. Today, so I'm told, the steel bands come lavishly attired and equipped courtesy of their multinational corporate sponsors, the marriages of capitalism and local culture. The Shell Oil Invaders and Mobil Corp's Casa Blanca? Somehow it doesn't ring quite right, given the militant history out of which the bands evolved. All motion is not necessarily progress.

Around mid-February, the calypso tents would go up at different venues around the city. In those days some really were giant circus tents. In the tents in nightly concerts, aspiring calypsonians would show off and test out their repertoires for the big contest. Calypsonians are not merely performers. They are poets, satirists, social critics, musical composers, as well as singers. Very much in the tradition of the African griot and tale-teller. In fact, one important category of carnival competition is extemporaneous composition. Each contestant is given a subject or theme around which to compose a calypso. On the spot, he is expected to create the words and music and to sing his instantly created calypso before a very critical audience.

This was Tante Elaine's favorite part of carnival. But we children never got to go to the calypso tents because the scandalous, irreverent, antiestablishment tradition of the form was very much still in evidence at that time.

One year, the governor had repeatedly threatened to cancel carnival or, as the people called it, Mas'. This naturally provoked everyone, especially the calypsonians. One night, a singer strode to the front of the tent and put up a detailed—anatomically correct—picture of a large jackass behind the stage. The picture of the animal excited considerable interest. What in Hades was a *donkey* doing in the calypso tent? Without explanation the brother launched into a rollicking song, the chorus of which went:

> De governor say no Mas'?
> Tell de governor he moddah's . . .

And he pointed to the animal as the audience shouted out the obvious rhyme. And:

> De governor say no Mas'?
> Tell de governor to haul he . . .

And he pointed at the animal and the audience, laughing, completed the line.

I have no idea whether that song won that year, but it certainly is the performance that all Port of Spain was laughing about and singing that week. No more was heard from that particular representative of the queen about banning Mas'.

Carnival proper began on the Saturday with Panorama, the daylong shoot-out, so to say, the mother of all steel band battles. The contest determined the year's champion and, I think, the order of march in the big parade, or Grande Marche.

Dimanche Gras, or "Big Sunday," saw the judging of the costumes of the troupes of dancing masqueraders and the crowning of the calypso king, as I recall.

Before sunup on Monday was *J'Ouvert* (day opening), the beginning of masquerade activity. This was the time reserved for Ol' Mas', the rowdy, raunchy, orgiastic element of carnival (as distinct from Pretty Mas'). The audience would be chased, daubed with mud in Mud Mas', and all kinds of madness and excess would take place. Ol' Mas' was not at all respectable. It was the time when revelers who'd been up all the previous night drinking would blow off steam. It's bacchanal, *oui,* bacchanal. Being as young as I was, I know *J'Ouvert* only from the shocked descriptions of my elders' conversations.

But the finale, or Mardi Gras (Fat Tuesday), was the family's. We would take benches and chairs to our friend Mrs. Brito's house. She conveniently lived on Charlotte Street, opposite the Rosary Catholic School, near to the entrance where the Grande Marche entered the Savannah. It was a perfect vantage point from which to view, comment on, and judge the entire parade. Almost daylong, with the steel bands, spectacular masquerade troupes, the calypsonians, and with masked individuals and groups of supporters dancing behind them.

We were too young to "play Mas'," and as the aunts pointed out, by not being in the parade we got to see everything much better anyway.

Unfortunately, I left Trinidad before I could assimilate and process all this. I've placed it all here in much more of a context than I had at the time. For what I had while I was there were simply experiences—impressions and sensations—which I'd been absorbing through my senses and by osmosis. I left at the age where I was just beginning to understand it all, but my impressions are indelible.

Trinidad was beautiful to me. It was love, it was security, it was community and protection. And my recollection of my childhood there is happy. Good times, secure times, in which I was totally at ease. I was free even as a young boy to roam the neighborhood with no restraints. We could walk around the Botanical Gardens, we could go to the Savannah. At night, when the moon was bright, all the lights would be turned out and we children would play in the moonlit garden. There was music, there was vibrancy, there was color, there was dynamism. I can honestly say that, as a young boy in Trinidad, I do not think I ever felt conscious of lacking anything.

Because I didn't know, or didn't at least really understand, the impact of belonging to a colonial subject people, I would not have changed Trinidad at all. I would have left it just the way it was.

CHAPTER III

A Tale of Two Cities

The letters are large, carefully rounded, a child's hand: *On January 16, 1952, my grandmother Mrs. Cecilia Harris Carmichael died. She was a blessed soul.*

The sentences are from a document my cousin Austin has sent to help anchor my memories to precise dates. It is a "family history" that his ten-year-old daughter, Petagay, compiled for a sixth-grade assignment. (Now an attractive and vivacious young woman, Petagay is a formidably dreaded, beginning literature teacher whose cheery visits to her ailing uncle never fail to make me smile. She bounces in full of laughter, high spirits, ideas, and excited talk of James Baldwin, William Shakespeare, Walter Rodney, and Toni Morrison. Petagay's upbeat presence and bubbling intellectual excitement are always a pleasure.)

She was a blessed soul, the little girl had written. That phrase leaps out in its childlike directness and simplicity. Also because the rest of the text is straight narrative, the milestones of family: names, places, dates, marriages, births, and deaths. That is the only editorial judgment to be found: *She was a blessed soul.* Why, I wonder, or how had our young historian been so taken with that language? Having been too young to have known her grandmother, she could only have picked it up from the oral tradition of her elders.

In any event Austin's purpose is served. The child Peta has given me the precise date of my departure for America—June 1952—six months after my grandmother's death.

The death was not nearly as traumatic for us children as it might have been. It was indeed our first encounter with the death of someone real close. However, we took our cue from the adults around us, who seemed to accept it with a stoic fatalism. She was old, much loved, and had led an exemplary life. Now she had gone peaceably to her Savior. His will be done.

Perhaps we were too young for the finality of it all to really dawn on us. Perhaps also we were distracted at the excitement of again actually seeing our father, who was coming home to bury his mother.

But even that reunion was not as dramatic—in the event it was quite anticlimactic—as it might have been. True, my father had left when I was five and had been gone six years, but I can remember no separation anxiety on our part. For one thing, the household in which we were left had been very nurturing. For another, my father had never been truly absent. We had pictures so we knew what he looked like. And even the house, the very walls around us, spoke eloquently and materially of his presence. As did the oral tradition: the neighbors' inquiries and recollections; the grandmother's and aunts' stories. And too there were our parents' letters filled with messages and admonitions, and the regular shipments of clothes, toys, books, and exotic "American" candies. All of which now contributed to our heightened anticipation and growing excitement for my father's return.

One by one the days went by. Finally, though, the funeral had to be held without him. Then it was said our father would be home the following day. Dutifully we fought off sleep deep into the night. When we could no longer keep our eyes open, we were sent off to bed. And when we awoke the next morning, our father was in the house. It seemed so natural, and he so familiar, it was simply as though he had never been gone from among us.

By the time his visit was over, it had all been settled. At the end of the school year, Mummy Olga would bring Umilta, me, and baby Lynette— at six years old, she was no baby—to our parents in New York. Of course, it would be an abrupt change from everything we had known, but we would have six months to get accustomed to the idea.

The ostensible reason for this momentous change—the one given to us anyway—was that Grandma's death had left a vacuum in child care and proper supervision in the household.

On reflection, though, I am not entirely certain that this was the only or even the main reason. I think it entirely more likely that our parents— and particularly my mother—wanted the family united, all her children around her. Of course, we were children and were not consulted on our preferences.

How did I really feel about so abruptly leaving the home, school, friends, community, in fact everything that I had known? There had to have been ambivalence, but I can honestly say that I remember no great anxiety. In any case, it was a fait accompli. We were going. To America and our parents, and particularly to my mother, who, for some reason, had not been as much of a presence in the aunts' daily conversation as had been my father. So I had, of course, a greater curiosity there. What would living with my real mother be like? I was, of course, not then familiar with the term *nuclear family*. The whole concept as defined in the West would have been contrary to the reality of the African extended family that I'd experienced at home or observed in the community. But that is what we Carmichaels were going to be now, a nuclear family.

I'm sure we must have heard in the general discussion a constant refrain about what a big, rich, "modern" country America was. How *lucky* we children were to be going there. Then too there was the considerable excitement of actually getting to fly in a real airplane.

"Boy, Stokely, you be lucky, *oui*!" was the verdict of my school friends, tinged, I realized, with no little envy. So naturally, I felt lucky. Lucky except for one thing, the wrenching prospect of being parted from Austin. Austin had been part of everything I had known from the time I first knew myself: big brother, playmate, mentor, playground protector, everything. We talked earnestly about our pending separation. Of course, we would miss each other. But, we consoled ourselves that it would not, indeed could not, be anything permanent. He'd come to New York and I'd return to Trinidad regularly. Hah!

On summer vacations we'd be together again. Nothing would change. Part of the time in New York, the rest in Trinidad. Summers would be perfect. That, however, was not in the cards or the family finances, and it would be many, many years before we were to meet again. But, neither geography, distance, or the prohibitive cost of travel could erode that initial closeness. Today, Austin remains not only a most trusted friend and confidant, but my brother in the truest sense of that word.

But what, I wondered, was America really like? The country I'd seen in the movies seemed very different from Trinidad. For one thing, with the exception of the occasional and doomed "redskins" in the westerns, all American people seemed to be white. And, as my father would occasionally later grumble after yet another provocation from the natives, "Boy, back home, if you went only by the movies, you'd believe this country didn't have no ugly people in it at all."

Much effort was expended in persuading us of our good fortune: America, in this account, was bigger, better, richer. It had *opportunity*, better schools, better houses, better clothes, better everything. Which was, of course, difficult to actually imagine. Finally, I concluded that America was exactly like Trinidad only much, much larger. Bigger and therefore better everything: cars, rivers, beaches, botanical gardens, carnivals, schools, everything. Everything just like Trinidad, only in the American version, new and improved. And you must remember since I had had absolutely no complaints about the original, the grander version must be heaven, straight?

Finally the big day. A rapid blur of memories. I remember most distinctly how surprisingly quickly the excitement of actually flying dissipated. The anticipation had built almost unendurably before we finally boarded the aircraft. Flying through the air had to be the most unimaginably beautiful feeling. I tried to imagine how thrilling the sensation: the height, the lift, the thrust, the soaring in the clouds, the speed, the incredible freedom of movement. A nervous anticipation spiced by a little fear.

Then we were all strapped in and I could hear the sound of the motors and feel the plane moving, first slowly, even ponderously, then faster and faster. The roar turned into a howl and the landscape outside the window rushed by. That was exciting.

"We flying now, Mummy Olga? Mummy Olga?" But Mummy Olga had her eyes tightly closed and might have been praying.

Then the engine's howl settled into a comfortable drone and suddenly all sensation of speed and even motion disappeared. Only a constant slight vibration from the propellers, an occasional side-to-side rocking, or a sudden lift or dip of the cabin told us that we were in motion. Soon my sisters were asleep. That did not seem right. I fought it. "Boy, you flyin'. You ain't be wasting it with no sleep." But the cabin was cramped. The journey seemed interminable. There was little to do. Sleep had its way. I think we changed planes once, perhaps twice. And we slept some more. Ho hum. How easily we humans become jaded.

They announce that we are landing at La Guardia Airport. I can see rows of yellow lights on the ground. In the distance, shimmering lights outline the New York skyline at night. Magical. Fantastic. Like carnival. Wow. New York. A new life. Our parents. Our mother will be waiting. Everyone is suddenly wide, tingly awake.

It really was true. New York was big. It was a cavernous building brightly lit even at three o'clock in the morning. A long, endless corridor stretched ahead of us. The line of people walked fast. After we got our luggage—from another huge room—we were in an even bigger one. At one end was a line of tall desks from which ropes extended forming corridors along which people carrying luggage formed lines.

Mummy Olga reached the desk, answered questions, showed documents. The white man smiled at the children. "Welcome to New York!"

Laden with luggage, we walked into another room, and thus began my American journey.

"Look for them now," Mummy Olga said. "Look for your parents. They be here to meet we, yes."

A small mass of people were lined up along the gate toward which we were headed. My eyes searched the huddle.

"Oh, Lawd, look see. See Dolphus and dem over dey."

Mummy Olga pointed toward an area of the crowd that seemed to be moving. A small group were waving handkerchiefs and seemed to be bouncing up and down. As we drew closer, I could see that most of the jumping was being done by a smartly dressed, stylishly pretty lady in a blue suit and two little girls. I recognized my sisters born in America; they had visited us in Trinidad. Soon my mother was hugging all three of us at the same time, with little Janeth and Judith squeezing in just a-squealing and a-hugging whatever they could reach, knees, bellies, whatever. There was laughing, crying, hugging, and everyone talking at the same time. Kisses flew around the group indiscriminately. Passing travelers turned their heads and smiled indulgently as they went by. Those Africans certainly are an expressive people.

The drive home seemed almost as long as the plane ride. Up close, the city seemed less magical. The streets all seemed indistinguishable. The buildings, all brick or stone, seemed drab and undifferentiated. One could easily get lost. It all looked the same and it went on and on and on.

One image was unforgettable. We must have been somewhere in Queens, on a long overpass over a thruway. In Trinidad, in my experience, cars rarely exceeded forty miles per hour. Suddenly, we were on this overpass and I looked down at a line of headlights just hurtling along out of the darkness. I mean they were just flying toward us. One behind the other and dangerously close for the incredibly high, reckless speed at which they were moving. It was amazing, unreal. These bright lights came zooming toward the overpass and disappeared underneath us with a sound like zap, zap, zap, marking their furious passage. It was more than a little frightening.

It seemed demented, suicidal, as if they were rushing to their doom. Wow. Did *all* cars in New York always go so fast? Were they racing cars? At this time of night? During our brief moment on the overpass, Umilta had seen it too. We exchanged a long, wordless glance, our eyes wide with wonder.

After a long ride, the car turns into a wide street, deserted at that hour. It stops before a towering building of brick or concrete.

"Well, this is it," my father says. "This where we living."

I look at 861 Stebbins Avenue in the South Bronx. This huge building is our home. Wow. America *really* must be rich. But something didn't quite add up. Something about it didn't look like a *home*. A place where people really lived.

"You mean," I ask him, "that this *whole* big house is for us?" The adults find that funny.

"No, Son," my mother explains. "Lots of families live here. We just have an apartment."

Well, that will be nice, I think. An *apart ment*. That sounds impressive, modern. Big as the building is, *a part* should be more than enough for us. All right!

When we got to the third floor, I could not believe it. There was one bedroom. This *apart ment* . . . three rooms in all.

"What," I thought, "you mean all of us going to live in this one little place?" But I kept my peace. Three rooms for eight of us. The four from

Trinidad, my parents, and my two sisters Janeth and Judith, who had been born in America. In Trinidad, Austin and I had our own little room up front. Now I would be sleeping on a couch in the living room. And, of course, it seemed even more cramped and disappointing after the grand expectations of American scale and wealth that had been conjured up by all the talk.

By the next morning, my curiosity and a measure of optimism had returned. From the break of day or even earlier, I had been awakened by street sounds—metallic urban sounds—car horns, engines of buses, trucks, the banging of forklifts, garbage cans, and what have you, such as were never heard in the Belmont I had left. By the time the household was stirring, I was dressed and eager to explore my new world. I asked my mother.

"Say what *explore*? Stokely, now this ain't Belmont, y' know. This the Bronx, New York. You can't go down there by yourself. You be so lost, boy. You can go with me when I go to the store. So you can learn the neighborhood."

Of all the early American impressions, of all the new information to be assimilated, by far the most important discoveries concerned my mother. As I've said, she was, in my mind, much more of a mystery than my father. So I was naturally filled with an excited curiosity about this smallish lady I was now meeting. She was pretty, petite, stylish in dress, and warmly and spontaneously affectionate in spirit, but with a no-nonsense decisiveness in her manner. I discovered right quick that she was also fiercely passionate in her convictions (even if not always right), with a determined, can-do optimism.

Mabel Charles Carmichael would become—and remain—a major influence in the lives of me and my sisters. This little dynamo of a woman was the stable moral presence, the fixed center around which the domestic life of this migrant African family revolved.

My father would have to work outside the home, and on occasion, outside the country, to support us. My mother worked at home to nurture, develop, and direct us. She was always there to praise or scold, admonish or encourage, or to fearlessly defend as the occasion demanded. We children quickly learned to see her as tireless, omnipresent, and all-seeing, the ever vigilant enforcer of order and family standards, whose displeasure was to be avoided at all costs. With Mother, the rules were always clear, expectations understood, her voice unquestioned, and justice impartial and swift.

Also it was my mother, if you remember, who was the American connection. Was it not she whom my father had followed here? And because she was largely responsible for our presence here, she had a strong personal investment in ensuring that the move be a success. So she was at some pains always to see only the best in things American, in a word, to wrap herself in conventional immigrant optimism. This was her impulse, save when it came to any kind of racist provocation touching her husband or her children. Then May Charles tolerated no illusions nor made any allowances. Then my mother would not only accept confrontation, she would seek it out. Hunt it down. Yes, she would.

"Neighborhood," indeed. For us children, the neighborhood consisted effectively of a few square yards of concrete sidewalk outside the building, for many clear limits were in force. We were told in no uncertain terms what these limits were. We could not play beyond the width of our building. We could not cross the street. On no account were we even to venture *into* the street.

Now I can see how carefully my parents had planned the timing of our move. But apparently there had been one contingency they either had not anticipated or could do nothing about.

See, Grandma Cecilia had died in January, the middle of the Trinidad school year and the New York winter. It was logical to wait until June to move us, when school would be over and the New York weather would have warmed up. Also, that way we children would have a summer to adjust to life in the new environment before braving the vicissitudes of the American school system.

But it also meant that, after the relative freedom of our Belmont neighborhood, we faced a long New York summer in a cramped, stuffy apartment where there was no "outside" in any real sense of that word. And the sidewalks of the South Bronx, though not as dangerous in 1952 as they would subsequently become, were also not as friendly and forgiving as the community ambience to which I was accustomed.

Now, in all the newness and strangeness of America, my first truly poignant, even disorienting discovery was unexpected. It had to do with, of all things, the moon. No kidding now, the moon.

As young children in Trinidad, we had looked forward to the full moon. We took it for granted, but I was soon to recognize how much it had meant. Under the brightness of our big tropical moon we had played gleefully in the transformed landscape of the garden and neighborhood streets. On Stebbins Avenue, where we now lived, I discovered that you could not see the moon. No moon at all. Imagine, no moon at all. That was inconceivable, most shocking and distressing. To me, this messed with the fundamental nature of the universe, the very heart and texture of reality itself. No *moon*? And along with that absence went the loss of the distant pulsings of Casa Blanca's rhythms on the night wind.

Whoi yoi, whoi yoi, whoi yoi. "*How can you sing King Alpha's song in a strange land . . . ?*"

Our restricted movement was another real shock. *Trauma* might not be too heavy a word, after the near complete freedom and security I had enjoyed on the island. The freedom to roam the community, to walk in the gardens and the Savannah, confident in the protection of every adult, a surrogate parent. Not to say that there was no sense of community in the Bronx, but it was a different kind of community. It had a different style and feel.

That first summer I spent as much time as I could "outside," which is to say, hanging out on my little square of sidewalk bounded on one side by the front of 861, on the other by the street, and at its ends by the sides of our building. Of course, little "playing" was possible there, so I mostly just hung out. I stood, looked, listened, and saw and heard a great deal. If Muhammad cannot go to the mountain . . . the mountain sure nuff came. . . . I saw fights, raucous squabbles and arguments, and even some petty crime. People seemed to have lots of indiscipline and what is now called attitude. But I heard no gunshots nor saw any gunplay. Those, mercifully, were still far in the future. There was great energy, but it seemed a brash, impersonal kind of undisciplined energy.

I had no language for "crowded ghetto," but that, of course, was what it was. And if I had been dismayed by the ratio of space to numbers of people in our apartment, I quickly learned that many of my parents' friends in the extended family were even more crowded than we, the classic immigrant reality. Though we Africans from the Caribbean seemed greatly outnumbered by the Africans born in America, I have come to recognize that the neighborhood was not so much a settled "community" as it was the confluence of two volatile streams of recent arrivals: the "foreigners" coming from the cane fields of the islands; the "Americans" coming from the cotton fields and small holdings of the rural South. Nearly all of them were first-generation immigrants valiantly trying to come to terms with a concrete urban vastness equally alien to both.

It was not as if the two groups were at each other's throats. Far from it. Beneath differences of style and accent, there indeed was a "community" of tolerance, respect, and the reality of concrete circumstances common to all. We were all black, poor, and recently arrived. There were cases of cooperation, friendship, and the kinship of shared experience. All in all, more united us than divided us. But simply, the adjustment was not easy for either group, and the overarching economic environment was not hospitable, fair, or particularly welcoming.

One morning I was looking on in astonishment as an older brother stole a crate of sodas from a delivery truck while the driver was inside servicing the machines. My expression must have reflected my amazement for I had never seen anything quite so brazen. As he ran past, the brother growled something at me. It sounded like:

"Whatcha lookin' at, fool. Want me to go upside yo nappy head?" Or

51

words to that effect. I couldn't understand exactly what he said. But from his tone, his meaning was unmistakable. In the interest of my health, I should mind my own cotton-pickin' business. And not even *look* at him?

So in the street . . . new attitudes, cultural styles, and rhythms, a new language, would confront me, a lot of disorder and indiscipline. These striking differences notwithstanding—they were, I sensed, differences of style and attitude, not of substance—I saw that more united than divided the two streams.

One real and effective force came from outside both emigrant African communities and was driven by a different engine, value, and vision. A new technology, instantly available if not omnipresent, was intensely fascinating. Seductive even. Television.

Now, we in Trinidad were not unfamiliar with the moving images, sounds, and counterreality of the audiovisual medium. In Trinidad we did, of course, have what our colonial mentors called "the cinema." However, the fare, being usually of British origin, was clearly no reflection of our reality or experience. Which no doubt is why we did not tend to "identify" with the images on-screen, which in any case were almost all white. Also, going to the cinemas, going *out* to the cinemas, was very much a special treat—a very occasional Saturday-morning kind of treat—which further emphasized its exotic, alien, and fantastic nature.

Television had yet to make an appearance there, so the reality of the box as a standard household fixture was to me, if not inconceivable, at least a great novelty. And in the children-packed South Bronx apartment, the magic of television was very present. What an incredible luxury it seemed at first: our own miniature cinema at home—instantly available. Given the long summer days, the limited options, and intimidating prospect of the streets, we ended up watching it a lot. It was television and more television.

And in particular that fall there was *Superman*. I had been familiar with Batman and Robin, who, of course, did not fly. But Superman, the man of steel, was, I think, on the tube nearly every afternoon. And he, or rather his flying, fascinated and entranced me.

Now I was not really a kid. I was eleven years old and nobody had *evuh* called me stupid. So this is patently not about my suggestibility or lack of good sense. It might be about constraint, boredom, and restriction of movement, coupled with too graphic an imagination. And it certainly is about the insidious, reality-distorting power even of that infant medium. We are not talking here about any sophisticated, digital megascreen in living color and surround sound. No cyberspace virtual reality. We are talking real primitive here: a simple twelve-inch, black-and-white box with a flickering screen and uncertain reception. And of course it was free of the gratuitous, egregious, technologically enhanced, special-effect-graphic images of violence ceaselessly pounded into the consciousness of today's youth.

If you are from working-class New York, then you know that many of these old apartment buildings are laid out on the principle of a hollow square. The front of each apartment facing out and the rear facing inward and forming with the other side of the building a kind of enclosed, square courtyard. Pulley-strung clotheslines ran across this courtyard from side to side. These were weather-frayed lengths of sash cord often worn so fragile that too wet a wash could bring them down.

One afternoon while my mother and Umilta were at the market, *Superman* came on. What I did next was certainly not from a sudden burst of inspiration. I had to have been cherishing and embellishing in my imagination for some time an image of the beautiful, perfect freedom of flight. Anyway, I draped a red bath towel around my neck, cape-style. I opened the kitchen window, climbed on the window ledge and placed my hand on the clothesline. I could see myself diving forward and gracefully gliding over to the opposite apartment propelled by the momentum of my dive as the pulley "flew" me across. I must have hesitated briefly to admire this image in my mind, because then a face appeared at the window opposite.

"Stokely, child. What you doing out there?" she cried.

"Oh, hi, Tante Jo. Wait there. I'm gonna fly over to you like Superman."

"No, Stokely," she said sharply. Then her voice became very calm. "I need you to do something for me, please, before you fly like Superman, okay, honey? Now go back in the kitchen, please."

Of course as an obedient and helpful child from the Caribbean, I immediately went back in. As soon as that lady saw that I was away from the ledge and my feet were firmly on the floor, she went off. I mean she just started to scream, Jack.

"My Lord, child. Are you crazy? But what a nearly distress on us here today, eh? You must be crazy, boy. How could you be so stupid? Best you take that silly cape off and go sit down. Wait till your mom gets back!"— etc., etc. I keep telling you, women have always been saving my life.

By the time my mother returned, I was quietly reading a book, the very picture of circumspection. For some mysterious reason, television seemed to have lost its attraction, at least for that afternoon. She calmly took me into the kitchen and yanked the clothesline, which obligingly came off in her hand, and explained how I would certainly have fallen to my death. I shouldn't be so gullible. Superman didn't exist, wasn't real, was simply a fiction on television. Human beings could not fly. Didn't I know that?

Of course I did, so why . . . ? Interestingly enough, there was one thing she didn't say: she never prohibited me from watching *Superman* again.

Since this was after our first and only Stebbins Avenue summer, I could not have been under the influence of television for more than a few months. I was not a stupid child, and as noted, the medium was in its infancy. So this was a comparatively tiny, flickering, black-and-white image that had so totally disoriented my sense of reality. What effect can the ubiquitous, inescapable, virtual-reality, video-game, contemporary version have on young minds today? Dumb question. I withdraw it. The answer glares out at us constantly in horrific daily headlines and on eye-witness newscasts over that very same medium each evening at six.

As I would discover, my experience with the Western media was not unique. Across the black world the response of my generation, my age set, to this egregious Western presence was more than a little ironic and frequently unpredictable. Take for instance the Tarzan movies.

Once a group of us in Guinea were discussing Tarzan. I described how my youthful misimpressions of Africans had been conditioned by them.

"Oh, I know those movies," Lamin said. "We used to watch them in Ghana too."

"Really? They showed them in Africa? What did you all make of the way they presented Africa?" I asked.

"Nothing at all."

"What? You weren't offended?"

"Not in the least. Why should we have been? To us they looked nothing like any Africa we knew. So we concluded that they were about black people in America. We thought America a very strange place indeed."

Despite what should have been—and undoubtedly was—the excitement of discovering the wonders of a new country, time hung heavily during that first summer. Even the novelty of television had quickly faded. Time dragged and I found myself wishing desperately for school to start. In America, education was free and better, my parents kept repeating. And it represented opportunity, boy. The kind of boundless opportunity not present in little, backwater Trinidad. Education was *modern* in America, the system was better. I could hardly wait and the anticipation only caused time to drag more heavily. Before the school question, though, there was the matter of the coat.

By about mid-August I was facing yet another major adjustment, which had nothing to do with either culture or technology. This one was elemental, purely climatic. I had begun to feel cold. My father laughed. "But it is still summer, you can't be cold yet. Wait till winter, then you really going see cold, boy."

"But I cold now. What I going do if it get any colder?" I complained.

"Oh, we'll dress properly. I'm going to get you a winter coat." But I was cold and kept bugging my poor father. "When am I going to get my coat? I need it now. I real cold, yes!"

Thus I became the first person on the block to start wearing a winter coat. Middle of August. Even though people were laughing at me, I wore that coat. How they to tell me how I was feeling? I was chilly. But my father's problems with the coat did not end there. By the time it got to November or thereabouts and it was *really* cold to me, I came in and handed him the coat. He looks at me inquiring.

"Thank you, sir, but I don't want that coat again."

He says, "Oh, and why not?"

"Because it doan work. The wind comes through."

So he laughs. "There's no coat we can find that some wind won't come through."

"So why bother to wear a coat if the wind will always come through?"

Now my mother really laughs. "Because, Little Man, if you take off the coat in winter, you freeze to death." Which all seemed to me as a choice between the proverbial black dogs and monkeys: either perpetual cold, death by freezing, or never leaving the house from November to June. What a country, yes?

So between cold weather, wind-porous coats, no moon, restricted movement, I wanted out of this mamajamma, Jack. I couldn't wait to get back to Trinidad. But with every passing day, the saving prospect of school loomed even larger and crept mercifully, if too slowly, closer.

Finally. All right, it's September. Time for school. I was more than ready. I had been well primed by our mother, who believed without question that America was the greatest country in the world and must therefore also have the best educational system. She pumped into my head, you must do well in school. Your job is to do well in school. You have to do well in school.

The school of my first experience of American education was P.S. 39 on Longwood Avenue, the very same elementary school from which a few years earlier another young Caribbean migrant had launched his now celebrated "American journey." Unlike Colin Powell, I was not to finish the fifth grade there, but it is where in September 1952 I began my American education.

At what must have been the crack of dawn, I was combed, pressed, and fully dressed in back-to-school finery. I can't remember if it was the classic West Indian white shirt and tie. I was champing at the bit, raring to pit my small-island self against the challenges of the finest educational system of the greatest country in the world. I knew that the students would be smarter and more sophisticated, the teachers stricter and more intellectually demanding, and the lessons "hard," infinitely more advanced and challenging. But I was determined not to let my parents down.

Of course, everything *was* different. Even the building, a massive, huge, and somewhat intimidating fortress of concrete and glass. And each class had its very own room, completely separate and discrete. I think I must have badgered my mom to escort me too early because I seem to remember sitting alone in a silent, empty classroom looking around with nervous anticipation.

Physically it was impressive. The entire wall at the front of the room was a blackboard. Facing which were neat rows of chairs, each with its own desk or writing surface attached. No long benches, chalk slates, and small blackboards set on tripods here. It seemed orderly, solid, and designed for very serious work. But no matter the degree of difficulty, I told myself, I was going to not just cope, but to excel here. I was as focused and serious as a sprinter facing the starter's gun.

Then pandemonium—literally "many demons." First, a sudden, loud grating sound somewhere between a loud buzzer and a jarring bell. Then almost immediately the door flew open and a wave of shouting, laughing, jostling energy rushed in. Students raced to particular seats, wrestling and jostling for possession. They were swearing, throwing spitballs, erasers, laughing, yelling, and even cursing. The apparent ringleader spotted me immediately. A muscular, stocky little brother, he told me his name was Jay.

"Wha's your name, dude?"

"Stokely."

"*Sto-ku-lee*," he echoed mockingly. "Boy, you sho talk funny."

"That's how we talk in Trinidad, boy. *You* does talk funny."

Then a white man in a suit came in, raising his hands as if for quiet. I stood, expecting the tumult and the shouting to subside. To my complete amazement, it got louder. An eraser whizzed by fairly close to the teacher's head. *I could not believe it.* I stood at my desk, my eyes fixed on the teacher.

"Siddown, fool." I thought I recognized Jay's voice from behind me. The teacher looked at me, smiled somewhat faintly, and nodded. I sank into my seat.

Talk about culture shock. This bedlam after the respectful, pristine, *echoing* silences of the schools I'd known, in which one could literally hear a pin drop on cotton. Stunned, I sank deeper into my seat, wrapped my arms around my ears, and let my head fall onto the desk in a timeless posture of withdrawal, amazement, and utter despair. "This?" I moaned. "Is this America?" Children throwing erasers at teachers? I'd never encountered children so noisy, so disrespectful, so destructive. How could one possibly concentrate in such a classroom? I don't believe I actually wept, but in that moment of utter desolation I sure felt like it.

Naturally order, or some semblance thereof, was finally imposed on or rather cajoled out of the class. Even the teacher's style seemed wimpy after the absolute magisterial authority of the Caribbean counterparts I'd known.

"All right, people, all right now. Please let's settle down now, boys and girls, shall we? Can we have some order here. Let me have your attention. That's better now. Gosh darn it, *settle down.*" So learning finally began.

Given my absolute confusion that first day when I had fully despaired of ever getting accustomed to the rougher ambience and dynamic of that classroom, it is remarkable how quickly my adjustment came. For one thing, the crushing academic challenge I had so feared simply failed to materialize. Quite the reverse, in fact. But before we get to the academic, check out the social.

Here my early acceptance was unwittingly brought about from an unexpected quarter, the aforementioned young master Jay, head ruffian-in-charge. On the first or second day, it became clear that we would have to fight or something much like that. The issue was my speech, about which he unfailingly made loud and unflattering remarks whenever I ventured to answer a question from the teacher. Finally, I suggested rather pointedly that he not do that. The class gasped and gave a long, gleeful *ooooooh* of anticipation. Whereupon Jay promised to whup my butt after school.

In Trinidad, I'd had relatively few school-yard fights because I was a fairly popular and articulate kid and could usually talk my way out of potential trouble without loss of face to either party. But also—perhaps the real reason—everybody knew that in combat I'd go off. Sure, you might whup me, but I'd be coming at you, Jack. I might even be crying, tears streaming down my face, even screaming "like a girl," but I be coming at you, fists flying, kicking, never quitting. Kick my booty, yes, but there would be a price. For which reason I think I was generally spared the attention of school-yard bullies, who usually sought easier prey.

But what now to do about Jay? I knew enough to realize that I couldn't start out my new school life by punking out. But what could I do?

The teacher, perhaps sensing my discomfiture, let me out about ten minutes early. Which was nice of him, but hardly a solution, as Jay's whispered "You lucky, suckah. But I'ma git you" made clear as I left the room. Jay's version of what Joe Louis had said about Jersey Joe Walcott before their second epic fight: "Pappy kin run, but he cain't hide." But I had no intention of doing either.

Once outside, I placed my books on a car, leaned up against it, and waited. But for what? That I didn't see clearly, but I sensed that running home would be about the worst thing I could do, a serious mistake. What then about the next day and the rest of the term?

So I waited, without any clear plan but affecting a studied and elaborate nonchalance. "But, I wuz cool," as the song goes.

Entirely too soon, school was out and the building emptied in a rush of noise and laughter.

Out comes Jay at the center of a knot of admirers, all laughing excitedly. From the flush of triumph on his grinning face, he seemed to be accepting their adulation for having run off the skinny, funny-talking new kid. Then they saw me and pointed me out to Jay, who looked over to see me leaning on the car, doing my best to appear unperturbed. He seemed surprised and a mite uncertain.

"Hey. Din the teacher sen' you home?"

"Yeah. But this in't ha' nothin' to do with him. This between you and me, boy."

Silence. Our eyes lock. Glares are exchanged. Silence. Game faces. We look each other up and down. Silence. Suddenly I realized that I didn't *have* to do anything. It was purely his move. More silence. The acolytes begin to woof, "Whup his butt, etc." But, for some reason, we don't fight.

I suspect the advantage of surprise and the power of confrontation worked for me. Certainly it puzzled Jay, but he did recognize that he had much more to lose than just a fight. But no fight happened and I think he was every bit as relieved as I was. What did happen, in fact, is that we became the best of friends. I guess that little Jay was more of a politician than I then realized. Like LBJ, he preferred to have me "inside dumping out, than outside dumping in." In any event, I was willingly enough drawn into his little orbit.

Now, he really was a wild little brother, and once we became good friends, I followed his lead, jumping into his little wild actions. What Tante Elaine would have called "all kinds of devilment." Hanging out at the back of the line, making noise, hitting boys up back their heads, grabbing girls in an ungentlemanly manner, and so forth. But there would be limits to my involvement in that kind of action.

Those came from my parents' constant injunction to do well. My biggest surprise, in that regard, was the discovery that not only could I compete academically, but that I was actually much better prepared than the American kids. In fact, I rather too smugly and hastily concluded that American kids were stupid. Yes, to my shame, I did. They didn't know geography. They knew little in math, while I *knew* my times tables. They couldn't write. Could barely compose or parse sentences. What? So I was just soaring through school.

In one area, though, I really needed to catch up, and my mother kept pressing me to study it: American history. I had no knowledge of it. But it was a fascinating story, and because it was my only real challenge, it became a favorite of mine. I devoured American history, which is of course to say, what passed for American history in a fifth-grade classroom circa 1952.

But I was not to finish the academic year in that remarkable classroom. So I have no idea what happened to ol' Jay. He may have become a CEO, a professional athlete, a successful criminal, a soldier, a cop, or an anonymous civil servant, now nearing retirement. Or he could more easily have been an urban casualty or a Black Panther militant. He was high-spirited, energetic, and daring. A "discipline problem" certainly, but he was neither stupid nor bad. In fact, he was quite lovable. I wish him well.

CHAPTER IV

"A Better Neighborhood"

My father's announcement took us children by surprise. My mother was part of the announcing, standing next to my father, her face a study in pride and determination. Any apprehension in her expression was held firmly in check beneath the weight of the first two.

My father explained to us that even before we'd arrived from Trinidad, he had been searching everywhere for a better home for us. Now, with the help of the Lord and our good mother, he had found what he was looking for. We would be moving in about two weeks, for our parents had bought us a house.

"Praise the Lord," Mummy Olga sighed audibly. "Praise His holy name."

It would be a better neighborhood, my mom said. We would have more living space. The streets would be quieter, less crowded, and the children would have more freedom. It was close to a school. My mother really emphasized that we would be moving to a "good neighborhood." I do not recall if she mentioned that it would be a white neighborhood, but it was.

The house was farther up in the Bronx, on Amethyst Street, in the Morris Park/White Plains Road area, not far from the Bronx Zoo. We would discover that the neighborhood was heavily Italian with a strong admixture of Irish. It was respectable working class, "ethnic," and very, very Catholic. On one side it bordered Pelham Parkway, across which was a predominantly Jewish enclave.

Ours would be the first, and for much of my youth, the only African family in that immediate neighborhood.

Because we were children, it never occurred to us to wonder why or how my father had been allowed to buy into that block. Nor how, on a single income—my father's, for our parents were very clear that my mother would stay home and mother us full-time—they could have scraped together the down payment. Or from what reserves of inner will and determination these two young immigrants had summoned the optimism and courage to take this major first step in pursuit of the American Dream.

I do recall the excitement of packing for the move, my sisters' and my gleeful anticipation of the promised space and freedom. How big would our house be? How fancy? Would we have our own rooms? This excitement lasted until we actually saw our new home.

It was a dump. I mean, it was a serious, serious dump. In fact, it was the local eyesore, and the reason—I now understand clearly—my father had been able to get the house with no visible opposition was because it was, hands down, the worst house on the block. It was so run-down, beat-up, and ill kept that no one wanted it. If that house were a horse, it would have been described as "hard rode and put up wet." A creature in dire need of a little care and nurturing. My dad was the "sucker" the owners had "seen coming" on whom to unload their white elephant. Which is one reason, I'm sure, the race question was overlooked. Who else could have been expected to buy such a wreck?

When we first saw it, we children were shocked. We looked around the house and at each other. I mean, even the cramped quarters at Stebbins looked like a mansion compared to what we were moving into. I mean, small, little, squinched-up rooms, dark, sunless interiors, filthy baseboards, a total mess and not at all inviting.

But our initial disappointment did not, of course, take into account my father—his supreme confidence in his skills and resourcefulness. He had indeed spent a long time looking for just such a house. Seeing not what was, but what could be. The neighborhood *was* quieter, and the house just three houses down from a school, and by the grace of God, sufficiently derelict and decrepit as to be available *and* affordable. Perfect. The Lord *do* move in mysterious ways.

My father had cased the joint purposefully and assured himself that the foundations were solid enough to afford him a base on which to build. He'd figured out *exactly* what he was going to do with this house.

Immediately when we moved in—my mother used to tease him fondly that he unpacked his tools before he unpacked his bed—my father set to work, even though it was January and cold. The remake took a long time, continuing in some way as long as he lived there. On those happy days when he had a construction job, my father worked on our house at night. On those all too many days when the union hiring hall failed to refer him to a job, he worked on our home day and night. Before he was through he had added rooms upstairs and down, knocked out walls to create more space, put in windows and doors. In a word, he completely transformed that wreck.

We learned later that as the neighbors looked on, amusement turned to skepticism, skepticism to wonder, and wonder to respect. They were, after all, working men and respected industry and competence. And as they watched the transformation from eyesore to one of the more attractive and well-maintained homes on the block, the neighbors recognized that because of my father the value of their property had not, as expected, plummeted by reason of our black presence, but had instead been *enhanced*.

The school three houses away on Hamilton Avenue was P.S. 34, where I and my three hearing sisters were immediately enrolled. The eldest, Umilta, who was deaf, attended a special school downtown. Naturally, for us, there would be the necessary period of adjustment—the new-kids-on-the-block syndrome. That we were African undoubtedly contributed something to this tension at first, but I must say clearly that I can remember no instances of overt racism from the neighborhood kids.

Whatever their elders' attitudes might have been, once we were accepted in "da hood" by the other kids, that was it. Once we became familiar presences on the turf, so to say, citizens in good standing of the neighborhood, we were to be defended against any strangers from outside, whatever their color. But there would be a period of adjustment.

Our mother was always at home and overwatchful with one eye tuned in on the street. She at first tried to keep us at home as much as possible, and for a long time she was never really completely comfortable with our visiting other children's homes. For this reason, my father built a clubhouse in our backyard for my friends. Our backyard became a focus of youth activity, which made my mother happy, as most of my time was spent where she could watch my movements and make sure I was not being subjected to racist insults.

I believe my status among the boys was determined early by my mom and a stocky, muscular kid named Paulie Henry. Paulie was Italian/Irish, and most bellicose. He would, as they say, fight at the drop of a hat—and drop the hat himself. One day early on, Paulie slapped around a friend of mine called Billy. I mean, ol' Paulie, like Stack O' Lee in the blues, had laid a hurtin' on poor Billy.

According to my mom, she came out and found me crying along with Billy. I guess, sensitive kid that I was, I was comforting Billy by helping him cry. Billy explained what Paulie had done and added that Paulie had promised to come back and beat me up too. In fact, he had gone to round up his boys to help him administer said beating.

"And where's this Paulie now?" my mother asked.

"Over in the school yard," Billy sobbed.

Before the words were well out of his mouth, my mother stormed into the school yard, trailed a little hesitantly by me and Billy.

"Which one of you is Paulie?" she demanded. Whereupon she declared in a loud and carrying voice—obviously she was sending a message beyond just the school yard—that *I* was not Billy. And *she* was not Billy's mother. So everybody, I mean, *everybody,* better understand that if they laid a finger on *her son,* she would come back with her husband's ax and set to chopping.

Upon which a chastened, deeply impressed Paulie hastened to assure her that this did not involve her son at all. That they had absolutely no intention in the world of touching her son. This was purely between them and Billy.

It had been a dramatic performance on my mom's part, and *quite* convincing. It certainly convinced Paulie and his gang, and even I was not entirely sure whether my mother had been serious. Which, I suppose, is exactly what she intended.

For it sure worked. I was probably the only kid on that block Paulie never fought with. In fact, he became a friend, and later, something of an influence.

In all of P.S. 34, there was but one other African family, the Stovalls. But they lived farther down in the Bronx, on the edge of the district. The oldest Stovall was a good athlete and, by reputation, rough, a "real toughie." I suppose as only the second African boy to come through, I basked in some of his reflected valor. Strangely enough, I never became real close with the Stovalls, perhaps because they didn't live in our immediate neighborhood. A case of the dominance of geography, "turf" over race, I presume.

In my class, the fifth grade, the acknowledged baddest dude was an Italian kid named Nicky. I had not been in school two weeks when, for some reason, Nicky challenged me. Again, the teacher gets wind of it and lets me out early. This time, though, there was no uncertainty on my part. I had learned with Jay precisely how to work this one.

In the end, it was almost a total rerun of P.S. 39 and Jay, as Nicky also decided it best that we not fight. Unlike Jay, however, we never became friends. Our relationship remained cool, but correct, a kind of peaceful school-yard coexistence.

Here at P.S. 34 I would find my peers undisciplined, less so than at Stebbins, but undisciplined nonetheless. Also just as destructive, breaking pens and pencils to throw at each other, dashing their books to the ground to fight each other. Which again raised the same question for me: Why were American children so undisciplined and even self-destructive? I still have no answer for that, but as I got more and more into the neighborhood, I would get to see this self-destructiveness at close hand.

By constantly reminding us that we were going to a better neighborhood, my mother had created certain expectations. Yet I would discover that just as much stealing was occurring in the "better" neighborhood, and this would come to touch me quite poignantly.

Despite my mother's efforts to keep us at home or in the backyard, inevitably, my being a boy and older, I would eventually begin to roam the neighborhood. This was almost always in the company of my new and close friend John DiMilio. John and I were inseparable, so close that the neighbors called us the Bobbsey Twins—one being fair and the other dark. They said, "Wherever you see one, you look for the other, he won't be far." We were constantly in and out of each other's home, and before long I was deeply immersed in the ambient local Italian culture.

What little sponges children can be. I loved the food, both the taste and the sound of it, those final vowels and rolling consonants: spaghetti, macaroni, pizza, calamari, antipasto, mozzarella, and so forth. Because of Umilta's deafness, our family had learned to sign to communicate with her. This might explain my fascination with the expressive vocabulary of gestures that was so much a part of Italian conversation. I picked up these gestures naturally, and soon I could curse fluently in Italian to the accompaniment of eloquent gestures, much to the amusement of the adults. "Yo, kid, wad-daw-yah, a wise guy? Gi-dudah-heyah!"

I must in truth have been a sight, a pint-size *paisano* in blackface. A real wise guy. Everyone knew me even if they did not know my name. The street name they gave me, because I was dark, was Sichie, short for Sicilian. (Later I would learn from Malcolm X the role of Africans in the history of that island and the extent to which the Moors had left their indelible imprint on Sicilian architecture and on the complexion of the populace.)

Naturally, I also picked up the prevalent political attitudes of the Italian community. They did not particularly trust the government, in particular the FBI and the IRS. Of the two agencies, the IRS was truly to be feared while the FBI, in vernacular translation "Forever Bugging Italians," was bush league. My neighbors had scant respect for either that agency or its director, noting that it had consistently failed to make a single racketeering charge against Al Capone stick, while the IRS had busted him on tax evasion.

In the Harlem barbershop where my hair was cut, I would hear an African version of this conventional street wisdom. "Better you kill someone than cheat on them taxes, baby. Yo kin get away with murder easier than taxes. Mes wit his taxes an' Uncle Sam *will* git you. Yes he *will*, swear befo' God. Look what happened to Capone."

I know my mother regarded my integration into the local culture with considerable ambivalence. On the one hand, she was pleased with my easy acceptance and local popularity. On the other, a caveat. Her mantra became "Remember now, you can't be doing like these little white boys. Something happen out there in the street and you *know* who will get the blame." And that familiar nostrum of black parents: "Your little white friends got it made. For you to make it, you will have to be three times better than them. You best remember that, now." That, as it turned out, proved not all that accurate, failing as it did to take into account the serious consequences of class, culture, and gender.

However, my mother's misgivings were well founded, for the youth culture of that block was even then at considerable odds with the values and expectations of the parents.

When I began to hang out after sunset, she imposed a 9:00 P.M. curfew, which, of course, I stretched as much as was prudent, which did not escape her notice. There would be frequent confrontation. Whenever I pulled in at 9:20 or 9:30, I'd hear about it in no uncertain terms.

One evening, fortunately for me, nothing very interesting was going down in the street. I went home early and retired quietly upstairs to my room. I read some and fell asleep.

At nine o'clock, my mother became incensed, "I know that boy's been running the streets. Well, when he comes in tonight, I am going to catch him. And he *will* hear *me.*"

Whereupon she fetches up some of my Dad's two by fours and nails and proceeds to batten down the front door as though in preparation for a hurricane. I mean it was a sho'nuff *barricade,* Jack. By about ten, she's worried. Ten thirty she's besides herself. She rouses my father. "That son of *yours* is out running the streets again. You better go find him."

"Course I'll go. But, May, you done nailed up the door," my father pointed out.

I hear my name and call down. "Did someone call me?"

"You *upstairs?*" my mother cried. "Stokely, you upstairs?"

"Yes, ma'am. Is something wrong?"

"No, nothing. Nothing at all," she cries. "Stay in your bed." But by then I'm coming downstairs, trying (without great success) to keep a straight face at the sight of the door.

"Oh, what happened to the door?" I ask innocently. "Is a hurricane coming?"

"Yes, Mr. Man. You go ahead and laugh. But the night I catch you, we'll see how you laugh then."

Did my mother have reason to worry? Absolutely. More reason to worry, in fact, than she ever suspected, even though she tried everything possible to keep me out of trouble. Everything possible. Just like John DiMilio's mother; just like Cookie Delappio's mother; just like Paulie Henry's mother. And many, many other mothers like them. They do their best to keep their children out of trouble in this society . . . and fail. They do all in their power to keep them out of jail, to keep them off drugs, away from the many dangers that are out there in America, and too often they fail.

That's why I laugh when I hear people say that it is the parents who are to blame. It's not the parents, it's the society, stupid. The society with its venal, backward, and predatory values. This is what must be changed.

So, what was it that my mother did not really know? Well . . . start with the bellicose Paulie, he of the ax-lady incident. Among his age group on the block, Paulie was a leader, in fighting, in stealing, in breaking into neighborhood stores, and such like antisocial actions. All potentially self-destructive. A nice friend otherwise, but this was just his undisciplined streak. Something I found so rampant in America.

I knew that some of my Italian friends were breaking into the little mom-and-pop stores around the neighborhood, and that Paulie was coordinating much of this. But, I thought they weren't very bright about it. Working in groups of three, they would break into a store one night. A couple of nights later, another group would break into the same store. They would keep breaking into the same stores until the police—apparently even less bright—would finally catch a few. I knew that, but figured it wasn't my duty to be preaching at them. So I left it alone.

What follows I am not at all proud of. But in a book like this, one has an obligation to be brutally honest. Perhaps it can serve as a lesson to others about the dangers of peer pressure.

Now, I'd heard about this petty thievery and simply did not understand it. As I said, fifty-six years old and still trying to *fathom* America. I'm pretty sure none of us were in dire need of money. I certainly wasn't. And I'm sure the others weren't either, even Paulie. Because once he broke into these little stores, all he could get is the change left overnight, $20 tops. It all seemed so stupid and risky to me, and for what? But as I told myself, it wasn't my business to be preaching to them. Possibly I didn't want to seem square.

Until that one night when I was hanging out and Paulie proposed that we rip off a store. And as he did so, he seemed to be looking straight at me. It was a test of some sort, that was clear.

I had to calculate rather quickly. I understood clearly the stupidity of this act, but there was the pressure to belong. It was very much "All right, are you down with us or not?" Very much as if, you punk out now and you won't be able to hang no more. We'll know who you are. That kind of pressure.

So I had to calculate, these are my friends, my boys . . . anyway, I calculated to do the wrong thing. But at least I was clever. I told Paulie, "No big thing. We can rip off a store. No problem. But it can't be a store around here . . . that's too close to home." So we went a little bit aways down from the neighborhood. Three of us. In those days these small neighborhood stores had little side windows above the doors. Since it was a quiet neighborhood, the owners usually left these little windows open. Paulie, being relatively small and muscular, could easily boost himself up with our help and climb in the window. Which was good, for I certainly wasn't going *into* that store. Paulie didn't mind, partly, I suspect, because we had to take his word about whatever money he found. Since the money didn't matter to me anyway, I didn't much care whether he shorted us on the take.

Anyway, Paulie went in. We stood watch outside. He got the money, which we split, and went home.

That really affected me because I had never thought I'd ever allow myself to slip to that degree.

That night I experienced what one might call a serious crisis of conscience. All the way home and before I fell asleep, all I could think was why? I certainly didn't need it. I kept thinking about my mother, seeing the pain and anger in her face. I wasn't worried about her anger, as in her beating me, 'cause as I figured it, I would be in jail where she couldn't reach me anyway. But the hurt, you know. I kept seeing her before me, all she had done, how valiantly she'd tried, how she'd worked so hard . . . and here was this huge failure I had stupidly brought upon her. The disgrace, that is what really touched me as I'm sure it touches many other youths.

That night we were successful but I told myself I would never, ever do that again. And I never did.

I often reflected on what the consequences for my life might have been had we been caught for this first criminal act, which would have been breaking and entering and petty larceny. All of us would have gone down together for sure, and it would have meant at least a juvenile record. I have no idea—forget the family crisis—where that first arrest would have led me. I know for Paulie exactly. His undisciplined streak led him to arrest after arrest after arrest.

Recently, I've been reunited with John DiMilio and he's confirmed that of that group of neighborhood friends only about two went to college and the rest have done some jail time on one charge or another. So, as it turned out, these little white, working-class boys did not have it nearly as "made" as my mother had initially thought. Course, I have been in jail, and not only in this country. But I'm thankful to be able to say that none of my arrests were on criminal charges. All were political.

Here too some say, "Well, you escaped. You made it. If you did, the others could too." No. No. No. It is not nearly so simple. I had or was lucky to find alternatives, and the movement may also have saved me. I'm convinced that the deck is so stacked that only a certain number can get through. I happened to be one of that certain number. That's all.

For one thing, I was really never as completely integrated into the neighborhood's young male culture as it might have appeared. In spite of my street "gang" activity, my fluency in Italian invective, and my popular name Sichie, clearly I was in that culture but really not of it. We were black and the neighborhood was white. Our socializing and our identification were with an extended family of Africans, at first mostly of Caribbean origin, but growing to include Africans born in the United States. On holidays, on Sundays after church, we would exchange visits for elaborate Caribbean meals, music, and conversation. Or there would be picnics in one or another of the city parks where we'd enjoy our music and games of soccer. So although we lived comfortably in a Little Italy, we depended for our social life and cultural expression and renewal on an extended network of friends and family that crisscrossed African communities in three boroughs of the city: Brooklyn, Queens, and Harlem.

On these visits the young Carmichaels dressed in their Sunday best and under heavy, heavy manners (our best impress-the-relatives behavior) earned accolades for excellent deportment. Which was, in one respect, a little ironic.

Because of Umilta, all five Carmichael children had learned to sign. This ability proved heaven-sent during those long visits with Caribbean adults, some of whom were firm believers in the Victorian dictum that "children should be seen and not heard." Dutifully we sat, silent as mice, while signing outrageous comments among us. Sometimes even venturing to make fun of the unsuspecting elders at the table.

"My Lord, look at that *hat!*"

"Yeah, it looks like a crow's nest, eh?"

At some point before we left, there would be some recognition of our admirable deportment. "Oh," someone of the seen-and-not-heard persuasion would gush to the delight of the proud parents and the muted giggles of the children, "your children are so well-behaved. They were so quiet all that time, they never said a word."

Yeah, sure. Thas only because you didn't hear what Umilta said about your funny ol' hat, Lady.

Another thing that distanced me somewhat from much of the petty outlawry of the neighborhood guys was that I loved to read and my parents encouraged this. These were two extremely intelligent and resourceful people, but without much formal education. They were literate enough, but hardly literary. So while they were convinced of the crucial importance of reading and encouraged me in it, they could not offer much guidance about *what* to read. My mother would buy all kinds of books that seemed to her "educational." She certainly bought a lot of encyclopedias, seduced no doubt by the salesmen's line about "giving your children every educational advantage." I also spent hours in the library enduring the taunts of the neighbor kids about being "a bookworm." With Olympian impartiality, I read everything and anything.

In addition, there was the threat of punishment. My mom was the first line, the cutting edge of family discipline—my father being held in reserve for really serious offenses—and she was particularly vigilant and strict with me, the son. But as long as I stayed at or near the top of my class, she would cut me some slack. So I contrived to stay there and pretty much did. Whatever I knew would please Mother, that I tried my best to do. Anything I knew would displease her, that I'd try to avoid. For this, she has earned my undying gratitude because, without her firm restraining presence, undoubtedly I'd have ended up in jail like so many of my neighborhood buddies. Thank you, May Charles, thank you, thank you. (In Africa, when you mean to thank someone seriously, you have to do it thrice.)

The other thing that contributed to my escape was that P.S. 34, the neighborhood school, went only to the sixth grade. For the seventh and eighth grades, we'd have to go to P.S. 83, which, while only about a fifteen-minute walk away, was something of a different world.

The year was 1954. For us, it marked the onset of puberty, the age when, as they say in the Caribbean, "A boy begin to smell him mannish." So the antisocial activity on the block became a little more ambitious, therefore potentially more serious.

Because P.S. 83 was a magnet school and a lot larger, a wider range of students would be feeding in from different elementary schools. Now there would be Jewish kids from across Pelham Parkway; more Irish and Italians from farther down Morris Park Avenue; and Africans, the same two from P.S. 34, the Stovall kid and me.

Since the school was larger, the kids from my neighborhood were split up in different classes. I imagine there must have been some kind of academic tracking in effect, for John DiMilio and I tended to find ourselves in classes with the more academically serious students from different neighborhoods. Some of the new students with whom I became friendly had rather more intellectual interests than my local circle. These new friends and I began to exchange visits, and this served to distance me somewhat from the neighborhood circle.

But in the evenings and on Saturdays we'd still hang out. The stealing continued but I steadfastly refused to participate. But that didn't mean I was completely uninvolved, because while I myself would not steal, I would hide the others' stolen goods for them. A nice distinction without a real difference, huh?

It *was* a contradiction and it preyed naggingly on my mind no matter how hard I tried to dismiss it. This was rendered even more troubling because my father was so scrupulously, resolutely, and unambiguously honest a man. "If you didn't work for it," he'd always say, "don't look for it. If you didn't sweat for it, don't even think of it." In all the time we lived together, I never knew him to deviate in the slightest from that principle. In fact, some of his fellow craftsmen would visit and sometimes talk about taking materials from the big construction jobs as, so they said, compensation for the discrimination they endured. Paying the bosses back, they said. Why didn't my father? But he was resolute: "If I didn't work for it, I ain't looking for it."

How I would ultimately have resolved this contradiction I do not know, but two events, coming at about the same time, intervened to make the decision for me.

I am pretty sure it was Paulie who first suggested we form a gang to be called the Morris Park Dukes. Never heard of them? Neither has anyone else. The Morris Park Dukes were never to etch their name in "glory" or infamy in the violent folklore of New York youth gang culture.

On Saturday the Dukes used to go to a movie theater on Boston Road and Pelham Parkway. The main reason for our going was to fight. You'd find some guy from another neighborhood who for some reason you didn't like and you'd both go to it. Innocuous perhaps, but certainly senseless: Go and fight someone you don't even know? Actually, this too was certainly copycat behavior influenced almost entirely by Hollywood's youth-culture, "urban jungle" movies of the time—*Blackboard Jungle, Rebel Without a Cause,* and so forth. What ever happened to Sal Mineo, who was very much a model and culture hero to my Italian friends?

Anyway, someone decided that we Dukes needed to take it to the next level. This meant making zip guns, the primitive, distant ancestors of the Glock nines, currently the weapon of choice in urban youth warfare. The manufacture of a zip was simplicity itself. First you steal the aerial from someone's car, preferably a car parked well outside your neighborhood. Then you procure a cap pistol and file its firing pin to a point. A suitable length of aerial is cut off, filed down, and inserted into the barrel of the cap pistol. Then you stretch a number of stiff rubber bands around behind the firing pin and in front of the trigger guard.

Now you position a .22-caliber bullet in the barrel under the pin. Pull the pin back and release it. If the alignment is correct—about one time in twenty—the pin will strike the detonator on the back of the shell and the gun will fire. Of course, *where* the bullet will go is anybody's guess.

So we decide to make zip guns. Why we were making them is, to this day, still not clear to me. I suppose we were to take them up to the theater on Pelham Parkway. I guess.

The next Saturday about twelve of the Morris Park Dukes went to a five-and-dime to buy the cap pistols. En route, someone was visited by insight: we the Dukes, we can't be *buying* no pistols. That's beneath us, a kid action. So just like that, we walked out of the store without paying. That evening we find cars with suitable aerials and break them off. When the owners woke up, their cars had no aerials. When the zips were made, some actually fired, most didn't. I can't now remember whether mine did. But this was the final act in my flirtation with the destructive behavior of our wanna-be gang.

Now that we had guns that fired—at least a few did—were we really going to shoot, possibly maim or even kill, some kid we didn't even know? I am sure the Dukes never did, but I sure wasn't about to tag along to find out.

Not long after that I went to a store—not the same five-and-dime—with one of my sisters, and when we came out, she proudly showed me something she'd boosted. I was outraged, absolutely livid. My sister cannot possibly be involved in something so *stupid!* What if she is arrested? What of the embarrassment to our parents? Instinctively, without hesitation, I order her to take it back. She refuses. "Look," I warned, "if you don't take it back, I'm gonna tell Mother." Apparently she did not believe me, so I did.

My mother took my sister back to the store, either returned or paid for the merchandise, and gave her a proper beating right there in the store. I'm fairly confident none of my sisters were ever tempted to shoplift after that.

That relatively trivial incident proved the straw that busted my camel's back. It forced me to face the real implications of all I had been doing, however halfheartedly, with the guys. No further rationalization was possible. The deep and abiding sense of guilt and shame that I experienced was awful. I mean, I can't remember feeling so absolutely wretched again. The hypocrisy of turning my sister in for shoplifting when I was doing much worse seriously haunted me.

I now think that those two accomplices—guilt and shame—are probably together the most corrosively painful scourges the human spirit can experience. Precisely because they always and only stem from one's *own* failure to keep faith with one's truest self. With one's private conscience, one's most cherished and basic principles, with one's sense of honor. For me it was an important lesson too painful to ever forget. I may not have known the word *integrity,* but that is what that was about. That simple incident first taught me that no matter how private or hidden the betrayal, one cannot live with oneself without integrity. The pain is too great. My late father had a much used saying that, because it seemed so unforgiving, puzzled me greatly as a young boy. It occurs to me that this is what it was about: integrity. "You can tell the truth every day of your life," my father would say, "and if, on the day of your death, you tell a lie . . . that is what will matter."

That very day I began seriously to separate myself from the antisocial behaviors of the street.

What is curiously inverted in the macho street code of my young friends is that they would, in all likelihood, have found my action quite natural and understandable. Not, as one might expect, an indignant "Jeez, whaad'ya say? Ol' Stokes ratted the kid out? Ged audda heah!" But an instinctive and complete understanding that considerations of family honor (and particularly that of the womenfolk) had left me no choice. For them, the women in the family, like "Caesar's wife," must be beyond reproach. Considerations of family honor that were, oddly enough, not seen to be threatened in quite the same way by our own escalating thuggish behavior in the street.

In September of 1954—a momentous year in contemporary black history—I went to P.S. 83, and I left in June of 1956. That is, I went to P.S. 83 just a few months after the Supreme Court's *Brown* decision and left just prior to the final victory of the African community in the Montgomery, Alabama, bus boycott. At the time, both events could not have seemed more remote from my immediate circumstances and for that matter to each other. But they were, in fact, closely related and both would significantly determine the trajectory of my life.

My two years at P.S. 83—the seventh and eighth grades—were important formative ones. From the perspective of forty-five years it is easy to see how the streams of cultural influence that were to imprint my personality, inform my consciousness, and determine the trajectory of my life had begun to emerge during those two years.

On the one hand, this period of my youth could—without too much irony—be called my most "all-American" period. At school I was completely surrounded by whites and, as far as could be seen, appeared to have been completely accepted by them. I was placed among the high academic achievers and pretty much flourished in that environment. So much so that in the eighth grade, a friend, Donald Sweetbaum, drafted me to run for vice president of the Student Council.

I was not at all sure I wanted to do that. I was very conscious of being the lone African in the class and I wasn't entirely ready to test—at the polls—how the class *really* felt about me.

But, when we sat down to discuss it, Sweetbaum was confident. "I know you gonna win, man, everyone knows you," etc., etc. Well, how could they *not* know me, I was the proverbial fly in the buttermilk. Then he clinched the argument: "Look buddy, how can you lose? I got the winning slogan." And he produced one of the more memorable jingles in American electoral politics before the advent of the Reverend Jesse Jackson: "Okeydokey, vote for Stokey."

Sweetbaum proved to have had his finger unerringly on the pulse of the electorate—*we* smoked the opposition. I'm glad for his sake that we then had no idea of the grand theft dough, the obscene sums of corrupt money political consultants would command from a terminally corrupt system today. Sweetbaum, an otherwise nice, decent kid, might have been drawn into a life of crime like the others we now see on TV.

Without question, P.S. 83 was a good, nurturing experience for me. The best proof of this would be that the school selected me among its candidates for the citywide competitive entrance exam for the Bronx High School of Science. The school's good judgment in my case was vindicated because I won a place in the "highly competitive, elite" Bronx Science. And this was 1956, a decade before any such notion as affirmative action was even contemplated. Therefore, I had earned this high academic honor purely on sheer *individual*, intellectual merit, untainted by any suggestion of demeaning "racial" preference. Well, you may believe that if you wish. (I'm sure my proud mother still does, and I got a bridge in Brooklyn I'd like to interest you in. . . .)

I was very, very clear, even at age fourteen, that my selection was heavily indebted to racial politics and the ongoing struggle and agitation of my people. Yeah, I had good grades, but I have no illusion that my being their sole African student didn't have something to do with the middle school's decision to nominate me. Or that Bronx Science did not understand clearly that they *had* to make room for at least a few Africans or risk being denounced for racism by the African community. Even in 1956, we had a word for it. We called it tokenism.

How did I know this? True, that this kind of discussion was really not a part of daily conversation at P.S. 83, given its racial composition. Actually, my nappy, nappy African hair, my "natty dreads," had saved me from that cocoon of willed "innocence" in which white America famously entombed its youth during the fifties.

See, when we first moved to Amethyst Street, we had gone to every neighborhood barbershop and failed to find a single barber who knew how to cut my hair. Or who would admit that he did. Which meant that, until I left for college, I'd have to go into Harlem every two or three weeks to have my hair cut.

At first the trips to the barbershop with my father—I believe it was on 145th Street between Seventh and Eighth Avenues—were a little disconcerting. I mean, simply because of the sharp difference in style, sound, feel, and *look* between Harlem barbershop culture and the Italian/Irish ambience of Amethyst Street. For one thing, everyone and everything, even to the pictures on the walls, was black, or at least not white. Then too the shop was popular, so I often had to wait my turn in the chair. This became the one time in my life that I actually enjoyed sitting around waiting for anything.

A constant stream of men came through the shop; some, from their accents, were from the Caribbean. Most though, from the soft, slow cadences and rhythms and the "bluesy folk" images of their speech, were from somewhere close to the heart of Dixie. Some men seemed to come in simply to talk and listen, for conversation that sometimes reached the level of art. There was the woofin', the jiving, the stylin' and the signifying and the dozens. No, there weren't the dozens, I mean, I ain't going to lie on my people now. This was a respectable establishment and the real "dirty dozens" would not have been appropriate, being entirely too "low-lifed." Now, there was occasionally a slight *flavoring*, a *hint* of the dozens, at least, the form of it. But only between two very good friends. And it certainly never got down and dirty the way the nasty dozens s'posed to be: "Yo' mamma doan wear no drawers," etc. But there was otherwise the full range and vast repertoire of African-American colloquial discourse.

Apart from the pleasures of the style, which reflected the African pleasure in language for its own sake, the content of the discussions was the real revelation to me. On a good day, a wide range of political opinion and commentary, and community, national, and international news was to be heard and dissected. There came into the shop old Garveyites, race men, street players, black Republicans *and* Black Muslims, nationalists of all descriptions, and the rappers, poets, and wordmen who seemed to talk simply for the joy of hearing their own voices.

That barbershop became for me a necessary corrective, an early window into an African-American worldview and sensibility, a crucially important counterpoint of reference for those.

Take for example the Korean War, excuse me, the "police action." I know that it was in the barbershop that I first heard the saga of Pork Chop Hill, that bloodiest of battles, where the white brass—MacArthur? Ridgeway? I forget who, but a white man anyway—cynically used hundreds of African-American troops, black men, as cannon fodder.

For a better example, during my two years at P.S. 83, two events would be of profound significance for African-Americans in my age set. They would not only affect race relations in the country but the psychology of an entire generation. But I can remember no organized discussion in school, in Sunday school, or any casual mention in the streets of the Bronx community of either the Supreme Court's *Brown* decision or, the next year, the lynching of young Emmett Till in Money, Mississippi.

But at the barber's, they were the central subject of discussion and analysis, the topic of debate, the source of anger and eloquence, the catalyst for poignant reminiscences, in short, for the handing down of collective history. For me, the barbershop was a necessary emotional and cultural corrective to the hospitable, quite comfortable but essentially alien vibe of the home turf.

•   •   •

When we first moved to Amethyst Street, our family had no car. This meant that church became a major chore for my mother each Sunday. The church we had gone to near Stebbins Avenue was John Wesley Methodist, a small church of a few Caribbean families. My father, always a devoted man, was in his element there, spiritually *and* culturally.

But getting there was onerous, particularly for my mother, who had to rise at the crack of dawn or before, cook the Sunday dinner, then supervise the preparation of five children. We then had to ride the bus or the train down to the church and back. So my mother decided to join a Methodist congregation within reasonable walking distance of our house. Westchester Methodist on the edge of the Parkchester district must have been the closest Protestant outcropping in that ocean of Catholicism. We children went to Westchester Methodist with my mother while my father would continue to worship at John Wesley Methodist among his own.

The congregation of Westchester Methodist, like all else in the immediate vicinity, was lily-white. So we Carmichaels integrated it. We were made welcome by the pastor and received warmly by many of the members, though for some time, some heads would continue to turn when we walked in.

I said "many" members received us warmly, because I can recall nothing from those members with whom we interacted except the kind of fellowship and hospitality one would expect from fellow Christians. If any in the congregation felt otherwise, they would, naturally, have kept their distance so we would not have gotten to even meet them.

We attended the Sunday School at Westchester and I would join the Scout troop. I have always, like my father, loved music. My mother, seeing this, had enrolled me for lessons with a local piano teacher. This was a short-lived investment in my cultural development, since it soon became clear that I was not destined to be a concert pianist. (Also, piano lessons were a little awkward to explain to Paulie and the Dukes.) But my brief foray into "higher" culture was by no means a total loss. Actually, I'd quite forgotten this until reading in a national magazine recently that I "played the piano at Westchester Sunday School." Which makes it sound as if I had been the resident pianist. What happened was that *once* I performed that beloved staple of all piano teachers for their beginners, Beethoven's simple and lovely melody, *Für Elise*. Proud mothers do tend to exaggerate, even forty-five years later.

In this Sunday school, I made many new friends—Ronald Zemati, with whom I also joined the Boy Scout troop, and Bob Johnson come to mind. Bob and I became really friendly and would visit each other's house. Nothing unusual in that except that Bob lived—as did many of the church members—in Parkchester, which at that time did not allow black residents. So when Bob and I would pass through Parkchester, there would be stares and raised eyebrows, which, naturally, we ignored.

If, however, we were with a group of young people from the Sunday school, *and* if I happened to be walking next to, or in conversation with, a girl, then heads and hackles would be raised, not just eyebrows. So, from a young age I clearly understood this aspect of American racism. Besides which my mother had, at about this time, begun to seriously caution me about white girls, and in particular that I should *never even think* about anything remotely resembling a white wife. If any such idea ever broached my consciousness, I should forget about it "like bullfrog forgot about tail" in the Caribbean proverb. The next year—after the revelation of the Till atrocity—a note of real anxiety and alarm crept into my mother's warnings on the subject. The issue would come up only once in high school, and I'll discuss that at the proper time.

Ron Zemati and I joined the Scout troop together, where once more I was the lone African presence. We went camping and on hikes, which provided a welcome opportunity to explore nature and the outdoors after being cooped up in the city. I learned a lot I would not otherwise have learned so I really enjoyed scouting a lot, becoming a Life Scout.

Among the merit badges that I earned was the one for religious knowledge. I was at that time, like my father, very religious and I really enjoyed reading the Bible for that badge. So religious, in fact, that I seriously contemplated a clerical vocation. Mummy Olga played quite a role in that. Still living with us, she was a religious woman. She was particularly taken with a blind radio evangelist, to whom she listened (religiously) every Sunday without fail. I cannot remember the preacher's name, but he calculated that if one read two chapters a day, one could read the entire Bible in a year and a half. This struck my aunt as a *most* excellent undertaking, particularly if I would read with her. So every night before bed we'd read our two chapters, and on Sunday evening we'd listen together when the preacher commented learnedly on the week's fourteen chapters. Mummy Olga would have been delighted had I fulfilled her fond predictions and gone into the pulpit. I always tease her that I came close and that she is responsible for my always quoting the Scriptures in my political speeches.

In rereading this account, my father, while a constant enough presence, seems but a vague one, hovering somewhere in the middle distance, indistinct, while my mother vibrantly commands the narrative foreground. This is true only in the obvious and limited sense that May Charles was very much, day to day, the center of our little domestic universe—while my father was out in the world securing our family's livelihood by the sweat of his brow.

That is exactly how they both wanted it. To them, this was not just the preferred arrangement, the proper ordering of our world, but the only conceivable one. In this, they were full partners, completely content and confident in this division of responsibilities.

As an adult I now understand just how precarious that daily bread had been. With the benefit of hindsight and adult experience, I can fully understand exactly how extraordinary a couple my parents were, but we always somehow knew that they were special (aren't all parents), but not *how unique*.

As individuals they would appear to be as strikingly different in their personalities as a man and a woman could be. As a couple, though, they were splendid, a perfect complement.

For one thing, I believe that until the last moment of their life together, they were in love. More than that, they were in the fullest sense of that word helpmeets: partners whose shared respect, trust, and confidence in the other was unqualified. Their major priority being, of course, their children.

Yet they patently did not see or engage with the world in anything remotely like the same terms. In a curious way, their individual styles and personalities were as different as their *essential* values were indivisible. My mother was, and remains to this day, voluble, passionate, impulsive, and excitable. Her spirit is fiercely confrontational. But she was also pragmatic, provident, and practical. She was an excellent seamstress, sewing much of our clothes. She also sewed for a small circle of customers for cash. So that in any financial crisis when extra money was needed, we could usually depend on May Charles to produce it from somewhere.

Adolphus, my father, was in contrast a deliberate man. Not excitable, quiet, thoughtful. Not physically very large, he was wiry and strong. He seemed to have boundless energy and was certainly one of the hardest-working men I've ever known. I've tried to emulate that quality in my own life and work. His face was spare, the skin taut over a prominent forehead and cheekbones with large, deep-set eyes that were steady and quiet. A face without lines or an ounce of superfluous skin or fat.

His demeanor was serious, but without being in any way stiff. His manner always seemed calm, almost relaxed. A very social man, he loved music and was an exquisitely graceful dancer. His words were always thoughtful. He was not verbose, but we always knew that whatever our father said in his quiet voice, he truly meant. We never disobeyed him. At dinner he'd always ask each of us, "Well, what did you learn today?" If someone came up shaky, he'd shake his head. "You know, the day on which you learned nothing is a wasted day. Enough of those and what've you got? A wasted life."

My sister Janeth (now Nagib) remembers that "because he said so little, we girls paid total attention to anything he did say." She also remembers that sometimes when they were small and had been bad, our mother would greet him with a litany of complaints about the girls' shortcomings in his absence.

"Adolphus, you've got to punish them." Sometimes he'd summon them sternly to the bedroom, take off his belt, and fetch the mattress a number of resounding whacks.

"What you all waiting for? Go ahead and cry."

What I most remember about our father is his ineffable calm, understated air of confidence. He knew his own worth and so was under no pressure to prove anything to anyone. Nothing, and in particular, no problem in carpentry or craftsmanship, ever seemed to intimidate him.

"Well, now," he'd say as he studied the problem. "There's always more'n one way to skin a cat." Sooner or later he came out with an approach—often not the conventional one—but one that would get the job done, and often more efficiently. When his fellow workmen visited, after a drink or two—my father did not drink, but he'd be hospitable—one or another of them would often get expansive: "Boy, you know your father's a great man?" And would brag about some process my father had devised to solve a problem that had stumped their foreman on the job.

But he never learned to like America. Never. Which was the greatest underlying difference between our parents. My mother was determined to make America work for us. The whole dream, for she was determined that in America we should not merely survive, but that we would triumph. In everything that America offered—hence the piano lessons, the better neighborhood, the big "white" church, and so on. We would, so far as her striving, upwardly mobile spirit was concerned, take our rightful place in the mainstream and seize whatever the American Dream had to offer that appealed to us.

My father had absolutely no argument with that. Except perhaps that he was more selective. I think somewhere in his consciousness lurked the notion that we were not only as good as anyone else, but possibly a little better. He was content with himself, with his people, his culture, and more than anything, with his principles.

For, as we children were to discover, something about him was very pure. Whatever he professed, that would he perform. Not only would he not lie, he never really expected that other people would. Again, my sister Nagib. She told me this recently, which had to have happened when she was very young:

"I will never forget the day our father discovered that white folks would lie. I heard them. He was in the bedroom talking with May Charles. It had something to do with his being able to join the union. He said, 'But, Mabel, he *lied.*' My mother said something. 'But, Mabel, the

man lied to me. The man *lied,* Mabel, flat out, he *lied.*' I will never forget,"
my sister told me, "the disillusionment in our father's voice that day."

The story I remember came a little later, after he was a dues-paying
member of the union in good standing. He had dutifully presented himself to the hiring hall for almost a month and was still waiting to be
referred to a site. Our mother, ever pragmatic, suggested he give the representative "a little something." She'd heard that was how it was done.
Everyone did it.

"You mean bribe him?" My father was incredulous. "That ain't right.
I don't have to bribe anyone. God is my bribe."

So quietly my mother got some money together, as usual. But given my
father's moral scruples, she couldn't do anything as crude as a bribe. A
present, though, was another matter, a gesture of respect and goodwill.
She gave the money to my uncle Albert who, as "Lord Hummingbird," a
calypsonian, worked on a tour ship. This was sometime after the war when
French perfume and silk stockings were at a premium but could be had
from the black market at the French docks.

When my uncle brought back the contraband, she called up the union
rep, saying she simply wanted to meet him and, of course, "here's a little
present for your wife."

Next day, my father came home beaming. "Told you I didn't have to
bribe anyone—God is my bribe." And he gathered the family together to
say a prayerful word of thanks. My mom prayed as thankfully as anyone.

I don't want to give the impression that my father was sanctimonious
or, as they say in the South, "plu-pious." He was nothing like that, but he
saw ethical principles in religious terms, and religious terms were for him
inviolate. He would, for example, say by way of rhetorical emphasis that
even if his children were starving, he would never work on Good Friday.
For, even as Abraham had been prepared to sacrifice his son on the mountain, so would he.

Except that we knew that the last thing he would ever tolerate was that
we, his family, should be in need. My father loved his family and had a
great sense of responsibility to them. He had to make sure that everything
we needed was there, and he would do anything to ensure our happiness
and well-being. To him, providing for us was his paramount responsibility. In capitalist, racist America, with six hungry mouths to feed, that was
a feat.

Even when he had a union job, he would sometimes drive a cab at
night. In the winter he'd drive the cab and also do occasional carpentry,
a room here, a door or window there. After work, he went to electrician
school to get a license. Sometimes in the winter he'd sign on as a carpenter
or electrician on a merchant ship and ship out. He was at home only to
sleep. "Why you working so hard all the time?" I asked.

"Only for you" was his simple answer. "Only for you." I have always believed this country forced my father to work himself to an early grave. And it was "only for us."

So, largely because of our indefatigable parents' resourcefulness during our childhood, our family was never poor, certainly not in the grinding sense that I would encounter poverty in Mississippi, Alabama, or even in Northern cities during my life's work.

The one time when we children would really feel the cold breath of want and hunger closing in on us was when my father fell ill and was hospitalized for some weeks. Then I discovered what it means for a family in a capitalist society to have a single wage-earner, and to have that person fall ill. Left to the rapacious forces of the market economy, the family is in *serious* trouble. You really go backward economically. That's what happened to us, but God moves in mysterious ways. . . . This is what my sisters ruefully refer to as our "time of milk and brownies."

As you might recall, Mummy Olga was a widow twice over. In Trinidad she'd had one particularly persistent and faithful suitor, Mr. Dowling Charles. We children knew that Uncle Dowling really wanted to marry Mummy Olga. But like in the Paul Robeson song, she always answered, "Oh, no, John, no John, no John no."

We children thought this most unfortunate 'cause we loved Uncle Dowling and just knew that he would have been the perfect husband for Mummy Olga, because he really cared for her, and the care extended to us. But perhaps after the premature deaths of two husbands, Mummy Olga got to believing the conventional folk wisdom—that she was one of those unfortunate women who were death on husbands.

Whatever the case, when Mummy Olga brought us to America, Uncle Dowling was not far behind. His stated reason for coming was to study to be a mortician, but we all knew he was following Mummy Olga. He wanted her, once he completed his studies, to return home with him as his wife, which Mummy Olga declined to do. (Maybe his choice of occupation contributed something to her resistance, I don't know.) But while he was studying, he supported himself by working in a little restaurant. It was such a tiny place that it bought supplies day to day, and their dessert menu consisted of one item—milk and brownies. When the restaurant closed at night, all that was usually left over was the dessert.

The restaurant was in Brooklyn, where Uncle Dowling reported for work every evening after school. During my father's illness, every night Uncle Dowling would ride the train all the way up to the Bronx with as much milk and brownies as could be made to fit into his briefcase. Until my father recovered, we had brownies and milk for breakfast, lunch, and dinner. Even today, whenever I see a brownie, I recall vividly, inside and out, their taste, their consistency, even their smell.

Uncle Dowling later returned to Trinidad. Sometime in the late seventies, I heard that our uncle was terminally ill. I was, at that time, prohibited from entry into any country of the British Commonwealth by a British ban. However, I was determined to say goodbye to this decent, caring man. And to do so in person. I'm happy to say this proved relatively simple to do on a brief "illegal" visit. It turned out that the ban decreed from "on high" was, at least in my case, very, very loosely enforced by my kinsmen below.

One winter when my father shipped out, one of the ports of call was Accra, Ghana. Independent Ghana. My father came back transfigured, almost glowing, and with many little African artifacts as presents for us. I will always remember the awe and wonder with which we looked at these beautiful and exotic objects that came from *Africa,* our motherland. Nagib recently showed me the elegant little ivory woman's head that had been her present. She's treasured her father's African present over all these years. What I've treasured are the stories about Nkrumah and his struggle for independence and my father's palpable pride and joy in the telling, and at having been among a free nation of African people. I was enthralled by these accounts and never even remotely dreamed that I might ever get to meet such a legendary figure.

One story my dad told with such dramatic description and feeling that the picture he presented etched itself indelibly in my imagination to this day.

It was the opening of Parliament in independent Ghana. Pomp and ceremony. The members are all seated. The gallery is full. World's press in attendance. An air of great expectancy. Everyone is waiting for the new government team to appear. Then they do. The Prime Minister, Mr. Nkrumah, leads his cabinet on to the floor of the hall. There's an audible gasp, surprise, outrage, pride, but mostly, astonishment. Then applause. Here my father's eyes glowed with pride and wonder and a tremor came into his voice.

To a man, the *entire* cabinet is wearing, not the British ceremonial top hat and tails, but the drab, shapeless, dehumanizing garb of British colonial convicts. The humiliating uniforms they had worn while in prison during the struggle.

"Boy, you hear me, those black men marched right out of prison and into power," my father exulted. Of course, my heart was touched by my father's obvious emotion. However, I could have had no idea then, that one day I would be able to share my father's pride in the telling of his story with the *Osageyfo* himself.

I was a sophomore at Howard when my father died. He had been a great lover of music of all kinds, particularly gospel and, of course, calypso. Often when I came in at night, he'd be sitting up in the living room listening to his music. "Come here, boy, listen to this!" and he'd put on something, maybe the latest Nat King Cole album. One evening I brought in a single that was the rage of Harlem, kind of a modified calypso by a young man in the Nation of Islam. "Okay, Dad, you listen to this. What you think?" He listened intently and had me play it twice. When he looked up, he had a tear in his eye.

"Bet you," he said, "they'll never play *that* on the radio."

The song was "The White Man's Heaven Is the Black Man's Hell," and the singer-composer was Louis X. You now know him as Louis Farrakhan. I'll never forget how his song brought a tear to my father's eye.

CHAPTER V

Bronx Science:
Young Manhood

"Yo . . . boy . . . Yeah, you. . . . What you doing up here? . . .
    Hey, kid. Didn't you hear me speaking to you?"
"Me, Officer? You weren't speaking to me, were you?"
"Yeah, I'm talking to you. What're you doing up here anyway?"
The youth gestures to the books under his arm. He flips back
    a cover to reveal a school logo.
"Coming from school, Officer, as you can see."
"Wha'?" The policeman stares at the book covers. "Those are
    your books? . . . *You* go to Science?"
"Yeah, afraid so, Officer"—mimics—"*I go to Science*. Some of
    us actually do, y'know."

In any culture, the growth during the period from adolescence to young adulthood is of major formative importance. As American culture is organized, this growth period corresponds almost exactly to the four years of high school, which are crucial in determining not only the adult personality but one's future.

That would certainly be my experience at the Bronx High School of Science, where in the fall of '56 I was an entering freshman. At Science, I would face a number of interesting challenges—intellectual, social, cultural, political—all of which would play a significant role in my development.

Within our family, the news of my selection to Science had been greeted with quiet satisfaction, entirely as if it were no less than had been expected of me. My parents knew that Science was an "elite" school, carefully selecting and preparing the city's brightest students for college. This fit neatly with a plan being developed by my father, who in his heart had never really left his beloved Trinidad.

My father's dream was entirely consistent with his values: a family plan for both parents, me, and whichever of my four sisters wanted to sign up. The son would study medicine while the daughters would become

83

nurses. While we children were completing our medical education, my parents would return to Trinidad, where my father would begin construction of the Carmichael family medical clinic, which he would personally design and build in preparation for the children's return to serve the community.

I guess for my father this would represent something of a triumphant homecoming: the family united and bringing back useful and necessary skills to his beloved community. Something of real and lasting value to justify his hard work in what was to him a long, cold exile. So, from that perspective, my admission to the elite Science school was right on time, clearly the first step. The extent to which we children had enthusiastically endorsed the plan can be seen in that, today, two of my sisters, Nagib and Judy, are nurses.

Bronx Science was an education in more ways than the school might have intended. I had known that the students were drawn from all five boroughs of polyglot New York and were said to be "very, very smart." So I expected high intelligence and academic rigor. But I hadn't expected—actually I hadn't given it much thought—the range of classes and cultures I found in the students there, once I got to know them.

Some were very affluent, the children of wealthy Park Avenue professionals and corporate executives. But the majority were just middle-class kids of college-educated parents, WASP, Jewish, Irish, Italian, and a few Africans born in America. Of some two thousand students at Science, about fifty or sixty were Africans from America. Some students were working class, or like me, first-generation immigrants from Asia, Africa, the Caribbean, or Latin America. That first day, the only kid I knew in the freshman class was Lefty Faronti, who was working-class Italian from my Bronx neighborhood.

The first challenge was academic. The one thing we all had in common was the knowledge that we were all supposed to be very smart. Naturally, I was eager to see how I would match up against New York's smartest. From the first day I could see that I was not the only freshman nervously sizing up the competition, eager for a chance to show off his smarts. And in truth, competition would be the rule at Science. It didn't take me long to understand that these whites were not necessarily any smarter than me, but that they simply—many of them—had intellectual backgrounds that I lacked.

On the first day, in one of the first classes, the first question we were asked was about our summer reading. How many books and which authors? Boy, was I glad, because I'd read a lot of books. My hand just shot up. Luckily for me, the teacher went in alphabetical order, because was I in for a shock.

I read a lot, voraciously but not at all selectively. My parents had not finished high school or studied in this country, but they knew I should read and insisted on it. But they didn't know *what* I should read. As I've said, my mom brought home tons of books, any books she concluded were "good," i.e., "educational." I read everything and anything, from *Reader's Digest* to the Hardy Boys and Horatio Alger–type uplifting books.

But these kids in the class had (or claimed to have) read authors about whom I'd never heard—Jack London, Ernest Hemingway, William Faulkner, John Steinbeck, and even names that didn't sound American. Later I would discover that they were in fact Russian and French. For instance, if memory serves, a boy sitting immediately behind me claimed to be reading *Capital* by Karl Marx. Long before they got to me, my hand was down for I was scribbling furiously, writing down all these unknown writers whom I would read as quickly as possible, for I resolved I had to know whatever my classmates knew. I ended up with quite a reading list that first day.

Obviously these kids' parents, like mine, encouraged their reading. Except that their parents, unlike mine, knew *where* and *how* to direct their children's reading. But if academic intelligence is, as I do believe, largely a matter of cultural background, I was soon to discover that I too had an advantage over most of my peers. From the regular intelligence tests that they used to give us, I came to understand that these students were no smarter than I.

I have no idea what these tests are like today. But when I was in high school, they consisted of three parts: vocabulary, reading comprehension, and math. And whenever we would take these tests, I'd whup the class. I mean, I'd whup 'em hands down. It's hard to say who was the more surprised, me or them. These were disciplined students with strong intellectual backgrounds who were *very* competitive. Yet, I was beating them?

By about my junior year I figured out the source of my advantage: my uncle Lew.

Within the family, the authority on things academic was Uncle Lew, my mother's uncle. Dr. Lewellyn Silcote was a physician educated at City College and Meharry Medical College in Nashville. Whenever he came to visit, we discussed my education and my prospects. Remember the only three avenues to economic independence thought available to African men then? Well, whenever we'd talk, I'd say, "I'm thinking of being a doctor like you." Uncle Lew would say, "In that case, study Latin. A lot of medical and anatomical terminology is based on Latin."

"What if I'm a lawyer?"

"Same thing. Just about all legal terms are in Latin."

"And if I decide to be a preacher?"

"There too, Latin again."

So I studied Latin and continued to do so all the time at Science. I studied Latin for four years. I read Cicero in Latin. I read Caesar in Latin. And of course Latin has a vast vocabulary. More important, this is the vocabulary from which much of the English vocabulary has evolved. Most of my peers at Science were studying French, which, relative to Latin and English, has a much smaller vocabulary.

So even were I a C student in Latin while you were an A student in French, if we took a vocabulary test, I should whup you, hands down. And since reading comprehension is based on vocabulary and recognition of usage and syntax, my wide if unselective reading was useful there. So I always dominated those two sections while also holding my own in math since it was logical and most times you could check your answers.

Thus I came to understand the cultural basis—or bias, if you will—of intelligence tests. Actually, I first began to understand this in the sixth grade just after my arrival in the United States. This was through spelling bees. In Trinidad, I'd always been number one in spelling. In America, even in the fifth and sixth grades I could never win. This was all cultural. Words like *neighbor* and *color,* I would invariably spell with the British *u.* Then too was pronunciation. I can still remember that I lost a spelling bee in the fifth grade over the verb *assure.* The principal who conducted the contest clearly said *ashore.* I didn't wait for the context; my hand was up and I spelled out "a-s-h-o-r-e." Then she said the context, as in "I ashore you of my good intentions." So naturally I corrected her with the proper (British) pronunciation: "No, ma'am, that's *asseur*" (as in *masseur*). Of course I lost. Funny how I've never forgotten that. I was sure I was right. But it did teach me that spelling also was less a function of intelligence than of culture.

(So much so that today I might be the world's worst speller. Living in Guinea, I now speak French. So I've been exposed to British and American spelling in English and to Guinean French. When I write in either language, I become confused among the three spellings. For example, the French *précédence* is similar in sound, but not spelling or meaning, to *presidents* or *precedents,* and so forth. Speaking, no problem; writing always requires great concentration.)

The Science experience over the next four years could not fail to have a profound effect on me in many, many ways.

Academically it was rigorous, completely a product of the Western Enlightenment: reason and the scientific method. The curriculum and approach were heavily focused on Western rationalism, scientific materialism, the physical sciences, and the scientific method, all of which I found logical and thus intellectually satisfying. This empiricism was as suited to the medical studies I then projected as to the study of social history and revolutionary theory and practice. Now the political would touch on the academic.

Even though the stifling effects of McCarthyism were still very much present in the late fifties, at Science—outside the classroom at least—the students had a vibrant political debate with some active, well-defined left formations within the student body.

My discovery of this student left was greatly aided by three unrelated, accidental elements: the rational organization of the school, the spelling of my name, and my love of soccer.

I assume its emphasis on rational order led the school to seat the freshmen in alphabetical order in all classes. Thus in my first class the fellow sitting immediately behind me was Gene Dennis. He was the one, I recall, who was reading Steinbeck and Karl Marx. In most classes my freshman year, Dennis sat either beside or behind me, so we got to know each other early and well. I liked the kid instinctively.

He was a very interesting guy, was Gene Dennis. He was a good student, serious and smart. But he was also funny and irreverent, friendly and natural. He was comfortable and easy to be around, unlike some of my other white classmates. Our friendship was sealed the second week when they asked who in the freshman class was interested in going out for the soccer team. I volunteered immediately.

"You play soccer?" Dennis asked.

"From birth, my man."

"Great. I play too. I'm going out for the team."

We both made the team. Although we didn't get much playing time that first year, we had to attend all the practices and dress for the games. So we saw even more of each other, and in our senior year we would cocaptain the team. So not only were we sitting together in class, but after school we rode the bus or train together to Van Cortlandt Park for practice and back down again.

Intelligent, humorous, and full of life, Dennis also had a thoughtful side, a depth of sensitivity and maturity whose source I only later understood.

(Only this year, 1998, did we renew contact and he sent me a book of his poems. One of these, addressed to his dad, was dated 1956, the year we first met. Here are a few verses:

> I did real good
> while you were gone.
> Took care of Mom,
> Was the man of the house,
> Bought her the presents
> you described in your letters,

the ones the censors
sensed
were all right.

Stood proud by the prison gate
Heard you shiver inside.
Watched your hair
bleach ice white
In the jail house light.

I did real good,
swallowed tears
In the park when
Richie beat on me
for being the Commie's kid.
Didn't let the FBI men
ask me questions
when they'd follow
me home.
While you were gone
I grew up fast
too fast
To be so old
at the age of twelve.

I hope you can
See the difference
when you get out
Tomorrow.
After all these years
I hope you can see
Behind my grown up eyes
and know.
I need you home so
I can be a kid
again.
If it's not too late.

Discovering this poem was a revelation. I was touched when I read those
lines, for he'd given no indication of that private pain in his manner or
conversation when I'd met him at school.)

As our friendship grew, I invited him home because my parents
insisted on meeting all our school friends. Of all those I brought home,

my parents and sisters liked Gene Dennis the best. They said he seemed the most comfortable and at ease in our home. "And," my mother added, "for an American kid, he has really good manners."

After a couple months of our sitting together in classes and soccer practice every day, Gene said, "Look here, man. I'm having a party Saturday night. Why don't you come down."

"Sure, anytime."

He wrote down the address, to which I didn't pay much attention at the time. That Saturday, though, I was sure he had made a mistake. The address was in Harlem. So I called Gene and delicately skirted the issue.

"Hey, man, is the party still on, 'cause I'm coming down, y'know."

"Course it's still on."

"Great. So . . . what time we talking about?"

"Say about seven-thirty, eight o'clock. You remember the address?" He repeated it. It was the same as I'd written, the middle of Harlem.

"You know how to get here?" he asked.

"Of course, I do." Now I really wanted to ask him how he came to be living in Harlem, but of course I did not. But I was more curious than ever.

By now I'd discovered the vast cultural difference between parties given by the white students and those given by "usses."

At that time at Science, few Africans would be at the parties given by whites. Often I'd be the only one. Usually people would be sitting around, often on cushions on the floor. Someone'd be strumming a guitar and folk songs would be sung. Sometimes classical European music would provide a soft background for conversation. Very little dance music would be played, and if it was, only a few people would dance.

It was at first a mild culture shock, but I adapted. I enjoyed the conversation and the soft music well enough. Those parties were pleasant, but they sho wasn't *fun* as in git down, big-time *fun*.

Gene Dennis's party would turn out to be very different from white parties. But had it been anyone but Gene giving the party I most likely wouldn't have gone. Why?

Because, a couple of weeks earlier this other student had invited me to his party. And he must really have wanted me to be there, because he kept checking every day, pressuring me almost. "So you are coming, aren't you?" "I am gonna see you Saturday night?" kinda thing. He seemed to really want me there. This party wasn't in Harlem, it was on Park Avenue.

There was a doorman and even the doorman was white. The elevator opened into the living room. I'd never seen *that* before. I mean it was opulent, roaring fireplace, sunken floors, high ceilings, heavy thick carpets, picture windows with a spectacular view of the New York skyline at night. I'd never seen anything like it except in movies. I was impressed. I would have been happy simply to spend my time looking at the view and admiring the artwork. But at some point we had to meet his mother and a group of her friends.

The mother was effusive. "Oh, Stokely, I've heard so much about you. How smart you are, your sense of humor. How handsome, what features you have, etc." The way she went on was embarrassing, it was clear I was the exotic featured attraction.

When I was leaving I said my good-byes and thanked the mother. One of her friends must have said something which I didn't hear. But I distinctly heard the mother's answer before the elevator door closed. It had a certain smugness I didn't like. "Oh, yes, of course," she said. "We allow Jimmy to hang out with Negroes."

Now, when Africans gave a party, it was big fun. Nothing but dance music, calypso, rhythm and blues, soul, whatever, and evrah-body be on the floor dancing, nonstop, righteously gittin' down. That was the point at African parties: to have you a good time, you just had to dance.

I had a great time at Gene Dennis's party though. It was a cultural synthesis between the two styles of party. First of all, it was indeed in Harlem, with almost as many Africans there as whites. *And,* they played good dance music and folks actually danced. But in another room, people just sat and talked. So you could dance, then get down and enjoy good conversation, a lot of it about politics. I really enjoyed myself. Far as I was concerned, it was the best party I'd been to that year. Gene and I became closer and it must have been obvious. . . .

A short time later at school an Italian classmate approached me belligerently. He demanded, in extremely vulgar language, "Why are you always hanging with that blank, blank, expletive, blank Communist Gene Dennis?"

"Gene Dennis? What you talking about, Gene Dennis ain't no Communist. Gene a blue-eyed all-American boy. Git outta here."

"See . . . that's how stupid you people are. That's just how they get you. They be nice to you and before you know it, boom, you in their power. You trapped. They got you. You duped."

I listened to this tirade in amazement. I could only stare at him while slowly backing away. It was my first, but by no means my last, encounter with that classic American formulation of Communist duplicity and cunning set against African gullibility. But of course I had to check it out.

I had a classmate called Michael O'Hare, who made a point of appearing intelligent and broadly well-informed. So much so that some considered him arrogant. I didn't think him arrogant. I just thought that O'Hare saw no reason to hide his light under a bushel: he was smart and didn't mind letting you know that he was. So I found him.

"O'Hare, what do you know about Gene Dennis?"

"Oh, only what everyone else knows, Carmichael. His father, Eugene Dennis Sr., is a high-level operative in the Communist Party U.S.A. He was jailed under the Smith Act. Your friend Gene is one of the bright hopes of the Young Communist League in America. Anything else you want to know?"

My jaw must have dropped.

"Nothing else, O'Hare." I grinned. "I was just checking to see how much you knew."

But it was—at least at first—a real problem.

So . . . my friend Gene was a Communist. According to my Italian classmate, a blank, blank, expletive Communist, which pretty much summed up the prevailing public opinion on the question around my neighborhood. (This was not as universal in the Harlem barbershop, where all kinds of radical opinion could be heard.) But Commie or not, Gene was my good friend. I really liked him. Instinctively I felt that there would be something vaguely dishonorable or even cowardly in turning against a friend who had done you no harm, had never offended you, purely because of the social pressure, which had nothing to do with our friendship.

But this was, after all, still the McCarthy period. Rabid anticommunism and paranoia were pervasive. I knew I would at least have to discuss this news with my parents.

Not having been born here, they had no deep understanding of the issue. Communism for them was simply something to be avoided. Americans said it was the enemy, so getting mixed up with or being associated with a Communist could do you real harm. So best to leave it alone. That would be about the extent of their attitude.

Before taking it to them, I wrestled with the problem and reached my own solution.

If he a Communist and the enemy, I figured, then they should jail him. They jailed his father, hadn't they? But Gene ain't in jail. He goes to Science. So that's on them. He's their problem, not mine. If he's a threat and trouble to them, then they should handle it. If they ain't put him in jail, then it sure ain't my job to jail him. Nor even to check his attitude, nor even to be a check on him for them. It's not my responsibility to do the state's work.* That took care of the problem for me, and when I discussed it with my parents, that's what I said: "If they haven't put him in jail, then it's not our business."

They were of course disturbed. They were aware of the prevailing attitude and instinctively didn't want their son to put his future at risk. They

---

*A few years later SNCC would face its own version of this question. Our collective decision then was not very different from my fourteen-year-old conclusion.

felt that maybe I should begin to put some distance between us. What really compounded their dismay was that they really liked Gene.

I see now that theirs was the classic dilemma: the demonization of the unknown, the abstraction at odds with the human reality. They were prepared to abhor and fear "Communism," but charming, decent Gene? It's like the kid who really hates and despises all gays and never tires of letting you know. But his music teacher? A wonderful human being and the greatest teacher he ever had.

Anyway, over the next four years, the friendship between Gene and me grew closer and my parents' initial concern shriveled away. But in one sense, I guess, my Italian classmate's prediction was accurate. I don't believe I became anyone's "dupe," but it wasn't too long before I was going to meetings of the Young Communist League, attending study groups, and eventually attending their rallies.

This association, which began in my freshman year, continued in some manner until graduation and was, for many reasons, an important element of my political education. Who was it that said, "Education is what you have left after you've forgotten everything you learned in class"?

While my association with the student left at Science did not begin my political interest, it certainly focused it in a certain direction—the tradition of European radical writing and revolutionary theory. For the first time I encountered a systematic radical analysis, a critical context and vocabulary that explained and made sense of history. It explained the inequities and injustice I'd long been conscious of in the society around me and prescribed (even predicted) revolutionary solutions.

That was wondrously exciting intellectually. Marxism offered me an approach, a coherent point of view from which to understand and engage society, in terms of the "forces of history." These people impressed on me that to bring about social change you had to study and clearly understand the forces of society. It's probably not really true that my political attitudes were formed here, but my interest in political struggle was heightened and I learned that a strong theoretical base required systematic study and that regular theoretical study is a constant political duty.

New York at that time had a whole youth culture on the left that seems no longer to exist in this country. There were many organized activities—debates, meetings, conferences, rallies, and even camps out in the countryside just as we had in the Boy Scouts. I participated in all these. I became familiar with names like Marx, Engels, Lenin, and Trotsky and other revolutionary thinkers, whom I read for the study groups. Out at camps in the New York or New Jersey woods, we'd discuss particular books, current political developments, struggles that were going on, what our attitudes ought to be, what tactics ought to be employed, and so forth.

In the evenings after the discussions, we'd have little parties. I will always remember these parties as ending with our singing "Hava Nageela" and dancing the hora.

At that time most Communist Parties followed the lead of the Communist Party of the Soviet Union. Stalin had given guns to Israel in their fight against the Palestinian people, so in socialist countries and Communist Parties worldwide, support for Israel was automatic; the Palestinian people clearly merited no political support at all. Therefore in my early days within the ranks of the Communist/Socialist Party, I regarded Israel as a socialist state, deserving of revolutionary support throughout the world.

At school I became identified—completely—with the left. I was always at their rallies, joining the arguments against the reactionary student groups. I participated publicly in all their activities. At demonstrations I was always forthright in defending their right to speak. So most students thought that I was a member.

But I joined neither the Young Communist League nor the youth wing of the Socialist Party, neither the Socialist Party of America nor the Socialist Workers Party. My reasons for this were interesting and not what you may think.

Of course, it was a repressive time of enforced conformity—the last half of the gray Eisenhower decade. The Smith Act was in effect. McCarthyism and the House Un-American Activities Committee were in full bay. They had already assassinated the Rosenbergs and jailed the leadership of the Communist Party. The FBI was harassing and the government was hounding one of my early heroes, Paul Robeson. Even Eisenhower would, before leaving office, warn of the sinister power of the "military-industrial complex" as the Cold War was at its chilliest. It was a time of loyalty oaths and witch-hunts. All of which constituted excellent reasons not to formally join any of these parties of the left. But those were, oddly enough, not my reasons.

You could say, I suppose, that my reasons for not joining were cultural. The longer I was around my Communist friends, the more complicated my reservations became, but at first it was simple: the religious question.

I was, like most Africans, very religious, coming as I did from a very religious family. And you know that one of my early career options was the clergy. However, most of the youth in the Young Communist League were—publicly anyway—devout atheists. They often made jokes about God, and while I appreciated these young comrades and respected them, those anti-God jokes—funny as some of them were—were initially shocking and very, very offensive to me.

However, at Bronx Science, with its scientific materialist orientation, my religious feelings gradually lessened.

And as my religious devotion waned, my scientific education and political orientation grew. But I was always clear that this religious waning was in *me,* not in the African community. I never fell victim to that confusion.

Now I can see clearly that this apparent contradiction between religious faith and science is almost entirely a Western phenomenon, but then the contradiction seemed real and insurmountable.

I instinctively understood that if my struggle was to be among my people, then any talk of atheism and the rejection of God just wasn't gonna cut it. I just knew that. My early political work in the rural South would confirm this. All our meetings were held in churches. They all began with prayer. When they approved, people would say, "Son, you doing the Lord's work." If they were ambivalent, it'd be a question: "Son, you sure that's the Lord's work?" And the preacher, fearing for the church insurance or his standing with the white folk, would say in denying us the use of his church, "Son, you know, that ain't the Lord's work now." Recruits would usually tell you, "If the Lord ain't in this movement, it ain't going nowhere," or, ". . . then I ain't in it."

I did not want to be alienated from my people because of Marxist atheism.

My other reservation would be more substantive, but it came more gradually but persistently as I matured personally and politically. This was the question—for want of a better term—of nationalism, of the cultural identity and revolutionary imperatives of the black world.

At first and for a long time, the encounter with all these revolutionary thinkers, theories, and rhetoric was eye-opening, intoxicating. It presented a new, comprehensive, "scientific" way of viewing the processes of history and social change. It was a worldview, a theory of History with a capital *H.* It was *universal* and all-encompassing. So far as revolution was concerned, it was the whole ball game.

So it's natural that it would not have occurred to me at first that it was really—in its worldview—quite narrowly focused.

The words *Eurocentric* and *hegemonistic* were not then part of my vocabulary or consciousness. I never overtly or consciously thought about the curious fact that all these revolutionary thinkers were European or that all their theoretical models were fashioned out of European historical experience. I accepted them as "universal." At first.

As I say, this consciousness of constriction of view and of exclusion came only gradually. I consider two incidents milestones in the growth of this consciousness.

The first incident revealed a subtle, unrecognized sense of exclusion that I was feeling at the time. An exclusion not of me personally but of my people and our history from the conversations of the left. At a political meeting, a group of us from Science were there, but I was the only African. Though I cannot remember clearly the debate, what I cannot forget is the intervention of a voice. A clear, ringing voice, a high tenor, precise in diction.

"My friends, what is at *issue* heah?" (*Issue* rhymed with *tissue*.) I turned and saw a tall, athletic-looking African pacing down the aisle toward the front of the hall, talking as he came. A handsome man, he was turned out in an elegant, eye-catching way. He may not have been wearing anything so dramatic as a cape, but in manner and gesture he *looked* as if he should have been. Part of the dramatic effect was because, as he paced deliberately and confidently to the front, that voice was marshaling his arguments with laserlike precision. Then he turned to face us and delivered an address, part admonition, part analysis, and part gentle scolding. It was eloquent and effective and displayed an easy mastery of the vocabulary, issues, and arguments of the left, all delivered in this clipped, British accent. He kept throwing out daring strategies for direct action and engagement at points where the system seemed vulnerable to pressure. Clearly this man was a radical activist, an intellectual *and a strategist* who apparently commanded the respect of the room.

I sat up. "Who the hell is *that*?" I asked Gene.

"Why," he said, "that's Bayard Rustin, the socialist."

"That's what I'm gonna be when I grow up," I whispered exultantly.

Later I would get to know and work with and ultimately disagree with Bayard. I now understand that this had been another of his patented, carefully crafted dramatic platform performances. But to me it was every bit as impressive as he had intended it to be.

I also think that this first impression was as great as I remember it because what I had been missing in these circles without necessarily being aware of it was a powerful and compelling black presence. Of course Rustin's eloquence, debating skill, analytic and strategic deftness, and practiced ease with which he captured the audience had all impressed me. But it was his *blackness* that had inspired. Of course there were African men in high positions in the hierarchy of the Communist Party, and by then I'd even met some of them at Gene's house, but it wasn't quite the same. They impressed me as stolid, dour, somehow distant, rather shadowy presences. Bayard was dramatic and obviously engaged.

Eventually I was further distracted from Communism by two literary influences from my other cultural life. Coincidentally, both were men native to Trinidad: C. L. R. James and George Padmore.

I've been describing the Bronx Science experience and my intellectual/theoretical apprenticeship in the mostly white circles of the young leftists. But that was only one stream of my cultural/intellectual growth. The classic overly simplistic model in the popular mythology is of the young emigrant arriving in "God's Country" to be progressively "Americanized" by exposure to "American" mainstream culture—the melting pot. Maybe, had I arrived in Nebraska or somewhere like that, this description might have been accurate. But this was New York, the Big Apple, and my acculturation there was at the hands of at least four radically different cultural streams.

In the Amethyst neighborhood, the local culture was white, Catholic, ethnic, working-class New York, relieved by excursions to the Harlem barbershop and my family's social and cultural life within the Caribbean community. And at Bronx Science I was exposed to the scientific materialist, rationalist tradition.

And then there was my introduction to and immersion in the culture of Africans born in America. My real introduction to African-American experience and sensibility first came via the popular culture through my love of music.

When we moved to Amethyst Street and I had my own little room at the top of the stairs, I started using my parents' old shortwave radio. You guessed it, it was the same shortwave radio that had been purchased a few years earlier in the vain attempt to tune in *Auntie Kaye's Children's Hour* and my ill-fated performance in Trinidad.

That radio replaced Casa Blanca in my nightly routine. I would go to sleep each night to the soft strains of music coming over the radio beside my bed. The radio became "mine" and rarely left my room. This continued from seventh grade until my graduation from high school, from 1954 through 1960. At the time I began to listen seriously, African music was breaking out of the church and surging out of the South, brought along on waves of Southern emigrants. It was making its way into the national airwaves and coming to dominate the popular musical culture of the nation in different ways. This was especially true among the youth.

Now, my father was a dancer and loved all kinds of music, especially calypso. But he also loved gospel and rhythm and blues, so our home was full of these records. I listened along with him and developed a taste for these musics too.

Two men would come to dominate my bedtime listening, sometimes even into the late hours when my parents imagined me long ago asleep. One was a white deejay called Symphony Sid, who played European classical music, jazz, and some pops, which he discussed eruditely. The other was Jocko, who, I believe, was one of the first African deejays in the New York area.

This is now 1997, thirty-seven years later, yet I can repeat exactly what ol' Jocko's rap was. He'd come on beating out a rhythm on the table and proclaim: Eat the yock/This is the Jock/Back on the scene/with mah record machine/Saying ooh bop a doo/How do ye doo/Take it off (artist's name)/Up in the air, les gooo . . .

I know Jocko meant well. But for all his influence Jocko taught us nothing. The music taught me worlds about the idiom and sensibility of black culture, but Jocko himself? Nothing at all. He might have told us to study hard, or even to shine our shoes. He might even have (God forbid) told us something political. But I imagine—it being commercial media—he was not being paid to do that.

From these two programs my knowledge of African-American music—gospel, jazz, R&B, soul—as well as European classical music would grow profoundly.

My uncle Stephen, a cousin of my mother's, was born in Montserrat, and his wife, my aunt Catherine, was born in the South. They lived in Atlantic City, where Uncle Steve had a small record store in the heart of the African community. During the summers that was where I'd spend the holidays.

At that time Atlantic City, at least for the African community, was nothing more than an outpost of the South. A way station on the northward migration. First I helped out in the store. Gradually I came to be left completely in charge. We sold the music that these folk coming out of the South were listening to. I can't remember the store carrying any white artists at all.

At first this was mainly gospel—the Five Blind Boys of Alabama kind of thing. And rhythm and blues or country bluesmen. Sam Cooke, for example, first sang with a gospel group, the Soul Stirrers, but would soon break away into soul ballads. This also was the era of Clyde McPhatter, Little Richard, the Upsides, Frankie Lymon and the Teenagers, Fats Domino, Lee Andrews and the Hearts, the Platters, the Inkspots, Big Joe Turner, and of course jazz—Ella Fitzgerald, Louis "Satchmo" Armstrong—and cabaret artists like Cab Calloway, Nat King Cole, and Billy Eckstine. To sell the music you really had to listen to it. Boy, was I happy in that environment. The proverbial red dog in the meat wagon had nothing on me.

I even made a contribution to the store's operations by persuading Uncle Steve that he could make more money if he played the records. Particularly on Fridays and Saturdays when the streets were filled with people. Finally, he was convinced. After that, a lot of youth would gather in the evenings and we'd all just dig the music and show off the latest dance moves. That was when I received my first groundation in our culture in America. It came from that music. And from these young brothers and sisters. Many had been born in the South and passed on stories they'd gotten from their elders.

While working in the record store, I saw how technological changes in the means of production could completely transform the culture in capitalism. A classic Marxist insight.

At first the store sold only 78s and the long-playing 33⅓ albums. The 78s were acetate, brittle, and fragile, and the albums were priced outside the range of children and working-class youth. This meant that the music was geared toward adults and was so marketed. Then came the 45 single. Of unbreakable plastic with a large hole in the center, these were cheap to produce and could be priced at, I think, nineteen cents, and were affordable by youth.

This would change the entire popular musical culture of America. I watched it happen. Much music that had previously been addressed to the elders and therefore incorporated adult themes, experience, and musical tastes, in short that was an adult music, would change radically. Now a significant part of the music began to be addressed to youth. A "youth market" was created and musical commodities were packaged to exploit it. Selling records in Uncle Steve's store, I could observe how the character of the music changed as the age of the customers went down.

As I said, the deejay Symphony Sid was erudite and commented in interesting ways on the music. He addressed an adult rather than a youth audience, quite unlike Jocko. So I listened carefully and learned a lot from Sid. One evening, I think I was in my junior year, I was listening to some jazz on Sid's program.

Then Sid promised us a treat: "Tonight I've got something special in store for you. A treat and a surprise. An extraordinary singer, a young woman from South Africa . . ." An African singer! I sat up in bed. At that time I'm pretty sure that I didn't know a single artist from the continent.

He went on to make it clear that although this sister was from South Africa and sang songs coming out of her African culture, much of what she sang could, musically speaking, be seen as jazz. I was hooked. It was a school night but I sat up. I refused to surrender to sleep before hearing this incredible new *African* artist.

Finally Sid announced the new singer. Her first song would be the old English folk song "Love Tastes Like Strawberries." When you listen, Sid instructed, listen to the clarity and purity of tone, the excellence of the diction, the exquisite pronunciation, and most of all, the extraordinary musical sensuousness and control. And, he instructed, try to remember that this is an *English* folk song, but listen to how she transforms it and takes it over.

"Without more ado, it is my pleasure to present from Johannesburg, South Africa, Miss Miriam Makeba."

Sid was right. If anything, his introduction had been understated. The voice, the arrangement, the effect, were just incredible. Unlike anything I'd ever heard. I was blown away. I mean *blown a way*, Jack.

But Sid and Miss Makeba were not done with the kid. Not by a long shot. The best was yet to be, because then Sid said now we'll listen to a song in her own language. Those of you who know the record will recall that she introduces the song in a soft, husky, irresistibly seductive voice: "This song, the name of which is 'Qongqothwane,' is unpronounceable by whites in my country. Because they cannot say Qongqothwane, they call it the 'Click Song.' "

Man, I went off even before the song. I went off at her gentle satire of the linguistic failings of the Afrikaners. Besides which, the song was great. I think it may have been the first African song I consciously heard. The melody working with the rhythm was infectious, at once naggingly familiar yet totally new and exotic. It made me tingle and tap my feet. Of course, I could not understand a single word, but the sounds of the language seemed hauntingly familiar. It was as though you knew the tune, and the sound of words you didn't understand at all, well enough to sing along, anticipating the end of each phrase perfectly. That was my first time with this feeling of seeming to recognize something I'd never previously experienced. But in Africa I would often encounter completely new scenes and situations that would feel in some inexplicable but strong way completely familiar.

I was gone. I mean in loove, Jack. What was her name? She's from South Africa, but what is her name, Jack? I was desperately trying to remember. Mercifully, Sid repeated "Miriam Makeba," the name of the album, and the label. I was at the local record store as soon as school was over the next day asking the clerk to order the record.

When it came, I could scarcely believe my eyes. The owner of that incredible voice was young and absolutely beautiful. Her rich, smooth brown skin seemed to glow. Her strong yet delicate features were those of a classic Xhosa beauty. And, the beauty of the African woman, she wore her hair natural. The only other female artist I knew who did not fry her hair was the magnificent Odetta, whom I had seen in the benefit concerts she frequently gave in support of the Southern struggle in Montgomery. Now here came Makeba, just young, impossibly beautiful, and natural. I was completely smitten.

I rushed home to play the record. The first person I saw was my sister Janeth, now Nagib.

"Janeth, look. This is the woman I'm gonna marry. I must marry this woman," I cried.

Of course, what I think I meant was, ideally I'd love to marry this woman. In a perfect world, this woman would be my wife. In a perfect world. In the real and imperfect world I'd have to content myself with buying every record she made and dreaming. It never occurred to me that I'd ever actually so much as meet her. And indeed when I first met her, it was anticlimactic and deflating. It was cold. A total nonevent, but I'm getting ahead of my story.

In my introduction to African-American culture my cousin Inez was as important as the record shop or the two deejays. Inez, who lived in Harlem, was the daughter of my mother's cousin and closest friend, Tante Geraldine. Inez was popular in her neighborhood. She seemed to know everyone within a five-block radius. She and I were always together running to parties. It got so that no one would bother me within those blocks because they knew me as Inez's cousin.

During my freshman year at Science, on one of my visits to Inez, I first encountered another of my early influences—the stepladder speakers of 125th Street.

As their name suggests, these speakers would actually exhort the people from stepladders set up on strategic street corners along 125th Street. And usually they would be as dramatic in appearance as they were colorful in speech.

The stepladder would be decorated with two flags. On one side the red, green, and black—the colors of African liberation. And on the other—apparently only because the law required it and usually at least one cop would be observing—was Old Glory. Queen Mother Moore, an associate of Garvey's, was a tall, regal woman who wore spectacularly colored African robes and looked every inch the queen. Charles X Kenyatta was a bearded, erect, warrior-looking brother. He wore a ranger-style bush hat with a leopard-skin band and one side upturned, and usually a khaki safari jacket with a machete in a leopard-skin sheath on his belt. And these speakers were nationalists to the max.

Many of them were remnants or offshoots of the Garvey movement like Carlos Cook. Here Queen Mother Moore would speak to me. Here May Mallory would speak. Here Charles X Kenyatta and Porkchop Davies would speak to me. Here, somewhat later, Malcolm X would speak to me.

As soon as the weather warmed up, they would appear. They would be talking about Africa. Her history, culture, liberation struggles, and bright prospects once independent. And about our need and *duty* as children of Mother Africa to look to her. It was all exciting and different. On 125th Street you would get information and a perspective nowhere else present in the society. Certainly not in the white media. And not at school or even in the discourses of the young Communists and Socialists.

The Harlem stepladder orators had a profound effect on me. In a very real way they were the oral historians of the community, our town criers, waking up the sleeping town and bringing news of distant conflicts. Our secular prophets, they were keepers of the flame, holding aloft our heritage as African people in exile, keeping the flame of reunion and unity alive, ceaselessly exhorting us to keep historical and revolutionary faith with our ancestors' long history of struggle and resistance. We should never forget that we come from a long line of warriors and strugglers.

They brought us regular updates on the African struggle for independence on the continent and in the Caribbean. Liberation was in the air: the remorseless motion of history, the onrush of revolution. And as they made clear, these were no mere *winds* of change, but roaring storms of revolution. It was all around us, they said, if only we would recognize and embrace it. And that meant struggle and organization, conscious and constant struggle.

I forget which one, but one speaker would always punctuate his exhortations with an anguished cry, a kind of chorus:

> Mah people, Mah people,
> If you only knew who you were,
> You could not live the way you do.

Over the years, those words have stayed with me.

On 125th Street they extolled African revolutionaries, Jomo Kenyatta and his Kenyan Land and Liberation Army, Kwame Nkrumah, Patrice Lumumba, Sékou Touré, men who had come to vindicate us as a people.

Every African will be free, they thundered. The Caribbean is going to be free. They will run out the colonial masters. The French will be run out. They will run the British out. The Portuguese will have to go. South Africa is going to be free. The inevitable movement of history, the fulfillment of prophecy.

One could not help but be moved by such oratory. And even what little information came through the white man's news media seemed to confirm it. Africa and Africans—all over the world—were on the move. The world could never be the same. The impression on me was profound.

Remember, within this period my father's ship had made landfall in newly independent Ghana. He returned to us full of a vision of African independence and black peoples' power, with many stories to tell. How, for example, President Kwame Nkrumah, whom the people called the *Osaygefo,* the Redeemer, at the opening of the independent Parliament, had led his ministers onto the floor dressed in the humble cloth cap and coat of a convict. The man who had once worn the costume of colonial humiliation and subjugation was now the leader of the nation, my father had exulted.

The effect of the speakers on me was more than political, it was rhetorical. That is, beyond the message there was the influence of style. Important elements of my adult speaking style—the techniques of public speaking in the dramatic African tradition of the spoken word, can be traced to these street-corner orators of Harlem. To them and the Baptist preachers of the rural South.

To be successful both had to be highly skilled in poetic and rhetorical terms, and flawless in crowd psychology. To hold, inspire, and work their audience, they had to be powerfully persuasive and quick-witted and surefooted.

Both had tough audiences. The task of the street-corner speakers was all the more formidable because their audience was neither captive nor passive. Either you captured and held their interest or they were gone. These speakers had to educate random groups of the unconscious in America about Africa. By no means an easy task. The African masses, colonized in America, were victims of racial and cultural propaganda and a near-total miseducation about Africa. The speakers had to find arguments that would render their audience receptive to a positive vision of Africa against the full weight of their social conditioning.

The Southern preacher's task was a little easier. He had on his side the weight of traditional religious language and music, an entire repertoire of techniques. Later, almost unconsciously I would take my speaking style from both traditions when talking to my own people.

These speakers also had to squelch hecklers, diffuse tension, and keep the meeting moving without its degenerating into either shouting matches or violence. (Remember the constant presence of "New York's finest.")

I'll give one example: One Saturday afternoon the sidewalks were bustling. The speaker was describing Africa's boundless potential and building an eloquent case for repatriation to a good-sized, attentive crowd.

Along comes this too slick brother, hair freshly fried, piled up in greasy waves held in place by a do-rag. He saunters up, his coat slung over his shoulder by one finger, Jackie Wilson style. He supercool. He listens for a while then snorts.

"Africa? Africa ain't s—. Africa can't even produce matches." The speaker ignores him and continues. The dude begins to really put Africa down in earnest. The crowd grows restive. You can see that some of the brothers are only inches away from going upside his greasy head.

"Brothers and sisters," the speaker appeals. "Pay no attention to this man." He makes a quick, eloquent gesture, taking in his eyes, ears, mouth, and smiles sadly. The crowd laughs and relaxes visibly. The heckler is "blind, deaf, and dumb."

Now the heckler is beside himself. He begins to spit out *every* racist cliché of American miseducation on Africa. Obviously he had learned well and forgotten nothing.

"I ain't left nothing in Africa. Sure ain't trading no Cadillac for no damn elephant."

The speaker saw what was fixing to go down. "I told you," he chided us. "You don't need to be paying any attention at all to this Negro. Did you all take a good look at him?" The speaker held out his hands palms upward. "Seems like its fixing to drizzle." He smiled. *"An' then, brother, your head be going back to Africa before your mind do."*

His timing was perfect. The put-down, signifying at its best, was a masterpiece of cultural and verbal economy that can only be understood if you know the crinkling effect of moisture on processed African hair.

The crowd cracked up, repeating the line: "Damn, he say his hair be going back to Africa 'fo his mind do." "Sporting Life" slunk away. The building tension was neatly and expertly diffused. The cop looked disappointed.

At the same time that I was listening to the message and admiring the skill and virtuosity of the stepladder speakers, I was also doing readings and beginning to go on demonstrations with the young leftists at Bronx Science. But more and more these would begin to seem like disparate and incompatible worlds. In some ways, they *appeared* quite compatible, both being about the dynamics of political struggle and revolution, but there were fundamental/innate contradictions.

Now any Marxist will tell you that synthesis is the final achievement in the dialectic. And as Junebug Jabbo Jones, the peripatetic African-American sage would famously declare, "If you cain't understand the principle of contradiction, you sho cain't understand diddly about black folks life in these United States."

As an adult I would ultimately be able to use the theory of Pan-Africanism to synthesize the contradictions between the nationalism of 125th Street and the dialectical materialism of the Marxist study groups. But at the time I moved quite comfortably between these two worlds, thinking, learning, questioning, but joining no party, whether that of Garvey or of Marx.

What was the chief contradiction? At first it was far from obvious, more a vague feeling than a clear idea. But it was persistent, and something I could feel long before I could name it.

As I've said, my introduction to a Marxist approach during my freshman year was intellectually exciting for two reasons. As a systematic, all-encompassing, scientific theory of history and revolution it presented a way—in which everything seemed to fit neatly—to understand the political world and the "forces of history." Besides which, its language and its logic were similar in approach to the scientific materialist method we were being taught to apply to the physical world at Bronx Science. This meant that, intellectually, both the physical and the political worlds were suddenly logical and coherent, functioning in accordance with clear "laws" and principles that were susceptible to study and understanding. That was compelling.

This was such an eye-opening discovery that, for some considerable time, criticism was unthinkable. (The term *Eurocentric* was, of course, not then in my vocabulary.) But just as with the religion question, I could sense that something important was missing from this seamless "universal" system. Somehow it did not seem to take into serious account the rhythms and historical presence of my people.

The first simple and concrete example I had was that of trade unions and "working-class solidarity." I could not reconcile the way my young white comrades talked about the labor movement and working-class empowerment with the discussions of my father and his friends about their treatment at the hands of the union and the white workers on their jobs and the Mafia.

On 125th Street I first discovered the missing element. And this discovery was every bit as exciting as the other. Here the speakers also talked about political struggle, liberation, and revolution, but in very different terms. This "history" not only included us, it was all about us. Africa, the African diaspora, the African world, and African revolutionaries were their subject and their concern.

At first these two worlds of mine rarely intersected, but when they did, there was a friction that threw off hot sparks. For me one of these points of friction was in deciding which political writers should be read, given attention, and studied. So far as the white leftists were concerned, no African revolutionary thinkers seemed worthy of serious regard.

On 125th Street, though, the names George Padmore and occasionally C. L. R. James were mentioned as important African writers who were revolutionary thinkers. But on the rare occasion when George Padmore's name came up among the Young Communists, the tone was dismissive, as if he were some kind of renegade, almost as if he were a traitor who had abandoned Communism.

One of the great political and cultural resources for me at this time was Michaux's famous African Bookstore on 125th Street, which I would visit every chance I got. Mr. Michaux saw that I liked to read about our people and took an interest in me. One day I asked Mr. Michaux about Padmore. He showed me a copy of Padmore's *Pan-Africanism or Communism* and explained that Padmore was a great Pan-Africanist thinker who was an adviser or mentor to Kwame Nkrumah. I was fascinated. I did not have the money at the time to buy the book, but I skimmed through it eagerly. Later I would study Padmore and become one of his greatest supporters.

Even today I always refer to Padmore as a seminal Pan-Africanist and encourage all Pan-Africanists to study and learn from him.

Later I learned with interest that Padmore was born in Trinidad—he died in Africa—and that his original family name was Seymour Nurse. Nurse is a prominent name in the African community in Trinidad. I also learned that during his boyhood in Belmont (close to where my father had built his house), one of his playmates was young Cyril James.

Whenever C. L. R. James's name came up among the white leftists I knew in high school, he was more or less pigeonholed as a "Trotskyite," hence a revisionist and apostate from the "correct" line. But to the speakers on 125th Street, C. L. R. James was an African revolutionary thinker. Later when I came to read his *Black Jacobins,* I was thrilled—moved and inspired. That book is a powerful historical classic on the revolutionary struggle against slavery in Haiti, which especially emphasizes the revolutionary roles, spirit, and character of Haiti's African masses in that struggle. I was just overwhelmed. I loved it. I strongly recommend this great book to young Africans interested in their peoples' legacy of struggle.

Still later I would discover another of Harlem's great treasures, the Schomburg Collection. When Malcolm X began to become a presence in Harlem as the dynamic young minister who was organizing Mohammed's Mosque #7, a story began to circulate that established the young minister's character.

According to the story, Malcolm was driving along and saw a group of young brothers shooting craps on a sidewalk. He stopped the car and approached the game. He either seized or put his foot on the dice. Of course, the players started to get into they bad bags. Malcolm froze them with that look he had. My young brothers, you know what this building is? he asked. Yeah, I thought so. You don't know, do you? This is the Schomburg Collection. It's got damn near everything ever written by or about black people. And what you doing? Instead of being inside learning about yourself, your people, and our history, you out here in darkness shooting dice. That's what's wrong with us, why Mr. Muhammad says, "If you want to hide something from the black man, put it in a library."

Now, I was not among those crapshooters. But the story impressed on me the importance of the Schomburg and I began to spend many a profitable hour there.

During this time, my home neighborhood began to change slightly, as a few more African families moved in. A couple of these families had sons my age, and two of them, Buddy Melvin and Vinnie DeLucier, became my good friends. Buddy went to DeWitt Clinton High School, while Vinnie, a devout Catholic, went to Cardinal Hayes. But on weekends we three were running buddies, walking partners, hanging out together, going to parties. We were disciplined students, but weekends we partied. Buddy was a great dancer; Vinnie was so devout a Catholic that he refused to dance the grind, it not being "right" to get that close to girls. (Perhaps Marx had a point on European religion after all.) But my man Buddy, now, he liked him a good time. My parents liked Buddy, and his parents liked me, so we spent a lot of time in and out of each other's homes. Buddy would come to play an important role in my social life at Science.

By the end of my freshman year at Science I had established the friendships that would follow me through the four years, and which pretty much established my place in the school's student community. I made some good friends based on things we had in common. Of like minds, we made common cause, so to say. These friends were smart, intellectually active guys who were serious enough, disciplined students but not overbearing about it. We tended to be more relaxed about our intelligence. Certainly, we did not buy into the teeth-clenched competitiveness and academic upmanship and posturing that obsessed so many of our peers. Also, we all were athletes in at least one varsity sport, political activists who instinctively despised injustice, street-smart, unpretentious youths who loved to party. We banded together and formed a little club called Kokista. I no longer remember where we got the name, or what, if anything, it meant. It had to have *meant* something, but all I remember is that we were Kokista.

The members were Gene Dennis, Larry Greenbush, Tony Pantorino, Kenny Stearn, and yours truly. The club had no real agenda. We just hung together, discussed life, politics, and girls in that order, organized parties, and simply had down-to-earth fun.

To a great extent, Kokista may simply have been our defense against the rigid, uptight, status-conscious atmosphere that pervaded the school. We were close, and up until today, some of us maintain contact.

Something happened sophomore year that greatly increased Kokista's visibility and prestige at school. Bronx Science moved up the Grand Concourse, literally into the "backyard" of DeWitt Clinton, Buddy Melvin's school. The two schools were right across from each other. They still are. But the student cultures of the two institutions could not have been more different. So far as the Clinton students were concerned, Science students were "intellectual, elitist, and more than a little effete."

Clinton, first of all, was a boys school. It was academically respectable, but had no pretensions to elite status, and its students liked it that way. You could say it was more "democratic." Clinton was in every way a rougher, more physical culture than Science, and the proportion of Africans there was far, far greater. They had talented, aggressive athletic teams and fights all the time. And now they felt that the wimps from Science were invading their turf. Inevitably there was tension.

The same old neighborhood madness: just because you're from Clinton and we from Science, we have to fight. Fighting was by no means the Science students' strong suit. They were apprehensive about walking to the subway and boarding the trains after school.

Fact is, some of them were plumb terrified. Enter Kokista. We had to lead the delegations from Science into the trains to face down any challenge. Gene Dennis was built like a fullback. Larry was a muscular, strong-looking guy, and Kenny Stearn was a competitive swimmer, huge and always in shape. I was tall, rangy, not intimidated, and with a mouth on me.

And my hole card? . . . Buddy Melvin. Buddy was on the fencing team at Clinton and was a rough, tough brother and very respected over there. So I'd always drop his name.

"Why you guys want to mess with us?"

"You go to Science."

"Yeah, but I just looking for my brother. He go to Clinton."

"Whose yo brother?"

"Buddy Melvin."

"Buddy's your brother?"

"Ahuh. Ask him."

"Yo, maybe this cat's all right," and they would forgo the ass-kicking. Or else I'd get Buddy after school and he'd ride with us.

He'd say, "Hey, don't you touch him now. He mah brother."

"Yeah? And what about them?"

"They with him. They okay too."

Despite our honorable new role as tribunes of the physically and martially challenged, Kokista was still seen as a rebellious, nonconforming element among the Science students. In that rarefied atmosphere, we were something like Science's version of the teenage "rebel without a cause" syndrome, the Northern urban version of the Southern "good old boys."

Except to Mr. Beckenstein, one of our social studies teachers. He was not at all impressed with our "youthful rebellion" as he called it. He reached out to all students and liked us. We thought he was real down and liked him because he took us seriously, got to know us, challenged us intellectually, and discussed the political issues of the day with us.

Once, junior year I think, my mother came to school for a parents/teachers weekend and met my favorite teacher. A minor disaster.

During their conversation, Mr. Beckenstein demonstrated his awareness of his student's progress by throwing out: "You know Stokely says he wants to go into medicine . . ." My mother nods and smiles, and the teacher continues, "But, you know, I think his real calling will be politics."

"Oh?" said my mother.

"Oh, yes," Mr. B. enthused, "that's where his talents lie. The thing that's in your young man's blood is politics." My mother smiled politely and said nothing.

But in the car going home, she exploded. I mean my mother went off on poor Mr. Beckenstein.

"But is that man crazy? Is he a racist or what? What is this politics trash? What can you ever do in politics? What is there for you? You see any colored people in politics in America? You see my trial now, eh?"

Of course from the perspective of the time (1958), my mom was absolutely correct. As far as she could see, there was no space nor role for Africans in politics in America. No role worthy of her son anyway. There was to her mind only Adam Clayton Powell. What was I going to do, displace him?

"Well, Mr. Beckenstein's a real nice guy," I mumbled, "and a really good teacher."

"Good teacher? Trying to stop you from being a doctor? At least we know you can be that like your uncle. But you ever heard of any colored politician? That man is steering you wrong, the ol' brute."

But I knew there was truth in what Mr. B. had said. Yeah, I was still doing science. To all intents and purposes I was still going to be a doctor. But politics . . . it was calling in my blood.

About that same time an incident happened that I've never forgotten. It taught me something that has been with me all my life.

A group of us were in front of the school talking about our classes. A couple guys from Kokista and some brothers. We were discussing math, no doubt trying to impress each other with our erudition.

This older African comes along and stops to listen. The brother looked borderline derelict: his clothes didn't fit, kinda disheveled, and his hair was matted as though he was trying to grow dreadlocks without much success. Of course, dreads were not yet in style, so the old brother simply looked untidy.

"What you young gennulmen talking 'bout?" He posed the question kinda aggressively.

"Oh, we just talking about the Pythagorean theorem, sir," we told him a little condescendingly.

"Hell, that don't even exist. That's right, there's no such thing as the Pythagorean theorem," he repeated. "See, that's ancient African knowledge. Pythagoras the Greek didn't discover that. He got it from Africans." And he walked away mumbling to himself. Of course, we were dismissive and we Africans a little embarrassed. Who was this hobo-looking old dude to be contradicting our teacher and textbooks?

We were still talking about it a few minutes later when the brother passed back.

"So you all didn't believe me, huh? Tha's good, check *everything* out. There is no such thing as the Pythagorean theorem, that's Egyptian. Okay? You go to the library and check these books." He reeled off a string of references, which I wrote down. I must admit that I was going through the motions mostly to humor him. "Thank you, sir, you know I gotta go check these." Figured I owed him the respect of at least appearing to take him seriously.

Sometime later I was in the library and came across the references in the back of my notebook. Sure enough, they existed. Every one checked out and, in fact, supported his story.

I was shocked. I mean astonished. Well, looka this. That old dude knew *exactly* what he was talking about. What I learned from that was never, *never* to underestimate or dismiss anybody. Not even the poorest, humblest, least prepossessing person. Especially with our own people. Ain't no way to know just by their appearance what they been through or where they coming from. "Thou seest that man's fall, but thou knowest not his wrassling."

That lesson would be reinforced time and again when as a young man I was organizing sharecroppers in the rural South. Especially with our elders. Knowledge and sometimes wisdom can come from the most unlikely of sources. The stone that the builders rejected . . .

And of course, in Africa, in the villages, the same thing. A proverb I heard stayed with me: "Truth is like a goatskin bag: each man carries his own."

CHAPTER VI

Howard University:
Everything and Its Opposite

As I began my senior year at Science, the question of college became paramount. Not whether I was to go, but where? Within the family, that I would go to college had long been taken for granted. Whatever else happened, the son was going to college.

Now, an aspect of male chauvinism was in that. Remember my father's dream of the Carmichael family clinic in Trinidad? It was simply assumed that *I* was to be the doctor. The idea that one or more of my sisters might have been better endowed intellectually, more academically disciplined, or had a greater aptitude for the healing profession never arose. (Two of my sisters are today registered nurses.) No. It was simply assumed that the family's only son would become the physician. I guess this was our Caribbean version of what is now called the "patriarchal attitude" as expressed in the only truly wrongheaded African proverb I know: "Educating a daughter is like fertilizing your neighbor's field."

No question my mother had some traditional ideas in this regard. During my "wild" teenage roaming, she had a barnyard analogy she never tired of. "Look," she would say, "I look at it like this: I've got four pullets and one rooster. You know I'm going pen up my pullets and let my rooster run free. If anyone else wants to let *their* hens run loose, that's their business. I'm not gonna pen up my rooster."

But having said that, I must point something else out about May Charles. After my father suddenly died during my second year at university, May Charles had to go to work. I've always been convinced my father worked himself to an early grave trying to take care of the family under American capitalism while fighting the racism of the workplace. My mom took the post office examination but quickly realized she could not support the family, much less educate them, on a beginning-level, weekly take-home pay of $59. So she shipped out as a stewardess on the SS *Argentina* so as to be able to help with our education, while Mommy Olga kept the home fires burning. Today May Charles will tell you with pride that all her daughters save the eldest, who had a disability, went through college successfully.

But for a time the choice of a college for me was problematic. The senior class at Science was full of college talk: nothing but the pros, cons, comparative strengths, and academic prestige of various schools. But after four years at Science—enjoyable and productive years to be sure—I was not at all sure that I wanted to spend the next four at a similar or even greater remove from my people and culture.

During my junior and senior years, my political life had become more active. And to my great delight most of the action was coming from the African community. Ever since Montgomery, Dr. King and his nonviolent actions had become more of a presence in the political discussion among New York progressives.

I and my friends in Kokista respected Dr. King a great deal because he had found a tactic that put thousands of people in motion to confront racism. And in Montgomery—the cradle of the Confederacy—the organized and unified African community had won big.

To be sure, the 125th Street nationalists did not support Dr. King. They attacked nonviolence, mocked his talk of redemptive suffering, and questioned the feasibility and desirability of "integration" as a goal. They felt Dr. King was "begging white folks to accept us," something white folks had never done in three hundred years.

I parted company with the nationalists on Dr. King. It seemed clear to me then that nonviolent mass action was an effective tactic. I supported any strategy that could move the Southern masses of our people to confront American apartheid. And any leader who could inspire them to this kind of direct action had my complete respect. In New York, at sympathy pickets and fund-raising events, supporters like Bayard Rustin would speak and artists like Harry Belafonte, Odetta, Ruby Dee, and Ossie Davis would perform. Our group from Science always attended these events. I was very, very proud that most of the political activity available to us was in support of my people's struggles.

In 1960, when the Southern student sit-ins began, CORE would picket department chain stores that discriminated in the South. We Science activists always supported those demonstrations.

We would also go to peace rallies called by the Ban the Bomb movement. The capitalist press always tried to portray the peace movement as Communist, a Communist front, or Communist-inspired. Of course there were leftists at these rallies. But the people I met were mostly very religious, committed pacifists, or folk simply concerned with global survival with no Communist or socialist politics at all.

So I was seeing a lot of political action, much of it in Harlem. But I never joined—formally committed to—any group, Marxist, nationalist, or religious. In my senior year, the Sharpsville Massacre occurred on March 21, 1960. The South African police and military fired on a nonviolent march of unarmed Africans killing sixty-nine and wounding over three hundred. I joined a large march from Harlem to the United Nations in protest. Earlier, I helped organize students for one of Bayard Rustin's "Youth Marches for Integrated Schools," which were mounted in Washington. I believe that this might be where I first heard Dr. King address a large group, but I can't really remember.

Early in my senior year the Young Communists at Science organized a bus for a demonstration against the House Un-American Activities Committee in Washington. I was on the bus. I am not sure whether I was the sole African on that bus, but if I wasn't, we sure were not many. This would not have been unusual in left political actions at Science, so I never gave it a thought.

The demonstration was in progress (I think at the White House, but it could have been the Capitol—official Washington, anyway) when our bus pulled up. We streamed off and approached the picket line, which was of impressive size given the oppressive political climate in the country at the time. As we approached the pickets, I saw something that would profoundly affect the direction of my life.

A section of the line was black. The marchers were not only all African, but they were all about my age. Man, I jes' rushed over.

"Hey, y'all. Who are you guys with? The Young Socialists? The Communists?"

"No, man. We're NAG," said a brother who introduced himself later as John Moody.

"Yeah? And what's NAG, my man?"

"That's the Nonviolent Action Group from Howard University. Why'nt you join us?"

I jumped in the line and the brothers and sisters told me about Howard and NAG. That they were affiliated with the Student Nonviolent Coordinating Committee (SNCC). That they had been campaigning in Virginia and Maryland and in D.C., the nation's capital. They struck me as smart, serious, political, sassy—and they were black.

All the way back to New York I was intensely excited. I was surprised at how excited I'd become to discover young Africans who were committed activists. But I was pretty certain that I'd solved the college question.

Everything I later found out about Howard confirmed the fit: Howard was a historic black school founded during Reconstruction to educate the children of "the freedmen." It was named for its first president, General Oliver Otis Howard, a Union general and abolitionist. More to the point, its medical school was said to have produced a majority of the doctors in the African community here and abroad.

In my mind, the choice of college had been a done deal from the conversations on that picket line at the White House. When we'd left, I'd said, "I'll see you in September." And while I would apply to and enroll at Howard University, it was NAG I was really joining.

But at first my parents weren't sure.

According to my mother, "During his last year in high school, Stokely started talking about Howard University. His father and I figured, because everyone said he was so smart, that he should go to Harvard. But every time we said 'Harvard,' he said 'Howard.' It was 'Harvard.' 'No, Howard.' Until finally we put the case to my uncle Lew, the psychiatrist, who was the family authority on all things educational."

Dr. Silcote's advice carried the day. He said that beyond a certain point the student was more important than the school. A serious student could get an excellent education at either place, as good an education at Howard as at Harvard. Besides which, he said, the friends you make in college tend to be friends for life. So Howard it was to be. Besides, it sure was a lot more affordable.

Howard University would open up vast new horizons for me. No doubt about that. Without question, I received a unique education there. And no question, it was qualitatively and substantively different from any education I could possibly have had at Harvard or anywhere else in the world.

At Howard I was educated as much by my fellow students as by the faculty; as much from the location of the school, the friends I made, and the spirit of the times as from anything to be found in the curriculum; as much from the character of the administration as from the quality of instruction; as much from the movement as from the university. But educated I was.

Because in our time—the opening four years of the 1960s—Howard University was an extraordinarily interesting place for any young African to be who was not totally brain-dead and who was concerned with his people and their struggle. And both conditions were to be found among students at Howard.

Howard presented me with every dialectic existing in the African community. At Howard, on any given day, one might meet every black thing . . . and its opposite. The place was a veritable tissue of contradiction, embodying the best and the absolute worst values of the African-American tradition. As Junebug Jabbo Jones (may his tribe increase) loved to say, "Effen yo' doan unnerstan' the principle of eternal contradiction, yo' sho ain't gonna unnerstan' diddly about Howard University. Nor about black life in these United States neither."

113

What's more, in every significant regard the Howard experience was the diametrical opposite to that of Bronx Science. Now, I am not putting down either school. I really enjoyed both, and I was, for good or ill, profoundly influenced by both, though in different ways. One obvious difference is age. I entered Science at fourteen and Howard at eighteen. But more than that, in terms of institutional culture, the character of the student population, the general social and intellectual ambience, it is impossible to imagine two more different schools.

Each school had a well-developed sense of its uniqueness. Each had an equally strong view of its institutional mission and constituencies. But nothing about these was even remotely similar. They could have been in different countries. Indeed on different planets. Which, if you think of it, is a reflection not on those schools, but of the country. Science had its face turned rigidly back toward Europe, while Howard, no matter how much some resisted or sought to play it down, had turned its face, however tentatively, toward Africa.

Howard's most egregious image in the African community was as an elitist enclave, a "bougie" school where fraternities and sororities, partying, shade consciousness, conspicuous consumption, status anxiety, and class and color snobbery dominated a student body content for the most part with merely "getting over" academically.

Was this true? Certainly to some extent, but while this aspect was for some reason very *visible*, it was, give thanks, by no means the whole story. Nor even close to it. There were, of course, the status-conscious, overindulged, whiskey-drinking children of affluent black professionals. But at least half the American students were from the South, and the great majority, whether from North or South, were poor, the children of black workers and strivers and most usually—as in my own case—the first in their immediate family to attend college. So, if they aspired to the attitudes, behavior, and values described above, they hardly had the means to afford them.

Adding to which a hefty percentage—greater than in any other American university—were "foreign" so-called. This meant Africans from either the English-speaking Caribbean or mostly anglophone Africa. These students tended to be slightly older, well prepared, and motivated academically, somewhat more cosmopolitan in outlook, and every bit as poor as the Africans born in America. So that when I checked into the new Men's Residence Hall in September, my roommate was Gurney Beckford, a small, dark, exceedingly earnest young man from the hills of Jamaica. Housing probably saw my place of birth as Trinidad and so stuck me in with someone else from "the islands." It was fine with both of us, we got on great. Gurney is still a good friend.

The new Men's Residence Hall was formally named Drew Hall that year. "Drew" being Dr. Charles Drew, the African (American) physician whose pioneering work in hematology isolated plasma and made blood transfusion possible. Dr. Drew had done this work while on the faculty of the Howard Medical School. According to the oral tradition on campus, Dr. Drew, whose work had saved countless American and other lives during World War II, and who had transformed the entire practice of Western medicine, bled to death after a car accident in the South where he was denied the prompt medical attention he had made possible and that might have saved his life. I'm told that this account has recently been challenged, but that is how it was told on campus when we were there.

I expect the Trinidadian birthplace was also the reason I soon received a letter summoning me to "the foreign students' orientation."

Of course I looked like, dressed like, and talked like a black New Yorker. But I could slip at will into the Trinidad idiom and accent of my parents and their friends. A first-generation immigrant kid who had not forgotten the language of the old country.

But my freshman dorm was an extraordinary place English-language-wise. There were brothers from Georgia, Alabama, Mississippi, every state of the old Confederacy, and areas urban and rural. There were my home-boys from Harlem, Brooklyn, and the Bronx, and brothers from Detroit, Philly, Roxbury, South Side Chicago. All Africans born in America, but what a diversity of slang and sound. Also, by the end of my first week I had beginning friendships with brothers from Jamaica, Barbados, Trinidad, Antigua, the Bahamas, and on and on. I had also met Igbo and Yoruba men from Azikiwe's Nigeria, Fanti and Ashanti men from Nkrumah's Ghana, and Luos and Kikuyus from Kenyatta's Kenya. All three heads of state had a personal relationship with Howard.

During 1960 a wave of African nations had attained independence, as would Jamaica, Trinidad, and a host of smaller territories in the east Caribbean in the following two years. Later, the *Osageyfo*, President Nkrumah, would correctly characterize this as being mere "flag independence." But to us at Howard that fall, blithely unaware of the looming threat of neocolonialism, it was an exciting, heady moment rich in promise. All Africa would be free. You could see it happening. Free to choose judiciously from the riches of its own traditional wisdom and the best of Western achievements to give the world a new definition of modernity and a higher humanism. Africa, we were fully confident, would solve the great human problems that continued to bedevil European civilization. We were so sure then, so optimistic, that we would live to see that. Now, I think it will take longer.

It seemed like almost monthly a new African embassy would open up with suitable dignity and fanfare. The diplomats always reached out to their nationals studying at Howard, who in turn invited their "American" friends. So we got accustomed to going with our friends to any number of annual national independence day celebrations at various African and Caribbean embassies. That time and place had a tangible, intoxicating air of Pan-African motion and internationalism. It was soul-stirring.

The administration at Howard, and to a certain extent the faculty, would reflect many aspects of the massive contradictions underlying the relationship between Africans in America and white America.

On one hand, the school pointed with justifiable pride to its historical role in the progress of the race. Not just by educating "Negro leadership" but claiming an honorable role at times in the actual struggle. For example, most of the lawyers in *Brown vs. Board of Education* were Howard Law School products. Outgoing president Mordecai Johnson had been a forthright advocate for African civil rights. President James M. Nabrit Jr., who replaced him the year after I entered, had been part of the legal team arguing *Brown*. So he came from an activist legal tradition.

The Howard Choir (in the tradition of the Fiske Jubilee Singers, which, in the 1880s, had rescued that school financially by famously touring European capitals singing the powerful music of their slave ancestors) could make you weep and exult with those same "Negro spirituals." Still, the dean of fine arts was so unreconstructed and unapologetic an Afro-Saxon that he absolutely forbid jazz in any form, not even from the elegant and musically sophisticated "Duke of E," in Crampton Auditorium . . . as long as he would be dean.

Howard was the only historically black school in the entire nation funded by the federal government. My position was, in simple justice, all black schools should have been, so that was no real cause for gratitude on our part. But that was not, could not at least publicly be, the position of the higher administration.

For some curious reason the congressional committees that controlled the university's budget seemed to attract a disproportionate number of Dixiecrat politicians. These Southern Democrats, the political beneficiaries and institutional protectors of white supremacy in the nation, were aptly described (some of them, anyway) as "the most mean-spirited, foulmouthed crackers who ever bought a fool's vote with whiskey." And they did not position themselves on those committees out of any sudden rush of goodwill toward black folk.

So annually Howard's president had to walk a narrow line drawn by the whim, caprice, or outright malice of these Dixiecrats. At budget time, a tangible mood of anxiety, high or muted, depending on the perceived mood of the Congress, seemed to emanate from our administration building. I don't remember a student who was not aware of this reality. And I don't know one that did not resent it. It was almost always one of the first things a new student heard: "Looka here, Uncle Sam pays the bills. Best you never forget that and always present yourself accordingly."

I can now sympathize with the fundamental difficulty of our administrators in having to go hat in hand to those racists. Those black men, when all was said and done, did have the responsibility to protect and advance as best they could the school's interests. But on campus that constraint translated into a series of attitudes, rules, and injunctions calculated to prevent any activity on the part of the students that was likely to offend "powerful white folk." These filtered down to us via the Student Activities bureaucracy, with whom we were, consequently, constantly at war.

As you might well imagine, we in NAG took a slightly different position. Inasmuch as this nation had enslaved Africans and continued to discriminate against them, thereby crippling them educationally, we felt that the *least* the nation owed the African community was excellent resources by which to educate ourselves. Educationally, we felt America owed us many more than one federally supported school. As a matter of historical obligation, not charity.

So far as "upsetting powerful whites" was concerned, we felt no obligation to be "nice" or "neat, clean, honest, and polite" as the formula went, just to get the budget. We felt, especially as we grew more confident in our organizing skills, that we students could organize effective pressure inside the nation's capital, in international forums, and before the world media, to ensure that the U.S. government met its obligations to black education. We understood that the Howard administration would need to stay aloof—publicly—but at least they should not hinder us. The world was changing, wasn't it?

But this was never the position of the administration. Which is why NAG was never a recognized student organization at Howard. Every year we petitioned. Every year the Student Government and the students supported us. Every year the initiative ran into the most skillful, stubborn, and barefaced obstructionism from the Student Activities bureaucracy. Processes were arbitrarily changed, suspended, or ignored; committees dissolved or simply did not meet all year; or else meetings were summarily adjourned before a final vote could be taken.

We would be furious, roundly denouncing the "handkerchief-headed, plantation-overseer mentality" of the Division of Student Life. But you know something . . . I'm now prepared to see a certain method in their madness. As the spiritual says, "You'll understand it better by m' by."

Because, you know, no one in the Howard administration ever once told us to stop. (Though they probably knew that it wouldn't do no good no how.) They never tried to coerce or threaten us with expulsion or other administrative sanction. Which was not the case with a lot of state-dependent Southern black schools. For example, President Felton Clarke of Southern University in Baton Rouge, Louisiana, that year, to his shame, expelled *all* his student activists, nearly fifty students. Two of whom, Eddie C. Brown and his younger brother "Rap," ended up with us in NAG.

The administration knew full well who we were. But by the simple expedient of denying us recognition, they gave themselves "deniability." By disclaiming knowledge or responsibility, they did not have to move on us, and they never did. I can imagine our president, like Ellison's invisible man's grandfather, "yessing the white folk to death."

[At this point an intervention for the record by our comrade-in-arms Tim Jenkins seems appropriate:

"I would quarrel somewhat with the characterization given of the past presidents as compliant tools of the Congress. The record shows that Mordecai (Johnson) repeatedly lectured the Southern bigots he needed for funding with his jeremiads against racism. The record will also show that during his tenure he repeatedly refused to fire a single professor condemned by HUAC. Or, during the forties, to expel the Howard students who sat in, in the cafeteria of the House and Senate. In this respect the Ralph Ellison quote may be something of a disservice to their historic contributions. This is not to say that there were not a host of subordinates who would gladly have thrown civil liberties to the wolves for job security along with other uglies of bourgeois ethics."

As Carmichael said, "every black thing . . . and its opposite." The best and worst of the black tradition. —EMT]

After spending the first two days registering, I set out to find NAG, which was not to be found.

"Nonviolent Action Group? NAG? Well, there is the NAACP. . . . No? The Alphas, the Kappas, the French Club. . . . No? Sorry, I can't find any such organization on campus."

Ultimately I found someone—Dion Diamond or John Moody, I think—who'd been at the anti-HUAC demonstration and could explain that NAG met every second Sunday off campus at the Newman House.

"But Howard's got an NAACP youth group, how come?" I asked.

"Course they do. But that's only because they never *do* anything, Jack. I don't think they even ever meet."

Which is how it was that on the second Sunday after my arrival I became a functioning member of SNCC, or at least its Washington, D.C., affiliate, the elusive NAG.

It is possible in hindsight to see some element of principle, strategy, and even political cunning in at least one of the university's actions that at the time had so infuriated us. Tell the truth an' shame the devil. But a host of other matters are not susceptible to any equally honorable explanation.

These came especially from middle and lower administration members and some faculty in the form of attitudes and policies that always angered us. I mean, they messed with our minds.

I'm talking an outmoded nineteenth-century missionary approach to "Negro education." We resented the patent condescension. According to which the educational mission was to "civilize young Negroes fresh from the cotton fields." It was to render us "cultured," i.e., polite and safe in word, thought, deed, and appearance so that ultimately superior white America might in its benevolence, one blessed day, accept "the Negro." Academically and culturally then, the imperative was to promulgate, uncritically, the curricula of American (read white) higher education and the attitudes and behavior of "the better class of white people." A few administrators would actually use such language to us without any evident embarrassment.

The assumption was that America had a "Negro problem," which was us. So that the *onus* was on *us* to improve *ourselves*. If only "the Negro" were less primitive and more responsible. If only they smelled less and glistened more, were more "cultured" and less crude, more industrious and responsible ad infinitum, then white America would gladly accept us. (Key word there, *responsible*. The white press used to brazenly issue orders thinly disguised as friendly advice to "responsible" Negro leaders. Responsible to whom or what?) Thus it was common on campus to hear Southern students harshly ordered to "learn to speak properly. Stop sounding so country." When in my sophomore year a NAG member (and my girlfriend) started to wear her hair natural, it precipitated hysteria among the dorm mothers. She was threatened with expulsion from the dorms and the school. Happily a young dean of women, Patricia Roberts, intervened and maturity prevailed. But this backwardness was widespread and ingrained and greatly resented by every student I ever spoke to about it.

An aspect of this thinking carried over into the curriculum and instruction. Too many of the faculty bureaucrats who set curricula seemed content to accept the establishment textbook version of American reality. A dispensation in which we were either absent or present only as a lingering but peripheral *problem* in American life. The Negro as social liability. For these loyal Afro-Saxons, the only serious criticism of the mainstream was for its incomprehensible exclusion of deserving and highly evolved Negroes like themselves. Correct that single, inexplicable shortcoming by affording them their due social recognition and public acceptance, and America was perfect.

Of course, the implication of these attitudes—that we students should strive for self-improvement while accepting respectfully all the values and practices of white America—required rationalizing racist humiliation.

This was precisely the kind of psychic self-immolation that was totally unacceptable to our generation of students. Totally unacceptable, Jack.

We were young adults. The "foreign" students—Africans born elsewhere—tended to be even a little older. Many were mature men and women who had worked for years before being able to seek higher education. At the first general residents' meeting in the new Men's Hall dorm, I can remember standing next to a dignified "freshman" from Guyana who looked older than my father, and being gradually suffused with deep embarrassment and outrage at what we both were hearing.

The dorm director was extraordinarily condescending and not real smart. I listened in disbelief and growing humiliation as he spoke to us as though addressing children. The highlight of his address was a catalog of insulting "housekeeping" expectations apparently predicated on the assumption that most of us were encountering flush toilets and indoor plumbing for the first time. To the men from Africa and the Caribbean, as to us, he was their first official introduction to Howard, and for them by extension, to African-Americans. What on earth can they have thought of us?

At the foreign-student orientation I again received a shock. It was a large enough meeting. Mature and intelligent men and women from Africa and the Caribbean receiving their first orientation to the school, the city, and again the African community in America. And here was an African administrator of Howard University in effect planting the fear of "American Negroes" in our consciousness. We were not really encouraged to associate with black "Americans"—cultural differences, they said—and were warned not to venture freely into the surrounding community because of crime. It was "us and them" at its worst. Howard was in a typical black urban community, with all the problems associated with that, but whatever their intentions, the presentation from Howard representatives was heavy-handed, crudely stereotypical, and a clear effort, I thought, to continue to divide Africans. I was furious. Had it come out of a white mouth, I'd have unhesitatingly dismissed it as racist. I resolved then and there to cultivate relationships with African brothers and sisters from outside the country and to try to pull them more and more into campus life and the social fabric of the African-American community. That became NAG's policy also.

But—praise the Lord—evrah thang an' its opposite . . . Mr. Ted Chambers, a short, infinitely sweet-natured African-American gentleman was coach of Howard soccer. He looked at me with astonishment colored by just the slightest skepticism.

"Son, you from New York? You play soccer?"

"Yes, sir. Captain of my high school team in New York."

His eyes really lit up. "Captain, you say?"

"Yes, sir. Bronx Science, three-year starter."

"Oh, can we use you! Go put these on and warm up. The tryouts start in fifteen minutes."

I ran off and put on the sweats and my own soccer shoes, which Science had allowed us to keep. I'd played all summer in Van Cortlandt Park because I knew the Howard team was supposed to be good. But when I ran back, the varsity was scrimmaging. I sat on a bench watching in astonishment and waiting for the rookies to show up.

Wow. This is such a great team, I thought. I can hardly believe this is the team I'm gonna play on. Wow. These guys were amazing: quick, incredibly skilled, they looked to me like young professionals.

"What's the matter?" Coach Chambers asked. "Why you still sitting on the bench?"

"Oh, Coach. I'm just waiting for the team to get off so I can—"

"Team? That's not the varsity, son. Those are the tryouts. Git on out there."

My jaw dropped. "*Those* are . . . tryouts?" He said yes. I got up slowly.

He approached, looking at me with concern. "You okay, son? Are you sure you play soccer?"

"Coach, I really do . . . but if those are the tryouts . . . can I carry water for your team?"

"If you can play, you should get out there."

I really wasn't a bad soccer player . . . in New York. Fact is, in Van Cortlandt Park I was considered a serious player, a rising star. So I did all right. Maybe even better.

"You did fine, son. You can make the team," Coach Chambers assured me afterward. I figured I probably could too. But clearly, to play with those dudes I'd have to devote way more time to soccer than I was prepared to. I was, after all, a premed student. I would have to study. But I went to every game I could and even played with the team in practice when I could.

Coach kept after me to join up. I knew why. I may have been the first African from America he'd seen in a soccer uniform. All his players were from the continent or the Caribbean. And they were simply excellent. The Howard team was one of the best in the nation, and the only athletic team of any accomplishment at a school that had no athletic scholarships at all. In the "American" sports—football and basketball—the courageous but outclassed Howard teams routinely had their heads handed them by teams of the best black athletes in the country . . . all on full scholarship with many on their way to the professional ranks. Today, those guys would all be at the white athletic factories, Notre Dame, Alabama, and the like.

But our soccer players were really, really dread. Today, half of them would be offered professional contracts. But here at Howard, they had no scholarships and everyone worked nights, went to school mornings, and showed up in the afternoons to destroy any team put before them on the field. And for the most part they were successful engineering, premed, and dentistry students too. My first two years they were national champions in the NAIA.

I got to know the players and brought my American-born friends to the games. The best of the players I practiced with were regularly named all-Americans. I remember Winston Alexis (Trinidad), Junior Sanguinetti (Jamaica), Aloysius Charles (Antigua), Alexander Romeo (Bahamas), Ernest Ekpe (Nigeria), and one utterly unbelievable soccer genius from Jamaica called "Dybie" Cooke. Back home, Dybie had been a regular on the national team. At Howard he drove a cab at night, went to engineering school by day, and never seemed to practice. Then at game time this short, stocky, bowlegged fellow would appear. Regularly, about four or five times during a game, seemingly at will, Dybie would nonchalantly collect the ball in front of his goal and traverse the full length of the field at a dead run, the ball seemingly glued to his feet. Starting, stopping, darting, feinting, as he dribbled his way effortlessly through the entire opposing team. This is no exaggeration, the *entire* opposing team!

The crowd would go absolutely wild, on its feet, giving out a collective roar that might well have been heard down at the White House and should have been. One did not have to understand anything at all of the game to recognize that you had just seen something magical. Just as later you would not have to know the intricacies of basketball to recognize Michael Jordan's genius or much about boxing to recognize the uniqueness of Muhammad Ali's physical endowments and craft. That was Dybie Cooke of Spanish Town, Jamaica. I wonder whatever became of that brother.

During my freshman and sophomore years, the Howard soccer Bisons dominated the NAIA. Junior year, they moved into the NCAA to go up against the wealthy athletic factories with teams full of imported talent, all on full scholarship and carefully recruited mercenaries.

By then I was totally politically engaged, but I made certain to be on campus the day we played the defending "big college" national champions. By this time the soccer team had worked its Pan-African magic on the student body. It was a rainy, overcast day. The stands were full of Africans born in America, Africa, and the Caribbean. It was a larger crowd than the winless football team had managed to attract, except maybe at homecoming. There's an editorial from the student paper, written after the game by its very "American" sports editor, Jimmy McCannon, that captures the moment rather well:

"Soccer is all right but it's a game for foreign students" is an old, cold argument that received a severe dowsing in the rain last Saturday as Westchester (1961–62) Large College national champions met the Howard (1961–62) Small College champions at a mud-drenched Howard stadium.

The Booters' great performance against the powerful Rams was indicative of the rise in the stock of soccer and the "foreign" student. . . . Most of the "fans" who braved the inclement weather . . . knew little or nothing about soccer, but fell in love with the speed, skill, and rugged action of the game. The crowd, which was drained of every emotion during an action-packed struggle between two very well-matched teams, was one of the largest ever to witness a soccer game here.

After the winning goal, pandemonium reigned. The crowd in a burst of passion streamed en masse onto the field and lifted their gory, mud-splattered scorers—Winston Alexis and Vernon Hazlewood—onto their formerly umbrella-protected shoulders. . . . In that instant a pride and unity created by their show of supreme skill made everyone connected to Howard proud.

Just as Jackie Robinson had made race a forgotten issue to the true baseball fan, our Booters dismissed in one unforgettable afternoon the tag "foreign." They belonged to Howard in every way and their adoring fans made them know it.

The men on that field representing us were no longer simply Jamaican, Nigerian, Antiguan, Trinidadian, or "West Indian." At the end of the game there were no "foreign" students or "Americans" on that field. The unity and belonging that enveloped the ecstatic faces that had shared a great athletic experience drew Washingtonians, Mississippians, Ohioans, and New Yorkers on the field to embrace fellow Howardites.

—Howard University *Hilltop*, November 16, 1962

Evrah thang . . . an' its opposite.

Ahm gonna lay down my sword and shield. Whether this was by inclination of the administration, by congressional dictate, the school's missionary origins, or by all three, I do not know. But I remember only two activities that were officially compulsory for all freshmen U.S. citizens: chapel on Sunday and the Reserve Officers' Training Corps.

I had no intention of entering the U.S. armed services, but in 1960 there was as yet no popular movement against the militarization of universities. So the only way I, as an individual, could resist was to get out of the marching, which I felt was a monkey show on campus, and also to raise the obvious contradictions in the military science classes.

We had a choice: the army or the air force. Since I had no intention of marching to and fro swinging my arms, I chose the air force, thinking there would be less parading about. But there was still too much.

So, the first day when we were lined up in our uniforms to march, Cadet Carmichael fainted. The second go-round I fainted again. The third time I fainted I was excused from parade, permanently.

In the class discussions I would raise questions about the ethics of having training in the arts of massive destruction at a school allegedly educating us for the advancement of humanity. This was no mere debating ploy. I was seriously troubled by the clear contradictions, so I kept raising that and similar questions.

Our instructor was a captain, an African born in America. After a few classes he understood that (a) I was genuinely troubled by the contradictions and (b) I was not likely to shut up.

"Okay, Cadet," he said, "here's what's going to happen. Take the exams, and any grade you earn, I will award. And of course, you needn't worry too much about attending the classes." That was cool by me. I needed a grade to graduate so I read the book and took the exams.

Some students—more than a few—not only disagreed with my position but were passionate and vocal about it. These brothers felt that it was our patriotic duty to serve. Some were planning to enter the military professionally. The interesting thing is many of them were from the South. So it was easy. "Look, Jack, I'd love to be a patriot too. And just as soon as this country ends segregation, ends racial discrimination, stops the denial of legal and political rights to our people, I'll run to enlist. I be the *first* one, blood, I promise."

A distinguished historian on the faculty named Professor Rayford Logan, had written a famous dissenting history of Reconstruction called *The Betrayal of the Negro*. So naturally I hastened to take his course, in which we read his *The Negro in American Life and Thought*. Either in that book or in his lectures, we learned about a consignment of German prisoners of war being sent south to prison camps in Mississippi during World War II. Their guards were a detachment of black MPs. When the train crossed the Mason-Dixon Line, guess what? These armed African (American) soldiers, in the uniforms of their country, guarding "their" nation's enemies, were at mealtime ordered out of the air-conditioned white dining car to the Jim Crow eating cubicle at the rear of the train. The enemy prisoners, being "Aryan," were welcome to enjoy the comfort of the well-appointed white-supremacist dining car.

Truthfully, I had no idea I'd said anything aloud until Professor Logan stopped speaking. Professor Logan was very austere. No one ever interrupted him.

"Yes, did you say something?" he asked, staring at me.

"Sorry. I hadn't meant to," I muttered.

"Well, young man, what did you not mean to say?"

"I said, sir, that if it had been me, I would have blown that train to hell."

Professor Logan merely looked long at me and nodded. "Thank you," and he went on with his lecture. After that I couldn't wait to be accosted by the Southern patriots about ROTC.

> Ah bin down in the Valley
> For a very long time
> But I ain't got weary yet.

With one important difference, those lines from a popular spiritual well describe my experience as a premed Howard freshman. Except that I got real, real weary down in that valley.

At Howard the liberal arts were taught on the upper quadrangle, the physically most elevated area of campus, the so-called Hilltop, where the Founders Library, the Art Department, Douglass Hall, Crampton Auditorium, and the Ira Aldridge Theatre were located.

Engineering, medicine, architecture and the physical sciences were taught in the lower area of the campus, hence, "in the Valley." As a premed student most of my courses, being natural sciences, were down in the Valley. Thanks to Bronx Science, these courses were not particularly demanding to me academically, many being, in effect, repeats of my senior year. The difficulties I would encounter in the Valley were of an entirely different order.

From my childhood, medicine was the career I and the family had chosen. It was one of the three—along with the law and the pulpit—said to offer a way of earning a living independent of white society's control. I had crossed off the other two in favor of medicine because it seemed to offer a clearer, essential, and more unambiguous service that was in short supply among our people. It also offered, as far as I was concerned, respect as well as a secure living, in that order.

In the Valley, with the exception of the engineers, the students all planned to become either physicians, dentists, or pharmacists, apparently in that order. A fair percentage were Africans from outside the United States. Most, but not all, of these students spoke in moving and idealistic terms of bringing modern medical care to their newly independent countries. A few, mostly from the Caribbean, seemed animated in their career choice mostly by the profit motive.

But the Africans born in America? They were, as Sterling Brown used to say, "a Negro of a different color." These guys—the clear majority—were forthright and to my mind more than a little vulgar. They bragged openly about the luxury cars, grand houses, and large incomes they were after. Their talk of the light-skinned, "good-haired" trophy wives they intended to marry really annoyed me. A wicked rumor on campus was that bourgeois-aspiring mothers of limited means would borrow, beg, or steal to send their light-skinned, attractive daughters to Howard. "Now, girl, you go bring me back a *doctah,* hear. Don't you dare come back without gitting you at least a *dentist.* Remember now, we can afford to send you at most for two years, so you got no time to waste."

Almost certainly that had to be an exaggeration, not without a certain malice, probably created by darker, smarter sisters. But the status-hungry premed freshmen sure seemed to play to it big time. All science students had white lab coats, which to the uninitiated looked much like doctors' hospital coats. These dudes—freshmen with seven years of school ahead of them, that is, if they even made it into medical school at all—would wear these coats all over campus, into the cafeteria, etc., proclaiming their matrimonial eligibility to all the aspiring doctors' wives. Around campus these freshmen boys would pretend to be medical students, ostentatiously addressing each other as "Doctah." An argument if I ever saw one for stringently socialized, fee-controlled medicine. Everything and its opposite.

This posturing and the shallowness of their professional motivation really got to me and a few other brothers like Al Chisholm. Finally, I just had to speak out in class. I attacked the acquisitiveness and shallow materialism. I reminded them of conditions in our communities, particularly in the rural South, and our peoples' need for dedicated physicians there. The response?

"Well, m'man, you sho welcome to go. Ain't nobody stopping you. Me? I wants me a practice in a large *faiine* city where I can make them large bucks, Jack."

There was Al, me, and a small group of like minds, so I did have allies in the Valley. But others had me pegged as a troublemaker. And not only the students. A few faculty in the Valley began to single me out.

"Carmichael, are you really sure you want to be a doctor?"

"Yeah, I want to be a doctor. It's not *medicine* I got problems with. It's the *profession* that gives me a cotton-picking pain." But by the second semester my involvement in the movement had increased so I was beginning to think seriously of answering, "You right. I don't want to be a doctor." This process would build. I don't want to suggest it was solely the distasteful materialism that drove me out. Nor was I, I hope, such a self-righteous-sounding prig. There was more. The movement had begun to exert a strong pull independent of anything else. I remembered Mr. Beckenstein's prediction—"it's in his blood." Soon I had to rethink my position seriously.

I reasoned that my attraction to medicine was mostly to serve human needs. I was seeing more and more clearly that our people's health problems were largely socially determined. Poverty, segregation, overwork, malnutrition, social deprivation of all kinds, were causing most of our people's physical illnesses.

As the idea of leaving medicine grew stronger within me, I reasoned that I wanted to treat people *before* they became ill, not after their health was fatally compromised by social evils. By the summer of freshman year when I returned from the Mississippi prison farm, my decision had been made, and that was the chief reason I gave the family.

I've made clear my feelings about the stunted and backward attitudes that prevailed among some faculty and administrators. But remember now, y'all, this is Howard. Every black thang . . . and its absolute opposite. And sho nuff, an array of excellent scholars and a tradition of black scholarship were also present as well as clear-eyed, dedicated teachers, many of them progressive. Sometimes both qualities combined beautifully in one and the same person: Sterling Brown and Harold Lewis come readily to mind. Give praise and thanks.

Because we in NAG had a slightly higher visibility as strugglers, and because we delighted in engaging all comers in intense political discussions concerning our people, we and the more intellectually progressive faculty had a natural affinity. In this, we were probably close to the last generation of Howard students to be so advantaged. Our benefactor in this, oddly enough, was American racism. Yeah, you read right, racism. The open and vulgar racist habits of American higher education. Because, before the full force of the then nascent civil rights movement made its presence felt, white universities not only rarely educated African students, they simply did not, as a rule, hire black scholars, no matter how distinguished the work or aristocratic the academic pedigree. (Look at the situation that confronted a young Du Bois, who was armed not only with a Harvard Ph.D., but also boasted advanced study at an "elite" German university.) Those practices that Dr. Du Bois had faced still prevailed in our time, but to our great profit.

For at Howard, we had the immense benefit of a number of venerable, pioneering, scholarly presences as well as brilliant young scholars and artists who today might undoubtedly be seduced by the wealth and "prestige" of the Yales and Stanfords of the academic world.

Some of these legends, although dead, lived on nonetheless in the ancestral tradition: Charles Hamilton Houston, Dean Kelly Miller, Dr. Charles Drew, and Alain Locke come to mind. Others had more recently departed for other earthly places. For example, Ralph Bunche to the United Nations and a Nobel Prize or Eric "the Little Doctor" Williams, whose *Capitalism and Slavery* was a massively influential correction of prevailing white myths about slavery and the development of European capitalism, who had gone on to the premiership of independent Trinidad and a knighthood. But they too remained lingering presences not only in the libraries but in the memory and folklore of the campus.

But others were still present and available. E. Franklin Frazier, whose most celebrated book, *The Black Bourgeoisie,* was an excoriating critique of the bankrupt values and affectations of that class, was alive when I got there. Also the historian Rayford Logan (*The Betrayal of the Negro* and *The Negro in American Life and Thought*), whom I've already mentioned. Another sociologist, G. Franklin Edwards, consulted regularly with the United Nations on strategies of development in the African world. There was the pioneering Africanist, native Mississippian W. Leo Hansberry. (I can still remember the pride and satisfaction we felt when, in my junior year, it was announced that the School of African History at the University of Lagos had officially been named The Hansberry School of African Studies.)

I also met Chancellor Williams, whose *The Destruction of Black Civilization,* which appeared after I left, is a courageous and original piece of scholarship. I can still remember with pleasure the hours I spent in the university gallery enraptured by the first collection of African art I'd encountered. I studied those striking masks and artifacts trying to imagine the stories they contained and to visualize the people who had made them and the cultures that had produced these artists. I can still remember the pleasure and wonder I felt just respecting, tasting, those sonorous, mysterious names out of our people's origins: *Yoruba, Bakongo, Igbo, Baule, Sunufo, Mandingo, Nubian, Ashanti.* Massive and crucial.

There was also the classicist Frank Snowden (*Blacks in Antiquity*) and the irrepressible poet/dramatist Owen Dodson, director for the Ira Aldridge Theatre, who regularly produced black playwrights and liked to transpose classical Greek playwrights into African contexts, *Medea in Africa,* for example. (Medea became an African priestess while Jason was a white explorer.)

Another of my intellectual influences was Professor Eugene "Oh, I got a letter from Bertie the other day" Holmes, a brilliant, irascible materialist philosopher who was a friend of Bertrand Russell's. The campus radicals loved a story about Dr. Holmes: Dragged unceremoniously before the House Un-American Activities Committee, Professor Holmes gave his occupation thus: "I am, sir, by profession a thinker. And you?" And thereafter declined on professional grounds to further dignify the proceedings with his participation. This had been during the height of McCarthyism. Was this account accurate? Maybe or maybe not, but we in NAG loved that story.

From the English Department I remember fondly Arthur P. Davis, critic/anthologist, and of course Sterling Brown himself—poet, folklorist, critic, editor, musicologist, griot, and teacher.

Those were some of the luminaries. There are doubtlessly more whom I've neglected to name. I studied with many of the ones named. But what was quite as important as actually taking their courses was their presence among us and what they represented. That they *were* there, and therefore their work and example existed for us. If you were bold, you could seek them out for conversation, but their example was so important—the example of consciously black intellectuals of the first order, who had devoted their professional lives to properly studying the African Presence at a time when we were otherwise being ignored or disparaged by "American scholarship." As important as any facts or methods we might learn from them in class was the reality they represented: splendid, stubborn commitment, a sense of duty and purpose. As scholars of black peoples they were custodians of tradition, keeping truth alive.

Then there were the young faculty, folks at the beginning of their careers who were closer to us in age and outlook. I can remember a number who encouraged, argued with, or counseled us as the occasion required, thereby enriching in numerous ways our intellectual development. Four young brothers especially took the time with us in this way. Elias Blake was an inordinately tall, slender, focused assistant professor of education. He was the kind of brother whom Rastas would describe as a "black-hearted man." I understand Bro Blake became president of a small Southern school, Clark College, a most proper place for a man of his dedication and energy. Conrad Snowden, a brilliant, articulate, young philosopher, was also a political and intellectual mentor to NAG. As was a brother in English named Clyde Taylor.

My freshman English teacher I've never forgotten. She was an instructor and a challenging teacher who was really down with black literature and our people's culture. But this teacher was unusual in one other important respect: she was young, stylish, and really fine. Her name was Toni Morrison. She and her tall walking partner, another young, equally fine and elegant sister named Eleanor Traylor, would turn heads as they walked across the quadrangle.

"Wowie, who be's them two *fly* sisters, mah man?" So naturally, their sections were always overenrolled with ardent young Howard men.* Who arrived in class to discover with some dismay that the young

---

*"Ms. Morrison had me in a bad way, bro," remembers Ed Brown. "I never *ever* went in for so much tutorial counseling in mah entire life. *Uh, uh, uh.* Just to be close to that woman, bro. As it say in the Bible, 'A woman did a wicked dance and cause a man to lose his head.' " —EMT

women were also smart and very serious teachers. A combination of assets that made for interesting classes indeed.

About eight years later my teacher and I met again when she would be my editor at Random House for both *Black Power* and *Stokely Speaks*.

So it was with considerable pride some years ago that I received the news in Conakry that my instructor/editor was now a Nobel laureate in literature. I was proud, because even though that prize remains a relic of northern European pretensions to cultural hegemony, they will occasionally stumble upon a worthy African writer (like Mahfouz, the Egyptian) who is grounded in their people's culture, struggle, and experience. Ms. Toni Morrison was clearly one of the committee's more inspired choices. Brother Chuck McDew sometimes says, "Even a blind pig will pick up a fat acorn evrah now'n den." I hear that Sister Morrison is on record as remembering me as "something of a rascal in class." Perhaps, no doubt. But they say what goes round comes round. Ms. M., don't look now, but your "rascal" just called you the blind committee's "fat acorn." Only metaphorically, of course.

There's one other class I have to mention. Professor E. Franklin Frazier, author of *The Black Bourgeoisie* (praised be his name) died during my sophomore year. Fortunately, I was able to sit in his class before that sad event.

That was a great class. Professor Frazier was funny and irreverent and I liked him. But I really disagreed with him on one issue: the presence of Africa and African cultural roots within the African community in America. Professor Frazier's position was that we were totally cut off from our African roots so that there were few if any significant African survivals in black culture in America. Here Professor Frazier had a long-term argument with a famous white anthropologist, Melville Herskovits, whose book *The Myth of the Negro Past* showed the strong influence of "Africanisms" in our culture. (This was a long-standing dispute. It was rumored among us that these two distinguished scholars once actually threw down: fisticuffs at a learned scholarly conference? I could well see ol' Professor Frazier gittin' it on down, but other folks said it wasn't true.) I never agreed with Professor Frazier, and after I read *The Myth of the Negro Past,* I was 100 percent with Herskovits. That's a *very* important book. Check it out for yourselves.

The Howard community benefited another way from extreme racism abroad and right-wing excess at home. These forces combined to create a small colony of excellent white scholars at Howard. (The law of unexpected consequences again?) The European scholars were refugees from the Third Reich's march across Europe and were, I assume, either Jewish or progressive, or both. Either Howard (and other historically black schools) afforded them a welcome that white institutions did not, or these scholars elected African schools as a gesture against the American version of the racism that had uprooted them. I recall them as gentle, civilized, and somewhat self-effacing presences. I gather that there had been many more during the war but most had retired by the time we arrived.

The white Americans, at least some of them, may have been chased to Howard by McCarthyism or, again, may have elected to serve there out of principle. (It sho wasn't Howard's salary or teaching load.) Two of this group stand out in my memory. The first, David Hammond, was an excellent botanist and a skillful and challenging teacher. The other was in fact a Frenchman, a political scientist who published the earliest clear analysis of the looming disaster being fueled by American arrogance and ignorance in Vietnam. His name was Bernard Fall.

In general my intellectual life became more balanced at Howard. Here professors would refer us to the kind of authors I had heard about only on 125th Street. Writers like Du Bois, Padmore, Richard Wright, and other Africans who were "hidden" in the curricula at Science and other white schools. One influential book had in fact been recommended by the disheveled man on the street corner. This was *Stolen Legacy* by George James. This book was particularly important to my understanding of the origins of Western thought after I moved into philosophy. Another book recommended to me by Professor Harold Lewis after my first visit to Mississippi was *Uncle Tom's Children* by Richard Wright. This is an honest and powerful book, almost scary. As I teased Professor Lewis, "It's a good thing you didn't show me this book before I went."

Professor Lewis also recruited some of us to the Little Forum, a reading and discussion group of which he was the faculty sponsor. The students participated in choosing the readings, and when a group of us from NAG entered, we wanted more serious social commentary, so the character of the reading list changed dramatically: C. Wright Mills's *Listen, Yankee* and *The Power Elite* come to mind. On his first visit to the U.N. soon after toppling the Cuban dictatorship, Castro had stayed in Harlem, where, according to street tradition, he was offered (and accepted) Malcolm X's offer of security by the Nation of Islam. Mills's fair treatment of the Cuban revolution confirmed me in my growing support, which continues to this day.

Arguably the area in which Howard affected my development most profoundly was in my direct experience of Southern black culture and the realities of life for Africans in the South. The university was in Northwest Washington on Georgia Avenue, a few blocks up from U Street and east of Fourteenth Street. At that time those two streets were the hub and axis of D.C.'s black business community. Black Washington was in effect an "up South" town. The people, the juke joints and nightclubs, the soul food restaurants and fast foods, the churches and the music, sacred and profane, were all straight out of Dixie. And Howard was located in the heart of this community. Half the students and just about all the support staff were Deep South. The cafeteria served soul food, and the style and accents of the staff were deep Dixie.

When I arrived, D.C. was the farthest south I'd been. I was familiar with Southern music—rhythm and blues, gospel and country blues, anything out of Memphis—from having sold it in my uncle's shop. And don't forget Symphony Sid and Jocko. Naturally I had heard and read about the South, but I knew nothing of it in actual life. Howard would give me my first direct contact with the lived experience of the South. From the Southern students I'd get a clear understanding of Southern life for our people: what segregation was like, the constant humiliations, the random brutality, the economic exploitation and ever-lasting *dependence*. Having studied Marxist-Leninist theory, I understood intellectually that material conditions affected a people's thinking and behavior. Howard gave me an actual demonstration of that effect. By and large I found the Africans in the South relaxed, friendly, and courteous, not at all as hard-edged and in-your-face as in Harlem.

Yet I knew that the Africans in Harlem had earlier migrated out of the South. What in Northern urban life had affected these Southern sharecroppers? Why had they become so hard and rough with each other up in Harlem, yet were so gentle with each other, so polite and courteous, in the South? Clearly, Southern culture was seriously eroded by the Northern urban environment.

All in all, the Southern African culture—as expressed at Howard— deeply impressed me with its courtesy, almost a courtliness, its hospitality, its humanism. When I went to the rural South, I would immediately again be impressed by these same qualities. Later in my political travels I would encounter the same qualities in the Caribbean countryside and the villages of Africa. African humanism?

My experience of Southern black culture at Howard and points south during this period played a great role in confirming me in my determination to struggle with and for my people. First learning about, then witnessing at first hand, the injustices and oppression that prevailed in the South was a large factor in this decision. As was the growing realization that our oppression was not Southern at all, it was *American*. But that was and could not have been all there was to that decision. In struggle one not only fights *against* something—injustice, oppression—but one must struggle *for* something equally real but positive. That's the other part of the equation.

In D.C. I was truly in touch for the first time with all aspects of the culture of Africans from the South. While at school I was also being exposed in a systematic and critical way to our intellectual tradition and the history of the struggle of those "many thousands gone," who as they proudly said always "lifted as they climbed." All of which could not help but have a serious effect on any young person searching for an honorable role for himself and his people in the world.

While I was sifting through all these new political and cultural experiences and impressions, trying to come to clear terms with my people's identity and cultural reality, figuring out my own relationship to it all and what it all meant, Sterling Brown (give praise and thanks) reached out to us.

I still cannot say for sure why he chose the students in NAG, but choose us he did, and I'm glad he did. Maybe, almost certainly, he understood the struggle we were engaged in better than we did. He, more than any other person, first helped me to understand the beauty of our people's language and the power of that extraordinary culture that sustained them through centuries of slavery and generations of apartheid.

Sterling Brown was a renowned poet, cultural historian, literary critic and scholar, folklorist, and jazz expert who was internationally celebrated. But just as important, he was a dedicated teacher, greatly beloved on campus because he reached out to students and the staff. "That Professor Brown, he a good-hearted man," the Southern staff would say.

He was not just another "expert on the Negro." His poetry and other writings presented the complex lives and hard-won wisdom of our people with clarity and understanding. His writing did not try to "give dignity" to the folk. He allowed their innate dignity and humanity to manifest itself in the poetry of their language and the power of their blues.

Besides which he was irreverent ("Jean-Paul Sartre ain't worth a fartre") and funny in deflating any pretentiousness that came his way. And pompousness was never in short supply at Howard. He had no tolerance at all for the inflated self-importance of the bourgeois assimilationist wanna-bes in which the place abounded. The types who lectured Southern students to "learn to speak properly." "Remember now," he'd say, "you cain't trust no three-name Negro. Especially one with them *numbers* on the end of his name."

Even before we in NAG got to know him, we'd heard on the student grapevine that the Leadbelly song "Bourgeois Blues" was the singer's response to his unhappy experience with D.C.'s black bourgeoisie, hence the lines:

> 'Cause it's a bourgeois town,
> Ooh, it's a bourgeois town,
> Where the only decent man is
> . . . Sterling Brown.

So even before spending time with him, we knew him for an ally.

Professor Brown took a liking to "the NAG kids." He would invite a group of us—Bill Mahoney, Tom Kahn, Courtland Cox, Ed Brown, Thelwell, Butch Conn, and me to his office in the evening ostensibly "to drink some likker, an' tell some lies." Those sessions were all oral history—tall tales, folk poems, literary and music criticism rolled in one. All of it of, from, or about our people. He was griot and respected elder brother, grounding us, so to say, in our African cultural heritage in America, in which he took such an uninhibited pleasure. Professor Brown was a living archive. He knew or had met everyone. Duke Ellington, Dr. Du Bois, Paul Robeson, Leadbelly . . .

Some weekends he'd invite us home, where his sweet-natured Miz Daisy would feed and pamper us. Then he could illustrate his points by playing us tapes and records or with readings from his remarkable library on black culture. He was informed, clear, and funny. You learned while you laughed.

But I'm reminded that he, by his example, taught us something else, something about struggle. See, professor had all the courtliness and charm of a Southern gentleman and an infinite sweetness and generosity of spirit, until that is, someone wrote or said something ignorant that denigrated his people or their culture. Wowie! Then that old gentleman became fierce. His weapons: superior knowledge, intelligence, and a biting wit. With him it wasn't his duty to defend our culture, it was his instinct.

["Prof was my first up-close example of how a committed black intellectual could be in this world. Here was a man with "superior" training. Degrees from Williams and Harvard. Urbane and light enough to pass. All the ingredients for the kind of intellectual "crossover" charlatans who abound today. Yet he clearly was totally content to immerse himself joyously in the study and appreciation of our people's culture and in service to we young blacks at Howard. And his unpretentiousness: he showed me that it was possible to do serious and important work without taking oneself too damn seriously or becoming self-important. "Mike," he'd say, "remember something unmentionable happens to the Negro when he begins to associate his three names with the adjective important." *I've never forgotten that. —EMT]*

Prof came along at exactly the right time for me (and I suspect for the rest of us). Because, although he never used these words, you could not fail to see and *feel* in everything he wrote, said, and did his undying love for our people and our culture.

In the turmoil of the struggle and the cultural confusions of official Howard, exactly what we were fighting *against* almost instinctively was always as clear as desert light. Prof helped us to see clearly at least one of the things that we really were fighting *for:* in the largest possible sense, to preserve and advance a legacy—our people's humanity as expressed in terms of their own devising. Psychic and cultural autonomy; the right to be and define ourselves without embarrassment, apology, or external constraint.

I shall always be grateful to that good man.

It must be abundantly obvious by now exactly what an interesting combination Howard and the nation's capital was then. The extent to which the Howard experiences in that remarkable historical moment were various and multiple. All things to all men? Many things to many men? Certainly many different things to many different folk. Every dialectic in the African world was there to be found. And we sure managed to find evrah last one. So your education came at you in waves from myriad and unexpected directions other than the conventional. Just about everything about that place at that time was educational, even the classrooms. It all shaped us.

CHAPTER VII

NAG and the Birth of SNCC

First there was Howard and then there was NAG. There can be no question as to the importance of the Howard experience in my formative life, but by far the most important element of that experience—morally, politically, culturally, and even emotionally—was the movement. And in our time the movement at Howard was NAG.

NAG was a close-knit community of distinctively individual young people, a few of whom were not students and a few others, though students, were not at Howard. In terms of geographic origins, experience, and personalities, we were as diverse a group of youth as one could expect to encounter, even though most of us were Africans from America. We had natives of the District, of the Midwest, New York, of the South, the Deep South and the Deepest South, of California, a couple Texans, and even one solitary eccentric African born in Jamaica.

But on Howard's campus we were a solid, highly visible community united by our interest in politics and, in the spirit of the times, by a conviction that youth could change the world. That we ourselves could change at least that part of it which most oppressed our people; and that consequently, it was our duty to try. Now, we'd all arrived at this place by very different routes, but that was the common ground upon which we met, embraced, strengthened each other, and went forward.

Much has been written about the physical courage of the movement generation. But that is obvious. My brothers and sisters could not have gone the places where they went, nor have done the things they did, without considerable courage. But physical bravery is merely the ability to make oneself face the prospect of danger, pain, or bodily harm, the certainty of jail, or the possibility of death. One can do all of those, and indeed they have often been done by fanatics, for quite despicable reasons.

Other qualities my brothers and sisters shared were as important as physical courage. One was a casual selflessness of purpose and a cheerful readiness to risk the things the society had programmed our peers to value most highly: education for personal advancement, jobs, careers, security, "the future," all that we'd all come to college to secure. *"Y'awl keep that mess up, git you an arrest record, and won't neither the government nor none of them white folks evah hire you for nuthen, hear?"* was something we heard constantly. Often from more practical fellow students.

To an upwardly mobile, aspiring nineteen-year-old, that prospect was as daunting as the physical danger, but, so far as I could tell, once in the movement few of us allowed ourselves to be held hostage by the threat to future status and material affluence. I respect my comrades as much for that as for their physical courage. For some of them have paid dearly. Being in a tiny minority with shared values we clung to, defended, and developed a loyalty and a love for each other that, as I've been reminded since my recent illness, endures to this day. Give praise and thanks.

At my first NAG meeting, at most thirty people were present and probably less, almost equally divided between men and women. The women were articulate and many were as vocal and assertive as the men, and NAG men were no shrinking violets. The "veterans" of course already knew each other and carried themselves with a confidence and *spirit* which came from shared struggles, but with so respectful and democratic a spirit that before the meeting ended we new recruits felt as though we instantly belonged. This was not accidental.

Cleve Sellers recently sent me what must be the only extant list of NAG membership during our four years at Howard. The list is certainly not complete. A number of folk must have come to a meeting or two, a demonstration or two, but left no record. But Cleve's list is certainly the core, the ones who followed through, made decisions, and did the work. It contains, over four years, a total of fifty-three names, of which twenty-one are women and eight are white. So on a campus of some eight thousand, NAG was statistically insignificant. Small wonder therefore that incoming freshmen were so warmly welcomed and accepted.

Of the eight whites on the list, four were men, three of whom, Tom Kahn, J. P. Harper and Butch Conn, studied at Howard. The other, Paul Dietrich, was older, about thirty, an intellectual, businessman, pacifist, and a socialist, quietly but openly gay. Paul owned Jazzland, a small club on Fourteenth Street within walking distance of the campus. Jazzland had visiting acts occasionally—I remember one group of big, baaad black women who wore suits, blew horns, and wore out some bebop—but the house musician was a bad brother called Lorenzo who played a mean jazz organ. Lorenzo was mildly epileptic, looked and played a little like a young Ray Charles, and when he got off in a riff, he'd become just possessed by the spirit and power of the music. So naturally NAG folks tended to drop in at Jazzland a lot after dark.

Most of the "veterans" during my first year were sophomores just a year ahead, so we'd be associated for at least the next three years. We freshmen would have four years together at Howard. A few new members came the following year—Charlie Cobb, Rap Brown, and Cleve Sellers—with whom I'd share some serious struggle. Cleve and Rap especially would soldier on through some very, very dangerous times in the late sixties. Both would be shot, jailed, and survive intact and strong. Rap and Cleve are two brothers who went the distance and then some more . . . and paid some heavy dues. Some heavy, heavy dues. Respect, nuff respect, my brothers.

From my first meeting I thought the discussion practical, focused, and unusually politically sophisticated. It was immediately clear that the organization was struggling on at least two very different fronts: one to organize the campus, the other to end racism in the nation. Each required different strategies and different kinds of organizing. The approach to organizing on campus, to influence student attitudes and political awareness, was different from the work off campus, where the focus was both local—discrimination within the District and outright segregation in Maryland and Virginia—and national, getting the attention of the Congress and the incoming Kennedy administration.

Depending on the campaign of the moment, each target required a different strategy. This meant that NAG planning sessions embraced student politics, national issues, and Southern segregation. Because we were in the nation's capital with the proximity of the African and Caribbean diplomatic corps and with their student presences at Howard, international questions were also a part of our discussions.

We were fortunate. No other group in the student movement—say the Nashville or Atlanta movements, or the New York or Boston friends of SNCC—faced the same range of political concerns regularly. Each area provided different issues that required slightly different strategic approaches. Colonized D.C., combining Northern, Southern, and national issues, was an excellent laboratory. One could not have gotten better political training if the situation had been designed for that purpose. Of course, at the time we never thought of it in these terms. We were simply devising strategies to deal effectively with the varied array of concrete political circumstances and issues which confronted us. If this proved first-rate training for young activists, that was pure accident, the gift of history and geography. In this, D.C. served us well indeed.

One of the least understood—or at least most generally misunderstood—constants of radical political struggle is its ever-loving *unpredictability*. Anyone planning serious involvement in struggle should be prepared for one certain thing: to be constantly surprised. Always. No matter how smart or analytically prepared you imagine yourself to be, serious struggle will surprise the cockiness right out of you. The most creatively conceived, elaborately organized campaigns can and will occasionally just fizzle out and fade away without effect or trace. I can think of many of them. While the simplest, most spontaneous, and insubstantial little tactic can take off into campaigns that affect history and your life in ways no one would have dared imagine, much less predict. That was how the Student Nonviolent Coordinating Committee started.

But first, one important warning. Looking back over a movement that has already become history can be misleading. It is now "history" so we *know*, or think we do, exactly what has happened. Right? No surprises. Having already happened, it takes on the appearance of inevitability. It not only happened, it *had* to happen and it *had to happen* precisely in that way. Utter nonsense.

First of all, it usually almost certainly did not happen in the way the official record says it did. Also, what that sense of "inevitability" forgets is the pervasive atmosphere of uncertainty that usually prevailed at the time. Surprises. Never being sure that results of a given action would be the result you intended. Never knowing what would, could, or *might* happen next. Complete uncertainty as to what dreadful and unanticipated development tomorrow might bring. Perhaps a lynching, a racially determined war in the streets? A presidential resignation or assassination? Or which trivial-appearing little incident would have consequences affecting your entire life. The beginning of SNCC was like that.

On January 31, 1960, four brothers, undergraduates at North Carolina A&T in Greensboro, sat down to eat lunch at the local department store. A bad lunch that the store would have been perfectly content to sell them . . . provided they ate it in the parking lot. But, those four young bloods *[Joseph McNeill, Ezell Blair Jr., Franklin McCain, and David Richmond]* sat down and changed a lot of lives.

When I first read about it, I quite understandably dismissed it. Politically inconsequential. Not serious. The black collegiate equivalent of white students stuffing twenty of themselves into a VW Bug, a telephone booth, or swallowing goldfish. John F. Kennedy, at that time, I think, hustling to steal the West Virginia primary from Hubert Humphrey, most likely did not notice the Greensboro Four either. And in the unlikely event he did, he probably saw it as I did, as inconsequential and fleeting.

But no Southerner—black or white—would have had my response. Of course, I would completely change my mind the first time I saw on TV young Africans calmly sitting at a counter while racist abuse, blows, and the contents of ketchup bottles, full ashtrays, and coffee cups were dumped on their heads. That made a believer out of me. Instantly.

But at first, I was a smart New York kid, a "serious student" of Marxist theory. So this Greensboro "stunt" seemed entirely too spontaneous.

The brothers were quoted as saying they "just wanted to see what would happen." Say what? Much too naive and insufficiently analytical, where could it possibly go? I thought smugly.

Well . . . the brothers did see what would happen. Nothing. After a couple hours they left and went back to the dorm. But when they came back the next day, it was with twenty-three brothers from A&T and four sisters from Bennett College.

Yeah, real fleeting and inconsequential.

Before the middle of the semester over six thousand students from seventy-eight Southern campuses or communities had sat in. Over two thousand had gone to jail. The black student sit-in movement had swept through the South. Nationally, some months later, by August 1961, over seventy thousand young people, mostly black but with many whites, had staged sit-ins. Over three thousand had visited Southern jails. Nearly all of my allies in NAG had been inspired into social activism by that trivial little experiment in "student exhibitionism" in that Greensboro department store.

Well . . . even though the tactic had flashed across the Southern landscape in spontaneous flare-ups, much like a brush fire on a drought-parched California hillside, without conscious intervention it would certainly have flared up and burned itself away, just like those brush fires do.

But even just the flare-ups had been spectacular. I cannot forget sitting one afternoon with some Kokista buddies in a cafeteria at Science looking with amazement and joy at a page of the *New York Times*. Fully three-quarters of that page was covered with little two-, three-inch reports. All with datelines from college towns across the South—Atlanta, Nashville, Jacksonville, Louisville, St. Augustine, etc., etc. Every story about young Africans sitting in, being attacked, arrested, or simply ignored. But whatever the response, those lunch counters did no business while my people sat.

"Oh, my God," I thought. "Negroes, like the spring, are breaking out all over."

They were. The people—thousands of anonymous young Africans—broke out and acted to change history. Bourgeois historians can argue endlessly about the precise causes, the spirit of the times or the motivations, but the fact is indelible. Those young brothers and sisters were acting on their own initiative and in their own interest. That's how history is made, people acting for themselves, sometimes with a little help from visionary and tireless organizers.

One of the most effective political organizers this country has ever produced must have read the same news stories we had. When the students erupted, Ms. Ella Baker, an African woman who had devoted her entire adult life to organizing grassroots African resistance to Southern apartheid, was working in an uneasy association with Dr. King and his Baptist ministers in the Southern Christian Leadership Conference. With some difficulty she persuaded Dr. King's ministers that "all that youthful energy, courage, and idealism should not be left simply to dissipate." Dr. King, who had visions dancing in his head of a SCLC youth wing to compete with the NAACP's, persuaded his board to appropriate $800 to bring the student activists together.

But Ms. Baker had a far higher vision, inspired in its boldness by her lifelong, unshakable faith in common people's, even the youth's, potential to lead themselves. She was authorized by Dr. King to call a conference at which the scattered student groups could meet each other and try to evolve a common philosophy and an organizational structure that could lend direction and continuity to this formless, spontaneous student uprising. Ms. Baker's meeting did all this . . . and considerably more.

Over the Easter weekend of April 15–17, 1960, 189 young people from over forty colleges and eleven states met at Shaw University in Raleigh, North Carolina, Ms. Baker's alma mater. There they listened to adult leaders including the Reverend Martin Luther King, the Reverend James Lawson, and Ms. Baker herself. The speeches were all good.

But, it was Ms. Baker's talk, "More Than a Hamburger," in which she invited the students to start thinking boldly about "transforming the entire social structure" of the South, that really turned the students on. Then she explained to the adult leaders present, *The younger generation is challenging you and me. They are asking us to forget our laziness and doubt and fear and to follow our dedication to truth to the bitter end.*" She challenged them to get out of the way, *"for these students have earned the right to direct their own affairs, yes, and even to make their own mistakes."* You can imagine how much the students would have dug that . . . because over the next few years we would do both seriously . . . our own decisions *and* our own mistakes. Certainly, certainly, *certainly,* Lord. Yes, we would.

Later we found out that during the conference Ms. Baker had walked out of a meeting with the SCLC ministers. The leaders were assigning themselves student delegations to be lobbied to get them to hook up with SCLC. Dr. King would deliver Atlanta; Wyatt T. Walker, Virginia; the Reverend Mr. Abernathy, Alabama; and so on. Ms. Baker refused to be a party to anything like that, feeling strongly that "the young people ought not be manipulated nor their energy and idealism co-opted." Those were important principles for Ms. Baker, which we never saw her compromise, *not once,* as long we knew her.

So by the time the conference ended, and almost entirely because of Ms. Baker, two important things had happened. The first thing was that the delegates had met numbers of young people like themselves. Young people who had previously only been names, faces, or arrest statistics in newspaper or TV news accounts. Now, these names had tangible reality, were friends and allies, and the importance of this cannot be exaggerated. In the workshops, the students were feeling their power, sharing their experiences, and it was purely, flat-out inspiring. To listen to a young sister from Rock Hill, South Carolina: "Then the mayor was outraged. He complained that we had conducted *nineteen* sit-ins during January. I told him, yes, we were ashamed. It should have been thirty-one." The accomplishment and wonder of a teenaged brother from Georgia reflecting, "*I,* myself desegregated a lunch counter . . . not some big man, not some powerful man, but little me. *I* walked the picket line. *I* sat in, and the walls [of segregation] came tumbling down."

The other and more important thing to come out of the Raleigh meeting was the creation of the skeleton of a structure, a "temporary coordinating committee," to maintain communications among and between the scattered campus movements. Ed King, a brother who'd led some bloody sit-ins in Frankfort, Kentucky, was elected chair. Later, that May 1960, just before the semester ended, the "temporary" was dropped at a meeting in Atlanta where the committee met with Mrs. Baker, the Reverend Mr. Lawson, and a militant and skillful young lawyer named Len "the Snake Doctor" Holt, who is certainly one of the great unsung heroes of our Southern struggle.

(I first met the Snake Doctor when he defended us in a Jackson, Mississippi, court during the Freedom Rides. Here was our lawyer, a young African, not much older than us, impeccably dressed, clearly better educated and more confident, articulate, and dramatic than the prosecutor, who kept turning his back whenever our lawyer spoke. At one point the Snake Doctor requested some court documents. The prosecutor, his back turned, threw them contemptuously to his feet. Bro Len silently bent down, picked up the papers, calmly made his presentation, and then— here's the part I've never forgotten. The young brother deliberately walks across that Mississippi courtroom, moves around to face the prosecutor, and *throws those papers in that cracker's face, Jack.* Len explained later, "Hey, we were never going to win in that court. But that didn't mean we had to accept any insults either." Being defended by the Snake Doctor was always an adventure and an inspiration in the South.)

That Atlanta meeting voted to remain independent as the Student Nonviolent Coordinating Committee elected Marion Barry of Nashville to the chair, and affirmed its commitment to nonviolence.

When school started that fall, the committee met again and elected Bro Chuck McDew as first chairman. All those pioneering students, Bill Mahoney, Diane Nash, Marion Barry, John Lewis, Julian Bond, Ruby Doris Smith, and the many, many anonymous ones whose names are not part of media records were interesting young black people. Bro Chuck McDew was one of the funniest and more interesting.

When his daddy sent him south to college from a small, industrial, midwest, rust-belt city, he was an all-state running back with simple all-American jock dreams. His intention, he said, was to "play four years, graduate, join the NFL, and live large." But being from the Midwest he'd played with and against white boys and he didn't reckon on the protocols of Jim Crow. He didn't know to say "sir" to white cops. Within a matter of weeks in Dixie, he was thrice knocked cold, had his jaw and arm broken, was hospitalized three times, and was jailed twice. He had a choice, either return north because "these here crackers is crazy," or join the fight.

He joined. Later Chuck converted to Judaism, in part because the only white religious leader to support the sit-ins in his college town had been the local rabbi. Bob Moses would famously describe Chuck as "a Negro by birth, a Jew by choice, and a revolutionary by necessity." So, you see, SNCC folk came cut in all shapes, sizes, and attitudes, yes, indeedy.

At the Atlanta meeting, Chuck, who still has a lot of preacher in him, sounded the call as SNCC's first chairman: "Instead of accepting the leavings of a sick and decadent society, we shall seize the initiative. . ." Which we did.

Thus in about nine months, thanks to Ms. Baker, an isolated and impulsive act of defiance, a tentative gesture coming out of a dormitory-room bull session, had evolved into an organization, or at least the bare bones of one. To have called it a national organization then would have been a big stretch, but I and my new community at Howard were members of a beginning student organization that would profoundly affect this nation.

From my very first meeting at Howard it became clear that NAG's battle was two-pronged—on the campus and in the surrounding communities. Both were instructive and each affected the other. For four years we would move between our struggle to expand the base on campus and the larger struggle in the streets. For simplicity and clarity, I'll talk first about the four-year campaign on campus, then venture southward.

Obviously NAG was an unprecedented entity in student life at Howard. It fit neatly into no familiar category. It was never a recognized student organization, but it wasn't one of those informal "homie" cliques either. You know, kids from the same city, D.C. or N.Y. or Philly who shared high schools, histories, and local youth cultures and who tended to hang out and party together at Howard. NAG came from *all over*. But despite our obvious individual differences and regional diversity, and our collective "oddness" so far as traditional student groupings went, we actually had much more in common than might readily have been apparent.

For the most part, NAG folk were good students. All of us were intellectually curious and read avidly, and a few of us were already quite accomplished. Tom Kahn, for example, was the author of an influential pamphlet on the civil rights movement called *The Unfinished Revolution.* Bill Mahoney published a novel, *Black Jacob,* while still an undergraduate. The Wheeler sisters—Jean and Sharon—maintained four-point grade averages most semesters during their four years, and a majority of us stayed on or near the dean's list.

But it was much more than a question of academics or "intelligence," because, among our peers at Howard, any number of equally smart students who were never members of NAG nor participants in the movement. And, of course, as people like to say, we were a generation favored by history. Which is true. History was kind to us. We had come along at an extraordinary historical moment that presented black youth with an unprecedented opportunity to engage society militantly.

But, more than academic intelligence, all NAG folk seemed to share certain personal qualities, which enabled us to respond effectively to that historical moment and to that campus. What bound us together was a great interest in and respect for our people and a passionate identification with the African struggle everywhere, whether in Mississippi, Mozambique, or Montserrat. And a sense that, as a consequence of the sacrifices of previous generations, we not only would not have to accept what they had, but could do even more.

One thing that reflects the spirit of the times among that generation of activist youth—white and black—is the recurrence of certain favorite quotations, ideas that spoke to collective human responsibility. These quotes were prevalent during my high school and early college years. Later in the decade these would be replaced by more overtly revolutionary slogans from people like Che, Malcolm, and Uncle Ho. But when I was a freshman, a lot of the people I knew would have some combination of these high-minded quotes up somewhere in their room. I remember three of these quotations.

One was from Dr. King's *Stride Toward Freedom* to the effect that "If a man hasn't discovered something that he will die for, he isn't fit to live." The second was from the white jurist Oliver Wendell Holmes: "As life is action and passion, it is required of a man that he should share the passion and action of his time at peril being judged not to have lived."

But the most common one—which I would later occasionally use to end speeches—was Rabbi Hillel's famous quote: "If I am not for myself, who is for me? And when I am for myself, what am I? And if not now, when?"

• • •

As I would soon discover, just about all of our Southern members had been—even from high school—questioning, resenting, and often resisting the racist protocols and practices of segregation in their hometowns. Many had attempted to organize resistance as best they could—often very lonely resistance—to the daily humiliations of the racism around them. Ironically enough, Dion Diamond (Virginia), Cleve Sellers (South Carolina), and Hank Thomas (Florida) had been sent off to Howard by parents anxious, with excellent reason, about their son's survival in the South. Ed Brown had been expelled from college in Louisiana for leading sit-ins. Sending them to Howard turned out to be a case of "Oh, please, Bre'r Bear, please don't throw me in that briar patch." Once on campus, every one of them headed straight into NAG, where they would turn right round and put themselves in harm's way in some of the hottest battle zones of the South.

All of which is to say that my new friends were strong-willed—read mule-stubborn—young adults who could live without peer acceptance. They did not mind—or had become accustomed to—being considered "strange" or "different." So the status conformism that dominated Howard student culture held absolutely no terrors for them.

But similarities in fundamental attitudes not withstanding, we were in no way intellectual clones of each other. Folks were stubbornly independent; therefore arguments and disagreements could be fierce, passionate, and unending. As Joyce Ladner famously said, "SNCC folk would argue with a street sign." Well, NAG folk would argue with the sign *post*. But the strident rhetoric never managed to conceal a deep mutual respect. Many of my comrades looking back over the years would admit to a feeling that I certainly shared: a relief bordering on euphoria. It was a lot like finding a long-lost family that you hadn't previously known about, but with whom you instantly recognized your kinship. And to this day you will hear the word *family* being used among us. Except, of course, that unlike biological family, this one was completely self-selective. This was a family that the times and the accidents of history had chosen for us.

The discussion at the very first NAG meeting I attended showed, as I've said, that we were simultaneously conducting two different struggles. Our ultimate aim was to participate in the struggle for human rights in the nation. Our duty, therefore, was to try to put large numbers of our peers from the campus into active participation in that struggle. This meant organizing our fellow students. But that effort is not, and should not, though it frequently is, be confused with trying to build "a student movement." Let's be clear here.

Narrowly defined, a "student movement" comprises only students acting in self-interest as a class. Consequently it engages issues affecting student life, i.e., student culture, student rights, entitlements, autonomy, and so forth. I don't mean in any way to disparage those issues. I remember from "Science" a leftist put-down: "One class-conscious worker is worth a thousand students," but that is not at all what I'm saying. Of necessity, NAG was involved in all of those "student" issues, *but never as an end.* We had to engage them to get to where we really wanted to go—the fight against racism in the general society. We were an organization mostly of students but we were not a student organization.

So even though we would completely transform the administration's stunted view of student rights and compel at least some respect for student activism, transforming Howard's institutional culture was never a primary (or even much of a secondary) goal of ours. But if we were to organize our peers for the larger struggle, we had no choice. To get to human rights in society, we had to begin with student rights on campus.

In the early sixties all American higher education was paternalistic and condescending toward students in ways contemporary students would not possibly believe. Traditionally, black schools, being at the mercy of a racist status quo, were even more problematic. In fact, they were downright authoritarian: "We don't understand *rights* here. What we understand here is *responsibilities.*" Student rights were what the administration said they were. Hence any struggle for the hearts and minds of the Howard studentry would inevitably have to begin with a serious butt-rubbing with prevailing institutional attitudes and practices. Inevitably a facedown with the administration.

There was much talk of widespread apathy among African students born in America during these times. That's not entirely fair. There was more fear than apathy. There was so much economic insecurity and racial intimidation where most of us came from; many Southern students were afraid to act because their parents were totally dependent on white folks for their living. Then too the administration (whether consciously or not) did everything to encourage that insecurity. The institution also actively encouraged juvenile social behaviors among students—a kind of prolonged adolescence—which discouraged bold political initiative on the students' part. What therefore was described as black student "apathy" was to some extent carefully constructed out of equal parts economic insecurity, intimidation, and an imposed paternalism. We didn't *want* to accept the racist status quo, but we were constantly being told that we had no alternative. But why *white* students of the time, the alleged beneficiaries of the American system, should have been so apolitical and apathetic in their behavior is, however, quite another story. One I will not recount here. In any case, all this was about to change dramatically.

Our efforts to organize a "student movement," although in one sense a diversion, were by no means a waste of time and energy. Because, in struggling for the mere right to exist and organize on campus, we gained experience, developed political skills, and tested techniques, all of which would prove invaluable in the wider struggle. So, in yet another quite unintended way, Howard was our laboratory, in this case for political education and even more important, political *praxis*. Take for example our perennial struggle for official recognition, which, of course, we never won. As we have seen, the university simply could not afford to let us win. So why would we continue to beat our heads against that particular brick wall? Why, indeed, expend all that time and energy? Because the campaigns served to maintain a high movement visibility on campus.

Students took sides, overwhelmingly in our favor. How could they not? So, by increasing student awareness and attention, the process became even more important than any possible result. And, in stifling our initiatives, the administration was frequently so openly manipulative that NAG always won by losing. Not to mention, of course, that the issues often involved fundamentals like free speech and freedom of association and of political action. We learned early that you can lose, but you are never defeated so long as you never abandon principle.

Besides, wrassling the administration to a standstill was excellent training and practice. Students had been accustomed to accepting in loco parentis, the principle of administrative parental authority. (This was when American parents still had authority.) The administration handed down *dictats* that students were not to challenge . . . openly. For instance, women had strictly enforced nightly curfews, but men did not. No student group openly challenged that double standard. Unthinkable today.

Prior to this time student defiance had been covert. It took surreptitious "social" forms, "getting away with" drinking, violating curfew, or flouting some other equally intrusive but ultimately trivial rule. I don't think it had ever before taken the form of *public* and *systematic* challenges to administrative prerogative.

So that is exactly what we did. And challenging the status quo was for us not only excellent training, but fun, big time. Because we always had to be impeccably prepared, this meant researching university rules and procedures and even civil law. Anticipating possible administration moves and figuring out in advance how to counter them. Learning the different techniques of negotiating from a position of no real power, when to bluff, when to fold, when to stall. This, of course, is a situation that we— and the whole black movement—would constantly face in the struggle in the larger world. As Bill Mahoney would sometimes say, "Today the administration, tomorrow the state."

NAG got pretty good at this kind of political maneuvering. Occasionally, on finding themselves outflanked in a meeting, our administrators would resort to naked authoritarianism, the "Because we said so" approach of harassed parents everywhere. Or they would simply adjourn meetings indefinitely. Naturally we would rush the story into the student paper and NAG's support with the students—and progressive faculty— would rise dramatically each time.

Sometimes we would be left little alternative but open—but invariably polite—defiance, upping the ante, "heightening the contradictions," expanding the scope and terms of the dispute even to the extent of threatening litigation. Later in quieter moments administrators would admit that they were simply unaccustomed to this degree of toughness and defiance from mere students. I mean even parents didn't usually threaten the university with lawsuits, much less students.

Of course NAG never actually sued Howard, but the mere threat established that we were adults, not children. And we did have the benefit of excellent legal advice and representation. An extremely canny litigator on the law school faculty, Professor Herbert Reed, advised and represented us in court whenever we were arrested.

Professor Reed didn't look like anybody's militant. He was a heavyset, rumpled, slow-talking Southerner with very much the manner and affect of an ol' country lawyer. Which could fool you. A clear, tough-minded black man, he was a great lawyer. I'm not sure he could or would ever have represented us against Howard. But he did brief us on the law and exactly what to say to fill bureaucratic hearts with dread. Professor Reed was yet another elder who gave us courage and confidence. Give praise and thanks.

From these experiences we took a number of lessons, not all of which will apply to every political circumstance, but which certainly worked with a resistant, if not totally hostile, academic establishment. So the lessons probably still do apply . . . if only for students in a university setting.

First: Be clear as to your goals and even clearer as to your strategy. Do not confuse these.

Second: Indeed be "neat, clean, and polite." But also hang tough, and the tougher you have to get, the more polite, correct, and *reasonable* your tone and demeanor must be.

Third: Do your homework and your research. Surprise them with the *accuracy* and *thoroughness* of your preparation, with what you know. Be prepared to outwork the suckers and let them see that you are.

Fourth: Be focused and uncompromising on *principle,* but be creatively flexible on tactics. That is, be consistent but never predictable. Always surprise them.

And the last thing: Never leave your sense of humor at home. Always find the ironies, laugh, and let them see you laughing. Especially when they don't know why you are. As Junebug Jabbo Jones (may his tribe increase) says, "What us Africans need most is a lot of patience and a sense of irony." Now these worked for us at Howard. They will work in a university setting where the institutional self-image tends toward reason and civility and where interests are not totally and irresolvably opposed. They will not, repeat, *will not* work, with say, armed barbarians or irrationally savage racists. Or with an inflexible government establishment whose "interests," as they understand them, give a low priority to justice for your people or the alleged guarantees of the Constitution. We would find that out to our great sorrow.

The two key student organizations for our purposes were the Student Council, which controlled funds, and the newspaper, which reached the whole campus. We targeted both successfully. In those days there were no such things as student radio stations or campus television channels. But NAG always had a presence on the newspaper, the *Hilltop*. Charlie Cobb and Mike Thelwell were on staff, but we all—Tom, Muriel, Hank, Jean, Courtland, Bill, Ed, myself—regularly contributed stories about the movement.

By the year (1962–63) Thelwell became editor in chief, the movement had completely captured that organ. The dean of men (let him be nameless) belatedly realized this and took what he apparently thought was clever and effective preemptive action. But, to be truthful, the dean might have been provoked to this.

A few weeks into the semester the sports, news, and feature editors, looking quite crestfallen, came in as a bloc and asked for a private meeting with Thelwell. They seemed oddly uncomfortable and embarrassed. They had, they told him, a confession to make. Right after their organizational meeting they'd been summoned to a meeting in the dean's office and had been instructed to report on the new editor. To their great shame, they had agreed. Why?

The editor in chief was, the dean told them, clearly a radical—possibly a communist—or crazy. For the good of the school, their duty was to observe and report to the dean personally any sign of instability, or worse, potentially subversive behavior, on the editor in chief's part. This agreement had been on their consciences ever since and they wanted him to know.

"So what were you supposed to be looking for, coded messages from Cuba?"

"Anything subversive. Besides, you know, 'you ain't right in the head anyhow.' "

"Well, what have you reported thus far?"

"Comaan . . . what d'you take us for? Course we ain't told him nothing."

"Nothing, huh? Pity that. 'Cause, y'know, that greasy-headed, chitterling eating Uncle Tom is quite right. You do have a responsibility to report . . ." Thelwell reached into a desk drawer for three envelopes, which he flourished. "In fact, I do want you to report to him."

"You want us to report you?"

"Please. Tell him that I showed you these three stamped and addressed envelopes that I keep always in my desk. Tell him I said that one was to my personal attorney, one to the American Civil Liberties Union. The third is to the National Student Association Committee on Student Press Freedom. Tell him that I brag *all* the time that I can't wait for the administration to try to censor the paper or arbitrarily move on the editor. Tell him I bragged how he would not only make me famous, *but* have not *one* but *three* heavy-duty lawsuits on his fat, nappy head in a New York minute. Tell him I said that."

The trio came back laughing, saying the dean had seemed grateful. He told them they'd done well; that their information was valuable; thanked them profusely and assured them that if they ever needed his assistance in the future, he would certainly be there for them. That was the last we heard from that gentleman all year.

"Oh, Bledsoe, you ain't nothing but a greasy chitterling eater," as Ellison's invisible man said about his college president.

But, of course, the *Hilltop* to which we all contributed became a sho'nuff overt organ of the student movement. Wherever there was a civil rights campaign, we'd write up the stories prominently. I was just shown a story I wrote in 1963 about the Baltimore campaign where Howard delivered five hundred demonstrators. (The buses were paid for by the Student Council—a cultural field trip we called it.)

Charlie Cobb, who had gone to work with Bob Moses in Mississippi, sent back regular field reports from the Delta. Hank Thomas spent his junior year in and out of Southern jails for CORE. He sent back a hair-raising column called "We Shall Overcome," to which I sometimes contributed. By the time he got back to campus Hank had the distinction of having been legally banished from the sovereign state of Alabama and placed under penalty of jail if he were ever so much as to set foot within that state's borders again. That's how crazy those crackers were. Junior year I wrote stories on the Baltimore and Cambridge, Maryland, campaigns for the "We Shall Overcome" column.

The other really important official student organization that would have to be infiltrated if NAG was to be effective was the student government, officially the Liberal Arts Student Council (LASC).

Under capitalism, money talks—in fact, according to your Supreme Court, money is *speech* whose freedom must therefore be protected. And the LASC was where the student money was. So we were always active in those elections, campaigning for the election of our members—Jean Wheeler, Tom Kahn, Phil Hutchins, myself—or our allies. So that at least some of the students' moneys could be directed away from such officially approved "social" activities as homecoming parades, ROTC's "Officer and His Lady" balls, and cotillion-like irrelevancies of bourgeois affectation and status inflation that Courtland called "niggeratti pretentiousness." Of course, the Greeks complained bitterly. According to them, the Student Council and the newspaper did not give enough emphasis to "social activity."

However, by my junior year we were able to elect Tom Kahn (who was white) treasurer, Phil Hutchins, who would ultimately be the last chairman of SNCC, vice president, and me a member. That was the year of the Route 40 and Baltimore campaigns. Somehow Student Affairs never quite figured out, or really wanted to figure out, what those bus rentals for "cultural field trips to Baltimore" actually were. Baltimore? Cultural? Give me an ever-loving break. Those were the years in which our gradual politicization of the student organizations burst into full flower.

I have been talking as if the level of serious student politics we brought to bear was unprecedented at Howard. And in the sense of open confrontation, it was. In the prevailing climate of authoritarian paternalism in which students were expected "to act like kids" and consequently did, and where the administrators' control was preemptory and unchallengeable, we were, probably, something new. We represented the first wave of a new student militancy that would crest in the late sixties. But we were not entirely without precedent.

For at Howard, we had at least one important recent predecessor, a consummate student politician, an "inside player" who'd operated very differently from us, but very, very effectively. I came the year after he graduated, but the NAG veterans, Tom Kahn, Hank Thomas, Mike Thelwell, and Bill Mahoney, talked of the outgoing LASC president with utmost respect. This brother's contribution to the direction and growth of the emerging student movement and the way he achieved it deserves to be much better understood.

[It was freshman orientation in '59. S.O.S. Same ol' same ol'. The usual procession of petty bureaucrats—vice assistant this and dean the other—subjecting the captive frosh to an unending, irrelevant stream of platitude after cliché, after bromide, after nostrum, after condescending inanity. The level of discourse was infantile, head hurting. Ms. Hamer had the right term for it: "It were very disencouraging."

151

Then, at the end of all this, the president of the student government was introduced, a skinny, craggy-featured young man in large, horn-rimmed glasses and a bad suit. I guess I didn't expect anything different since he was only a student, on the same platform as the administrative mush-mouths, and seemed quite obviously to be an afterthought on the program.

But, bro, it was a breath of fresh air. The student leader was brilliant, a man among boys. He was wonderfully articulate, clear, purposeful and sharp strategically. Nothing rhetorically militant but controlled and pragmatic in his language. And he was talking real politics, his plan to use our government to establish student rights and affect the struggle in the society. I couldn't believe it. He was clearly the most intelligent and effective speaker on that platform. It was far and away the best political talk I'd heard since setting foot in the country. . . . And remember, this was in the middle of a presidential campaign. Now, it could be that the speech sounded so great only because of the crap that had preceded it. But it was the first thing I heard that made me proud to be a Howard student. I realized for the first time the real possibilities of American student politics. —EMT]

Timothy Jenkins graduated the year before I arrived but I would meet him in Nashville after the Freedom Rides and the next year in Greenwood, Mississippi. He must clearly have been a new breed of student leader to the Howard fossils, as he apparently was a new Negro to the leadership of the National Student Association, where he played a shrewd and effective role at the time of the sit-ins.

What is significant about this brother is that he chose to go inside the system, but always with purpose. I've always told young people who ask, "Yeah, it's possible to work honorably within the system, but *only* in service to a serious movement outside." You gotta have a radical alternative outside that you can serve from inside. That was Tim.

He was from Philly, so on campus they called him "the Philadelphia Negro." He was said to be an honest brother, but "slicker than pig grease" (only they didn't say "grease"). He was known to be shrewd and tart of tongue, help us, Jesus. When Ms. Baker's first meeting with the sit-in students took place in Raleigh, the Howard student government quietly contributed some significant travel funds. That was Tim.

As an undergraduate he had traveled abroad. He'd lived with a Serbian family in Sarajevo where he said he'd had his "first exposure to white tribalism." He'd visited revolutionary Cuba with a NSA delegation. Which inclined him to run for vice president for international affairs in the National Student Association. So before the convention in 1960 he started his campaign.

What happened next was supremely ironic, though none of us knew the details at the time.

As was later revealed, an influential faction of the NSA leadership was covertly being subsidized and "handled" by the CIA. These CIA "assets" became concerned that this clear, unapologetic, nonshuffling, nongrinning, effective Negro might prove "uncontrollable" in charge of international affairs. But Tim's campaign had been skillful. At NSA he was the rare black student leader and much too popular and persuasive a candidate to be simply "dissed." However, the CIA faction thought that domestic affairs were relatively tepid, not so "sensitive" compared to international affairs. So they brokered a political solution in which Tim Jenkins emerged as VP for *national affairs* just as SNCC was aborning. Suddenly national affairs were what was happening and our brother could not have been better placed, in his words, "to represent those Southern kids on the front lines" within the national student establishment, as well as to channel all kinds of foundation resources to the Southern movement.

But Tim was so consummate an "inside" player that few in the NSA establishment knew that he was also at the same time on the executive committee of the early Students for a Democratic Society, when it was still affiliated with the League for Industrial Democracy. There he worked to build an alliance between radical white students and the Southern black movement in ways that we will discuss later.

It should be evident that Tim Jenkins did not look or behave like the conventional image of the "militant" black student. But no students I can think of had a more positive effect on the development and direction of our movement during its formative years. My point is, in some circumstances, there can be a role for clear and effective black activists *inside* the system. At least that was true *then*. I'm not so sure about *now*. Later, it even seemed to make a certain pragmatic sense when Tim, then in law school at Yale, said he was joining the Republican Party. He told us then that "a lot of influence" could be wielded by a skillful and honest African operating within that party. But history surprises us all, does it not? Tim joined the Republican Party of Rockefeller, which turned into the party of Strom Thurmond, Jesse Helms, and Clarence Thomas. Help us, Jesus. Some would say there's not a dime's worth of difference between them, but in a small, practical way there really was. But it might not be enough of a difference.

So, NAG did have at least one effective political predecessor in student government, one who managed to divert "insider" resources to the struggle. If so, NAG was, in effect, only continuing in that tradition when we moved into student government. Looking back, I guess those Howard students who felt constrained to remain aloof from the struggle back then can now take some comfort that they were at least represented in the struggle by some portion of their student activity fees. During my college days the struggle on the campus would prove both instructive and valuable, but that would come later.

As an eager freshman I was much more concerned with getting into the struggle in the streets. That's where I really wanted to be. It would not be long before I'd be fully involved. Fully involved, almost consumed.

CHAPTER VIII

Nonviolence—
Apprenticeship in Struggle

Premed freshman Carmichael had arrived at Howard fully prepared to embark on the road to medicine. Cleve Sellers recently reminded me just how well prepared for that I had really been. Thanks to a contribution from the faithful Mummy Olga, I was, in practical terms, probably the best medically equipped freshman. Almost certainly the only one to arrive fully armed with stethoscope, rectal thermometer, and little triangular rubber hammers used to bang knees in order to check reflexes. Yeah, I sure was ready, Jack.

The medical hardware had been Mummy Olga's proud contribution. She was working at Harlem Hospital, where she admired the young African interns, no doubt fondly imagining her son among them. She had somehow managed to come by these items (I won't say she liberated them, Mummy Olga being far too good a Christian for that), which she proudly produced just before I was to leave. Her little surprise. I hadn't the heart to tell her that it would be at least five years before I'd be needing anything like that. ("But hi! It in't doctor you go study? I thought you was going study doctor, *oui*?")

Mummy Olga's equipment notwithstanding, what increasingly preoccupied my mind from my first NAG meeting was not listening to heartbeats, but the anticipation of my first demonstration in the South. Course, I'd walked many a CORE picket line in New York. But this would be the South. The real movement. The hostile crowds and cops I'd seen on TV. The war stories from the NAG veterans only made matters worse. I simply could not wait for my own baptism by fire. The discussions, and the planning and training sessions, were interesting, but they only served to whet my impatience for action. Would I, could I, maintain nonviolence in the face of attack? What would my first arrest feel like?

Next to veterans like John Moody, Hank, Courtland, Bill, I felt like a rookie, eager to earn his stripes and fully belong.

•   •   •

155

My freshman year I regarded as a training period, greatly respecting the more experienced leadership and considering myself in training under them. One brother in particular I regard as having trained me, by his example of courage, calm determination, and evident strength of character. Because he was a slow-talking Southerner, and not ideologically glib, some NAG folks regarded Hank Thomas as "kinda country." But even they had to concede his moral power. I just thought he was one of the most impressive young black men I'd ever met.

He was a big, strong ol' dude too, a rangy six foot five with an athletic build. In fact, he'd turned down a football scholarship to Wisconsin in favor of an academic scholarship to Howard. And those Howard coaches really wanted him to play defensive end for the Bisons, but he was totally committed to the struggle. I really admired Hank. Whatever he said he would do, you could absolutely count on. I came to believe that this quality is particularly strong in Southern black culture. I would encounter it over and over in Mississippi and Alabama. In the youth *and* in their parents. Ed Brown had that quality, as did his brother Rap, now Jamil al-Amin. As did Bob Mants, Annie Pearl Avery, Dory Ladner, James and Willie Peacock, Randy Battle, and so many others.

Also, I learned a lot from Hank about growing up under segregation, in St. Augustine. The schools there were completely segregated but many of the teachers were very conscious black people. Students were taught speeches by Frederick Douglass and Dr. Martin Luther King and sang the "Negro National Anthem" by James Weldon Johnson. During the Suez Crisis, a large picture of Gamal Abdel Nasser, "who looked exactly like Mr. Mason, the biology teacher and football coach," appeared in the hallway. At Ghanaian independence, President Nasser was joined by President Nkrumah, "who looked to us exactly like Mr. R. J. Murray, our principal, so," Hank told me, "we learned about the African struggle and completely identified with these African leaders."

After my experience at Bronx Science this made quite an impression: the international black consciousness that these Southern African teachers were quietly nurturing in those segregated schools. Later I would constantly hear similar things from other African students from the South.

I once met a brother who grew up in St. Augustine with Hank. This guy (Benjamin) told me that Hank had amazed his peers when at fifteen he single-handedly struggled with segregation in the movie theaters. The teenagers did not have much in the way of entertainment, so "the movies were a real big teenage thing." Hank refused to accept segregated seating, so he was thrown out. He announced that he would never again pay money to be disrespected, so "he never set foot again in a movie theater until he left for college. We were all amazed, and admired him, but, man, we weren't about to deprive ourselves of the movies. Hank stood alone in that."

I would also learn a lot, often at considerable personal risk, from another Southern brother, who was exactly the opposite of Hank. This brother was from Virginia and was as slight as Hank was big, as swift, verbal, and volatile as Hank was calm and deliberate. Dion Diamond was so skinny that Courtland used to say, "Put Dion and helium in a room and Dion would rise."

Dion was superclean, a campus fashion plate—no small feat on a campus where "vining and styling" was a major occupation—and intense to the point of being hyper, with a mouth on him that would not quit. You did not want to git into no dozens with this brother. No you did not. Then too he always managed to surround himself with fine sisters, "dusky Southern belles," while styling, signifying, and talking macho trash. But feisty and aggressive? Help us, Jesus. It was nothing for Dion to talk down towering football linemen and just humiliate them with his quick wit and razor tongue. Seen him do it more than once. He'd simply talk some big ol' dude down. We figured it was only a matter of time before someone would mess up his face for real, but it never happened that I know of.

Truthfully, at first I didn't quite know what to make of Dion. What was this skinny shrimp doing with all them fine sisters anyway? And he always looked an inch away from getting "in yo face and on yo case" with his wasp-smart, mouthy self. But I got to like Dion a lot, even if he did get us into tight situations. He was, as I would discover, dangerously fearless and dedicated.

Of course we were all activists, but Dion and Hank were nonviolent shock troops. As was Cleve Sellers, who entered in my sophomore year. The word *activist* described Cleve. In fact, his parents had sent him to Howard in part because, as a high school organizer and "troublemaker," he'd become marked in Denmark, South Carolina. He'd organized high school student resistance to the point where he was thought to be targeted by the Klan. Not only were there anonymous threats, but his parents were advised by "respectable" whites that it would be best to get Cleve out of town. At Howard, Cleve and I would become close friends and soldier together through many a struggle.

A rather more cerebrally oriented element in the group could, for want of a better word, be called "intellectuals," though one of them claimed to "reach for his gun" whenever he heard that word.

Tom Kahn and Paul Dietrich were white, deeply committed pacifists and, as everyone understood, gay. They were—apart from Bayard Rustin and Jimmy Baldwin—the only gay people we were aware of who were in the movement. Somehow it was never an issue. It was simply the way they were. They neither hid nor proclaimed it, so there was nothing to discuss. I don't think anyone felt it necessary even to give it much thought. I can't—nor can anyone I checked with—remember any sense of avoidance, denial, or curiosity within the group. It was simply a given, something of no pressing importance and, above all, private. Anyway, it was not really anyone else's business. So what was there to discuss? There were just too many important public issues for the group to be concerned with somebody else's sexuality.

Tom, being a Howard student, was more centrally influential than Paul in campus politics. He was also our channel to Bayard. Tom had graduated high school young, at fifteen or sixteen, then made his way to New York, where he'd been involved in radical politics until, at twenty-one, he'd come to college. A pacifist and socialist, he was one of a small group of white radical youth who'd become protégés of Bayard Rustin's, with whom he was said to be close. Tom was a shrewd strategist with by far the most experience of us all in radical political organizing, having, as it were, studied with Rustin. His influence on NAG campus strategy would be profound.

Paul Dietrich, also a pacifist and radical, had a Chinese partner said to be a son of one of Chiang Kai-shek's warlords. In addition to Jazzland, his popular little jazz club in the African community, Paul was also partner in a large, fashionable Chinese restaurant on Connecticut Avenue. Occasionally Paul would treat NAG folk to a good meal there. One evening Paul came over to our table just grinning and gestured across the dining room to a large, noisy table of old white men.

"Recognize any of them?"

"Hell, no. A bunch of ol' white geezers in bad suits. Why?"

"Look again carefully." He smiled mysteriously. "Know your enemy. That red-faced one is Eastland. Next to him, Stennis, both of Mississippi, and Russell of Georgia." He named a few more Dixiecrat congressmen and members of their staffs. As he explained, these luminaries would, in "the Southern way," go duck hunting in the fall. The game was brought to the restaurant to be converted into a variety of exotic Chinese dishes, after which their Capitol Hill colleagues were invited to a duck feast. Our African presence across the room did not seem to affect their segregationist appetites.

"So, Paul, consorting with the enemy, huh? Tell the truth. You do anything to the food?"

Paul was indignant, or affected to be.

Courtland Cox was from Trinidad by way of New York, but I hadn't known him in high school. Another big dude, Courtland was always thoughtful, deliberate, and given to aphorisms. "Blackness is necessary.

But it is not sufficient" is the one everyone remembers. Courtland always went out of his way to give the impression of being serious and organized. He still does.

The movement brought him some extraordinary experiences all before the age of thirty. I recently saw a picture of Courtland back in 1963 at a table with Roy Wilkins, Whitney Young, Dr. King, James Farmer, and A. Philip Randolph planning the March on Washington. He was representing SNCC while still a Howard undergraduate. Later in the sixties, Courtland sat on the Bertrand Russell commission on the Vietnam War. Later, at the initiative of C. L. R. James, he was named executive secretary of the secretariat for the Sixth Pan-African Conference, where he had to negotiate with heads of state, African governments, and contentious liberation organizations. His surprising conclusion: "You know back when Dr. Du Bois and George Padmore were organizing the Pan-African Conferences and all black folks were still colonized? Well, it had to have been a hell of a lot easier then."

As he explained, now they had to deal with governments as well as their oppositions, complex protocols, and outsize egos. If the opposition was given the slightest recognition, the government would boycott. If the opposition was not officially recognized to their satisfaction, then *they* would denounce the congress. Where countries were still fighting for independence, there would sometimes be two, three, or more rival groups, each insisting that it alone represented the liberation movement. It was incredibly complicated, "an old-fashioned, down-home mess." But still they managed to have a congress. "I'm sure it was easier before we were allegedly 'free,' " Courtland complained.

Two other comrades with whom I have maintained contact over the years are Bill Mahoney and Mike Thelwell. Both were into writing fiction. Mahoney was an olive-skinned brother from New Jersey with a strikingly Asiatic countenance. A strong face whose prominent cheekbones suggested Native American ancestry. The first time I saw him was in the dorm working at the front desk and, as always, reading a book. His very first words to me were something about Hegelian dialectics. No showing off. That was just the way his mind worked most of the time.

In 1963, Jim Forman sent Mahoney back to D.C. to work with Thelwell in setting up a Washington office for SNCC. Talk about an odd couple. Thelwell says that when he met him at the bus station, Bill came off the bus with a wooden box on his shoulders. "Where's the rest of your luggage?" Thelwell asked. "This is it," Bill said. In this wooden box were books, a blue work shirt, a pair of jeans, a few socks, and some drawers. And that was it, Bill's worldly goods—a change of clothes and a lot of books.

For some reason women were attracted to Bill, who often did not seem to notice.

One sister, Jeanie Bell, got his attention though. Jeanie was a smart, organized, effective, bighearted woman who worked for a union. She was also attractive. Without her the Washington SNCC office would have been empty. She got her union to contribute used desks, filing cabinets, mimeograph machines, typewriters, you name it. Anyway, Jeanie fell in love with Bill and took him in. She had a real nice apartment too. This was no student crash pad. So Bill's wardrobe, diet, and address immediately improved along with his love life.

Then Jeanie had to attend a union convention out of town. She was gone only a week. When she returned, she came into the SNCC office. "Oh," she said. "Bill wrote me." "Must be true love," we said. She produced the letter. On SNCC letterhead, it read like a field report. "Look at how he ends the letter," she said, laughing almost tearfully. Her true love concluded after reporting matter-of-factly on movement events, "Yours for freedom, William J. Mahoney."

Bill is one of our casualties, having been severely damaged psychologically, he believes, by agents of the government. A number of our people have symptoms sufficiently similar to his to at least raise the serious possibility that something may indeed have been done to them, possibly while they were in jail. Even so, we have stayed in touch. Every year in Conakry I can depend on receiving at least two lengthy, complicated letters from Bill raising knotty philosophical and political questions.

His partner in the Washington office, Mike Thelwell, was NAG's sole "foreign" student. An African born in Jamaica, Thelwell first appeared on campus bearded and wearing an army fatigue cap. He was so vocal and tireless a defender of the Cuban *barbudos* that on campus people knew him as "Castro." When people would ask him if he was from "the islands," he'd pull himself up to his full height. "The *islands* indeed? I'm from the *continent* . . . of Jamaica." That always cracked me up. The brother's all right, but still, he's got his pompous Caribbean side. These are friends I made from my first semester. We learned a lot together, and together we'd experience serious struggle, as you will see.

At the time, we paid no real attention to one important aspect of NAG. However, as Cleve's list indicates, fully half of the core membership were women. This seemed entirely natural to us, in no way remarkable. So much so that we never thought even to add up the numbers. (Nor, in fact, to count the whites.) We all wanted our people's freedom and were together equally involved in the struggle. What could have been simpler, clearer, or more natural? We didn't think in "gender" terms.

Our sisters asked no quarter and gave none. They neither requested nor expected special treatment as women. And we didn't offer it. There was no women's caucus within the group. Ruth Howard, Muriel Tillinghast, Karen House, Jean Wheeler (Smith), Karen Edwards, Cynthia

Washington, Mary Felice Lovelace, and their sisters were simply NAG members, fellow rebels, our comrades in struggle, constant, bold, always ready to step up, perhaps even taken for granted.

Women faced a very different set of cultural assumptions than did men on that campus. Some institutional proscriptions, cultural expectations, and social conventions affected women and did not even remotely extend to men. Of these, the dorm curfews were only the most obvious. In fact, only after an incident with a sister daring to wear her hair natural did the men in NAG even begin to think seriously about how these double standards affected our sisters. For us to understand exactly how serious and tough-minded our sister comrades had to be even to *think* of choosing radical political involvement in the first place. And then to stay involved for the long haul as many of them would do when we moved off the campus and into Southern Freedom Houses.

In the "feminine" culture of the Howard women's community, a heavy conformity was demanded. Conformity to social conventions of "fashion," of "feminine delicacy," to the decorativeness and frivolity of "the Southern lady." In short, to a set of superficial, severely limiting "women's" roles that were invidious and pervasive. In defiance of such reductive, deeply entrenched attitudes, our sisters chose to be intellectually serious, politically engaged, self-defining young women, and to do so publicly. In so doing, they had elected to be part of a small, militant minority. Not an easy thing at any age, much less at the age of nineteen and against the weight of a stultifying, all-enveloping campus tradition. In that environment, merely to join NAG was already—for the sisters—a declaration of independence, a stubborn, public act of will and moral conviction that we men never had to take on in anything like the same way. And this was even before facing the other rigors of the movement: arrests, violence, and the hostility of white mobs.

It is no wonder then that our sisters proved such dependable and admirable partners in struggle. I'm embarrassed that back then we men never sufficiently appreciated the psychic *cost* of their commitment. Or, if we did, we certainly never gave it public recognition. Except, you know something? On reflection . . . I'm not at all sure just how kindly these bold, independent-minded sisters of ours would have received any such attempt at special treatment on our part. They might very well have handed us our heads.

At first, D.C. was not really too different from New York. I'd worked some with New York CORE in the Northern struggle. The D.C. CORE chapter, led by Julius Hobson, an older professional man, was not large. We saw Julius Hobson as an experienced struggler, a good strategist, an uncompromising militant, and a man of selfless devotion, one to whom we were prepared to listen and whose direction in matters of struggle we would accept. Within D.C., Hobson would engage de facto segregation and discrimination in areas that are still problematic today: education, housing, and employment. At the demonstrations Hobson staged, NAG students would be, in effect, his foot soldiers on the picket lines.

Julius Hobson had a strong reputation as a fighter, so naturally he was demonized in the local press as a dangerous radical, a black militant. Which, of course, only endeared him all the more to us. Clearly, all he was doing was attacking injustice and confronting the establishment with the contradictions of their own hypocrisy. He taught me a lot that first year.

Occasionally, if a large demonstration was needed, we'd go over to Philly on a weekend. This also was training, but I mention Philadelphia for a different reason: one of my greatest abiding regrets from this period.

Only when Paul Robeson died did I learn that all during the late sixties this magnificent black artist and fighter for humanity had been living quietly in that city. We never knew. I wish we had, because for all of us in the movement he was a legend. A veritable demigod in his endowments of courage, intelligence, principle, and character. In NAG we played his records and talked about him all the time. Sterling Brown spoke of him movingly. We admired his great dignity, militancy, and stubborn integrity. The way as an artist he embraced the struggle, celebrated the common people, and embodied and expressed the power and beauty of African culture in America all over the world.

Paul Robeson was an exemplary black man, a true Pan-Africanist in his lifelong affinity and identification with African culture. He said often and proudly that his father had always told him, "We are descended from the Igbo people." When he was thirty-eight, he declared his identity, as an artist, with the oral historians of traditional Africa: "Had I been born in Africa, I would have belonged, I hope, to those families which sing and chant the glories and legends of the tribe. . . . I would have liked in my mature years to have been a wise elder, for I worship wisdom and knowledge of the ways of man." Such clarity so young. To us he was a wise elder and a great example.

And all this time he was so very near and we somehow never knew. Had we but known, NAG would certainly have sought him out to pay respect. We would have marched to wherever he was in Philly with our picket signs, serenaded him with freedom songs. Just to praise and thank him for his example and inspiration to our generation. I believe, I know, that his great warrior's heart would have appreciated that. It certainly would have done me good. It simply never occurred to us at the time (1961–63) that this legend of our culture and struggle could have been so very close.

[I believe Ture must have forgotten—because he would certainly have known at the time—that SNCC had later found occasion to express our debt and grat-

itude and that Bro Robeson's last recorded public appearance (1966) had been at a SNCC benefit. I know it would have consoled Ture had he lived to read the following:

"In his closing years Robeson dropped out of public awareness and was largely ignored by the leadership of the Civil Rights Movement, except for the militant young leaders of the Student Nonviolent Coordinating Committee. At a gala celebration of his sixty-seventh birthday (1965) Robeson was deeply moved when keynote speaker John Lewis, then chairman of SNCC, proclaimed, 'We of SNCC are Paul Robeson's spiritual children. We too have rejected gradualism and moderation.' " Indeed? —EMT]

The first year I was at Howard my friend Larry Greenbush from Kokista at Science was at American University, also in D.C. Larry didn't like the place much, and he'd seize every chance to go home to New York on weekends. Often I'd go with him. AU had many affluent students with cars, so we had no difficulty getting rides. Sometimes chipping in for gas, sometimes not.

On those rides I developed a deep hatred—one shared by many—for Route 40, which at that time was the main route out of D.C. Once Route 40 entered Maryland, everything was segregated, *evrahthang*. On those rides we'd leave as early as possible on Friday afternoon, which usually meant before supper, so the food question would inevitably arise. On Route 40, to buy food, I'd have to go round the back. The white students would say, "No problem. We'll buy the food and bring it out. We'll all eat in the car." A logical enough solution, but one that I always declined. Larry would also refuse to buy from segregated establishments: "Nah. I'll wait till we get to Jersey. Ain't hungry anyway." But I knew he was at least as hungry as I was. Larry was, after all, a big nineteen-year-old who loved to eat.

Strangely enough, we could never discuss or talk easily about it. So we simply sat silently in the car waiting for the others. Each pretending not to be hungry. But of course I knew why Larry was never hungry. And he certainly knew that I knew. But it remained unspoken between us, both of us strangely embarrassed to silence by the painful absurdity of a racism that had nothing to do with either of us. But I believe we grew closer in those silences.

It would take NAG some years before we could properly attack Route 40, but we were always looking rancorously at it. It was a constant irritant to those of us from Philadelphia, New Jersey, and points north. How this humiliation to Africans born in America (and their friends) became an international issue and a target of the movement is an interesting story. And to us, quite instructive. The year I went to Howard, 1960, was celebrated as "the Year of African Independence," and by 1963, the number

163

of new African, Caribbean, and Asian embassies in Washington had mushroomed. These comprised the "nonaligned" bloc, a third force in international affairs, and the Western democracies (formerly colonial masters), led by the United States, were contesting with the Soviet Union for influence with these nonaligned nations.

Naturally Asian and African diplomatic personnel traveled frequently between their Washington embassies and their U.N. missions in New York. This meant that black and brown men and women, some with the rank of ambassador, would be driving up to roadside greasy spoons in cars with diplomatic license plates and insignia. But were the Route 40 crackers impressed? No, sir! They knew "niggers" when they saw them. They rarely failed to insult the diplomats, embarrass the Kennedy administration, and delight Soviet propagandists. Every time it happened we exulted.

The Kennedy administration—check this out—the U.S. government prepared and was about to release an announcement of a new policy. Harsh penalties would be imposed on any Route 40 establishment that embarrassed the administration by refusing service to dark-skinned *foreign diplomats*. Think about that. That announcement was canceled when someone in the administration *[most likely Harris Wofford —EMT]* pointed out to the State Department that such a distinction was not likely to sit well with millions of American citizens who were black. This apparently had not occurred to them. Can you believe that?

This did not stop the State Department from privately calling in the restaurant owners to encourage them to learn to distinguish between Africans from the continent and those born in America. At least so it was rumored in Washington. We had no reason not to believe it.

So when CORE called for sit-ins along Route 40, we were more than ready. There was a lot of press because of the international aspect. It was the only civil rights campaign I was ever on that had—however obliquely implied—the public endorsement of the Kennedy administration, which had greeted the CORE announcement with vaguely supportive mutterings about national interests.

Which might also have been why it was some of the easiest campus organizing NAG ever did. Or it could just as well have been that a lot of our peers nurtured their own humiliating memories of Route 40. Whatever the reason—probably a combination—the Howard delegation that arrived at the staging area—a large Baltimore church—was some five hundred strong.

Students from schools across the Northeast—Brandeis, Harvard, Yale, Cornell, New York University, and Johns Hopkins—answered CORE's call. When we and the Morgan State students arrived, the church was already half filled with white students (good ol' CPT?). I suspect that many of these white students were youthful "New Frontiersmen," inspired by JFK's injunction to "ask what you can do for your country" and eager to put an end to their president's international embarrassments. Of course, what with the admission policies and high tuitions of those schools, their half of the church was pretty much lily-white. Almost totally. Somehow these delegations had managed to get there before we did, even though we were coming from a mere forty miles up the road.

However, the moment when Hank Thomas and Muriel Tillinghast led in our delegation was curious, highly dramatic. Every head in the church turned toward us as this line of serious-faced, young Africans kept filing in and gradually filling every pew on our side. The sitting students broke into applause, which, considering the issue, was more than a little odd. Once seated, however, we returned their applause.

This odd, surprising moment was quite affecting but also ironic and more than a little ambiguous. But mostly moving. A house of Christian worship, filled with young Americans neatly divided down the middle, one-half black, the other white, saluting each other with polite applause before setting out together to engage segregation. And brought together probably as much by the foreign-policy interests of the government regarding independent Africa as by outrage over domestic racism. As the *Reader's Digest* liked to say, "Only in America." Of course I applauded vigorously too. But my applause was for my old friend Larry, who was by then long gone from D.C.

Toward the end of freshman year I'd finally get my chance to head to the Deep South. As they say, be careful what you wish for. . . . The CORE Freedom Rides that spring changed my life, as they did the direction and character of the student movement. This was when I decided, definitely, to be seriously involved in this struggle. From now on, serious commitment.

Just two days ago I watched a group of young Africans on American TV talking about nonviolence and the "olden days" of the movement. They "respected" the movement, they said, but had difficulty identifying completely because they themselves were not "passive." They all agreed that they could not imagine themselves being "so passive." "No, no, no," I shouted at the screen. "*Passive* is exactly the wrong word." In fact, you'd be hard-pressed to find a more inaccurate term. But that is a widespread mistake and is much more than a problem of language.

Nonviolence is—in terms of human evolution anyway—an unnatural response in certain situations. No question. In American cultural terms, particularly the cowboy, mountain-man, outlaw, carbine-and-six-gun culture of the American frontier, popularized over the media, nonviolence is clearly aberrant, a cultural contradiction. But that is irrelevant.

Because, as *technique* of social struggle, nonviolence is anything but passive. Quite the reverse. (How can you have a "passive" movement? That's a contradiction in terms.)

Now, on one level nonviolence *is* a philosophy of life, an ethical principle, a way of being in the world verging on the religious. On another level, however, it is merely a strategic approach to struggle. But on both levels it is a very stern discipline. And no discipline is ever "passive." That's the first thing. Which is what Dr. King (peace be unto him) had meant when he explained to me, "Stokely, you have to understand one thing. The beauty of nonviolence is that you never let any outside force, nothing outside of yourself, control what you do." Check that out. That's discipline, Jack, and self-control. I will come back to this aspect.

Nonviolence as a strategy of struggle, as personified and pronounced by Dr. King, gave our generation—particularly in the South—the means by which to confront an entrenched and violent racism. It offered a way for *large* numbers of Africans to join the struggle. Nothing passive in that. (Remember now, only a limited number of people and a certain kind of person can successfully be recruited for a riot or armed struggle. Think about it.)

One must remember that the patron saint of nonviolent political struggle, Mahatma Gandhi, successfully used the technique to liberate an entire subcontinent from the imperialist grasp of what my Rasta brethren call properly the "brutish empire." It is useful to remember the correct term, which is *nonviolent direct action.* It is the *direct action* aspect that my friends and I gloried in. It was directly confrontational, even aggressively so, only in a nonviolent way. Nothing passive about this.

But this is not really the same thing as pacifism, with which it is often conflated. Pacifism is the total personal renouncement of any and all forms of violence in human life in all situations, whether personal or state-sponsored. This aspect of pacifism is ethical and religious in effect and can often appear passive. But the deepest aspect of this, called radical pacifism, is aggressively activist, envisioning a world in which the armed violence of the state—the military—is replaced by "armies of nonviolence." Nonviolent techniques will replace armed, military conflict as the means for negotiating political disputes between nations. A book by Krishnalal Shridharani, an Indian theoretician of radical pacifism, called *War Without Violence* is the radical pacifists' key text. A noble, visionary idea, but (not having read the book) I have great difficulty envisioning such a circumstance, a universal nonviolent substitute for war.

Part of our training in NAG was in elementary techniques of nonviolent confrontation. How to maintain discipline under physical attack. The various responses and positions by which to protect yourself and others while under attack. We were also introduced to the history and theory. In this, Bayard Rustin was our great teacher. As a committed pacifist and the quintessential radical activist, he could instruct us in the principles as well as the tactics and techniques of nonviolent direct action. Bayard had been one of two radical pacifists—Glenn Smiley being the other—sent in 1955 by the Fellowship of Reconciliation (FOR) at the outset of the Montgomery bus boycott to train the young and inexperienced Martin Luther King and the Montgomery Improvement Association in the *techniques* and *psychology* of nonviolent mass action.

Which had been only fair. There was considerable justice in this. As I discovered, Bayard had been arguing passionately, indeed agitating tirelessly, for many, many years that the only hope for combating racism while avoiding race war in America was through nonviolent direct action. He had been—with mixed results—trying to get the FOR to commit to training the African masses in America in the techniques and philosophy of nonviolent struggle. Thus, in 1955, events in Montgomery would seem to have made a prophet of him.

Rustin wrote an important essay on this topic called "The Negro and Nonviolence," which we studied in NAG. The piece, which is addressed to the FOR, the national organization of radical pacifists, begins with a catalog of incidents of racial violence and injustices suggesting an impending racial cataclysm. When first I read it in 1960 at Howard, it felt alarmingly contemporary. What is sobering is that now, nearly forty years later, it still retains much of its contemporary feel. Check it out:

> Even in normal times, changes in social and economic patterns cause fear and frustration, which in turn lead to aggression. In time of war, the general social condition is fertile soil for the development of hate and fear, and transference of these to minority groups is quite simple. Organized violence is growing in the North and South. The Ku Klux Klan is riding again, employing more subtle methods. Negroes and whites in Southern iron ore mines, as well as in Mobile, Alabama, shipyards, are going armed to work.

Bayard then lists ominous violent racial events from across the nation: on the job, in the streets, within the armed services, cases of "Negro soldiers and civilians being killed by whites." He next describes a building black response with numerous cases of groups arming themselves amid a widespread sentiment to respond in kind in an organized way. "Growing numbers of Negroes see mass violence looming."

All of which presents the pacifist community, "those of us who believe in the nonviolent solution of conflict as a duty and an opportunity," the need to point out the practical necessity for "nonviolent direct action as the only way, consistent with the end he desires, that the Negro can attain progress."

While conceding the difficulties—"nonviolence as a method has within it the demand for terrible sacrifice and long suffering, but, as Gandhi has said, 'freedom does not drop from the sky.' One has to struggle and be willing to die for it"—he then argues that the approach is entirely consistent with the religious culture, moral sensibility, and highest traditions of the black community.

> Certainly the Negro possesses qualities essential for nonviolent direct action. He has long since learned to endure suffering. He can admit his own share of guilt and has to be pushed hard to become bitter. He has produced, and still sings, such songs as "It's Me, Oh Lord, Standin' in the Need of Prayer" and "Nobody Knows the Trouble I've Seen." He is creative and has learned to adjust himself to [difficult] conditions. But above all he possesses a rich religious heritage and today finds the church the center of his life.

The essay concludes with an eloquent appeal to his fellow pacifists to stand with the black community in the coming struggle.

> Those of us who believe in nonviolent resistance can do the greatest possible good for the Negro, for those who exploit him, for America, and for the world by becoming a real part of the Negro community, thus being in a position to suggest methods and to offer leadership when troubles come.
>
> Identification with the Negro community demands considerable sacrifice. The Negro is not to be won by words alone, but by an obvious consistency in words and deeds . . . we can add to world justice by placing in the hands of thirteen million black Americans a workable and Christian technique for the righting of injustice and the solution of conflict.

That just blew me away, when, as a nineteen-year-old freshman, I first read it. Blew me away, Jack. The only word that came to me was *prophetic*. Especially when I noticed the date—October 1942. Fourteen years before the Montgomery boycott produced Dr. King. "Wow, that's how long this brother's been on the case. Just about as long as I've been alive. Oh, wow." My admiration for Bayard's activist spirit, vision, and endurance just grew.

Clearly that 1942 essay was a strategic proposal addressed to the Fellowship of Reconciliation urging them to put their radical pacifist nonviolence to the test against American racism. It seems they did try. I suspect that the establishment of CORE in 1946 was their answer. With, until the Freedom Rides, quite modest results. It is not difficult, therefore, to imagine Bayard's high excitement upon reading in 1956—fourteen years later—of the adoption of nonviolent principles by the Montgomery leadership and community. No wonder he rushed down to place his practical and tactical expertise at the disposal of the visionary but inexperienced young minister.

That was Rustin the theoretician and strategist. I would discover that he was also, in his younger days, one of the more skilled practitioners, one-on-one, of the psychological discipline of nonviolence. This too is worth a careful look, it being quite different, not theory but a practical application of specific techniques.

The most obvious and common situation for the nonviolence technique is the publicly staged engagement—demonstration or sit-in—where there are witnesses and an audience, preferably the press and the police. The cops, even when hostile, cannot really stand around in the presence of witnesses and watch the situation escalate into murder. It's as simple as that. In these situations you can occupy the moral high ground merely by maintaining nonviolence and keeping your dignity. Your attackers will inevitably appear brutish and irrational, the mob. You win the battle of the image, especially if TV cameras are present.

However merely maintaining a strategic nonviolent posture on public demonstrations does not entirely encompass what Dr. King meant by discipline and control. He was talking about actually taking control of a situation and an opponent, actually imposing your will even as he rains blows down on your unresisting head. This is, in effect, more than merely disarming your attacker. This controlling of the situation entails a nonviolence of word, deed, and demeanor, a nonviolence of spirit if you will. Basically, it is simple. You merely had to eliminate everything in your behavior—word, deed, look, gesture, or body language—that might provoke or nourish the impulse to violence, the evolutionary conditioning to battle, in your opponent.

All these techniques are illustrated in another of Bayard's essays from this period, which we studied in NAG. "Nonviolence vs. Jim Crow" is actually a textbook illustration of all aspects of nonviolent technique: moral, psychological, religious, physical. It perfectly illustrates Dr. King's notion of nonviolent discipline: "You never allow anyone or anything outside yourself to dictate your action."

The essay is an account of Bayard's arrest in Nashville for the crime of refusing to move to the back of the bus. During the incident he is repeatedly and brutally beaten and verbally abused by the arresting officers. If you aren't being properly analytical, it will look like just another case of a Negro head-whupping at the hands of Southern cops. That he is finally released by the district attorney, who addresses him "kindly" as "Mr. Rustin," may seem a very small victory won at an excessively high price. Yes and no. And certainly not to Bayard. For him this is no random incident, it is a planned and successful demonstration of nonviolent technique by a master. Observe:

Recently I was planning to go from Louisville to Nashville by bus. I bought my ticket, boarded the bus, and, instead of going to the back, sat down in the second seat. The driver saw me, got up, and came toward me.

"Hey, you. You're supposed to sit in the back seat."

"Why?"

"Because that's the law. Niggers ride in back."

I said, "My friend, I believe that is an unjust law. If I were to sit in back I would be condoning injustice."

Angry, but not knowing what to do, he got out and went into the station . . . for about thirteen miles north of Nashville I heard sirens approaching. The bus came to an abrupt stop, and a police car and two motorcycles drew up beside us with a flourish. Four policemen got into the bus, consulted shortly with the driver, and came to my seat.

"Get up, you_____nigger!"

"Why?" I asked.

"Get up, you black_____!"

"I believe that I have a right to sit here," I said quietly. "If I sit in the back of the bus I am depriving that child"—I pointed to a little white child of five or six—"of the knowledge that there is injustice here, which I believe it is his right to know. It is my sincere conviction that the power of love in the world is the greatest power existing. If you have a greater power, my friend, you may move me."

How much they understood of what I was trying to tell them I do not know. By this time they were impatient and angry. As I would not move, they began to beat me about the head and shoulders, and I shortly found myself knocked to the floor. Then they dragged me out of the bus and continued to kick and beat me.

Knowing that if I tried to get up or protect myself in the first heat of their anger they would construe it as an attempt to resist and beat me down again, I forced myself to be still and wait for their kicks, one after another. Then I stood up, spreading out my arms parallel to the ground, and said, "There is no need to beat me. I am not resisting you."

At this, three white men, obviously Southerners by their speech, got out of the bus and remonstrated with the police. Indeed, as one of the policemen raised his club to strike me, one of them, a little fellow, caught hold of it and said, "Don't you do that!" A second policeman raised his club to strike the little man, and I stepped between them, facing the man, and said, "Thank you, but there is no need to do that. I do not wish to fight. I am protected well."

An elderly gentleman, well dressed and also a Southerner, asked the police where they were taking me.

They said, "Nashville."

"Don't worry, son," he said to me. "I'll be there to see that you get justice."

When we reached Nashville, a number of policemen were lined up on both sides of the highway down which I had to pass on my way to the captain's office. They tossed me from one to another like a volleyball. By the time I reached the office, the lining of my best coat was torn, and I was considerably rumpled.

Finally the captain said, "Come here, nigger."

I walked directly to him. "What can I do for you?" I asked.

"Nigger," he said menacingly, "you're supposed to be scared when you come in here!"

"I am fortified by truth, justice, and Christ," I said. "There's no need for me to fear."

He was flabbergasted and, for a time, completely at a loss for words. Finally he said to another officer, "I believe the nigger's crazy!"

At the courthouse I was taken down the hall to the office of the assistant district attorney, Mr. Ben West. As I got to the door I heard a voice, "Say, you colored fellow, hey!" I looked around and saw the elderly gentleman who had been on the bus.

"I'm here to see that you get justice," he said.

I left the courthouse, believing all the more strongly in the nonviolent approach. I am certain that I was addressed as "Mister" (as no Negro is ever addressed in the South), and I was assisted by those three men, and that the elderly gentleman interested himself in my predicament because I had, without fear, faced the four policemen and said, "There's no need to beat me. I offer you no resistance."

I won't comment on Bayard's use of psychological techniques, those are obvious. Except to say not everyone could have used them as effectively as Bayard did. Bayard was an impressive physical presence. He would have been impeccably dressed and would, in the rural South of the time, have appeared obviously educated, intelligent, articulate, and "cultured," for a "colored" man.

Those, plus his personal dignity and natural flair for dramatic improvisation, were as essential to the outcome as any of the moral issues. And although he was obviously improvising as he went along, it was not entirely spontaneous. The broad general terms of his responses were standard nonviolent techniques, carefully controlled and developed for effect much like in a theatrical performance. He, the victim, actually controlled the audience's responses. Notice how, while he was ostensibly speaking to the cops, he was really addressing the onlookers. Bayard was good at that. Not everyone can do it.

The two things that most surprised me when I first read it were the prosecutor's letting "Mr. Rustin" walk and the four conscientious white men who intervened on his behalf. I better explain that. Were I to say this in a speech (or let it stand as written), the next day's headline would read, "Kwame Ture doubts that white men have consciences." Which would be stupid. In my time, I been called a lot of things, but nobody ever called me stupid.

However, one further step in the theory and practice of nonviolence I—no doubt a spiritual failing on my part—was unable to follow. It is here that we begin to hear talk of "soul force," *agape,* or love force and the moral redemption of the aggressor. According to these principles, disarming the violent impulse by complete nonresistance is only the first imperative. You must then seek to establish a moral human contact by looking the aggressor gently in the eye. And, speaking nonaggressively, addressing him as "friend" or "brother," expressing not anger but "reason," a "spirit of love and forgiveness" and your "common humanity." That's the theory anyway. I found the practice to be a lot different.

Truthfully I was never into that kind of spiritual evangelism. I never saw my responsibility to be the moral and spiritual reclamation of some racist thug. I would settle for changing his behavior, period. Moral suasion, legal proscription, or even force of arms, whatever ultimately it took, that's what I'd be for. I've always been content to leave saintliness to the more spiritually evolved among my brothers and sisters. Besides, to tell the truth, I've never really seen that human contact stuff to work. Well . . . actually . . . the closest I ever came was once in Cambridge, Maryland.

We were having a sit-in. One minute I was sitting on a stool at the counter of this rinky-dink diner. Next thing I know I'm lying on the floor and somebody over me is cursing, ranting, raving, and kicking repeatedly at my midsection. This guy is really pumped, I mean the dude is raving. Then quickly he runs off. I never even got a good look at him, much less engaged in any "brotherly" eye contact or loving reasoning. The only contact I recall was between my head and the floor, his boot and my belly.

But that night we're in the mass meeting in the church when this white boy comes in and apologizes to the group and to me personally. He wanted us to know how really sorry he was. First and only time I ever saw that. Some of the folk were really moved, saw in it the hand of God, y'know. The guy, his name was Eddie Dickerson I believe, turned out to be decent enough. We ended up sending him to New York CORE for training. Next time I saw him was in a picture. He was sitting in a restaurant in the South and the owner was smashing eggs over his head and kicking him. Anyway, I don't make any claim to having converted Eddie with nonviolent soul force. All I did was roll into a ball to protect my stomach. So . . . I've always had honest doubts about the conversion of sinners by the moral force of nonviolence. For me and most of my friends it was merely a valuable if limited strategy.

I was surprised that four Southern onlookers came so unequivocally to Bayard's defense because that patently did not conform to our sense of the South in 1960. Not with anything I read in the press, saw on TV, or heard from my friends. Nor would it conform to my own experience only a few months later. Also, I was particularly puzzled because the incident had taken place way back in 1942, the year after my birth. In, to my understanding, the bad ol' days of rabid Southern bigotry. So it didn't add up. Could the South have been getting worse, being more violent, more racist, more mean-spirited in 1960 than it had been twenty years earlier? This really puzzled me. So much for "progress," eh?

Well t'ain't really much of a mystery. See, the South had in fact changed for the worse. In reality, the Dixie that we would go into within a few months was in many ways a much more violent place than twenty years earlier. Why this should have been so is interesting, though I won't pretend that we understood it so clearly at the time.

It's actually quite simple. The events Bayard described took place years before the Supreme Court desegregation decision of 1954 (*Brown vs. Board of Education of Topeka, Kansas*). The effects of that decision must be understood clearly. The decision didn't—and still hasn't—desegregated American schools. But it profoundly, profoundly affected the South— white Southerners and the African communities—but in very different ways.

The court's decision was greeted with a resounding silence from the national leadership and the two other branches of the federal government. Eisenhower, the president, never said a mumbling word in support of the court's decision, contenting himself with grumbling that his appointment of Chief Justice Earl Warren was the "biggest damnfool decision" of his presidency.

And the Congress. No clear unified response there either. In fact, the very first response was from Senator James "Big Jim" Eastland, plantation owner from the Mississippi Delta. Almost the next day, "Ol' Jim" rushed to the Senate floor to denounce "this political legislation by a political court which the South will nevah obey." He issued the classic Confederate call for "interposition and nullification," which in this vacuum of national leadership set the stage for everything we in SNCC would later encounter in the South.

It was a field day for every Confederate patriot, racist demagogue, and opportunist politician in the South. They saw the schools decision as the first serious crack in the Southern edifice of legal segregation. They proclaimed the sacred, patriotic, and ancestral duty of evrah red-blooded good ol' boy to rush to the defense of the Southern way "as oah foahfathers did at Antietam, Manassas, Bull Run, and the Battle of the Wilderness, we must prove worthy sons of gallant fathers," etc., etc. The press for the most part was hysterical. The Jackson, Mississippi, *Clarion Ledger* predicted "blood flowing in the street which must be laid on the steps of the Court."

Membership in the Ku Klux Klan, which had been in serious decline, shot up to its highest level in fifty years. In the Mississippi Delta, a plantation owner called together a new organization—the White Citizens Council—four months after the decision. The council's sole purpose: to organize resistance—and it spread like kudzu across the Southern landscape. *[Exquisitely symbolic of the deterioration of race relations, or their illusion, in the region is that Robert "Tut" Patterson of Itta Bena, the founder of the White Citizens Council, had in boyhood been "best friends" with Aaron "Doc" Henry, a leader of the Mississippi Freedom Democratic Party and the NAACP. —EMT]*

Previously "moderate" politicians saw which way the wind was blowing. George Wallace (Alabama), who would become governor, and Governor Orval Faubus (Arkansas) changed into rabid defenders of segregation overnight. A year after the decision, our age mate, fourteen-year-old Emmett Till, would be butchered and thrown into the Tallahatchie River in the Mississippi Delta town of Money. His acquitted murderer, "Big" Milam, told a reporter that when he saw a picture of Till standing next to a white girl in a group of black and white kids with whom he'd graduated from junior high school in Chicago, "My friend, that's when I knew I had to kill him. That's what the war is all about down here." Milam was subsequently elected sheriff in a neighboring county.

Simply stated, what happened was that between 1954 and 1960 the thug element of the South took control. With the full encouragement of the media, the complicity of the capitalists, and the opportunism of the politicians, "ol' Bubba" took over. In fact, Bubba became the political leadership. A desperate "us versus them," "iffen yo' ain't with us, yo' agin us, a traitor" garrison mentality arose. An atmosphere of beleaguered, tight-jawed conformity enforced by intimidation and reprisal, fear and threat, descended over Dixie. One brave white woman journalist in Mississippi, Hazel Brannon Smith (peace be unto her courageous spirit) wrote in a 1959 editorial, "Today we live in fear . . . it hangs like a dark cloud over us, dominating every facet of public and private life . . . almost every man and woman is afraid to do anything that would promote harmony and goodwill between the races."

Now that was the white South of my generation's experience. Tense, hostile, armored. Naturally we thought it had always been that sharp-edged and vicious. That's why we were all amazed by Bayard's defenders on that bus. I still doubt that in 1960 those same decent men would have been able to summon up the moral courage to come to the defense of any Negro challenging even the slightest manifestation of segregation in the way Bayard had done. His superb skills and nonviolent virtuosity notwithstanding. Sad. Unfortunate. Ironic. But true. But in our time the South was showing its worst face to the world. A time in which "the best lack all conviction, while the worst are full of passionate intensity."

That essentially was the result of *Brown vs. Topeka* in the white South. It had a very different effect in the African communities there. The legal implications of the decision were not lost on us either. In our churches, schools, Masonic lodges, beauty parlors, barbershops, and juke joints, our people understood—or hoped they understood—that finally the highest court had decided that, at least in one area, we were entitled to the fairness and equity promised in the Constitution. And a central tenet of black Southern aspiration had always been the importance of education. That was why those Reconstruction congresses of freedmen had set up some of the first public education systems in the nation. And that this was a beginning.

Consequently this decision was clearly seen among black people as the highest achievement of the "judicial strategy" that the NAACP had doggedly been pursuing for fifty years. It was a splendid victory. And now that finally the high court had spoken, justice must surely follow. Glorah hallelujah. The Arc of the Universe, it curve toward freedom. It do. A nation not of men but of laws. Praise His holy name. And for the first time since 1896, the law was on our side. Thank you, Jesus!

But what our people saw instead was, all around them, the mobilization of Confederate rancor and resistance. Klan parades. Physical, psychological, and economic intimidation, lynchings and beatings. Mobs mobilized against young children. Previously rational white "friends" becoming silent or turning racist. The proliferation of Klan and Citizens Council propaganda. From the rest of the nation and the national government, silence. Things were in fact worse. All motion is not progress.

Our people did the only rational thing: they began to arm themselves. Returning Korean War veterans organized community self-defense: "Put not your trust in princes nor in sons of men, for in them is no salvation." The preachers could have added, "Nor in courts of justice or in legal proclamations."

The biggest irony—the law of unexpected consequences—was that the *Brown* decision really was the highest achievement of the judicial strategy.

But it also brutally exposed the severe limitations of a purely legalistic approach. A great victory, true, and it wasn't that nothing happened: things actually got worse. Clearly something more was needed, additional strategies, a different approach. But what exactly? Race war? Into this vacuum stepped—the next year, 1955—the Montgomery Bus Boycott, Martin Luther King, the faith of the black church, Gandhian nonviolence, and civil disobedience. The merger of two foreign philosophies, one (nonviolent direct action) from India, the other (civil disobedience) from the far reaches of New England transcendentalism, with black religious culture. Once these were cobbled together by Dr. King, it gave the Southern African community a moral philosophy to justify resistance and the techniques to execute that struggle.

Cool. But why, especially in the face of the ominous, armed white mobilization around them, would our people respond so massively? Because in Mrs. Hamer's phrase, they "were sick an' tar'd of being sick an' tar'd." And because also with the judicial strategy, our struggle had been entirely in the hands of our heroic but invisible lawyers. Quietly, doggedly, against the grain of legal precedent and sentiment, they had trudged from courtroom to courtroom hidden and unseen: a struggle by proxy. The general community was neither involved or even always aware.

But with this new way—nonviolent, mass-based direction action—the entire community, everyone who would, could be a part and hope to survive. Everyone brave enough could share in the struggle for his or her own liberation and be seen to do so. It was public and you didn't need education or money or to be a lawyer. So in Montgomery the community—ordinary folk—came together, stood strong, stayed off the buses, and walked for a year. They strengthened each other and watched their own strength grow. Folks were fired from their jobs. *[White housewife: "Beulah, good as we've been to you, I jest know you aren't involve din this boycott foolishness, now, are you?" Beulah (righteously): "Oh, no'm, Miss Anne. I sho ain't in that mess. Me? I jes' stays offa them buses an' leaves dat fool'ness alone. Yes, I do." —EMT]* People arrested. Some beaten in the streets. Cars burned. Houses (Dr. King's among them) bombed. Police harassment. The Klan paraded. Fired shots in the dark. Planted dynamite. The White Citizens Councils issued proclamations. Across the entire South, Africans watched and prayed. Took collections in church. Sent money. In Montgomery the community, the common people, stood firm. It was the faith, courage, and endurance of the ordinary people that pushed the leadership at every step. A movement was born. Rise an' shine an' give God the glory. Glorah. Glorah hallelujah. Praise His holy name.

That, in the proverbial nutshell, was the background of what we would be facing in the South before my freshman year was over. Now, what we're talking here is history. History as I lived it and understand it.

But I've never told anyone I was an academic "historian," so it is probable I have neglected to mention something quite important. So be it.

In January of 1960—I was still in high school then—the administration in Washington changed. Democrats replaced Republicans. A "vigorous, progressive, young" president, so they told us, took over. He proclaimed a new challenge of energetic and progressive activism when Americans should "ask not what your country can do for you; ask what you can do for your country." It was a great speech . . . until you really studied what he was saying. But many of us heard what we wanted to hear. And some of us believed him. So, soon indeed, we would test the sincerity of those words about defending freedom and paying any price.

CHAPTER IX

The Great Leap Forward:
The Freedom Rides

Much has been written about the Freedom Rides. I am not sure what I can add. But as a participant from almost the beginning, I would like to tell the exact truth of those events. Like so many events in the struggle, the rides began in considerable ambiguity and uncertainty. The most lasting consequence of the rides was the change they would set in motion regarding the role and form of SNCC. In this way, the rides changed many lives, my own included.

When, in 1961, we first heard the plans for the CORE project that the world would come to know as the Freedom Rides, our response was mixed. At first a long silence, then incredulity, which turned rapidly to skepticism.

"They going do what? Oh, man. From *D.C.* to *New Orleans*?"

"Ah says to hush your mouf. Say whut? Is dey crazy?" Then a long, pensive silence as people visualized what was being proposed. And, I think, silent because no one wanted to be the first to say out loud what we all were thinking.

The plan, however, was simplicity itself. In any sane, even half-civilized society it would have been completely innocuous, hardly worth a second thought or meriting any comment at all. CORE would be sending an integrated team—black and white together—from the nation's capital to New Orleans on public transportation. That's all. Except, of course, that they would sit randomly on the buses in integrated pairs and in the stations they would use waiting room facilities casually, ignoring the white/colored signs. What could be more harmless . . . in any even marginally healthy society?

CORE's purposes were twofold and quite clear. Practically, the intent was simply to "test" the implementation of a fifteen-year-old Supreme Court ruling mandating the integration of facilities for interstate travelers. For fifteen years there had been flagrant noncompliance with "the law of the land" as handed down in the *Morgan* case (*Irene Morgan vs. Virginia*, 1946). Then, in 1960, the *Boynton* case (*Boynton vs. Virginia*) had reinforced that finding. So now not only were there *two* Supreme Court decisions, but the implementation machinery existed in the form of the Interstate Commerce Commission. No legislation was necessary; all that was required was John F. Kennedy's proverbial "stroke of the pen," which, though long promised, had not been forthcoming.

The new Kennedy administration had come into office mouthing rhetoric about the national government's responsibility toward the constitutional rights of *all* Americans. CORE's plan would test their sincerity and their resolve, for in JFK's famous phrase, was not "sincerity always subject to proof"?

The second purpose was more symbolic, even sentimental: a celebratory recapitulation of a "Journey of Reconciliation" through the upper South that CORE had undertaken back in 1947.

There would be two major differences this time. Legally, this trip should have been less controversial since it did not involve civil disobedience, being in full compliance with federal law rather than in "defiance" of unjust ones. But of course legality was never at issue. Also, while the Journey of Reconciliation had prudently confined itself to the so-called border states of the "upper South," this one would be headed through the Deep South, into the very "heart of Dixie," a region that had changed considerably since that first journey and entirely for the worse. The South was now literally an armed camp, racially polarized, politically tense, hard-edged.

For some of us there was still another complicating factor. In accordance with Gandhian practices, CORE would be "informing the competent authorities" of their intention and itinerary. In this case the U.S. president, attorney general, and the director of the FBI, as well as the chairman of the ICC and the CEOs of Trailways and Greyhound. It is tempting, in historical hindsight, to report that NAG immediately and unreservedly embraced this plan. But we didn't. Not at first.

Of all the other organizations in the movement we were closest in temperament to CORE. We shared their activism, admired their militancy. Their members were our friends, our allies, our brothers and sisters. We supported each other's demonstrations. But this . . . this Freedom Ride? What was the CORE national office thinking? We had some serious questions. Were we prepared to go? Did it make political sense? Was the issue worth the risk?

"Ah, man, it ain't nothing going happen. It's just some American citizens riding a damn bus, man. The Kennedys got no choice. They gotta uphold the law. Ain't nothing going happen, you'll see."

"Shoot, in Mississippi? In Alabama? Is you crazy, Negro? Nothing going happen? Them folks be lucky to *survive*, bro."

"I'm witchu, Jack. Hell, I'm part of this movement too, but I'm mah mammy's only son and sho nuff too [expletive] young to be dying for no [expletive] seat on no [expletive] bus, you dig. It ain't worth it, y'all."

But being NAG, rationality prevailed, and the proposal was analyzed, dissected, taken apart, and plain worried to death. Two major and unresolved areas of concern surfaced. We could all agree that *all* racism had to be attacked and constitutional laws enforced, but this strategy? The more political ones—led by Tom Kahn—questioned the conceptual framework: the viability of any strategy whose success or failure was totally dependent on factors beyond our control, in this case, the behavior of the enemy. For it to work, they'd have to be the dumbest crackers in the world. All they had to do at each stop was meet the riders, escort them safely out of town, and repeat that all the way to New Orleans. The Freedom Ride would have disappeared without trace or effect. I wouldn't be writing this.

Later that summer Tom would write:

> I think we have to recognize that the Freedom Rides were a fluke—a bomb whose fuse we never lit. When it exploded, the noise was louder than anyone had expected. We owe the impact of the rides . . . to the irrationality of segregationist officials. Had they not been so insane as to permit and encourage mob violence and bus burning . . . the Freedom Rides would have been just another . . . nonviolent project. This it seems to me, is the most obvious weakness of the Rides . . . I don't mean they should not have taken place . . . only that a project whose significance and impact are attributable to circumstances entirely controlled by an irrational enemy should be recognized for the peripheral undertaking it is."

So much for strategic coherence. Others of us were morally queasy about a strategy whose *success* required that your people's lives be placed in serious jeopardy. I mean, if the racists have "the sense that God gave a bedbug," as Mr. Turnbow would say, then nothing would happen and the project would have, in one sense, failed. If, however, and only if, our people were seriously brutalized, then *that* would represent success? That didn't ring quite right.

Another issue we questioned was the Gandhian practice of informing the "enemy" authorities. That was Gandhi in India, this is the U.S. of A. What some of us feared—later proven beyond any doubt—was that a letter to J. Edgar Hoover was tantamount to a telegram to the Klan. Wasn't that a little much like setting up your own people?

There were no answers that evening, just these troubling questions. What it boiled down to was simple. For fifteen years the law had been clear and ignored. The machinery for implementation had long existed. No one did squat. Black people continued to be humiliated and abused on interstate travel. So what alternatives were left? Only nonviolent direct action. Brave and committed people would have to place their bodies—their physical survival—on the line. Was this not at the heart of nonviolent direct action as we all understood it?

Ironically, a project intended to test the resolve and values of the Kennedy administration instead tested us. It had the immediate effect of forcing us to a sudden and painful self-examination, challenging, if only theoretically, our own personal commitment. I say theoretically because at that point we weren't yet being called upon to make a decision. It wasn't our project, so we didn't *have* to do anything . . . yet.

But the discussion brought home to us something important and chilling: the extent to which raw violence was really *always* the last line of defense, the ultimate weapon of Southern bigotry. That the survival of segregation's oppressive social arrangements was predicated on the threat of violence and the generation of fear: "Bring that mess on down heah, nigger, and we will kill you." As simple and vulgar as that. We had now come face-to-face with the reality that the entire edifice of racial oppression in Dixie was propped up—with the clear complicity of the national government—by the violence of both the mob and the state. Often in the South a distinction without any real difference. And most important, the realization that if we were serious about going forward with this movement, we would all *personally* have to confront this, sooner or later, faceup.

Which is probably why we were a quiet, thoughtful group leaving that meeting that evening. Hank Thomas, deep in thought, seemed even quieter than usual. I was thinking seriously too. I could see no compelling reason to make any decision just yet, but I could sense that one would be coming. Shortly after that, Hank told us that he had called CORE headquarters the next day, volunteered, and had been accepted.

Everybody had long respected Hank's quiet dedication and courage, and when I heard what he'd done, my admiration for him only increased. But for many of us in NAG, the questions persisted and arguments continued. Once Hank had joined up, the questions were no longer so abstract. The thought of one of our own on that bus made it real. CORE's plan was not yet public, but for the next few weeks the "ride" was all we talked about.

Whatever doubts persisted, though, were kept inside the family. Publicly on campus we expressed full support and awe and admiration for the riders' courage. Which was quite true. Besides, wasn't it the government's clear responsibility to protect the lives and rights of law-abiding American citizens traveling peaceably in their own country?

Then it turned out that D.C. was not only the staging area, but that the group would gather there for an intensive week of bonding, training, nonviolent workshops, and situational role-playing prior to setting out.

The night before the volunteers' departure, Paul Dietrich gave them a dinner at his Chinese restaurant and invited folks from NAG to join them for coffee afterward. I remember this dinner clearly, and that meeting the actual volunteers was a bit of a shock.

As it happened, there were thirteen riders—James Farmer, CORE chairman, and twelve volunteers—so the grim symbolism was obvious: Jesus and his disciples at the Last Supper, or more cynically Christians walking fearlessly to face lions. Neither image was really exaggerated because a markedly religious, indeed spiritual, mood prevailed at that table. This was years before the counterculture fixation with exotic and self-dramatizing dress. This group was conservatively dressed, almost formal. They looked nothing like media-image militants or revolutionaries. My impression was of quiet seriousness and complete respectability, an abiding gentleness and determination, a strength of spirit. Conversation was muted. At that table no one raised his or her voice. This was not at all like NAG's meetings. SNCC's two representatives, Hank and John Lewis, seemed clearly the youngest.

I was actually shocked how elderly, more like parents, some of the CORE veterans seemed to me. The one married couple—a soft-spoken college professor and his gentle wife *[Dr. Walter and Mrs. Frances Bergman from Michigan]*—looked to be in their sixties. Paul whispered that a big, graying, distinguished-looking gentleman had been a navy captain commanding destroyers in World War II *[Commander Albert Bigelow, USN, Ret.]*. The warrior had become a pacifist, commanding a small boat, *The Golden Rule,* into the South Pacific to obstruct U.S. nuclear testing at Bikini atoll. Another wiry, older white gentleman *[James Peck]* had been arrested on the original Journey of Reconciliation in 1947. Clearly he had kept the faith. I also remember a young black minister *[the Reverend Elton Cox]*, a middle-aged white lady *[Charlotte DeVries, a writer from New York]*, and six other younger folk, mostly Africans. *[In addition to John Lewis and Hank Thomas of SNCC, there were Ed Blankenheim, Joe Perkins, Jimmy McDonald, and Genevieve Hughes from CORE.]*

That evening was my first meeting of John Lewis, and like everyone else in SNCC, I was overwhelmed by his courage, his quiet determination, his conviction in the rightness of the cause. He was a seminary student, if not already a minister, always soft-spoken, and dressed in a suit in the cut of a Martin Luther King. I was extremely proud of John as our chairman and representative.

When we joined them, Paul said that we had just missed an extraordinary moment. James Farmer had signaled for attention and addressed the table. He had told the gathering that although they were leaving in the morning, people still had time to reconsider. No one was obligated to go. It would be better, he said, for anyone who had developed the slightest doubt or second thoughts about the serious step they were about to take to withdraw then. For their own consciences and the good of the project. There would be no shame in that, no dishonor.

Perhaps, he said, it might be too difficult for anyone experiencing doubts to come forward publicly in front of the "family." But anyone who wished could come see him privately afterward, he'd understand. Or if even that was too embarrassing, one could simply not show up at the bus station in the morning.

On May 4, 1961, a group of us went to the bus station to see them off. All thirteen were there. Everyone tried to maintain a cheerful facade, smiling, joking, trying to disguise the foreboding we all felt. As we watched the buses drive away, I was filled anew with admiration. But I was also sick with fear . . . for them.

For the first week we followed their progress through reports from the D.C. CORE chapter. Nothing happened in Virginia. They were through North Carolina. Nothing serious. We began to be cautiously optimistic. In the Rock Hill, South Carolina, bus station, John Lewis was knocked unconscious, as was Albert Bigelow when he stepped between John and his assailants. But by May 12 they were in Atlanta and we thought, if this is the worst that happens, it will be better than we dared hope. Then came Alabama.

Before they left Atlanta, the Reverend Fred Shuttlesworth called from Birmingham to warn the riders that the Klan in that city had been organizing publicly for a week. Even before they reached Birmingham, all hell broke loose. This violence, we must be clear, was neither random nor spontaneous. It was carefully planned and orchestrated. In the town of Anniston and then in Birmingham, the buses were met by armed mobs, obviously prepared and waiting in ambush.

When the first bus arrived in Anniston, Professor Bergman was knocked unconscious by a blow to the head from a baseball bat. He subsequently suffered a stroke and was paralyzed for life. James Peck was also brutalized but was not permanently damaged . . . then.

The second bus was surrounded by a mob shouting threats and armed with clubs, chains, and guns. The riders told the driver not to stop. The tires were stabbed and blew out on the outskirts of town. The mob, following in cars, threw incendiary bombs into the disabled bus and tried to seal the doors. The riders managed to get out, some suffering from smoke inhalation. Hank Thomas was on that bus. What saved them, he told us, was that the fuel tank exploded, forcing the mob away from the door. His lungs were burning from the smoke when he staggered out, coughing.

A man approached him solicitously. "Boy, you all right?"

"Yeah . . . I think so," Hank began, whereupon the man produced a baseball bat and clubbed him down.

Uniformed police on the scene were said to be "fraternizing" with members of the mob. That evening on TV at Howard, we and the rest of the country saw that bus burning on the side of the highway. But after much difficulty, another bus was secured, and the group went on.

At the Birmingham bus station the mob was much larger and more savage. None of the riders escaped injury. James Peck was left for dead in a pool of his own blood. His head wounds would require fifty-six stitches and he would suffer permanent neurological damage.

Asked why, after the violence in Anniston, no police were at the Birmingham station, Bull Connor, the police chief, explained that it was Mother's Day. All his officers were with their dear old mothers. Later it was disclosed that the police had cut a deal with the Klan: once the bus arrived, the Klansmen were to be given ten minutes free and clear with the "outside agitators."

The next day the group—those able to travel—were met by an even larger mob when they arrived back at the Birmingham bus station. Since buses were clearly out of the question, they decided to fly to New Orleans. That proved no easier. The mob followed them to the airport, where they were again surrounded. Every time a New Orleans flight was announced, the airline received a bomb threat. It was chaos. But at least the police kept the mob off our friends. After some twenty harrowing hours and only after the intervention of a Justice Department official (John Seigenthaler, special assistant to the attorney general), they finally made it onto a flight out.

At Howard we followed these events, heartsick with horror and impotent anger as our worst fears were not just realized but exceeded. All of us had grown up watching Southern mobs on TV—Montgomery, Little Rock, New Orleans. But this was much different. This time the people being badly hurt and in danger of being killed were folks we knew and respected. The political leadership of an entire American state had not merely abdicated to mob violence, they clearly seemed to be encouraging and orchestrating it. And until the Kennedys dispatched John Seigenthaler to negotiate the riders' escape from the Birmingham airport, the federal government had been invisible.

At least invisible to us. It turns out that there *had* been federal involvement, albeit an ambiguous one. In Anniston, Birmingham, and elsewhere, the FBI had given the Freedom Riders' itinerary to the local police. Presumably for their protection? Yeah, let's be charitable. However, the FBI also had hard, specific information that some of these local cops were active Klansmen, so they had to know that the Klan would get the riders' itinerary. The FBI also had prior knowledge of the planned violence.

[As Burke Marshall, at the time head of the Civil Rights Division of the Justice Department, said on the television documentary Eyes on the Prize:

"The FBI had information . . . it turns out that was quite specific about what was going to happen in Birmingham. They may have had similar information about Anniston, but I'm not sure. But they clearly had advance information from Klan sources that the Freedom Riders were to be attacked in the Birmingham bus station and that the police were going to absent themselves. The Bureau did not pass that information along to anyone in other parts of the Justice Department. They didn't inform the Civil Rights Division. They didn't inform the Attorney General." —EMT]

We also later learned that Robert Kennedy—at least after the pictures of the burning bus flashed around the world—had been blistering the phone lines to Alabama governor John Patterson, who, a year earlier, had been the Kennedys' man in Alabama. (Patterson had been chairman of the Kennedy for President Committee in that state.) There you see clearly what we were up against—the hybrid nature of the Democratic Party. An allegedly "progressive" young president in bed with the segregationist governor of a racist state. The deadlock of vulgar political expedience on both sides. Given the razor-thin margin of JFK's victory in 1960, the last thing the Kennedys wanted was to alienate the Confederate vote. At that time, remember, voting in Dixie was strictly "white folks business." This political consideration (on the part of the Kennedys) was to emerge again with far-reaching consequences for our young organization.

Instead of affirming the riders' rights and enforcing the Constitution as he was sworn to do, Bobby Kennedy issued his call for "a cooling-off period." Which was wishy-washy enough. But I've never been able to forget or excuse his blaming the violence on "extremists on both sides." That really got to me. *Extremists? Both sides?* I don't recall that anyone in the media called him on the extreme absurdity of that moral equivalence. The image of that small group of lawful, peaceable, gentle, supremely decent people I'd met, set against the hate-shouting ignorance of bus-burning, club-swinging Klansmen? In any event, the call went up from liberal quarters to stop the rides. After all, nobody wants to see innocent people murdered.

James Farmer came under incredible pressure. In Atlanta he'd received news of his father's death and had temporarily left the ride to fly to his mother's side in D.C. and so had missed the violence in Alabama. Now he was presented with a conflict between his politics and his conscience.

The last thing that this decent, humane pacifist, whom I would soon get to know quite well, wanted on his conscience was the death of another human being. Fundamentally also, he was patriotic, intent on improving his country, not, as the Kennedys were implying, debasing its international prestige. However, he was now being told he was in danger of doing both. He was receiving a veritable deluge, obviously orchestrated, of phone calls from allies of all stripes, liberals and various "highly placed" individuals all appealing to his patriotism, his humanity, and his sense of "responsibility." Somehow it seemed to escape the callers (and the media) that they were calling the wrong "leader." That it was the president's responsibility to safeguard the integrity of the nation's laws, to maintain the peace and the physical security of its citizens, thereby protecting the nation's image in the eyes of the world. Brother Farmer protested that the riders had broken no laws, burned no buses, and that to end the rides would be to capitulate to lawlessness, bigotry, and violence. To no avail.

Finally CORE announced the indefinite "suspension" of the Freedom Rides and were praised for their wisdom and responsibility. Brother Farmer also received at least one more phone call, this one of a slightly different nature.

In Nashville, the SNCC students were as horrified as we by the ugliness of the brutality. But for them the implications of the CORE decision, understandable though it was, were much worse. We got a phone call from Diane Nash, calling on behalf of the Nashville group.

"Hey, you watching this mess?"

"Whad'you think?"

"Sure is bad, ain't it?"

Diane was a persuasive young woman. It was not just ugly bad, it was ominous. If the Freedom Rides were stopped because of violence, and only because of violence, then the nonviolent movement was over. We might as well disband SNCC. Our movement is over. Give the racists this victory and it sends the clear signal that at the first sign of resistance, all they have to do is mobilize massive violence, the movement will collapse, and the government won't do a thing. We can't let that happen.

"You right. But what can we do?"

"I just spoke to Mr. Farmer. Told him that if CORE was unable to continue, we would. There's no choice really."

"What'd he say?"

"What could he say? Asked if I fully understood the danger. That, y'know, it could be suicide. I told him that was the risk we had to face. Is NAG with us?"

"Call you back after we talk."

Whoee! Gut-check time now.

Diane was always a clear, militant, uncompromising sister. Committed to the philosophy of nonviolence. One of the most admired people in SNCC. And real, real pretty too. The coolly pragmatic Tim Jenkins once famously said that Diane and most of the Nashville group "were addled by righteousness." On this call, though, she was dead-on right.

That urgent meeting was very different from the first discussion a month earlier. All the strategic and political second-guessing that had seemed so momentous just months before receded into the distance now that the survival of the movement was at risk. Just one more instance of how politics can surprise you. In fact, the first wave of volunteers from NAG included some who had initially been most skeptical of the political wisdom of the tactic. Paul Dietrich who had been moved by the muted drama of that last supper in his restaurant, left immediately. Dion, Travis Britt, John Moody, Bill Mahoney, and I arranged to move up our final exams. We followed as soon as we were free. SNCC's strategy was to keep the bodies coming and to fill all the jails in the South if necessary.

May Charles was funny. I guess today you'd call it in denial. She was just so sure it had to be a bad joke.

"Don't run them kinda joke, boy. Think you can fool your mother so? I know you. School's over. I hear the noise. You calling from the bus station downtown. So you can walk in jes' now and laugh at me. I know you, Stokely."

"May Charles, this is for real now. Something I gotta do. I only ask one thing. If the press should contact you, just tell them you're proud of me, okay?"

"Get out of here. You chatting nonsense. How I to tell them I'm proud of stupidity? You mad? Fighting for people who don't even care about you."

"May Charles, I'm fighting for all of us. Anyway, say you proud. Don't embarrass me, please . . . I beg you."

Sometimes when students from the South joined the rides, their parents would have to denounce them publicly. They were no longer their children. They didn't agree with that foolishness. Couldn't understand what had got into that girl's head. Course that was fear. And survival. Telling the white folks what they wanted to hear. Which of course was promptly and prominently published in the local papers. Do you suppose those whites really believed that okeydoke? Talk about delusional.

My dad was different. He knew what I was involved in and was quietly proud. I knew that. But he hadn't realized the *extent* of my involvement. He was concerned about my academics. I assured him that I'd be careful, and that I would stay in school until I graduated. Then I got on a late flight to New Orleans. May Charles hadn't been crazy. She had heard background noises, but I was calling from the D.C. airport, not the New York bus station.

• • •

It was about 9 P.M. when I made that call home because CORE had arranged for a night flight that would arrive in New Orleans at about 3 A.M. The thought was that at 3 A.M. the airport would be relatively deserted, few cops and no mob. Travis Britt, a NAG senior, I believe, from New York would be traveling with me.

At the airport Julius Hobson met us with another volunteer, Gwen Greene, from the Baltimore civic action group. I knew Gwen and her sister Connie from demonstrations. NAG would sometimes support their actions in Baltimore, and they would come to D.C. to support ours. Everyone really liked the Greene sisters; they were devoted strugglers— militant with sunny, ebullient personalities and radiant smiles. I was both happy to see her (I liked Gwen) but a little apprehensive for that same reason. But our sisters-in-struggle were always up front, neither seeking or expecting special treatment. If I'm not mistaken, on the Freedom Rides, women would ultimately outnumber men in the Mississippi jails.

This was at least a week since Diane Nash's history-changing call. While I had been moving up my final exams, waves of students had been moving into Mississippi by bus, where they were immediately being arrested.

By the time I could get away, the decision had been taken to test the railroads. Which is why we were to fly to New Orleans and join a group going into Mississippi by train. We would be the first group doing the trains, and it was not clear just what that would be like. We all were a little nervous. Julius Hobson gave us our instructions, and they were precise. Almost cloak-and-dagger, like operatives going behind enemy lines.

The flight would get in at three o'clock. We should carry our bags on and get off early. The authorities weren't supposed to know we were coming, but what with tapped phones, you could never tell. So we should act as if we were traveling separately. He described exactly the CORE worker, Rudy Lombard, who would meet us. What he looked like. What he would be wearing. We should simply follow him out to the parking lot, but separately and without giving any indication that we knew him.

Rudy was accompanied by another worker, Oretha Castle. We were nervous but the airport cops paid us no attention. Once outside in the warm, humid Louisiana night, Rudy and Oretha greeted us like family. I remember the shock of recognition I felt breathing that air so warm and soft, with a familiar sweetish smell. It took me a second or two to identify it—from my childhood. It was the smell of the tropics: Trinidad. Also I had an immediate warm feeling for the CORE workers. Which turned into respect as I saw how they operated: cool, efficient, and organized.

Rudy and Sister Oretha drove us into the city to the African community where we were put up in some run-down projects. All the way my neck swiveled side to side trying to take everything in as the sun rose.

This was the farthest south I'd been, the real deal. The feel of the air, the fruity, swampy smell, the surrounding lush vegetation. But you know what really represented Deep South to me: my first sight of tall trees festooned with beards of Spanish moss. The mere sight of those moss-bearded trees etched against the rising sun said *Louisiana, plantation, slavery, bayou, swamp, lynching* . . . the mythical South. Just seeing those trees sent a tremor through me.

Then we came to the city and the projects. I knew housing conditions in Harlem, but the conditions of the projects in New Orleans were absolutely appalling. We were all shocked. But the people living in these abysmal conditions were warm and kind. They took real good care of us and even embarrassed us by treating us like heroes.

Rudy and Oretha brought us our tickets and clear instructions. CORE had publicized the change of target, and already a crowd was reported at the railway station. So we could expect at least one mob. What else wasn't clear. It was thought unlikely that the Klan would try to bomb or derail an entire train. But who knew? Once in the station, moving into the trains, we'd be on our own. "We'll be on the scene, but nowhere near you. You guys will have to get through the mob by yourselves. Good luck."

See, you must understand what had been happening with the buses. Within days of Diane's call, Southern (and some Northern) students had begun converging on Birmingham, determined to continue the rides from the scene of carnage where the original group had been brutalized. From Nashville, Diane dispatched the first seven students by bus. Being who they were, two of the students sit right behind the bus driver and decline to move when ordered. Wednesday, May 17, they arrive in Birmingham, where Bull Connor arrests the two and places the others in something he calls "protective custody." For two days in the Birmingham jail the brothers and sisters sing freedom songs and go on a hunger strike. A little past midnight Friday morning, Bull Connor himself arrives and without explanation takes the students out of the cells and into police cruisers. They have no idea where they are really being taken. The police say they are "being taken home."

The police drive them through the darkness 120 miles to the Tennessee border, where they are deposited at a railroad crossing on the highway. They are told that "a bus or train will be along directly," at which point they should return home. A bus or train? More likely, the Klan, the students think, as the cops drive away. They feel completely exposed and defenseless. They know their arrests as Freedom Riders have been in the media. Who else knows about their whereabouts now? They do not trust the relationship between the Alabama police and the Klan. They agree that they can't stand there on the highway, so they walk across the tracks until they see a small, ramshackle house. One of ours, or God help us, poor whites? They decide to risk it. A cautious voice calls fearfully through the door. It's after three o'clock in the morning.

"Who ye be? Who dar?" Hearing black voices responding, an elderly African man peers out cautiously into the darkness.

When the old man let them in, he wouldn't turn on a light and spoke only in whispers. When the sun came up, he went to buy breakfast, which took him a while. He explained that since he and his wife didn't buy large quantities of food at one time, he'd divided the order and walked to three different stores to avoid suspicion.

Later the students managed to call Diane. When the car she sent from Nashville arrived, the driver asked, "So where we going? To Nashville or back to Birmingham?"

As they were leaving, the old lady had hugged each in turn. "Gawd bless y'all. Y'all some brave chilluns. Yo' doing de Lawd's work."

But we know, don't we, that it was that anonymous, isolated, vulnerable old couple, like so countless many other Southern Africans we would meet in the struggle, who at great risk to themselves recognized and performed "de Lawd's work" that morning.

Once back in Birmingham, they sought refuge at the Reverend Shuttlesworth's house,* where they met up with Ruby Doris Smith, a Spelman College freshman, who had made her way from Atlanta, and some Northern volunteers who had come to continue the rides. Bill Mahoney and Paul Dietrich from NAG were with this group.

---

*Once we were out of jail and able to compare notes, the adult figure that commanded a respect bordering on awe from the students was the Reverend Fred Shuttlesworth, the movement's point man in Birmingham. Everyone had their Reverend Fred story. It was Reverend Shuttlesworth who scouted the Klan and warned CORE of their preparations there. It was Reverend Shuttlesworth who walked into the station and carried the unconscious James Peck to the hospital. It was Reverend Shuttlesworth who would spend the night with the besieged students at the bus station that Friday night. In Montgomery, two days later, it was Reverend Shuttlesworth who met James Farmer and conducted him through the hundreds of angry whites surrounding the Reverend Mr. Abernathy's church where Dr. King and the new group of student riders were trapped.

In the movement, many of us worried about Reverend Shuttlesworth's survival. We figured that sooner or later the racists would murder him. Indeed, his home was bombed and there were countless threats and attempts, but Reverend Shuttlesworth soldiered on. Someone suggested sentimentally that perhaps even the Klan respected his courage too much to kill him.

That Friday the Reverend Shuttlesworth accompanied the students back to the Birmingham station. That entire night a mob surrounded the station, periodically lobbing in stink bombs. This time police were present, holding the mob at bay with guard dogs. Not unreasonably, none of the bus drivers would agree to drive the group.

"I got me but one life, and Ah be damned effen Ah'm giving it to no NAACP or CORE," one driver said not unreasonably. Of course in that time and place all the drivers were white. So our comrades spent the night surrounded in the bus station. It was scary, a standoff. "But at least if we couldn't leave," a student said, "the crackers had to stand there all night too."

The next morning a driver was found, and under massive security the group left for Montgomery. Floyd Mann, the conscientious, highly professional director of public safety of Alabama, reported, "When the bus left Birmingham, there were sixteen highway patrol cruisers in front and another sixteen behind with a helicopter flying overhead looking for potential trouble."

However these state forces disengaged once the bus entered the municipal jurisdiction of Montgomery, and the bus drove into an apparently empty bus station. A young brother named Freddy Leonard, whom I later met in jail, was on that bus and told me what it was like getting off that bus. The station was absolutely, eerily empty when they arrived at high noon, he said.

"An' then all of a sudden, just like magic, white people! Sticks and bricks! *Niggers!* Kill the niggers."

Floyd Mann reported that, once the Freedom Riders alighted, mobs of white people appeared "from everywhere" and "law and order had broken down." He later reported that he'd had "confidential information" that the Montgomery police planned to be absent from the station that morning. Mann almost certainly saved some lives that day. Seeing that the Freedom Riders were being brutalized with baseball bats, he "had to threaten to take some lives." He put his pistol to the heads of some of the bat wielders and threatened to shoot. He also fired a shot into the air. He undoubtedly saved some lives, but as usual our side took the casualties.

Sitting in our cell, Freddy Leonard and I would become close friends. Freddy told me that what had saved the Africans was a white student named Jim Zwerg from Wisconsin. He was brave, Freddy said, because when the mob saw him, they were so enraged at this white man, they forgot about the Africans for a moment. They just engulfed Zwerg and nearly killed him. John Lewis was knocked cold. So was William Barbee. Barbee and Zwerg were damaged for life. Freddy was convinced that only the sound of the shot that "some white feller" fired saved them.

Bob Zellner, a white Montgomery student who had agreed to deliver a message to one of the group, arrived a few minutes after the bloodletting was over.

["It was the weirdest thing I'd ever seen in my life up to then. The platform was deserted. I mean empty, man. Not a living soul. And silent? Mah Lord, an eerie, eerie silence. The middle of the day and dead quiet. My footsteps were the only sound and they seemed to echo.

"But the scene, ol' buddy, was like a movie set of a battle scene. But no bodies, only pools of blood on the concrete. Silence. An empty bus, door ajar, a window broken in. Silence. Sticks and bricks scattered around. And clothes. Here a sneaker, there a skirt or a pair of jeans. A broken suitcase or two. Dead silence. And everywhere textbooks and notepads scattered around. That affected me 'cause I knew it was students my age. And an open Bible lying in a pool of blood. I remember there was some kind of construction going on so there was one of those plyboard construction fences. Well, embedded in that plyboard was a brick, flung with such venom that it just embedded itself in the wood. I stood there looking around that echoingly silent, littered, bloody scene in amazement. I just knew that people my age must have been killed. It was a bad, bad, feeling."]

No more than a few months later, Bob Zellner became the first white from the Deep South battle zone to join the SNCC staff. He would be arrested as many times as me or more, and the Klan would put a price on his head.

I had been taking exams in D.C. while all this was happening, so at the time of my Southern train ride, I hadn't yet heard the grisly details. As promised, a mob was waiting for us at the train station. I'd seen large, vocally hostile crowds at demonstrations in Virginia and Maryland, but nothing like this.

It seemed large. They were shouting. Throwing cans and lit cigarettes at us. Spitting on us. And swinging, actually fighting each other to get in a good lick at us. Travis Britt, who had courage, led the group. He was magnificent, plowing through that crowd. I was on the outside, Sister Gwen Greene on the inside. To this day I don't know how, but under Travis's leadership we got through and onto the train. Some of us were bleeding, but we all got on, wiped off the spit and blood, and the train set out.

That journey through the mob had been utter chaos. So much happening at the same time that it's all a blur. One thing I remember clearly. Usually in scenes of chaos and violence I find myself fixing on one specific thing. I try to concentrate on that object while ignoring the rest.

I remember this little old white lady with a cane. So old that cane should better have been a walker. But there she was, face contorted, shaking with rage and infirmity. Was she a passenger en route somewhere who stumbled on the scene, or had this ancient person come out to defend the

Confederacy? Anyway, I fixed on this old lady and she on me. Our eyes locked, and the one thing she clearly wanted most was to bust my black head with that cane. Hate was in those old eyes. As I approached, her rage grew visibly. She was trembling so much I began to fear she was about to fall out with a heart attack before I got close enough to hit. I was nineteen years old. I couldn't believe that the color of my skin could evoke such hatred in another person. This old woman was shaking so bad that the blow from her cane wasn't hardly a blow. But I got some serious licks from others in the crowd.

I don't remember if we were by ourselves in the coach, but luckily no one on the train attacked us. Mobs were waiting for us at every stop, doing everything they could to get at us—crashing the doors, trying to run over the guards and conductors. But they weren't traveling so they couldn't get on the train without a ticket. That probably saved us. They tried to break the windows. They tried to throw rocks and cans through the doors as soon as they opened. It was really a battle. Nineteen years old, I was tasting frontline battle seriously for the first time, though I had no idea yet what Freddy Leonard and the others had just gone through in Birmingham and Montgomery.

We arrived in Jackson, entered the "white" waiting room, which was, to tell the truth, only tolerable. But the "Negro" one? I took one look and made up my mind then and there that, campaign or not, I would never go into one of those. And I never have. It was squalid, stained, uncleaned, unswept, just horrendous. It seemed to be kept that way intentionally as an insult to black people's senses and dignity.

Into the white waiting room comes Captain Ray and his cops with his famous "move on or you're under arrest."

While we were waiting to be processed, I was discussing Thoreau with another student. This seemed to bother one of the cops.

"What there you talking 'bout theah, boy? You going be picking cotton. Tha's what y'all be doing."

I looked at him. "Yo *mamma* be picking cotton fo' I do." His face reddened. The students started laughing, picked it up, and dropped some serious dozens on him.

"*Oowie*, Stokely says his *mamma* going pick cotton."

"Tha's cold. Wonder if his mamma could?"

"Think his mamma smart enough?"

"Dunno, man. My mom pick cotton. You think his momma could hold up, picking cotton?"

"Judging by him, I would'n think so, man."

That pretty much set the tone of the young students' response to Mississippi authority. It also indicated the difference in attitude and demeanor between us and the older generation of CORE activists and ministers, who really were pacifists. Our overall posture was, of course, nonviolent, but our attitude was not pacifist. We would show these cops that we weren't asking nor giving quarter, so they would select us for their special treatment.

SNCC's strategy was simple. If they kept arresting us for defying segregation laws, we'd fill the jails in Mississippi under the slogan Jail, No Bail, which was the same for the Pan Africanist Congress of Azania (South Africa). By early summer, when the Freedom Rides were discontinued, some 445 students, pacifists, clergypersons, and other people of conscience of all races and from all over the country would come together in Mississippi prisons. Many would be forever changed by the experience, the students especially. I believe that women were in the majority of those political prisoners.

We were in with experienced activists, some revolutionaries, clergy, and college professors, so the jail term was like a university of social struggle and moral discourse. Many students would fall away and return gratefully to their regular lives and careers. Others, a small hard core, would emerge determined, tempered, and more focused on continued struggle than when they'd gone in. That was certainly my experience. Most of us would go on to become SNCC's first full-time organizers. Others—usually the spiritual pacifists out of Nashville—would gravitate to Dr. King's staff. Others signed up with CORE. Most of the ones who did not commit full-time to the movement continued to be active in some way. But for those who joined up full-time, whichever organization we went with, we remained a close brotherhood and sisterhood of shared experience. For us, that prison experience would be life altering, a rite of passage, a turning point.

The first thing I learned in that Hinds County, Mississippi, jail made a lasting impression. After the explosions in Alabama, the Mississippi segregationists knew two things. That we were coming and that white Mississippi had to avoid the negative international publicity that Alabama had earned. Still, the "pride and sovereignty" of the great state of "Mississippah" was involved, and they couldn't afford to let the Freedom Riders openly flout their segregation laws and escape unscathed. The outside agitators had to be damaged. But after Alabama, the "good white citizens" could not be seen doing the damage, so Bubba had to be restrained in the presence of the TV cameras. Instead, the authorities gathered a dozen or so of the toughest black prisoners, lifers and long-termers with violent records, and made them an offer they didn't think they could refuse. The hard-core prisoners would be given civilian clothes and taken secretly to the bus station, and all they had to do was stomp down the agitators, really mess them up, in return for easy time, reduced sentences, maybe even a small cash payment.

"How 'bout that, Sam? Ain't no one much care whut you do to them Communists an' race-mixin' mongrels. Heahs yore chance to whip some Northern white-trash haids, no questions asked. Now how 'bout thet?" To the authorities' surprise, however, those African men said no. Except for one, there were no takers.

When I heard that, I almost cried. My spine tingled and my eyes almost teared. We're talking about a state that did not convict *any* white man for murdering even the most prominent black citizen. In two years, Medgar Evers would be a case in point. A white corrections officer could expect more hassle for taking an out-of-season deer than for shooting down a black convict. Especially those long-term hard-timers with manslaughter or even murder on their record. And these brothers, these jailhouse desperadoes, knew exactly how totally at the mercy of the penal system they were. And they still had the courage and principle and clarity to say no, even if they mumbled.

"Expects not, Cap'n. Nahsuh, sho don't thank Ah kin do that, suh."

The first chance I got I asked a trusty about it. "Don' know directly anything about that, bes' you ask white folk. White folk, he know." Now how was I supposed to do that? "White folk" turned out to be an older, dark-skinned prisoner of few words. I asked him.

"Yup. Sho is. Tha's the word anyway."

"You sure? Do you know any of the brothers?"

"Yup. Knows 'em all. Mos' of 'em anyway. Dey be's some hard mens. Dey *all* have the name of a mean man."

One of them was his good buddy. I said I'd like to meet him. To thank him. "You gotta go to the farm fer that. An' I heard he ain out in the county no more. He done gone, boy. White folk bin an' done taken him off."

He didn't know where. But he *hoped* his friend was in the hole in Parchman.

"You *hope* your friend's in the hole?"

"Yep. I sholy do hope that."

I've always thought those nameless, principled "hard mens" to be heroes of the movement and shudder to think of the price they must certainly have paid. My people, my people.

As the numbers of political prisoners grew, we were segregated from the Africans in the general population. We were put in a block on the first floor and met for a few hours a day in a rec room. The Freedom Riders spanned generations and ideologies. There were a number of older black ministers. James Farmer had himself been a theological student. The Reverend James Lawson, the mentor in nonviolence to the Nashville students, was there. Another minister, the Reverend C. T. Vivian, was really defiant. He was calm, dignified, nonviolent, but made no concessions to the racists. When they called him "boy," he told them, "My denomination normally ordains *men,* not boys." He had a bandage around his head for omitting to say "sir" to the racists. Among the students from Nashville, three brothers were seminarians: John Lewis, Bernard Lafayette, and James Bevel. They were students of Reverend Lawson's in nonviolence and were serious about "Christian love" and the redemptive power of "the beloved community." Reverend Lawson was a committed pacifist who had studied Gandhism in India and served a prison term as a conscientious objector during the Korean War. This group would hold a nonviolence-workshop-cum-prayer-meeting during rec period. The NAG folk—Bill Mahoney, Hank Thomas, Dion Diamond, John Moody, me, Freddy Leonard, and a few others would generally abstain from the prayer and hymn singing, preferring to discuss the politics of our situation quietly off to one side.

At night, the entire group would sing freedom songs, which united all factions and outraged the authorities. At night we could hear the women Freedom Riders singing over in the female unit:

> O Freedom, O Freedom,
> O Freedom, over me.

And we'd sing back:

> Just like a tree that's planted
> by the water,
> We shall not be moved.

Apparently the entire prison was hearing us serenade each other, and the other black prisoners would pick up on it too.

One of the women leading the singing had a remarkably beautiful voice, unusually powerful and pure. "I know her," said Freddy Leonard. "She from Nashville. Her name is Joy Reagon."

"Is she as fine as her voice?" I asked.

"Yes, she is. In fact, finer."

"*Whoee,* boy, then when I gets out, I'ma ask her for a date. See if she can be fine as she sounds."

"No, you ain't," said Freddy. "No, no, no. I'm going *marry* that woman, boy."

Joy Reagon I never met. She remained for me a hauntingly beautiful, pure voice coming into my cell out of the Mississippi darkness.

They say that freedom
Is a constant struggle . . .

But I did meet her brother Cordell, who was also a freedom fighter in SNCC and also an extraordinary singer with the SNCC Freedom Singers. But guess what? Freddy Leonard did indeed marry Joy Reagon. Obviously ol' Freddy was a man of his word.

Then the brothers upstairs got involved in the singing. As we continued to sing freedom songs, Big Hank Thomas was our song leader. The prisoners on the floor above would sing back their work and prison songs. That was some incredible music. Some of those prisoners could really sing, and their song leader was simply amazing. This brother had a powerful, vibrant baritone and a unique roots singing style. Especially when he'd line out the words of the dirgelike "common" meter songs, and from calls around the block the other brothers would respond and draw out the lines in the old-fashioned "long" meter style. It was beautiful and haunting and unlike anything I'd ever heard, taking us, it seemed, out of the cell and all the way back to Africa. The nearest thing I've heard to this brother's style is a kind of Wolof male singing I've heard in African countryside villages.

This brother, rotting away in a Mississippi cell, was a world-class talent. He'd have been a sensation singing in the Village. The prisoners' songs were moving and defiant, especially the ones about prison life.

See that man a yonder
On that big white hoss
Yeh, yeh, yeh, yeh,
Doan know his name but
Dey call him boss.
Yeh, yeh, yeh, yeh.

Weren't for that man an'
His shaggy ol' houn'
Yeh, yeh, yeh, yeh,
Be in New Orleans fo'
D' sun go down.
Yeh, yeh, yeh, yeh.

See that man a yonder, he
A dangerous dude.
Yeh, yeh, yeh, yeh,
Had me a pistol, Ah'd be
Dangerous too.
Yeh, yeh, yeh, yeh.

Of course to the prison administrators this situation was intolerable. Black musical culture across class and gender (also race, since the white Freedom Riders were singing along too) was uniting the African prison population with the political prisoners. If we didn't stop the damn singing, the mess cart would stop coming on our block. This little cart dispersed gum, sodas, and snacks. The junk food was no big deal, but the cigarettes were to many of us. Because of soccer I didn't smoke and never developed that habit. But many Freedom Riders were chain-smokers. For them it was a real crisis. Not to worry or stop the concerts, though. The brothers upstairs let down a bag on a string. We put in our orders and the money. The bag came back and the smoking and singing continued.

This lasted—for me—little more than a week. More political prisoners kept coming in almost daily. We were filling at least this jail. Besides which our presence, unity, and quiet defiance was "bad for prison morale, a destabilizing influence." Had to have been the guards' morale. It certainly wasn't the prisoners. Consequently, we were informed, we would be moving to Parchman Penitentiary, where they would know "how to handle troublemakers."

In truth my heart fell. I knew Parchman by reputation. It was in the Mississippi Delta. It and Angola (the Louisiana State Penitentiary at Angola) were reputed to be the two most brutal prisons in all the South. There must be dozens of blues and prison songs about those two. Parchman was famous in song and legend as a hellhole. I knew exactly what we were going: to a concentration camp and serious torture.

We continued to sing, but now perhaps in a tone of bravado masking an undercurrent of real anxiety. At least so I thought. Also, we were anxious about the sisters. Were there women in Parchman? No one knew. Some of the brothers' girlfriends were over in the female wing. "Man, them crackers at Parchman better not mess with my lady, man. I don't play that." Empty posturing, of course, but I suppose it made them feel more like men and hid their anxiety.

In retrospect, I suppose the Hinds County jail experience was not the worst. The food was barely edible but at least we weren't beaten. And for the time we were there, our influence on the local African prisoners had been remarkable. All in all, a psychic victory.

I think the head jailer may have had something to do with the relative restraint of the jailers while we were there. Clearly this was not their usual behavior, for at first the local black prisoners simply couldn't believe that we could defy the racial protocol of the prison system and not be immediately beat down.

Anyway, the night before we were to leave, the head jailer came to visit. I'd seen that man before. When we'd first come in, he'd issued a warning. In his jail he'd not tolerate Communists and troublemakers breaking the rules. We'd find that out. Give any trouble and he'd be forced to rule with a ruthless hand.

Once the singing and "fraternization" started, he returned and tried to exert authority by threats and withdrawal of petty privileges. And we would argue with him, nonviolently of course. Which I think had made an impression on him. Because he'd given us a lecture. Perhaps, he said, we weren't really evil Communists. "Y'know, y'all ain't real bad boys, you ain't killed, robbed, or raped nobody." So maybe we were just misguided. So he set out to set us straight by explaining what we didn't understand about the Mississippi way of life. He himself did not hate "Negrahs." Why, as a boy he used to go fishing with them. And Negroes in Mississippi weren't *mistreated*. They were treated *fairly* (some would apparently confuse *fair* treatment with *mis*treatment) and preferred the present arrangements. The usual stuff.

So the last evening he comes and grasps the bars of the cell hard. I mean, I could see his knuckles turn white. He is clearly agitated and begins to talk about his life, his beliefs, and his maid, Annie. "Annie was *gude*. She raised my five kids." The family loved Annie dearly. When she died, the family wept. They all went to her funeral. Every year they place a wreath on her grave. So we should see that we had it wrong on race relations in the South. "Yeah," Bill Mahoney muttered, "but we can't ask Annie, now, can we?"

Then he got real personal, even passionate. I didn't know what to make of it. Tears rolled down his cheeks. He began to shake. He was, he said, a Christian man. He believed in God and the Southern way of life. Nothing would change that ever. He was really emotional.

"Now y'all caused me a heap of trouble. But you are human beings. You ha' your beliefs and I ha' mine. But I wish you to know, in mah heart, I dew not wish you any harm." And he turned and walked away.

It was heavy. That kind of naked emoting always is, so I tend to distrust it. But I think this man was sincere or at least sincerely troubled. Why else had he felt it necessary to come?

"And Pilate washed his hands," one of the Bible students said. And in truth, the jailer's last statement, with the prospect of Parchman facing us in the morning, was less than comforting.

You are human beings. . . . In mah heart, Ah do not wish you any ha'am.

Now, when my group had arrived at the county jail, the earlier group had not been there. That's when "white folks" had told me about the offer to the "bad mens" and their refusal. The Freedom Riders had been transferred to the county farm, where the Reverend C. T. Vivian had been beaten down for neglecting to say "sir." C. T. Vivian was always a very proud black man who made no concessions to racism. And he was sharp of tongue.

Later in SNCC I would hear the story of another "Freedom Rider" who had a very different experience at the county farm. His name will appear nowhere in CORE's records so I want to tell his story now.

When the Freedom Rides reached Alabama, Jesse Harris was a seventeen-year-old high school senior, I think from Jackson but it could have been McComb. He saw the reports, had been greatly moved by the courage of the riders, and so decided that *he* would meet them when they got to Jackson. So Jesse made his way to the bus station, waited until the bus pulled in, followed the riders into the white waiting room, and was arrested with them.

While he was being booked, the cops discovered that Jesse was local and not formally a part of the group, hence completely unprotected. CORE had no idea of this local boy's existence and arrest. I know I hadn't until a year or so later. The Jackson courts, of course, did not welcome the idea of this kind of defiance catching on among "their" local Negro youth. While we "outsiders" were sent to the city jail in Jackson, Jesse, alone and by himself, was sent to the county farm and out to work in the fields.

The first day when the "Walking Boss" gave him an order, Jessie answered simply, "Yes." *[C. T. Vivian had answered simply, "No."]*

"Gawd damn it, boy, you from Mississippah, you're 'sposed to know to say 'Suh' to a white man." Jesse told him that he said "sir" only to his father or to elders whom he respected. The guard slapped him and swore that he'd teach him how to talk to a white man. He sent for "Brown Bessie," a thick broad leather strap greatly feared by the prisoners. Jesse was ordered to lie on his belly across a nearby log. After the beating, weakened from pain, Jesse stood up, shaking, on trembling legs.

"Niggah, I reckon you know to say 'Suh' now, huh?"

Jesse looked the white man silently in the eye. Then he stepped up to the log and laid down again. The "walking boss" decided that "this nigger's crazy." And told him to get up. I suspect that even that racist didn't have the heart to continue the torture. As far as I know, Jesse never said sir.

Later on the SNCC staff I would meet Jesse Harris. He was a tireless organizer and director of the Maccomb project; Jesse was greatly respected by all of us at SNCC. When the movement in Mississippi dissolved around him, Jesse Harris became a minister for the Nation of Islam in Jackson. He exemplifies the spirit that I came so much to admire in the best of our people in Mississippi.

[Charlie Cobb:

"Jesse was real cool, an amazing brother. I remember he used to caddy for the

white folks at the Jackson Country Club. He taught himself the game. Once he told me how he used to win money off the men he caddied for. That shocked me, y'know. Hustling crackers in Mississippi. *He said, 'But, Charlie, I used to do it all the time. Did it frequently. But, oh, Charlie'—he grinned—'you had to play a very careful game.' I guess so. Ol' Jesse was tough, shrewd. I really liked the brother. But you know, Jesse disappeared. Some time ago I was trying to find him. Went to his old neighborhood. Talked to his sister, his friends. The neighbors. No one had seen Jesse in two years. No idea where he might be or what might have happened to the brother. He'd simply disappeared. A brother with a lot of heart." Nuff respect, Jesse. Peace be unto him.]*

Parchman farm, oh, Parchman farm. I'd heard folk singers in the Village singing about Parchman all during high school. Now I was nineteen years old and heading there myself, into the legend. I sure hoped those songs were exaggerated.

They came for us by night, presumably for security. The enveloping darkness did not make me feel secure. What was this ominous place we were going to? What was lurking unseen in the surrounding darkness? A highway patrol car led the way. The ride was fast and rough. Sudden jamming on of brakes. Equally sudden drag-race starts. We were thrown around too much for there to be any singing. I can't remember much about the journey of about two hours. My first sight of the Mississippi Delta, which was to be my first organizing assignment, was simply of a vast, eerie, formless darkness surrounding our bus. It was like being adrift in dark space. I had no idea the role this strange, haunting place would play in my political development and my growing sense of my people's lives.

The Delta is an unnaturally flat, low-lying area of land, pool-table flat. So flat that in daylight this treeless, featureless flatness stretches before you like the sea all the way to the horizon where land and sky merge. So flat that Ed Brown, who would head our project in Holmes County, swears that he could ride a bicycle to the store while coasting all the way. Then turn around and ride back home and still be coasting all the way. It is an area of rich, black, alluvial soil, some of it wetlands and cypress swamp reclaimed by the labor of enslaved Africans, an arrangement still very much in effect when SNCC got there.

The Mississippi Delta was the location of the immense *Gone With the Wind*–type cotton plantations worked by thousands of Africans before the war. Parchman had been an antebellum slave plantation growing cotton. Cotton itself being an African immigrant from the equally fecund Nile Delta of Egypt, from which the area took its name.

Parchman Farm is, of course, the state penitentiary. It is a working farm and is the only operation of the state government that regularly turns a profit. It was designed, organized, and run along the lines of an ante-bellum slave plantation for *humanitarian* reasons in the 1890s. Say what, plantation slavery as a humanitarian reform? I'm serious, check it out.

See, to meet the state's labor needs in the 1880s, allegedly "free" Africans were scooped up, framed, and "leased" to plantation owners to serve out their sentences. No longer being slaves, i.e., valuable property, their lives were expendable.

And the postbellum venture capitalists were even worse than the plantation owners, if you can imagine that. These adventurers were looking for quick fortunes draining and filling swamps or in turpentine camps deep in the wilderness. In the swamps and forests, conditions were inhuman, unimaginably brutal. The work was dangerous and accidents frequent. Also the men were starved, brutalized, murdered, or simply worked to death. The death rate in these camps was astronomical, at times over 30 percent. The survivors, emaciated and often sick, returned "in such wretched misery, the mere sight of which would touch the most obdurate and cruel of hearts." A scandal ensued. A reform move-ment organized the state penitentiary at Parchman plantation, along the *organizational lines of antebellum slavery, as a humane improvement.* Don't take my word, check it out for yourself. Go to primary sources, not the Internet.

In Parchman, the working prisoners are called gunmen. Not, of course, because they are armed, but because they work "under the gun." In this case, the rifles and shotguns carried by the "riding and walking bosses." Today prisoners aren't usually chained together, but that used to be normal.

Except for the leasing of prisoners (which was stopped in the 1940s), it had operated essentially unchanged since its founding in the 1890s. There was only one major difference from slavery. Progress? Improve-ment? That depends on your point of view. When we were there, poor whites also worked the fields under the gun. *That* wasn't true during slav-ery. Racial progress? Your call.

At Parchman, we were taken to the basement of a long, low brick build-ing where we were made to strip and stand around completely nude while waiting to be processed. From a group of off-duty guards came a chorus of crude and hostile comments. Some of these guards carried what I at first thought were long nightsticks. But these seemed to be of metal with three sharp points—like a trident—at one end. One or two of the guards grinned and made menacing gestures toward us. I would soon learn that those were cattle prods. Well, Parchman was a farm, I guess it had cattle. The metal cylinders contained powerful batteries, and the three little points were terminals emitting a strong electric charge. We would meet these cattle prods again, a favorite tool of law enforcement in parts of the Delta and Alabama.

When those points touched your skin, the pain was sharp and excruciating, at once a jolting shock and a burn. You could actually see (three puffs of smoke) and smell (the odor of roasting flesh) your skin burning. I'm surprised the animal rights movement hasn't yet made an issue of their use.

The man in charge of the processing was a massive, red-faced, cigar-smoking cracker in cowboy boots and a Stetson who strutted and stomped about blustering out orders and "promises." Deputy Tyson obviously fancied himself a wit.

"This is not a threat, it is a promise. I kid you not." It was quite a performance. In less foreboding circumstances (and if we weren't buck naked like our ancestors [Africans] while being enslaved), it would have been tempting to dismiss Tyson as a buffoon or a caricature from a bad movie. But complete nakedness and vulnerability curtails one's sense of humor. To protect us from the other prisoners, so we were told, we were going to be locked down in maximum security in the safety of death row.

They lined us up still naked in single file.

"Ah heahs you boys likes t'march," Deputy Tyson chortled. "So now y'all can jes' follow me. Ah'm Martin Luther Coon." We followed the Stetson, the broad behind, and a cloud of rank cigar smoke down long, narrow concrete corridors.

The cells were no more than six by nine feet, concrete, windowless, with two steel racks for bunks, a sink, and a commode enclosed by steel bars. As we came in the row, we noticed three large, boxy metal structures on the walls outside the cells but gave them no attention. We were two to a cell, which we left only for a weekly shower. I was in the first cell and my cellmate was Freddy Leonard from Nashville. We became not only friends, but allies. We were almost the same age but he looked at most fifteen. (I saw him on a TV program a few years ago and Freddy still looked like a teenager.) He had an open, honest face, a cheerful and mischievous disposition, and an easy grin. You couldn't not like Freddy. He was compact and muscular and had the heart of a young lion. We were the youngest Freedom Riders and got on well together.

In the cell next to ours was James Farmer, who took a paternal interest. He was himself a preacher's son, a former seminarian, a pacifist, and really a gentle, good-hearted man. He told us stories about his early days in struggle and we learned a great deal from him.

One of James Farmer's stories I've never forgotten. It amazed me and Freddy and illustrates something I'd been learning about the philosophy of pacifism.

When CORE was founded in Chicago, it was an offshoot of the pacifist organization FOR (Fellowship of Reconciliation). CORE's first target was a skating rink that discriminated against Africans. That was illegal in Chicago, after the manager turned away a black group from CORE, then admitted their white comrades, they had the goods on him. They filed charges and the manager was arrested. This caused great anguish and hand-wringing within the group. Eventually they took up a collection and bailed the manager out. We were incredulous. Why would they do this?

For two reasons, Mr. Farmer explained. One, they felt the manager, a working man trying to keep his job, was only a tool, in fact also a victim of racism. The poor guy didn't make the policy. And more important, many felt strongly that the police represented the "coercive power of the state" and its implied "monopoly of violence." Calling on the state to arrest the manager was a hostile act incompatible with true pacifist principles. So after some soul-searching, they bailed the guy out.

Which turned out, as Mr. Farmer explained, to be a good decision, politically speaking. Why? At the next FOR board meeting, Mr. Farmer gave his report on CORE. On hearing of the arrest, some FOR board members were sufficiently upset to entertain the notion of ending their support for the young organization. They were mollified only when it was explained that CORE had indeed bonded the manager out. Young Mr. Farmer got off with a stern lecture on proper pacifist ethics.

To Freddy and me that seemed not only excessive, but to miss the point. It was obvious to us, then and now, that Africans in America had the clear right and duty to use all means available to fight their oppression. Later, when I studied the abolitionist movement, I saw the split between Frederick Douglass and William Lloyd Garrison on that very issue: militant force or only moral suasion in the fight against slavery. But back in that cell I did not yet know that this story, which seemed so curious and incredible, was actually a pattern of things not only in the past but in the future of our struggle.

Which shows that the trajectory of our struggle in America is really cyclical, full of ironies and contradictions that seem to recycle themselves ad infinitum. That Greek philosopher Heracleitus was wrong in our case: Africans in America seem always to be crossing and recrossing the same river.

Given that the political prisoners were in lockdown 24/7 and confined two per cell, it might be expected that time would hang heavy. Not at all. No way, José, not with this group. What with the range of ideology, religious belief, political commitment and background, age, and experience, something interesting was always going on. Because, no matter our differences, this group had one thing in common, moral stubbornness. Whatever we believed, we really believed and were not at all shy about advancing. We were where we were only because of our willingness to affirm our beliefs even at the risk of physical injury. So it was never dull on death row.

The first battle of wills with Tyson came early. We didn't win. About the second day, we began singing our freedom songs. In marches, Tyson: "Y'all gon' ha' to stop that singin'. We ain't having none of that [expletive] heah." Next visit. "Ah'm warning you. You gonna lose yore mattresses." The steel ledges had a pattern of perforations, and even through the thin mattresses you felt the sharp edges of every hole when you tried to sleep.

When we didn't stop, Tyson came for the mattresses with some guards and trusties. Freddy and I decided we wouldn't surrender ours, nonviolently of course. When they snatched mine out from under me, dumping me on the floor, Freddy decided to wrap himself around his. The guard yanked Freddy and the mattress into the corridor but couldn't pry it loose. The guard swore. "Boy, you must not know where you is. Gimme that. Awright, go git 'em, Shorty." A muscular prisoner jumped in and stared whaling on Freddy. Of course he got the mattress. It was humiliating. Shorty was black. I knew the brother didn't have a choice, but did he have to appear so willing a tool? Afterward, to my astonishment, Freddy defended him, saying he wasn't so bad.

"What you talking about? He like to take yo' head off."

"Hey, he coulda hurt me real bad, man. But he was pulling up. I could feel it, man. Besides, I know it hurt him worse than it hurt me. Every blow he came down on me, Shorty was crying, man. That's why I gave him the [expletive] mattress."

So now we were left with the cold steel bunks and the thin shorts and singlets. But it's midday in Mississippi. The cell block is warm enough, hot even. After lunch, the preachers decide to praise their God with prayer and hymn singing. I think they thought that since the jailers professed to be good Christians, they'd not interfere with their worship. But Tyson wasn't having any of that either. He orders them to stop.

Well, the preachers inform him that they are going to praise their God. That like Daniel in the lions' den, like, I forget their names—Shaback and Shebago Shadrach, Meshach, and Abednego in the fiery furnace, they too would make a joyful noise unto the Lord under any circumstances! So if the state of Mississippi needed the money, which clearly it did, they could auction off the mattresses. *They* were going to praise their Lord!

"Is that raht?" Tyson said. "Ah see, said the blin' man. Wal, tell you whut. Y'all can give yore hearts and souls to Jesus, 'cause yore asses gonna belong to me." He slammed the door behind him. Deputy Dawg (as Hank christened him) was never noted for originality.

The service began with renewed fervor. Freddy and I even joined in the more militant hymns. Then the deluge. A fire hose. They hose down the entire row.

"Hallelujah! He washing away our sins," someone hollered.

"Next time, bring some soap!"

But we are all soaked. There's water on the floor. The walls are dripping. It's uncomfortable, but not too bad. The service continues. Then there is a loud humming noise. We assume Tyson's trying to drown out the singing. So we sing louder. But as the sun goes down, we discover that the machines are either air conditioners or exhaust fans creating a powerful draft. (I doubt that the state would have lavished air-conditioning on death row, but as the night went on, it sure felt like it.)

Since our clothes are wet, the concrete floors are flooded, the bunks are cold steel, and the commodes attract and keep the cold, we can't touch anything. Freddy and I kept walking in circles all night, tight circles, trembling and freezing in the night of a Mississippi summer.

I think Tyson kept those machines going for twenty-four hours. Needless to say, the preachers forgot about praising their God in those conditions. Sneezing, coughing, and some swearing replaced hymn singing that night. Sheback and Shebago, whatever their names were, they are forgotten too. No more singing and praising God at night.

Round midnight, cold and miserable, I couldn't help it. I shouted.

"Yo, Bevel. Reverend Bevel. We're freezing an' it's all your fault. You just had to go tell Tyson about that fiery furnace, huh?"

Cold as we all were, people had to laugh. 'Cause there was some truth in that.

As many preachers and religious people as there were in that jail, there were real differences even among the faithful. Of the young Nashville seminarians around the Reverend James Lawson—James Bevel, Bernard Lafayette, John Lewis—Bevel was by far the most interesting and unpredictable.

Short, muscular, shiningly bald-headed with a heavy, dark beard, Bevel had the burning eyes and visionary intensity of a Russian mystic. He was always, I mean *always,* arguing—passionately—some highly original, far-out position or the other, and I, for one, was never quite sure: Was that constant gleam in his eyes fanaticism or mischief? Was Bevel entirely serious, crazy, or just putting you on? But he could be depended on to take it on out to the edge, whatever "it" might be at any given time.

Prior to the hymn singing, there had been a discussion of the possibility of seeking bail for the group. This Bevel had ridiculed as totally lacking in faith. Dismiss all thought of bail. Righteously fill the jails. Absolutely no bail; when it was time, God would show the way out. All that was necessary was faith. And to praise God like Paul and Silas. Had they forgotten the spiritual, now a freedom song?

Paul and Silas was bound in jail
Had no money for to go to their bail
Paul and Silas began to shout
Jail door opened
And they walked out.

Had Bevel been serious? Who could ever tell with Bevel? All I know is that no jail doors opened that night and instead the Lord had sent a flood.

Don't be misled. I liked Bevel. He was a soldier, always unpredictable and often funny, but a soldier only in the Lord's army. Another time when they were working with Dr. King, Bevel and Bernard Lafayette found themselves in a small-town Alabama jail. Bevel begins his Paul and Silas rap again. What Bernard hadn't noticed, but Bevel had, was that the jailer had failed to secure the cell door. So Bevel suggests they pray themselves out.

"My brother, I *feels* the power today. The grace an' presence o' Almighty God. Oh, yes, Ah do. Ah feel it. Let us pray, Reverend." After some devout outloud prayer—"Ah want you to come to us, Lord, like you came to Paul and Silas"—on the line, *"jail door opened,* ol' Bevel rises.

"Open your heart and open your eyes, my brother. Behold, the power of faith," and he smites the door open before the astonished eyes of his friend Bernard. That was classic Bevel.

Freddy and I figured that being the youngest, and in the first cell, we should be the first line of resistance. So we determined never to cooperate, to resist as much as possible while maintaining nonviolence, but pushing that posture to its limits.

That's when Tyson introduced us to something I've never seen mentioned in anything I've read about torture in America's prisons. Something they call wrist breakers.

These were viselike metal contraptions that were applied to the wrist. One metal clamp went under your wrist, another fit over the top. A bar above the top clasp had a threaded hole into which a T-shaped rod—also threaded—was screwed. By screwing it down on the upper clasp, the pressure on your wrist could be increased unbearably. It was essentially a small vise. The pain was excruciating. If you tried to ignore the pain, they'd twist it laterally so that you would feel your bones in the joints of your arm about to break. Involuntarily, your whole body would have to follow your arm. You'd leave your feet and flip over like a fish. If they continued to twist, you'd find yourself rolling over on the floor following the pressure on your arm.

The first time I saw it I said, "Hey, I'm never gonna do that. Even if they break my arm." When they put it on me, I said to myself, "I'm not gonna flip," and planted my feet. The pain became intense. Next thing I knew I found myself on the ground revolving. "Yow," I said. "How did that happen? When did I flip?"

But being nineteen and arrogant, Freddy and I learned nothing the first time.

"Next time," Freddy woofed, "I ain't flipping. They going *have* to break my arm."

Course I was not to be outdone. "Me? Well, I going show them they can't *even* break mine."

Next time Tyson pulled Freddy outside the cell first, while I remained locked inside. They tightened the wrist breaker, and sure enough poor Freddy flipped. "Had enough?"

Freddy held up his wrists and turned them over. "Hey, you ain't even broken them yet."

Tyson got mad, but he knew that breaking Freddy's arm would be too much. He swore and threw him back into the cell.

Then my turn. After I'd flipped a couple times: "Had enough?" After Freddy, what could I do? I stared at him. He flipped me again. "Enough yet?"

I lay there and began to sing a movement song: " 'I'm going tell God how you treat me, one of these days.' " The entire row joined in. I think we won that one, barely . . . on points.

The next one was a loss, though self-imposed. This was the ill-conceived hunger strike. One of the white comrades, a Gandhian whose name escapes me, had started a hunger strike. His personal witness. I don't even recall a specific issue. It may have been a generalized "noncooperation with evil" taken to its limit. Or there could have been a specific demand. I don't remember. But this fellow had been on a hunger strike for some days. The suggestion arose that in solidarity we should all join in. Then came the debate, a long discussion, the mother of all arguments.

Our cell was united and solidly rejectionist: no hunger strike. Freddy and I were adamant on that. Here we are being whupped on almost every night by these jailers, and you want to talk about a hunger strike on top of it? No way. We need our strength to face these pigs. Generally the other NAG folk and the politicals were opposed, the ministers, pacifists, and Gandhians for. They argued for unity. Unless we all participated, it wouldn't be effective. They had to be able to say we all were on strike. Not some, it had to be all. It was a Gandhian technique, etc., etc. We argued. We discussed. We disagreed. We ultimately wore down.

Finally, Freddy and I were the only holdouts, and being the youngest, we'd clearly have to give in sooner or later. Which we did, but we never agreed with the tactic. I know that a number of others didn't either. But the process is important. Notice what had happened. What had begun as purely an individual witness, a personal statement, had become, through righteous rhetoric and group pressure, a group tactic, binding even on those with serious objections. We would encounter this dynamic time and again in the struggle. Sometimes the result would be positive, but it could often be just the opposite.

Freddy and I didn't want to be the only cell eating while our colleagues starved, but we had our conditions. Freddy said, "Awright, y'all, I'm in. Told you not to have no hunger strike, but I'ma go along. I promise you I won't be the first to break it. But I'm sho nuff going to be the second one."

"I'm with Freddy," says I. "I don't agree with this either. Except I'm not gonna be the second or the third. I'm going to be the last."

Next morning we told the trusties to take the food back. The whole block was on strike. They were puzzled, never having encountered that before. Tyson came and told them to leave the food. When they came back for the plates, Freddy and I checked carefully. All were untouched.

Suppertime, a miraculous transformation. The food, which had always been disgusting, suddenly looked appetizing and smelled great. Fried chicken, peas, greens, and corn bread still steaming and with what looked and smelled like butter. They placed the trays in the slot in the door where we could see and smell the food. The penalty for knocking over the trays was solitary confinement in the hole, so we couldn't even do that. We had to endure the smells. And it got worse (and the food better). Roast beef, mashed potatoes, pecan pie. I hope the other prisoners got to enjoy it when the trays went back untouched.

Then in a couple of days the stomach pains began and didn't stop. I now have the greatest respect for Bobby Sands, the Irish patriot who went for sixty-six days on hunger strike. The arguments now became louder and more contentious, the conflicts sharper. Freddy figured it was the pain. And all this great food sitting under their noses. "When they start shouting and screaming on each other," Freddy theorized, "it distracts them. They forget the pain and don't smell the food." I'm sure he was right, but for the next few days death row did not sound like an oasis of verbal nonviolence.

Freddy and I maintained that the whole thing was stupid and useless. The pacifists talked about Gandhi's fasts. We didn't want to hear that. We weren't Gandhi. We were soldiers in a fight. It was absurd and counterproductive to weaken ourselves. That was doing the racists' job for them. Why help them? Our job was to survive, not starve ourselves to death. Many of my attitudes toward struggle were shaped by those discussions.

From our cell we could see the trays come in and go back out. For a few days all that good food remained untouched, to Freddy's increasing frustration. Then, on about the fourth day, Freddy leapt up, pointing and shouting. "Look, look, that one's empty. Someone done ate."

"I don't know who," Freddy sang out to the others, "but someone just ate. I don't care who it was, but Freddy Leonard's gonna be the second."

Whoever it was apologized. He had been sick, a medical condition, etc. Freddy said he didn't care anything about that. He, as promised, was going off the strike.

"Hey," he said between bites, "the strike's broken, man. Forget them, go ahead and eat, bro."

"No, man, I'm the last one." But I was mad.

"Why?"

"I've got my reasons. You'll see."

By the fifth day, the strike was just about over. Next day, the only two not eating were me and James Farmer, the voice from the cell next door. He claimed the strike was doing wonders for his waistline. By then I'd gotten to appreciate "Mr. Farmer" as I called him. And I learned a lot from him about organizing. Course we couldn't see each other except once a week when he'd pass in front of my cell on his way to and from the showers. But Freddy and I got to see everyone passing and what condition he was in.

Anyway, Mr. Farmer and I kept up the strike for one more day. He wanted to be the last striker. Because, I think, he was the CORE leader and had supported the tactic. But I said no, I would be last. On the seventh day he broke his fast. Freddy said, "All right. You can go now." I declined. I wanted to say something to them before I ate. I waited until after supper that evening. I had my little speech all prepared.

"Friends, most of you don't know me. My name is Stokely Carmichael. I'm in with Freddy Leonard. You may have heard of us. We're the youngest in here. Myself, I'm a very young man but I intend to be fighting the rest of my life so I'll probably be in jail again. So probably will some of you. So this may not be the last time we are together in prison. That's why I want you to remember my name. Because if we are ever in jail again and any of you even mention the words *hunger* and *strike*, I'm gonna denounce you properly. I'll be the first to denounce you. You can tell everybody that. That if they are ever in jail with Stokely Carmichael, never ever mention anything about any hunger strike."

All that night I thought about breakfast. Now that I was free to eat, the night seemed interminable. Of course with the strike over, the next day the food had reverted. It was again awful and, for good measure, so oversalted as to be barely edible. Thus ended the hunger strike.

June 29, my twentieth birthday, found me in that cell. It would be the first of many I was to spend in Southern jails. It got so that people in

SNCC would say, "Hey, it's Carmichael's birthday. Keep your distance from him today unless you want to be arrested too."

Shortly after that, Mr. Farmer was bonded out. *[In James Farmer's account, from the start CORE's legal strategy had been to bond people out by their fortieth day in jail. If they served longer than that, under Mississippi law the appeals process was no longer available. —EMT]* Then, without consulting SNCC, CORE decided that the Freedom Rides had made their point: no more riders were to be sent in and the ones in jail were to be bonded out. Freddy and I and the six people with us were opposed. We thought we should just go ahead and fill the jails. But to no avail. We were all bonded out.

According to the deal that CORE had made, once out of Parchman all Freedom Riders were immediately to leave the state. But some strong members of the local African community were having none of that. They would not have us slink silently out of the state like criminals. No. No. No. The bread of fellowship must be broke. Appropriate words be said, proper ceremony observed, and the occasion marked and duly acknowledged. Was this strictly necessary? Of course not. But it was right. In that atmosphere of racial tension and threat, this took courage. It would have been prudent and safer for the local people to keep their distance from us "outside agitators." But these brave people weren't about to turn their backs on us.

So when we were released, delivered by bus to Jackson, and told to get out of the state, a committee of these bold local people were present to receive us. They took us to Tougaloo College, where a lavish reception had been prepared. The gym was all decorated and there was a sign, "Welcome Freedom Riders."

Now, we all were hungry and had all lost weight. I was like a walking stick, I mean gaunt. Even I knew that I had to be looking bad, but I had no idea the spectacle I presented until later when I saw, and failed at first to recognize, a picture of myself coming out of that jail.

In the college gymnasium we were greeted, praised, thanked, and above all, fed. But not before a particularly eloquent minister gave thanks. He thanked God for sending us, us for coming, and God again for bringing us safely out of the house of bondage, suffering, and evil. There was singing, music, dancing, and food. Welcome tables heaped with food, delicious, clean, Southern cooking, skillfully prepared and lovingly presented.

A youth committee of brothers and sisters our age were in charge of hospitality. Among them was one sister who just sparkled. She seemed very much in charge: responsible and just the slightest bit imperious. But, oh, she was beautiful to me, gracious and radiant. I forgot hunger and the apparition I must have appeared and sought her out.

Her name was Mary Felice Lovelace and her parents taught at Tougaloo. She was an art student at Howard. At *Howard?* I was incredulous. She was on campus? Lived in the dorms? And I'd never *seen* her? *Her?* She was intelligent, black, militant, and beautiful. How could I not have noticed her? That just didn't seem possible.

[According to the young lady, it wasn't. She has a differing recollection of history. She told writer Charlie Cobb that during one of Washington's infrequent snowfalls the previous winter, Carmichael and Ed Brown had been pelting passing coeds with snowballs in front of Slowe Hall. Infuriated when Carmichael caught her flush, she jumped in his face and lectured him on the error of his ways in no uncertain terms. To such effect, apparently, that the offender completely blocked out the entire incident. At the Tougaloo reception she thought she recognized him, but couldn't associate the earnest, "heroic" Freedom Rider with the grinning campus hooligan. —EMT]

I told her about NAG. She said, oh, definitely, she was in. We danced a lot and agreed to meet on campus in the fall. Mary Felice Lovelace would be my first and—during my college years—my only love. She was smart, talented, and tough-minded, but loving. I was always proud to be with Mary and thought we were destined to spend our lives together, but the movement would intervene.

We got out of Dodge that evening. In New York, we were met at the airport, driven to the CORE office to meet the press. I immediately called May Charles and told her I was free and in New York. Naturally she started to cry. Then to laugh. Then she couldn't wait. She was just excited, bubbling over. Immediately she went to sit in the window looking for me to appear on the street.

CORE was planning to send us home in cars, but I got tired waiting and took a train. She saw me while I was well up the block, but wasn't sure it was me. Then she really started to weep.

"Oh, my God. Look at what they have done to my son."

She asked, but I'd never tell her any details. "Oh, nothing to it, Mom. It was okay." But seeing how I looked, she never believed me. She immediately began to fatten me up with every "strong" dish from the Caribbean she could think of. When she informed all her friends and relations that "Stokely look like death, Where is thy sting? Grave thy victory?" well-meant Caribbean nourishment flowed into our house from all quarters of the extended family.

I lay at home for most of July, resting. Occasionally the CORE office would call to ask me to take a speaking engagement for them. People, it seems, wanted to hear from a "Freedom Rider" and I guess James Farmer remembered the "kid" in the next cell. Whatever the reason, they kept asking me, and I began to gain experience in public speaking for the movement.

These were usually fund-raisers, though, and as was the case with Willie Sutton and banks, CORE had to go where the money was. Thus I found myself in some truly opulent surroundings talking about Parchman Farm, poverty, and oppression to sympathetic rich white folk, quite as though there were no connection. Some of these apartments reminded me of that penthouse party during freshman year at Science.

It was disjunctive, almost schizoid, and as it turned out, a token of things to come. Later, with us in SNCC, the same contradictions would surface. We'd be sending young field-workers, some of them coming out of hardscrabble sharecropper poverty, into trappings of enormous wealth and power, there to tell moving tales—we called them "war stories"—of our people's suffering and resistance. It was classic Americana, shades of runaway darkies and Northern audiences.

During this period I met another brother who was a great influence on the movement and who would be a great example of constant commitment: Harry Belafonte.

The effective and consistent contributions of Harry Belafonte to our peoples' liberation struggle in our time is not fully or widely enough understood or appreciated. When I met him, this "star," pioneering popularizer of Caribbean music, was already an influential presence in our struggle. Activist, counselor to leaders, strategist, diplomat, fund-raiser, mentor to youth, Belafonte was an all-round key player in our struggle in this country, the Caribbean, and across the length and breadth of the continent. He has done this quietly, effectively, and admirably, without any need to seek the limelight.

He has not merely responded when asked but has taken creative initiatives where necessary. To my knowledge he has been a principled and positive force. His example of devotion and commitment among artists has enhanced the struggle in our time. Like Paul Robeson before him, whom he greatly admired, and Miriam, my first wife, his art was always in service to our culture and our struggle. In struggle, Brother Belafonte is one who came early and stayed late. Yes, he is. And of course, in personal wealth and his career, he paid a price.

In our music-loving Caribbean household, he was a culture hero. My family, especially my father, were most impressed when I told them whom I'd just met.

One day Harry was meeting with a group of Freedom Riders from the New York area. He invited us to be his guests at a concert in Forest Hills that night. Queens? Oh, man, to a city kid that's the far side of the moon. I was planning to hang with my boys in the Village that evening. So

I was getting ready to beg off when he mentioned that Miriam Makeba would be appearing with him.

Say what?

"Oh, Bro Harry, what time? How do I get there? We're gonna get to meet her, right?"

That evening I took such a long time and such inordinate pains getting dressed that my sister Janeth [Nagib] noticed.

"Stokely, where you going? Why you dressing up so? Posing in front of the mirror an' all, eh?" I told her it was nothing. I was going to meet Miriam Makeba is all.

"Ooh, Stokely en't telling the truth," she squealed. "Say he going to meet Miriam Makeba."

My schoolboy fantasy was back like a big dowg. Not only was I going to meet her, I was going to make an impression, Jack. Sweep her off her feet. Yes, I would. After much thought and trying on for effect, I settled on a silky Harry Belafonte shirt. The kind with flared collars, a deep V neck, and billowing sleeves with my best slacks. I was clean and, so I thought, looking great.

That evening I couldn't take my eyes off her on the stage. She was wearing a sheath dress with a long slit in slinky material in an orange-and-yellow Matabele print. A tall hat in the same print set off her large, expressive eyes, her soft, rich skin, and the finely chiseled beauty of her classic Bantu face. In the stage light she was truly exotic, sensual, and feline in motion with that richness of her voice. She was kickin', and if I was blown away, and I really was, I could see I wasn't the only one. She captured that audience. But I was cool. I *knew* I was gonna get her attention. She was going to notice me. Yes, she was.

And I did. Soon as our eyes met, I saw her start. She looked at me again and her face changed. I knew she was mine. Something flashed between us. We both knew. We both could feel it. . .

Hah. I wish.

When my turn came to meet her, I pulled myself up to my full height, squared my shoulders, turned on my most dazzling Belafonte smile, and looked ardently down into her eyes.

I took her hand. "Miss Makeba, you were incredible."

"Oh, thank you so much. Very kind." She gently disengaged her hand, turned, and reached out to the next in line. I stood, empty hand extended with that dumb grin on my face. Some impression. Eight years later when we met again in Conakry, she had absolutely no recollection. None. The best-laid plans of men . . . and boys.

But I recovered. Toward the end of a pleasant month at home where I was a minor neighborhood celebrity, the phone rang. My mother handed it to me. It was Nashville SNCC. There would be a political seminar during August. They were sending me a plane ticket.

"Cool," I said. "Cool. You know I'll be there. Count on it."

"Be where?" my mother asked, alarmed. "Where you think you going again?" Her voice was sharp, tense.

"To Nashville—" I never got to finish explaining.

"No. Oh, no. Over my dead body. Oh, no. Look what they did to you. After you not mad. Oh, no." All I could do was wait for her to catch her breath. It took a while.

"I'm sorry, but I gotta go—" And she was off again. And it wasn't theatrics either. May Charles was deeply, truly afraid and she let it all come out. She wept. She raged. She screamed.

"May Charles, this isn't something I want to do. You have to understand, I'm going. I got no choice. It's something I *have* to do."

Gradually she calmed down and went into the bedroom. I could hear muffled sobbing, but when she came out, she was calm. She walked past without a word and started to iron my clothes.

"But I won't be needing good clothes," I protested.

"Yes, you do," she said. "At least, if nothing else, you'll be looking decent."

That I think was my mother's Waterloo. The point at which she realized—and accepted—that nothing was going to stop me from participating fully in this struggle. At whatever the cost. However she'd made peace with herself on the issue, she had. When I left for Nashville, it was with, however fearfully, her blessing.

CHAPTER X

Nashville:
A New Direction

On the surface it looked like any other academic seminar meeting in a university classroom anywhere in America. Nothing (except perhaps that, highly unusual in that time and place, the visiting "faculty" were thoroughly racially integrated) distinguished it from any other "interdisciplinary graduate workshop," as the organizers described it. And indeed it was resolutely and rigorously academic. It boasted an extensive list of required readings, mandatory class attendance, and required "a term paper in a special area of choice" from all participants.

I don't recall that formal academic credit was offered, but if it wasn't, it certainly should have been, because, to put it simply, it seemed like summer school by another name. So why was I so all-fired determined not to miss it and so jump-up impatient to get there? Because for four weeks that August, Nashville would become the hub of a newly confident, evolving student movement, and that Fisk University seminar room would be at the center of it all.

I felt honored and excited merely to have been invited. I recognized a good many of the names of the scholars who would be coming to speak to us, including some high-powered progressive intellectuals of the time: Dr. August Meier, Kenneth Clark, C. Eric Lincoln, L. D. Reddick, Herbert Hill, and, I was proud to see, a couple of our Howard stalwarts, E. Franklin Frazier and Rayford Logan. These luminaries came for expenses and a princely honorarium of $25. Also there would be some of the activists we most respected: Ms. Ella Baker, the Reverend James Lawson, and a promised "roundtable with Dr. Martin Luther King." Which alone was reason enough to be excited. A few other names—Harris Wofford, Red Sarrat, Clarence Mitchell, Henry Van Alestyne—I did not recognize. These turned out to be Washington insiders, some from inside the Kennedy administration itself. As I would learn, their presence was not accidental.

One unit on this scrupulously complete program excited much laughter and joking from everybody. "Hey, Chuck. Whose idea was this? *Sex?*

And *Race?* In the *South?* We need to learn about this?" "You trying to say they related? Surely you jest." I can't recall who the scholarly expert for that unit was, but there it was on the program, sho nuff. Our planners, bless they hearts, was nothing if not earnest and thorough.

What was most exciting was the prospect of being among other strugglers again, and getting to know those young activists whose names I'd been hearing but whom I hadn't really met—even though some of us had been in the same jails. In Nashville, we'd get a chance to see and really connect with each other.

Actually I couldn't really think of these folks as my "peers." Of course, anyone with Freedom Ride jail experience was considered a "veteran." So at nineteen years old I was a "movement veteran." But I was still among the youngest in age and experience, if only by a year or two. If I were a "veteran," then the people I was meeting were "generals." People I really looked up to. Diane Nash certainly. Ruby Doris Smith came out of Atlanta with Oretha Castle, whom I'd met as an experienced struggler in New Orleans. Also another impressive sister from Nashville named Lucretia Collins, all committed fighters.

In Nashville I would first meet most of the emerging leadership who would play crucial roles in the organization, the Southern struggle, and therefore in my early political life for years to come.

That's when I first met Tim Jenkins, the student government president I'd heard so much about at Howard. John Lewis was in the seminar as were Chuck McDew, Charlie Jones, and Charles Sherrod (a charismatic seminarian who had just been hired as SNCC's first official field secretary). Lester McKimmie, a devoted brother who would later work closely with me in D.C. in the Black United Front, was there, as was my Parchman cellmate, Freddy Leonard. From D.C. there were John Moody and Dion Diamond from NAG and our close ally Reggie Robinson, leader of the Baltimore student movement.

I quickly realized that the real architect of the seminar was Tim Jenkins. He had seen a need, thought up the project, and used the insider influence of his NSA vice presidency to secure funding for it.

Tim Jenkins explained when we met, "Even before the Freedom Rides I didn't think we could allow the energy and excitement of the sit-ins simply to dissipate.

"After the rides, it was even clearer that the student movement, if it were to survive at all, would need a new, sustainable program and focus. And I certainly wanted to nudge it down off that lofty, ethereal plane of 'the beloved community,' and the excessive religious zeal of the pain-and-suffering school of struggle."

He got no argument from me on that, Jack.

Today, Tim adds, "I felt that what the movement really needed at that point was not idealism or inspiration but information. Hard, pragmatic information about how the political system actually worked . . . or failed to work. Where the pressure points were. What levers were available that students could push. Where allies might be found. Who the real enemies were. What exactly was the nature of the beast we were up against? That was the purpose in Nashville."

As I was soon to find out, a more specific agenda than information sharing was present in Nashville. McDew, Tim, and Chuck Jones were convinced that the young movement needed to identify national interests with goals that were compatible with our own (which were at that time quite unformed or at least only being formed)—interests whose resources could be tapped into and brought to bear. That was the big question for me: Did such "interests" actually exist in the nation? And, if so, how could mere students even approach them? And why would they take us seriously?

By the time we came together in Nashville, Tim and the others were beginning to believe they had located just such an interest. A powerful interest indeed, and here's the thing. *They,* apparently, had come to *us.* And this powerful interest? The Kennedy administration, no less. Say what? I couldn't believe what I was hearing. What did they, could they, want with us? Incredible. But apparently true, and as it turned out, quite a story.

Even while some of us were still sitting penned up in Parchman, Bobby Kennedy's emissaries had begun sending out feelers to the student movement? Git outta here. What was he up to? Was he now talking to "extremists on both sides"? Maybe it was "ask not what your country can do for you; ask what you can do . . ." time, huh?

I wasn't about to cut him any slack at all, Jack. On Parchman death row, we had talked about him like a dog. Hey, wasn't it because of *their* failure to enforce their own laws that we were sitting in that hellhole in the first place? And for what, buying a ticket and riding a bus? C'mon. Gimme an ever-loving break, bro. That hadn't been everyone's reaction, but it was most people's and it sure was mine. But, I couldn't wait to find out what in the world the attorney general of the United States could possibly want with us.

Actually his interests turned out to be clear enough. Naive, on at least one crucial issue, but clear.

It seems the administration was determined to "minimize any further possibility of again being blindsided by unexpected racial crises." According to official Washington, the Freedom Rides had been an "unmitigated disaster." We had succeeded only in "damaging" American foreign policy interests; "tarnishing" America's image in Africa and Asia; "embarrassing" the administration internationally *and* giving a "propaganda victory" to the Soviets. A total disaster, *unmitigated*.

Yeah, well . . . that was *their* perspective. I wasn't buying any of it. Not for a New York minute. Which is not to say that all this hadn't happened. It had, but all politics is perspective. From where we stood that interpretation—which, incidentally, was also what the media was running—was outrageous, a total inversion of reality.

Yeah, they had reason to be embarrassed internationally. Excellent reasons, but these had nothing to do with us. It was their inability or reluctance, demonstrated to the entire world, to discipline their renegade Southern provinces by enforcing federal law and stated government policy within their own borders. That was the embarrassment. And that was on them, not us. They were merely embarrassed, but we had *suffered* because of their timidity.

And was the country's international image "tarnished"? No doubt there either, and well it should have been. For it wasn't tarnished by anything we did, but by the unregulated, irrational, racist violence that the administration was seen to tolerate against black people and their allies. And the "Soviet propaganda victory"? That too. Hey, all the "leader of the free world" had to do to deprive the Soviets of that "victory" was to be seen around the world to be *living up* to the nation's own lofty rhetoric about democratic freedoms and human rights for *all* its citizens. Y'know, there is a name for this kind of moral inversion and we all know what it is.

So how did the administration propose that such international political embarrassments be avoided in the future? Well, that's where certain "serious domestic political concerns" of the brothers Kennedy, which would come to affect us, *seriously* came into play. These concerns involved the next presidential election (1964) and "Jack's razor-thin margin of victory in 1960." *Razor-thin?* Try less than half of one percent of the popular vote. But here again was a serious matter of perspective, because the administration's take on this was the exact opposite of ours. A difference in perspective that had a lot to do with the upsurge of movement militance during JFK's short tenure in office.*

*In the election of 1960, JFK had received a late, sudden and unexpectedly large majority of the black vote. More, if memory serves, than any other Democratic presidential candidate except FDR, and far more than had been predicted by pollsters. See, JFK, the candidate, had absolutely no civil rights record going into the election and consequently no visible support in African communities. Nonetheless, this late black surge. Naturally, we saw that as the margin of his very thin victory, which it was. Had those black folk not voted or gone the other way, Nixon would have been president. So, we felt, the president owed the black community something, at the very least respect, a fair hearing, and our civil rights.

They, however, saw the returns very differently: as a sign that, for 1964, they

JFK's narrow margin was why the administration strategists were now so convinced that on no account could they afford to alienate the "Bubba vote" any more than they might already have. Further public confrontations with the leadership of the Dixiecrat wing of the party had to be avoided at all costs. And since they had almost certainly already lost significant Southern white support because of the Freedom Rides, then perhaps, maybe, the registration of at least a portion of the South's 4 million disenfranchised blacks might help offset that loss. On both counts they felt they needed us. Naked political self-interest? Of course. But, hey, that's the name of the game. And so far as the politics of American presidents usually went on the question of our rights, it was an unusually enlightened self-interest.

Hence the overtures to the movement: it would be, they argued, in everyone's—the nation's, the government's, the Negro's—best interest if the "extremists" in SNCC and CORE could be persuaded to abandon confrontational direct action tactics to concentrate their efforts, quietly, on voter registration. Everybody wins.

For them, the proverbial two birds with one stone. This tactical change, they felt, would buy them "a cooling-off period with no surprises or unsightly washing of the nation's dirty racial linen in public," while hopefully a new base of "Kennedy voters" would be created in Dixie. (We knew this was *naive* from the git. No way would those Southern crackers welcome Africans voting.)

---

needed to placate their party's Southern wing and its white Bible Belt Baptist constituency, which had looked with suspicion on Kennedy's Catholic faith. Same facts, different priorities. This would be a constant in my experience with American politicians.

The story behind the late black crossover is kinda funny, instructive, and ironic. The week before the election, Dr. King was being held in a Georgia county jail with a bad reputation for violence. JFK was persuaded—against the advice of his brother, Bobby, who was said to be livid when he heard—to make a phone call to Mrs. King "simply to express concern." Daddy King was so moved by this small gesture that he made his famous declaration: "I've got a bag o' votes to deliver to the man who cared enough to wipe the tears from my daughter-in-law's eyes." Or words to that effect.

Clerical networking took place, and the Sunday before the election, endorsements of JFK rang out from Baptist pulpits across the black nation. Much is ironic in this story. Not the least of which is something Dr. King told me when I got to know him . . . *doctrinal sectarianism* might not be too strong a term.

Before the phone call, his father and his friends and allies in the Baptist alliance, "all them old Baptist preachers," he said, "had absolutely no more intention to either endorse or vote for Kennedy than the man in the moon."

I wondered why.

"Are you kidding, Stokely?" Dr. King asked. "You forget, the candidate was a *Catholic!*"

And for us, voter registration would accomplish two things also: the jump-starting of a drive for full citizenship for "the Southern Negro," which had been betrayed in 1877. And, if we "militants" would only cooperate, we would be pleasantly surprised to find how supportive the administration could be. Of course, being in jail, I wasn't at any of those meetings with the administration. But, so I'm told, a raft of promises were dangled: financial support, legal protection, and even none too subtle hints of draft deferments for registration workers. And on one occasion, this was presented by the attorney general himself, in person, live and in color!

[Ture's reading and recollections of this crucial transition period are precise and accurate so far as they go. A more recent account—by the excellent social historian Taylor Branch—fills in gaps in young Carmichael's direct experience and expands our understanding of the full extent of the Kennedys' role in this transition. —EMT]

Branch writes, ". . . They [the Kennedys] immediately stepped up efforts to create a well-financed, tax exempt organization to register Negro voters in the South . . . the clandestine pursuit resembled the campaign to secure tax benefits for those who had helped ransom Bay of Pigs prisoners . . . Kennedy himself intervened with IRS Commissioner Mortimer Kaplan to secure that exemption for the Voter Education Project . . ."

The Kennedys' idea was to bring all the civil rights groups *"under uniform rules and a central budget."* The wild cards were, of course, SNCC and CORE, the two activist organizations responsible for the Freedom Rides and with whom the administration had the least contact.

". . . On June 16," Branch relates, "Attorney General Kennedy received a delegation from the Freedom Ride Coordinating Council . . . they hoped to receive federal help [protection] for the Freedom Rides. . . . But what they instead received was a counter point from the Attorney General. 'The Freedom Rides were no longer productive,' he said. [They] . . . could accomplish more by registering Negro voters . . . if they would agree . . . he'd do everything . . . to make sure they were fully supported and protected . . .

He mentioned the confidential work . . . [going on] to secure tax exemption and large foundation grants.

"This was too blunt for Charles Sherrod, who was on his feet . . . sputtering indignantly at what he regarded as a bribe. . . .

" 'You are a public officer, Sir. It is not your responsibility, before God or under the law, to tell us how to honor our constitutional rights. It's your job to protect us when we do.' *[Go deh, Sherrod, sho do sound like SNCC to me —EMT]* Wyatt Walker, fearing he might attack Kennedy in the frenzy of his sermon, pulled him [Sherrod] back to his seat by the pocket of his pants.

". . . Kennedy and his aides pressed their points then and later. They went so far as to extend confidential promises that the administration would arrange draft exemptions for students—so long as they confined themselves to quiet political work. Harris Wofford put the choice to them most graphically: they could have jails filled with Freedom Riders or jails filled with white southern officials who tried to obstruct federally protected voting rights."—Taylor Branch, *Parting the Waters*

After leaving those meetings, people had sought advice from elders. They had to. Was the administration serious? Could they be trusted? What should the students be doing? One person they had consulted was Harry Belafonte. He advised them not to reject the idea out of hand. You first need to get yourselves organized to think it through. Figure out the politics, then make your decision, he told them. He then made a generous personal contribution to begin that process *[a reported $10,000]*. Folks were just overwhelmed, and I believe that marked the beginning of Bro Belafonte's long relationship—as adviser, benefactor, and big brother—to the young freedom-fighting organization.

To say that these administration signals took us students by surprise would be the grandmammy of all understatements. Folks were, depending on their inclinations, in turn suspicious, flattered, surprised, confused, or all of the above simultaneously. Remember now, at that point, SNCC wasn't even a real organization. A vigorous, exciting movement sure, but an organization? Not hardly, no way.

So all the time we were in Nashville discussing "Should we?" what was really in the back of everyone's mind was "Can we?" As a practical matter—with no staff, no full-time field organizers, not even a real office—in short, no real organization—were we in any position even to be dealing on that level? A different group of folk might have been intimidated. We probably should have been, had we known better. But with these guys? Nothing intimidated us. SNCC would become famous for not having sense enough to be intimidated. But a lot of intense late-night discussions and soul-searching took place, and it was all very exciting. Things were moving fast. You could just *feel* in the air that something big, new, was fixing to happen. It was not only exciting but even a little scary, and I was just overjoyed to be part of it.

Night after night of long, intense, interminable discussions as young people sorted out their ideas, values, beliefs, fears, commitments, and priorities. Were we really ready for this? Occasionally leaving campus to sit in at a department store was one thing. Full-time organizing in the Deep South was entirely something else. What about our educations?

Folks wrestled with that. Some prayed. We all sang: "Guide mah feets, Lord / While I run this race. / Lord, I don't want to run this race in vain." Or: "Wade in the water. / Wade in the water, chillen. / Wade in the water. / SNCC's gonna trouble the water," and the haunting, long meter "We'll never turn back."

I learned how interesting and brave my new comrades really were. After what we'd seen with the Freedom Rides, nobody, but *nobody* had the slightest illusion about what might be awaiting. Was *all* this really our responsibility? And if not ours, then whose? If not now, when? Each of us had to search his or her own character and conscience.

One idea really took hold. I can't recall who first said it. Or if anyone did. It probably just evolved. But it became a kind of mantra. As students we have a unique responsibility. At this stage of life we are at our most free. The freest we will ever be. We have neither family, career, mortgage, or any other adult responsibilities to tie us down. If we can't afford to do this now, when will we be? *If not now, when?* If you're serious, you gotta do it now or git off the pot.

For me those sessions were important. I think that was when we began to bond into "a band of brothers." I know that I certainly started to feel the strong respect and love for these brothers and sisters which has lingered all my life. Tactically and politically I had no problem with the voter registration proposal. I was with Jenkins and McDew . . . we couldn't just continue sitting in indefinitely. We had to take it to another level and I was all for the new political direction. Thanks to Rayford Logan *[The Betrayal of the Negro]*, I was very clear on the history. After the betrayal of Reconstruction, it was the systematic disenfranchisement of our people that had started the whole mess. That had paved the way for almost a century of Jim Crow exploitation, discrimination, humiliation, and lynching. And the nation's betrayal of its own professed principles.

So the vote, if not the answer, was certainly the start. We could finish what Reconstruction had started. With Africans voting, the South would be a different place, unrecognizable. So it didn't seem much of a choice to me. Besides, when was the last time the political interests of any American president coincided with the political empowerment of black people? Hey, while our interests weren't identical, they were at least compatible, so I hoped.

One thing though. And this is where the administration seemed really naive: nobody in Nashville had the slightest illusion about any "cooling-off period." If the crackers had gone stone-mad, butt-kicking crazy merely over a few seats on a bus, why in the world would anyone expect them to sit still for black folk voting? Uh-uh, this was gonna be dangerous. But if the feds—the powerful federal government—were gonna be seriously involved this time . . . maybe none of us would have to die.

To me it was an offer we couldn't afford to refuse. Not if we were serious, anyway. And I knew that I was going to be part of it, no matter what. Obviously this would mean a different level of commitment. For a start, people would have to drop out of school, if only temporarily. (Actually, most never made it back.) And I'd only just finished giving my father my word that I'd finish school at all costs. That was my, and a lot of other folks', largest question, our educations. But I was in. That was definite.

While this discussion was raging, all kinds of folk kept coming through Nashville. I particularly remember two brothers who were to be important in this new organization. One was an articulate, irrepressible, boyish-looking guy from Atlanta who always seemed to have an infectious grin on his face and a twinkle in his eye. Julian Bond passed through but didn't stay long. Seems, if memory serves, Julian had other things on his mind just then since the young lady with him was his bride-to-be and they were in the process of eloping. Julian now insists that there had been a wedding but not quite an elopement. A subtle distinction but I guess he should know.

The other brother who dropped in was a young journalist/school-teacher from Chicago named Jim Forman. He didn't stay long either because he was working with a struggle heating up in a town called Monroe, North Carolina. First time I saw this stocky, curly-haired, almost baby-faced older brother, he was stopping folks—to jawbone them passionately—about support for this brave community and their remarkable leader, Robert Williams. Last time I remember seeing Jim—some forty years later *[Hartford, 1986]*—the brother was still buttonholing folk and talking up some new strategy of struggle. Indefatigable Jim Forman.

In a few months, Jim would sign on as the first full-time employee and executive secretary for SNCC, which at the time was more of a dream than an organization. James Forman, more than any other single person, would manage the nuts-and-bolts transformation of SNCC at its most crucial time. Administratively, Jim turned a loose association of contentious, widely scattered, diffuse student groups into an effective organizational force at the cutting edge of the black struggle for human rights in the South. That was no easy job and it would consume him completely. Hey, we never were a hierarchical, leader-centered group like SCLC nor a centralized bureaucracy like the national NAACP. But for a while we were the most spiritually unified, focused, creative force in the movement. And it was Jim had everything to do with creating the administrative base and scraping together the support to make that possible.

In later years I would hear people who were not there say many things about Jim, and indeed, he and I would come to our own parting of the political ways. The necessary organizational role Jim undertook would almost inevitably place him at the center of political controversy, confusion, misunderstandings, and even slander. That comes with the territory. If you can't stand the heat, git from in front of the stove. But, as much as humanly possible, against overwhelming odds and some incredible pressures that I myself would later come to understand fully, Jim Forman was an anchoring, stabilizing presence at a time when the organization needed such a presence. You should read his book *[Making of Black Revolutionaries]*.

The task Jim undertook at that crucial moment was not only difficult and demanding, it was well nigh impossible. Without James Forman's devotion, strength, responsibility, resourcefulness, and innate decency, the character of our infant organization—if indeed it survived—and consequently the history of the movement would have been very, very different. Tell the truth and shame the devil. Our people owe Jim Forman a lot.

But back then in Nashville, all Jim was talking about was this Carolina town called Monroe and a local NAACP leader called Robert Williams. In a short time, this brother would become a great inspiration and a lesson to us in SNCC, as well as a symbolic and ideological leader to a number of radical groups across the spectrum of the black struggle. That story was crucial in how we came to understand the struggle we were involved in.

After they were released from Parchman that summer, Paul Dietrich and Bill Mahoney were among a group of about ten, mostly white Freedom Riders recruited by Forman, to come to Monroe. The group's presence was to show white support and bring their experience in nonviolent protest into the mix.

When Paul and Bill got back to D.C., they had an interesting tale to tell. For one thing, both were absolutely convinced that Robert Williams's insistence on armed self-defense was the only thing that had saved their lives. And Paul was a devout pacifist.

These Freedom Riders along with a small group of local youth had run up a small picket line in the center of Monroe. The picket was in support of a range of community issues. It was a Saturday and the downtown was crowded. A large crowd formed. Gradually the crowd turned into a mob. Verbal abuse turned into occasional blows as agitators whipped up the crowd. What police were present did nothing to control or disperse the mob. In fact, the cops were verbally hostile to the picketers.

[Bill Mahoney later told us: "I just knew we were dead. Man, we were completely surrounded by angry white folk. People started jumping out of the crowd to take a swing at us. Next to me, Paul (Dietrich) was knocked dizzy by a vicious blow to his ear. While I was supporting Paul, someone slugged me over

my eye. People on the line were bleeding. The threats got louder. It was clear that it was only a matter of time before they would swarm over us.

"I had been watching this old, old toothless man in overalls getting hysterical. His face was all red and convulsed. He kept screaming, 'Kill the niggahs. Goddamn, kill 'em. Go on, kill the niggahs.'

Then I saw the old man's face suddenly change. He started pointing over my head. 'Gawddammit,' he cried. 'Them niggahs got guns. Them goddamn niggahs got guns.' The old cracker started jumping up and down, pointing and weeping and shaking with rage. 'Gawddamn,' he wailed. 'Them niggahs got guns.' "]

Suddenly there was movement in the back of the crowd. Car horns blared and the crowd surged and parted. A small squadron of taxis led by a car filled with black men came into the square. The men in the lead car jumped out carrying rifles. Facing the crowd, they called the picketers into the cabs.

"Yes, they did," Mahoney said, "and I'm convinced that's the only thing that saved us."

At first glance, Robert Williams, an obscure local NAACP leader from small-town North Carolina, might seem an unlikely candidate for a symbolic, revolutionary leader to a host of radical groups in the late sixties. Equally unlikely was his elevation to the pantheon of heroes of the resolutely nonviolent student movement that we were in 1961. Unlikely, that is, if you believed the national media, in whose account Williams was an unstable personality, a dangerous radical, an advocate of armed racial violence, and a hunted criminal whom the NAACP had been forced to expel for "political irresponsibility."

But in this, Williams was different only in degree from a lot of people I've since worked with in our struggle and greatly respect. I've noticed that the corporate media aren't really dependable in their depiction of our black leaders who refuse to compromise our people's rights, or of the truth of our condition, or of those who dare to step outside the narrow boundaries of acceptable struggle that this system tries to impose.

With few exceptions, most of the figures I truly honor have been, and usually at the highest point of resistance in their lives, demonized by the press and hounded by the government. However, once safely in their graves, they might rate an honorific postage stamp (Malcolm X, Dr. Du Bois) or even a national holiday, as with Dr. King (peace be unto their names). Or, being older and physically impaired, like the great Muhammad Ali, their images might be recycled into those of secular saints or national treasures. Conveniently forgetting of course that when, at unbelievable personal sacrifice, Ali made his principled stand against a stupid, vicious war, he was the most vilified and hated black man in white America. So Robert Williams is in excellent company. Even so, I wouldn't bet on his getting a postage stamp anytime soon.

But consider this. Roll of honor or list of public enemies? In the previous generation, my father's great hero, the Honorable Marcus Garvey, and Paul Robeson, as well as Dr. W. E. B. Du Bois, all at some point were demonized, jailed, or hounded into exile. And of people I've known, worked with, respected, and learned from—Julius Hobson, Cecil Moore, Malcolm X, Gloria Richardson, Assata Shakur, Robert Williams, Muhammad Ali, Jamil al-Amin (H. Rap Brown), and even Dr. King himself—*all* at some point, whenever they were seen to cross that media-imposed line of "responsible" black protest, were subject to vicious character assassination by the press.

We had first encountered Williams's name in my freshman year, early in the Kennedy administration, in a way that could not help but get our attention. It was during the U.N. debate on the Bay of Pigs debacle.* Engaged in a desperate exercise in diplomatic damage control, U.S. ambassador Adlai Stevenson piously announced he deplored "the betrayal of the Cuban revolution," and he reserved his government's right and affirmed its will to send assistance—military when necessary—to any people struggling anywhere for human rights and democratic freedoms. So there!

At the end of which, the Cuban representative, Ambassador Raul Roa, rose to read a letter he'd just received. Apparently, he'd been asked by the representative of another people struggling against oppression to convey an appeal for just such American military assistance. To wit:

Mr. Ambassador:
Please convey the following appeal to Mr. Adlai Stevenson: Now that the United States has proclaimed military support for people willing to rebel against oppression, oppressed Negroes in the [American] South urgently request tanks, artillery, bombs, money, and the use of American airfields and white mercenaries to crush the racist tyrants who have betrayed the American Revolution and the Civil War.
We request the world's prayers for this noble undertaking.
Robert Williams, President, NAACP
Union County, Monroe, North Carolina

I'm told the delegates and the spectators in the gallery erupted. I know we at Howard howled. Reportedly Ambassador Stevenson and the U.S.

---

*The spectacularly unsuccessful U.S.-sponsored invasion of revolutionary Cuba, a sovereign nation.

delegation were conspicuously not amused. We had no way of knowing Roy Wilkins's reaction, but it was a sure bet that the very conservative head of the NAACP didn't find it funny. But after that we in NAG became curious about this brother. Later, what Bill and Paul had to report about their experience in the Monroe struggle turned us into strong Robert Williams supporters. For us he became a kind of counterexample to unvarying nonviolence. Turns out Williams'd been fighting racism across the board for a real long time—dating to the time of the Montgomery bus boycott—but with a somewhat different approach. He had tried all avenues—voting, negotiation, lawsuits, demonstrations—and finally insisted on the most fundamental of all human rights: the right to self-defense.

That U.N. letter impressed us with Williams's audacity. His willingness to cross boundaries, to step out of "his place" to confront and embarrass the government with its contradictions and hypocrisy before international forums. Bayard Rustin—speaking I'm sure from experience—used to say, "One thing they do not forgive: under no circumstances shall any Negro dare criticize America from a foreign country." Paul Robeson had found that out at great cost. As would Jimmy Baldwin and Malcolm later.

The more we found out about Robert Williams's struggle, the more there was to admire. You know what stood out about him? His outrageous and extreme self-respect. He wanted nothing more and refused anything less than full human respect for his people: the full, equal rights of all free human beings. That was it. Which, of course, in that time and place made him "crazy." The Monroe story is important for this generation to know and understand clearly because it was a great lesson to us.

Not long after Williams had begun to organize the Monroe community to assert their rights *[circa 1958]*, the state struck back. They announced a vindictive, federally funded urban renewal program clearly designed to dismember the black community. As Williams tells it:

"They came through the community where we lived. The stable section, where 90 percent of blacks owned their homes, some valued at over $35,000. 'Course this was where the leadership was, the militants, the voters, the guns . . . the resistance. Those sections where the housing was poor, where black homes didn't even have indoor toilets, they completely bypassed. No urban renewal there. Naturally we protested, but they were having none of that. And there were federal funds involved too. We decided to file suit.

"Then the president visited India. There he made a huge pronouncement. He and the United States wanted all the people of Asia to have decent housing and adequate food. We saw the opportunity. We sent a telegram to Prime Minister Nehru. We described the threat to black people's houses in Monroe and asked Prime Minister Nehru to convey the message to President Eisenhower. We signed it from the NAACP. Apparently the Indian leader delivered the message effectively with spectacular results.

"We expected Eisenhower to denounce the telegram as a fraud. Or that he would jump all over us when he got back. But instead, a strange thing happened. When he came back, he asked this African-American, Dr. Snowden, who worked in Housing, to contact us and assure us that he was every bit as interested in our houses as he was in houses for the people of Asia. That we could rest assured that there would be no urban renewal in Monroe until the law was fully complied with. . . .

"That stopped the program dead in its tracks. It just bogged down . . . finished. Of course the local officials never forgave me for that. We were always embarrassing them."*

That's what I mean by his audacity and his instinct for the contradictions within the establishment.

But Williams's work and reputation had really begun a few years earlier. A marine veteran of the Korean War, Williams came out of the service with a mission. He returned home to Monroe and immediately began to resurrect the local NAACP chapter, persuading his fellow veterans and ordinary country folk to join. By all accounts, it was not a typical chapter. It consisted of a "rougher element": domestic workers, tenant farmers, sharecroppers, and of course Williams's brother veterans. Its militancy was a constant thorn in the side of the state NAACP leadership.

The next year, Dr. Albert Perry, a prosperous, young black physician, was elected president of Monroe's new interracial Council on Human Relations. Composed of "representatives of both races and all faiths," this new organization was created by various local churches to promote public awareness and understanding of problems affecting good feelings between the races in Union County. The two presidents, the tough ex-marine and the idealistic young physician—black men both—would find themselves at considerable risk and, working together, pushed to the limits.

Dr. Perry's ordeal began in the summer of '57 after a black teenager drowned while swimming in a farm pond. The African community was upset at the absence of safe facilities for its youth. Dr. Perry and Robert Williams represented the community's concern to the city council and the recreation commission. The white officials were sympathetic. Indeed, a swimming pool for blacks was envisioned, but for some time in the future "when funds became available," they chuckled.

Fine. But, until then, could not black kids have some access to the town pool? Perhaps, on the basis of, say, one, maybe two days each week?

*_Black Scholar_ interview, May 1970.

Sorry. That wouldn't be feasible.

Why not even one day a week?

Afraid that wouldn't be possible. You know . . . the expense.

Expense?

Well, you can see, can't you now, that this would mean draining and cleaning the pool each time? Surely you understand that?

The two blacks left. Next day Williams escorted a group of kids to the pool only to be refused entry. On the basis of which the NAACP filed suit. According to the local media, this was a hostile act that could conceivably result in the closing of the pool, thus depriving white children of a safe place to swim.

That's when the Klan became really active. It began to have regular meetings, at which Dr. Perry was, for some reason, the main focus of their venom. The day after the first big Klan meeting, a phone caller informed Mrs. Perry that her husband had been sentenced to death. After which, death threats became a nightly occurrence in the Perry household.

The Perrys reported each threat to the police, who simply dismissed the reports, often with overt hostility. The Perrys decided they would not be run off. The men of the community volunteered to protect their doctor and his wife. Each night, a "shift of some fifty fellas" would stand armed watch around the Perrys' home. The next night another fifty would take over. Armed men escorted Dr. Perry to his office and home again. "I was very well protected. I was never by myself for one moment."

The threats continued as the Klan upped the ante. They took to ending their meetings with a show of force: a caravan of cars, shining their lights, blaring their horns, firing guns, and shouting insults while parading through the black community. Often the parade was led by a police cruiser, and always it drove by the Perry home a few times. Dr. Perry recalls that the car interior lights were kept on so that the robed and hooded Klansmen were clearly visible. In some of the cars, women and children could be seen. The siege of the Perrys lasted from August to October 1957.

After a Klan meeting broke up the night of October 8, a particularly large and noisy motorcade, preceded by a police cruiser, entered the black community for the last time. As the lead car passed the Perry home, the night erupted with sudden and sustained rapid fire from over fifty guns, most of which seem to have been those short, loud, efficient M3 carbines of Korean War vintage. And the shooting was not coming from the Klansmen. In an unpublished eyewitness account by novelist Julian Mayfield, "The fire was blistering, disciplined, and frightening. The motorcade of about eighty cars . . . disintegrated into chaos with panicky robed men fleeing in all directions. Some abandoned their cars to flee on foot. One carload turned into a dead-end street where they were cut off by Robert Williams and a detachment of armed men."

The terrified driver begged "Mr. Williams" to please let them go. They just didn't know what they were doing and promised never to come back into the black community again. Yes, sir, they fully understood how close they had come to being killed.

In the end, no deaths were reported, only because Williams's troops had been instructed not to kill anyone unless absolutely unavoidable. This time, we fire "high or low." Whether the terrified Klansman who had begged for his life would have honored his promise never to return cannot really be known. The Klan suddenly became scrupulously law-abiding after the city council belatedly passed an ordinance prohibiting late-night motorcades. Henceforth, travel within city limits after nightfall, in groups of more than three cars, would require a permit. The invasions of our communities ceased.

Having failed to take Dr. Perry's life or run him off, the racists next went after his reputation and livelihood, accusing him of performing an illegal abortion on a white woman. They succeeded in framing, convicting, and jailing the young doctor and taking away his license for a time. What was particularly disgraceful was that the entire community—black and white—and particularly his medical colleagues, knew that, as a devout Catholic, Dr. Perry had always refused to perform any abortions or sterilizations, even when they were legal. (Under state law, these procedures were permissible under certain conditions.)

Yet we are to believe that this very religious man had suddenly decided to perform his first abortion, not a legal one but a criminal one, upon a *white* woman reportedly of dubious reputation? That he undertook to violate a lifetime of religious principle, civil law, *and* Southern racial taboo in the climate of hatred, death threats, and harassment that was surrounding him? Give . . . me . . . uh . . . bureak. Please.

After his conviction by what would almost certainly have been a lily-white jury (which in that climate would have included some Klansmen or Klan sympathizers), Dr. Perry fought for his reputation, career, and freedom for two years, all the way to the U.S. Supreme Court

Apart from whatever contributions the loyal and generous local folk were able to offer, Dr. Perry was left to bear the considerable expense of his legal defense by himself. He discovered that the impeccably circumspect NAACP did not "as a matter of policy" take "sex cases." (A curious policy. It explains, among other things, why the Communist Party had been left to carry the fight to save the nine "Scottsboro boys" from legal lynching in Alabama. Or why, in too many cases, brothers were left without defense before the accusations of white women desperately try-

231

ing to salvage reputations and status, or before the hysterical fantasies and neuroses of culturally repressed Southern belles. Or why, when a black man like Dr. Perry refused to be intimidated or run off, the system's last dependable resort was the sex, race, and white womanhood card.)

After the dismissal of his last appeal, the woman whose testimony had convicted him recanted to Dr. Perry. She was going crazy she said. It was on her conscience . . . promises and threats had been made. But she was now willing to testify truthfully. But it was too little too late. The doctor was off to jail.

After his parole (July 1960), Dr. Perry's professional difficulties continued. But the brother was neither beaten nor broken. Listen to how this decent, supremely wronged man evaluated his experience. In 1961, he told Jim Forman:

"Anything I've said about the rights of man I believed then and I believe now. I have not changed . . . I've been a doctor. I've practiced medicine in this county for nine years. I've now been without my license for two years. I've been a convict in a state penitentiary. I've been an exile from home. And it hasn't changed me. . . . The community's made me feel good . . . most people think of what I did as a sacrifice. . . . Well, I think we all should sacrifice something, all of us. . . .

I think most people, black and white, know it was a frame-up. . . . Surely, I think I must do my part. I don't think I'll ever get through doing my part."

I never had the honor of meeting Dr. Albert Perry, but I cherish the utmost respect and admiration for the brother's spirit. But still, nobody has ever been made to pay for what was done to him so long ago. Even now, someone should still be made to pay.

While the railroading of Dr. Perry was still going on, a series of unrelated racial incidents brought Robert Williams his first notoriety in the national media and his (first) suspension by the NAACP leadership.

First came the infamous—or world-famous—"kissing case." Boy, talk about showing your worst face to the world. At the time I was a junior in high school. I well remember the surge of absolute outrage that swept the black community when this story broke. It was every bit as intense as the response to the acquittal of Emmett Till's murderers in Mississippi had been a few years earlier. Here's what went down.

One evening in October 1958 in Monroe, a young girl [seven years old] mentioned to her parents that in the course of playing "house" she had either kissed or been kissed by one of her little playmates. I have no idea what this child could have thought as she watched her father storm out of the house, shotgun in hand, in search of the alleged kisser. Or when she saw him joined in this undertaking by a posse of similarly armed neighbors. Or at hearing her mother declare to the press that she would have killed the boy herself had she the chance. Providentially, before any of these wrathful vigilantes found him, the kisser *[David "Fuzzy" Simpson, aged seven]* and his accomplice *[James Hanover Thompson, aged nine]* were arrested by the Monroe police. These perpetrators would spend the next six months in juvenile jail.

Upon their arrest, the boys' mothers—both of them domestic workers—appealed to Robert Williams for assistance. He notified the NAACP and asked them to intercede on the boys' behalf. However, a week later, when they were tried, convicted, and remanded to reform school, the boys had no legal representation present. The sentencing judge *[one J. Hampton Price, Juvenile court judge]* kindly reassured the mothers that with good behavior the boys might be released before their twenty-first birthdays.

Later, once the story broke nationally and after Robert Williams had traveled to New York to further publicize the outrage, the NAACP retained Attorney Conrad Lynn to represent the boys. They had by now been in juvenile jail nearly three months, during which time their mothers had not been permitted to see them.

Then the incident became an international embarrassment after the story ran in the European press. International committees were formed. Prominent foreigners uttered denouncements. Petitions from thousands of indignant Europeans reached the White House. The North Carolina attorney general is reported to have publicly complained that he might be forced to release the boys because of the "propaganda." Whatever the reason, after they had spent some six months in jail, the state quietly released the two boys (pint-size sexual predators?). Neither explanation nor apology was given. Again, Bro Williams had taken the country to the court of international opinion. Also an important precedent had been set: the NAACP, however belatedly, had taken its first "sex" case.

The next year (1959) came three incidents in rapid succession, which broke the proverbial camel's back. A black woman working in a hotel was kicked down a flight of stairs by a guest. In a new spirit of militancy, the sister pressed charges. Shortly thereafter a mentally impaired black man *[James Mobley]* was arrested for the attempted rape of a white woman. Mobley was brain damaged after being injured in a workplace accident.

Next, a white man *[Louis Medlin]* was arrested and charged similarly: with attempted rape. Except that this victim was black. That the white man was even arrested is in itself interesting. That the woman was six months pregnant might have had something to do with it. The man had entered her house and attacked her in the presence of her son. He then pursued her into the yard, where the attack was witnessed by a white neighbor, willing to testify. Perhaps not least, though, the anger in the black community was so intense that Williams had been hard-pressed to prevail on his men not to go after the alleged attacker in force. Whatever the reasons, charges were preferred.

"Since he's been charged," Williams is reported to have argued to his troops, "we must at least give the courts a chance."

However, all three trials concluded within days of each other with predictable results. The hotel guest who had kicked the black woman down the stairs walked. The brain-damaged black man, convicted and jailed. Within hours that same afternoon, the white man *[Medlin]* was cleared of all charges.

Having counseled his followers to give the system the benefit of the doubt, perhaps Williams felt particularly ill-used, even betrayed. In context, his statement from the steps of the court seemed—to me and my friends in the movement—both logical and perfectly justified. Not at all unreasonable. He said, in part:

"If we cannot take those who do us injustice before the court, it becomes necessary to punish them ourselves. . . . We cannot rely on the law. We can get no justice under the present system. . . . Since the federal government will not halt lynching in the South, and since the so-called courts lynch our people legally, if it becomes necessary to stop lynching with lynching, then we must be willing to resort to that measure. We must meet violence with violence."

The media coverage, predictably, was sensational and essentially devoid of context. Myself, I had no problem with Bro Williams's position then and I have no problem with it now. We come from a long line of patient people, but inevitably there comes a point . . . Among my peers in the movement, as for a great many in the African nation, Brother Williams had simply been stating forthrightly what we all were feeling. We may not have adopted his position on self-defense then, but within the ranks of the young movement was a great deal of sympathy for it. Not so, however, from the NAACP leadership, which promptly engineered Williams's suspension. I believe they would have expelled him if the rank and file would have gone along. Anyway, once the suspension was up, his people immediately reelected him.

By the time I met up with Paul Dietrich and Bill Mahoney that fall (1961), Robert Williams had become a hunted fugitive and taken political asylum in Cuba. The triggering event had happened while they were in Monroe, at the very moment they were being rescued from the mob at the courthouse by Williams' men.

News of the mob had spread through the city and surrounding black communities. And as is usually the case, the news was well attended by rumor: a Freedom Rider had been killed. The demonstrators had been mauled. Injuries and deaths had occurred. An angry crowd of black men, many armed, had gathered around the Williams home. He had just about succeeded in calming and dispersing the crowd when a car driven by a white couple blundered onto the scene. In his version, he took the frightened couple into his house for their own safety because the crowd was angry and volatile. After about an hour they drove away. The couple later claimed they had been detained at gunpoint. The government charged that Williams had held them "as hostages." There's no question that guns were present at the scene, but Williams insists they were never menaced or coerced, and that once the crowd dispersed, the couple had left of their own free will.

Howsomever, Williams, his wife, and Mae Mallory, a sister from New York, became fugitives. Bro Williams would spend ten years in exile in Cuba, then China and Tanzania, before returning to America in 1970. All of which served to invest his name with the patina of legend.

So there I was in the summer of 1961 with the generals in Nashville in the middle of the debate over the future of the movement. Trying to think through the next stage of our struggle amidst everything that was happening. But of course it wasn't all theoretical debate. We were, after all, activists, so we just had to have an action project. The Nashville leadership obligingly came up with one. At a large supermarket on the edge of the African community, the shoppers were almost completely African, but none of our people were employed there. Reportedly, the staff didn't always show respect or courtesy to the shoppers. So this store was a natural target. As soon as the sessions ended in the afternoon, we'd throw up one of those Don't Shop Where You Can't Work picket lines.

A few of the NAG brothers were on the line—Dion Diamond, John Moody, Reggie Robinson, and I'm not sure who all else from D.C. may have come by. But, apparently, our attitude and presence were noticeably different from those of the Nashville core group. Though nonviolent, we weren't *exactly* passive in the way we carried ourselves, especially the sharp-tongued Dion. Other young people and adults from the community were beginning to come out on the line, and they, unlike the leadership, hadn't had the rigorous training in Gandhian philosophy the Reverend Lawson had been offering for almost two years.

Crowds of white hecklers began to gather every evening. When these whites would shout threats and racist insults, the new folks would tend to stare them down or even answer in kind. But technically we were maintaining nonviolence on the line.

Dion and I spent a lot of time together. We were staying in a little African-owned hotel close to the Fisk campus. Between the hotel and the campus was a small movie theater, also African-owned. We passed it every evening. The sister taking the tickets was strikingly beautiful. A young sister, our age or younger, she was sooo fine. A radiant, warm smile, velvety black skin, and a soft, deep voice with slow, musical Southern cadences. And there she was every evening when we passed.

We noticed her. She noticed us. Dion and I eventually got to know her. We'd tease her just to see her smile and hear the music of her laugh. Dion, being Dion, got competitive.

"Yo, man. The sister digs me, man. It's *me* she smiling at. Ain't that right, sister?"

"Oh, mah sister," I'd say, "have mercy. Don't hurt this fool. Leave him in ignorance. Let it be our little secret."

She'd smile and pretend to be embarrassed, unable to choose between "two such fine gen'lmen."

Then a group of brothers off the corner started to mutter. They it seems had eyes for the sister too. The usual American stupidity. Turf and territory. Attack any stranger coming into town rather than, as said in Africa, welcoming the stranger from another village. These youths got a little bolder every evening.

"Dion," I warned, "them boys getting ready to touch us."

"That's only 'cause they don't know us, man. Once we tell them who we are, they ain't gon' touch us. You'll see." He brushed it off.

So . . . one night I'm rapping serious to the sister, hoping to get a date, when the block boys came up and mumbled a bit rough. So I told them, look, I know you wondering where I came from. What I'm doing here an' like that. Well, I'm from New York. You know we ain't got none a' this segregation (expletive) in New York. Yet here I am fighting these crackers and the po-lice. An' y'all who live here ain't doing squat. But it's *me* you wanna fight. Uh, uh, uh. Why me and not Mr. Charlie?"

That stopped them short.

"Y'all the ones down there at the store?"

"Yeah, we the ones down there."

"W'ell, you know, we be up for that. Excep' one thang, man. We don't go for none a' that nonviolence stuff. Y'know?"

Dion had come up and was listening.

"Hey, Stokely," he whispers, "let's organize these brothers." So the conversation begun. Finally we told them. Well, you don't *have* to practice nonviolence. We ain't goin' ask everybody to be nonviolent. *We* are nonviolent. That's our choice, but you ain't gotta be, so long as you find a way to struggle. That's all. Nonviolence is hard, it ain't for everybody. But the fight is everybody's. You don't have to do what we do. As long as you fight. We're not gonna tell you *how* to fight, as long as you do. Everybody's gotta be in the fight.

So the brothers began to talk and to organize themselves. When we saw them, they'd ask about the demonstrations and keep saying how they wanted to do something. We said, "You gotta do what you the spirit say do." After that, the vibes on that block changed. The young lady in the booth told me they'd even started to speak up for me. She said they told her, "He's a real down brother, girl. You need to check this brother out."

Anyway, a few days later—a Friday evening I think—we were picketing and the crowd was large, loud, and real hostile. Threats, insults, very loud. And a lot more police than usual. But the cops were just standing around "a-watching an' beholding" as Mrs. Fannie Lou Hamer would say. But doing squat while the crowd got louder and bolder. You could feel that something was fixin' to happen.

The ringleader was one big, *loud* ole boy who had everything evil to say. Each time I'd pass by I'd look dead into his eyes and just grin at him. A special nonviolent picket-line grin I'd developed for the Nazis in D.C. Then, I'm passing in front of the store window when I sense in my peripheral vision a shape bearing down fast. I start to move away while turning to see. Before I can turn, he charges into me and slams a forearm upside my head. I staggered, thrown back by the force. As I fell, my legs flew up like a scissors kick in soccer, and my boots shattered the plate-glass window. Boom. As I hit the ground, I rolled away as sheets of glass came crashing down where I'd been lying.

The whites started pointing at me and yelling, "He did it. He ain't nonviolent." The hoods rushed down on us followed by the cops, making arrests. Of course, you know who got arrested. Just as the police van was beginning to move, pandemonium broke out. There was an entirely new sound. I looked back and saw cops and white folk scurrying around, dodging bricks and bottles. The mob scattering in panic.

Turns out it was the young brothers from the corner. Apparently they'd found their own way to struggle. When the brothers saw us arrested and being thrown around by the cops, they came down throwing bricks and bottles and whatever else they'd stockpiled.

While we were being booked, John Lewis and some of the Nashville leadership went off on me about the window. Dion and others pointed out that I'd done nothing, merely nonviolently allowed the assailant to knock me down and into the glass. Somehow, Dion and I were designated "troublemakers" and put in the same cell. According to the cops, we were "leaders of the disturbance." How they arrived at that I didn't understand. Probably because of the window and Dion's irrepressible mouth. He simply would not be cowed. Dion's fearlessness would soon give me courage.

I've had a lot of experience in jails since this time. But this one? Whoa, it was unforgettable. This one was very, very strange.

We're in the cell, unable to get to sleep. About two o'clock in the morning we hear footsteps approaching. I turn over to see a young white cop staring at us. He's holding a pump-action shotgun, which he loads. As he does this, he's staring at us and cursing. Dion and I exchange glances. Now what?

"So you the two ____ ____ ____ little sons of bitches who started this, huh? Wal, tonight you some dead niggers. I'ma kill yore black ____ ____ ____."

He cocks the gun, cursing all the while. His eyes are bloodshot and staring as he moves the gun back and forth, first on me, then on Dion.

We are frozen. Dion in one corner of the cell, me in the other. The gun swings from one to the other. The cop is ranting and cussing. I'm stiff as a board trying to watch the guy's eyes, his trigger finger, and the yawning muzzle of the shotgun at the same time. I watch as it swings away and back over to Dion. Then I hear Dion's mouth. I cannot believe my ears.

"Come on, you cracker so-and-so, shoot. Pull the damn trigger. Ain't nobody scared of you. Shoot. I'm ready to die if you bad enough. Shoot, white man. Do it." Dion just goes off, and as I see from the corner of my eyes, *he's steadily advancing on the gun.* A veritable torrent of language flowing out of his mouth, defiant, challenging, nonstop language. Talk about putting me through changes. One minute I'm sure I'm dead, the next I'm absolutely certain that I've gone out of my mind. I can't believe Dion. I remember thinking, "F' God's sake, Dion, shut up. Please. This man's drunk. He's crazy. You fixing to get us killed, Dion."

The cop stares at Dion, begins to tremble, and swings the gun back over to my corner. What could I do? Having no choice, I start up too.

"Yeah, cracker, go ahead. Pull the ____ trigger. We ready to die. Are you? Pull the trigger."

The policeman really started to shake then. Which was, if anything, worse. Now two voices are coming at him. Silently he lowers the weapon, turns, and walks away. I sink down on my bunk, listening to the footsteps recede. I can't describe the range of emotions. Fear. Anger. Disbelief. Relief, then exultation, then anger again. At Dion. I will not repeat exactly what my first words to him were—in effect, Dion, you crazed so-and-so . . . that's my life you messing with. You understand that your crazy self damn near got us killed?

"Me," said Dion. "Me crazy? Negro, we alive, ain't we? Did he pull the trigger? Boy, you should be kissing my feet for saving yo' shiftless life. Best you never forget this, Negro. When in doubt, jes' follow me. Always follow the kid."

For some reason, I found myself laughing. "You de man, bro, I'ma follow you. I'ma follow you."

Crazy-assed Dion Diamond.

•   •   •

As we got out of jail, there was a big meeting at which the Reverend James Lawson presided. A mass meeting of just movement people, in his church in Nashville. It seems that just about everyone was there. The point of this heavy, heavy meeting, as we soon discovered, was to try Dion and me for causing the violence at the demonstration. Both of us, but especially me, even though Dion had had a bigger mouth in organizing the brothers off the block.

It was all very solemn. A real tribunal. John Lewis was the most outspoken, but the entire Nashville leadership was quite vocal. They were just calling me out by name. Very stern lectures. There was even talk of expelling me from the nonviolent movement. *That* got my attention. Hey, now, this be serious, Jack.

I sat quietly, trying my best to look calm. But my mind was racing, organizing my defense. Actually *expelled* from our people's struggle? I was worried. I mean really nervous. I said nothing, trying my best not to show how utterly wretched I felt. So miserable in fact that it never even occurred to me to question whether this group even had the right to expel me. I thought that if these guys who I respected so much, this splendid new family, were to decide they wouldn't have me, then what could I say? I knew I'd continue to struggle, but with whom? I never stopped to think that NAG was probably too ornery to let anyone else expel one of us. They'd probably take me back.

So I had a bad couple of hours. Twenty years old and expelled from the first movement I'd found that really touched my soul? I prepared my defense and waited.

But slowly, oh so slowly, the tone of the meeting began to swing when SNCC people from the other cities and the younger people began to speak up.

"Listen, yo," they began to say, "we really don't have the right to tell the whole community how they must fight."

"Yeah. We can use nonviolence as our means, but that's only us. If other folks want to use other means, should we, can we stop them? That's elitist."

"Maybe, but on our demonstrations we can."

Wow. My hopes began to revive as different voices began to be heard. I could feel the kangaroo court atmosphere gradually lightening.

Then ol' Freddie Leonard jumped to his feet.

"Hey. The fact is a lot of us agree with Stokely. In fact, we *wanted* to throw some bricks and bottles too. We getting real tired of our mamas being insulted and our heads being whupped. Tha's right." There was a chorus of *Ahmen*s and *Ride on*s.

Finally, the Reverend Mr. Lawson adjourned the meeting. I think that when he and John Lewis saw that the sentiment of the meeting had changed and seemed about to challenge the principles of total nonviolence, they forgot about condemning me. They just adjourned the meeting and forgot about it. If memory serves, that was about the end of it.

But I learned a lot. Naturally, I was most relieved. And I want to make something clear, I had no resentment toward either the Reverend Mr. Lawson or John. I mean, you simply had to respect their courage and their principles, even if you didn't embrace them all quite so absolutely. And the incident taught a valuable lesson that I've always made a point to observe. When you're involved in action with another group on their turf, you have to be absolutely sensitive to their political discipline and values. You've got to. Got to. Unless prepared to do that, don't become involved. Absolutely. I've been guided by this principle ever since.

While we were in Nashville that August, something happened in Atlanta. A small thing, quite unremarkable. A serious, quiet-spoken, serious, Harvard-educated young teacher from New York got on a bus for Cleveland, Mississippi. Robert Parris Moses was accepting an invitation from a remarkable man named Amzie Moore to come into Mississippi to work on voter registration. The only defense Bob carried with him was a direct number to the civil rights Division of the Justice Department. In undertaking this little trip Bob was going against the conventional wisdom of the older civil rights groups. Mississippi was, they felt, a closed society that had either murdered, intimidated, or run off every black who had ever tried to organize resistance there. They told Bob that it was far too dangerous and primitive a place to send organizers into. Not with any hope of survival, much less success.

Bob is reputed to have said (something I can well believe), "But that is only a hypothesis, untested. Someone has to test it. That's the scientific method." So he went in alone. Bob not only tested the hypothesis and survived. He succeeded in building one of the most dramatic grassroots, populist organizations in recent American political history.

When the Nashville seminar broke up, Reggie Robinson and Chuck McDew would go to join Bob. I was quite torn, but promises to my family prevailed. I headed north for my sophomore year at Howard.

CHAPTER XI

To School or Not to School

Much was pulling me back to Howard that fall. When I got back from Nashville, I'd again reassured my father that, whatever happened in the movement, I'd first finish school. Besides, I relished the atmosphere of intellectual ferment on campus. True, I was still wrestling with the career question: medicine or something else, politics? But I enjoyed some of my courses, respected many of my professors, and really enjoyed the Caribbean and African friends I was making. Most of all I really looked forward to hooking up with the NAG circle and catching up with movement news. Now a sophomore and a movement "veteran" I was a very different person from the entering freshman of a year ago. I'd "been down into the South," done hard time in jail, and had stories of my own to tell. Besides, and very important, there was that self-possessed young lady from Tougaloo who had seemed to stay on my mind all summer . . . So there was a lot to engage me at Howard. And yet . . .

During that first semester my attention was seriously divided. Bob Moses, whom I was yet to meet, was in Mississippi in a place called Amite County. Two D.C. friends—Reggie Robinson (from Baltimore) and Travis Britt (who had led us onto the New Orleans train)—had gone to struggle with him there. Also Dion had stayed south to work for SNCC and Hank (Thomas) was taking the year off for CORE. The front lines of our struggle were in the Deep South. I'd had my first real taste of it and definitely wanted more. But I had promises to keep. So I was back in school, but for how long?

Mary Felice Lovelace seemed as happy to see me again as I was to see her and felt no need to hide it. I always liked that about Mary, she was very direct. Even though she'd stayed on my mind all summer, I found her even more attractive than I'd remembered. Hey, I did find her prettier than I'd remembered, but that isn't what I mean. I'm talking about her manner. She was smart, with a quietness and reserve that could be mistaken for shyness but really was confidence. She was funny and warm and affectionate. But also serious, fiercely loyal, and on matters of principle, very single-minded. In fact she could be quite stubborn. And she was black and proud of her people.

That fall Mary had a studio course all afternoon on, I believe, Wednesdays. I was free then and ended up spending every Wednesday afternoon holding her paints and handing her brushes and keeping her company while she painted. That way, we got to know each other and soon became inseparable. We were each other's first love, and all during my college years, she was my only love. We remained close until the movement drove us apart and she married John O'Neal. John, also in the arts, was creative director of the Free Southern Theater (a cultural outreach of SNCC) and a funny, really decent brother whom I've always respected.

[Ivanhoe Donaldson, SNCC field secretary:

"I remember Mary and John's wedding. Man, I was never in my life so relieved as when that preacher pronounced them man and wife. A lot of SNCC folk were there and you could feel the nervous tension in that church. My heart stayed in my mouth the entire time. I was absolutely sure that Carmichael and his guys were gonna stage a raid. That any minute he'd come storming up the aisle to snatch Mary. I was so nervous I was almost shaking." (This may be the only time that Ivanhoe has gone on the record as being scared. —EMT)*]*

Mary's presence was a strong incentive to my staying in school. But even so, it was far from a done deal. That first month I kept wavering with every new report from Amite County.

The first thing I heard was that Bob Moses had had his head busted in the street. When I heard the details of that, my respect for Bob increased. Later we would come to understand that his response to the attack was typical of him.

It had taken him about three weeks to identify five or six brave souls in the community willing to come to a voter registration class. On his way to the meeting he was attacked and his forehead was split open by a blackjack. Bob got up, went home, washed his face, dressed the wound, put on a clean white shirt, then hurried to the meeting. After which he went to the police and proffered criminal charges against his attacker (the sheriff's son-in-law). Of course the cops couldn't believe that a nigger, even a crazy Northern one, would actually bring charges against a white man.

[Bob later explained:

"I know that the people already had excellent reason to be nervous. So if I appeared at the first meeting covered in blood with my head gaping open, that would have been the end of voter registration in that community. I pressed the charges simply to establish that we had that right. And to show that I wasn't going to be intimidated either by the attack or the law."]

When I heard that, I knew that sooner or later I was going to stand alongside this brother in struggle. With each new report, it kept building.

The next news was that Travis, after taking a group to attempt to register, had been beaten unconscious on the courthouse steps in a town called Liberty. My suitcase got packed and unpacked one more time.

Then, a week later, when the next group went, the SNCC worker—John Hardy—was knocked unconscious, pistol-whipped by the registrar while his back was turned. That same week some people fishing in the Big Black River pulled out a sack weighted with stones. Inside the sack was the decomposing corpse of what had once been a black man.

All of this within the first month of Bob's arrival in Amite County. The fate of SNCC's first Mississippi project was clearly hanging in the balance. So why were we in school? Shouldn't we all be heading south to reinforce Bob's hard-pressed troops?

Then, very shortly, the terrorists changed tactics and upped the ante. If you notice, except for the corpse in the river, all the violence had been directed toward the organizers, the "outside agitators." But seeing that SNCC was not intimidated or likely to be driven out, the Klan decided to send a brutal message to the local folk. Mr. Herbert Lee, a respected farmer with whose family Bob had been staying, was murdered in broad daylight and in the presence of witnesses. A member of the NAACP, Mr. Lee was a leader, along with E. W. Steptoe, of the voting drive in Amite County.

It was September, cotton-picking time. Mr. Lee had taken a load of his cotton to be ginned. He was sitting in his truck in a long line of neighborhood farmers, black and white. The killer—E. H. Hurst—a childhood playmate of Mr. Lee's and his next door neighbor, was a state representative and a known Klansman. Hurst got out of his truck, pistol in hand, walked up to Mr. Lee, and after a few words, shot him in the head. The body lay for hours in the dust where it had fallen. That same day a coroner's jury brought back a finding: justifiable homicide. Some black farmers who had been present were coerced to testify that Mr. Lee had threatened Hurst with a tire iron.

There it was, the one thing that Bob had feared the most had become a reality. This was a crucial moment for him and for SNCC. A soul-searching time, a morally and spiritually harrowing time. Bob was willing to risk his own life, but was he prepared to risk the lives of the people he was organizing? "If I hadn't come, those children would have a father tonight," he said. What was our moral responsibility in such situations? It was an issue we in SNCC would have to confront time and again, wrestle with and ultimately resolve.

And where was the federal protection—"voting is a federally protected right"—the government had assured us? A short time later Bob got an unequivocal answer to that question. Here is how it happened.

Louis Allen was a neighboring farmer, a quiet Christian man, not much involved in the movement. "Ah called mahself keeping out of that mess," he said. He had been at the gin that day, sitting in his truck behind Mr. Lee's. He'd seen the murder. The police had ordered him to say that Mr. Lee had brandished a tire iron. It was a lie, but he had been in fear for his life. But, he said, he was a Christian man and his conscience gave him no peace. It was a sin to tell a lie on the dead. He knew Mr. Lee for a decent and brave man. He respected him. So he was sick at heart for his "false witness." "It was a sin and a shame to slander the dead," Mr. Allen said, "so let the fur fly with the hide. I'm gon tell the truth."

But to whom? Certainly not the local police. So whom? Bob accompanied Mr. Allen to the FBI office in Memphis. They held out no false hopes. If it came to a hearing in Mississippi, they said, they could not protect any witness. Besides, what was the use? No Mississippi jury was going to convict a white politician anyway. Best Mr. Allen keep his mouth shut and learn to live with his conscience.

Which might have been honest. Except that by the time Mr. Allen got home, there were threatening messages: "Nigger, you a dead man. We know where you been." So much for federal protection. Maybe (and I don't for a minute accept that) the feds couldn't protect this honest citizen, but did they have to rat him out? After he was badly beaten by a sheriff's deputy, Mr. Allen abandoned his property and fled the state. A few years later *[January 1964]*, he quietly ventured back to complete the sale of his house. He never made it out again. Like his friend Herbert Lee before him, his body was found lying shot to death, in the dust of his front yard. Another early lesson for SNCC. Another moral burden for Bob.

All this during my first semester back. It was not at all clear that I was going to be able to resist the pull of that violent, primitive place. At home over the Christmas break we had another long family discussion. I again agreed to stay the course in school. Which I would do. But, at the end of each academic year, the moment my last exam was turned in, I would be on my way to Mississippi.

We would all receive another important early lesson from a really sweet young brother in the incoming crop of freshmen. A lesson in political survival, the viciousness of my hometown police, and the callousness of the courts.

The young brother's name was Khalid Sayeed. A Moslem out of Harlem (I think Nation of Islam), Khalid would be NAG's first political casualty. When he first started showing up to meetings, this brother really stood out. First of all he looked all of fifteen years old. Then too he always wore a suit and large horn-rimmed glasses like Malcolm's. A quiet, thoughtful brother, he also stood out in NAG because he was so unvaryingly polite and serious, almost formal in his manner.

At first, Khalid'd just show up at meetings, saying little but listening and watching every discussion carefully. If a book or essay was mentioned, Khalid would have it read by next meeting. He took in everything, *evrah thang*. I can still see his serious, expressive eyes behind those glasses turning to each succeeding speaker like someone at a tennis match. I began to sort of look out for the brother, partly because he looked so young, was so serious, and also because he was my homeboy from Harlem.

In fact all we veterans kinda adopted him as a younger brother. From his name and deportment we figured he was from a Muslim family and was at our meetings trying to sort out the different ways one could be a black man in this country. Because, naturally, NAG's confrontational integrationist posture would have been at considerable odds with the Nation's ideology. Whatever the case, Khalid had been a constant, quiet presence at all meetings and volunteered for any mundane task that came up.

Pretty soon he was at all our demonstrations. I recall his being badly gassed with us in Cambridge, Maryland, later on.

Then, at one of our early meetings one year, I think it was the semester after the March on Washington and the Cambridge campaign, someone missed him.

"Hey, someone's missing . . . Where's Khalid?" No one could remember seeing him.

"Dig, man, the brother is Muslim. Could be he's had second thoughts about the movement."

"Maybe he isn't in school. Folks do flunk out, y'know."

"Hey, not Khalid. That brother was seriously booking."

"Well, we gotta check it out."

At the next meeting, someone, I think Courtland Cox, reported, "Khalid's not in school. The brother is in jail. Yeah, that's right, the slammer. Remember those idiots, call themselves militants, who got themselves busted, talking about blowing up the [expletive] Statue of Liberty?"

The meeting seemed in shock. There were groans, shouts, and anguished expressions. Say what? Oh, *hell*. No. Not that sweet little brother, oh, man. But a newspaper clipping outlined this so-called plot. Sure enough, among the arrested was "Khalid Sayeed, student, 18."

People were angry and grieved. At first,. our anger was directed mostly against whoever had involved the young brother in this harebrained nonsense. "Man, the [expletive] Statue of Liberty? What the [expletive] was the point of that?"

When the trial opened, that anger only increased, though it changed direction significantly. We were able to follow it because it received prominent, sensationalist front-page coverage in the *Washington Post* and the *New York Times*. The chief prosecution witness turned out to be the one in the group with the most "militant" rap. Under cross-examination the witness admitted to having supplied the idea, some guns, and the explosives. On the stand at the beginning of his testimony, this Negro identified himself by his "slave name" and occupation: he was a New York City police detective.

The naked entrapment was, even in the *New York Times* report, blatantly obvious. Yet all the accused were convicted and given long sentences, clearly we thought, to "send a message to young black militants." The detective/provocateur was warmly commended by the judge.

I don't know what ultimately happened to our young comrade. (Courtland says he thinks he remembers that there was a successful appeal of some kind. I sure hope so.) Nor do I know what happened to that contemptible, conscienceless excuse for a black man, the cop provocateur. But I do know what should have happened to that traitor, were there any justice at all. I think I know the message they intended the case to send to young Africans. It was, however, not the message we took. Just the opposite, in fact. Simply recounting this travesty I can again feel the outrage, the murderous rage that settled on us as that trial unfolded. With us, all they succeeded in doing was creating some embittered black youth. I have never forgotten what it taught me about excessively vocal militancy and police agents in our organization.

At the end of that first semester there was a meeting—in Atlanta, I think—and some folk from NAG went. But our family always spent that holiday together so I went home, despite the thoughts of Mississippi swirling in my head.

When I returned to school after the Christmas break, I don't think I had even finished unpacking my mother's ironing when Pride, an African down the hall, called me to the phone. I was hoping it was Mary Felice, but Pride said, "No, my brother, I think it's your mother." Which seemed unlikely since I had only just got back. "I guess I must have forgotten something at home," I thought. It was a Sunday evening, January 21, 1962.

I could hear and feel the upset in May Charles's voice. Finally I heard what she was telling me. My father had died that afternoon.

I could not believe my ears. Adolphus Carmichael was barely forty years old, a wiry, industrious man full of energy and life. His death took everyone completely by surprise. I maintain that he was worn down and driven to an early grave by the pressures of racism and capitalism in this country. My father literally worked himself to death providing for us.

[Mabel Carmichael remembers:
"Stokely had just gone back from the Christmas break. When he came

back for the funeral, he never looked at the body. Never once. 'May Charles,' he said, 'I want to remember our father the way I left him last week.'

"*My husband died on a Sunday. He'd worked late that Saturday. Sunday morning he stayed in bed, which for him was unusual. Then he told me he really didn't feel like going to church that morning. Which was very unusual 'cause he was a lay preacher, a real pillar of that little church. He asked me to bring him a glass of water. When I came back, I began to laugh and tease him.*

"*His mother had been a very good-looking woman and sometimes he'd joke, 'Boy, if I only had my mother's nose, you'd be sorry. These women really wouldn't leave me alone then.' So when I brought him the water, he was lying there looking especially handsome to me. I said, 'You're always saying you wanted to look like Mumah. Well, right now you look just like her.' He smiled, took a sip, and gagged.*

"*The ambulance was there in a matter of minutes. The EMTs ran in with oxygen. They ran in and put on the mask. One of them said, 'He made it.' I began to pray, 'Oh, thank God. Thank you, thank you, Jesus.' The man looked up at me.*

"*'Who are you, lady?'*

"*'I'm his wife. Oh, thank you. Thank you, Jesus.'*

"*'Oh, lady,' the man said, 'I'm sorry. That's not what I meant.' "]*

My father's sudden death was a crisis for us all. *Shock* would be about the best word. Total and unexpected. First, complete surprise and disbelief. A bad dream, not real. Then numbness and disorientation, like sleep-walking.

A shock for all of us, and of course one can't quantify such things, but I think it was hardest for my mother and maybe my baby sister, Janeth (now Nagib), who had particularly glowed and flourished in her father's love.

Besides suffering the loss of her first love and helpmate while still a young woman, my mother now had to face the financial vacuum created by his death. Which she did. She saw that we kept the home our father had made us and that the children were educated. Coming home from the funeral, she told me, "And as for you, go right back to school. That's what your father wanted. I'll manage."

Which finally resolved the matter of school for me. There was no longer a choice: movement or no, I'd have to finish at Howard.

I returned to school and immersed myself in study and the politics of the campus and neighboring states. I think the movement distracted me from brooding too much about my father. I would experience, for example, serious and brutal campaigns in Cambridge, Maryland, and Danville,

Virginia, during my time in school. Carloads of us from NAG would regularly drive south for SNCC meetings.

That semester after my father's death, if memory serves, I took "Introduction to Philosophy" with a brilliant young brother named Conrad Snowden. After that course, I was hooked. I loved the clarity and logic and especially the intellectual discipline—in short, the habits and elegance of thought that was philosophy. So I changed my major. Besides, since I'd already had most of the required science, I figured I could always return to medicine after graduation if I so chose. But the movement would take care of that.

To help the family, I, like most other Howard students, had to work. But even here, in the kinds of work I did, the movement was a factor. Unlike most of the guys, I never drove a cab at night, waited tables, or manned the lobby desk in white apartment buildings.

The National Council of Negro Women had a support system to help activist students stay in school. Ed Brown, Courtland Cox, and I received work scholarships for which we counseled and advised youth in the high schools. I can't remember the name of our school, but I recall it had a basketball court upon its roof.

Also, an important NAG adviser and supporter was a craggy-faced Yankee named Warren Morse. A socialist, Warren was an official in a fast-growing local union (AFSCME) and hired us for his organizing drives. Ed, Courtland, Butch Conn, and I would get up at 5 A.M. and spend a few hours before classes handing out leaflets and talking to workers as the early shift changed. Warren made a point of hiring NAG folk. After I graduated, Phil Hutchings got my job. Warren was our ally and supporter. He has remained a good friend. After he retired to the mountain wilds of Vermont and I was based in Conakry, we continued to correspond regularly.

In yet another unusual work-study. Professor G. Franklin Edwards had designed an experiment/course in which some of us participated for academic credit, and as I recall, some kind of tuition waiver. Professor Edwards had designed a study examining the nature and causes of different kinds of resistance among black youth. On the one hand, the "positive" political resistance presumably represented by the sit-in student types, i.e., us. On the other hand, the self-destructive, antisocial resistance expressed in youth crime and juvenile delinquency. The study entailed, among other things, bringing representatives of both groups together to examine how they related. We met inside the Norton Reformatory, the District's high-security youth jail by another name.

I'm not sure what the study revealed. But Ed, John Harper, Courtland, and I had no difficulty becoming quite friendly with the young "criminals." Especially with one remarkably intelligent young brother, said to be a particularly "vicious" murderer. As far as fundamental attitudes, we found little that separated us. The real difference, so far as we could see, was just opportunity and education. That's all. I remember that I told a group of those inmates about the "hard mens" in the Mississippi jails. The ones who'd refused to attack us. They liked that story. One of them said, "Don't surprise me, man. I think same thing would happen here too. Dudes may not say it, man, but they dig what you guys be doing. You all be representing us, man."

It was always sad to leave the brothers locked up inside while we headed on back to campus. There but for the grace of God . . .

Despite all this work, the bulk of the financial burden of my education remained on May Charles's shoulders. Only this year did she produce a bunch of Howard receipts and explain how she'd managed to pay them. That year, an uncle of hers in Canada had died leaving $3,000 to each of his young relatives. May Charles deposited her share toward my education. Each semester, after she'd paid that bill, she would struggle to replenish the little cache before the arrival of the next one.

CHAPTER XII

The Hearts and Minds
of the Student Body

Now that it was clear what I'd be doing for the next three years, I turned my attention seriously to campus politics. Since we had no "official" presence on campus, NAG knew that we'd have to infiltrate recognized student organizations. I've already mentioned the newspaper. The real plum, though, because it had money and a degree of legitimacy, was the Liberal Arts Student Council. As "Deep Throat" rasped to the journalist, "Follow the monay," which is what we did.

We targeted the council. Tom Kahn shrewdly got himself elected treasurer. An ally, Vernon Gill, became president with our support, while a couple of other NAG people (Karen House, Jean Wheeler, Muriel Tillinghast) and I were elected to the council.

The idea was to find, as Tim Jenkins before us had done, progressive, politically effective ways to use the student activity fees that the council controlled. One such effort we called Project Awareness.

Project Awareness was certainly the most visible political initiative we were able to launch with the Student Council's resources. In ways we had not anticipated, it also proved one of the most personally affecting to us in NAG.

Tom Kahn, at that time one of our most experienced activists and a shrewd strategist, was treasurer of the council that year. As "floor whip," I got quite good at organizing the votes. So, we got the council's unanimous approval for Project Awareness.

Student Affairs, however, greeted the proposal with suspicion, correctly sensing NAG's fingerprints all over it and consequently assuming subversive intent. Well, they were half-right. But really, nothing was subversive about the project, unless free speech and open discussion of ideas is subversive. Or perhaps it was simply that the proposal included none of the approved and traditional uses of student funds: balls, cotillions, beauty contests, or homecoming parades. It proposed to raise campus awareness of social issues by staging debates between well-known advocates on opposing sides of controversial questions.

We were, of course, careful to couch the proposal in the most high-minded of academic values. Freedom of inquiry, open debate, full discussion, and from the most rigorously *nonpartisan* posture. Hence the debate format.

Even so, the idea completely confounded the bureaucracy. (The new director of Student Affairs, Carl Anderson, was young, more forward-looking, and an honest brother. But, poor guy, his job was to represent to us the views of the old-generation deans, something that he managed to do with impressive integrity.) This, after all, was unfolding at a "Negro college" within a shout of the Capitol and in the dark shadow of McCarthyism. The bureaucrats delayed the proposal, stalled, obfuscated, and eventually bucked it all the way to the President's Office, where President Nabrit, to his credit, approved it *in principle*.

However, each debate had to be individually approved. Although I can remember no speaker actually being rejected outright, in each instance so many questions were raised, clarifications requested, and such general nervousness evinced, that never until the last minute was it clear whether any program would really happen.

That taught me a lot about the *dependency* in which white America needed to keep our community. Naturally we were enraged. Not at the nervous Nellie administrators, but at the totalitarian political racism of a system that *needed* to impose this kind of dependency, control, and fear upon our elders. I was venting about this to a brother from Alabama in the cafeteria one day. The brother, whose name I think, was Laverne put things in historical perspective for me:

"Hey, mah man, that ain't so bad. My daddy went to Tuskegee, man. An' he told us that there the administration warned students *not* to walk around campus *with they books in they hands, man.* Yeah. Check this, brother man. The white folks might not like seeing no niggers with no *books,* you dig? And the faculty? Man, some of them had decent cars? But whenever they had to drive out of town, man, them dudes put on *chauffeur caps.* Tha's right, chauffeur caps, bro, so the crackers wouldn't know them fine cars belonged to them. Them cars was too good for black folk. Shoot, mah man, now heah you come talking about *socialism and free speech* an' ain't nobody come to lynch yo' black butt? Or put you out of school? That's American progress, my brother." It may have been progress or it may only have been geography.

Hearing stories like that daily, we in NAG vowed that ours would be the *very* last generation of Africans in this country expected to buck dance, shuffle, or Tom for white folks' approval. Bet on it, the very last. We were real clear on that. And, of course, quite wrong.

Unexpectedly though, our first debate (between two white men on a black campus)—the venerable and respectable socialist Norman Thomas and an ultraconservative columnist called Fulton Lewis III—proved a huge critical success. "Socialism or Capitalism?" was a sho-nuff public relations coup so far as the administration was concerned. The Washington media, which usually paid scant attention to Howard beyond some occasional patronizing advice, not only came on campus but were full of praise. The press liked the "high intellectual tone" of the debate and Howard's "courageous affirmation of academic freedom." Once white folk approved, administrators visibly preened and, for a few days, even smiled warmly at us on campus. Which did not mean, however, any lasting reduction in the level of administrative anxiety and vigilance. When we proposed the debate "Integration or Separation?" between two black radicals—NAG's political mentor Bayard Rustin and Nation of Islam minister Malcolm X—administrative anxiety resurfaced at full flood.

And, help us, Jesus! Or better help the beleaguered bureaucrats, for next year we proposed to bring a prominent, card-carrying member of the *Communist Party USA* onto campus! The subject was "Is the Soviet Union a Progressive Society?" Herbert Aptheker, radical historian and editor of *Political Affairs,* the theoretical organ of the CP and a historian of black people, was to debate Saul Mendelson, also a historian and a member of the National Committee of the Socialist Party. Whoee! Trouble, blues and trouble.

Talk about anxiety and confusion; as the *Hilltop* made sure everyone knew, "Dr. Aptheker would be the first known Communist to speak at the university under official auspices." As you can imagine, it wasn't easy. The poor bureaucrats squirmed and wriggled and bucked it all the way up to President Nabrit, who courageously approved it. *Approved* is almost certainly the wrong word. He allowed it to happen. The dark shadow of McCarthyism was still long in the city.

Tom Kahn immediately congratulated the university "for its far-sighted commitment to academic freedom. Its endorsement of the right of students to hear a diversity of views places Howard in a category with Harvard, Oberlin, Antioch, and other top schools that have traditionally been havens of free speech and open inquiry." Yeah. Well. But those were private schools, not a black institution under the thumb of every jackleg know-nothing Dixiecrat demagogue. President Nabrit was a brave and principled man, but his momma didn't raise no fool. His response to Tom's encomium was a masterpiece of Washington-speak. To wit:

"This is something that *Howard* is not participating in. However, we would be interested to see what develops. These things require much thought and an involvement of many factors. *Howard* has no position on the matter and neither do I." Be interesting to decode that, but bottom line: the debate went forward. One other person stands out. Professor Emmett Dorsey, head of the Government Department. For both controversial debates—the Aptheker and the Malcolm X—when everyone else was running for cover, Professor Dorsey agreed to be our moderator.

The Malcolm/Bayard debate has, of course, now become legendary. To this very day, whenever—and wherever—I meet people who were at Howard with us, that is what they seem to remember first. Just a few years ago, party business took me to Nigeria. I needed transportation in a small town in the east. A middle-aged professor gave me a ride.

"Bro Ture," he said shyly. "Don't you remember me? I marched with you in Washington. I was at Howard." Truthfully, I didn't remember the brother. Then his face lit up and he smiled. "I'll never forget," he said, "the night you guys brought Malcolm X to campus." Neither have I. And I've had similar conversations with Howardites I've met all over the African world—Jamaica, Trinidad, Ghana—over the years.

At that important time for us in NAG, Bayard was very much a real presence, a political mentor. We admired his freewheeling activist spirit, his radical tenacity and resourcefulness under pressure. And his tactical dexterity and debating skill as a public speaker. At that time we also accepted his analysis of the movement—essentially a socialist critique calling for a united front among American progressives, particularly the labor movement and the black struggle. (Later, of course, we would have serious ideological and tactical disagreements, but even in our disagreements I've always respected Bayard's long-term commitment to struggle.) Bayard's was radically different from Malcolm's public position at that time, and I think we expected Bayard to win the debate hands down. What actually happened was different and instructive.

Project Awareness was NAG's only *official* public project, funded and approved by the university. So it had, as we intended, a visible effect and presence in university life, but its unintended effect on us in NAG was even greater. To understand this, one must understand something else about the realities of the time as it affected us young Africans, and not only at Howard.

Then as now, if you were young and black (forget gifted) in this country, you were always looking for honorable terms to define yourself and your relationship to the society. What in this "white republic" truly represented you? With what or whom could you identify? And where did one look to find them? If one did not find these figures and values within one's immediate circles—family, friends, school, or church—you were not going to find them anywhere else, certainly not in the public media. Until the movement came along, we Africans—unless athletes or musicians— were rarely to be seen, except on the local news being accused of crimes. (I'm constantly being told there's been great progress made, but from what I've recently seen of the U.S. media, you coulda fooled me. Must be a different definition of progress.)

Back then when an African appeared in the programming, it was usually one stereotype or the other: a servant, a grinning clown, a buxom Aunt Jemima. Occasionally a responsible Negro spokesman—a Roy Wilkins or a Whitney Young—might make an appearance. But whatever he, and it was invariably a he, had to say would be addressed to the sensibilities and expectations of the white establishment—corporate and political—never to us. It was a kind of preemptive self-censoring. Which is why Bro Malcolm could make such a good rhetorical living dogging these "so-called Negro leaders," as he called them.

So our generation never expected to find much that represented what Dr. Du Bois had called "our spiritual strivings" in the American media. The exclusion of racial minorities generally, and militant and intelligent black voices in particular, was near total. We used to say in NAG, "A free black mind is a concealed weapon." And someone would always add, "Yeah, an' the media going make darn sure it *stay* concealed too."

This exclusion was so complete that *Jet* magazine even ran a small weekly column alerting Africans to every TV program that was going to show a black face, any black face, that spoke a single line or sang a song. It was usually a short column.

But then there was sport.

Twice a season when the Washington Redskins played the Cleveland Browns, the dorm TV room was jam-packed, and not because of the color symbolism of the teams' names either. And *evrah-black-body,* no matter where he came from, was a Cleveland fan. Why? Because of the peerless, the incredible, the transcendent Jim Brown. An African who was so absolutely and undeniably superior in what he did that even the racist press called him "superstar." And besides which, beyond athletic dominance, Bro Brown was a socially conscious, outspoken black man.

But in this media-imposed white curtain, there were two notable breakthroughs. Whenever *Jet* gave a heads-up that either of two young black men would be on, you had to push and wedge your way into the TV room. Standing room only, bro. And James Baldwin and Malcolm X (peace be unto them) never disappointed us. Clearly, especially as you look at the procession of grinning, styling, empty, obscenity-spewing black faces merchandising commodities on the media today, sometimes less can indeed be more.

Even though Jimmy and Malcolm, superficially at any rate, appeared dramatically opposed in their messages—which come to think of it was probably the reason they were on TV in the first place—they were important to us for the same simple reason. Unlike the "responsible" spokesmen, unable or unwilling to risk offense to white patrons whose support they hoped to win, Malcolm and Jimmy were free black men. They spoke the truth as they saw it. They never apologized for us. They attacked, eloquently, every demeaning definition imposed on our people. They made no concession to racist arrogance or ignorance. They never backed down. And they took no prisoners.

Clearly, obviously, and demonstrably smarter than their white interlocutors, they refused to play Mr. Bones or Mr. Tambo,* but took them to school, put them under heavy manners, and instructed them sharply and sometimes, much to our delight, painfully. In the dormitories at Howard—and I'm certain at other black colleges—young Africans of our generation had our attitudes informed by their examples.

I don't know if these two brothers ever fully understood just how much they meant, how crucially important, how painfully necessary, their kind of bold representation in those times was for our age set. I certainly hope they did.

We never tired of watching them. Well, y'know, they weren't on that frequently, so every time was an event. And whatever the program or setting, the scenario was always the same. Either a media "personality" or a collection of them, all white and by their own definition experts on everything. Certainly more intelligent, better informed, and more sophisticated than their "Negro" guest, whom they fully intended to instruct and lecture on the realities of the "American race problem," official version. Their condescension and smugness would be palpable . . . at first.

Then of course came the show we had all gathered to see and come to expect: the ambush and dismemberment. The visible wilting and melting away of their arrogance as Jimmy or Malcolm carved up and demolished the edifice of unexamined clichés, platitudes, and evasions by which they pretended to describe racial realities in the country. This rarely failed to happen. And what was sweetest about it was this: the more supercilious the host, the more satisfying was his pubic discomfiture on national TV. Hey, what is going on here? This is not, repeat, is not *happening*. Why, this ungrateful burr-head never even went to college. Here, I put this (expletive) darkie on TV and this is the thanks I get?

Two different things were going on. The first was an illustration of two observations Jimmy Baldwin had made when he came to talk to us at Howard. "Black Americans have the great advantage of never having believed the collections of myths to which white Americans cling." And: "White Southerners delude themselves that they know the Negro. Nothing could be further from the truth. Negroes, on the other hand, know white people very well because we have had to observe them very carefully. Our very lives depended on it."

*Stock buffoons from blackface minstrelsy.

The other factor was the abiding superficiality of the media "experts on everything," who had, before the show, most likely devoted all of fifteen minutes of thought to the issue of race. Then they would presume to lecture highly intelligent black men who on those questions were living experts, having confronted, analyzed, and reflected on racism their entire lives. So what could you expect? Had it been a boxing match, any competent referee would have declared "no contest" and stopped the carnage. But we ate it up, Jack. Yes, we did.

Project Awareness introduced us not only to Jimmy and Malcolm, but also to other prominent artistic, intellectual, and activist figures from the older generation. I'm talking now about folks like Harry Belafonte, Sidney Poitier, John O. Killens, and Ossie Davis. The kind of folk you respected greatly but never imagined you'd ever get a chance to meet.

What was surprising about this was that without exception these accomplished elders seemed glad to meet *us*. They seemed to approve of what we were doing, to take us seriously and even to respect us, or at least what we, as "sit-in students," represented to them. On occasion, much to our embarrassment (and barely concealed pleasure), one of these celebrities might say, on meeting us, something like "Aha. So you are the guys I've been reading about, the ones raising so much hell? I'm real proud of you guys." Something like that.

Well, you can imagine how that made us feel. But happily the *activists*— Jimmy, Harry, Bayard, and Malcolm—never *said* things like that. They *showed* us their care and support. By taking time to talk with us. By their advice and mentoring. By their evident concern: the willingness to raise bail when necessary, to rise to our defense as needed. To us the value of this support across generations was beyond measure. So whenever I meet students, any young people really, who are serious about struggle, I always try to do likewise. To advise, strengthen, and encourage them in any way I can.

The debate would be the first time I would be seeing Malcolm X up close. Bayard we already knew. Sometimes when we had a large demonstration, he'd come and afterward always lead a discussion. Sometimes he'd bring an African leader. I recall at the time of Zambian independence Bayard brought the new president, Kenneth Kuanda, whom he introduced by his praise name, the Lion of Zambia, to speak to us in NAG. So we knew Bayard well. But Malcolm, the racist demagogue regularly demonized all over the white press, who was making his first appearance at Howard, was a real novelty.

We met him when he got to campus. Thelwell interviewed him for the newspaper, then brought him over to a little dinner we had organized for our guests.

Upon his appearance in the small dining room the atmosphere abruptly changed. Suddenly the room became totally silent but strangely charged. The clatter of silverware, the hum of conversation, everything just stopped. All heads turned to the door.

There he stood, smiling almost diffidently in the doorway. Tall, slender, his horn-rimmed glasses glinting, the expression of his lean face alert, carrying himself erect, with a formality, a quiet dignity, in his posture, yet beneath it an unmistakable warmth. Without doing a thing for a moment he simply commanded the entire space.

"Salaam aleikum, brothers and sisters," he bowed. "Sorry if I'm a little late, but your young editors turned me every which way but loose. They were without mercy."

He politely declined to eat with us, explaining that for religious reasons he ate only one meal each day. He sat a little apart taking cup after cup of black coffee and our endless questions. Malcolm had a *presence,* something you could not miss but neither could you quite name. It was a noticeable life force, an energy field, an aura, a . . . *something* quite unlike that of any leader I'd ever seen until I had the honor of meeting (peace unto him) President Ahmed Sékou Touré. El Comandante Fidel Castro Ruz is a leader who also radiated a similar personal magnetism. Now, Dr. King had great charisma . . . once he started to speak. That was the power of *nommo,* the African spoken word, God's trombone, but before Dr. King unrolled that magnificent voice and revealed the eloquence of his moral force, he could be standing in the room and you might easily not notice him. But if Malcolm or Sékou Touré or Fidel Castro stood completely still and silent in a large, crowded room, you—everybody—knew it, Jack. Yes, you did.

There Malcolm sat, drinking coffee and answering our questions, and with every answer his stock rose, as much because of his manner as his answers. He was unfailingly courteous, treating each questioner and his or her question with wit, care, and a great respect, which put everyone at ease . . . only somewhat at ease, not entirely. Because at the same time he always radiated a ripple of tension, a banked power, and a quality of alert, guarded watchfulness that really was like a great cat's. And everyone present could feel it.

One small but electric moment made an impression on me. The only administrator at the dinner was Dean Patricia Roberts. (Peace be unto her spirit.) That she was there at all tells you why we all admired her. The dean was an attractive lady, close to Malcolm in age. Dean Roberts challenged something Malcolm had said and a sharp, if formally polite exchange ensued which both seemed to enjoy. Then, Malcolm made a sally, I forget exactly what, and gave the dean a long, challenging look accompanied by his slightly ironic grin. Their eyes locked for an instant. Then Dean Roberts, before she looked away, actually seemed to blush and emit something that sounded suspiciously like a soft giggle.

Dean Roberts was one self-possessed, strong, consummately cool African lady who rose to unprecedented heights in U.S. establishment politics. A career in which she encountered presidents, heads of state, cabinet secretaries, and such other highly placed miscreants. I'll wager none of them ever succeeded in inducing Patricia Roberts Harris to blush and lower her eyes. *Ever.*

The opinion of the overwhelming majority of the audience was that Malcolm won the debate. We were surprised, because as I've said, NAG expected Bayard's position—which we generally shared at that time—to prevail. But it was, no question at all about it, Malcolm's evening—emotionally, rhetorically, and dramatically.

Bayard (peace unto his name) subsequently told his biographer, Jervis Anderson, that he had organized the Howard debate at Malcolm's request. According to Anderson, during a conversation on a Harlem street corner, Malcolm had lamented that although he was being invited to speak at Oxford, Harvard, and other "great" white colleges, Howard, the "capstone of Negro education," had never dared invite him. Bayard allowed as how he could organize a Howard appearance for Malcolm, but (for reasons we know) it would have to be in a debate format.

I'd never heard this version until recently, but it certainly seems to explain a puzzling impression that some of us had at the time.

I can't remember who spoke first. But I do remember Bayard doing two things that were totally uncharacteristic. One, he spoke quickly and almost perfunctorily when his turn came. There was none of his theatricality or his usual fire or for that matter his analytical rigor. In fact, I doubt that he even used all his allotted time. He ran down his usual democratic socialist, integrationist class analysis of the American scene. The reasoning and the logic were there. The passion and fire seemed missing, there were two moments of transcendentally Rustinian gamesmanship. Having concluded what seemed a hurried, rather cursory initial presentation, Bayard paused, then fished out and consulted his timepiece. "I believe," he announced, "I should stop heah. Because I am fully cognizant that the ministah has by far the more difficult and untenable argument to construct."

Second, after Malcolm had spoken, Bayard again graciously—but uncharacteristically—conceded his rebuttal time "to the ministah because it seems quite apparent that it is he whom this audience really needs to heah at considerably greater length." Say what? No one has ever seen

Bayard yield time, microphone, or a platform in any debate before—or since, come to think of it.

But this should not in any way detract from the brilliance of Malcolm's performance. Not in the least. On that platform that evening Malcolm was so remarkable that I can say that he won the debate. Clearly. *Clearly. He* "won the debate." However, Malcolm did not "convert" me or anyone else in NAG that evening.

See, if you had to characterize NAG's politics at that stage, you'd have to say we were radical reformists . . . but evolving. We were secular and militantly confrontational within the framework of a nonviolent activism. Our intention? Merely to push, prod, and pester American social practice into greater conformity with the nation's high-minded, much ignored constitutional rhetoric and its "democratic" principles. No more, no less. Being "young and idealistic," we still thought this possible. A hard struggle, yes. A long one, yes. Painful, certainly. But at least . . . possible. Or so we hoped. And definitely worth fighting for. So we did not expect to be converted to some fundamentalist theological worldview and a political and social solution based on racial separation. Notice I said *social,* not *cultural.* So we weren't converted. But I for one certainly learned something of lasting importance from Malcolm's performance that night.

Over the past two and a half years I'd been immersed in much that— inevitably—was informing my view of the world. I'd been exposed to the excitement, the hope, the optimism—and the real problems—of emerging Africa. To a sustained conversation—politically, culturally, intellectually— on blackness. I'd experienced Southern black culture and Howard "genteelity." I'd done time on a Mississippi prison farm and walked many a picket line in hostile country. But intellectually my general political worldview was still anchored in the principles of my high school Marxism, essentially a European theoretical context, albeit a "revolutionary" one.

But what Malcolm demonstrated that night in Crampton Auditorium on the Howard campus was the raw power, the visceral potency, of the grip our unarticulated collective blackness held over us. I'll never forget it. A spotlight picked him out as he strode, slim, erect, immaculately tailored, to the mike on an otherwise darkened stage. When he uttered the traditional Islamic greeting of peace, *salaam aleikum,* the answer came roaring back at him from the center of the hall. *"Wa aleikum as salaam."*

[On reflection, Ture and I now conclude that the Nation, as was its custom, had brought in a large number of the faithful and occupied the center of the theater. Hence the initial roar. After that, the students were caught up in the general responses from all over the hall. —EMT]

Then Malcolm went into his introduction of himself. I think I remember it exactly after thirty-five years. It was classic theological nationalism.

259

"Salaam aleikum. I come to you in the name of all that is eternal"—pause—"the black man."

This time, the deep roar came from all over the hall, and it was visceral.

"Before you were American, you were black." Roar.

"Before you were Republican . . . you were black." Roar.

"Before you were Democrat . . . you were black." Biggest roar.

After each variation a roar of affirmation. The hairs tingled on the nape of my neck. The audience just erupted around me, I mean *erupted.* It seemed entirely spontaneous, a sound somewhere between a howl and a roar. As if this gathering of young Africans—from the continent, the Caribbean, America—were freed to recognize their oneness, to give loud affirmation to something they were being educated, conditioned really, to suppress and deny: our collective blackness.

Malcolm's talk was, as I recall, well received. He recapitulated his reading of American history with his unsparing indictment of its recurrent racism and brutality. In this, Malcolm's oratorical approach was as simple as it was effective. A single, repeated powerful line of indictment followed by a capsule of historical evidence. To wit:

"The American white man is the world's greatest racist." (Ref: African slavery, Indian genocide, Chinese exclusion, Japanese interment, etc.)

"The American white man is the world's greatest killer." (Ref: Hiroshima, Nagasaki, Plains Indians, police and Klan violence, etc.)

"The American white man is the world's greatest liar." (Ref: Violation of constitutional guarantees, Native American treaties, etc.)

"The American white man . . . world's greatest . . . rapist, thief, deceiver." (You fill in the blanks.)

After which—this one was always sensitive for me—he attacked the "unmanliness" of leaders who would watch white men brutalize their women and children while professing "nonviolence"

"We are nonviolent with those who are nonviolent with us. But we are not nonviolent with those who are not nonviolent with us."

'Course, with this, all the brothers in the room who'd never been on our picket lines suddenly found justification for their absence. But it was powerful. I recall being most impressed by the philosophical way he concluded, saying in effect:

"My stand is really the same as that of twenty-two million so-called Negroes. It is not a stand for integration. The stand is that our people want complete freedom, justice, and equality. That is, respect and recognition as human beings. That is the objective of every black [person] in this country.

"Some think that integration will bring this about. There are others who think that separation will bring it about. So integration is not the objective. Nor is separation the objective. The objective is complete respect as human beings.

"The only difference among so-called Negroes in this country is not in the objective, but in the method through which this objective should be reached."

Obviously those are not Malcolm's exact words on that night. But they are close and they are Malcolm's words *[delivered elsewhere]*. They state the gist of his closing argument at that debate as I remember them. As I recall, upon his conclusion almost the entire room was on its feet, I first among them.

That this message should have been so enthusiastically received by an audience most of whom were being so heavily programmed for "integration" and upward mobility in the American mainstream may have seemed something of a contradiction. But, as Junebug says, "If you don't understand the principle of eternal contradiction, you ain't going understand diddly." Certainly the crowd's response did not prefigure any sudden influx of Howard students into the Nation.

It was simply refreshing for young Africans to hear someone stand up and so fearlessly describe the real America black folks knew and experienced daily. Especially in a setting usually so relentlessly cautious, guarded, and overly sensitive to the delicate sensibilities of the same white ruling class responsible for perpetuating our people's oppression. In fact, I cannot remember the media's response to this debate or if they were even present.

The other program I remember most vividly was during the next academic year, 1963. No debate, but a symposium. This one was no way as controversial, but proved no less profound in what it taught me.

The subject was literature, more precisely, the role of the black writer in struggle. What I hear they call today "the culture wars." Naturally we invited Jimmy and his friend Lorraine Hansberry *[Raisin in the Sun]*, actor/playwright Ossie Davis, the novelist John O. Killens, and Ralph Ellison *[Invisible Man]*. Our elder brother, friend, and mentor Professor Sterling Brown agreed to moderate. At the last minute after announcements had gone out, Mr. Ellison sent his regrets. Ms. Hansberry (peace unto her spirit) also was unable to participate, but this was truly for reasons of health. Not too long after that, the sister danced and went to join the ancestors.

There was another capacity audience and the evening had a movement/Howard focus. Jimmy Baldwin was coming off a speaking tour on behalf of CORE, so he was focused on struggle and at the peak of his eloquence. Ossie Davis was a Howard alum whose play *Purlie Victorious,* a comedy on the absurdity of segregation, was just ending a successful

Broadway run. John O. Killens, whose classic novel *Youngblood* was one of my favorites, had a son at Howard who wrote for the *Hilltop*. Killens had also written the screenplay for the movie *Odds Against Tomorrow,* in which Harry Belafonte starred. The tone of the evening's rhetoric was militant and engaged.

Killens: "America is in many ways desperately sick and the Negro is the doctor who might save her. . . . America, I [the Negro writer] am your conscience."

Jimmy Baldwin: "It is the responsibility of the Negro writer to excavate the real history of this country . . . to tell us what really happened to get us where we are now. . . . We must tell the truth till we can no longer bear it."

Again, another great public relations success for the school so far as the white media were concerned. But the most thorough and perceptive coverage came in the *Washington Afro-American,* a weekly then edited by a militant young editor named Chuck Stone.

As our group was leaving the auditorium, a tall figure wearing shades and a trench coat with upturned collar rose from a seat in the last row and started to slip out. Why was this tall brother wearing shades at night?

"Hey, that's Sidney Poitier!" Courtland Cox said.

"Man, you crazy."

But it was. "When I heard that all these cats were going to be together in one place . . . you know I just couldn't miss it" was what he said.

Ed Brown, Courtland, and Butch Conn shared a little apartment on Clifton Place, and somehow—we hadn't presumed to plan anything for such distinguished visitors—we all ended up there. Being D.C., the liquor stores were long closed, but Ed, of course, knew a bootlegger.

Another anonymous drop-in was at the symposium. I never saw him myself but others did, and later Malcolm X confirmed to me that "whenever I hear that this little brother is going to speak in any town where I am, I always make a point of going to listen, because I always learn something." Malcolm made no secret of his admiration for Jimmy Baldwin. "I believe," he once told Jimmy, "that if I am the warrior of this movement, then you are its poet." Whoee, let the church say "Ahmen."

The impromptu gathering afterward was the most memorable part of the evening. Our older writer brothers reasoned with us like family. We glowed, strengthened by their regard and evident concern. And these accomplished elders all seemed so at ease in that small, raggedy student apartment. Remember now, this was November 1963. We had three years of struggle behind us. So was the March on Washington and Dr. King's Dream. John F. Kennedy had recently been gunned down. The national mood was sore, tense, and uncertain, as was our mood. One theme kept recurring from these men of respect. Essentially this: "In our generation we could not do what you are doing. We're glad that you can, proud that you do. But we worry for you. You young people need to be very, very careful. We ain't asking you to stop, but are you quite sure you really know the things this country is capable of?" Turns out we didn't then, but it wouldn't be long. . . .

The high point of our reasoning came as the sun was rising after we had literally talked the night to death. It fell to Jimmy Baldwin to summarize with his usual clarity.

"Well, here we are, my young brothers and sisters. Here's how matters stand. I, Jimmy Baldwin, as a black writer, must in some way represent you. Now, you didn't elect me, and I didn't ask for it, but here we are. . . . Everything I write will in some way reflect on you. So . . . what do we do? I'll make you a pledge. If you will promise me, your elder brother, that you will never, *ever* accept any of the many derogatory, degrading, and reductive definitions that this society has ready for you, then *I, Jimmy Baldwin, promise you I shall never betray you.*"

There was a brief silence. Then a loud "Yeah." I know most people's eyes had tears in them. I think every one of us there took that pact seriously.

Recently me 'n' Mike Thelwell discussed that moment. Thelwell said, "Y'know, Jimmy was probably the one who took it most seriously. He never betrayed us. You remember this?"

"This" was a newspaper clipping from 1968, five years later. If I'd seen it at the time, I had no recollection. And I think it's something I would certainly have remembered. Black Power was under vicious media fire. Brother Rap was being hounded with "incitement to riot" charges. I had just returned from Africa and had had my passport lifted by the government. I was being mercilessly pilloried in the press for allegedly calling for "revolution." Jimmy was writing from Paris and the headline read, "Baldwin Batting for Carmichael." Brave, loyal Jimmy. I saw immediately how the column recapitulated much of the discussion that night five years earlier.

I first met Stokely Carmichael in the Deep South when he was just another nonviolent kid, marching, talking, and getting his head whipped. Those times now seem as far behind us as the flood, and if those gallant, betrayed boys and girls who were then using their bodies to save a heedless nation have since concluded that the nation is not worth saving, no American has any right to be surprised.

. . . I've never known a Negro who was not obsessed with black power. Those representatives of White Power who are not hopelessly brainwashed will understand that the only way for a black man in America not to be obsessed with the problem of how to control his destiny and protect his home, his women, and his children, is for that black man to become in his

263

own mind, that something-less-than-a-man which the Republic—alas—has always considered him . . . and when the black man, whose destiny and identity has always been controlled by others, decides and states that he will reject the identity imposed on him, and control his own destiny, he is talking revolution.

. . . Now I may not always agree with Stokely's views or the ways in which he expresses them. But my agreement or disagreement is absolutely irrelevant. I got his message. Stokely Carmichael, a black man under thirty, is saying to me, a black man over forty-six, that he will not live the life I've lived or be corralled into some of the awful choices I've been forced to make. And he is perfectly right.

Yes, indeed, small, slender James Baldwin was a constant brother, a warrior spirit. He kept the faith with our generation.

Check this. As the struggle developed in the sixties, we began to hear more and more about a "generation gap" in America. As technological developments change the general experience of each generation, that "gap" seems to be widening. But, between my age set and our adults? Sure, there were inevitable "generational" tensions. The usual suspects: differences of style, musical tastes, language, perspective, tactics, and attitudes, yes. But there was a bedrock, a solid platform of understanding and respect. I do not recall or believe that usses were ever *alienated* one generation from the other. There was *never* an unbridgeable gap of understanding and sympathy. To us that was a particular affliction of white America we Africans were happy not to have.

But now, when I listen to our youth and to people my age, I get the impression that this American disease may seriously be threatening our community. I truly hope not. We Africans don't need it and cannot afford to let it happen.

Because my age set, the generation of the sixties, needs desperately to see in our young people the serious commitment to struggle that our elders were happy to recognize and encourage in us. A generation that came of age in struggle and that now commands resources our parents never dreamed of should, and I believe would, embrace—joyfully—and support a coherent, creatively radical movement among our youth. And I know how much our youth, as we were, would be inspired and encouraged if they could feel the support and respect from their adults that we enjoyed. Far too much history needs to be passed on and better understood, and way too many dangerous and crucial new struggles are to be waged, for our generations to be alienated from each other. But, I can see that things are not so clear for youth today, the enemy not so exposed and easily visible. As the Mystic Revelations of Ras Tafari sing:

The enemy is around you
Seeking to devour you.

That's why today's youth, who are no less daring, no less venturesome, and no less interested in our people, our struggle, and our heritage than we were, truly need our guidance and our support. They live in confusing times. We need clarity and each other. Pass it on.

We received a unique political education on that campus "proudly there on hilltop high," as the alma mater phrased it. Certainly not the education my parents had envisioned—think of May Charles going off on poor Mr. Beckenstein back at Science for suggesting that politics was "in my blood"—but nonetheless an invaluable education in the contradictions and ironies of black American politics.

Certain questions, persistent ambivalences, kept coming up in one form or another. Questions that, at first anyway, never seemed to get answered definitively. Some came with the territory of being nineteen years old. Some from being nineteen and an activist. Still others came from being nineteen, activist, *and* African born in America. And particularly with being that age and of that race in that time.

Only now do I see clearly that one source of these ambiguities was our constantly being told by adults of the unprecedentedness of our generation. So that for us there were at first no models or guidelines. As the movement gathered strength, any fool could see that the society would either have to change seriously or kill us all. That was clear. Whether the society wanted to our not, it would not, could not, remain the same. That too was clear.

But in what ways would it actually change? That was the problem. Real change? Token change? One persistent view we kept hearing: "You young folks will have such *opportunity*. Such interesting opportunities. I envy you all. Many, many more opportunities than we ever had. How I envy you. Now is the time to be young. You are a favored generation."

Yeah. But boil it down to gravy, what did that really mean anyway? That we conform to all the attitudes, values, and style of corporate America? Try for graduate school at Harvard *[Mrs. Carmichael remembers that after leaving Howard, Stokely was offered a full scholarship to earn a Ph.D. in philosophy at that august institution. —EMT]* and hope, assuming that this would really be a viable option, to integrate an otherwise unchanged establishment? Or did one have to continue standing outside, as my grandmother would have said, "pelting stone and flinging rock." Or was there yet a third way, an honorable way, to be "in it but not of it" as Tim Jenkins was proposing?

Some of the age set, those of our peers you never saw on a picket line, took the first path. They buried themselves in the library and positioned themselves to take advantage of opportunities that the movement would open up. Many of them did well for themselves, allegedly proving that "the system works." But for many of us a whole lot more was seriously wrong with America than the mere fact of our exclusion. Remember the rhetorical question "Who wants to integrate unto a sinking ship?"—i.e., a fundamentally brutish and unjust system? This was the issue, our brother Jimmy would say, "the fearsome conundrum," that we—all of us in the movement—would have to wrestle with during these years.

The first case involves Dean Patricia Roberts. We respected her even before the Malcolm debate because the year before the debate, Mary Lovelace (the first love of my young manhood) had decided to wear her hair in public as the good Lord made it. This was at least two and a half years before the "Afro style" would sweep the African community. Of course I thought Mary looked absolutely beautiful.

But, those colored Victorian spinster ladies, the dorm mothers? They panicked. There can be no other word for it. Strangely threatened at the sight of a head of natural African hair, they absolutely panicked. And having panicked, eminently respectable, usually motherly ladies become real mean, yard-dawg mean.

"Chile, are you crazy? Don't even *think* of leaving this dorm with that wild African bush on your head."

"Girl, best you go put a scarf over that rat's nest."

"If your momma know what you're doing, she'd die of shame."

"I'll even give you the money to get it done."

No, she couldn't go among "decent people" looking like that. It would disgrace "her family," "the school," and "all black folk." If that crazy girl did not get some sense, there would be nothing for it but to expel her from the dormitory.

Of course, all this did was get Mary mad and the rest of NAG up in arms. Today it seems absurd. It is easy now to laugh at this level of false consciousness and backwardness. But then it was a sho-nuff crisis and a battle of wills.

Even if I hadn't been in love with Mary, I'da been angry. But I was in love, and as Ed Brown said, "madder than the preacher when the mule kicked his momma." I was all for throwing a picket line around the women's dorm. But mad, really, at whom? At the deepest level it was pathetic. At those suddenly hysterical old ladies so completely alienated from themselves? Helpless captives to an aesthetic imposed by racist arrogance? Most pathetic was that they truly believed they were actually acting in Mary's best interest. That they were protecting the values and the precious few hard-won gains of "the better class of Negro people." Until young Dean Roberts intervened. Both Mary and her Afro stayed in the dorm. After that we regarded the young dean as a strong ally among the bureaucrats.

Sidney Poitier was then America's first sho-nuff "black matinee idol," the Denzel Washington of the early sixties. His name meant box office and the brother made a point of only accepting roles that portrayed our people with dignity. Handful though they were, the few black actors of the time who occasionally made it into film—Harry Belafonte, Yaphet Kotto, William Marshall, Woody Strode, Ivan Dixon, later to be joined by Jim Brown—had that principled sense of responsibility. This of course was before the wave of blaxploitation films showed us graphically that not all motion is progress. Particularly for black folks in Hollywood.

Poitier's movie *Lilies of the Field,* for which he would win an Academy Award, was about to open nationally. Prior to general release a series of showings were scheduled in major cities, the proceeds to benefit the civil rights movement. So naturally NAG was invited to the D.C. fund-raiser in a fancy downtown theater. We could not otherwise have afforded the price. It was a major social event. The star would be in attendance and the liberal establishment—black and white—turned out in all its finery.

A group of us in our jeans were standing in the lobby feeling a trifle uneasy amongst the affluent, elegantly turned out Washington players and wanna-bes. Then in swept Poitier himself surrounded by a crowd of dignitaries, assistants, and media types. When he saw us across the lobby, he stopped, took a second look, pointed at us, broke into that incandescent matinee idol smile, and strode over to hug and greet us, much to the amazement and envy of the assembled dignitaries. We even were a little surprised too. It was an extremely nice gesture. I was impressed that the brother even remembered us from the Malcolm debate. But he was always good that way. The next year he and Belafonte would come to Mississippi to support SNCC's summer project.

Then, and this is the real story, in comes Dean Roberts, looking fine. She too comes over, and of course, we start to signify.

"Oh, Dean Roberts. Ooh, best-looking lady in the *house.* You looking good, Dean. Sho is good to see you out supporting the movement. Sho hope you keeps on going, one step at a time."

"Keeps on going? Exactly what's that supposed to mean, guys?"

"Well, Dean Roberts, progress, yours. Having made it to a respectable movement event like this, with affluent white folk *and* a Hollywood celebrity and all, maybe you'll make it onto the picket lines one day. There's demonstrations next weekend in—"

"Come on. You guys know how much I support the struggle. But we have to make intelligent choices here. Some of us work best from the inside. I am much more valuable to you working where I am than out carrying a sign. You understand that some folk have to stay on the inside, pulling strings, don't you?"

It was a strange moment. We had been teasing, but the dean was serious. I was not sure whether she thought we completely believed her, or even whether she completely believed herself. In Washington, people were always hinting at influence in high places and their quiet work "behind the scenes," which, of course, by its very nature could neither be seen nor verified. I figured this to be more of the same, the usual D.C. bougie cop-out. Besides, what kind of *insider* influence could a mere Howard dean have in the racist beltway politics of the time? We all liked and respected the dean, but we'd heard it all before. So I was skeptical.

Well, as it turns out, I sure was dead-up wrong on that one. I discovered this nine years later when the incoming Carter administration announced its cabinet, and there was our dean, the first African woman cabinet secretary *[Patricia Roberts Harris, Secretary of Housing and Urban Development].*

"Well, well, well," I said. "Looka that. So it wasn't no jive after all, huh? The sister had really been playing some serious, 'hardball insider' politics all along. Obviously with a result like this she had to have been playing tough too. I'm convinced that the dean would have continued to fight hard for our people from the inside. I'm sure of that. But I've often wished we could have talked. So much had happened since that evening in the theater foyer. I've often wondered how the dean (peace be unto her) would have evaluated her choices and what she must have learned and been able to accomplish for our people from her high position on the "inside."

[A Hilltop *report of a demonstration was written a few weeks after the movie preview by NAG leader Muriel Tillinghast. It pointedly mentions "a popular lady administrator who cannot be named" whose presence on the picket line greatly encouraged the Howard women. —EMT]*

One of the memorable experiences that touched on this inside/outside question came later that spring *[March 1963].* The campus paper had created a brief stir in the D.C. media with a story about a gymnasium under construction on campus. This story would bring the movement squarely onto the placid campus. Big time. Why this should have been the case is interesting and instructive. Consider: The year is 1963. The funds for the gym come from the federal government. The contract is awarded by the General Services Administration. John F. Kennedy is still president for another few months. Brother Bobby is attorney general. The administration, self-proclaimed "leader of the free world," is constantly being embarrassed internationally by evidence of the domestic racism being turned up by the movement. So much so that they have evolved a formula that is trumpeted daily into Africa, Asia, the Caribbean, and into black America. It goes something like this:

"Unfortunately, some *pockets of prejudice* continue to exist in some areas of American society. However, the *official* policy of the U.S. government is one of full democracy and racial inclusion. The federal government is in total and vigorous opposition to all lingering vestiges of racial or religious discrimination in American life. Racial discrimination within all federal institutions is strictly prohibited."

So . . . whatever racist mischief Mississippi states' righters might be up to, one does not expect to encounter racism or even tolerance of racism within the federal government itself, right?

However, what the student newspaper reported was that our new gym was being built at a black school, under federal contract, *by segregated labor.* Of the ten or so local labor unions working there, only three—the carpenters and the laborers—were integrated. The two *laborer* locals were for some unfathomable reason virtually all black. But all the building trades *craft* locals—the ironworkers, steamfitters, sheet-metal, plumbers, and electrical workers unions—in the District and Baltimore were lilywhite.

The *Hilltop* reported that an official of the electrical workers had offered this explanation to the Civil Rights Commission: "Nigras are all afraid of electricity," while a plumbers union spokesman told investigators that "Jews and colored folk don't want to do plumbing work because it's too hard."

We'd all known the story was coming, but I was hot, especially because of my father. It brought back vividly the many bitter conversations I'd listened to between my father and his friends about their experiences in the building trades in New York. So while the racism should have been expected, it was shocking and insulting to encounter it on our campus. *And* under federal auspices.

What made it even worse, if that were possible, was that D.C. was a majority black city. One where the only real industry was the building trades, from which our people were systematically being excluded. The ironies and insults abounded. The *Hilltop* also reported that our administrators had raised the issue in the past, only to be completely "dissed." The paper reported:

> University officials told the *Hilltop* that the university had no control over the awarding of contracts for university buildings. The federal government, through the General Services Administration, is responsible for letting the contract and supervising all stages of construction until the finished building is turned over to the school.

There had been, it was disclosed, numerous meetings between the university and representatives of the unions and contractors in an attempt to correct the situation in university construction programs in the past.

Quite obviously to no avail.

A separate story in the same issue announced the funding of a university project to "improve social conditions" in the rapidly deteriorating surrounding community, where black male unemployment approached 40 percent.

The *Hilltop* editorials took no prisoners:

> It is difficult and painful to believe that a situation so antithetical to the professed goals of this institution . . . so utterly subversive of the principles and ideals upon which Howard University is predicated is allowed to continue.
>
> . . . The G.S.A., in awarding this contract as it did, is guilty at best of negligence, at worst of a cynical and cavalier insult to this university and everything it represents. . . .
>
> . . . President Kennedy should know that "sincerity" is indeed subject to proof . . . if within the bureaucracy of his administration . . . there is a policy of "softness" towards segregation he is wasting his time and ours.

The newspaper and the student government sent pained, indignant, but detailed letters to the GSA, the President's Committee on Equal Employment Opportunity, and the contractor, and we waited.

Boy, on this issue all the students were hot. Most of their career aspirations were based on the feds following through as promised to open up job opportunities for them on federally funded projects across the nation. The ironies abounded. Almost all of our newspaper's ads came from defense corporations with fat federal contracts proclaiming themselves "equal opportunity employers."

So students were aroused. How could they not be? The hypocrisy was clear. The racism of the unions, clear. The complicity of the federal government, clear. The disrespect for us, the school, our administrators, and black people in general, blatant.

But here's the real irony, for NAG, in purely political terms, it was the perfect issue, and we worked it like a Delta mule. So why didn't we feel triumphant? In this case, Muhammad didn't have to go to the proverbial mountain . . . the mountain had indeed come to Muhammad. Like it or not, the movement had draped itself firmly around Howard's ivory tower. "Dang, y'all done brought that mess right up on campus now, ain't you?" Yes, we had.

• • •

While we waited for a response to our letters to the two federal agencies, mobilization on campus went on. The agencies did not reply to us, but to the media: "they were unaware" . . . "they were investigating," etc. Except that we found a year-old report from the Civil Rights Commission that had clearly documented the racism in the Baltimore/D.C. unions. The Student Council passed a resolution calling for universitywide demonstrations. Vernon Gill, LASC president, sent copies of the resolution to the media and the two federal agencies. We waited.

Then a funny thing happened, which to this day I can still neither explain nor understand. Word came—quietly. I can't remember who brought it but I can remember the lowered tones in which it was delivered. The executive chairman of the President's Committee on Equal Employment Opportunity—a black man—would meet with us. Say what? With us? A buncha students? Why? We hadn't sought such a meeting because, truthfully, it hadn't occurred to us. So who was this guy anyway and why did *he* want to see *us*?

We were told that he was "the most powerful black man in the federal government," that's who, Hobart Taylor Jr. A Texas lawyer, he was a protégé of Lyndon Johnson's, "LBJ's eyes and ears" on the committee with responsibility and full authority to enforce compliance on all federal contracts. He had the full support of the vice president, and as the committee's first black chairman, his appointment was proof of the administration's seriousness about ending discrimination on federal contracts. Wow. Impressive.

And he wanted to meet us? But why? Couldn't be that the brother was going to ask us to cool it, could it? Nah. He'd have to be crazy and you didn't become the "most powerful," etc., by being dumb. *[We had yet to encounter Clarence Thomas. —EMT]* So . . . why? It could only be a victory. You know a courtesy, to give us a briefing before the announcement. We should be honored. Think so? Well, what else could it be? But why was the meeting scheduled for 8 P.M.? Well, he a busy, important man.

Now, of course, I understand that it was of a certain genre of Washington meeting—one of those clandestine gatherings that never appear on any official's schedule, but which one reads about years later.

So, full of anticipation and questions, us goes, a group of us. I remember Tom, Mike, Cleve, Ed Brown, Courtland, and I don't know who all else. But we presents ourselves at some massive federal building at exactly 8 P.M. Obviously expected, we're met and whisked inside in no seconds flat, through echoing, deserted corridors of power and into a large, imposing, otherwise empty office, where "the most powerful black man" is sitting at a large desk.

He turns out to be a stocky, open-faced, affable, youngish brother wearing a sharp suit and a welcoming smile. We exchange pleasantries, shake his hand, congratulate him. "Brother Taylor, it's really good to see one of us so well placed," etc. "Yeah, it sho do do mah heart *gude* ta see one a'usses messing in such high cotton," Ed growls at his most folksy. We joke that this may be the most black folk ever to gather in that room. Almost certainly the first all-black meeting there ever. Almost like a building occupation, huh? Mr. Taylor seems relieved that we're smiling when we say that.

And then down to business. We listen for the announcement, which does not come. In fact we can't really understand what the brother is saying. It is not that his language is lawyerish or obscure. Each sentence is clear enough, but oddly oblique, nothing is adding up. But we all get the idea that we are being sent a message. That the brother is clearly trying to tell us something. But what? I even begin to be a little paranoid: "Why is the brother talking so strangely, can the place be bugged?" I find out later that I'm not the only one who had that thought.

Looking back, I now recognize the source of the problem. It was as if two different people—two masks—were talking to us. One being a loyal older brother and a committed black man, the other being the chairman. One trying to show us reality, the other repeating the official line. But by the time he's finished we are thoroughly confused, so we ask directly. It's been over thirty-five years so I can't remember exactly who asked what, but it went like this:

"Okay, Brother Chairman. You are telling us that current federal policy is against discrimination in government contracts, right?"

"Yes, absolutely . . . the executive order . . . oh, yes."

"Great . . . executive order, the policy. But is there the will? This *is* serious, right? I mean, it will be enforced, right?"

"The will? Oh, definitely . . . there *are* people in this administration who are real serious on this. Real serious. Generally speaking, yes."

"Good, good . . . And this is the agency that has that responsibility, and the authority, to enforce the policy?"

"Yeah, uh-huh. We do . . . we have."

"The authority to enforce compliance?"

"That's right. We sure do. Well, theoretically anyway."

Silence.

"Theoretically?"

"Theoretically, yes . . . it's complicated . . . there are powerful forces . . . but theoretically, yes . . . statutory authority, yes."

"Okay, brother. Then what about the Howard gym? We got the policy, we got the will, and we got the agency, so . . . ?"

"Well, as you know, that's being investigated."

"Investigated? But that's a matter of record . . . the Civil Rights Commission report . . . do you have any doubt?"

"Doubt? Me? No. I know it, you know it, the government knows it . . . Negroes are excluded. No doubt."

"And that is against policy, right?"

"Right."

"And, you do have the responsibility to enforce policy? I mean, that's your main job, right?"

"Right."

"So . . . will you pull the Howard contract?"

"Well, no . . . *that's* not going to happen."

"But you do have the authority . . . you could . . . I mean, if the facts warranted, you *could* pull a contract, right?

"Well, theoretically anyway. That would be extreme, though. Complicated . . . there'd be repercussions . . . there are considerations . . . powerful interests . . . important people. . .who'd not be happy."

"But can you at least threaten? Y'know, make some motions, scare them a little?"

"Maybe . . . perhaps . . . we'll see."

"Can I ask this? Has the committee ever . . . ?"

"Intervened? On a contract you mean?" Pause for reflection. "Well, can't recall that it has. Not yet, anyway."

"Why not?"

"As I said, there are some important people who wouldn't be very happy."

And so it went. Round and round it goes, where it stops, nobody knows. Finally, a light shined. So we go back over the territory.

"Just to make sure we understand. You're telling us that government policy prohibits discrimination on federal contracts?"

"Absolutely."

"That the exclusion of Negroes on the Howard contract is not in dispute?"

"Absolutely. On that and every other contract in the District."

"And that you—and this agency—have the responsibility to enforce . . ."

"That's right."

"But that there is nothing you will, can, or intend to do?"

"All of the above . . . at this time."

"Why?"

"Well, there are some very powerful people . . ."

"Powerful people? Who? Where? In the administration?" Slight nod. "The party?" Barely perceptible nod. "In business?" Nod. "Well, who *are* these people?"

"Let just say, some very powerful people."

We thanked him and left, wondering just why he had called us in in the first place. Somehow, though, no one thought to ask that question.

"Damn, that was weird."

"Wasn't it? Kafkaesque."

"What the hell was it all about?"

"Beats the crap outta me. But, y'know, I think the brother was really trying to tell us something."

"Yeah. I got that feeling too. But what?"

"I kinda somehow feel sorry for the dude, y'know?"

"Sorry? For the most powerful Negro in Washington? Yeah, me too."

"Man, that was some weird. So much for working on the inside, eh?"

"You sure got that right, bro."

Soon though I'd get another slightly different lesson on the subject. We went back to campus to inflate the rhetoric and mobilize the students.

The Student Council president, an ally named Vernon Gill, said that since the feds had failed to "acknowledge or answer letters sent in the name of the Howard student body," the council was calling for a "massive demonstration" at the building site on March 22. Not only that, the Student Council had set up a committee of mobilization, and many fraternities, sororities, and the student councils of all five schools had pledged support. So if there was no reply by March 16, demonstrations would commence on the 22.

All of which was totally unprecedented. This was the *official* student government and a host of recognized student organizations. And the action would be on campus. Consequently, our administrators couldn't deny or finesse Howard student involvement on this one. What would they do? And, more to the point, what would the Kennedy administration do? As the days ticked by, we kept issuing statements. Nothing happened.

At about eleven o'clock on the day of the demonstration, which is supposed to begin at one, a few students are beginning to gather on campus. Thelwell and I are in the newspaper office going over the issues and planning strategy. Along with Gill, both of us are supposed to speak at the rally before the demonstration. NAG has already decided that it will be a dignified, peaceful march for the benefit of the press, not a confrontation. We don't want student "civilians" hurt or arrested. By then, after campaigning all over the South, we considered ourselves "soldiers" in the struggle, or as a song had it, "in the army of the Lord."

Then a phone rings and we are informed that the president's office is looking for us. President Nabrit wishes to see us. The quick-witted editor *[Muriel Pettaway]* who took the call said she would try to find us.

On that campus the president was a remote, lofty presence. Neither of us had even so much as spoken to him face-to-face before. Uh-uhm. This can't be good. Man, he's going to try to get us to stop. No, he won't, he knows we can't do that now. Yeah, but suppose he *orders* us to? Damn, why don't we just don't go? Say they couldn't find us. We go *after* the demonstration. We can't do that, it's sneaky, we ain't kids, goddamn. Yeah? But why do we have to go *now*? We go *after* the demonstration, it's easier to get forgiveness than permission. You know that. Yeah, but that would be disrespectful. Besides, Nabrit isn't the enemy. We gotta go now. Why would he wait till the last minute? He's smarter than that. He knows that this way we would almost have to defy him. Well, we have no idea what kinds of phone calls he's been getting. Remember, *there are powerful people . . .* and there's always the budget. So we don't go. We gotta. No, we don't. Not now. What if he tells us to fold? He won't. He might. Let's hope he doesn't because we can't. Look, we won't be disrespectful or defiant. We'll be polite but very clear. And take the consequences? What choice do we have?

"Yo, tell the president's secretary we're on our way."

So we put on our game faces and walk across the campus, past where students are beginning to gather. Neither of us have been inside the president's office before. The door to his inner office is closed. The secretary says he's expecting us. We should knock and go in. We pause, look at each other. Thelwell seems to be stifling a sudden grin. What's funny? We knock and open the door.

The president is at his desk, signing letters. We stand there till he looks up. "With you in a minute," he says.

We can read nothing from his face. Then he rises and walks toward us.

"Young men"—he has a husky, Southern voice—"you all done . . . why I think you done jes' right. You done exactly right." He holds out his hand. I take it. Thelwell looks about to faint from relief.

"These folk, shoot. I tell 'em. I keep telling 'em. All this talk about civil rights . . . why it don't mean a dadburn thing as long as a man can't get hisself a decent job to support his family. Hell, y'all done jes' exactly right." Both of us are speechless. A little embarrassed. We just shake his hand and mumble modestly.

"And," he said, "that demonstration y'all planning. I guess you can claim a victory. By now one of these should be waiting for you over in your office. He handed us a document. The letterhead said U.S. Department of Labor.

Washington, D.C., March 27
Secretary of Labor W. Willard Wirtz acted today to require contractors and unions building the gymnasium at Howard University to comply with the nondiscrimination clause of the construction

275

contract. If they fail to do so, the Secretary said, he will ask the Justice Department to enforce compliance.

. . . Secretary Wirtz acted in his capacity of Vice Chairman of the President's Committee on Equal Employment Opportunity and in accordance with the executive order issued by President Kennedy in 1961.

. . . we are now convinced that persuasion alone will not produce the action required.

. . . He referred to attempts to influence contractors and unions to end discrimination at Howard University and in government construction in the District. Investigation, he said, has shown that . . . qualified Negroes are available to do such work and to enter craft apprenticeship programs.

The secretary gave the unions ten days to begin compliance or the matter would be referred to the Justice Department.

Walking back across campus, I asked Thelwell. "What were you grinning about . . . at the door?"

"You noticed? It was literary. You wouldn't understand."

"Negro, don't be playing that."

"*Invisible Man.* You know, send this Negro a little further."

So we had a rally where about two thousand students showed up. We did what politicians always do. We claimed a victory. The matter was never referred to the Justice Department and no one ever explained to us the changes agreed to. But it was a splendid victory . . . on the inside. I believe the electricians may have taken on three Negro apprentices that year.

CHAPTER XIII

Mississippi (1961–65):
Going Home

They say that freedom is a constant struggle.

When we left Parchman prison in July 1961, many of us knew that we would be coming back. If not to prison, then certainly to the Magnolia State.

We had been learning a lot at Howard: that was our laboratory. We learned even more in NAG: that was our on-the-job training. But Mississippi was my real education and SNCC my alma mater. In black Mississippi I was blessed. Mississippi first taught me the pain and the joy of struggle. It crystallized my politics, opened up my eyes, and taught me how to organize.

SNCC introduced me to the brotherhood of shared danger within bonds of loyalty. Yes, it did. But the struggle in black Mississippi first brought me face-to-face with the best in my people: their patient courage, quiet nobility, and the beauty and power of an enduring culture that had brought them whole through centuries of slavery, poverty, and unspeakable oppression. In meeting them, I would meet the best in myself. Yes, indeed.

In high school I'd read this phrase somewhere: "The South is every Negro's Old Country." I can't recall which famous black writer said that, but at the time I figured it applied only to Africans born in America. Because even folks born in Harlem or Newark would have grown up with their family's Southern stories and memories. Made sense. But of course it had to be different with me. My extended family being Caribbean, our ancestral stories had a calypso rhythm, an island accent, not a blues beat. The South wasn't my old country, so I thought.

So why was I engulfed by an almost nostalgic sense of recognition and homecoming? The place neither looked, sounded, nor really even *felt* like the Trinidad of my childhood, but I sure felt very strongly that I'd come home. I could feel it. But I couldn't *explain* it. It was a gesture, facial expression, an attitude, a personal style and spirit, and these almost always in older people.

The first time I heard anyone else try to describe that exact feeling of *recognition* was Mrs. Hamer, some years later when she came back from Guinea. And guess what? My second time having that same feeling as strong was four years later when I first was in Guinea myself.

There in the Mississippi Delta's vast, almost eerie flatness of cotton lands; in its small hamlets and rural churches, on its dark, dusty plantation back roads; from its fetid jails and the cattle prods and blackjacks of brutal "po-lices"; in the drive-by shootings and midnight bombings of night-riding Klansmen—I saw the best and worse of which human beings were capable.

When I say I learned a lot in Mississippi, that's the Lord's truth. But you know, the truth is, I probably *unlearned* twice as much—which is just as important, in some ways perhaps more important. So this chapter is not an account of SNCC's Mississippi campaign. That can be found elsewhere. This is more about what I learned and unlearned there and the people from whom I learned it. Because, by the time I would leave Mississippi *[early 1965]*, I would be clear on what my life's work was to be. I had discovered what I was—an organizer—and that the movement was my fate.

Greenwood . . . Leflore County . . . the Delta. By the time the school year was over in June 1962, Bob Moses had moved his operation from Amite County into the Delta. One could call Bob's move, as we did, a "strategic withdrawal" or a "tactical relocation." In SNCC we never used the word *retreat*. But, truth be told, Bob and his organizers had sho nuff been run out of SNCC's first Mississippi beachhead down in Amite County. The jailings, beatings, bombings, and finally the murder had, as intended, paralyzed the local community. For the moment nothing more could be accomplished there, so Bob'n them had to move. But we would be back.

Chuck McDew, last one out and locking the Freedom House for the last time, left a note for the Klan, "po-lices," or other interested parties: SNCC DONE SNUCK. But only to resurface in the heart of the place they called the Delta. And this time, SNCC would not be moved. Bob and his troops had learned a thing or three. As they say, experience runs a hard school. Which is how it came about that the new base to which I reported that June 1962 was in the city of Greenwood in the county of Leflore.

The Greenwood SNCC office was four blocks over from the black high school. Which must still have been in session because no sooner had we arrived at the office when a group of high school students came trooping in, all laughing and excited. Soon as they saw us strangers—a carload of us had driven over from Atlanta—the teenagers became shy and fell silent and wide-eyed. So I went over to talk and ended up with a place to stay. The place that would become my home for the next three years whenever I was there.

I was captured by a rangy, long-legged fourteen-year-old, dark and pretty with smooth, lustrous Wolof skin, an animated expression, and huge, expressive eyes. Miss June Johnson decided that I was to stay with her family and nowhere else. When I met the family, I discovered that her mom, Mrs. Lulabelle Johnson, took care of the twelve children of the family. Yet there was always a bed and something to eat for me in that house. That was only the first of many lessons that would, one day, inevitably steer me back to Mother Africa. I became close to the Johnson family, the parents, the grandmother, and the children. In fact, I felt like a family member, and all the Johnsons became stalwarts of the movement in Greenwood. Over the next four years, Mrs. Johnson would take care of a great many SNCC people coming through Greenwood. She always called me her son.

[June Johnson remembers:

"The high school to which I went was the Broad Street Regular High School which was right down the street from the SNCC office.

"No way we could have gotten home without passing by, so we would detour right in. . . . One afternoon Stokely was there. . . . I thought he was very demanding. I thought he was abrasive. I saw that he was profound about his blackness and I thought he was very sincere and very committed to what he had come to Greenwood to do.

"So he began to talk to us about school, and what did they teach us about our history? We pretty much told him and he began to tell us what you need to say to your teachers. What you need to say to your principal. He was very challenging, very intimidating. So in order to develop a working relationship with him, we told him we were country kids growing up and weren't accustomed to people talking to us that way. Like we were grown and that we weren't allowed to talk that way to our teachers and ministers. That if we did, we'd probably get kicked out of school. . . .

"So he developed classes for us. And not just history, he had people helping us with our maths. So we'd have these sessions at night and Stokely was always on our case about our hair, about frying our hair and about our history. And he'd talk to us about why it was important for us to become part of the movement and help people in Greenwood to become registered voters because they could empower themselves and get out and challenge the racist system. . . .

"See, how Stokely came to live with us was because . . . My mother was resisting the movement when it first came. So I was in a serious battle with my mother because this was something I really wanted to do. I'd heard them [the parents] talk about how they were abused and mistreated by these whites in the town. How my mother had to work from five o'clock in the morning to five in

the afternoon for fifteen dollars a week. With twelve children, and my father (Mr. Theodore Johnson) was in the cotton business. He was a cotton binder. So because I wanted to be in the movement, I was mad about bringing everybody home. See, if I latched onto them and brought them home, demanding that my folks feed them and put them up, that gave me leverage to be in the movement, and that' how I got involved.

"Yeah, and that made a lot of us at home. We don't know how, but everybody had a place to stay. But my mom? She thought the sun rose and set itself on Stokely, because Stokely had a charm with older people. He had a charm about himself and my mom took a deep love for Stokely. And because Stokely worked very hard, she took good care of him. She'd make sure he'd get at least one hot, balanced meal every day. My mother would save and hide food for him so other folk wouldn't get it. She would do that. Yes, she would. Because Stokely was determined."]

The Delta itself was not to be believed. Day after day you could sit in the middle of it and not believe what you were seeing or hearing. The landscape was my first experience in *unlearning.* It was unlike anything I'd ever encountered. Quite literally one vast, flat, unbroken cotton and soybean plantation. A friend from Howard I took on a tour of the Delta wrote about the experience:

> In its precise geographic meaning, [the Delta] refers only to the wedge of land between the Mississippi and Yazoo Rivers but [it] extends in popular usage to most of the northwestern quarter of the state. The area of the Delta coincides almost exactly with the Second Congressional District of Mississippi, the home of Senator Eastland, the Citizens' Council, and of the densest population of Negroes in the state. . . .
>
> What can be said about this place that will express the impact of a land so surrealistic and monotonous in its flatness that it appears unnatural, even menacing? Faulkner comes close to expressing the physical impact of the region: ". . . Crossing the last hill, at the foot of which the rich unbroken alluvial flatness began as the sea began, at the base of its cliffs, dissolving away in the unhurried rain as the sea itself would dissolve away."
>
> This description suggests the dominant quality: a flatness like an ocean of land, but within the vast flatness, a sense of confinement, a negation of distance and space that the sea does not have. And there are the rivers—in the east, the headwaters of the river called Big Black, and sluggish tributaries, the Skuna, Yalobusha, and Yocona, which flow into the Tallahatchie, which in turn meets the Sunflower to become the Yazoo, which was called by the Indians "the river of the dead." The Yazoo flows south and west until it meets the Mississippi at the city of Vicksburg.
>
> . . . I once entered the Delta from the west, from Arkansas, over a long,

narrow old bridge that seemed to go for miles over the wide and uncertain Mississippi. It was midsummer and a heat that seemed independent of the sun rose from the land. The slightest indentation in the road's surface became a shimmering sheet of water that disappeared as you approached it. The numbing repetition of cotton fields blurring in the distance wore on one's nerves and perceptions. This has been called the richest agricultural soil in the world. So it may have been, but it also is tough and demanding— no longer boundlessly fecund, it now yields its fruits only after exacting disproportionate prices in human sweat and effort. An old man told me, "For every man it enriches it kills fifty," and some folks joke that "the Delta will wear out a mule in five years, a white man in ten, and a nigger in fifteen."

Which describes only the physical impact of the place, not the primitive economic and racial realities of the society. *Unlearning.* I had understood going in that the Delta was "impoverished," in fact the "poorest section of the poorest state in the Union."

Hell, no. No, no, no! The Delta was in fact very, very rich. It produced great wealth. It was agribusiness on a gigantic scale, highly productive, heavily government subsidized, and based almost totally on the equivalent of slave labor. Our people's slavery.

I must be fair, it wasn't *really* slave labor. Plantation workers, all black, were paid . . . $3 a day from can see to cain't. In 1961, the Delta was rich; it was only *the people* who were poor. Dirt poor. Nineteenth-century poor. *Third world,* to use the favorite term of the U.S. media, poor.

Working on voter registration, I would meet some black folk who did not officially exist. This is 1960s America I'm talking about. I'm talking about people who had been born, lived, worked, married, had children, and would die on the white man's land where they were born, without their birth having been registered anywhere off that plantation. No agency of the state had any official record of their existence. I don't know how widespread this was, but I did meet people in that situation. Some of them had never ventured farther than twenty miles from the plantation of their birth. Until, that is, the owners began to speed up mechanization so as to turn them off the land.

Education? Hey, in some of these counties the *first* schools for blacks had hastily been built in 1954 *after* the *Brown* decision. They didn't even bother to call these squat, ugly concrete-block structures schools: they were designated Negro Attendance Centers. Truth in labeling, Mississippi style.

Medical care? I can still remember a SNCC field report from Panola, a county that was really just one large plantation. The SNCC workers were distressed by the running, chancrelike sores on the faces and limbs of black children. The adults on the plantations felt that when the children entered the fields to work the cotton, the "pizen" (insecticide sprayed by planes over the cotton) entered any little scratch or break in the children's skin and ate away the flesh like acid. We also discovered that people could typically pass their lives on these plantations without once being examined by a doctor or trained nurse.

(In 1963 SNCC had a conference in D.C. The D.C. staff sent all our local people for complete workups from the Medical Committee for Human Rights. Mrs. Hamer, who, until joining the movement had spent her life on a Mississippi plantation, had always had a noticeable limp, which she told us was the result of childhood polio. However, the results of the first complete physical examination of her life—this great-souled woman was then in her forties—revealed she'd never had polio at all. She'd broken her hip as a child. The fracture had never been examined, diagnosed, or set, hence the limp and constant pain she would live with the rest of her life.)

I'm talking about human conditions so primitive and brutal for black people that visitors from the North invariably responded with shock, pain, and disbelief. "Oh, my God, this can't be happening in America. No, not in the twentieth century!" Hey, better believe it.

The elaborate and expensive machinery was nothing *but* America: the crop-dusting planes, the massive tractors, the huge cotton-picking machines, were twentieth-century corporate America in spades.

And this was no hidden aberration lying below the radar screen of America's social conscience. This arrangement was not only *tolerated,* this exploitation was heavily *subsidized* by the federal government, making every American taxpayer, white and black, complicit in the brutalizing of their kin. Then there was the complex network of ownership uncovered by Jack Minnis's SNCC research department. These plantation factories must have been very profitable investments. One was owned by the corporation supplying electricity to Boston, Massachusetts. The majority stockholder of another was Her Majesty, the Queen. Yeah, you heard me. None other than Elizabeth *Regina,* Queen of England, Empress of India, and by the grace of God, majority owner of one of the largest Mississippi plantations only slightly evolved from outright slavery.

Until I left Mississippi in 1965, this eerie, brutal landscape that seemed so completely oblivious to the passage of time would be my base.

Yes, suh, I were "jes' a-learning and unlearning" as Mr. Hartman Turnbow might have said.

But the most important thing Mississippi first taught me was to really love my blackness. Not that I *ever* hated it, but *really* to love it, that's whole 'nother question.

Like everyone else in America I'd been hearing how beaten down, backward, and "slow" the "Southern Negro" was. They'd been "'buked and scorned," oppressed so long and so hard, they'd had all humanity, all pride and resistance, beaten out of them. They'd been reduced to shuffling, scratching their woolly heads, content to bow, grin, and drawl "Yassuh, boss" to any white man. Sounds familiar, right? Besides which, having retreated into a "pie-in-the-sky" religiosity, the Southern Negro would wait for death or the Lord to deliver them. Not exactly promising raw material for militant struggle.

Consequently we "idealistic" Northern students would have to "save" them. We were, in effect, modern missionaries bringing "enlightenment" to the "benighted Negro." Now I'd never exactly believed any of that crap. That had not been my experience at Howard, nor in the New Orleans project, nor the Mississippi jails. But it was in the air. It was implied in the ignorant questions of smug white reporters. It was, and continued to be, the subtext of the media coverage. But it was flat-out nonsense. Utter nonsense.

I met heroes. Humble folk, of slight formal education and modest income, who managed to be both generous and wise. Simple, homespun, unlettered, hardworking, self-respecting men and women, Sterling Brown's people, who took us in, fed us, instructed and protected us, and ultimately *civilized*, educated, and inspired the smart-assed college students.

I could go on for a long time about the courage of our "local peoples." But why reinvent the wheel? You can now consult some excellent books on that subject.*

To be as we were, young and black, and to have the opportunity to work with and get to know women like Mrs. Fannie Lou Hamer, Mrs. Annie Devine, Ms. Victoria Gray, Ms. Susie Ruffin, Mama Quinn, and Ms. Lulabelle Johnson was more than a privilege. It was a benefaction beyond price. I count myself and my SNCC friends very, very lucky indeed.

Because of women like these, some strong men, and the spirit of community we found there, an amazing thing happened, something one would have thought impossible and quite unbelievable. How is it possible to live surrounded by extreme privation, amidst the most brutal *material* poverty; in an atmosphere of unrelieved tension; with your life in real and constant danger; and yet day after day find yourself at your most focused and fulfilled, your spirit at peace? Every day to find terror bal-

---

*Ture particularly recommended five books: Anne Moody's *Coming of Age in Mississippi,* John Dittmer's *Local People,* Charles Payne's *I've Got the Light of Freedom,* Kay Mill's biography of Fannie Lou Hamer, and Elizabeth Sutherland Martínez's *Letters from Mississippi.* —EMT.

anced by exhilaration? But incredibly enough, it happened, it did. Ask any-body who was there.

When dosing me with her bitter bush medicines, Grandmother Cecilia used to encourage me, "Boy, what don't kill you will surely strengthen you." Well, some of us were surely strengthened, a few of us it killed. Many others bore no visible wounds but were permanently damaged. We call those our walking wounded. *They don't come by ones . . . they don't come by twos . . .*

[June Johnson remembers:

"Stokely had a charm about himself with older people. And he had the utmost respect for ministers. Now, it was all right for him to do what he had to do. I mean, he was profound to white folks when they called him boy. He made it very clear that there were no boys around. He was not afraid of the police. He had to make young people know that in order to be free you had to pay a price, a serious price. And that there was nothing wrong with going to jail and he went to jail many times in Greenwood. Many times.

"But in spite of what his vocal was in terms of this and that in public, there was a certain way that he carried himself amongst the people. Stokely had a mild demeanor that he could sit down and be very patient, calm, and intellec-tual and talk through with ministers and what have you. But he wouldn't accept to be disrespected, and then he didn't allow you to disrespect local folk. He didn't allow that. No, he didn't. Now, it was all right for him to do what he had to, but he didn't accept seeing outsiders come in and be disrespectful to the local people. He was very much a local-people person. He was very much for the people . . . always."]

The strong men keep coming . . . strong men coming on . . .
the strong men, strong men . . . coming.

So very much to unlearn . . . I figured, of *course,* that I already knew all about our history. Why, I even considered that was part of my *mission,* to teach the youth our true history.

Well, sitting at night and listening to some remarkable older men talk about their lives—the things they had seen and done; things that had hap-pened to them and their families; the many, many, many different kinds of struggles and strategies they'd tried; the economic heroism of their very survival—was an education. An education in endurance and resource-fulness. These were some brave, smart, solid, centered, infinitely hard-working men, who understood their lives fully. What emerged from their stories was that their people's poverty was not accidental or inevitable. And that the racism around them was *not* simply random acts of irrational prejudice by individual whites. That the evils of Mississippi racism were the expression of a systematic, public policy by the state designed to effect and perpetuate the subjugation of black people. That in an American state, the government was, and had been, waging open warfare—physical, psychological, economic, and military—against half the population because they were black. *And,* that this warfare had been conducted for one hundred years openly, within full view and with the complicity of white America, from the president on down. "Ain' gon' lie to you, son, that's the way it be here."

Yeah, you say, so what's new? You're not saying you didn't know that? Course I knew it, *abstractly,* from books. But I never began to *really feel* it until I looked into the eyes and lined faces of men like Amzie Moore (a truly great African), Mr. Dewey "Big Daddy" Greene, Mr. Hartman Turnbow, Mr. E. W. Steptoe, or Mr. C. C. Bryant and listened to their voices telling their stories. *Then* our history became real to me.

Sometimes the one thing that is the most glaringly obvious is the thing everyone overlooks. Something so blatantly obvious no one seems to see it. Well, I'm sure y'all remember the racist mantra that was (is?) conventional wisdom of white America or Jim Crow? It go somethin' like this:

When two races are unequally endowed but occupy the same area, the only logical, wise (and kind) thing to do is to separate them. Thus each could develop at its own pace. The superior race will not be dragged down or polluted by the inferior, while the less competent one can also proceed in its own limited way, without being overwhelmed and made to continually confront its own inferiority by forced competition, which it can only lose, with the superior race.

Even if you're too young to have heard that particular version, I'm sure you bin hearing its contemporary version from the current generation of right-wing racists who seem to have hijacked the political discussion in white America.

Now I can't think of any African I ever knew who believed that bulldooky. But one heard it so often from "educated Southerners" that I had to assume that they, and white folk in general, must really have believed it.

Then one evening I'm unable to sleep and everything I've been seeing and hearing about the "great state o' Missipah" is running around my head. The entire, elaborate structure of discriminatory laws and statutes. The succession of "Mississippi plans" designed to keep the Negrahs in their place. Because, make no mistake about it, the single, central organizing principle, the major civic concern upon which the social, economic, and political arrangements of the entire state were predicated, was white advantage and black subjugation. And that was clear. The hierarchy of social status, the protocols of racial etiquette and exclusion, the codes of manners and behavior, were *all* racially determined and painstakingly designed to crush my people's spirit. An entire apparatus of law and practices created for one purpose: to encumber and impede black progress. No other earthly reason. None. Like South Africa under apartheid.

"Oh, wow," I yelled. What could have been more obvious? *Them crackers don't even think we inferior at all.* They *can't.* The entire organization of the state was indisputable proof of that. If you so sure a people are inferior, you don't need to spend the time, energy, and obsessive effort creating this barricade of economic and educational impediments and political restrictions. For what? To keep an *inferior* race "in their place"? Surely, if you *know* they inferior, then you simply leave them to stagnate, anchored in place by the weight of their own incompetence. So that's not it. They scared of what might happen if we had a fair shake. *Aie,* by their deeds shall ye know them. From that moment of insight (it takes great insight to uncover the obvious) a lot of things began to fall into place for me.

Language, and especially the spoken word, has always had a serious hold on me. From my earliest childhood I've been just fascinated by words and the sounds and rhythms of words and our people's voices. I still am. Our people take pleasure in wordplay and in the rhythms, tones, and music of spoken language. Usses jes' loves to play with our language. Where do you suppose Dr. King's eloquence came from? And I wasn't the only one in SNCC who came to appreciate the soft cadences and slow music of Southern black speech. In fact, we used to make jokes when, after a month or so, some visiting white graduate student—even a doctoral candidate or two—would begin to sound like "unlettered and ungrammatical" sharecroppers. Imitation, they say, is the highest form of flattery.

For me it was a pleasure and instructive to listen carefully to the skillful way our people use language. Once, I remember, I was talking to this older man, a field hand, outside his little house. A car came into view raising a cloud of dust in the distance. "Oh, oh, son, best you step inside the house for a spell." I stood inside the door and listened as the plantation owner blustered and berated the brother about outside agitators, gratitude, and voting. The brother assured his employer that he knew nothing "'bout that mess." He had "no more use for it than a rattlesnake." Their last exchange was classic. It went something much like this:

"J.T.," the boss asked earnestly, "answer me this: Have we evah abused or mistreated you?"

"Weal, Cap'n, Ah *cain't* really *say* as you has. Nahsuh. Nah, you knows, I sholy couldn' *say* nothin' like that, Missa Charlie."

"Good, good. An' ain't Ah always treated you fair? Ain' Ah *always* been right with you?"

"Cap'n," the brother said thoughtfully, as though searching his memory, "you know, *I got to say* you has. Yessuh, I sho gotta say that. I *could nevah* look in your face and say yo' hasn't been good t'me. Nahsuh, Ah sho would never do that, suh."

"J.T."—the boss beamed, confirmed in his own benevolence—"you a good ol' boy."

"Mighty kind of you, suh," J.T. agreed. He watched the car drive out of sight, then turned to me. "Son, tell me one more time where that meetin' is to be."

When I first heard Mrs. Hamer talk about how disgusted the people were, I had no idea at the time that her description would become such a part of popular vocabulary. "We be sick an' t'ard of this mess. Fack is, we sick an' t'ard o' being sick an' tar'd. But we keeps on, an' we keeps on, *'cause we got to keep on keeping on.*" And again in Atlantic City at the 1964 Democratic National Convention, when she told the Democratic leadership, "We didn't come heah for no two seats, for *all* of us is tired." I seriously doubt that Hubert Humphrey or Walter Mondale recognized the many layers of meaning, the complex levels of political wisdom and ironies, compacted into that simple little sentence.

The day I told Mr. Hartman Turnbow how three generations of movement women—Mrs. Hamer, Annelle Ponder, and June Johnson (my little sister)—had been beaten in the Winona jail, his face grew overcast, his voice thoughtful.

"Y'know, son," he mused, "water seek de low places but power seek de weak places." Another time he told me, "Soon as the leaves turn color in the fall, evrah peckerwood in Holmes County an' his pappy, they calls theyself goin' a-hunting. They be after them li'l ol' squirrels and rabbits. With them, huntin' be a tradition an' a practice. But, y'know somethin? Iffen them li'l critters had some guns of they own? Why, I bet you the very next day they be mighty few white men's lef' in this county be calling theyself hunters. *So effen Ah had me Bob Moses' job? Why, Ah'd git me some guns an' Ah'd sweep all the way from Holly Springs raht down to Biloxi.*"

Mr. Turnbow never staged his march from Mississippi's most northerly town to the sea, but after he tried to register and "some white fellers" tried to burn him out, "Ah were not being nonviolent. Ah had me my rifle an' Ah commenced a-popping." When the sheriff accused him of attempting to start the fire himself, Mr. Turnbow asked, "Sheriff, now why would Ah try to burn mah own house an' Ah don't even have no insurance on it?"

A few days before or after his friend Mr. Herbert Lee was gunned down, slight, wiry Mr. E. W. Steptoe went to the Liberty courthouse to register. The sheriff, gun conspicuously in hand, challenged him. "What business you got heah, Steptoe? State your damn business." Mr. Steptoe, looking from the gun to the lawman's eyes, said mildly, "Wal, Sheriff, *if Ah lives,* Ah reckon I'm goin' reddish to vote." And he stepped right on past the hulking lawman.

My people, oh, mah peoples.

We had a Freedom Day in one of the Delta towns, the first one in that county. One old lady, dressed in her Sunday best and exuding determination and pride, had walked the line in the blazing sun all morning. After taking and failing the test, she was asked by a reporter how she felt.

"Right proud," she said. "Why, suh, Ah feels downright proud." Because, as she explained, even though "we ain't what we *want* to be, an' we ain't what we *goin'* to be, Ah thanks God Almighty that *we sho ain't what we was.*"

I've got the light of freedom, I'm gonna let it shine.

And, of course, there is the Reverend Mr. Hulme and the governor. It was before my time but had deservedly become legendary. Only days after the *Brown* school decision, the governor *[Hugh White]* called in seventy black leaders to denounce the court's decision and to belatedly propose an "education equalization" scheme, by which he proposed to begin to close the *$115 million* differential that separated the state's spending on black and white education. One hundred and fifteen million? Tells you something about "separate but equal," huh? The meeting ended with the Reverend Mr. Hulme's famous response.

"Guvnor, you shouldn't be mad at us. Those were nine white men who rendered that decision. Not one colored man had anything to do with it. The real trouble, Guvnor, is that for too long, *you've given us schools in which we could study the earth through the floors and the stars through the roof.*"

And we should not lightly dismiss that forty acres and a mule either. Later, Kwame Nkrumah would tell me, "All liberation begins with land." Working the Delta, we began to see clearly how the withholding of those forty acres had been no trivial blow. In fact, almost exactly a hundred years later, the lasting, visible, painful consequences of that betrayal were still indelibly etched in our people's condition. Of the many, many betrayals and disappointments Africans had suffered at the hands of this republic, I began to see how Congress's failure to make good on its promise of those forty acres to the freedmen was arguably the most far-reaching and injurious. No doubt about it.

Organizing in the Delta, it was easy—and painful—to see just how our people's history—and by extension that of the entire South and the nation—would have been vastly different had those forty hard-earned acres bought and paid for by centuries of stolen labor been distributed.

Organizing in those counties where some black families held and worked their own land was so much easier, a pleasure. In certain parts of

Holmes County—Mileston for instance, or in a wonderful little community called Mt. Beulah, where *all* the land was owned by Africans—you immediately felt the difference in people's confidence and manner. The way they presented themselves.

Folks didn't shuffle, they stood straight and looked you in the eye. Their eyes didn't flicker uneasily over your shoulder to see if the man was watching. These communities had a spirit of self-sufficiency, of independence, and of collective capability and cooperation. Wherever our people could, by their own effort, coax a living however modest from their own land, you found determination and inner psychological strength.

And across the state, leadership often came not from those whom Mrs. Hamer used to call derisively "the preachers and the teachers," but from men (and one notable woman, Mrs. Laura McGhee) who owned land.

And then there was the church. True, on occasion Mrs. Hamer would denounce fainthearted "preachers and teachers." And I was coming from Harlem where a favorite target of the stepladder nationalists was "Reverend Pork Chop" and it was common to hear Christianity, "the white man's religion," denounced simply as a snare and impediment to black liberation.

Let the record show, though, that most of our meetings took place in small, rural churches. And that in the summer of '64 in Mississippi alone, over thirty such churches—most of whose insurance had suddenly been canceled—were burned to the ground. Crimes for which, by the way, no one has ever been charged.

So that what I came to see was that our people's "religiosity" was neither simply (as some opinion had it) passive escapism nor the tight-jawed and self-righteous sanctimony of self-proclaimed "saints." What I came to see very clearly was that with our people the religious impulse at its finest was something much more profound. Morally and socially effective, it incorporated a living vision of history, self, and struggle. A vision that was central to their survival, both spiritual and psychic.

Folks used to think I was joking when I'd say that one reason the Mississippi Project was one of SNCC's most successful was in no small part due to the fortuitous accident of Bob's last name. Until, that is, they sat in a crowded church and heard Mrs. Hamer leading the singing of her signature freedom song. And heard her, when she reached that verse, sing:

> Who's them sisters dressed in black?
> Must be the hypocrites turning back.
> Who's them sisters dressed in red?
> Must be the children Bob Moses led.
> Go tell it on the mountain . . .

Then, even the most obtuse could not fail to feel the recognition of biblical inevitability that would ripple among the older folk and the more devout of the youth. At such times I'd joke to myself, "If only my folks had had the foresight to name me Joshua, this movement would be unstoppable."

For these folks the movement was inevitable, the long-awaited fulfillment of prophecy. They *knew* it was coming, the only thing they didn't know was *when* . . . for "no man knows the day or the hour." When some nervous old preacher, justifiably worried about exposing his church building to the danger of a movement meeting, would ask querulously, "Son, you sure this be the Lord's work?" I could resort to the Old Testament to make an incontrovertible case. I did a lot of organizing out of the pages of the Old Testament.

"Oh, yes, Reverend. T'ain't just the Lord's work, it's the Lord's *will*, Reverend, the Lord's will. As the good book say, 'Come let us labor in the vineyards of the Lord, for behold the harvest is great though the workers be few.'"

Because this *African* Christianity of our people was a living faith selectively based on the highest values of ancient scriptures. From the depths of slavery, against the intractable evidence of their bitter experience, our ancestors had reached their imagination deep into the sacred books of the ancient Hebrews (a very *African* world by the way) and plucked out an enduring metaphor of their condition and a view of history. A long view, which our people enshrined in the doctrine and liturgy of their church and the poetry of their sorrow songs. Those same spirituals that Dr. Du Bois had called "the most beautiful expressions of the human spirit this side of the seas. The singular spiritual heritage of this nation." *Let the church say ahmen!*

So my "peoples" were strong in faith and certain of their ultimate deliverance. For in faith all things are possible. And overarching this narrow world was the infinite grace and certain justice of God's purpose, the gradual and unchanging arc of whose universe curved toward freedom.

So my people articulated a God, the God of Abraham, Moses, and the prophets. A God of justice and of ultimate and righteous retribution. A God who absolutely forbade oppression and was not mocked. A God who bound the captives' wounds, "There is a balm in Gilead," they comforted themselves, "to make the wounded whole." A God who cast down the mighty—"Pharaoh's army got drownded," they exulted—who raised up the lowly, yea making the crooked straight and the rough smooth. For were we not also God's children? "In time, chillun, all in God's time," they counseled, "'cause even the sun do move, no lie can live forever, and the arc of his universe, it curve towards freedom. *It do, it do.*"

So my people were sho nuff armored by faith—a faith not in principalities or powers, not in the goodwill of princes nor in sons of men, but in the ultimate justice of divine purpose, that irresistible motion of the universe that manifests among men as history. And the Lord helps those who help themselves. So a faith in their own strenuous and collective effort: "Lifting as ye climb. Walk together, chillun, don't you git weary." Seize the time when it come.

Yeah, you say, so that's the tradition. You probably learned that in the chapel at Howard. Mayhaps, but what I *saw and felt* in Mississippi was that these ideas were real, still living and informing the people's view of reality and themselves as much as they infused the language of their songs. So that, let us say, at a meeting in a lonely church—never mind that the Klan or the sheriff's men were driving by flashing their headlights—when we sang "Guide my feets, Lord, while I run this race, for I don't want to run this race in vain" or "Go down, Moses, way down in Egypt land, tell ol' Pharoah, let my people go," and "Wade in the water, chillun, God's gonna trouble the water," it was prophecy being fulfilled and history made manifest around us.

Not in spite of, but because of the danger, and through those ancient songs, the music, we were at one with our ancestors. You felt their presence. At these times when we would sing these songs, I'd always get an almost eerie feeling that, somehow by the power of that music, time was eclipsed. I think we all shared something of that feeling. But I know I'd feel in those moments of peril that our mood and circumstances were exactly the same as our ancestors'—those nameless Africans, enslaved in this strange land, who out of faith and the troubles they were seeing had composed words of such enduring inspiration. And through the words and the music we felt their presence. How else could the words of those old songs, essentially unchanged, feel so right and work so well? "How can you," as the Mystic Revelations of Ras Tafari would ask, "Sing King Alpha's song in a strange land?"

It was an experience that we could not have bought and is never to be repeated or forgotten. It is little wonder that our most effective local organizers all could sing and summon up where necessary the rolling cadences of a song sermon. Some like Sherrod and Bevel were indeed young seminarians. Sam Block (peace be unto him), Willie (now Wazir) Peacock, and Hollis Watkins were all beautiful singers. I never was much of a singer myself, but I did learn to preach a little bit. . . .

Hitting a straight lick with a crooked stick.

That was one of Sterling Brown's favorite lines. It was his metaphor for the folks' artful way with a story. When he used it, Prof meant a style of indirection, cunningly saying one thing to signify another.

It didn't take me any time to see how deeply ingrained in the people's style of discourse this approach was, especially in public situations. It became clear that some older folks took great pride in constructing stories that took a crooked path to hit a straight lick on whatever issue was being discussed. Almost as if it were intellectually beneath them to simply jump on the naked issue without first "dressing it up some." Some of the younger Southern people seem to have mastered that style and skill—Bob Mants and Ed Brown in particular come to mind.

Later when I'd encounter almost the exact same storytelling approach to discussion among village elders in the hills of Guinea, it would feel familiar and comfortable. In Mississippi, you saw this best in "mass" meetings, most of which rarely had more than thirty people in attendance. I recall one meeting "out in the rural" where the community had come under severe pressure because of the eviction of people from the surrounding plantations. People whose homes were already crowded were taking in families less fortunate, a child here, two there. But clearly that could only be a desperate holding action. The crisis was real, growing, and coming ever closer.

The movement was appealing for federal intervention in terms of emergency aid. Good luck. We were also collecting food and clothes in the North, but this too could only be a drop in the bucket. So the meeting was unusually well attended and the mood very, very somber. "What is we gon' do?"

As was the custom, everyone who felt so moved got up to testify. I remember two speakers. First was, I think, a preacher, a stout, bull-shouldered, older gentleman with a close-cropped head and a deliberate way of talking. After him a large lady would pick up on the man's effort with a story of her own.

What is we gon' do?

"Wal," he said, "it put me in min' of a time when things was mighty hard . . . fer the rabbits." Then in a deep, unhurried voice that commanded the meeting's attention, the deacon tells a story. The hounds were hunting the poor defenseless rabbits to near extinction. So hard-pressed they couldn't even sneak into the fields to nibble a little grass. Driven to distraction, the rabbits called a mass meeting. Unable to find a solution, they decided to commit mass suicide. Yassuh, to drown theyself. So they locked paws and started for the river. A long line of rabbits moving as one in the moonlight. They topped a rise and came face-to-face with the hounds out looking for rabbits to chase.

But when them ol' dogs saw this long, unbroken line of rabbits, shoulder to shoulder, advancing on them steady, them ol' hounds turned tail and took off running. Ran so far and ran so fast they were outen the county before sunup. Rabbits had no more trouble. Not a bit.

Hit a straight lick . . .

Folks were laughing and applauding, but not everyone. "Now, Elder Jones, I know you ain't saying we gotta go drown ourself, now, is you?"

"No, you know he ain' saying any of that," the large lady intervened. "He saying something else. Y'know, hit remind me of these two little boys.

"See hit was these two brothers walking along jest a-chunking rocks at evrah thang they meet. Evrah thang dey see, nothing but a rock up side dey haid. They come upon a cow. The biggest boy, he went upside that ol' cow's back with a rock. The cow jumped up, holler moo, and run off. The li'l one laughed. You know how boys is."

So the path of destruction proceeded to their great amusement. They hit a mule, a donkey, a pig, a rooster, and a duck, each of which gave the appropriate bray, cackle, or quack, ran off or flew away. "Then they comes to this big, I mean it was a big, ole hornets nes'."

"Ooohiee, looka that," said the little one, "Le's bust that sucker wide open." He drew back his arm, but his big brother grabbed it.

"No," he said, "no. We ain't gon' chunk that un."

"We isn't? Why isn' we gonna bus' that one?" the younger asked. "Le's do it."

"Nah. Uh-uh, we's sho ain't gonna bust that un," the older brother said. "An' the reason we ain't gonna do none o' that is . . . *because dey's organized.*"

. . . *Wid a crooked stick.*

The men used to tell a different kind of story when they were "drinking likker an' telling lies." Out in the plantation quarters the likker in question was an evil-looking, oily, yellowish stump likker the man called "gosh" or "slap-yo-mammy." This moonshine smelled bad and had a metallic taste, but the stories were good. A good many of these tall tales concerned a slave named John, more properly High John the Conqueror. Now, High John he was a "be" man. He be there when times was good and he be there when times was hard. He be always outwitting the white folks and successfully stealing pigs or chickens, which he'd share with the hungry folk. Ol' High John, High John the Conqueror.

High John's owner was a gambling cracker. He'd rather bet money than eat shrimp, and High John was clever enough to win him a lot of money. Now, on the neighboring plantation was a slave named Goliath. This Goliath was a massive, bullet-headed, bull-necked nigra, meaner than a jailhouse dawg and strong as ten mules. His master had a standing bet of one thousand gold dollars that no one could beat this slave fighting. He'd killed more than twenty strong black men.

So High John's master's eyes got big for them thousand dollars and he set to thinking. "Boy," he called one of the slaves. "Go fetch me John."

"Boss, High John done gone fishin' and say he don't want no nigras disturb him."

The master didn't like that one bit, but he knew High John. "He said that, now did he? Well, I guess I jes' have to go disturb him my own self. Boy, fetch me mah horsewhip." And off he stomped looking mighty angry.

Down to the creek there was High John lying on his back in the shade holding a cane pole twixt his toes.

"John," said Ol' Massa, sweet as milk, hiding the whip behind his back. "Yo' know that Goliath nigger?"

"Reckon Ah do," said John, looking at his line. "Reckon Ah do, Cap'n."

"Think you can whup him fighting?"

"Doesn't thank," said High John, who was not one to waste too many words on white folk.

"You doesn't, uh, don't think you can?" Ol' Massa asked.

"Doesn't thank," said High John. "Ah knows."

"You don't think. You knows? Knows, I mean know what?" Ol' Massa asked. He wuzn't right bright, y'know.

"I *knows* that boy ain't goin' fight me," John explained.

"Oh, yes, he is," Ol' Massa said. "'Cause I already done bet Colonel Jackson one thousand dollars."

"You done whut?" High John looked at him. "Well, makes no never mind. That boy ain't goin' fight me."

"Well, you best be right," the boss man said, "'cause, n——, if you lose me my money, you gone wish he'd gone on an' killed yo' black ass."

"Yo' money safe, Cap'n. That ol' boy don't want no smallest part o' High John. I kin win yo' that money, but you may not like how Ah'm gon' do it now."

"You win me that money, boy, you be all right with me. I won't fergit you. Boy, but you damn sure better be right. Heah me?"

"Bet yo' life an' live fo' evah, Cap'n. That boy ain't gon' want no part of me. An' Ah knows you ain't gon' fergit me, neither."

And High John pulled his straw hat back over his eyes and make pretend he sleeping.

Day of the fight all the white folks gather at the fighting place. All the blacks be watching from a good distance 'cause none of them cared to get too close to that crazy Goliath. He were a fearsome sight. He were seven foot tall, even though he had bowlegs, and went about fo' hundred pounds. His li'l ol' pig eyes were bloodred, his skin were coal black. He had an iron collar and a long, heavy ol' iron chain round his neck. On both sides this chain was fixed to a sturdy tree. Live oak on the right. Hickory tree on the left, and evrah time Goliath jerked them chains them big ol' trees would creak and bend like they fixing to break clean. He jes' a-foaming and a-bellowing and a-smacking hisself upside the head. Pow. Pow. Pow. He were a fearsome sight, yes indeedy.

The fight s'posed to be at noon. The sheriff, who was holding the two bags of gold, pulled out his watch.

"Five minutes," he announced. "Yore boy ain't heah in five minutes, the purse go to Colonel Jackson."

High John's missis she start to fume and fuss at Ol' Massa. Jus' a-fussin' an' a-fuming. "Tol' you going lose owah money. That shif'less John done run off so now you done lost a slave too. An' if John do come, it's the same thang. That ugly ol' Goliath n—— going kill him sho. Oooh, I cain't bear to even look at him. You crazy ol' fool," an' she jest would not stop.

Be half a minute to go an' the sheriff be looking at his timepiece and counting down. Ol' Missis so angry until she cry living eye water and she ain't stopped fussing even one little bit. "You dad-blasted ol' fool. Done lost us our money and one shiftless darky."

Suddenly Ol' Massa give a mighty shout. "Great Gawd in the mornin'. Here come John. We got us a fight. We got a fight." He so excited his face gits all red and he jump into the air and slapped his Stetson down in the dust. Everybody—even Goliath—turned to look where he pointing.

And sho nuff heah come ol' John. Had him on a top hat and a white linen suit and he be riding a white horse. It was Ol' Massa's best suit, his bes' hat, and his favorite thoroughbred racing horse. An' there come High John, horse be jes' a trotting an' a-cantering, John he be jes' a-stylin' and a-bowing, greeting the folk jes' like he was a congersman.

"Howdy do. Good to see ya. So good o' y'awl to come. Howdy. Good to see ya now."

Jes' coming through the crowd a-bowing and a-smiling and tipping his hat polite as you please. Yas, suh. Ol' High John. High John the Conquerer. Even ol' Goliath forgot to roar and beller, he stood jes' a-watching an' beholding like the rest of folk.

Ol' Missis, she could not believe her eyes or her husband's bes' suit or his bes' hat or his purebred racing horse.

"N——," she screamed. "You shiftless, no-count, nappy-head, chicken-stealing, snuff-dipping—"

She never got to even finish. High John jumped down offen that horse an' walked over to her.

"Woman," he roared, "ain't I done told you not to evah call me outen mah name?"

And he opened his hand and *kapow. He smacked that white woman down in the dust.* Y'hear me, chillun?

There was a dead silence, broken by this loud crash. When Goliath, crazy as he was, saw High John smack that white lady, it scared him near to death. He tore down them trees, broke off them chains, and took off a-running. Nobody know where he go.

"Negra bad nuff to smack Ol' Missus," he muttered, "whut he gon do to po' me? That *mus'* be the baddes' negra God's got."

Ol' High John look at that boy a-running. "Colleck yo' money, Cap'n," he say to Ol' Massa. "Diden Ah tell you that boy doan want no part o' me?"

Ol' High John. High John tha Conqueror.

[This, I know, was young Carmichael's favorite of the High John stories. —EMT]

CHAPTER XIV

A Band of Brothers,
a Circle of Trust

A great deal has been written about SNCC, not all of which is accurate. By far the best of these accounts are the witnesses from folk who were there. More of our movement brothers and sisters should make a serious effort to write their stories before it's too late. There is still a lot of history—much too much—that we carry around only in our heads. The latecomers, outside observers, and foreign correspondents who have done most of the writing can't help but impose their own political preconceptions and Monday-morning-quarterback hindsight. Some of this, surprisingly, is quite good, a lot just plain wrong, and some outright malicious. We must tell our stories. I won't say we "owe it to history" if only because I've been hearing and ignoring that for a great many years.

I came onto the SNCC staff just as the organization was beginning to take form after the Freedom Rides. The time when folks first began to drop out of school to work full-time in the South. I watched the organization grow, evolve, and disappear almost as quickly as it had grown. I was there and know what happened, much of the how and why, and exactly the way things went down. Or at least, I have strong views on that process, and of course, I make no claims to being a historian, so what follows is in no way intended to be a "history of SNCC." It is *my* experience, what I learned from it then, and what I've come to understand since.

That SNCC was unique—an organization of American youth that actually played a central role in transforming the political history of the South and the nation—is now commonplace. Everyone says that. But the things that were most unprecedented about the organization seem either to have escaped most observers or to have been egregiously misunderstood.

Let's begin at the gitgo. With Ms. Ella Jo Baker (eternal peace be upon her). When Ms. Baker called that first meeting of sit-in activists, nobody attending, but *nobody,* could have envisioned anything like an *independent* organization. What you saying? We're talking about college "kids," black Southern college students, operating off their campuses on weekends.

That's what we all did. Nobody had any idea that they could create and maintain an *independent* political organization. Or become full-time freedom fighters. None. None of them were even *thinking* in those terms. Ms. Baker planted that seed. I can still hear Julian Bond talking about how floored he and the other students at the Shaw University Conference were at the notion of an independent organization run by students.

Then, once the issue was discussed and the conference voted to be independent, reality set in. How was it to be structured? How administered? Who would pay for the office? The phone? Where would the money come from to bond folks out of jail? To pay lawyers? That might explain some the attractiveness of the Jail, No Bail slogan. Then again, how would people live? Would there be salaries, and if so, where was *that* money to come from? And that was just the practical part. The nuts-and-bolts, dollars-and-cents, pay-the-bills part (which, thank God, Jim Forman would take on his shoulders and wrestle with for almost the entire life of the organization). The part about whether an *independent* organization of mostly African Southern students could survive even for a month, part. At their most wildly optimistic, folks gave the organization five years to live.

[Chuck McDew remembers:

"We didn't really know exactly what we were going to do, but we knew we were going to change the face of America. We talked in terms of five years for a couple of reasons. First, we felt if we go more than five years without an understanding that the organization would then be disbanded, we run the risk of becoming institutionalized or being more concerned with trying to perpetuate the organization and, in doing so, giving up the freedom to act and to do. So we talked about five years, period. The other thing we said was that by the end of that time you'd either be dead or crazy. . . . We'd seen people burn out already. It hadn't been a full year and we were seeing that already. . . .

". . . We were taking it on faith. None of us had ever done it (putting together an independent, militant organization), so we really didn't know how to do it. Chuck Jones—another of the three founding 'Charleses,' of McDew, Sherrod, and Jones—put it this way: 'Man, we just plain jumped off that cliff blind and learned to fly on the way down.'"]

It was Ms. Baker who provided the metaphorical wings. Her calm, rational presence and evident confidence in us gave *us* faith. We could do this.

But it really was the CORE Freedom Rides—which we had made ours—and the Kennedys' sudden interest in black voter registration that promised us what little start-up money we had, or thought we would have. Though, as Jim Forman would be quick to point out, let the record show, that the bulk of this liberal VEP (Voter Education Project) money that the Kennedys had been dangling before the movement continued to go to the older "adult" organizations. And this long after it had become crystal clear that the organization with the most staff working full-time and most creatively on voter registration was SNCC. I guess we students were a cheap date. A hundred dollars of VEP money could pay the salaries of ten of our field secretaries for a week. I doubt whether the NAACP or SCLC could have hired two people for that.

At the same time, other questions equally or even more fundamental had to be engaged. Questions we had to ask ourselves and continue to ask ourselves over the life of the organization. Ask and be prepared to have the answers change and keep on changing as the organization grew in size and influence and as political conditions changed around us. We may have all arrived at the same jumping-off place, but we had reached that place from very different starting points and by slightly different routes. So we had to find common ground on which to agree.

Just what is SNCC? Organizationally? Politically? Philosophically? What are its goals, purposes, and means? How do we understand ourselves? What is our role? How would SNCC be different from the NAACP? From SCLC? Were we kidding ourselves and really just trying to found an *institution* after all? Something intended to outlive us? Thanks largely to Ms. Baker, those questions got answered in ways that allowed us to bond together seamlessly, at least for then.

But, as I've said, these questions would also persist over the life of the organization and even beyond. Because, up to today, wherever ten or twelve SNCC veterans are gathered together, these questions will certainly raise their gnarly old heads, *fresh* and contentious as ever. For if, as Chuck Jones put it, we had to learn to fly before hitting the ground, we also had to decide the style and trajectory of that flight: Just what kind of bird were we, buzzards or falcons?

The answers we came up with gave the organization its identity and evolving character. Which of course had everything to do with the people we were or imagined ourselves to be. The urgency of these same questions had made those endless all-night discussions—which had begun in Nashville—so exciting and intense. I'm not going to even try to recapitulate those debates now. What is important is that they came out of the absolute necessity to define ourselves as we went along and to keep doing that. The process this gave rise to and became a large part of the organizational culture.

In fact, before long, left intellectuals began analyzing SNCC's "ideology" of "participatory democracy" and our "antileader philosophy." Both concepts were held up as SNCC's prescription if not for organizing society at large, then certainly for running a radical political organization. Especially *participatory democracy,* that became the New Left mantra, their answer both to "representative" democracy *and* democratic centralism. We always laughed at these theoretical formulations.

Because this wasn't SNCC "ideology" or any kind of advanced social "theory." I mean, we never proclaimed that the organization *had* to proceed by consensus rather than majority vote. Or, as C. (Junebug) Cox would ask, "Where is it carved in stone that decision-making *has* to entail all night debate until consensus is attained? I have seen no graven tablets." Well, it just happened that way. Why? Because it had to. Because it could not conceivably have happened in any other way. I don't understand why people couldn't see that. Check out the situation.

You've got twenty or thirty very different young people in the room. All have taken time out of school because this is where they want to be. Nobody is being paid to be there. Each is in some way a rebel. These be some stubborn folk. Most are leaders back at their schools. None are particularly good at taking orders or allowing themselves to be intimidated. And if they don't *believe* in something, you can flat out forget it. But they do believe generally in what the group is trying to do, which is to fight injustice and end racism. Many will have shared dangers together. So they like and respect each other, particularly the courage and commitment. The level of *education* varies, but the level of *intelligence* is high. Unusually so. But the level of involvement is even higher. There are some strongly held views. Some will become "famous." A few will become politicians. A number will officially be declared "geniuses." Some will go on to distinguished careers. Some will never make it back to school, and some will never fully recover from the stress and danger. But as a group they are some very, very interesting young people.

So far as the young organization is concerned, nothing, but *nothing,* is written in concrete. So how are decisions to be made in such a gathering? Decisions that folk will honor and be bound by? The notion of an authority figure, leader, or group of leaders issuing orders is laughable. No person or group has authority to "fire" anyone. Close majority votes won't work because what if the minority seriously disagrees? Nobody is gonna risk his or her life for a program or policy with which he or she seriously disagrees. I think you begin to see the dimension of the problem.

All you could do is talk it out. Whatever time that takes. And because folks really respect each other and the purpose that brought them here . . . and because the issues are deadly serious and decisions have to be made . . . and because people are indeed earnest and the talk is interesting, folk hang in. Most everybody contributes something to the discussion, if only questions at first. Gradually, very gradually, shared understandings, an analysis, and language acceptable to everyone begin to emerge. Then someone, sometimes but by no means always Ms. Baker, summarizes. "Okay, now, are we agreed that? . . . Can we say the following? Do I hear objections?" Bingo! Consensus. Joy, happiness, hugs. A sense of unity, accomplishment . . . relief.

But its being SNCC, there's always going to be one: "But I thought we said . . . I still don't understand why . . ." Groans, muffled curses, and we have to back up and start over from whatever the point of objection was.

But, y'know, for quite a while it did actually work like that. If only because there was no other way it could have. Of course, I never claimed to have been the most patient African in the world, and sometimes my impatience would show. But once, very gently, Ms. Baker pulled my coat. "Stokely, you know, you're going to have to learn to be more patient."

"But, Ms. Baker, some of these people jes' loves to hear themselves talk. I know them, they be testifying and posturing . . ."

"So . . . let them. They will get to the point. Not everyone can be as quick as you, Stokely, but everyone is as important."

"I know that, Ms. Baker, but still . . ."

"Of course it's important that we all *agree*. But it's just as important that we all *understand*. However long that takes. *We have to work with people where they are.* Now some folks don't say much. But you watch them. They are listening very carefully. And thinking. Some are dealing with these questions for the first time. But they are learning and soon they'll be speaking. In SNCC, they have to feel free to speak and that's important however long it takes."

Ms. Baker was right, and as you can see, I've never forgotten that conversation. It became an article of faith for me in all the organizing I've done during my life. Because what came out of that process was more than an organization or even a philosophy. It was really a "culture," a way of dealing among ourselves and with the people we were trying to organize. Somewhere along in there—very early—we took to calling ourselves "a band of brothers and a circle of trust." *[Later amended to "a band of brothers and sisters."—EMT]* Which I believe we were. But "participatory democracy" was neither theory nor ideology, it was simply necessary. There were real issues to resolve, a clear role to define, a collective identity to agree on.

So far as structure, we had only two officers: a chairman who "spoke for" the organization, and an executive secretary, who did the administrative work. There was also an executive committee of, I believe, some twenty-one people, which was supposed to "set policy," but that was a joke. Not because we didn't respect the committee, or because it never met or took a vote, that I remember, but because no one was ever quite sure who was on it or who wasn't. It did not matter. Whenever the executive committee met, whoever happened to be around and felt like it simply sat in and spoke his or her piece. I can't remember any staff member present ever being challenged nor, come to think of it, any "policy" that it handed down. I mean in early SNCC.

"Offices" didn't matter but we really respected our officers. Jim *[Forman, executive secretary]* because he worked so hard, was deeply committed, resourceful, and really fought *hard* for the survival of the organization—politically and financially. John *[Lewis, chairman]* because he was brave and had paid some serious dues. Besides, he seemed to actually like going around reading speeches that reflected what we were about. That, at first, was about all the "national" structure that we needed or wanted.

How we understood ourselves and our roles evolved naturally out of those legendarily long meetings. Here are some of the hard questions we wrestled with and the conclusions we arrived at. Of course, and lucky for you, the long, winding discussion that got us there cannot be reproduced here.

What is SNCC really?

We are a collection of mobile organizers. We go wherever there is a need, when we are invited, stay only as long as we are wanted, and serve the people's needs as they tell us. *So, we do anything?* No. We help the community do as much as they are willing to do, within reason and "SNCC principles," as long as it serves the struggle. *Serves the struggle?* To empower the people to represent themselves and liberate the community.

What aren't we?

SNCC is not a membership organization (NAACP) trying to organize local chapters or build an institutional membership base. We organize the people to speak in their own interest and try to leave behind us strong leaders and organizations forged in struggle. We are not one-shot mobilizers (SCLC) who come in to lead and speak for the community. Mobilizing hundreds of people in mass demonstrations and arrests, then leaving the community to pick up the pieces when media attention shifts. Our way is to live in the community, find, train, or develop representative leadership within strong, accountable local organizations or coalitions that did not exist before, and that are capable of carrying on the struggle after we leave. When we succeed in this, we will work ourselves out of a job. Which is our goal.

We were not as naive as this sounds. In fact, we used to joke that to the extent we were successful, it would be precisely those organizations we helped create that would one day run us out of town, our militant presence having become an embarrassment. Either so they could assert their autonomy or move to mend fences and enter pragmatic negotiations with the local establishment, which by that time would have no reason to like us. In fact, excellent reason to hate our guts.

Well, then, who are we?

People young enough, free enough, as yet without the family and career obligations, which will surely come, and bad enough to be able to devote full-time to the fight against racist injustice. *But why?* Because we may never have that degree of freedom or the opportunity again. But for whom? For our people—our parents who could not do it and for our children who will not have to.

And for how long?

How long? Not long. Remember "free by '63"? Yeah, and "still alive in '65?" For as long as it takes or as long as you can. Folks drop in, folks drop out, but the struggle goes on. Everyone's contribution is important. We say we work with people where they are. Some can give a month, some a year, some everything. Some will come to a meeting, others will go to jail. Some will slip a dollar in your hand, others put up their house for bail. We work with people where they are—from each according to his ability . . .

On nonviolence.

Talking about SNCC principles . . . I mean, can we talk about nonviolence? What's to talk about? That ain't negotiable. We nonviolent, period.

Yeah, but what does that really mean? At all times and in all ways? See, the other night I was at Mr. Steptoe's. When it got dark, the family brought out their guns. Asked me if I wanted one. What's SNCC's position then? What was I supposed to do? What does the organization expect? *Whoee*, long, *long* discussion.

Conclusion: SNCC is officially nonviolent. This organization will not buy, store, or distribute weapons. SNCC workers will not carry guns. But we certainly cannot and will not be asking folks living in the teeth of the Klan to unilaterally disarm. You want to take that responsibility: to ask folks not to defend themselves? How can we?

Fine, but what if they offer us a gun? Well, bro, tha's between you, Jesus, and your conscience. Do you even know how to handle a gun? Can you shoot straight? Do you help defend the home or do you be nonviolent? That's entirely on you.

That seemed right to me and most folk. But a few people wondered openly if that was in "the true spirit of nonviolence." Dr. King says that "the *tactic* of nonviolence without the *spirit* of nonviolence can be a form of violence." I also knew that I wasn't about to check on my people up in the Delta to see if anyone going out on the highway after dark was carrying something heavy. Especially after the terrorists sprayed Bob and Jimmy's with a semiautomatic rifle outside Greenwood.

On red-baiting and political respectability.

People are reporting that "liberal supporters" are saying that they hear that SNCC accepts "help from Communists." That "it is immoral to work with Communists." Say what? What exactly do they mean?

Well, that we can't be working with certain unions, certain lawyers, *and* certain individuals. Well, like who exactly? A few names are mentioned. What? When I call so-and-so, they are always ready to help. *Always.* No questions asked. Or, man, *she* has always been our most dependable supporter, always helpful. Or, hey, *that's* who is handling my case in Alabama. Long, earnest discussion. Conclusion?

We can't afford to be hostage to any such sectarian history. First of all, it just isn't right. Second, we can't afford it. What'd we look like asking folks for they political history and checking for ideological purity? That ain't SNCC. SNCC will work with anybody who supports our programs, shares our goals, honors our principles, and earns our trust. Period. Cheers, applause. That became our stated policy. It did not please the totalitarian liberals, and the CIA assets in the national media would continue to red-bait the organization. That was not only absurd, it was counterproductive. It merely increased our contempt for that kind of political litmus test. Whenever reporters would raise it to me, I'd tell them, "Hey, you don't worry about the Communists, worry about SNCC. We way more dangerous, Jack."

There is no question—which may be the single thing everybody agrees on unequivocally—that the person most responsible for this process was Ms. Ella Jo Baker. No question. Her mere presence was crucial to the dynamic and tone of these early meetings. She was so patient with us, very patient. She paid us the respect of taking us as seriously as she took the struggle. She was always clear. Always focused. I've never heard her raise her voice. And in return, our respect for this extraordinary woman was so unconditional that we would not even think of showing her the disrespect of raising our voice or swearing in a meeting. Her mere presence disciplined those meetings.

When I think back on those times, I'm amazed to realize that Ms. Baker was then roughly the same age I am now. Amazing.

The sharpest image I retain of Ms. Baker from this period: It's one, two, or even three in the morning. The meeting has been going all day. People are bleary-eyed, disheveled, sprawled out all over. Some twenty-year-olds have even nodded off. And there's Ms. Baker sitting erect. She is wearing a dignified but stylish blue suit, stockings, and if memory serves, a small, elegant hat. She would not be out of place in church or at a NAACP board meeting. She seems quite alert and her eyes follow each speaker intently. But you can't really see her entire face because she's wearing a surgical mask against the thick cloud of smoke from the many chain-smokers in the room. At the end of the meeting she's looking unrumpled, fresh, and still alert.

Of course, a number of other adults supported and advised us. I've mentioned Bayard Rustin at Howard and Harry Belafonte's early and constant encouragement. At those early meetings another important adviser was a young history professor from Spelman, Howard Zinn, who wrote the first book—and still one of the best—on SNCC's early days [SNCC: The New Abolitionists]. Then there were the local folk. In Mississippi, Amzie Moore was Bob Moses's great mentor, though I suspect that Bob's leadership style was patterned—whether consciously or not—on Ms. Baker's. The Reverend Ed King, a young, white clergyman from the Mississippi establishment, was a stalwart ally and was made to suffer greatly for his "treason" to the Southern way. Later, after I became chairman, Dr. Martin Luther King was helpful to me personally with advice and support. In southwest Georgia there was the remarkable King family, A. D. and Slater King. In Selma, Alabama, an extraordinary family of warriors called the Boyntons. And in Lowndes County, Alabama, Mr. Jackson and his family.

But Ms. Baker was far and away our most influential adviser, a constant presence, counselor, and role model; she was in many ways the organization's principal architect. For, even beyond the internal culture—how we organized ourselves and related to each other—Ms. Baker's influence was profound and far-reaching. The organization's political orientation, moral outlook, and organizing principles owed much to her guidance. But this guidance was so natural, so gentle and unobtrusive, as to have been almost imperceptible at the time.

See, all her adult life, Ms. Baker had been an organizer. She had become very, very good at it. As a young woman she had been a traveling "orator," traversing the South to set up local chapters of the NAACP. This, I believe, was back in the forties. Later she would serve as director of chapters for the NAACP. This is when, I believe, her affinity and respect for people at the Southern grass roots really matured. After that she had been, in effect if not in title, the experienced organizing intelligence giving form to Dr. King's young SCLC. My impression is that Mrs. Baker was as disillusioned by the male chauvinism as by the hierarchical fixation on status in the leadership of both groups. Also by a certain elitism; and a bureaucratic disregard for the intelligence and ability of local people "at the grass roots" that flowed from those attitudes. So naturally Ms. Baker would consider it her duty to help this new, youthful organization in which she was so invested to avoid those tendencies. Because she clearly understood the danger of becoming that against which you are fighting, she was never doctrinaire. About the most inflexibly dogmatic statements she ever permitted herself were "a strong people don't need strong leaders" and "we who believe in freedom cannot rest." She never did.

Ms. Baker never ever pulled rank, traded on the authority of her greater experience, or wielded that authority to try to impose a direction on our youthfulness. That was just not her way. Nor did she adopt the transparently condescending liberal pretense to equality of "Gee, kid, I don't know any more than you, we're all here learning together," which some teachers affect. She respected herself and us far too much for that. She knew way more than we did and we all knew that. What she was was our trusted adviser, our teacher, and an "authority" figure. No question about that. So naturally we took all our tough questions to her. But we never got a dogmatic or in fact almost never, a direct answer. Usually she preferred to answer with another question and then another, forcing us to refine our thinking and to struggle toward an answer for ourselves.

"Ms. Baker, should we . . . ?"

"Well, certainly you *could* . . . but what is the result you really want to achieve here? If you do thus and so, how do you think so-and-so is likely to respond? If you do X, what will that say about this organization?" Then she'd be content to sit back and listen carefully as we wrestled with the issue, groping our way toward a shared understanding. I'm not sure that Ms. Baker always agreed 100 percent with every conclusion we reached. In fact I know at times she did not. But I know she truly believed *we* had to make our own decisions so long as the process was open, inclusive, and rigorous. We all learned a lot about organizing—I know I certainly did—from being around Ms. Baker. And it wasn't just process either. It was also substantive. Our definition of SNCC as a group of organizers, for instance. Or our faith in and respect for the local people. Our egalitarianism and notorious distrust of hierarchical leadership.

A number of other myths about our organization need to be corrected one hopes once and for all.

There's the question of "whites" in SNCC and the "black nationalism" that drove these "good white liberals" out. In the typically reductive, simplistic, media-driven version of history, SNCC began as an "integrated" group devoted to a mystical Christian vision of a communal "beloved society," before the rise of an intolerant "black nationalism" ruined this interracial Eden. Or there's its opposite, an equally inaccurate revisionist version. According to which "race relations" in SNCC were never really all that good. The organization had always, from the git, been riven by racial/sexual tensions and jealousies so that the apparent color-free harmony had always been just a myth. Some commentators even allege both at the same time. Gimme an ever-loving break. Both are equally pernicious. I believe I can shed some light here. As usual, the truth is far more interesting than that conventional piffle.

If I say that SNCC was never an "integrated" organization. That no "white Americans" were ever on the SNCC staff—certainly not the field organizing staff. That, if they joined, "whites" never survived in SNCC more than a month. That "nationalism" was no exotic import from Northern ghettos, but indigenous to the Southern communities out of which we came. That the organization was "nationalist" from its first day. . . . You'd say, "Aha! There we go! Ture either has completely lost it, is being deliberately provocative, or is crudely trying to rewrite history again." 'Fraid not. All I'm doing is telling the truth.

Start with the "beloved community." Honestly I never knew what that meant. I always did have real difficulty getting my head around it conceptually. What exactly—in practical terms—did it describe? Of course, I understand that the term comes out of a race-free, Christian, pacifist vision of lions lying down with lambs and swords beaten into plowshares, and grounded in Gandhian nonviolent activism. I also know that it had currency among spiritual pacifists, the social gospel seminarians out of Nashville who had studied with the Reverend James Lawson. Nobody had any real objection to the term as I remember. *But* I certainly never used it and can't remember anyone from NAG ever doing so. Nor Ms. Baker or Mrs. Hamer nor any of our local staff, nor the local people from the communities for that matter.

However, the Reverend Mr. Lawson is credited as the principal author of the very high-minded founding document coming out of the first conference. I believe the term *beloved community* first appears in that statement and was subsequently recycled.

However, everything I understand about that meeting suggests also a realistic concern with practical political questions from the very first. Also a strong identification with the African liberation struggle from the git.

Was I quite serious in saying there were no "whites" in SNCC? Aha, you say. So what about Jane Stembridge, Bob Zellner, Sam Shirah (peace be unto him), Dinky Romilly, Mary King, Casey Hayden, Betty Garman, Bill Hansen, Jack Minnis, Penny Patch, Ursula Junk, Mendy Samstein, Danny Lyon, and a number of others? What were these guys, tokens? Department-store mannequins? Black folk in whiteface?

Gimme a break. They were friends, allies, comrades, SNCC staffers, and brothers and sisters in the struggle. But, as usual, you're not listening. I never said no whites ever *joined* SNCC.

[Some did and one heard all kinds of amazing stories about that: Sam Shirah's Sunday-school teacher had been George Corley Wallace. Chuck McDew said that "when Bob Zellner joined SNCC, it ended three generations of family Klan membership." The Freedom Singers give a concert in a small town in backwoods Minnesota. An eighteen-year-old high school graduate is so moved that next day she sets out to hitchhike to New York, convinces the SNCC office there that she has a contribution to make, and ends up working very well in

307

Mississippi. A young German exchange student at a small Midwestern Catholic college (Ursula Junk) hears the call. With the mother superior's blessing, she leaves for Mississippi and devotes a couple of years organizing women's co-ops for the Poor People's Corporation. —EMT]

So how could I say there were no "whites" in SNCC? Because upon joining us, those comrades stopped being "white" in most conventional American terms, except in the most superficial physical sense of the word.

To start with, for these young "white" Americans even to seriously *think* about joining the struggle in the conditions that prevailed meant that they were unusually conscientious and socially aware young people. Then, quite apart from the danger, the ones who joined were "whites" who had no problem working happily in a black organization with black leadership and that worked mostly in rural black communities at considerable risk. That alone would separate them from the general run of their white countrymen—then and now—and entitles them to our respect.

And, while all of us would be changed by the experience, our "white" staffers had at least three particularly attitude-changing experiences that "white" Americans almost never have: working with blacks in complete equality; being on the receiving end of white racial hostility; *and* being immersed in the highest expressions of black culture while meeting the black community at its very best. What thinking young person could avoid being changed by even one of these experiences, much less by all three together?

Socially and politically our comrades of lighter complexion stopped being "white." When they experienced the full force of racist hostility from Southern white politicians, police, and public opinion, compounded by the indifference or paralysis of the national political establishment, whatever class and color privileges they might have taken for granted were immediately suspended. At moments of confrontation they were at as great a risk as any of us, and as "race traitors" were sometimes in even greater jeopardy.

"Boy, best you hush yo' damn mouth. Fur as Ah'm concerned, you lower'n any [expletive] nigger, heah? Ah'd shoot you easy as Ah would a rattlesnake."

Or, the flashlight shines into the car and stops on a young white woman.

"Aha, now looka heah. Gal, ain't you got no shame? Tell me somethin', wicha these niggers you sleeping with? Or Ah bet you doin' them all, huh?"

On the one hand, American bigotry at its ugliest. And on the other, just the opposite, the same cultural realities that were affecting and educating us all: the warmth, texture, language, style, music, spirit, and moral strength of black Southern culture all brought together in struggle and resistance. This was a remarkably sharp juxtaposition. And it was exciting and transformative, a unique moment in American history, and we all were changed by it. Entirely a matter of perspective. Seriously. So I meant it and as a sincere compliment when I said there were no "white" people on the SNCC staff.

Or that SNCC was never an "integrated" organization in any conventional sense of that term. You know the usual integration: a group of blacks adopting the attitudes, lifestyles, vocabulary, and values of "mainstream" (read *white*) American culture, hoping to become assimilated and begging acceptance in a white world. The movement—SNCC, at any rate—was far, far better than that. In fact, the cultural dynamic was exactly the reverse of that melting-pot model of "integration," which was exactly the cultural imperialism we had fought at Howard. Integration meant black folk trying to become "white." In SNCC, "white" folk became "black."

All of us—regardless of color—who struggled inside that organization were forever changed, by the times and by the experience. Being young, how could we not have been? So those of us within that circle of trust became family and remain so to this day. Because for a brief moment it had been possible to believe—and, in SNCC, it was as true as it is likely ever to be in this society—that race, class, and indeed even gender did not really matter. We had far more important external things to concern us.

But this is America and we would not be permitted to escape the society's crude realities forever. It would become clear that SNCC's spirit—internally—was like a dream within a bubble, a thing insulated, but only for a time, from the realities of class, color, status, and education in the larger society outside. You see this most clearly when you look at the fate of different branches of this "family" since the movement days. The difference between the lives and careers of the local staff—the Annie Pearl Averys, Jesse Harrises, Willie Rickses, MacArthur Cottons, Randy Battles, etc.—who were the real cutting edge of SNCC, and those of the educated "middle class" blacks and most of the "white" members of the family once the high tide of the movement crested and receded in the South.

But for a time we were not conscious of this. Why? Because if SNCC was, as the press took to calling us, the "shock troops" of the Southern movement, these local African youth were the shock troops of the shock troops. Nuff respect. But after the "heroic days," the issues of class, color, and education, which for a moment had seemed to disappear within SNCC, reasserted themselves in peoples' lives in the society outside.

•　　•　　•

Of all the remarkable and surprising people I met in the Mississippi struggle, none was more interesting and influential than Bob Moses. By the time I finally met Bob in Greenwood in the summer of 1961, he was already in my mind something of a legend. During that academic year he was to us, watching from Howard, not simply just the head of the Mississippi project, but had become almost a symbol of the SNCC spirit. I mean, anyone who was doing the things we'd been hearing had to be not only a great leader, but more than that even, a sho-nuff *hero*. And of course, to look the part. I mean, you could always tell at a glance who the "hero" in a movie was, right? There always was that certain look. So you just know that this Bob Moses had to be larger-than-life: at *least* as dramatic and articulate as Bayard, as charismatic and physically imposing as Malcolm, and as eloquent and inspiring as Dr. King. At least, that's clear. So you knew I just could not wait to meet this paragon.

So that morning we gits to the Greenwood office. Folks be coming in and out. Field secretaries, Sam Block, Willie Peacock, "Do Right," John Hardy, James Jones. Some local teenagers. Lots of energy and excitement. I met a lot of folks. But no Bob Moses. After a while I realized this and asked where he was. "Man, I really want to meet that brother, y'know." The teenagers nudge each other and giggle.

"Hey, he say he want to meet Bob." Titter, titter. Whatever was funny was lost on me. "Hey, he be right back, man. You gone git to meet him, sho nuff." Giggle, giggle. "In fack, here he come now." I turned to the door eagerly. But the only person there was this stocky brother I been talking to briefly. We'd exchanged a few sentences, as I seem to recall, about Camus's *The Rebel*. A quiet brother, almost nondescript in baggy overalls, a white T-shirt, and brogans. He had an open, roundish brown face with faint freckles and wore thick, round glasses that gave him a studious, even owlish appearance. His voice was deliberate, low-key, almost muted, but his eyes were focused, always intense, always serious, and kind. Everything about this brother seemed utilitarian, serviceable. Even the no-frills way he dressed. That was Bob.

I hadn't realized who I had been talking to because Bob had absolutely no swagger about himself, no posturing, no ostentatiousness, no self-projection. Just this quiet, attentive seriousness to whomever he was talking to. His manner was always the same, almost self-effacing. Which does not necessarily mean humble because, as we know, ostentatious humility can and usually does mask the most outrageous of egos. But with Bob it was as though he were not at all interested in impressing you with his brilliance or importance. Or for that matter even what impression he was making or failing to make. In fact, quite the reverse, as if he were trying to transcend and efface his presence so as to concentrate on the problem, the idea. And to get you to move beyond the superficial and focus on *ideas* too.

Bob always listened—and the thing is, you could actually see him listening—far more than he ever spoke. And whenever he did speak—whether in a meeting or from a platform—it was softly and thoughtfully, almost haltingly, as though he were deliberately screening all emotion and rhetorical flourish out. I cannot remember hearing Bob ever utter a slogan of any kind. Nor, come to think of it, raise his voice or issue an order.

He had left a teaching job to come south, and in a basic way he remained a teacher very much in the style of Ms. Baker. Rather than giving orders or answers, he was good at defining issues, what became known in SNCC as "raising questions." Usually ethical questions.

"It seems to me what we need to ask ourselves is, are we willing to endanger the lives of other people, the local people, who work with us?"

"We are nonviolent, but do we *have the right* to ask Mr. Steptoe to remove the guns from his home where his family is sleeping because SNCC people happen to be there that night? Can we take away a man's right to defend his family?"

Jes' a-raising questions.

As you have probably surmised, I came to admire Bob a lot. I mean a lot. He had been a doctoral candidate in philosophy at Harvard when we met. I was changing my major to philosophy. Bob's example of clarity and rationality influenced me in that decision. When I got to know him, we'd sometimes discuss philosophy. I remember one night in a Freedom House we sat up almost till sunup discussing a tough philosophical problem. That was Bob. He taught me a lot of philosophy.

[Moses remembers one such session:

"One particular night Stokely and I spent several intense hours going over the proof of Goedel's completeness theorem for first-order quantificational logic, which I'd studied in graduate school. You know, one of those philosophy-of-math courses. It's a difficult proof to understand. That evening showed a side of Stokely that was not in public view: a demand for understanding and clarity about difficult, abstract, highly technical logico/mathematical material. I was deeply impressed by his insistence on mastering the proof, especially in that setting."

Hearing this I couldn't help suppose that the Freedom House in which this discussion took place was one of those bugged by the Sovereignty Commission. Can you not see those watchdogs of Southern freedom reviewing this tape?

" 'Gittin' anythang good on that tape, Bo?'

" 'Hard to tell, Cap'n, mighty hard. Listen at this. What you reckon them nigras be saying? They must be talkin' Communist, huh?'

" 'No, son, that's code. They talkin' code, boy. Best we send it on to the FBI for decoding, y'know?'

" 'Oh, yeah. Tha's right, Cap'n, les' do that. Boy, there sure ain't no flies on you, Cap'n." '—EMT]

Bob was really, as we used to say, "into" existentialism, particularly

Camus, believing strongly that we are what we do. Not what we say or what we might even *think* we are. But what we actually *do.* How we treat others. What we accept or condone for ourselves and others. What we resist. If you exploit others, you are an exploiter. If you oppress, you are an oppressor. If you sell out principle, you are a prostitute. It is only in the act of rebellion—not in talking or posturing—that you become a rebel. And there is a human moral imperative to rebel against all injustice. Simple enough, right? Well, try to live by those precepts. Bob really seemed to try and, far as I can see, still does. To the extent that Bob was a leader in SNCC, he was so by example, and his authority came from the respect that example earned from us.

The other thing that was really important to me was this: you could not be around Bob long and fail to see how much he really loved our people and was totally committed to our liberation. Obviously our styles and personalities are very different. But as a young man and budding organizer, I was influenced by Bob Moses in fundamental and I think lasting ways. Many of us were, to some extent. Because, boil it down to gravy, Bob was, first of all, a phenomenal organizer. Thoughtful, smart, infinitely resourceful, and most important of all, effective. In Mississippi, with his ability to inspire and instill courage in all kinds of people, myself included, he was able to create something really remarkable.

[Endesha Mae Holland:

"Bob was so gentle . . . so kind, you couldn't ask for anybody better. He planned strategy. He got people out of jail. He calmed nerves. He soothed feelings. He made everybody feel like they had a part to play. I 'member one time he pointed to me. He said, 'Now, Ida, now you been to jail before. You know how to go to jail.' I was so proud. I was glad to say, 'Yes, Bob, I do know.' I was so glad to be used for something. While the whole town was looking down on me, the movement said, 'You are somebody.' "]

In fact, I missed the famous March on Washington because of Bob. We had gone up with the group from Mississippi, but then Bob asked me to come with him on the day of the march to meet with some radical white students who wanted to talk about how they could be involved. It was a big SDS convention, I think somewhere in Virginia, but I'm not sure. We didn't know what might happen in D.C. on the day, it could have proved dramatic. (It didn't, but I did miss Dr. King's Dream in the original.) Yet I didn't hesitate a New York minute. I was just too honored to be asked by Bob to accompany him. I remember watching Bob talk to those white students and being just incredibly proud that this brother was our leader. Bob and I argued that activist white students, if serious, should come off the campus and undertake to organize poor communities of whites. If, for example, they would set up SNCC-like projects, say among the miners in

Appalachia, that could be the basis of an alliance, organized by students, between poor whites and poor blacks. The meeting was enthusiastic about the idea but I cannot say what, if any, follow-up there was.

[Our brother's account of this student meeting on the day of the march is the only lapse of memory I encountered in the many hours of taped memoirs he left with me. Months after completing this chapter I leafed through Danny Lyon's magnificent book of movement photographs.

In the foreground of a crowd shot before the Lincoln Memorial there stood a group of SNCC stalwarts singing. Clearly recognizable were Hollis Watkins, Willie Peacock, Jim Forman, Annell Ponder, Courtland Cox, and next to Julian Bond in the foreground is Bob Moses. A few pages on it hit. Whoa now! By Carmichael's detailed account, Bob isn't supposed to be there. He's at an SDS meeting in Virginia.

Moses confirmed his presence at the march. He also remembered he and Carmichael's being at the SDS meeting, but was certain that this meeting was in 1964. Clearly, then, Carmichael's memory must have conflated the two events. But then, where was he on the day of the march?

I distinctly remembered, as did everyone I checked with, his being at the field headquarters on the Mall the day previous. (He'd been driving a car loaned to the march by a local company. A D.C. cop gave him a ticket. To his unconcealed amazement and glee, a captain strode over, remonstrated with the officer, took the ticket, and tore it up. "Well, look at this," Stokely said, grinning. "I guess Bayard really done made the revolution."

But no one could remember seeing him on the day and none of us knew where he was. Nor could we imagine anything that could have lured him away from so dramatic a political event. That, we agreed, simply wasn't like Stokely. So, where could he have been? A mystery. A great puzzlement. We concluded that there must somewhere be a sister—once militant and powerfully alluring, perhaps still so—who could, if she so chose, shed some light on his whereabouts that day. —EMT]

The next spring (1964), Bob would give me the greatest honor and responsibility I'd had in my young life. When he came to D.C. to organize support for the Mississippi Freedom Summer, Bob asked me to serve as director of the Second Congressional District (the Delta) during the Freedom Summer. I was moved, overwhelmed as much by the responsibility as by Bob's confidence. To be appointed to that job, and by Bob? I couldn't believe it.

It's the summer of '62. The movement in the Delta has survived its first year. And well enough to spread out of Greenwood and into the small towns, rural areas, and plantations of neighboring counties. Indianola is the county seat of Sunflower County, home of Parchman prison and

James Oliver Eastland, millionaire cotton planter and powerful Dixiecrat chairman of the Judiciary Committee of the U.S. Senate.

The flat Delta earth is baking underneath the afternoon sun. It is hot and stuffy in the rickety, old retired school bus. The faces of the eighteen or so people—SNCC worker Charles McLaurin and some local people— carry a sheen of sweat and fear. The police cruiser has trailed the bus since it left Indianola. The driver drives carefully, scrupulously observing the speed limit and all traffic laws. The cops continue to follow and everyone is tense.

The local people are from the town of Ruleville. They are the second group from there to make the trip to Indianola to attempt to register to vote. The registrar has been abusive. The sheriff threatening. All have failed the test. Now they are worried, wondering whether they have not been foolish. Whether it was worth the risk after all.

A siren screams and behind them blue lights flash. The bus pulls over. The driver is called off. The people can see him being interrogated. The fear is almost tangible. Without motion the heat becomes unbearable inside the bus. Then the silence is filled with a rich, powerful contralto voice, singing:

> Ain't gonna let nobody turn me round
> Turn me round, turn me round, turn me round
> Cause I want my freedom, I want my freedom,
> And I want my freedom now.

The singer is a shortish, rotund, brown lady named Fannie Lou Hamer (peace be unto her). When she reaches the second stanza—

> Ain't scared of nobody
> Cause Ah wants mah freedom . . .

—the lines are literally true because everyone has joined in. Mrs. Hamer would say later that she had burst into song to "encourage the peoples 'cause Ah could see that evrahbody was a-feared an' I just didn't know anything else to do." That inspired burst of song—and what happened after she returned home that afternoon—would change Mrs. Hamer's life. Her boldness and the inspired intervention—not to mention the great resonant voice—had caught Charles McLaurin's attention. Was not this evidence of the grassroots leadership spirit that SNCC was committed to finding and nurturing in the Delta?

At the courthouse the registrar had required Mrs. Hamer to interpret a section of the Mississippi Constitution about "de facto law." She had failed, she said, because "you know I knowed 'bout as much any 'facto law' as a mule knows 'bout Christmas." She had also been required to name her employer.

When Mrs. Hamer reached the Marlowe plantation where she'd worked as a timekeeper for eighteen years, her husband, Mr. Perry Hamer, was worried. News of her aspiration to citizenship had reached the plantation before she had. The owner had been looking for her all afternoon. The bossman was succinct. Either Mrs. Hamer removed her name from the list of applicants or she should remove herself from his plantation.

"Well, Mr. Marlowe," she said, "I didn't go register for you. I registered for myself."

That night Mrs. Hamer sought shelter in the Ruleville community. Shortly thereafter, night riders shot into the house where she had been staying.

[According to Kay Mills's excellent, very thorough biography of Mrs. Hamer:

"The next morning the boss told Mr. Hamer to tell his wife to come back home. Things would be like they always were. She replied, 'That's just what I'm trying to git out of. Things be like they always was? I want change.' Years later, Marlowe's son Dave said his father hadn't meant to throw her off his place. . . ."

"When she reached Ruleville that night, Mrs. Hamer went to the Voting Rights meeting. She said she had been thrown off the plantation and had no place to go. 'I jes' thought I'd come on out here and tell y'awl.' Her friend Mary Tucker spoke up.

" 'Don't say you ain't got nowhere to go so long as I have a shelter. If I ain't got but one plank you can stick your head under there too.' And she said, 'Thank you, Tuck.' And Joe McDonald said 'If you ain't got room, I got room,' and we just put our arms around her.' " —EMT]

That's how it began. Of course, Mrs. Hamer would become a symbol to a great many people across the nation. And I suppose, something of a symbol to us in SNCC too, but in a particular way. We knew and loved this stout, earthy, kindhearted lady. Yes, she represented something important to us. But she did not merely represent an *idea,* some SNCC *theory* of grassroots leadership. The twentieth child born into a family of sharecroppers, Mrs. Hamer *was* the grassroots, the "local peoples" SNCC is always accused of "romanticizing." I'm talking here about Mrs. Hamer's spirit. Her warmth. Her values. A fundamental decency and generosity. Her simplicity and absence of self-importance or pretentiousness. She simply embodied in her jes'-plain-folks way all the qualities and values we were coming to admire in the local peoples.

She was smart and really funny, and by virtue of her history and experience, politically very astute. Unlettered though she was politically, she had a shrewd understanding of political and economic power and the injustice of its effects on poor folk in this country because she had lived it. She had been induced by the bossman to pick her first cotton at the age of six, for candy.

With no formal education beyond the sixth grade, she was powerfully and wonderfully eloquent. Though untrained, she was an artist, a great singer. And a very forgiving human being. 'Buked and scorned all her life because she was black, she was unfailingly sympathetic—and helpful whenever she could be—to the suffering of poor whites. This in spite of the history she told me. In her childhood, her entire family worked in the fields. One year they seemed to be making some progress. After a good crop her father managed to buy a pair of mules and a cow. They woke up one morning to find the animals dead. Poisoned by an envious white neighbor. The family never recovered economically.

More than a symbol, she was day to day a real leader in her community, and as real to us as member of the family. And if she was also a symbol, she was a symbol of the best in our people, and the best of what SNCC wanted to think the struggle was all about. Simple as that.

When white men in the Winona jail savagely beat three generations of black women, they had no idea how close they came to triggering a race war. Those were three of the most loved and respected of the movement's women. *[Mrs. Hamer was forty-four, Annell Ponder was in her twenties, and Stokely's teenaged "little sister," June Johnson, was fifteen. —EMT]* There were brothers in Greenwood who had the means and certainly the intention. Especially after Medgar Evers was murdered in Jackson the next day.

That one was close, I mean narrowly averted, and I'm not talking hours. I'm talking minutes. Brothers were about to roll on that two-bit jail. Maybe they should not have been dissuaded.

The facts are well-known. Our sisters had been returning from a voter education workshop. The bus stopped in a mean, ugly little town called Winona, and four of our sisters entered the white rest room and were arrested. When Mrs. Hamer got off the bus to inquire, she was arrested too. The cracker cop who informed Mrs. Hamer that she was under arrest kicked her as he did so. In her cell she could hear them beating the younger women.

"After I was placed in the cell, I begun to hear sounds of licks and screams . . . the sound of licks and horrible screams, and I could hear somebody say, 'Nigger, can you say, yes, sir?' She never would say yessir and I could hear when she would hit the floor . . . them licks jes' asoundin'," That was Annell Ponder screaming. She never said *sir*.

"After that I heard some real keen screams, *real keen,* and after that was when they passed my cell with a girl. She was fifteen years old, Miss Johnson, June Johnson . . . the blood was running down her face."

Then they came for Mrs. Hamer. Two black prisoners* were ordered to hold her down and beat her with a studded leather strap. Mrs. Hamer asked, "How could they do that their own race?" Turns out they could. The whites oversaw the work, threatening the black men whenever they appeared to lighten up.

"I began to scream and one white man got up and began to beat me in mah head, telling me to hush. Another white man—my dress had begun to ride up high—he walked over an' pulled my dress back down as they beat me. Then he pulled my dress back up and they continued to beat me." Mrs. Hamer came close to death in the immediate aftermath of that beating. She said that the nightlong ministrations of Euvesta Simpson pulled her through. But whenever we talked about it, Mrs. Hamer would merely wonder how people who called themselves Christians could treat other human beings in that way. A question she managed to ask her tormentors before she was bailed out. She was still asking it with genuine bewilderment years later.

Another day I'll never forget was when I drove Mrs. Hamer to a small town called Sunflower City. We had no sooner left the car and started walking down the street when a white man passed us going in the opposite direction. An ordinary-looking white man, bald head shining, wearing khakis.

But Mrs. Hamer froze stock-still and caught her breath audibly. Something strange happened to her face as she turned and glared after the man. The change was so sudden that I was startled. Her usually benign expression was gone, replaced by something I'd never before seen in her face and never ever saw again. This look of revulsion, contempt, and anger was so intense that I at first took it to be a sign of physical distress. A heart attack, perhaps? It couldn't be something totally out of character, like a hate stare?

"Mrs. Hamer. What happened? Are you okay?" I cried.

She took a deep breath and shuddered. "That's Big Milam. The cracker who murdered that poor boy Emmett Till." That was the only time I ever saw anything other than compassion on Mrs. Hamer's countenance.

Another thing I remember about Mrs. Hamer is her elation and joy when she returned from Africa in 1964. *[A SNCC delegation visited Guinea on the invitation of President Sékou Touré, which had been arranged by*

---

*This case was actively pursued by the Justice Department, and five police officers were actually brought to trial on federal charges. The two black prisoners found the courage to testify to being threatened and bribed to participate in the beating of Mrs. Hamer. The Mississippi jury acquitted the police. It is not known what fate befell the prisoners when they were returned to Parchman Farm after testifying against the police. —EMT

Harry Belafonte. —EMT] Here was this daughter of Southern share-croppers speaking neither French nor any of the African languages yet talking on and on about how completely at home and connected she had felt. She had been thrilled and couldn't stop talking about black folks running things. Pilots flying planes, etc., etc. And she was sho nuff in love with Sékou Touré (peace be unto him).

"Oh, Stokely, the president came to visit. Oh, he was sooo handsome, all in his white robes, an' he was so kind." Despite the language gap, she had spoken with everyone she'd met. "Oh, Stokely, those people be jes' like us. The way they fix they hair, some of them. How they stand, how they walk, even the way they carry they babies." Like many returning Africans, she could not exactly explain the powerful feelings she'd experienced, but understood that it was real.

"But, Stokely. It was so *strange* . . . I jes' *feel* that I got family there . . . I mean people my own blood . . . who I'll never know."

When I was leaving the Delta, I went to say good-bye. She gave me a big hug.

"Stokely, you know that so long as I got a house in Mississippi, you got a place to stay. If there ain't but one chicken wing in the pot, you got half."

Mrs. Hamer was a great-souled sister.

I've said that Mississippi first taught me to really love my blackness. Which it surely did. But it taught me something else important. That what I really was and wanted to be was an organizer.

Organizing in those circumstances was rough. It was a constant hassle, challenging and demanding. The most demanding work I'd ever done. But it was also the most satisfying work, fulfilling and at times just outright inspiring. I'd never felt anything like it. It brought out the best in me, qualities I had not known I had.

The thing that remains with me most strongly from that time, when everything else—the violence, the cops, the politics—recedes, is an incredible sense of community, of closeness and warmth, that we had. Which is all that made the movement possible in the first place. Within the organization we had some remarkable models like Ms. Baker and others I've mentioned. But as organizers we had to work with the entire community. The ordinary folk, from the older people, the preachers, the mothers and fathers, to the young folk, the teenagers, and even the little kids. As an organizer, you had to work with *evrahbody.* You had a role and an identity with the entire community. A slightly different role with each group. That was a revelation and a real pleasure to me.

You had to earn and keep the community's confidence and respect. So you couldn't set yourself up as some "leader" or be trying to tell folks what to do. Or asking people to do anything you wouldn't first do yourself. I mean, here you are, all of twenty years old, and you are social worker, teacher, political adviser, as well as "son" and eager student to the elders. To the youth, you are peer, friend, big brother, role model, tutor, mentor, and even sometimes coach and playground supervisor. I loved it all.

We were trying to organize an entire community, but the core of the movement community was really a particular group of strong families, grandparents, parents, and children. The Johnsons, whom I've mentioned; the Greenes, Mr. and Mrs. Dewey Greene Sr. and the children, Dewey Jr., George, and their sister Freddie. The McGhee family, who asked and gave no quarter, Mrs. Laura McGhee and her warrior sons, Silas, Jake, and Clarence, the giant paratrooper. And there were other families whose names don't come to mind.

[Endesha Mae Holland:

"It was so beautiful to see women like Ms. Lulabelle Johnson and Ms. (Laura) McGhee. They would walk with such pride. They shoulders be back and their titties be sticking out a looooong way in front of them. Mama say you could see they titties a whole block before you see them. An' they be walking with such pride. They be jes' marching. An' I can remember myself tryin' to walk with that heavy step they used. Look like the earth would jes' ketch their feet and hold them up. These women would walk they walk, y'know, and when they gets up in front of this human blockade of po-lices, they start talking they talk and singing them songs. 'I ain't scared o' nobody, 'cause I want mah freedom . . .'

"Oh, chile, it jes' made me so proud."]

As I would quickly discover, these were families in which the parents had never surrendered. Had never accepted the limitations racism tried to impose. Who never allowed their kids to believe for a minute that their possibilities stopped at maid, cook, or cotton chopper for white folks. Parents who instilled and demonstrated self-respect, no matter how materially poor their circumstances. People who had been hearing about the bus boycott and Dr. King, the sit-ins and Freedom Rides, so before we got there, they had been touched by the spirit of the times, even down there in what Bob Moses called the "heart of the iceberg."

So they knew or expected or hoped that the movement would one day be coming. But they also knew—in fact had lived—the history. So these "Freedom Riders" as they called us, if and when they came, would have to show them something real before they would jump out there or allow their children to. But, once that happened, look out. There would be no turning back. As the song went:

> I done pledged my life to the fight,
> and I never will turn back,
> Lord, Ah must go,
> Ah shall go,

> *Ah will* go
> . . . To see what the end will be.

What I learned from the younger generation was different. The Greenwood project had not been started by Northern "liberators" but by two local college students—Sam Block and Willie Wazir Peacock—recruited by Amzie Moore. These two brothers first showed me the ropes, taught me the territory and how to go about organizing amongst the folks. For one thing, both Sam and Willie could sing more than a little and preach some too. Valuable skills indeed for a Delta organizer. They taught me much more besides.

Sam had come into Greenwood first. All alone. People talked about that time with wonder. As soon as the whites figured out what Sam was about, they took action. First they threatened the old man who had rented him a room. Regretfully and almost in tears, he asked Sam to leave. Sam understood that since his cover was blown, no one in the community would dare shelter him and he wouldn't put them on the spot by asking. So he slept in an abandoned car for the next three weeks. But every morning he was out organizing on foot. That alone got my respect. But there was more. Next, they arrested Sam, I forget for what nonsense.

The local judge ordered him out of town, adding that if he had good sense, he'd leave the state too.

"No, Judge," said Sam. "You know I ain't about to do none o' that." As he was leaving the court, the sheriff put in his two bits, warning him as to how he didn't expect to see him anywhere in Greenwood again. "Wal, Sheriff, in that case I guess you just gon' ha' to pick up and go. 'Cause I'm sure not going no place."

That's when the local folks got brave enough to give him shelter again. After that, Sam slept in a different house every couple nights. You can see why he was respected in that community, was ol' Sam Block.

He and Willie inspired many of the young men of Greenwood, some of whom became SNCC organizers. I'd be spending most of my time with these guys. They taught me a lot, and I guess I taught them something too. You could say we learned from each other.

George Greene knew everything there was to know about car engines. He was into stock car racing. I think he'd had some training and wanted to be a race driver. He taught us those skills, high-speed turns and "fishtails" and generally how to take evasive action at high speeds. You couldn't really call it defensive driving because it was essentially aggressive. George had me practice until I was fairly good, or at least competent at it. Later on when SNCC began to get a few cars, George would soup them up so as to be able to outrun the Klan or, if necessary, the cops.

In 1964, when I became district director for the summer project,

George fixed me up a car. I mean mah man *fixed* it. He souped that engine, reinforced the suspension some kinda way, and I believe even did something to the brakes. I'm not sure what all George did or how legal any of it was, but I was driving something very like a race car, a stone bomb. Despite the traveling I had to do that summer, I always felt real confident in that car. Even a little cocky. What with the Klan patrols, the cops—local and state—and just your average redneck citizen with his rifle rack in the rear window, you always felt vulnerable on the highways. But with George's driver education and the bomb I was driving, I felt right secure, thank you very much. I knew nobody—cop, Klan, or whoever—could keep up with me unless I wanted them to. But it couldn't outrun bullets. By the end of the summer I'd have reporters gawking and exclaiming over all the bullet holes in that car. Thank you, Bro George, and George, May Charles, my dear worrying mother, thanks you too.

I was away on a speaking engagement, so Silas McGhee was using that car the night the white folk shot him in the head. He recovered, but when I heard, my first thought was that seeing Silas in the car, the terrorists had shot him thinking he was me. I felt just awful. But then I realized that they probably hated Silas worse than they did me. The McGhee boys, Silas, Jake, and the big paratrooper, Clarence, along with their mom—had seriously been waging a war of their own with a mob at a movie theater in Greenwood for weeks. That was one family that never "took low" for anyone. There was no quit in them.

The more time I spent with the young people of Greenwood, the angrier I became. Deeply angry. I first noticed then something I've since seen again and again among our people all over the world: the criminal deprivation of opportunity—whether from racism, poverty, or both—and the waste of potential among our youth. You see such spirit, such curiosity, energy, intelligence, and real talent in our young people being denied the opportunity to develop. Incredible human potential being wasted by social injustice, and the denial of resources, nothing else. Where the society is underdeveloped and poor, it's bad enough . . . but in the "richest, freest country in the world"?

But for a moment, even if in a limited way, the movement gave some young people the chance not just to assert their human and political rights, but to discover and express their talents as well. The best example of this from Greenwood was fifteen-year-old Ida Mae. Whose mama ran a juke joint that was said to be somewhat disreputable. Ida, like other teenagers, used to hang around the office a lot. Bob Moses set her to work typing, something she had never done, and pretty soon she was—much to her own surprise—not only typing regularly, but listening, conversing, learning, and reading everything she could lay her hands on. Her bubbling excitement over Richard Wright's *Uncle Tom's Children* was just unforgettable. She was blown away, she said. Not only was the book about black people, but black people in *Mississippi. And,* it was written by a *black man* from Mississippi. She was just overwhelmed. "I didn't ever imagine no black person could do anything so great." So I told her about Ms. Margaret Walker down in Jackson. She wanted to go to Jackson to talk to her. Maybe she did, I don't know.

See, when Ida Mae was twelve, she was doing domestic work for a white family. One day, the wife told her to take the husband a drink of water. When she brought it to the bedroom, the man pulled her onto the bed and raped her. At fifteen, by her account, she was an apprentice prostitute. "When I saw all them SNCC workers coming through, seeing they was new in town, I thought mebbe I could turn me some tricks." Then Bob put her to work. Seeing her intelligence and curiosity, a volunteer helped her get into a Midwestern college, something she had never even wildly envisioned. Some years ago, someone asked me whether I remembered Ida Mae Holland. Yeah, why? Because she is now Endesha Mae Holland, Ph.D., one of the leading dramatists in the country and a professor somewhere in the New York University system, tha's why.

Whenever I went back to Mississippi, I'd hear stories like that. Another was about a young girl from a sharecropper family who went to a freedom school and was inspired. She went on to earn a doctorate and was heading up a community health organization somewhere in the Delta. Or, the little brother from Holmes County who as soon as he was old enough organized the little town he came from and was elected mayor at nineteen. Oh, there are stories. And they were good to hear. But what about the thousands of others just as able?

[The young woman is Dr. L. C. Dorsey, executive director of the Delta Health Center in the black town of Mound Bayou.

The young politician must be Eddie Carthen of Tchula, which is quite a story. In the early seventies, I took a group of students to a conference in Mississippi, and we literally ran across a very articulate young man sitting under a tree and who appeared about the same age as my students. He claimed to have been elected mayor of Tchula. Apparently, the incumbent white mayor—who had been in office some twenty years—flatly refused to vacate town hall. Instead the mayor elect was arrested on some pretext. Though legally elected, I don't remember if he was ever allowed to officially take office. It was a long, complicated series of events so utterly outrageous it was hard to believe. But the young man did not seem either crazed or delusional. Later, folks in Jackson confirmed the story. Before we left young Carthen, one of my students asked him where he'd learned so much about politics.

"From the movement," he said. "When I was fourteen, I went to the Freedom School, tha's where I first learned about politics." —EMT]

CHAPTER XV

Of Marches, Coalitions, Dreams, and Ambulance Chasing

A harassed-looking Bayard strode into the office visibly and dramatically agitated.

"Heah I am," he complained, "working frantically against all odds, *tearing* mah hair trying to fashion a social revolution, and *all* you young SNCC Negroes can think about is . . . is . . . is *ambulance chasing*? I need you *heah. History* needs you, *heah."*

Classic Rustin. Only Bayard could move in the same sentence from highly theatrical distress (torn hair) to grandiosity (social revolution) to an acid put-down (ambulance chasing) to emissary of history. That was one of the reasons why working with him was never dull.

I think the date of that little outburst was probably June 11, 1963. It could have been no more than a day or two after the Danville, Virginia, atrocity. Bayard was then trying to negotiate the politics while beginning to organize the logistics of what would come to be known as the August 28 March on Washington for Jobs and Freedom. Several friends from NAG (Tom Kahn, Ed Brown, and Courtland Cox) were working on Bayard's staff for the mobilization.

On June 10, one of the most methodically brutal police assaults on unarmed, peaceful demonstrators of the entire movement had taken place in the Virginia town of Danville. Earlier the Danville movement had appealed to SNCC for help, and we'd sent four organizers there. Young, brave Dottie Miller (later Zellner), Avon Rollins, Ivanhoe Donaldson, and Bob Zellner had answered the call for workshops in techniques and the discipline of nonviolent protest.

After negotiations with the city authorities went nowhere, the Danville movement staged a march and pray-in on the steps of City Hall. It was chilling. Really outrageous. I mean, here was a group of peaceful, respectable, dressed-for-church demonstrators, thoroughly trained in the discipline and spirit of nonviolence, led by two Christian ministers kneeling in prayer on the steps of the Danville City Hall. For this act of defiance, the police unleashed fire hoses, followed by squads of cops swinging nightsticks. It was nightmarish. Obviously the Danville police had been impressed by Bull Connor's tactics in Birmingham a couple months earlier.

The police response had been swift and savage. I mean brutal, and coldly methodical too. First, blasts from fire hoses swept the people into the streets, tearing off clothes and rolling people along the pavement. Then, before they could regain their feet, a wave of cops and, I believe, deputized garbagemen, swinging clubs beat them where they lay. It was the worst systematic brutality we'd yet seen, not excluding Dr. King's Birmingham campaign, which had dominated the international headlines earlier that spring. But of course, the national media had not been in Danville.

Naturally—as with the Freedom Rides—the immediate impulse on all SNCC projects was for folks to drop everything and rush to Danville to reinforce our battered brethren. "We cannot and will not allow violence to . . . etc." Hence Bayard's ambulance-chasing dig. It worked. Ed and Courtland did not defect to Danville, but stayed to help Bayard fashion his "social revolution."

[Danville is a small (45,000) Virginia city on the banks of the Dan River. A third of the population (15,000) was black. It was a textile and tobacco town, home to Dan River mills. Danville took particular pride in two distinctions: having the "largest single unit textile mill in the world" and of having been "The Last Capital of the Confederacy." It was also a classic company town; the Dan River corporation, being by far the largest employer and taxpayer, pretty much ran the city government. Their mills employed eleven thousand Danville residents. Of this workforce, some eleven hundred were blacks and only in the most menial jobs. The highest-ranking, best-paid black employee was a machinist at $80 a week. In town, blacks were segregated in housing, education, municipal employment, public accommodation in restaurants and hotels, and even were denied use of the city library, allegedly the site of the last full meeting of the Confederate cabinet. —EMT]

That spring, a new organization, the Danville Christian Progressive Association, led by three prominent clergymen *[the Reverend Lansdell Chase, the Reverend Lawrence Campbell, and the Reverend Alexander Dunlap]*, began to petition the city for relief, especially in education and employment. They asked for jobs as police officers, firefighters, meter readers, and clerks. They also mentioned streetlights, paved roads, and garbage collection in the African neighborhoods. Rebuffed completely, the ministers Dunlap and Campbell led a march on June 5 in which two hundred people were arrested. That's when they appealed for help from SNCC. And that's when it got ugly.

The police attack on June 10 left "drenched and bloody bodies lying in the street" according to Dottie Miller's field report. Of sixty-five demonstrators, forty-eight needed medical attention at the segregated hospital. When Danny Lyon, the SNCC photographer, arrived at the hospital, it was by his account like a MASH unit:

"Wounded people were sitting on the floor in the halls. People with lacerations and fractures were lying on stretchers waiting to be stitched up. Forman kept telling me to take close-ups of the wounds. I photographed a man whose shirtfront was completely covered with his own dried blood. His broken arm was in a sling. Next to him stood his friend, one eye swollen closed, his head split open in two places; sutured shut, the swelling rose about two inches from his scalp. These people had been kneeling in prayer at City Hall."

Before the march, fifteen SNCC organizers had been sent into Danville. In her memoir, *Freedom Song,* Mary King describes a town on military alert, patrolled by local cops, state troopers, military personnel with helicopters, and a militia of deputized municipal workers, mostly untrained laborers and garbagemen carrying clubs. Fear and harassment were constant.

Clearly the "Last Confederate Capital" took its historical inheritance seriously. In fact, after SNCC called for a boycott of Dan River mills products (supported in New York by the ILGWU*), the enduring presence of "history" there became manifest. When a local grand jury brought back indictments of "incitement to violence and war" against our workers, it was a capital offense based on a statute dating to 1832, during the panic in the aftermath of the Nat Turner rebellion. This prohibited "inciting the black (slave) population to violence and war against white citizens." The prosecutors did not see the irony. Had nothing changed in 130 years?

But Danville was only one place. That summer of the March an estimated fourteen thousand people were arrested in similar nonviolent protests across Dixieland.

Bayard's little performance had summarized exactly the ambivalence and the tension the movement was experiencing in the spring of '63. Bayard and the venerable A. Philip Randolph (God's peace on them both) had first raised the idea of a march that winter, December 1962. Their idea had been to focus all the energy and the movement's scattered resources on the national government, which had been dragging its feet. The Kennedy administration was entering its third year and had done nothing effective, at least that we could see. Then all that spring, nonviolent protests had been raging *all* over the South! Apparently spontaneously,

*International Ladies Garment Workers Union.

communities were organizing themselves to engage the injustices and the humiliation that surrounded them.

And I do mean *all* over the south. Black people were *happening,* Jack. It was a black nonviolent *intifada.* SNCC was getting daily requests to send organizers everywhere. Even up to within forty miles of the nation's capital. Even before the request from Danville. Earlier that spring SNCC Atlanta had asked us to help train a spirited movement in a hardscrabble little town called Cambridge on Maryland's Eastern Shore. All spring semester, groups of us had been going from Howard every weekend to work with a sister named Gloria Richardson and her people in Cambridge. Cambridge was one mean town, but Gloria and her people were great, spirited, and serious. Reminded me a lot of folks in Mississippi.

So . . . black people were happening, Jack. If you cared at all about your people, it was an exciting, hopeful spring to be alive and active.

Now the bad part. SNCC was entering its third year in voter registration and had staked out the hard places. Those "black belt" counties in the Delta of Mississippi, Arkansas, Alabama, and southwest Georgia. We had agreed that CORE could have Louisiana. We were working where Africans were in the majority and the vote could theoretically make a real difference. Which is why the repression was so desperate. As Mr. Turnbow said when I explained this, "Power seek tha *weak* places, water seek tha *low* places, but SNCC done seek the *hard* places, seem like t' me."

In every one of these places our staff and the local people had been seriously terrorized. And the federal government—the Justice Department, the FBI, those Kennedy liberals who had promised so much—where were they? Nowhere to be found. Worse even, for wherever we did see an FBI presence, it was rarely easy to determine which side it was on. The Atlanta office constantly tried to make sure the Feds knew. We phoned, wrote, and telegraphed the Justice Department. We notified liberal congressmen. We complained to the press. All to little avail. To say we were disappointed in the administration and JFK's "new frontier" would be an understatement. Scratch *disappointed* and try *betrayed* and *abandoned.*

[The following telegram from September 14, 1962, bears witness. It is quite representative and could easily have been sent in September 1961 or September 1963 and every month in between. Only the names and places would have needed to be changed. —EMT]

DR. MARTIN LUTHER KING
C/O SOUTHERN CHRISTIAN LEADERSHIP CONFERENCE
330 AUBURN AVE.
ATLANTA, GA.
  PLEASE URGE THE UNITED STATES JUSTICE DEPARTMENT
TO CONDUCT FULL INVESTIGATION AND APPREHEND THOSE

WHO KILLED UNIDENTIFIED NEGRO MAN IN GOODMAN, MISSISSIPPI. INVESTIGATIONS ALSO NECESSARY ON SHOOTING OF MARY LANE BURKS AND VIVIAN HILLET IN RULEVILLE, MISSISSIPPI. ALSO SHOOTING OF CHRISTOPHER ALLEN, JACK CHATFIELD AND PRATHIA HALL [SNCC STUDENTS FROM THE NORTH] IN DAWSON, GEORGIA AND BURNING TWO CHURCHES IN DAVISON AND ONE IN LEESBURG, GEORGIA. A WAVE [OF] TERROR AND KLAN REACTIVITY IS SWEEPING SOUTHWEST GEORGIA AND MISSISSIPPI. FEAR WE CANNOT PROTECT OUR FIELD SECRETARIES AND POTENTIAL VOTERS WITHOUT DIRECT INTERVENTION OF FEDERAL GOVERNMENT.
                    CHARLES MCDEW, CHAIRMAN, SNCC

Which is why the idea for a march on Washington made sense when we first heard it in December 1962. Yeah! Let us unite and focus all this activity in one place. Let's bring nonviolent direct action to the seat of government. Sit-ins in the halls of Congress. Campouts on the White House lawn. Let them either enforce their laws and professed "policies" in the South or be "embarrassed" again before the world. Let the nation and the world see what we've been seeing. Who they going to lock up? Us? When they can't seem to lock up the Klan? By then I was ready to take my chances. I really wanted to sit in, in Senator Eastland's office.

I know there were people around Dr. King and many in CORE and certainly SNCC who, with our supporters, could have turned out at least two thousand hardened veterans ready to face jail in Washington if necessary. Hell, we were already getting our heads whupped, our churches burned, and our people shot while the national government did diddly. Let them arrest the movement on the steps of the Capitol before the eyes of the world. Course, not everybody felt that way.

Bayard and Mr. Randolph's plan was to present a united front of the civil rights leadership. But Roy Wilkins (NAACP) and Whitney Young (Urban League) (peace be unto them), the "inside" players, were having none of it. No, Suh. Bad idea, this "march." Unwise. Untimely. Impolitic. No march, and certainly, certainly, *certainly*, Lord, *no* direct action. That would embarrass the president. Damage delicate relationships with supporters in Congress. Alienate powerful liberal allies. Anger the general public. Trigger white backlash. Utter madness, bad idea.

Since we had seen precious little hard evidence of presidential "goodwill" or "powerful liberal allies" or "congressional supporters," we wondered whether these "so-called Negro leaders" (Malcolm's term) might not be having delusions. I mean, endanger the administration's civil rights bill?

In 1962, the White House had been floating a "moderate" civil rights bill as its legislative priority. But—and I remember this clearly—when Congress reconvened that winter, January 1963, the media reported that the civil rights bill was now on a "back burner." The administration's legislative priority was now a *tax cut.* Sound familiar? So what was there for the march to endanger? Besides, far as I was concerned, the bill was a red herring anyway. What was needed was not any *new* legislation, especially not a "moderate" bill, but some real political will! As in serious *enforcement* of the laws that already existed.

Given the arguments of Young and Wilkins, the march idea was stalemated. It could go nowhere all winter long because Bayard and Mr. Randolph remained committed to a united front. Then came the spring. Birmingham police brutality and the specter of race war captured the national attention. Wilkins and Young began to feel a little heat from thousands marching in the streets. Well, maybe a *certain kind* of march, a carefully orchestrated and controlled *gesture* . . . nothing too militant or threatening, then maybe . . . And then presidential priorities began to shift again.

In June, in fact the week after the Danville police atrocity and Bayard's little performance, President Kennedy addressed the nation in prime time. It was a good speech, no question. He talked for the first time about the moral issues in the implicit injustice of racism and with a new sense of moral urgency resurrected his civil rights bill.

I should say a little more about that speech. It was announced that the president would "address the nation" on the *question of civil rights. All three networks would be carrying the speech live and in prime time. Whoee.* Either this was going to be important or else the White House and the media were hyping it so we would think it was important. It was also rumored that his "wise men"—or most of them—opposed the speech. In the climate of the time, that got your attention. So millions of Americans, white and black, tuned in. Given the administration's record, I was sure it would turn out to be just another cop-out. But I was surprised. It was accurate, clear, and truthful. The clearest, they said, since Lincoln's second Inaugural Address (1864) a hundred years earlier. That's a long time for presidential silence, friends. I think this speech has to be what accounted for JFK's great popularity among ordinary black folk in the South. It was probably also what—as much as anything else he did—earned him the enmity of whites there. (When the news of Kennedy's shooting reached Jackson, the staff reported that Africans stayed off the streets, where gangs of good ol' boys celebrated with loud cheers and rebel yells.) But what did Kennedy actually say that night?

He began by declaring civil rights "a moral issue as old as the Scriptures and as clear as the American Constitution." Simple and self-evident truths that no American president had had the vision to see, or the courage to say, for a hundred years? Apparently not, so he deserves that credit.

Then when I thought he might ask us to be patient and nonviolent again, he addressed his white countrymen:

> If an American, because his skin is dark, cannot eat lunch in a restaurant open to the public; if he cannot send his children to the best public schools available; if he cannot vote for the public official who represents him . . . who among us would be content to have the color of his skin changed and stand in his place? Who among us would then be content with counsels of patience and delay? One hundred years of delay have passed since President Lincoln freed the slaves. Yet their heirs are not fully free . . . from the bonds of injustice . . . from social and economic oppression. And this nation, for all its hopes and all its boasts, will not be fully free until all its citizens are free.

Historic? Perhaps. Certainly. But it was no more than we'd been saying all along.

In Jackson, Mississippi, that night after the speech, Byron De La Beckwith shot down Medgar Evers from ambush. Some days after the speech, JFK met with the national civil rights leaders,—who were now discussing the march with new energy—to suggest strongly that any confrontation in D.C. would doom his legislation. Congress would respond ill to any "intimidation." Any violence or disruptions in the streets of the nation's capital would only strengthen the hand of the racists in Congress. Would "alienate" and lose the "goodwill of the American people," among whom he clearly did not include us or the people we worked with.

So, another one of those "tough" political calls. Wilkins and Young supported the administration's argument. Bayard and Mr. Randolph, supported by the activists, did not want to abandon the march. Keep it alive if only as a threat. Finally they agreed to scrap the idea of *any* direct action or confrontation with the administration. It should be a giant rally *in support of* the administration's legislative program. Once the White House gave cautious, tentative approval, that was the turning point. Check it out. The very establishment that had been the *target*, the fully deserved target of the demonstration, was now giving *permission?* And then only if we promised to be good?

Enter now the "liberal establishment." Suddenly all kinds of "powerful and respectable" organizations (not the AFL-CIO, though) found it possible to support the march publicly. Bayard had his coalition, but there would be a price. From now on everything, but everything, would have to be approved by them, or indirectly by "representatives" of the White

House: the program, the speakers, the route of the march, the slogans, the signs to be carried, and of course, even the speeches. What, in fact, the Negroes would be allowed to say. At least in our case that was true.

Thereafter this "coalition," the so-called Big Ten, would take full credit for the passage of the civil rights bill of 1964. Quite as if the hundreds of aroused communities, the thousands of demonstrators in the streets and jails, the fire hoses and police dogs of Birmingham, had had nothing to do with getting the attention of the president and Congress in the first place. And, most galling of all, was this self-righteous attitude, that by supporting the bill, *they* were bestowing a great favor on the Negroes. That we ought to be grateful to them for granting us rights that other Americans—even ones off the ship only last week—took for granted. Gimme a cotton-picking break!

Which is not to say that Bayard and Mr. Randolph do not deserve honor and credit. They surely did. For their initiative and persistence had forged the alliance that made the march possible.

And the march itself? It was a spectacular media event. The first real political "media event" of the sixties. That is to say, a "political event" choreographed entirely for the television audience. And, by the way, look again at the pictures. That was no 250,000 people as reported by the D.C. police. It had to have been at least twice that. Easily.*

Dr. King may indeed, as he said he intended, have "subpoenaed the conscience of the nation" with his great speech. Later, when they received the leadership, the Kennedys were said to have been moved by the "dignity, peacefulness, and grandeur" of the spectacle. And undoubtedly that "river of black and white humanity" flowing through the city to stand before the Lincoln Memorial had a certain "grandeur." All true. A grand and moving spectacle.

But it is also true that in cold political terms, the march changed nothing. At least in the immediate aftermath. Next day, business as usual. Cops all over the South were back to whupping heads and taking names with a vengeance. In the Congress, the civil rights bill somehow managed to again fade into the background and out of discussion. Once more, apparently, a dead issue. So much for your powerful liberal coalition. A year later the bill would pass. But credit for its passage belongs even more to

---

*Jervis Anderson reported, "Seymour Perves, the march's publicity director, distrusted all police estimates of black political gatherings. . . . 'I went crazy with that figure,' he recalled. 'I was standing next to Randolph, and I leaned over to him and said, "Brother Randolph, I happen to know there are at least four hundred thousand people here." But Randolph was a man of principle. He said it would be improper to announce a figure larger than what the police gave him.' " —EMT

those four young girls murdered in a Birmingham church three weeks after the march. Or to the morally depraved racists who planted that bomb. Or maybe to Lee Harvey Oswald or whoever actually fired that rifle in Dallas two months after that.

Yeah, tell the truth and shame the devil, 'cause, as they say, the truth shall make ye free.

[Had Ture thought of it, he could well have extended credit for passage of the legislation much closer to home. The civil rights bill, HR 7152, was signed on July 2, 1964. By then our three workers on the Summer Project (see next chapter) who were murdered in Neshoba County, Mississippi, had been missing for almost two weeks, during which time the Mississippi struggle had completely dominated the national media attention. —EMT]

All of which is important to understand properly because a lot of mythology, folklore, and historical rewriting surrounds this subject. Even if we did not and could not have understood it clearly at the time, the political tensions that dogged the march from the beginning were not incidental. They were fundamental. And one "minor" event on the day itself would be prophetic: the censoring of John Lewis's speech. Which, according to the conventional wisdom of the establishment, had represented "irresponsibly radical attitudes of a politically naive student element," which had always been "disruptive" of the "movement" and which later would "destroy" it. Utter, utter nonsense. Let's be clear on that.

First of all, when John's speech was censored, this so-called grand movement coalition was all of two months old. Something cobbled together with the permission of the Kennedys. Bayard's coalition materialized only *after* the compromise resulting from the Kennedy meeting in June. "Once Kennedy agreed," Tom Kahn told me, "all kinds of liberal support miraculously appeared. The morning after, it was like a different world."

I mean, for three years, all over the South and elsewhere, thousands of black people and conscious whites had been in the trenches, peacefully and nonviolently agitating for rights supposedly guaranteed to *all* by the Constitution. And we had been battered by the violence of the mob and the state. All this time the conservatives had attacked us relentlessly, as did much of the nation's media, and not just in the South either: the great liberal *establishment* had sat on their hands. True, they did not leap to attack us like the Southern racist and their Northern right-wing allies like William F. Buckley and Judge Bork. But they essentially stayed aloof, silent as the grave, unable, apparently, to decide whether black folks were actually entitled to the rights of American citizens or if their effort to gain them deserved their support. So where was all the "moral leadership" then? Where was the coalition? *Hey . . . check . . . it . . . out.*

The march (August 1963) was their first public act affirming the basic moral right to simple justice for our people. Yeah. And they hung in until the voting rights act (1965). Then, as soon as we raised the call for Black Power (1966), they split. Where have they been since and where are they now? Of course, there have been honorable exceptions, but in general? So don't talk to me about no "liberals" or the "grand civil rights movement/coalition" either. Okay?

The response to John's speech was therefore very much a sign of things to come. Very much so. For that speech was no rabid diatribe of radical excess. Hey, SNCC had carefully put that speech together to accurately and truthfully reflect our experience. It may not have been pleasant, but it was all true. Maybe our experience was not so pleasant either, no American Dream. So kill the messenger, shall we?

John pointed out that even as he spoke, nine of our people were under indictment in Albany, Georgia, not by Dixiecrat politicians but by the federal government. The very same Justice Department, he pointed out, that was unable to do anything about four field secretaries—all young students—who, for peaceful picketing, were in jail, denied bail, and being threatened with death penalties in Americus, Georgia. Which side, he wondered, was the federal government on?

He talked about hundreds of our people in jail for voter registration. He talked about the thousands of *my* people in the Mississippi Delta evicted from plantations or working for starvation wages, $3 or less for twelve hours of work. Would the Kennedy bill help them? Would it protect women and children from fire hoses and police dogs?

Also, John pointed out, the "glaring contradictions" of the American political system "in which the party of Kennedy is the party of Eastland and the party of Javits [Senator Jacob Javits, R-NY] is the party of Goldwater." "Where," he asked, "is our party? The party which will make such marches unnecessary?"

The future deputy minority whip of the House of Representatives went on to deplore American "politicians who build their career on immoral compromise and ally themselves with political, economic, and social injustice and exploitation." I'm sure John has not forgotten those words. The speech concluded with a direct appeal for more "ambulance chasing" when John called on Americans in the thousands to "stay in the streets of every city, town, village, and hamlet until the unfinished revolution begun in 1776 is complete."

I saw nothing unreasonable or objectionable there, do you? Still feel that way myself. The real question is, what kind of "coalition" are you in when you cannot even publicly describe your own experience or openly raise and agitate for your deepest concerns? So that whole speech issue can be seen in retrospect as a clear portent of things to come—the stifling restraints of premature "coalition."

One other point of correction. History has it that SNCC was "pressured" into accepting censorship. Not true. SNCC made no concessions to liberal sensibilities or establishment pressure. John, Forman, and Courtland *did* accept certain changes, but not in order to curry favor with the powerful or appease liberal sensitivities.

[Courtland Cox was in the room and remembers it this way:

"Poor Bayard. Man, he hadn't really slept for at least a week. Continually running around putting out fires around the clock . . . dealing with everything from the politics to the logistics, to the press and the police . . . from the White House and the 'allies,' to Roy Wilkins and Malcolm X . . . making sure there would be enough medical personnel and portable toilets. I mean preparing for every contingency. And then on the morning of the march this? It all seemed such nit-picking, totally unnecessary. I mean some of those objections . . . the word revolution, *and even our association with the African struggle. 'One man, one vote is the African cry, it must also be ours.' They even wanted that out? So at first we told Bayard, 'No way. Over our dead bodies.'*

"[Bayard] understood perfectly. He was between a rock and a hard place. But he was cool. He just went into the crowd and brought Mr. Randolph, who said to us:

" 'Young men, I've waited twenty-two years for this. . . . Would you young men accommodate an old man? I've worked all my life for this.' That's why we negotiated a few changes. For had we walked out, as we were quite prepared to do, that would have been the headlines: 'SNCC breaks unity on March. Movement divisions exposed.' We just couldn't have that.

"Man, I just looked at that old gentleman. That venerable old warrior at least seventy-five years old, who had fought for our people all his life. . . . And here we were a third of his age. . . . How could we do that to him?

"But I'll never forget. Mr. Randolph supported us on Africa. And on revolution? *He said, 'Nonsense. Revolution* is *a perfectly acceptable word, which I myself use whenever it is appropriate.' End of argument."]*

I've always felt that it was not really the language or even the ideas that were being objected to. And it could certainly not have been the facts. Those were indisputable. So what was offensive had to have been the *tone* and the spirit of the speech. I think it just wasn't sufficiently *humble,* and above all, it didn't sound *grateful.* You dig?

Sounds crazy? You right, it is crazy. But for reasons best known to themselves, white folks seem to need and expect us always to be grateful. See, I'm convinced that it couldn't have been the actual changes, which, after all, were slight and subtle, that had been the issue. It was the idea that we *had* to submit to changes on demand. You could say it was both symbolic and psychological. Nonetheless, we went through the motions for Mr. Randolph and Bayard.

You know the Boers in South Africa had a term in Afrikaans for that attitude, *baaskap.* That was the guiding principle behind apartheid. *Baaskap,* that which must be maintained at all costs. What it meant was unchallenged control, dominance, ownership, literally white "bosshood," white supremacy. SNCC had encountered the idea all over the South: in the jails and the courthouses, on the plantations. I guess we met the Northern liberal version of *baaskap* at the Lincoln Memorial. But it never has worked, not in South Africa and certainly not at the march. Because here's how Mr. Randolph (peace be unto him) opened the speeches in his keynote address:

"Let the nation and the world know the meaning of our numbers. We are not an organization or a group of organizations. We are not a mob. Nor are we a pressure group. We are *the advance guard of a moral revolution* for jobs and freedom. The *revolution* reverberates throughout the land, touching every city, every town, every village, where we are segregated, oppressed, and exploited."

Revolution: a perfectly acceptable word. I myself use it whenever appropriate. . . .

The day before the march, the scene at the planning area on the mall was highly organized chaos, mind-boggling. An air of excitement, of anticipation, of feverish preparation for something unprecedented and major. But what exactly?

In one area enclosed by a mobile picket fence, guarded by a detail of police (bomb threats had been phoned in), teams of volunteers at long wooden tables toiled busily away at a variety of tasks. Staff communicated with each other by means of walkie-talkies. Some teams were stapling poster board placards (bearing the five officially approved slogans) to slender handles. Volunteers from local churches were making thousands of sandwiches for box lunches. Others were packaging assorted merchandise, officially approved souvenirs—march mementos, pins, pennants, etc.—for sale to the expected multitudes. Others were stacking official march programs with rules of conduct and the line of march and so on. A great many cops and city and federal officials, obviously under orders to be cooperative and welcoming, bustled about smiling and looking for ways to be helpful.

Lots of NAG members were working. I found Ed and Courtland.

"Wow," I teased. "All this sweetness and light, bro? It hurt mah eyes. Y'all done got the federal government on our side at last, huh?"

"Yeah," Ed growled. "Looks so to you, do it? Wal, I hear they also got every cop in the District standing by. Capitol Hill po-lice, federal marshals, they even calling dudes back from leave, mah man."

"Yeah, not to mention the troops massed with tanks and stuff just outside the District. And just in case, I hear they got paratroops on alert in

North Carolina. Be here in an hour if they decide they need 'em. Sweetness and light? Look more to me like terrified and ready, bro."

Inside the work area there were government production teams, USIA, Voice of America, etc., posing the volunteers (interracially, of course), shooting miles of film, interviewing workers. "What does this mean to you?" "Why are you here?" "Smile now, this is going to Russia and Africa," they said. "You couldn't have a demonstration like this in Moscow or Havana now, could you?" No kidding, more than one guy actually said that.

Aha, I thought, so that's the line, huh? American democracy at work. Forget the grievances that brought people there. A Cold War propaganda victory for the government and "democracy."

I can hear some of you: "Well, but isn't that true?" Wrong question. Misses the point entirely. First of all, I didn't know then and still don't know what the march had to do with Russia or Cuba. Besides, I knew the newsreel films the government was fixing to distribute all over the world wouldn't include shots of the troops and tanks massed on the edge of the city or the paratroopers standing ready. Nor candid shots of civil rights workers inside the Parchman death house.

So even before the issue with John's speech the next day, we were already uneasy. By what perverted reckoning does a protest against American inhumanity to black folk suddenly transform into an endorsement of the very system that oppresses us? Or the government that tolerates it?

Gimme a bu-rake!

Case in point. The morning of the march, news came that Dr. Du Bois had died in Ghana. That grand old man who, almost single-handedly for sixty years—the entire course of the century—had been the intellectual architect of the struggle for our liberation in this country and the world was dead. Had he been in the country, would the *coalition* have afforded the doctor his richly deserved place of respect on that platform before the Lincoln Memorial? I truly doubt that.

Related to which, a message of support and warm fraternal good wishes to the African-American people in their struggle arrived at the march headquarters. It came from Chairman Mao Tse-tung on behalf of the Chinese people. Dr. Du Bois especially had been greatly respected by the Chinese people and government as he was in many nations across the world, so that message may have been a tribute to the grand old man by the Chinese government.

Now, whatever your politics, greetings to the righteous struggles of African-American people from the head of state of the world's most populous nation are significant and should be received that way. Right? I mean, anyone presuming to speak for our struggle must be able to recognize this and find a way to respond with appropriate courtesy and dignity. That, as they say, ain't rocket science.

Well, apparently not to Bro Roy Wilkins of the NAACP, who could have elected to remain silent, but did not. He chose to issue an insulting statement—gleefully reported in the *New York Times*—repudiating the chairman's message of sympathy, support, and friendship from the Chinese people. Now *that*, I thought, was extreme, not John's speech. It was rude, unnecessary, and ungracious.

I don't recall the exact language as quoted, but I do remember the tone. It had to do with American Negroes knowing who our friends are. Our not needing or appreciating support from international riffraff, Communist dictators and such. When and if, however, the Chinese people enjoyed democracy, then maybe . . . Something like that. *[Apparently the CORE leadership felt the same way. Brother James Farmer's rejection of the Chinese expression of support, however, was issued from a Louisiana jail. An irony that could not have escaped* nos hermanos chinos, *as Fidel would refer to them. —EMT]* In SNCC we found that truly embarrassing. Not so much for what it revealed about the *mentality* (for Bro Wilkins was by all accounts a very intelligent man) of those Malcolm used to call "the so-called Negro leaders," as for what it said about the puppet status to which they had been subjugated within the U.S. political system. "A place for every nigger and every nigger in his place," as the Southern governor used to say.

Some folks suggested that the brother had not really written that statement, that it may in fact have originated with the State Department or even the CIA. But, even if true, would that be better or worse? Your call.

Talking about democracy. Earlier that spring as the registration drive picked up momentum in the Delta, the authorities moved to crush its spirit by making a serious example. In the tiny rural town of Itta Bena they arrested a group of workers after a voter registration rally. Then they arrested fifteen more in Greenwood. These were all local youth, including some of Bob's first recruits from Amite County—Lawrence Guyot and two high school students, Curtis Hayes Mohammed and Hollis Watkins. The other workers arrested were from the Delta. Some of them served the time (four months) in the Parchman death house as we had. Others were sent to the Leflore County prison farm. And all for trying to register American citizens to vote. The important point is that these were all local black youth, who were consequently not protected by national media attention as the original Freedom Riders had been. Or by the Kennedy Justice Department. As a result, the thugs in the prisons felt free to torture them and did so. I assume they intended to send a message to other local young people to stay away from voter registration.

They tried to make them believe they were about to be killed. Or that some of their friends had already been killed. Some were hung by their wrists from handcuffs. They were all kept naked in their cells for forty-seven days. Another punishment was the "hot box." This was a small zinc box completely exposed under the Mississippi sun in which you were kept until you passed out. All for registering voters? And our federal government knew that this was happening and was powerless to intervene? Gimme an ever-loving break.

I was in Greenwood the day the brothers were released and I could see they were in bad shape. Ol' Guyot had lost one hundred pounds. (He could afford that better than any of us, 'cause usually he hovered up around three hundred pounds.) That wasn't Larry's best year. First the cops in Winona had beaten the bad out of him when he'd gone to see about Mrs. Hamer and the three women. Then four months in Parchman. Guyot was funny, though. They say when he came back from the beating at Winona, face all swollen and bruised, he headed straight to the meeting that night. When his turn came to speak, he strode up to the front of the little church and stood glowering wordlessly at the people in a challenging way. The church became silent. Guyot glared at the people. Then his fist shot out pointing at the people.

"Immanuel Kant," he thundered, "wants to know. Do you exist?" That's Guyot, another bro who came early and stayed late. He is still organizing in the D.C. community. *[Guyot remembers the Immanuel Kant quote differently. He thinks the incident happened a year later after he got out of jail in Hattiesburg. —EMT]*

I think that just about all those guys just out of jail came up for the march. Jimmy Lee Pruit was from Itta Bena. He was eighteen years old and had passed out in the hot box. On the way to D.C., the SNCC car he was in broke down in some small Carolina town. No mechanic would fix it so they had to abandon the car. But Jimmy Lee gets to the march. The marshal stops him because his sign isn't authorized. Jimmy is stubborn, he ain't giving up the sign. It's his sign. The only one he came to carry. Finally, they have to refer the case upstairs. The head marshal listens to Jimmy and makes an allowance. He can carry his sign. The disputed sign? It read, "Stop Criminal Prosecutions of Voter Registration Workers in Mississippi."

Enough said. But it was a magnificent spectacle.

Cambridge, Maryland was—might still be—a nondescript, hard-bitten, little town some fifty miles or so from the nation's capital. It was also, during the spring and fall semesters on both sides of the March on Washington, NAG's local Mississippi. Many brothers and sisters from Howard, and the Maryland black colleges, served their apprenticeship in grassroots community organizing there. It was close enough so we could drive over on weekends. It was where many of us—Cynthia Washington, Cleve Sellers, Stanley Wise, Bill "Winky" Hall, Khalid Sayeed, Muriel Tillinghast, John Baptiste, Reggie Robinson, and Johnny Wilson—got to experience a protracted campaign and the emotional satisfaction of working with a strong, spirited community of black people rising up to face down their oppressors and refusing to back down.

To get to Cambridge from D.C. you had to drive over the longest, highest bridge I'd ever seen. That bridge was kinda *ominous*. It was incredibly high and miles long so that at first you felt like you were driving up toward the sky, and when it started to descend, that you might be leaving the known world for a region that time had passed by. Cambridge's social arrangements and attitudes were classic and reminiscent of Mississippi or South Africa.

In this hardscrabble town with a stagnant economy, working-class life was not easy for anybody and almost impossible for poor blacks. Although Cambridge was smallish, it sure had a well-defined ghetto. The dominant impression was not just of depression, but of neglect: rows of weather-beaten wooden houses already dilapidated and steadily deteriorating. In 1963, the population of the town was fourteen thousand, of which a third was African. Unemployment among us was 29 percent, and much of what employment there was, was—as in the Delta—seasonal. So that 30 percent of our people who were employed worked for thirty weeks—or less—each year. Sixty-six percent of all African families had incomes of less than $3,000. You get the picture. Some white working-class neighborhoods seemed almost as bad, but of course we did not enter those communities if we could help it.

To compound its economic woes, the town was rigidly segregated and highly discriminatory. Municipal employment and city services—health care, housing, and education—were either segregated or flatly excluded Africans. For example, the long-promised housing development for the African community: even though the federal government was providing the money, the mayor's office had twice managed to delay or postpone the construction. Blatant stuff like that.

The white political establishment was not just entrenched in a racist past, but was outright hostile and arrogant about it. They didn't even try to disguise their racism. They were unwilling to concede anything to the movement, not even the *appearance* of respect. It was as though the very idea of having to sit and talk to "their" blacks who were suddenly getting "uppity" was an intolerable insult to their personal dignity and to the natural order. They were giving up nothing but hard times, Jack, and they didn't try to hide it.

Inevitably, after talks got nowhere and the movement took to the streets, the police conduct mirrored the politicians' attitudes. That's when CNAC (the Cambridge Nonviolent Action Committee) turned to SNCC, and as the closest SNCC groups, NAG and the Baltimore students went in.

The other distinct aspect of white Cambridge was a clearly organized faction that regularly used violence against the movement. Not just the loud, aggressive crowds that usually surrounded demonstrations. Those we were accustomed to. (Remember, it was in a Cambridge sit-in that the young man had attacked me, then come to the church to apologize.) No, now there began to be regular reports of gunfire at night . . . shots into people's homes out of the night and physical attacks on blacks traveling alone or in small groups after dark.

I have no proof that this vigilante violence was either organized or condoned by the authorities, but I saw no attempt to stop it either. In the face of the political hard line and police hostility, the black community felt exposed and unprotected. A group of African men under arms began to patrol the community at night. And soon, when the sound of random gunfire was heard at night, it meant that shots were being exchanged.

That spring (1963), tensions increased in the town. In one notable incident that June, the police appeared to behave both professionally and impartially. Two white men had turned up shot on the outskirts—or just inside—our community. Later that same night some businesses owned by whites went up in flames, apparently torched. The next day, or soon thereafter, a mob of nearly four hundred armed white men chanting racist slogans marched on the black community but were stopped by police blockades on every road leading in. Tension on both sides of the color line rose. By this time, I was down in the Delta, but a SNCC project staffed by NAG folks was in place in Cambridge.

On July 14, carload(s) of whites drove through the main street in the African community firing into houses. They ran into organized defense. Sustained fire was returned from various points, off roofs, out of windows, behind cars and trees, etc. That exchange of fire lasted more than an hour.

Of course that got the attention of the national press, who were remarkably evenhanded. The media duly reported Cambridge to be a "war zone," lamented the "breakdown" in race relations, and righteously deplored the violence on *both* sides: that of the whites who had come through our community shooting and the blacks who had dared to fire back. Media indignation grew when, the next day, Gloria, the CNAC leader "refused to repudiate black violence."

Actually, she had deplored *violence* and called for a serious investigation. She'd also affirmed CNAC's commitment to nonviolent protest. However, while she strongly condemned the invasions and the violence by the invaders, she pointedly declined to condemn the defenders. "When you are attacked by a rabid dog," she said, "you don't run or throw away the walking stick you have in your hand." Which was enough to earn her a chorus of condemnation—totally spontaneous and well informed, I'm sure—from "responsible" Negro leaders, as well as various liberal "friends of the Negro," including the president of the United States. But Cambridge had gotten his attention.

Even though, or perhaps because, JFK was clear that the violence showed that "[the] Cambridge [movement] had lost sight of what demonstrations were all about," his Justice Department suddenly sprang into action. The attorney general called an emergency meeting in Washington on July 22 to address precisely the issues that CNAC had been trying without success to raise for half a year. Are we to believe that this sudden administrative urgency had nothing to do with the awful specter of an armed black community determinedly defending itself against white attack? Perhaps. Or with the March on Washington now definitely coming their way in a month? Perhaps. But a "high level" meeting was hastily organized.

I should say something about the Cambridge movement and its leader. The city of Cambridge—in its political and racial arrangements—was at once completely typical yet unique. One curious contradiction: Cambridge was, in terms of apartheid and black powerlessness, as racist and feudal as any rural Mississippi county or any Transvaal county town. In that way, it was typical. But unlike in Mississippi or South Africa, blacks in Cambridge could and did vote. Passing strange, eh? The "dictatorship" of the majority?

The other anomaly was that the "militant" leader was a woman. And Gloria Richardson was a real leader. She was one tough-minded, tough-talking field general who marched at the head of the troops on every demonstration unless she was in jail. Gloria was another of the movement's many remarkable women. We liked her a lot.

It is hard to believe that Gloria, a slender woman with shoulder-length hair and a café-au-lait complexion, was then in her early forties, for she seemed much younger in style and spirit. In the fitted jeans she often wore, with her easy, direct manner, and in her passionate commitment to the struggle, she seemed like one of us. And in fact, reporters often mistook her at first for just another student. Yet the loyalty, respect, and affection with which the local people—at least those active in the struggle—regarded their leader was unmistakable. But she drove the politicians crazy. And she was accustomed to abusive phone calls and death threats nightly. Even some elements of the black community—the local NAACP leadership and the small class of local black professionals—found her too controversial, "confrontational," and something of an embarrassment.

Why this should be so was curious, for her own family was of that class. She had studied theater at Howard and was a sorority sister there—an AKA—which should tell you all you need to know about her social background, and a lot about the social/racial history of Cambridge.

Although blacks voted, our community there was powerless and seriously oppressed. Yet a small, snug class of colored professionals coexisted and seemed to have made their peace quite comfortably with things as they were. Gloria had been from that group. Not only were there lawyers in her family, her grandfather was a politician. He was the first Negro to serve on the Cambridge City Council (1912), and he had held that position for *fifty* years. But to what end? Given the concrete conditions we found there, you could accurately say that Cambridge blacks must have had "representation without representation." This situation seems to have been a direct result of the town's history. Up until the Civil War, the great majority of the Africans in Cambridge were enslaved, but a small community of "free colored" were permitted a few more "rights" than the slaves. They or their children could not be sold and no law prohibited them from seeking education. The more I heard, the more it sounded like "the coloreds" in South Africa to me.

As with all SNCC projects, the rank, file, and leadership in Cambridge were ordinary folk. And the organization was democratic so the grassroots people doing the work were free to express long-suppressed feelings in the political discussions. Which they did. Gloria respected that and represented their decisions (as in the referendum) honestly. For this she caught a lot of flak from the white establishment and the press, but worse, elements of the now discredited old-line black "leadership" were not slow to join in the criticism. Tell the truth, God laughs.

About a week after the famous Cambridge shoot-out, a high-level meeting took place in the Justice Department in D.C. When Gloria and her delegation (the CNAC group was accompanied by SNCC observers John Lewis, Reggie Robinson, and Stanley Wise) arrived at the meeting, there were, to their great surprise, no representatives of the Cambridge city government present.

Instead, they found members of the Maryland political leadership: the governor's chief of staff, the Maryland attorney general and assistant attorney general, and a soldier introduced as General Geltson, commander of the state National Guard. Nobody from white Cambridge. Not a soul. *Nada.*

These two groups were joined by Bobby Kennedy and Burke Marshall (attorney general for civil rights) and a black gentleman in a suit.

At the meeting's end an agreement in principle was worked out between our side and the Maryland officials. It was a good agreement. All the previously nonnegotiable injustices were addressed in a rational and fair way. It was agreed:

1. To begin the complete and immediate desegregation of public schools and hospitals in Dorchester County.
2. Construction (at federal expense) of two hundred units of public housing in the Cambridge black community. (The African gentleman in the suit turned out to be Robert Weaver, head of the Federal Housing Finance Agency.)
3. Employment of a (one) Negro in the Cambridge office of the Maryland Department of Employment and a second Negro in the post office there.
4. Creation of a Cambridge Human Relations Committee.
5. Amendment of the Cambridge town charter so that places of public accommodation could be desegregated.

As I said, nothing ground shaking or radically disruptive; in fact, quite reasonable and moderate. Our folks left that first meeting exultant, wondering what all the hassle and unpleasantness of the last six months had been about. Once there was the political will, previously insurmountable problems became quite manageable, right?

The next morning a delegation from Cambridge—the mayor and key members of the City Council—were somewhat truculent, but agreed to sign on condition that CNAC would agree to suspend demonstrations. CNAC says no problem. As long as there is observable, good-faith progress being made toward implementation, reasons to demonstrate will no longer exist. Demonstrations are, after all, not fun. People have better things to do, etc.

Whereupon "The Treaty of Cambridge" was formally signed by both parties with some distinguished witnesses indeed. (Messrs. Robert F. Kennedy and Burke Marshall, the attorney general and assistant attorney general of the United States). Well, I guess, as every schoolchild knows, "wars" are always and only concluded by "treaties," right?

The ordinary people of Cambridge were euphoric and very proud. This was real progress, more than they had really expected. More than in the last fifty years. And they *themselves* had done it. By standing up for themselves. By defending their human rights. It had all been worth it. The risk. The danger. There was *some* justice in the world after all. It was, the SNCC folks said, very moving. Our first clear victory. And the first unambiguous sign of the system working for us.

As far as I know, those elements of the agreement that were the responsibility of the federal and state authorities proceeded in good faith. The goodwill of the town government officials was another matter.

They were victim to a sudden onset of democratic scruples. Su they announced that before the town charter could be amended (end apartheid), the change had to be *democratically* approved by a citizen referendum. Say what? The same citizenry—some at any rate—who'd been firing into our community? In the prevailing climate this seemed a transparent and cynical ploy to change the agreement after the fact.

Gloria and CNAC screamed foul and the membership voted not to participate in any referendum on their rights. A decision that was widely and roundly criticized as at best "bad politics" and at worst "bad faith," with Gloria in particular being singled out for great abuse. Hey, I thought the community was absolutely correct on the principle and the *politics*. Still do.

First of all the politics. Given the demographics and the intense racial polarization, the referendum could never have passed. No way. That's why they *had* it in the first place. Even had they *wanted* to, not enough whites could have summoned the courage to cross over. That was clear. And on the principle? Even if some whites would have crossed over, which of *you* would be prepared, and are you now prepared, to subject your fundamental rights and dignity as a human being to the whim and caprice of your neighbors' vote? No, you wouldn't. Nor will *you* ever be asked to. But *we* should? C'mon . . . gimme a break.

When, to no one's surprise, the referendum failed that fall, demonstrations resumed and were met with increased violence. Violence, in this case, in support of "democracy." Think about it. This time, black folks were not only angry, they felt betrayed. Cambridge, Maryland, became a dangerous place. Soon martial law was declared and the town occupied by four hundred national guardsmen under the command of Brigadier General George W. Geltson.

By the time we gather back at Howard the semester after the March on Washington (September 1963), the situation in Cambridge is stalemated. The movement is dug in but there is no progress at all to report. At every turn, the city government stonewalls. They aren't giving up an inch and certainly not to a "rabble" of "their" uneducated field Negroes and a bunch of students and outside agitators led by Gloria.

Gloria was holding the movement together with the help of SNCC staff, and students from NAG and other schools came in regularly to help with workshops, registration, and petition drives or to march in demonstrations, but with no victories and little progress to report, local people were getting tired and discouraged. The intoxicating sense of progress and accomplishment of the previous summer was a distant memory.

Ironically, the single thing that still united the black community and kept the movement strong was the presence of the National Guard, which cordoned off the black community every night. They were supposed to be "keeping the peace" or even defending the community, but black folks felt besieged. The young guardsmen were, after all, armed Maryland white men. People in the community were certain that when off duty, the guardsmen fraternized with the local whites. Our folks didn't feel secure, they felt *occupied,* as in occupation, military.*

The next spring, the 1964 presidential primaries begin. George Corley Wallace, the rabidly segregationist governor of Alabama, national symbol of Southern white resistance, and candidate of the Ku Klux Klan, declares his candidacy. Not only that but he's going to kick off the Maryland campaign—you got it—in Cambridge. Talk about a calculated provocation, fishing in troubled waters. Outside agitators?

Gloria tells us that Wallace, apparently with the full cooperation if not the invitation of the authorities, will be speaking to a white-only audience at a local skating rink. What is usses gone do? She tells us that as far as the people are concerned, it's an insult and a deliberate challenge. They know we gotta respond in some way. Can they count on NAG support?

So some of us—Courtland, Ed, Cleve Sellers, Thelwell, and others—begin going over to discuss strategy and help organize whatever action is to take place. Some people question whether the movement shouldn't simply ignore Wallace. That redneck demagogue be there for a night and he'd be gone . . . Yeah, but if we do that . . . Another of those interminable discussions. People have strong feelings on both sides.

Once we get to Cambridge, however, it becomes clear that doing nothing is not really an option. No way the community could just ignore Wallace's visit. Not after Birmingham, and the four young girls in the Sixteenth Street Baptist Church. Certainly not after everything people in Cambridge had been subjected to and are *still* going through. No way. They wanted the movement to do something effective. But what? There really weren't a lot of clear options. A bad hand any way you read it.

Few real options, and as usual, no easy ones. But we had to do something. That was clear.

Once we start organizing the community, certain other things become clear. People seemed proud of and fiercely loyal to Gloria. And they are embattled. I mean, by now it is not at all uncommon to see guns being worn and even offered. Now, don't you even venture out at night, they advised. And if you do, best you carry you something. Don't go out there without you got you a piece, son.

Our rally is in a fraternal lodge and folks really turn out. A number of

*People from the Cambridge staff or community really ought to write down the details of our people's experience under this occupation, which went on for quite some time, well into the next year. There was nothing else quite like it in the entire movement.

NAG folk, along with activist white students from area colleges and a couple of SNCC photographers from Atlanta, have come in. And of course the national media is out in force, looking for a sensational story.

After the speeches the people form a line in the darkness outside the lodge. There are over six hundred of us but you can't really see everyone in the dark. The reality of marching in darkness through hostile white territory is suddenly very real and sobering.

Gloria takes her place in the lead. A group of us—a lot of NAG women are on that march—from NAG fall in behind her. We set out and march down Race Street, at most five blocks.

Ranks of guardsmen in full battle dress, carrying carbines with fixed bayonets and standing in close order, completely block the road. A few carried enormous airfield searchlights. Behind them you can see and hear a large crowd of whites. Silently we march up within fifteen yards. Gloria moves up and engages the general. It is so quiet we can hear every word. He orders her to disperse the march. You have no permit, he says. Does George Wallace need a permit? she ask.

She stands for a moment. A slender woman looking at a solid wall of soldiers towering over her. Then she pushes a rifle aside, tries to step through the ranks, and is immediately arrested. I believe a picture was taken at that exact moment that would appear on front pages across the country. Two brothers (John Baptiste and Khalid Sayeed) go to her side and they too are arrested. When the general bellows at us to disperse, we all sit down.

The troops begin to put on gas masks. We have expected that and carry damp cloths to protect our faces against tear gas. The standard drill is to get low, cover your face, breathe through the damp cloths, and wait for the gas to disperse. We are ready. No big thing.

A SNCC photographer, Cliff Vaughs, moves up to get a picture of the troops in the masks. They grab him. I hold on to his ankle as the soldiers yank on his arms. Poor Cliff is airborne. Danny Lyon gets a picture of that. And then this curious figure moves out of the ranks of the soldiers. He too is masked, has two large metal cylinders on his back, and a long, hollow metal tube in his hands.

[In Danny Lyon's immortal words, "He looked like a vacuum cleaner salesman from outer space." Cleve Sellers recalls, ". . . a strange uniform. He looked like an astronaut. His uniform was iridescent, giving off a faint, eerie glow." From descriptions of the gas's effect it appears to have been an incapacitating chemical agent being experimentally developed for the military during the sixties. It seems to be the same gas used in today's military to "neutralize" the area around downed aviators before masked rescue teams are sent in. That night in Cambridge, one death—that of an infant in its crib—resulted from its use. —EMT]

The man with the canisters points the tube *[allegedly a flamethrower converted to this purpose —EMT]* at us and a thick, wet, clinging cloud of white smoke billows out over us. The cloud envelopes those of us in front first, and after that I can see nothing. Instantly my eyes, nasal passages, throat and lungs are afire. I cannot breathe. I remember thinking, this is it now, I'm dying. Then, nothing . . .

[Danny Lyons:

"Stokely Carmichael, then twenty-two years old, was seated in the front of the line of demonstrators and the gas was sprayed directly into his face. He must have suffered terribly. That night most of the staff went to visit him at the hospital."]

I may have been lucky, for the next thing I remember is waking up in a hospital bed the next morning. I have no recollection of how I got there. I later learned that, in the total chaos, Cleve Sellers had found me lying unconscious and that he and some brothers had commandeered a car to drive me to hospital. I have no doubt, given my childhood respiratory problems, that those brothers saved my life that night.

I can't tell you what went down after that because I was completely out of it. But others were conscious and what they described was total chaos. People choking, retching, trying to run away, and passing out. People screaming in fear and agony, vomiting and soiling themselves because they'd lost control of their bladder and bowels. Reports of guardsmen advancing on hysterical citizens, firing their guns as they came. *[Since no gunshot wounds were officially reported, the guard must have been aiming high. —EMT]* Pure chaos and brutality.

[Cleve Sellers:

"The gas made our wet handkerchiefs burn like fire. It also burned our nostrils. When we attempted to breathe out of our mouths to save our nostrils, the gas attacked the insides of our mouths and throats. My throat and stomach felt as if I had gulped a mouthful of burning acid. The gas threw us into total confusion. We forgot about demonstrating, Governor Wallace, and the skating rink. Everybody jumped up and started running. I took about fifteen steps and collapsed.

I held my aching head up and tried to peer out of my burning, tearing eyes. The guardsmen were about thirty feet from me. They were moving forward shoulder to shoulder with their bayoneted rifles extended like spears. They grunted in unison before taking each step: 'Ah-HUMP-CLUMP, ah-HUMP-CLUMP, ah-HUMP-CLUMP!'

"I ran about a half block before the guardsmen began to fire their rifles. They were grunting, shuffling, and firing in unison: 'Ah-HUMP-CLUMP-CHOW! Ah-HUMP-CLUMP-CHOW! Ah-HUMP-CLUMP-CHOW!' My throat was on fire. My legs felt like rubber bands and my mind was hallucinating.

"I managed to clamber over the fence. I thought I had reached safety. I was wrong. I was running in the street again. The guardsmen were still behind me.

They were still coming—and still shooting. All of a sudden, the street was bathed in a bright light. In my confused state of mind, I paused to catch my breath and figure out what was happening. Looking back in the direction of the guardsmen, I discovered the source of the light. The guardsmen had turned on the searchlight and pointed it in our direction. It was blinding. All I could see were the silver bayonets of the advancing guardsmen.

"I am certain that a lot of people would have been seriously injured if a small group of black men had not started shooting at the guardsmen to slow them down. It was like a scene from a western movie. The men would run a few steps, crouch on one knee, and fire; run a few steps, crouch on one knee, and fire.

"I ran to the CNAC office, which was filled with people. Most of them were too sick to talk. Stokely was the sickest of all. He was in terrible shape. Tears were flowing from his eyes, his stomach was still retching, and he was only partially conscious. I tried to talk to him, to ask him how he felt, but he didn't even recognize me.

" 'Come on! We've got to get him to a hospital before he chokes to death!' I yelled to a group of men standing nearby.

"Grabbing Stokely by his underarms, we dragged him to a car. He was too weak to do anything except moan. We were outside the black community before I realized what we were doing. Oh my God, I thought. Here we are driving, black and unarmed, through a hostile white community during a race war. My head began to clear up—fast."

When I awoke the next morning, I had no idea where I was. The sun was shining. A nurse was in the room so I figured it was a hospital. I found I could stand, so I asked for my clothes.

"Why? You can't go anywhere," she said.

"I'm okay," I said, thinking her objection to be a medical one.

"Maybe, but you are under arrest. You can't leave."

"Lady, I'm grateful to you for taking care of me. But ain't nobody arrested me. How can I be under arrest? I'm outta here."

"Way-all, the police brought you. But, I guess I can't stop you. Hey, I'm not a cop."

So I gits back to the office and most of the leadership is in jail. At first I see only some volunteers and some young community people, except, of all people . . . General Gelston. And he's blustering and lecturing them about outside agitators, Communists, and knowing what's good for them, etc., etc., when I walk in.

"You," he cried. "What are you doing here? You're supposed to be under arrest."

"What are you doing here?" I ask. "You're a war criminal. Chemical warfare against unarmed folks. You should be in jail, not me. Unless you have a warrant, *you* better leave." Which, to my great surprise, he does. I still don't know why. But so did I, before he could come back with reinforcements.

Oh, yes, by the way, George Wallace received 43 percent of the vote in the Maryland Democratic presidential primary, which should tell you something about that electorate and the referendum debate.

CHAPTER XVI

Summer '64: Ten Dollars a Day and All the Sex You Can Handle

They say in Mississippi, no moderates have we met.
You either be a Freedom Fighter
Or Tom for Ross Barnett."
—SNCC freedom song

Just for the record: I did not at first support the Summer Project. In fact, for all kinds of reasons, a lot of people on staff were not at first supportive either. And I always retained an ambivalence. But once the decision was made, I was a good soldier like everyone else. We worked ourselves like rented mules to make it happen. And once we were swept up in the momentum and excitement, we'd have rather died than see it fail.

In many ways, the Mississippi Summer Project was a turning point for a whole generation of us. It was certainly the boldest, most dramatic, and traumatic single event of the entire movement. It certainly had the most far-reaching effect: for national party politics, for that activist college generation, for the state of Mississippi and the movement there, and especially for SNCC as an organization. After the summer, none of those would be the same.

What was my initial objection? Primarily this: That it was way too ambitious. That it would be a serious mistake for the organization—*our* organization—to extend itself so far beyond our own internal capabilities and resources. That there were organizational dangers in taking on any project that, like this one, depended on large numbers of outsiders. A project entailing *five times* as many volunteers as there were staff in *all* of SNCC, as well as involving a good many other organizations, each with its own agenda on whose resources we would have to depend to fund much of the project? It seemed real risky in terms of the organization's identity and even its independence.

As usual, there was great debate within SNCC. The other major projects (southwest Georgia, Alabama, Arkansas) felt—and rightly so—that such a huge project would suck in all SNCC's resources and attention. But if Mississippi can bring it off, they decided, more power to them. The local Mississippi staff had different concerns, but that was mine, that we were in danger of overextending ourselves.

We were in Washington when I first heard that Bob and the folks in Mississippi were proposing to invite a thousand volunteers—lawyers, doctors, teachers, and students—into the African communities of Mississippi during the summer of '64. They were to set up community centers, freedom schools, libraries, health and legal services, *and* work on voter registration and community organizing. *Wow.*

When we first heard it in D.C., it was in many ways like Diane's call for Freedom Rides all over again. At first, this long—I mean looooong— silence as people tried to visualize exactly what this would mean. How it would work. Whether, in fact, it *could* work. *Oh, wowie.*

Hey, by now you must have some slight idea what working in that place was like. So it should not be too hard to imagine what our responses at Howard were based on. Hey, we'd come through the Freedom Rides. I'd been in the Delta. We'd witnessed the March on Washington. We'd been to Cambridge, to Danville—we'd seen, so we thought, *evrahthang*. But this . . . Bob'n them calling for a *thousand* volunteers? *In Mississippi? Oowie, git back!*

Say what? A *thousand*? You kidding me. Where they gon' come from? Where they gon' put them? Hey, can they *actually* bring that off? Isn't there going be certain bloodshed? *Uh, uh, uh,* he'p us, Jesus. Is they crazy?

If you thought about it conceptually, it had to be either an act of madness or a daring stroke of genius. A few said that was "a false dichotomy," it wasn't necessarily either/or, that it could and probably almost certainly was both. Either way, it would call for a phenomenal effort in organization. You pays yo' money an' you takes yo' choice. Which, at first, folks did on either side. Forget about the size and scope, concentrate instead on specific tasks. That way it would become manageable. Which is what I tried to do.

I'm certain that had such a proposal come from anywhere or anyone else, it would have been dismissed as an impractical, even dangerous fantasy. You must recall that in the atmosphere of those times, the air was full of grandiose, "militant" schemes and rumors, most of which dissipated into space no sooner than they were uttered. (Remember the New York World's Fair Drive-In Campaign?) But this was Bob Moses talking. And he never ran his mouth loosely. *If* Bob said it could happen . . . "Bet yo' life and live for evah . . ." Besides, we were SNCC. We did the impossible. By the time the decision was final, we were already working hard.

• • • •

Some context is necessary here. By fall 1963, the Mississippi movement was stalemated. It had been a long, tedious war of attrition. We thought we'd seen *everything* that state was capable of throwing at us, run dead up against all the machinery of repression and techniques of obstruction at the state's disposal. The "closed society" had gone into a systematic war mode. It began at the courthouse level. There, local officials, the registrars, the sheriffs and the cops, presented a unified first level of resistance. They were backed up on the next level by the White Citizens Councils—the business community and especially the plantation managers, who systematically fired any black who tried to register and evicted hundreds *before* they could even try. In winter 1962, the counties cut off the federal surplus foods to twenty-two thousand blacks. By tradition, these "commodities" were all that kept people from starving over the winter while they waited until they were needed for the seasonal work when the cotton-planting season began. That, exploitative though it was, had been the arrangement for generations. Now the state claimed not to be able to even *afford* the cost of distributing the food. Soon, though, they would find contingency funds for all kinds of bizarre weaponry, most of which would never and could never, we hoped, be used.

The legislature had created a Sovereignty Commission, a spook-and-dirty-tricks agency to threaten and defame citizens while bugging and infiltrating spies into the movement. In this, the local media were willing agents. The few newspapers that tried to stay aloof were starved of advertising, boycotted, and run out of business. To go back and read the Mississippi newspapers of that time is an education in the abuse of freedom of the press. They created, circulated, and kept recycling a stream of the most scurrilous lies, slander, abuse, character assassination, of any and everyone even close to the movement. Then too there was the constant hate and fear-mongering. We were not only anti-American agents of atheistic Communism being run and funded out of Havana, we also were deranged, diseased, drug-crazed degenerates, mongrels, and sexual perverts.

[Case in point. Ursula Junk, the German exchange student mentioned earlier, recently obtained her Sovereignty Commission file. In those days, Ms. Junk was a famously chaste and devout young Catholic woman on the verge of taking sacred orders. She was therefore considerably astonished recently to find herself identified by the McComb police as a German prostitute imported from Munich, whose black stockings were necessary to conceal the syphilis sores that were said to cover her legs. —EMT]

I mean this was the kind of stuff that, if you were a segregationist and you believed it, gave you no choice. It *clearly* would be a patriotic act, a civic duty, to exterminate vermin such as we were alleged to be. Obviously, as in the case of Medgar Evers, some had already acted on that impulse. How many more deaths like that could we expect?

And this insanity was everywhere. I mean *evrahwhere* and at all levels. A steady stream of it came out of the governor's mansion, whether from Ross Barnett or Paul Johnson, his successor. *[When Johnson succeeded Barnett, he praised his predecessor because "under his able administration, 116,000 Negrahs fled the state." —EMT]* In Washington, the Mississippi congressional delegation, led by Senator "Big Jim" Eastland (millionaire cotton planter), faithfully recited it into the *Congressional Record* and to fellow travelers in the national press corps. And all this was *before* the Summer Project announcement.

All of which is to say that not many black voters—probably no more than maybe three hundred total—had been registered in two and a half years of hard work. And for those few, the black community had been made to pay a fearful price. That is how matters stood in August '63 when someone came up with the inspired (or perhaps only desperate) idea of a parallel "freedom" election during statewide elections that November. Since every official avenue is blocked, why don't we just run our own election?

A freedom vote? That's nuts. What good is that? Only the state can run elections. We can't be electing nobody our own selves.

True, but we can show that if they *were* allowed, our people would indeed participate. So, what'll that prove? That an' fifty cents'll buy you a cup of coffee in New York. Maybe. But it will also destroy Eastland's myth that "Ouah Nigrahs are happy. They have no interest . . . , etc. Plus, even if it's only a "mock" election, it will give the people the experience of an election campaign and casting a vote for the first time in eighty years. See, we'll run a full campaign. Candidates, posters, rallies, meetings, the works. We'll take it across the state into counties we haven't yet been able to penetrate. Think of it as an organizing device.

Doc Henry (peace be unto him) agreed to run for governor on a freedom ticket with Ed King, a white Mississippian, as lieutenant governor. *[Aaron Henry, state NAACP president and the Reverend Edwin King, Tougaloo chaplain and scion of the Mississippi establishment. Shortly thereafter, the Reverend Mr. King was run off the road at night and nearly killed. His face carries the scars to this day. —EMT]*

The tactic turned out a great success. Our candidates traveled the state. Well, almost the entire state. Some counties and towns were still considered too dangerous. But after the election the movement had a statewide list of contacts, which became the basis for the Mississippi Freedom Democratic Party.

On election day, polling places were set up in churches, beauty salons, barbershops, country stores, just wherever our people were to be found. There were even mobile ballot boxes in cars. And very important, it was a unified effort. The entire Mississippi staff along with SNCC organizers from other projects and all our local community activists pitched in. It *felt* like an election. And except for the small fact that it had no official legal force, it *was* an election. Over eighty thousand black Mississippians cast their first vote for a political candidate.

Before 1964, the freedom election was the largest openly and conventionally "political" demonstration we'd ever tried in Mississippi. There were the expected harassments, arrests, a few beatings, and the usual stream of threats, *but nobody was killed or seriously injured,* and there were no bombings that I recall.

A statewide campaign like this was unprecedented and stretched the staff thin. A young Stanford professor, Allard Lowenstein, volunteered to organize a group of student volunteers to come down and work on the campaign. Bob accepted the offer and forty students from Yale and Stanford came into the state for the three weeks leading up to the vote.

[Lowenstein was a politically ambiguous figure. A former NSA leader, reputed CIA asset, and a future congressman from New York, he kept popping up in and around the movement here and in Africa. At this time he was teaching at Stanford. Years later, in one of the more tragic and ironic incidents of the time, Congressman Lowenstein (D-NY) would be shot and killed by one of the Stanford students he had recruited for the freedom election. —EMT]

From all accounts, these volunteers made a real contribution in many ways. In others, it was a learning experience for them and us. Some things they did well. They had technical skills and some prior sense of what an election campaign entailed. That was good. But though they were supposed to have been briefed, some—not all—seemed to have no idea of movement reality. For their own safety and everyone else's, the local staff had to keep explaining brute reality to them. You could call it a mutual learning experience.

The thing that was most instructive, though, was the violence. During the three weeks the volunteers from elite private universities were in the state, nobody—local person or volunteer—was badly hurt. I mean, despite this being the most visible, active, far-ranging, and provocative political activity SNCC had yet attempted, the level of violence had not noticeably risen. In fact, had seemed to diminish? Odd.

Except, of course, that these volunteers—some of them anyway— were among the most well-connected young white people in the country. The true beneficiaries of the system. A few were said to be from extremely wealthy and powerful families. Some were the children of politicians, I think in one case of a U.S. senator. And naturally, the national media had followed them into the state. Also, there was suddenly a visible if temporary FBI presence at the rallies. Bob later explained to me, "That was the first time that I realized that the violence could actually be controlled. Turned, y'know, on and off. That it wasn't totally random. I realized that somewhere along the line, there was someone who, even if they didn't actually order it to happen, could at least send out word for it to stop. And it would . . . at least for three weeks. That was a revelation."

That was one part of it. You can see why people have claimed that this freedom election was the model for the Summer Project. And it may have been, if not the model, then at least a precedent. But there had also been a real downside to the experiment.

A few of the volunteers—not many but a few—were almost sent home. I'm not sure, maybe one or two were in fact asked to leave. Why? Apart from a misguided and dangerous sense of entitlement and class pre-rogative, acting as though nothing could happen to *them,* a few seemed incapable of respecting the experience and accepting the authority of local staff. Whether this was because the staff was black, young, or merely local, I don't know or much care. But it was antithetical to everything that was most important to SNCC. And it is also why so many of the local staff at first resisted the idea for the Summer Project.

One of our best project directors was a brother named Dickie Flowers. He was smart, sassy, disciplined, and very effective. Dickie was well respected in SNCC. Forman said that Dickie came to him quite dis-tressed before the Summer Project. "Look, Jim," he said, "I'm the proj-ect director. You know I know what I'm doing. Yet when those volunteers were here, I all the time found myself saying I'd been to damn Morehouse. Jim, now you know I ain't been to Mo'house or no house."

Apparently, as it turned out, even Bob himself had some quite serious reservations. In fact, in his usual manner, he'd at first held off taking a public position. Folks assumed this was to avoid undue influence and to allow the staff and community leaders to debate the pros and cons and arrive at their own decision. Which was only right: it would be a major undertaking and these were the people who'd have to make it work and ultimately to bear whatever consequences resulted. This, after all, in a state where just two and a half years earlier most people had been scared to give a bed to a freedom fighter. Most churches afraid to open their doors to the movement. Now we were talking about housing a thousand volunteers?

But there was more to Bob's silence. Today Bob admits that at first he was not at all sure about the plan. Another one of those critical moments of decision in which we had no clear guidelines or precedents or guar-antees. Another one of those "learning to fly on the way down" situations. But since it was unthinkable to abandon the local people we'd put in motion at great risk to themselves, and to whom we had given commit-ments, Bob knew we had to do something different.

[Bob Moses remembers:

"You know what really made it clear for me? They murdered Louis Allen. That's what made the difference. See, in '63, after they killed Medgar, Bob Spike

[the Reverend Robert Spike, Director, Commission on Religion and Race, National Council of Churches] came to me and said he would begin to organize a visible national religious presence in the state. So he brought sixteen clergymen to the Freedom Day in Hattiesburg, where there was all that police violence. Remember, that's when Rabbi Joseph Lelyveld and others were badly beaten. . . . It was after that, at a meeting in Hattiesburg, that the Summer Project idea was raised. Guyot will remember that. Reverend Spike was there too. I said nothing at first. I was still trying to come to grips in my own mind with all the implications. There were so many. . . . And you know, the law of unexpected consequences. Then, during the meeting, the news came that Mr. Allen had been murdered. I went out to where the family was, spoke to Mrs. Allen. On the way back, it became clear that we had to do something, something big, that would really open the situation up. Otherwise they'd simply continue to kill the best among us. I'm not even sure what direction the discussion was heading when I got back to the meeting. But that's when I began to argue strongly that we had to have the Summer Project." —EMT]

That spring semester (1964), with the exception of the action in Cambridge, all NAG's energy was focused around the situation in Mississippi. It was still winter when we heard about Mr. Louis Allen.

We knew we couldn't let that go. So we decided we had to symbolically place the responsibility where it truly belonged, on the Justice Department. So we organized this march. We had this small coffin that we were going to carry through the march and then deposit on Bobby Kennedy's desk.

> *[There's a street in Itta Bena called Freedom.*
> *There's a town in Mississippi called Liberty.*
> *There's a Department in Washington called Justice.*
> *—sign in the Greenwood office —EMT]*

A lot of folks were at that march, mostly SNCC supporters from the area colleges. There had to be at least a thousand, maybe twelve hundred, marchers, black and white. Pretty impressive. So there we were, a group of us parading the coffin at the head of the march leading down Sixteenth Street to the Justice Department. Someone said, "Hey, there's Bro Malcolm." And sho nuff there was the brother standing on the sidewalk reading our signs. He was by himself and we shouted at him to come join us. He merely smiled and shook his head. But I could sense that a part of him really wanted to.

We gits to the Justice Department to find a line of cops out front. Before we can figure out what to do, the doors spring open and two security guys come out pushing wheelchairs, the occupants of which are dumped unceremoniously on the pavement. Tom Kahn and Courtland Cox had gone before us to Kennedy's office, and when they weren't permitted to see him, they had spontaneously decided to stage a sit-in. The wheelchairs were, I guess, Kennedy's nonviolent alternative to calling the cops. Then the attorney general came down to talk with us. All I remember is how small, skinny, cold, and harassed he looked in his shirtsleeves. But neither I, nor anyone else I've spoken to, can remember a word he said to us that day. I guess we weren't smart enough to understand that it was "history."

[Ed Brown:

"It was a nice long line, bro, a pretty good turnout. Nearly half the marchers were white. We were singing. Mahoney and myself were carrying this coffin at the head of the march along with Carmichael and Thelwell. We feeling pretty good, having pulled together a pretty impressive march, and we going to confront the feds. Then there was Bro Malcolm with that enigmatic smile of his. It was the first time we'd seen him since the debate with Bayard, so we strut over, all full of ourselves. He, as always, was very warm. So I say, 'Bro, you really should come with us. We going put this coffin on Robert Kennedy's desk.' He laughed and declined. One of us pointed to the march with ill-concealed proprietary pride. 'So what you think of our demonstration, Bro Malcolm? Pretty nice, huh?'

"The brother looked at the line of marchers and he just grinned. 'Wal, since you ask me, my brother, I'll tell it to you like this. Now, if I see a long line of cats and mice all marching toward the same hole? If the cats ask me "how we doing?" I gotta say it sure look like you doing fine, right fine. But now, if the mice ask me . . . well, now, you know I gotta give 'em a different answer.' That sorta knocked the cocky out of us, but we couldn't stop to argue. We figured that ideologically he had to say that anyway, y'know. As we were running off to catch up he called after us, 'Remember now, just because you see a man throwing worms into the river, don't necessarily mean he a friend to the fish.' But I did feel that the brother looked a little lonely standing there by himself. I knew he had to be getting a little tired of standing on the sidelines because of the Nation's strict ban on political activity. But for that, I felt the brother would have been happy to come with us to confront the Justice Department that day . . . because, after all, the march wasn't about integration, it was about equal protection of the law. I also felt that with the brother it would only be a matter of time . . . Malcolm was fundamentally an activist."]

After that march, and with the exception of the little excursion into Cambridge and the continuing food drive, our attention turned to the Summer Project. Once the project was decided, that was foremost in our minds. If SNCC, particularly Moses and the local people, were calling for a thousand volunteers in Mississippi, we'd do our best to see they got fifteen hundred. We'd do whatever it took.

Bob made a couple of trips into D.C. testing the political waters for the Mississippi Freedom Democratic Party challenge at the Democratic National Convention. On one of those trips he asked me to be coordinator for the Second Congressional (Delta) District that summer. I was floored. Ah *means* speechless, almost. Immediately, whatever reservations remained in my mind went on a back burner. Funny, huh?

What caught my interest most was of course the politics. The national politics. The idea of taking a Freedom Democratic delegation into the Democrats' convention. The idea of bringing the struggle before the nation. Challenging and exposing the Dixiecrats' arrogance and racism before the whole world. That really got to me. Bob didn't even have to point out (but he did) how central to the whole strategy the Delta would be, with its population being about 70 percent black. I was in and I was pumped, Jack. Had Bob and the folks in Mississippi asked me to organize West Hell, I'da packed my bags. Yes, indeed.

[Bob Moses:

"The Delta was very important, very. Now what we were faced with, of course, was how we were going to have somebody who could handle all these sophisticated volunteers and the local people. And not just the grassroots but the Amzies too. In other words you had local people that you worked with at the grass roots and (who were) really not part of the network of experienced organizers of resistance. Then you had Amzie Moore and Aaron Henry and a small network of people who had been out there for years and were very sophisticated. There you have a picture of what it would take to negotiate all these different levels.

"It's not just political sophistication. It's more than that. Which is, on the one hand, a feel for the common person which allows you to move freely among them and really be accepted by them . . . a real bond between you and them. So, Stokely had that. But you could have that and not have the ability to work with the white Northerners, all these sophisticated students, and command their respect. But that's yet a different situation from working with the Amzies, right? So Stokely was able to move back and forth among all those levels. Not many people could handle that.

"You look back at what happened in the Delta that summer and Stokely's being able to deliver . . . 'cause Stokely really delivered. And his being able to deliver a delegation which in the first analysis was able to stand up to all that pressure in Atlantic City was just, just remarkable. And it wasn't just Stokely. He brought with him, y'know, that Howard crew. Teams of people who had already learned how to work together and build trust. Really quite remarkable."]

Specific roles flowed from our being at Howard and located in the nation's capital. One task was recruitment, which those of us on campus took on. The other major task had to do with the federal government, the "liberal establishment," and the Washington press corps. Specifically, how to get their attention and the kind of government action that might save lives that summer. That fell to the SNCC Washington office, which Bill Mahoney and Mike Thelwell had set up six months earlier.

Let's talk about recruitment. SNCC wanted to have as many Africans as possible amongst the volunteers. There, NAG could help, for our members were experienced strugglers, veterans. For them, it would be another moment of truth, a time to stand up and be counted—like Cambridge or the Freedom Rides three years earlier. So the Howard (NAG) contingent was the largest black unit. That part was easy.

The biggest problems we found recruiting additional non-NAG volunteers across campus were family and finances. Some Southern students' families just freaked out, Jack. I remember once two church ladies came to git their daughters and chased me with a shoe fixin' to beat my nappy head flat. Yes, they did.

But the main problem was really economic. SNCC was asking people to bring at least $500—partly to help with living expenses, as their hosts would likely be poor, and partly to be available to bond themselves out of jail. A lot of our students not only didn't have $500, but needed to earn their next year's school fees over the summer. That excluded a lot of our people who really wanted to come. I mean a lot who really, really wanted to answer the call. SNCC was able to raise some "scholarship" money, but it wasn't nearly enough.

It's hard now to realize just how precarious the financial condition of most of our students was in those days. Of course, its being Howard, there were some very affluent Negroes. But *they* mostly weren't interested. The ones who really were interested tended to be poor. Maybe today it would be different. I sure hope so for the country's sake. Now more African students might be able to afford to go. But this financial reality in '64 would ensure that the majority of the student volunteers would have to come from the more affluent sectors of white society and private schools.

By then, SNCC had about six really active centers of campus support across the nation. In addition to the SNCC offices in New York and in D.C., Ann Arbor, Chicago, Madison (Wisconsin), the Bay Area of California, and Boston had active campus-based groups. All these bases turned their attention to screening candidates for Mississippi. The process was pretty similar everywhere. By the end of the summer, seven hundred students who had previously been sympathizers would now become activists on a very different level. In truth, we ended up actively discouraging many more people than we accepted. When folks would come in all bright and eager, we had to make sure they understood. First, you'd tell them war stories. Try to scare them to death. "You do understand, don't you? It's entirely possible, very likely even, that not everyone who goes down will be coming back. Why would you want to put yourself in that situation?"

"Hey, this is America, you can't mean . . . ?"

"Yeah, Jack, we do mean . . . Maybe you best go think seriously about this."

In many cases, that would be enough and you'd not see them again.

For those who came back, it got rigorous. See, you had a clear general sense of what you were looking for. You could usually recognize it, but it was not easy to define in words. People at ease with themselves, in control of their lives. Sober, intelligent, self-controlled, disciplined folk who were clear on what they were getting into and why. People, we hoped, who could handle a kind of stress they had never before imagined, much less encountered.

It was generally selection by elimination because *what we didn't want* was much easier to define and usually easier to spot. You couldn't have folks going for the wrong reasons. Folks likely to be a danger to themselves and everyone else. We had to find out who people were and why they thought they were going. No missionaries going to save the benighted Negro or martyrs looking for redemption through suffering. Be on the hard lookout for the stench of personal virtue. No mystics. No flakes. No kids in rebellion, looking for attention or to get back at Mom and Dad. No druggies, beatniks, or premature-hippie types—too irresponsible. Plus folks in Mississippi wouldn't know what to make of them. Nobody flunking out of school and looking for a place to crash. No self-righteous ideologues or zealots out to make a personal statement to the world. *Well, tell me, what exactly would you be doing this summer if you didn't go south?* A most important question.

I'd say that we probably accepted no more than a third. We didn't insist on honor students, but that wouldn't hurt. You didn't have to be class president, or head of your sorority, but that wouldn't disqualify you either. Editor of your school paper? Let's talk. That you got on well with your parents would also work in your favor. We ended up with an impressive group of young Americans at their most idealistic. Interesting people, serious people, political activists, Peace Corps volunteers, seminarians. No pun intended, but in 1964 the country's "best and brightest" were headed for Mississippi, not Southeast Asia, and were genuinely to "ask not what your country can do for you; ask what you can do for your country." Y'all remember that?

But it was a schizoid time, no question. Unreal. Because at the same time this was happening, another side of America—its worst and most hypocritical—was showing itself within the Washington establishment and the "great state of Mis'sipah." And, the thing is, you could hardly tell the difference, except, and not always, in the style of their rhetoric.

• • •

Truthfully . . . by then I'd thought nothing further could possibly surprise or scare me so far as Mississippi was concerned. I simply could not even imagine that conditions there could worsen. Boy, was I ever wrong.

Once the project was announced, reports from the Jackson office made it clear that a climate of intense war fever was being systematically ratcheted up within the state. You couldn't tell whether this was simply an official campaign designed to intimidate and scare us and the project away, or whether these people actually believed the stuff they were writing and saying. Either way, though, the evil stuff the state and the media were putting around was *all* that the Mississippi public was hearing about the project. Nothing else. It was an *official* and unchallenged incitement to mayhem.

It's not just that, as soon as the project was announced, the violence and harassment increased. That they burned—what was it?—five, six churches where freedom schools were to go. That was normal. Completely expected. No surprise.

I'm talking about something qualitatively and *quantitatively* different from anything we'd yet seen. I'm talking about a deliberate, systematic, unchallenged campaign of disinformation put out by the local media, much of which originated with the governor (through his Sovereignty Commission) and ran through the legislature, down to local mayors and petty politicians, drawing in every freelance racist in the state. Every day it was something more extreme and outrageous, and nobody in authority was challenging it.

Here's what the population was exposed to daily, starting about in April. Tell me if this isn't fear-mongering at its worst, a calculated exploitation of people's anxiety and confusion to whip up anger and bloodlust. In Washington, we read the clippings and looked in vain for one voice of reason and moderation, or even of accuracy.

The political rhetoric had suddenly taken a militaristic tone and a siege mentality: invasions, encirclement, and armed preparedness. A mood of unspecified jeopardy and insecurity. The media's standard term for the project was the "invasion" by "thousands" of degenerates and terrorists, capable of unimaginable debauchery and evil. All the more frightful because it was never really specific. And this never changed. Never.

The Jackson mayor, Frank Thompson, who must have smelled stark naked political opportunity, led the charge. Every couple days he announced—and vividly described—some new security measure. First, he added one hundred new cops to a force of two hundred. Then two horses (*horses?*) and six attack dogs, whereupon he announced proudly that the "Jackson police force is now twice as big as in any city of similar size in the nation."

That apparently did not satisfy the mayor or reassure his constituency. He then announced *in detail* the purchase of weaponry. The cops got *200* new shotguns. Then a "stockpile" of tear gas and the issuing of gas masks to every officer was announced. (Nice photo of this.) The mayor purchased and posed next to (photo op) three military troop carriers and three tractor-trailer-type vehicles to haul away "demonstrators" *and* two half-ton military trucks with mounted searchlights (nighttime operations?). He then announced that the fairgrounds had been converted into a stockade capable of holding "thousands." At which point he pronounced himself satisfied. "This is it," he assured the citizens. "They are not bluffing but we are ready for 'em. The invaders won't stand a chance. We can handle twenty-five thousand."

Political leadership, Mississippi style. *Oh,* man, how could I have forgotten "Thompson's tank"? This grotesquerie was his pride of purchase, an armored *six-and-a-half-ton* "battlewagon" complete with bulletproof glass, machine gun ports, and four or six built-in tear-gas-gun emplacements.

That was the city of Jackson.

The legislature was not going to let itself be outdone. The governor called it into emergency session, and the stream of legislation that emerged was equaled only by the heated rhetoric with which each measure was introduced. To prepare for the invaders, they doubled the size of the quasi-military state highway patrol and gave it "emergency" authorization in all jurisdictions. They too stockpiled guns and ammunition. They created mechanisms for a statewide dusk-to-dawn curfew. They outlawed freedom schools. Made it a crime to distribute leaflets *[if the leaflets advocated a boycott. —EMT]* It was hysterical but I can't remember all the craziness. They passed a raft of weird, clearly unconstitutional contingency measures just short of outright secession. *[In one town, it became illegal for a white outsider to live with or "otherwise molest" a black citizen. —EMT]* All of which was, of course, duly and sensationally reported in the press.

If this was the state's respectable "leadership," what of its demagogue element? Hey, I couldn't detect much difference. It was equal opportunity self-promotion. That spring, two groups *[the White Knights of the Ku Klux Klan and United Klans of America —EMT]* launched competing recruitment drives across the state. Organizational competition? Sounds familiar, no? Their message:

"These invaders don't want equality . . . they want what you have . . . your homes and your wives and daughters . . . they coming into your houses . . . evrah white Anglo-Saxon Christian man bettah be prepared to arm himself . . ." One group kicked off its drive pretty dramatically with cross burnings in *sixty-four counties on the same night.* They distributed bumper stickers: YOU ARE IN OCCUPIED MISSISSIPPI.

It was not reassuring to know that the population was being incited from every side. Nowhere in this frenzy was the slightest breath of reason and sanity to be heard. Sad, very sad. But in the circumstances, not unexpected.

The thug element, whether inside a Klan mask or the governor's mansion, had completely taken over next door in Alabama. Six months earlier a prominent, successful white Birmingham lawyer named Charles Morgan had publicly condemned the Sixteenth Street Baptist Church bombing in which the four little girls had been killed. For this offense, he and his family were run out of the state, lucky to escape with their lives. So the echoing silence now from the forces of decency in Mississippi was understandable. But it was not reassuring. "The best lack all conviction, while the worst are full of passionate intensity." Not necessarily. It was just that any slight difference that had ever existed between the mob and the state in Mississippi had completely disappeared.

[The following language, from an "official" publication of the United Klans of America (July 4, 1964), reflects the tenor and mood as well as a carefully cultivated sense of victimization and conspiracy:

"We are in the midst of the long, hot summer of agitation promised to the innocent people of Mississippi by the savage blacks and their Communist masters."

Followed by a prayer of thanksgiving:

"On behalf of our persecuted people, we thank thee that our Satanic enemies, the domestic Communists who occupy the seats of power . . . have failed to provoke the violence which would bring down martial law and complete dictatorship on our great state."

Followed by a sacred pledge:

"To preserve law and order, the only way it can be . . . by the strict segregation of the races controlled by Christian Anglo-Saxon white men, the only race that can build and maintain just and stable government."

To which end they pledged to:

"Defend the rights of our posterity from . . . atheistic priests, brainwashed black savages and mongrelized money worshippers. We advise all priests and mongrels that we will not travel your path to a Leninist hell, but will buy you a ticket to the eternal if you insist." Let the Church say, Ahmen!—EMT]

In D.C. we read these reports with amazement and alarm. That state, it appeared, was even crazier than we knew. And as far as we could see, the madness was not being reported in the Northern media the way it ought to have been. Which put us in a strange place. On the one hand, we're getting more and more worried about our people already in Mississippi. At the same time, more people, obviously attracted to the pay and benefits, keep coming in to ask about going down. (One racist newsletter described our volunteers as *"human jetsam coming because they were promised ten dol-*

lars a day, free room and board and all the sex they want from members of both races." I mean, who could resist. As they say in Mississippi, "You cain' beat that with a stick.")

In Atlanta, Julian Bond and Mary King kept trying to get some national coverage of the Mississippi madness. The Washington office was trying to do the same with the Washington press corps. More crucially, they were desperately trying to get some signal, gesture, statement, something out of the national government. Some sign of moral leadership and an indication of concern. Something to signal the Mississippi politicians to cool it. There are all kinds of ways—public or clandestine—to do that. We would have been satisfied—overjoyed—just to hear someone in authority say that the education of children and the registering of American citizens as voters were not criminal enterprises. That the rights of American citizens engaged in these peaceful and legal activities would be protected by their government.

But the only statement from any federal official was from the sainted J. Edgar Hoover, who announced that the FBI had no intention of "wet-nursing" the project participants. Which, whatever the director's language had been, became this headline in Mississippi: "Hoover: We Will Not Wet-Nurse Troublemakers." Talk about sending signals. Whether Hoover was speaking simply out of his own well-established racism or officially for the Johnson administration was never clear. However, *that* was the only statement from any prominent member of that administration, and no public correction was made by his alleged superiors. No disavowal, no reprimand.

All that spring Mike Thelwell and Bill Mahoney wore holes in their shoes trudging all over Capitol Hill talking to every congressman or congressional assistant who would listen. Could a group of congressmen call for a congressional hearing? Well, could they write a letter to the president? To the attorney general? Perhaps officially visit the state. Hold a press conference? *Anything? Before* more people got killed? Some congressmen were concerned and sympathetic but, they explained, for some reason they weren't in the leadership. Finally, in desperation, the Washington office organized our own hearings on violence and voting in Mississippi. They got a panel of distinguished Americans—jurists, religious leaders, and intellectuals *[Judge Justice Pollier of New York, Representative Don Edwards (D-CA), himself a former FBI agent, Professor Robert Coles of Harvard, Professor Howard Zinn, and some others —EMT]*. They invited the press and public. Witnesses from Mississippi included Mrs. Hamer, Mr. Steptoe, Mr. Turnbow, Bob Moses, Ann Moody, and other local folk. The hearings got some press attention, and bound transcripts of the testimony and the panel's recommendations were circulated around official Washington. These distinguished Americans had concluded that on the basis of the testimony, a dangerous but entirely avoidable crisis and potential tragedy was looming in the state. They called for reason and restraint on both sides and judicious preemptive actions from the administration. That too was ignored.

I remain convinced to this day that the slightest intervention—public or private—indicating firmly to the Mississippi authorities that acts of terrorism and lawlessness would bring serious federal consequences would have saved lives. But that would have required a "profile of courage" from someone in the Johnson administration.

[I continue to believe that a tragic, supremely bureaucratic irony was at work here. I suspect that all the material coming out of Mississippi was routinely kept away from the one person in the administration who would instantly and intuitively have understood and known what to do. And how to do it.

LBJ would have recognized and known how to read the signs. He spoke the language of those "good ol' boys" and would have known from long experience how to get their attention. I believe had LBJ been apprised of the ominous developments he would have been able to cajole, jawbone, threaten, and scare the pants off those Southern politicians in terms they wouldn't dare ignore. And that he might have done so out of more than political self-interest. —EMT]

Now, we did have some support. The Commission on Religion and Race (of the National Council of Churches) under Dr. Spike (peace be unto him) for one thing. Also thousands of progressive people sent us their individual contributions after James Baldwin sent out a national fund appeal. But what about the "liberal" establishment? Who can unravel that mystery? Even whether such a creature actually exists? But an attitude in certain circles, I can't say how widespread it was, surprised and deeply, *deeply* angered us.

One Midwestern young lady forwarded us a letter from a family friend and Washington "insider" explaining to her parents why she should not be allowed to volunteer. Young "Janie" should not be fooled, he said. This "scheme" was not at all the "altruistic-undertaking-by-idealistic-young-students" being represented. At best it was an elaborate political hoax. (Here, he must have meant the challenge to the Democratic National Convention.) At worst, evidence suggested that it was a cynical stratagem designed by "hardened political operatives" to embarrass the government by exploiting the decent impulses of naive college students so as to lure them into danger and possibly to their deaths. Behind the scheme was a strong suggestion of "Communist influences," ruthlessness, and unpatriotic motives. That letter has since been lost (had copying machines existed in those days, I know more copies would have survived). The only language I'll swear to now is the "hardened political operatives," "Communist influences," and luring innocent students into jeopardy to embarrass the government. But the tone and message was exactly as I've described it. It made us furious and bitter.

It struck me as indecent, a craven betrayal. I mean, we'd come to expect this from J. Edgar, or the Mississippi Sovereignty Commission. But from the heart of the Washington liberal network, the "educated, progressive" forces? How widespread was that attitude? Was this the word being whispered around official Washington? Weren't all of us in SNCC "innocent college students" only a year or so ago? Were we too being manipulated, or were we the "hardened" political operators and manipulators? Were we sitting safely somewhere while putting "America's youth" at risk? We, of course, were not "America's youth," right? That was all so untrue and so unfair. I felt we should have confronted the writer in person, but we never did.

It began to emerge that this line really was being pushed by someone. Because versions replete with quotes from "informed observers" and "well-placed sources" began to appear in columns. Generally they evaded any government responsibility and were contemptuous of us in SNCC, of black people in Mississippi, and of the moral intelligence of America's youth. This attitude would have consequences later on. I remember particularly the journalistic prostitutes Evans and Novak, but there were some others. At the time we did not know of the practice of the spook agencies planting stories and feeding disinformation to their assets in the media. But that certainly would explain the total inversion of reality in some of these stories.

I recall that some other columns pointed out that what we intended was legal, constructive, and in any sane society, quite innocuous. That it deserved the full protection of the law, but those were the minority.

[I distinctly remember the mood becoming more ominous with every passing day and each bizarre new report from the state. Were we really recruiting lambs for the slaughter? Would the country actually stand by and see people murdered for teaching schools and registering voters? I spoke daily with staff people in Mississippi. I don't remember a single person there worrying about their own survival. They were concerned for the local people and the safety of the "civilians" coming in, the volunteers. Rather than cynicism I heard a subtext of misplaced, wistful hope for the system. A kind of patriotism of faith. No one wanted to believe that any administration would let a slaughter take place, especially if they had advance warning. Our job in the Washington office was to make sure they had it.

Some people on the Hill cared. But invariably they were not part of the "leadership," hence no congressional hearing. The Dixiecrat committee chairmen were too strong and the administration wasn't interested.

I remember one day in particular. I was briefing Congressman Robert Kas-

tenmeier (D-WI). I was by now thoroughly horror-struck at what seemed likely to happen. I described the project and then—almost compulsively—began to relate in detail what had been going on in the state.

As I spoke, the congressman slumped lower and lower in his chair. I grew concerned for him but I couldn't stop talking. Then his head bent forward, as if he were gradually being beaten down by the weight of what he was hearing. His head went lower and lower. By the time I was finished with the harrowing account, the poor congressman's head rested on the desk, his arms folded over his ears in a protective shield as though to block out the grim picture. That's how heavy it was. —EMT]

I want to say that I don't know whether any private interventions— what they called in South Africa "constructive engagement"—were made to the Mississippi authorities by the Johnson administration. Or whether, as it looked to us, they merely stuck their heads in the sand hoping the impending crisis would disappear. If there was intervention, it couldn't have been very effective, because the media campaign to spread hysteria in the state had not lightened up as "D day" came closer. No kidding, that language was actually used down there.

In about two weeks after school was out there was to be an orientation at a little college in Ohio. *[Western College for Women, Oxford, Ohio. The orientation was funded by Dr. Robert Spike's Commission on Religion and Race. —EMT]* Most of the students we'd recruited in D.C. felt it wisest not to go home for those two weeks. So after the dorms closed a lot of folks ended up crashing at our place. Cleve and I decided we'd use the time for a little pre-orientation training to prepare the troops for what they would be facing. So our apartment turned into a mini–Freedom House. It was good getting to know the new people. Getting folk to be up-front about their fear and their reasons for going. Only a few had ever been on a picket line and faced a hostile crowd before, but they were clear. Nervous, a little scared, but clear. It's our people, our struggle. It's time I did something.

[Cleve Sellers:

"I remember the first time I almost took one for Carmichael and we hadn't even left D.C. yet, Bro. One very warm evening we were all sitting on the front porch chilling. Carol Martin and Doris Wilkerson, two volunteers from the same town, were particularly worried about how their mothers, also best friends, were taking the news of their daughters' summer plans. Worried, as it turned out, for good reason. Because, Bro., all of a sudden these two grim-faced, well-dressed black ladies came marching up the block. They stopped in front of me.

" 'Are you Stokely Carmichael?' one demanded.

" 'Wal, ma'am, all depends, y'know, on who's asking.' I smile at them, trying to be funny.

"Big mistake, Bro. Huge. That lady went into her purse, pulled out a high-

heeled shoe and measured my nappy head, with some sho-nuff bad intentions.
Stokely comes forward and tries to charm the mothers. They ignore him.

" *'You two. Go inside. Get your things. You're coming with us.' There was a*
long argument. The girls in tears, but stood their ground. At one point, the moth-
ers even summoned the police who could do nothing but sympathize because the
girls were not minors.

"Finally the mothers left, but with the universal parental parting shot.

" *'Okay, since you grown enough to go to Mississippi, then you grown*
enough to not bother even trying to come back home. You hear?' Both young
ladies not only went to Mississippi but, thank God, came back safely to proud
and relieved parents."]

When we got to the little women's college people were coming in from
all over. A buzz of excitement, of expectation, was in the air. It was a first-
day-of-school kind of excitement. New students coming in, checking out
the scene, meeting folks, wondering who all these people were. Except
here was an electricity that college never had.

I've seen accounts of tension between the volunteers and the veterans.
The volunteers not feeling welcome. Mutual suspicion based on race.
Staff being cold, almost hostile. All that stuff. That's not at all what I
remember. No way.

Was there tension? What'd you expect? Course there was. Were people
nervous and edgy? Wouldn't you be? Was this based on race? Not really.
I mean, yes, the Mississippi staff was mostly black, Southern, and poor,
and the volunteers mostly white, Northern, and middle class. But so were
many of the orientation staff, ministers from the National Council of
Churches (NCC), and so on. So it wasn't as if these "sheltered" young
whites were suddenly surrounded by "alien" black faces.

In truth, many of the volunteers, like most white Americans, had
never really been around black people in any significant way. And the
Southern staff was not in the habit of assuming *anything* about strange
white folk. *And,* they'd had varying experiences with the freedom election
volunteers. And there were a lot more white folk this time. *A lot more.* As
more and more arrived, people were looking them over and wondering
just how they would fit in. Given the climate they had left in Mississippi,
people had a deep foreboding. But race per se was the least of it.

So, was the SNCC staff standoffish and superior, excluding the eager
young whites? Hell, no.

The tension and discomfort folks felt would have been perfectly natural
even if this were a school social, some icebreaking freshman picnic. And
this was no picnic. People were driving up in cars with plates from New
York, California, New Hampshire, New Mexico, Vermont, Nevada, you
name it—an eclectic mix of people. Volunteers, even when from the
same school or city, were in many cases seeing each other for the first time.

So the volunteers, even when of the same class and race, were essentially a group of strangers. Not an especially comfortable situation for most young people. Add to that a certain inevitable anxiety. While the staff not only knew each other, they evinced a real closeness. An unspoken bond of shared experience that could seem—especially if you were real egotistic—a little exclusive.

I think that a lot of the exaggeration about *racial* tension came from the media. They were of course all white and probably felt real discomfort in our black presence. The press also really contributed to this "racial difference" in their own inimitable way by making it immediately clear what story they had come to report. What and who, so far as they were concerned, represented the real importance of the event.

They ran through the campus looking for photogenic "all-American" types for interviews. Some networks even selected subjects to follow up during the summer. I can't recall that a single staff or local leader was so selected. Nor even a Northern black volunteer.

Strange mentality, the American press. Why on earth would some nineteen-year-old suburban freshman be a more interesting subject than a Mrs. Hamer, a Jesse Harris, or a Mr. Steptoe either in political terms or even for simple human interest? Boy, only in America.

We from NAG bridged both groups. We knew the staff and had been working with white students in the capital area ever since the Route 40 demonstrations. Besides which, the volunteers were real familiar to me. They mostly looked and sounded exactly like the white kids I'd gone to Bronx Science with for four years. I recognized them immediately.

[*The clearest, most intelligent discussion of the recurrent black/white tension between staff and volunteer occurs in* (white volunteer) *Sally Belfrage's admirable memoir,* Freedom Summer. *Ms. Belfrage, who worked in Greenwood in close proximity to Stokely and his people, wrote:*

"*Implicit in the songs, tears, speeches, work and laughter was the knowledge, secure in both them and us, that ultimately we could return to a white refuge. The struggle was their life sentence, implanted in their pigment, and ours only so long as we cared to identify. . . .*

"*They resented us and this was as difficult for some volunteers to assimilate as it was understandable: the volunteers wanted gratitude . . . and couldn't understand why there was a tendency to use them simply as the most accessible objects of Negro anger . . . which acted to diminish any self-important, bloated white pride.*

"*It humbled, if not humiliated, one to realize that finally,* they will never accept me. *Which then raised the question: why, then, am I here? If they are not grateful for my help, if we are supposed to be struggling for brotherhood and can't even find it among ourselves . . . ?*

"*. . . Yet those* (volunteers) *who exonerated themselves could see no contra-*

diction between their innocence and their . . . desire for gratitude. . . . Why grat-itude? The struggle was as much ours as theirs, and to expect thanks was . . . to feel superior to that battle.

*". . . But we didn't have to come, did we? We could have stayed at home, gone to the beach or earn badly needed money for next semester. . . . And here we are. We came. Among the millions who could have realized their responsibility . . . we alone came. Don't we earn, if not praise, then at least some recognition? . . . **I want to be your friend, you black idiot,** was the contradiction everywhere evident."*

Then, perceptively, even prophetically, Ms. Belfrage observed:

"SNCC is not populated with Toms who would wish to be white. They are not the ones who fill closets with bleaches and straighteners, who lead compromised existences between reality and illusion. They embrace their color and are engaged in working out its destiny. To bend to us was to corrupt the purity of their goal. To understand us meant to become like us, and the situation was too tenuous for the risk. . . .

"Once I heard a white man say to James Baldwin, '. . . I feel victimized by some of the things you wrote. . . . I feel personal guilt for your condition. But it isn't my fault. What can I do?' Baldwin answered, 'That you are guilty and I bitter is the state of things. It may not be your fault. It is not my fault. It is not enough to feel guilty. Change things.' "]

For a couple of days we had an intensive seminar/crash course on the history and culture of the movement, the situation in Mississippi, and plans, programs, hopes, expectations, and rules of conduct for the summer. We had the usual role-playing, singing, film clips, and a succession of speakers. Bob Moses spoke, local folks and staff ran workshops. Perhaps because of the NCC influence there was a strong spiritual/ethical tone. The usual suspects. My old friend the Reverend James Lawson, the Reverend Vincent Harding, and Bayard all spoke on Christian pacifism. The volunteers seemed equally divided: some were quite spiritual and others were like me, basically political in their orientation.

Then, the day before the session was to break up and we were to ship out to Mississippi, a representative of the volunteers' government, a lawyer from the Civil Rights Division of the Justice Department, addressed the group.

John Doar was a tall, intense young lawyer, and the Justice Department's point man in the state. He knew the state, he knew us, and we knew him. He'd even paid some dues. His federal status did not make him popular with the whites or necessarily immune from physical attack.

The day of Medgar's funeral in Jackson, Doar had stepped between a crowd of angry, rock-throwing black folk and a phalanx of state troopers with drawn guns. He is credited with averting serious bloodshed that day, and justly so. People in the movement thought of him as a decent man and honest. Certainly John Doar was not the enemy.

Problem was, though, he wasn't an effective ally in any visible way either. See, he'd come down to Freedom Days. He'd observe, interview people, take notes, gather evidence, then return to Washington leaving people with the impression/hope/expectation of federal action. But then nothing would happen. At least nothing that we could see.

Folks didn't quite know what to make of that. Or more specifically, of him. Had he in fact reported and recommended the actions we'd been led to expect? And then been overruled by his bosses, Kennedy and Burke Marshall, whom we knew to have very political connections and agendas? Was Doar an honest man caught up in a politically corrupted system? Or did he speak one way to us, another to the Mississippi politicians, and still another to his bosses in the Justice Department? Doar, the classic insider/team player could not, or would not, say to us, "Hey, guys, there's really enough evidence and clear statutory and constitutional grounds. You know that. I know that. I made the recommendation and argued like mad for it. But Kennedy and Marshall shot it down." That we could have understood, and believed. But he never said that.

I can't remember everything Doar said in his speech, but judging from the volunteers' reactions, it must have sounded like a litany of federal impotence. What followed was a barrage of questions that proved he had not addressed their single greatest concern. Then someone asked directly, "What will be the role of the federal government in protecting our lives?" And the room became very, very silent.

Whether Doar's answer was that the federal government "will or can not guarantee anyone's safety" or "cannot protect you," I can't recall exactly. Whatever the actual words, the message people took was that their government would be absent, not involved. That, so far as their government was concerned, they would have to take their chances with a hostile state, defenseless, precisely mirroring the situation of the black population of Mississippi for the last seventy years.

You could feel a sudden, palpable deflation in that room. Then anger and disappointment. Bob Moses stepped onto the stage to stop the booing. "We don't do that," he told the volunteers, then said that he thought Doar was only being honest with us.

Given what we'd been struggling against in Washington, I was not really surprised by Doar's remarks, but it did seem that so much else might have and should have been said. I have never been able to figure out why Doar was even sent, if that was all he was instructed to say. Was he in fact only a bureaucrat sent, as a matter of policy and strategy, merely to scare people off?

Or, as Bob and others seemed to feel, was he simply being personally honest? Having been left hanging out there so often, did he now feel he could not take personal responsibility for raising false hopes? Would not again mislead people with the kind of inflated assurances we'd been fed after the Freedom Rides? Well, whatever the motive: scruple or policy, the result was the same. A tragedy for everyone concerned. Remember now, the press had been in the room.

Of all the speeches the press heard that day, that statement of Doar's became *the* story across the country. Frantic parental calls ordering their offspring home began to pour in. Could that have been the intent? If so, however, there would be other quite unintended consequences.

Having received word that the deacon board of a small rural church in Philadelphia, Mississippi, that had agreed to host a freedom school had been beaten and terrorized and the church completely destroyed by fire, Mickey Schwerner, the CORE project director, was deeply concerned. He decided to leave the orientation early to be back with his people. He had left before Doar's speech. With him went James Chaney, a street-smart Mississippi brother who was a key organizer, and an idealistic young volunteer from New York named Andrew Goodman.

Doar's statement, suitably dressed up for Mississippi consumption, arrived in the state with a vengeance, threatening the safety of our workers. I have no idea what the tone of the radio or TV coverage was, but I did see some of that day's newspaper headlines. Incendiary. The press leapt on Doar's remarks like a tick on a fat dog. Vindication. "Fed Tells Invaders: 'We Will Not Protect You.' " Or "No Federal Protection for Invaders/Commies" or words to that effect. You could look it up. And that's only the headlines, the tip of the iceberg. They would certainly also have published commentary, responses from politicians to the report. Even more vindication. Praises for the good sense, however belated, by Yankees in "seats of power." Finally, seeing through the web of Communist deceit, the federal government was now signaling its intention to stand aside, freeing the good people of Mississippi to defend their "way of life" by whatever means necessary. I am certain that this could never have been John Doar's intention.

In the middle of this campaign to demonize us "invaders," this use of Doar's statement was criminal. And, in hindsight, predictable. It not only removed the only remaining restraint but seemed to imply federal license to murder. For some socially marginal good ol' boy, subject to months of demagogic incitement, that would have seemed a patriotic duty. And a clear signal.

This was the media climate into which our three friends drove that day. After arriving in Meridian, they went to check on the folks who'd been beaten and whose church was destroyed and were never seen again . . . alive.

[Before he died, Cecil Price, the deputy sheriff who delivered the three to the Klan, reportedly told a black coworker that he'd been "brainwashed." —EMT]

As I recall, we were training the second group of volunteers when we received the news: the three had gone to inspect the churches and failed to return.

Periodically the reports were updated. A routine was in place. Immediately the staff had begun calling all the hospitals and jails in the area. In Atlanta, Julian and Mary King started calling friendly politicians and media people asking them to investigate. This kind of attention could save the life of workers being secretly held in jails. At first none of the police would admit to holding the three. Next day the police in Philadelphia admitted, well, yes, they had been arrested, but had since been released and had driven away. Most likely they'd left the state. A day later, a group of Choctaw hunters found the burned-out shell of their car in the Bogue Chitto swamps. After that, Bob first told the group that we had to face that Mickey Schwerner, James Chaney, and Andy Goodman were in all likelihood dead. You could see how painful it was for him to admit that, even to himself.

[Bob Moses:

"We (the staff) wanted to believe they were still alive somewhere while being scared that they weren't. Once the car turned up, I was sure they were dead. So then, what d'you do? It was especially tough because of Rita Schwerner, Mickey's wife, who was there. Because of her I really didn't want to come out and say that. But then there were the volunteers. They had to be told the truth. Of course, as I discovered, Rita probably knew. Very early that morning old tough-minded Ivanhoe (Donaldson) had gone to her room and invited her for a walk. As they walked over the deserted campus, with Ivanhoe trying to comfort her, finally he'd said firmly but very gently, 'Rita, you know he's dead.' "]

Of course, Mississippi politicians rushed to put their spin on it. The governor and the local sheriff *[Lawrence Rainey, later indicted]*, denounced a plot "to get attention and defame" Mississippi. The three were probably in Mexico drinking beer and laughing as they watched the commotion on TV. "Governor Paul Johnson informed the press that 'those boys are in Cuba.' " In Washington, James Eastland called for an FBI investigation of this "civil rights fraud." According to *his* information, the workers had been reported missing *before* they disappeared. No one appeared to question how the senator knew exactly *when* they had disappeared. One influential *Washington Post* columnist, to his eternal shame, actually accused us of intentionally setting up our brothers to be sacrificed. I'll never *ever* forget that.

[After the gutted car was found, Joseph Alsop, "dean of the Washington press corps" and establishment insider, wrote: "It is a dreadful thing to say, but it

needs saying. The organizers who sent these young people into Mississippi must have wanted, even hoped (emphasis added) for martyrs." The unprincipled hacks Evans and Novak rushed in with identical innuendos of their own. —EMT]

Now, after the fact, official Washington has discovered authority for all kinds of previously impossible activities. Presidential phone calls to the Mississippi governor; a huge FBI office established in Jackson; a battalion of sailors dispatched to beat the bushes. The previously only "investigative" FBI suddenly discovered the authority to make arrests when, in Itta Bena, agents found and arrested three men who had held two newly arrived volunteers at gunpoint. That single act, widely reported, probably saved many of us in those early days. But it came too late for our three comrades.

In Oxford the mood was at once somber and chaotic. I could see, we all could see, that Bob was devastated. His absolute worst fear. First Herbert Lee, then Louis Allen, now this? I remember Bob always used to say that this movement compressed and speeded up time. That we lived the normal experience of a year in about two months, sometimes less. By that calculus, his three years in Mississippi amounted to thirty years' experience. In that moment, every one of those thirty years showed their mark on his face and in his eyes. You could see that the brother took it hard. For a brief period he seemed almost paralyzed. As though a curtain had come down and he'd withdrawn deep into himself. He sat motionless, staring silently into space, as though meditating or in a deep trance. He stayed like that for hours before he came back to us.

We did all we could to support the brother. "Yo, Bob, you did everything that was humanly possible. This ain't your fault, brother." Of course he knew that. But it needed to be said. *[Only days earlier, he'd written the president outlining the situation and his concerns: "We are asking that the federal government move before the fact . . . I hope that this is not asking too much of our country." —EMT]*

We all suffered with Bob, grieved for our three brothers, and felt helpless. It was a terrible, terrible few days. Could we even trust the government to seriously investigate? And the worst for me was not the fear, but the impotence. There had to be *something* more we could do to help the brothers. And for ourselves. For Bob. But what? I discovered that a lot us on staff were feeling that way too. Meanwhile the orientation continued. That at least was something to do.

I really gotta say something here about those volunteers. I know it's been said but I want it on the record. During the next three days they were impressive. Won my respect, yes, they did. Lookit, man, it was heavy. First

of all, any sense of youthful invincibility they might have had was now history. Any feeling of security and preferment was long gone, Jack. This was no longer, if it ever had been to any of them, another chic undergraduate summer adventure. This was ugly. It was real. It was life-threatening. It was a shock. Welcome to the movement. Now you could see it in their eyes. At that point a wholesale exodus would have been natural. Anxious parents were burning up the lines, ordering, pleading, cajoling, bribing (Remember that trip to Europe we talked about?) their offspring to come home. One or two parents personally drove out to retrieve them. One father, so I'm told, came, listened soberly to his son, shook his hand, hugged him, then drove off alone.

What was truly impressive, and to tell the truth quite surprising, was how few left. At one point I recall Bob's being alarmed that no one was leaving. It seemed unnatural. When he spoke to us, he emphasized that people were not only free to leave, they should *feel* free. Leaving carried no stigma. In fact, it would be a perfectly rational, understandable human choice. Few, if any, takers. Why didn't more of these young Americans say, "You know, this ain't really worth my life. I'm going home"? I really can't say. And in a year or two, many of these same people would be denounced as unpatriotic cowards for refusing to go destroy a small country halfway around the world. Those volunteers earned my respect, yes, they did.

The other extraordinary thing one could not help be moved by: the uncommon grace, courage, and dignity of the parents and families of the missing men. I mean, in the midst of their uncertainty and anxiety, in the midst of their loss and sorrow, these people *[Mrs. Chaney, the Schwerners, and the Goodmans]* displayed such courage, such clarity, and such dignity. They were just inspiring. There absolutely had to be something more we could do.

The night outside was pitch-black. I mean *dark*, Jack. Remember the line "blacker than a thousand midnights in a cypress swamp"? It was sorta like that and I was happy as a pig in mud. Very little traffic, so Charlie Cobb and I were gonna sneak into Neshoba County under cover of darkness.

We had a mission, and in case we were stopped we had our cover story down pat. We were schoolteachers headed to Florida on vacation. We thought we were slick too. We even had some high school textbooks (intended for the freedom schools) in the car to support that story. We also had $100 concealed under the floorboards. But unknown to either of us, a few pieces of movement literature, which should not have been there, were also in the bottom of my bag.

So far as I was concerned, the darkness and the deserted road were all to the good. In Meridian we would hook up with three other teams to go into the county to find out what had happened to our missing comrades.

(At this point, we weren't sure their disappearance wasn't going to be "covered up" in some way. We would try to see that it wasn't.)

In SNCC we didn't abandon our brothers and sisters. We didn't leave our wounded on the field. Even if we didn't succeed in finding our comrades or what had happened to them, we at least owed it to them to go look. Like me, Charlie had also initially been opposed to the Summer Project. He'd worried that the cost would be too high. Now we both were scared that this might be only the opening salvo: the first in a series of such murders during a long, bloody summer. Another reason why we could not allow this to be covered up.

But in concrete terms? Neshoba was in the Third Congressional District, which by agreement was CORE territory. Charlie and I had worked the Delta, so we didn't really know the area, except by reputation. We were going into a place said to be a Klan stronghold, violent and yard-dawg mean. We figured on one advantage: the local people, who, as with Emmett Till's murder, might have information. Things they'd heard or seen that they would not easily share with strange white men. We heard on the radio that the gutted remains of the station wagon had been found by a band of Choctaw hunters. What else might they have seen? Many Choctaws looked entirely African to me. We hoped maybe we could blend in with them on the reservation and take advantage of their knowledge of the terrain. Admittedly not a fully formulated plan, but we were again learning to fly on the way down. (We never did hook up with our Native American brothers, but it wasn't necessary. The black community received us and watched our backs.)

We were driving an old Buick with D.C. tags. It had recently been donated, had not yet been registered to SNCC, so nothing connected us to the "invasion." I was driving carefully and we hadn't been stopped. Now under cover of the deep Mississippi darkness, we figured we were less than an hour outside Meridian. At the CORE community center there—which Mickey and Rita Schwerner had set up—we'd meet up with the three other SNCC teams.

We were just going (carefully) through this deserted little town when the engine started to cough, jerk, and lose power. Charlie looked at me. I looked at Charlie. The car jerked and coughed.

"Man, we've gotta check this out. I'ma have to stop." The brother did not look happy.

"Maybe it's just a wire that's come loose."

"Yeah, but I still gotta stop."

"Well . . . if we must, pull under that streetlight up ahead."

We sat for a moment listening and looking around. The street was empty. Everything was still, reassuringly quiet.

"Okay. We gotta be quick and get the hell outta here."

So we opens the doors and jumps out and come face-to-face with this Southern belle. Talk about timing, Jack. Just as we swung the doors open and hopped out, we hear this frightened squeal. At that precise moment a white woman had stepped into the light. (Wonder where *she* was coming from at that hour.) She takes one look, her eyes all big, her mouth hanging open, and takes off running into the darkness.

We knew then we had to git outta there fast. We give the engine a quick glance. "Let's keep going as far as we can before this car stops. If it stops, we can figure out what to do then."

"I do think it's too late, my brother," Charlie says. I look up and sho nuff there's flashing lights bearing down. Turns out we were only a block from the police station. The cops are suspicious. Clearly on invasion alert. So, I takes the offensive.

"Officers, we're teachers on our way to Florida. We're having car trouble, but will be on our way in a minute." Oh, no, they gotta "investigate."

"Investigate what? We've broken no laws. There's no reason to hold us, Officers."

They search the car and us. Then they consult. Search the car again. Take us to the station house.

"Officer, I know my rights. Either you have to arrest us or let us go." They arrest me. Turns out I've misplaced a letter of permission from the owner. So I'm arrested on suspicion of car theft. Charlie is told to go.

"Officer, I'm not leaving my friend," Charlie says.

"You aren't gonna separate us," I chime in. "We both stay or we both go."

"I'm not leaving my friend. You will have to arrest me too," Charlie says.

"Boy. You must not know wheah yo' is. Best you git your _____ going before we git real mad." Charlie doesn't budge.

[Charlie Cobb:

"What I remember most is the darkness, that woman, and that the jail was real, real bright. Painfully so and the cops wore shades. I figured whatever was going to happen to me would have to happen right there. The evil that you know . . . I wasn't going out into that darkness. No way. I'm thinking why suddenly won't they arrest me for refusing an order? Why do they want me in the street? In SNCC you never leave jail alone after dark. That's what happened to the three missing guys. I remember that one time in the same situation Guyot refused to leave. He told a cop, 'Either arrest me now or I'm going slug you in your jaw.' They arrested him. But I wasn't ready for that just yet. So I just stayed put.

"Meanwhile, you know Carmichael, he's arguing. Demands his phone call. No deal. By now it's late, after midnight. The town should be long asleep. I'm

not sure but maybe they find some leaflets in Carmichael's bag. Now they get real hostile. A group of guys with guns show up. What's this, relatives of the woman? The local home guard sniffing out invaders? (I have seen published reports that "armed civilians were gathering" outside the jail after the discovery of the movement literature. If so, they were nowhere in evidence when Charlie was thrown out of the jail. —EMT) *Those guys leave, but now I'm certain I'm not leaving. They put Carmichael in a little cell overlooking the street. He signals me to stay put.*

"*The cops have a problem. Arrest is not an option 'cause that's exactly what I want. Finally, they rough me up some and physically throw me out the door. I don't see the men anywhere. But I don't know when they might come back. In the car, I retrieve the money. Now what? Should I go back to post Stokely's bond? No. That's just too much like what happened to the missing workers. So I bring the car right outside the jail, where I can see Carmichael's cell and whether they try to bring him out. I lock myself in, put a tire iron on the seat besides me, and cower in the car, praying for sunrise. That was the loneliest, scariest few hours of my life. In the morning I bond Stokely out. That damn ol' Buick ran fine all the way to Meridian.]*

All that night I just kept fussing. They must have thought I was crazy. I wanted them to know I was watching to see if they went out after Charlie, but they never left the station.

Next day, when we reached Meridian, the other teams were pacing the floor, debating whether to report us missing. (We were supposed to be clandestine.) Ol' Cleve, I recall, was threatening to come search for us or the Buick. Ivanhoe Donaldson, his teammate, said, "Yeah, Cleve, take the car an' then what? Expect me to come searching for *you* on foot? Then what? Someone else comes searching for me?"

Man, I'd never been hugged so hard in mah *life,* Jack. Which told me how edgy folks' nerves were, convinced we'd fallen victim to the terrorists too. I'm still not sure why we hadn't because, according to the local people, Durant, the two-bit town where the car had chosen to stop, was infamous, even in that county, and "knowed for mean." A place routinely to be avoided by black folk at high noon much less after dark.

The other teams had come in without incident. Dona Richards (Moses), Bob's wife, had volunteered. As Ivanhoe said, "Dona *insisted* and who was going to stop her?" With her was Euvesta Simpson, the sister who'd tended Mrs. Hamer after her beating in the Winona jail, and Gwen Gillon, a gutsy little sister. Brother Ralph Featherstone, a young D.C. teacher, was in Mississippi for the first time, as was Cleve.

Louise, the fine sister in the office who brought us up-to-date and gave us a list of contacts and phone numbers, was visibly emotional. At times she was barely able to control her voice. When she was explaining procedures in case we were stopped, Ivanhoe, who was driving one of the cars, stopped her. "Don't worry, my sister, that ain't in the script. We ain't going be *stopped*. They going have to *catch* us. At a hundred and twenty miles an hour, more if the car will do it." Ivanhoe was like that.

We studied maps of the county. Looked over the local papers. In a grim way that made it real. Being there and seeing our missing friends described as "race-mixing agitators and mongrels," and worse, was very different from hearing it over the phone back in Washington. I thought, "Yeah, boy, you sho nuff behind enemy lines now." We made our plans and went in after dark in two cars.

What was left of the church was another dose of reality: this little clearing deep in some piney woods reeking of smoke and kerosene. Ashes, charred embers, sheets of rusted zinc, smoke-blackened, all twisted and billowed from the heat. Nothing to be done there. Nothing useful to be found. None of us said much. I was thinking that the last people to look at these ruins were probably our missing friends. We left quickly and quietly.

Our contact was a farmer and obviously a good one. His house had inside plumbing and he owned some land. He was a leader of the congregation of the burned church. Behind his house, a spacious new barn smelled of hay and animals. That's where we hid and slept during the day.

He and his wife were sure our men were dead. "Them same peckerwoods as burnt Mt. Olive church killed those boys." He thought they did it as a warning to the local community because of the freedom school. We were welcome to stay and search as long as we liked. But they clearly didn't hold out much hope. "No telling where those bodies be by now."

That couple was good to us. Very good. The lady fed us an incredible meal. I mean she really *fed* us. And wouldn't hear of accepting any contribution from us. Her husband was organized and clear.

The fewer people, black or white, who knew we were there, the better, he warned. The area be so tensed-up, it was best not to be seen nosing round. Even normally peaceable white folk were liable to be shooting first. So best we stayed in during daylight. There'd be security though. A couple of rifles be covering the back lot and barn all the time. But it was best for all concerned that nobody saw us.

During the day some local men he trusted would be helping us. It wasn't hunting season, but you could run coon anytime. Usually folk ran coon at night, but weren't no law against doing it in the day neither. So the mens be roaming the woods with their long-eared ol' coon dogs and their rifles and shotguns. He didn't figure even the Klan wanted no truck with black men hunting and toting rifles.

We had to talk about that. It meant we'd be searching at night. One of the reasons we were even there was to show the flag. To show the community *and* the whites that the movement wasn't to be so easily scared off.

Hard to do that in the dark. Then, the local men were armed. Should we, those of us who could use them, not also carry guns? We decided that none of us would.

I get asked a lot, "Knowing what you know now, would you again do the kinds of things y'all did then?" I always say, "Absolutely. I'd do it again. Wouldn't change a thing." But y'know truthfully? The one thing I would do differently? I sure would not venture into those swamps and woods again unless I was well armed. And I'm talking superior firepower too. Tha's right, serious arms.

So we went out. This county was very different from the Delta. This was woods, scrubby hills, and swampy bottoms with thick brush and marshy reeds. Clouds of mosquitoes and deerflies that flew into your eyes and mouth. Your face and hands, any exposed skin, were covered and stung. And it was *dark*. Briers and brambles scratched your face and hooked your clothes. We'd been warned of rattlesnakes in the hills and moccasins in the swamps. Unseen things slithered away underfoot, and each time you listened for the rattle and tensed for the strike. It was hot, very hot, muggy, and dark. When you got home before daybreak, man, those ticks and chiggers be all over your skin and in your muddy clothes. And over it all, the constant fear of detection by white folks.

After that first night, I think we all realized how impossible it really was. But nobody wanted to be the first to say it. If I were the one missing, I'd want to know that my comrades cared enough to look. I think I wasn't the only one who must have felt that way. So we tried to rest up in the barn to go out the next night.

[Cleve Sellers:

"Although we were supposed to sleep during the day, it was nearly impossible. We were too tense. The broiling heat and soupy humidity didn't help. The tension that kept us awake by day took on a different character when the sun went down. The daytime fear was diffuse, it produced restlessness and fatigue. The nighttime tension was precise. It heightened the senses. I could hear, see, smell, and feel things that I was oblivious to in daylight. I even imagined I saw things in the pitch black.

We were transported to the area to be searched in an old pickup truck, traveling on narrow, rutty back roads. The driver never used his headlights. At times he'd flick on his park lights for a second to get his bearings. I never ceased to be amazed at his skill, his knowledge of those back roads and apparent ability to see in the dark.

"The procedure was always the same. We'd pile from the truck and fan out. Walking slowly and rarely talking, we'd search swamps, creeks, abandoned houses, and orchards, ruinate barns, tangled underbrush, and unused wells, probing with long sticks. We couldn't use flashlights. In one section there was a fire tower. To avoid detection by the fire watch we even discarded all shiny metal

objects like belt buckles, which might have reflected light. At times we had to pass near to white farmhouses. All farms have watchdogs. We sneaked by ready to run at the sound of a sudden barking that would alert the household. That never happened, thank God."]

We went back out a couple of nights. Of course, we never found our people. But we did find out a lot about ourselves and about loyalty and what real courage was. That old farmer, his wife, son, and two daughters whose church had been burned. They sheltered, fed, and guarded us. And their friends who drove us out and picked us up, knowing the risk to themselves and their families. I think Mickey Schwerner and his team would have been proud to see the loyalty their local people showed.

But of course by then our brothers were under thirty tons of red dirt in a farm dam. And finding their remains cost the FBI a $30,000 payment to a Klan informer. Hey, we didn't have thirty pieces of silver, much less $30,000, and which Klansman was going to confess to *us*, even if we were offering $30 million?

After a few nights we could see it was hopeless and getting more dangerous. Besides, our continued presence was putting our host family at risk. I really wish I could remember that brave family's name. So when we heard on the radio that the FBI had taken over the case and that troops *[actually five hundred sailors —EMT]* had been sent in, it gave us an honorable out. Besides, we all had a project to go run.

It was also becoming clearer that Mickey Schwerner, James Chaney, and young Andrew Goodman hadn't died entirely in vain. Yes, it was an absurd, ignorant, vicious waste of three good young lives. But the belated attention of the administration and the media presence that followed it undoubtedly saved a great many others. Only why did it have to come so late? And at such a price?

[Two of the bodies found in the Pearl River were nineteen-year-old black students who'd been expelled from Alcorn A&M for campus protests. Local Klansmen confessed to having kidnapped and murdered them on their way home six weeks earlier. I believe the Klansmen were acquitted. When their disappearance had been reported to the local sheriff, he had dismissed it: "Them li'l niggers pro'lly gone to Chicago." There had been no investigation. Had two white New Yorkers not disappeared along with Jimmy Chaney, the bodies of Charles Moore and Henry Dee might never have been found.

The most heartrending film footage of the funeral of James Chaney in Meridian shows his eleven-year-old brother, Ben, consumed with grief, weeping inconsolably. Everyone said that his big brother James had been his hero and the center of Ben's existence. That was easily apparent from the intensity of the young boy's grief at the funeral.

Some years later on a visit to Mississippi, I thought of the young boy. "Whatever became of young Ben Chaney?" I asked.

"Oh, you haven't heard? He's in jail."

"Goddamn, for what?"

"Murder," they said.

A few years later, I learned that the young man had been acquitted of a murder charge in New York. I pray that he has also regained some peace and equilibrium in his life. —EMT]

CHAPTER XVII

They Still Didn't Get It

I was vice president of the State Conference of NAACP branches. I did everything I knew how. Every time we moved, we had to move according to law. Unless we were advised to do certain things, we didn't do it. But, when SNCC came, it didn't seem to matter what these white folks thought. When SNCC moved, SNCC moved in SNCC's way. I tell you one thing, SNCC gave courage and determination to blacks in Mississippi.

—Amzie Moore, *Voice of Freedom*

That was one hell of a summer. It began in tragedy that was unnecessary, predictable, and avoidable and ended in farce. Or maybe not farce, but in the longer term, a greater political tragedy. And I know that to this day those "smart" Democratic politicians in Atlantic City didn't have a clue. I mean, the so-called leadership. Not a clue as to the chance they'd had and exactly how badly they'd blown it with everything that happened afterward: if not with that election, then certainly with black people, with the white youth of the country. Still not a glimmer. And four years later in Chicago? I guarantee they still didn't get it. Never quite understood that it had all really started in Atlantic City, where they had rolled over and "dissed" our people from Mississippi. *[The Mississippi Freedom Democratic Party delegation to the National Democratic Convention. —EMT]*

The Democratic Party leadership had a chance to reach out to embrace the future, and instead they reached back to try to preserve a shameful past. This backward-looking racist response was among the flat-out dumbest political miscalculations the Democratic Party leadership ever made, and that's saying a lot for, the Good Lord knows, they've made quite a few. And it sure came back to bite them big time, didn't it? We'll get to that.

All the time we were searching in Neshoba, I had been thinking about my responsibilities in the Second Congressional District. In fact, I'd been thinking about little else ever since Bob had asked me that spring. I'd known I would need all the help I could get there. A movement is only as good as its organizers. I was confident—whatever happened that summer—that we'd have good, dependable organizers in the Second District.

Even at Oxford I'd checked out the volunteers carefully. Listening to them . . . the kinds of questions they asked . . . what they said . . . how they'd said it . . . their manner, attitudes, their political smarts. How their spirit struck me. Whenever someone particularly impressed me, I'd get into a conversation with him or her. If my snap impression held up, I'd say, "Ask for the Delta. We can use you in the Delta." You'd be surprised how much you can learn about people from even a short conversation if you pay attention. I ended up recruiting some good folks there. Of course, the staff who would be running other projects were doing the same thing.

The district office would be in Greenwood, my old stomping ground. That was great. I loved that county. We had a real base there, some strong families. And the young veterans who would move "out in the rural" to start new projects and teach the volunteers how to survive. These were my people.

The project director for Greenwood would be Bob Zellner. Ol' good-hearted, "cracker" Bob, smart, experienced, and devoted, was almost certainly the only white person SNCC could put in such a crucial position. The local people accepted and trusted him completely. A Southern thang, I guess. He did a hell of a job on a very hot seat, as everyone knew he would.

But the volunteers, most of whom I'd be meeting for the first time, were still the big question. How many would we have? How, in the crunch, would they fit in? After Oxford, I figured that if they showed up at all, that would be a big point in their favor. They would have made it through two tests. First, the tough recruitment screening, then the tension and excitement of orientation. So you knew they had courage. But having courage was not nearly the same thing as being able to fit into a movement culture in the black community of the Mississippi Delta. That would require discipline, humility, as well as the ability to adapt. How many Bob Zellners can you expect to meet? Well, we'd see.

But even there I had a big hole card, sixteen "volunteers" I already knew well. These were experienced strugglers, who knew how to organize, and most of all they were black. These were the folk from NAG. Three carloads had driven down from Howard to Oxford. I'd told Bob we were a team and he assigned them all to the Delta. So it would be a question of mixing and matching the elements—the local staff, NAG folks, and the white volunteers.

Four of us—Cleve, Ivanhoe, Charlie, and I—drove up to the Delta together from Neshoba County. Ivanhoe was project director in Moss

Point. By the time we got to Greenwood, Cleve had decided to go with him. Charlie would be working with freedom schools all over, but I teased him that Ivanhoe didn't want him anywhere near his project since the night in Jackson Charlie nearly got Ivanhoe killed. According to Ivanhoe, two cops pulled them over: "Y'all them NAACP niggers, huh?" Either Charlie had felt a professional* respect for accuracy or resented the association. "Well, actually, we're SNCC," he corrects the cop, who immediately goes off, but not on Charlie. He snatches Ivanhoe, throws him down, sticks a gun in his ear, and keeps shouting that he's gonna blow his (expletive) head off, until his partner restrains him.

In Greenwood, the scene around the office was indescribable. The community in the immediate vicinity was literally humming and buzzing with activity. Constant traffic. A busload of volunteers unloading. Local adults coming to welcome and collect their volunteers. Kids standing around gawking at the incoming strangers. Boxes of books and equipment for community centers and freedom schools being unloaded. The occasional carload of local white men driving by and shouting insults.

The community looking at the arrivals, the rookies looking at the community. Every now and then a few more cars arriving. Each new group looking hot, rumpled, curious, and a little dazed. Excitement and anxiety, anticipation and uncertainty in every face. What was this place? Just what had they gotten themselves into? For most of them, the next two and a half months would be the sternest test of their lives thus far. How would they do? This heah was for real now, Jack.

For the most part, I'd say they did just fine. For the overwhelming majority—white or black—it would be a life-changing experience politically and culturally. In black Mississippi, the whites experienced at firsthand a side of America they'd not seen and could scarcely have imagined. They learned something about their country, about black culture, and about themselves. Their presence changed black Mississippi, but clearly black Mississippi changed them even more. They might have come for different reasons—adventure, idealism, even to write about it—but most went back better people than they came. That much, I'm sure of.

[This seems to be the testimony of the volunteers themselves in their letters home. See Elizabeth Sutherland Martinez's classic Letters from Mississippi. *These letters in perceptiveness, freshness of detail and description, variety of events and situations, and range of experience are unlike anything I've since encountered in civil rights literature. Collectively, they constitute an irreplaceable record of an extraordinary moment in American social and cultural history at midcentury.*

Some volunteers returned to campus or community with an enhanced

---

*A professional respect: Charlie later became a distinguished journalist.

activist zeal. Many, if not most, went on to careers of service and advocacy in medicine, the arts, religion, education, or politics. Of course, their presence on the project suggests that these inclinations were probably present before the fact.

Perhaps SNCC should have anticipated this development. Alan Schiffman, a Princeton doctoral candidate in philosophy who decided to stay on in Neshoba County, explains, "I'd learned such an awful lot in a short time. It became clear to me that nothing in graduate school was likely to compare in intensity or importance. Besides, I really loved the people in that community. They were so generous, so centered, and so strong. They just didn't take no crap. I felt most comfortable there, such fond memories" —EMT]

In fact, at the end of summer almost two hundred offered to take a year off and to stay on in the state. Truthfully, I hadn't anticipated that. Certainly not that many. It would create serious, serious problems of too rapid growth and institutional identity for SNCC in 1965.

In Greenwood, the first thing I found was more people looking for assignments than I'd expected. In southwest Mississippi the Klan violence was so heavy that volunteers assigned to Pike and Amite Counties were at first held out and sent to the Delta. Check that out. The Delta? For safety?

In a matter of days everyone had a project and a job. Folks were briefed on security measures, community values, Southern sensibilities black and white, expected behavior, movement values, and shipped out. That was my job. One thing I remember . . . a rush of satisfaction when the car left for Tallahatchie County. You know, that vow I'd made to myself and Bro Emmett Till. That night two years earlier when I first saw the bridge and highway sign to Tallahatchie. "One day we gonna open you up."

That for me was the real beginning of an amazing ten weeks. More incredible stuff happened. And compressed into such a short time. My job as director—really a traveling troubleshooter—took me everywhere, I mean evrahwheah, across the Delta, county to county, project to project. I always emphasized security, discipline, and building political power. I visited freedom schools, spoke at precinct meetings and county caucuses, in churches, under trees. I was at freedom days and funerals. Everywhere. I saw a lot and learned a lot. About myself and especially the dangers and demands of leadership.

It was the greatest responsibility and challenge I'd yet had. I was amazed at how people—especially when under stress—responded to a title. By virtue of being "district director" I was seen as having instant authority. People were disposed to like and trust you just because. And to depend on you. Yeah, of course, they'd accept, even seem to need, firm decisions and instructions. But in return they also seemed to expect you to produce instant solutions to every problem. People depended on you to inspire confidence. You inspired confidence by showing confidence.

Yeah, they expected clarity and decisiveness at all times. But the decisions had to be seen to be fair and intelligent. No stupid moves. No bombast, no empty guarantees: no overstated promises that you couldn't keep and which people knew you couldn't keep. You had to be *credible*. To keep trust, you had to perform. To keep authority, you had to earn it, over and over. To lead not by fiat but by example and work. Of course, some of my own rules I wasn't able to keep.

"We're not here to go to jail. We're here to do a job. Which cannot be done in a cell. Your duty is to stay out of jail if at all possible, okay.?" I ended up in jail four times.

But, for the most part, I think I was able to rise to the demands of the job. Mostly it came naturally. First place, I really loved the job and the challenge. Then I was actually too busy to feel fear. A luxury I simply didn't have time for. So I showed none. And the confidence thing? There I was a true believer. Because I was genuinely confident that we'd succeed. I literally could not imagine failure. I guess people were able to feel that confidence. I simply could not imagine anything more important and necessary that I could have been doing. So of course my enthusiasm and energy were always high and clearly visible.

To the extent I was successful those were the reasons. Some things you can't fake. But mostly, y'know, we fed off the people, staff, community folk, volunteers, the kids. Sure, every day there was some new crisis or atrocity. But, also twice, three times a day there was something else to marvel at. Acts of courage, generosity, decency, even humor. Something more to admire and respect. It kept you humble and committed. You couldn't let folks like this down. Simple as that.

Also, every organizer really needs a sense of humor. And trust me, there was a lot to laugh at. Innocent misunderstandings across class, culture, and race. The absurdity of racism. The dependable and amazing stupidity of the "authorities." And of course if you could make people laugh—especially at yourself and themselves—it really helped. After a while, that became second nature.

(True story. One freedom day about seventy black folk are outside the county courthouse hoping to take the test. Along come these crackers with a monkey on a leash with a sign: "I want to redish too." They and the ape are admitted to the courthouse only to emerge to announce that the ape, being unable to read, had failed the test. From her scowl, this seemed to agitate one of the older black ladies on the picket line. Folks thought she was insulted by the monkey. "What monkey? I ain't seen no monkey. It's thet pitiful-looking, li'l ol' *white* lady what's bothering me. If them peckerwoods knowed she couldn't read, they shoulda left her home in her bed. Po' l'il ol' ugly thang.")

As the summer went on, the parts of the job I found myself looking forward to with purest pleasure were my visits to freedom schools. These were probably the most unambiguous successes we had. I tell you, that summer I saw what real education—for students and teachers—could be and mean. It was a joy to see. As well as sometimes painful and angering.

See, going into the summer, my emphasis was on the political. Heavily. Now, of course, I'd always understood the importance of education. That's clear. In Greenwood I'd spent a lot of time talking to June Johnson and her friends and the younger kids about their schools, about books, ideas, our history. So I understood—and deeply resented—the callous, criminal deprivation of education to black youth in the Delta. So I knew the schools were necessary. The idea was logical and appropriate. But I can't say I was real excited about it at first.

But, boy, was that to change, Jack. Fast, quick, and in a hurry. Because forget the idea, the reality was something exciting.

See, I'd known that the students would be turned-on. How not? Learning all the things about their world, their country, and their history that the state's Bantu educational system deliberately kept from them?* And especially in an uncensored, student-centered, creative classroom situation. So we'd made the curriculum political and cultural. A lot of black and African history and culture. A lot of discussion of Mississippi politics, the challenge, etc. Exposure to a lot of poetry, plays, and music with strong encouragement to create and perform their own. So I knew the students would have to like it.

But honestly? No way could I have expected the intensity of the enthusiasm, the excitement. By students and parents.

In one school in the district, the day after school opened a couple of teachers were awakened by a knocking on their door. It was dawn, not yet full light. The two women peer nervously out into the semidarkness afraid of what they might see. It was not the Klan. Only their students grinning and calling on them to start school. It wasn't yet six o'clock.

[The following is from a volunteer freedom-school teacher named Pam in Holly Springs, a town not in the same county as Mound Bayou, but quite evidently subject to the same policies of Bantu education. —EMT]

---

*Mound Bayou was an all-black town. The policy of the school board in that county at that time: "Neither foreign languages nor civics shall be taught in Negro schools. Nor shall American history from 1860 to 1875 be taught." Enough said. — EMT

Dear Mom and Dad,

The atmosphere in class is unbelievable. It is what every teacher dreams about—real, honest enthusiasm and desire to learn anything and everything. The girls come to class of their own free will. They respond to everything that is said. They are excited about learning. They drain me of everything I have to offer so that I go home at night completely exhausted but very happy. . . .

. . . Every class is beautiful. The girls respond, respond, respond. And they disagree among themselves. I have no doubt that soon they will be disagreeing with me. At least this is one thing that I am work-ing towards. They are a sharp group. But they are under-educated and starved for knowledge. They know that they have been cheated and they want anything and everything that we can give them.

I have a great deal of faith in these students. . . .

Love, Pam
—Letters from Mississippi

Now I can't be sure of the actual figures, but my sense is that among the volunteers, women may have outnumbered men by quite a bit. (Even though I'm sure we must have asked recruiters to try to sign up more men.) Many on the staff saw that as a mixed blessing. Not through any fault of the women's, but because of the deeply engrained, almost psy-chotic Southern male attitudes about "white womanhood." Which, I'm afraid, most of the women volunteers were going to represent.

This was cause for real concern, Jack. Young white women in the black community would be seen as a provocation and a flash point for violence. That was reality. A security risk to themselves and everyone else in communities in which lynching was by no means a distant memory. And in the climate of hostility folks could see being created. "Ten dollars a day and all the sex you can handle . . ."? Everyone was nervous on the woman question.

One expedient was to try to "hide" the women in libraries and freedom schools as opposed to sending them canvassing door-to-door. (Course some women did do canvassing, but in all-women or all-white teams.) Naturally, a few women complained initially about our "compromising" with racism and keeping them out of "the real action." But it soon enough became clear that much of the "real action" was to be found in the schools.

(Besides, after answering one or two of the incessant phone calls accusing them in the most vulgar language imaginable of every conceiv-able "depravity" with hordes of black men, even the most militant women understood clearly why certain precautions were necessary. This black-man/white-woman sexual obsession was pervasive. Check this. Some cops

in Jackson are harassing a volunteer who reveals that in real life he's a med student. What could be more harmless and respectable, right? To these cops it was obvious. "A med student, huh?" One sneered. Obviously that volunteer could be in the state for only one reason. "You here to give abortions to all them white gals pregnant by nigrahs, huh?")

However, one dividend of the strong female presence was that we were able to open more schools than originally planned. Even then there was unmet demand.

Down in Hattiesburg, where the three churches in which freedom schools were scheduled to go had been burned in one week, the schools opened a few weeks late. The teachers optimistically prepared for one hundred and fifty students and prayed that half that number would turn up in defiance of the terror. On opening day they found themselves calling for ten more teachers to accommodate the six hundred would-be students who appeared.

Remember what I said about those forty acres and a mule? During this summer when I traveled all over the Delta, that had become clear: the serious difference that owning some land made to the spirit of the people. Those folks in Neshoba who helped us so much in the search? Landowning farmers. Time and again I would see the same thing. Any little community where people owned some land, whether in Holmes, Bolivar, or Leake County, the same spirit and community strength.

The community called Harmony was such a place. All summer there'd been a struggle with the local power structure and the Klan. Same ol' story. Harassment and resistance. All summer. When the county tried to close the schools by evicting the people from a community center they had prepared, they simply located the school in a church and built and guarded a new center. Then the county tried to open the "Negro" schools in the middle of the summer, a move intended to close down the freedom schools and avoid the court-ordered integration of first grade in the white schools. The Harmony community parents simply voted total boycott of the Negro schools. It went on and on all summer, a constant struggle. Harassment, resistance, and of course, education in action.

[We have a running account of this struggle from the letters home of several volunteers. —EMT

July 1

About 12 miles away is Harmony (pronounced Hominy), a Negro farm community of about 300–400 population. The people have been active for a long time in the NAACP. They were the first in Mississippi to file suit for integration of schools and consequently there was terrorism last year. . . . Although few of the people have had much education themselves,

they know the value of it. They speak intelligently and articulately. The first time I began to get excited and optimistic . . . was when we arrived . . . There was a welcoming committee of about 40 people . . . We didn't arrive until near noon, but the people had been there waiting since eight. All kinds of speeches were made to tell us how much we were welcome. It was great.

We are on a farm . . . the most beautiful you could imagine—red, red dirt. They hardly buy any food—even their lard is home made. . . .

. . . We have four old school buildings—run-down, wooden frame, few windows left—filthy. They are old for one reason. There has been no school in Harmony since 1961 . . . But the people had entirely cleaned out one building, put in homemade chairs and tables and arranged the library . . . Today we worked cleaning out what will be our (school) building. . . .

Love, Judy

. . . Then the sheriff came with about six white men, who were introduced as the "Board of Education." . . . After we had finished cleaning the school, they told us we should not use it; it is county property. We (the community leaders) told them it is private property . . . We are getting a lawyer and will fight in court. (The case was lost.)

July 29

Everyday this week . . . the men of the community hammered and poured cement. At noon, about 7 or 8 women all gathered at the center with fried chicken, fish, salad, and gallons of Kool-Aid. . . . It is a thing of beauty to see us all work together. Tuesday and Wednesday was the laying of the sub-floor. Two men cut the wood, two or three teenage boys and girls lay the wood down and hammered it in. . . . It (our new school building) should be up by Saturday, or at latest Tuesday. The land was given by a local man for "the sum of one dollar."

August 6

The men (and some of us when we have time) work on the building up to 10 hours a day with a 100° sun beating down and the humidity so high one's clothing becomes soaking wet after only a few minutes work. The building is guarded at night, because these people, after having had their homes shot into and having a couple of crosses burned in the middle of their community during the last few months, do not intend to have all their hard work go up in flames right away. . . .

August 5

About 4 men or teenagers armed with rifles and pistols stand guard. Every local car that goes by has to honk a specific number of times. . . .

If anyone does attempt to bomb or burn the center, they haven't got a
chance. . . .

August 10
    The decision came Saturday night . . . the shocking news: the 3 Negro
schools of Leake County are opening Monday, August 10th, three full
weeks before the white schools. . . .
    The parents and students of Harmony were really riled up and voted
to boycott totally and use this as a "strike" for demands: equal student-
teacher ratio, heat in winter . . . no firing of Negro teachers for registering
to vote, no hand-me-down desks, books and buses . . .
    . . . And so today, the kids didn't go to school. . . . We spent three hours
in Freedom School with all the children, ages 4 through 19. It was excit-
ing and wild—we had the older teenagers each take two or three 2nd and
3rd graders and explain why we are boycotting. . . .

Canton, August 30
    We were sitting on the steps at dusk, watching the landscape and the
sun folding into the flat country . . . a 6-year old Negro girl with a stick
and a dog, kicking up as much dust as she could with her bare feet . . . we
could hear her humming to herself, "We shall overcome" . . . —Letters
from Mississippi]

I just loved going to talk about the movement or to conduct lessons in
those classes.* But I also saw something that has stayed with me all my
political life. All real education is political. All politics is not necessary
educational, but good politics always is. You can have no serious organizing without serious education. And always, the people will teach you as
much as you teach them.

Even with everything that was happening all across the state, organizing
the Freedom Democratic Party (FDP) was, of course, my priority, the
real challenge. We faced not only the formidable task of explaining the
concept—the party and the challenge—to the people, but a hard deadline
by which a host of specific things had to be done.
    This party had to be organized statewide and a delegation selected by
mid-August. Not only done right but scrupulously documented with
records kept for the lawyers. Every smallest step required by the state and
the national party had to be precisely followed and documented.
    In organizing terms, what exactly did that mean? Well, in the Second

---

*The book *Stokely Speaks* has a transcript of a class on black language that
Carmichael conducted in one of the freedom schools.

Congressional District, there were what, maybe twenty-two counties? In each of those the smallest party unit was the precinct, maybe four, six precincts per county. Because the Delta is literally one large cotton/soybean plantation and congressional districts are based on population, the Second District had by far the most counties spread over a much larger area than any other. But that kind of evened out, because some of these counties had small populations and as few as two or three precincts. In each of those precincts we had to sign up members in this new party and get them to do two things. Try to attend the white (regular party) meeting, then, being turned away, come to our own meetings. The time and place of which had to be advertised to prove that we were open to all.

The precinct selects delegates to a countywide caucus. From the county, officers and a delegation to the district convention are selected. Then from each of the five congressional districts, about forty delegates to the state convention in Jackson where the delegation *[forty-four delegates and twenty-two alternates]* is selected for Atlantic City.

Yeah, you say, but isn't that not more or less what happens in all fifty states? Gimme a break. In every state there is party history, infrastructure, experienced officers, full-time party employees, workers, an apparatus in place, and a familiar process that merely has to be activated every four years. And even with all that, the process is still a major undertaking. With us, none of that existed. We not only had to create it all, but given our insurgent status we couldn't cut any corners that might give the Democrats a technical out.

[This description of a precinct meeting by a volunteer in Vicksburg, which although a city and not in the Delta, still captures the initial experience:

Fear reigned at first—but soon people were excited about the prospects of the party and neighbors were talking to neighbors about the "New Thing." Block parties and mass meetings were being held. . . . Spirits grew. Hundreds of people risked their lives and jobs to come. Representatives were elected. . . . Resolutions were introduced, minutes were kept . . . The precinct meeting was one of the most exciting events of my life.
—Letters from Mississippi*]*

And we had to create it among folk who had been kept away from political participation for over seventy years, and who were painfully aware of the risks involved. And to whom we could not—at least not in good faith—make any guarantees. "So, tell me, after we do all this, then what?" We certainly could not promise victory at the convention. But, you know, the people really understood that. "No way to tell what them white folk liable to do, huh? But at least we kin try. Make them have to do *something,* right?" And momentum slowly started to build. I spoke at a lot of those early meetings, night after night, one small country church out in the cotton fields after another. I always talked about political power in the Delta. Who had it. How they got it. How they used it. And how, praise the Lord, without any doubt, we were going to get our fair share. And the FDP's challenge was the first step.

[A volunteer's report of the first Greenwood project meeting suggests that Carmichael, even then, was moving toward the political ideas that would transform the movement two years later:

Greenwood, June 22
   The meeting tonight was really something. Over two hundred people were there and they were very hip. We all introduced ourselves. Stokely . . . gave a good speech . . . He didn't give them any of this better-street-lights crap, but talked about the question of power. Power is not abstract if you know how Eastland (Senator James O., a Delta plantation owner) *controls the appointment of every single* (federal) *judge in the whole damn county . . .* —Letters from Mississippi*]*

Usually I'd give my little speech and step back and watch the people begin to act politically. It was wondrous to see. In the midst of everything else that was happening, the staff had to maintain focus and discipline and follow this detailed process through in ten weeks. Just thinking back, it really was quite amazing—just to get it done. The staff and volunteers deserve a lot of credit for some truly amazing organizing in pretty trying conditions. No question.

But, you know, the best work from the greatest organizers in the world, which we certainly were not, would have meant absolutely nothing—nada, squat—without some truly incredible community people. Not just brave, but hardworking, resourceful, dedicated people. Actually some quite ordinary, dry-long-so folk who rose remarkably to the occasion. I think it was that summer, night after night, meeting after meeting, that I really came to understand where Ms. Baker's great faith in ordinary people came from. Her unfailing confidence in the democratic political instincts of the grass roots. I saw that time and again, and it was, well . . . inspiring. That's the right word for it.

No, no, I'm not getting overly sentimental or too general here. Statistically I know we're talking about a small percentage of the black folk in the state. So what? That only makes the ones that showed up even mo' bettah. That's precisely the point. When you're involved in dangerous struggle for the people—assuming of course a moral struggle—you will always, always, be surrounded by remarkable people. The best of our-

selves. Think . . . about . . . it, Jack. So whenever I walked into another precinct or county meeting, I just knew I'd be in the company of heroes.
[From several volunteers:

Greenwood, July
What a meeting it was—a totally unorganized group of people had come together for the first of many steps in organizing a local political party. And it was truly democratic. Hundreds of people came to each precinct, compared to the five or ten Mississippi whites who show up for their precinct meetings . . .

Greenwood, August
Of even more significance than the precinct meetings was the County meeting. Here all the delegates from Leflore County met, and a real convention was held with candidates vying for election—with serious discussions of issues and of problems facing the community, the county. You should have seen me after the meeting. I was so excited that I kept running around outside. I was overwhelmed by the history . . .

Moss Point, July
*. . . The County convention . . . It was just amazing seeing these people, many, or rather most, of whom have never had any experience at all in politics running the meeting, electing the people and passing resolutions for a state platform. These people, housewives, unskilled workers, many, but not all, uneducated, are fantastic. People who have never spoken publicly before get up and make the greatest speeches . . . —*Letters from Mississippi]

And the political instinct was wondrous to see. No one said, "You gotta balance the ticket." So many women. So many preachers, so many this or that. But you know by the time we got to the state convention it was balanced. By the time we got to Jackson I was proud of the group from the Second District.

The "politically unsophisticated" people in their collective wisdom knew who could be trusted. Who deserved the honor. Who had earned the right. Who had a clear head and strong heart. The delegation was a cross section of service and merit, across sex and age, status or education. I mean you had the old warriors—Dewey Greene, Sr., Amzie Moore, Doc Henry, Robert Miles—who'd kept hope and dignity alive during some long, dismal, savage years. The valiant women—the Mrs. Hamers, Mrs. McGhees, Mrs. Johnsons—mothers of struggle. And too, the next generation, a few young college students, clearly intended to keep the struggle going.

[Young Leslie Burle McLemore, a Rust College senior, would write his Ph.D. dissertation on the Mississippi Freedom Democratic Party, found the first

department of political science at a black Mississippi college, and is at this writing president of the Jackson City Council. —EMT]

Distractions were everywhere, not just cross burnings, church bombings, drive-by shootings, the usual crap, but weird stuff, stuff you couldn't have imagined. Greenwood was the center *[the national SNCC office moved to Greenwood for the summer]* so there was a constant flow in and out. For instance, Bob and I had to handle security for visitors, y'know Belafonte and Poitier, Dr. King, the politicians . . .

Dr. King was my biggest headache. The Klan swore publicly that he wouldn't leave Mississippi alive. I had heard that his people hadn't wanted him to come. SNCC can't protect you, they argued. SNCC will git you killed. So I took it as my personal responsibility to protect him in the Delta. A matter of honor.

He arrived escorted by carloads of FBI. I told him, "Dr. King, I know you nonviolent, but don't worry about a thang. An FBI car will be in front and in the rear. Your car be in the middle, and it will be nonviolent, no problem. But the cars immediately in front and immediately behind you? Those'll be our people, Dr. King, and usses going to be ready for anything." He didn't argue. We stayed real close every minute he was out and moving around. They would have had to kill a lot of us to get to him. And they would have paid a heavy price. Dr. King was cool. He talked about the need to build the party and left without incident. Not a peep out of the Klan. That's something I take pride in.

[I've seen reports indicating that LBJ was every bit as concerned and as active as was our narrator. In addition to lighting a fire under a resistant J. Edgar Hoover, the Johnson administration had leaned heavily on the Mississippi governor and on Senators Eastland and Stennis, holding them responsible for Dr. King's safety, which suggests that a similar urgency from the administration in June might have saved our colleagues in Neshoba County. —EMT]

But guess what the most serious distraction in Greenwood was? Early in the project, the first freedom day *[when large numbers of people descend on a courthouse to try to register]*, they arrested over a hundred people—volunteers, staff, local teenagers, me. That was a distraction, yes.

But the biggest problem Bob had trying to keep Greenwood from exploding was the civil rights bill. That's right, passage of the civil rights bill damn near brought the project in the Delta to a halt. Look, if there had been riots or street warfare in Greenwood, the national office and the district office couldn't have functioned. The volunteers would have had to be pulled out. The local Africans on staff would have had to make a hard choice or be caught in no-man's-land between the two warring sides. It would have been a sho-nuff mess.

See, once that bill got close to passing, you began to see even more carloads of white men, guns bristling, cruising the city. Some were flat-out Klan. Some were supposed to be deputized, armed "auxiliary" police. You couldn't tell the difference. People said they recognized Byron De La Beckwith [*murderer of Medgar Evers, only recently convicted —EMT*] armed and riding as an "auxiliary" policeman.

In our community there was high excitement and discussion, especially among the youth. A pretty large group really wanted to jump in the white folks' face. To exercise their new legal rights. You really couldn't blame them. But we had to take the position: Not now. Leave it for the time being. Now is the time to be focused. Work on the party. Stick to the plan. Be disciplined. Don't let the crackers distract you. The adults supported us in this, but the youth were restless.

Of course I was uneasy with it. It was strange for me and Zellner to have to counsel restraint. Say what? Telling folks not to confront racism? Especially when they now had—allegedly—for the first time, the legal right to put racists in jail? Yes, indeed. Politics do require a lot of patience and a sense of irony, jah. It do. But it was working. One faction—a loud faction of the youth—was real restless. But discipline was holding. Tribute to Bob, the project staff, and the community elders.

Then an amazing thing happens. Exactly the last thing we needed. An outside group, all kinds of press in tow, comes through, intent on "testing compliance with the new law." Dr. King and SCLC, right? No star, dead wrong. It's the national NAACP, Jack! Yep. The NAACP national office practicing direct action? Must be the revolution, huh? Talk about role reversal. Of course they don't consult anyone. Why should they, we the grass roots. So they streak through. And with their press and FBI entourage, of course, they get served. In places none of our folk could afford or think of going to. Upon which they utter platitudes to the press about "a great and historic moment" and split as fast as their cars will take them.

After that how we s'posed to rein in the local youth? Best we could do was to try to keep it disciplined and nonviolent. Which is why my next arrest was at a local white café. Yeah, the civil rights bill guarantees public accommodation. Uncle Roy [Wilkins] gets fed and splits and I'm in jail again. Historic moment.

After which a certain element of the youth simply refused to be intimidated. They started to jeer and exchange threats with the carloads of gun-toting whites. Guns were brandished and occasionally fired. Rocks and bottles were thrown. Then, one night businesses and homes in the community were shot into. Of course so was our office. We began to hear threats of retaliation in kind. Amid this tension, Bob and his project staff decided to try to organize the militant youth.

Somewhere in all this the McGhee family got involved. Silas McGhee decided he wanted to go see a movie at the LaFlore Theatre. They sold him a ticket, he entered and sat down. But when the movie started, some of the whites went crazy and the cops had to come and take Silas out after only five minutes of the movie. That's how it began.

The rest of July was a running battle between the McGhees, the theater, the mob, and the cops. A few days after the movie theater event, Silas was snatched off the street by a carload of Klansmen, who took him out in the woods. He managed to fight them off with a shovel and escape. But now the McGhees were really mad.

Silas and his brother Jake kept going back to the theater. Five or six times. Each time when they tried to leave, a mob greeted them.

One night a couple SNCC cars had to drive through the mob to retrieve them. The car's windows were shattered and the McGhee brothers were injured by flying glass. At the hospital our people were trapped inside by carloads of gunmen patrolling the highway outside. Finally, in the early morning, a reluctant sheriff agreed to provide an escort. If memory serves, that same night we held the Greenwood precinct meeting.

Another night Jake and Silas went back to the movies, but this time when the mob formed, a towering (6'8"), linebacker-built paratrooper in full dress uniform appeared and faced down a member of the mob. Turned out it was their older brother, Clarence (Robinson), a decorated Korean War veteran on active duty at Fort Campbell, Kentucky. A trained American fighting man, taking leave to come defend freedom, democracy, the Constitution, and his younger brothers in his hometown. Then he got himself jailed for assault.

That was the night Bob Zellner and Mrs. McGhee went together to the jail to see about Clarence. Even today all I got to do is mention the McGhees to Bob and his eyes and grin get big.

"Oh, man, I'll never forget that night. When this cop jumped in Mrs. McGhee's face and shoved her? Ooiee, bro. I swear, that little bitty lady threw the fastest, prettiest straight right I've ever seen. Knocked that sucker clean down, flat on his back and woozy as a floozy. Yes she did."

The McGhees of Greenwood, warrior sons of a warrior mother. But it wasn't but a week or so after that when the Klan pretty near succeeded in stopping Silas for good. I was away and Silas was using my car to take people to a meeting. He was sleeping in the car when some night riders shot him in the temple. Give praise and thanks, the brother survived. But that was one shooting that really got to me. Silas—who I liked and respected a lot—was a year younger than me.

That gives you some sense of the atmosphere in which the FDP was put together. So I don't care who or what you were, you could not help but be moved by the state convention in the Masonic Temple in Jackson. Just the sight of the hall. All these proud people sitting purposefully under their county signs: Neshoba, Leflore, Sunflower, Amite, Pike, Tallahatchie County. Just even the names themselves, every one resonant with memories of sacrifice, bloodshed, and struggle, were a mark of accomplishment and pride.

When the Neshoba delegates walked in, the room stood and applauded. I guarantee there was not, could not have been, any state convention in the country that equaled ours in any way. Not in spirit, not in fervor, and certainly not in singing. Mrs. Hamer leading "Go Tell It on the Mountain." Ms. Baker's keynote address: "We who believe in freedom cannot rest . . ." Until, Ms. Baker said, the life of every black mother's son is as important as the life of every white mother's son. I looked at Mrs. McGhee in the Leflore County delegation, then Mrs. Chaney in the Neshoba delegation. *[Later, Bernice Reagon and Sweet Honey in the Rock would compose a powerful song around those words of Ms. Baker's. —EMT]*

The people cheered Attorney Rauh when he outlined the politics of the convention and told them justice and history were on their side. Then the forty-four delegates and twenty-two alternates to Atlantic City were selected. Once again I was amazed and impressed by the choices. That group represented generations of resistance and survival, true leadership and courage. Every strength—life experience, character, courage, wisdom—you'd care to name, except maybe wealth and college degrees. I would have matched them person for person with any state delegation you could produce in Atlantic City.

Look, by that August when we left the state to drive to Atlantic City to support the delegation, the staff, as Mrs. Hamer would say, "was all wore out." All of us were physically exhausted from the sheer burden of all the organizing work. Many more of us than we knew then were totally burned out. Emotionally scarred, spiritually drained from the constant tension, the moments of anger, grief, or fear in a pervading atmosphere of hostility and impending violence.

But we were running on hope and maybe faith. At least the local people were, those brave souls on the delegation and the communities that had elected them. They were the ones with the faith. (The press in its usual wisdom would quickly pronounce and dismiss them as naive, politically unsophisticated, uneducated, simple.)

Faith in what? In the truth. In the justice and decency of the American people, once they knew the truth. Once the president and the people really understood what we went through daily in Mississippi, they'd want to do right, wouldn't they? And by now the country—the good people, the decent majority—had to understand what was going on. How could they not?

Hey, all summer the world press had streamed into the state and set up camp. Television, newspapers, magazines, the works. On TV, one Mississippi story after another. The people had seen their friends, their neighbors, their leaders, their children, their volunteers, all telling the story to the world.

And the country had come in to see for itself. SNCC's Northern support offices had organized waves of visitors. Thursday was Parents' Day. Every Thursday, a different group of proud but concerned parents would fly in. Doctors and lawyers arranged to spend a week or two of their summer vacations with either the Medical Committee for Human Rights or the Lawyers Committee. Under the auspices of the National Council of Churches, groups of prominent religious leaders and clerics of all faiths and denominations came to observe. Congressmen and other politicians prodded by conscience or constituent pressure came through, looked around, and made suitably supportive statements at the obligatory press conference. Movie stars and celebrity entertainers dropped in, some even giving free performances in small, isolated country towns.

(One hot afternoon I remember picking Mrs. Hamer up for a meeting. She got in the car and gave me a puzzled look. "Stokely, seems I heard this name before. Who is it? "The woman's name seemed vaguely familiar but I didn't immediately place it.

"I'm not sure, Mrs. Hamer. But why?"

"Wal, jes' a while ago this little white lady wearing some blue jeans come walking in my house. I never seen her before. She wanted to know was there anything she could do to help me. She jes' wanted to help. Wal, I had this big pot of beans on the stove. So I told her I had to go to a FDP meeting an' didn't have nobody to tend the beans. They was to feed the workers an' I didn't want them to burn while I was gone. She was jes' *so* glad. She said to just show her what to do. Which I did an' handed her the spoon. I left her in the kitchen. You think that's all right?"

"Guess so, Mrs. Hamer. Why not? Anyone should be able to keep beans from burning. What was that name you said?"

"She say her name is Shirley MacLaine."

I told her I thought the "li'l white lady" she'd left in the kitchen stirring her beans was quite possibly a fairly famous movie star.

"A real movie star, huh? Ain' that something. Uh uh uh." Mrs. Hamer contemplated that for a minute, then smiled. "Ah guess the Lord sure do move in mysterious ways, eh?"

"Why you say that, Mrs. Hamer?"

"Why, honey, He musta knowed that that was my last sack o' beans an' how hungry you young folk be getting. But a *movie star* now? Sho hope she doan let mah beans burn.")

That was what that summer was like in black Mississippi. People had been struggling there for years before we got there. In isolation with no support and little visible progress. Now with this project, the Mississippi movement had broken through. Conditions in the state were finally being exposed to national attention.

So by the end of the summer, far as our people were concerned, the entire country had to know. The national Democrats, even the *president*. Why, honey, didn't he send his personal representative? *[In June, Allen Dulles had briefly come to Mississippi as the personal emissary of Lyndon Baines Johnson. —EMT]*

Seems like the whole country—everybody and their mamma—had come, not just to the state but even to people's own insignificant, small towns. Weren't that something? Those three boys hadn't shed their blood in vain, no, suh. So how could the Democrats not know? And when they got to the Democratic National Convention, if they met folk who still claimed not to get it, why then they'd be mighty happy to bear witness their own self. Tell it like it is. Be mighty proud to testify. That was *their* job.

By now a great deal has been written about what happened at that 1964 Democratic Convention in Atlantic City. There is no need to tell that story all over again. The facts are "on record." But what about their meaning? The process and the consequences? That's still in dispute. Some important aspects I've never seen explained, and I'd like to add my two cents to that kitty.

For example, what was the Mississippi Freedom Democratic Party really? It was a bold, creative response to the political realities that confronted us in Mississippi and the South. A desperation tactic, certainly. A political party? Yes, but not in any usual sense. As American political parties go, this one was absolutely unique. Who ever heard of any political party in which no more than 5 percent of its members could even cast a ballot? Yet it accomplished remarkable political results. And it was the single most incredible act of organizing in the entire civil rights movement. I certainly learned a lot from the whole experience.

I remember when Bob first raised the idea that SNCC could organize a party with the black community that would be open to Mississippians of all races and would go to Atlantic City and try to challenge the lily-white "regulars." Folks thought he was nuts. Or fantasizing.

Just consider. Forget for a moment the hostility and terrorism such a party was likely to attract and just consider the sheer work of the organizing and self-education it would require. Not only would we have to learn and follow precisely the involved rules and practices of the local party, we'd have to find people in every beat, precinct, and county who were willing to present their black selves to every meeting of the all-white party and try to participate in selecting the delegation. Do you fully understand what that meant then? Our people knew who would be guarding those doors. It was a daunting prospect.

This, folks, was the party of E. H. Hurst *[the murderer of Mr. Herbert Lee]* and of "Big" Milam *[who admitted killing Emmett Till]*. The party of James O. Eastland and Ross Barnett. The party of the local plantation owner and all the local blacks' employers, of Klansmen, White Citizens Council members, registrars, sheriffs, and petty small-town bureaucrats who had absolute power over black lives and jobs. The party that had disenfranchised their grandparents in 1877 and had schemed ever since, using every tactic—law and terror—to keep our people away from the ballot box by any means necessary.

That was the party we would be asking our people to find the courage to confront. Then, if they survived that, they'd need to have their own meetings—parallel and public—at every level up to the state convention to select their own delegation. Then, assuming we accomplished all that, a way would have to be found to get our people to Atlantic City. At this time the Mississippi Project didn't have $500 in the bank and SNCC paychecks like death, according to Shakespeare, "would come when they would come."

Then, while all this was happening in state, folks had to be working nationally to try to generate enough support within the Democratic Party so our people would not simply be dismissed and ignored one more time. The conventional wisdom: *"Oh, man.* What makes you guys think the party will ever recognize you as Democrats? Where's your charter? Or that they'll concede that this challenge has any legitimacy? It'll never happen, bro. And, that's if—an' this a big if—y'all even get that far. If, in fact, those po' folk y'all setting up for God knows what even *manage* to get *out* of Mississippi at all. Never happen, Jack. Good luck. But I will say this, it bold. It's crazy, but y'all bold."

And as usual, the conventional wisdom seemed right. It was impossible. Any rational person would not even have started. Forget danger, just the work. The massive organizing. The thousand and one petty details—every one crucial—that had to be attended to. Then the national politics. The job of education. The state conventions to be targeted, hoping the leadership would allow us to address the delegates. Finding reliable allies who could be trusted to represent our interests—the struggling, powerless black people of Mississippi—inside the convention.

We all know what happened.

Look, there were no issues (except us) in that convention. No issues at all, none. Remember now, it wasn't in any sense a classic presidential nominating convention. It was a coronation. That of King Lyndon, the Great Restorer. The only real issue being whom he was going to anoint as his running mate, and second, as it turned out, being what to do with us. The two were not unrelated.

Remember now, John Kennedy (unto him peace) had been shot down. *Whoee!* Grief, uncertainty, and great anxiety across the land. Opening salvo of a coup? Right-wing conspiracy? No, not at all. Order is maintained. Into the Oval Office steps the big Texan and the center not only holds, it doesn't even miss a beat. In fact, the administration seems to work better. The nation is relieved and grateful. Because, in memory of the martyred leader, the new president "jawbones" Congress, twisting arms and whuppin' heads, to get through the legislative agenda that had bogged down under Kennedy. Within the party, Johnson is supreme and the country is said to be grateful. Remember?

Barry "Extremism in the Pursuit of Liberty Is No Vice" Goldwater had already wrapped up the Republican nomination. And as their convention had literally read the moderate wing out of the party and insulted, spat upon, and jeered at the *fourteen* black delegates, more than half of that party had already been totally alienated. The few *[only fourteen, lowest number of blacks at a Republican National Convention in living memory. — EMT]* traditional Negro Republicans who had survived the right-wing capture of the delegate selection process were made to feel downright unwelcome. Jackie Robinson is said to have wept. Another said, "I now know what it felt like to be a Jew in Nazi Germany." He needn't have reached so far for the simile; "a black person in Mississippi" would have served even better.

So all that Goldwater would carry into the election would be the far right of the nation, a large part of which was certain to be the white South. That's all, Jack. Nationwide in 1964 a small minority.

Recall also that over the summer, the same week that our comrades' bodies were being dug out of that Neshoba County earthen dam, the civil rights bill had been passed with LBJ's strong support over a Dixiecrat filibuster in the Senate. From that moment on, far as the Democratic Party was concerned, the racist Southern vote was long gone. In Barry G. ("in your heart you know he's right"), the Dixiecrats had a Republican they could vote for with conviction, and as it would turn out, the first Republican Party they could embrace. Even we—politically naive though we were said to be—could see all that clearly. So how could the political pros, the "Democratic heavies," not know this? From their behavior in Atlantic City, evidently they didn't understand or they refused to believe.

Our lawyer at the convention was Joe Rauh from D.C., a force in the liberal wing of the party, and he was instrumental in the challenge getting as far as it did within the national party. That's true and one must never be ungrateful in politics. Initially, he opened some doors on the inside. That spring when Bob Moses had come to D.C. to talk to political people there about the idea of the convention challenge for the first time, just Rauh's name clearly opened doors.

We were in an initial meeting over at the Institute for Policy Studies with the kind of political people who would even come to a meeting with us at that point, the usual suspects: low-level congressional aides, a few labor union officials, some ADA types, mostly young "progressives." Bob explained the idea for the challenge—the people from Mississippi go to the convention and challenge the national party to renounce racism and exclusion. To become democratic. A long silence, then.

Wow, bold idea, Bob. But hopeless. Never get off the ground. Long shot. Fageddaboutit, the leadership will never . . .

Then Bob says quietly, "Well, y'know, I was just talking to Joe Rauh—"

"*What,* you *talked* to Joe?"

"—and he said he thought we could be seated. That there was a real chance of that."

The meeting's atmosphere changed immediately, Jack. Immediately. It was now "Oh, my God, *Joe Rauh said that*? Really? *He did*? Hmmm, so Joe said he thought you could be seated, huh? Well, now, maybe we just better take another look at this, eh?"

I'd been in D.C. four years and had never even heard of the guy. But when I saw the effect of just the mention of his name, I figured I'd better find out who this guy really was.

[Joseph Rauh Jr., a Washington insider, was chief counsel for the United Auto Workers, adviser to Walter Reuther, and a close personal friend of Senator Hubert H. Humphrey (D-MN). He was also a leader in Americans for Democratic Action (ADA), the Democratic Party's left wing, and a longtime activist for progressive causes within the liberal establishment of the Democratic Party. —EMT]

After the meeting Mr. Rauh agreed to be the official MFDP lawyer for the challenge, and as a result we saw more doors beginning to open and attitudes among Democratic liberals began to change noticeably. And I mean *noticeably.* No one was saying it was a sure thing. Hey, it was still a long shot. But now it was a *real* long shot, not merely a fantasy one. A world of difference in Washington politics. Now it was "If Joe Rauh is your lawyer, there has to be more to this than meets the eye."

Also, over the summer, Ms. Baker had moved to D.C. and, working with Northern friends of SNCC groups, had managed to identify and cultivate some real support in a number of state delegations *[about ten state conventions adopted resolutions of support —EMT].* So we were able to go to Atlantic City with some firm allies and strong advocates inside the convention.

And *outside*? Hey, we now had a real presence around the country because of the avalanche of press attention to the state of Mississippi over the summer. Besides, the convention had no real burning issue, and the press always needs issues, so naturally they came to us. We were a good story and we were easy to find and always available.

On the boardwalk outside the convention hall, staff, local folk, and Northern supporters had set up a round-the-clock vigil. Volunteers on their way home from Mississippi detoured through Atlantic City, some bringing their parents. Occasionally the families of the murdered workers came by to stand with us. There were giant pictures of our three martyrs and the burned out shell of the station wagon from the Bogue Chitto swamp on display. The folks kept singing. Mrs. Hamer and Bernice Reagon came by to lead the singing, and members of the delegation came by to make speeches and thank the people. Visiting politicians came to pledge support. At times the crowd reached three, even four thousand people.

Oh, we were a sho-nuff presence and highly visible. Every delegate going into the arena had to pass our vigil. It was all unusually powerful and moving, and many a delegate stopped, looked, listened, and volunteered his vote before going on in.

You know where I was. You know I stayed on the boardwalk, Jack, talking to the people who stopped by. So I wasn't in on all the meetings and wheeling an' dealing on the inside. But I remember someone brought a little portable TV so we could follow some of what was going on inside. I'll never forget what I saw on that TV when Mrs. Hamer stepped up to the mike before the Credentials Committee the day before the convention was to open. She had just begun to talk about her beating in the Winona jail when the network cut to a White House press conference.

LBJ got on and announced some program or policy so trivial that I can't even remember what it was. If he was asked about the convention, the MFDP, or his vice presidential choice, I know I would have remembered everything he said. So either he wasn't asked or more likely didn't answer. Anyway we never saw Mrs. Hamer's testimony, but that didn't matter. The Credentials Committee sure did.

[Subsequent accounts by White House aides report that the president had been closely monitoring the proceedings in Atlantic City. When Mrs. Hamer began to talk, President Johnson, at least in one account, is said to have exploded, "Get that ignorant (or illiterate) black woman off the air." (In some reports we heard, LBJ's final adjective was not the word black.) *Hence the hastily called presidential press conference. However, the attempt to keep Mrs. Hamer's story from the American people was only temporarily successful. Later that evening at least one network aired her testimony in its entirety. Delegate supporters reported that their delegations received a flood of telegrams from*

indignant constituents that evening. There were similar reports from the White House. —EMT]

That was the situation the night before the convention formally opened. What happened that night and the next morning has been subject to heated debate. Distrust, suspicion, rumors, and accusations of treachery, sellouts, bad faith, and manipulation have flown back and forth. I warrant that there is no one person knows everything that went down. But I will tell you what I do know. But first a little background.

After LBJ stepped up to replace Kennedy, the vice presidency had been left vacant, so as we neared the convention, the politicking among the various factions supporting different candidates was fierce. Of course, in the end, none of the warring camps had any real leverage on Johnson's decision. The president and the president alone would, at his pleasure, anoint his running mate. And on that point the famously poker-faced LBJ was silent and inscrutable as the Sphinx, clearly enjoying the growing anxiety of the aspirants.

When the MFDP appeared on the distant horizon, the camp promoting Senator Hubert Humphrey for vice president was jockeying hard. And that camp was led by Joe Rauh, our lawyer. So, was Mr. Rauh's support of the MFDP purely an act of conscience, or did he see us as a possible pressure point in the larger campaign for his friend and ally Humphrey? Probably both.

Inside the Mississippi movement speculation was rife. People said the reason the liberals literally picked up the MFDP and brought it into the convention—a convention otherwise without issues—was to use it as leverage: a negotiating card in the hand of the Humphrey supporters in the struggle for the number two spot on the ticket.

It is easy and tempting to say—as many do—that those forces cynically used us to advance their real intent, then cut the deal and dropped us. They picked us up, brought us in, put us in play. Then LBJ says, "Y'all dragged this mess in. Y'all *better* fix it. Ruin *my* convention an' old Hubert can forget about the vice presidency the way Texas bullfrogs forget their tails, heah me?" So they did.

[After Atlantic City, at the Leadership Conference on Civil Rights, Joe Rauh and Clarence Mitchell made our lives miserable (Jan Goodman and I represented SNCC and the MFDP). Nonetheless, on this question, I find myself wanting to record a few words in defense of my old nemesis.

The notion that Mr. Rauh ("and the liberals") seized upon the challenge purely as leverage with which to advance Senator Humphrey's ambitions in an otherwise issueless convention, then dropped us once that purpose was achieved, is a common belief among movement people. It is, I think, a little too pat. Too neat and too simple. Political motives are usually much more complicated and events more ambiguous than that.

Mr. Rauh had for many years been fervently committed to an eventual Hubert Humphrey presidency, so that goal would always have been foremost in his strategic and political calculation. This was no secret: he was always the first to admit this. However, I believe that after getting to know and work with Bob Moses; witnessing the Jackson convention; seeing conditions in Mississippi and meeting the people he was to represent; the MFDP became personal to him, much more than merely another convention issue or bargaining chip.

Certainly his political frame of reference was different from and even incompatible with ours. But within those terms I believe he observed certain principles. He saw, conducted, and described himself as an "honest broker." And we were his clients. I believe that he would not wittingly have debased the professional obligations implicit in that arrangement.

But, in Atlantic City, seasoned operative, veteran of high-stakes convention politics though he was, Bro Rauh was taken by surprise by the intensity of forces he himself had helped put in motion.

With long-standing interests in conflict with more recent commitments, he found himself between the proverbial rock and hard place. I believe he tried, fairly and honestly, to reconcile his divided loyalties and to negotiate a just result. That proved impossible. But I do not believe that in any sense Joe Rauh can fairly be said to have "sold" us out. —EMT]

No matter how we'd gotten there or why, we knew that night on the boardwalk, that the convention as a whole still had to vote on our challenge. And that when they did, we would win big. Responding to heavy, heavy pressure from the White House, the majority would call for the seating of the all-white Dixiecrat delegation. As a gesture toward us, the report would include *strong* language declaring that no racially exclusive delegations would be seated in future conventions. That was supposed to be our victory.

First, though, another vote had to be made. Congresswoman Edith Green of Oregon (eternal peace be unto her) had circulated a minority report that proposed seating both delegations, dividing Mississippi's delegate votes equally between them, each delegate counting as half a vote. And the delegates from both camps, to be seated, would have to pledge their support for the national ticket in the coming election.

Now, as I've said, the issue of votes was, in practical political terms, purely symbolic. The incumbent LBJ was going to be nominated by acclamation, so any division of the Mississippi votes wasn't going to make any real political difference. It was purely symbolic, but that was some heavy, heavy symbolism, Jack.

The Green proposal was entirely acceptable to our people. They had no interest, despite the treatment they had received at their hands, in kicking the white Mississippians out of the convention. What they wanted was inclusion. Full participation as equals. As proud Freedom Democrats, the equals of everyone else in the convention. That, they knew, would be a historic political leap forward for black Mississippi. Simple justice and on national TV. (Even if, this time round, they each had only half a vote and nothing to vote for.)

Course now, the white Mississippians did see the matter quite differently. There were congressmen, judges, all kinds of state officials, even a plantation owner or two on their delegation. These local, petty, white supremacist tyrants sharing a vote with *their* nigrahs? Political equality, even if only symbolic, and on national TV? No cotton-picking way, José.

Apparently this prospect was equally horrifying to the party leadership. Those Mississippi Negroes could not be allowed to "stampede the convention." They simply could not allow the minority report to come to a vote on the convention floor.

They swung into action, Jack, overnight. Everyone of our "rock solid" supporters they could put pressure on they did. And, as we discovered, these were all loyal party activists, vulnerable at some point along the patronage food chain. What amazed us was how *overnight* the leadership could find the *one* person to whom a delegate could not afford to say no. One small businessman said that his banker called him at midnight—remember that crucial expansion loan . . . ? Another's boss called—that promotion we've been discussing? One strong black lady from either the New York or California delegation, I forget which, was in tears. Her husband was up for a judgeship, his life's ambition. His sponsor called, she had a choice: us or her husband's career dream. And so it went. We needed eleven votes, went to bed with fifteen firm commitments, and awoke the next morning with six left standing. There would be no minority report for the convention to vote on. Crisis control, LBJ style.

Then came the famous "compromise." I guess you could call it the Mississippi Compromise of 1964. The leadership knew it had to throw us something, a sop to our supporters, a public relations gesture. So the Freedom Democrats, we were told, would be given two "seats at large," which, as the people were quick to see, represented nowhere and no one. The leadership even named the two delegates—Doc Henry and the Reverend Ed King. The rest of our delegation would be "honored guests." And they pledged never to seat any "lily-white" delegations in the future. They would create a Civil Rights Committee on the Democratic National Committee to ensure this. That was to be our victory. Our people should take it, express joy and gratitude, and go home.

Course it backfired. The white delegation, mortally offended—at what I don't know—walked out in a huff anyway, calling on their Confederate brothers to walk with them. The local people of the MFDP knew tokenism when they saw it. Maybe if they hadn't struggled so hard, risked and endured so much, and hoped so fervently, they might have gone along with the condescension. But as Mrs. Hamer put it, "We didn't come here for no two seats, for *all of us* is t'ard." The MFDP rejected the compromise.

Now, all of this went down on the morning of the opening day of the convention, and it caused a lot of confusion and rumor, and growing bickering between our "allies" and us. What with the crowds, the press, the camera crews, the politicians, the constant stream of bad information and misinformation, the scene looked to our people like Babylon and the Tower of Babel combined.

All that our people really knew at this point was that their challenge was suddenly over. All these new friends, the good peoples, who had promised their votes were now not even going to get a chance to vote? Sure seemed like Mississippi all over again.

"Stokely, so this is what y'all calls democracy?"

"No, Mr. Turnbow, it's politics . . . as usual."

"Wal now, sure tain't the same thing, now is it?"

"No, suh, it sure ain't."

So what to do? We had a meeting. One of those looong SNCC-style meetings. But this particular meeting was incredible.

Outside, the press was restless, impatient for the story. Inside the convention managers wanted a show of unity. The president would be coming in a day or so, and his advent needed to be seen to be triumphant. The white Mississippians were packing their bags, so it became important, for the appearance of unity, for our supporters watching on TV across the nation, that the MFDP publicly accept the compromise. Have a press conference. Declare victory. Grin. Show gratitude. So they called in the big guns.

Suddenly the first in a long line of friends and advisers began to materialize. "High-ups"—politicians, civil rights and religious leaders—started showing up to advise and explain political reality. That was a *parade,* Jack. A few I knew. Some I recognized, others I saw for the first time. Reuther, Humphrey, Dr. King, Bayard, I think Roy Wilkins, James Farmer, Dr. Spike, assorted congresspeople, religious leaders. A lot of rhetoric, high drama, and surpassing earnestness.

For the party. For the president. For the *country* . . . We gotta have unity. . . . All depends on you . . . the most important decision of your life . . . a great victory . . . be *political.* You gotta accept. . . . For God's sakes, don't blow this . . .

Some—Dr. King, Dr. Spike, maybe even Bayard—say, "Here's what we think, but finally, it's not our decision, it's yours." But mostly I remember unrelenting pressure: "You simply can't afford to make a serious mistake now."

Many of the delegates were quite confused and uncertain. And who could blame them? This barrage of friendly advice and concern was probably too much. Ultimately self-defeating. Why were the people, only last week voiceless, faceless, powerless, now suddenly so important to all these VIPs? What could they really want? Why did they care so much? If this was such a splendid victory, why didn't it feel like one? The only faces the delegates knew and trusted were those of Bob or Guyot *[Lawrence Guyot, chairman of the MFDP]*, the staff, and those volunteers who had lived with them all summer. And more important, their leaders: Doc Henry, Ed King, Mrs. Hamer, Mrs. Devine, Ms. Gray, Mr. Steptoe, Mr. Miles, Ms. Ruffin.

I believe, rather I know, that if Bob or the rest of us had *told* them what decision to make, they'd probably have done that only because they trusted us. I answered any question about all that was happening as best I could, given the available information. (I was growing more convinced by the minute that, at that point, their decision probably made no real political difference one way or another. But I didn't think it useful to say that just then.)

It seemed to me that the most important thing was that those people leave there knowing that they, and they alone, out of their own intelligence, judgment, and experience, had made their decision themselves. Autonomy. They had earned that right.

When Hubert Humphrey was introduced, heavy emphasis had been placed on his long support for civil rights, as a "true friend of the Negro." In his appeal Humphrey had mentioned the importance of the MFDP's decision on the nomination of the vice president. Mrs. Hamer was clear, the disappointment palpable in her voice: "Mr. Humphrey, I've been praying about you an' I been thinking about you, and you're a good man. But are you saying you think that your [getting the] job as vice president is more important than the rights of our [400,000] black people in Mississippi? Senator Humphrey, the trouble is, you scared to do what you know is right. Senator, I'm going to pray for you some more."

Humphrey had the grace to blush and was actually silent for a moment. I don't remember what answer he gave her. *[Some reports claimed that at that moment the senator was seen to weep. —EMT]*

The peoples listened closely and politely, asked the important people a few thoughtful questions, and thanked them for coming. Then they deliberated carefully among themselves, took their decision, announced it, and gave their reasons. They had not come for two seats at large or to be "honored guests." The compromise was not acceptable, so they would go home.

I was proud of my people, real proud. Of their dignity. Their clarity. Of the way they had stood up under incredible psychological pressure. The way they saw through the blandishments of the snake-oil salesmen. They had struggled too long and come too far to be chumped off like that. The Democratic Party could, and would it seemed, try to treat them the way the state of Mississippi always had. But they were certainly not going to grin and profess to be glad. They could have stayed in Mississippi and done that.

I was also especially proud that among the strongest and clearest were my ladies from the Second Congressional District—the Delta.

Course now, the politicians and the media saw it somewhat differently. Oh, man! In the name-calling, finger-pointing, and denunciations that followed, we heard and read endlessly how the *"apolitical* SNCC *radicals"* had "cynically manipulated" the "simple, 'politically naive' people" into a bad political decision. Yeah, yeah, yeah. Gimme a cotton-picking break.

As if the people—especially *these* people—were incapable of cutting through the rhetorical overkill to see that they were being shafted one more time. Yeah, the people running the attack on us were furious, but not, as they claimed, because we had *manipulated* the people. But precisely because we had *not*. They were spitting mad because we hadn't joined with them and used our influence on the people to help sell them a bill of goods.

From the passion, the venom, the pettiness, and most of the media commentary, you'd think that we had somehow managed to ruin their convention, divide the Democratic Party, jeopardize the president's election, and splinter the civil rights coalition. Such nonsense, such nonsense . . . such utter, utter nonsense. Help them, Jesus. I still don't think the decision made an ounce of political difference. But to our people, the principle was absolutely important.

If we had gone into the convention as the little pets, the clients of the liberals, we came out as outcasts, sho-nuff political pariahs. Someone, I think Ivanhoe, said, "We're the new Communists." You know how whenever black folk got fed up and took to the streets, you always heard talk about "Communist" agitation? As though black people lack sense enough to know they're oppressed until and unless some Communist runs up to tell them? That, according to totalitarian liberal opinion, was our role with the Freedom Democrats at the convention.

First of all, the Southern racist vote had been lost long before the Mississippi delegation walked. So, had Johnson's managers allowed the convention to vote democratically, the Democratic Party would have lost nothing. Not a cotton-picking thing! But it would have gained much.

It would have sent a powerful message of hope and justice to black folk, and of decency, principle, and fairness to the nation, particularly its youth. A signal of encouragement, especially to a generation of idealistic young Americans of all races, the assurance that they had a political home within the system, a major party worthy of their respect. Instead, millions of the most active American youth were alienated. Instead of looking to the future, the leadership had turned back to try to embrace a messed-up past. A serious failure of vision, principle, and leadership that would come back to haunt the Democrats and the nation in '68 and beyond. And they still didn't get it.

Second, the election: In 1964, Barry Goldwater's brand of ideological conservatism had seemed demented *["That jackass is nuts." —LBJ]* to the vast majority of the American people. It sounded exactly like the reckless, narrow-minded, chauvinistic, militaristic, neoracist, ultracapitalist extremist concoction that it really was. (It would take decades of propaganda, disinformation, protracted and ruthless boring from within, along with the Nixon/Reagan Southern strategy, before that ideology could fully capture the Republican Party and push the national political debate to the far right.)

In 1964, Goldwater had but two chances, slim and none. Johnson's landslide victory was assured and near total. In the election, Goldwater would carry only a few Western states and some of the white South (which, defecting from the Democrats, would become the base for rebuilding the Republican Party into the conservative monster it has since become). But that was yet to come. In 1964, Johnson did not need the Bubba vote. He could have gone with us and lost nothing. And, perhaps, gained the future.

Leaving Atlantic City, the staff and the delegates were exhausted. But we didn't exactly limp back to Mississippi, our tails between our legs. No indeedy. In fact, the opposite.

Many on the delegation were justifiably apprehensive. Wondering exactly what reception would face them on their return. Would the night riders be rampaging? Homes burning? The state officials be seeking vengeance? The volunteers would be gone. So too the national press corp. And for whatever it had been worth, the big FBI presence in Jackson. So there was real anxiety. But also defiance and a certain pride.

Yeah, they hadn't been seated, but they had not been ignored either, had they? Indeed, hadn't they forced the president and the nation to take notice? Yes, they had. And the whites hadn't been seated either. Or, at least you could say they hadn't *sat* either. Could even say they had been run off. So you could fairly call it a draw. Our people had fought them to a standstill. They hadn't given in an' they sure hadn't given up. What we gotta do is go home an' commence abuilding up the party. Keep on keepin' on.

I was thinking sort of the same thing, but about the organization.

SNCC in Mississippi would now have to seriously regroup. It would have to reorganize and draw down from the unreal scale of Freedom Summer to a program sustainable with local staff and resources. Many of my comrades from NAG—Muriel Tillinghast, Jean Weaver, Ruth Howard, Ed Brown, Courtland Cox, Ralph Featherstone—would also be staying on. There was momentum in the community. We needed to build on it.

But a lot of folk, truly exhausted, were on the verge of cracking up. In recognition of this, Harry Belafonte arranged and personally paid for a visit to Guinea.

["They had been on the front lines so long and had endured so much, been doing so much, that I feared burnout. It was clear to me that they needed to get completely away at least for a short while. They all deserved to go, but that was, of course, not possible. We could only take those most in need of a complete change of scenery. A tough choice. I thought that in Africa, the newly independent nation of Guinea had just the right spirit. The people and its young leader, Sékou Touré, had a vision and energy then that reminded me of SNCC." —Harry Belafonte]

Ironic, huh? Everything, as they say, is timing. Here I was, dreaming of Africa since my father's return from Ghana when I was a kid. And as a teenager, listening to the street-corner nationalists in Harlem. Now here was a chance. But really, I was not "wore down" like a lot of other folk, and serious work needed to be done in my district. What with drawing down and building on the Summer Project. That had to be a priority, so I asked Bob Moses and Jim Forman not to consider me for Africa.

A few weeks later, I was in the Greenwood office talking to staff, visiting projects, trying to figure out which ones we should strengthen, which to close, and what programs to emphasize, when Lawrence Guyot, chairman of the MFDP, called.

"The MFDP executive just met, Bro Stokely. Great news, my brother. Stay exactly where you are. Be right over to talk wicha. The 'peoples' need ya, my brother." A deliberate tone of mystery and barely suppressed glee and mischief was in Guyot's voice. Charlie Cobb had it right: "When ol' Guyot gets into that Southern backslapping, good-to-see-ya-fella, king-fish political-boss bag, it's best you keep your hand on your wallet."

Even so I was surprised. He walked in, this broad, poker-shark, bluffing-for-the-pot grin of his plastered over his moon face, squeezed my hand, pumped my arm—"You a great American, Bro Stokely"—and announced that the MFDP needed SNCC help to campaign across the state for the Johnson-Humphrey ticket.

After dropping that little bombshell, he sat back, glasses glinting, grin widening, all three hundred pounds quivering with excitement and glee as he peered intently into my face, clearly waiting for a response. But

I wasn't gonna play his game by repeating stupidly, "You want SNCC to campaign for LBJ?" So I pretended I hadn't really heard.

"I'm sorry, my man, what did you say?"

We stared at each other.

"As the only loyal Democrats in this state, the MFDP is going to campaign for the national ticket."

He stared some more, panting and wheezing with suppressed laughter. I still couldn't believe my ears. Obviously Guyot was now stone crazy. But actually, even if he was crazy, "If this be madness there be method in it." As Polonius said about Hamlet.

[Another little known aspect of the brother: He always was quite taken with Shakespeare's language. Only recently, Harold Bloom told me that Carmichael once had turned up at Yale and very politely asked to sit in on one of his lectures on the Bard. —EMT]

CHAPTER XVIII

The Unforeseen Pitfalls
of "Success" American Style

Stokely, whatever is going to happen with all you young people
in SNCC? You all just going to keep wandering about, goin' from
pillar to post with never a firm place to lay down your heads?
—Mrs. Annie Devine, MFDP challenger,
Fourth Congressional District

The record will show that in the 1964 presidential election in Mississippi,
Lyndon B. Johnson and Hubert H. Humphrey appeared at the top of a
MFDP slate of candidates. So I guess we did end up running the only
campaign for the national ticket in the state. We had this poster. Across
the top in big letters, it said:

VOTE
MISSISSIPPI FREEDOM DEMOCRATIC PARTY

For President, Lyndon Baines Johnson
[over a picture of the president]

For Vice President, Hubert Horatio Humphrey
[another big picture]
[under that, our candidates for Congress]

Mrs. Fannie Lou Hamer, 2nd District
[picture]

Mrs. Annie Devine, 4th District
[picture]

Mrs. Victoria Gray, 5th District
[picture]

I thought it a real good-looking poster. And I thought it ironic and audacious: boldly co-opting, as it did, the national ticket onto our MFDP slate for a freedom election.

As best we could, we covered the entire state, not just the black community, with these posters. They seemed to have quite an effect. Judging from the way they were torn down, defaced, or riddled with bullet holes, our posters must have enraged somebody. We kept putting them back up.

I figured three distinct groups were involved with the posters. The few moderate Democrats in the state removed them to reclaim their presidential ticket and so not to further alienate white voters. (Didn't work.) Moderate racists were content to scrawl obscenities, while the hardcore—Bubba and ol' Billy Bob—just had to reach for their pistols and shotguns. Most bullet holes were clustered around the top of the ticket. Voting with their trigger fingers?

Ours were the only Johnson/Humphrey posters I remember seeing in the state. But for some reason our appeal to the national campaign headquarters for an appearance by either or both candidates at a giant MFDP rally in Jackson never received the courtesy of a reply. Odd, clearly bureaucratic bungling. We understood the heavy demands on the candidates' time, but couldn't they at least have sent Lady Bird or Mrs. Humphrey? Especially after we mailed them a few campaign posters as proof of our good faith and hard work. I figured for every poster we put up the ticket lost five votes. But, hey, we were loyal Democrats.

At least they never asked us to take the national candidates off our ballot. Which was good because fortunately Johnson and Humphrey did win the freedom election. Which was all they won in the state, because Goldwater and Miller cleaned their clocks in the state-run so-called election. But it was hardly our fault that only 6 percent of our people could vote in that closed affair, was it?

After Atlantic City the atmosphere back in the Delta had been strange. I felt, after the pressure and intense discipline all summer, a kind of deflation. Objective conditions hadn't changed. If anything, they were more dangerous. Yet there was a limpness. Like a taut bowstring suddenly going slack, or a balloon collapsing as air escaped. But that was only within the organization. The mood in the community was quite the opposite.

One volunteer said it was like a movie. Watching a large army breaking camp at the end of a campaign. Confusion, random movement, and a landscape littered with debris. His friend said, with greater cultural precision, that it reminded him of the last day of summer camp. Both perceptions had some truth. Except, of course, that in any halfway decent army frontline troops would be rotated out with fresh replacements coming in. We didn't have that luxury. The same ol' troops had to keep soldiering on.

It actually was quite an emotional scene, especially the parting of volunteers from their hosts and students. What was surprising, though, was the number of volunteers who weren't leaving or were leaving only to make arrangements with their parents and schools in order to come back.

Even among those leaving for grad school or to start careers, you heard expressions of ambivalence or regret. Leaving was "harder than expected." The job wasn't finished. Their students had cried. They had come to love their communities. They felt, they said, strangely guilty about going back to their "real lives."

The ones returning were the ones so affected by the summer's experience that they could not bring themselves to flat-out leave. So they decided to sign up, most of them for a year. That kind of commitment had certainly not been their intention in June, so clearly something had happened to them. That wasn't entirely surprising to me. I'd seen some signs in a few cases that this might happen. But the numbers were a surprise. And from some people I simply wouldn't have expected.

Why did so many young, white Americans feel so strongly? I knew why I was staying and why my brothers and sisters in NAG were. But these relatively privileged and sheltered white youth? I've thought about that. It was not just the novelty or the excitement and the drama. It was something more profound: self-discovery. Hey, I learned something important about myself that summer too. We all did. I think these young, white Americans found and used qualities in themselves that they had not had to call upon before. Confronted situations they had never expected to encounter. Learned some ugly truths about their country and felt they had a chance to do something about it. Young people have an innate sense of justice. All they need is a chance to express it. I know that. But mostly, I think, they felt useful, needed, and truly appreciated. Many, I suspect, for the first time. And it felt real good to them. The deep human satisfaction of serving humanity and trying to make real change.

Part of it too was stepping out from under the narrow social, political, and cultural constraints—the individualistic, status-seeking materialism and muted racism of middle-class America. The project had been a unique event in that respect. A situation quite abnormal in American social arrangements of race and class. Bringing together two strata of the society that were never supposed to meet in friendship and equality. And that never did again in quite the same way, so far as I am aware.

But nobody in SNCC had planned for so many recruits. And all at the same time. How could the organization assimilate them? How could it turn them away? These were some of the most compatible of the group. Decent white folks, but white folk nonetheless. What would their status be? Would they be on payroll, therefore SNCC staff? How would that affect decision-making? The character of the organization? SNCC's way was, whoever does the work participates in decisions. Clearly SNCC could not think of excluding the newcomers from decision-making. Creating, in effect, second-class citizens without a vote within the organization. But what would be the long-term consequences of this sudden influx of bright, articulate, middle-class, young Northerners? (Hey, if you came from New Mexico or California, you were as much a "Northerner" in Mississippi as if you came from New York or Vermont.) I don't know that these contradictions were ever, or could ever have been, resolved neatly.

The MFDP too was facing some self-evaluating. It may have been feverishly put together in three months, but it had a strong base. Across the state, it had a county-by-county structure under responsible, elected leaders who enjoyed the respect of their communities. The state executives were acknowledged movement leaders. So the party could really take root and grow. They had had a taste of battle and were ready for more. For them, Atlantic City was not a defeat, it was a revelation. They could carry the fight to the highest level and survive. And everyone—leadership and rank and file—was eager to keep up the pressure. But how?

In politically normal circumstances you'd build on that structure from the ground up and channel the enthusiasm into local races—beat supervisor, county agent, tax assessor, even sheriff, and so forth—gathering experience and training candidates. With a little help, the party could certainly have mounted effective local campaigns and gotten its political feet wet in that way, whether or not it won first time out. (That Mississippi now has the largest number and proportion of black elected officials in the nation suggests some of this has come to pass.) So why didn't the party do that then? Why was Guyot talking instead about another national campaign and such a far-fetched-sounding one? Simple. The MFDP was not even remotely in a normal political situation in one important respect. Ninety-five percent of the party members could not vote.

But with SNCC's help, the MFDP could run another freedom election. Challenging the congressional elections would again dramatize that small fact: the systematic denial of the most fundamental democratic rights of a citizen. The MFDP again making a way out of no way.

I supported the freedom election mainly because it was action. An organizing tool. Something for the staff and the community to get behind immediately. Remember, the civil rights bill that had passed that summer had been eloquently silent on voting rights. That was the big issue left, and this freedom election was the first step in a larger strategy, the Congressional Challenge. Which was a really far-out, radical, legal, and low-percentage political strategy devised by the MFDP's new lawyers, Arthur Kinoy and Bill Kunstler, to project the question of voting rights into the halls of Congress.

The Freedom Democrats had decided to challenge, if possible, the seating of the Mississippi delegation to the U.S. House of Representatives. There were, however, some problems.

The only people who could bring challenges were candidates who were generally challenging election results and claiming the seats themselves. Such claims are settled by a House vote, usually along partisan lines. Bear in mind that the five Mississippians were Democrats in an overwhelming Democratic House with a collective seniority of something like 235 years among them. So we're talking about unseating some extremely powerful, deeply entrenched Dixiecrat committee chairmen.

The strategic complexity of the Congressional Challenge was never properly reported or generally understood at the time. Perhaps because in many ways the rules of the challenge had to be as arcane, fluid, and insubstantial as the rules of the House itself, which are as notoriously arbitrary and unpredictable as the capricious, ever changeable "will of the majority."

That's one thing I learned. In such matters what is real—forget justice or legality—is whatever a majority says is real. "The House is the only judge of its membership."

So, for example, the right-wing canard that we were childishly "asking" or "expecting" the House to seat three black women from Mississippi purely on the basis of a "mock election" was a deliberate distortion that the media—and our former allies—obligingly picked up and circulated. Of course the House could have seated, should a majority have so chosen, the proverbial "yella dawg." It had the sole power to seat whomever it chose. But we neither asked nor expected that.

What we set out to do was infinitely more subtle, carefully researched, and politically sophisticated, even if as improbable. Listen: Only claimants to a contested seat had "standing" to bring a challenge before the House, which the body could entertain or dismiss as it chose. Because the FDP had been able to run candidates in only three of Mississippi's five districts, we could challenge only three of the five congressmen.

So although our three ladies—Mrs. Gray, Mrs. Hamer, and Mrs. Devine—went through elaborate motions of asserting their claim to the seats, even going so far as to present themselves to the door of the chamber on opening day and seeking admission, fully understanding by prior agreement that they would be turned away, it was all theater. Going through the prescribed motions according to the script.

So our goal was never really to have the MFDP candidates seated (clear justice though that would have been). Nor did we ever plan to bring that issue to a vote. What we hoped to do was force a vote on a "fairness resolution," which would set aside the state's election and hold the seats vacant while the challenge ran its course. In other words, a vote on the denial of the vote to Mississippi's black citizens and the illegality of its electoral system. And we didn't expect to win that vote, if we could get it. Leaving the seats vacant would have been fair. It would also have been historic. For the first time since Reconstruction, the Congress would have denied representation even if only temporarily to a Southern state for disenfranchising its black citizens. But we didn't expect it to.

What we dared hope for on opening day was simply enough support from the floor—against the vigorous bipartisan opposition of the House leadership *and* the Johnson White House—so that they could not simply dismiss the challenge out of hand. For enough member support to keep the challenge alive and moving forward in the prescribed parliamentary channels. This was an elaborate process involving the gathering of evidence, committee hearings, and finally a full House vote on the committee's report.

Nothing was written. It was all dependent on the will of the body, a matter not of law but of raw politics. Could we expect this white men's club to even permit a vote against three of its members who were heavily insulated by seniority and protected by the leadership and the White House? Also, Congress was a far more centralized, rigidly controlled arena than a convention. This new effort was therefore strategically far more complicated and at every point completely at the mercy of powerful, entrenched forces entirely beyond our ability to influence. Chances? Slim or none. Unless, of course, our upstart, inexperienced Washington staff, by now a pariah among the liberals, could perform miracles in the two months before Congress opened. Not very likely. *[Hah! —EMT]*

Those were just our problems *inside* the Congress. *Outside* Congress, our erstwhile liberal allies in Washington were no longer even talking to us and were vigorously and gleefully denouncing the new challenge. Clearly we had failed to understand, they gloated. We still didn't see that the MFDP had reached the gates of the Atlantic City convention only by riding on their broad and generous shoulders. On the strength of *their* patronage and influence. Well, we'd now learn. Capitol Hill was their territory. Without them to open doors, not a single congressman would even talk to us, they predicted confidently. No member would be found dumb or suicidal enough to try to lead our challenge onto the floor. And if one were found, the leadership would never recognize such a cockamamy scheme. And if (fat chance) it did, we'd be lucky to get more than the one vote from the lone member sufficiently deranged as to introduce the challenge in the first place. They couldn't wait for us to fall flat on our collective face and learn political reality the embarrassing way. What we were trying to do was totally impossible.

Except for what happened on January 4, 1965, when the new Congress convened. When Congressman Ryan (peace be unto him, William Fitts

Ryan, D-NY), our lone "maverick," rose to challenge the seating of the three Mississippians, the Speaker did not at first appear to see him. Then some sixty members of both parties rose to their feet behind Congressman Ryan. Too many for the Speaker to overlook. It was insurrectionary, a mini-rebellion of the membership.

The Speaker seemed astonished. "Why does the gentleman rise?"

"To challenge the seating . . . ," Congressman Ryan replied. The Speaker then had to ask the Mississippians to stand aside while the rest of the House was sworn. Consternation in the visitors' and press galleries. First hurdle cleared. But that was only the beginning.

Then Congressman Ryan, joined by James Roosevelt (D-CA), offered the fairness resolution, proposing to keep the seats vacant until new, open, federally supervised elections could take place in the three contested districts. Representative Green called for a polling of the House, and again enough members rose to force a roll call rather than a voice vote.

That was the second big hurdle cleared. Then, once there was a recorded vote, something totally unexpected happened. An astonishing 149 members of the House of Representatives found it necessary to vote to unseat the Mississippians. Of course we lost, and they were then sworn, but we'd kept them out for almost two hours and their seating would be "provisional" while the challenge ran its course in the House. On that vote, the leadership had come within seventy-one votes of losing control of the House. (If seventy-one members had switched their votes to us, we'd have won.) It's hard to say who was the more shocked: the Speaker, the Washington liberal establishment, or the Mississippi power structure.

When those 149 members voted for the challenge, black Mississippi was delighted. Truthfully, I was a little surprised at first. But I really shouldn't have been. I'd come to D.C. with five busloads of our people. Before Congress had reconvened, teams had spread out on the Hill trying to lobby members. The morning of the vote we had to do something with these 250 people. No way we could get them all passes into the House gallery, but they needed to be part of the action, to be doing something. But what? Then, someone remembered the underground passages connecting the various House office buildings to the House chambers. That's where we took the people.

On opening day, as congressmen and their aides made their way through these tunnels, they turned a corner and found themselves passing between two lines of silent, working black men and women from Mississippi. The people, spaced about ten feet apart, stood still as statues, dignified, erect, utterly silent. The double column of black people must have lined over sixty yards of the tunnel. On both sides. It was pure theater, bro.

The congressmen had come by in little groups, each group, a congressman and one or two aides, deep in conversation. They'd turn the corner, and for a moment the sight of our people would stop them dead in their tracks. We didn't move or say a mumbling word. Then the group would walk between the two rows, but now suddenly very silent. It's hard to describe the power of that moment. I looked into the legislators' faces as they passed. Most could not take their eyes off those careworn, tired black faces. Some offered a timid greeting, a smile, or tentative wave. Others flushed and looked down. All seemed startled. Some clearly nervous, even afraid. All seemed deeply affected in some way. Our people just stood there and looked at them.

For these lawmakers using the tunnels that morning, that impassive, profoundly physical presence was an unexpected confrontation with reality. That grave, mute presence became the most effective and eloquent of testimonies. To those passing congressmen, the issue of Southern political injustice could no longer remain an abstract statistic, distant and dismissable. In the reality of the people's presence that dismal history became tangible and immediate with an inescapably human dimension. As they went in to cast their vote—for or against—those legislators would have to see and feel again the force of that black presence and those unsmiling faces. Of that I was convinced.

I believe that many of the Democrats who voted for us may have been in Atlantic City and were denied a vote there. Under the steady, silent gazes of the people in that underground tunnel, their consciences were awakened and the Republicans (the ones whose votes we got) remembered that they belonged to the party of Lincoln. I think the people's presence had a lot to do with those 149 votes.

The liberal *lobby*, at least the faction led by Joe Rauh and Clarence Mitchell who had been bad-mouthing the challenge, could not quite hide their embarrassment and dismay. Yeah, we hadn't won the vote, but then we hadn't expected to. We'd prayed for fifty votes, hoped for forty, and would have been overjoyed with thirty. Gimme a break, we weren't the fools they said we were. We'd gotten everything we'd hoped to get and more.

Put that way it sounds like a great victory, huh? Right. Let us be quite clear now. That is the kind of distortion that comes from insider thinking and insider politics. In those terms the compromise at Atlantic City was also a "great victory," right? The Mississippi congressmen saw this vote as a defeat. The liberal lobbyists saw it as an embarrassment. The MFDP lawyers *[William Kunstler and Arthur Kinoy]* and Thelwell and Jan Goodman in the Washington office were of course elated. Of course it was an accomplishment. But a victory? Hey, step back and take an objective look. What had really happened?

For over seventy years the State of Mississippi had, as a matter of policy, trampled the basic political rights of nearly half a million American citizens. That wasn't a secret. Everybody knew that, the people, the president, the Congress. Would this nation have tolerated any of that for a second if those half million citizens had been Irish, Jewish, or Catholic Americans? We know the answer to that one.

So now the African people of Mississippi had confronted the Congress with the opportunity—indeed the duty—to repudiate this blatant violation of our rights and their Constitution. What happened? By that vote, the House leadership and a majority of members had, in effect, endorsed Mississippi state racism. How's that a victory? Give credit to the minority of conscience, those 149 members who had been moved to take a clear moral stand. More power to them! But what does that "moral victory" really say about American democracy? So I wouldn't call it any "victory." But to the extent it was a loss, it wasn't our loss. That's for sure.

Instead of being summarily dismissed, we'd forced a roll call. And instead (as the totalitarian liberals had predicted) of one vote at most, we'd gotten 149. And this not only without any help at all from them, but despite their vigorous attempts at sabotage. They should have been ashamed. The NAACP national leadership hadn't supported us. In fact their Washington lobbyist led the "pay-no-attention, the civil rights leadership isn't touching that foolishness" camp. But most of their local chapters had written or visited their local congressional representatives. The AFL hadn't done anything, but several progressive locals had.

[To begin the campaign we'd called a meeting in Washington to brief potential supporters nationwide. About a hundred activists representing various organizations showed up. The usual suspects: students, sandaled intellectuals, tweedy academics, clerics, black activists, essentially a middle-class and professional gathering. In the midst of this, two guys, obviously working class, stood out. Clearly they knew no one in the room. They stood together wearing bad suits, heavy-soled brogans, and crew cuts, looking uncomfortable indeed.

After our candidates spoke, I gave a detailed explanation of the complicated challenge process and the discussion began. Long, involved, speculative questions. The two did not join in the posturing and theorizing. I kept smiling at them trying to figure who they might be. I knew they could not be the Man, for not even the FBI could do such a piss poor casting job. (We later discovered that the FBI had been present. They leaked better minutes of the meeting to the Washington Post *than we had in the office.)*

"C'mere, kid." The little one with the broken nose and cauliflower ears motioned me over. "Nice job, kid. Good presentation. Very cleah."

He didn't seem any older than I, but I let the "kid" pass and thanked him.

"We from the UE (Union of Electricians). Jim Matlas sent us to check youse out."

"Oh, welcome, brothers."

"We leaving now, kid, seen enough. Whadda ya need?"

I told them votes and money.

"The AFL supportin' youse? . . . Tha's what I thought. Scab bastids." He thought for a minute, then named two Pennsylvania congressmen, Representative Green and another member whose name I forget.

"Whaddaboud dese two guys. Dey wicha?" I explained that neither gentlemen had been returning our calls.

"Izzat right? Creeps won't return your calls, huh? Figures, da finks. Arright. Doan worry aboud it, kid. You got 'em. You got 'em. An' doan worry, dere'll be a contribution from the union too." And with that they left.

That was a Saturday afternoon. I got to the office that Monday at about nine.

"Mike, you late," Jan Goodman greeted me. "Congressman Green's office's already called for you four times. And another Pennsylvania congressman's called a couple times too."

Two class-conscious workers—and a strong union—are worth a thousand students, I thought. In about a week, the UE check came. —EMT]

The Leadership Conference on Civil Rights hadn't supported us, but many church organizations within the conference had. I learned something from that. Not every congressional district in the country has labor unions. But they all have churches. And in those days, many of those churches had active social action groups, which had supported us. Unfortunately most of these church groups seem to have been infiltrated and hijacked by the lunatic right in recent years. Very unfortunate for the country.

What we did have going for us was a widespread popular indignation across the nation. The volunteers, their parents, friends, and all the people who had come through Mississippi that summer. Delegates who'd been denied a vote in Atlantic City and simple decent citizens who'd been outraged and shamed by each new revelation. The MFDP Washington Office working with the Friends of SNCC network had done an incredible job mobilizing these popular forces to bring pressure on the House membership. And, as the vote showed, it had worked beyond the expectations of all the media experts and Beltway "insiders."

If the Washington liberal insiders were embarrassed, the Mississippi power structure was traumatized. I mean *traumatized,* Jack. One of the challenged congressmen was reported to have experienced a "slight" heart attack and was under doctors' care. He recovered. "Our beloved state has been betrayed," thundered the *Jackson Clarion Ledger.* "One hundred and forty-nine members of Congress voted to deny three of our duly elected representatives their seats and the State of Mississippi three-fifths [they didn't see the historical irony] of our representation in the U.S. House of Representatives." *Unthinkable. Shameful.*

The governor (Paul Johnson) hastily circulated a letter to all state offices—voting registrars, law enforcement, judiciary, everybody—urging "restraint, courtesy," and a cessation of violence at least while the state was under this "cruel spotlight of Congressional scrutiny." See, the size of the vote meant that the challenge would now have to go forward in Congress. The seating of the three was "provisional." Only the "fairness" resolution vacating the seats had been voted down. The state officialdom was shaken. I mean in serious shock, Jack!

The governor, the senators, the challenged congressmen, and a bunch of local officials meekly accepted subpoenas from MFDP lawyers, numbers of whom had volunteered to come into the state to take their depositions. The MFDP were informed that their lawyers would be more than welcome in the courthouses, the state house, even the governor's office, for that purpose. "Mighty hospitable of y'all, gentlemens," said the MFDP executive. "Mighty kind. But y'all be right welcome in *our* community too. Be mighty 'bliged if you'll come on over." They didn't want their people to have to go into those state buildings and courthouses with their histories of white power and black humiliation. Going there might intimidate our people. Let's see if we can't get them over on *our* territory. We been going to them for years, hat in hand. Now let's see if they won't come to us. And they did, Jack!

These suddenly chastened white Mississippi politicians and their lawyers came, polite as you please, to the Masonic temple or to small Delta churches, packed to the rafters with their black fellow citizens. I said, now look at this. Southern chivalry, Jack. I mean it was courtesy titles *all ovah* the place. "Yes, *sir;* no, *madam; Mr.* This, *Mrs.* That." Man, the peoples had them a field day. Some claimed they'd racked their brains for questions to ask, "jes' to hear that white man say 'yes, ma'am' or 'no, sir' to me one more time."

The MFDP and their supporters kept that challenge going through the Congress for nine months. By September, the voting rights bill was in committee. The final vote dismissing the challenge was in September. So technically, the MFDP lost. The challenge was dismissed. But I tell you what, it helped pass the voting rights act. In fact, quiet as it's kept, the Congressional Challenge was a major factor in the passage of that important legislation.

A lot of the members who had voted to dismiss the Challenge sent earnest letters to constituents trying to justify their vote. They were, they explained, firmly committed to the voting rights bill, which would finally take care of this national disgrace once and for all. *[Really? What would they now make of the Florida presidential election of 2000? —EMT]*

Consequently, they argued, it seemed unnecessarily disruptive to kick out any sitting members at this time. That was their out on the challenges, but the voting rights bill passed.

After Mr. Louis Allen's murder, Bob had said that we needed something bold to jump-start the Mississippi movement. Well, you could say, Freedom Summer did that in spades. But with some unanticipated long-term consequences for the organization. A project of that size is bound to have consequences, but *whoa*.

People who said "Mississippi ain't never goin' be the same" were right. But only in specific ways. In black Mississippi certainly, some oppressive—carefully constructed and brutally enforced—psychological barriers had been breached forever. Once the people saw their friends and neighbors on TV publicly fighting the white power structure of the state to a standstill, that genie was out of the bottle forever, Jack. But in hard political and economic terms, conditions were, of course, still as grim as they ever were. That work remained (and much unfortunately still does) to be done.

But what really and fundamentally would never be the same was SNCC. Whether or not we fully understood that then, it was true: SNCC could never go back to being the organization/family it had once been or perceived itself to be. The organization would have to change. Our understanding of ourselves would have to change. Both internally and externally the organization would need to face a whole new set of issues and decisions, and not only in Mississippi. But the extent of that would only gradually become clear as we began to assess our new circumstances. And that at a time when, emotionally drained, the staff was not really in the best shape for that kind of fundamental decision-making.

Internally SNCC was in flux. Over the summer, Mississippi had commandeered organizational attention and sucked in staff and resources from other states. Our projects in Alabama, southwest Georgia, Arkansas, and Cambridge, Maryland, had almost been placed on hold. (For example, most of the NAG organizers who would have worked in Cambridge that summer were with me in the Delta, leaving Bro Reggie Robinson to help Gloria Richardson keep the movement going there.) Even the national office had been moved from Atlanta to Mississippi. And now many of the key people were in Africa. Organizationally then, SNCC was temporarily decentered. And in human terms too.

Some of our most experienced fighters, bone tired and burned-out, needed to drop out for a while. They—usually very responsible people—began to "float" between projects or off on their own. Others, no less stressed, were doggedly running in place, trying to hold the pieces together and maintain some order and direction in what was almost a vacuum.

Then too there was the matter of scale. SNCC now had a heightened presence and visibility nationally. As a result, the organization would soon be confronting unfamiliar problems of growth and affluence: "success, American style." What terror couldn't accomplish, a temporarily fat bank account might? Only in America.

Thanks largely to heroic efforts of Friends of SNCC groups in New York and California, SNCC, for the first time in its existence, had some dollars in the bank. At least to us it looked like some very long bread, Jack. Someone said over two hundred and fifty grand. Unreal. "That ain't SNCC, man." Unbelievable. But true . . . for a hot minute.

But overnight the staff—which means the organization—was fixing to double in size. *Overnight,* Jack. Say what, add almost two hundred new people to the payroll. (A payroll that, as it was, frequently never came.) How could such a huge new obligation ever be sustained? As it turned out, the cost would prove the least of SNCC's problems where that was concerned. There even was serious discussion about hiring a professional fund-raising agency. That was rejected. Too corporate. Too potentially corrupting. Fund-raising should stay political, the way it was with the Friends of SNCC. Then too SNCC now owned property, a fleet of new cars, the famous Sojourner Motor Fleet (SMF). A building would come later.

Now that's a story. How did SNCC come by some twenty-three spanking-new light green Plymouth Savoys? A Kremlin subsidy channeled through Fidel Castro, as the Klan and some Dixiecrat congressmen maintained? (In which case they would have been Ladas, not Plymouths.)

The way we got them was actually exactly the opposite—American market capitalism in action. So, how did SNCC come into possession of twenty-three brand-new, midsize, medium-priced products of the American automobile industry? The United Auto Workers fronted for us, that's how. As part of its labor contract, the union was entitled to purchase "product" at cost. A progressive, mostly black UAW local in Detroit bought the cars and sold them to us. What amazed us was the numbers. The retail price of these cars to the American consumer was, I believe, something like $3,600. SNCC paid almost $800 each, or about two-tenths of the sticker price. *That* apparently was what they cost General Motors to build. So *eight-tenths* of the sticker price was inflated by merchandising: advertising, middlemen, and corporate profits? I couldn't believe those figures. But we got the cars.

Getting them at all, and at that price, seemed miraculous. But with SNCC drivers, keeping them running and insured turned into a major, major expense and headache. Someone in Atlanta went and painted the SNCC logo, black and white hands clasped, on the sides of the cars. The field staff who would have had to drive those targets in the Deep South were outraged. As was the insurance company, which flat out refused to insure any car flaunting so provocative an insignia, so off they came. Keeping track of the cars was another question. I wouldn't be at all surprised if in some Southern rural counties the last survivors of the Sojourner Motor Fleet were still hauling passengers. Just like in the third world. I'd sure like to think so.

Course every project wanted one of these babies. Prior to the SMF, what we'd had, and been glad to get, was old family cars that were just about on their last oil change. In progressive families, when it came time to replace the family car, instead of trading them in the owners would send them to SNCC, pleased that old faithful would be devoting whatever mileage was left in its worn pistons to the cause of freedom.

But these new cars, Jack. After George Greene and his boys got finished souping them up, the Klan cars didn't stand a chance out on the highway. Luckily, the insurance company didn't know about that.

Also, with our new prosperity came the beginning of a new press scrutiny, which became more much critical and most times flat-out unfair. It was, I now see, the opening salvo of the generation gap that would characterize press coverage of the politics of the late sixties. And it wasn't just a reevaluation of the organization.

As though to compensate for the praise they had been so free with during the summer, elements of the national media now began to reevaluate the SNCC volunteers in an ugly way. Maybe, after all, they were (especially the women) merely spoiled, overindulged, rich white kids looking for a "black experience." Which by their definition had to be sexual. I found this to be all-round insulting, to our people as well as to the women volunteers, and transparently stupid. Maybe the prurient racial/sexual hang-ups that we'd associated with Mississippi cops and the Klan were really a national sickness of white American culture after all.

I mean, gimme a break. Why on earth would any affluent, young, white college woman, intent on a summer of sexual adventure across the color line, choose a destination with a violent history, hostile natives, high risk, crowded and "primitive" living conditions, little privacy, hard work, constant tension, and a nervous host community vigilant for and intolerant of any sign of sexual impropriety? Over places like the south of France, the Village scene, or some Caribbean tourist trap where they could have their "black experience" in relative luxury, safety, and exotic surroundings?

Almost thirty years later we were at a reunion/conference in Hartford. There, veterans of the movement were rehashing all aspects. On one especially good panel, I thought, SNCC women—black and white—talked about their experiences. I was pleased to see that what they remembered and understood was exactly what I remembered. Then, at some point, this white guy, a psychologist as I recall, gets up. And says in effect, "This is all very interesting. I'm married to a Summer Project volunteer myself. And there's one important thing I haven't heard discussed all confer-ence—*the sexual exploitation of white women.*" The movement people—staff and volunteers—looked at each other in silent amazement for a minute. Then everyone started laughing or woofing at the guy. "Yo, man, go ask yo' wife." "Hey, come interview me, I'll tell all." It was disheartening.

Hindsight is truly wonderful. Looking back, things tend to seem so much clearer that you feel like a dummy for not having seen them in the first place. That fall, winter, and spring, I remember pure chaos within the organization, as though too much was happening too quickly. But it's pos-sible that it could have felt more like chaos than it actually was. Because, in hindsight, I can see patterns behind all the motion and confusion, a certain logic and inevitability that was not at all clear at the time.

As I've said, there had been rapid changes within SNCC. Also, the country's political landscape was shifting seriously. There were, though we could not have known it, the beginnings of some unprecedented, extraor-dinary developments in the political culture of the country. We in SNCC would find ourselves at the center of much of this ferment, having to try to deal with both—the internal and the external—at the same time.

[In 1965 the national "political landscape" would indeed shift dramatically. Among other things, we would witness the assassination of Malcolm X in New York; in Alabama the last massive march of the civil rights coalition; in Wash-ington the passage of the voting rights act; and in Los Angeles, the first in a series of explosive and disruptive urban insurrections. All of which would have far-reaching effects on SNCC as an organization and on the evolution of Carmichael's political thought. —EMT]

This period, as I can clearly see now, was only the beginning. This fast-forwarding of events would continue over the life of the organization. Bob Moses used to say that in the movement time was compressed: that in Mississippi we lived a normal year's experience in a month's time. Well, that escalation was fixing to go national on us.

From the beginning SNCC had needed and was able to define itself as it went along. Now, at the end of the summer, the need for this kind of self-evaluation had become crucial. We needed almost constantly to assess our changed situation, our resources, our direction, and our will. We needed general agreement on changing goals and direction as well as on the programs and policies that would get us there.

Hey, no problem, call a staff meeting. That's always worked in the past. So when folks got back from Guinea, that's exactly what we did. Three or four times. But the staff meetings sure weren't the same. The earlier staff meetings were relatively small. Then people tended to know each other, have similar experiences and a common vocabulary. People who worked in offices sat in with the field staff and left feeling deeply involved at a frontline level. Given time enough, we could usually reach something approaching a consensus and leave the meeting with a feeling of closeness, agreement, and direction. It wasn't easy but it had been possible. And most important, everyone left with a sense of unity and of participation, of understanding and having contributed to how and why a given policy had evolved.

Now a staff meeting was a very different animal. Veteran staff would arrive as usual from southwest Georgia, Alabama, Arkansas, to find a multitude of new faces, the Mississippi volunteers. Then Northern staff from the New York and Washington offices would arrive. Then first-time volunteers and staff from Friends of SNCC in California, New Jersey, Michigan, Boston. These were from college towns. People who had worked hard, sending money, support, publicity, and volunteers into the South. Most were serious people with a long-term political commitment to the work of the organization who had earned the right to participate fully. But among them there had to be some faddists, getting on the bandwagon of what they saw as the newest "hot" political thing going. And, I'm afraid, one or two must secretly have been in government employ.

SNCC had no mechanism for handling meetings of this size and composition. SNCC's usual process of decision-making became unworkable. A recipe for confusion. Yet, the moment you say that, you gotta think again. Because some of it was creative confusion. But much was just that: confusion. But the issues were real enough. And the internal needs of the organization were alarmingly real and constantly changing.

What and who is the real SNCC? With this large, diffuse group, how do we handle decision-making? Obviously by vote, but who can vote? More important, who cannot? And who's going tell them you ain't got the right? How do we structure and administer this sprawling organization? Can SNCC staff be fired? If so, who can do it? And by what process? I can't believe we're even asking a question like that. What does that say about what SNCC is becoming? What we need to be discussing is program. With the passage of the civil rights bill, what should our political program now be? What happens when the voting rights act is a reality?

One group, led by Jim Forman—mostly black Southern staff and most NAG folk—argued for a more centralized administrative structure, clear and enforceable policies, and greater accountability from staff. I agreed in principle, but the devil was in the details. Besides, I couldn't really think of anyone in SNCC with either the desire or the personality to impose that kind of bureaucratic control.

Another group—the "Freedom Highs"—were opposed on principle. "That's nothing but a bureaucratic coup. Creating an administrative hierarchy. C'mon, that's not SNCC. That's the NAACP. SNCC is freedom of ideas and conscience. The only way we can continue to do what we've done is by being free 'to do what the spirit say do.' Bureaucracy will crush life and creativity out of SNCC." The discussions went downward from there.

An awful lot of time and energy went into these debates, which only grew more divisive and heated. I remember some long, inconclusive, and frustrating meetings in which the only thing that became indisputably clear was that the present system (or lack of it) simply wasn't working.

Some very smart and intellectually forceful people were in those meetings. All kinds of position papers, analyses, and proposals got circulated and discussed. A few were prophetic—the question of the Vietnam War, and student responsibility to oppose it; the status of women, and a women's movement. But some were strange, Jack.

One argument for "full participatory democracy" called for "all SNCC staff, volunteers, and *community people* to constitute a permanent and continuous decision-making body." All staff? Unemployment was high, but most community people had jobs or work. Presumably the sole purpose of SNCC would now be the *process* of making truly democratic decisions. Who then would implement them? Jesse Morris answered with a proposal for a powerful decision-making executive committee with membership to be limited to black Southern staff with less than a high school education. Folks didn't know exactly how to take that proposal. Jesse was a bright, enigmatic brother, and one could not always tell how serious he was being. Jesse is the brother who came up with the idea of the Poor People's Corporation to provide income to people being displaced. The PPC taught crafts and supplied materials to unemployed people and sold the products in PPC stores in New York and California. Jesse organized that operation and kept it going for years.

SNCC had clearly outgrown the old ways, but the conventional alternative that sounded more and more like a hierarchical bureaucracy was none too appealing either.

It was frustrating for everyone. But it was most painful for the Southern field staff, for those young Africans whose lives had been given new meaning and possibility by the very movement that their courage and sacrifice had made happen. Now what *was* this, this . . . debating society with so many new, strange-sounding white folk and its array of little cliques and alliances forming and reforming? They wanted back the SNCC they had joined and created. The audacious SNCC with the clear sense of direction and purpose they'd come to know. I'm talking about the Mary Lanes, Curtis Hayes Muhammads, the Annie Pearl Averys, the Peacock brothers, the Randy Battles, Jesse Harrises, Hollis Watkinses, the Willie Rickses (Mukasa), and so many others who had been our shock troops and (no pun intended) the soul of the organization.

I don't think I'm exaggerating all this, but I am compressing it a lot. Besides, the fractious atmosphere I'm describing was almost only at those meetings where the entire organization came together. Out on the projects the work went forward more or less as usual.

[Indeed, it was at one of these fevered meetings that the brother uttered his allegedly "majorly sexist" sound bite re "the position of women." The one line, grossly misrepresented, egregiously and gleefully recycled, by which and apparently only by which he is remembered in certain politically correct feminist circles. Oy vay!

When invited to revisit that moment for clarification in this book, the brother disdained to do so, a palpable impatience apparent in his voice.

"Hey, Thelwell, I said it, period."

But having been present at its utterance, therefore aware of the context and the subsequent perverse and ongoing misuse of the line to discredit not only Carmichael but all of us, I persisted.

"Look, man, I actually didn't even remember saying it. It was the next morning that Cleve told me that I had. 'Really?' I asked. 'I said that?' 'Oh, yes, you did, brother,' Cleve said. That's how I know I did."

Clearly, on that score, the brother felt no pressing need to justify himself in these pages. And, I imagine, especially not before the councils of the ideologically self-righteous. Nor do I feel any such need on his account, since the testimony of his life is eloquent on that issue. What follows, therefore, is included simply in service to the truth of the historical record.

It happened at the Waveland meeting where Mary King and Casey Hayden's pioneering position paper on the role of women in the movement had first been circulated. The first informed account of the incident would come years later in Freedom Song, *Mary's invaluable movement memoir.*

Mary King:

"Even if our meetings were intense and there were hostile interchanges, afterward there was always music, with beer and dancing late into the night, and our basic affection for each other would flow across the wounds of the day's diatribes. Waveland was no different.

"One night, in the charged atmosphere of the retreat, a group of us gravitated toward the pier with a gallon of wine . . . we talked and laughed among ourselves . . . seeking humor to salve the hurts of the day.

"Stokely Carmichael, handsome, gregarious, and sinewy, had an elongated frame and an easy smile that flashed across his face warming up the environment around him. . . . Stokely had the ability to joke like a professional stand-up comedian, a facile wit accompanied by an amazing capacity for sustained humor that reflected his high intelligence. He had been called Stokely Starmichael the summer before in Mississippi because of his natural celebrity. Cracking jokes one after another, he usually made fun of himself and the people of Trinidad more than of anyone else. It was the same this night. Casey,

Mendy Samstein, Carole Merritt, a beautiful black woman ... and several others of us were beginning to mellow after the traumatic meetings. We were soothed by the gentle Gulf winds that were still warm in November, the lapping waves, and the wine. . . .

"Stokely started one of his monologues. He led slowly and then began to warm up. One humorous slap followed another. We became more and more relaxed. We stretched out on the pier, lying with our heads on each others' abdomens. We were absorbed by the flow of his humor and our laughter. He reveled in our attention as we were illuminated by the moon. Stokely got more and more carried away. He stood up, slender and muscular. . . . He began to gesticulate dramatically, slapping his thighs and spinning around . . . silhouetted against the moon like a Javanese shadow puppet . . . he made fun of himself and then he dressed down Trinidadians. He started joking about black Mississippians. He made fun of everything that crossed his agile mind. Finally, he turned to the meetings under way and the position papers. He came to the no-longer-anonymous paper on women. Looking straight at me, he grinned broadly and shouted, 'What is the position of women in SNCC?' Answering himself, he responded, 'The position of women in SNCC is prone!' (Of course he meant supine. —EMT) *Stokely threw back his head and roared outrageously with laughter. We all collapsed with hilarity. His ribald comment was uproarious and wild. It drew us all closer together . . . even in that moment, he was poking fun at his own attitudes.*

*"Casey and I felt, and continue to feel, that Stokely was one of the most responsive men at the time that our anonymous paper appeared in 1964."** ✷

I can personally attest to the accuracy of Mary's account. I too remember well the prevailing mood of tension, uncertainty, and emotional fatigue that Mary describes. What I do remember distinctly—in fact will never forget—is the moment it changed. And how surprised and impressed I'd been at the art *in the brother's performance on that long dock. For it was exactly that—a performance.*

My surprise and delight was at its sheer energy. The skill in improvisation: the dead-on mimicry, the procession of subtly developed, irreverent, wickedly clever, politically incorrect lines, delivered with impeccable comic timing. I recall a sly wit and a bubbling good humor that, as Mary describes, was infectious.

As a comic routine, it would not have been out of place on any public stage in the country. (Maybe not in Mississippi.) But on that particular evening, in that company and in those circumstances on that Gulf Coast jetty, it was quite extraordinary, cathartic even.

Out of nowhere and all of a sudden there was Stokely in flight, doing a series of comic routines built around characters and situation. To me, some—one in particular—seemed entirely too polished and skillful not to have been professionally

✷Freedom Song, pp. 451–52.

developed and rehearsed, though I couldn't see how they could have been. In others, so it seemed to me, the quality of driven intensity to the performance bordered on possession.

Over the years I'd known the brother, more than occasionally, to play the clown. But this was craft of a different order. Where, I marveled, was all this coming from? Upon what atavistic sources was the brother drawing? Because it did seem cultural: very much in the calypso/African tradition. The spontaneous improvising of ironic commentary against the prevailing communal follies of the day.

The bit that first caught my attention was his dramatization of a disastrous pulpit audition. A seminary-trained, ostentatiously overeducated young preacher giving a trial sermon to a rural congregation in his hometown. The accents were Trinidadian, but the cultural dynamic could just as well have been rural Mississippi.

Carmichael did all the parts, miming gestures and expressions, reproducing voices and accents. As with the multidimensional performance repertoire of an African tale-teller, the total effect defies representation on the page. The subtle vocal nuances and comic effects can only be suggested as the teller moved back and forth between pulpit and congregation.

First, the barely concealed pride of the mother fanning herself expectantly in the ahmen corner. Then a veritable Greek chorus of foot-tapping sisters, barely able to restrain their eagerness to "git happy in the Lord."

Enter the young minister full of ego and erudition. He is a tad foppish and very "refined." He delicately mops his brow, then stands immobile, hands clasped, preening himself in their admiration. A discreet clearing of the throat while he waits for their complete silence and total attention.

A fine entrance, but the follow-up? Mixed reviews at first. Instead of the down-home preaching the sisters anticipate, the popinjay delivers a lecture. No matter how the sisters try to help him up, he refuses to whoop and holler in the spirit, and clearly nobody is goin' git happy in that church. Instead, he insists on lecturing in this dry-as-dust academese with a distressing pedantic delivery. The mother's pride slowly turns to dismay. The sisters' raised eyebrows and quizzical expressions rapidly become audible indignation and signifying.

"But, dis ain no preachin', chile."

"Mi dear, best wake me when the preachin' start, eh?"

That was funny enough: the intergenerational clash of cultural style and expectation, old-fashioned sensibilities versus an educated, acquired snobbery.

Then it really got wicked as an unexpected dimension was introduced.

As he warms to his task, the young preacher's mannerisms, already prissy, become positively effete. Also, we begin to detect a faint lisp, which becomes more pronounced as he gets into the lecture. The text, which seemed at first quite innocuous, becomes less so.

"My real thubject today ith"—pause—"Jethus' love for mankind." He *pauses, glares challengingly at the congregation, nods primly, dabs at his pursed mouth daintily, and repeats, "Jethus' love of man . . . kind. Yeth indeed."*

Troubled looks, visibly growing apprehension among the sisters. Can there be an unspoken agenda emerging?

"Far as the gothpel of St. John tells uth . . . clearly . . . Jethus had a beloved dithiple, yeth he did." Emphatic nodding. Points a long finger into the text. "Yeth, indeed, it seth so right here, John . . . wath . . . hith . . . beloved dithiple. Aha!" He glares down at the church.

"An' and moreover" . . . long, triumphant, smug stare—"the gothpel tells us, it seth, 'When Jethus saw him enter'—pause, nod—" 'he fell on hith neck' "—arched eyebrows—" 'and he kithed *him.' " Long, challenging, triumphant smirk.*

"Oh, yeth, he did, Jethus kithed him." Yeth indeed.

Case closed. So there.

After that came the press conference. Topical with more familiar types, it was funny enough. But I found it less original and its targets too easy. A dumbish, smugly white journalist shooting the usually aggressively misinformed questions to a civil rights worker who is either putting him on or is, himself, not right bright. That is never quite clear, but it is a comedy of errors: the blind leading the bland. The reporter's manner becomes more overbearing and pompous as his questions become more absurd and the answers more inept. It had to be obvious to all present that this satiric blade was cutting both ways. Or so I thought. That was the context of the infamous sequence by no means either the most outrageous or the cleverest. In fact, at the time, I found it forgettable and promptly did so. Until, that is, I saw it taking on a life of its own. Goddamn incredible, I thought. Of all the funny lines the brother said that night, is that the only *one some idiot remembered? Depressing.*

This sorry tale does, however, have one encouraging footnote, which concerns Carmichael's obituary in the New York Times. *When the brother died in 1998, I awaited the* Times *obit with unusual interest. It proved quite a document. Covering almost two-thirds of a page, it managed in that journal's inimitable manner to get every name and date right and every meaning and truth wrong. Not unexpectedly it recapitulated every last cliché of establishment opinion to deny the slightest political influence, consequence, or significance to the brother's contribution. So much so in fact that a major question leapt out: Why would the editors devote so much space to a life, in their assertion, of such surpassing irrelevance?*

But I found, or rather, was pleased not to find what I was looking for: any mention of this old "the position of women" canard. As the only disparaging myth that was missing, its absence was quite conspicuous. I had particularly looked for it because I knew of an intervention by two admirably principled women who just happened to be white intellectuals.

After Ture's illness became terminal, Mary King and Francesca Poletta—

a young Columbia sociologist who has done extensive research and some perceptive and original scholarly writing on SNCC—contacted the Times *obituary department. They gave them the facts and evidence on this issue and a stern injunction not to once again recycle and perpetuate this crap. Obviously, they prevailed, for given the tone of the piece, the absence of that myth was notable. Mary, Francesca, nuff respect. —EMT]*

This period of internal inclarity happened at a crucial time in the history of the movement and for SNCC as an organization, the worst time possible. Things were changing rapidly. *[For example, at one of those staff meetings, word reached us of Malcolm's assassination. —EMT]*

For one thing, though we found this out only later, our heightened political visibility had earned us unwanted attention from a new set of enemies. Apart from the alienation of the older generation of liberals who should have been our allies and defenders, the feds had begun continuous and hostile surveillance. The FBI started plotting to "neutralize" us and actively infiltrating agents to that end—apparently even Military Intelligence was involved. So now the federal government was picking up the dirty work that the Mississippi Sovereignty Commission and the Alabama Anti-Subversive Agency, the so-called Red Squad had been doing rather ineffectively all along.

By the end of spring, for a number of reasons, I would ask to transfer out of Mississippi. Having graduated from Howard, I was now a full-time SNCC organizer. Like so many other SNCC parents, my mother was eager for me to get into graduate school immediately if not sooner. No way. I knew my life's work would be the struggle for my people's liberation. However, Mississippi, where I'd served my apprenticeship, was clearly not the best situation for what I thought was now necessary.

[The continuing-education question seems to have been recurrent. Mrs. Carmichael remembers one instance from the period: "I don't know exactly who made the offer, but it was from Harvard. A full scholarship for him to do a master's and Ph.D. in philosophy. At first he didn't tell me. But when he did, I said, 'Boy, remember I could hardly afford Howard, and this is Harvard. Are you crazy?' So he told them that he wanted to travel for a year. Then later he told them, thanks, but they should give the scholarship to a needy student. I said, 'Now I know you crazy.' He said, 'May Charles, we can settle this. You bring any Ph.D. you can find anywhere and let us argue in front of you, and you'll see who will win. I don't need a Ph.D. for what I have to do.'" —EMT]

After he returned from Africa, Bob Moses seemed to be withdrawing. As leader (a concept he was never comfortable with) of the Mississippi project for three years, he'd endured unrelieved pressure. Incredible pressures. His example of resourcefulness, tenacity, and humanity had made him a kind of political and spiritual guru to the staff. Something else he had certainly never sought. Each new murder, beginning with Mr. Lee's, up to the Neshoba killings, had been another moral and psychic shock to his spirit. The emotional and physical demands of being the steady rock holding up the weight of the Summer Project had upped the emotional ante. The behavior of the political establishment and the liberals was another bitter lesson. Through all this, Bob always seemed to accept responsibility for everyone—staff, local people, the volunteers. So I could understand, as we all could, how the brother might have reached the limit of human endurance. How any human being would need to lay that burden down. I think we all felt deeply for the brother. He was loved. But we could do little, for Bob was a very private person.

One night he came into one of those staff meetings and said he was not, and had never sought to be, a "leader." From that moment on he wanted to be considered merely another field secretary. To emphasize that, he was no longer to be known as Bob Moses, but Robert Parris, his mother's maiden name. Then most startling to everyone who knew him, he said, as though to finally lay to rest the baggage of his old identity, that he would no longer talk to whites. Then, leaving a troubled silence behind him, he walked out of the room. And eventually out of sight and contact. Later I heard he was in Africa, where he would spend ten years teaching in a village school.

[After Bob walked out of that meeting at the Union Theological Seminary in Atlanta, he would never again be present in a SNCC meeting. He drifted for a while, becoming an active force in the emerging student mobilization against the war in Vietnam. Speaking at a number of early national rallies in Washington and New York, he related American behavior in Vietnam to racial conditions in Mississippi. "Don't use Mississippi as a lightning rod, use it as a looking glass."

Feeling both targeted and exposed when—at the age of thirty-one—he received a draft notice, Bob went underground and eventually to Canada. (Probably lucky for the military, which may well have found itself hard-pressed to handle a draftee of Bob's character, political clarity, unbreakable will, and moral intelligence.)

In a recent conversation, the brother confided something quite provocative as well as revealing about his frame of mind during that period of political uncertainty. While underground, he reflected on the assassinations of JFK, Malcolm, and others. Bob says he posed himself a hypothetical: Just supposing that these assassinations represent the opening salvo of a systematic right-wing offensive to decapitate the movement, who would be the next logical targets? The key figures to be neutralized to stop the movement? "I had quite a list, but my short list had five names: Martin Luther King Jr., Robert F. Kennedy, Stephen Currier (of the Taconic Foundation), Reverend Bob Spike (of the National Council of Churches), and James Farmer (of CORE)." Of the five, only Mr. Farmer died of natural causes. Before the decade was out, Dr. King and Robert Kennedy would be shot down within weeks of each other. Mr. Currier was lost in a plane crash (Edward, the remaining Kennedy brother, would survive a similar plane crash), and Dr. Spike was found murdered in a motel.

Bob left Canada for Tanzania, where he married a SNCC colleague, Janet Jemmott. The couple spent two years teaching in a village school and started a family. After the Carter amnesty, the Moses family returned after a ten-year exile. Janet became a physician and Bob used a MacArthur "genius" grant to develop a revolutionary early-intervention method for teaching algebra.

"Mathematical literacy is to black youth in the information age what voting rights were to black sharecroppers in the civil rights movement." Using organizing techniques developed in SNCC, Moses and his associates have grown the Algebra Project into a national organization extending into school systems across the nation. They have also created a Mississippi Foundation, which works in social development. All of which is discussed in his recent book written with Charlie Cobb, Radical Equations: Math Literacy and Civil Rights. *Moses is not only one of the most extraordinary figures in an extraordinary generation, but he is still one of the nation's most effective organizers. Nuff respect. —EMT]*

That affected me deeply. I felt a responsibility to carry on the work Bob had given so much of himself to. But in Mississippi? Not necessarily. Now, up to this point, the MFDP was without a doubt the best—most fully realized—example of SNCC's organizing vision. Seeing ourselves as catalysts for strong local organizations. Not building empires or seeking to perpetuate ourselves institutionally. Organizers who brought technical resources—information and training—to communities and then left. The idea being to leave behind us strong, representative grassroots organizations with indigenous leadership. Communities capable of carrying on the struggle in their own interests.

As I said, we used to joke that to the extent we succeeded, those very groups we'd helped develop would be the ones who would one day have to invite us to leave. The trick for us would be to recognize that day coming one day before the people did. With the party in Mississippi, I thought I could see that time approaching. But it wasn't simple. On the one hand they did have a solid base and strong leadership. They certainly were capable of charting their own direction independent of SNCC. The Congressional Challenge, for example. But they were a young organization with no full-time support staff. That was us. Clearly we had to provide any technical support they requested until they no longer needed us. But doing so without pushing our ideas of what their best interests were or their programs ought to be could be tricky. The relationship was ambiguous, with real potential for tension. The party was at the same time independent and dependent. Fiercely independent in policy-making, yet materially and technically dependent in practice.

And even though I had completely understood the tactical necessity of its organizing itself as the Freedom Democratic Party for the convention, I felt that on the local level this was a serious contradiction. How could Africans even think of "integrating" a party with the racist history of the Mississippi Democrats? That to me was premature.

With a potential base of 45 percent of the population, should black folks in Mississippi—and the South—not be building strong, independent voting machines? Machines that, if not capable of electing statewide candidates outright, could at least determine who would not be elected. SNCC was in the Delta or in southwest Georgia and the Alabama black belt in the first place because of the numbers. It seemed to me that once the right to vote was achieved, the 4 million Africans in the South needed to organize separate parties truly responsive to their communities. Later, with those statewide organizations functioning properly, coalitions and alliances would undoubtedly be necessary, possible, and productive. But initially I thought it would be a disaster to allow the new black vote to be co-opted into the existing racist parties. Absurd.

The MFDP was one model, but we needed at least a second one. As someone famous said, "Let a thousand flowers bloom and a thousand schools of thought contend." Right? Right. In Reconstruction the black vote was concentrated inside one party under white leadership. We all know what happened. So I was looking around outside the state.

CHAPTER XIX

Selma:
Crisis, Chaos, Opportunity

> The Negro meets no resistance when on a downward course.
> It is only when he rises in wealth, intelligence and manly
> character that he brings on himself the heavy hand of perse-
> cution.
>
> —Frederick Douglass

Looking back, 1965–66, Lowndes County, Alabama, was a turning point
for me, and for SNCC.

As soon as the lawyers finished deposing our people and the state officials in Mississippi for the Congressional Challenge, I figured it was time
to move on. SNCC was in transition and I sensed it was time for me to
try a somewhat different direction.

But leaving my people, old and young, in the Delta was harder than
I'd foreseen. I hadn't honestly expected the outpouring of warmth and
affection, I mean the *extent,* y'know, and so openly and emotionally
expressed.

"Stokely, so long as I got me a roof over my head in this heah Mississippi, you got you a place to stay. An' if it ain't but two chicken wings in
the pot, you know you got one," Mrs. Hamer said, and I heard variations
on that everywhere I went. Even from a few places that I hadn't really
expected. It would have been really hard had I been leaving the movement
or even the South. But I was only going across the state line into Alabama.

Alabama. Whoa, boy, now that was a tough one. I'd been talking to
Forman about setting up a project where I could implement certain ideas
coming out of the MFDP experience. Where SNCC could use the things
we'd been learning in the Delta. We decided I should check out Alabama.

I had one more SNCC national staff meeting. I'd been on my way to
report for assignment to Silas Norman, the Alabama project director. I'm
almost certain it was on the way to that meeting that I heard it. On the car
radio.

"Former Black Muslim leader Malcolm X has been shot and killed . . ."

I can't remember who all were in the car, but we listened to the report in dead silence. Who *had* killed the brother? The report said the shooters were black. That one had been captured. Yeah, sure, I thought. How convenient. I didn't for a moment believe that. It wasn't the whole or the true story. I knew that. Instinctively.

Then it began to hit me. Malcolm dead? How can that be? That warm, vital, truth-telling, strong-hearted, force-of-nature black man? *Dead?* They—whoever did it—made a bad mistake killing that brother. A real bad mistake. Then I wondered how far the thing stretched. Who else might be next?

Since his return from Africa, Malcolm, now free of the political and ideological constraints of the Nation, had been reaching out to movement leaders. There had been at least one high-level secret meeting. I knew that. Some of us had been talking about a role for him with SNCC. The voting rights bill was coming. I knew we in SNCC would have to begin looking seriously to the ghettos in the North, for the kind of grassroots organizing we'd been doing in the South. Malcolm would be key. We weren't sure how it could work, or if such a thing was even possible, but it wasn't as strange as people seemed to think.

Malcolm had always, always, been respectful and supportive of us in SNCC. Of all the civil rights groups, I knew he felt closest to us, to the SNCC spirit. Hey, after a long talk with Malcolm, even John Lewis had come back from Africa sounding like a Pan-Africanist revolutionary. It had been SNCC who had invited Malcolm to Selma, when he spoke in the Brown Chapel. Sure his presence there had upset some people, but the grassroots Africans in Selma had been really responsive.*

Also, man, a month or so earlier, when Mrs. Hamer and a group of Delta teenagers had gone to Harlem, we'd arranged for the group to spend some time with the brother. He made a hell of an impression. The youth came back elated, just *elated,* talking about nothing but Malcolm. Even good Christian Mrs. Hamer had a crush. "Stokely, he so handsome

*I asked Ture about written accounts that local "Southern" blacks had been turned off by Malcolm's "Northern nationalism," that only the few "Northern" militants in SNCC had responded to Malcolm's message and posture. Ture's response: "I wasn't there. I was still in Mississippi. But of course I followed it thoroughly. I followed the SNCC grapevine, and if you look at the films—they have films—the crowd went wild. *They're* lying, the films are there, they speak for themselves. There's a film of Malcolm speaking in Selma and you can hear the crowds go wild. I studied that film. Even Malcolm would never forget. That's the speech where he said, 'I'm not telling you to do anything you wouldn't think of doing yourself, so I've not told you anything new.' And the Africans went wild. But anyway that's just trying to rewrite history." —EMT and so kind." Almost the same things she had said about Sékou Touré. Malcolm and Mrs. Hamer had spoken in a church where his introduction had been so clear and respectful, so *lovingly* respectful of Mrs. Hamer. He'd challenged a roomful of Harlem militants. "Y'all brothers always rapping about how bad you are. All that talk. Well, this little lady here's bad. She can teach you—all of us—about courage and struggle." Now they'd killed him. Like his friend Lumumba.

Though I can't recall who else was in the car, I distinctly remember saying that those killers would regret this. That killing Malcolm was a bad mistake. See, Malcolm was the only figure of that generation, the *only* one, who had the natural authority, the style, language, and charisma, to lead and discipline rank-and-file urban youth. The only one who commanded that kind of respect.

Over and over you saw it. Time and again. Many times you saw a crowd of angry Africans fixing to tear the place up, and the only person who could reason with them, cool them out, was Malcolm. That was because the masses knew and trusted him. Now they'd killed him. Bad mistake. Even though the media was saying that the shooters were black, I assumed that the government—New York police, FBI—which had him under watch 24/7, was at the heart of it. I still think that. There's entirely too much about that assassination that's never been satisfactorily explained.

[Peter Bailey:

"I really started to follow Malcolm after that church bombing where the four little girls were killed. There was a big rally in Harlem in front of the Hotel Theresa. Jackie Robinson, who had been a childhood hero of mine after he opened up the major leagues, had put it together. Malcolm spoke first. Then after about eight other prominent leaders spoke, Jackie Robinson thanked everyone for coming. 'The rally is over. Please go home.' The crowd, unsatisfied, started shouting, 'We want Malcolm. We want Malcolm.' They wouldn't leave. They started getting belligerent, jumping on cars, stopping traffic. Brother Malcolm, who'd been just leaning up at the Chock full o' Nuts, got back on the platform. 'Brothers and sisters, let's don't do this,' he said. 'The rally was for a very impor-tant cause. We've had it. I think everyone should now go home.' Immediately, immediately the crowd quieted down . . . just faded away . . . called off the ruckus . . . jumping . . . screaming . . . yelling . . . stopped. Within minutes the air cleared. I never seen anything like that in my life. He had a certain integrity that people responded to." —Voices of Freedom]

I wanted to go to the funeral, but in the end I wasn't able to. The Selma staff who'd invited Malcolm a month before felt strongly that out of respect SNCC should send a delegation. All the Selma staff wanted to go. I wanted to go too, but I was now working under Silas Norman, and Silas and Jim Forman in effect ordered me to Selma to hold the fort. SCLC was already moving in and they needed someone experienced on the ground. I was it. Forman kept me briefly in Atlanta to discuss strategy, then sent me into Selma.

Jack Minnis, the director of SNCC research, had developed excellent, very detailed information on the Alabama power structure: which capitalists owned what, their historical relationship to the terrorist network, and so on. I studied that and was well briefed. It was Jack *[Courtland Cox once called him one of the most intelligent people in SNCC, which is saying a lot given the level of intelligence in the organization. —EMT]* who would find the old Alabama law that would be key to how we organized in Lowndes County.

Alabama could have been Mississippi all over again, and in many ways it was. Enter Lowndes County and you back in the Mississippi Delta, Jack. Miles of cotton plantations, a huge black majority, an aging population, serious poverty, and serious, *serious* political and economic oppression. The same Wild West ambience, whites in cowboy boots and Stetsons wearing handguns with rifle racks in the pickup trucks. No difference visible to the naked eye.

But elsewhere there were important differences. Alabama had much larger cities and heavy industry, unheard of in Mississippi. The earth around Birmingham (the Pittsburgh of the South) had deposits of coal and iron ore. Pittsburgh, my *tochis;* what Birmingham at that time really reminded me of was Johannesburg, South Africa: black miners doing the most dangerous and dirty work for a fraction of the pay of white miners, many of whom were trained in explosives and racism; once militant and progressive unions now hopelessly compromised; a racist, capitalist establishment referred to locally as "the big mules"; a history of violent class warfare; and an instinctively violent police force, used in the thirties to break unions and bust workers' heads, now content to brutalize the black movement. Rigidly segregated, this was South African–style apartheid. P. W. Botha would have felt right at home.

Wonderful town, Birmingham. But that was not my destination.

Selma was a different place. Very different. No less oppressive or brutal, but so very different. For one thing, I really liked that African community. See, if I say that racism in Selma was as ruthless, the segregation as complete as any I yet seen, but that the black community was more together—psychologically and culturally a proud community—than many I'd seen, it must certainly sound like a contradiction. But that was the Lord's truth. Could be that the strength was a consequence of the severity of the racism, or that the oppression was so severe because of the cultural strength of the Africans. Or both?

Whatever the case, many movement people have said that Selma people were the "most African" blacks in the South. I could see exactly what they meant. The community was poor and economically oppressed, true. But it was also self-contained and self-sufficient with businesses (small but our own) and black professionals, and strong in black religion and culture, with even two tiny church-affiliated colleges, Lutheran College and Selma University.

On first entering Selma, my distinct impression was that I sho nuff was back in antebellum Dixie. The twentieth century seemed to have missed Selma, a small riverfront town/city on the Alabama River, almost completely. Visually, it seemed to exist in its own time cocoon, a time warp. Eerie.

Jack Minnis's research explained some of what I was seeing. During slavery, Selma had been the commercial, merchandizing, and processing hub of the surrounding cotton belt, the Alabama delta. Hence the rows of huge, weathered, old, wooden warehouses with long wharves jutting out into the river. The only evidence of modern technology being the infamous Edmund Pettus Bridge across the river into Dallas County.

Of course, in primitive, antebellum capitalism, one of the most lucrative commodities was African bodies. A large part of Selma's commerce was the importation of Africans for the surrounding plantations. Shiploads of Africans passed through Selma, the area's largest slave market. The features and culture of Selma's black population (a little over 50 percent in my time) reflected that history.

Whites, of course, had their own peculiar sense of history. They never forgot that during the Civil War, the town had almost completely been razed by Union troops, a goodly number of whom were said to be black. And, especially galling, that during Reconstruction, *their* former slaves had sent an African to the U.S. Congress. And when I read that Nathan Bedford Forrest, Confederate icon, slave trader, terrorist, and founder of the KKK, had lived in Selma, much about white attitudes and actions in Selma became much clearer.

Selma's whites were obsessively determined—after the "humiliation" of Reconstruction—that black power would never again raise its nappy head amongst them. Period. So it didn't surprise me to find that they proudly claimed "Bull" Connor (of Birmingham infamy) as a native son. Or that they were equally proud that theirs had been the first Alabama town to establish a White Citizens Council.

Then there was Bull Connor's local imitator, Sheriff Jim Clark, whose contribution to modern crowd control was a mounted posse whose equipment of choice was the bullwhip and the cattle prod. This posse was said to include members of the landed gentry, no doubt combining fantasies of the Confederate cavalry with the slave patrollers. And I had thought Mississippi was crazy.

The city was in Dallas County. In 1961 my old friend Reggie Robinson from Baltimore had scouted Selma as a possible SNCC project. In 1962 we sent in the first field secretary, the Reverend Bernard Lafayette. The night Medgar Evers was murdered, the Klan sent an assassin after Bernard. Bernard maintains to this day that his nonviolent discipline and demeanor saved his life. I suspect that his nonviolence might have been aided considerably by the neighbor who ran out, shattering the silence with his shotgun. I was surprised to read that one of the things SNCC launched here was a bus boycott in 1964. A bus boycott in 1964? Well, a bus driver had shut the door on a pregnant African and dragged her to her death beneath the bus. But now the issue was the vote, and for reasons already stated, the Selma resistance was fierce.

The one thing SNCC did *not* have to do in Selma was identify and develop grassroots community leadership. As I said, this was a self-contained community, and its Dallas County Voters League had a mighty impressive group of leaders. Some proud, fearless black leaders who, against all odds, had never quit and never backed down. Nuff respect.

They were mostly professional people: ministers like the Reverend Mr. Lewis and the Reverend Mr. Reese; Dr. Jackson, who I believe was a dentist; tough-talking, indefatigable attorney J. L. Chestnutt; and of course, the president, Mrs. Amelia Boynton, a former teacher and widely respected leader.

A word about that family. Mrs. Boynton was a gracious, elegantly spoken lady. A teacher deeply committed to her people's uplift, Mrs. Boynton had been president of the Dallas County NAACP. When the NAACP was outlawed in Alabama, she didn't miss a beat. She merely led the membership into the Voters League and became president of that. She was demure, highly "cultured," and quite unintimidatable.

The entire Boynton family were warriors. The plaintiff in the Supreme Court case *Boynton vs. Virginia,* which integrated interstate bus travel, was her son. Her husband also had been a highly respected leader, who managed—with the ingenuity of his widow—to continue the fight literally from his grave.

When Mr. Boynton (peace be unto him) danced and joined the ancestors, an injunction against the congregating of more than three Negroes *[the language was "three persons," but it meant us —EMT]* was in effect in Dallas County. No kidding. But crowds of people were certain to come pay their respects to the fallen leader. So the announcement of the memorial service for Mr. Sam Boynton said quite prominently, "Memorial Service, Voting Workshop and Rally." When my time comes, that's the kind of memorial service I'd like to have.

Stuck in their antebellum time capsule, Selma whites did not welcome the passage of the civil rights bill of 1964 any more than the ones in

Greenwood had. In Selma, the immediate effect was to increase the intensity and meanness of their resistance.

This was the situation into which SCLC came. SCLC had always maintained that the local leadership invited them in "because SNCC was in over its head." That's self-serving nonsense. Over our heads, huh? The Selma black community had always celebrated a community holiday, the Emancipation Proclamation Day, which, of course, was not an event celebrated by white Selma. Dr. King was invited to give this day's speech. I've always suspected that like the guest who was invited to dinner and hung around, SCLC solicited a longer visit. With their traditional hit-and-run tactic, they were always in need of a new arena, and which Southern black community could refuse Dr. King? Especially an embattled one, like Selma.

Now we would have had no problem working with SCLC had their approach been compatible with SNCC's values. Especially since the first organizers they sent in were Diane and Jim Bevel and Bernard Lafayette, all former SNCC folk, who ever since Parchman Farm during the Freedom Rides had been paying serious dues in struggle. We understood each other. The problem was in the SCLC approach of massive, temporary mobilization and press agentry as opposed to creating powerfully organized communities capable of sustaining political struggle. Organization vs. mobilization was always a serious problem, because every day-to-day tactical decision was affected by the strategic approach. Every one.

SNCC had steadily and purposefully been building on the base already in Selma. Yeah, the resistance had been crude and brutal, but that actually helped the growth of the organization. We were expanding the *organized* mass base. Something viable and ongoing.

Here comes SCLC talking about mobilizing another two-week campaign, using our base and the magic of Dr. King's name. They going bring in the cameras, the media, prominent people, politicians, rat-tat-tat, turn the place upside down, and split. Probably leaving most of the strongest people sitting in jail.

That was the issue, a real strategic and philosophical difference. Try explaining that to the press, eh? Good luck. Hey, our approach minimized *their* role, but SCLC's entire strategy centered around the media. So of course stories about "young SNCC organizers, jealous of Dr. King," began to appear nationwide. Which, as I'm told, are still being recycled by historians. Nonsense. Utter off-the-wall bull and nonsense. Nobody was "jealous" of Dr. King. We respected him. But we did have principled and tactical disagreements, that's all. And Dr. King understood and respected that. He never ran to the press with any of that nonsense. Others in SCLC may have. But Dr. King, never.

Here's where the stuff hit the fan. We, jointly with the Dallas County Voters League, organized a freedom day (a large voter registration effort by numbers of people) at the courthouse.

Dependably, Sheriff Clark went nuts. He actually physically assaulted Mrs. Boynton. The story spread like wildfire in the community. Pictures on TV of Mrs. Boynton being thrown around and dragged by her neck. The idea, much less the sight, of this genteel, impeccably dignified lady whom everybody respected (she reminded me of Ms. Ella Baker in her manner) being manhandled by that redneck barbarian was the last straw. I mean folks were riled up, Jack.

The next day Clark pushed another black lady *[Mrs. Annie Lee Cooper —EMT]* on the line. The wrong black lady. She was big, strong, and mad. She refused to move, saying, "Ain't no one scared of you, Clark." He grabbed her, she hauled off and slugged him. I mean really slugged him. Some folks say more than one time. It took a bunch of deputies to hold her down while Clark busted her head with his nightstick.

The Selma teachers—you heard me, the *teachers*—took it on themselves to march as a group on the courthouse a few days after that. In black Southern communities, the teachers are both "middle class" and vulnerable. None of us had ever seen a group of teachers, so identified, do something like that anywhere else. That's what I meant when I said Selma was a special community. All their students were thrilled. Just so proud of their teachers.

All of which suggested to SCLC that the perfect thing to do with all this community momentum and energy was to organize a march to Montgomery, some fifty miles through the most backward and violent country in Alabama. To do what? Petition the governor, a certain George Corley Wallace. Gimme a break, Jack. Y'know there is a saying among engineers: "If all you have is a hammer, the whole world will look like a nail to you." That was SCLC exactly. SNCC was moving in an entirely different direction. SCLC was depending on the federal government all over again, something we were over and done with. To us, that had gotten real tired. Then also, it involved SCLC's calling in Northern supporters to "march with Dr. King." Not only did that bypass the local organizations, it was a provocation to violence. SNCC had already finished with that one too.

People think of the Selma to Montgomery March as being for voting rights, which, of course, in the larger sense it was. But the real catalyst, the immediate trigger, besides Clark's behavior in Selma, was the murder of a very decent young brother from a respected local family. Actually, immediately before the march, there had been two murders, both of young men active in the struggle: Sammy Younge Jr. and Jimmy Lee Jackson.

The first murder was of Sammy Younge Jr. (peace be unto him) over in Tuskegee. Sammy was twenty-one years old, a navy veteran, and one of the Tuskegee students working with SNCC. The gas station attendant who, without any provocation at all, shot him down for attempting to use a "white" rest room, walked. I'm not even sure if he was ever charged with any crime.

It was then that SNCC issued its first antiwar, antidraft statement (January 1966). We also began to say publicly that until our lives were protected and our rights respected at home, no Africans had any business fighting America's wars. Period. And that was even more true when they were clear-cut imperialist wars like Vietnam. No young Americans, Africans or no, should fight that kind of war. We should not, in Dr. Du Bois's famous words, "accept from America equal right to do wrong."

The next murder, the one that triggered the march, was that of a brother named Jimmy Lee Jackson (peace be unto him), in Perry County, neighbor of Dallas County. When SCLC joined us in the Selma campaign, the violence of the resistance hardened into a standoff in Dallas County. So Dr. King and them tried to spread the campaign out into the surrounding counties. Try as he might, though, one county Dr. King was never able to get into was Lowndes.

It was incredible, but SCLC could not find a black church in Lowndes County, not one, that would offer a pulpit to Dr. King. Can you believe that? Dr. Martin Luther King Jr., no pulpit? Actually, Bevel did tell me that there was one. But Dr. King never made it. On the day he was supposed to preach there, the pastor who'd extended the offer came into Selma, weeping, Bevel said, "living eyewater." He'd been run out of the county. By the Klan, right? No, Jack, by his deacon board. That's right, the deacons of his own church ran the reverend out. I've got to admit that when I heard that, it did cross my mind that Lowndes County might not exactly be the most strategically hospitable place for our next project. But of course it had been the terrorists. We later found out that the Klan *had* terrorized the deacons into running off their pastor.

SNCC had done some organizing in Perry County, where people trying to register had encountered the usual violence from the mob and the state. But Perry County people were strong, Jack. The most memorable was one old farmer, Mr. Cager Lee. He and his family were just stalwart. One strong African family. Those people just kept on keeping right on going, back to the courthouse. Whenever a group went to register, there they were.

Jimmy Lee Jackson was Mr. Lee's grandson. An SCLC preacher came to speak one night at a Perry County church, and when the people left the church after the speech, the state troopers ran amok, just chasing and whupping people everywhere. It was a police riot, pure and simple.

When a trooper attacked his mother and Jimmy Lee stepped between them, the trooper just shot him, twice. Jimmy Lee Jackson died a few days later. Of course, there was no investigation of this murder either. It got cursory press attention nationally and, despite SNCC's efforts, no response from the federal government. To the media and the national government, the lives of "Southern negroes" Jimmy Lee Jackson and Sammy Younge Jr. were apparently expendable.

With the proposed march to Montgomery, we had predicted, and dreaded, chaos. A bunch of media hoopla and confusion. But truthfully, we expected nothing like what we ended up with.

In the end, we had not one march—but three. Or more accurately, "the march," after two abortive attempts all within two weeks. It was madness.

The first and last one are the ones in the history books, but the middle one had the greater political effect internally. That first attempt, "Bloody Sunday," lives in infamy in the video archives of the world. On that Sunday afternoon, the gathering was pretty big but still a local affair. About what you'd expect for Jimmy Lee. People were still stirred up behind the murders and Jim Clark's violence to our women at the Selma courthouse.

Those present were the Selma leadership, people from the local African communities around Selma, and the local activists—mostly young, with a lot of Tuskegee students. And those SNCC organizers who felt they were morally bound to stand with the community.

All along, George Wallace had been issuing pronouncements, one after the other: he was not going to allow any "illegal" march in his state. Jim Clark and the Selma politicians were saying the same thing, while over in Lowndes County, the Klan had made it known that the march would enter their county at its own risk and anyone fool enough to come in would not leave alive.

The first question was whether the march would even be allowed to leave Selma, and if not, how exactly did the state and local cops plan to stop it? My real concern, though, was what would happen once it got into "bloody Lowndes." What security was SCLC planning for the people it was fixing to lead in there? Or, were they going to place their hopes on the intervention of the Good Lord and the federal government? Or perhaps in *agape,* the redemptive power of love?

No, sir, I did not support this move at all. Nor did SNCC nationally.

Hey, trying to distinguish between the Alabama cops and the Klan was, as we say in Africa, choosing between black dog and monkey. The security of our people was my concern. I did not see that being properly addressed. Which is why I could not support it and did not march.

John Lewis, representing, according to the press, SNCC, co-led this attempt. Of course we know what happened: "Bloody Sunday." On the Elmund Pettus Bridge the marchers were met with overwhelming force. Al Lingo's storm troopers (including no doubt Jimmy Lee Jackson's murderers) were as usual ruthless, but relatively disciplined. It was a *controlled* brutality, reminding me of Cambridge, Maryland. The massed state troopers first fired tear gas canisters into the marchers, who were tightly packed on the bridge. Then the troopers advanced in a solid phalanx, swinging nightsticks and ax handles, breaking heads and limbs, systematically pushing the marchers back across the bridge and into Selma. The marchers' eyes streaming, some bleeding and dazed, they broke ranks and were trying only to escape, trying to get off the bridge. The march had been turned around. It was over. Period.

Had they left it at that, the State of Alabama might well have gotten away with their brutality one more time. But, as usual, racism is its own worst enemy. The racists found a way to rescue an ill-advised movement strategy that was on the verge of total failure. We can only suppose that Jim Clark and posse, not to be outdone by Lingo, and on their own turf, just had to claim their share of the "glory" and bragging rights.

Just when you thought the whole sad and distressing debacle was done, here came the Confederate cavalry charge. I mean just running over and into the people in full view of the TV cameras, rebel yells clearly audible, using their long clubs and bullwhips on defenseless black heads.

The gratuitous brutality and unconcealed racism in that footage, flashing across the nation and around the world, succeeded in embarrassing even George Corley Wallace, let alone the administration in Washington. Even Southern segregationist congressmen found it necessary to appear in the media distancing themselves and "the decent, God-fearing people of my state" from "this deplorable behavior."

After everything I'd experienced, everything I'd learned in the movement, I'd considered myself beyond illusion. No longer capable of being surprised at anything racism might do. But this . . . this atrocity surprised even me. Thirty years later I still find myself . . . *[quite obviously experiencing deep anger. —EMT]*

Naturally Bloody Sunday rendered, at least for a New York minute, all doctrinal and strategic differences moot. For many in SNCC it was déjà vu all over again, the Freedom Rides revisited, the "violence-cannot-be-allowed-to-stop-the-movement" reflex.

That Sunday night the scene in Brown Chapel was like a wake in a MASH unit. Everywhere you could see dazed and bandaged people, but also a real undercurrent of determination, but mixed with a different kind of anger. Some folk seemed to embody the spirit of the song "We'll Never Turn Back":

> We have hung our heads
> and cried,
> Cried for those like Lee
> who died,
> But we'll never turn back . . .

Others were, for the first time, talking openly of getting guns and taking lives. But there were also new people in the chapel. People who had never marched or demonstrated, and who had had no intention of doing either, now turned out. "This time we going to Montgomery. They sho cain't kill us all."

The next few days were true chaos, motion, excitement. SNCC staff started to come in with local folks from all over the South. So did media from what looked like all over the world. Dr. King pledged to personally lead the next march, set a date, and issued a national call to conscience for his fellow clergymen to join him on this "historic crusade of conscience." The clergy responded in numbers, Jack, black and white of all faiths and denominations.

Ever since Dr. King's letter to the American clergy from the Birmingham jail, an activist spirit had manifested itself in the national religious community. People of faith began to pour into Selma. For two of them from Boston, a Unitarian minister and a young Episcopal seminarian, this would be their last Christian witness, at least in this world. Secular Northerners also angered by the brutal images on the bridge answered the call.

Now there finally was federal intervention, though not the kind SCLC had envisioned. The State of Alabama, temporarily relinquishing its states' rights rhetoric and posture, went into the hated federal courts seeking an injunction against the march. *Which they got.* The court—naming Dr. King and other leaders—issued an order enjoining the movement from marching. Go figure.

The SCLC leadership, maintaining that the federal government was its ally, were reluctant to violate a *federal* court order. But the people they had invited and pledged to lead kept pouring into Selma by the hour. With their marching shoes on. It was a sho-nuff mess. SNCC folk—and many Northerners—were saying that neither Southern violence nor the federal courts must be allowed to stop the people's right to free and peaceful expression. Crisis of conscience time for SCLC.

On the actual day, the crowd was real large. Immense. Local folk in numbers, Jack, and the Northerners, mostly clergy in clerical dress, the church militant, and SNCC veterans—all formed up behind the leaders. Dr. King and a host of prominent figures led the line and they set out over that bridge one mo' time. On the other side a massive military formation of the state's police machinery, in what looked like battle dress.

Now what, Jack? Does the state dare brutalize these visiting dignitaries the way they did the local Africans? And will it be, this time, with the explicit mandate of a federal court order giving them color of law? Will the feds finally make an arrest in Selma, this time of Dr. King and the non-violent marchers? And, let us not forget, the whole world is watching or will be once *this* footage airs.

It was very different, but this march got no farther than the first. It got to the center of the bridge and turned back, nonviolently.

[Silas Norman, Director, SNCC Alabama Project:

"You will remember the pictures . . . John Lewis with a knapsack on his back going down under the state troopers' batons. After that incident, I decided that I could no longer sit back and be philosophically opposed to the march. On the second march I emptied my pockets and prepared to offer my body as a living sacrifice. We started across the bridge for the second time. As we got to the end, state troopers lined up on every side. I noticed that they were not moving towards us this time.

"And I will remember that Dr. King—he was a row or two behind me—said, 'Let us pray.' And then the march proceeded to turn around. Well, Jim Forman was close to me. We were all sort of baffled. Jim kept saying, 'What's going on? Let's go ahead.' There were hundreds of people asking, 'What's going on? What's happening?' We had no idea. We discovered later that there had been some agreement with Robert Kennedy, with the government, that the march was not to proceed. Personally, I did not participate in that march again. I felt we'd been betrayed and I no longer wanted to participate. I felt that I could better spend my energies working with people in the movement in small groups in Selma."—A Circle of Trust]*

So you know that was anticlimactic, Jack, for *evrahbody.* But the disappointment from the visitors—and even anger—was palpable and understandable. Here they had dropped everything at SCLC's urgent summons and rushed down. Hey, these were not movement folk, accustomed to a life of quick adjustments, suddenly changing plans and surprises.

Then too, for most of them this was the most daring and dangerous step they had ever taken. They *wanted* and deserved to be proud of themselves. It was also their first experience of the excitement and moral intensity of the movement and they wanted to contribute, even to risk something for a clear moral cause. They wanted confrontation.

So you know there had to be some serious letdown and conflicting feelings, Jack. First, inevitably a natural human relief at being spared a trampling under the horses' hooves, perhaps a broken head or worse. And then, of course, immediately followed by embarrassment at the relief they were feeling at having been spared the confrontation they had sought. Folks were confused, let down, and leaving. Dr. King had thanked them profusely and asked those who could to stand ready to return.

The Reverend James Reeb had just finished placing his bags in a car for the trip to the Montgomery airport. A couple of colleagues, reluctant to waste the trip, told him that they had arranged to stay over for a few days. Impulsively he retrieved his bags and joined them.

The group went to supper in a black café and, after eating, left the café and took a wrong turn into white Selma, a small but fatal error. Passing a bar [The Silver Moon Café], a known Klan hangout avoided by local Africans, they were attacked. The Reverend Mr. Reeb (peace be unto him), clubbed in the head, died in a car en route to a Montgomery hospital. Another good man's life taken senselessly. The tragic and ironic aspects of which, of course, were not lost on the media.

The media were also feeling cheated. They had had neither their march nor a repeat of Bloody Sunday, so where was the story? Well, the visitors' small mistake in direction gave them a story to pounce on. The media had their story and the movement another martyr.

So much of a story in fact that LBJ was moved to send a message of condolence to Mrs. Reeb, with a government plane to transport the widow and the corpse home. Which, of course, was no more or less than ought to have been expected from the leader of any halfway civilized country. But the Reverend Mr. Reeb's tragic and senseless death had not been the first movement-related murder in the area in a matter of weeks. The march had been called, remember, in response to a local African man's murder. Where was LBJ's and the nation's response then?

[This quote from Carmichael in the press indicates the brother's feelings at the time: "Now, I'm not saying we shouldn't pay tribute to Reverend Reeb. What I'm saying is, if we are going to pay tribute to one, we should also pay tribute to the other. I think we have to analyze why LBJ sent flowers to Mrs. Reeb and not to Mrs. Jackson." —EMT]

Editor's note: During this campaign in Alabama, the level of violence directed at clearly identified religious figures puzzled us for a number of reasons.

The first attack was, of course, on the clergymen in Selma that resulted in the Reverend Mr. Reeb's death. This was followed, after the march, by the murder in Lowndes County of Mrs. Viola Liuzzo, a devout Catholic laywoman, though she was not so identified by her killers, one of whom (Gary Francis Rowe) happened to be in the employ of the FBI. Later that summer in Hayneville, two white clergymen were gunned down in the presence of witnesses. Immediately after firing, the gunman had reportedly put his weapon down, walked over to the courthouse, and placed a call to Colonel Lingo, head of the state police.

"Al, best you git on up here," he announced, "I jes' shot me two damn priests."

At the trial, despite this admission and the testimony of eyewitnesses, after less than two hours of deliberation a jury returned a verdict of not guilty.

But even before this second incident, some things about the murder of the Reverend Mr. Reeb seemed culturally dissonant. In the Washington office we'd tried to puzzle this out. We understood that the Selma march had a much larger, more highly visible and identifiable representation by white clergy than was usual in the movement. We also understood that this contingent, conspicuously displaying vestments and insignia of the church, intended their presence to be seen as a Christian/moral/religious witness against local racial attitudes and social practice. We further understood that this public repudiation of the cherished "Southern way of life" by white officials of the church would be a severe shock to local sensibilities. In effect, a clerical rebuke to the Southern version of the natural moral order.

What seemed dissonant to us was not merely the lethal violence directed against clergy, but the willingness of the public to condone and tolerate it. This from people accustomed to describing themselves as "honest, God-fearing Christian folk" and referring to their region proudly as "the buckle on the Bible Belt." That was puzzling us until someone from the Alabama staff sent us a page from a local newspaper with a note. A revelation.

I can't remember which staffer had sent us the newspaper page, but the accompanying note said that it explained much of what the staff had been seeing all during the march. For example, one of the most common signs waved by hecklers had been "Rent your priest suit here."

You know we gotta be some baad-ass nigrahs, Bro, the note said. To walk all damn day wet and cold in the rain, mess around all night, then be up at six to hit that road again. Yeah, I wish.

The accompanying news story must have been seen locally as correcting the default of the "Northern" press corps.

As I recall (I did not then have the foresight to save the page), it was a tabloid-sized center spread. I assumed it was from a small-town weekly somewhere in the vicinity of the march, but it could just as well have been from the Sunday magazine of a local daily. It was presented—very dramatically—as the findings of a reporter who claimed to have infiltrated the march and was now exposing its inner workings.

Unshaven, scruffy, and sporting a civil rights button, our man nervously slipped among the marchers only to be surprised at the casual acceptance—even goodwill—with which he was received. Emboldened, he first worked his way close enough to a group of nuns so as to overhear and later join their conversation. His second surprise: the ladies' conversation did not display the gentle spirituality one would expect from brides of Christ.

In fact, he was horrified, as much by the demotic coarseness of their language

as by the vulgarity, irreverence, and anti-Americanism it expressed. Much of which, he said, was not suitable for reproduction in a family newspaper. Soon the women revealed the obvious: they weren't really nuns at all, they confided proudly, but unemployed New York (the adjective might have been "Greenwich Village") actresses, hired to parade down the highway in religious regalia.

Next, as I recall, he walked with two jolly, avuncular, middle-aged priests who—no surprise—also turned out to be hired actors. Throughout the day he reported being constantly offended by the marchers' casual and uninhibited familiarity across lines of age, race, and sex. But alas, for the poor fellow, it was to get much worse.

That evening he entered a large tent where a hot meal awaited the group. After the meal, off came the costumes. Out came the playing cards, the whiskey, unspecified "drugs," and loud music of a decidedly unspiritual character, which inspired sexually suggestive interracial dancing. What followed, led in general lasciviousness, exhibitionism, and looseness of language and behavior by the erstwhile nuns, could only be hinted at, being best left to the readers' imaginations. Not having the stomach to witness the debauchery that was clearly a-building to an orgy of some sort, our man sneaked away to file his report.

I truly regret not having saved that page since the foregoing has had to be reconstructed from memories now four decades old. But I can vouch for the accuracy, if not of every detail, then certainly of the broad plot and the prurient tone and tenor of the piece. I certainly remember the outrage and despair I felt reading it. If they believe this, I thought, then there's nothing they might not do. Were I some hardscrabble, fundamentalist Christian segregationist, I could easily see myself feeling a moral duty to exterminate the kind of human vermin willing, at one fell swoop, to violate the purity of the race while dishonoring the symbols of the faith.

What I was amazed at was the calculated cynicism and cunning, the unerring precision with which the writer had targeted and exploited every last one of the most fundamental and primitive of local biases and sensitivities. I've since seen (in Jamaica) identical techniques utilized in the very same way. These teachings were described in a program called "Destabilization and Psychological Warfare," developed by U.S. military intelligence.

Given subsequent disclosures of the FBI's disinformation campaign against the movement, which heavily involved the placement of fake "news stories" with cooperating editors, one has to wonder about the actual provenance and authorship of this story. Whatever the source, I believe there can be little question about its brutal effect.

Then too, the rape unto death. Some reporters accompanying the march had been accosted by a group of local white youth. Why, the locals demanded angrily, wasn't the Northern press reporting the real story? What story? The young white woman everyone was talking about. The one who on the first night

had been raped by so many blacks that she had fallen into a deep coma. Rushed secretly to a Selma hospital, the poor girl had died that morning. Why were they, as white men, conspiring with the march leadership to suppress that story? —EMT]

[I've since encountered another variant of this Southern folk tale. In this one, the comatose young woman is a prostitute, as evidenced by the thirty-six hundred dollars in small bills found tucked in her underwear. She was assumed to have worked herself into unconsciousness servicing the lust of black marchers. —EMT]

All this time we had a lot of discussions. I had definitely not been for having no march, bro. Too many serious contradictions. But I didn't think it politic for us to oppose it publicly either. We were between a rock and a hard place one more time.

At meetings, I had advocated my position, at first a minority of one. We should not get in a position of fighting Dr. King publicly, I said. We should try to see how best to use the situation. There is no way we can stop this march. Exactly what we dread, the chaos, disruption, is going to happen anyway. And when the marchers leave, as they will, we'll have trouble and a deflated community on our hands. Either we are capable of trying to create order out of that, or we leave Selma with them after the march. For those who stay, that will be our task. If you can't shoulder it, get out of the way. If you can, let's get it on. But there's nothing you can do about the march.

I said, the people *looove* Dr. King, don't oppose him. We need to figure out how best to use the march and to pick up the pieces afterward. Eventually people began to take that position. Then confusion: Atlanta put out a statement that SNCC was not participating. Then they said that staff as individuals could follow their consciences. Then Jim Forman came to Montgomery and called for night marches—in effect competing with Dr. King for media attention. I strongly disagreed with that one also. All told, it was not our finest hour.

John Lewis, our chairman, was clear. *He* was going to march. Not as chairman of SNCC? people asked. Well, he said, he was also on the SCLC board. Folks wondered just what that meant.

One brother in the meeting, Bob Mants, had supported John's position on marching. But after that Sunday meeting where I was advocating my position vigorously, Bob began to approach me closer and closer. I kept advocating. This march is nonsense, but we can use it. Finally Bob asked me exactly how I proposed to do that. So we talked it out. And he too, after a while, said he wasn't going for that marching stuff either. Especially after that second one where hundreds, if not thousands, of people had ultimately felt confused and betrayed.

I asked Bob what he was going to do. He said, "We going into Lowndes County together, bro, I'm with you."

I said, "All right," and that's what we did. Bob Mants and I worked that march, Jack. Me'n Bob were in it from the beginning. We organized Lowndes county together. We became real close during that entire campaign, shoulder to shoulder, like brothers. Closer than brothers. In fact, Bob's still there in Lowndes, an elected official.

CHAPTER XX

Lowndes County:
The Roar of the Panther

Ever since getting to Selma, I had been looking more and more closely at Lowndes County. It seemed more and more a logical place for the ideas that we were developing out of the MFDP experience.

Once you crossed the infamous Edmund Pettus (who he?)* bridge in ten miles, you were in Lowndes, and once you finish Lowndes, you in Montgomery. The precise march route. But as far as struggle was concerned, Lowndes was a wasteland, terra incognita. Hey, there had been strong, organized struggle in Montgomery. The bus boycott had "shocked the world" (like Bro Ali) and produced Martin Luther King Jr. Selma, mean as that place was, had seen serious struggle. But in Lowndes, nothing, nada, squat. And the way people talked about the place, you could understand why. So as far as movement was concerned, this was virgin territory, bro, with no organizational rivalries to deal with, precisely because it was a terrorist stronghold. Which, of course, was a problem, but also in a strange way, an advantage. Crisis equals opportunity. I asked Minnis for specific information on Lowndes. I discovered it was even worse than folks were saying.

One of the poorest counties in the nation, it was feudal, Jack. It actually made the Mississippi Delta look advanced. About eighty families owned 90 percent of the land. Of a population of fifteen thousand, *twelve* thousand were Africans, not a *one* of whom could vote. Hear me, not one. Half of our people were below the poverty level, most of the other half at or barely above it. Mostly agricultural day laborers and share-croppers. Fully half of the women commuted to Montgomery for house-work at $4 a day. Many of the men also worked in Montgomery. Sounds like South Africa, huh? And talk about rural. The largest town was Fort Deposit, the Klan stronghold, with all of thirteen hundred people and the largest concentration of whites. I'd say almost fifty-fifty. The county seat, Hayneville, a place I'll never forget, was even smaller. We concluded,

---

*Actually, Confederate general Edmund Winston Pettus.

therefore, that "bloody Lowndes" afforded every opportunity we were looking for.

So with the march, how did we turn a negative into a positive, as Sékou Touré would always advise me later? Well, Highway 80 traversed the length of the county. We knew that there was no way the march could go through without the aid of local people strong enough to let them pitch their tents on their land. People brave enough to come out, cheer them on, offer a little food or some water, etc., etc. So what Bob Mants and I did, we trailed that march. Every time local folks came out, we'd sit and talk with them, get their names, find out where they lived, their address, what church, who their ministers were, like that. So all the information, *everything*, you'd need to organize, we got.

We told them we'd be back. I promised them the movement was coming to Lowndes. That Lowndes County was going to have its own movement. Of course they were skeptical. Didn't really think we'd be back, y'know? That's when we first met a brother named John Hulett. Another man was with him *[Mr. R. L. Strickland, who would later emerge as a leader —EMT]* didn't seem to believe us.

He wasn't at all convinced. He said, "Young fella, you one o'them non-violence folk, huh? An' you reckon on coming back? Wal, in this county, turn the other cheek and these here peckerwoods'll hand you back half of what you sitting on. If you do come back, you all gon' have to find a different way to come in here, young fella."

I told him we were coming back, by any means necessary. He just looked at me and smiled.

When the march left Lowndes, so did we. Bob and I returned temporarily to Selma. March got close to Montgomery and all these preachers, politicians, and celebrities came streaming in to march into Montgomery on the last day. We missed all that. Many were well-meaning, conscientious people, strong movement supporters. But others were organizational types who wanted to be able to say, "I marched to Montgomery with Dr. King." And they still be saying it today too, Jack. Every time I hear that I laugh. If everyone who claims that they'd "marched with Dr. King" had marched, the tail end of that march might just now be entering the city limits of Montgomery.

But when we went back into the county, people remembered us. We already had good contacts across the length and breadth of the county. You have any idea how long that would have taken as an organizer? Without the march? Dr. King handed all that to us on a platter, and we took it. Hey, as soon as we arrived, we got a house. We just walked into a house. Here's where you will stay. Here's where you'll eat. These folk will look out for you. Here's the guns that will protect you. I'll never forget that.

[There had in fact been a history of militant political activity on the part of blacks in the county. For example, the two elderly gentlemen who undertook to sit up nightly with their long rifles guarding the house where the SNCC workers slept. These two men were veterans of a sharecroppers union from the 1930s which had a history of armed self-defense. —EMT]

That's the reason Lowndes County went so fast. Within one year we had that county completely organized. In one year.

You know I never respond to lies. My father taught me that. Never respond to lies, he'd always say. "Something ain't true, Son, why you going waste your time with it?" So I don't. But one little myth I will refute. People keep saying that they read how I went into the county. That I was dropped off late one night carrying only a list of names, a sleeping bag, and a snack. Some say a Bible. Gimme a break. That's romantic. It's also silly and as Fred, the brother they murdered in Chicago *[Fred Hampton, chairman of the Chicago Black Panther Party, assassinated by the FBI —EMT]*, would say, "Custeristic." Well, Custer was a white man an' my momma didn't raise no fool. Had I been silly enough to try that, I probably and deservedly wouldn't be here today. And if not the terrorists, the people—who are neither silly nor romantic—would likely have run me out themselves, period.

What did happen was that a few days after the march, four of us went in broad daylight to test the waters *[Carmichael, Bob Mants, Judy Richardson, and Scott B. Smith]*. We wanted also to take advantage of whatever excitement the march had generated. We came to this little town called Whitehall, where we had some names to check out. As we came through, the high school—the black school—was letting out. But they didn't even dignify it with the name *school*, much less *high*. It was the Negro Training Center. We decided to seize the time, give the students some leaflets to take to their parents. The youth gathered around, all excited. Still excited about the recent march. Some accepted material, others were scared.

Then a young brother drove up in a school bus and asked for material to distribute. So you know we took *his* name. *[The sixteen-year-old bus driver was John Jackson. Today he is, and has been for years, mayor of Whitehall, a progressive little town. —EMT]* The cops pulled us over. Rah, rah, you under arrest. Against the law to distribute Communism near a school.

"School? We didn't see any school. Thought that was a training center." Anyway, they backed off and we left.

[Bob Mants:

"This was the first and only time Carmichael probably ever used his head. We were all there shaking, with perhaps the exception of Judy. We had these two radios in our car with long whip antennas. (Good ol' Sojourner Motor Fleet. —EMT) *Carmichael picked up the two-way radio as if he were talking*

to the Selma base. Problem was we were out of range, but the police didn't know that. He told them—talking so that the sheriff and state troopers could hear every word—exactly what to do if we weren't back at a certain time, giving the cops' car number. That perhaps saved our lives, because they let us go.

"... I still suspect very strongly that had it not been for that incident at the school, it would have been at least two, three, four months before we moved into Lowndes to organize. What happened was, with the students and teachers getting out of school, the word had spread. Them civil rights workers were in here. The next morning when we rolled back in, people were waving. 'You all right? Y'all all right?' After that incident at the school, they knew we had to be bad. We were back out there the next morning." —A Circle of Trust

John Jackson:

"I was sixteen years old and driving a school bus making fifty dollars a month. . . . I was crazy enough to stop my bus to take some of the leaflets. I went home and talked to my father. We had an abandoned house which my brothers had just left, so I said to my father, 'Them boys are going to get killed trying to make it back to Selma. And George Wallace will hang them if they try going into Montgomery. So they need a place to stay.' My father came with me to meet them, and I think he kinda liked those fellows, or like me he about half-crazy. So he said, 'Hey, boys, y'all could take this house over here, there's no one staying in it.' They were kinda glad because they used to have to get the hell out of Lowndes before dark." —A Circle of Trust]

So, Jack. Population fifteen thousand, twelve thousand African. Not a single one registered. Check that, *one* was. Mr. Hulett, who would become chairman of the party, had succeeded in registering about a month before we got there. That tells you all you need to know about the county *and* about Bro John Hulett.

At this point, SNCC had been struggling around the vote issue going on five years, with what results you've seen. But that one we gonna win. That's clear. Then what? How should we, could we, how must we, move to maximize the effect of that victory? In the South? In the nation? How could we stretch and remake the electoral system to do justice to our interests? Africans were and would always be a minority nationally. So what would this vote that people had sacrificed so much for, some even died for, really mean? Only a fool would think that winning the right to vote would *automatically* free anybody. Remember, Africans in Cambridge, Maryland, could vote and you saw how much good that by itself had done them.

Voting could be a new start. But only if we organized ourselves and used it skillfully and cleverly. And even that would have to be geared to different situations depending on local demographics. So, clearly, there could be no single or simple answer. No one-size-fits-all approach. The cultural attitudes of the majority were, and continue to be, against us. History was against us so far as our position in the society was concerned. Our poverty was against us. Our numbers were against us so far as electoral politics were concerned. But *clearly* we had to go there to see how far electoral politics could take us. But what exactly should our (SNCC's) role be in this next stage? That was the question we faced.

Certainly in the South a potential 4 million new black votes had to be a powerful force for change. We could retire a few African-killing sheriffs. Vote out a particularly racist congressman or two. But was that to be all? Could there be a way to maximize the potential power of our people's votes? How? By being co-opted into either or both white national parties? I didn't think so. We'd seen that in Reconstruction and we all know what happened then.

So I thought, maybe in Lowndes County, with our overwhelming majority, SNCC could show a dramatic way if the local people were willing and brave enough. A way that could work all over the black belt in the South. Since none of the other organizations had any presence at all in Lowndes, we had a clear field. No time need be wasted on interorganizational foolishness. Here, at least in demographic terms anyway, was a possibility. If we were serious about advancing our people's struggle to improve their conditions, we had to explore it. This possibility would soon attract some of the best organizers SNCC had.

The recruiting of people and the setting up of a grassroots organizational structure went quickly. Mr. Hulett, our lone registered voter, was key. He had organized and became president of the Lowndes County Christian Movement (LCCM) for Human Rights. He was an interesting brother, intelligent, committed, with great personal integrity and courage. Married with seven children, he commuted daily to Montgomery to work. He may (at twenty-seven) have been too young to have been involved in the bus boycott, but he knew people who had been involved. He was familiar with organized protest there, but never in Lowndes. So he was ready, had been ready, to step out and provide serious leadership once we got there. In fact, he'd been agitating before we got there. I never did find out exactly how, in the climate we found there, he had, on his own, managed to register. Mah people, oh mah people.

[John Hulett:

"Lowndes County was considered a total rural county. Very poor. Bad roads. The school system was very bad, the worst almost in the nation. There were no jobs available except farming and sharecropping. Most of the young peoples who finished school, they immediately left the South and went north, to try to live, and even to survive.

"Most black peoples had to live in fear. We had a sheriff during that time

461

that I can never forget. At nighttime, the young men, if they walked the road and saw car lights coming, would just run in the bushes and hide until they come by. . . . Because they thought the sheriff was coming by and maybe would do something to them. During that time we had a new beginning. We decided ourselves what group we were going to work with. The people of this county chose Stokely Carmichael and his group. They helped us to organize and gave us a kind of leadership and the encouragement that we needed to go through with." —Voices of Freedom]

The organization grew steadily, but real political progress was slow. In six months we succeeded in registering only two hundred or so people. Though hundreds made the effort. This was the work I truly loved. The meetings in rural churches with people who seemed to step out of the pages of black history. The singing, the eloquence, the determination and hope in their faces, the spirit. People who carried so much vulnerability in their eyes, who knew exactly what they were risking by being there, but being there anyway, steadfast.

Then in August 1965 two things happened. First, the voting rights act became law. Soon as that happened, I asked Jack Minnis to check out the laws on independent parties in Alabama. Jack was good. In less than a week he called back. He'd found this old forgotten law enabling independent parties on the county level. We figured with their one-party state, the politicians, almost all Democrats, had forgotten it. There wasn't even a Republican opposition to speak of. So, to them it must have been unthinkable that anyone would think of trying to start an *independent* party in Alabama. Much less *their* "nigrahs." And in Lowndes County? Forget about it. So the process was actually quite simple.

All any group had to do before the primaries was hold a convention and nominate a slate of candidates. If your slate received more than 20 percent of the primary vote, you were in business. You could then call yourself a party, whose name and symbol would have to be on the ballot for the election which would then become necessary. The Democrats were arrogant and complacent. I'm not sure whether they had ever had to bother with an election after the Democratic primary, since there had been no organized opposition since 1880. So technically it was surprisingly easy.

All right. There it was. The primary was next May. Ten months off. In Mississippi we'd had five months to organize an entire state. Here we had nearly a year to do a single county. We were psyched, Jack.

Next thing was that Lowndes County became the first county in the South where a federal registrar was assigned under the new law. Of course, this partly was because of the clear record of voting discrimination and resistance there, but probably more so because of the particularly brazen murder of a white worker less than a week after the passage of the bill.

Once we got Jack's information, Mr. Hulett promptly resigned from the Christian Movement for Human Rights and became chair of the Lowndes County Voters League, later to be known as the Black Panther Party. That was an interesting discussion. Some people were clear right off: "Yeah, we going build our own political thing here, in our own party."

[Mr. Hulett:

*"Stokely Carmichael and Courtland Cox and others got together and told us, according to Alabama law, if we didn't like what the Democratic party or the Republican party was doing in our county, we could form our own political organization, and it could become a political party. . . . They asked me would I take over the political aspects and resign from the Lowndes County Christian Movement, and I did. And we were able to pull our people together to form our own political organization." —*Voices of Freedom*]

But many others had to be persuaded. For some interesting reasons, they didn't at first think an "all-black" party could be any good. For one thing, they automatically saw voting as inclusion. Hey, having been kept out so long, of course they wanted in. To them, a black party seemed like the same old segregation. That was natural.

The other reason was sad, a question of self-confidence. They had been so conditioned for so long to think that politics was "white folks' business," in which blacks were not allowed or competent. They assumed that the white folks who ran things had knowledge, experience, and education that their leaders lacked. So how could we do the job? However, once we showed them the educational background of most of the white local officials, they realized what a hoax that was. And with the political education workshops, their confidence grew.

But what really did it was when someone said, "Hey, this ain't no 'all-black' party. Ain't nobody stopping white folks from joining if they want. You know any who want to join?" That cracked them up. Besides, all you had to do was show them the Democratic Party's slogan, "White Supremacy for the Right," and its symbol, that ol' white bantam rooster. Then they said, "Yeah, thems the same folk that's been doing all the shooting and killings. Who would want to join up with them anyway?" Quickly they became excited at having their own thing, a party that really represented them.

Later when we proposed the black panther as our ballot symbol, some thought it might seem too aggressive. I think it was Jennifer Lawson who came up with the design *[others say it was Ruth Howard —EMT]*. But then we explained to the folks that the panther was a powerful animal but reclusive. It avoided humans unless provoked. They liked that. "Yeah," they said, "and it sure can eat up any ol' white fowl too."

[John Hulett:

"The black panther was a vicious animal who, if he was attacked, would not

back up. It said that we would fight back if we had to do it. When we chose that symbol, many of the peoples in our county started saying we were a violent group who is going to start killing white folks. But it wasn't that, it was a political symbol that we was here to stay and we were going to do whatever needed to be done to survive.

"Those of us who carried guns carried them for our own protection, in case we were attacked by other peoples. That's what the purpose of that idea was. White peoples carried guns in this county and the law didn't do anything to them about it, so we started carrying our guns too. I think they felt that we was ready for war, but we wasn't violent. We wasn't violent people. But we were just some people who was going to protect ourselves in case we were attacked by individuals." —Voices of Freedom*]*

Once the federal registrar came into the county, the plantation bosses got even meaner. It was like the Delta back in 1961, an attempt to drive out the African population before they became voters. African workers were run off the plantations for registering. Sharecropper families were run off the land, their crops abandoned in the fields. It was cruel to see. Most of the evicted people left the county, but some brave souls stayed. I wish more families had, because the tent city we set up really turned a negative into a positive.

A black farmer volunteered some land and we moved the families into tents. Then we used all the techniques SNCC had developed in Mississippi. We set up freedom schools. We had literacy and political education classes. We played tapes of Malcolm. Taught African history. I remember we developed comic books to teach local politics. The role of the tax assessor, of the sheriff, and like that. These comics were very effective.

We, of course, didn't have the resources to bring in every family they evicted. And besides, many were afraid to stay. But I wish we could have kept every one in Tent City. Once the people were out from under the oppressive plantation system, they just blossomed and developed confidence. Every day you could see it growing. When night riders started driving by firing guns, the men and boys posted sentries along the road and returned fire. The night-riding stopped. The people organized themselves, worked communally, and just ate up the education. It was beautiful to see. For a while, Tent City was a fine little community. But, of course, it could only be a temporary measure. Then, I guess, the plantation bosses and owners realized they needed their workers and tenants. They devised a different strategy and the evictions stopped. I always look back at that little Tent City with great pleasure and satisfaction. I only wish we could have taken in and serviced two hundred more families. The evictions would have backfired totally because in Tent City the people became really organized.

[Josephine Mays:

"My brother Willie registered to vote, and the man told him that he had to leave. So he moved to Montgomery, and after that my mother, she moved to Montgomery too. And after I moved to Tent City I become a registered voter.

"It was a great experiment for me in Tent City. . . . Now we could make a start for ourself, and get out and register to vote and help others become registered voters. And to find (out about) the world for themselves. . . . So much was going on. We got involved with lots of activities to help black peoples to get jobs and learn how to do things for themselves. Like we bought land, and then after we got the land we built a house, something that we had never had before of our own.

"The white peoples would come round. They would pull up to the side of the road and they would call us hoodlums and niggers and things like that. They would shoot at us and try to scare us, but we wouldn't let them bother us. We hung in there anyways." —Voices of Freedom*]*

I'd already learned in the Delta that what really challenged and satisfied me was organizing my people. That would be my job as long as my people were oppressed. I knew that. And here I was with my own project. Soon Lowndes County became a magnet for some of the best organizers in SNCC. I never set out to recruit them or raid other projects, but our momentum and direction attracted them. That was no accident.

A lot of folks from Mississippi had become frustrated with the Democratic Party orientation of the MFDP, and by the prevailing atmosphere of uncertainty within the organization. So they began to look at Lowndes County and saw that we were disciplined and had a clear program that could use their talent. In a time of transition, it seemed like one of the few viable programs with a clear focus that SNCC had.

After Bob Mants, Judy Richardson, Scott B. Smith, and I first went in, Ruth Howard and Courtland Cox from NAG followed. Then Jennifer Lawson and Janet Jemmott *[not NAG]*. Then too, in neighboring counties we had other NAG folks: H. Rap Brown in Wilcox County worked with us, and Cynthia Washington in Greene County, while ol' tough-talking, no-nonsense Annie Pearl Avery, still packing her pistol, came to Hale County. We were a close-knit staff, unified with a clear direction. A talented, tough-minded group of young people.

One night early that summer I went to a meeting in Brown Chapel in Selma to speak about our work in Lowndes. Some students from California were in Selma for the summer. After I spoke, this smart, articulate sister came up. This sister was together, bro, political, a grad student at Berkeley. I could see immediately that she was devoted to our people. And besides, she was beautiful. She had a vibrant spirit, a beautiful Afro, and a smile that could light up a huge room. A strong, beautiful black woman, you couldn't help loving the sister. At least I couldn't. I felt an immediate attraction.

[Apparently reciprocal. Gloria House:

"I have a great deal of love, admiration, and respect for the people I came to know and love in SNCC. I did then and still do. I still feel as if we are a beloved community even after all these years. . . . The first night I was in Selma I went to a mass meeting. . . . And who should be the main speaker but Kwame Ture. I was introduced to Kwame after the mass meeting and, of course, fell in love with him immediately." —A Circle of Trust]

So this sister was all excited about the meeting, the spirit, the singing, the enthusiasm, and the unity. As I said, black culture was strong in Selma; the singing especially was always powerful. So I told Gloria she ought to come to some of the meetings in Lowndes if she really wanted to experience black culture at its full power. That was the beginning of a close, loving relationship. After the summer Gloria came back to work in Lowndes and we were lucky in each other there for a while, until the demands of the movement separated us. But we were lucky there for a while. Sometimes, rarely, in struggle, that can happen.

A few whites were working in Selma and some of the other counties, but not in Lowndes. This was not because we had any formal policy of excluding them, we simply did not encourage them. At that time, it really was like operating behind enemy lines. We discussed the question among ourselves. The general feeling was that we couldn't, on principle, exclude anyone who genuinely wanted to struggle against racism. On principle. But as a *practical* matter, under the objective conditions, we found it would have been foolhardy, even irresponsible, to bring in whites.

While I was inviting the new sister, Gloria, a white volunteer had joined us. He said he too was interested in experiencing a Lowndes County meeting. I knew and respected this guy Jonathan a lot. He'd been in Selma awhile and would always seek me out for serious discussions whenever I was there. I appreciated his intelligence and his seriousness. In this he was a little different from the usual white activists you met. He was somewhat more thoughtful and analytic. Tried to think things through, didn't trot out glib slogans but was looking for lasting solutions. We had some real good talks. He was shocked and pained by the racism, injustice, and poverty he was seeing. And he really seemed interested in black culture.

I remember we were almost the same age. I don't think he was a Southerner, but I knew he had graduated from some military school down South *[Virginia Military Institute]* and was an athlete. Now he was studying for the priesthood, I think in Boston, and I used to tell him, "Stay in the church, man. White America is going to need priests like you."

I thought Jon was an impressive guy, very responsible. Would have been an asset to most projects. But not in Lowndes County. He understood that, accepted it, but always wondered if that wasn't too much like allowing the terrorists to define our actions.

So when the three of us were talking, I may have said he could probably come with Gloria and them to a meeting, but they'd have to return to Selma that same night. Or I may not have, I can't really remember exactly. But what I should have said very firmly was, please, stay the heck away from Lowndes. Hindsight again.

Just after the voting rights bill passed, some local youth planned a demonstration in Fort Deposit, which was a Klan stronghold. Some stores there had been abusive to local youth testing the new law, and the youth now wanted to do a picket. A few carloads of people came in from Selma. Among them were Jonathan and a Catholic priest *[Father Richard Morrisroe]* who had recently come into the state. After some discussion we decided they could come as observers. I was a little uneasy even about the picket itself, which would be, if memory serves, the first direct action not directly related to voting in the county. But, I thought, hey, a public demonstration in the middle of the day. The media will be there. What can happen?

[Ruby Sales:

"One of the things that we were very conscious of is that, sometimes in that kind of situation, white presence would incite local white people to violence. So there was some concern about what that meant . . . to jeopardize the local black people. The other question was who should be in the forefront of the movement. People like myself thought it should be the people themselves in Lowndes County, the local black people, who should be in the forefront. I had some serious concerns about what it meant to allow white people to come into the county and what kind of relationship that set up in an area where black people had historically deferred to white people, and whether or not that was in some real ways creating the very situation that we were struggling very hard to change. More fundamentally, I was very afraid of unleashing uncontrolled violence because of Lowndes County's history . . . and the fact that since I had been in the county I had encountered more than one violent incident . . . but ultimately it was decided that the movement was an open place and should provide an opportunity for anyone who wanted to come and struggle against racism to be part of the struggle." —Voices of Freedom*]*

Well, it was a short demonstration. The Klan was waiting. We were immediately surrounded by a mob larger than the demonstration. That was one time I was not sorry to be arrested. A group of us were taken to the Hayneville jail—mostly local kids, a couple students from Tuskegee, a couple staff, along with Gloria and the two whites from Selma, who were especially singled out by the jailers for verbal abuse.

We were arrested on some trumped-up charges, but the bonds were steep. And the place was fetid, Jack. Unbelievably foul, even for a Southern jail. I heard that some of the local people had come down to check on us but were threatened at gunpoint and turned away without any information on us. We were effectively incommunicado.

We figured we could bond out one maybe two people to go organize bond for the rest. Someone suggested the father. But he said he was more useful inside and probably better off, not knowing the territory and all. I agreed to bond out with Scott B. Smith. We were to come back with lawyers, bond money, and a community escort. I said two or three days, four at the most. Folks gave me messages for their families to tell them where they were, assure them they were well and in good spirits, etc., etc.

It took a few days longer. We'd just rounded up some lawyers. Attorney Chestnutt from Selma and SCLC was sending somebody from Montgomery. Atlanta SNCC was sending the bond. But we were a day too late. The day before we were to meet the lawyers to go to Hayneville, they were released. Now, the group had been defiant, keeping up their spirits by singing and refusing to Tom to the jailers. But this was not a surrender by the jailers, it was an ambush, a stone setup just as in Neshoba County the previous summer.

[*Ruby Sales:*

"The jailer told me that we were being released on our own recognizance. That raised a red flag to me because it was just very incongruent with the blindness of their racism that they would release us on our word, when they didn't think we even had a word. The other thing that bothered me tremendously was that there was no one to meet us, because I knew enough about Stokely Carmichael and also the local people, like the Jacksons, that if we were being released from jail, their commitment was such that they would be there to meet us. So that was another red flag for me. But the deputy and the sheriff told us to stop asking questions and get out. So finally we left, but we just didn't feel comfortable because there was no one around. There was a kind of eerie feeling as if suddenly the streets were deserted, and we could not locate a black face anywhere." —Voices of Freedom

Gloria House:

"Of course we were suspicious of this. No one from SNCC had been in touch with us. We had not been told that bail had been raised; we had no information from anyone, and we thought, this doesn't sound right. But they forced us out of the jail at gunpoint. Being forced out of jail at gunpoint—you know something worse might be waiting for you outside, so you sort of hang on to that jail. Well, we did. We were standing around outside the jail and they forced us off the property onto the blacktop, one of the county roads, again at gunpoint.

"Since we had been in jail and really hadn't had anything fun to eat or drink—we had been eating pork rind and horrible biscuits and whatever— some of us thought, 'Let's walk to the little store here and get a drink, have some

ice cream.' We headed to a corner store. Just as we turned onto the main street of Hayneville, gunfire broke out, and we realized the gunfire was coming in our direction. The youngsters, of course, started running everywhere, and some of us just fell on the ground. Ruby Sales and I had been walking with Jonathan Daniels, and we fell there on the ground. Jonathan was hit and we think he must have died immediately. Father Richard Morrisroe, the only other white member of the group, was also hit. He did not die, but he moaned and groaned and moaned and groaned in a horrible way that none of us who were there will ever forget. It seemed to me it was hours before anyone appeared on this road in Hayneville. Everyone had been informed, of course, that something was going to happen, so this curiously deserted main road was silent because that's the way it was intended to be. We thought we were all going to be killed."—A Circle of Trust*]*

There they were out on the street on foot in a strange town with no one to meet them. They were trying to reach the black community and a phone. Three or four of the sisters were approaching a store when a gunman came out shooting. They say Jonathan and Father Morrisroe threw the sisters aside and took a full load of buckshot. I could see Jon doing something like that. When the shooting stopped, Jon was dead and Father Morrisroe seriously wounded. By the grace of God, he survived.

[Ruby Sales:

"As we approached the store and began to go up the steps, suddenly standing there was Tom Coleman. At that time I didn't know his name; I found that out later. I recognized that he had a shotgun, and I recognized that he was yelling something about black bitches. But my mind kind of blanked, and I wasn't processing all that was happening. Jonathan was behind me and I felt a tug. The next thing I knew there was this blast, and I had fallen down. I remember thinking, God, this is what it feels like to be dead. I heard another shot go off and I looked down and I was covered with blood. I didn't realize that Jonathan had been shot at that point. I thought I was the one who had been shot. When the second shot went off, I heard Morrisroe crying for water and I realized that he had been shot. I also thought that Joyce Bailey had been shot. And I made a decision that I would just lie there, and maybe if I lie there, then Coleman would think that I was dead and then I could get help for the other people. He walked over me and kicked me and in his blind rage he thought I was dead. Joyce Bailey had escaped and she ran back around the store to the side near an old abandoned car and she was calling out our names. 'Ruby, Jonathan, Ruby, Jonathan.' I heard her and I got up. I didn't stand up, I crawled, literally on my knees, to the side of the car where she was, and when I got to her, she picked me up and we began to run across the street, and Coleman realized that I wasn't dead. At that point, he started shooting and yelling things, and Joyce and I were running across the street for dear life and we were screaming and yelling and there was nobody."
—Voices of Freedom*]*

The gunman was a violent racist, brought in under Klan contract, so it was said, to target the two whites. Though from his actions, he clearly was seriously trying to kill the sisters too. That one was arrested after the Justice Department brought pressure. Same ol' same ol'. Some of us went back for his trial and watched him be acquitted by a jury of his peers. After that shooting, the black community saw that they had no choice, either quit or defend themselves. So they made the necessary preparations to do that.

Jon's murder grieved us. His wasn't the first death we'd experienced. But it was in some ways the one closest to me as an organizer. I'd thought they might have been gunning for me that night when they shot Silas McGhee in my car. That brother survived. But this one . . . Now I *knew* the kind of pressure I'd watched Bob Moses endure. I don't mean I understood or sympathized. Everyone had understood. But, now I *felt* what Bob must have been feeling, the pressure, the weight of the responsibility, the sorrow.

But we couldn't let that stop the work. That's precisely what the killers intended. However, from then on, a little too late, the project staff took the strong position, nonnegotiable, that to allow whites in would be tantamount to inviting their deaths. That became our policy. And we armed ourselves.

[Mrs. Mabel Carmichael:

" 'Course I remember. I was still living in the Bronx then. My son came in unexpectedly. I thought he was in Alabama, but he said he had a responsibility, something he had to do for the movement. I had never seen my son like that. Silent, grim, like a heavy, heavy weight was pressing on him. Even when his father died, that had really hit him, but this was different.

"He said that as project director he had to go tell the young man's parents how their son had died. It was when he asked me to ride with him that I knew how hard it was on him. That's the only time he ever asked me to go with him on movement business. He told me the young man was his friend. That he'd told him not to come.

"I think it was somewhere upstate (actually Keene, New Hampshire). *That entire trip I don't think he said two sentences. He didn't even play the radio. You know that's not like him. I think I've blocked a lot of this out. I don't know what he said to the parents. They seemed to be real good people. The three of them went into another room. I believe Stokely was crying. He never told me what was said. The trip back in the car was just as silent. I do think that this was the hardest thing my son ever had to do in the movement. At least that I ever saw." —EMT]*

The *Osageyfo* used to tell me, "The only people who never make mistakes are people who never do anything." I've made mistakes and I'm sure I'll make some more 'cause I'm not finished working. We made a mistake with Jonathan. One that I always remember with regret.

But it sure backfired on the racists. Organizing the party became much easier after that. Now all of the people could see that the Democratic Party—"Hey, them ain't nothing but some night-riding, cross-burning, no-count, low-life snakes"—was not for them.

Could be that I channeled my anger into work, but I became tireless, almost driven. I was determined that this evil system had to be destroyed, and that only the people themselves could do it.

With a federal registrar in the county and firm agreement on the party, the greatest problem we still had was the threat of terrorism. Which increased, especially as our registration grew and the primary approached. These terrorists put it out that no blacks were gonna vote in that county. They swore they'd shoot the entire place up before they'd let that happen. But our people simply refused to be run off. And, man, were they serious too. Serious as a heart attack. They made what preparations they could.

One thing I'll never forget. On election day, Bob Mants and I were cruising the polls. Now there was some law about bringing firearms within—I forget—one hundred, two hundred yards of a polling place? We had stressed that in all the meetings. Up comes this old lady. I mean she had to be eighty years old, Jack, all proud and determined-looking, dressed for church and going to vote for the first time in her life. And she was going to vote for the Panther, then go home. I mean, that ol' lady came up to us, went into her bag, and produced this enormous, rusty, Civil War–looking old pistol.

"Best you hol' this for me, son. I'ma go cast my vote now. I'ma vote for the Panther an' go home." Yes, sir. *Yes, sir.* They would come, these old church sisters, bring out their pistols and stuff, put it right there, and step on up to the polls, yes, sir.

The people had no choice but to take the threats seriously. Just the week before the primary, we were scheduled to hold our nominating convention in the Hayneville courthouse. The sheriff, who must have been implicated in Jonathan's murder said, "No way. No *[expletive]* nigger convention is gonna happen in *my* courthouse." He deputized what must have been every Klansman in the county and some from outside. We said, "Well, we coming. It's our legal right, by any means necessary."

[One source puts the figure at 550 deputized white men. At his trial, Coleman, the assassin, had been described as a "part-time deputy sheriff," so he may well, almost certainly, have been among them. This was a common practice. I can recall having been horrified by a report from Mississippi the previous year, where a local sheriff was reported going into bars and deputizing and arming whites who had been drinking all afternoon. —EMT]

471

It seemed like a real crisis was looming. Of course we were concerned. But you know the people would not back up an inch.

About a week before the primary one of those Justice Department men had come by. Luckily—for him—Bob Mants wasn't there. So the guy comes up to me.

"You know there's likely to be a lot of violence out here with that convention."

I said, "Yeah. Looks that way."

So he comes up with the same old line: "Well, don't you think you people ought to go slow?"

So I told him to go tell the racists to go slow.

Here the federal government just passed this voting rights act. Here I am organizing my people to exercise their democratic rights, and this representative of that same government comes to tell us "to go slow." What's that "go slow" mean, we shouldn't exercise our rights? I asked him that. Also I reminded him that we weren't the ones who'd started any violence. Not once. I told him, you should go tell the terrorists to go slow. You best cool out the whites, we ain't chilling *nothing,* Jack. Tell them, we going straight ahead.

He looked at me like I was crazy. "But there's apt to be a lot of bloodshed."

"Yeah, but this time it won't just be our blood."

"Don't you have any responsibility here? What responsibility do you have?"

"The responsibility I have is to tell you to tell your people, they get the first shot. That's all they get. The first shot. After that I promise you, when we finish with this county . . ."

He stood gaping at me as though I were speaking Swahili.

So I repeated, "You understand now—they get the first shot." Then I just walked away. Actually I was polite as always, y'know, but I wasn't going to let him waste any more of my time. I said, "Thank you very much for coming. But I have to go now. I've got to go organize my people for war." So we just went on and organized. There wasn't one shot fired that day. We held our convention in Hayneville, but we did move it to a local Baptist church.

[According to other sources, federal and state authorities intervened to propose the compromise location acceptable to both sides. The First Baptist Church of Hayneville, where the convention was held, was a few blocks from where Jonathan Daniels was slain. —EMT]

In the primary vote we qualified easily, so that on the election day we had a slate of candidates led by Mr. Hulett and Mr. Strickland. None were elected. What we discovered on election day was that the plantation bosses had completely reversed their tactic. They had quietly registered numbers of their captive workers. A few months earlier they had been running them off the plantation for registering, now they were running them off if they didn't. Go figure.

On election day, they trucked their field hands in to vote against the Panthers. But of the two thousand newly registered blacks, over nine hundred withstood the threats and cast their votes for the Panthers. The peoples had them a party of their own, bro.

Five years after that convention, Bro Hulett, an African who in 1965 could not vote, and who could remember having to duck "like a deer" into the bushes when the sheriff's car approached, was elected sheriff of Lowndes County. Brother Charles Smith became a county commissioner. In the next election, Messrs. Hulett and Smith headed a slate of eight Africans. They won every seat they contested. Today John Jackson is mayor of Whitehall. Mission accomplished, at least partly anyway.

People often ask me, "So whatever happened to the original Black Panther Party?"

I tell them that it demonstrated exactly everything I would later argue in my book *Black Power* on the question of premature coalitions. See, after years of independent organization and growth in numbers and confidence, the party voted to affiliate with a completely new, reconstructed Alabama Democratic Party. The Klan element in Alabama having followed David Duke *[and the Louisiana Klan]* into the Republican fold.

Didn't I feel/take any responsibility? Gimme a break. The incredible chutzpah of that Justice Department gofer. What about the *government's* responsibility? I'm sure he left thinking that that Carmichael Negro is crazy and bloodthirsty. Probably reported that to his bosses in Washington too. Well, tough. I didn't mind if they thought that. Wanted them to, in fact.

"Go slow"? Gimme a break. How could we possibly go any slower? We'd broken absolutely no laws. We'd initiated no violence. None. So why come demanding that—one more time—we should give up our fundamental rights as citizens and human beings. No way, Jack. I hoped he'd go back and report, "Those blacks ain't cooperating. They're giving up nothing. We better lean seriously on the people creating the violence." Which, as it turned out, was more or less what went down. Not a shot was fired.

But what if the government hadn't moved? If once more they had failed to exert federal authority? If those peckerwood terrorists *had* taken the first shot?

You'd better believe we'd been concerned about that long before that Justice Department man showed up. We'd spent a lot of time arguing it out. Our people were determined, brave, but they sure weren't soldiers.

473

Many were old, and the majority in most meetings were, as always, women. The county demographics were just like the Delta. Most young adults had been driven out in search of work or less oppressive conditions. We were left with a lot of older folks—valiant old folks to be sure—but old folks nonetheless, young teenagers, kids, and some adult men like Bros Hulett and Strickland.

So it would be unconscionable to leave them exposed to Klan violence or to expect them to go to war. Who knew what the Klan and the police would bring up against them? So if the government wouldn't enforce the laws, to protect them, we figured we had to. And find people who'd help us do that. That was clear.

We heard about a group of veterans from Baton Rouge, Louisiana, the hometown of Ed and Rap Brown, called the Deacons for Defense and Justice. I think it was Rap Brown who told me about them. Those brothers were organized, trained, and had some serious firepower. Their mission was defending black communities from the Louisiana Klan. We made contact. Once they heard what was going down in Lowndes, they said, "Yeah, we coming." That was the start.

Then we explained the situation to SNCC and proposed that they allow us to take a delegation into the big Northern cities. To talk with brothers and sisters willing to come down to help defend the population. SNCC, after surprisingly little argument, approved. I was chosen to go.

We went to New York, Chicago, Detroit, Philly, the Bay Area, etc., etc. Most of the big cities. We spoke with the militant, nationalist elements. Also at that time these cities had many clandestine formations. We spoke to as many as we could find. We even contacted gangs, as well as regular groups like the Nation with trained units, like the Fruit of Islam. Every city sent a contingent, every one, however small. Paid for it. Brought their own arms too. Got quietly into the county. All in all, you could say thirty to fifty people. Maybe more.

Those who came, came to fight, not just as security. I'd say most had military training. Some had served in Vietnam and had brought back their weapons. We didn't parade them, of course. But we introduced them at the mass meetings, had them greet the community and say a few words of solidarity. You know black Southern communities are very formal, with a certain etiquette just like in African villages. "Brothers and sisters, you ain't alone in this. We bring greetings from the brothers and sisters in Detroit. We came prepared to do whatever is necessary." The people loved that. They just went wild at the meetings. And it was known to the whites that we'd brought in reinforcements. But they had no idea how many.

Bob Mants and I were in charge of deployment 'cause we knew—more or less—the terrorist strongholds. So what we did was secretly post our fighters as close to these places as we could hide them. With instructions. Not to act until acted upon.

We had this slogan among ourselves: "The white folks get the first shot. After that, it's ours." Of course, no one has any idea what would or might have gone down. But give praise and thanks, the terrorists didn't take that first shot. It would have been grim, Jack.

But this is important historically. I think we had six, seven fighters out of California. That delegation was led by an impressive brother named Mark Comfort, who I think was a Vietnam vet. He was a serious brother, low-key and dedicated. Before they returned home, they asked for a meeting. Not just Mark's California delegation, but groups from New York, Philly, Detroit. In essence, they said, we like this Black Panther Party idea. We want to take it back and try to spread it. We said, it's the people's. We ain't got a patent. Feel free. If local conditions indicate, go for it.

But when Comfort got back to the West Coast and brought the idea up, there sprang up, I don't know, maybe ten, twelve different groups all claiming the name. So they asked that SNCC send out someone to help resolve the issue. I was sent by SNCC to investigate and try to resolve the situation. And, its being SNCC, to do some fund-raising while I was there. I wanted Bob Mants to come too since he also knew some of the groups, but SNCC said both of us shouldn't be out of Lowndes at one time.

My thought was to try to bring all these groups together into a unified Black Panther organization and to discuss exactly what political program they were going to organize around. Never happened. My brother, the contradictions out there were rough. Uh-uh, I mean *rough*, Jack. We sat and we discussed and discussed. Discussed with them collectively. With them in groups and individually. But no way. No way. It became clear real quick that no one coming in from the outside could hope to solve these contradictions. It was just impossible. Histories went back years between these groups. Members once of the same group had split into factions and these were competitive, if not openly hostile.

Two brothers from Oakland were representing, far as I could see, no established group. They were together so I guess they represented themselves. They were militant and political and one of them, Huey, seemed very serious. When I first met them, he was the one that impressed me. He didn't say much, whereas his partner, Bobby Seale, rarely stopped. He be steady running this rap. But when Huey P. Newton said anything, you could see that it was something that had been carefully thought out. Something he'd reflected over, something relevant to the discussion. So you could see that he was listening seriously to what was going down. Also, the brother was unassuming, almost humble in his manner. And, very important, he had a good sense of humor and smiled easily. I liked the young man. Although so quiet, he impressed me over a lot of the others who were more vocal.

But the intergroup contradictions, wow. So I reported to Atlanta. Hey, no way can we bring these groups together. And we certainly can't arbitrarily choose which should be the legitimate Black Panthers. None belong to SNCC and none have asked to join. I had one last meeting and asked them to make one final effort to unify, which they promised to do. I then left to do some fund-raising in Los Angeles. I spent a week, ten days tops, in Los Angeles.

I got back to the Bay Area to find everything miraculously resolved. Now it wasn't unity by any means. But the issue of the Panther name was settled. All the groups, one by one, said it's okay, they were no longer interested. They no longer wanted to form a Black Panther Party. The brothers from Oakland, Huey and Bobby, seemed to be the only ones still interested.

I said, now looka this. Wonders never cease. Hey, I knew I was good, but not that good. And my momma sure didn't name me Solomon *[biblical king of the Hebrews of legendary fame for his wisdom in resolving disputes —EMT]*.

But I knew Comfort. We'd spent a lot of time together in Lowndes. I knew his seriousness. We had confidence in each other so I knew I could depend on him to tell me exactly what was going down. Which he did.

He said, okay, what happened was that Huey and his boys just flashed their guns on everyone.

"At a meeting?" I asked.

"No, man, one by one on an individual basis. It was nothing but a cold-blooded bogart, man." Now this brother Comfort was solidly built. You could just look at him and see that you didn't want to bring no gorilla mess to him on any level. I know he had been trained in the military. Maybe, I'm not sure, even with battlefield experience. And I know he had some trained cadres around him. So I didn't think he was intimidated.

"If we struggle over the Panther name with these dudes, it will go to gunfire, man. Warfare over this is silly . . . That makes no sense at all. But they hell-bent on being the Black Panther Party and ready to go to war over it."

He explained Seale's and Newton's backgrounds in an Oakland street gang. "They think they've advanced beyond the gang mentality because they've adopted revolutionary slogans now. But that gang mentality is still very much there, and black people could end up killing each other over a humble. That's stupid." So that was why he was withdrawing. It simply wasn't worth a gun war.

Which essentially meant that Bobby and Huey became the Black Panther Party in California.

Then after I got back to Lowndes, we received a very correct letter from Huey, respectful and eloquent, formally requesting permission to use the Black Panther as the name and symbol of a revolutionary party they planned to organize. We never formally gave permission. What we said was that since we didn't own the symbol (who'd heard of intellectual property rights in those days?), it really belonged to the people, so they didn't need our permission. But it was respectful of them to ask. We told them we hoped and expected that their new party would always defend the community and be unfailingly respectful of *all* black people. They vowed it would.

Here's another little piece of history not generally understood correctly.

A few weeks after the Lowndes election SNCC called a general meeting in Memphis. This was going to be a big 'un. Forman had announced that he was stepping down as executive secretary. In that position Jim had a lot of power and influence. But he had really earned it. Jim had been at the heart of building the organization. The epicenter of every crisis. He had been tireless. Tireless and dedicated. Now his health was compromised, bleeding ulcers, blood pressure, etc., etc. The brother was worn down. Said he needed to step back. Everyone was talking about that. Who would, who *could*, replace Jim Forman.

For almost two years, since January 1965, SNCC had been in flux. During the time I was in Alabama, it had gradually but decidedly changed in its political focus and organizational character. With the civil rights bills of '64 and '65, the national legislative agenda of the Southern movement had been achieved. Now what remained was the implementation of those laws. Was that SNCC's mission in the South, or was that more properly the business of local communities? That was one question. Only one question of many in the ongoing necessity of defining ourselves and the true character and mission of the organization in 1966. Now many of us were looking to see how and whether SNCC could bring our organizing experience and techniques into Northern cities. Could what we'd learned in the South be effective in the North?

This was true especially for those of us from NAG, which had allowed us to work in the North and the South at the same time. So we knew all the work we'd done in D.C., the rent strike and all. So that definitely was in our minds, more and more.

I had been seriously looking to move back to D.C. It seemed the perfect place for me to continue organizing. I knew the city, at least the black sections. I'd cut my political teeth there. It had an African majority and was a colony, which was probably why it *was* a colony, a colonial territory occupied, taxed, and governed by the federal government, as far as the local African community was concerned.

So I was looking at D.C. as a place where SNCC could do some real organizing. That was what I was talking about en route to the Memphis meeting: the nation's capital should be SNCC's first major Northern project, a kind of pilot project demonstrating and refining all we'd learned about organizing at the grass roots. But first we had to put our minds to the subject of the Memphis meeting.

Except for an elected twenty-person executive committee, which rarely met, SNCC had always only had two elected officers: John Lewis, chairman, and Jim Forman, executive secretary. Now Jim, who'd exercised executive authority and done a phenomenal job, was voluntarily stepping down. He could have had the job for as long as he wanted, or the chairmanship if he had wanted that. But he was stepping down. John Lewis was planning to stay on. Just about everyone in the organization, including me, liked John personally. *Personally,* what was there not to like? John was a regular guy, uncomplicated, friendly, and brave, always willing to put his body on the line. He'd certainly taken his licks. I'll never forget Paul Dietrich, fellow Freedom Rider (who had given the Freedom Riders the Chinese dinner party), saying after the March on Washington, "Wow, this is the first time I've seen John without a bandage on his head." Yeah, the brother had certainly paid some heavy dues.

But so had a lot of other folks. And I had become aware of a growing sentiment on the Alabama staff that John no longer represented them *politically.*

I'd been hearing the talk, so I knew that a number of his actions in the last year had angered and confused some people. Now there was a real undercurrent—some people, I believe Stanley Wise was one, were even talking of running against John. But I truly wasn't paying that much attention. SNCC had never, to my knowledge, voted any of its two executive officers out. And I thought that if it came to an election, the general sentiment in John's favor would prevail, easily.

Only when I got to Memphis, Tennessee, did I discover how strong that feeling against Lewis was among Mississippi staff also. There were a number of things. Now, when he'd returned from Africa (December 1965) where he'd met African freedom fighters and reasoned with Malcolm, he'd seemed in touch with the direction of the organization. In fact, he'd sounded like a born-again, Pan-Africanist freedom fighter. Sounding a lot like Malcolm, he clearly saw SNCC's struggle as a struggle for liberation and self-determination and an irreducible element of an international black struggle. I said, "Go, John."

[The destiny of Afro-Americans is inseparable from that of our black brothers in Africa. It matters not whether it is in Angola, Mozambique, South-West Africa, or in Mississippi, Alabama, Georgia, or Harlem. The struggle is the same. It is a struggle against a vicious and evil system that is controlled and

kept in order for and by a few white men throughout the world. —John Lewis, December 1965]

But recently he'd seemed to have drifted back to that mystical "beloved community redeemed by suffering" again. Some of his actions began to seem, if not capricious, then strangely willful, quite at odds with the people and the organization he nominally represented. Not cool.

When, for example, SNCC decided for excellent reasons to have no part *organizationally* in SCLC's march on Montgomery (people could as individuals follow their inclinations), John suddenly appeared identified as "SNCC Chairman" and jointly leading the march with Hosea Williams from SCLC. Folks didn't understand or much appreciate that.

Then, after the voting rights bill, there was a summons to a totally cosmetic, public relations "White House Conference on Civil Rights," which SNCC decided to boycott. We saw it as a transparent ploy to co-opt the new black vote for the Democrats. But our chairman took it upon himself to present himself to the White House with the "respectable" Negro leadership.

But what really crossed the line with the entire Alabama staff was an episode during the run-up to the Lowndes County primary elections.

Into the thick of this struggle, John Lewis comes into the state, I think with Dr. King. Did not inform SNCC people working there. First thing any of us knew, there was our chairman all over the Alabama press calling on Africans to vote in the Democratic primary, while we were trying to get them to vote in the separate, independent primary. Needless to say that was pumped by the press all over the state, but especially in Lowndes County. Ol' Bob Mants was hot, I mean he was *incensed*. I mean, Bob had come into the state with John, whom he respected, had loyally stood with him on the Edmund Pettus Bridge, and was nearly killed for his pains. Now this from John? The brother was hot. I think that tore it with John so far as Bob was concerned.

I had to question whether John had fully understood the implications of that act. For the staff. For our program? I still wonder. 'Cause it was hard to believe that he, knowingly and deliberately, would publicly undercut our work so blatantly. But what does it say if the chairman is that far out of touch with his organization? Just as earlier I thought he had completely misread the staff's strong feeling of betrayal with the fiasco at the Pettus Bridge. That second march attempt when SCLC had led thousands across the bridge only to kneel, pray, and turn them round. Course I didn't have the strong sense of *personal* betrayal that Bob had, though I too was quite annoyed.

However, when we got to Kingston Springs, Tennessee, I discovered that this current was far stronger and more widespread than just the Alabama staff. Many among the Mississippi field staff were saying,

"Yeah, John's a nice guy, but he shouldn't be chairman. He just isn't representing us." This wasn't no undertow, Jack, it was a groundswell. But still I thought, should this even come to a vote, which I doubted, most folks will vote their sentiments rather than their politics; John would survive on sentiment.

However, when the question of the chair came up, there were a few prospective candidates. I recall Stanley Wise being one. The discussion was long. They discussed and discussed and discussed. As the issues got sharper and the political cleavage more evident, it became clearer and clearer that John Lewis really did not understand, or perhaps care to understand, the feelings within the organization.

Cleve Sellers and a couple of people came to me. "Okay," they said. "There's a clear discussion. A clear question of direction and policy. You represent our position. You know it. You're the logical person to run for chair."

"Oh, hell, no," I said. "I don't have time for this. I'm going to D.C., remember?" Coming to this meeting, the last thing in my mind had been running for any elective office. I'd never held or contested any elective office in SNCC, not even the executive committee. I was a field organizer, content to be that, happy as a bee in a sunflower field in August.

"Man, that's irresponsible," said Ivanhoe, who would scold you in a minute, yes, he would. "There's a crisis in the organization. You gotta, you're the obvious choice." Anyway, they drafted me.

[Cleve Sellers:

"That's accurate. It was a bunch of us who argued Stokely into running. As I recall there was Ruby Doris (Smith-Robinson), *Muriel* (Tillinghast), *Ivanhoe* (Donaldson), *Roy Shields, Jesse Harris, and this brother, I can see his face but the name escapes me, a project director from Meridian. There were some other Mississippi folk too." —EMT]*

As I recall, Ruby Doris had already been elected to replace Jim, and Cleve had been elected to a new executive position—program secretary—specially created to bring some order to field operations. Then came the vote between John and me. They discussed and discussed again. Wore it down. Wore it *out,* Jack. I think the first vote came about two o'clock in the morning if memory serves. I'd been paying attention but I hadn't realized just how many people had drifted away. John won, narrowly.

I told Cleve, "Well, sentiment won. But it's okay. I'm not going to fight John. This was useful. The issues have been clarified. The political direction is clear. He *must* have learned something from all this. It'll be okay."

Tell the truth, I was ambivalent. On one hand I knew the issues were important and not about to go away. On the other, I was relieved. Organizing was what I really wanted to do. So I was getting ready to make it on out when Worth came in. *[Worth Long, member of the Alabama project staff, now a distinguished folklorist and movement historian. —EMT]*

Worth turned the whole thing around. A passionate speech. Oh, no, this is totally incorrect. First of all, it does not reflect the general mood and direction of SNCC. What we want to do and what we should be doing. It doesn't reflect the majority of staff. It may not even be legitimate. Folks aren't here. If you really want to make this decision tonight, we gotta go round up the people, give everyone a chance to participate.

So at two o'clock in the morning they start to wake folks up. Calling in the folks who had drifted outside. Only then did I realize how many folks had not been present for the vote. When they came in, they say, "Oh, no. We didn't realize you all were voting. That can't stand. We gotta reopen the process. This is an important decision."

Then, the debate started, Jack. This time on process.

Cleve an' them came to me. "Don' say anything at all," they said. So I was silent. Ruby Doris and Cleve volunteered to step down to allow new elections across the board. John refused. That was his first mistake. It alienated a lot of folks. Not just the ones claiming to feel excluded, but even some of his supporters who felt he was obstructing full and fair discussion *and* full participation.

[Willie Ricks Mukassa:

"I happened to be chairing that session. When the people started talking about a re-vote, John got up to talk about it. As he came up, he whispered, 'Save me. You gotta save me, Willie.' I said, he crazy. How he expect me to 'save him'? How am I going do that? Especially, African, when Fay Bellamy got hot. Bro, that sister lit into John like a duck on a june bug. Man, she turned him every which way but loose." Cackling laughter. "It was after that they decided to vote everything over again."

Fay Bellamy:

"Mukassa said that? Well, you know, I am proud of that. See, I liked John personally, thought he was a nice enough person and all that. But in some important ways didn't seem like he had a clue. Some folks were saying that he was certainly brave enough, but a bit of a handkerchief head, y'know? What'd I say? Well, it's been a while.... What I remember was he wasn't representing us. He may have represented SCLC. Or Dr. King. Maybe he was representing himself. But he sure wasn't representing us. He wasn't paying attention to what the organization was doing. Wasn't participating on projects, wasn't doing the job a chairman should. He was making speeches, fronting in the press but ... Every time LBJ called, he'd rush his clothes into the cleaners and be on the next plane to Washington. You had to wonder where his head really was."]

I still thought it likely that John would win on sentiment: that even though people could now see that where he was politically was not where they wanted us to go, they'd still let sentiment sway them. "Yeah, so maybe he's not the best chairman, but I still like John, y'know?" I said as much to Cleve: "Yeah, man, we got the politics, but he get the sentimental vote, but it's okay."

But then he made his worst mistake. I simply couldn't believe it. Bad judgment, Jack. A most unfortunate statement. Shot himself in the mouth.

He got up and said—which was quite true but most people didn't know it—he said that when he'd come into SNCC it was *because he was invited in as chairman. Oy vay.* In that context? Very ill advised. The statement had at least three implications, each worse than the last.

First, that the position somehow belonged to him.

Second, that absent the chairmanship he would not have dignified the organization with his presence all these years.

Third, that if he was no longer chair, he would leave SNCC. *Then* what would we do?

Man, you know SNCC people: how they felt about titles, "leaders," and anything that even remotely looked like an ultimatum. First of all, it was unseemly, counterproductive, undignified. This desperate scrambling around to hold on to the position. For that was all it was, a position, a title, for blessed little power was involved. I thought perhaps he'd been spending too much time around Roy Wilkins and the professional "Negro leaders." Why else would he make such a silly, self-defeating statement? I never understood that. Still don't.

[Editor's note:

At this point I suggested that John's motive was no longer so inscrutable. That in the light of subsequent events in his political career and with our brother never having been known for subtlety, that may in all probability have been precisely what was intended. And that this element of character—unbridled ambition, an instinct toward the establishment, and a certain lightness of principle—were all fully revealed in the surpassing ugliness and opportunism of the campaign for Congress he mounted in 1976 against his erstwhile best friend, Julian Bond.

"That may well be, Thelwell." Kwame gave me a quizzical look, too quizzical, I thought. "Even so, so what?"

"So why don't we just say that?" I snapped.

"Because, Thelwell, I thought you understood this is not going to be that kind of book," he said slowly with an exaggerated patience bordering on condescension.

"'What I understood was that it must tell the truth, Thelwell, for history,'" I mimicked. "Besides, I've read the congressman's book, you haven't."

"So?"

"He's not real generous or even fair to you. Whenever you appear, you're either deluded, disruptive, destructive, duplicitous, bent on violence, or childishly

egotistic. The book is not only transparently self-serving, it's real mean-spirited toward you."

"So we should be the same toward him? Gimme a break." He grinned that grin.

Stung now, I played my hole cards, both of them. "Hey, far be it from me to be more royal than the king. I know I merely the griot here, and kings have been known to wimp out before. But you really ought to read that book. The congressman's got a little mantra you'll just love. He keeps saying piously, 'Every time I had to choose between the black thing, or the right thing, I chose the right thing.' Decode that for me."

"You not making this up? The black thing or the right thing, huh? He actually said that?"

Aha, I thought, I knew that'd get his attention.

"Repeatedly. Repeatedly." I looked as sorrowful as I could. "And it must have sounded real good to him too. For he said it at least four times, fo' times."

There was silence between us.

"Okay, Thelwell. We'll hold that one. Leave it the way it is for now. Junebug used to say, 'Inside every Negro there lurks a potential black man.' Lemme think about it. Later, when we get to that chapter in the book, we can fight about it. . . . By the way, you have that book with you?"

So we left it. I do know that the brother read the congressman's book, but we never had the chance to discuss it or "fight about" this chapter. Consequently, having no idea of anything he might have wanted to change or add, I've left it as he did. To append the above discussion is my editorial decision, entirely without prejudice and only in the spirit of full disclosure. As Stokely said, "We all liked John." —EMT]

CHAPTER XXI

"Magnified, Scrutinized,
Criticized . . ."

"Well, Stokely, tell you what. I'll be in town on Sunday. Why don't you come to lunch then? After church. I can see that there's a lot of talking we need to do."

"Be an honor, Reverend. But I wanna be clear now. In order to git some of that good Baptist cooking, I gotta go to church first?

Chuckles. "Well, no, Stokely. I wasn't saying that at all. But y'know, that isn't such a bad idea. The Good Lord knows you going need all the help you can get. Besides, I'll be preaching."

"In that case, Dr. King, you know I'm goin' be there."

During my time in Atlanta I would become close to Dr. King. That invitation to lunch was the first of many. The first thing he asked when I got on the phone was, had anyone read me my rights yet? "My rights, Reverend, how so?"

"I thought not. Well, I guess it's up to me. From now on, Stokely, anything you say will be taken down and used in evidence against you . . . and the rest of us."

That was the first of many, many times that Dr. King would warn me that my role had changed and that anything I said or did would reflect on my organization and our people's struggle.

"You're not what you used to be, Stokely. You now represent SNCC. You have to be very careful. Your every word will be magnified, scrutinized, and criticized. By friends as well as by enemies. And believe me, Stokely, it won't always be easy to tell one from the other, the sheep from the goats."

I told Dr. King that I didn't really expect the job to be too different from the work I'd been doing all along in SNCC. It was just a matter of proportion. I'd perhaps be having more press conferences than other SNCC workers. But, like other organizers who'd also had their fair share

of meetings with the press, I'd done that. Nothing new. Maybe now there'd be more microphones, that's all.

He laughed. "Stokely, that only tells me how much you have to learn."

After that Dr. King and I would become closer and closer during the time I was in Atlanta. On Sunday, when we both were in town, I'd sometimes get invited to eat with the family. We always talked politics. I'd say Dr. King took me under a brotherly wing to advise and sometimes chastise me. He seemed to like me. Despite a few tactical disagreements over the years, my admiration and respect for Dr. King only increased. He was deeply devoted to our people's welfare. And he was honest, always.

[Andrew Young:

"Martin always saw Stokely as a young man with tremendous potential and ability. He liked his spirit and dedication.

"I know that, in return, Stokely's admiration, indeed love, of Dr. King was deep and genuine. I think Dr. King may well have recognized a lot of himself in the younger man, in particular, a stubborn moral courage, honesty, and a selfless willingness to serve our people. Of the many media distortions of his record, none seemed to affect Carmichael except one. The crude conventional formulation about 'young militants led by Stokely Carmichael' turning against Dr. King. That really annoyed him, whenever we came across it. 'But, y'know, it doesn't really matter, Thelwell. Dr. King knows that never was true.'"—EMT]

One thing about Dr. King's courtesy call surprised me. When he said he wasn't at all surprised by the election. That he'd always had a feeling that one day I would "be called to serve SNCC" in that or a similar position. Why was I surprised to hear him say that? Because John Lewis was a seminarian and also was on the SCLC board. Consequently, I'd sorta assumed that Dr. King, if he thought about the election at all, might be expected to have been partial to John. But he seemed quite happy with the result and I didn't get the impression he was just being diplomatic.

That first week I got quite a few other courtesy calls, something I hadn't expected. But Dr. King's was the most important. Another one came from my old prison teacher, Jim Farmer. Mr. Farmer (peace be unto him) was funny. He said he too had been watching my "career." He had confidence in me but wasn't quite sure whether to congratulate me or to commiserate. Did I know the West Indian proverb about the high-climbing monkey? I told him my grandmother used to say it all the time.* He sounded a little wistful when he said he'd be praying for me. And that I'd need to develop "some calluses on my soul" real quick. Remember the line, he said, "uneasy lies the head"? I said that didn't apply since SNCC didn't have no crowns no how. He laughed. "If that's really true, more power to you young people."

---

*"The higher the monkey climb, the more he expose he behind."

It was good of Mr. Farmer to call, but I wasn't worried about watching my back since I didn't plan to get too attached to the position. In fact, just the opposite. I planned to go back into the field, preferably in D.C., as soon as the job I was elected to do was accomplished.

[Mr. Farmer had only recently relinquished the leadership of CORE, a position he'd held since CORE's inception some thirty years earlier. This may explain the somber note Carmichael detected in his call. CORE's changing of the guard, a concession to a so-called youth movement, may also explain some of Roy Wilkins's subsequent behavior during this period.

In 1984, writing about his experience in the Parchman death house during the Freedom Rides, Mr. Farmer had written:

"The new riders had come from all over. One, a tall, skinny kid in his senior year (sic) *at Howard University, possessed an infectious smile and enormous charm. We instantly felt we'd known him always. But he seemed so pliant and easygoing, so quiet and so shy* (sic), *that I told myself he'd never make it in this world. His name was Stokely Carmichael." No comment necessary. —EMT]*

But now I had to think seriously about this new role. It really did seem to me to be just more of the same: the work I'd been trained to do in SNCC. Except in different proportions, that's all. Hey, I'd been doing mass meetings, three or four a week, with hundreds of people. Press conferences, speaking at fund-raisers up North. Every organizer did those, so public speaking was no problem. True, I'd have to leave my project, but I planned, as chair, to be in the field all the time. So I couldn't see that my life would need to change in any fundamental way.

But the *organization?* That would have to change, inevitably, no question. That really had become clear even from the discussions during the elections. My job was to articulate those changes, project the new mission of SNCC into the national political debate, and get back to organizing as soon as possible. Simple enough.

Besides, I was surrounded by a good team. The internal administration of those changes—the real heavy lifting, day to day—was on Cleve and Ruby Doris. They saw the need for the same changes I did, so our position was thorough, thorough, thorough. When you read historical accounts of that election, they make it seem as though I, by my lonesome, somehow maneuvered it all. Rather than a group of serious, dedicated organizers, some of the best ones in SNCC, who had a common vision. Our team represented that vision. I mean, the real power within SNCC had always been the executive secretary, formerly Jim Forman, now Ruby Doris (Smith-Robinson). She was hardworking, clear, and decisive. Ruby's seriousness and dedication had earned her a natural authorit within SNCC that everybody respected. Ruby and I went back a lo time, to the Freedom Rides. We trusted each other, so that was ea could take my marching orders from Ruby Doris any day. Any da

Of the three, Cleve's job—program secretary—was in some ways the most challenging and not only because it was new. Until a year before, no such position had existed in SNCC, so Cleve had to define the position as he went along. The program secretary was created to bring order to near chaos, to impose discipline and coherence to the way personnel and resources were managed across an organization that had grown much too rapidly. Naturally, some folks, even people who liked Cleve personally, opposed the position on principle. To them, the notion of *structure* was anathema and especially when, as was inevitable, it conflicted with some part of their "personal freedom." So conflict was built into the position, yet the organization had reelected Cleve, so obviously most people felt a need for the position and a certain confidence in him.

Cleve and I had been at Howard. Together we'd been through a lot. He was like a younger brother to me. I knew Cleve and would trust him with my life. But while I felt the utmost confidence in our team, I was under no illusion about the task we were facing.

I knew that the changes we would have to implement were logical and inevitable—independent politics, independent organization, the emphasis on pride and culture, strong resistance to the war. They were also irreversible, so that people like John Lewis and others would probably leave the organization, but that a strong, if smaller, core would be left to soldier on to the next stage. I was clear on that.

I also knew instinctively that those positions would, almost certainly, cause tensions inside the movement and in the society. I understood from experience that the press, never too nice to SNCC, would now denounce us. That the FBI would step up its harassment and that draft boards would play a role in that. That funding the organization, which had never been easy, would now become even more difficult. I had begun to realize all this during the discussions in Tennessee even. Now, thinking seriously about it, it seemed clear that we were likely or certain to become an exposed target. But honestly? I did not anticipate the *intensity* of the flack and the sniping that the organization would receive.

When we got back to Atlanta, the new team had our first press conference to outline the organization's new direction. We decided to stress continuity and logic. It was a large press conference. The press had a lot of questions. But somehow I can't seem to remember a single question they asked. Not one. What I do remember clearly is how little they seemed to understand, as though they were stuck in 1960 with the student sit-ins and we were speaking in unknown tongues. An impression confirmed when we saw the stories they filed. Most lacked both context and logic. And missed that the new direction was simply a necessary response to current political realities.

It was as though the unity and progress of the civil rights movement was under threat from "young, black militants" who had suddenly materialized inside SNCC—apparently from outer space and speaking, as I said, no language known to the American media. And the efforts at clarification made by Julian Bond and SNCC's small, hardworking publicity staff seemed to fall on deaf ears. Portents of things to come.

I saw then that the major part of my job—projecting publicly a new role and identity for SNCC—was not going to be so easy. But, of course, I never thought it would be impossible. I said, later for the press, I'll just concentrate first on the other part of the job. For that I needed to spend time with our staff and projects in the field. To evaluate conditions on the projects: the work being done, the morale of staff, the needs, the problems, etc., etc. Most important, to get a clear idea of exactly how folks wanted to be represented. So that's what we started with.

So for the first month Cleve, Stanley Wise (peace be unto him), another brother from Howard, and I visited every SNCC project across the South.

We were in Little Rock, meeting with the Arkansas project staff, when someone ran into the meeting shouting that James Meredith (the African brother who had been met with a riot when he integrated the University of Mississippi) had been assassinated on a Mississippi highway just outside Memphis.

I heard someone moan, an unearthly, almost animal sound. Loud, anguished, hardly human. I know I felt cold, suddenly numb from the top of my head to the soles of my feet. Weary to the bone. Another man done gone. Then the room was filled with anger and frustration.

Apparently Meredith, always a strange, almost eccentric brother, had embarked almost single-handedly on his own "March Against Fear." He meant to march through Mississippi to demonstrate to the people that white violence was nothing they had any longer to fear. A noble intention and a bad idea. With predictable results.

Now the brother was dead, uselessly and senselessly. Worse than useless, because the only message our people would get would be the one the assassin wanted them to get. Exactly the opposite of the message poor Meredith had intended. To survive the Ol' Miss riots only to end up shot down from ambush along some Mississippi highway?

[Apparently the would-be assassin—Aubrey James Norvill—was still angry about Meredith's role at Ol' Miss years earlier. "I only want James Meredith," he had declared when he stepped out of the bushes and fired four times at Meredith, completely ignoring Meredith's four companions. —EMT]

We were still arguing about what action we could and should take when we learned that Meredith was alive in a Memphis hospital. Since Memphis was only a few hours' drive, we decided to go pay our respects. The three of us went. Our mood during the drive was grim, bordering on

desperation. We were angry and tired, tired, tired. Tired of folks being brutalized or killed with impunity. Tired of the indifference and complicity
of the nation. Tired of mealymouthed politicians. Tired too especially of
half-baked, knee-jerk ideas from our side. Particularly of these wretched,
pointless marches, appealing to whom? Accomplishing what? What we felt
in that car was an all-encompassing anger and frustration, as much with
movement futility as with the racist violence.

At the hospital we met Dr. King and Attorney Floyd McKissick of
CORE in Meredith's room. Remembering Bro Farmer's strange phone
call, I couldn't help smiling when I saw Bro McKissick. Meredith was
still weak. He seemed dazed and distracted, so ours wasn't a long visit.

Outside, Dr. King told us that Meredith had agreed—more accurately,
had been persuaded—to allow the civil rights organizations to pick up the
march from the place (Hernando, Mississippi) where he'd been shot.
CORE and SCLC were committed. What was SNCC's position? I said
SNCC didn't have one. After that mess in Selma, you know I wasn't about
to commit the organization to another march just because Meredith had
gone and gotten himself shot. What sense did that make?

The argument was familiar. Too familiar in fact. The old "the movement can't allow violence to stop us" argument all over again. Yeah, well,
that was getting real tired. Stop us? How *us*? Which *us*? SNCC hadn't
agreed to any such march. What if the idea had been a dumb one to begin
with? I told them we'd have to take the proposal back to the SNCC executive committee and I wasn't at all certain what response was likely.

"Can you do that in twenty-four hours?" Dr. King asked. Turns out
Roy Wilkins (NAACP) and Whitney Young (Urban League) were flying
into Memphis for a meeting the next evening. Could we have a SNCC
answer by then? The three of us looked at each other. One thing is certain, we said, we sure can't have it *before* then.

At first we were unanimous. Have nothing to do with the madness. But
after a while that wasn't so clear. The march would be going through the
Mississippi Delta. My old congressional district, where both Stanley
and Cleve had worked in '64. Our turf. Our people were bound to be on
the line. How could SNCC let the other organizations march through and
we be absent? No way we could explain that to the local people we'd
worked with, especially the youth. No way. That was obvious.

Your rock and hard place one mo' time. Because, on the other hand,
what exactly was a "march against fear" anyway?

I mean in political terms? A symbolic act, a media event, a fund-raising
operation? It was all of those and nothing. Meredith had consulted
nobody in the movement. Apparently he'd wanted neither help nor
advice. Now we were to be stuck with his ill-conceived, almost stillborn
infant? No way would SNCC fall for such off-the-wall okeydoke. And

they'd be right. Resources were scarce and getting scarcer. I could already hear Ruby Doris: "Another march? Is y'all crazy? Now I know for sure, Howard University really done ruint mo' good Negroes than whiskey." *[No, sister, that was* Harvard. *—EMT]*

But guess what? The more we talked, something else slowly began to emerge, slowly, slowly. None of us had had much sleep, maybe that was it. But maybe, just perhaps the idea's very weakness—its vague, ill-defined, amorphous quality—could be its greatest value. What if we could give it some serious political meaning? Hey, after all, it was going through our counties. MFDP country. Our folk would be doing the marching. SNCC projects would be doing the organizing. We could turn it into a moving freedom day. Doing voter registration at every court-house we passed. Have a rally every night. We could involve the local communities. Address their needs. A very different proposition from the previous promenades of the prominent.

The more we talked the more excited we became. We called Atlanta and asked Ruby to set an executive committee meeting for the next morning and at sunup caught the first thing flying south.

I didn't sleep much that night, and not merely because Stanley was snoring like a big dowg. But because I began to see that this could be my first real test as chairman. I wasn't interested simply in a media platform from which to *proclaim* SNCC's new direction. I'd already seen how that didn't work.

Hey, *telling* them hadn't worked at the press conference. We'd need to *show* the media. I wanted this march to *demonstrate* the new SNCC approach in action. To incorporate it: in the planning, in the personnel, the organization, the decision-making, and especially in the orientation and message. In everything the local communities and leadership would have to be centrally involved. Everything.

That way we could showcase our approach. We wouldn't just *talk* about empowerment, about black communities controlling their political des-tiny, and overcoming fear. We would *demonstrate* it. The march would reg-ister voters by the hundreds. Local people would organize it, would help decide on objectives, and, to the extent they could, provide resources and generally take responsibility.

Our base in the Delta was certainly capable of organizing that. The local community and *their* interests would be the constant focus. It could be their march, period. I didn't see how SCLC and CORE, the activist groups, could object. Or even the NAACP, for that matter, since so many of the strong local people were also NAACP members. The real problem figured to be the SNCC executive committee, at least so we thought. We knew they were fed up with marches.

By the time we got off the plane in Atlanta, it was all surpassingly clear to us. All this was definitely possible, but could we bring it off, and especially in the time we had?

The executive committee meeting was just great. Though we didn't see it then, the meeting turned out to be exactly what we needed. Our presentation, so I thought, was a veritable model of clarity and vision. So naturally it was met with near total skepticism. Not necessarily at the goals, but at the feasibility, the implementation. Many of the objections were obviously valid. The questions pointed and practical. They forced us to back up and refine our thinking and polish our arguments. By the end of the meeting we had both concept and language down pat. We would be the best-prepared voice in the Memphis meeting.

What the SNCC executive committee finally said was, fine, do it if you bad enough. *But,* don't you be committing SNCC resources to no march now, hear? Course Mississippi project resources and people can be used, but don't be calling Atlanta for any more help. Understand? Hardly a ringing endorsement, but it was all we wanted. But, y'know, they were in effect really saying what we were: let the local Mississippi communities carry the ball. We called down to our project directors in the Delta to start organizing a meeting and hit a flight back to Memphis.

[Cleve Sellers remembers:

"We were very clear . . . it was time for the black community to take responsibility for the march's success. We wanted them to share not just in doing the actual marching, but in providing the leadership and resources. We'd seen Selma and Birmingham, the entourage of press and visiting leaders leaving behind a vacuum, a few corpses, sheer confusion and frustration, and a very pissed-off white community prone to violence. We felt very strongly that, this time, the Meredith march could be a showcase for doing campaigns very, very differently from the way they had been conducted across the South in the recent past. Local initiative, local empowerment."]

In Memphis, the next real test would be the "summit" meeting that night. Everything would hinge on how that went: whether the march even went forward. Whether it would be something politically useful in which SNCC could participate.

The notion of "taking over" or even "leading" the march wasn't in our thinking. All we wanted was to give it direction. I honestly couldn't think of any valid objection to what we were proposing. Nor any reason why all the organizations couldn't participate amicably in it. While I wasn't exactly sure what to expect from the "summit," I did think we were ready with a plan that made sense and that this would be obvious to all parties.

"So, bro, you expect any problems?" Stanley asked. Stanley always was a worrier.

"Can't think of any. Hard to say. Why?"

"Well, y'know, it'll be your first summit. Representing SNCC among the big Negroes . . ."

I honestly hadn't thought of it in those terms. My concern was with the issues.

"Shoot, big Negroes? Hey, don't forget . . . *they* ain't never been to no SNCC staff meeting either, Jack. *That's* their problem. We'll just stay on the issues, period. If necessary, turn it into a SNCC staff meeting and see can they hang. You *know* we got the issues."

"I know that," Stanley said, "but I'm more thinking of the politics and the personalities."

As it turned out, we both were right. About two in the morning after the dust had settled, Cleve grinned at me. "So you really weren't kidding, huh? Damned if you didn't sho nuff turn it into a SNCC staff meeting."

"Hey, don't knock it," I said. "It worked, didn't it?"

Yeah, I guess you'd have to say we did all right. But sometimes you can win the battle and lose the war. Still, I can't see how we could have done otherwise. One thing, though, it wasn't really a SNCC-type meeting. Not at all. Know what it did remind me of? It was exactly like those meetings we used to have with the Howard administration. Exactly. How so? Remember how they'd walk in in their suits, all paternalistic, self-important, overconfident. Figuring us for naive kids they could intimidate with the majesty of their authority. So utterly dismissive. And completely under-estimating us so that they'd walk in completely unprepared. Then, come to find out we'd be the only ones present who'd done any homework at all. And we'd eat their lunch. I swear that was the dynamic in that motel that evening. Exactly, Jack. I couldn't believe it. Could not believe it. I mean, mah man, we were the only ones there with anything resembling a coher-ent, defensible analysis. It was good ol' Howard all over again.

What exactly happened? Weal . . . going in I figured Dr. King would be key if it came down to a struggle, because I had no idea what Bro Young and Bro Wilkins's position was going to be. Figured they'd be together, whatever it was. I assumed—correctly—that they were coming mainly because they didn't want Dr. King to again have center stage all alone with the national media, the way he'd had it on the Selma march. That much was clear. Also, I figured that they would favor a public relations approach. The least controversial, most conventional, media-compatible, acceptable-to-the-establishment-and-administration approach possible. Now, we had no principled objection to any of all that, as long as the local political goals and activities were included prominently, and I didn't see that they were mutually exclusive. For, I honestly couldn't see anything possibly offensive to *anyone* in what we were proposing. So I didn't see that any ideological division of the movement needed to happen. Especially since I planned to present our proposals in the most moderate and reasonable language possible. Which I did . . . at first anyway. No problem, or so I hoped. But what if there were differences at the table?

Well, Bro McKissick was a Southern brother and an activist. According to the press he—like me—had been elected by a "militant" faction in CORE. And CORE's experience in the South was close to ours. For that reason I was confident that he'd see the *operational* logic of our position. Besides which the brother had paid some large dues. For years, Jack. Hey, the brother had integrated and been the first African to graduate from the Law School at the University of North Carolina. So I figured him for a fighter, a serious, honest brother and a natural ally. And I was right.

So I figured that in any real division it'd most likely be CORE and SNCC on one side with the NAACP and the Urban League on the other, with the deciding vote possibly falling to Dr. King.

So the plan was to avoid "division" at all cost, right? Well, the first person we ran into when we got to the motel before the big meeting was the brother from the Deacons. *[Deacons for Defense and Justice, an armed self-defense group out of Bogalusa, Louisiana.]* The brother seemed upset. As soon as he'd heard what had gone down with Meredith, he'd rushed up from Bogalusa, offering to provide security for the march. He felt he wasn't getting straight answers (or the proper respect). He had been told that we would be taking up his offer at the meeting and he should wait. We knew the Deacons from over in Lowndes. We owed them. Besides, they were as brave, well-trained, and as disciplined a group of brothers as you could hope to find in the country. Businesslike, no posturing, no rhetoric. Plus, we needed *them,* not the other way around.

So much for avoiding controversy. At least now we knew what the first tough issue was going to be. Negroes with guns.

"Hey, bro," I said. "No sweat." I told him if the Deacons don't patrol the road, SNCC don't march. If SNCC don't march, there ain't no march. We set out for the meeting.

"Man, I can't believe you just said that," Stanley blurted out. "That's what you call sound negotiating tactics? Respecting the Deacons is one thing. But, man, jamming us into a corner with them before the meeting even starts? I mean, Dr. King—"

"Don't worry about Dr. King, Stanley. The reverend may surprise you yet. Besides, everybody knows this is an issue the movement is going to have to face sooner rather than later. You're not saying you'll feel more secure with the Mississippi Highway Patrol out there all by themselves, are you?" (On the first day of the march, I would discover how prophetic that question was.)

We finally got to the meeting room. Big conference table. Dr. King was already there with Bernard Lee, his assistant, and Bro McKissick. I told them that SNCC had sent us as a delegation with precise instructions. No problem. They said that the "big two" were on their way. Now, I'd heard many, many stories from Bayard about how impossibly difficult and prickly Roy Wilkins could be over questions as much of rank and status as of actual politics. From Bayard's stories, he sounded like a bad trip. "Tell me again, Rustin, why should I even meet with you? Whom or what do you represent? You represent nobody."

I'd also heard that he regularly tried to condescend even to Dr. King in these meetings and was downright dismissive of CORE, so how he felt about SNCC I could easily imagine. I decided I wasn't going to wait for him to patronize me. I'd beat him to it. At all cost, young man, avoid controversy.

Wilkins and Young came in together, suitably attired and carrying official-looking briefcases. Whitney Young was smiling affably. He seemed a pleasant enough brother. Bro Roy, now he didn't even crack a smile. I met them at the door, Jack, just a-beaming an' a-smiling, as Mr. Turnbow would say, jes' a-beaming an' a-smiling. Cleve and Stanley were right behind me, all earnest, polite, and properly respectful. I grabbed Bro Wilkins's hand and started pumping away, giving him my broadest smile.

"Mr. Wilkins, Mr. Young. A pleasure, gentlemen. An honor to meet you. An *honor*, Mr. Wilkins. Just looking forward so much to working with you, such an *honor*." Later, Cleve said, "Damn, bro, I thought you was going ask for his damn *autograph*."

For a moment, Bro Wilkins seemed disarmed, looking surprised and suspicious, giving me this tight, little smile. He was a taller man than I'd expected. I saw Dr. King, who was watching us, catch himself and quickly hide an amused grin behind a broad smile of welcome, but I could see he was cracking up inside. This spirit of goodwill lasted until we started to sit around the table. Brother Wilkins was steady giving Cleve and Stanley a sour look.

"Martin, didn't you say this was to be a meeting of the *leadership*?" The brother was still glowering at Stanley and Cleve, who refused to catch his eye.

"I said of the national organizations, Bro Wilkins. Each group has one vote."

"Martin, you know we talk with generals. Not with rank and file."

"Oooh," I said. "*Generals*. Well, Dr. King, that sure nuff eliminates us. You know, SNCC doesn't even have colonels, much less generals. We all just bare-butt foot soldiers in SNCC." However, I didn't move. This time Dr. King didn't hide his grin.

"Y'know, Stokely's right, Roy. The young people are very democratic. Neither Floyd nor I had any problem with it."

Bro Young was silent; Bro Wilkins turned the sour look on me. "Well, *John* certainly never felt a need to surround himself with an *entourage* either," he snapped.

"That was his biggest problem," Stanley muttered.

I figured that a quiet answer turneth away wrath, so I accepted the blame. Oh, Mr. Wilkins, you so right. Oh, dear, I believe this is really all my fault. I'm so *new* to all this, the SNCC executive probably figured I'd need help. Guess being my first time out an' all, they didn't trust me *alone* up here with all y'all *generals*. So they sent a delegation. Not an entourage, sir, a delegation. It's just that I have so *much* to *learn*. I just dripped diffidence, even humility. Even Whitney Young seemed to be suppressing a grin.

"Hell, less git started. We got work to do," McKissick growled.

"As long as you all understand now. SNCC has one spokesman and one vote. That clear?" I think Bro Wilkins considered that a gracious concession.

I tried to look properly grateful. "Yes, sir. Thank you, sir. Understood, yes, sir."

Everyone could agree that, if possible, the Meredith march should go forward. That ideally it should be a joint project of the major organizations, equally represented. It should be a genuinely cooperative effort of equal participation, with each organization contributing according to its strengths. Agreed. After that it would merely be a matter of designing the march and the message. Everyone agreed, now the fine-tuning.

Somehow Dr. King fell into the role of moderator. He looked around the table. I said SNCC had no money, but we knew the territory. And had infrastructure on the ground. We had the troops. We could deliver bodies, the "rank and file." However, we did have a few ideas that we'd like to put to the meeting at the appropriate time. So far so good. Then came the NAACP's turn.

Bro Wilkins said that the NAACP and Urban League had been in discussions. Serious, high-level discussions. Their presence was to ensure that the march was politically successful. That it was *properly* organized and conducted *intelligently* so as to be taken *seriously*. To that end they had identified potential sources of financial and political support. All at the highest national level. The *very highest* levels. They were prepared to deliver these important political allies and funding support. National figures now, powerful organizations. But, of course, there had to be conditions. Nothing problematic, but once these were met, the money and support would be there, guaranteed.

All that these important allies required was the right invitation from the organizations. We'd have to guarantee that our powerful supporters not be embarrassed in any way. That the march's tone would be respectable, its political message responsible. No criticism of the Johnson administration, for example. Bro Wilkins didn't anticipate any problems there. However, without firm assurances from all of us, the Urban League and NAACP were not about to risk this hard-earned political currency with LBJ and the Congress or their credibility with the supporters. That was the deal. Simple political realism. Surely we could understand that.

As he spoke, Whitney Young kept nodding in vigorous agreement. Dr. King agreed in principle, but said some details needed to be clarified. But generally he saw no reason why we should not be able to reach a broad agreement among ourselves that would be acceptable to these potential supporters.

I hadn't heard anything new or surprising. Business as usual, insider politics. A combination of the March on Washington and Selma to Montgomery all over again. As if we had learned nothing and nothing had changed in the last couple years. But still, I also hadn't heard anything that was *necessarily* incompatible with our goals/interests either, assuming good faith all round. So I was cautiously optimistic and careful to be scrupulously polite. But clear and systematic. Step by step.

I was careful not to criticize the NAACP's position, much less attack it head-on. For instance, I never *directly* said that the old models failed to address present realities. I simply stuck to time, place, and context. This was the Mississippi Delta. A violent and primitive place. Why had Meredith been marching in the first place? Why was he shot down? Why even a march against fear? Who and what was he trying to address? How could those concerns be served by another national media production? Could some visiting dignitaries flying in from New York to walk the last four miles and then leave help a sharecropper family overcome years of intimidation and fear? Or, could a march be designed so as to give local communities the confidence to assert themselves? To help them organize, register, vote, and defy the forces trying to keep them intimidated? That was our interest: Could this be accomplished by a national media spectacle? Not likely, but the march could become a powerful organizing tool while remaining a joint effort of the movement. We could talk politics at mass rallies every night. SNCC staff and local people could organize those rallies. We should do voter registration in every town with a courthouse. Urge local leaders to run for office. The local communities should be the entire *focus*. Local leaders should speak on every platform.

I was getting ahmens from McKissick. Dr. King was nodding. I don't know whether he'd been thinking in quite those terms exactly, but he was an honest man. He had a real feel for the condition of our people in the South. He knew that what we were saying was true. Apparently all Wilkins managed to hear was that SNCC wanted to exclude whites from the march, perhaps even the movement. But others were saying, yes, why couldn't there be a local focus? Was a call for national leaders really the only or the most effective strategy at this time?

The other major issue was, of course, security, more specifically the Deacons. I said SNCC supported their participation, period. Bro Wilkins perked up. I knew he was hoping that this would be the wedge that would separate SNCC from CORE and SCLC. So I had to hit that one hard. Look, I said, if this were a parade in New York or a promenade around the Reflecting Pool, that'd be fine. But this here the Delta, y'all. Meredith had had no security. And the only reason we not at the brother's wake tonight is because instead of buckshot, that racist pumped four blasts of *#4 bird shot* into his head. The only reason. This movement doesn't need more martyrs, certainly not more white ones. And SNCC thinks it would be immoral and irresponsible to put people—black or white—out on those highways without all the security we could offer. *We* needed the Deacons, not the other way around. We weren't doing them any favors.

Those two were the sticking points. The argument went back and forth, over and over, round and round, and of course, the gloves came off. Some hard and stupid things were said, but, swear 'fo God, I tried to remain polite long as I could. But it wasn't too easy.

Both Dr. King and Attorney McKissick, who'd been deep in the mess in the South, understood where SNCC was coming from. I know Dr. King was still sore inside, grieving over the two people killed on the Selma march. McKissick said the Deacons had come out of the violence that CORE workers and communities had been subject to in Louisiana. They were disciplined and law-abiding. He had no problems with their participation. Dr. King said that as long as it was clear that the march was thoroughly and fully committed to nonviolence and the Deacons understood and pledged to respect that, their mere presence on the march wasn't necessarily a contradiction.

[Andrew Young:

"I wasn't in that meeting but SCLC was aggressively nonviolent and Martin personally and spiritually committed to nonviolence. But he did make a practical and ethical distinction between self-defense involving defensive violence and retaliatory violence. His attitude was that he could never condemn a man for defending his life, home, and family. He often said that he would himself never resort to violence, even in defense of his life, but he would and could not demand that of others. That was a religious commitment with one's God in the privacy of one's conscience, which folks had to make for themselves. He saw the Deacons as a defensive presence, not a retaliatory one."

Floyd McKissick:

"Someone said they grew out of CORE operations and community organizations in Louisiana. So you tell them to go home, I said. I refuse to tell them to leave. I think they've earned the right to be on the march. I think we should tell them, as we tell everyone else, that we believe in nonviolence. But I'll not tell them to leave 'cause they've earned the right to be here. And to protect themselves and other people. I don't believe in one standard for whites and another standard for blacks." —Voices of Freedom]

It went back and forth. Finally, Bro McKissick said, "I'm nothing but a po' country boy, y'all, and it's getting real late. I'm going on to my bed, but I'm with Stokely on both counts. G'night, y'all." So now it was a standoff. SNCC and CORE on one side, the NAACP and Urban League on the other.

All night Dr. King had played a patient, conciliatory role, seeking, if at all possible, unity. He'd listened carefully and judiciously to both sides. He tried to steer a middle course, to reconcile differences and find common ground. Seeking at all times to be fair and practical. I think at first he really had favored sending out a national call as he had done in Selma. If his position changed in the discussion, it was certainly not because he "caved" to pressure from the "young militants," but quite the opposite. He followed his conscience and saw the logic of emphasizing local initiative. Tha's all.

Hey, how could we, even had we wanted to, *pressure* Dr. King? Gimme a break. I personally have never, *never* known Dr. King to be other than honorable, a man of courage and conscience. He was always under a lot of pressure, but it wasn't from *us.*

Any pressure, and there was considerable and crude pressure, came from the "moderates." Loss of funds, of the support of powerful friends, of *respectability,* loss of credibility, etc., etc., etc. Yet finally Dr. King stood with us on both counts.

Maaan, was Bro Wilkins mad. Jack, he was madder than Mose when the mule kicked his momma. Bro Young, as I recall, didn't say anything, but Uncle Roy went off. I mean he went off. Dr. King was being irresponsible and would regret it. He was irreparably damaging the movement, etc., etc. And as for me, I was impudent, inexperienced, arrogant, and ignorant of history. I didn't understand the movement or the delicate dynamics of coalition. Didn't even understand politics. A foolish young upstart, dangerous to himself and the movement.

The two *[Messrs. Wilkins and Young]* put on their coats, made an elaborate show of shuffling their papers and snapping their briefcases shut with dramatic finality. Then they sat there glowering. I almost laughed out loud. I mean, they were like little kids waiting for someone to implore them to stay. Then they got up. If Dr. King persisted in this folly, they would have no alternative but "to wash their hands" of this project.

"Yeah," Cleve muttered, "like Pilate before you." I shushed him.

No one asked them to stay.

That was the meeting. None of that had to happen, none of it. But there was no give-and-take with Bro Wilkins. None. He clearly had no respect for the experience or contributions of mass activism, or the intelligence of any of us, not just SNCC. In his mind, whatever the movement had accomplished—the legislation—was entirely because of the insider contacts and skillful influence of the NAACP. It never occurred to him that they had never been able to get *any* legislation—not as much as an antilynching law—until masses of black people had taken to the streets in nonviolent direct action. To him it seemed totally unacceptable that any of us would presume to suggest, no matter how tactfully, the slightest divergence from any program laid down by him. We were—all of us, even Dr. King—underlings. Not very political, I thought. I couldn't help wondering if he was equally imperious in the gatherings of the powerful and the wealthy he was so pleased to be invited to. Somehow I didn't think so.

However, had they kept their word, we'd all have been grateful and movement history quite different. What do I mean? Well, I can't really prove that they ran to the press to denounce us. But had they "washed their hands" of the march in private and kept their mouths shut about what, after all, were principled disagreements *within* the movement, the sensation-seeking press may not have run hog wild the way it did in reporting the march. Because the tenor and language of the questioning at the press conferences Dr. King, Attorney McKissick, and I held to explain the goals and purposes of the march were quite unrelated to anything we were actually saying.

"There are reports of divisions in the movement. . . . Any truth to the rumor that militants have captured . . . ? Dr. King, are you abandoning nonviolence? . . . Is integration no longer a goal? . . . Are whites to be excluded? . . . Have your priorities changed?" Now who told them all that?

Some of this questioning, at least so it seemed to me, echoed rather suspiciously—in tone and language—the thrust of the brother's denouncements as he'd left the meeting. Could be coincidence. Maybe he and the media just naturally saw the world the same way. Unfortunate. But I could not dismiss the thought that someone had found it necessary to rush to the press with their displeasure. If so, it's more than unfortunate, it's sad. Rule or ruin. In whose interest, finally? I really hope they didn't do that, because finally it would be no different really from some "slave" running to report their brothers to "ol' massa."

Sad also, because I wanted very much to be able to respect Bro Wilkins. We owed him that much. He had been in the trenches (however elevated) for our people for a long, long time. The NAACP, led by Dr. Du Bois, had kindled and kept our struggle going through some very dismal times. Its judicial strategy had struggled doggedly against great odds and had succeeded in making important contributions. No question. None among us had the slightest interest in trying to deny that. So why was the brother so obsessively insecure, so narrow and so rigid? Toward all of us, and especially Dr. King? I can only attribute it to a personality failure, because I'm convinced that he had to have understood the logic and spirit of our position way better than he let on during that meeting. How could he not have, long as he'd been a black man in America?

Anyway, as I recall, that is what I thought at the time. I thought about it again many years later when someone sent a copy of his memoirs to me in Guinea. It all came back when, to my amazement, I found a number of places where a much younger Roy Wilkins had been taking positions quite similar to the ones he'd attacked so bitterly in that meeting at the Lorraine Motel. Odd. However, all being said, the brother did struggle for our people. Peace be unto his spirit.

[I was intrigued by that comment but did not follow it up in our conversation. I later consulted Mr. Wilkins's memoir, Standing Fast, and was able to find two passages that seemed to fit Bro Ture's recollection. The first, interestingly enough, after a trip into the Mississippi Delta during the thirties:

"Right after I returned from my expedition to the Mississippi Delta, I sent a letter to Arthur Spingarn, Chairman of the NAACP's Executive Committee . . . arguing that it would be an extraordinarily fine thing for the NAACP to hold itself up as a defender of the rights of Negroes everywhere and under all circumstances. As things were, I pointed out, we tended to be isolated in New York and out of touch with the very people we needed to serve. I knew very well that the NAACP's strategy of carefully selecting lawsuits and political issues and working from on high in Congress and the Supreme Court had produced many tangible benefits. But from the vantage of those muddy camps on the Mississippi, such tactics looked less meaningful than they did from the snug offices of 69 Fifth Avenue." —EMT]

"So on Sundays, when the family set out, Austin and I were clean, Jack." At rear: Mummy Olga holding baby Janeth. *Center front:* sisters Lynette, Umilta, and Judith. *On the wings:* cousin Austin Letrin and, *far right,* "little man." (Courtesy of the Carmichael Family)

"I believe that until the last moments of their lives together, they were in love." Adolphus and May Charles Carmichael after their reunion in New York City. (Courtesy of the Carmichael Family)

"Why are humans better than animals? Because we have kinsmen." Igbo proverb. Kwame Ture in Miami (ca.1989) with his nieces and nephews.
(Courtesy of the Carmichael Family)

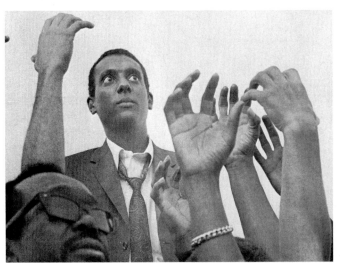

"For every fund-raising appearance we accepted, we scheduled a political one in the community . . . especially in cities where there had been insurrections." Carmichael urges people in Watts to work for "their own city," with control over the police and schools. Los Angeles, California, November 1966.
(Magnum Photos)

"*Cliff Vaughn moves up to get a picture of the troops in the masks. They grab him. I hold on to his ankle. Poor Cliff is airborne.*" When the demonstrators are gassed, Carmichael is hospitalized. Cambridge, Maryland, 1964. (Bettmann/CORBIS)

"*Trudging along, mile after mile, discussing every blessed thing under the sun.*" Left to right: Dr. King, Floyd McKissick of CORE, and Carmichael leading the March Against Fear into Canton. That night, encircled by state troopers, the nonviolent marchers were gassed and beaten in a fearsome display of police brutality. Canton, Mississippi, July 1966. (Bettmann/CORBIS)

"*We're gonna make this our Mississippi. Even if we got to tear it down and build it back brick by brick.*" Carmichael exhorting Marchers Against Fear at the rally at the state capitol concluding the march. Jackson, Mississippi. (Flip Schulke/CORBIS)

"We shall not be moved." SNCC chairman Carmichael instructs demonstrators to sit down in the streets after being stopped by police en route to the state capitol. Montgomery, Alabama, 1967. (Bettmann/CORBIS)

"Hell, no. We won't go. They expect us to run in Harlem and fight in Hanoi? They must be crazy." Carmichael speaking on Black Power and the Vietnam War to black students at a Southern college. Hampton, Virginia, 1967. (AP/Wide World Photos)

With two great ladies of the African struggle in the United States, Mrs. Rosa Parks and old comrade Diane Nash. Conference of Southern Civil Rights Movement, Ann Arbor, Michigan (ca. 1980). (Rehanda Green [Omowele])

"We had many discussions. I had to be honest about certain disagreements but the leaders were always very gracious." With Truong Chinh, chairman of the National Assembly of the Democratic Republic of Vietnam. Hanoi, North Vietnam, October 1967. (Bettmann/CORBIS)

"What impressed me was his simplicity and sincerity. He was always modest and candid, freely admitting mistakes, problems, or shortcomings." With Fidel Castro at the founding conference of OLAS, Havana, Cuba, 1967. (Julius Lester © 2003)

"Before I could even change my clothes, Madame Du Bois hurried me to the villa to meet the Osageyfo Dr. Kwame Nkrumah." The Eighth Anniversary of *Le Partie Democratique de Guinea,* Conakry, Guinea, 1967. (Courtesy of the Carmichael Family)

"Our first and only child was a son. To me, this alert, vigorous baby had the aspect of a warrior." At home with second wife, Marliatou, and infant son, Boabacar Biro, Conakry, Guinea, 1981. (William F. Campbell)

"After that Sékou Touré went out of his way to show greater confidence in me. I can never forget that." Al-Hadji President Ahmad Sékou Touré at the Organization of African Unity Summit, 1980.   (Alain Nogues/CORBIS)

"We could have restored him, no question. The masses loved him and even in death, those CIA stooges in the military were scared of him." President Kwame Nkrumah triumphantly carried by supporters at independence (ca. 1958). (Bettmann/CORBIS)

"*I could scarcely believe my eyes. The owner of that incredible voice was young and absolutely beautiful.*" Miriam Makeba at the beginning of her American career, 1958. (Leo Rosenthal/Time Life Pictures)

"*African names, African dress, African rituals and music were evidenced in ways they never had been during my youth.*" During a triumphant return, Ture is delighted by the virtuosity on the tenor pan of eight-year-old pannist Atiba Williams at a reception in his honor, Port of Spain, Trinidad, 1996. (Bert Alette, courtesy of *The Port of Spain Daily News*)

"*Mummy Olga never ever beat us, but would she scold. Lord have mercy. Ha! And the sorrow and disappointment in her gentle eyes was worse.*" Ture greets his aunt Olga at the airport, Port of Spain, Trinidad, 1996. (Marlon Rouse, courtesy of the *Trinidad Guardian*)

Coconspirators back in the day. Stokely Carmichael and Michael Thelwell after a presentation on Black Power at the University of Massachusetts, Amherst, 1972. (Courtesy of *The Springfield Republican*)

"It must tell the truth, Thelwell, that's all. Tell the truth." An ailing Kwame Ture with Ekwueme Michael Thelwell reviewing an early chapter of Ture's memoirs in the Convent Avenue apartment of Dr. Gerri Price, 1997. (Courtesy of the Carmichael Family)

"Thank you for asking. The first time you kicked me out of Africa no one asked me where I wanted to go." Where it all began. With mother and David Brothers at slave shipping castle at Elmina, Ghana (ca. 1990). (Courtesy of the Carmichael Family)

CHAPTER XXII

"We Gotta Make This Our Mississippi"

We gotta make this our Mississippi,
Jes' as water seek the low places,
Power seek the weak places.
—Hartman Turnbow
MFDP leader,
Tchula, Mississippi

Once a reporter said to me, "You know, Mr. Ture, they say journalism is the first draft of history."

Something about his self-important smirk annoyed me. "Yeah," I said, "Napoléon had something to say about that."

"Oh, what'd Napoléon say?" he asked.

"You mean you don't know? C'mon, I thought you guys knew everything. He said history is nothing but lies commonly agreed upon. You saying you the first draft of that?"

"Mr. Ture, you calling me a liar?"

"Oh, no, but I may be calling you a historian."

I mean it's passing strange how just about everything I've read about this march manages to completely miss the point. That reporter was right about one thing. It started with the press. Now I'm not saying that they printed straight-up lies, or that they outright made up stuff. No. No. No. But they may as well have. It's more what they *didn't* report, what they *couldn't* see, didn't see, or more likely, didn't *want* to see. Or equally what they *were* looking for and what they *wanted* to see. A failure of communication on our part and of understanding and emphasis on theirs. Whatever.

Hey, we read that the Deacons were there with (oh, horrors) *guns*. But not that after Meredith, no one else got shot and nobody was killed on our march. We read that whites were excluded. Not true. The "leaders" weren't invited but quite a few white supporters did march. We read that

501

the numbers were down, meaning that support had "waned," but not that thousands of black folk turned out along the way, and that almost *five thousand* of them registered to vote in Mississippi for the first time. First draft of history, huh? What we miss in nearly all historical accounts is the most important aspect. The incredible spirit of self-reliance, of taking responsibility, of taking courage, which local people demonstrated. That it really had become for all those local people *their* real march against fear. Somehow that got missed? Gimme a break.

What the press saw, or thought it saw and reported stridently, and what has subsequently been recycled in second and third drafts of history, is that young militants turned on a beleaguered Dr. King. That an ideological struggle took place between SCLC and SNCC, between Dr. King and the "young firebrand" Carmichael. Gimme a break. That's not how it went. No way. The only part even remotely true was that SNCC people and SCLC staff jostled considerably. I'll explain that later.

I remember a great deal about that march with great satisfaction and pride. But the one thing that absolutely stands out about that campaign is the way our relationship with Dr. King deepened during the days we spent together on that march. In fact, the fondest memories I cherish of Dr. King come from that time. We'd always respected him, but this is when I, and a lot of other SNCC folk, came to really know him. I know Cleve, Ralph, Stanley, and others felt that way too.

After that Lorraine Motel meeting, we set up a planning meeting with our Delta projects. We put together teams for specific tasks, divided up responsibilities for every community along the line of march. Our network of local contacts was activated to mobilize folk for voter registration, handle logistics, find sites to pitch the tents, feed the marchers, and set up the mass meetings. Folks swung into action and in a matter of days we were ready to go.

We had meetings with the Deacons to clarify their responsibilities. No problem at all. They were just splendid. Young brothers, mostly veterans who had trained the others. They were very clear, very disciplined. They would patrol the perimeters of the march and at night guard the campsite. During the day they would also walk the ridges along the highway and investigate any possible ambush sites, beating the bushes and stands of trees along the road, and very politely check out anyone they found loitering there. In fact, the only violence our marchers did experience came at the hands of the so-called law—the Highway Safety Patrol.

Within days we felt ready to set off. We gathered outside Hernando, the place where Meredith was taken down, and formed up. No more than 150 or so marchers met us there. Mostly SNCC staff and young local folk physically able to undertake the walk of nearly 150 miles. I'd say most of them had been students in our freedom schools two years earlier. Also a lot of the young people I'd worked with in Greenwood. It was good to see them again. There was also a contingent of Highway Patrol—about a dozen—ostensibly there for our protection. First crisis.

Man, no sooner had the march started, these men started shouting and bellowing orders at us. They were ordering us off the road surface. This one trooper was just shouting and turning redder. I guess his idea was that we should walk more than a hundred miles over the tufts of grass and overgrown weeds on the roadside. When we didn't leave the roadbed, this big rednecked policeman came charging at us. I saw him coming with his hands stretched to bull-rush us. I was in the middle with Dr. King on my right, Attorney McKissick on the left, our arms linked. Certain he was going to shove me, I tensed up, bracing myself to meet the charge. I was set to ram my chest forward and—nonviolently, at the point of impact—hopefully break his wrists. I stuck out my chest and almost fell. Nothing.

Man, that cop went right by me to slam into Dr. King, knocked him down. I couldn't believe it. I yanked free to go after him, got one arm free, but Dr. King had my right hand and was not letting go. I was fighting to get to that cracker. But Dr. King hung on to my arm shouting, "Get Stokely, somebody, lay on him." People were screaming. A bunch of folks piled on top of me. After they cooled me out, we continued the march. We walked on the highway.

All day SNCC people kept saying, "Man, you really messed up." I said, "Yeah, yeah, I know." That evening there would be a meeting to discuss the day's events and plan for the next day. I expected that folks—especially SCLC—would come after me at that meeting. But none of them did. Because, I think, they'd all seen the cop push Dr. King. So it was left to Dr. King to chastise me:

"You know, Stokely, as we've discussed, you have greater responsibility now. You have to be very, very careful now that you represent SNCC. You can never forget you're now the head of an organization . . . ," etc. He corrected me firmly but gently.

I apologized. "I am sorry, Dr. King. This is the first time I've broken discipline on a nonviolent demonstration. But you, Dr. King, look around this room. We all know each other. I've been in battle with everyone here. You all know me. You all know I've been on the front line and I've never broken nonviolent discipline, right? I've been beaten, knocked unconscious. I've been sent to the hospital. And until today, I've never broken discipline. I'm sorry, Dr. King." Folks were nodding support. When I saw that I got bold. I said, "Dr. King, this is the first time. And the only reason I did was because that cracker charged into you. I know I kinda lost it then, but, Dr. King, you can tell those good white folk out there that, if they want nonviolence to stay alive, they had better not touch you. Better not lay a hand on you. Because, Dr. King, the moment they touch you is the moment nonviolence is finished, done."

Dr. King understood. Everyone understood that that was true. Once they touched Dr. King, nonviolence was dead.

Even with the presence of the Deacons, the debate on self-defense was far from over . . . among us. 'Cause, by day and by night the harassment never stopped, ceaseless. And, of course, the state troopers were a joke. They intervened only when some of our people were about to retaliate.

All day, man, passing pickup trucks and cars would veer over, speed up, and zoom by, inches from where our people were walking. Folks had to jump off the highway. Not once did the troopers issue a ticket or a warning, not once. So you know dudes were talking about bringing out their pieces.

Then at night when we pitched the tents, crowds of armed whites would gather close as they could get and shout insults and threats. The leaders would ask the cops to disperse them or move them back. That never happened. Except once. If memory serves, in Belzoni. Three, four cars full of gunmen drove up, within feet of the tent. The Deacons challenged them and there was a facedown. *Then* the cops intervened and backed them off. So of course there would be folk saying, "What we waiting for, till they kill some of us?" Oh, yeah, the debate went on.

Add to that, every night when the voter registration teams reported in, more harassment. In these little towns they were stoned with rocks, bottles, what have you. They be followed by groups with guns and clubs swearing to kill them. Cars veering over at them, chasing them down the highway. Those teams went through hell, man, yet they registered a lot of folks. But it was nerve-racking and you'd have folks saying the teams should be allowed to carry weapons. Before someone got killed. But the leadership counseled restraint, nonviolent discipline. But the debate went on . . . inside the tents every night.

What brought it out into the open was Philadelphia. After that, the debate boiled to the surface at a rally where the press was present. After that, national headlines: "Movement Divided on Nonviolence." Actually, there was no debate on nonviolence, that was clear. The debate was on self-defense.

See, the march was approaching Yazoo City, near Jackson, on the anniversary of the Neshoba County murders. We had to pay our respects to the memory of the three martyrs, but it was too far for the entire march to go. So we decided that the march leaders would drive over with a group of marchers, hook up with the local folks, and have a public memorial service. Dr. King would conduct the service in front of the courthouse after we marched from the black section.

Wow. We gits there and the local folk tell us that a mob has been gathering at the courthouse from early morning. They said that *[Deputy Sheriff]* Cecil Price and a few of the cops on duty at the court had been indicted for the murders. As were some others in the crowd. We discussed, but those local Neshoba County people were clear: "Ain't nothing to discuss, we going." So we set out. It wasn't a long march, but I wasn't sure we'd make it. Every block there'd be an attack. First came the rocks, bottles, and firecrackers. Followed by small gangs with fists and clubs. Cars swerving into the marchers. Only when a fight broke out would the cops do anything. Dr. King's presence and constant calls for discipline kept most marchers nonviolent. But even Dr. King was hit by a bottle.

We get to the courthouse only to find a screaming mob, at least a thousand white men. I really wasn't sure we'd even get to complete the service, much less make it out with everyone alive. But somehow we did. Dr. King was just steadfast. That night, after we left, the Klan drove into the black community shooting. The community fired back seriously. I hear they peppered those night-rider cars. So they took off, only made one pass.

That night at the usual rally the debate flared up. Dr. King was hot. *[Press reports call it "one of the angriest speeches of his life."]* He talked about the state of Mississippi and its vicious racism. Said that Philadelphia was the worst situation by far, the most violent that he had ever faced. But, he said, the only reason no one was killed was because the march had maintained order and discipline. McKissick supported that. But others took a different position. Willie Ricks said nobody was killed because we showed them that we could defend ourselves when attacked. I think this was the first rally where the brother from the Deacons *[Ernest Thomas]* shared the platform with the leaders. Among other things, he issued a warning to the white folks between here and Jackson. Anyone who messes with this march be putting their life on the line. The brother sounded serious too. That was what triggered the headlines. But I do seem to recall that we got to Jackson without further incident.

But the Mississippi police were a constant provocation, all march. The next time they nearly caused a riot was in Greenwood. Early on there'd been a slight confrontation over the Deacons. But since it was legal to carry loaded weapons as long as they were not concealed, they had to back off. Not happily now, but they backed off and withdrew most of the troopers, leaving only four. That was fine with us. But when we got to Greenwood, they were back in force.

Greenwood was like a homecoming for me. Everyone in the community knew me. Even the whites. I'd been in jail so much even the police chief knew me. The African community really turned out. There was going to be a huge rally in the Brant Street park in front of the black high school that June Johnson and her friends attended. We were to pitch the tent there. A lot of our people, hundreds, were gathering in the park. The march was gathering momentum. I could see it was going to be our largest rally.

Local leaders were becoming really involved. Even Charles Evers (who had replaced his brother Medgar as head of the Jackson NAACP) had come to Greenwood for the rally. I guess he must not have heard or didn't care about the organizational "hand-washing" from on high.

And there Bro Evers was, talking loudly about his feelings on being in Greenwood, a place he'd vowed never to set foot in, because it was the hometown of Byron De La Beckwith, his brother Medgar's murderer. Medgar's killer, armed and deputized, was rumored to have been seen among the groups of armed whites and cops patrolling the area. Which, naturally, created some serious undercurrents of anger in the people. And I knew that some elements in the Greenwood community had been ripe for a confrontation with the vigilantes ever since Freedom Summer. SNCC had managed to avert that then, but now?

About then, June Johnson, my little sister, came rushing up. She was visibly angry and agitated, and she'd been looking for me all over.

"Stokely, I gotta talk to you. Now. In private." I'd never seen June so emotional. She had tears in her eyes. But she had reason.

Turns out she'd recognized one of the state troopers. He was the white cop who had directed the beatings of June, Annell, and Mrs. Hamer in the Winona jail the night Medgar Evers was murdered. The one who'd taken the blackjack from the prisoner and brutalized Mrs. Hamer. *Oy*, trouble, blues and trouble, Jack. June was one of the most popular and admired teenagers in the community. Once that news got out, nobody but nobody could stop some brothers from going home after their guns. And who could blame them? But the human and political consequences . . . All the anger I'd felt when the beating went down came rushing back.

June was absolutely certain and offered to point the sick bastard out. I didn't trust myself to be in his presence. "I'll handle it, babe, be cool."

I found the Safety Patrol commander; maybe it was Birdsong, I don't recall. But I told him, "You leave that sick, twisted, sadistic [expletive depleted] out here and it's going to be on you. *On you.* My people find out who that bastard is—and what he did—and this mess is over. You under-stand you got about ten minutes, if that." Of course the news got out to some of the brothers, but by that time that trooper was nowhere to be found. Birdsong got him out of there. Another crisis narrowly averted.

After talking to the commander, I was called over to the school. The local Greenwood cops were trying to prevent the workers from raising the tent. The school board had given us permission and stood their ground. It was their school so it was an issue of community control, black power if you will. I told the workers to put up the tent unless the local community leaders stopped them. Words were exchanged and I was dragged off to jail. But the tent went up.

By the time I got out of jail, I was in no mood to compromise with racist arrogance. The rally had started. It was huge. The spirit of self-assertion and defiance was palpable. I looked over that crowd, that valiant, embattled community of old friends and fellow strugglers. I told them what they knew, that they could depend only on themselves, their own organized collective strength. Register and vote. The only rights they were likely to get were the ones they took for themselves. I raised the call for Black Power again. It was nothing new, we'd been talking about nothing else in the Delta for years. The only difference was that this time the national media were there. And most of them had never experienced the passion and fervor of a mass meeting before. That was the only difference. As I passed Mukasa *[Willie Ricks]*, he said, "Drop it now. The people are ready. Drop it now."

[Cleve Sellers remembers:

"Stokely, who'd been released from jail just minutes before the rally began, was the last speaker. He was preceded by McKissick, Dr. King, ★ *and Willie Ricks. Like the rest of us, they were angry about Stokely's unnecessary arrest. Their speeches were particularly militant. When Stokely moved forward to speak, the crowd greeted him with a huge roar. He acknowledged his reception with a raised arm and clenched fist.*

"Realizing that he was in his element, with his people, Stokely let it all hang out. 'This is the twenty-seventh time I have been arrested—and I ain't going to jail no more!' The crowd exploded into cheers and clapping.

" 'The only way we gonna stop them white men from whuppin' us is to take over. We been saying freedom for six years and we ain't got nothin'. What we gonna start saying now is Black Power!'

"The crowd was right with him. They picked up his thoughts immediately.

" 'BLACK POWER!' they roared in unison.

"Willie Ricks, who is as good at orchestrating the emotions of a crowd as anyone I have ever seen, sprang into action. Jumping to the platform with Stokely, he yelled to the crowd, 'What do you want?'

" 'BLACK POWER!'

" 'What do you want?'

" 'BLACK POWER!'

" 'What do you want?'

" 'BLACK POWER!! BLACK POWER!!! BLACK POWER!!!!'

"Everything that happened afterward was a response to that moment.

★Some accounts have Dr. King away speaking in Memphis that night. —EMT

More than anything, it assured that the Meredith March Against Fear would go down in history as one of the major turning points in the black liberation struggle." —Sellers, The River of No Return]

We left Greenwood with more new black voters on the rolls in two days than we'd been able to accomplish in four arduous and bloody years. On the march, the crowds remained large and enthusiastic. Local leadership was praised, brought forward, and encouraged to run for local office. Gathering strength all the way, we came down out of the Delta and got to Canton, not far from Jackson. Canton was the home of Mrs. Annie Devine (peace be unto her wise spirit), one of the FDP candidates in the Congressional Challenge.

After Greenwood, the troopers' behavior had become—if you can imagine this—even more surly and provocative. I guess not having suc- ceeded in provoking a riot, they decided to riot themselves. So on this night they rioted. The same issue as Greenwood. Again, we had permis- sion from the black community to put up our tent in their school yard. Only difference is that by the time we got into Canton, night had fallen. We had to work in darkness. At first we did not know that they had sur- rounded the school in large numbers. Could not have been less than a hundred of them. It was nothing but a planned, vicious ambush, designed, I imagine, to demonstrate white power at its most brutal. We are working by flashlight, trying to erect the tent. Tired, hungry people are milling around. Suddenly the scene is lit up by searchlights out of the sur- rounding darkness. A bright, white, blinding light. A voice amplified by a bullhorn commands us to disperse. It was dark. We had no place for 150 marchers to go, and they knew that.

I told the voice that we had permission and nowhere else to put the people. I told the people to stand their ground. Next to me, and clearly illuminated by the lights, Dr. King made an anguished appeal for calm and reason. "I am tired, so tired of violence," he said.

"Dr. King," I cried. "Please get down. You're too good a target here."

Some SCLC folks had started to pull him down and to encircle him with their bodies when the cops fired in the tear gas.

I took a direct hit in the chest from a canister and was knocked to the ground. Semiconscious and unable to breathe; my eyes tearing. My ribs felt as though crushed. Gas in my lungs was always my weakness. It felt like Cambridge, Maryland, all over again. Choking for breath, I could hear screams, shouts, and Dr. King calling on people to remain calm amid the sickening thud of blows. They were kicking and clubbing people lying on the ground to escape the gas. Men, women, children, it made no differ- ence. Then they were gone, leaving us to tend the wounded and raise the tent. So obviously it had simply been a demonstration of naked brute force for its own sake.

[*June Johnson:*

"It was awful. Worst thing I ever saw. People was choking everywhere. They gassed Dr. King. Nearly killed Stokely. Whupped on every black head they could find. The only blacks that didn't take a beating that night was the Deacons."]

First draft again? According to the press—God bless 'em—Greenwood was when SNCC first issued the call for Black Power and changed the character and direction of the movement. Also, according to those accounts, this was when the "ideological struggle" between SCLC and SNCC, or between Dr. King and me, became public. A struggle expressed as a battle between shouted slogans, "Black Power" versus "Freedom Now." Wrong on both counts, wrong, wrong, wrong, and worse, trivial: as though Dr. King and I were high school cheerleaders. They sure do have a habit of reducing the black community and our issues to absurdity.

First of all, SNCC had been talking about political change and self-determination for years. The entire march was predicated on that. So nothing was new there. Given the history and the prevailing tension in Greenwood—the school yard confrontation, De La Beckwith's rumored presence, the sadistic cop, etc., etc., it may have been somewhat more emotional, that's all. But, as usual, the press saw what they could see and heard what they could hear.

[*Arlie Schardt,* Time *magazine:*

"The media coverage of the march was interesting because there was a tendency, I thought, to overplay it. There were a couple of reasons for that. One is that there were a lot of reporters who were new to this beat who were coming in from a lot of papers around the country as the march began to pick up momentum and as this Black Power theme began to get some publicity. The second reason was that the theme was never really clearly articulated. Or at least what it meant was never clearly defined. And so it was open to very broad interpretations. There were some whites, for their own reasons, who wanted to take this as a signal of real black hostility and enmity, and there were others who simply didn't know how to read what was being said. Therefore it was left open to the idea that this was a dramatic change in the civil rights movement in which blacks were telling the whites, 'Get out and forget it. We're on our own,' and that it was anti-white. But there was a lot of confusion because there was no unanimity about this." —Voices of Freedom]

Now, as for the "struggle" between Dr. King and I on the march? Utter, utter nonsense. In fact, it was exactly the reverse. The fondest memories I have of Dr. King come from that march, and I'd say that, despite the very present danger, the happiest, or at least the most relaxed, I'd ever seen him was on those Delta highways. It was the first real time he'd spent with us or us with him. I know that a lot of us in SNCC ended up seeing him in a very different light. During those sweltering Delta days Dr. King became to many of us no longer a symbol or an icon, but a warm, funny, likable, unpretentious human being who shared many of our values. Dr. King had a great, mischievous sense of humor. Most people don't know that.

[One of these media accounts that accords fully with Carmichael's recollection of the dynamics of the call for Black Power ran in the Southern Courier *of June 25–26. Writing from Greenwood, David R. Underhill reported on the battle of the slogans. —EMT]*

Some of the march leaders have tried to keep the new chant from taking over. As the line was moving toward Belzoni, Robert Green, one of the SCLC's top men when the Rev. Martin Luther King, Jr. is absent, started shouting, "What do you want?"

"BLACK POWER!!" was the answer. After a few rounds of "BLACK POWER!!" Green said, "Let's have a little 'FREEDOM!' " Then there were a few rounds of "FREEDOM!"

. . . *[Carmichael says:]* that black power in practice would be "Negroes taking over the government of the counties where Negroes have a majority." On the march, Carmichael has not said whether Negroes should hold every public office in these counties, but he has said they should hold the most important offices, at least.

Some of the other SNCC members on the march say black power means every office for Negroes, and some say whites would be allowed a "token representation, which is all they deserve where they are a minority."

Carmichael says black power is not black nationalism or black racism, as many people, Negro and white, have charged. "Every ethnic group in the country's history has taken over where they had a majority. Nobody called it anti-white. Now we're doing it too, and people call us anti-white. Why?"

Negroes must take over where they can, according to Carmichael, because this is the only way they will be able to stop intimidation and murder, to stop working for $3 a day, and to stop everything else which has kept them down.

They must also do it, Carmichael says, because black power will make Negroes proud of being Negroes.

In Greenwood, Carmichael said, "You ought to get the nappiest-headed black man, with the broadest nose and the thickest lips, and make him sheriff. This isn't anti-white. It's just a way of sayin' we're not ashamed of bein' black. We need to be proud of bein' black. We need it bad."

Many of the CORE members of the march, and most of the many people from Chicago here, agree generally with SNCC's position.

Some SCLC leaders on the march have spoken indirectly against this position. . . .

News that "Dr. King is coming" always brings out a large cheering crowd. But King's speeches are beginning to show that he isn't counting on just his name to keep the people coming and listening. He always talks about nonviolence and about the Negro freeing the white man while freeing himself, and he has never used the phrase *black power*, except to criticize it.

In Athens Monday King said black power is too easily confused with black nationalism.

But even though King does not like the phrase, he has started saying almost the same thing the SNCC leaders mean when they talk about black power.

At the Greenwood tent site, after Carmichael and Ricks had talked about black power, King said, "We've gotta organize ourselves into units of power."

And at the courthouse in Greenwood, he pointed at some of the police and said, "We're going to put black men in those uniforms." He also spoke strongly of putting black men in all the major local offices. Then he said, "We need power" to do these things.

See, of all the "adult" leaders, Dr. King had always best understood and supported SNCC's work and approach. Back when we most needed support, he had praised the Summer Project as one of the "most creative projects" of the movement. Well, there were reasons for that. True, he'd never spent time in the field with us, but Dr. King understood and really loved our people's culture. Hey, he was deep down—in one large part of himself—a product of that culture. And Dr. King had undying love for our people, undying love. On the march, that side of him came out beautifully. Especially in those night meetings in those little churches. You could just see him respond to the people's singing, to the eloquent little speeches, to the preaching, to their spirit. You could see how he enjoyed being among his people.

Another thing people forget is that Dr. King was only about ten years older than most of us. He used to remind me that he was just about my own age when he was first called to lead the Montgomery bus boycott. Remember, he was thirty-nine—same age as Malcolm—when they killed him. So he really understood us better, more sympathetically, and was much closer to us in spirit than people think. Much closer.

The main thing is that I got the strong impression that being out there on the road with us, and with his people, was almost like a holiday for Dr. King. That being away from the office—the phone calls from advisers, supporters, the internal politics of even his own staff, from the constant pressures, often from his own government, and the demands and constraints of leadership—was a great relief to him. As if he were out of a straitjacket. We sensed that this was the aspect of the movement that he liked best, where he was most free to be himself. And that out here, marching, talking, sleeping in the tent, he was relishing that freedom.

Another thing people tend to forget about Dr. King is his courage. You hear some ignorant types talking that because Dr. King was nonviolent, he was somehow, y'know, wishy-washy. That's so stupid.

Before I got to know him, when I'd see him in meetings, etc., when he wasn't speaking, he'd sometimes seemed to me somehow strained, under pressure, vaguely distracted. Certainly not happy. Well, as we've since discovered, he was under tremendous pressure. Think about it. Since his late twenties, during his entire public life, that brother had lived in the awareness of his impending death. Dr. King knew he wasn't going to survive the movement. It began back in Montgomery when he received an average of forty death threats per week. For the rest of his life—fourteen years—that never stopped. Never stopped. Never stopped. Every Klan and Nazi group had a bounty on his head. Martin Luther King was the number one target for every racist with a rifle, shotgun, or stick of dynamite. Being the prime symbol of black aspirations meant being the prime target of white hatred. The brother lived with that.

Now he never said it to me, but I've heard that he said he did not expect to live to see forty. And he didn't. That's the pressure Dr. King lived with all his public life, yet he never backed down and he never backed off. I mean, there he was with us, out on those exposed highways, with the only security he could trust being the Deacons, looking more relaxed than I'd ever seen him. Appearing to enjoy himself. And then to see him with the people. Amazing, incredible, inspiring.

Oh, man, there we'd be trudging along, mile after mile, discussing every blessed thing under the sun. Movement politics, national politics, nonviolence, integration, black culture, our people's condition, different approaches to struggle. Every thang but everything, Jack. And the only differences we ever had were on strategy and tactics (he said we were impatient), never on goals or values. Never.

Then we'd be approaching a crossing, a small settlement, even the outskirts of some plantation, and there they'd be. A small or large crowd, waiting, God knows how long in that sweltering heat, just to see Dr. King. Soon as they spotted him, a stampede. "There he be. Martin Luther King. I see him. I see him." They'd stop the march. Folks just wanted to get close, to touch him, hear a word from him. I bet you go back into those communities today, there'll be folks to point exactly where he stood, tell you what he was wearing, and repeat every word he said to them. Who he hugged, whose hand he shook.

He always responded with a few inspirational words: "A new day's coming . . . we ain't what we want to be, and we ain't what we gonna be

. . . but a new day's coming. Register *and* vote. . . . How long, not long . . . a new day bright with the sunlight of freedom after the long dark night of segregation. Out of the deep, lonely valley of oppression to the high mountaintop of human dignity. We each have our role to play. You can begin by registering *and voting.*"

To some these may sound like clichés, but not to those people. Not in that time or those places. For most of them, especially those off the plantations for whom just standing there defiantly where their bosses could see them waiting for Dr. King, this was their first real act of self-affirmation. For me it was moving, the evident love of the people for Dr. King. And he for them. And I could see in his face and his eyes how deeply touched he was.

One time I was really moved too. I mean *literally* moved, Jack. I was walking next to him and a small group was waiting, some old ladies. These old women, about six or seven, were under a tree lining a spot just to see Dr. King. They were looking, looking, shading their eyes as we came up. All I heard was "I see him, I see him," and boom, I'm flat on my back. I mean, those old women ran up, *knocked me down, Jack,* and stepped on over me, just to get next to Dr. King. I don't think they even saw me, until the last one running by.

As she stepped on over, she looked down, surprised. "Oh, my! Son, you all right? You ain' hurt, is you?"

"No'm. I ain' hurt. Entirely my fault. I should know better than standing between Dr. King and his people."

"You sure got that right, son," she said, and kept on moving.

So where did all this talk of dissension and rivalry in the press come from? Well, after Greenwood there was some controversy. But that was entirely between organizational staff. What happened, as I recall, was that in the early stages of the march, Dr. King and Bernard Lee had been representing SCLC all amicably and brotherly while the other SCLC leaders were off on some kind of staff retreat. Now SCLC staff came rushing in jostling for positions and cloaking it in political terms.

Once the media hysteria about Black Power and racism started, these guys suddenly appear to "rescue" their leader, take over, and redirect the march. As did Charles Evers, who clearly had instructions from the NAACP national office to repudiate SNCC and Black Power. Some of that did happen. But it wasn't really a response to anything that was actually happening but a knee-jerk response to the media's simplistic reports. Another case of the leadership allowing the media to bogart the movement and to dictate what the leadership's public position ought to be. Dr. King understood that clearly. He never repudiated Black Power. Never. Despite pressure, even from his own staff, he never yielded to the hysteria. You can check. That's a myth that he attacked us. He was careful about that. The most he ever said was that the language was "unfortunate," being subject to "misunderstanding by our white brothers and sisters."

In fact, I got him good on that one. The first time I got invited to lunch after the march, the press was still having a field day with their black racism nonsense. So I walk in with this long face, the very picture of desolation.

"Stokely, I can see something's troubling you." Dr. King was immediately concerned. I just shook my head real pitiful.

"Are you sure you all right?"

"Oh, Dr. King, Dr. King. I'm confused. I just don't know . . ." Naturally he asked if he could help. Did I want to talk about it? He put on his best pastoral counseling face, all creased with concern.

"Well, Dr. King . . . I guess you can explain this. It sure beats me. I just can't see it."

"Well, what is it, Stokely?"

"It's this Black Power thing, Dr. King. The press been killing me. Just killing me, Dr. King. Be calling me everything but a child o' God. Seems like they love to hate me. But you, they jes' looves you. I don't get it."

"I'm not sure they love me, Stokely. But what's the issue?" I knew I had him then.

"Well, Dr. King, I was in Ebenezer this morning. Great sermon, by the way. But, y'know, I didn't see one white face in the congregation. Not a one. And your choir. How many blond sopranos you got? And good white folk on your deacon board, how many? Or, come to think of it, on the SCLC staff? That's what I can't understand."

"Sooo? I'm not sure I'm following you, Stokely."

"Well, Dr. King, here you head of a religious institution and a social organization, all black. Why, you the epitome of Black Power, not once but *twice* over. Yet the press, they looove you while they whuppin' my poor nappy head flat. Can you explain that?"

He cracked up. "Well, Stokely, it's simple. Maybe I just don't talk about it. Besides, since when do you expect our media to be rational?"

[Andrew Young:

"Black Power itself was something Martin disagreed with tactically. In fact, what he said all the time was 'Jews have power, but if you ever accuse them of power, they deny it. Catholics have power but they always deny it. In a pluralistic society, to have real power you have to deny it. And if you go around claiming power, the whole society turns on you and crushes you.' It was not black power that he was against, it was the slogan Black Power, because he said, 'If you really have power, you don't need a slogan.' " —Voices of Freedom]

I learned a lot from Dr. King just from observing him. In the struggle I've been lucky to meet or been close to some extraordinary human beings, all of whom instructed me. I've met famous revolutionaries: Dr. Fidel Castro Ruz, Colonel Muammar Qaddafi, even, briefly, the great Ho Chi Minh. I've studied under Dr. Kwame Nkrumah, President Ahmed Sékou Touré, and Madame Shirley Graham Du Bois. I knew Bayard, Malcolm, Mrs. Hamer. But at my most important, potentially confusing, and formative stage, Dr. King was a true mentor, who instructed me by example. There was one particular occasion where I was able to observe Dr. King's truest self in his natural environment. I can never ever forget. It was a rare privilege.

One Saturday night, I'd say about eight months after the Meredith march, I was working in the Atlanta office. It was late, round about midnight, and the phone rang.

"Young man, what you doing in the office so late?"

"The people's work, Dr. King. Workin' for the people."

"Well, as it happens, so am I, Stokely. So am I."

"Reverend, I'm surprised, shouldn't *you* be doing the Lord's work?"

"A distinction without a difference, Stokely. Haven't you learned yet they are one and the same thing? What are you doing tomorrow?"

"Same thing. I'll be still working for the people, Reverend."

"It's the Lord's day, Stokely, why don't you act like a good Christian and come to church?"

"Oh, Dr. King. You should see the work I have. Y'know, we SNCC heathens . . ."

"Stokely, this is one time I really want you to come."

Something in his voice told me to stop talking. This was no casual invitation to church and lunch afterward.

"All right, church. Where?"

"The Ebenezer."

"Something special happening, Reverend?"

"Well . . . I'll be preaching."

"Hey, now, you know I'll always come hear *you* preach 'cause you always could make me tap mah feets."

He didn't laugh. "I really do want you to be there tomorrow because . . . tomorrow . . . before my congregation . . . *I'll be making my statement on the war.*"

After a long silence, my voice came out sounding very quiet. "I'll be there, Dr. King. I'ma be in the *front row* of that church."

I recall starting to say, "God bless you, Reverend." But I didn't. That was his line and it might have sounded strange coming from me. He might not have understood how much I really meant it. I now wish that I had said it.

We hung up and I sat thinking. Then I called Cleve. "Hey, bro, I got some news. Usses going to church tomorrow."

515

· · ·

See, the war had been one of the hottest topics of discussion between us during the march. As it had continued to be every time I saw Dr. King afterward. Ever since we'd made our statement on the war SNCC had been out there isolated from the other civil rights organizations. The press had beat up on us, vilified us really, and a lot of the brothers suddenly started to receive draft notices. Dr. King knew this because I'd made a point of telling him. Where were the other organizations on the question? I'd ask.

Dr. King, as a Christian and a committed pacifist, believed all war to be immoral, "the most terrible and destructive vestige of humanity's primitive past," made more horrific by modern technology. Something humanity should have long outgrown, and which we must continue to struggle to render obsolete. But he was also especially convinced that the immorality of this particular war was compounded by a political mistake of national arrogance and stupidity. Because it was unnecessary. America had no vital interest whatsoever in that country. Vietnam posed absolutely no threat to this nation. So that it was positively immoral for this government to be sending young Americans halfway round the world to kill and die there. Even worse, to be slaughtering hundreds of thousands of our fellow human beings who had done us no harm. Killing them in their own country and destroying the country to boot.

He also felt that LBJ was fundamentally a decent president who really did want to use the power of the office and the federal government to address the serious social and economic problems of poor Americans. He felt, in this, the president was a potential ally who could be even better than FDR, except for his tragic weakness on the war. "It is a real tragedy," he felt, "as much for the country as for the innocent Vietnamese." We have to save LBJ from himself and his advisers.

Naturally, we agreed. We said, "Dr. King, why don't you help the president and us. Help the country. Help the Vietnamese. Say all of that publicly. Use your moral authority and the prestige of the Peace Prize. Hey, if we say it, they dismiss us. They can't dismiss you."

"I only wish it were so simple," he said almost sorrowfully. "But I have to be careful so as to be effective when I do. I will . . . but when the time is right."

As the peace movement, largely white and students, grew, he became more uncomfortable with that position. I know they pestered him. I mean, here he was a Nobel Peace Prize laureate, the icon of domestic nonviolence, more or less standing aloof from the peace movement. I know that Dr. King found this a profound moral contradiction as well as a political problem.

So why did Dr. King stand back? Two reasons really. One I clearly understood, but the dimensions and intensity of the other I was not really aware of at the time.

I understood that the struggle for black people's rights was at a critical stage. A delicate balance: the tantalizing prospect of unprecedented progress on the one hand, and the threat of a reactionary backlash on the other. Dr. King was publicly identified as the movement's leader and spokesman, and he felt that his *primary* responsibility was to his people's advancement and welfare. He felt the political reality was that the advancement of black people's legitimate rights was totally dependent on the goodwill of the administration and the white majority of our fellow citizens who supported the war. That being so, how could he, as our most visible *public* leader, acting out of a *private* and *individual* moral conviction, jeopardize the rights long overdue our people, and for which hundreds of thousands of us had made real sacrifices and were still struggling? His was, after all, a minority position of individual conscience. Indeed, according to the polls, the majority of older blacks—the nation-at-risk reflex—were unreflectively supporting the government in its war. So, of course, I could sympathize with Dr. King's ethical dilemma.

What I was not sufficiently aware of was the truly enormous weight and intensity of unrelenting pressure to which Dr. King was daily being subjected at the time. As we now know, LBJ had his own well-founded doubts about the war. His administration was extremely nervous—paranoid even—at the prospect of the peace movement spreading. (Which explains what we were experiencing in SNCC.) So they deployed surrogates of every stripe to persuade, pressure, or threaten Dr. King in order to keep that "Nobel Prize Negro" in his place. Other civil rights leaders— Roy "We will fight for this country no matter how many of us they lynch" Wilkins—the totalitarian liberals, the Atlantic City and beltway insider crowd, all mouthing threats disguised as platitudes about "the best interest of the Negro people." Apparently all Dr. King's advisers and most of his staff were dead set about his coming out against the war. They called themselves pragmatic, but fundamentally they were simply much more conservative than he. To them, the peace movement was not quite respectable.

"You gotta be responsible. Don't 'squander' your position on these radical youth. You will only destroy this organization; hurt fund-raising; alienate our white supporters; bring the press down on you; anger LBJ, the administration, and the FBI. Don't do it, it's political suicide."

Now that's some pressure, Jack. I suspected some of this was going down, but could never in my worst nightmare have envisioned the extent. Evidently no one said to Dr. King, "I understand it's your moral duty." So it must have been a painfully lonely struggle indeed. Now I understand much better the source of the strain I often sensed in the brother, but which he never shared with us. Now he was going to make his stand. That was when I called Cleve.

[Dr. King had apparently made earlier statements on the war during April, including his famous Riverside Church address. —EMT]

Ebenezer was full with an air of expectancy, as it always was on those Sundays when Dr. King was to be in the pulpit. Cleve and I sat in the middle, a few rows back, where he could see us. Somehow, in the middle of that church, I felt very close to Dr. King that morning.

But y'know, Dr. King didn't really preach that morning *[Sunday, April 30, 1967],* nor did he lecture. He taught. I'd heard Dr. King speak many, many times before and I heard him after. I've heard him preach, heard him exhort, heard him orate. But, African, that morning was extraordinary. I've never seen him better.

Hey, not just because of the politics either, for it was more than a political speech, or even a demonstration of leadership. Certainly more than a sermon, more than a moral reasoning or a history lesson. 'Cause it was all these and more. I have no idea how long he spoke, could have been an hour, could have been two, though I doubt that. But you could have heard a pin drop in that church, except where at key points the people just had to "holler one time."

That Sunday morning, Dr. King had an aura, a kind of inner glow. He was leader, pastor, teacher, shepherd, and most of all, a brave, anguished human being talking with the people who loved him. A man speaking from his heart, out of the depths of his conscience and his conviction, out of his spiritual striving. It was *all* the best elements of Dr. King combined in one moment. That is the King speech that people really should know. Folks should get that speech and really listen to it. Not read it, now, but *listen* to it.

See, first of all you gotta consider the setting. This was his spiritual home turf, his natural environment, the sanctuary of Ebenezer Baptist. You know that Sunday morning service in *any* big, black Baptist church in the South is high art. A great show, a pageant of style, ritual, and spectacle, of music and poetry. You have these enormous, elegantly robed choirs rendering the magnificent ancestral music of our African-American heritage as only our people really can.

And in that setting you had the brother whom the congregation loved, trusted, and revered without reservation. They loved him for his love and respect for them, which he had demonstrated in many ways over many years. And especially for his loyalty. They knew he could have gathered riches doing many other things. He could have accepted the pulpit of larger, richer churches. He never did. They knew Dr. King did not have a mercenary, acquisitive bone in his body when he said that the Nobel

Prize money did not belong to him individually, but to the movement. No one could question his commitment to justice, his love of his people, or his honesty. So they were prepared to receive what he told them.

In that long speech, he taught. He brought them along logically, step by step, and let it all hang out. The people followed every word, understood completely, and responded. It was magical. He spoke political truths in plain terms, which coming from me would instantly have been dismissed as irresponsibility. Instantly. "I must conclude," he said, "with great sorrow, that my government is one of the greatest purveyors of violence in the world today."

He talked to them about the philosophy of nonviolence. Of how it had to be applied everywhere in the world as a vital force in world politics and struggles between nations. That it could not be segregated to the struggle of our people in the United States.

He talked to them in terms they understood, about applying their own experience to the war, showing them the similarities in the life situations of a Vietnamese peasant in a rice paddy and that of a black sharecropper in a cotton field.

Then he talked to them of prophets and kings. Of his belief in the existence of two kinds of laws. The laws of God and the laws of the state. Divine law and the laws of man. And how in obedience to God's higher law it was sometimes necessary to stand up, even against your own government. Even though in their struggle against segregation the federal government had been, however reluctantly, their ally. But if the time came when, in service to a higher law, one had to go against even the government of the United States, there would be no force on which one could call for help but God.

So that church understood clearly that his taking this position would be most unpopular, leading him into confrontation with the powers of this world.

I even remember exactly how he closed. On an honest note of public self-criticism. "There comes a time," he rumbled, "when caution becomes cowardice. I do not know and cannot care what others may do. But as for me . . . I'm gonna study war no more." And he turned away.

Cleve and I were on our feet even before the rest of the faithful. I do believe I recall seeing a tear gleam in Cleve's eye, I do know that his draft board in Denmark, South Carolina, had begun chasing him with draft notices. Before the dust settled, Cleve would do time for refusing to go to Vietnam.

CHAPTER XXIII

Black Power
and Its Consequences

When you throw a stone into a pigsty . . .

I came to the chairmanship knowing exactly what I was elected to do, and that it would not be easy.

After the successes of the Meredith march I felt we'd made a real breakthrough. At least to the extent of commanding the attention of the media, and therefore the nation. (Course, as we've seen, given its biases, that is a double-edged sword. Live by the media, die by the media.) But I had reason to feel that things were on schedule so far as advancing SNCC's program within the national movement and to the larger political community. So everything seemed according to plan. The next big task: begin to organize the African community nationally.

We knew that the real challenge was going to be the North. The movement would now have to turn its attention to the Northern ghettos where the problems were as great as in the South. But would what worked in Mississippi work in Chicago? It was not going to be easy. Looking back, one has to say that the challenge has to this day still not been effectively addressed. At least not in the way we'd hoped and expected.

But the immediate challenge would be to help the organization adjust internally to the changed political reality and to develop strategies and programs to address those changes and move forward. That too was expected. I therefore anticipated no surprises. And, fundamentally there were none. During my chairmanship, nothing in the job I was elected to do, or my role in the organization, changed. Yet the year I spent as chairman was different, categorically different, from anything I'd expected. How so?

Well, it was the volume and the pace of events rushing up on us. Everything seemed to go on fast-forward. The prevailing political environment hardened and the demands of the job intensified incredibly. The organization became a target and I a lightning rod. Much of this had to do with the media and the government. Some had to do with us and mistakes we made. But a lot came from certain elements of the movement and some from our liberal "allies." Everything happened so fast it seems I spent the entire year in constant motion. Flying across the country, speaking, meeting with community groups, meeting the press, on national TV, on college campuses, in churches. It was constant motion, constant motion. I could not spend the time I had expected with SNCC in the field, or perhaps I did. Except that the "field" had expanded. Oh, yes, it was exciting and challenging, but I don't remember that it was a particularly good time.

In Mississippi, everyone used to tease a chirpy, bright, young volunteer named Lucy. For this young woman every conceivable occurrence, no matter what, was always "a learning experience, a learning experience." Well, Lucy, you could say that the chairmanship was exactly that, "a learning experience, a learning experience."

[Apparently this period was so full of activity that Carmichael was not able to recall or recount all its details and range. The week after he stepped down from the chairmanship, Life *magazine (May 19, 1967) ran a sensitive portrait of Carmichael written by Gordon Parks. The editor's note that introduced the story, though less balanced than the Parks story, captures some of the frenetic activity from the media's perspective:*

"Flailing at the white society he condemns, the young man galvanizes his audience with the strident call for 'Black Power.' At twenty-five, Stokely Carmichael, leader of the Student Nonviolent Coordinating Committee— 'Snick'—is damned, lionized, and simply discussed more than any other Negro leader. He speaks in Nashville, the Negroes there riot, and the Tennessee House of Representatives calls for his deportation. He parades in Harlem on the second anniversary of the death of Malcolm X. He's in Bimini for a tête-à-tête with 'my congressman-in-exile,' Adam Clayton Powell. He's in Puerto Rico making common cause with the nationalists who seek independence from the U.S. He stands in the United Nations Plaza, pouring invective on Johnson, McNamara, Rusk, and the Vietnam war—'Hell no! We ain't going!'"—EMT]

I've mentioned some courtesy calls from movement elders. Yet another came from a powerful elder somewhat outside the pale of the conventional movement. After the "Black Power" march, we were surprised and intrigued to receive overtures. Intermediaries suggested that the Messenger *[of the Nation of Islam]*, the Honorable Elijah Muhammad, would be pleased to receive a delegation from SNCC for "conversations."

We assumed—correctly it turned out—that the Messenger's interest was in the new Black Power orientation in SNCC. We respected the work of the Nation at the grass roots, but there were contradictions. First, we felt strongly about the death of Malcolm and his problems with the Nation's leadership. Also, we had no idea how the Nation operated on the inside, but clearly some fundamental organizational differences existed between them and SNCC. Two more different cultures could hardly be imagined. SNCC was into freedom of individual conscience and democratic participation. The Nation, best we could tell, was authoritarian, dogmatic, and fundamentalist. There was also serious disagreement over what Cleve and I called their narrow nationalism, the blanket condemnation of *all* white people, the so-called blue-eyed devils. Clearly antithetical to SNCC's composition, experience, culture, and associations. What would there be to discuss?

Well, the Nation was about developing black institutions and certainly seemed to have a real presence at the urban grass roots. Since SNCC intended to move into that territory, we should at least explore opening channels. So Cleve and I agreed to go to Chicago.

I recall the headquarters as a huge building covering almost a city block. My impression was of varied operations—offices, the newspaper, perhaps a school—but we were taken directly to the well-appointed living quarters of the family. There the atmosphere was formal yet relaxed, subdued, people spoke very softly. With one notable exception we met only family. I remember various offspring and Captain Sharif, I believe, a son-in-law of the Messenger and commander of the Fruit of Islam *[the Nation's security arm —EMT]*.

I'd seen pictures of Mr. Muhammad, but in person, wow. Physically he seemed almost frail. The Messenger was a slightly built, almost petite, light-skinned black man with a distinctly Asiatic cast to his features. He spoke slowly and softly. His speech retained strong traces of rural Georgia. He did most of the talking, conducting us through the story of his divine appointment and his mission to build the Nation to redeem the lost-and-found black man in the wilderness of North America. *["My recollection is that there was a lot of talk about divine intervention, a lot. And much fulfillment of prophecy and some stuff about a mothership," Cleve Sellers recalls. "Very un-SNCC stuff."]*

Hey, we already knew the history. It wasn't the message that fascinated me, it was the messenger. How could this tiny figure with the soft, uninflected voice and precise, almost delicate mannerisms have accomplished all this? It didn't add up. There had to be a lot more to the Messenger than met the eye. The son of dirt farmers in Georgia, of little or no formal education, capable at best, at least according to Southern racist calculation, of being a deacon in a backwoods church. Yet, starting from nothing, he had built this powerful organization, given hope and a vision to many, outlasted and outwitted all rivals, and commanded the unquestioning loyalty of thousands of followers. I wasn't at all sure exactly what I was looking for, but I studied him carefully, in my mind comparing him to Malcolm.

He certainly was not an imposing physical presence and didn't seem at all charismatic. Clearly, in his understated way he had natural authority and was accustomed to great respect, which he accepted quite casually. His eyes were guarded, but watchful and focused. Occasionally he asked probing questions and seemed to listen carefully to our answers. But mostly he was teaching, instructing me 'n Cleve. I could hear something of the black church in the soft murmurs of affirmation, the "yes, sir"s and "that's right"s that occasionally filled in the pauses in his talk. He was very gracious to us. But in the end I have to say he remained a mystery to me. But we were young then; perhaps today I would have seen more.

A banquet had been prepared and the Messenger seemed to enjoy watching us eat, murmuring slyly, "It looks to me that this here movement must be starving these fine young men." The high point came when we were joined at the table by the heavyweight champion of the world and the whole mood lightened. Ali came in smiling, full of energy and fun and exuding confidence, charm, and high spirits. I liked the brother immediately. Because, beneath that jovial public exterior was clearly a proud, serious, conscious young black man, far more intelligent and thoughtful than the media ever gave him credit for, who cared deeply about his people. Our paths would cross many times, many times, especially in the struggle over the draft. Later when he fought George Foreman in Zaire, I was living in Conakry. He sent me a ticket to come in and we had a great time, but that's another story.

When Cleve and I talked about the visit, we agreed that meeting the champ had been the high point. Far as the Nation was concerned? The visit simply confirmed our opinion that SNCC would have to try to build Black Power and advance our people's interest while avoiding narrow nationalist regimentation or religious fundamentalism.

[There is a footnote. Clearly a version of this visit survives in the oral history of the Nation as is attested by the following from Eric Ture Muhammad in 1998:

"In 1966, (one of) Baba's first official acts as chairperson of SNCC was to visit the Honorable Elijah Muhammad and the Nation of Islam. It was then that Mr. Muhammad instructed the Fruit of Islam to protect Kwame Ture [then Stokely Carmichael] wherever he was found in the world. He referred to him as his Fruit of Islam." —EMT]

Dr. King's judgment about the "unfortunate choice of language" proved to be prescient and, if anything, understated.

Who could have thought it? I mean, two simple, clear, very commonly used English words. One an adjective, the other a noun. Basic. Nothing the least obscure or academically pretentious about them. Nothing mysterious or even slightly ambiguous either. Just two ordinary, unthreatening, everyday words in common usage, *black* and *power*. What could be simpler?

But in combination? He'p us, Jesus!

The conjunction of these individually harmless and inoffensive words became shocking. (As in Brother Ali's "I'm gone shock the woorld.") Apparently incomprehensible in combination, the phrase became a source of confusion to otherwise intelligent and sophisticated Americans. A concept, so it appeared, entirely beyond the cognitive reach of the white national media and public. Talk about inaccessible. Then, with the media's incomprehension combining with its global reach, the concept, invested with all kinds of fearsome implications, would reach across oceans into the Caribbean, Africa, and even Europe.

Suddenly rendered menacing, sinister, and subversive of public order and stability, the two words would, in short order, have me denied entry into France and Britain, declared persona non grata, and banned in thirty territories of the former Brutish Empire, including even the country of my birth. They would make me the object of vilification and, on more than one occasion, put my life at risk. I know this all must sound crazy, but I'm not exaggerating one little bit. It's all true. Crazy, yes, but true.

Before the dust settled, this verbal combination would inspire scholarly debate, learned dissertations, hysterical denunciations from press and pulpit, and require us to write a number of explanatory essays and a book. We would discuss them on college campuses, in churches, and from all manner of public platforms and media forums; on national network television as well as local channels. Yet even today, I keep reading that "one major problem was that SNCC (or Carmichael) failed to define the term clearly."

Ow. Now that do hurt, because it sure do seem to me that I, along with a lot of the folk in SNCC, spent my entire term as chairman doing little else but defining Black Power. I assume, therefore, that it wasn't that we "failed" to define it. No, no. Clearly, what we failed to do was to produce a definition that the opinion industry wanted to hear.

Well, here we go again. But this be the last time . . . for sure.

Yeah, the movement was changing. Had to change. Struggle is, after all, a dynamic, complicated, and organic process. And not all motion is progress. But, c'mon, gimme a break. We certainly did not change the entire direction of the black movement or the attitudes of black America merely by combining two simple words at a rally in Greenwood, Mississippi. That's silly and absurd, even for the American media.

As you've seen, the movement had been growing and changing. It had changed, was changing, needed to change, and would change, independent of any single thing SNCC—or anyone else—said or did. Period. That's inevitable. That's politics. And regardless also of anything the establishment, much to their evident regret, said or did. Though, as has since been revealed, they sure did do a lot to confuse the issue.

West Indian proverb: "When you throw a stone into a pigsty, the one that bawls is the one you lick." Well, let's take a look at who was doing the loudest bawling. The usual suspects: the *New York Times;* the national newsmagazines; many liberal journals—the *Progressive,* etc., etc.—and of course the establishment wing of the civil rights movement. (I even had a couple of public debates on the subject with NAG's early mentor Bayard.)

With Black Power, even the conservatives—the William Buckleys of the world—who had bitterly opposed every aspect of the integration struggle and had denounced both civil rights bills were heard to squeal indignantly, "What, now they *don't* want to integrate? What *do* these people want anyway?" To which I'd say, hey, make up *your* minds. What do you conservatives want anyway? To marry *our* sisters?

But the language and tone of the *liberal* outrage was instructive. The usual hand-wringing and pious condescension, public distress that the black movement was about to irreparably damage itself and our long-suffering people's prospects of "acceptance." For example, one famous public intellectual, James Wechsler of the *New York Post,* worried that we "were killing the dream" . . . that "the cause of Civil Rights was floundering" . . . "the visions of the freedom movement are imperiled" . . . "some deeply dedicated *[but obviously confused]* men are setting the stage for the destruction of the noblest cause of our time." And so it went. As if, had it not been for those two misaligned, ill-chosen words, American society would have transformed itself into a thoroughly integrated, multiracial, color-blind utopia. Gimme a break. There is a term for this kind of nonsense, which I won't use here.

After the NAACP convention that year, we knew we had to respond seriously. See, when these delegates from all their branches gather, you looking, for the most part, at the active *local* leadership in many of our communities across the country. The older generation, yes. Our parents, in some cases. But collectively, they were some of the people who kept the struggle going. One had to respect them, whatever the national office was or wasn't doing.

So when Bro Secretary Wilkins led the attack, the effort was clearly to cut us off from an important part of the African community. The secretary called us racists. Black Power, he said, meant antiwhite power. It meant black separation. (I guess in his mind the country was racially unified.) It meant "the ranging of race against race" on the irrelevant basis of skin color. Everything the NAACP had fought against for so long. "We will have none of it."

When Bro Wilkins was followed by our old friend the vice president, it became clear that Mrs. Hamer's prayers for Mr. Humphrey had gone unanswered. I assumed that the vice president represented the Johnson administration line and he'd come loaded for bear:

> Racism is racism . . . the dogma of the oppressor . . . we must reject racism whether it comes from a throat which is white or a throat which is black . . . we must reject apartheid. Integration must be recognized as the means to the ends we are seeking.

I can remember thinking as I listened to this dishonest claptrap. And it wasn't just ill-informed or out of touch, it was *dishonest.* "Now tell me who is deluded and who are the real ideologues out here?"

Obviously this massive chorus of outrage and distortion was not really about anything we'd actually said, but about its implications. Because, remember now, at that point we'd not said anything "revolutionary," unless electoral politics in the South, with black people voting racists out and seeking office themselves was revolutionary.

After the NAACP convention, the SNCC executive committee decided that we had to make a clear statement to try to cut through the hysteria and inject some rationality into a discussion that was steadily getting crazier by the minute. The committee decided that SNCC needed a position paper and they mandated me to develop one. Mike Thelwell and I spent a few days poring over and analyzing the wave of attacks. Where they came from; which interests were involved; what they said; what they meant; why were all these different groups experiencing this sudden need to rush onto the record with gratuitous good advice for "the Negro"? As it were, to save us from ourselves one more time?

Of course, not everything was an attack. A few conscious writers understood that a period of black self-determinism was both necessary and inevitable. And that it did not necessarily have to threaten whites. I recall, especially, I. F. Stone, an honest, decent little guy with big horn-rimmed glasses who wrote a political newsletter out of D.C. But such voices were a minority. *[Izzy Stone was one Washington journalist who always came to our press conferences and gave us fair and intelligent coverage. —EMT]*

Among black intellectuals, there was some division, not always along generational lines. As I recall, only two African intellectuals commanded any real attention among opinion makers in white liberal circles. *Two.* I don't remember any black faces among the conservatives. One was Dr. Kenneth Clark, a psychologist, and the other was Bro Jimmy Baldwin. Neither attacked us. Dr. Clark was distressed by the implications. He predictably came down strongly for integration, grieving in a kind of high-minded way for a fading utopian dream of a raceless society. But Bro Clark didn't do any name-calling. Jimmy was always clear and stalwart. Strong. I remember he said the Negro has always been used to mark the bottom for this society. Now when the foundation begins to shift, the universe itself begins to tremble. Deal with it. I don't remember his exact words but that was the idea. I can't recall any other black intellectuals of the time who commanded any serious respect, attention, or influence in circles of white opinion. So much for "integration."

We concentrated on the torrent of attacks. You always learn more from your enemies. Patterns emerged. A number of things became clear. For one thing, these attacks were not really about anything we'd actually said. They were about the *implications* of what we'd said. What Black Power might and could mean. And, of course, what they *thought* it might mean or do. Clearly, the combination of those two words had struck a nerve.

What was even more evident was that—tactically—these attacks were preemptive strikes. Disinformation intended, collectively—so it seemed to us, by its volume—to drown out any free or open discussion of the *idea*, the strategy among our people. To *impose* their definition. So, what was the discussion they were so anxious to head off? What was it they didn't want us to be talking about? What interests of theirs could such a discussion among us threaten?

Posing the questions in that way forced us to be clear. The issues were of two kinds: political *and* cultural. The political was obvious: the movement's beginning to rethink the goals and the means of our struggle. To consciously begin to organize among ourselves and find the power to affirm and control our legitimate political rights and our full human dignity. Self-determination. No longer pretending to accept, with a grin and a shuffle, whatever grudging crumbs and concessions the white establishment might feel disposed to toss our way. Thankee, massa. Thankee, boss. No, no. To *assert* and *demand* everything that is ours by right, nothing less. That was the politics.

But, of course, you can't divorce politics from culture. The underlying and fundamental notion was that black folks needed to begin openly, and had the right and the duty, to define for ourselves, *in our own terms,* our real circumstances, possibilities, and interests relative to white America. To determine what the relationship was. Simple as that. To consciously and publicly free ourselves from the heritage of demeaning definitions and limitations imposed on us, over centuries of colonial conditioning by a racist culture. Cultural and psychological self-determination, that's all.

Hey, if this was the discussion that this torrent of disinformation and intimidation was intended to derail, then I had some real bad news for them. They were way too late, Jack. This discussion—however suppressed—had long been under way among our people. In fact, it had never stopped, never stopped, from the first Africans' arrival in chains, never stopped. Still hasn't. So even had we wanted to, SNCC could claim no credit for having started it. At best, the most I can say is that with the unwitting help of the media, we helped bring it out onto center stage. That's all. And one way or another, that was going to happen, would have happened anyway. These ideas and feelings had been building up, building and percolating upward from the grass roots of our struggle for years, especially all during the sixties.

So what Thelwell and I decided was that we needed to give the argument focus, to make it plain. To discuss both the politics and the culture. The essay we produced that weekend—"Toward Black Liberation"—was generally accepted as SNCC's first position paper on Black Power.

In that essay we set out to analyze and crystallize everything that SNCC had learned about our people, our culture, our struggle, and American society into a single argument. We also had to define the need for and possibilities of Black Power and to project a realistic program and a new approach for the next stage of the political and cultural struggle: it was already clear that the movement would have to move out of the South and into Northern cities; what was that going to entail?

Naturally there were things we missed. Most important, there was, for example, no detailed, realistic economic analysis in the essay, nor did we really anticipate the intensity and viciousness of the media's and the government's covert response (COINTELPRO). And who in 1966 could have imagined the way the lunatic right would capture the Republican Party, bogart the national political debate, and set the right-wing political agenda that white America would accept for the next thirty years? Hey, in 1966, Nixon was a political has-been ("You won't have Nixon to kick around anymore") and Ronald Reagan was a grade-B movie actor. Who could have imagined?

But even so, if you read our essay today, much of it, especially the discussion of our situation, was right on: accurate, logical, even prophetic. And we did give a clear new direction to the political discussion within the movement. A lot of folk, one could say an entire generation of black people, picked up on it. But as I said, we didn't start the discussion.

I had expected—hoped for—the political response. But I must admit that the range and the *intensity* of the cultural aspect surprised me a little. I mean, the extent and the passion with which our artists and writers, and especially the musicians, just picked up the ball and ran with it. Ran with it, Jack. And too, there was the Black Arts movement, which just seemed to emerge in the North—as the cultural expression of Black Power— among young writers and artists. Young brothers like Gil Scott-Heron, Amiri Baraka (LeRoi Jones), Larry Neal, Sonia Sanchez, and them. As I said, these ideas and feelings had been percolating upward within all elements of our community. Had been for a long, long time; now they broke into the open.

I really dug the popular music aspect—soul, rhythm and blues, even funk a little—of this uprising of political and cultural consciousness, and not just because it reached millions of our people. As a young boy, it had been popular music and jazz that had been my first avenue into African life in America. We are an African people, so it was natural that from the beginning, from the spirituals right on up, music would be our weapon and our solace.

Indeed, certain jazz musicians had always incorporated a high social and cultural consciousness into their work. And in the early sixties, artists like Sister Odetta, Oscar Brown Jr., Max Roach and Abbey Lincoln with their *We Insist! Freedom Now Suite,* or Nina Simone's "Mississippi Goddam" and "Young, Gifted and Black" had reflected the Southern struggle.

But now something slightly different. Political consciousness moved into the popular arena. Soul, rhythm and blues, stuff that had been purely commercial, dance music, entertainment. I think Bro Sam Cooke (peace be unto him) might have got in first with "A Change Is Gonna Come." After that we talking about people like Marvin Gaye, "What's Going On," Brother Curtis Mayfield, "We're a Winner," "Keep On Pushing," "People Get Ready," Sister Aretha Franklin's "Respect," and of course, the King of Soul, Brother James Brown's "Say It Loud (I'm Black and I'm Proud)." This music reached people we couldn't otherwise reach. How effectively, I can't say. But from it, one sensed an exuberant mood in the community.

We began by analyzing the thrust of the attacks. A number of threads ran through them all, for one thing the language of political abuse: "racists," "Klansmen in blackface," "demagogues," "hate mongers," "adventurists," etc., etc. But the single recurring constant was the sanctification of "integration." The funny thing is that we'd not yet even discussed, much less attacked, that concept in any systematic way. Yet out of nowhere, all these suddenly devout integrationists, many of whom had been dragging their feet on civil rights, popped up to defend the true faith and attack us. Yet in practical terms, integration was nowhere to be found in the land. Clearly, like "communism" in Marxist dogma, "integration" was pure ideal, not a reality but the highest value devoutly to be wished and to which the faithful should aspire. So we decided to start with this suddenly very sacred cow.

What we discovered was that apparently no one in the movement had taken the time to seriously analyze the unexamined assumptions underlying the concept of integration or its practical feasibility as a strategy. It was weird. A generation of us had simply come along, found it enshrined in movement rhetoric, and accepted it without serious examination. A good in itself. Hey, if the racists and the Klan were agin it, then we were automatically for it. Knee-jerk, no critical thought. Now, because of the attacks, we began to really ask some serious questions.

From the beginning, fundamental contradictions had been present but pretty much ignored. One example: This incident in Aberdeen, Maryland, still rankles. This was during the Route 40 campaign. The one and only time I ever set foot in that town. A restaurant sit-in. An integrated group of students have occupied every seat and are not being served. So we sit there.

Then in storms this heavyset blond woman, face flushed, obviously upset, and shaking with rage or something. She's got the attention of everyone in the place.

"I want to know," she demands loudly, "what's wrong with y'all?" She's talking to the group but she's looking dead at me. Our eyes lock. The woman is obviously enjoying her little drama.

"Why don't *you people* want to stay with *your own kind*," she shrills. "Why you all want to come around folks where you not wanted? Huh?" The nonviolent rule was that you never responded in kind to hecklers, but this woman's tone got to me. It must have been her smugness. Her self-satisfaction and easy assumption that we were there to associate with *people like her.* "Well," she demands, "why don't you want to stay with your own kind?"

"Lady, since you asked, I'm going to tell you. But you listen now, 'cause I'm only going say this once, okay?" I guess she must not have intended it as a real question 'cause she shut up and seemed quite shocked to be getting an answer.

"Lady, believe me, we aren't here 'cause we think the food is good, or because your company is attractive, okay? We here for one simple reason and one reason only. *You,* collectively, do not have the right, none of you, to tell us where we can go or cannot go. Simple as that. I refuse to allow you or any one else to dictate and define *my* rights. That's all. It's a matter of principle. Once we establish that principle, I guarantee you'll never see my face in this place again. You better believe it ain't about white folks' company. You can believe that."

I don't remember that the woman said anything. I'm not sure she even understood. But hers was a common enough misconception, very common. We even heard it from some Negroes at Howard, as if the only reason to resist segregation had to be because you wanted to be amongst white folk? Nonsense. Certainly not for the people I was working with. We simply refused to accept any arbitrary limits imposed on us by American apartheid. That's all. Simple as that. Le's move on.

So, what did integration really mean? In cultural terms? In psychological terms? As a practical goal not for individuals but entire communities? For the formation, preservation, and development of black institutions? Was integration really the opposite of segregation? Was it an end in itself? Was it really an honorable or practical goal for our people? The solution to our problems? Finally, was it feasible and what would an integrated American society really look like?

The answers we came up with surprised us. Not only by their unassailable clarity, but by how very obvious they were, once you stripped away the pious rhetoric and mystification, and also by the extent to which we'd always known and suppressed certain truths that should have been obvious and up front.

The unspoken, unexamined, and unacceptable assumption of the "integration" being preached was that nothing of value or permanence could be created by black people in association with ourselves. Simple as that.

The American "melting pot" meant us—as a people—assimilating, despite racist resistance, the culture and values of the mainstream, hoping to pass over into and be "accepted" by the white community *on their terms.* To blend in, call no attention to differences—in effect, to sneak into white acceptance. Clearly a form of cultural suicide. So that is what we said.

Then we said that the solution to our problems had nothing to do with our "acceptance" by white America and less with "universal brotherhood." Our struggle had to be about power. And since SNCC was neither crazy nor stupid, it had to be clear that we weren't talking about overthrowing the system and black folk taking over the country—so why all this weeping and gnashing of liberal teeth? This was simply about the power to affirm our black humanity; to defend the dignity, integrity, and institutions of our culture; and to collectively organize the political and economic power to begin to control and develop our communities. It was patently *not* about abandoning our black communities and rejecting our black culture, but about developing the one and embracing the other.

Simply put, our goal and direction could not be about deserting our communities as refugees to white suburbia, but toward liberating, controlling, and developing our own communities. Not about abandoning our culture and rich heritage in order to "integrate" into an American "mainstream," then, as now, self-consciously defined as culturally "white" and Eurocentric. This was about pride, self-respect, and autonomy, in fact, part of the universal human struggle of all people everywhere for self-determination, pure and simple. The devil, however, was in the details. How to develop the unity and the strategies to make this possible in a strange land? And in the face of the pervasive white-controlled media manipulation?

It was patently not about either hating or loving white people. That quite simply was not the issue. That it really had nothing to do with them was something they could not seem to grasp. Being pro-black didn't mean you're antiwhite. As I used to say, just because you're building your own house doesn't mean you have to tear down the house across the street.

Indeed, we explicitly talked about trying to build the political bases from which at the appropriate time we could enter into coalitions with whites as respected partners and allies rather than as patronized beggars and clients.

That essentially is what we wrote in that first SNCC statement on the question of Black Power, back in 1966. Was it just "a jive black rap" by "dashiki-wearing demagogues"? Hate mongering and whitey bashing? I'll let you judge for yourselves thirty-five years later. Here are a few brief passages.

On the white media:

> Our experience with the national press has been that where they have managed to escape a meretricious special interest in "Git Whitey" sensationalism and race-war-mongering, individual reporters and commentators have been conditioned by the enveloping racism of the society to the point where they are incapable even of objective observation and reporting of racial *incidents,* much less the analysis of *ideas.* But this limitation of vision and perceptions is an inevitable consequence of the dictatorship of definition, interpretation, and consciousness, along with the censorship of history that the society has inflicted upon the Negro—and upon itself.

On the basic necessity of self-definition as a means toward liberation:

> Our concern for black power addresses itself directly to this problem, the necessity to reclaim our history and our identity from the cultural terrorism and depredation of self-justifying white guilt.
>
> To do this we shall have to struggle for the right to create our own terms through which to define ourselves and our relationship to the society, and to have these terms recognized. This is the first necessity of a free people, and the first right that any oppressor must suspend. The white fathers of American racism knew this—instinctively it seems—as is indicated by the continuous record of the distortion and omission in their dealings with red and black men.

In trying to clarify the real effect of power and race in the society, we came up with a concept we called institutional racism. Thelwell is always saying we should take credit for coining the term. Maybe, but who needs it?

There have been traditionally two communities in America. The white community, which controlled and defined the forms that all institutions within the society would take, and the Negro community, which has been excluded from participation in the power decisions that shaped the society, and has traditionally been dependent upon, and subservient to, the white community.

This has not been accidental. The history of every institution of this society indicates that a major concern in the ordering and structuring of the society has been the maintaining of the Negro community in its condition of dependence and oppression. This has not been on the level of *individual* acts of discrimination between *individual* whites against *individual* Negroes, but as total acts by the white community against the Negro community. *Institutional racism.*

For example, when unknown racists bomb a church and kill four children, that is an act of individual racism, widely deplored by most segments of the society. But when in that same city, Birmingham, Alabama, not five but five hundred Negro babies die each year because of a lack of proper food, shelter, and medical facilities, and thousands more are destroyed and maimed physically, emotionally, and intellectually because of conditions of poverty and deprivation in the ghetto, that is a function of *institutionalized* racism. But the society either pretends it doesn't know of this situation, or is incapable of doing anything meaningful about it. And this resistance to doing anything meaningful about conditions in that ghetto comes from the fact that the ghetto is itself a product of a combination of forces and special interests in the white community.

We also discussed forthrightly the nature of the colonial relationship between the ghetto and American power. How much has changed today? You decide.

It is more than a figure of speech to say that the Negro community in America is the victim of white imperialism and colonial exploitation. This is in practical economic and political terms true. There are over twenty million black people comprising ten percent of this nation. They for the most part live in well-defined areas of the country—in the shanty-towns and rural black belt areas of the South, and increasingly in the slums of northern and western industrial cities. If one goes into any Negro community, whether it be in Jackson, Mississippi, Cambridge, Maryland, or Harlem, New York, one will find that the same combination of political, economic, and social forces are at work. The people in the Negro community do not control the resources of that community, its political decisions, its law enforcement, its housing standards; and even the physical ownership of the land, houses, and stores lie outside that community.

It is white power that makes the laws, and it is violent white power in the form of armed white cops that enforce those laws with guns and nightsticks. The vast majority of Negroes in this country live in these captive communities and must endure these conditions of oppression because, and only because, they are black and powerless.

We tried to bring some clarity to the discussion of the concrete circumstances facing our people in communities across the land. And to the evolution of American apartheid, North and South: Is this rhetoric or demagoguery? What progress has thirty-five years achieved?

I do not suppose that at any point the men who control the power and resources of this country ever sat down and designed these black enclaves and formally articulated the terms of their colonial and dependent status, as was done, for example, by the apartheid government of South Africa. Yet, one can not distinguish between one ghetto and another. As one moves from city to city it is as though some malignant racist planning unit had done precisely this—designed each one from the same master blueprint. And indeed, if the ghetto had been formally and deliberately planned, instead of growing spontaneously and inevitably from the racist functioning of the various institutions that combine to make the society, it would be somehow less frightening. The situation would be less frightening because, if these ghettoes were the result of design and conspiracy, one could understand their similarity as being artificial and consciously imposed, rather than the result of identical patterns of white racism which repeat themselves in cities as distant as Boston and Birmingham. Without bothering to list the historic factors which contribute to this pattern—economic exploitation, political impotence, discrimination in employment and education—one can see that to correct this pattern will require far-reaching changes in the basic power relationships and the ingrained social patterns within the society. The question is, of course, what kinds of changes are necessary, and how is it possible to bring them about?

Then the inevitable, long-delayed examination, in objective terms, of the implications of the concept of integration, its desirability as a goal, as well as its practical value as a social strategy. You tell me, what has been the achievement of this strategy after nearly forty years?

According to the advocates of integration, social justice will be accomplished by "integrating the Negro into the mainstream institutions of the society from which he has been traditionally excluded." It is very significant that each time I have heard this formulation, it has been in terms of "the Negro," the individual Negro, rather than in terms of the community.

This concept of integration had to be based on the assumption that there was nothing of value in the Negro community and that little of value could be created among Negroes, so the thing to do was to siphon off the "acceptable" Negroes into the surrounding middle-class white community. Thus the goal of the movement for integration was simply to loosen up the restrictions barring the entry of certain Negroes into the white community . . . only a small select group of Negroes. Its goal was to make the white community accessible to "qualified" Negroes, and presumably each year a few more Negroes armed with their passports—a couple of university degrees—would escape into middle-class America and adopt the attitudes and life styles of that group; and one day the Harlems and the Wattses would stand empty, a tribute to the success of integration. This is simply neither realistic nor particularly desirable. You can integrate communities, but you assimilate individuals. Even if such a program were possible, its result would be, not to develop the black community as a functional and honorable segment of the total society, with its own cultural identity, life patterns, and institutions, but to abolish it—the final solution to the Negro problem. Marx said that the working class is the first class in history that ever wanted to abolish itself. If one listens to some of our "moderate" Negro leaders, it appears that the American Negro is the first race that ever wished to abolish itself. The fact is that what must be abolished is not the black community, but the dependent colonial status that has been inflicted upon it.

Naturally we had to engage the vexed question of independent organization as one of the means toward the liberation of our communities. I still can't see what was so controversial about this concept.

The single aspect of the black power program that has encountered most criticism is this concept of independent organization. This is presented as third-partyism, which has never worked, or a "withdrawal" into "black nationalism and isolationism." If such a program is developed it will not have the effect of isolating the Negro community but the reverse. When the Negro community is able to control local office and negotiate with other groups from a position of organized strength, the possibility of meaningful political alliances on specific issues will be increased.

I won't describe my emotions now on rereading these next sections. The passage was our attempt to evaluate our *[the movement's]* accomplishments as of 1966. All I'll say is that it gives me no satisfaction to have been accurate then and apparently prophetic now. I'm most saddened that, for reasons I'll discuss, we (SNCC as an organization) were never able to devote the kind of energy and resources to the organizing project in the Northern urban areas that I had hoped we would do. On the brain drain:

What has the movement for integration accomplished to date? The Negro graduating from MIT with a doctorate will have better job opportunities available to him than to Lynda Bird Johnson. But the rate of unemployment in the Negro community is steadily increasing, while that in the white community decreases. More educated Negroes hold executive jobs in major corporations and federal agencies than ever before, but the gap between white income and Negro income has almost doubled in the last twenty years. More suburban housing is available to Negroes, but housing conditions in the ghetto are steadily declining. While the infant mortality rate of New York City is at its lowest rate ever in the city's history, the infant mortality rate of Harlem is steadily climbing. There has been an organized national resistance to the Supreme Court's order to integrate the schools, and the federal government has not acted to enforce that order. Less than fifteen percent of black children in the South attend integrated schools, and Negro schools, which the vast majority of black children still attend, are increasingly decrepit, overcrowded, understaffed, inadequately equipped and funded.

This explains why the rate of school dropouts is increasing among Negro teenagers, who then express their bitterness, hopelessness, and alienation by the only means they have—rebellion. As long as people in the ghettoes of our large cities feel that they are victims of the misuse of white power without any way to have their needs represented—and these are frequently simple needs: to get the welfare inspectors to stop kicking down your doors in the middle of the night, the cops from beating your children, the landlord to exterminate the vermin in your home, the city to collect your garbage—we will continue to have riots. These are not the products of "black power," but of the absence of any organization capable of giving the community the power, the black power, to deal with its problems.

SNCC proposes that it is now time for the black freedom movement to stop pandering to the fears and anxieties of the white middle class in the attempt to earn its "good-will," and to return to the ghetto to organize these communities to control themselves.

That essentially was the analysis. We concluded with a political/demographic projection and posed a choice to the nation. Ironically enough, a projection "over the next three decades," which would bring us roughly to this moment *[1997].* So now would be about the right time to assess which choice this nation did make. C. L. R. James once said, men make history, but only so much history as it is possible for them to make. Societies, however, make decisions that then become history. A rational society makes rational decisions, a humane culture makes humane history. And we know America is, of course, both rational and humane, right? It's now thirty-five years later, the "next three decades" we spoke about. . . . What has been the society's choice?

> The revolution in agricultural technology in the South is displacing the rural Negro community into northern urban areas. Both Washington, D.C., and Newark, New Jersey, have Negro majorities. One third of Philadelphia's population of two million people is black. "Inner city" in most major urban areas is already predominantly Negro, and, with the white rush to suburbia, Negroes will in the next three decades control the hearts of our great cities. These areas can become either concentration camps with a bitter and volatile population whose only power is the power to destroy, or organized and powerful communities able to make constructive contributions to the total society. Without the power to control their lives and their communities, without effective political institutions through which to relate to the total society, these communities will exist in a constant state of insurrection. This is a choice that the country will have to make.

That, eventually, was the message we took across the length and breadth of the country during my period as SNCC chairman. Despite all efforts to distort its message, to create confusion and unnecessary controversy, and to discredit us as racist, black people really responded. The proverbial "idea whose time has come"? Well, we'd sure see, wouldn't we?

Actually a lot sooner than could have been expected. This was incredible. Right at the height of this raging media-generated controversy about Black Power, a major movement action that, in any halfway rational society, should have settled the question was taking place. It didn't. No one noticed, or at least made the connection.

Yet this campaign that was dominating the national news coverage could not have better demonstrated the practical and political differences between the two approaches—Black Power and integration—had it been designed for that purpose. And no one in the media, not one, made the connection. At least not anywhere that I saw. It was incredible, a kind of willed blindness. So what am I talking about?

Well, this. As you know, right after the Meredith march, Dr. King and SCLC went into Chicago. Not unexpected. Walking down those Delta roads, we'd discussed how the movement would have to take on the Northern cities. I was quite naturally curious to see how well SCLC's hit-and-run mobilization techniques from Selma and Birmingham would fare

537

in the North. Chicago would be a serious test. The sheer scale of the city, its ethnic neighborhoods, its politics, the infamous Daley machine, the entrenched industrial capitalism. How responsive would these be to SCLC's nonviolent, mass mobilization marches and cries for integration. I wasn't sure. A brother in engineering once told me, "If the only tool you have is a hammer, then the whole world will look like a nail." I wished Dr. King well, but I wondered what tactical changes he was preparing for his first Northern campaign. I had my doubts.

Chicago seemed at first anticlimactic; nothing much seemed to be happening either way until SCLC confronted the housing issue. Then everything crystallized. Housing was central to our thinking on Black Power. We were arguing that black people had to find creative ways to transform our urban communities, beginning with the property. To summon the will; fight for resources; seek control of the housing, the schools; to rehabilitate our own space and create livable, functioning communities of our own. No one said it would be easy, but at least that was the direction. All right, if you insist, a turning inward. Yeah. But creatively, and *intelligently,* looking inward, while still engaging the system—city, state, nation—for what the community needed and deserved. That's what we were proposing. And the result, this knee-jerk response about racism, divisiveness, separation, etc., etc.

On the other hand, SCLC's Chicago project program, exactly the opposite of ours: integration and something they called "open housing." The tactic: nonviolent marches into the surrounding "white ethnic" suburbs, presumably to "open" them up so inner-city blacks can move in? Hey, there are people already living there. *Aye-yai-yai,* I thought. Right issue, wrong approach, wrong strategy, wrong solution. I didn't see what good could result, but honestly? I never, never expected the size and ferocity of the white response. It was ugly and you know very sad. Because it didn't really have to happen at all.

I mean SCLC and CORE start leading these marches, and what happens? Mobs of angry working-class whites, mostly youth, young men, the parents probably being at work. We talking crowds of four, five thousand now. With baseball bats, lead pipes, racist signs, KKK, swastikas and other Nazi insignia. Angry, contorted faces. Screaming all kinds of racist slogans. Hundreds of cops struggling to keep the groups apart. I mean it was ugly. I mean these were larger crowds than anything Dr. King had faced anywhere in the South.

I looked at those images on TV and three things were clear. As an organizer I knew that crowds of that size don't just spontaneously gather, no way. Someone, and not just the locals, had been doing some serious organizing. That was quite clear.

Two, I'd never been in those Chicago suburbs, but I sure recognized those faces. They were from my old neighborhood. Guys I'd gone to junior high school with in the Bronx. I'd been in and out of their homes and never seen a swastika or a Klan poster. So I knew Nazi organizers and other hard-core racists had to be in there fanning the flames. Which is not to say there wouldn't have been racism anyway. Of course there would be. Immigrants step off the boat and immediately start assimilating American racial attitudes. But from my experience that would be a latent racism feeding on distance and ignorance.

For example, the Italians on the street were quite skeptical when we moved in. Not openly hostile, but not welcoming either. However, once my father rebuilt the house, thereby improving *their* property values, there was at least tolerance, sometimes even genuine friendship. So, yeah, there certainly would be, in these communities, shall we say, a level of latent racial antipathy present to be exploited in the right circumstances. And these were the perfect circumstances.

These were working people. Their identity revolved around four things: family, home, church, and neighborhood, in no particular order. I knew that those neat little houses, as with my father, represented their only life savings, their most tangible material accomplishment, the American Dream. And the neighborhood was not just turf, it was their *identity*, representing family, church, school, the local bar, everything.

Any perceived threat to any of these, real or imagined, and we talking war. Be the easiest thing in the world to whip up a mob to confront any "invasion." It all seemed utterly pointless to me. How could these marches help the African community? Who was going to be the first to "integrate" such an aroused neighborhood? And to what end? Or was there going to be a wholesale migration from South Side Chicago to Cicero? Gimme a break. I kept waiting for someone to point out the obvious. In vain.

I don't recall any real discussion, any comparison of the two alternatives, anywhere in the media. It was as if the two approaches had no relationship or connection to each other so far as the public media was concerned. Go figure.

So soon as I could, I made a point of going to Chicago to see Dr. King. As I recall, he was still staying in a hotel, 'cause we met in a hotel suite there about one o'clock in the morning. We talked for a good while. I shared everything I was thinking about the open-housing campaign. He listened, asked a few questions, but didn't say much. When Dr. King listened quietly, you knew you had his attention. Then we talked about Vietnam. I think it was only a few months after that he had come out against the war. And as we've seen, he never publicly attacked Black Power. But then Dr. King never publicly attacked any other civil rights group. Never did.

● ● ●

Where one thing stands, something else will stand beside it. That's an African proverb I've always liked. This ancestral wisdom deals with duality and contradiction, complexity. Nothing is ever entirely one thing or even simply what it seems. Another, different thing will stand beside it and behind it. A particular thing will often include its opposite.

There is a question people are always asking me: "How did the chairmanship change your life?" I always answer that it didn't. It affected it, but it didn't *change* my life. Hey, it affected my life because my job changed. But it didn't change me. Not in any significant way. I just had a larger stage for what I'd been doing in SNCC. Period. Of course now, I learned a great deal. I learned a lot more about organizational politics; the pettiness of which some "leaders" were capable; about the media and its lies; and, oh, yes, about the country: the government and *its* lies.

But that doesn't mean that I, personally, changed. In fact, the opposite. All of that merely served to clarify for me exactly who and what I really was—just another organizer. Which is why I stepped down from the position after a year to go back to organizing.

The major frustration I had was spending so much time on the road, in planes, on public platforms. This was necessary but it meant that I wasn't on a project working closely with our people, seeing the people grow in their organized strength. I found out right quick how much I missed that. How much that kind of organizing meant to me and was the work I really loved doing.

In fact, even the time I could spend in Atlanta working with Cleve and Ruby Doris on the day-to-day running of the organization was much less than I'd expected and wanted. So these burdens fell heavy on Cleve, Ruby Doris, and the executive committee at a time when there would be some heavy internal challenges to face. I wasn't at all comfortable with that, but it really couldn't be helped.

See, after the "Black Power" march, a number of things happened that really took over my time. The first was that SNCC's fund-raising base was shrinking. Seriously. Not entirely unexpected. Actually this had begun from the time SNCC came out against the Vietnam War. *[At the time, Brother Ralph Featherstone put it quite aptly: "Man, SNCC went from sugar to shit in six months." —EMT]*

Then, with the Black Power and the urban uprisings, and especially with SNCC beginning to address the problems of our people in Northern cities, our Northern base of support really began to shrink. Hey, we weren't naive; after all, we'd experienced some of that after Atlantic City when the totalitarian liberals turned against us. But that was a joke compared to what we were now seeing. We'd anticipated a "backlash," but perhaps not the extent or the suddenness of the liberals' alienation. No question, the media misrepresentation and attacks contributed greatly to this alienation, but the necessary growth in our politics made it inevitable anyway. Let's be real.

For example, for some time the staff had been contracting. Some of this was just natural attrition; old organizers, white and black, were burning out and falling away to try to get themselves together. Or to go back to school. But more than that, a lot of it was expected—right on schedule. Remember now, the huge, sudden expansion had come after the summer project when unexpectedly large numbers of volunteers had signed on. Most of these good white folk had planned at most to give the movement a year and then return to their lives and careers. Most had done that. Perfectly natural and expected. However, the perception, widely circulated in the media, and pushed by our political critics, was that Black Power was running whites out of the movement.

As I said, we'd have been fools not to expect the "white backlash" that the media had been threatening us with ever since the sit-ins in 1960. But from the "progressives" and allies? Gimme a break. But we were clear about this in our discussions. Very clear. The organization would be foolish to think that it could represent the interests of the black masses honestly and without compromise while expecting to receive the major part of its funding from white benefactors. We knew that. No way. This had long been a potential contradiction; now it surfaced seriously. We knew we had four choices.

1. Allow ourselves to become a puppet organization completely subservient to the attitudes of the contributors. No thanks.

2. Since many supporters were "progressives," we could try to engage them in serious discussions, to bring them along, educate them about the real political positions of the organization and try to hold at least some of that base. A chancy proposition. Yet it is important to say that a core of loyal and fair-minded white supporters did stand firm with us. Not the majority by any means, but quite a few strong, honest folk. Chuck McDew called them the "righteous among the nations." Give thanks.

3. Maintain our integrity and independence of mind and action as long as possible, then simply go out of business as an organization. Just pack it in. Why not? SNCC had a proud history of accomplishment and struggle. It had never envisioned itself as a self-perpetuating institution anyway. If SNCC no longer existed as an organization, our people would just have to find other arenas of struggle. Which many did and are still doing, many people.

4. Fight hard to preserve the organization as the logical vehicle for Black Power. This meant adapting to the next level of struggle while trying

to develop an independent fund-raising base within the black community. Even if this meant cutting back on the scope of operations, but surviving as an independent black organization free to follow the logic of the struggle. That was my first commitment.

I still believe that the last was possible, and not just theoretically, even back then. Hey, the NAACP did get its basic operating funds from its membership. But of course that base had taken fifty years to develop and the organization still needed significant outside funding. SCLC got significant funding from its base in the black church, and even *they* needed outside funding. We had no such natural base, but SNCC was always a guerrilla operation with relatively modest needs. To develop a similar base would require a total, full-time effort on our part, and much more time than we would have. But we were accustomed to operating on a shoestring. A fraction of the other groups' operating costs. So we could perhaps survive.

Naturally, as you might expect, we ended up doing a little bit of all, except, of course, the first: craven submission. But those were the realities that dictated how my time as chairman was spent.

Once Black Power became the hot media topic of the moment, I instantly found myself in great demand as a speaker. We tried to use that for two purposes: to clarify and spread the political message while raising sorely needed organizational funds. And even this wasn't really new. Almost everyone in SNCC was sent out on fund-raising speeches. That was normal. A lot of different folk usually did that. But now, thanks to the media, mine was the name and face associated with Black Power in the public mind. That, and the title *chairman*, i.e., *official* spokesman, along with the fact that suddenly my name on a poster could fill a hall, meant that I commanded higher fees than other staff people. So that quite apart from the politics, I was rapidly becoming marketable property, show business capitalism. This was real sudden, a kind of instant media celebrity. Of course, it was unreal and much about it I did not at all like. But it came with the job. And SNCC sure needed the money. Contradictions again. *Where one thing stands, something else . . .*

Even so, we made sure that for every public-relations-type fund-raising appearance we accepted, we scheduled a political one in the community. A speech at a black college or a community rally in the inner city. Especially cities where there had been insurrections, like Watts, Detroit, places like that. So there I was making a great many speeches— I mean a lot, Jack. Sometimes traveling all day and speaking every night. Often two, three speeches the same day. Yeah, so folks say I love to talk? Maybe so, but certainly not like this, bro. This was unreal, hectic, ironic. I'd estimate that I had to have spoken—I mean in person, now, not counting the expanded media audience—to over two hundred thousand black folk over that year. Easy. At the same time, I met some strong people, all over the country. Real strong. Folks who would continue to struggle with me my entire life. For example, that's when I met Brother David "Light the Fire" Brothers. And, everything I saw of our people's condition across the country convinced me even more that we were doing the right thing.

Contradictions? Okay, I'll show you contradictions. Somehow I'd become this media attraction, right? Now the cameras and writers are following me everywhere. Suddenly anything I *say* is news. I mean I'd even appear on a TV program and newspapers would report *that* as if it were news. Unreal.

[Our brother was indeed following an incredible speaking schedule at this time, from national media such as Meet the Press *and* Face the Nation *to small-town church halls. The most complete record of these appearances came to us courtesy of the American taxpayer. Mr. Hoover's FBI appears to have collected and preserved every last press clipping from every Carmichael appearance, no matter how small the town or the audience. Where there were no press clippings, we find field reports from agents of the Bureau in the audience. —EMT]*

You think, "Well, good. Use the media to spread the message. Where's the contradiction?" C'mon, get serious. It doesn't work that way. For one thing I was being consistent. Saying more or less the same thing over and over. What they call "staying on message," huh? But where's the story in that? The press doesn't like repeating itself. They looking for something new, exciting every night. Anything to "spice" up the story. So what kept getting reported was whatever they thought they could sensationalize. Usually out of context. Whatever was or could be made to sound confrontational or controversial got featured, usually to the exclusion of serious supporting arguments or context. Of course, I take some responsibility in this. While I didn't set out to offend anyone, I certainly wasn't about to bend over backward merely to *avoid* giving offense either. I was going to tell the plain truth. If someone wanted to take offense, tough. So the message, as reported, was sometimes garbled, sometimes distorted in the reporting. Especially in the headlines. Sometimes even if the reporting was reasonably accurate and fair, you'd get these lurid scare headlines that didn't reflect anything in the story underneath. Accidental, general incompetence, or deliberate sabotage? Your call. But, hey, I saw entirely too much of a pattern for it to be entirely accidental. In fact, so much of a pattern that when occasionally we did find an accurate account that was fair and intelligent, *that* was what looked like the accident. Usually these would come from some reporter who shortly thereafter would somehow always *seem* to get reassigned to some other story, and pretty quick.

What became absolutely clear was that no serious radical movement can afford to get too cozy with the corporate media. Much less depend on trying to use it to spread the message. But neither could they be avoided. That's one reason we wrote the book *Black Power,* to make the argument directly, free of media interpretation and distortion.

Of course one temptation—pressure really—was toward self-censorship. Sanitizing everything you said—tone, language, message, everything—so as not to give "offense." Qualifying every statement so that the media could find little to sensationalize. Of course one could play that game, but then you end up saying nothing, or talking code, like just every other mealymouthed American politician. Hey, I remembered only too well those Negro leaders who used to come on TV when we were in the dorms at Howard. We'd sit there and watch them talk right over and across us, addressing the white establishment. Saying only what was permissible, expected, and inoffensive to white folk. Keeping themselves, and us, firmly in our place.

No way, Jack, that one was *clear.* That I refused to do. What's the point of saying anything if you ain't going tell the truth? I know most black people appreciated that. And not only the youth either. We heard that from a lot of people in the older generation too, those who hadn't been worn down to the point of being unconscious. A lot of folks.

[Many movement observers believe that Carmichael was at the height of his effectiveness as a public speaker during this period. Especially in capturing and expressing with passion and conviction the mood and aspirations of an entire generation. Adrianne Means, a Howard University activist, heard him speak:

"When Stokely started talking, it was exactly as if I were talking. He was speaking for me. Articulating everything I'd been feeling and thinking . . . about the attitude we, as young black people, should have toward ourselves and the country. . . . No more pleading and begging for our rights, but coming together, organizing to take what was rightfully ours. The fact that here was someone, and someone of prominence, articulating everything that I was feeling so powerfully really inspired me."

To my considerable surprise, I'd have the same experience in 1968 at a black writers conference in Montreal. Having been out of SNCC for some years, I'd never heard the public Carmichael in action, so I was curious. I expected no surprises in the political message, and there were none. What I had not anticipated, however, was the effect of his passion and eloquence. Consequently, I was surprised and somewhat embarrassed to find myself suddenly on my feet among the much younger students, close to tears and shouting with an intensity of feeling every bit the equal of theirs. Not my usual style. I've often wished to be able to review a tape of that speech to see whether the effect would be repeated and to analyze just how it was achieved. Later I would discover an admission from the great C. L. R. James that he'd had a similar reaction to mine upon hearing Carmichael speak publicly.

I was actually in the act of writing this note when the mail came. In it was a letter from a radical novelist I'd never met, Hans Koning. The note was a reminiscence of Carmichael's wedding to Miriam Makeba, from which the following line leaped out: "I've always thought that he, and Churchill, were the greatest speakers of our time, each word like a brick in a wall they were building."

I was struck by the timing of the letter's arrival as by the irony of the association, since the two speakers—the black nationalist and the British imperialist—did, after all, have a name in common, remember. —EMT]

But you know what was interesting? How often, after some TV program, people in the media would feel free to offer professional advice. Look, you are a media personality now. Don't waste it. You're convinced you have a message, then don't blow it. You gotta *cultivate* a different image. *Polish* your *image* . . . protect it. TV is a "cool" medium . . . be cooler, less confrontational . . . less angry . . . cultivate the right image . . . be more effective. Stuff like that, all the time. I thought that was mighty kind of them, protecting us from ourselves.

Image. C'mon. Hey, this wasn't about *image.* Was I up there trying to sell sneakers or move product? First of all, I wasn't trying to be either "angry" or "confrontational." In fact, 90 percent of the time I was real sweet: calm, logical, polite. You can check the film. But I could be provoked. I sure wasn't gonna be patronized or sit still for silliness or insults to my people either. No way. And certainly, *certainly, Lord,* I wasn't about *cultivating* some *image* to make whites more comfortable. Hell, no. I took the same position on speaking that Malcolm took on nonviolence:

"We are calm and nonconfrontational with those who are calm and nonconfrontational with us. But we are not . . . ," etc. So, of course, the *image* from that time: young firebrand, angry militant, fiery radical, etc. Hey, I can live with that, they tell more about the press than about me. Like "Give 'em Hell" Harry Truman, I told them the truth and they thought it was hell.

So image was no problem. The real problem I saw was somewhat different. It was how anyone in that media limelight could easily become confused. And indeed, later I would see it happen to a lot of folk. People start to get all this media attention and they begin to think they important. People recognize you anywhere you go. Autograph seekers be approaching you. (Or at times, loud, bellicose types looking for a confrontation.) So if you so inclined, and if you not careful, you begin to feel sho nuff like *you* the celebrity. As if you *personally* have become important. *You* personally, quite independent of any job, title, role, independent even of the movement. It's this media culture. It is insidious, and if you allow it, can be seductive. I've seen "leaders" created by the media become addicted to the attention and make themselves pathetic trying at all costs to stay in the limelight. That's not the only reason or even the main reason I decided to step down from the chairmanship when I did. But it certainly contributed. You cannot conduct serious political organizing in the media. The revolution will not be televised.

One thing I can say absolutely though is that I never, never compromised the political message. And that I always tried to represent the struggle and our people with the dignity they deserved. That's why you won't find any vulgarity or obscene language of any kind in any speech I made. At about this time, some militants got into the "filthy speech" mode started by a group of radical white students in the Bay Area. SNCC never did.

I mean, what would I look like getting up before serious black people cussing and swearing? Be the surest and quickest way to turn them off. That stuff may have seemed cool and "hard-core" to middle-class white youth, but I considered myself to be representing the best of our people and a serious struggle. After that, what would I say to Ms. Baker, Mrs. Hamer, "Prof." Brown, Dr. King, or most important, May Charles? I always felt I had to represent—even when we didn't always fully agree with them—the people who had formed me, as much as I did the younger generation. That's why you won't find me resorting to any of that off-the-wall, filthy speech okeydoke at any time. Check . . . it . . . out.

However, I did find myself developing different styles depending on the audience and situation. I had a standard-English speech reserved for the merely affluent and curious. Many times these people would say or write that they had expected an "antiwhite diatribe" or a "raving militant rap." Only to be *so* pleasantly surprised to get a reasoned argument that—even if they didn't agree with it—was "thought provoking." Pleasantly surprised, gimme a break. What'd they expect—flagellation therapy? That wasn't my thing.

Then too I had a harder, more analytic, and ideological argument for more serious political and intellectual forums. These would be the speeches collected in the book *Stokely Speaks: Black Power Back to Pan-Africanism.*

Then there was a down-home, nitty-gritty idiom in a style I mostly borrowed from the Harlem street-corner nationalists and the Southern black preachers. This I saved for the brothers and sisters on the block. But the political message stayed the same, whatever the audience, language, or occasion. Only the style changed.

I stayed heavy on black pride and self-determination. Black unity and self-confidence. *Undying love for our people. Undying love for our blackness.* Also, more and more against the obscenity, the naked arrogance of sending young black men to be cannon fodder in the Vietnam atrocity. That was the crowning insult, given everything we were going through right here in this country at the time.

"This Vietnam War ain't nothing but white men sending black men to kill brown men to defend, so they claim, a country they stole from red men. How can McNamara deny the racism when proportionately more black boys are dying in his stinking war? Well, I got news for Mr. Mac. No Vietcong ever called me nigger. Hell no, we won't go. So any fighting I do I'm gonna do right here. Ain't gonna fight in Vietnam and run in Georgia. Our grandfathers and great-grandfathers had to run and run. This generation is plumb out of breath. We ain't running no more. Ain't going fight in Hanoi and run in Harlem. We ain't running no more. No more. No more. Period."

[Editor's note:

During this period Carmichael would emphasize and constantly revisit the theme of self-definition. By the time (1968) he and Hamilton published the book Black Power, *they could note with pride a change in the popular vocabulary of black self-description:*

"Many blacks are now calling themselves African Americans, Afro-Americans, or black people because that is our image of ourselves. When we begin to define our own image, the stereotypes—that is the lies that our oppressor has developed—will begin in the white community and end there. The (black) community will have a positive image of itself which it has created. This means we will no longer call ourselves lazy, apathetic, dumb, shiftless, etc. Those are words used by white America to define us. When we accept those adjectives as some of us have in the past, then we see ourselves only in a negative way, precisely the way white America wants us to see ourselves. Our incentive is broken and our will to fight is surrendered. From now on we will consider ourselves African Americans and black people who are in fact energetic, determined, intelligent, beautiful, and peace-loving."]

No question, bro, this was some interesting times. No question. I mean interesting as in the Chinese curse ("may you live in interesting times"). Even if I wasn't organizing on a project, all that traveling and talking was indeed organizing. Of a different kind maybe, but organizing nonetheless.

SNCC's financial survival and our struggles with the media were by no means the only challenges. Politically, so much was going on so quickly that everything seemed to be just rushing up in your face all at the same time. Piling on and piling up, Jack. Zap. Zap. One new crisis after another.

Not to suggest that everything was a crisis, though. Far from it. Some things were just plain fun. As I would travel around, all kinds of people would show up, old friends from the past, from Howard, from Bronx Science, would show up. Usually this would merely be pleasant, touching base, reestablishing contact. But sometimes such a meeting would be quite consequential—the one with my freshman English instructor, for example. I won't swear but I think it was after a debate I had with Bayard in New York on Black Power, and who should be in the audience but Ms. Toni Morrison.

Now an editor with a big publisher (Random House), she wondered whether it wouldn't be valuable to expand the Black Power paper into a full-length book. A full discussion of the concept, free from media distortion. Hey, the sister was preaching to the converted. She didn't have to convince me. Only problem, my schedule was brutal. But we hooked up with an excellent brother, Professor Charles Hamilton, a political scientist at Lincoln University. We produced the book *Black Power*. More than a collaboration between Brother Hamilton and me, that book was in many ways a collective SNCC project. A lot of folk—Elizabeth Sutherland Martínez, Ivanhoe Donaldson, Courtland Cox, Jim Forman—all contributed to different sections.

I remember there was considerable public interest when the book came out (1968), but I couldn't really tell you anything about sales or earnings. All my royalties went to SNCC. I think for a while that book might have paid all our salaries. But certainly it must have done all right, because two years later the publisher and Sister Morrison brought out a collection of my political speeches. By then I was back and forth between Guinea and here. *Stokely Speaks* was collected and edited by Ethel Minor, a very dedicated, conscious SNCC sister. The sister used to work with Malcolm, and later she would do a lot of work with us in Guinea. A strong, capable sister, Ethel did an excellent job on that book. Nuff respect.

Traveling and organizing as I was doing, I could see firsthand the extent to which the society was in ferment. I mean serious ferment, Jack. People forget but there really was this growing sense of impending crisis across the country. Particularly with us in the inner cities. The urban scene was rough, and particularly among our youth.

That was one noticeable difference, a big one. See, in the old days we would come out of the South to "relax" in the "relative calm and safety" of the North. Not anymore, bro. Hey, now the tension and sense of danger was as heavy and pervasive in Chicago or Los Angeles as it ever had been in Mississippi or Alabama. In one sense, worse, in fact.

The difference was that this was random, kinda chaotic. You couldn't always identify who might be an enemy or where immediate danger might come from. Everywhere I went, social conditions at the grass roots—employment, housing, health care, education—were deplorable. I mean, bad. Look, for so many young brothers leaving high school—and I don't mean dropouts, I mean graduates—the only choice was the military now or jail later. I'll never forget what some young brothers from Brooklyn told me one evening. They'd just graduated. They said at their high school graduation—from Boy's High—the last speakers, after the graduation was over, were a captain from the local precinct and a marine recruiting sergeant. The cop said, "Gentlemen, no point fooling ourselves. We all know how it is out there. Either you go with him [the Marine recruiter] now or you come to me later. Your choice."

Now, when I'd come into a city to speak, the police presence would be everywhere. Intentionally visible and oppressive. Seems most cities had a tactical police force—paramilitary cowboys is what they were. SWAT teams. And following—or anticipating—urban insurrections, real aggressive and tense, nervous. And a nervous cop is nothing to joke with, makes me nervous. The feeling of encirclement and pressure on the community was suffocating. As though our communities were under siege. Suffocating. So, at the grass roots the mood was volatile, simmering like something about to erupt. Brothers were saying, "Hey, this is war, bro, and we ain't gonna be messed over jes' like that no more. No mo'."

What made it feel dangerous was that, unlike the South, here there was—too many times—no clear, solid center. I mean no single accepted community of leadership and resistance you could identify. Instead, all kinds and varieties of militant groups, frequently armed and competing, were popping up like mushrooms. Full of sound and fury, bro, and recognizing no single, respected figure of authority. Seeing this, I first began to fully understand exactly how much the struggle of the black nation had lost when they'd murdered Brother Malcolm (peace be unto him). Those open rivalries and ideological differences were just hanging out there to be exploited by our enemies. Which, indeed, they would be, ruthlessly. Like with U.S. and the Panthers later.

But, you know, having said all of that, I got to say something more. Because there also was this powerful spirit of audacity, of self-confidence, of resistance, a "les' get it on, sucker," "in yo' face" determination that was exciting to see. The problem was to channel it in a positive direction in an effective, disciplined organization. The problem was always *organization.*

I've said the media was following me everywhere. My error. What I should have said was the media, the police, *and* the FBI. This was when the heavy surveillance and the dirty tricks began in earnest. Especially from the FBI. At no pains to even try to conceal their presence, they became like my second shadow. Nor was there any longer the pretense of neutrality, or that they were there to "observe" or "discourage" racist terror. Uh-uh! They had chosen their side and we were now the target. And those were only the obvious ones, the ones we saw. It has since been revealed that most groups were heavily infiltrated by undercover plants.

[Mrs. Carmichael remembers her home being under constant surveillance: "I told people that I didn't bother to lock the door when I went out anymore.

Nobody would break into my house 'cause everyone knew the FBI car was always sitting across the street watching."]

Naturally I found myself spending time—I do mean a lot of time—reasoning with these young, urban Northern brothers where I went to speak. As often as not trying to mediate unnecessary rivalries, which—some of them anyhow—seemed on the verge of open warfare. Much of this looked to me like nothing but a new version—complicated now by ideology—of the same old turf wars I remembered from my teenage days. But, of course, I recognized this clearly as a function not of Black Power, but of *powerlessness* and desperation in communities under relentless pressure. Vicious and unrelenting pressure.

I was able to reason with them because the activists accorded me a certain respect and a degree of authority. I suppose because I was SNCC chairman, a veteran of the Southern struggle (some of the groups I knew from when they had sent representatives to Lowndes), and as the media-designated "spokesman" for Black Power. It was strange, all of a sudden I was at the age of twenty-five like an elder statesmen to militant youth. I counseled unity above all. Avoid tribalism, avoid sectarianism, warlordism. I stressed the need for a united front, for clarity, i.e., the need for serious *study* and above all the enduring need for *organization*. The need to put together a clear, disciplined, coherent, democratic, mass-based, grassroots organization of our entire community. The tight organization of our people. None of this vanguard-party nonsense.

I would observe all of this carefully and of course report everything back to SNCC. By then, we all knew that the movement would have to turn northward. But on the basis of everything I was seeing, it was going to be an entirely different proposition from organizing black folk in Mississippi or southwest Georgia. Entirely different. What worked in the rural South was not going to be effective in a large urban area. No way. The concrete conditions and the culture were too different. We would—as an organization—have to be prepared to go in in a very different way. Exactly how was the challenge. In Chicago, Dr. King had been finding out, to his great sorrow, that the Northern movement would need to have a different character requiring new approaches.

So it became clear to me that what I was doing—moving from city to city, spreading the message—was not, long term, the most effective use of my time and experience. As soon as possible, I would need to *demonstrate* the message practically. To settle on a major city and organize the kind of unified, purposeful, accountable power base I was talking about. My mind was still set on colonial D.C., and some months later that's where I would go to begin that process.

•   •   •

It was more than ironic, actually, had it not been so potentially lethal, at times even funny. Between the overt hostility of the local city cops, the constant machinations of the FBI, and armed rivalries in the community, the simple act of coming to give a speech became an adventure. Lines, which in the South were always real clear, became blurred or nonexistent. How so? Well . . .

More than once I had to ask myself, "Man, did you survive five years of Klan threats and terror only to come to be blown away by tribalism amongst your own?" Or more likely, by some government agent ratcheting up and manipulating the tribalism. Which did in fact happen. Yes, it did. Quite often. I mean, more times than I care to remember, I'd arrive in some city and be met by a delegation of serious brothers, all of them obviously heavy.*

"Greetings, Brothah Chairman. Welcome. We the security detail for your visit, my brother. Everything be cool, brother. We got your back."

I wouldn't be finished thanking them before another group in military formation would come stepping in. Jaws all tight, gritting on the first crew while at the same time conspicuously ignoring their presence.

"Armed Front for Community Defense, Bro Stokely. The Front be the group taking responsibility for all security matters, *my brothah.*"

What now, cut down in a cross fire between elements of my own "security"? I developed a calm manner, a soothing touch, and a diplomatic sixth sense to defuse and disarm these situations. And it always worked, as long as it stayed among ourselves. Because at heart these brothers genuinely wanted only to fight for our people and be respected. Usually only when the cops or the government provocateurs got involved did situations become deadly.

There were so many strange and bizarre stories, I can't even remember most of them. It's hard to believe the weird stuff that went down during that time just from traveling around speaking. Odd. Weird.

The Nashville story, the "riot," is kinda typical. All the elements combined in that one. Seems funny now, but it sure wasn't then.

SNCC had planned a regionwide student conference on Black Power over a weekend in Nashville. The conference for black college students involved speeches, workshops, and of course recruitment. The focus was on the local political situation and heavy on political organizing.

So . . . a SNCC team goes in to organize the conference. Good organizers. A member of this team was a dedicated, hardworking sister named Kathleen Neale. This sister was militant and had this immense Afro, blazing red hair.

Heavy = armed, carrying, packing heat.

Our organizers must have done too good a job publicizing the conference because about a week before it was scheduled, all hell breaks loose in the Nashville media. All kinds of politicians and "civic leaders" are all over the press denouncing SNCC, black militants, Black Power, the conference, even me, who is hundreds of miles away. They demand all kinds of strong (and illegal) actions to prevent the conference from taking place. The police are called up on highest alert. The citizenry is aroused and frightened. Thousands of black militant students are going to converge on the city, etc., etc. Okay? All of which, naturally, only served to publicize the conference and ensure standing-room-only attendance.

I was scheduled to deliver the conference keynote. But I also had a long-standing and lucrative speaking engagement at a white university, Vanderbilt. More official hysteria and attempts to cancel that. But the student government there stands firm. A clear academic-freedom issue. I also had another speech at a school about a hundred miles away the next day.

A West Coast New Left magazine *[Ramparts]* had sent their new black reporter to do a story on Black Power. So for about a week, this brother, Eldridge Cleaver, had been traveling with me. So we goes together to Nashville. We gits to the SNCC office. Where the brother takes one look at our sister Kathleen (and she at him) and boom, pow, that's all she wrote, Jack. Revolutionary love strikes again. The next year, I believe it was the next year, Sister Kathleen married Eldridge. *[Much to my sorrow. —EMT]*

The scene in town, particularly among the students, is vibrant with political excitement. The first night, I speak at Vanderbilt. The auditorium is huge and packed, Jack. A largely white student audience. But, so the organizers say, there are more Afro-Americans in the hall than they can remember. A lot of highly visible security and, of course, the cameras. I can feel the tension in the hall.

But it's all anticlimactic. I speak forthrightly. The brothers and sisters cheer. The whites are attentive, respectful. The talk generates spirited discussion. There are some sharp questions, but no hostility. In fact, everyone is real polite. The sponsors are delighted. For them, it's a great evening. I takes SNCC's check and split. No problem. I have no idea what, if anything, the press reported.

The next morning, Saturday, I give the opening address at the SNCC conference and leave in the afternoon for the other speaking engagement out of town.

That night, there is an incident in a nightclub in the black community. Nothing to do with our conference. As I understand it, some drunks were thrown out. They return later, mad, armed, and looking for trouble and a fight breaks out. So far, nothing that doesn't happen in a hundred American cities every Saturday night. Alcohol, testosterone, and hooliganism, usually nothing to do with race. Not good, but it do happen.

Except that this time, when the Nashville cops, having been primed for a "riot" for the last week, come in ostensibly to restore order, they storm into the community. In large numbers and with unnecessary force. Flashing lights, shouting orders, whupping heads, and taking names. Stupid. Counterproductive. The blacks who were fighting each other unite against the cops.

As one witness told me later, "They call theyself clearing the streets. But the way they come in, man, it weren't nothin' but brute force and ignorance. Brute force an' ignorance, my brother." As I say, I was not there, nor was there anyone from SNCC. But the people were angered. Brothers decide to defend themselves. Bricks and bottles fly. Tear gas and gunfire come back from the cops. At some point there is return fire. According to the police, they came under sniper fire first. According to black eyewitnesses, the police opened fire first. However, some Africans apparently did exchange fire with the police, who were forced to withdraw and regroup in the face of unexpected resistance. They were not pleased.

Hey, I was over a hundred miles away, so I really can't say what did happen. My recollection is that it was all over in a few hours and I can't even now recall if there were casualties on either side. How many or how serious.

However, the next day the community is occupied and the media are calling it a major riot. The "sniper fire" is attributed to "black militants." I arrive back the next night to discover a warrant is out for my arrest. Incitement to riot, criminal anarchy, something like that. I also discover that I'm the object of a "citywide manhunt" and an "all-points bulletin." Which surprises me more than a little since, in my ignorance, I've just driven right through the city, into the community, past any number of patrol cars, without even being stopped. So it was hard to take it seriously at first.

"Hey, this ain't no joke, bro. Stop laughing. These cops out there seriously searching, following and harassing black folks going home from the conference. Expect them to start busting into folks' apartments any minute now."

"So, why don't I just split?" I ask.

"Because they got the bus stations and the airport under surveillance, that's why."

"So I can drive out."

"Hey, they patrolling every highway out. Stopping cars. Every young African with an Afro."

"So, I'll take my chances."

"No, you won't, my brother. These crackers stop you on the highway, what's the odds they bring you in breathing? You weren't here, so you don't know what went down, okay? Black folk plain ran their butts out the community and they holding you responsible. Git serious."

I got right serious, Jack. Especially when I remembered my first time in a Nashville jail with Dion and that cop outside the cell with his shotgun. I became very cooperative, quick, soon, and in a hurry.

Then the everlasting SNCC discussions. The first step is to stash me someplace secure until we can devise a plan to get me out. Turning myself in was not an option we discussed. Every suggestion had something wrong. I remember there was talk of calling "respectable" older folk where the cops might not think to look. Rejected. Bad idea. Phones may be tapped. Besides, those folk probably be too scared to be harboring no fugitive anyway. But we got to get the brother out of here fast. Every car that drove by, people froze.

There was one very, very light-skinned sister in the meeting. She seemed nervous and unsure of herself. She kept raising her hand tentatively trying to say something. But she wasn't very assertive and people kept talking over her. Turns out she was new to the movement. I noticed and said that people needed to show more respect and let everyone speak. That sister over there been trying to say something.

The sister said shyly that she'd just moved into a white apartment building that week. A lily-white neighborhood, and since the cops were only tearing up the black community, why don't they sneak the brother in there? Pandemonium. A lot of objections. Impractical, dangerous, etc. But that ultimately was what we did. Stashed me in the white community. The white-looking sister drove me over and smuggled me up the back steps.

After that, the question was getting me out. According to the radio, the cops were confident I was still in Nashville and would soon be "flushed" out. As if I were a quail in thick brush, a game bird.

Now the question was getting me out. People started calling on the elders. Professional and respectable types. Ministers, progressive professors over at Fisk, anyone who they thought might be able to help. No dice. Nobody would touch that one.

Some people started muttering against "respectable Negroes." One brother was just cussing out one of his professors, a leftist novelist over at Fisk. "Man, that jive, handkerchief-head Negro jes' scared. Man, wouldn't even talk to me." I told the brother to cool that. First of all, what do you expect them to do, all the propaganda that's been in the media? Besides, do you have any idea what that brother may have gone through during McCarthyism? Hey, the brother probably thinks his phone still tapped. Someone else suggested they try one of her professors, an African. The same brother grumbled, "That old African, what he gon' do?"

"I'll call him," I said. All the professor said was "Let me give this some thought. Call me back in an hour." When I did, he said, "So where do you want to go, my brother?" I said Atlanta. Done, he said. You got it. Don't tell me where you are. Have someone bring me the address. I'll come get you.

Next morning. The professor sounded buoyant. "All set, my brother, you have a reservation. I'll be there in a half hour." I got the impression the brother was enjoying himself immensely.

"Hey, I'm not sure you can come where I am," I said.

"Why?"

"Race. You'll stand out."

He laughed. "But that's precisely the point. I *want* to stand out. Don't worry. You'll see." But truthfully, I was beginning to wonder if this African were not some kind of flake.

The bell rings. I open the door. There stands a beaming African born on the continent in full traditional dress, with a gleeful twinkle in his eye, wearing a wide smile and carrying a small suitcase. He was enjoying himself. The brother has a brisk manner. "Hmm, you're a little tall for these robes but no problem. You have a reservation in my name so you'll be traveling as Chike Onowachi of Nigeria. You are my elder brother and you don't speak much English. I'll escort you in, speaking loudly in Igbo. All you have to do is nod and mumble. Okay? Leave the talking to me." He reaches into the suitcase and produces robes and a red hat. "Put these on." He dusts some white spray on my temples and eyebrows.

"Look at yourself." He laughs. "You look just like an old *eze.*"

"Now you'll walk into the airport leaning heavily on this stick. I'll take your other arm." So, that's what we did, walk through with Brother Chike keeping up a running conversation with himself in Igbo. A lot of cops are in the airport and not many young black men. I saw cops nudge each other and grin at the two old Africans in their bright robes, chattering away in their strange language. (Later, when I asked him what he had been saying, he said, "Mostly proverbs. And whenever I passed a cop, I said, "Stupid *oyibo*, the one you seek is under your nose.")

When I got to Atlanta, I went straight to our lawyer's office. Howard Moore, who was married to Julian Bond's sister, was SNCC's lawyer in Atlanta. At some point, Howard defended all of us. He was an audacious brother, fearless. Also funny. "As your lawyer, I should talk to the Nashville authorities, shouldn't I? Let's mess with their heads, shall we?"

"I'm calling about my client. I understand you looking for him? May I speak with your chief?

"My client? Stokely Carmichael. Can I speak with the chief? . . . How ya' doing, Chief. . . . Yes, I represent him. . . . Oh, yes. He's with me now, right here in my office. He tells me he just found out you want to see him. . . .

"Oh, really? Advise him to turn himself in, huh? Well, now, what are the charges? . . . Hmmm, I see. Sounds mighty serious, Chief, mighty serious. . . . Oh, *very* serious. I see. I see. Feelings runnin' high among your men, eh, Chief? . . . I see. I think you absolutely right, Chief. Something unfortunate could happen. Of course, I'll tell my client—the chief says you should turn yourself in now before his men find you. . . . Yes, Chief. Certainly I should accompany him in. . . . Yes, yes, I see. Certainly. . . . Wal now, I suppose I could . . . but, tell you what, Chief. We got us a little problem right heah. . . . Well, there's me, my two assistants, and the client. That'll be, les' see, four return tickets. Are you going spring for those? . . . Oh, Chief, I'm sorry. Didn't I tell you? . . . I practice law in *Atlanta*. . . . Yes, suh, that's where we are. Oh, I'm so sorry, Chief, I thought you knew that."

I guess the Nashville police wouldn't spring for the tickets. Must not have really wanted to get me.

[*According to some written sources I've seen, the Tennessee legislature then passed a resolution calling for Carmichael's deportation. Since he was a U.S. citizen, the legislative intent must have been a revival of the medieval practice of banishment.*

Throughout our conversations Ture always insisted that the chairmanship—with its high visibility, constant pressure and demands—did not "change my life" in any significant way. In his view the job was merely more of the same, slightly intensified. But there was a price. Occasional glimpses recorded by associates reveal, or at least suggest, another aspect of the young Carmichael.

SNCC colleague Jim Monsonis recalls an evening in 1963, when Stokely was still an undergraduate:

"I had to attend a meeting in Washington and arranged to spend a night at his place. I'm not sure whether off-campus or on, but it was a pleasant, comfortable room. We spent the evening hashing over movement issues and strategies. What I remember most clearly, however, is that throughout the evening a steady stream of students came by for academic help. One with a philosophy argument he didn't quite understand; another had a math problem; a third sought advice in writing a paper. In each situation Stokely was a master teacher, a side of him I hadn't seen before. He was able to explain things clearly without talking down so that student left with good answers and their dignity intact. I'm not at all surprised he was offered a Woodrow Wilson Fellowship for further study. Had he continued on that track, he would have made a superb teacher. Come to think of it, he remained a teacher all his life."

Professor Charles Hamilton remembers going to Carmichael's apartment while they were working on his book during his chairmanship. Work proved impossible. The phone rang nonstop: the media. SNCC Atlanta. Each call a different city. A question here. A crisis there. Finally Carmichael looks up out of the clamor. "This is too much. Too much is happening too fast. Man, I'm too young for all this. I need to read more. To study. To reflect."

In 1967, right after Carmichael stepped down, Gordon Parks would report, "Long before he announced that decision he had talked about the doubt he had of his leadership role. 'I'm an organizer,' Stokely said. 'I want to get back to what I do best. I'm too young for this job. I don't know enough about the outside world. I need time to read. Reflect. I think perhaps more than anything I'd like to be a college professor someday.' "

As fate would have it, the next year chance, Cold War politics, and overt actions of the federal government would conspire to give him a remarkable introduction to the outside world and time and opportunity to read and study. —EMT]

Over the years I've been attacked from many different quarters for various political stands I've taken. That's to be expected. Welcomed, in fact, when you stand up for justice and try to tell the truth.

Madame Du Bois and I had many conversations about Dr. Du Bois. One thing she said has stayed with me: "Du Bois lived a good life: He fought all the right fights. He made all the right enemies." Making the right enemies. A pretty good way to judge a life, right?

There's been one issue in particular—the question of justice for the Palestinian people—on which I seem to have made my most implacable enemies. So be it. I'm proud of my support over many years for the human rights of the Palestinians.

This issue first surfaced publicly in 1967, just as I was stepping down from the SNCC chairmanship, but the roots were planted much earlier. A lot of nonsense—misinformation and disinformation—has been written about this.

At Bronx Science, I attended study camps with the Young Socialists and Young Communist groups. We sang folk songs at these sessions. Here I learned to sing "Hava Nageela" and to dance the hora. During the fifties, these young-left groups were unquestioningly pro-Zionist. Stalin had given arms to Zionist factions in 1948, and Israel was said to be progressive and socialist. End of story. There was no discussion at all of the rights of the Palestinian people. None. Not in those circles. So it never occurred to me then, that there might be another side to the story.

It was the early sixties before I encountered—in the pages of *Muhammad Speaks*—any discussion of Palestinian rights and resistance. This was before there was any mention on the American left of the injustices being done to the people. And as for the corporate media, forget it. Unless it was to characterize the Palestinian resistance as "terrorists." But, of course, issues of justice do not disappear. The U.S. media may try to sweep them under the rug, but they will eventually surface. Yes, they do. But even back then, it didn't take a genius to sense that something important was missing from the media coverage of the Middle East. That was clear.

Later, the movement presented us in SNCC with many urgent and immediate problems that focused our attention locally. This would begin to change after the 1965 assassination of Malcolm X. In SNCC this change was due almost entirely to the work of one courageous activist sister. I can truly say that my commitment to the disciplined study of Zionism in a systematic way can be attributed to this sister's influence.

[In the two accounts of this period that I have, one a long letter from 1991, the other an interview with me in 1998, Ture carefully avoided identifying this sister by name. I believe I understand his concern. —EMT]

Our sister had studied Latin American affairs and Middle Eastern history in college, after which she took a job in South America. There she met Palestinians who had been expelled from their homeland by the Zionist military. She began to investigate the issue.

Upon returning to the States, influenced by Malcolm, she worked with the Nation of Islam. Upon his expulsion from the Nation, she followed Malcolm into the Organization of Afro-American Unity. After his assassination, the sister joined SNCC, where she organized a study group on the question of Palestine. I was working in Lowndes County and was part of the group. It was at first a small group, but serious. Rap Brown, known today as Jamil al-Amin, was a member, as was Ralph Featherstone (peace be unto him), a capable and committed brother from D.C. A few years later, Bro Ralph would be blown to bits by covert forces, most likely connected to the FBI.

The group read a book a month and met for discussion. We read everything we could find, not just pro-Palestinian or anti-Zionist materials. We found, to my surprise, that a great deal of the most incisive and persuasive critical writing was by Jewish writers who, from the perspective of the moral traditions of Jewish thought, opposed the militaristic expansionism underlying Zionist policies.

We also read the principal Zionists—Herzl, Ben-Gurion, Begin, documents from the Stern Gang, etc., etc. As a matter of fact, these Zionist ideologues provided the strongest evidence against Israeli policies by openly revealing the naked colonialist intention at the heart of the Zionist enterprise. That was my second surprise. The third, and this was the shocker, was discovering the close military, economic, and political alliance between the Israeli government and the racist apartheid regime in South Africa. Now this was a real shock since I knew that during World War II, the Afrikaner nationalists had fervently supported the Third Reich and had cultivated close associations with and had even organized themselves along the lines of the German Nazi Party.

The brutal racist system that Afrikaner nationalists imposed on our people in South Africa was an adaptation of the master race ideology of Adolf Hitler and German fascism. Pure and simple, the worst state-sponsored racism the world had seen since the Third Reich. All decent humanity condemned it rightly. Of course, we knew that while piously condemning apartheid verbally, America and her European capitalist allies were quietly profiting from it in economic and military terms. That was shameful. But, I have to say, discovering that the government of Israel was maintaining such a long, cozy, and warm relationship with the worst enemies of black people came as a real shock. A kind of betrayal. And, hey, we weren't supposed to even *talk* about this? C'mon.

From all accounts, the basis of this unsavory alliance proved even stranger. In the racist, fundamentalist theology of the Boer, Afrikaners and Zionists were both "chosen people," thus authorized by divine covenant to occupy and possess the homelands of other people not similarly favored by God. *Divine covenants* in the modern world? Gimme a break. In any event, however fanciful the basis, the results of the military cooperation were real and concrete enough, chief among them the arsenals of tactical nuclear weapons stockpiled by Israel with South African assistance.

Our group was no secret cabal within SNCC. One of SNCC's mantras was "knowledge is power." So, as we learned, we shared our political education with other field secretaries. We discovered that many SNCC people already harbored serious doubts about the media's official version of events in that region of the world. I even had discussions with Jewish supporters of SNCC who were conflicted and morally troubled by aspects of the geopolitical behavior of the state of Israel.

By the time I became chairman, a caucus in SNCC had been reading a book a month for two years on the Zionist question, entirely due to the honest, persistent, humble, and unassuming work of our sister. But there had been no organization-wide discussion of the issue. Therefore no official organizational position on the issue existed.

I intended, during my chairmanship, to bring the issue before the staff to determine the will of the group: whether we should take a public position and exactly what that position should be. But many urgent battles—Black Power, Vietnam, resistance to the draft—intervened. Then that orderly process was short-circuited, and did not take place in the correct sequence. What happened was this:

My last act as chairman was to work with our sister in drafting a position paper, possibly for distribution in the SNCC newsletter, intended as the basis for internal discussion. This was a hard-hitting position paper, much of it in the form of sharp questions against a background of incontestable historical facts. This is what later came to be known in the press as SNCC's "anti-Israel" position.

[Charlie Cobb:

"This was when we were beginning to look more seriously at the liberation struggles, particularly in Africa. But the 1967 Arab-Israeli War was very much in the air. What I recall about that position paper was a very general ongoing conversation in the Atlanta office. Folks would stop by, read it, make comments or suggestions. It was all very casual. On the level of "Hey, these folks once had a country. Now they don't, they're all scattered and displaced. There's something very wrong about that." That is, until it ran in the newsletter. Then it got intense."]

Of course, the newsletter was picked up by forces outside SNCC, fed to the press, and the rest is history. The most incredible wave of vilification erupted. And you know SNCC, once this barrage of denouncement and attack was unleashed, almost overnight, we weren't about to go embark on no "damage control," Jack. Nor was SNCC about to "apologize" and repudiate the paper. Which, for one thing, was entirely accurate. So as a result of the *[preemptive? —EMT]* attacks, the document became in effect the SNCC position.

There was a press conference. I was no longer chair but I was present as Jamil and Featherstone defended SNCC's right and duty to express a position. The press was hostile and immediately began their attack. Jamil and Featherstone demolished them with facts and figures, dates and documentation. The brothers were in no way defensive, they went on the attack effectively. But needless to say the reporting did not reflect that.

What this "overkill" offensive launched immediately by organized Zionist forces demonstrated was that to raise any questions, however legitimate, about Zionist policies and actions was seen as a declaration of war. Unthinkable, verboten, in U.S. political discourse at the time. Not to be permitted. So war was declared on SNCC.

Would it have been different if the organization had been able to formally discuss the issue before all the hysteria? Probably not. I'm sure the overwhelming majority—even consensus—would have been in support of justice for the people of Palestine. On the moral issue, no doubt at all.

Where there would have been serious—indeed, necessary—discussion was on the political question. The political wisdom of the organization's taking a public position at that time. Was it necessary to take on another fight, that one in particular, and at that time? Why did SNCC need to have "a foreign policy" anyway? No other civil rights organization had a position on the Middle East, and there were clear reasons for that. A good deal of their financial support came from mainstream liberals, quite often from progressive elements of the Jewish community. In those circles, anything other than unquestioning support of Zionist policies was unthinkable, taboo. Apparently, the Palestinians were nonpeople. The blatant injustices they endured at the hands of America's client state were never to be discussed. And the Palestinian resistance? Simply "terrorists."

So obviously there would be a price to pay. It would have come down to priorities. But as Dr. King said, "There comes a time when silence is tantamount to consent." But in any event that discussion never took place. Had the process not been short-circuited, I'm sure the overwhelming sentiment would have been to make a statement, a moral statement, on justice for the Palestinian people while trying hard not to offend or alienate our Jewish friends on a personal level. Such a statement, one intended for public distribution, would almost certainly have been more nuanced. In properly diplomatic language, which the talking paper definitely was not. But you crazy if you think the *language* would have made any difference politically. This was an orchestrated declaration of war, Jack.

[Faye Bellamy:

"When folks were discussing the paper in the office, I can remember thinking, 'This here is crazy. Politically it makes no sense to abandon one base before developing a new one.' But people didn't seem too concerned about that. At least not in my hearing. So I didn't raise the question. No, actually I did once briefly with Ivanhoe. He said that if SNCC ever became too concerned purely with its survival, it would no longer be SNCC. No longer honest. Where was it written that SNCC should last forever? Words to that effect. After that, I didn't raise the question."]

I've often said, looking back, that it was all inevitable, SNCC being what it was. Look, when we took on white supremacy and the Klan, we were attacked. But we survived. We took on the president and the National Democratic Party and survived that. When we opposed the war and the draft, we were really attacked, but survived even that. But dare to open our mouths on Zionism? That one, you don't mess with and survive. That was the lesson the Zionist thought police meant for us to learn in 1967. But we are still here. On this one, history will certainly be the judge. That, you can depend on.

Since those (1967) events, I am proud to say that I have never ceased to speak out and work for justice for the Palestinian people. Consequently the attacks—on me personally and increasingly on my people—have been incessant. Here I mean scurrilous accusations of "anti-Semitism," by which you are meant to understand a primitive and bigoted hatred of all things Jewish. The Jews as a people and Judaism as a religion and culture. Gimme a break. That ol' dawg just won't hunt. It is the height of intellectual dishonesty and more of an insult to your intelligence than it is to me or my people. However, it is one thing to try to discredit me, it is quite another to besmirch my people. Now that I do not play.

Everyone knows my people to be deeply spiritual, loving their God and respecting all religions. There is no way any antireligious speaker can get a hearing from these folk. No way, Jack. Besides which, especially in the United States, my people recognize a deep religious bond with Judaism, one that springs from the Hebrew scriptures of the Old Testament.

Of course there is a strain of ugly anti-Jewish religious bigotry in the United States. But have you known a single African ever to burn or bomb a synagogue, desecrate a Jewish tombstone, print swastikas on a Jewish door, or establish any restrictive quotas? C'mon, stop the nonsense.

For myself? I feel absolutely no need to respond to transparently politically motivated charges of personal "anti-Semitism." I am content to let my life and public record speak for itself.

My party, the All-African People's Revolutionary Party, and I continue and will continue to struggle in support of the just cause of the Palestinians. In this process I've worked and corresponded with a great many observant Jews, some of whom were Israelis, with even a few rabbis among them. Decent and honorable people who refuse to dehumanize their Palestinian neighbors; deplore the military occupation of Palestinian lands; and are heartsick at the spiraling and unnecessary cycle of violence that has resulted from these policies. These decent and honorable Jews resist the militaristic policies of the state as much for the harm they do to Palestinians as for the mortal threat they see them representing to the highest moral values of traditional Judaism.

It was at an international conference in Libya in 1976 that I first heard G. Neuberger say, "If one is a good Jew, one cannot be a Zionist. If one is a Zionist, one cannot be a Jew." I myself would not presume to originate such a judgment, though I have quoted it. What I will say, however, is that clearly one can be a good Jew without being a Zionist, and that being anti-Zionist does not make one *necessarily* anti-Semitic. For I have seen with my own eyes the terrible human cost—to both Jew and Palestinian in the Holy Land—resulting from the militaristic posture of the cabal of right-wing Zionist extremists there. I've seen pain in the faces of displaced old people and children in the refugee camps. I've heard anguish in the voice of a Jewish mother contemplating the actions of her government. "How can they do these things? Did we learn nothing from history?"

In my formative teenage years I read voraciously. One of my favorite authors was Isaac B. Singer. What I was most impressed by was the love for his people and their culture his work revealed. A number of close friends were Jewish. We visited each other's homes. I experienced Jewish religious culture at the seder table of a friend whose father was a rabbi. Many of these friendships endure to this very day, as has my respect for the culture.

Take the question of anti-Semitism—hatred of Jews. First sign of any criticism, and apologists for the Zionist state throw the charge around like small change from a drunken sailor's pockets. That's unwise and counterproductive for two main reasons. One: Something happens. Say Israeli armed forces commit—as all occupying armies tend to do from time to time—an excessively violent act against unarmed civilians. World opinion is outraged. "See, see," you shout, "they hate us because we are Jews." C'mon. You know that is denial and evasion. At least admit that decent, right-thinking people may legitimately be turned off by some very questionable actions done by the state in your name. That is something that should certainly concern you. As indeed it does concern many, many Israelis and Jews of conscience.

The other danger: We all know that a pathological hatred of Jews does exist and has been mobilized to truly malevolent ends in our lifetime. Pogroms in Eastern Europe, near genocide—the slaughter of millions of innocent human beings—by Nazi Germany. But that is precisely why—like racism—the term must not be trivialized and cheapened by being thrown around too loosely. Such misuse diminishes the power of the term, robbing it of the true horror of its historical meaning. I don't believe that can be what you intend.

Y'know media labels—*anti-Israel, pro-Palestinian*—are silly and simplistic. Intended, I'm convinced, to obscure the issues more than anything else. In my own case, I'm not pro-Palestinian. I'm pro international law, human rights, and simple justice. Am I anti-Jewish? No, I'm strongly anti colonial occupation, population displacement, military aggression, and injustice everywhere.

So I can tell the world: I am not now, have never been, nor can ever be anti-Semitic or anti-Judaic. However, I am, and will be unto death, anti-Zionist.

CHAPTER XXIV

Around the World in Eighty Days

All the World's a Stage?

A couple weeks before SNCC's next general staff meeting in Atlanta (spring 1967), I told the executive committee that I'd be stepping down. I told the brothers and sisters that I wanted to go back to what I did best, grassroots organizing.

I thought I'd pretty much done the job I'd been elected to do. I also felt that I'd become something of a media lightning rod, attracting too much unnecessary negative fire to the organization. I acknowledged that some of the positions that had become publicly associated with me had been beyond official organizational policy. I accepted responsibility for that. These positions were mostly on U.S. foreign policy and international revolutionary liberation struggles, and it wasn't that SNCC people necessarily disagreed with what I had said, but that SNCC didn't have an official policy on some of these issues. And many thought it wisest that we didn't. "Where is it written that SNCC got to have a public position on everything in the world?" But I had opinions, and the media was quick to attribute them to the organization. Proof of Dr. King's warning: "Everything you say, Stokely, will be taken down and used as evidence against us."

Course being SNCC, not everyone agreed and there was a long discussion. But I was certain it was the right decision for me, and for the organization. I felt I'd used up all my political capital pushing Black Power. Then, the discussion focused on exactly what role the chairman should have in the future. Everyone agreed it should be less visible, less public, less controversial. After all, SNCC's pride was that we had no "leaders."

I felt that since we'd succeeded in establishing the concept of black self-determination in the political debate, the new chair should be able to operate beneath the radar of constant media scrutiny and challenge. *Should,* because that wouldn't necessarily be automatic. SNCC had become too much of a target and any chairman was likely to continue to be one as well. But I felt that the organization could help the leadership by establishing clear guidelines and expectations for them.

At the meeting I explained my reasons to the full staff and supported H. Rap Brown for the chairmanship. Rap was Ed Brown's brother. I knew him from Howard. He'd been NAG chairman, had worked in Cambridge and with us in Mississippi. Later in Alabama he'd done an excellent job in Greene County, where he'd earned the respect of the staff and local people. Rap had a reputation as a serious, strong brother. He had a calm, deliberate manner and a presence that inspired confidence. He was elected.

I sensed that in Rap's chairmanship people wanted a calm, solid presence. Someone strong and committed enough to represent the staff and who, without the political baggage that I carried, could step back from the media spotlight and tone down the decibel level with the press. I know that this was Rap's intention when he took the office, and I thought, given any kind of a fair chance, Rap might just be able to bring it off. What we would discover, however, is that neither the media nor the government had the slightest intention of allowing him—or the organization—any space at all. Rap and SNCC would walk straight into the illegal government conspiracy known as COINTELPRO.

That's another thing that's deliberately overinflated and misrepresented. People ask—at least used to ask—"What about SNCC's expulsion of white folks?" I don't know about the word *expulsion,* but what about it? "Do you have second thoughts, personal regrets?" I mean, come on. Personal regrets? Hell, no, because there was nothing personal about it. It was political, that's all. We move on. That's all.

By 1967, and not just in SNCC, the direction, the *political* direction, of the movement had changed. In politics you adjust to change and keep moving. No one understood that better than the people in the movement. It was again the white media and the totalitarian liberals who blew it out of proportion. They had their axes to grind. Looking for something—any stick they could use to beat SNCC down with. This, the role of whites, was just another one. But by then it was really a nonissue.

If you look at it correctly, SNCC had always been a black-led organization. And there had never been many whites on the field staff. Before the Summer Project you could count them on one hand. Of necessity; it was flat out too dangerous.

There was Bill Hansen, project director in Arkansas. A friend and ally. All my years in Africa we corresponded regularly. Still do. Mendy Samstein in Macomb. Mendy was one in a million. Sam Shirah, a real Alabama boy; you know George Wallace had been his Sunday-school teacher? Sam (peace be unto him) I hear was later murdered. Jack Min-nis, a very good struggler, wasn't in the field. He was in the Atlanta office. And there was Bob Zellner; we've talked about Bob. A real soldier. Came early, stayed late. In fact, Bob and Dottie Zellner were the last white organizers in SNCC. I used to tell him, "You always turning things around. Used to be us Africans who were the last hired and first fired. In SNCC you were the first [white] hired and the last fired."

Let's be clear. For me, integration was never a goal, a principle, or an absolute value. It was never our reason for existing. It was for a while a consequence of the work, an at times pleasant, at times problematic by-product of struggle, but never a *goal*. The goal always was liberation, the ending of our people's oppression, period. And everyone in SNCC understood that clearly.

Well, in some places it was a little different, southwest Georgia, for instance. There Charles Sherrod, the project director, took the position that on *principle* all projects should be integrated. But that was never my position. In some situations it worked fine. In the Atlanta office, especially early on, a core of smart, committed white allies could and did make valu-able contributions. No question. To the work and even to the culture of the organization at that time. Also in the Northern offices.

But in the field? The negatives always outweighed the positives. The presence of white women, for instance. That drove white Southerners plumb crazy. Killing crazy. Which is why in Mississippi and Alabama, the women field organizers and the women project directors had to be all sis-ters. I'm talking about some extraordinary young African women, mostly local, but some strong sisters from the North too.

So for me the major question with whites in the field was security, tac-tical. As a practical matter whites in rural black communities simply stood out too much. No way they could blend in or be disguised. The local racists see somebody white in our communities and immediately, boom: civil rights worker. Target and focus for hostility and violence on everyone.

On the Summer Project. Of course, some brave young whites did extremely valuable work. More power to them. But at what price? Three lives. Same thing on the Selma march. Two murders. In Lowndes County we established a policy: no white workers on the project. The first and only time we relaxed that and you saw the result. A very, very good man dead.

After that, my position was clear. Whites should organize in white com-munities. Especially in poor white communities, where a lot of work was needed and almost none was being done. That's why I had always sup-ported the Southern Students Organizing Committee as strongly as I did. *[Patterned on SNCC, this was a group of progressive Southern youth attempt-ing to generate a movement among poor whites. —EMT]*

This was my position when I moved into the chairmanship and it was my position at the "Peg Leg" Bates meeting. By then, no new white workers were coming into the organization, and if memory serves, only about seven or so were left on the staff. This was the result of the changed political climate nationally and natural attrition. So the role of whites in the organization was not really a pressing issue. In fact, hardly an issue of any kind.

However, an organized faction came into the "Peg Leg" Bates meeting determined to make the question of the role and presence of whites an *ideological* one. That was not just silly. It was diversionary and destructive because it was unnecessary. It prevented the meeting from getting to the host of urgent programmatic questions the organization needed to deal with. Instead, it generated anger, confusion, frustration. . . .

[If the foregoing has an episodic, incomplete quality, that is because it is not a discrete statement. It is cobbled together out of passing references, culled from various of our conversations on other matters. So that while it is an accurate representation of what the brother said on the subject at various times, it is not the thoroughgoing analytic account he gave to other issues. For example, we do not have his detailed impressions and account of the meeting at which whites were "expelled." In this I didn't sense a reluctance so much as impatience, even boredom: "Why even belabor that dead horse now?" I got the impression that he felt that, given the time we had, he wished to put more important questions on the record. Compared to which this was a distraction, an artificially inflated, media-manufactured issue.

I would have been content to leave it that way except for one thing. After his death a student brought to my attention a document I had never previously seen. Taken from a Web site on the sixties, this document was presented as the "Student Nonviolent Coordinating Committee Position Paper: Basis of Black Power" by Stokely Carmichael.

Absolutely wrong on all three counts.

Just as the alleged Holy Roman Empire was neither holy, Roman, nor an empire, this travesty was not a SNCC organizational position; nor was it really about Black Power; and it patently was not the work of Carmichael. It was not his style, not his language, and the positions it expresses were contrary to his attitudes. Over the years one becomes accustomed to encountering all manner of reimaginings—some silly, some malignant—of SNCC's history. But this was so perverse that I concluded it needed to be addressed and corrected in this book.

Rather than addressing Black Power in any meaningful way, this document was a crudely argued tract assailing the presence of whites—in the movement generally and in SNCC in particular. While it does attempt to appropriate the language of Black Power to those ends, it does so in terms so ill-informed, absurd, and vulgar as to suggest a parody of an attitude we used to call derisively "bone in nose" nationalism.

I felt that Carmichael would not have been other than deeply angered to see his thoughts and attitudes so misrepresented to this generation of students and distressed to see his name associated with either the attitudes or vocabulary of this tract. And, far from being a SNCC position, this document, in its insulting pop psychological stereotyping not only of whites, but ironically, however unintentionally, of blacks also, manifested a near complete ignorance of SNCC history, culture, and experience.

The level of its political discourse can be gleaned from the opening:

> *The myth that the Negro is somehow incapable of liberating himself, is lazy, etc., came out of the American experience. In the books that children read, whites are always "good" (good symbols are white), blacks are "evil" or seen as savages in movies, their language is referred to as a "dialect," and black people in this country are supposedly descended from savages.*
>
> *Any white person who comes into the movement has these concepts in his mind about black people, if only subconsciously. He cannot escape them because the whole society has geared his subconscious in that direction. . . .*
>
> *. . . Thus the white people coming into the movement cannot relate to the black experience, cannot relate to the word "black," cannot relate to the "nitty gritty," cannot relate to the experience that brought such a word into existence, cannot relate to chitterlings, hog's head cheese, pig feet, ham hocks, and cannot relate to slavery, because these things are not part of their experience. They also cannot relate to the black religious experience, nor to the black church, unless, of course, this church has taken on white manifestations.*

Nor could I believe that the extraordinarily strong-minded black people I knew in SNCC would recognize themselves in the following:

> *Negroes in this country have never been allowed to organize themselves because of white interference. . . . Blacks, in fact, feel intimidated by the presence of whites, because of their knowledge of the power that whites have over their lives. One white person can come into a meeting of black people and change the complexion of that meeting.*

Nor is it possible to imagine a more perverse and complete inversion of the psychological and cultural dynamic that prevailed in SNCC than the following:

> *Whites can only subvert our true search and struggles for self-determination, self-identification, and liberation in this country. Reevaluation of the white and black roles must now take place so that whites no longer designate roles that black people play but rather black people define white people's roles.*

. . . It must be pointed out that on whatever level of contact blacks and whites come together, that meeting or confrontation is not on the level of the blacks but always on the level of the whites. This only means that our everyday contact with whites is a reinforcement of the myth of white supremacy.

And so it went. Whatever its political or intellectual failings, the document did achieve a certain historical effect after it was leaked to the New York Times *and prominently reported as representing the style and thought of the new leadership. (Many SNCC people insist that it was leaked by a disgruntled former officer, who must certainly have known better.)*

In fact the document was the issue of a militant team sent into SNCC by a small, clandestine formation of nationalist revolutionary intentions based in Philadelphia. Many years later I would listen with slack-jawed amazement as that mission was blithely described by someone claiming to be a founder of the group:

"Oh, we respected SNCC for the way they lived and worked among the masses as Chairman Mao said. However, we concluded that they lacked the correct ideological orientation. So we sent in a group—one intellectual and three gunmen. Their mission was to purge whites and establish a correct revolutionary ideology."

The folly of the times, I thought, arrogance and ignorance in the guise of "ideology." I assume the position paper to have been the work of the "intellectual" rather than the "gunmen," but then, one never knows.

Cleve Sellers:

Stokely was just furious. Once we learned what was going on, I'd never seen him so angry. See he knew Max personally from the Lowndes County elections. His was one of the groups that had sent fighters to defend the community against the Klan terrorists. Stokely had respected that, considered him a brother. But to find out that he'd sent agents into SNCC to promote this "narrow nationalism" that was causing these problems? He took that as a personal betrayal. We considered that a hostile act. But by the time we had grounds to remove them, a lot of confusion and division had already been generated."

Carmichael's reported anger would not have been hard to understand. Although its headquarters had always been in Atlanta, SNCC had never established an organizing project in that city. This changed right after Julian Bond's election and repeated ejections from the Georgia legislature and amidst the ongoing discussion of the necessity for urban organizing that attended the call for Black Power. It seemed doubly appropriate therefore that the group's first excursion into urban organizing should be in its own backyard. An area called Vine City, Atlanta's most neglected and depressed slum, was in Julian's district. That seemed the logical place to start. With Carmichael's strong approval, the contingent of infiltrators had been put on staff to establish an urban pilot project there.

The ideological militants on the Atlanta Project staff seem to have been singularly ineffective in organizing the community for a number of reasons. Chief amongst which may have been that their energies and priorities were directed inward, toward "correcting the ideology" of SNCC itself. Hence, the position paper on the Internet so erroneously attributed to Carmichael.

Matters would come to a head at the staff meeting of December 1, 1966, at "Peg Leg" Bates's estate in upstate New York. This was intended to be a staff retreat for a much needed general review of the organization's overall situation, prospects, and programs. Which never happened. Over three days the organization was able to discuss none of these pressing questions. How was this possible? This is, in my experience, the only SNCC meeting that most participants seem to have difficulty remembering clearly in any detail. A kind of collective exhaustion or blocking out appears to have taken place.

The racial question was placed first on the agenda, so the leadership intended, to be quickly disposed of so as to get to the substantive programmatic issues facing the organization. Their sense was that this need not be a long discussion. The position that was to be articulated by Carmichael to open proceedings was felt to be the sentiment of the overwhelming majority of the staff, black and white.

In his opening remarks, Carmichael saw no need—political or strategic—to sunder time-honored relationships with sincerely progressive whites. Operationally, he proposed a strategic division of labor within the organization, with the remaining white allies organizing in white communities, as practical, logical, and consistent with SNCC's experience and current direction.

Apparently someone had miscalculated badly or failed to recognize the driven ideological fervor and hard-edged determination of the minority. Because what then happened—the human and political dynamics of it, that is—defies rational explanation. At least in a more conventionally structured, authoritarian political arena. Or even in the freewheeling but purposeful organization I remember so fondly.

After almost three full days of a discussion variously described as "wearing," "exhausting," "painful," "pitiful," and "horrendous," the agenda had not moved beyond the first item and at least forty people had abandoned the meeting in anger and frustration. Quite evidently the separatist minority had succeeded in holding the proceedings hostage to their position that nothing could be discussed until their "fundamental" question was decided. Why this should have been allowed to happen remains for me an abiding mystery on which it is tempting to speculate. But I shan't.

What is beyond dispute are the facts. By the time the question was called, only sixty-one folks were still participating. Of the vote itself, the numbers are eloquent and perplexing: Nineteen voted for the motion to "expel." Eighteen voted against, with twenty-four, including the seven remaining whites, opting to abstain. So forty-two did not vote for the motion.

Nineteen of sixty-one is hardly a ringing endorsement. If we consider that before the attrition set in, the meeting had begun with better than a hundred, the percentage carrying that vote approaches that of George W. Bush's percentage of the national vote in the 2000 election.

Why so inconclusive and ambivalent a result, especially on so sensitive a subject, could have been allowed to stand defies explanation. It bespeaks a level of exhaustion, psychic demoralization, alienation, and a species of personal and political confusion that even at many years' remove is saddening to contemplate in an organization once so vigorous, bold, and clear. This meeting must truly have been painful to endure. —EMT]

D.C., "the capital of the Free World." Yeah. A city with a black majority administered by congressional committees mostly of white Southerners. A classic internal colony. With no representation in Congress, no local government worthy of the name, the population was as effectively disenfranchised as black people in Mississippi. I couldn't wait to take it on.

But I wasn't gonna rush in hollering slogans. As Mr. Turnbow once said, "Y'all gon' ha' to sneak in, slow, slow. Jes' slide on in, jes' a watching an' beholding." I moved back and quickly started studying and analyzing the situation. SNCC researcher Jack Minnis gave me a file on D.C.'s local government, federal preserve, congressional relationships, employment, everything, and I began speaking to everyone I could. Met with all groups, grassroots on up, youth gangs, church, civic, my old professors, whatever, talked, reasoned, studied, discussed, kept far from any media.

Sure, there were a lot of groups, but no real program. Local community organizations had different programs, different emphases, connections, commitments, capabilities, and leadership. Nothing that *collectively* addressed the overall interests and issues of black folk. There was some kind of national party apparatus—Republican and Democrat—but truthfully, I couldn't see what they did besides eat patronage and try to deliver votes to the national ticket every four years.

The black organizations, far as I could see, never got together to discuss their common interests as black people or to explore where joint actions and strategies might be possible and useful. To see where we could agree and find common ground, and where we'd simply have to agree to disagree. But privately, among ourselves, and with respect. That just never happened. Black people in D.C. were fragmented and unfortunately still are. And of course, there was no unified, community wide discussion of the District's colonial status.

I knew I couldn't just rush in and call for these discussions. SNCC had an office in D.C. run by an able brother, Lester McKimmie, now Baba Zulu, who was Southern and had come up through the struggle. Bro Les was shrewd and committed, so we worked well together. Quietly we began initiatives toward more regular consultation and cooperation among the groups. Low-key. Nothing binding, just general fraternal discussions among black folk, something that looked like an informal leadership council. A forum where people could touch base, see what, if anything, might emerge. A way to avoid misunderstandings and cross-purposes and, at best, to have the community speak in a unified voice, at least on some issues. (A few other cities—Boston, Chicago, Los Angeles, among them— were also trying to do this at that time.)

And, y'know, we were making real progress, slow but good enough. Then an unexpected invitation came that, in more ways than one, changed the direction of my life.

In May, I accepted an invitation to London to speak about Black Power during the month of July. It didn't seem like an opportunity we could afford to pass up and I would be gone at most two weeks. The London conference was called "The Dialectics of Liberation." I understood it to be an "international" gathering of leading revolutionary thinkers and activists, discussing issues and approaches pertaining to struggles for liberation across the globe.

Actually, things in D.C. were moving along so well that my initial impulse was to decline in favor of the SNCC leadership. But by then Rap was already locked in struggle with the government. We talked about it. We were moving so carefully and deliberately in D.C. that I figured I could afford to take a couple or more weeks without ill effect. I decided to go for three reasons.

First, so much disinformation had been flung around the concept of Black Power that I thought somebody ought to be at this conference to make necessary clarifications.

Also, SNCC was eager to make contact with revolutionary brothers and sisters, especially the freedom fighters from Africa. We considered ourselves part of that same generation of the same struggle.

Then again, "Black Power" formations had begun to emerge in the African/Caribbean immigrant communities in Britain. This seemed a perfect opportunity to establish contact and exchange ideas with these emerging forces.

The visit proved interesting and productive, but the conference itself was not at all what I'd expected. Some black and brown faces were in the audience (especially the sessions where I, and later C. L. R. James, spoke), but I'd come expecting and eager to meet revolutionary activists, especially Africans, from the front lines of the third world struggle. But the speakers' list was European leftists, literally, to a man, heavily "theoretical," and seemed weighted toward intellectuals and academics. George

Ware and I discussed it. I said, bro, this be a waste of time. I've come here to waste my time. We concluded that the conference was not going to be worth much.

Here I was really eager to meet fighters, only to find armchair theoreticians. But it was more than that. I found that, as usual, the discussions tended simply to exclude black people's concerns and perspectives. Nor can I recall women or women's perspectives. Not only was I a minority on the program, but I began to feel like a footnote, a token representative of black struggle. And this at a time when the only real struggle was not in Europe but in Africa, Asia, and Latin America. In no way did the program adequately reflect this.

And once the presentations began, the speeches, at least those I heard, tended toward abstract psychology. About "alienation" and the "individual," the psychological "dialectic" of *individual* liberation. Very Eurocentric. Business as usual among white bourgeois intellectuals even when they call themselves revolutionary. Not necessarily even *deliberately* excluding us as much as being oblivious, not even recognizing the existence and relevance of our perspectives, concerns, or analyses. Or even that the black world *could* have valid perspectives they needed to respect. Same ol', same ol'. The casual assumption that they defined and owned the terms of the discussion. *[I discovered that the conference had indeed been called by four psychiatrists concerned with "radical innovation" in their professional field. —EMT]*

But I did meet a lot of the activist brothers and sisters in the African/Caribbean community in London. For instance, I did a long interview for the BBC with an excellent brother named Andrew Salkey (peace be unto him). An African born in Jamaica, Brother Salkey signed two excellent anthologies of Caribbean short stories he'd edited, which I still have in my library in Conakry. (Certain "friends" have tried to capture those books over the years, but I'm happy to say they are still in my library.*) It was always a great relief to work with conscious black journalists. Such a difference, a pleasure. (Like the year before when Brother Gordon Parks had traveled with me and did the only fair and intelligent story I remember from that time.)

In London, students, community activists, and intellectuals gathered at Africa House. I spoke and spent time there, meeting young people—mostly students—from all over the Caribbean and Africa. There were also some Asians and progressive whites—an exciting mix. At that time this

---

*Carmichael/Ture was famous for his generous impulses. He was perfectly capable of "bestowing" handsome presents only to show up a year or two later innocently inquiring, "When are you going to return those books from your countryman that I *loaned* you?" —EMT

was the center for Pan-African political discussion in London. I gathered that any African head of state, or liberation movement leader, coming through London would stop in here to report to and reason with his own people. Over the years (once that silly ban was lifted), I'd usually stop in at the Africa House whenever I was back in London.

If memory serves, I first met there the brother who made himself my guide into the African-Caribbean enclaves around London: Brixton, Notting Hill, etc. Bro Michael X was from Trinidad. He was a black-consciousness militant, quick-witted with a real mastery of that sharp, in-your-face, verbal comeback that in Trinidad they call *picong*. And the brother always had a sly, biting political edge to his wit.

I was there, talking with some students, when I noticed this short, muscular, redbone-looking brother coming toward us. You couldn't help noticing him. Something about him set him apart from the students. Something a bit too flashy in his clothes or his style? Or his walk, not exactly a swagger or a strut, but vaguely and unmistakably "street."

"Oh, oh, there's that Michael X," a Jamaican sister said, not entirely approvingly, adding with a grimace, "The press calls him the British Malcolm X." I'd heard about the brother. I began to really check him out. By some accounts he was of "unsavory character" and something of a player. And, as I quickly learned, a performer. When our eyes met, he broke out this beaming, wide smile and threw his arms wide.

"Oh, God, Brother Carmichael, is you? You the very man I come to see, boy. The very man, oh God, boy, oh God, boy."

There was nothing British—much less Oxford—in the brother's accent. It was pure San Fernando, back o' bridge. I felt it might have been deliberately exaggerated to mark not only our common Trinidad origins, but his own class distance from the "bourgeois" students standing around.

"Yeah, boy, I does need your advice for true. I believe I jus' mess up bad bad, man. Oh, God, boy, listen this." By which time he had, as intended, commanded the attention of everybody and launched into a story about a meeting he'd just attended with "some decent, very respectable people, boy" on solutions to "the growing racial problem in Britain."

These "respectable people" included an Anglican bishop, assorted vicars, an Oxford don, some retired colonial civil servants, and a sprinkling of highly respectable and accomplished colored folk, even a black baronet. The latter being Sir Learie Constantine, a great West Indian cricketer who'd been knighted.

These good people, deeply distressed by the increasing racism being directed at the growing immigrant community by the British public, had been meeting over tea to explore initiatives to try to counter this.

"So now they come up with this plan which they think is good. But see they doesn't want to go forward with it before, and unless, checking it with the masses, we common folk, eh? So they does invite me to tea. I guess I the street militant, yes. The bishop's wife, she ask the name of my organization. I say, 'RAAS.' She look shock. 'That's the name of the organization, ma'am. RAAS [The Racial Adjustment Action Society]. 'Oh,' she say.

"They all now looking at me right strange. So I say, 'Well, yes. I certainly agree that this racism is deplorable. Quite unworthy of the British people, yes. But I glad such distinguished people taking an interest, eh. Gives one hope, eh, what? I real honored to be there.' I cock my little finger, sip my tea, and try to look serious an' respectful.

"Well, they say. After much thought and discussion they arrive at a proposal which had possibility. They had concluded that the situation was sufficiently grave, that the *sovereign* herself should intervene. Oh, God, I thinking, the queen? What that ol' bat goin' do? You ever hear she talk, boy? Give a speech, eh? But I jest sip my tea and look interested.

"Yes, we believe that it is incumbent on Her Majesty to set the tone. An example to the nation. A gesture simple yet direct. Dramatic and unmistakable yet appropriate. But what form should this take?

"'Well, yes,' I say. 'Is a brilliant idea for true.' But in truth, boy, I now wondering the same thing. What form? They all smile and nod agreement.

" 'Well,' the bishop wife say. 'As you know, Mr. X, the very best ideas are sometimes the simplest.' They pretty sure they have such an idea, but they want to run it by me, so, as it were, to benefit from my unique and valuable perspective.

" 'Okay,' I say. 'Be happy to help if I can.'

" 'What we were thinking, *are* thinking,' say the bishop, 'is that perhaps, we here acting as a body, might, privately of course, *prevail on Her Majesty to adopt a black child*. Would that not be salutary? A splendid example, what?'

"They all looking at me now. I now looking pensive, boy. I sip my tea, screw up my face, and grunt, 'Yeah.' I mutter. 'A black child, uh-huh.' Finally they say, 'Well, Mr., ah, X, what do you think?'

" 'Oh, is brilliant,' I say. 'Absolutely inspired.' They begin to beam and smile.

" 'Only one thing,' I say. 'It might could be better.' They all stop smiling and look puzzled. 'How so?' they ask.

" 'Well . . . I thinking now. The queen, she still quite a young woman, yes?'

" 'Yes, relatively speaking. Perhaps, but why . . . ?'

" 'Well, instead of advising Her Majesty to *adopt* a black child . . . why don' we . . . why ain' we just go ahead and ask her to go on and *have a black baby*, eh?'

"Talk about a long silence, boy. Then . . .

" 'Good heavens, man. You can't . . . you can't mean actually . . . actually . . . um . . . *giving birth*?'

"I say yes, tha's exactly what I saying. Ain' you looking a striking example of racial tolerance? This'll be an example not just to the nation, but to the world.

"Boy, the meeting break up just so. I doubt they go ask me back. But tell me, Bro Stokely, you think I wrong?"

Then he cracked up, enjoying himself shamelessly. That was our first meeting. I'd figured the story was a tall tale in the Sterling Brown tradition, but later other people would assure me that such a meeting had indeed taken place.

The brother was born Michael DeFrietas in Trinidad. He'd been influenced by the struggle in the States and particularly by the visit of two Muslim brothers from the United States. He said that after meeting Malcolm X when he'd come to debate and defeat William Buckley at Oxford University, he'd changed his name to X and formed the first Black Power organization in Britain, the one he called RAAS. He also said he'd hung with Ali, when the champ had come over to fight the previous year. He swore Ali had given him the trunks he had worn the night he'd put a serious whupping on a brave but hapless British heavyweight named Henry Cooper. Which could have been true, because when he wanted to be, Michael X was a likable, charming guy. And he could talk a hungry dog off a meat wagon. Yes, he could. And he was perceptive, always swift in picking up and deflating racist assumptions and postures. He was especially good at putting on or putting down the white press.

He said he'd taken Ali into the immigrant communities around London, and he invited me to "tour" with him and his boys. "Boy, come see how Black Power be ripping like brush fire through we communities, yes. You have no idea what you boys started, mate, no idea. I show you something I know going surprise you, yes." He was right.

I wasn't at all surprised to see militant African/Caribbean youth embracing the call. These youth were second-generation and weren't about to accept the condescension and abuse their parents had endured. No surprise there. What did surprise me was to hear Black Power resonating and to see the raised fists in the *Asian* communities, especially among Pakistani youth.

But when Michael explained it, it made perfect sense. British racism was at no pains to distinguish between different immigrant groups. Since World War II, the "subject peoples" of their empire had started to stream back into the "mother country." "Colonialism in reverse," Michael X called it. "An', boy, the natives are restless, you hear?"

First it was Malcolm, he explained. Being Muslim, he'd had a big effect with his call for self-defense by any means necessary. This especially because white-racist skinhead youth gangs and thugs from a neofascist formation called the National Front had taken to ganging up on Asians. Paki-bashing, they called it.

Then when Ali came through, he also made a point of reaching out into the Muslim communities. Hey, but God is great. The Asian youth couldn't believe he'd come to greet them. Here comes the heavyweight champion of all the world, black, sassy, and lo and behold, a Muslim, like them, and royally kicking white butt all over the place. So Pakistani youth were inspired by Ali's presence and deportment. They organized to defend their communities and started yelling Black Power. Made sense. Good for Brother Ali.

Back to the "Dialectics" conference. The hall was full. But the audience was noticeably different from the earlier session, with a heavy representation of our people—black and brown faces, mostly activists, students and intellectuals. I knew they'd come expecting me to represent our perspectives, which had been so casually ignored.

Looking at the program, Michael X had made that irrepressibly clear. "Looka dis, oooh, looka dis. We ain' here, boy. Ain' you see that? *We ain' here*. You doan see is going be up to you to represent all of we, boy? You better be up to it, hey."

Of course I was clear. I knew that our people had turned out expecting me to change the focus and perspective of the discussion. To interject the issues around colonialism and its consequences, which is to say of race and power in the world. To talk about the arrogance of European assumption of intellectual and cultural hegemony, which was the basis of their political imperialism and economic exploitation of most of the world's people. I'd have to show how all the issues involved in the Black Power debates in the States—cultural autonomy, self-determination, self-definition, and political empowerment—applied equally to the anti-colonial liberation struggles being waged around the world. Obviously that required going dead up against the entire weight and momentum of the Eurocentric bourgeois intellectual, individualistic direction of the conference.

Intimidating prospect? Be serious. I mean I had two things going for me. Not only was I accustomed to fighting from a minority position at such "intellectual" events, but more important, I was right. I was on the side of history, Jack. At its root the world struggle was not being waged over issues of "individual alienation" nor even narrowly defined questions of class struggle or solidarity, but about national independence, cultural integrity, and racial respect. So that's what I talked about.

The news of John Coltrane's (peace be unto him) death had reached me the night before. That could not be ignored. So I began with that announcement and asked the room to rise and observe a period of silence for this great black artist and cultural warrior. A few people seemed surprised, vaguely discomfited. But in truth, I really wasn't asking them. It was a matter of respect. They stood. That established, I went to work.

[The speech, from which the following are excerpted, can be found in Stokely Speaks *and is well worth looking up. It is perhaps the most clear, complete (and eloquent) bringing together of Carmichael's political thinking and abiding concerns during this turbulent, contentious, and decisive period. —EMT]*

Now since I've been at the congress, I've been very confused, because I'm not a psychologist or a psychiatrist, I'm a political activist. I don't deal with the individual, I think it's a cop-out when people talk about the individual. What we're talking about around the United States today, and I believe around the third world, is the system of international white supremacy coupled with international capitalism. We're out to smash that system. People who see themselves as part of that system are going to be smashed with it—or we're going to be smashed.

[Carmichael then goes into a wide-ranging discussion of cultural imposition versus cultural integrity.]

The people of the third world are going to have to stop accepting definitions imposed on them by the West. . . . I'm always appalled when some white person tells me that "progress is being made." I always ask, "Progress for whom, in whose terms?" We will have to tell you when progress is being made. You cannot tell us progress is being made. You cannot tell us, precisely because, progress for us is getting you off our backs. . . . As a young man in the West Indies, I always felt that the only thing a white man could do for me was to leave me alone . . . but we studied your literature in school and Rudyard Kipling's "White Man's Burden," where he said they had to come save me because I was "half savage, half child."

[On European condescension and arrogance.]

I'm always amazed when I pick up a newspaper and read that "England today decided to *give* the West Indies their independence." That's totally absurd, you cannot *give* independence to anyone. You cannot *grant* anyone their independence. If it's independence, they just take it; and that is what white America is going to learn. No white liberal can give me anything. The only thing a white liberal can do for me is help civilize the other whites, because they need to be civilized.

I just went, as systematically as time permitted, into the history of the confrontation, political, cultural, moral, between the West and the rest of us. It was a long presentation and afterward the questions flew hot and heavy. Of course then the brothers and sisters jumped in. I thought it an absolutely necessary and healthy discussion, the first since the conference had started. But of course I'd later read how "Carmichael and his troops" had succeeded in dividing the conference "along racialist lines." Absurd. Hey, shoot the messenger? If anything, I'd broadened the scope. Internationalized the frame of reference. You might even say, the brothers and sisters had liberated the dialectic with a healthy dose of reality.

After that talk, the Cuban high commissioner came, congratulated me, and asked whether I'd be interested in attending an international conference in Cuba. I said of course I would, I'd be honored. He said I should think about the politics before being so quick to accept. What politics? I was eager to learn as much as I could and really wanted to see the progress of the Cuban revolution. The U.S. passport was not valid for travel to Cuba, but he explained that was no problem: if I gave him a paper with my particulars and a photograph, those would be acceptable as travel documents by his government. There would be no need to stamp my passport. I thanked him for his consideration. I said it was an honor to accept the invitation. But I had too much respect for the accomplishments and idealism of the Cuban revolution to think of insulting the people of Cuba by sneaking into their country. I'd be honored to have a Cuban stamp in *my* passport. He said that was gallant and honorable but maybe not politically too smart. Perhaps I should think about it further. I thanked him. But, c'mon, get serious. I had been under surveillance for a while. You think the CIA didn't know where I went, whom I spoke to, and presumably what I said, anyway? And that being so, I wasn't about to sneak around like some kid, or better, a runaway slave.

The next day, I believe, C. L. R. James addressed the conference. My memory is vague as to whether he had originally been scheduled to speak or was a last-minute addition. It is hard to imagine that a group of radical intellectuals could have scheduled such an event in London and omitted so major a black revolutionary thinker and literary intellectual. But given everything else, maybe they had. Strange are the ways . . .

Again the hall was full. And again we were well represented in the audience. There was an air of expectancy, because the revolutionary elder statesman was also to talk on Black Power. I was sitting next to Michael when this slender, erect, almost frail figure with a startling shock of snow-white hair made his way to the microphone with a stately dignity. The room erupted, Jack. Spontaneously the entire room was on its feet applauding the venerable old brother. It was the single most moving moment of the whole trip.

Michael was beside me, applauding as fervently as I was. As we're clapping, he growls out the corner of his mouth, "We mad, I tell you. Here we applauding the very man they bring to cut we throat, yes. To bring the correct revolutionary line to put we nationalists in we place, yes."

"You just paranoid," I said.

"An' you call yourself a black militant? How any black militant can *paranoid*, eh? That impossible." We stood and applauded anyway.

Of course C.L.R. was most generous to us. Very gracious and went out of his way to say some kind things about me. Of course, the old man understood everything. His talk on Black Power was elegant. It was clear, forthright, erudite, closely reasoned, and anchored in history. Had there been any basis to Michael's suspicions, then the scheme, if there had been one, had sadly backfired. Totally. I turned to Michael. "See, you, I told you just plain paranoid, bro."

A couple of days later when the order from the Labour government arrived *[Home Secretary Roy Jenkins, a socialist —EMT]* ordering me out of the country and declaring me persona non grata, Michael smiled mirthlessly. "Well, boy, you paranoid yet?"

[Here again, Carmichael's account to me of the James talk is extremely self-effacing. He would say no more than that C.L.R. had been "uncommonly gracious and generous" to him. I was unable to find a text of our elder statesman's remarks at the conference. But I believe we may derive some sense of the tone and content of his "graciousness" toward Carmichael on that occasion from a speech James delivered only a few weeks afterward while Carmichael was still in Cuba. —EMT]

Mr. Chairman, ladies and gentlemen, Black Power. I believe that this slogan is destined to become one of the great political slogans of our time. Of course, only time itself can tell that. Nevertheless, when we see how powerful an impact this slogan has made, it is obvious that it touches very sensitive nerves in the political consciousness of the world today. This evening I do not intend to tell you that it is your political duty to fight against racialist consciousness in the British people; or that you must seek ways and means to expose and put an end to the racialist policies of the present Labour government. . . .

But . . . I want to say a few words about Stokely Carmichael. I think I ought to say Stokely because everybody, everywhere, calls him Stokely, which I think is a political fact of some importance. The slogan Black Power . . . is undoubtedly closely associated with him and with those who are fighting with him. But for us in Britain his name . . . means more than that. It is undoubtedly his presence here, and the impact that he has made in his speeches and conversations, that have made the slogan Black Power reverberate in the way that it is doing in political Britain. . . . And I want to begin by making a particular reference to Stokely. . . . And I do this because on the whole in public speaking, in writing . . . I usually avoid, take great care to avoid, placing any emphasis on a personality in politics.

I heard him speak in Canada at Sir George Williams University in March of this year . . . and I was so struck by what he was saying and the way he was saying it (a thing which does not happen to me politically very often) that I sat down immediately and took the unusual step of writing a letter to him, a political letter. After all, he was a young man of twenty-three or twenty-four and I was old enough to be his grandfather and, as I say, I thought I had a few things to tell him which would be of use to him and, through him, the movement he represented. I will now read to you parts of the letter.

"I was glad to hear you because I wanted to know for myself what had lifted you up to the pinnacle on which you now stand. . . . You are just twenty-four and you are not only one of the people on the American continent who is to be reckoned with, but you are a world-famous figure, at twenty-four. . . . I am profoundly aware of the dangers of being in such a position at such an early age. I propose therefore in this letter to deal of course with the movement because everything depends on that, but also with the specific dangers that beset you as a leader. . . .

"One of my most important and pregnant experiences is my experience both personal and otherwise of West Indians and people of West Indian origin who have made their way on the broad stage of Western civilization. . . . They are Marcus Garvey, George Padmore, Aimé Césaire, Frantz Fanon. These are West Indians who have played a role on the world political stage that is not even properly understood by their own people. . . . And you are one. I suspected it when I was reading some of your writings and having heard you I am absolutely certain of it. . . ."

We need not go further into that now. I went on to say (it was a rather lengthy letter) that there were certain doubtful points in his speech which he should bear in mind. . . .

. . . I received a reply in which he took up the points I had made and said he recognized their importance. That was in March and April of this year, 1967. The year has not ended and now he speaks with a scope and a depth and range of political understanding that astonishes me.

Bienvenidos a nuestros hermanos e hermanas negros de los Estados Unidos.

I wasn't at all sorry to see the last of Britain. But the brothers and sisters and conscious white allies were outraged. They regarded the government's action against me as outrageous—a political, almost personal, affront to them. (Michael X: "They doan respeck we at all, boy, at all, at all, yes.") And more so a betrayal, coming as it had from a "Labour" government that many had supported, now cravenly acting as a U.S. puppet. Demonstrations were being organized as I left.

"Well," I said, "it's your issue, Jack. You all deal with it." I was already looking forward to Cuba, where, as I joked, the climate was certain to be better. *In every way, Jack.*

In fact, the British expulsion order shows the classic stupidity of the reactionaries. True, the black and immigrant communities had been beginning to organize to engage the racism they were encountering. Now the government moved that organization along by presenting them with a clear issue, a provocation. It wasn't anything I did or said that caused the demonstrations in London and the Midlands. It was that silly order. Hey, I was leaving in a couple of days anyway. Go figure.

The Cuban revolution was then, what, eight years old? The government and people of Cuba were busy, busy trying to liberate their society from the inherited historical distortions and injustices coming from slavery, the racism of a plantation economy, capitalist exploitation and a colonial relationship with *los imperialismos yanquis.* The United States. A process I very much wanted to see for myself: a colonized and exploited society transforming itself independently according to rational, fair, and humane principles. And, naturally, I wanted to check it out free of the propaganda interventions of the U.S. media. Surely that was my right?

Many of us in SNCC felt that logically the United States should, in good faith, have been doing everything to aid that transformation: to help the Cuban people take back control of their country from the military and the U.S. Mafia in order to transform the society. Instead, to its shame, and in the name of capitalism, the United States was endlessly plotting and scheming to isolate the country and destroy the revolution.

Forty years later they still haven't succeeded in destroying the Cuban revolution. All this country has managed to do there is a lot of harm, gratuitous and pointless harm, and causing needless suffering to the Cuban people. This country has a lot to answer for in this world. One of their "founding fathers" said, "I weep for my country, when I consider that God is just." He was right.

This was an excellent time for me to be going to Cuba because the revolutionary government was launching a bold initiative to counter U.S. attempts to isolate them. At the time, Washington controlled an essentially puppet formation they called the Organization of American States (OAS), a grouping mostly of U.S. client states, many if not most of them right-wing military dictatorships. (So much for democracy.) So with that one, American hypocrisy was obvious, unconcealable, "boldface for true," as they say in Trinidad.

Having defeated one U.S.-sponsored invasion *[the Bay of Pigs]* and survived the "U.S. Missile Crisis," the Cubans were now hosting an international conference to create a very different regional alliance, OLAS, the Organization of Latin American Solidarity. A development, of course, viewed with alarm in official Washington. Expected. But only when I got there did I discover the frantic extent of U.S. efforts to obstruct, sabotage, and otherwise discredit the effort. They had tried everything to prevent delegations from their South American puppets from attending. Then we show up.

The day I arrived, I think, or the day after, the Cubans captured infiltrators sent by the CIA to assassinate Castro and launch a popular uprising during the conference. American *intelligence*? *Popular* uprising? Gimme a break. It was deluded, embarrassingly incompetent, laughable.

The only governmental representation at the OLAS conference was observer delegations from revolutionary countries: Algeria, Guinea, Nasser's Egypt, etc., etc. And just about all the liberation movements were there: the Vietnamese, the ANC, Southern Africa, etc., and of course the European socialist bloc countries.

But the congress itself was of progressive forces from Latin America: radical political parties, the guerrilla groups actively fighting at that time, people's organizations, radical trade unions, and the like. (For example, I was delighted to see that Trinidad was represented by trade unions from the oil field workers. A cousin on my mother's side *[Weeks]* was a trade union and Black Power leader there.) One North American organization that had a small observer delegation there was SNCC. I was not officially a member of the delegation, but I remember we all depended on Elizabeth Sutherland Martínez, director of the New York office and a good friend who was fluent in Spanish.

It was an incredible moment, more than just exciting. It was eye-opening, inspiring, and mind-blowing. I mean, here were brothers and sisters from around the whole world, Jack, especially the "third world," who were struggling to liberate humanity from colonialism, economic exploitation, and the absurd and pernicious principle that corporate profit, individual selfishness, and greed can be an effective basis for social organization and decent human interaction. I felt, we felt, we were among friends and allies of shared commitment, many of whom expected to be arrested when they returned home. So many different groups and faces, all in some way struggling against injustice and inequality, and to improve humanity. Hey, I knew there had to be among them contradictions and ideological and tactical differences, but the *general* shared purpose and direction was clear. These were SNCC's kind of people. The SNCC group was surprised at the general awareness and respect among the delegates for the African struggle in the United States, and for SNCC in particular.

And, of course, Havana was a beehive of activity. What with all these delegations arriving, it seemed by the minute, our hosts were extremely busy. Nonetheless we were impressed by their efficiency as well as the warmth and graciousness of their hospitality at all levels. All levels. And even more so by their enthusiasm and high spirits. A people excited and united about something important to them: from schoolchildren to the highest officials to the ordinary citizen, the man and woman in the street. No one was too busy or too important to welcome and receive us. *"Bienvenidos a nuestros hermanos e hermanas negro de los Estados Unidos. Venceremos [We shall overcome]."*

Nowhere did I see signs of racism or of extreme poverty. Be clear now, I did see signs of the lingering *effects* of racism and poverty. Those couldn't be eliminated in eight years, but no signs of *present* racism. Okay? And no beggars or hungry-looking people in the streets. And you know I looked, Jack. What I did see was a society in motion. A people with energy, confidence, idealism, and *hope*. And of course, *pride*. Hey, they'd soundly defeated the invasion sent by *los asesinos yanquis,* reclaimed their country, and were turning their society toward justice. But they were clear. The real work and struggle was still ahead. "There are still very many grave problems, *compañero.* But we invite you. Come back in ten, fifteen years and you will see what we have done."

I had many such discussions. People were confident. They could and would engage the entrenched problems: poverty, racism, economic injustice, literacy, poor health care. The same problems that beset, and still beset, my people in the richest country in the world. I wondered why the United States with all its wealth and resources could not summon up a similar enthusiasm and commitment to social justice at home. My heart and respect went out to the Cuban people at a truly hopeful, exciting, and dangerous time.

So, yes, I was deeply impressed. More than that, I was *inspired* by the humanistic idealism of their revolution. Yes, indeed. My support for which has never wavered over the years. Never wavered. I was also deeply affected by the physical, tangible presence of all these cadres, warriors for change from all over the world. For me, the international struggle became tangible, a human reality, names, faces, stories, no longer an abstraction. And our struggle in Mississippi or Harlem was part and parcel of this great international and historical motion. It was both humbling and inspiring. I felt recommitted, energized.

Naturally, amid all the bustle and excitement, the international media was all over the place *[167 representatives of the international media were accredited to the conference —EMT],* the *yanquis* being, as usual, especially visible and vocally aggressive. Many recognized me and wanted interviews or had questions, many of them offensive. Why was I there? Why was SNCC? As though we had no right to be. My impressions of Cuba? Of Castro? Of the conference? How did we expect our presence to be understood "back home"? I refused to be provoked. I was there as an individual. The SNCC members were there as observers—with nothing of importance to say to the media. Period. Thank you. What about you? I asked them. What do you make of the CIA infiltrators? The Cuban government had made two groups of recently captured U.S. agents available to the press and the delegates at press conferences, much to the evident embarrassment of the Yankee media.

Apart from observing the Cuban social revolution, I had another strong interest in making this trip. I wanted to see Dr. Fidel Castro Ruz in action and, if possible, even to meet him. In high school, we'd followed his long-odds campaign against the corrupt and brutal military dictatorship. Remember the famous story when a reporter called the dictator Batista a "sonuva bitch" and the American secretary of state said, "Yes, but he's *our* sonuva bitch"? Says it all, doesn't it? Or was that Somoza in Nicaragua? Same difference.

Everyone in Harlem remembered Fidel Castro's first victorious trip as a head of state to the United Nations in New York when, provoked and insulted in a midtown hotel, he'd moved his entire delegation uptown to the Theresa Hotel. Harlem loved Fidel. After that, the U.S. government rebuffed his further overtures, causing his subsequent alliance of necessity with the Soviet Union. The U.S. government, in its arrogance, acting—one assumes—on behalf of Mafia interests, handed the Soviets the Cuban revolution on a platter. Smart politics. So during my youth Castro was the most controversial—admired as well as demonized—political figure on the world stage. And clearly the boldest and most charismatic. Course, I did not really expect to have the honor and opportunity to meet him to talk to.

When I first heard him speak at a public meeting, I saw immediately where the confidence and energy I had been noticing in every Cuban I met came from. This first Castro speech was at a collective farm, and the leader of the revolution was talking to the *campesinos* about agricultural production. I recall, if memory serves, that his subject was *cattle breeding* and meat production and that he was not speaking from notes or reading a TelePrompTer. You would never have guessed the subject from the passion and intensity in his voice or the audience's response. Or from his enthusiasm and humor, for he had those country folk cracking up, Jack. Something, I believe, about a "great bull" the government was importing to improve the bloodlines of Cuban cattle. Much laughing and cheering. His confidence in the people was obvious. You didn't have to understand Spanish to see and feel the real affection and respect he had for those country people. Or the love and loyalty they returned. I mean without understanding two words (there was a translator), I could see the communication flowing between the leader and the people. You could sense that he was in turn challenging and inspiring, teaching and cajoling, teasing and *educating* them. And they responded, hanging on every word, shouting answers to his questions. I'd never seen any political leader with that kind of identification and empathy with the masses. Well, check that, maybe Dr. King and Malcolm. But then, they weren't heads of state, were they? For some reason I found myself thinking of a Mississippi Delta plantation and tried to imagine an American president talking to the workers there. I honestly couldn't. What would he have to say to them about their lives, and in what language?

Once I had the opportunity of talking to Dr. Castro, something else was unmistakable: a formidable intelligence. He was just on top of everything, Jack. Every aspect affecting the revolution. I mean, on *top.* Every aspect: facts and figures, clear, detailed analysis. I mean, from world affairs, which you'd expect, to health care, education—preschool to university—nutrition, housing, even to *African* culture in Cuba. Encyclopedic knowledge, easy recall, facts, figures, details, at his fingertips. That alone was amazing.

I saw it as an indication of more than intelligence, of a fierce, passionate, *personal* dedication to the new society he and his countrymen intended to create. He obviously had a clear, complete vision of the new and humane society he wished to bring about. Coupled with a practical, realistic understanding of the obstacles: exactly what, in human and material terms, would be required in every area to achieve these goals. As though, he, Castro, would *will* it into existence. That was most impressive.

My first impressions of him *personally?* Well, the first thing you going to notice, he's a big dude. I mean, physically imposing. But, y'know, there was nothing overbearing in his presence. Yeah, of course, he was in charge, *El Comandante.* You could see that, what with the aides an' all. But this was a natural authority. An *easy* authority. He never raised his voice. Always calm, serious, attentive, even humble. But you could somehow sense his determination, his will, and you could *feel* his energy. I recall a sister whispering, "Why, he has such kind eyes." Then I noticed. Yeah, it was true, he did have compassionate eyes.

What impressed me was his simplicity. He was always modest and candid. No bombast or claiming cheap or inflated victories. He frankly admitted problems and shortcomings, even failures, the limitations of the government and society. "I have to say that at present that does not go well . . . we shall have to improve . . . we do not as yet have the capacity . . . but we are working at it." And he had the confidence that nothing was beyond the people's capacity and will to overcome. He had faith in his people. That too *really* impressed me. But what I tend to remember best, of course, is always the political.

So this I clearly remember. The right-wing U.S. press was calling him a dictator and yelping constantly about elections, elections, *free* elections. That was a joke, Jack. Just from his people's response to him, a cotton-picking joke. No question at all, he'd win any election in the high 90 percent, easy. Then, I guess, they'd say, "It was rigged, a 'Communist show election.'" Gimme a cotton-picking, ever-loving break, Jack. Here's a dictator who moves around his country and people freely, without visible security? I mean, no platoons of black suits wearing shades with wires coming out they ears, hey? He seemed quite secure in his people's loyalty. And check, this was when the CIA was sending wanna-be assassins regularly. Remember the exploding cigars? Last time I looked the brother was still on the case.

Remember now, when I first got to Cuba, I'd been hoping, but not expecting, to have the honor of meeting Castro, however briefly. To my great surprise, with everything that was going on, he made time for us. He even took a group of us into the Sierra Maestra, the mountains from which he, Che, and his gallant little band of *barbudos* had fought their way to power. He put the SNCC folk in his jeep to ride with him. He pointed out battle scenes and described the battles that had taken place. Strategies, numbers, weapons, casualties, etc., etc. Victories as well as defeats, lessons learned. He remembered where and when brave comrades gave their lives and seemed to mourn them as he called their names. "A brave boy, a patriot . . ." He freely admitted mistakes, including his own. In fact, he may have talked more about those than about the triumphs. Because "of course you learn from victories. But those tend to confirm the correctness of your thinking. You can become arrogant, overconfident. You'd better learn more from those mistakes you are lucky enough to survive. In revolution, if you don't study and learn from your mistakes, you and your *compañeros* won't be around very long." His ultimate explanation of his improbable victory, so few against so many? "Better intelligence from the people. And, remember, we were fighting for our country's future. They were only fighting for their miserable pay and a dictator they hated."

One thing I remember asking him about was a legend among Harlem nationalists. All Harlem had been moved by his coming there, as a new head of state. He'd granted an interview with a group of militants. The brothers, so it is said, came in woofing. After giving the brother proper "revolutionary" greetings, they launched into a lengthy description of some rather ambitious "revolutionary" military intentions. After listening patiently to their plans to "wage armed struggle in the belly of the beast," he crossed to the window and peered out. The brothers sat awaiting his response, no doubt hoping for approval. He kept looking. Finally they asked what he was looking for so intently in New Jersey. "The Sierra Maestra, the mountains. I don't see any mountains out there."

When I asked, he merely laughed. "*Verdad,* there were no mountains to be seen."

The conference was another education. Just in the array of countries present—Vietnam, Algeria, Egypt—and of course, a whole different vision of human possibility. I was humbled to learn that I'd been made an honorary delegate and given a place on the program to address a plenary session. Why? I assumed the suggestion came from the ambassador, the comrade who had come to my speech in London and invited me down. Of course, they probably wished to mess with the U.S. government, but that was secondary and I had no problem with it. What else could it have been? Of course, I understood clearly that this wasn't about Stokely Carmichael, or even SNCC. I understood that I was there for one primary reason: the Cubans' respect for the historic struggle of our people. That I was standing on the shoulders of Dr. Du Bois, Paul Robeson, Dr. King, Malcolm, Mrs. Hamer. That's what I tried to represent. *[The brother's remarks can be found in* Stokely Speaks. *—EMT]*

Naturally, I developed the obvious similarities between the experience and situation of the people of Latin America and that of the African-American people. Y'know, oppressed by the same forces—capitalism and gringo imperialism—and thus sharing the same struggle. I described the black American community as an internal colony within the United States. I called for unity of the oppressed and the victory of the world revolution. And, of course, I expressed my respect, solidarity, and undying support for the courageous Cuban people and their revolution. True then, true now.

Now, I was not representing SNCC, of which, remember, I was no longer an officer nor even a member of the delegation. Nor was I representing black America or *any* America. It was a personal analysis and a call to struggle. I considered it a carefully reasoned speech, moderate in tone, careful in language, that said nothing that wasn't demonstrably true. And certainly, nothing that I hadn't said before many times.

Hey, but of course the American media went off and the government wasn't far behind. Oh, man, stupid, blustering speeches in Congress, all kinds of posturing with all manner and kinds of ridiculous legislation entered to much fanfare, purely for effect, never to see the light of day.

After the speech I met with the press. Watching the behavior of the U.S. media I remembered Bayard's unwritten law: "The one thing you cannot do is criticize America from a foreign country." Foreign country, hey, try revolutionary Cuba.

[Apparently this encounter with the American press led to a corrosive New York Times *editorial, datelined Havana, written by James "Scotty" Reston (August 2, 1967):*

"Stokely Carmichael is playing an incredible game down here. He is not only condemning his own country abroad, he is misleading Fidel Castro . . . about the condition and power of the Negro in America (sic). *The facts are plain. His black power policy has not gained popular support among the Negro community in the United States. . . . He is strutting around Havana as a symbol of the American Negro, most of whom have rejected his leadership. . . . Carmichael is too intelligent and cynical not to know what he is doing." —EMT]*

The Yankee press didn't trouble to hide their hostility. As though it was their duty to bully me back into my proper, nappy-headed place. I think I can say they did not succeed. But I was polite and answered all their questions.

I made it clear that I was there as an individual. That the SNCC delegation, which had not spoken, were there as observers. Speaking for myself, I had nothing but admiration for what I'd seen in Cuba. Did I support the *Communist* regime? I supported the goals of the revolution and its accomplishments. Why? I will always support the closing of casinos; the ending of the prostitution of Cuban women and children; the running out of the mafiosi; the building of schools and hospitals; don't you? On the conference? Of course I support its goals. Why? Because I support *all* the international liberation struggles for national independence and against colonialism, cultural imposition, and multinational capitalist exploitation. I've always said that, so what's new? Well, you can imagine the headlines. In fact, you don't have to imagine, you can go check for yourself.

[At the conference, the brother had begun with a statement of common interests. —EMT]

We share with you a common struggle, it becomes increasingly clear; we have a common enemy. Our enemy is white Western imperialist society. Our struggle is to overthrow this system that feeds itself and expands itself through the economic and cultural exploitation of nonwhite, non-Western peoples—of the third world.

We share with you also a common vision of the establishment of humanistic societies in the place of those now existing. We seek, with you, to change the power bases of the world—mankind will share the resources of their nations instead of having to give them up to foreign plunderers; civilizations will be able to retain their cultural sovereignty instead of being forced to submit to foreign rulers, who impose their own corrupt cultures in those civilizations they would dominate.

[On the common enemy.]

Our people are a colony within the United States, and you are colonies outside the United States. It is more than a figure of speech to say that the black communities in America are the victims of white imperialism and colonial exploitation—in practical economic and political terms, it is true.

We are moving to control our African-American communities as you are moving to wrest control of your countries, of the entire Latin continent, from the hands of foreign imperialist powers. There is only one course open to us: we must change North America so that the economy and politics of the country will be in the hands of the people, and our particular concern is our people, African-Americans. But it is clear that a community based on the community ownership of all resources could not exist within the present capitalist framework.

[On race and nationalism.]

Black Power is more than a slogan; it is a way of looking at our problems and the beginning of a solution to them. It attacks racism and exploitation, the two horns of the bull that seeks to gore us. . . . Because our color has been used as a weapon to oppress us, we must use our color as a weapon of liberation, just as others use their nationalism as a weapon for their liberation.

[On the U.S. urban insurrections.]

The true potential revolutionaries in this country are the people of color in the ghettos, those who have developed insurgence in the African-American and Latin communities, where past rebellions have taught important lessons in dealing with the government's armed reaction to our uprisings in the internal colonies of the United States. No doubt these are reported to you as "minor disturbances initiated by a few malcontents"—but these are major rebellions with numbers of participants who are developing a consciousness of resistance. These rebellions should not be taken lightly.

Who knows or even cares what the U.S. media reported of the speech. But the next day, the very next day, Jack, the Cubans brought me a wire service report. See here, the Yankees fixing to take your passport. They showed it to me. Sure enough, some State Department higher-up, I think his name was McClosky, something like that, was saying that my passport would be seized once I returned.

I said, "So they going take my passport for coming to Cuba, huh? Hey, let's really give them something to take it for." He said, what you mean?

So I got out the passport and showed him where it said something like "not valid for travel to the following countries." I said, "See all these prohibited countries here? Well, you have representatives from every one except China here. If these *gringos* going take my passport for coming *here*, let them take it for *all* of 'em. Please explain, though, that I have no money. But that if they invite me, I'm certainly willing to come." He said okay and left.

When he came back that evening, he said nothing. I asked whether any countries had invited me. He just blinks his eyes. "You were serious?" He blinks his eyes some more. "I could see you were angry, but I didn't think . . . you were . . ."

"Serious?" I asked. "You didn't think I was *serious*? Lemme explain something, Jack. When my people were slaves, they had to get a pass from some white man to go anywhere. *Anywhere.* Even to go visit their family on another plantation. A white man's written permission to go *anywhere.* That's over, Jack. I will never again allow any white man to dictate to me where I can or cannot go. Never." He blinked again.

The next time he came back, he said, "You were invited by everyone. Where do you want to go first?"

"Vietnam, of course. I must start there because they are at war." Oh, man, the Cubans. We have a lot to thank them for. Especially us Africans. Africans born in America and Africans born all over the world. We have a lot to thank the Cubans for. You know that Cuba had more medical personnel working in Africa and the Caribbean than the World Health Organization? Every time Africa has sent out a call, Cuba has answered, and as I always tell my people, you can never be ungrateful in politics.

That day was the final plenary session of the conference, and Comandante Castro was to close the conference. He made a magnificent speech, just magnificent. He had a good time exposing the idiocy and incompetence of U.S. foreign policy and the CIA's bungling. Then, quite unexpectedly and humblingly, he asked me to stand before these revolutionaries of the world and asked them to pledge to protect me. And they did. I was overwhelmed.

[Which is as much as the brother cared to say for the record about Prime Minister Castro's references to him. For whatever reason, this modest, abbreviated account fails to do justice to a speech that was classic Castro—defiant, witty, merciless—and perhaps at his most inspired. Standing before the assembled revolutionaries of the Americas, representatives from world socialism, the African and Asian liberation movements, and the world media, the young leader had himself a good ol' time at the expense of the Colossus of the North. The U.S. government's "criminal" and incompetent interventions, the bumbling ineptness of the CIA, as well as the complicity and bad faith of the U.S. media were all targets for the leader's ridicule.

His audience just loved it. Frequently interrupted by applause, laughter, sustained applause, cries of "Hit the Yankees hard, Fidel," and hoots and jeers at each new instance of imperialist arrogance and ineffectuality, it could not have made the U.S. press corps in attendance happy. Particularly since the prime minister relied heavily for his ironic efforts on direct quotes from U.S. officials and the media's own dispatches.

Beginning with the U.S. attempts to disown the captured infiltrators and to discredit the Cuban government's parading them before the conference, the Cuban leader had some well-chosen words for the good faith and professionalism of the American media, before moving to the meaning of Carmichael's presence, as follows. —EMT]

They are absolutely incapable of judging anything . . . that news agency [AP] is always serving imperialist interests, always concealing something, always defending something which is not good, even if by mistake, distorting everything. . . .

We Latin Americans know these facts only too well. All the representatives present here know them well. These facts are known, above all, to those who have to suffer these lies, this reporting, which while serving the worst imperialist causes, is the only information available to whole nations on this continent. And that is part of the imperialist mechanism, because those lying, truculent, fraudulent news agencies are part and parcel— part and parcel!—of the imperialist machinery. They are part and parcel of the instruments used by imperialism to carry out its policies.

Courtesy compels us to treat individuals with politeness, but courtesy does not compel us to refrain from stating some truths which are only too well-known. [Applause] . . .

But here is a case which expresses the essence of imperialist thinking. It is an article from the New York *Daily News* entitled "Stokely, Stay There." We would indeed be honored if he wished to remain here . . . ! [Prolonged applause] But he himself doesn't want to stay here because he believes that the struggle is his fundamental duty. But he must know that whatever the circumstances, this country will always be his home. [Applause]

The article states: "Stokely Carmichael, the Negro firebrand, is in Havana, capital of Red Cuba, after having stopped off at London and Prague, and we suggest that he remain in Havana, his spiritual home.

"As pointed out, we urge Stokely to remain in Red Cuba until this miserable island is rescued from communism, and then he can head for some other Red country. If Carmichael returns to the United States, we think that the Department of Justice should throw the book at him."

And in conclusion, after more of the same sort of thing, it states: "While we are busy in Vietnam, we can hardly crush Castro—although the government could, and should, stop discouraging Cuban refugees who plan Castro's destruction."

Stop discouraging? Stop discouraging Cuban exiles who plan Castro's destruction? Discouragement indeed! Discouragement indeed! "But let's stick a reminder in Uncle Sam's hat to trample Castro underfoot with all the force necessary to destroy his communist regime just as soon as we win the war in Vietnam. . . ." [Jeers and boos]

Observe how they express themselves, with what unbelievable exasperation, with what contempt, they speak of "a Negro firebrand," of "the miserable island," of "trampling underfoot." Because it must be said that the imperialists are annoyed by many things, but most of all they are annoyed by the visit here of a Negro leader—of a leader of the most exploited and most oppressed sector of the United States—by the strengthening of relations between the revolutionary movement of Latin America and the revolutionary movement inside the United States. [Prolonged applause]

In the past few days, innumerable articles about Stokely's trip have been published in the U.S. press; some very insulting, others more subtle. They have elaborated a whole series of theories. Some say, "Stokely is fooling Castro," "Castro is fooling Stokely." . . .

And they have gone still further. Some theorists have stated: "How strange that this country is not racist, and Stokely is a racist. . . . How strange! How strange!" Their aim is to create the impression that the Negro movement in the United States is a racist movement.

It is logical that the exploiters, who for centuries practiced racism against the Negro population, now label as racists all those who struggle against racism. . . .

That is what we must reject—as injurious and slanderous—the attempt to present the Negro movement of the United States as a problem of racism. We hope they will give up the illusion that anyone has deceived anyone. The drawing together of the revolutionaries of the United States and those of Latin America is the most natural thing in the world, and the most spontaneous. And our people have been very receptive to and very capable of admiring Stokely for the courageous statements he has made in the OLAS conference, because we know that this requires valor, because we know what it means to make such statements within a society that applies the most cruel and brutal procedures of repression, that constantly practices the worst crimes against the Negro sector of its population; and we know how much hatred his statements will arouse among the oppressors.

And, for this reason, we believe that the revolutionary movements all over the world must give Stokely their utmost support as protection against the repression of imperialists, so that it will be very clear that any crime committed against this leader will have serious repercussions throughout the world. And our solidarity can help to protect Stokely's life. [Sustained applause]

A couple of days after the conference, the Cubans put George Ware and me on a Cuban Airlines flight. George was stopping in Europe, I was continuing on to Vietnam with a connection in Madrid. Forty minutes into the flight, the captain announced, "*Compañeros y Compañeras,* we have been called back to Havana briefly. We regret the delay."

Now what? We thought the CIA counterrevolutionaries might have been planning to blow up the plane. But back in Havana, George and I were taken off the flight, which then continued. Cuban intelligence had reported an American reception committee waiting in Madrid to seize me and my passport and presumably escort me in chains and under guard back to God's country. Give praise and thanks for the excellence of Cuban intelligence.

We were transferred to an Aeroflot plane, which was carrying the Soviet delegation back home. This was my first time flying seventeen hours nonstop, from Havana to Minsk and then on to Moscow. The delegation included many brothers and sisters from Central Asia, and we had some interesting discussions about relative colonialism.

I had no time to form any impressions of Moscow. We spent two days there before continuing on to the Chinese border and a Chinese flight to Beijing, where I would meet a person who would become very influential in my political and personal life.

See, I was traveling with Cubans and we were coming from Russia. At this time, the Sino-Soviet dispute was hot and Cuba was seen by the Chinese to be solidly in the Soviet camp. In fact, the one conspicuous absence at the OLAS conference had been that of the Chinese. Also, the Chinese Cultural Revolution—Red Guards and all—was in full swing in Beijing. And remember Robert Williams, who'd been so valiant in Monroe, North Carolina? Well, after being framed by the FBI, the brother had been given political asylum in Cuba. When the Cubans restricted his political activities, Bro Williams had moved to China, where he'd made ideological criticisms of his former hosts. Consequently, the political climate was not easy to navigate, and various factions tried to pull me in. Fortunately, Madame Shirley Graham Du Bois (peace be unto her), who was much loved and appreciated by the Chinese, was in Beijing at the same time and proved a great help to me while I was there. And afterward too.

Bro, the morning I arrived, there was a knock on my door. I wasn't expecting anyone. A Chinese man bowed and handed me an envelope. I almost fell out. It was an invitation to dinner from Madame Du Bois.

Course, I immediately accepted, Jack. I knew who she was, had read some of her books, but I'd had no idea she was in China.

She was everything I'd expected and much, much more. Not a tall woman, actually about May Charles's size and coloration, she was an elegant lady with a real presence. Very serious. She was charming, brilliant, alert, very disciplined, and political. But, y'know, although she was very serious, she wasn't somber. She had a delightful, irreverent sense of humor and an African-American sensibility and perspective. Over the years, we would become very, very close. I called her my political mother. She called me her son.

That evening we just talked. We talked about so many things, about everything. She briefed me on the Cultural Revolution, Chinese politics, the Sino-Soviet dispute, and the activities of our countryman Robert Williams. She wanted to know my impressions of the state of the movement in America, the London conference, and of course, OLAS and my impressions of Comandante Castro.

What would I do after Vietnam? I told her about the U.S. government and my passport. I'd decided to try to join one of the African liberation organizations and, like her husband, just let the Yankees keep the wretched passport.

"Please, *please* don't do that," she said. "Just put it deep in your back pocket and sit on it." She said that her husband—she called him Du Bois—had never relinquished his passport, that the U.S. government had refused to renew it.

Then Mrs. Du Bois said, "Do you know Nkrumah?"

I said, "Of course, who doesn't know Nkrumah? I've read all—"

"I meant, have you met him? Would you like to?"

"Would I like to? To meet Kwame Nkrumah? Madame Du Bois, I'd give my right arm . . ."

"Well, then, you shall. You need to. You should. I'll see that you do. You'll hear from me."

[In June 1997, Kwame Ture wrote the following in a letter to David Du Bois at the University of Massachusetts–Amherst. —EMT]

I was humbled by your students' papers. As you know, changing life-long attitudes in a two hour discussion is not easy. At this time it has to be a major task for all revolutionaries. In a word, we are forced to try to "out sound bite" the capitalist media. If, after all, they can "give you the world in twenty-two minutes," plus commercials, we are compelled to scream "Black Power," to scream "Pan-Africanism" and let that mean all. But we were humbled to see the honesty of your students in facing contradictions which challenge life-long opinions. That made Martin Luther King come alive with his oft-repeated "truth crushed to earth shall rise again." Or as the Egyptians say, "struggle is like a rubber ball: the harder it is smashed into the dirt, the higher it rebounds into the sky."

My Brother, I have ever to be grateful to your mother. And you need not worry about the present, your mother has etched her life's work into history, leaving an indelible mark. Centuries from now, she will be remembered and researched. A great woman becomes even greater after her death and the longer she is dead, the greater she becomes. Your mother is already assured of this. When one speaks of Pan-Africanism, she is there. Of Nkrumah's early model in Ghana, she is there; of our struggle in the States, she will be there. Of authors who wrote for history, she is already in all this. She will be a cross reference of struggle.

Excuse the bad penmanship. My right hand is injured. I'm in Honduras at an alternative clinic for cancer. My health improves. I will be in Ghana in two weeks, July 11–15th. Again, thank you.

I actually thought we would not make it to Vietnam. At times during that flight I was convinced that my bones would lie, never to be found, somewhere in the jungles of Southeast Asia. Then I consoled myself that I was doing revolutionary work, so what difference did it make where I died? As Che said, "wherever death might surprise us." After that, I didn't really think about the plane crashing anymore.

When I'd said good-bye to Madame Du Bois, she'd said, "Not goodbye, my son. Farewell, for we shall certainly meet again." The plane was a Chinese cargo plane allegedly bringing medical—though some could have been military—supplies from Beijing to Hanoi. There were no passenger seats, nor seat belts, and this was the heart of the monsoon season. Oh, man, the plane bucked and pitched, lumbered and rolled; sometimes it fell straight down in air pockets or was tossed, spinning, in what felt like a hurricane.

I sat on this little fold-down seat between the cockpit and the stacked cargo and reflected on everything that had happened since I'd left D.C.: London, Havana, Moscow, Beijing. C.L.R., Fidel, Madame Du Bois. A host of activists and revolutionaries. Now I was en route to Vietnam. That incredibly valiant little country that had defeated the French and was now fighting America's military power to a standstill, Jack. I knew that "Uncle Ho" had lived in Harlem, washed dishes in a New York restaurant, and written an essay on lynching, which I'd read. A lifelong patriot, a dedicated revolutionary and organizer, he'd done time in jail, been exiled, and never once wavered, never once become discouraged, never taken a backward step. I wondered what it would be like to talk to such a man.

Among the European expatriate professors at Howard had been a Frenchman named Bernard Fall. Before most people in the States even knew where Vietnam was—back in the Kennedy administration—this Frenchman was writing about the Vietnamese's twenty-five-year struggle for independence from France.

I'll never forget a lecture he gave on the battle of Dien Bien Phu. The arrogant French generals—trained at Saint-Cyr, the French equivalent of West Point—were contemptuous of the "primitive and backward peasant army." It was poorly trained and ill-equipped. They always referred to the Vietnamese commander as "Schoolteacher" Giap, because that had been the general's profession before he studied war and took up arms to liberate his people.

The French strategy was to concede control of the countryside to the patriot army. At a place called Dien Bien Phu, a hundred miles deep in the jungle, they built a massive, "impregnable" base. A technological fortress, a monument to modern communications and state-of-the-art military equipment, it would be supplied entirely by air. There were no roads in, the place was entirely surrounded by jungle. They amassed squadrons of jet fighters, bombers, American helicopter gunships, and cargo planes that could airlift artillery and arms into battle. They massed elite forces, paratroopers, commandos, the Foreign Legion, the cream of the French army. They had the full panoply of Western military technology, much of which was supplied by good ol' Uncle Sam. What was their plan?

From this "impregnable, inaccessible" fortress, they would defeat the "peasants" from the air. Bombing raids, artillery bombardments, followed by the rapid deployment of airborne troops in their helicopter gunships. What could these primitives do in the face of all this? The ragtag, upstart "People's Army" and their "schoolteacher" didn't stand a chance.

Well, the schoolteacher had something for them. Without an air force or the kind of long-range artillery that would allow him to even think of attacking the impregnable, remote fortress, what could he do? What did he have? His people and the jungle, that's what. Those people made hundred-mile-long foot trails on the jungle floor. Hidden under the canopy of leaves, they transported ammunition, supplies, and mortars on their backs, by foot. They dismantled huge artillery pieces, and teams of porters carried and dragged them through the jungle. Relay teams, many of them women, pushed bicycles, each loaded with four artillery shells, weighing as much as those pushing them, a hundred miles over these jungle tracks. They transported and stockpiled ammunition, rice, and dried fish around the French fortress to supply and feed thousands of fighters. They stealthily lifted the artillery parts and ammunition to the hills surrounding the fortress and reassembled them. The French in their arrogance and overconfidence had not a clue that they were surrounded. Not a clue, Jack. So much for French military intelligence.

I have no idea how many months or even years this must have taken.

Or the will and determination, the sheer physical effort, the raw man-power it must have required. But Schoolteacher Giap and his people did it. The rest is history.

By the time these "generals" and what was left of their troops surrendered to the village schoolteacher, the "Battle of Dien Bien Phu" had shocked and humiliated the entire West.

Of course we can say the French were ignorant and arrogant. But one could almost excuse them, because what the Vietnamese People's Army did was humanly impossible. At least to the Western mind. But *once* they had done it, what in God's green earth was America's excuse? And especially when you consider that the United States had absolutely no justification, no national interest at all, in invading those people's country. Instead of learning from the military humiliation of the French, Uncle Sam is going to *avenge* it? Why? Gimme *ah* break.

During that perilous flight, I prayed for the plane to stay in the air just so I could meet these extraordinary people and the leaders who so inspired and organized them. We were scheduled to arrive in Hanoi at about midnight. I assumed this was to ensure that we entered North Vietnamese airspace at night so as to avoid American jet fighters. I'm not entirely sure of this, because I didn't think the Americans would be criminal enough to attack an unarmed civilian plane from a neutral country. But we did come in under cover of darkness.

Because of the storm we were hours late. It was 4 A.M. When we landed at Hanoi, the airport was in total darkness. No lights at all to be seen at the airport, because of the American bombing. So we landed in what looked like total darkness. But the plane hadn't come to a halt when out of nowhere all these people just materialized. I mean, out of nowhere, Jack.

A troupe of the most beautiful little girls, about eight years old, beautifully dressed, smiling radiantly, shyly but proudly presented us with flowers. Had they been up all night or had they been awakened and dressed up to come give us flowers? I didn't know, but they didn't look sleepy; they looked proud, happy, robust. Then a spokesman welcomed us and explained how sorry they were to be receiving us in such conditions. That really shamed me. I mean, the Vietnamese apologizing to me for the war conditions under which they were forced to live. Could you imagine that? I mean, which government had imposed these conditions on them?

An incredible people. That already showed me something. But even on the ride into the city I saw things that told me that America was never going to defeat these people. No way. We were approaching a river. A really wide expanse of open water. Then by the time we got to the water's edge, a bridge that had not been there would suddenly appear. And once we'd driven over, you looked back and the bridge was gone. The U.S. bombing had forced them to improvise a system of mobile pontoon bridges, made in sections. Oh, man, they were just so efficient and resourceful. As I would go around, I'd see many little things like that.

Even the youth. I'd meet fourteen-year-olds. In America, they'd be kids. But these "kids" would give me the entire history of Vietnam. The entire history of the struggle they were involved in. The aims, the objectives of the socialist revolution, the problems the revolution would have to overcome. They blew my mind.

Another example: I knew that the Vietnamese patriots made effective use of the strategy of united fronts. This was one of the key ways they were able to come together. That's what we need as a people in the United States, even now. (Our party—the All-African People's Revolutionary Party—has been trying to organize a Black United Front in the States since 1969 and we haven't been successful yet.)

So I asked the Vietnamese about their experience with united fronts. They were beautiful. They brought out all their people who'd done that work and made them available. They brought a brother who spoke English and who'd written up a report for us, about fifteen pages.

I was staying on the second floor of a little building in the center of Hanoi. This cadre was reading and explaining his report when we heard sirens.

"We are sorry, comrade," he said. "They are coming to bomb. We must go to the shelters." I could hear the sound of approaching planes, so off we went. Now, the Vietnamese are small in physical stature, so among them I towered like a giant, an African giant. Also they can sit on their haunches, almost like they're sitting on their own two feet, for hours.

So getting into the shelters—essentially tunnels leading underground—was no problem for them. They just stooped real low. I had to crawl in on my hands and knees. Meanwhile the sound of planes is getting louder. So we get to an underground room where people are sitting. They ask, am I comfortable? I say yes. They keep asking again and again, are you comfortable, comrade? I assure them. Then the brother moves the lantern next to him, produces the report that he'd stuck under his shirt, and continues the briefing from the place he'd stopped, unperturbed. Blew my mind, Jack. Outside, I can hear bombs.

But that's not even it. He's continuing to read, which is cool with me. I'm rolling with the action. The explosions sound even closer. He reads and explains. Then there is a deafening blast. It sounds right on top of us, as though it were a direct hit on top of us. The earth shakes. Dirt from the roof streams down on us. Some trickles into the pad. The brother calmly leans over and blows (blow, blow) the dirt off and continues his report. Whoa, bro. After that . . . I'll never forget that long as I live.

That bomb hadn't hit the shelter. It had, in fact, destroyed a hospital a block away. When the bombing stopped, the Vietnamese took me to see the wreckage.

During our discussions I had one slight, recurrent problem with the cadres. The leadership was clinging to Marxism-Leninism as the only path to socialism. As I explained in an earlier chapter, I had serious questions with the Marxists over nationalism, and I knew my people would always have a problem with Marxism and religion. But the Vietnamese leadership was receiving me as a representative of the African struggle in America and assuming that I shared their ideology. So I had to be honest.

I explained that, yes, I came from a people who came out of a long history of struggle recognized around the world, and whose struggle was intensifying daily. But that my people had not adopted that ideology, so that even if I felt that Marxism-Leninism was the correct approach (which I did not), I would not be representing my people's struggle honestly if I pretended that this was their position. They thanked me for my honesty, but said they could see, regrettably, that I still had "a lot of growing to do." But I held my position firmly, especially, y'know, on the nationalism question. Then something happened that blew me away. On that question in particular.

Quite unexpectedly one day I was invited to lunch with Prime Minister Pham Van Dong. They took me to his residence, and he met me at the gate with a warm embrace. A gracious host, he was a worldly, sophisticated man who spoke perfect English. Unlike Ho Chi Minh, he'd never been to America, but he knew the struggle there clearly and had a serious understanding of the contradictions.

Then, just as we got to an unpretentious but elegant little room where we were to have lunch, I heard a sound approaching: the clatter of wooden sandals against tiles. I knew. I couldn't yet see anyone but immediately I knew. I just became uncontrollable. I could see a slight figure coming down a dim hallway, and before I could see enough to recognize him, I just ran. I embraced, hugged, and kissed him before catching myself and releasing him.

"Oh, I'm sorry, sir. I'm sorry. It's just such a great honor. I forgot myself." But he was cool. I was overwhelmed, couldn't really believe that Ho Chi Minh was inviting me to lunch.

He sat next to me with Pham Van Dong across the table from us. That's one lunch I'll never forget. My mind was racing. I mean, here I am, twenty-six years old, what am I going to say to the venerable Ho Chi Minh? I knew I'd have to record, remember every word for posterity. Luckily, both leaders spoke excellent English.

"You know I spent time in Harlem?" he asked.

"Yes, sir. I know you did. I'm familiar with your writing on lynching."

He seemed surprised. I also wanted him to know that I wasn't unprepared, and that we knew and appreciated his role.

"Yes, sir. Africans in America know of your struggles here in Vietnam and also your work in Harlem. That's why we feel a responsibility to support your just struggles here."

That's when he told me that he'd been in Harlem during the time of the young Garvey. That he had thought Garvey to be a great man. That he'd heard Garvey speak and had even once made a modest financial contribution to the Garvey movement. Hey, you know that blew me away. I mean, here I'd been getting from the other leaders just the opposite of what I was now hearing from Ho Chi Minh himself.

So we went on to discuss other matters, then he suddenly leaned closer and asked, "When are you African-Americans going to repatriate to Africa?" I froze completely. Never forgot it. 'Cause I'd been hearing the completely opposite line from the other Vietnamese.

I said, "Well, sir, we are not there yet, but that remains the ultimate goal. But it will surely be in the future, as the contradictions continue to develop." Then we discussed the role of nationalism and culture in the struggle.

Ho Chi Minh was a great man. He clarified many things for me. He had a real appreciation of our struggle in America. We discussed, of course, the role of African-American troops in Vietnam. He then said something that only really hit me in the next country I visited. He said that they recognized clearly the contradictions within the U.S. army and explained their tactics toward the African soldiers. He said that their policy was to try, as far as possible, to avoid killing Africans, preferring to try to show them the contradictions and win them over to the side of justice and history.

When we were about to part, he asked me, was I married? I said, only to the struggle. Then he asked me if my mother was still living. I said, "Yes, sir, very much so." Then he gave me a silk scarf to bring to her. Hey, whatever else I might lose in travel, *that* I knew I was going to bring back to May Charles. I didn't care how, but you know I was going to bring that back. May Charles still has that scarf today.

I was extremely honored. Extremely honored at the opportunity to represent our people's struggle in Vietnam. The Vietnamese showed us every consideration and respect. I realized then there was no other honorable choice. My duty was to remain faithful to them in their just struggle, and to encourage my people to do so. I vowed never to waver or compromise in my efforts to expose American imperialism's criminal war against those people.

So I was walking on air leaving Vietnam. It was all so clear. The bombing was going on while I was there. They had shown me the American planes they'd shot down. I saw the wreckage, the fuselage; they weren't lying. I saw their patriotism on every level. I saw also their courage, determination, and their conviction of the inevitability of victory. And they weren't deluding themselves about that either. That impressed me the most.

I mean, look at all the forces arrayed against this little country, yet they remained convinced they could and would win. And they did it. So you just knew that whatever struggle you were in, so long as it was just, no matter what the odds, victory was possible. So when I left Vietnam I was on a cloud.

Of course, the things I hear and read nowadays about Vietnam are deeply troubling. Neocolonialism, global capitalism, Nike sweatshops, cultural imperialism. The ironies of history are full of grief, my brother. To see how a people so valiant, gracious, resourceful, patriotic, and *undefeatable* could summon up the strength and valor to defeat a military superpower and still lose the peace, at least temporarily. A bitter, bitter lesson.

The American government and people owe that nation deep, abject apologies. And reparations. Serious reparations for war crimes. America should repair the lasting human, social, economic, and environmental damage they inflicted on that country for no reason. And not by accident, but as a matter of policy. For any other country, say Serbia, it would be recorded as war crimes against humanity. Gimme a break. What Germany did in Europe during World War I was child's play compared to what America did in Vietnam. And the Germans were made to pay heavy reparations. Simple justice. I weep for this country if there is any justice in history.

Africa our home. That is where I went after Vietnam. I left Vietnam humbled and inspired and went home to a continent locked in struggle. Liberation wars, the winds of change, the Cold War, great-power interventions.

I don't think it necessary to describe my mood. All I'll say is that the plane didn't feel necessary. It was merely a concession to the conventions of physics. I was flying for real, Jack.

My first destination was Algeria. We'd all followed the Algerian liberation struggle. I'd read Fanon many times and of course cheered their righteous victory. So my anticipation was double, twofold. Not only was Algeria a bona fide revolutionary country that had thrown off colonialism by force of arms, it was *African*. The timing was perfect and I was in no way disappointed. The euphoria of liberation was everywhere. Algeria at that time was a secular society in the throes of social transformation and trying to reclaim its culture and history. An exciting time to visit, and the visit was more than I could have expected. I have a lot to thank the Algerians for.

I mean, America forms you in such limiting ways without your even being aware of the limitations. I was no exception. I'd had no exposure at all to non-Western cultures, much less Islamic ones. In America, your exposure came, if at all, through films. And all you got of these were snake charmers and belly dancers. That's about all. So I didn't even know about Islamic prayer, right? That's how ignorant I was.

Now, back then, a gesture common among Africans from America when traveling in Africa or the Caribbean was to kneel on the tarmac and kiss "the sacred soil" of this black country. That was a common gesture among "usses" back then.

When my plane stopped in Libya en route to Algiers, it was time for the midday prayer, but of course I didn't know that. So I look out the window and see a bunch of folks kneeling and pressing their foreheads to the earth. Oh, I say, oh, look. They "kissing the sacred soil" just like we do. Wow. And not just once either. I thought the people praying were passengers who had just stepped off the plane. Pitiful. That's how little I knew of other cultures. Or languages for that matter.

I had an important meeting with the Vietnamese while in Algeria, and of course at that time I spoke no French. Zilch. Not two words. So the Algerians were kind to send an interpreter for me. Elaine Kline was a young, Jewish woman, born in Brooklyn, who'd somehow become associated with the Algerian revolution. Naturally, I'm a little embarrassed to say, as soon as I meet her, I immediately think CIA. So I'm watching her like a hawk, Jack, listening carefully to every word. Now, I have no French, but having taken Latin, I have a vague general sense of the common vocabulary shared by English and French, so I'm trying to monitor the translation. At one point I say, "I humbly request of the comrades such and such a thing." And I hear her say *"Il demande"* in French. Man, I slam my hand into the table and glare at her. "Look," I say, "I ain't *demanded* nothing. I *requested* very humbly."

She looked at me the way a teacher looks at an obnoxious child. "Sir. In the context in which I'm using *demander,* it means precisely 'request.'"

Man, did I feel foolish. I apologized, but continued to listen carefully. After the meeting as we were walking out, I went over to apologize to the Vietnamese. But they said, "No, no. You are being vigilant. We like that, we like that." Later, I got to know Elaine's politics better and developed full confidence in her. I came to see her as a free agent who'd attached herself to the Algerian struggle out of conscience and genuine conviction. A decent, committed struggler.

I ended up spending about six weeks in Algeria, which was great for my cultural education. Madame Du Bois had arranged for me to be invited to the Eighth Congress of the Parti Démocratique de Guiné, where we would meet and Madame Du Bois would introduce me to President Nkrumah. But that was some six weeks off, so I stayed in Algeria for that time.

The Algerians were really, really beautiful. They took me everywhere and showed me everything, and I learned a lot.

They had only recently, a matter of five, six years or so, won independence from a century of French colonialism, and only after a bitter struggle. So the entire society had an air of possibility. A real mass enthusiasm was everywhere. And everyone knows the cultural arrogance of French colonialism—"our ancestors, the Gauls . . ." So there was great emphasis on the local cultures. The Algerians were high on their culture: language, music, traditional poetry, the arts. The masses just loved it. So they would have all manner of public cultural performances in the evenings, to which I was always invited. I could see and feel, just as in Cuba, the role that indigenous cultures could play in nation building.

I've always loved music, and there I'd hear North African music all the time, everywhere, twenty-four hours a day. Much of it was revolutionary music, music of struggle, like our freedom songs, and I began to appreciate North African music. Though very different from black African music, there were resonances. The North African music with the strongest rhythmic base was Moroccan. I gradually got to the point where, if I listened to a song and concentrated, I might be able to tell this one is from Libya, this from Egypt, this from Algeria. One very popular singer was absolutely dominant: that sister, the great Egyptian singer from the villages, Om Kalthoum. The Algerians just loved her. I myself got to really appreciate the power and beauty of her singing, the feelings she communicated even if I didn't always understand the words.

That was the culture. Then there was the political struggle. I learned a little about that too. Something Ho Chi Minh had told me only really became clear in Algeria. One good thing for me was that the liberation was only recently won, so all the freedom fighters were still around and I was able to meet them. Now, I was a young man and these were experienced warriors, veterans who'd been fighting for years. They wanted to help me by sharing their experiences. While I was meeting these fighters, many of them field commanders during the liberation war, the same thing would happen over and over, time and again. Of these FLN commanders, some fifty, sixty of them had served in the French army of occupation in Vietnam.

And just about every time Vietnam came up, these grizzled veterans would just light up, Jack. "Oh, I owe so much to the Vietnamese. It was there that I first became aware of my duty to fight colonialism. The Vietnamese caused me to see that. The Vietnamese are a great people

. . . a great people." Turns out that a surprisingly high percentage of those liberation front commanders had been captured by the Vietnamese People's Army. And the Vietnamese really worked on them, sought to drop some political clarity on them, y'know. "My brother, why are you here? How have we offended you? Are we in your country? We're fighting the same man who has his heel planted on your soil. You shouldn't be here fighting *us*. You should be at home fighting the common oppressor. Together we can get rid of him."

And now some thirteen years later, these former colonial conscripts turned liberation warriors are praising the Vietnamese for educating them. And have liberated their own country, which is now in a position to offer support to the Vietnamese, who still have to be fighting—this time against the Americans. And here all these Algerian commanders are thanking the Vietnamese for the gift of consciousness. Talk about the ironies of history, Jack. But it showed me *clearly* that everything was part of the same struggle. I remembered then what Ho Chi Minh had said about their policy toward the African GIs in the U.S. army.

In Algeria I was treated royally, almost like a *rais*. That, I discovered, was due to SNCC, and it was more than a little ironic. This was 1967, remember. So, of course, the Six Day War was very much in the air. And naturally the Algerians were passionately supportive of the Palestinians. I discovered to my surprise that they knew that SNCC had recently taken a public position on Palestinian rights and justice for the Palestinian people. I knew that at that very moment SNCC was catching everlasting hell in America for that position, but it endeared SNCC to the hearts of the Algerians. They were amazed that a black organization inside the United States would dare to publicly support justice for the Palestinian people. I mean they were just thrilled the brothers and sisters had the consciousness and the courage to take that stand. Most of them thought that SNCC was the first African organization in the States to support Palestinian rights. I explained that this wasn't really true. The first *civil rights organization,* true, but not the first African organization.

I pointed out that the Nation of Islam had been the first. I could vividly remember in '64 seeing a picture of Malcolm X meeting publicly with a PLO representative. I pointed out that about the only place we could read accounts of events in the Middle East that represented the Palestinian position was in the Nation's newspaper. Not even in the newspapers of the American left could you read that. But, of course, SNCC was the one in the civil rights movement to take it public. So SNCC was greatly respected in Algeria.

When the time for me to leave for Guinea grew close, I was invited to a high-level meeting. They were beautiful, these Algerians. They said, okay, you say you are moving on to Africa. But isn't Algeria Africa? Hey, we're all Africans. We will be honored to support your struggle in the States. We see it as our historical, revolutionary, and fraternal duty. I mean they just came out and said, if at any time SNCC wishes to establish a presence in Algeria, here is what we're authorized to offer. They offered everything, everything, Jack. An office, residence, operating expenses, telephones, passports, diplomatic recognition, diplomatic immunity, and even military training. I could hardly believe my ears. They were so generous, and so principled. Because, remember, during their war of liberation, they themselves—the Front for National Liberation—had to be recognized and helped in their struggle by friendly countries. People forget that it was in Ghana that Fanon wrote *Wretched of the Earth.* Ghana allowed him the time and space to do that, treating him almost like a diplomat, while the Algerian struggle was going on. Revolutionary Algeria understood it to be their duty to recognize and support other legitimate struggles.

They offered us every courtesy—the same ones they would later extend to Eldridge Cleaver and the Panthers—and of course we thanked them sincerely for their generous, fraternal offer. I said I certainly thought it likely that SNCC would at some point accept it and conveyed the offer to Atlanta. Then I continued on to Guinea.

But almost the minute I got to Guinea, I said, this is it. The minute I got to Conakry, I said, "Oh, man, I'm home." I mean, the Algerians had mass demonstrations, oh, yes, they did. They had mass enthusiasm. But in Guinea, they were *disciplined.* In Guinea, they had organization, they had patriotic enthusiasm, and they were disciplined.

CHAPTER XXV

Mother Africa
and Her Suffering Children

As exciting as Algeria struggling toward social and political transformation undoubtedly was, as fascinating and instructive as I found the culture, and notwithstanding the overwhelming graciousness and consideration I was receiving from everyone there, I eventually found myself becoming decidedly restless. Even as the time for the end of my visit drew closer.

Hey, be clear now. I certainly don't want to appear ungrateful. In 1967, revolutionary Algeria was a fascinating place. There was a lot to see, and even more to learn.

And especially because of everything I could see of their young leadership cadres—the ones with whom I mostly dealt were some very, very impressive young people. They were committed, bright, very knowledgeable-about-the-world, well-educated, serious young activists, honest and tempered by the long war for independence, who seemed clear on the struggle ahead: the formidable task of building a humane and progressive modern society out of the nation's Islamic heritage, the traditional cultures, and the ruins of French colonialism.

These young Algerian cadres really impressed me. From them, I got the same sense of confidence and determination I'd seen in Cuba. A clear-eyed, unsentimental sense of possibility and struggle. So why then was I feeling restless? The answer, in one word, was Guinea, my next destination.

See, thus far, this strange, unplanned journey of mine had been extraordinary. Unbelievably fortunate, eventful, rewarding. Hey, I'd seen the indomitable Vietnamese people locked in struggle. In Cuba, I'd had the opportunity to see the energy and dedication of a revolutionary people and to attend and feel the spirit of justice and resistance in a continentwide gathering of deeply committed brothers and sisters seriously struggling for radical change all over the Americas. Now, I'd caught a long glimpse of Free Algeria, Frantz Fanon's adopted country. It was a lot, Jack, quick, fast, and in a hurry. Of course it had to seriously affect my view of the world. Huh? *Seriously,* what you mean?

Of course I knew I was inordinately fortunate, especially for a young African from America. This clearly was—I knew that then, but I can *really* see it now—a remarkable moment in history. What I mean is this: Right before my eyes I could see the world stirring. I mean, I was not only seeing history move, the motion of history actually seemed to be speeding up, bro. Everywhere I went an exciting sense of movement. And I knew my people in America had to move along with it. I truly became aware of being part of a uniquely favored historical generation. A worldwide generation entrusted by history with opportunity for struggle and progress, in which we *all* had a responsibility.

I could see also that rich, gluttonous, smug, self-satisfied, shortsighted America was really not, as it imagined itself to be, the center of the universe. Was in fact a major obstruction and it didn't really have to be that way. That around her, beyond her, despite her, the world—*usses*—the so-called wretched of the earth—was everywhere rising up. We are human beings. Deal with it. Deal with us. America could so easily and naturally have placed itself in the forefront of the struggle of the world's people.

This was more than exciting. It was inspiring, in fact, life changing. And the more I saw, the more I wanted to see. To see it *all*, bro. To take it *all* in, to reflect, study, to assimilate, to understand, to be clear. So the more I saw, the more my interest grew. It was inexhaustible, but so was my energy. That's what I meant by restless.

Misgivings? Second thoughts? Whatchew mean? Of course not. Hell, no, Ah will go. Hey, this is my first trip outside America—as an adult. What could there be to regret? Well, maybe one thing, but I wouldn't really call it a regret. I was seeing and learning so much so fast that I needed to remember. You know, to bring back to the brothers and sisters. I knew I was exceedingly, impossibly fortunate. I found myself over and over wishing more of us could be there to see with me the things I was seeing. I wished *everybody*—well, *almost* everybody—in SNCC could have been there. To analyze, to discuss. To share perceptions, insights, questions. *That,* I really missed, those loooong, all-night SNCC discussions. Is that a regret?

So anyway, I'm in Algeria and growing restless—for what? For revolutionary Guinea, bro. Black Africa. The ancestral motherland. Having seen all these revolutionary societies, I wanted now to see how the struggle was going down in the ancestral home, among my kinfolk, flesh of my flesh. And Guinea was the place.

Hey, you don't think it was an accident that when Harry Belafonte set up the SNCC trip to Africa, the host country would be Guinea, do you? A former French colony, rather than, say, one of the anglophone (English-speaking) countries? No accident there, bro. I remember Harry saying in a meeting that, yeah, it's a small but very proud country with an *African* revolutionary spirit in the people and the leadership. He talked about the vision and the boldness of the young leader Sékou Touré, who'd invited SNCC, saying that Touré's approach was in many ways similar to SNCC's. I wanted to see what that meant. (And of course he mentioned Touré's charisma. I can remember teasing Mrs. Hamer mercilessly that she had a crush, big time, on her "handsome young president." "Oooh, Stokely, he's so *black* and so *handsome*.")

Mrs. Hamer: "Oh, hush, Stokely. You know how I love my Perry Hamer, all six feet two of him, right on down to the soles of his big, flat, ol' size-twelve shoes."

But what I most remembered was being in high school when Bro Touré led his people to independence. I think every conscious black person my age or older remembers what happened then.

After the French defeat in Vietnam and with another looming in Algeria, de Gaulle had second thoughts on the question of empire. In 1958, he offered France's West African "possessions" (no kidding) a referendum to choose between partial independence within some kind of French commonwealth arrangement, or full political independence. Only "tiny" Guinea opted for independence.

When the Guinean people voted for independence, the French colonials were outraged. I do mean *outraged*, Jack. The French did everything in their power to cripple the society before leaving. It was brutal, ugly, and petty. They sabotaged *all* government agencies: destroyed records, took away files, locked offices, destroyed what equipment they could not take, even going so far as to tear telephones off the walls. The French technicians took the plans for all electrical wiring, telephone lines, and sewage systems in the city of Conakry.

They left the national treasury empty and expelled the young nation from the French West African commercial union (Communauté Française Africaine), hence leaving the country without a national currency. Dig the viciousness of that. They left the government without a medium of currency (the CFA franc) by which to trade internationally—to purchase as much as a gallon of gas from another country, *or* pay the civil servants, police, and teachers at home. You dig? Can you imagine that?

Independent Guinea was *meant* to fail. Or, more accurately, to be sabotaged. It was inevitable, a matter of months at the most. This was France and its allies at their mean-spirited and spiteful worst. The Western community of nations—the United States and France's European allies—sat on their racist hands smugly waiting for this impudent little black nation to implode. Hah. One thing I remember was a quote attributed to the young leader at that time (I think in *Time* magazine of all places): "If the choice is to be between riches in slavery, or freedom in poverty, then Guinea chooses freedom." Or even "if the price of freedom is to be poverty . . . then Guinea will always choose freedom . . ." or words to that effect.

But Sékou Touré, his party, and his people had not faltered. Ten years later, little, valiant Guinea was still very much alive. Fighting, but definitely alive. And check this. Not only had it survived, but it had been there to receive and welcome the *Osageyfo*, President Kwame Nkrumah of Ghana, when reactionary stooges and traitors, bought and paid for by the CIA (your tax dollars at work), had staged their coup in Ghana, the year before my trip, waiting until the great patriot was out of the country.

What had most impressed me was the sensitive and principled way Sékou Touré, his government, and his party did it, in the true spirit of Pan-Africanism and the highest values of our traditional cultures. President Nkrumah was not given charity, political asylum, or the humiliating refugee status usually accorded deposed leaders in the usual protocols of international diplomacy.

No! The government and people of Guinea not only received our heroic brother with appropriate honor and respect, but Sékou Touré *officially* declared the deposed leader copresident of the Republic of Guinea, pending his legitimate return to the leadership of the people he had so skillfully led into independence. Wow, bro. All progressive forces on the continent and across the diaspora shouted affirmation. Our spirits were moved. Hey, that's a *very* African gesture, we said, give praise and thanks.

I certainly cannot recall any similar gesture of respect, brotherhood, or solidarity between two politicians anywhere else, much less two heads of state, can you? Yeah, you sneer, it was almost certainly merely honorific. Meaningless. Hollow. Well, once I spent time in Guinea, I could see for myself that it was anything but honorific. Of course President Touré and his advisers ran the government and party day to day. But President Nkrumah wasn't simply trotted out for ceremonial occasions. He, first of all, was very much the senior adviser to President Touré, seriously consulted on matters of policy and national direction. He was also offered specific areas of responsibility according to his inclinations and interests. It was a truly inspiring relationship between these two African patriots, like nothing I've seen, read, or heard about in history or contemporary politics.

One of the first accounts I heard once I got to Guinea, and something not widely known outside the country, might partially explain this uncommon sensitivity on the part of the young Guinean president.

People told me that in 1958, after the French looted the Guinean treasury and destroyed the infrastructure, leaving the government to collapse, President Nkrumah was the first to intervene to save the young nation.

Within days of the French departure, some say the very next day, President Nkrumah either sent a delegation or, as some say, came in person to advise and support the young government. Most importantly, he brought a check in the amount of 10 million pounds sterling, drawn on the foreign reserves of the Bank of Ghana. A loan without conditions or interest to buy the young nation a few months breathing room and give them some foreign exchange. Kwame Nkrumah was always and to the end a true Pan-Africanist.

That story taught me something fundamental. You might say the first and most important of many lessons I was to learn from both men. "You can never be ungrateful in politics" (or in life). That's something that President Nelson Mandela—the *Madiba*—continues to teach us every day in his constant, loyal, and principled support for those who supported his people's struggle: Libya and Cuba. Perhaps it's an African thang; you just wouldn't understand. Hey, I know that today 10 million pounds sterling might look like chump change to the gluttonous multinational plunderers of global capitalism. But in 1958, to a newly independent African nation grappling with the inherited contradictions and underdevelopment of colonialism—in this case, Ghana—Nkrumah's conscientious, brotherly act was a significant sacrifice, a principled and generous demonstration of Pan-African solidarity. A sacrifice that was, by the way, enthusiastically supported by the Ghanaian masses. One that, as subsequent events prove, Ahmad Sékou Touré never forgot.

Now, nine years later, the ruling party, by its rightful name the Democratic Party of Guinea for the African Democratic Revolution, was having its Eighth Congress. There would be observers representing allies from the various liberation struggles, from progressive African states and nationalist political parties across the continent.

While I was in Guinea, I was to hook up with Mrs. Du Bois, who would be attending the Pan-African Congress, and meet the great man himself, the *Osageyfo*, Dr. Kwame Nkrumah.

But, had I the faintest idea of all that actually awaited me in Guinea, I would have been even more restless to get there than I already was. The time came, I sincerely thanked the Algerians, I thanked them *seriously*, and continued on to Guinea.

Almost the minute I got to Guinea, I said, this is it. The minute, Jack. I said, *yes*, this is it. My people are disciplined. They are organized, purposeful, and disciplined. Example? All right, let me give you an example of discipline.

Remember de Gaulle's ultimatum? When he gave the choice, yes or no? You know he himself went to all the colonies selling the scam. In every colony, every colony, even the greatest puppets like Ivory Coast and Senegal, there were popular demonstrations against de Gaulle. The only colony—the only one, Jack—where there were no hostile demonstrations was Guinea.

In Guinea, nothing but courtesy, ceremony, respect, and African etiquette, the beating of drums, traditional dances, joy and celebration in the streets. The Frenchman must have been quite pleased. And yet Guinea was the *only* place that voted no. All the countries where there had been demonstrations against de Gaulle voted yes.

That was tradition. You in our country. We must make you welcome. Show you the elaborate courtesy due a powerful guest. But how we vote on our nation's future is our business, Jacques. Which may explain the viciousness with which the French then trashed the infrastructure.

Some years later, about 1976, I think, I'm in D.C. I had—out of revolutionary duty—to attend a reception in the embassy of a very, *very* reactionary African country. I haven't gotten five feet inside the door and I'm surrounded, bro. I mean literally. Attacked from all sides, without pity, about my choice of Guinea for the country of my return.

"What's Guinea? Why you choose Guinea? Is Guinea the only country in Africa? It's a dictatorship. It's a *bloodstained* dictatorship. Why Guinea? Etc., etc., etc. Naturally, y'know, I'm under attack so I'm gonna respond right and left, back and forth. This went on for a good two hours. I'm still just barely inside the door. A host of people just looking on. I mean it got hot, Jack.

All this time a young diplomat from another African country had stood listening to both sides. He listened intently but said nothing. Finally, he said, "I've listened carefully to both sides. Well, I've been fortunate enough to actually visit Guinea. I'm a footballer. Our national team did a tour of West Africa. In every country, didn't matter whether we won or lost, there was disorder. But when we won, security had to take us off the field. The crowds threw things. Seemed about to attack us. In Guinea, we won. Badly defeated the national team. The crowd stood and applauded us as we left the field. I've never forgotten that. The only place."

That's what I'm talking about. But it should be clear. This was not some imposed "totalitarian" discipline. It was self-discipline. Something coming out of indigenous culture and tradition.

During Sékou Touré's time, the reactionaries would routinely send agents to infiltrate various communities to destabilize the regime. Saboteurs, undercover, so they could plant bombs, assassinate local leaders, stuff like that. How did these communities defend themselves? They simply resorted to traditional practice.

See, with Guinea, the capitalist media always gave everything their little "totalitarian" spin, all right? Did it in Cuba too with the local committees to defend the revolution. You know, "neighbors spying on neighbors, folks denouncing their enemies," etc., etc. They couldn't do that to Guinea 'cause the local people simply reverted to tradition, no muss, no fuss.

See, in traditional villages, if any stranger came in, even a friend, to visit another, you would formally bring and present them to the chief and elders. Automatic. So the Guineans simply recalled and emphasized that tradition. Every stranger had to be formally presented. Everyone knew who they were, where they came from, and whom they were visiting. Anyone not so presented stood out. So it became difficult for them to lie undercover to carry out their terrorism.

'Course the reactionaries tried to label it undemocratic, dictatorial, etc., etc. But the masses, they were enthusiastic. It was something they were familiar and comfortable with. It was completely in harmony with their tradition. So it worked. See, traditional African societies were extremely disciplined. That discipline was second nature. Self-discipline, not anything imposed from outside. I want to emphasize that.

One of the things I really liked was that the PDG's (Partie Democratique de Guinea) approach was always based on the practices and values of the local culture. Which is why they were so successful in local organizing. And the country was *organized*, Jack. Soon as I set foot in it, I began to realize that. And every day I saw it more and more. Mrs. Hamer really responded to that aspect, the empowering of the local folk. She told me, "All my life I've lived in America and no president ever came to see me. I go to Guinea, and the first day, the president himself comes to where we staying to say hello. And you know what, Stokely? It was *ordinary* people like me, who were running *everything*. The ones who were left back and never had no chance. Now they have the chance to run they own country."

Look, Africans in the diaspora return home for many different reasons. I returned home for revolution. It should be uppermost in people's minds that at this time Guinea was the most revolutionary and innovative country in Africa. That's what motivated my return. Not the "culture," not the climate, not the vegetation, the "beauty" of the landscape, or to discover my "identity." Later I'd come to know and appreciate those. But what attracted me first was the unified spirit, the political structures, the level of organization, at the grass roots, bro, the ideology, the national pride and dignity and of course the combativeness of the country in fighting against injustice.

[Under some gentle insistence, the brother's response to which you might detect in the tone of what follows, our brother condescended to discuss some of the "peripheral tra-la-la." —EMT]

Now, of course, Africa is a beautiful continent. But I do not think that I, a poor humble revolutionary, not a craftsman of words, can describe

Africa's beauty better than others who, for centuries, have already described it, okay? I know that East Africa is considered more beautiful in a spectacular, scenic way, but West Africa is itself extremely beautiful in its own unique way. Myself, I just *love* the mountain forests in the Guinean interior. One of my favorite places in the world.

Also, Guinea has almost the same climate as the Trinidad of my child-hood. And the same two seasons, wet and dry. And the vegetation? Almost identical. Fruits and vegetables that I'd not seen in America and almost forgotten, I'd now see again. My taste buds would now come alive, reminding me that once, long ago, I knew this taste. Time and again I'd take something to my mother, who'd say, "Yes, we had that in Trinidad, but we called it something else." So having been born into that variety of tropical fruits, and the climate, it was good to encounter them again. Sud-denly the moon became a presence in my consciousness once more.

But more than these, it was the *social* environment. What was every-where overwhelming was the quality of human interaction. A certain warmth and security you felt among people that is so absolutely missing in America. Except, of course, sometimes among Africans in the rural South—where I had last experienced it.

The politeness, the sensitivity, the respect—the overwhelming human contact. That's not abstract, bro, I give you an example. Having been col-onized by France, Guinea's national language was French. Now for some reason, Africans born in America seem to have a fear of going into non-English-speaking African countries. Yet that turned out to be one of the most positive things for me. How so? I want to tell you that when I first went into Guinea, I could speak not a word of French. (Well, maybe *oui, monsieur,* and *mademoiselle.* No more.) I mean in high school we'd read Cicero in Latin, Caesar in Latin, but of French I had not one word. (And the African languages, Soussou, Mandingo, or Fula, you know you could forget those.)

And that's the interesting thing. I had no French and most Guineans no English. But I never once felt excluded or at sea. People would bend over backward to communicate with me. To ensure that I fully understood what was being discussed. It was just so incredibly considerate; an aspect of human sensitivity that seemed so natural. The extraordinary lengths to which *evrah* one went to communicate, to explain, to make sure I under-stood and felt included in whatever was going on. Without a common lan-guage between us, folks had to be so *expressive.* My brothers and sisters found the most inventive and creative ways to communicate. They made it fun, a contest: who could find the best way to get through to this bar-barian kinsman from across the sea. It was all so touching that it may, in part, have backfired. I was enjoying this so much that for too long I may have delayed making a serious effort to learn French. In fact, what French I picked up was mostly by osmosis.

What, in retrospect, was strange was communicating with President Touré. President Touré was an exceedingly perceptive man, almost prescient sometimes. But his comprehension of English was rudimentary (though I did begin to suspect he understood much more than he let on. I'll give an example of this during the Portuguese Aggression of 1972). But the odd thing is that even before I had any French at all, only twice did I have to use a translator in speaking with the president, one-on-one. For face-to-face communication I *only twice* used a translator, and that was because those discussions were politically sensitive. I know this sounds crazy, but it's true.

True, in the early days when he gave a speech, I had to get on the earphones and get it in English. His speech at the Party Congress, for example. But when we had face-to-face meetings, for something we needed, for instance, our communication was excellent. How so?

Well, I spoke simple, almost broken English. Simple sentences. He must have done the same with French. But it had to be more than that. Something about the nature of the communications. Perhaps it was like two doctors (something I saw in Cuba last year) who are without a common language. Say, a student doctor and an older master physician. No common language, but what they really know—the human anatomy and its functions—that is always the same. That doesn't change. Some terminology may be the same or similar in both languages, or can differ greatly, but their shared *understanding,* their knowledge, is the same, so they can communicate well even if across two languages.

In our case, our "science" was that of revolution. The terms, references, and ideology were in different languages, but you could somehow sense the meaning.

Again, you must remember that I went to Africa for revolution. I knew that what happened in Africa would affect all black people everywhere. And at that time, the overt battle for the continent's future was raging. In fact, revolution was raging around the world, and revolutionaries from all over the world found their way to Conakry to consult Sékou Touré and Kwame Nkrumah. President Touré was inclusive and considerate. Every event of that kind, he'd ensure that I was there and that I was given some appropriate role to play so that I wasn't just sitting in. Just about every event, every guest that came, I was totally included. I learned a great deal from this. *[I am not sure whether our Brother was aware of this as he spoke, but his account of his inclusion in these meetings is a classic description of the process by which youth were educated in traditional African societies. —EMT]*

•   •   •

My first day in Conakry was eventful. It was midday, steamy hot when I arrived. After I went through airport formalities, I was taken to the Hotel Basiere, which was close to the airport. I saw immediately that Conakry was no huge, modern city, no skyscraper skyline, y'know? It reminded me of sleepy old Port-of-Spain. Lots of low buildings of weathered wood or two-story concrete ones. The town was on a bay surrounded by steep, forested mountains. The airport sat on a spit of land jutting out into the Atlantic. There were mangroves in the water along the shore and coconut palms and mango trees towering over the houses. All of which combined to give the town a familiar appearance: old-time colonial Caribbean. But what really surprised me, with a sudden nostalgia, was not the scenery; it was the smell. As we were entering the town, I put down the windows and felt the warm, moist air on my cheeks. The car was instantly filled with a salty, fishy smell of a warm sea, a woodsmoke smell from the cooking fires, and that of lush tropical vegetation. It was a long-forgotten smell of childhood.

The first thing I did in my room was check out the shower. I was hot, I mean sticky, Jack. I had just dropped my bags and was heading into the shower when there was a knock on the door. There, to my surprise, stood Madame Du Bois, crisp, cool, and elegant.

"Madame Du Bois, how are you?"

"I'm fine. How was the trip? Good. Come on. President Nkrumah is waiting."

"Madame D., I just this minute stepped in. I've been traveling. I'm filthy. I can't go meet Kwame Nkrumah like this. I have to shower, change clothes, etc., etc."

"No time for that. You don't keep a president waiting, young man."

"Madame D., at least let me wash my face. Change shirts . . ."

"Even that will take time. Y'know, for a revolutionary, you mighty finicky, young man. All right, be quick." All the five minutes I was doing that Mrs. Du Bois stood outside the bathroom urging me to hurry.

We drive through the town and come to a scenic section on the shore called Kolaya. The car stops before a tall gate guarded by soldiers, behind which I can see this white villa. We drive into a little courtyard, walk across a wide, open veranda overlooking the ocean, and enter a large room that opens onto the veranda.

There, rising to greet us, was the *Osageyfo*, Dr. Kwame Nkrumah, copresident of Guinea. He was wearing a loose-fitting white suit with the collarless tunic called the *nyerere* jacket. President Nkrumah was not tall, was physically quite a little man. What I remember most is his smile and his eyes. His smile was radiant and welcoming, gracious. His eyes were alert, piercing . . . a golden brown color that at times seemed to glow. Very

... compelling. *[Many people have remarked on the* Osageyfo's *eyes as being his most striking feature. In Jamaica, eyes of this glowing brown color are called, among the peasantry, maroon eyes. The fighting Maroons of Jamaica were mostly of Ghanaian descent. —EMT]*

At this meeting he did most of the talking. For me, it was like being again in Ho Chi Minh's presence. I was overwhelmed and could scarcely say anything even in answer to his direct questions. Luckily, Mrs. Du Bois was there to bail me out. That first time she supplied most of the answers. In subsequent meetings we'd have wide-ranging discussions, talking at length about Vietnam, Cuba, Algeria, the continent, etc., etc. But at this first meeting he talked about our people's struggle in the United States. His discussion was, however, much more detailed and current than was Ho Chi Minh's. He had a sophisticated understanding of the dynamics, the players, the interests, and the contradictions. But the thing is, this is now my second discussion of the racial situation in America with leaders outside of America, both of whom had clear and precise positions on our situation. What did Nkrumah say? One of the first things he said was that, whether we knew it or not, the struggle of the Africans in America was inextricably linked to the struggle in Africa, and theirs to ours. And that those of us who were conscious of this connection had the responsibility to articulate it tirelessly to those who were not yet conscious. That is something that I have tried to do consistently.

On the way back to the hotel, Mrs. Du Bois sprang her second, way bigger surprise, and this one was a monster, Jack. She was explaining about the Party Congress. How it would be both celebratory and forward-looking. Celebratory of the party's accomplishments in its first nine years of independence, indeed of the nation's very survival. It would then project the next stage, the principles and blueprint for achieving the socialist cultural revolution and advancing the continental struggle for Pan-Africanism.

Hence there would be many foreign observers present and a great many cultural events, because one of the things the party emphasized was the traditional cultures. But the most anticipated event, the one everyone was talking about, Mrs. Du Bois said, was the concert by South African singer Miriam Makeba.

"Oh, wow," I thought. "I don't believe this. This is *nice.*" But I was casual, noncommittal.

"Oh, that's cool," I muttered. "She's a great singer. My favorite."

"She's already here. Have you met her?"

"Once, years ago . . . briefly. She couldn't possibly remember."

"Well, would you care to greet her now? To renew acquaintances?"

I was there for revolution. I tried hard to sound nonchalant. "Wouldn't mind . . . but only if it's . . . uh . . . y'know, convenient."

I don't believe my poker face fooled Mrs. Du Bois for a minute. She said, "Well, shall we, then?" and gave directions to the driver.

Seven years earlier when we had shaken hands, I'd been an infatuated nineteen-year-old college freshman coming off the Freedom Rides. She, ten years my senior but looking all of nineteen, was then Harry Belafonte's brilliantly talented, beautiful, young African protégée, fully embarked on what would be a meteoric career in American show business.

Now Miriam Makeba was a bona fide sensation, an international entertainer of the first magnitude. I mean big time, Jack. Hey, but I was no longer nineteen either, had grown some, had done a few things myself, and was coming from a meeting with Kwame Nkrumah himself. So where was all this sudden adolescent rush of nervousness coming from? Be cool, fool.

When I stuck out my hand, she ignored it even as she brushed aside Mrs. Du Bois's attempted introduction. "Oh, but I've been reading about *this* brother," she said, giving me a quick sisterly hug. "I've seen you on TV."

"I've been seeing you on TV too," I said. "You're my favorite singer."

In person she was even more attractive than her public image. She had an easy warmth and graciousness that was as natural as her hair. She moved with an unstudied grace and an unpretentious dignity that was, well, almost regal. I once heard a line somewhere that she brought to mind: "an aristocracy not of birth, but of spirit." That was her. My clearest early impression has not only stuck, but grown over the years. It was of an incredible outward gentleness, almost a softness, that overlay but didn't quite conceal a powerful inner strength. It is a combination of gentleness and great strength that I've seen mostly among African women. It is very attractive. I couldn't take my eyes off her. Up close she was beautiful in a way none of her pictures could do justice. There was a radiance, a vibrancy of spirit, that film simply could not capture. I was shook, Jack. Shook, but, hey, not speechless this time. This also was a brief visit, for there was going to be a big reception later that evening at the Palace of the People. And you know the ladies had to go git ready, bro.

"I'm so glad you're here," she said. "We must find a chance to talk, yes?"

"I'll look for you at the reception," I said.

"And I'll be looking for you." I would discover that she was always direct. I liked that a lot.

Hey, you know what I was thinking about the rest of *that* afternoon, Jack. Of all the incredible things that had been happening during this trip, this had to be, hands down, the most unbelievable. I mean, to meet this beautiful, entirely remarkable woman again. And in Africa too! And, even more incredibly, this time she clearly seemed quite interested in getting to know me? Oh, wow. At least I sure hoped so.

The reception was sheer torture at first. Then it turned into something like a dance, then a game, almost fun. She was, of course, in demand, always surrounded by a crowd. I was constantly being introduced to people who were quick to help me over the language barrier. So it became a matter of tearing myself away, weaving through and around throngs of people just to exchange a quick word. A smile here, a meeting of eyes there, or a help-less shrug.

"But this is impossible," she said. "Give me a moment. I'll arrange something." She did. She was a resourceful woman. I liked that about her too.

Once we were able to really talk, that was it, Jack. I discovered that this attractive, apparently so gentle, mature woman was a very political crea-ture, in fact an uncompromising militant where her people's freedom was concerned. On that she was *clear*. In this, she was tireless, always on call for the countless liberation struggles everywhere on the continent. More than other human beings, she was eyewitness to the rebirth of a continent: She sang in Nairobi at Kenyan independence, in Luanda, at Angolan independence, at the inauguration of the Organization of Africa Unity in Addis Ababa. For Samora Machel in Mozambique. On and on, so it went. Always crisscrossing the continent and never able to touch down once in her homeland.

Looking at the youthful, serene, seemingly untroubled beauty of this woman's face, one could never imagine all she had already endured and survived. First, the daily humiliation, grinding poverty, and brutality of apartheid in South Africa, where as a young child she'd accompanied her mother into jail for a year. Her mother's crime? Brewing and selling "native" beer to support her children after her husband's untimely death. She had survived the murder of family members by police: two of her uncles were murdered at the Sharpeville Massacre. She had endured the pain of exile and the constant harassment from the illegal government and, most recently, had survived a serious onslaught of cancer in the United States. Looking at her calm confidence, though, one would never guess all that this African woman's life had been. She was a survivor. And a beautiful spirit.

All of this came to enrich her art, gave it great power, making it dif-ferent from anything else in the American musical scene at the time because she so loved and respected her people's culture. Totally com-mitted to the integrity and dignity of her heritage, she never exploited the material. She celebrated it. Miriam Makeba—Zenzi, Mama Africa—never, never cheapened or dishonored her ancestral culture for money or career. No, she did not. Not for her any exotic sexual exhibitionism, no cheap display of "primitive African sensuality" pandering after wealth, fame, or acceptance from the white audience. Instead, she celebrated and honored her people's culture and embodied their struggle with dignity. And incredibly enough, made it all work. At least for a while. When we met again, she was at the very highest level of her profession. An international star, without compromise of principle.

I found her an irresistible combination: a strong, beautiful African woman. A magnificent, supremely gifted artist with purpose, entirely without self-importance or pretentiousness that I could see. Nothing of the prima donna about her. A warm, witty, conscious black woman with a shy, impudent sense of humor. A loyal friend. Who could resist? Hey, I couldn't believe it was really happening, bro, much less *resist?* Whoa now.

Our relationship began in Guinea, but it wasn't easy. I mean, just the logistics. Especially for her. See, we were both official government guests. But she had musicians and a teenage daughter to take into account. Also a lot of official obligations, for which she was always accompanied by a lady translator. Me, I was relatively free—that is, until the American embassy tried to hijack my passport and I was given my own security. It wasn't easy to snatch a few hours to talk, but we managed. Made it an adventure even.

Over the years, Zenzi would pay a great price indeed for her principles. And certainly, an even greater one for her marriage to me the next year. I've seen her get angry and determined, but I never heard her whine. I've seen her beset, buffeted, and battered; but I've never seen her bow. I learned a lot about love and courage from this woman, and about life. I have much to thank her for. Respect. One love.

Earlier this year (1998) we met again—after twenty years apart—when I finally was able to pay my first visit to Azania ("Free South Africa"). The visit was not exactly the triumphant experience that so many of us in the diaspora had worked for and dreamed of for thirty years. But it was great to see her. And she was glad to end her years of exile, to be home at last. Her fighting spirit and impudent wit were still very much in evidence. As was, from this story I heard, her effect on men of superior judgment. It seems that after an appearance she was paid an elaborate, flirtatious compliment by President Mandela. In which, there was an implied proposal of marriage. Zenzi didn't miss a beat.

"I thank you, Mr. President. I am honored, Mr. President, but *Madiba,* you must remember that all my husbands have been younger than I." The president cracked up as did the audience.

In Africa, motherhood is honored, especially among our women. It is seen as one of women's highest achievements. Consequently, across the entire continent, north, south, east, or west, *mother* is a title of great respect. So that after first giving birth, a woman will be given a new praise name registering this fact and conferring a new status. Hence, Mama Tiki, Mama Lamin, Mama Kwame. The woman becomes known in the community as mother of Tiki or Lamin's mother or Kwame's mother. For some time now our sister has been known all over the continent as Mama Africa. Miriam Makeba, Mama Africa, is not some press agent's invention. It is the name conferred on her by the masses, the common people. It is the name by which her people call her. Mama Africa, Mother of Africa. Seems just about right to me.

I think it was just about the start of my third week in Conakry. Mrs. Du Bois and I were finishing breakfast on the veranda of the hotel. We had been looking out to sea, the Atlantic, and talking about the slave trade. Had ancestors of ours crossed these very waters? Then, Mrs. Du Bois said, "That's an American embassy car approaching. Wonder what that means?"

We found out right quick when a Negro in a suit came up to our table and handed me a letter.

"Don't *touch* it, Stokely," Mrs. Du Bois said sharply. This turkey was there for me to "surrender" my passport. Say what? At the word *passport,* Mrs. Du Bois leapt up, shrieking. I mean, she was screaming now.

"No, Stokely, no. *Don't do it.* That's exactly what they did to Du Bois." Mrs. Du Bois just went off, Jack.

"I remind you, Mr. Carmichael, that this is an official government document, property of the United States."

"Yeah, yeah. And this is a free black country, *brother,* in case you hadn't noticed." Gimme uh break. Can you believe these people? But Mrs. Du Bois ran the dude off. I mean, she ran him off, bro. She lectured that Negro like she was his mammy. He actually seemed to slink away.

After Mrs. Du Bois reported the incident, President Touré gave me security. I think he may also have registered an official diplomatic protest. At the hotel the desk clerks were replaced by plainclothes policemen. First cops I ever liked. The officer on at night was an alert, politically inquiring brother. Obviously one of their more promising young officers. He spoke a little English. He came from a small village, loooooved Sékou Touré, and supported the revolution. Very bright, he was a bit younger than I and we became quite close. We talked serious politics and I came to like the young brother a lot. Years later, we'd meet again in ironic circumstances.

The embassy never tried again, so the worst result of the passport incident was to my private life. The security hampered my mobility. Didn't stop it, now. Just made it more difficult.

• • •

Yes, as a matter of fact, I do remember my first meeting with Sékou Touré. In fact, there's a picture of it. I always wanted to get that picture. Never did though. It was during the Congress. During my first week. A big event in the National Stadium. This was September/October so it could have been National Independence Day. Seventy thousand people, national dress, very festive.

Just as I was coming up the steps to enter the stadium, the copresidents arrived. President Nkrumah calls me over, presents me to President Touré. Touré shook my hand and places me between the two of them and we walk in together. Once we enter and the people saw the copresidents, a sound went up, Jack. You can't program, coerce, coach, rent, or buy that kind of massive sound. It *was* visceral, bro . . . spontaneous, intense, powerful. It made your hair stand up, Jack.

Once the pressures of the Congress were over, I was to have many meetings with the *Osageyfo* and a few with President Touré. My meetings with President Nkrumah were almost daily. I always, *always* learned something. We discussed many things: the coup in Ghana, his eventual return to power there, the African-American struggle, Pan-Africanism. Mistakes he'd made in Ghana. "The only people who never make mistakes are people who never try to do anything. The thing to do is to learn from your mistakes," he always said. Of course he was checking me out carefully. I knew that. Example? Okay.

Our third or fourth meeting. As I'm leaving, he casually hands me this manuscript. "See what you make of this." In the car I find it's the manuscript of his next book, *Handbook of Revolutionary Warfare*. I started reading in the car, all afternoon and through the night. I read it carefully too. Apart from my interest in its author, this was the first thing I'd seen in English in quite a while. Just reading my own language was a pleasure. I stayed up all night.

Next morning, he didn't mention the manuscript. So I thanked him for allowing me to read the book. Said how important I thought it was. He was gracious. Thanked me, and just brushed past it to discuss something else. I realized then that he thought I couldn't possibly have really read it yet. Thought maybe I'd skimmed through, y'know?

So soon as I saw an opportunity, I began to raise certain aspects of the book, particularly about the All-African People's Revolutionary Party. We began to discuss the book in a systematic way, step by step. I pulled out the manuscript and quoted from specific sections that I'd marked. And he saw that I not only had completed the book, but had read it seriously. I think this impressed him.

"But you must have been up all night. Aren't you tired?"

"Yes. But as a matter of fact, I'm enthusiastic, very energized, thanks to the energy you've given me. Because in this book, you solve certain theoretical organizing problems I've been wrestling with."

"Which ones?"

"The party. How and toward what objectives to organize a revolutionary party in the United States. And you've clearly outlined the objectives and process here for us."

"But for Africa, for Africans . . ."

"We are Africans, sir. How can you prohibit us from joining the party?" I said I'd be willing—honored—to devote a lot of time to working to establish at least the basis for organizing branches of the All-African People's Revolutionary Party in the Western Hemisphere. He was skeptical, saying the program was really addressed to the continent. He hadn't really been thinking of the diaspora as part of the party.

"Yes, sir," I said. "I understand that. But is it not you, yourself, who taught us and have written that it was Africans in the diaspora who gave birth to the concept of Pan-Africanism and who kept it alive?"

He laughed. "True. So?"

"Well"—I knew I had him then—"if we kept Pan-Africanism alive during the darkest days, through all the Congresses, now when our people take it to a higher level with a party, why should we be prevented from playing a role, however humble? Wouldn't that be a great historical injustice?" Then I played back everything we'd talked about concerning the interrelatedness of the black struggle. Long silence. He looked at me intently. Then he smiled.

"All right. I'll give you the permission/mission to begin organizing the basis for the All-African People's Revolutionary Party among our people in the diaspora." And so I have tried to do.

When I was first introduced to Guinea, I had no idea this country would become my home and base for over thirty years—until the end of my life. During my first few weeks there, I still thought I would make one more stop in Africa, then return to the United States.

That stop was Tanzania. At that time Tanzania, under the leadership of the *Mawlimo*, Dr. Julius Nyerere, was the only other remaining solid African base of support for the liberation struggle. No way was I about to return to the United States without going there. Just about every one of the liberation groups had offices and cadres, and some even bases of fighters, training in Tanzania.

I go in to say good-bye to President Nkrumah.

"Well," he said, "your plans . . . what will you now do?"

"Tanzania, sir. I'm exploring the possibility of joining one of the liberation groups, getting into the struggle there."

"Oh, oh. Very good. That should be useful for you. Instructive. However, I was thinking that perhaps you'd like to stay here and work with me . . . as my political secretary."

I froze. A loooong silence. So long, in fact, that he began to look at me as if to say, is something wrong? Something I said? It became awkward as I stood there speechless. In fact, I'd started—just managed to stop myself—from shouting, "Oh, wow, yes, sir. An honor." Why didn't I? 'Cause I caught myself. No, Jack, you can't have heard *that* one right. Start whooping and hollering accepting an offer that hasn't been made? Embarrass yourself and the *Osageyfo*? You'll look like another brash, self-important, and egotistic American fool to him. And he'll have the embarrassment of having to put me right. . . . I mean, who was I to be political secretary to the legendary Nkrumah? . . . So I caught myself. Then I had the presence of mind to say, "Sorry, sir, I didn't quite hear that." So he repeated it.

I had heard right.

[In this account, the young Carmichael appears merely greatly surprised by President Nkrumah's sudden invitation. An invitation behind which, I believe, it is possible to detect the fine, caring hand of the indefatigable Shirley Graham Du Bois. Also, according to legend, that of the venerable C. L. R. James.

How, or whether, the brother ever came to understand that presidential invitation any differently over the years, I cannot say. Another of the many questions I failed to ask. In retrospect, however, it seems a logical, even predictable event in a series of such events bespeaking a larger pattern of concern for young Carmichael's survival and development by a remarkable constellation of revolutionaries and radical intellectuals of an earlier generation.

Surely Fidel's extraordinary public appeal for Carmichael's protection to the assembled OLAS revolutionaries and Nkrumah's invitation to come work and study in Guinea indicate the elders' deep-seated, well-founded awareness of the dangers awaiting the young man in the America of those troubled times.

I recall that, at the time, the more paranoid among us—myself included—were convinced that, absent Nkrumah's invitation, the brother, in all likelihood, would not live to turn thirty. Subsequent published documents from the FBI's COINTELPRO files confirm that he was indeed targeted with extreme prejudice. So much for paranoia. But, in perhaps saving his life, the elders also defined it.

More to the point, I also recall that many of us felt that upon his return the brother was, in some subtle, indefinable, but very definite way, different. Not exactly changed, so far as his politics were concerned, but different in some profound, personal way.

It is now clear to me that he had been deeply affected by his travels. And particularly by his acceptance and adoption by these revolutionary elders. And that this, implying as it did formidable political responsibilities, would define the tra-jectory of the rest of his life. As it did.

Though he never says as much in this book, it seems clear to me that subse-quently his every major life decision was so as to keep faith with that duty from the elders. A matter of personal honor. —EMT]

But you know my mind was racing, Jack. I certainly hadn't expected anything like this. I knew that in a liberation movement I would learn a lot that I wanted to know. But by just being around and working closely with Nkrumah, I'd learn the African revolution, even if just by osmosis. So I accepted on the spot. Unconditionally. On the *spot,* Jack. I told him I had to go to Tanzania and return briefly to the States. But that I'd be back in a month or two at most and would be honored to serve him in whatever ways I could.

Many people have asked about that. You know, what about SNCC? About organizing D.C.? How come you didn't say, "Of course, sir, I'm honored. I'd love to do it. But I'm gonna need some time to consult my organization"? Fair question, but it's really two different questions. First of all, D.C. It was an internal colony with an African majority. It *needed* to be organized and I really wanted to do it. But wouldn't it have been the height of egotism to feel that I was the *only one* in SNCC or the country who could organize D.C.? Besides, right then, I may in fact have been the last person who *could.* I'd been getting the news from there. The way the press, the Congress, and the covertly sinister agencies had been having a field day denouncing me. I'd heard of the covert destabilization movement launched by these agencies, especially the FBI, and I expected to be jailed on some trumped up la-di-da on my return. So my association with the D.C. program might be a political liability—the kiss of death.

Number two, moving to Africa. Perhaps having been born in Trinidad, and having always followed the independence struggles in the Caribbean and Africa as much as the American struggle, I had a somewhat different perspective from many of my colleagues in the civil rights movement. I have never felt that America was *the only* or even the *primary* arena of our struggle. Less so after these travels. I had always thought the struggle was one. No righteous struggle anywhere in the African world was alien to me. I felt strongly that it was simply a matter of where and how at any given time one could make the greatest contribution. To spend some years struggling in Africa was in no way to be abandoning the movement in the States.

So far as consultation. Of course, I saw myself consulting SNCC. Maintaining close contact from Guinea, setting up a truly active rela-tionship, cross-fertilization between the struggles on either side of the Atlantic. Some of which did indeed go on. Besides, I couldn't really imagine anybody in SNCC objecting to one of us going to work closely with Kwame Nkrumah. Is you crazy? But . . . if they had? Hey, I'd have accepted any disciplinary action from any organization—expulsion, whatever—to be the political secretary to Kwame Nkrumah, you kidding?

But overall, I had no idea, then, of what would *actually* happen to the civil rights movement in America. I was so certain that the Black Power movement would inevitably grow stronger and clearer. That the relationship between Africans in America and the struggle on the continent could only grow closer and deeper. Consequently, I assumed my decision would only be a "change of location" within the same struggle, simple as that. But, as it turned out, I was only partly right in this.

Oh, the two presidents . . . been waiting for that. You have no idea how often I've been asked that. I get tired . . . I get asked that a lot, Jack. Very different men, bro, strikingly different personalities, some of it cultural. I'm talking background and experience here, you know, those formative experiences that condition how someone views and approaches the world? In those aspects, two Africans' stories could hardly be more different. And at times their initial . . . their *instinctive* . . . approaches to a situation or problem would be from radically different perspectives and references. But they would inevitably seem to end up at the same place.

Their personalities were very different, and yet on the important things? Their vision and ambition for Africa and commitment to black people worldwide? The selflessness of their devotion to the people's struggle, the personal sacrifices they made, their integrity? In these they were as one, Jack. Totally united, complete agreement. That was quite remarkable to see. So different and so identical at the same time. It was precisely as if each were a different—but necessary and complementary—part of the same being. Bring them together and they complete the whole. Sounds weird? Hey, I saw that time and time again.

Example. How's this? After those ignorant stooges deposed Nkrumah while he was in China, they *knew* they could not let him ever set foot back on Ghanaian soil. His mere presence, even under arrest—the British had tried that—they saw as a serious threat. Because they were convinced that the masses would rise up. *Which is why the plane landed in Conakry.*

Now, Sékou Touré was hot, Jack. His initial impulse was to march the Guinean army immediately into Ghana and restore the democratically elected president. But Nkrumah—here's the difference between them—prevailed on him not to.

Oh, a host of reasons, Jack. On that one I think Nkrumah may have been correct. First, the OAU (Organization of African Unity) and their hard policy against "aggression" against other states. Besides, the French stooges at the OAU were always trying to isolate Guinea as an exporter of revolution. And equally important, Nkrumah wanted to avoid unnecessary bloodshed among his people. When he returned, it would be because his own people brought him back. He wanted the masses to repudiate and humiliate the army stooges. Which, had he lived . . . I am convinced would have happened.

Even by their praise names you could tell what kind of men they were. Now we ain't talking no "nickname" here. Or those ostentatious titles some stunted African "leaders" give themselves, grandiose, pompous, meaningless. I'm talking about something different. A praise name is the descriptive name the people put on you, which reflects the popular perception of what you essentially are, what you are about. What defines your life. Your qualities and accomplishments, yes, but also your *spirit*. In their time, an African person will get many names. Not all of them necessarily flattering. But generally one will stick, come to dominate, to take over in the popular consensus. That's what I'm talking about.

For President Nkrumah, that was, of course, *Osageyfo,* literally the "redeemer of the nation," or more simply, in the street, the "redeemer." *Osageyfo.* It fits. Now, with President Touré, his most popular praise name, and the one I think he most identified with, translates as "the defender of the poor." That also fit. The people started calling him that during his days as a militantly effective labor leader, and it carried over perfectly to his policies and emphases as leader of the nation. Defender of the poor.

My name, Kwame Ture, is not a praise name in that sense. It's my legal name. Besides, I selected it myself. Sort of. I was discussing some theoretical strategic questions with Sékou Touré. On one question there was a difference of analysis between the copresidents, and I tended toward Nkrumah's position.

"On this one, sir, I think I'm with your copresident."

"No surprise. You're always taking the old man's side. I don't see why you don't just simply go on and take his name too?"

(We called President Nkrumah the old man. But in an African context, unlike in the West, this is an address of the highest respect.)

Since no name is meaningless in Africa, I knew that the suggestion was nowhere as simple as President Touré made it sound. It was accepted that Nkrumah had chosen me—for whatever reason—as a kind of political son, his own sons being at the time very young and with their mother in Egypt. During the coup, President Nasser (peace be unto him) had sent a plane to receive the family and bring them to safety in Egypt. However, President Touré's casual suggestion required a little diplomacy.

"You know I'd be honored to do that, sir. I will ask the owner of that great name. But, you know, sir, everyone in Conakry says that I have two [political] fathers. I know that if my name doesn't reflect that, people will not understand. They may even laugh at me, asking, 'Oh, so has his other father now disowned him?' You want me to be shamed in the street?"

He cracked up. "I see you've learned well." He understood precisely what I was saying.

Since that day my name has been Kwame Ture. I hope I've tried to live up to the responsibility it carries.

When I said there were significant differences in the *individual* backgrounds of the copresidents, I didn't mean just in nationality or national culture. There was much more to it, which few people understand.

Francis Kwame Nkrumah was born into a Christian family in a tiny rural village in colonial Ghana. He was not from a nationally dominant group like the Ashanti Kingdom or the Fanti Federation. His people were few in number and, in national terms, politically and culturally insignificant—a subgroup of, I think, the Ewe people. (The minority status of his people may well have affected Dr. Nkrumah's view of national authority so far as traditional rulers were concerned; his copresident's ancestral antecedents were just the opposite.)

Small and slightly built, the boy Nkrumah was inordinately intelligent and thoughtful. He thrived by his intellect. He shone in missionary school and, despite considerable economic difficulty, managed to complete secondary school with honors and get himself to America in search of higher education. He worked his way through a small black college in Pennsylvania called Lincoln University. He spent years learning American politics and experiencing the conditions and daily struggles of his African brothers and sisters in America.

Then his thirst for knowledge led him to London after World War II. There he did graduate study and associated himself with a vibrantly political group of African/Caribbean students and intellectuals. In the African student organization, for example, he would work with future leaders like Jomo "Burning Spear" Kenyatta (leader of Kenya's independence movement and its first president), the great Nnamdi "Zik" Azikiwe (leader of the Nigerian independence struggle), and many others. Also Nkrumah had worked with Pan-Africanist intellectuals George Padmore and Dr. Du Bois in planning the 1946 Pan-African Conference in Manchester. After which he returned to Ghana, organized the party that led the nation into independence in 1957 (he always called it "flag independence"), and set about the task of building a meaningfully independent modern nation.

Given his travels and associations, inclination and education, at least part of the *Osageyfo*'s constituency was the modern intellectual of the European left. He not only knew America and Europe firsthand, but his

Samory Touré—said to be grandfather of Sékou—had for eighteen years organized all three groups and led the stubborn, uncompromising *Guinean* resistance to French imperialism. To all Guineans, whether Sosso or Fulani, Samory was the symbol of national pride and courage, a national hero. To the French he was the embodiment of native recalcitrance and backwardness in his "ignorant" rejection of French "progress." Because of his leadership, "troublesome" Guinea had always been the least-favored West African colony of the French, a persistent thorn in their side.

More than that, people would tell me that Sékou, grandson of Samory, had come to power "sixty years to the day" after the death of his grandfather who had fought the French to a standstill for eighteen years. This coincidence had to be portentous. (The president himself never referred to Almamy Samory as more than his "ancestor.") But to the masses, Sékou was the reincarnation of the great patriot warrior, the fulfillment of prophecy—the completion of a circle of history. Almamy Samory Touré, returning in the person of his grandson to take the nation into the independence for which he had fought for eighteen years and given his life trying to preserve. The justice of history. (Hey, you can't beat that with a stick. Any American politician would kill for such a political pedigree. George Bush, the grandson of George Washington? *Whooie, murdah!*)

So you can see that for my two fathers, their birth circumstances/ancestral origins were crucial, and a major difference between them. One was born at the very center of national culture, politics, historical legend, and consciousness; the other, from a small, peripheral group outside the mainstream of national influence. But both ended up in the same identical revolutionary place in the contemporary histories of their nations. Another of history's imponderable ironies?

The next difference was in their formative experiences. Unlike Nkrumah, Sékou Touré would not live, work, and study for twelve years in the land of the *wazungu* (whites). He almost did as a young man, and why he did not is also instructive. Here is a story I heard on my first visit. Oral tradition again.

The sixteen-year-old Sékou Touré was also a brilliant student, effortlessly so. Head and shoulders the best in his class, he was on the fast track for a prized colonial government scholarship to a French university. Prime material—like Léopold Sédar Senghor before him—for evolution into that greatest accomplishment of French colonialism—the black Frenchman. But this was not to be. For one thing, this youth was neither appropriately humble nor properly grateful. Unlike the ascetic, supremely cerebral, and physically slight Nkrumah, young Sékou was physically robust, an athlete, and a charismatic and rebellious leader among his

political thought was informed by the intellectual currents and
courses prevalent on the left at that time. He was thoroughly
in the vocabulary of capitalism and imperialism and armed w
oretical approaches and analyses of nationalism, Pan-Afric
Marxism. As president, many of his advisers would be draw
Western political/intellectual world. Some kinsmen would say,
much so.

A story to illustrate: This concerns one of the more interes
of the period, the only traditional ruler in the first independen
Nana Kobina Nketsia IV, paramount chief of Segundi-Tagrat
nobility, a patriot and nationalist, was the only traditional lead
by the British during the agitation for independence. He also l
ter's degree from Oxford, where, as he liked to put it, he wa:
man in the history of Oxford University the subject of whose c
was himself." (An explication of the elaborate, yearlong c
sacred ritual, secular ceremony, and symbolic historical re
attendant to the investiture, in this case, his own, of a tradit
among the Fanti.)

So the chief was a "Western-educated" man, yet strongly i
Akan traditional belief and practice, and with impeccable natic
dentials in struggle. It is he who, after some differences with a
"expert," is said to have famously exploded in cabinet: "Mr.
must I remind you that, after all is said and done, Karl Marx
ancestor?"

Ahmed Sékou Touré, Defender of the Poor, on the other han
have a similar Western exposure. This brother was African to the
proud of it. I mean I cannot *ever* remember seeing him in a We

Born to Mandinka parents in the Guinean town of Faran
Touré was Muslim. The Mandinka, a powerful branch of th
speaking (Mandingo) peoples of the Western Sudan, are posse
proud military and political history and a major cultural for
temporary Guinean society.

Modern Guinea is entirely a creation of European colonial
ing. Historically it had been part of Greater Mali, the powerful
the Western Sudan founded in 1492 by Sundiata Keita, cultu
all the Mende-speaking peoples. Three powerful culture gr
Mandinka, the Sosso, and the Fulani, who had been united in I
coexisted in modern Guinea.

As a Mandinka, Sékou Touré could claim nominal descent
line of the legendary King Sundiata, the lawgiver and culture h
entire region, but moreover his own family name also resonated
ern Guinean history, through the figure of Almamy Samor

peers. In class one day he challenged the official colonial version of history (our ancestors the Gauls?). The subject was the Emperor Napoleon.

"Sir, please explain this," he challenged the headmaster. "You tell us that Napoleon, a soldier who usurped the state, is a noble figure, a great national hero. But we never hear about Sundiata Keita, whose empire was bigger, lasted longer, and was more humanely run than Napoleon's. How come so? And worse, my ancestor, Samory Touré, he who unified Guinea's people, defended our country and our culture, you always dismiss as a backward and bloodthirsty savage. Was my ancestor in your country attacking your women and children? To us, Napoleon is the savage, Almamy Samory a true national hero." *Oh, whoee,* sacrilege, Jack. (Of course these are not, can not be, the young brother's exact words, but these are the arguments attributed to him in the tradition.)

The stubborn youth would neither back down nor back off. Not only did he defend his position, but grew downright bellicose as the debate heated up. His fellow students got brave and supported their champion so that a mini-insurrection ensued in the classroom. The headmaster was not pleased. This was an assault on French (and his own) authority. Net result, a blackball. What had been a glowing recommendation for the scholarship to France became something else entirely. "Totally unsuitable" . . . "a malcontent, troublemaker" . . . "disrespectful" . . . "a potential subversive." "I do not advise . . ." Words to that effect. If the colonial authorities had anything to do with it, young Sékou would never set foot in a French university. Consequently no scholarship, no Paris, no Sorbonne. It is interesting to speculate what might have been the fate of the handsome, charismatic young African in postwar Paris. But as a result, after high school young Touré went to work as a labor organizer. The rest is history.

Labor organizing took him across the length and breadth of his country. Into every province, every small town, village, and culture. His knowledge and love of traditional culture, respect for local peoples, hatred for economic injustice and colonial condescension, all grew during this period. As did his legendary organizing skill and common touch. I suspect that this is where that fierce populism, the respect for "ordinary people like me" that had so impressed Mrs. Hamer, really began. As did that "SNCC-like" spirit that Harry Belafonte had detected in this grandson of Samory, the Defender of the Poor.

But as we have seen, character and the demands of history can brush aside almost polar differences in background, education, temperament and personal style to bring two men to the exact same place. When I met the copresidents, far, far more united than divided them. They were one in combativeness, an indomitable will to overcome all odds. In an unyielding devotion to Africa: in a shared vision and confidence in the continent's destiny. A faith in the ability and potential of the masses of our people. And most astounding, an incorruptible, impeccable personal rectitude and honesty. My two fathers may be—along with the sainted Nyerere— the only African heads of state in contemporary times who went to their ancestors much as they came into the world. That is, without leaving vast personal estates and Swiss bank accounts behind. At his death, Sékou Touré did not own even as much as a house in Conakry. That kind of personal integrity is almost unheard of in politicians anywhere, and especially, much to our sorrow, in modern Africa.

And most of all, both men cherished, projected, and exemplified for me an undying love for our people. *Undying love for the people. Undying love.* All the things I would learn from them, politics, ideology, revolution, how to organize, study, and prepare, were invaluable. But of all the things I learned from them, it is their *values* that most endure. The integrity of their example: the fearlessness, the selflessness, the incorruptibility, the undying love for our people. Give thanks. All honor. All respect. One love.

I left Conakry promising and expecting to return in about two months. In fact, it would be more than a year, almost two in fact, before that could happen, but I was always fully committed to returning.

Miriam had already left for a big concert in Kenya. We agreed to meet in New York, and I left about a week later for meetings in Tanzania and with the liberation groups. Before the *Osageyfo*'s invitation—in fact while I was still in Algeria—I'd written to every legitimate liberation organization to check out the possibility of serving with them. I really wanted to participate as a frontline fighter. But that was up to them. I was willing, I said, to serve in any way they felt my contribution would be most useful. Only one group replied. PAC (the Pan-African Congress of Azania) said, yes, they could accept fighters and would be willing to discuss it. A warm brotherly reply. So that's whom I sought out when I got to Tanzania.

The Dar es Salaam I saw was, at that point, a hotbed of international intrigues. It was a real trip, bro. At first, not understanding properly many of the things that were going on, I made many errors. At least one of which would come back to bite me. For years.

[Now this question I did ask, twice: So what was this error, bro? Somehow to discover on reviewing the tape that, instead of a direct answer, what we had was a detailed description of the "snake pit of international intrigue and left sectarianism" that was Dar circa 1967. A milieu in which he had naively trusted "the wrong people," probably sent in by the CIA, and had been set up. But of the error itself, not a word.

However, after consulting the collective memories of assorted members of the age set, I'm confident (99½ percent certain) that we've succeeded in identify-

ing the error to which Ture had referred. (The one with the legs and teeth.) We all recalled (however variously) widely circulated reports of a speech in Tanzania in which Stokely Carmichael had allegedly repudiated "Communism"/"Marxism"/"Socialism" as being "irrelevant"/"incompatible"/"unsuited"/"alien" to "black people"/"Africa"/"African liberation"/"African culture." Select one from each section or all of the above. That's the problem with collective memory.

What the actual sequence of words reported was (this varied from source to source), I cannot say. Even less so for the words the brother did indeed utter. We agree that this was the general gist.

I myself have a strong recollection of having first seen it on the front page of the New York Times. *This would be entirely consistent with James Reston's tantrum of a column from Havana, "Stokely is fooling Fidel," etc. However, I've not been able to retrieve the* Times's *Tanzanian story.*

In any event, some version of the above had been widely, even gleefully, reported in the U.S. media as Carmichael's sudden and shocking "repudiation of 'Communism'/'Socialism,'" which had excited a vigorous ideological counterattack from various factions of the African liberation struggle. Some had the temerity to suggest that this was a cynical, crudely vulgar attempt on Carmichael's part to weasel his way off Uncle Sam's "enemy list" before returning "home."

Well, whatever his actual language might have been, the one thing it manifestly was not was some craven recantation intended to appease the American government. That was the last thing on his mind or in his character. Gimme uh break. (I wanted to use that on my own.)

In fact, it is not at all difficult to reconstruct what most probably, almost certainly, had happened.

By that time Carmichael's position, one that he maintained to the end of his days, on Marxism-Leninism was pretty much established. An indispensable method for historical analysis, but also distressingly and constrictively Eurocentric as a perspective on social evolution. Consequently, to try to impose or dictate the adaptation of rigid Marxist dogma on non-European peoples, especially Africans, struggling for liberation, was itself a species of colonialism. Moreover, he was coming from Algeria and Guinea, from extended discussions of the African cultural socialist revolution at the Party Congress. A "Mr. President, Karl Marx is not our ancestor" ambience.

Therefore, it is not at all hard to imagine Carmichael, fresh from long discussions with Nkrumah and Touré, leaping into heated ideological dispute, particularly with the notoriously doctrinaire, lockstep Marxists from the Soviet client groups from southern Africa (the ANC of South Africa and the MPLA of Angola). And, once engaged, uttering whatever it was he did say that enabled his ideological opponents (and the U.S. media) to discredit his revolutionary sincerity.

"It's the kind of thing any nationalist might have said," reflected Olombe

Brath, dean of the Harlem nationalists. "And we don't know what he said, only what they reported. The real problem was the timing. How those reports would be received in Havana after Fidel had just got done defending Black Power against charges of racism and personally pledged to defend the brother. That was the problem."

Indeed, Castro is reported to have been deeply disappointed, indeed to have felt personally and publicly betrayed. And, of course, as we shall see, the CIA was quick to exploit the opportunity to try to discredit Carmichael on the international left. Since it is impossible to imagine another "error" in Tanzania as consequential as this one, I can only assume that this is the one to which Ture was referring on the tape. —EMT]

At this point, two-thirds of the continent was by now at least nominally independent. "Flag" independence. And in the rest, the imperialists were desperately digging their heels in, trying to stop history. So liberation had to become a question of armed struggle, protracted people's wars. These were the hard-core imperialist racists: the fascist Portuguese dictatorships in Angola, Mozambique, and Guinea-Bissau (a close neighbor of Sékou Touré's Guinea), and of course the white settler colonies of South Africa, South-West Africa (Namibia), and Rhodesia (Zimbabwe)—all were arming, digging in, and waging war against their black populations.

The Tanzanian government and people were just heroic, very principled and generous. They extended recognition, shelter, and as Tanzanian means permitted, material support to all liberation forces, across the board. At great sacrifice, too, because this meant that the country was frequently bombed, infiltrated by terrorists, and even militarily attacked on many occasions. This is one reason President Nyerere is so widely and deservedly beloved all over Africa. Of course, the government was careful not to discriminate between the rival claims to "legitimacy" of the various groups, regardless of their origins and sponsors. And this would prove a major problem for me.

In some places the nationalist movement had divided naturally along unavoidable doctrinal lines. Example, in South Africa: PAC had spun off from the older ANC on the question of militant direct action and later armed struggle. Unfortunate but understandable, almost SNCC and the NAACP in a different context.

In other places unfortunately—Angola and Mozambique—the independence movements had been infiltrated, manipulated, in some cases bribed, and split into factions by foreign interests usually imperialist if not always capitalist. The competing factions would be recognized, armed, funded, and "advised"/manipulated by these foreign sponsors, good ol' Uncle Sam among them. Where there had been a single independence movement, you now found two or three factions often and unfortunately divided along tribal lines. At first the sponsors would be of the Socialist Bloc, sometimes the Soviets, occasionally the Chinese. But later sometimes you'd even discover a group being funded by the CIA and the KGB simultaneously. Talk about a mess, boy.

So in Dar you found offices and political operatives representing *all* these formations. Must have been, I'd say, anywhere from ten to seventeen different organizations at any given time. Each with its spokesman, ideology, armed wings, and of course, foreign sponsor. Talk about clientelism. Most had honest leaders committed to struggle, but it was a situation ripe for corruption, and unfortunately a few hustlers, poseurs, and charlatans were to be found among the leadership ranks. It happens in struggle and these figures do great harm.

One or a couple of groups were paper organizations, flat-out charades, scams, criminal enterprises only out to "chop money" at the expense of their people's liberation. This, to me, is about the basest, the lowest, the foulest corruption to which a human being can sink. Pimping your people's freedom. A special place in hell for them. And even to this day, Africa is still paying a fearsome price. Jonas (at different times client of China, the Afrikaners, the Rhodesian Special Forces, the U.S. government, and the darling of the right-wing Reagan Republicans) Savimbi's nasty tribalist, genocidal, racketeering little war is still torturing the Angolan people. To this very day *[1998 —EMT]*.

Then, as I discovered, the various group representatives were only the tip of the iceberg in the tower of political Babel that was Dar circa 1967. Because, very much present, if not always visible, in this chaotic political mix were the various clandestine espionage agencies of the foreign sponsors. The city was a veritable snake pit of intrigue, deceit, betrayal, and corruption compounded or engineered by the agents of these countries. I mean Uncle Sam's CIA spooks, inept as ever but with very deep pockets; BOSS (Bureau of State Security of the apartheid racists); Portuguese military intelligence; Israel's Mossad (what was their interest?); the Rhodesian Special Forces; and the KGB all made their not-so-hidden presence felt. I also heard that Cuban intelligence had a presence there. There were almost certainly others; I can't imagine that the MI5 of a fading Brutish Empire, America's Cold War running dog, wasn't also present and active. What an ever-loving mess I walked into. It wasn't that I hadn't known all this stuff *theoretically.* But the *reality* on the ground, that was something else, Jack.

Now, I'm not arguing equivalence here. Clearly the interests and motives of the Soviets, Chinese, or Cubans cannot be equated with those of the South African racists, the Portuguese fascists, the Rhodesian settler colonists, or the Americans. But the Socialist Bloc was not disinterested either: its Cold War foreign policy objectives were primarily self-serving, and the interests those countries advanced, while assuredly far more compatible, were not at all always identical to the interests of the African people either. In many cases, the Socialist Bloc were the lesser of the evils. And Africa is still paying the price for that.

I must say here, however, that most people in Dar felt that the Cubans—who had a large and active embassy there—tended to be honest, genuinely revolutionary, and free from any narrow, nationalist self-interest in Africa. Of course, they, themselves, were susceptible to pressures and influence from the Soviets, but the *compañeros* had the reputation of being decent and keeping their word. Some years later, the Cubans, at the invitation of the threatened Angolan government, would gallantly stop the arrogant South African military cold at the battle of Cuíto Cuanvale, when the Boers with CIA support invaded Angola. The Cuban revolutionary army completely outmaneuvered, outthought, and outfought the South African invaders. A crushing defeat for the Afrikaners. Africans have a lot to thank the Cubans for.

In my experience, in Dar people and things were not necessarily who or what they seemed. One of those you-can't-tell-the-players-without-a-scorecard situations. And those weren't hard to come by, but no two scorecards were ever the same. I mean, from the moment I got there all kinds of folk are in my face. Some I now know to have been sent by the CIA. Each running a strong revolutionary line and professing *devoutly* to agree with my positions so as to win my confidence, and of course, so I'd more readily accept whatever they had to say. Each volunteered an orientation. "Here's what's *really* going down, brother. Lemme pull your coat." Then they'd run it all down for me, a detailed picture of the entire scene. Characterizing and identifying the players, the interests, the histories and tendencies of the various groups. Very considerate, very complete.

Of course, after a while I peeped the game. They were there either to recruit me or at least to totally influence and even dictate *all* my subsequent perceptions of whatever I might see or whomever I might meet. And of course, what I would say publicly. It was an effort to program me. Clever, which is why they all tried to get to me early. By the time I recognized it, I'd already made a few errors. But I do learn quickly. (This is a common and effective ploy that I would see again in Guinea. It was the stock-in-trade of the propaganda arm of the U.S. embassy in Conakry. Soon as a group, visiting journalists, students, observers, or whoever came in, there was the obligatory "official briefing" almost before they got off the plane. After which, Jack, forget it. Everything they saw, heard, or thought they understood about the society was already colored, determined, and distorted by official government disinformation.)

The only relief from this unceasing intrigue and deviousness that I found there was with the young cadres of PAC (Pan African Congress). I never saw them indulge in crude factionalism. Never heard them denounce even the rival ANC (African National Congress). In fact, PAC cadre were always careful to honor and acclaim the ANC leaders Mandela, Tambo, Chief Luthuli, as ancestors in struggle, patriots, and honorable fighters for black people with whom they happened to have a few principled differences. But they were not the enemy. They were allies. The PAC were disciplined, clear on their positions, but never dogmatic in trying to impose them. They would struggle fiercely over ideas, but never attack the character or motives of the other group. Mature. Very principled. This was refreshing.

I came to attribute much of this to the leadership and example of a remarkable Zulu couple, David and Elizabeth Sebako. The couple had obviously made a lot of sacrifices for the struggle, and their commitment was total, but very healthy. David Maphumza Sebako (Baby Elephant) was the PAC head of mission in Tanzania. He had been the only one to reply—a warm, brotherly reply—to my letter. He was young, intelligent, shrewd, and a fighter. Clear, uncompromising, with his love and commitment to our people evident in everything he said and did. And over the years I knew him, he was always, *always* principled. In the late seventies the Sebakos moved to New York, where David was the PAC representative in the United States. He was an extraordinarily effective representative of his people's struggle against apartheid. He organized massive consciousness in Afro-American communities across the nation, and "Bro Phunzi" is widely respected and beloved among our people in America.

In Tanzania this couple impressed me greatly. Africa needs more leaders like these, I thought. When, some years later—I think 1979—I learned that this bighearted, able brother had been shot down, ironically, by one of his own, I was deeply, deeply saddened. (According to the grapevine, the killer was either deranged or an agent.) The same feeling of loss I felt when I heard that another most excellent brother, Walter Rodney, had been killed in an explosion in Guinea.

The David Sebako I knew was a truly noble and effective brother, a patriot who made an enduring contribution to his country's freedom struggle. I hope the ruling party there will find the generosity and decency to acknowledge that in some appropriate public way. It would be to their enduring credit to do this. While they are about it, they should also take the opportunity to officially recognize the contributions of Mangaleso Robert Sobukwe (PAC leader) and Bantu Steve Biko (of the Black Consciousness movement), both of whom died in apartheid jails. It is only right. It also is what David Sebako would have done, were the positions reversed.

Another thing about PAC: they were young and daring. They were also deeply involved with the Black Consciousness movement emerging among African youth in the townships at home. Since the Black Consciousness movement was almost identical—in its analysis, goals, perspectives, and rhetoric—with the Black Power movement in the States, we had firm common ground there. So it was a natural alliance.

The Sebakos were welcoming, warm, and friendly and invited me to stay with them. We became close. One day I heard excited chatter and laughter in the office. I walked in and there's Zenzi, all happy to be among her country folk.

"Whoa, lady, what you doing here?"

"I didn't expect to see you either."

Turns out, Tanzania had been the first country to issue Miriam a passport when the illegal Boer regime had made her a stateless refugee, so whenever she was anywhere close, she always made a point of stopping into her "second home" to pay respects. She had impulsively decided to take a short holiday in Dar. We had a good time. Most nights, brothers and sisters from her homeland or neighboring Zambia and Zimbabwe would gather to cook, sing songs, and dance. We'd eat, sing, and hang out. No factionalism, no sectarianism. Nothing but goodwill. A reunion of young frontline African freedom fighters grounding with each other and their culture. Zenzi had that unifying effect. Those few days remain my fondest memory of Dar es Salaam. By the time she had to leave again, we had become a solid couple.

Before I left Tanzania, the news came that Huey P. Newton had been wounded in a shoot-out in Oakland, California, in which a white police officer had been killed. Ever since my trip to California in 1966, to try to straighten out the Black Panther name squabble, I'd been in intermittent communication with Huey and Bobby. But, of course, not during my travels. I was sorry to see this thoughtful young brother wounded and in jail. But I can't say I was really surprised. I spoke at a "Free Huey" demonstration in Tanzania before I left.

At this point, I decided that I'd seen all I needed to see in Africa at this time. It was time to go back to the United States, face the authorities, see my mom, tie up loose ends, and prepare to take up President Nkrumah's offer. I figured I'd spend at least two years studying with *Osageyfo* in Guinea. With that in mind, I headed back to "God's own country."

CHAPTER XXVI

In That Ol' Brier Patch

Come let us labor mightily in the vineyards of the Lord,
For behold the harvest is great, though the workers are few.

Guess ol' McRufty, McClusky, or whatever his name, was real determined to have that passport. I handed my documents to the immigration officer and had to struggle to keep from laughing out loud. From his expression you'd have thought a rattlesnake had popped its head up out of the passport and gritted on him. I didn't see him do anything, but he sure must have. In seconds, Jack, I'm surrounded by suits and uniforms. They were polite, I was polite.

(Good cop) "Mr. Carmichael, would you kindly step this way, please?"

"Why? Gentlemen, am I under arrest?"

"Arrest? Oh, no. At present we merely wish to talk with you."

"In that case, gentlemen, I'm sorry. That is really not convenient."

"Sir, I don't think you understand . . ."

"No, no, sir. *You* don't understand. I haven't seen my family in a while. I really do have to be going. My documents, please."

"I'm afraid that will not be possible, Mr. Carmichael." (Some legal mumbo jumbo, section this, number that.)

"Hey, let's be clear now. Let the record show I ain't 'surrendering' nothing. You're arresting my passport over my strong protest. And we both know that is illegal. Any further conversation will have to be with my lawyers. *Gentlemen.*"

(Bad cop, sneering) "Guess you won't be doing any more foreign travel anytime soon, huh?"

I just grinned at him. "Looks that way, mah man. Funny though, Britain trying to keep me out, France trying to keep me out . . . Y'all want me in. Thank y'all most kindly. Guess you want me here doing my work, eh?"

After Africa, the city I'd grown up in looked and felt foreign to me. Familiar yet strange. Like a place I was seeing for the first time. Noisy, mechanical, cold, impersonal, alienating. Everything seemed exaggerated.

But it was great seeing my family. Of course May Charles cried. Later I learned that the FBI had really been harassing her. Sending in strange Negroes whose names I didn't recognize, all claiming to be "friends of Stokely's." Probing for information. "Heard from Stokely? Where he going next?" Cars in front of the house. That kind of nonsense. I didn't like them annoying my mother. But May Charles was unfazed. "Hey, I tell people, now I don't even have to lock up when I go out. J. Edgar Hoover is watching my house, honey."

I had another reason for flying in to New York. Zenzi was based there. She had a long-standing regular gig at the Village Gate when she wasn't touring. She had returned to the city a couple of weeks before I did. In Tanzania, I'd asked her to bring back some letters and a package for May Charles. Of course my family was amazed to hear her voice on the phone when she called to arrange delivery. Even more so when she arrived in person and proved so warm and unaffected. But, I suppose, by then nothing I did really surprised the Carmichael women.

I didn't have time to worry about the government's little games. I mean, what was this passport seizure supposed to do? Intimidate me? Demonstrate their power and control over me? American *baaskap*? What? All it meant was that I wouldn't be returning to Guinea as quickly as I had planned, that's all. Hey, I had plenty to occupy me in America. Until the passport situation was resolved with the lawyers, I'd just keep on working. It was an "Oh, please, Bro Bear, don't throw me into that ol' brier patch" situation all over again. Nkrumah always said, "A revolutionary makes a positive out of a negative." That's what I'd do. Go to D.C., push the United Front, for which we'd been laying the foundation. Also I'd start talking up and building the bases for the All-African People's Revolutionary Party in the United States. I'd reestablish as heavy a speaking schedule as I'd had as SNCC chairman. Only now I'd connect Black Power more to the Pan-African struggle, specifically the movement against apartheid in South Africa and the efforts to return Nkrumah to Ghana in triumph.

So that's what I presented to the SNCC exec and everyone was cool with it. For the present, I said nothing publicly about the *Osageyfo*'s invitation. Why? Look, I'd been dead serious about what I'd said about slavery, about never again allowing whites to dictate where and when I could travel. No way. But still, the easiest thing to do was to liberate the American passport. If they insisted on impounding it, I knew I had other ways to go anywhere I needed to, but those options would be more complicated. I wanted the passport back, both as a practical matter and as a matter of principle. But I figured, petty and childish as the government had shown itself to be, the less it knew of my plans the better. If they knew of my intention to take up the Nkrumah offer, the harder they'd probably try to hold on to the passport, so why give them that added incentive? And if I was really effective in my work, it would sooner or later occur even to them, hey, is it really in our interest to prevent this nappy-headed black militant from traveling? Maybe he less of a problem for us *outside* the country. So, we'd see. Because, I had every intention of being effective. The other thing, of course, was I could use the time with the new lady in my life. Zenzi and I picked up right where we'd left off in Tanzania.

"Dang, bro, that must have been some short speech, huh? You mean it's really been *two weeks* already? Seems like you just left. You must not have liked London, huh?" Lester McKimmie's (Baba Zulu) sarcasm may have been heavy-handed, but he and the D.C. staff had been working. Quietly cultivating the need for greater communication and cooperation in the D.C. community. We discussed what my role was to be. Whether or how the media attacks on my "disloyalty" might affect my reception with the other organizations. Hey, bro, you just another SNCC field secretary now. Only way to find out, full speed ahead. So we went forward.

I hadn't been in D.C. a week when Bobby Seale or Eldridge Cleaver, whom I'd met when he traveled with me for the *Ramparts* story, called up. Hey, well, at least one organization wasn't put off by my hostile press. Turns out the Panthers were becoming even more of a media pariah than I was. They were trying to mobilize a national campaign around Huey's trial, would I help? According to them, none of the other civil rights organizations would touch the issue. So they were approaching SNCC. Well, what kind of help? Could I make some Free Huey speaking appearances?

I told them I'd be willing, personally. But I'm just another field secretary now. You gotta clear it with the SNCC leadership. That's when discussions between SNCC Atlanta and the Panthers began. But I was in D.C. and I wasn't privy to those discussions. To this day I have no idea exactly what was discussed, between whom or to what result. I'd actually thought the discussions were only about SNCC support for the Free Huey campaign.

It had to be months later—I believe in a phone call from Jim Forman— that I learned more. I was as surprised as everyone else to hear that a "merger" or an "association" was being formed between SNCC and the Black Panther Party. And that the Panthers had "drafted" three of us from SNCC. Forman to be minister of foreign affairs, Rap to be minister of justice, and I to be prime minister. That is, of course, if I accepted. Hot dang, a *cabinet* position at twenty-six?

I really can't tell you anything more useful about those discussions.

But you can probably figure out my own feelings by the fact that I insisted absolutely, as a condition of acceptance, on the insertion of the word *honorary* before *prime minister.*

I'd left for the London conference at the beginning of June and this was now what, December? I'd been gone six months, but now that I was back in harness with the brothers and sisters in D.C., it felt as if I'd never left. Funny, while I was traveling, what with everywhere I'd been and everything I'd seen, it had seemed like a lifetime. America had receded, seemed distant, even a little unreal. Yet now that I was back, the trip seemed very short, indeed a matter of weeks, a month at most. Being back among the brothers and sisters felt real good. It confirmed my feeling. Our struggle is one. Struggle here, struggle on the continent, the location didn't really matter. I knew I would always go wherever the struggle sent me.

We figured the work on the United Front was as ready as it was going to be. SNCC sent out invitations to one hundred black organizations in the District. We invited *evrahbody,* from the NAACP, Urban League, CORE, SCLC, the Nation, to small community organizations, the Masons, social organizations, the Greeks, local youth groups, everybody and their momma. We followed up with phone calls.

A preliminary discussion, a family meeting. No media. Please do not involve the press. There's nothing we need to be announcing at this time. Yes, Carmichael would be present. In fact, he would be moderating. Far as I could tell, everyone, well, *almost* everyone, we invited maintained complete media silence. And just about every organization sent a representative. Of course, you can't really expect to keep a meeting of this size and significance entirely secret. Soon the *Washington Post,* the afternoon paper, the *Star,* and the *Baltimore Afro-American* were on the phone. We were polite, but wouldn't even confirm the time and place. Or even that there was to be a meeting. "Soon as there's something to report, promise you, you'll be the first to know. Bye."

May have been the wrong tactic. Hey, you know them. *What,* the Negroes are meeting and they *don't* want us present? Carmichael *and* the NAACP? What d'you mean only rumors? Something's definitely up. Find out what. That's why we hired you. Use those "sources" you brag about. If something serious is up among the Negroes in this city, we expect to know.

The white media would be seriously deflated to discover how little credibility or effect they actually have with us. In fact, the reverse. Here they had been seriously demonizing me for the past six months. Here they'd been calling me everything but a child o' God, and the meeting was full, Jack. I mean *full.* I know some folk came because they knew me. But a lot more came because they felt instinctively that anyone the media hated so much had to be doing something right. The Malcolm effect. And still others came simply to see the devil the media had created, One sister came up to me with a big grin and asked, "Bro Carmichael, I just have to know, what you do with them horns? And do you got a tail?"

Our first meeting, at the New School for African American Thought, was just beautiful, very spirited. I was proud of our people. The spirit and tone of the meeting was just splendid. I spoke for SNCC. What I proposed was quite simple. The gathering represented the black organizations in the District. But their combined memberships were a mere fraction of our people's number. I proposed initially a collective campaign to broaden that base. We'd send organizers into every African community urging people to get involved in one or more organization, their choice. The first step.

Then we'd continue to meet and talk about follow-up programs. To that end, the first order of business would be to select a steering committee from among ourselves, and to constitute the Black United Front of Washington, D.C. The steering committee would meet regularly, call meetings of the group as necessary, and work out the details and implementation of programs. It was experimental; we'd have to feel our way. But our people would be organized.

From the first, I was getting *ahmen*s and nods of approval. I stressed voluntary association, democratic procedures, tolerance of differences, mutual respect, organizational freedom to participate in some programs and abstain from others without any public criticism. I urged everyone to pledge not to discuss the Front with the media at that time. And above all, constant communication and no public attacks on each other.

The response was enthusiastic. When I opened up the discussion, people were serious and seemed genuinely committed to making the thing work. Agreed with the need to thoroughly organize the city. With a massive attempt to enroll every black Washingtonian in one or another activist or civic organization. The steering committee—a good, representative one—was elected. The committee scheduled its first meeting within a week. I took it as a good sign that the first committee meeting was to be in the offices of Sterling Tucker of the Washington Urban League.

What I remember was a great spirit of unity and real excitement. Yeah, we can do this. We need to do this. Let's git together and get it on, Jack. Folks got right down to work. They came up with an excellent committee. All the major organizations, activist leadership across the board, ghetto grass roots as well as the bourgeoisie. Many were people I'd worked with. Mrs. Willie Hardy, a tough, respected community leader. Marion Barry (formerly of SNCC), who had a powerful youth group, Pride, Inc. Julius Hobson (CORE), who had schooled us in direct action when I was at Howard. My favorite philosophy professor from Howard, David Eaton;

Nathan Hare, a sociologist who'd been fired from Howard for militant activism; the Reverend Mr. Fauntroy, SCLC Washington representative and a member of the City Council; the Reverend Channing Phillips, who'd given the MFDP use of his church and had set up the nonprofit Housing Development Corps; Chuck Stone, who'd been editor of the Afro-American newspaper and Adam Powell's press representative; and other leading clerics. All activist, all serious.

Yeah. I was enthusiastic. I began to have visions of every D.C. community being as organized as those in Guinea. All our people, registered and voting. Their leaders in constant communication, talking and cooperating. Not easy, but certainly possible. I still ask, why not? Two things to which I didn't pay enough attention at the time, I guess.

The only missing invitee had been the Reverend E. Franklin Jackson, the Democratic National committeeman. And the only nominee to the steering committee who declined to serve was the local NAACP chairman, H. Carl Moultrie. Was that accidental? I dismissed it as their usual establishment caution. Once the idea took off, they'd be happy enough to scramble aboard. Of that I was certain. The *Washington Post* report of the first meeting I remember as tentative, and predictable; funny but not unfair. Funny and tentative because for once the Negroes weren't talking. So there was a lot of "It is thought that," "the membership is apparently," etc., etc. Clearly the brothers and sisters were honoring the pledge of silence. And those who spoke were careful to stress the unity and harmony. Predictable because of the ominous tone of the questions. Why a "closed" meeting? What did it mean that no whites were present? Why would "the radical Carmichael" call together "militants and moderates"? Middle-class Negroes and street people? One informant—the only one—identified as a moderate, hastened to point out that "Carmichael made it clear that he was not intending to organize an anti-white coalition." As I recall that question never even arose in the meeting. As indeed, why should it have? The story ended up grumbling that most people attending would not talk with the media, neither to confirm or deny what had gone down.

[Actually, the language of that paragraph was more favorable! To wit: "The unity that came out of the meeting was manifested in the reluctance of most of those attending to discuss in any way what had happened." The Post *also quoted Carmichael as refusing to say more than "it was a beautiful meeting. You'd have been proud of black people. We were really together." One participant was quoted as saying, "Stokely was very good. Very receptive to various points of view. There was general agreement that he handled the meeting very well." Another said, "The moderates were pleased to discover that Carmichael was (sic) a human being." No kidding? —EMT]*

•   •   •

The general media tone—relatively benign, stressing community unity and harmony—was not to last the week. Before the first steering committee meeting can take place, Bro Whitney Young of the National Urban League breezes into town and gives the media the red meat for which they had been slavering. Young attacks my role and motives. Suddenly I'm again a lightning rod and the hounds are off and running.

[Next day, the Washington Post *informed the city, "NEGRO COALITION LEADERSHIP RIFT BREWS." "A leadership tug-of-war between moderates and radicals began emerging . . . indications are that the chairmanship of the Steering Committee . . . would rotate, probably every two months. . . . However, Stokely Carmichael . . . was reportedly in line to be named first chairman."*

A second banner headline in the same paragraph read: "D.C. NEGRO LEADERS WORK TO MAINTAIN UNEASY COALITION." This story said that a steering committee of "moderates and radicals" would meet to "set goals for their black united front." That while "Black Power and anti–Vietnam War rhetoric had been kept to a minimum by Carmichael," the "moderates present felt that Carmichael was making a special conciliatory effort to keep them within the unity structure" and that, in the words of another moderate, "Stokely seems to want a bridge back to respectability in order to enable him to acquire a broad enough base to operate" and that "the moderates only felt they had to cooperate" because of "the Black Power people. We did not want them alone to carry the banner of Negro unity."

The story said, "Whitney Young, Executive Director of the National Urban League, was in Washington yesterday.

" 'If Stokely wants to run this, we won't hold still for it,' Young said. 'If he is trying to establish himself as a leader of leaders, we won't go for it.' " —EMT]

So now suddenly there is public division. Sad and unnecessary. Why? When I met Bro Young in Memphis before the Meredith March, I'd felt that he'd been relatively reasonable, at least compared to Bro Wilkins. Young was no neophyte. He certainly understood how the game is played. So why this? Of all the things he could have said—No comment, it's too early . . . Not privy to the discussions . . . We are watching developments with interest . . . Guarded optimism . . . We support anything that might help unify our people . . . etc., etc. He knew the game. So why come all the way to D.C. to sow confusion among our people?

[The Post *then quoted Lester McKimmie as saying, "SNCC is disturbed over the statement issued by our brother, Whitney Young. . . . We feel that it is essential at this time for our people to be united on every level, from the masses to the black bourgeoisie . . . a united front is one of the ways to begin the hard and long task of organizing our people."*

SNCC concluded, "Brother Whitney Young is flesh of our flesh and blood of our blood. We continue to see him as a brother. We pay tribute to the work his

organization has done and is still doing. . . . Any member of SNCC would be happy to serve on any committee of which our brother Whitney is chairman."
—EMT]

We tried to keep it clean. Disciplined and noninflammatory. But the tone of harmony had been disrupted. Unfortunately, Bro Young's snipe was not to be the last of the disruptive ploys. It was immediately followed by an alarmist, transparently dishonest media offensive begun by two white reporters preying on white anxieties. These two syndicated hacks were the same running dogs who, before the Summer Project in 1964, had accused Bob Moses and SNCC of cynically and deliberately trying to engineer the murder of innocent white students so as to create movement martyrs. This time what they came up with was even more stupid and vicious. This time I was the whipping boy. But to understand it we have to back up a few months, to when I first got back to D.C.

Just about the time I arrived back, Dr. King and SCLC had announced plans for a Poor People's Campaign. SCLC intended to round up a representative group, some five hundred or so, of the nation's poor. Africans, Native Americans, whites, Hispanics, evrahbody, and bring them to Washington to talk to the emperor about the plight of America's poor. The plan was to dramatize economic suffering in the country and demand a genuine war on poverty. A war at least as vigorous as the one being waged against Vietnamese peasants who'd done this country no harm.

I—and SNCC—felt that the issue was precisely the right one. In fact, Dr. King was adopting elements of SNCC's approach. He had probably learned something from the way the local Mississippi people had *made* the Meredith March work. The new plan was dramatic: five hundred poor people would camp out in the capital of the richest society in the world. In spirit, the project looked very SNCC-like and we wished it well.

We had only two reservations, organizational as well as tactical. Could the much smaller SCLC staff, whose strength was in mobilizing massive, relatively brief, hit-and-run, direct-action campaigns, sustain the level of detailed, coordinated *organizing* this project demanded? Organizing the housing, the health care, the feeding, the educational programs, the child care, and daily lobbying? How long could they sustain all that? In the event, the SCLC staff did a good job establishing their village.

And, tactical? Well, assuming they succeeded in establishing their village and putting the case dramatically to the White House and Congress and before the nation and the world, what would happen if, as we feared, LBJ and the Congress simply stonewalled them, how would they then get their people out? They sure couldn't just pack up their tents and slink away without something tangible from the government, some claim to victory, no matter how slight.

And without that, how long could they hope to maintain morale among all those poor folk crowded together in a makeshift camp? To us, the demands seemed vague and much too general. The people could be stuck there for months. That is if, in fact, the establishment would even tolerate their unsightly and embarrassing presence in the middle of the nation's capital for that long.

Naturally, the press evoked the Bonus Marches of 1920. Hundreds of starving veterans had pitched camp in Washington demanding the "bonus" promised them by "a grateful nation" when they were being urged to enlist to go fight the kaiser. You remember how that ended, don't you? Troops commanded by an ambitious young officer, the cryptofascist Douglas MacArthur, demolished the camp and busted the heads and limbs of their former comrades-in-arms. And those American veterans were *white* men, Jack, albeit poor white men.

It concerned us, the real possibility of a serious tactical error on SCLC's part. Precisely the right issue, but a potentially flawed tactic. But of course we wouldn't publicly criticize SCLC on this.

But then the white media got involved, preying, as is their wont, on white fears. Also, I suspect, hoping to discourage Dr. King by alienating his white supporters. Dr. King, they condescended, undoubtedly meant well but this was dangerous and unwise. American cities had recently been racked by "riots incited by black militants." When this campaign bogged down, as it must, wouldn't local black militants and angry ghetto youth create chaos and violence in the very shadow of the White House? The angry black mood, the long, hot summer, etc., etc., etc. Besides, hadn't that "firebrand" Carmichael recently relocated to D.C.? Hadn't his colleague H. Rap Brown "incited" a riot in Cambridge, Maryland? You get the drift. Put two and two together and get six. This racial fear-mongering always works largely, if not only, because of white guilt and ignorance. Also, in this case, because the American political classes are notoriously gutless. Remember how Congress had fled Washington and called out the army, air force, and marines at the fearsome prospect of a nonviolent march back in 1963? *[Recall also the congressional courage so prominently on display during the anthrax scare of a few years ago? —EMT]*

When Dr. King came into D.C., I went to see him. Of course, I assured him that I and SNCC would never do anything to embarrass him or jeopardize the campaign. He said, "Stokely, you don't need to tell me that. I know you." I told him that Washington SNCC would organize the local community—the street people and youth gangs—to make sure they were cool. He said he'd appreciate that. I remember that he had seemed, even for him, unusually tense and stressed. As I was leaving, he held on to my hand, looking worried. "Stokely, please be extra careful, now. Avoid any unnecessary risks. Promise me." I recall laughing and saying something about being accustomed to danger, that it wouldn't feel normal without it. But Dr. King repeated his warning. He seemed unusually somber to me. Very soon I'd have reason to remember his mood at our last meeting.

SNCC issued a statement saying we understood the necessity for the Poor People's Campaign and strongly supported its goals. We publicly pledged to Dr. King our support in keeping the peace. That was to take at least some of the pressure off Dr. King by undercutting the hysteria the press was trying to generate amongst local white folk. It seemed to work for a while; at least it cooled out the talk about the black militant threat. Until, that is, the United Front meeting from which the media had been excluded. Then the alarm was ratcheted up again. Clearly, the initial reports of unity, harmony, and secrecy in the African community must have alarmed someone.

Suddenly the media revives the old line about the danger to the Poor People's Campaign posed by Carmichael and local "black militants." Presumably we militants, directed, no doubt, by the Kremlin, would lead an army of ghetto youth and Dr. King's poor folk in razing the nation's capital. Course, had they indeed sent in troops to brutalize the poor folk, there's no telling how the D.C. black community might have reacted. But talk about fear-mongering. C'mon, gimme a break. The idea was so patently unreal and stupid it could only have originated with FBI disinformation—the conduits being the same two syndicated whores who'd slandered Bob and the SNCC Summer Project. Except that in this new, revised version, the vehicle for subverting Dr. King's campaign was, presto, the Black United Front??? No kidding, that literally was what they said. If their intention was to evoke a sense of impending doom, panic white folks, and intimidate "moderate Negro leaders," it didn't really seem to work. Most black folk—unfortunately not all—and sensible whites simply ignored it as the foolishness it so obviously was. The Front continued to meet, but the spirit of unity was a little tarnished.

[*Hard as it might be to believe, Ture's characterization of this attack is actually quite understated. The "syndicated hacks" in question were Rowland Evans and Robert Novak of the* Washington Post. *Tell the truth and shame the devils. In the SNCC Washington office, we considered them the newspaper's token and misguided gesture toward hiring the handicapped. It required the two to produce the column, we said, because one could neither read nor write, while the other could not think. Unfortunately, they never quite managed to organize the division of labor properly between them.*

When I located the column in question, it literally beggared belief. Affecting to express the deeply seated "fears" of "top officials" of the administration and of "moderate Negro leaders," it is classic of divide and conquer, pandering to

McCarthyite paranoia, white racial anxieties, as well as a general alarmist fear-mongering.

Even for two such shameless hacks this column was a masterpiece, a milestone in the decline of American journalism, some fifty years in advance of its time. In the incisiveness of analysis, elegance of thought and subtlety of language, it anticipates, indeed exceeds, the political gangsterism and rhetorical inflation of the contemporary political talk show. So much so that it really deserves to be reproduced here in its entirety, to be read and savored in its full absurdity. However, I rather doubt that the authors will permit us to afford you that unabridged pleasure.

In addition to scaring whites, the purpose here was twofold and quite transparent: at one fell swoop to diminish both Dr. King and Carmichael, while publicly driving a wedge between the two while warning "moderate Negro leaders" of the dangers they incurred by associating in any way with Carmichael. While on the surface an overt, politically intemperate frontal assault on a sinister, opportunistic, and ideologically dangerous Carmichael, the column is also contemptuously dismissive of poor Dr. King. Dr. King is portrayed as hapless, inept, confused, weak, "desperate," and "declining" in influence and, with his well known "history of surrendering control to better organized extremist elements," easy pickings. Extremist elements such as whom? you cry. Why, SNCC, of course. Is that not exactly what happened, so the authors claim, on the Selma March when "SNCC forced Dr. King to the wall and seized control"? Of course, no such thing happened in Selma or anywhere else. Obviously the writers meant the Meredith March, and as you have seen, nothing remotely like that happened there. Forced Dr. King to the wall, indeed!

In the Washington Post *the headline was quite explicit in its fear-mongering: "OFFICIAL FEARS GROW THAT CARMICHAEL WILL SEIZE DR. KING'S 'MARCH OF THE POOR.'" The lead was equally a typically vulgar assertion of Beltway insider information at the highest levels, to wit: "Fear is growing among top officials in the White House and Justice Department that Dr. Martin Luther King's April 'March of the Poor on Washington'* [sic] *will result in a stunning victory for Stokely Carmichael." These "top officials" and fear-ridden "administration strategists" who are, of course, never identified, see "King's ill-considered campaign" as "a golden opportunity for Carmichael to gain primacy among Negro leaders." Nice work if you can get it. Presumably official Washington was trembling in fear and loathing at the prospect of young Stokely's capturing the hearts and minds of "the Negro" leadership class. And how is this miracle to be accomplished? Hey, pay attention, because "King's ill-considered campaign exactly coincides with the new Leninist phase—in many ways the most dangerous phase—of Stokely Carmichael's swift ascent to the top." That's how. Swift ascent to the top? Whatevah, don't ask.*

However, we know that master manipulator Carmichael is all the more dan-

gerous after "his travels in the Communist world." From whence the devious fellow has returned "quietly implementing V.I. Lenin's tactics" of co-opting and subverting harmless "non-revolutionary social reformers—such as King." Oh, the fiendish cunning, the wickedness.

Well, you may sneer if you feel so inclined. But that will only be because you fail to understand that poor, hapless Dr. King, after his "failure" in Chicago and his now "desperate condition within the movement," is now "particularly susceptible to Carmichael's embrace" (those perverts).

We are alerted to this danger by the cynical decision of "Carmichael's new Black United Front to endorse the aims" of King's Poor People's March. And even had they not thus revealed their sinister intentions and low cunning, the mere "formation of the Black United Front" was already a dead giveaway. Clear evidence of the "Leninist line" on which the brother was now firmly embarked. You still don't get it, huh? Nothing could have been more obvious. As our two custodians of political morality triumphantly reveal about "Carmichael's tactics": "He is explicitly following Lenin's famed 1920 injunction to the British Communist Party not to attack the Labor Party but to 'support' the democratic socialists 'in the same way as the rope support the hanged man.'" So around Carmichael, Dr. King would be indeed well advised to watch his neck. Hey, as Carmichael would be the first to enjoin you, don't take my word. Go check it out for yourself. —EMT]

The convergence of all this was that a new discordant note and an element of mistrust were created within the steering committee. But the Front and the committee continued to work despite a few defections. Most groups were steadfast. I even, at one point, offered to withdraw if that was the will of the group. No one would hear of it. But it was also clear that those in our community who nurtured fantasies of wielding "insider" influence with the Democratic administration—the usual suspects and we know who they were—did not wish the United Front to succeed, with or without my involvement. Very sad. And, as an entity, the Washington United Front did not long survive. But of course, many of the sincere members continued to be effective and committed to our people's interests. Today, the need for unity across class lines in our communities is even greater. I continue to work for that.

[This is a conviction in which the brother has never wavered. Indeed, his very last act of nonviolent protest in this country was in service to that ideal. In late spring of 1998, the year of his death, almost paralyzed by cancer and against the passionate advice of family and friends, Bro Ture traveled from New York to Baltimore to stage a sit-in. The site, ironically enough, was the national offices of the NAACP. The purpose: to enlist our old SNCC comrade Julian Bond in a politically sensitive meeting toward such a united front.

Julian was away from the office, and what ensued had to have been unprece-
dented in the history of direct-action protests. Certainly the strangest sit-in in
Ture's career.

The NAACP staff—especially, so I'm told, the sisters—greeted the wheel-
chair-bound militant with an outpouring of respect, consideration, and affec-
tion. They shook his hand, hugged and kissed him, posed for pictures with him,
sought his autograph, proffered food and drink, and generally saw to his every
comfort as best they could. From time to time, NAACP president Kweisi
Mfume emerged from his office to confer with the lone protester. According to
Eric Ture Muhammad, who accompanied the brother, "I ain't never in my life
seen no sit-in quite like this one." —EMT]

At the same time, the pace of other movement demands had not slack-
ened in the slightest. In fact, the media's best efforts notwithstanding, I
was in even greater demand as a speaker. So I found myself doing as
much traveling and speaking—sometimes for SNCC, occasionally for the
Free Huey campaign—as I had during the year I was chairman. Only now
in my speeches the issues of Pan-Africanism and the African liberation
struggle combined quite logically and seamlessly with the struggle to
build Black Power in America.

There was one major difference. Now, whenever possible, Miriam
accompanied me on these speaking engagements. And as often as possible, I'd catch her performances in clubs or concerts. We were seeing each
other a lot and supporting each other's work. I never, never got tired of
watching her perform. Not just a great singer, she was a consummate
entertainer. And she certainly was a political asset at my speeches, big
time. I'd introduce her from the stage. She'd stand, smile, bow, and the
folks would go wild. The better we got to know each other, the more
impressive and admirable I found her to be. Our feelings for each other
inevitably grew stronger.

I remember her explaining the meaning of her African name, Zenzi.
She was, she said, the sixth child of her mother, conceived after her
mother had been warned that another pregnancy could prove fatal.
Which nearly was the case—for both mother and daughter. After a difficult labor, neither mother nor the frail baby seemed likely to survive.
Which reminded me a lot of May Charles's accounts of my own struggle
for survival at birth.

Like May Charles and me, the Xhosa mother and daughter had been
attended by the grandmother. The old lady kept muttering *uzenzile,*
uzenzile, at her near-comatose daughter. This is a common Xhosa expression of reproach, reserved most usually for children, but also for adults
who ignore warnings only to bring disaster upon themselves and others.

Literally, it means you brought this on yourself. This is your own stubborn fault.

During her convalescence, Miriam's mother heard *uzenzile* so often that she decided to name her new daughter Zenzi, a variant of the term. All African names have meaning, Miriam explained. "Story of my life, *uzenzile*. Any trouble that comes, I tend to bring on myself." She laughed ruefully.

By then I knew I loved this woman. She said she loved me and showed me so in many, many ways. But the question of marriage never entered my thinking. Or maybe, I just never allowed myself to seriously entertain it. This was only partly because of what I'd answered to Ho Chi Minh when he'd asked: "Sir, I'm married to my people's struggle." I had no real expectation of surviving to a "ripe old age," so marriage was not really an option I thought about. Nor was it because of the difference in our ages. That simply wasn't an issue for either of us. Never was. Nor was it because we were always overcommitted and always on the move.

It was more, if anything, the politics. Thanks largely to the media, I'd accumulated this incredible trash pile of negative political baggage in the public mind. At least in the minds of those Dr. King used to call "our white brothers and sisters." That didn't bother me, in fact the reverse. But, on the other hand, Zenzi had a brilliant career that was simply flourishing. As an entertainer, she was very popular with all segments of the public and at the pinnacle of the entertainment industry in America. I didn't know whether a formal, public association with me might not jeopardize everything that this brave, supremely talented woman had struggled so hard to achieve. The more popular an entertainer is, the more the public feels that he or she is somehow accountable to them in their personal life. Presumptuous, but unfortunately true.

For that reason, I would never have been the first to mention marriage. No way. Hey, if it ain't broke, don't fix it. And things really were beautiful between us. But then I started to pick up certain subtle but clear signals. In fact, in her book, she even says she implanted the idea. Maybe so, but whatever the case, we were soon talking about marriage.

Zenzi was, deep down, a traditional African woman. If we truly loved each other, which we did; if we were going to continue to be together, and we were; if we made each other happy, which we did; then we should be married. Period.

What about possible consequences for her career? Was she prepared to risk all that? For us? Hey, she'd already been hearing this from people professionally close to her. It hadn't caused her to stop seeing me, and the relationship hadn't affected her career. So why should marriage? Besides, it really wasn't anybody's business but our own, was it?

Initially we told only our families and a few close friends, but we were already an item in some gossip columns. No one's business but ours, right? We quietly got married before a judge, justice of the peace, some bureaucrat in a civil ceremony at New York's City Hall. (Not all her friends were apprehensive, however; President Sékou Touré was just delighted. But then, President Touré was more like family to Zenzi anyway. He ordered the Guinean mission to the United Nations to host a big reception for us for a month later and the Tanzanian embassy joined in.)

It was, I'm sure, the next day after the ceremony, the next *morning*, Jack. I never will forget this. All that evening and morning Zenzi'd been so happy, just radiant. She went into the next room to get the phone. I was sitting on the bed. Never forget it. She came walking into the room, her face expressionless, frozen, like someone in shock. "Zenzi, what's wrong? What's wrong with you?" I thought someone might have died. Her daughter, Bongi, was pregnant. She didn't say a word. Just came and sat next to me on the bed. I put my arms around her. I could feel her shaking. "Baby, *what's wrong?* Tell me." I was convinced something terrible must have happened to her daughter. "Honey, whatever it is, you gotta tell me."

"My manager just informed me that all my shows have been canceled." Her voice was flat.

I couldn't believe it. All I could do is repeat stupidly.

"*All* your shows?"

She just shook her head. "All our dates. All of them."

We sat in silence.

"Zenzi, I'm sorry. I'm so sorry." What else was there to say?

[*Miriam Makeba remembers, in* My Story:

All my friends and associates can see how happy I am and they are pleased for me. So is Bob Schwaid, the tall, dark-haired white man with glasses, who is my manager. But when he phones, he sounds very disturbed.

"Miriam, they are backing out."

"Backing out, who?"

"Everybody, they are canceling your bookings, right and left."

"But why?"

"I think you know why."

I feel that tenseness inside. So, I think, it is starting, again.

I ask Mr. Schwaid, "But don't we have contracts?"

"Sure we do. But this is show business. Their attitude is, 'Go ahead and sue.'"

Not everybody cancels my shows. Some realize that I'm Miriam Makeba first and Mrs. Stokely Carmichael second. I'm a singer, not a revolutionary. I keep reminding the press of this. But interviewers won't leave me alone about my husband's politics.]

I knew it was me they were aiming at. She didn't have an enemy in this country. But I hadn't expected this. I'd figured, at most, some people would criticize her. Racists might boycott her shows, maybe stop buying her records. But this? All at once? It had to be an organized campaign. No question. All her bookings, all at once? It had to be organized across the industry. A full-blown conspiracy.

I could never have imagined my enemies would be so ruthless or so thorough. And so quick. I mean, the *day* after we got married? How low could you go? That's something I don't play. I would never go after someone's wife or family just because I couldn't get at them. It was industrywide and clearly intended to crush my new wife. Not just her career, but her spirit.

Who had the motive, that kind of network, and the cunning? I didn't think the covert agencies of the government had that kind of influence over the entire entertainment industry. *[Perhaps, but as the behavior of the Internal Revenue Service would later make clear, the federal government played a role in the continuing harassment of Ms. Makeba. —EMT]* They'd have needed help. The Mafia? You heard stories, but what did the mob have against us? Besides, that wasn't their style. They'd send muscle. Break a leg or a head. So who else? Only one organized interest group comes to mind. But I have no hard evidence. And we don't want to indulge in conspiracy peddling, now do we? But it's pretty clear.

I could see in her face that she was devastated. I felt terrible because I knew I was the real target. But you know something? She never once expressed any regret to me, or anything associating me with the loss of her American career. I'm sure she must have had some feelings about it, but she never once expressed them to me. That's the kind of woman Miriam Makeba is.

That morning, sitting with Zenzi on that bed . . . I'll take that moment with me to my grave. You feel so helpless because the cowards hide in the shadows. Never showing their hand so we could expose them. Perhaps I was naive to have been so utterly surprised. But for whatever reason, I was. Surprised at the ruthlessness and thoroughness, the organization of it. But perhaps we should not have been surprised. There had, in truth, been an early warning before we were married. The first time Zenzi had been penalized for our association had been less damaging in the long term, but emotionally almost more painful to her, because it came at the hands of a black puppet in the Caribbean. Zenzi had been enthusiastic after her first visit to the Bahamas. Not only from the climate of friendliness of the people; she gloried at the sight of independent black people running their own government. Exactly what her people were fighting and dying for at home. Because she wanted to make a real contribution, she decided to open a boutique there featuring African styles and cultural artifacts.

The local authorities were just delighted, cooperative, very welcoming. Why not? A celebrated African artist investing in an African nation in the Caribbean? Zenzi threw herself into the idea with her usual energy and enthusiasm. She invested considerable money: finding a place, hiring folks, importing the merchandise. The opening was a highly successful fashion show, the proceeds of which she donated to an institution for the blind. My little sister Janeth (now Nagib) was one of the models. Everything went splendidly. She was very happy. However, that same day, the local press ran a story about our engagement.

When she is summoned to the prime minister's office the next day, she simply assumes the man wishes to congratulate her and offer his support. After all, the country needed investment, right? Instead, Lynden Pindling summarily informs her that her business permits are canceled and that suddenly she was no longer welcome in the Bahamas. Period.

Astonished, she asks for an explanation of this sudden about-face. "Well," he says, "we hadn't known of your engagement to the American revolutionary Stokely Carmichael. He is persona non grata in the British Commonwealth, of which the Bahamas is a part."

That shameless, callous, cowardly, greasy-chained, money-grubbing, bootlicking black lackey, calling himself head of an independent black nation? He was nothing but the overseer of a Caribbean plantation. Miriam had been deeply hurt when she returned from that betrayal by one of us.

Unfortunately, Miriam was made to suffer a great deal because of our love. I will always have a tender spot, knowing as I do the suffering she endured during our marriage. But if those jackals and hyenas intended to crush her spirit, they failed. Utterly. The American career they could destroy, but they couldn't touch that woman's spirit. I never once heard her complain.

I had been planning on going to Africa anyway, and Miriam had a standing invitation, oft-repeated, to make Guinea her home. So we just began to direct our energies toward that move.

"There are other places I can sing. America isn't the world." She was right. I mean, she truly was an international artist. She was extremely popular in Europe, beloved in Africa, highly appreciated in South America, Canada, Japan. So we directed our energies toward that. We'd go back to Africa. She'd recuperate and continue her work. Meanwhile, we still had the official wedding reception to arrange for a week later. With the involvement of the Guinean and Tanzanian missions, the entire African diplomatic corps in New York began to talk up the event. After all, my bride was claimed by all Africans, even the reactionary states. The African-American press picks up on it too. Soon, it's looking like the social event of the season. That already seemed a little much to me. But then, next thing I know, the marriage is suddenly a "symbolic union between black America and the continent," the motherland with the diaspora.

Press hype, of course, but y'know, in cultural and political terms, a popular consummation. We were cool with it—after all, we were committed Pan-Africanists—but, gimme a break, that's one hell of a burden to load on one marriage. All said and done, we were just two mule-stubborn black people who happened to love each other. No more, no less. Unifying black America and the African world? C'mon, sounds nice, but be serious.

As it turned out, even this symbolic ceremonial thing (we were already married, remember) had to be postponed. A couple weeks before the event—April 4—Zenzi's daughter had a son in New York.

That same day in Memphis, they murdered Dr. King.

I was in D.C. Miriam was in Los Angeles. She'd just started an engagement at a big nightclub in Hollywood, the Coconut Grove, the only major venue that hadn't canceled on her.

"Are you all right, Stokely? I'm coming home. No way can I go onstage tonight. We have to be together at a time like this. Be on the first plane flying east."

She was upset, sobbing. She'd sung at fund-raisers for SCLC and knew and admired Dr. King very much. But, as I found out, she'd been almost out of her mind with worry that mine might be the next name on their hit list.

Then, by the time she got back that evening, inner-city Washington was in flames, Jack, and under military curfew. At least black Washington was. So it was a few hours later before I could get home to her. When I opened the back door, she just fell into my arms sobbing. "How'd you get through the curfew? I was sure something bad had happened to you."

Poor Zenzi. She'd been pacing back and forth all evening, hearing sirens and occasional gunfire. It seemed to her like South Africa all over again. She had been listening to the radio for the one announcement she most dreaded. By the time she heard me at the door, she had almost managed to convince herself that her new husband was lying dead somewhere in the streets.

I was in no way responsible for the burning of D.C. Hey, Jack, if I had been, why would I deny it? Then or now. Far as I was concerned, this country had coming whatever it got that night. *In spades.*

When the news came, a group of us from SNCC went into the community. We went from store to store, asking all businesses to close as a sign of mourning and respect. Which everyone did. Immediately. People were in deep shock and grief. But you could actually see and feel grief and loss turning to anger. And I do mean rage, Jack. Folks were spilling out into the streets all worked up, and the rest is history. No one could have stopped it—you kidding?—no one. Nor did I particularly want to. Hey,

I was as angry as anyone. Finally, finally and at last, this country had killed Dr. King. Just as the brother had always known they eventually would.

[*Cleve Sellers remembers, in* River of No Return*:*

It took me about a half hour to get myself together. It probably would have helped if I could have cried, but I couldn't. . . . Rage and numbness dominated my emotions. Sitting alone in the corner, all I could do was stare blankly at the walls and try to swallow the huge lump in my throat.

Stokely was very upset. He is volatile and tends to have little control over his emotions when he is angry. His eyes reflected pure rage. . . .

Somewhere near 8:30 P.M., Stokely stood in the middle of the paper-cluttered floor and made an announcement. "They took our leader off, so out of respect, we're going to ask all these goddamn stores to close down until he is laid to rest. If Kennedy had been killed, they would do it. . . ." Although the situation was not yet ominous, I was very tense. I wondered whether Dr. King's assassination had been part of a nationwide plan. They may have decided to get all of us at the same time and get it over with, I thought to myself. If they kill Stokely, Rap, Huey Newton, and the rest of us, the movement will be thrown into total disarray. Stokely shouldn't be out here where anyone who wants to can easily gun him down.

My thoughts were interrupted by the shouts of a black teenager standing in the periphery of the fast-growing crowd.

"Stokely, you're the one," he screamed.

"Dr. King's dead, ain't no way but Stokely's," yelled another. . . .

Many began to pick up rocks and bottles. When we passed the Republic Theatre, one young boy in the crowd stepped forward and rammed his fist through one of the glass doors. . . .

. . . During the next half hour or so, the inevitable began to happen. Enraged by the senseless assassination, people in the community began to stream into the streets. They were looking for some way to let out their frustrations. We tried for a while to keep them from moving before they were prepared to deal with the police. . . . But by 11:00 P.M., it was obvious that we could do nothing to dissuade the people. They intended to have some kind of revenge. . . .]

Cleve was in D.C. Dr. King had been his spiritual adviser on the conscientious objection hassle with the draft. Cleve served time for that principle. He'd grown to even love Dr. King from the Meredith March. I couldn't even look at Cleve, the brother was in such pain.

A group of us from D.C. SNCC drove—as we'd done so often over the years while I was at Howard—down to Atlanta for the funeral. This trip was the strangest of them all. Almost surreal. Inside the car, rage, grief, uncertainty. We couldn't leave the interstate. Every hundred miles or so we could see clouds of black smoke hovering in the distance. Cities and towns burning, Jack. According to the radio, many of them under martial law. Beware the anger of a patient people. Mourning the murder of their leader, the only way left to them.

We decided we couldn't under any circumstances leave the highway. Last thing we needed was a carful of young blacks—especially when they found out who we were—caught up in some Southern small-town curfew. Because, all over the country, black America was telling the nation: This time you went too far, killing this good, decent man, this man of peace. When you killed Dr. King, you killed nonviolence. Man, all the way to Atlanta, every station that came over the radio, more reports of riots, insurrection, disorder. Black folk signaling America, when you killed Dr. King, you killed nonviolence.

Hey, the people were absolutely right. What would we have looked like, as a people, if we had just lapped our tails between our legs and done nothing? What else was there for us to do? What would we have told our children? That we grieved and did nothing? Yeah, of course Dr. King would never have approved. But don't you think that, perhaps more than anyone else, he at least would have understood? In deep, deep sorrow maybe, but surely he'd have understood.

[According to press reports, in the immediate aftermath of Dr. King's murder, over seventy-five thousand National Guardsmen were called out in 110 American cities to quell or guard against uprisings as black America registered its outrage. —EMT]

As I recall, every news bulletin, every plume of smoke off the highway, every cop car or army truck with armed white men, seemed to shake Zenzi a little more. What is happening to this country . . . ? Why, this is 1960 South Africa all over again. She recalled Sharpeville. Sixty-nine unarmed Africans in a nonviolent demonstration shot dead by security forces. Hundreds wounded. Among the dead, two of her uncles.

My thoughts . . . who, why, and why *now*? Was it intended to stop the Poor People's March on Washington? Before we "militants" took it over and plunged the nation's capital into race war? C'mon, did those beltway apparatchiks actually *believe* their own propaganda? They couldn't be that crazed and vicious. Or could they? Whatever the cause, Dr. King was dead.

My mind kept flashing on that sermon/declaration of his on Vietnam that Sunday morning at the Ebenezer. It had been clear to me that he'd called to invite Cleve and me to that sermon as a way of thanking SNCC. Because we'd really pushed him on Vietnam. Hard as we could. Could that be why they'd killed him? I had to remind myself that all his public life Dr. King had been anticipating assassination. Death threats daily.

I recalled our last meeting. How harried and stressed Dr. King had appeared that day. Our last parting. Only, of course, I hadn't dreamed it was the last time. The concern on his face: "Stokely, promise me you'll be more careful."

One thing I knew then and firmly believe today. This was *not* no lone assassin, nonsense. Powerful forces were involved. There have been too many unexplained coincidences and contradictions to come out since. Why were the cops withdrawn? What was that Special Forces team from Military Intelligence doing in Memphis? On and on, etc., etc. One day it will all come out. Of that I am certain. One day it will come out.

The funeral was powerful, haunting. Sorrowful but strangely beautiful. Very moving. I gotta say SCLC did that right. Yes, they did. Black folk understand how to do funerals. It's in the culture. Deep in our culture, bro. The ritual, the spectacle, the sorrowful dignity. The sorrow songs. The choir, the soloists, man, they *did it* for Dr. King.

Only thing, which I suppose couldn't be helped. Ain't never been so many high-up white folk in that church, before or since. Celebrities, politicians. Powerful white folk. First one I saw was Hubert Humphrey, and the next, Bobby Kennedy, who, if you recall, had authorized the FBI phone taps on the brother. While thousands, I mean thousands, of poor black folk were sweating outside in the sun, many of them crying. People who loved him and whom he loved. Greater love hath no man than that he lay down his life . . . For a moment, I thought we should stand out here with Dr. King's people. Then I saw the "important" guests all going in. I said, hell, no. Ain't nothing going keep us out. We belong in there. So we crashed, four of us from SNCC and Zenzi.

Then we marched with the people to the grave, saw the brother buried, and came on back to D.C. We all knew one stage of the movement had gone into the grave with the brother. We all knew that.

In retrospect, the Panther/SNCC "alliance"—*flirtation* might be a better word—was a comedy of errors. Except, of course, it was not at all funny at the time. In fact, it narrowly missed being the flat-out tragedy for black people that the government was trying its best to set up. So, bad as it was, it could easily have been a lot worse. A lot worse, Jack.

But hindsight comes easy. Most armchair judgments fail to take into account the pressures of the times. And those were some very, very strange times, bro. And even back then, a lot of people—in SNCC and our supporters—were questioning this sudden Panther connection. A lot of questions and legitimate confusion. What *is* this anyway? What does it mean? How can it work? Which already tells you something, doesn't it?

As I explained, I wasn't party to those discussions. But what drove them was pretty clear. And not all that unusual in politics. Each organization—more accurately, the leadership of each—felt that the other group could offer it something it needed. Pure self-interest. Sometimes it works, more often it doesn't. As it happened, in this case, both were mistaken in what they thought they saw in the other that they needed or felt they did.

In the South, SNCC had accomplished everything it was set up to do. Jim Crow, as our parents had known it, was dead. All that was left was the organizing of the funeral. SNCC, as an organization, could either disband, stay South and try to build on the gains there, or move to the North, where the action was heating up. I was one of those who thought we had to make the move into Northern urban centers. There was important work to be done there. Which is why I was in D.C. But not everyone agreed.

A lot of our Southern field organizers were gonna stay home and build on what they'd helped accomplish. My old organizing partners Bob Mants and John Jackson continued successfully in local politics in Lowndes County. Ed Brown stayed in the Mississippi Delta and was very effective. He organized the Delta foundation and other economic cooperatives that even today still bring economic alternatives to the local community. Julian Bond went into Georgia politics. He had to be elected three times *and* have recourse to the courts before the Georgia legislature would seat him. Charles Sherrod—SNCC's first full-time field secretary—stayed in southwest Georgia building a wide-ranging organization. And so forth.

Others of us, myself included, felt we had to begin national organizing to achieve Black Power. Which is where the Panthers seemed a possibility. I know this was what motivated Jim Forman and whoever else was talking with the Black Panther Party. See, two radical groups seemed to have had some success organizing at the grass roots in the Northern cities: the Nation of Islam and the emerging Panthers. Especially with Malcolm gone, the Nation of Islam had seemed entirely too apolitical and fundamentalist in orientation. On the other hand, the Panthers were political, a youth-oriented movement, and very much in yo' face. They were militant and seemed to tap into the same energy and momentum that SNCC had done. Of course, the Panther rhetoric was "abrasive" and their public image mixed, but they were very attractive to urban youth. Perhaps for those very reasons.

What SNCC offered was six years' experience on the front lines. Also a certain legitimacy in struggle. Perhaps the young Panthers could benefit from our organizing experience and our mistakes? If so, perhaps the Panthers could be our channel into the Northern urban struggle? A long shot but worth exploring, delicately.

All this, we must remember, was against a backdrop of internal demoralization, exhaustion, and incredible external pressures. SNCC as an organization was feeling. Struggling hard but reeling. The backlash—highly orchestrated, I might add—coming from Black Power and SNCC's alleged "expulsion of whites," compounded by our stand on Palestinian rights, had given our former liberal allies, now reinforced by the forces of organized American Zionism, two weapons with which to drum us out of the "liberal consensus." And they used them relentlessly. This had seriously crippled fund-raising. While our direction was clear enough, what we needed was viable programs and a new base.

And the Panthers, what was their interest? At the time they were beginning to have high media visibility, albeit of a dubious kind, and a growing national image. As a consequence, the Black Panther Party was spreading rapidly among Northern African youth who'd grown up listening to Malcolm, seeing SNCC on TV, and feeling deprived of their opportunity to be involved in the kind of struggle SNCC and Dr. King had waged in the South. But the Panther leadership lacked real political experience. This was an organization literally with no history and no precedent in American politics. Like SNCC in its early days, they found themselves in midair, "learning to fly on the way down."

I know that Huey, at least, saw SNCC members as elder statesmen, experienced fighters who had maintained a cohesive, functioning organization under heavy fire. SNCC, therefore, must know how to organize and efficiently administer a militant, youth-oriented black organization, right? The Panthers, I assume, were interested in tapping into SNCC's political experience and internal organizing skills. Hey, it may well have looked that way from a distance, but I had to laugh.

I mean, if you've been paying attention, you know that SNCC was the last place to look for a classic model of organizational efficiency. Besides which, much of the organizing experience and institutional memory had been dispersing. So from the git, the perceptions of both groups, while not totally illogical, were simply inaccurate. That became clearer once I began visiting the various Black Panther Party chapters springing up around the country. Hence my insistence on the "honorary" appointment.

Whenever I was in Oakland, I'd always go pay my respects to Mrs. Newton, Huey's mother, before visiting him in jail. She was a sweet lady, in many ways a real Southern lady. Huey appreciated my visits to her. My first impression—that he was a thoughtful and serious young brother—was reinforced in those jailhouse meetings. I definitely thought he was a brother we could work with. He seemed to understand and respect the work SNCC had done in the South and to hope the party would come to play a similar role in the Northern cities.

I pointed out that that was not very likely if their most visible community program remained armed patrols monitoring police behavior in the streets. No way you going get anybody's aunt or the deacon board of the local church to turn out behind that kind of "vanguard" action. He said he understood that. He explained that the patrols, though absolutely legal, had simply been armed propaganda intended to be temporary. To affirm our community's legal right to self-defense against police abuse. But, he explained, their first real popular program in the community had been to organize regular buses to take mothers, wives, sisters, and children from Oakland to visit their men incarcerated in distant prisons all across the state. That program had been very successful. Also, he said, the party was organizing resistance to evictions, counseling welfare recipients on their rights, setting up education programs in the community, especially in black history. But, of course, the only thing the media picked up on was the guns.

We agreed that this image would only isolate the party out *in front* of the community, whereas, where they needed to be was *deep inside* the day-to-day fabric of the neighborhoods, organizing our people at all levels. He said he intended to redirect the drift toward a paramilitary posture back toward community service. All that could result from militarism was an isolated youth group of warrior types, more like a gang than a political party. What our community needed was real organization. I felt the brother was serious and clear. And that perhaps SNCC could help him develop effective programs to *organize* the community. We talked a few times.

Then on my next visit, Cleaver, who, with Huey in jail, was assuming a larger role within the party, informs me that on the instructions of the lawyers, I was no longer allowed to visit the brother. I said I found that strange, because in SNCC *we* gave instructions to our lawyers, not the other way round. But our meetings stopped. I wondered about that. But I never saw Huey again until in court at his trial.

During the trial and after he was convicted, the Free Huey campaign spread into the college campuses. Opposition to the war had radicalized white youth. SNCC being closed to them, many of them saw the Panthers as a newly available avenue into militant struggles in the black community. As did the radicals of the New Left. Cleaver brought with him a close relationship with *Ramparts* magazine, the self-proclaimed crypto-Maoist voice of the new white left.

[Ramparts: *A once moderate magazine of Catholic social concern that was taken over, funded, and run as an ultraradical, neo-Maoist organ by affluent, young, white California radicals. A development as mystifying as it was sudden and short-lived. Instant revolutionaries. —EMT]*

Ramparts began to run features on the Panther leadership and proclaimed the party the "revolutionary vanguard." The establishment media followed suit, presenting the Panthers as the militant black wing of the American youth rebellion, the black shock troops of the white New Left and the "counterculture." I thought it a fundamental error to allow any white media—establishment or radical—to define a black organization in that way. Whether it's the left's revolutionary fantasy or the right's racist nightmare: angry young Negroes with guns. Either one posed the same danger to the membership. Both or either image would serve only to distance and alienate the organization from the adult community they were supposed to be organizing. I could see the party becoming less and less of a community-based organization and more and more of an urban youth formation, a black, working-class SDS and one not far enough removed from the classic urban street-gang model.

There were just too many contradictions, Jack, serious contradictions. The similarities between SNCC and the Panthers were as obvious as were the differences. Both were organizations of black youth, true. Both were fiercely committed to ending the conditions oppressing our people. Of course. There were idealistic, brave, and intelligent youth in both. Given. Both groups were unprecedented in American political history, understood. So it would be logical to assume there could be a natural fit, right? False. Utterly. In fact, no two organizations could have been more fundamentally different. In origins, in style, in organizational culture, in ideology.

I mean as sudden and improvised as SNCC's emergence had been, compared to the Panthers', our trajectory looked like a gradual, highly rational, orderly evolution. Theirs was more like an eruption. No fault of theirs.

SNCC had been fortunate in ways that the Panthers were not. To start with, the Panthers did not have the benefit of the highly experienced, politically activist adult mentorship that we had. No Bayard, no Ella Baker, no James Lawson, no Dr. King. Also, in our early days, SNCC was anchored in, nurtured by, protected by, and disciplined by adult social networks and a culture unique to the rural Southern community. We were educated morally and aesthetically by the traditions, etiquette, and vocabulary of the Southern black church. The Panthers were, for the most part, the product of an alienated, urban ghetto culture. Early SNCC members had evolved out of a radical pacifist activism. SNCC also had—this in retrospect, for it certainly did not seem so at the time— the luxury of shared experience, whether a jail cell or picket line, which had built strong bonds and mutual trust among us even before a SNCC existed. Also the habit, the very necessary luxury, of free and open debate, of endless discussion.

The Panthers never had, far as I could see, that kind of incubation period. Not only were the times very different, but the party seemed to spring full-grown out of the fertile political imagination of Huey P. Newton. They had almost no history before the media thrust them instantly into national attention. The dominant culture out of which they emerged was the youth gang culture of the Oakland streets. Which, in fact, was what made them so very attractive to the white media. Their "colors," the leather jackets, blue shirts, and black berets, the militaristic style, militant rhetoric, and guns either visible or implied were all variants of urban gang culture and style. Which, in turn, was also what made the party almost irresistible to alienated urban youth looking for the means to struggle against the daily provocations, injustices, and dead-end frustrations of ghetto life. Hence, the party's extremely rapid growth, which by itself would have brought inevitable organizational problems anyway. But there was more.

Their theatrical militance and high visibility would make them the approved target of every big-city police force they came up against. What, a black street gang with politics? No way, José. We can't have that! I mean, for the cops, it was literally open season on any brother wearing black leather and a beret. Hey, this was a time, remember, when few cities were without their enforcers: hastily thrown together paramilitary "tactical" police units—mostly white Vietnam veterans—created ostensibly to guard against urban insurrections. A Northern urban version of the slave "patrollers" guarding white interests against black insurrection.

And if that were not enough for the young organization, their problems would only be compounded by the revolutionary fantasies of the *Ramparts* editors and the white New Left. Far as I was concerned, "revolutionary vanguard" was just another name for black cannon fodder, cold as that. Because if, rhetorically speaking, J. Edgar Hoover was running behind the New Left radicals, he wasn't far behind. He, in turn, declared the Panthers to be "the greatest threat to the internal security of the country" and directed the Bureau to turn their COINTELPRO to the destruction of this newest threat. Which they did.

[The FBI's COINTELPRO—as has been clearly revealed subsequently—set out to destroy the Panthers by any means necessary, no matter how vicious.

In August 1967, Hoover had created the notorious counterintelligence program to counter "black nationalist hate-type groups," among which he identified SNCC and the very churchly SCLC. The purpose of which endeavor (COINTELPRO), Hoover wrote, was primarily to "expose, disrupt, misdirect, discredit or otherwise neutralize the activities of black nationalist hate-type organizations and groupings, their leadership, spokesmen, membership and supporters and to counter their propensity for violence and civil disorder." In that memo the director instructed his agents to "prevent the rise of a 'messiah' who would unify and electrify the militant black nationalist movement." He explained that Malcolm "might have been such a 'messiah,' he is the martyr of the movement today."

He specifically identified the very churchly Dr. King and Stokely as "aspirants" to this role. In a follow-up memo the director opined that "Stokely Carmichael appears to have the charisma to become such a messiah." A characterization that took on a distinctly ominous tint when he went on to outline another goal of the program as being "to make it clear to black youth that if they aspire to be revolutionaries, they will be dead revolutionaries."

The Hoover declaration on the Panthers to which Carmichael refers came in September 1968, right after Newton's conviction. The nation's "chief law enforcement officer" wrote: "The Black Panther Party is now the greatest threat to the internal security of the country. Schooled in Marxist-Leninist ideology and the teachings of Chinese Communist leader Mao Tse-tung, its members have perpetuated numerous assaults on police officers and engaged in violent confrontations with police throughout the country."

It is variously reported that of the 295 disruptive and illegal actions subsequently directed at black organizations under this program, 233 were directed at the Black Panther Party. —EMT]

This was way beyond government "dirty tricks." This here was some vicious, ruthless, and illegal stuff intended to create confusion, mistrust, and suspicion in order to set up confrontations designed to get folks hurt or killed. And in some cases, they succeeded. It was two FBI "information gatherers" who killed Panthers John Huggins and Bunchy Carter in the shootout in the UCLA cafeteria. *[The shooters, two young brothers, George and Larry Stiner, who were being run by an FBI handler named Brandon Cleary, were convicted for the murders and sent into the California penal system, from which they "disappeared" without explanation a few years later. Their fate or whereabouts has never been revealed. —EMT]* It was an FBI-organized raid that assassinated Fred Hampton and Mark Clark in Chicago.

But it was largely character assassination, false accusations, the forging of incriminating letters, etc. I myself would at one time or another be the target of all of the above. They would even stoop to dragging my wife's name into the faked letters. I've since seen FBI memos proposing that my name be signed to a false report addressed to an FBI agent and that this be planted in a movement car. Or that with the assistance of "a cooperating bank," a fake bank statement showing "substantial regular payments" be created in the name of Huey P. Newton and mailed anonymously to Panther headquarters. The idea being, of course, to make us appear to be government informants and possibly get us killed.

The FBI had been shadowing me for years, so that was nothing new. But what I was now seeing was of a different order: the evidence—rather the effects—of all this covert action, this destabilization, was visible in every Panther chapter I visited. A mood of growing paranoia, an air of interpersonal mistrust and suspiciousness. But at the time, I of course had no real idea of the extent of the government's role in generating this atmosphere.

Later this all—most of it anyway—would come out *[the Church Commission hearings of 1970 —EMT]*. What emerged was not merely lowdown, vicious, and ugly, it was also illegal. The government framed innocent people. Got others killed. Killed some themselves. Almost succeeded in getting me killed. All of which is clearly established in official congressional records. And guess what? Not one of the government's criminals have ever done a day of jail time for these crimes. Jail time? Gimme a break, Star. I'm not aware that any of these FBI criminals have as much as been reprimanded or even demoted, much less fired. What does that tell you?

The "national" leadership of the Black Panther Party was a small, ingrown group, primarily out of Oakland, around the founders Bobby Seale and Huey P. Newton, who were joined about this time by Eldridge Cleaver. Cleaver developed the newspaper, which was soon being sold across the country. Unfortunately, the newspaper to a great extent defined the public image of the young organization.

[Cleaver, recently paroled from prison, had achieved a certain literary eminence among left intellectuals with a collection of prison writings, Soul on Ice. *White intellectuals tended to praise the book. Blacks were generally skeptical of his treatise on rape as "a revolutionary act." He was at this time the black presence at* Ramparts *magazine and the* Ramparts *presence in the Panthers. —EMT]*

Cleaver more than anyone else set the tone of the paper, which was strident, confrontational, and extremely militaristic. It also published sensitive orders from the Central Committee to the membership. I'm talking about the kind of sensitive stuff no responsible organization puts down on paper, much less publishes where every cop in the country can read it. The Oakland group approved new chapters, issued political guidelines and policy directives, and shipped newspapers out to be sold. The administrative style seemed to me highly centralized and authoritarian, especially since the internal structure was hierarchical and the titles militaristic, "field marshals," etc., etc. But there was (and indeed could be) little real Central Committee control on the ground. I mean, there was no way the national leadership in Oakland—even if it had been the most politically and administratively experienced leadership imaginable, which it was not—could have controlled and directed this sprawling octopus. I mean, just in terms of sheer distance and rate of growth. Even without the government penetration with agent provocateurs. Hey, the organization wasn't just growing; it was proliferating, erupting. Apart from culture and ideology, this growth was a sho-nuff administrative nightmare. Which, I suspect, was one reason for their reaching out to SNCC in the first place. Ironic, no?

[By the end of 1968, there were twenty Panther chapters in cities from Los Angeles to New York. There is no way to estimate the membership along with fellow travelers and supporters. In fact, in 1968, faced with this uncontrolled growth and a growing awareness of government infiltration, Bobby Seale announced a moratorium on accepting new members. —EMT]

However, the media attention, the murder of Dr. King, the Panthers' militant posture and stylish bravado combined to make the party very attractive indeed to that generation of inner-city African youth. Northern, urban young people as eager to become involved in our people's struggle as we had been six years earlier. Only six years? In those times, six years was more than a generation, it was an epoch.

So the organization grew entirely too quickly and randomly. I also noticed that each new chapter took on characteristics reflecting the particular political history of that city. The New York Panthers—where I felt most comfortable politically—tended logically enough to be nationalist and Pan-Africanist in orientation. In Chicago, extraordinarily strong youth-gang formations—numbering in the thousands, they say—played a definitive role. In Detroit, I don't recall any strong Panther formation, most likely because of the presence of radical leftist organizations of young black workers in that city. In Los Angeles, the chapter reflected the strong personalities first of Bunchy Carter, a formidable gang leader who'd come into the party from the prison system, and later of "Geronimo" Pratt, a highly disciplined, impressive Southern brother who'd come into the movement from Vietnam, where he'd been a crack soldier, highly decorated. A serious brother, very sincere. And so it went. Every city, every chapter, a markedly different character.

[Alprentice "Bunchy" Carter would, along with John Huggins, be murdered by two FBI informants in a shoot-out set up by the FBI in a UCLA cafeteria. Geronimo Pratt would serve more than twenty years for a murder he did not commit. A murder for which, at the time of his trial, the FBI had wiretap evidence proving that Pratt could not have committed it. —EMT]

That by itself may not have been insurmountable. But this influx of new members meant that the local leadership in the different cities didn't *really* know each other, or, for that matter, the Oakland leadership. They shared no personal histories, no time for the bonding that is so essential. (Which, come to think of it, also describes my own relationship with the Oakland group.) This increased the possibility for misunderstanding, distrust, and suspicion, which, as we now know, was being contrived and manipulated *relentlessly* by the government's covert actions. Even worse, there could be no effective internal machinery to thoroughly screen recruits coming in. So there were quite a number of people who were *sent* to join by FBI, police, or both, with instructions to report and disrupt.

[In the fourteen cities where chapters were opened and the FBI had offices, Hoover instructed the FBI office to "exploit all avenues of creating further dissention in the ranks of the Black Panther Party." By developing "imaginative and hard-hitting . . . measures aimed at crippling the Black Panther Party." I've seen subsequent studies that identify ninety proven FBI informants/provocateurs within the ranks of the Panthers. —EMT]

Put all these factors together, Jack, and what you had was a disaster waiting to happen. And it didn't require any great gift of prophecy to know who would pay the price. It would not be the New Left intellectuals, the Berkeley radicals, nor the *Ramparts* theoreticians. It was gonna be us again, black youth. I pointed this out to the leadership of the Panthers. And I said it publicly and I said it often. A lot of brave African youth would pay the price for the leadership allowing the media, and their white "radical allies," to define them in ways calculated to bring fire down on the heads of the members. It was unconscionable, allowing our youth to become the surrogates of white leftists acting out their revolutionary fantasies through black proxies. Hey, the "vanguard party of the revolution" simply meant to me African cannon fodder by another name. It wasn't in "advance" of our people, it was far out and away, distanced, split off from them, exposed and vulnerable. *That* was the most serious difference I had with the "leadership." I felt that posture to be a serious political error, irresponsible, and to use their own term, "Custeristic."

But there's something else that needs to be said. Nowadays, it is easy and fashionable to dismiss the Panther leadership simply as inept and borderline thugs. That's much too convenient. It is true that serious mistakes were made, for every last one of which a stiff price was paid. And, as I've said, the leadership often left much to be desired in terms of experience and judgment. But for most of the early formative years of that organization, it was under unrelenting attack, covert and open, by gun, subversion, and misuse of law, on the part of the federal government and local police. It was common and heartrending to hear over and over again eighteen- and nineteen-year-old Panthers say simply, "I don't expect to survive." And you heard that a lot, Jack. Constant harassment took its toll. Much of the party's energy, posture, and thinking had to be reactive and defensive, which in turn defined their policies and behavior.

One result was to harden the Oakland homeboy mentality, the turning inward. They never opened up that inner network to really embrace some creative and impressive community leaders from cities like Chicago, New York, or Los Angeles. So the leadership never really became "national," and that hurt the organization. And at any given time, one or more were in jail. Which is not to say that *any* leadership, no matter how representative, experienced, stable, or creative, would have been able to change all or most of what went down. No way. But I think some serious mistakes might have been avoided had they broadened the leadership base and heeded advice from those who were a little more politically experienced. True, at the time, the country itself was more than a little crazed, and the police and feds were out of control. But at least *some* things were avoidable, and that's on the Panther leadership. As the Xhosas say, *uzenzile.*

I was involved with the Black Panther Party for about a year. Why? Because I thought there was real potential there, valuable initiatives that deserved to be defended and advanced, if possible. When I concluded that this wasn't about to happen, I left.

All right, okay, the perceived wisdom is simplistic. As when we now hear—mainly from their former New Left patrons—that the Panther leadership was nothing but street thugs, and the party, at core, a criminal enterprise and a paramilitary street gang. End of story.

Hey, that tendency when present was always a minority element, usually around one or two gangster/warlord wanna-bes. Besides, how many of those jackanapes types—already firmly in the clutches of law enforcement *before* becoming Panthers—were *sent* into the organization for exactly that reason? I mean, I was once briefly assigned a Panther "bodyguard." Turns out this brother was not only borderline psychopathic and potentially homicidal, but quite evidently in the employ of the government. So the "criminal" element, which of course became the primary focus of the media and former "friends," was a constant problem.

But this element was constantly in tension with a whole other aspect that much more accurately reflected the character of the membership. And which, of course, is rarely mentioned. Most Panthers did *not* join because they wanted to ambush cops, rob banks, or flash guns on other black people. Early Panther code: "No Panther will use drugs or alcohol when about the business of the Party. . . . No Panther will point a gun at a member of the Party or community. . . . No Panther will take as much as a needle from the community without payment . . . full and fair payment."

Those, the rank-and-file members, are the brothers and sisters I respected and tried to represent. They were as devoted, sincere, hardworking, and idealistic as anyone in the movement. And they were brave. They truly wanted to serve the people and uplift our communities. Most were grassroots. Some high school dropouts, some college students. A few, whose problems were war-related, were recovering addicts, some homeless. Others were well trained, politically conscious Vietnam veterans. Also, as is always the case with us, many of the party's most devoted and sincere members were sisters. And, as in the Southern movement, these were the ones who day to day did the heavy lifting. As usual, our sisters were the backbone of the organization and as usual have never been sufficiently recognized. Nuff respect.

These brothers and sisters, the grassroots rank and file, were the forces responsible for every significant accomplishment of the organization. They lived among the people, ran the educational programs. Fed the children. Canvassed the community for the various campaigns. Fought off the military onslaughts of the police and FBI. And paid the price for their courage and idealism. They were in the community, tried to serve the needs of the masses and articulate community concerns. They patently were not about military posturing to impress the media or white wannabe revolutionaries.

Twenty-nine died at the hands of the police. Over one thousand were arrested; some are still in jail. I have nothing but respect for these brothers and sisters. I only wish that there had been some way I could have more effectively advanced their values and protected their interests with the small, ingrown, under pressure, circle of policy-makers. I regret . . . very much . . . that in the prevailing circumstances this was not possible.

First of all, a lot of the chaos and paranoia we now know to have been deliberately induced. But these efforts also found fertile ground in the limitations and insecurities of the leadership. And the internal culture also fed into that. From a SNCC perspective, the organization seemed to me entirely too hierarchical. With a quasi-military chain of command even. Not enough serious political education instead of slogans. Also, there apparently was no time, and absolutely no provision, for full internal discussion within the organization. Instead, "mandates," "orders," and "directives" were handed down whether or not folks agreed with or even understood them. You can understand that this aspect would bother me quite a bit.

In this climate, to raise questions, even legitimate and sincere ones, was too often seen as disloyalty or as challenging authority, an error to be corrected with physical or ideological intimidation, expulsion, or both. I myself never witnessed any of this, but brothers and sisters did tell me that occasionally, in some chapters, "discipline" could be ordered and enforced by goon squads. C'mon, "beat downs" may be a common gang tactic, but they are no way to build loyalty, unity, or even discipline in a radical black political movement. They had no business in our organizations, especially among bold and defiant young brothers and sisters who were already facing intense *external* pressures. Any tendency toward physical discipline was a primary threat to the health and survival of a unique, potentially very valuable movement—a movement that, God knows, already had no shortage of political enemies, and some very dubious friends.

•　　•　　•

So my ambivalence grew. I was reluctant to give up on the great possibilities I saw in the Black Panther Party. I met many committed brothers and sisters there, who would remain lifelong friends and allies. David Brothers *(Light the Fire)*, chairman of the New York Panthers, has been such a friend. Brother David is, as the Rasta brethren would say, a truly black-hearted man. Brother David, now old but still very clear, is still active. It is truly heartwarming to see even today the spontaneous respect with which he is always greeted by Panther veterans we happen to meet. It is always "How you doing, Brother Chairman." "Brother Chairman, you all right." And the party offered valuable programs that our communities needed and that therefore deserved to be preserved and further developed. There was a political consciousness and militant spirit that, properly disciplined, could have been of immense value to urban youth and the community. Which in fact was precisely what the government was so anxious to prevent. These were things that one was obliged to fight for. On the other hand, there was the irresponsible adventurism; a rigid, politically confused ideological direction; and the strong-arm tactics, which combined to suggest that the organization might not be salvageable. Not wanting to accept that, I resisted that conclusion perhaps for too long. Once I allowed myself to admit it, I began to separate myself.

What triggered that? Well . . . there were many things. It was more like a growing awareness. But the final straw was a reported inexcusable incident in the New York SNCC office. I and all of us in SNCC were angry when we heard that a group of "West Coast Panthers" had invaded the office, held Jim Forman at gunpoint, and threatened his life. C'mon, that was it, Jack. Time to reevaluate the relationship.

I mean if the Panthers could be *that* ignorant of history, so confused, and with so little respect as to bring that kind of thuggery to a man like Jim? A brother who'd devoted his life and exhausted himself in our struggle? How'd Jim Forman get to be the enemy? You knew it was time to move on then. That episode really exemplified the utter and dangerous confusion of the times. At the time of the incident, we all understood that these particular Panthers were Cleaver's enforcers, acting on some beef or other between Forman and Cleaver. But, given the disinformation and dirty tricks, who knows for sure? They could easily not have been Panthers at all but hoods in black leather jackets sent in by the COINTELPRO criminals. Or if Panthers, they could have been renegade jackanapes acting out on their own. Or, as folks believed, Cleaver *may indeed* have ordered it. Somebody must know what actually went down and why. I, and most of us, am still not sure. But, whatever the case, it was inexcusable.

And beyond the incident, what really shook and insulted me was hearing that Jim thought that I may have been somehow involved. What?

Hey, I know Jim had been deeply affected, psychologically, for it had been an ugly ordeal. That I could easily understand. After everything he'd survived, from racists in the South, to come to be possibly blown away by his own people? That would be a blow for anyone. But even so, to *imagine* that I could ever be party to something like that? After everything he and I'd been through together? Of course, Jim and I have long since cleared that up. I mention it only to illustrate the utter insanity of the times and the effect on human relationships. And it signaled the beginning of the end for me and the Panthers. *[Forman himself has since denied that the incident ever took place. —EMT]*

Meanwhile, the feds had apparently seen the error of their ways and quietly released my passport. My wife's troubles continued. She'd had a contract for three albums per year with a recording company, all of which had always done very well indeed. Now the company—without the courtesy of a letter or even a phone call—simply allowed the time for the next recording session to go by. But by then, nothing surprised us. More evidence of the orchestrated conspiracy to make her a nonperson in the American entertainment industry.

South African students would tell us of their surprise and disappointment on arriving in America and not being able to find any of her records in the stores. (Of course they were banned in South Africa.) Also, the federal government now involved itself in the campaign against her. The IRS developed an aggressive interest in all her past tax returns. This was more than strange because she had always been superscrupulous where her tax obligations to the American government were concerned. There was less and less, professionally speaking, to keep her in the United States. Shortly after the wedding reception, we'd begun shipping home furnishings and personal effects to Conakry. Once that process was complete, we followed.

[In this section, Ture frequently refers to the government's dirty tricks but never at any length or in much detail. I have not examined the complete FBI file on the brother, but from the little I've seen, the file in its entirety must be voluminous and quite revealing. According to people who have inquired, the Bureau admits to having in excess of twenty thousand pages on the brother. The Bureau must also have opened one on Ms. Makeba if the surveillance/harassment to which she was subjected is any indication.

Ms. Makeba, from My Story:*

> *The FBI, which has been following Stokely everywhere he goes for a long time, now begins to follow me, too. Every day there is a car in front of the house. The car is always behind, even when I am alone. I have a feeling they must hear what we say inside the house, because when I get to where I am going, there are FBI men there, too. How do they know where I am going if they do not listen to our*

conversations? It can be Stokely's mother's house in the Bronx, or it can be the airport. They are there. These faceless white or black men in their suits sitting in their cars and looking at me. When I arrive in a city, they come to meet me. They are easy to spot because they are conspicuous. I know the difference between strangers who look at me because they saw me on TV or like my music and these men who look at me because they are studying me. After I rent a car, I see them at the desk getting the address of the place I am staying, and when I get to the hotel, they are there. When I leave my key at the desk, they ask what room I am in. I guess it is so they can bug it. We call them our "baby-sitters," but I am really scared. It is nerve-wracking and it is something I never would have expected in America. This is really nasty treatment from a country that is supposed to be free.

I tell Stokely I feel as if I am in prison. We even have the impression that some-one is listening when we are making love. He says, "Never talk to them. Don't look at them."

This harassment-cum-surveillance was however only the merest tip of the iceberg. The files reveal a covert campaign of surpassing ugliness. It involved character assassination by way of planted rumors, forged documents, and letters.

I saw documents proposing that the Bureau use its "criminal contacts" in the black community to circulate allegations that "Carmichael is a CIA agent." (When this particular FBI fabrication surfaced, it was picked up and dissem-inated most vigorously, ironically enough, by the Black Panther Party leader-ship, the then Marxist African National Congress supporters in this country, and later by the KGB.)

Another proposal was to use the same channels to circulate the idea that Carmichael has "sold out" and "become bourgeois" as evidenced by the $70,000 house he and his wife had purchased in D.C. Those proposals were obviously implemented, because the house-purchase story appeared in the Washington Post and circulated widely in movement circles. The couple had purchased no such house.

We have mentioned the fraudulent report to an FBI handler that was to be left in a car used by Carmichael and Panther field organizers. In the prevail-ing atmosphere of paranoia and distrust Ture described, that deception could certainly, as intended, have resulted in bloodshed.

But the absolute nastiest of these proposals coming after the Carmichaels' move to Guinea was one designed to "discredit Carmichael in Pan-Africanist circles." The agent proposed that through French contacts, the Bureau get its hands on the kind of paper and typewriter in common use in Guinea. To what end? you ask. Watch. Then a letter purporting to be "from Carmichael to a black nationalist friend in New York" would be composed. The contents? The letter would complain bitterly about a purported affair between Sékou Touré and Miriam Makeba. The tone and language would be that of a new husband unhinged by jealousy and humiliation and in danger of losing control. It would

673

declare that "he could not stand it any longer" and that if it didn't cease, he would be driven to take drastic action to bring the matter to a close. Carmichael's name would be signed to it.

And the disposition of this little fiction? Much thought had been devoted to that also. The letter should be crumpled and walked on repeatedly, to give it the appearance of street litter. It would then be mailed to the Guinean mission to the United Nations by an anonymous "friend" who would claim to have found it blowing on the sidewalks of New York. The "friend" would explain that he was bringing it to the mission's attention because of the defamation and implied danger to the president.

Since the Guinean president had been the target of repeated assassination attempts by enemies, foreign and domestic, there can be no mistaking the intent of this little plan. Whether it was ever approved or implemented is not clear. But in another report, an agent gleefully describes a phone call placed to Mrs. Carmichael at midnight. The caller warned Mrs. Carmichael that a fictitious "Black Panther hit squad" was en route from California to New York for the purpose of "assassinating her son."

The tactic was successful beyond expectations, the agent gloated, because "three days later Carmichael and Makeba were on a flight to Guinea." Since this move had been contemplated and planned for a long time, this credit to his race reminds me of nothing so much as the proverbial fly sitting on the backside of a stampeding water buffalo, looking back at the dust churned up by the buffalo's hooves, puffing himself up and boasting, "Oh, see what a cloud of dust we raise!"

One assumes that these are representative examples of the field agents' "creative and hard-hitting counterintelligence measures" solicited by the director. —EMT]

Consciousness more than anything else is what separates humanity from all other animals. Consciousness is attained by the acquisition of knowledge. This is a continual process in a conscious life. Now information is not the same thing as knowledge. All conscious people, and especially we Africans, have the responsibility to struggle through the barrage of information and misinformation from the capitalist media so as to properly understand the social, political, and economic conflicts that affect us. Thus to understand our historical duty to advance the transformation of our people and societies to a better, more humane way of life. This is a lifelong responsibility. It begins with consciousness.

Perhaps the first weighty thing *Osageyfo* said to me—in our very first meeting—was about consciousness and the unity of our struggles. Whether we knew it or not, he said, the Afro-American struggle is inextricably linked to the struggle in Africa and vice versa. Those of us who were conscious of this had a responsibility to make the connection clear to those who might be unaware. The single best weapon of the enemy, he said, was a lack of consciousness among our people. The *Osageyfo* was right in this. Which is one reason the various media of the capitalist system wage so unrelenting a war to control, define, and deform our consciousness. To keep our people confused and divided: the miseducation of the Negro continued.

There is another maxim the *Osageyfo* was fond of: action without thought is blind; thought without action is empty.

Over thirty years, the All-African People's Revolutionary Party has naturally evolved, but one can say that those two ideas have undergirded our approach and mission over the years.

In 1968, in his *Handbook of Revolutionary Warfare,* President Nkrumah called for the formation of a continentwide people's party as a permanent vehicle for advancing the African struggle. He envisioned "a political party linking all liberated territories and struggling parties under a common ideology, thus smoothing the way for continental unity while assisting the prosecution of the all-African people's war." In other words, a revolutionary African united front.

The *Osageyfo* had already written that "all people of African descent whether living in North or South America, the Caribbean, or any other part of the world are Africans and belong to the African nation." So, hey, it was easy for me to persuade him that Africans in the diaspora had a real role to play in this effort. But of course that would necessitate consciousness, organization, and unity of purpose on our part. This is when he honored me with the mission to begin this work. From that moment this responsibility would become a constant and central activity in my subsequent political life. The mission: work to build the party using a simple message, *"We are an African people."*

All African-descended people living in 113 countries on the continent and in the diaspora are at the bottom the same people. In fundamental ways we share history, culture, and common enemies—racism, imperialism, neocolonialism, and capitalist exploitation. At present we suffer from disunity, disorganization, and ideological confusion. Imposed conditions that we must struggle through to attain organization, unity, and clarity so as to be able to advance the key goal—the total liberation and unification of the mother continent under African socialism. However, this is only the first major stage of the struggle. Of course, this is ambitious, a vast ongoing enterprise. A general vision, direction, and commitment. The cumulative work of many lifetimes, an incremental and continuing struggle. We understood that clearly. But we were young and, as they say, "a journey of a thousand miles begins with the first step."

•   •   •

In 1968, the first work/study circle of the new party met in Conakry. The first American circle began to meet in the United States before my return to Conakry that same year. At the time I was based in D.C., beginning my work with the Panthers, when I learned of my "expulsion" from SNCC. For some time our political emphases had been growing apart, which happens in politics. That is understandable. But I certainly did not appreciate first hearing about this from some reporter calling for my reaction and reading to me from a press release out of Atlanta. Some days later the letter came. That wasn't cool. Course there were many levels of politics involved, but it's water under the bridge now, long since resolved.

[I've never seen the SNCC letter officially notifying Carmichael of his expulsion, which had been signed by the then chairman, Phil Hutchings, himself a NAG product and a friend. However, Mrs. Carmichael did show me a letter she had received from Phil at the time. He characterized the measure as purely a political matter and assured her that it in no way diminished the strong personal affection and respect he felt for her son and herself. —EMT]

By then I'd already started drawing together brothers and sisters who I felt would be interested in the Pan-African party. Mostly people I knew from SNCC and the Panthers, these were serious, committed, disciplined, and dependable sisters and brothers. Folks I knew to be hard workers and among some of our best organizers.

When discussions began, everyone understood clearly that this would be a major commitment. We were laying the base of a permanent party in an ongoing struggle, the end of which none of us would live to see. That was clear.

Considering our organizational backgrounds, it was inevitable that our thinking about the methods and the approach to the party's operations would be greatly determined by the lessons learned from the SNCC and Panther experiences. And of course, by the *Osageyfo*'s precepts on consciousness, thought, and action.

For example, the media. We'd all seen the effects of the white media during my chairmanship. And worse, what premature media exposure had done to the Panthers: negative notoriety, much too rapid, uncontrollable growth, and of course, unwelcome attention from the police state. So we knew that media attention was treacherous. At *best*, a double-edged sword. So it was no accident that the party had been in existence in America nearly three years before issuing its first press release. We deliberately opted for slow, steady recruitment beneath the media screen to carefully establish a firm base.

The other lesson was of course the vanguard-party approach: we understood that to be a conceptual and strategic error. Often by sincere and well-intentioned revolutionaries, but a strategic error nonetheless. Because no successful struggle can be waged by a party in advance of the people. You simply can't fight the people's fight for them. The masses must be involved, organized, and brought along to make their own struggle. Only the people make history.

Thought without action, action without thought? Neither. The party emphasized a balance of work *and* study. In the Panthers I'd struggled with the leadership to emphasize and institutionalize serious political education for the membership. But by then it was too late. Circumstances working against that were already in motion.

With the new party, from its inception, we *organized* around political education. Since the struggle was about political consciousness in the community, our first responsibility was to educate ourselves seriously. So we began by setting up a rigorous and thorough political education process that was mandatory.

To this very day every new member, after an initial orientation on the goals, principles, expectations, and ideology of the party, is assigned to a work/study circle, which is the basic unit of the party. The core reading list has grown to some twenty books and pamphlets. These cover African political and cultural history, Pan-Africanism, political philosophy, and revolutionary theory. The writers include C. L. R. James, Frantz Fanon, George Padmore, Kwame Nkrumah, even some Karl Marx, and others. At regular discussion sessions, members are expected to keep abreast of contemporary political events and issues as well as the basic readings. This commitment has never changed.

[In September 1998, after a greatly weakened Ture had returned to Conakry for the last time, I called down to check with him. I was told that he now weighed under one hundred pounds, was in constant pain, and had become very weak physically. So much so, they said, that that morning he had to be propped up in bed so as to be able to conduct a meeting of his work/study circle. Within days he was dead. —EMT]

But of course, thought without action is effete, and politically meaningless. So along with serious study, disciplined and *sustained* work is the duty of all our members. Our work takes many forms. Building the party. Working with other compatible organizations, organizing the community around particular issues, or mounting occasional independent mobilizations on specific issues. Working diplomatically, at international conferences and with progressive governments and revolutionary and progressive movements in many countries around the world. Our work has been continuous on many, many fronts.

The primary and fundamental emphasis of the work has been the need for our people's *organization*. Not ad hoc mobilizations but permanent, effective, systematic organization. This is necessary because:

. . . without organization there is no way to channel all the energies of all the people who want to work for our betterment and improvement.

. . . organization is necessary because without it we leave ourselves open to the oppressors' tactic of "divide and conquer" or "divide and rule."

. . . organization is necessary as a tool to make democratic decisions about our future direction.

. . . organization is necessary because without it we let issues dictate what direction we go in. The enemy (capitalists) constantly creates issues for us to respond to. The end result is that we go in circles and never really get to the root of the problem.

. . . organization is necessary because oppressed people have never defeated their oppressors without it.

So clearly lack of effective organization is our greatest enemy. What is the nature of the organization we need?

. . . permanent organization because without it there is no guarantee that the struggle will continue beyond the current phase. We also need to plan for generations ahead because our development spans forever.

. . . organization that allows for us to correctly interpret the true nature of our oppression and how it affects the political, economic, and cultural reality of our lives and to educate the people as to what we are fighting against and what we are fighting for.

. . . organization that is capable of mass mobilization when necessary to keep the collective energies of the people working for the right objectives.

. . . revolutionary organization that seeks a total transformation of society from the backward way of having a privileged few who own and control almost everything to a new kind of society where there is no exploitation of the masses of the people.

This has been a continuous struggle in which there have been victories, accomplishments, and of course setbacks. That is the nature of the beast. The struggle goes on. *La luta continua.*

[Quite obviously the foregoing is not presented as a history of the work and fortunes of the All-African People's Revolutionary Party. It is merely Bro Ture's comments on its origins, principles, and motivating mission. Before his return to Africa for the last time, the brother did tape a brief history of the party.

Having been present when he instructed that it be sent me for that purpose, I know that Bro Ture intended that account—or at least elements of it—to be incorporated into these memoirs. For whatever reason, I have never received that material. Consequently we have no discrete, summarizing reflection by Bro Ture on this important aspect of his life and work—particularly the party's work, struggles, and accomplishments and the lessons he derived therefrom. Doubly regrettable because, as will be clear from scattered references and incidents in his

narrative of his later years, the party's work continued in interesting and con-
sequential ways on a great many fronts in many countries. It is entirely likely
and devoutly to be wished that such a history will one day appear. Nonetheless,
it would have been instructive to have the brother's uniquely informed per-
spective here. —EMT]

CHAPTER XXVII

Conakry, 1968:
Home to Africa

This time, Jack, I'm kicking and screaming to the world.
This Africa belongs to me as much as it belongs to you.

Our return to Guinea to live as a married couple was low-key, very businesslike. Nothing at all like the bustle and fanfare of the first visit what with the huge international conference and all the cultural events and receptions. People went out of their way to make us feel welcome, but it was simple, efficient.

It was welcome. Here are the arrangements we've made. Here is where you'll live. Your household effects have already arrived. Let us know what help you need getting settled. Boom, boom, boom. Very efficient. I liked that.

President and Madame Touré were warm, welcoming us "home to Guinea" on behalf of the government and people. We should from now on consider ourselves Guineans and the country our home.

Of course we were honored. But honestly, I took that as a formality. I had been thinking of Conakry more as a base for a few years. A place to study, learn, regroup, and then move wherever struggle sent me. Even back to the United States perhaps. As it turned out they were quite right. Guinea would become my home, and not for a few years either, but for life.

Madame Andree Touré was a spontaneously kindhearted woman, traditionally African. She was always most kind to us and invaluable to Miriam with all the domestic problems of getting settled. Madame Touré became—and remained—a great ally and confidante of my wife's and a friend to our family. It was not for nothing that the people always praised her for her legendary kindness.

President Nkrumah was similarly businesslike. I was presented to members of his staff and we got immediately into a detailed discussion of my duties. Clearly he'd been giving it serious thought. We have much work

to do, but of course, you'll need time or perhaps a few weeks to get accli-
matized. "Next week, sir. I'm eager to get started."

He smiled. "Everything in its time, young man. I see that you are
impetuous." And that was it, we were officially home in a revolutionary
African country. I with a new marriage, a new society, a new life.

The first issue for us was a delicate one. Zenzi and I were starting our new
life together in a new society. Naturally we were looking forward to
establishing ourselves socially, as just another couple in Conakry, but we
didn't want special treatment. People were hospitable so there were
many invitations. More perhaps than for just any new couple in town.
Zenzi, as an internationally famous *African* artist, was something of a
celebrity. I, myself, also had a certain status as an *American* freedom
fighter. So the invitations poured in. Neither of us wanted that kind of
spotlight attention for those reasons. Then we were living in a government
guesthouse in a guarded compound, with a government car and driver,
at first. This was of course President Touré's hospitality, and necessary, he
felt, for reasons of security. Of course, that was generous and something
of an honor. But there was a downside. It was also constricting as wherever we went there was this official government-driver-cum-security.

Naturally we had to reciprocate the invitations we were receiving, and
some people—especially when we'd meet ordinary people and invite
them home—you could see some of them felt a bit uncomfortable in an
"official" residence. And, of course, this was government funds, the people's money. And we'd come to support the revolution, not to profit from
it. So we wanted out of this situation as soon as possible, Jack. We wanted
our own place where people could really relax and play the music as loud
as they liked.

The more politically attuned brothers and sisters couldn't understand why we wanted to move so soon. Nonsense. You need to get accli-
matized. Accept official Guinean hospitality. We want you to have
everything you need, etc., etc. Then, of course, there was President
Touré, who might well feel that we were rejecting his hospitality and protection. We certainly didn't want to seem in any way ungrateful. So it was
a little delicate.

But the ladies finessed it. Miriam sought the advice of Mrs. Touré and
it went from there. As soon as it was appropriate, we worked out an
arrangement. Our first place was in a section they called Camayenne.
Over the years we lived in three different sections of the city.

In all my years in Conakry I met with the press only twice. The first time
was upon our return. I explained that I was there to join copresident

Nkrumah's staff and to support the African struggle in any way I was asked. I thanked President Touré and expressed my strong and enthusiastic support for the Guinean revolution. So everyone in Conakry knew that I stood unequivocally with the revolution, which did not please the U.S embassy and its local sycophants or those local elements with colonial mentalities. In fact that is when the FBI and CIA began a vicious campaign to discredit me internationally.

Guinea is not capitalist. Nor is it communist. Guinea is not France. Guinea is not Europe. Guinea is Africa. And Guinea is socialist. The task for the revolution is to find an African path to the fullest development of our people, our culture, and the nation. We are free to take what is best in the traditions and experience of our people. Also to take what is valuable and humane from the accomplishments of Europe even while learning from their moral failures and mistakes. Using the lessons of our culture and our history, and the best of Europe, the African revolution strives to build a just society worthy of human beings.

This is not the task of a single generation, one leader, or one government. It is the task of the entire people over many lifetimes in which everyone has his or her duty to perform. It is a great task with many difficulties to overcome. It requires unity and sacrifice. But it is not beyond the will, the courage, and the intelligence of our people. Only the people make history.

Our task in this generation is to begin. To clearly set an irreversible direction. To lay the framework and build the base. We must not falter. We cannot lose faith. We must not grow weary. This is our historical and revolutionary duty. We shall not fail.

That in effect (in my words) is the general vision of the African revolution held by Sékou Touré and the party. In one way or another, I heard some version of this many times from both presidents, from loyal cadres in the field, and from the youth and from the elders. Political rhetoric? Perhaps, but not empty rhetoric. Everywhere I looked I saw a serious, honest effort to implement that vision against relentless odds, some natural, others imposed. Against the machinations of formidable outside enemies and internal treachery as well as the natural inertia resulting from years of colonialism. But I believe to this day that the masses of the people generally understood and fervently supported that mission. It certainly was what I signed on for then. And it is what I still believe is necessary even in, or *especially* in, the changed and degraded circumstances facing Mother Africa and her children today (1998).

Impossible idealism? Hell, no. Idealism, perhaps, impossible, not at all. Sure, in hindsight and cynicism it is now easy to dismiss every decent and courageous attempt and creative initiative, given the state of the world today. Especially if one lives in America at the mercy of relentless media propaganda. That's what they want you to believe: that all is hopeless. But free your mind. Think about it clearly, and you will see that this revolutionary path, difficult and challenging though it proved, is still the only honorable direction available to us. The only course offering any real possibility or hope for Mother Africa and her suffering children. True then, even more so today. There is so much propaganda and rewriting of history. But we need to understand clearly what did happen and as important or more, what did *not* happen. The story I was witness to for almost forty years.

First, what did not happen. Look, had the continent come to so-called political independence in an unimaginably moral, peaceful, and benign world, the internal challenges facing Africa would still have been formidable. No question. But imagine, if you can, a rational and humane international order governed by principles of goodwill, tolerance, brotherhood, decency, and justice, expressed in acts of international generosity and cooperation. Hard to imagine, huh? Even in this benign fantasy, the purely internal challenges of African development—issues of geography, climate, culture, education, health, economics, the legacies of colonialism—would still have been vast. Of course. Certainly. And that's in the *best* of possible worlds where Africans were free to choose rationally and to plan wisely and systematically. But, of course, the world as it was in the second half of the twentieth century did not allow us the luxury of such choice. Well, what *did* it offer? Let us see.

The so-called Cold War for one. The hegemonic designs of two morally bankrupt "superpowers" seeding the African landscape with their proxy wars. Guns, land mines, and surrogate armies are not aids to development. Tanks, planes, and bombs are not foreign aid. The stubborn, destructive wars of resistance waged by settler colonies do not make for stability. Nor does predatory, multinational, corporate neocolonialism spreading corruption, ripping off resources, and distorting economic development. Or political intervention and destabilization creating and supporting brutal dictatorships so as to enable the continued foreign exploitation of Africa's wealth, nor the destabilizing effect of the pop culture imperialism of the West. These are not abstractions. Nor are they excuses. Africa has no need of excuses. These are facts. Once they overthrew the revolution, I saw them all.

Let us get the context clear here. Guinea is a medium-small African country of some ninety-five thousand square miles with a population between 6 and 7 million. With a short Atlantic coastline, it is a rugged land, with densely forested mountains, high plateaus, and a proud, very independent people.

When Zenzi and I returned in 1968, the People's Revolutionary Republic of Guinea was exactly ten years old, and all the effects of the

Cold War politics I've mentioned and colonialism were plain to see on the society.

Historically, Guinea had been part of much larger African political states—the Mandingo Empire of Mali; then later the Fulani Empire of Songhai. Now it was bordered by *six* different nation-states. Every one the creation of European imperialist whim, totally arbitrary, without geographic, cultural, or economic logic or reason. Right there, the best argument for Pan-Africanism if any were needed.

Along the coast (where Conakry is located), its neighbors are Sierra Leone and Guinea-Bissau (formerly Portuguese Guinea). Inland, it has Senegal and Mali to the north, Liberia and the Ivory Coast to the south.

Physically, I found the landscape magnificent. From the coast, the land rises sharply into the Fouta Djallon mountains. Three great rivers—the Niger, the Senegal, and the Gambia—rise in these mountains. The climate is tropical, the land fertile, and the rainfall abundant, so the dramatic mountain slopes are covered by dense tropical hardwood forests. The center of the country is a high plateau with savanna-type grasslands.

The country had, of course, been colonized, but not really penetrated, by the French, for a number of reasons: the ruggedness of the interior; the stubborn resistance of the people led by Samory Touré; the durability of their cultures; and most important, the absence of obvious, easily extracted and exported mineral wealth.

I remember only one line in a book by a nineteenth-century English explorer. Can't now recall the writer or the book's title, but one line engraved itself indelibly in my memory. The Englishman was somewhere in Cameroon. About one section he writes, "This is the most miserable, wretched, and godforsaken country I've yet seen. In two weeks I've seen *nothing from which a man might hope to take a profit.*" Reading that, I thought, good. Excellent. That's a blessed part of Africa. You check it out.

It seems that only in Africa is potential "wealth" really a curse. In every region of the continent "blessed" by vast deposits of extractable mineral wealth—gold, diamonds, oil, whatever—the people have suffered. First by foreign exploiters, then by their local surrogates. Greed combined with easily stolen wealth has been disastrous, retarding or deforming healthy social and economic development.

That principle operated in Guinea's favor. Most people were farmers growing rice and other grains on the grasslands, and bananas, yams, and a wide variety of other tropical foods. Large herds of cattle were raised on the plateaus. So we had a population largely self-sufficient in traditional ways, but not "developed" in modern Western terms, which explains the truly African quality Zenzi and I found so attractive in the society and culture.

But modern development also requires foreign exchange, which in turn requires exports through which to enter the world market. Coffee, rice, and palm oil were produced for export. Fishing could be developed, and the valuable hardwood forests made timber a possibility. Also, some minerals were present: modest deposits of diamonds and uranium in commercially exploitable quantities, and most important, vast reserves of bauxite, which properly utilized could fuel development. But absent obvious mineral wealth, the early colonists mostly stayed away. The traditional society was not deformed.

So, that was the picture at independence. A country "poor" and "small" but fundamentally self-sufficient, with possibilities within its resource base. Of which the single greatest, most impressive resource both to be developed and in turn to drive development was, hands down, the people. Not commodities, not minerals, but its proud, independent, highly disciplined, energetic, and capable people. In that decision, Sékou Touré and his party were absolutely right. As in their emphasis of the importance of women in every aspect of this national mobilization for development. The extent to which Guinea's women were both the strong backbone of the revolution as well as its beneficiaries is another aspect that is conveniently forgotten today.

There was another visible and impressive effect of the economic isolation France and its allies imposed at independence hoping to bring down the regime. Left to its own devices to collapse, the society did not. The people rose to the challenge out of their own resources. Nobody talks about that.

The regime put a great deal of energy, scarce resources, effort, and planning in educating and developing the people. They emphasized a range of grassroots community-based programs in health, agriculture, for women, the youth, the arts, etc. Food prices for the poor were subsidized. The nation was organized from the grass roots up. Promising village youth were identified and given opportunities unheard of under colonialism.

Encouraged by government programs fostering self-sufficiency, farmers grew more food, fed the nation, and prospered. Local craftsmen using indigenous materials, traditional techniques, and ingenuity produced clothes, shoes, domestic implements, furniture, and tools of all kinds. There was also a very aesthetic cultural dimension. Artists and musicians resorted to the rich heritage of their traditional cultural forms. Making a virtue of necessity, the people were producing out of their native resources much of what they consumed. A thriving and evolving domestic market was very much in evidence. The deluge of cheap, imported junk that is generally dumped into Africa, deforming the local economy, displacing local craftspeople, was conspicuously missing. And I saw nothing that suggested that the ordinary people did not fully understand and support these efforts. Nothing. In fact, the reverse. Most Guineans, especially the women and the youth, were enthusiastic.

But, as we would discover, not *everyone* was as supportive. There was some real scarcity and hardship, especially of imported goods. No nation is or can be completely self-sufficient in the modern world. I mean, what is America's trade balance today? Check it out. Nowhere do I read about these accomplishments launched by the revolution. Nor do I read about the visionless, corrupt, venal regime that has so demoralized this brave society since.

You hear a lot of propaganda today about failed experiments, misman-agement of the economy, government incompetence, and poor planning. Who am I to say that none of that happened? Show me a country where it doesn't. But that is all you hear about when Sékou Touré's Guinea is dis-cussed today. That assumes that the leadership had limitless options and choices at their disposal and simply took the wrong ones. Utter non-sense. Governments must choose a strategy of development. Or select judiciously among several strategies, mixing and matching as they go to fit objective conditions. We judge them on the consequences of the choices they make. In this case, the choices they were *permitted* to make. I mean, we saw what happened with their first "choice" as an independent people. When the people of Guinea in a free and open election exercised their right to *choose* their relationship to France. What happened?

"Oh, so you *chose* independence, did you? You thought it was a real choice, did you? Well, you shall see."

Boom. Locked treasury. Ransacked infrastructure. No currency or medium for foreign trade. No international credits. No foreign exchange. Now go on. Be independent. So we see how illusory that "choice" really was. Nkrumah's gesture we've discussed. It was generous, but at best, a stopgap buying the government a few weeks. So the next "choice." A close association with the Soviet Union. No question, at that critical moment the Soviets rescued Guinea economically and we must always be grate-ful. But left to choose selectively, would that have been the choice?

I mean, check out the details. Since the Bretton Woods capitalist cabal never did recognize the Russian ruble as an acceptable foreign cur-rency, there is no medium of trade between the two countries. This one really blew my mind, Jack. The economic relationship between two sov-ereign nations in the twentieth century begins on a system of *barter*? Give me a break. So many tons of bauxite for so many cars or so much med-icine? Talk about choice again.

But to survive, the new nation has to earn foreign exchange, even if it is on terms set by the capitalists, right? So what does Guinea have to sell that the world needs? The most marketable commodity they have is the vast undeveloped deposits of bauxite. Process it into aluminum and you have a product. Brings us to the next choice. What happens? The Soviets build Guinea—for a price—a massive aluminum processing plant. Again, one must be grateful. But in truth it is ponderous, heavy Soviet technology already close to being obsolete. Is that really the most appropriate technology for Africa? The most viable economic option? But how real a choice did the government actually have? And so it went. You get the point. Multiply these "choices" by one hundred and then talk to me about "mistakes" in economic planning. Especially when you look at what replaced it.

So we see that this mythical range of options exists only in theory. In the world of power politics and economic domination, a small, emerging nation—trying to break out of a malevolent exploitation—does what it can and what it must. Making, as Nkrumah taught, a positive out of a negative. And that is just the distractions and obstructions caused by *economic* pressures. The political pressure, overt and covert, never stopped. In fact, as long as Sékou Touré was alive, it was constant, ruthless, and growing. By the time we got there, the revolution was surrounded and grimly fighting for its very survival.

The efforts to isolate Guinea in West Africa were unrelenting. Propaganda. Subversion. Destabilization. A succession of foreign-sponsored plots and attempted coups. Constant attempts to assassinate Sékou Touré, at least three while I was there. It reminded me of what I saw on my first visit to Cuba.

First the isolation. At independence, Guinea had two stalwart allies. Two other leaders in West Africa had a Pan-African vision and commitment. Modiba Keita of Mali, Kwame Nkrumah of Ghana, and Sékou Touré of Guinea announced the formation of a West African Federation for cooperative development in economics, politics, and defense. Within six years, President Touré was the only one left standing, the other two leaders having been deposed by military coups sponsored by Western governments. France was responsible in Mali and the United States was implicated in the Ghana coup.

So when we got there, Guinea was therefore the last remaining outpost of revolutionary nationalism. The only surviving beachhead. Isolated, embattled, the party resolved that its historical and revolutionary duty was to defend the revolution by any means necessary. And they were right. Which is why the people were organized and trained for national defense. And why an efficient security apparatus had to be created. With the overthrow of the two allies, the Guinean revolution-in-the-making was diplomatically isolated, surrounded, and besieged. The French client states—particularly Senegal and Ivory Coast—harbored pockets of counterrevolutionaries trained and subsidized by French intelligence, who plotted and infiltrated constantly.

Guinean officials traveling to regional conferences reported being constantly courted with offers of money. The lavish lifestyles of their foreign counterparts were displayed and contrasted with the austere conditions the Guineans endured in a deliberately and rigorously egalitarian Guinea. Inevitably, some were seduced.

On one occasion, a loyal officer named Boiro was, I believe, returning from just such a foreign junket when he was approached by some brother officers. Upon his refusal to join their plot, Boiro was pitched out of the plane. The subsequent investigation uncovered the murder and the plot. The prison established specifically for political prisoners was named in honor of the martyred officer. Camp Boiro's first inmates were his murderers.

Camp Boiro became controversial. Of course, it became a propaganda focus for Touré's enemies, and it was projected as evidence of the "brutal repressiveness" of the regime. I have no doubt that conditions in Boiro were harsh. And no doubt that most of the horrific stories were either deliberate fabrications or grossly exaggerated. What I do know is that it was necessary to defend the revolution by all means necessary. Subsequent events have only confirmed me in that opinion.

Free choice or forced necessity? You decide.

Operationally, being attached to copresident Nkrumah's staff, I was part of his entourage. At any given time, this numbered anywhere between forty and sixty loyalists. Some had been with him in China and returned with him to Guinea. Others had left Ghana after the coup to come and share Nkrumah's exile. These were people committed to returning their *Osageyfo* to the office to which he had been elected by his people. That became my mission also. During those times, a constant influx of supporters from Ghana came for consultation and planning.

A small staff lived in the villa with the "Old Man" to see to his needs and security. Others, like myself, were scattered across the city.

Within the entourage, four of us hung together and were known as the youth group. A brother about my age, Francis Wuff-Tagoe, had been studying journalism in New York when the coup had happened. He had hastened from New York to offer his services to his leader. Naturally we were joined to each other, he being a competent journalist and a committed brother whose main duty was preparing a daily summary of African and international political news for the Old Man.

The third member was Lamin Jangha, who arrived about six months after me. A wiry, athletic, intense young brother just out of high school, he'd made his way some one thousand miles from Ghana to offer his services. I took an immediate liking to the young brother. Everyone liked him. He was spirited, smart, passionately committed, daring, and very determined, as his arrival in Conakry testified. Over the years Lamin and I would become close, traveling together on missions all over Africa and the Caribbean.

Our fourth member was Thomas "Papo" Amono, and his was quite a story. Before the coup, many Ghanaians studied in the Soviet Union. In Moscow, Papo organized a small group that persuaded the Russians to fly them to Conakry to join their deposed leader. Of that group, Papo stayed the course. He was fearless and effective in the operations in Ghana and became a tireless organizer in the All-African People's Revolutionary Party. Like me, he continues to live in Guinea and is part of my extended family.

In any case, the four of us—Francis, Papo, Lamin, and I—and of course, Zenzi, became like a real family within the group.

Lamin's story is not only interesting but instructive on the spirit of the times in Africa. He is Wolof, born in Gambia. At thirteen, he was among one hundred Gambian youth selected by the Gambian independence movement to study in Ghana, which was newly independent.

Always the Pan-Africanist visionary, President Nkrumah understood clearly that the transformation of Africa would require a generation of well-educated and politically trained workers, organizers, and leaders. He set out to help create this force. One of the first programs he instituted was intended to properly educate and train such a force among that generation of African youth, not just Ghanaians. He made scarce Ghanaian resources available for that purpose.

Thirteen-year-old Lamin was so inspired by the energy and revolutionary patriotism in Ghana that he did not want to leave. When after a year his group was preparing to return home, he and his best friend went for a farewell stroll through Accra. The boys were determined to complete their education in revolutionary Ghana and were trying to figure out how to make that happen.

Wandering aimlessly through Accra, the youths' attention was attracted to a colorful map of Africa on a wall. They talked their way inside and were received by the owner, who was the editor of the party newspaper. Impressed by the boys' intelligence and militancy, the editor agreed to intercede on their behalf and to act as their sponsor. The editor immediately went to Flagstaff House to apprise the president of the youths' situation. Nkrumah instructed that those Gambians who wished to remain in Ghana for education be given scholarships through high school to university level. Thus Lamin was completing his last year in high school in Ghana when the coup happened (1966). First he was heartbroken, then outraged. He decided to graduate, then to make his way to Guinea to work for the *Osageyfo*. How the youth was able to organize that is a whole 'nother story, but a year after his graduation, here he was in Conakry.

There was a Guinean brother who in the early days would be important to my education. One morning I was at the villa when a young officer came striding up, snapped off a salute, and greeted President Nkrumah.

"Ah, Lieutenant Kouyate. I want you to meet Stokely Carmichael."

The brother was in fatigues but they were parade-ground crisp. An exceedingly tall, very dark brother with an alert expression and a smile that lit up his entire face, this young officer would become a close friend.

The brother was impressive—correct, professional, and highly competent. He spoke English well and was the military liaison to the Nkrumah entourage, so we saw a lot of each other. In fact, he supervised my military training. From the duties assigned to him, he was obviously highly regarded by his superiors. Not only was he the official military liaison with the liberation groups operating from Guinea (at that time just about all of them), but this youthful officer was also the Guinean representative to the Subcommittee on Liberation of the Organization of African Unity, at that time of independence struggles, the single most important committee of the OAU. And we were roughly about the same age. This really impressed me.

That was not just Lieutenant Kouyate's assignment, it was his vocation. He was passionately committed to the liberation of the continent and in constant touch with all the groups. So I could learn a lot from him. And did. He spoke many languages; his English was good, but he was never satisfied with it. It was classroom English, somewhat correct and stilted. The brother really wanted to speak English like a black American, so he listened to soul music *all* the time. Then he would come up with long lists of words, phrases, idioms, for me to explain. So I taught him Ebonics and he instructed me in the nuances of local behavior, what was expected and what was taboo. So apart from my military training, we had a lot in common. This brother also had a sincere admiration for Sékou Touré and was fiercely loyal to the mission of the revolution. We became very close. I thought him an admirable young revolutionary warrior.

Hey, look. I went to Guinea because there was a lot I needed to learn from President Nkrumah. So of course I wanted and intended to study. That's clear. But also I was there to fight for Africa, Jack. And especially to do anything necessary to restore Nkrumah to the leadership of Ghana. I made that clear often. So often, in fact, that the Old Man often found it necessary to caution me against what he called my "youthful impetuosity."

"What every true revolutionary needs is a sense of irony and a lot of patience. You must learn to curb your impatience and youthful impetuosity."

"Yes, sir."

"I mean, tell me, do you believe in the inevitability of the African revolution?"

"You know I do, sir."

"Very well, so you know it will come?"

"Yes, sir, without a doubt."

"So it can only be then that you must think that *you* should be the one to make it?"

"That would be egotistic and presumptuous, sir. A true revolutionary is never . . ."

"Very good. But y'know, you do remind me of a man standing on the shore watching a boat approach. Now he *knows* the boat is coming. He can clearly see it coming. But he is impatient. He must wade out to meet it. Which in no way speeds up the boat's arrival. At best, the man is soaked; at worst, he drowns. The boat's progress is not affected in the slightest. All impatience is selfishness and egotism. Remember that."

"I see, sir, thank you."

Then he hands me these books. About five books, tells me to read them and bring him a report. On something or other, I forget what. So I takes the books. But you know I was mad, Jack. Here I come to fight, this man gives me books? By the time I gits home, Jack, I'se hot. Actually pulled back my arm to throw the books against the wall hard as I could until I remembered they were the *Osageyfo*'s books.

I wrote the report. Truthfully, I just threw something together. A little five-page report. Next day, when I take it to him, he raises his eyebrows and takes it. He's sitting at his desk. He invites me to take a seat by him, but before even glancing at the report, he takes out his pen. Y'know that old British schoolmaster's red pen?

Then he starts in to reading. I'm sitting there watching that red pen flashing. I mean just flashing everywhere, Jack. Crisscrossing the page, back and forth, up and down, marking up errors, ridiculous errors, careless errors, stupid errors. Marking them in red. When he hands me back the report, you could see nothing but red ink everywhere, Jack. He looks at me steadily.

"Oh, I thought you said you came here for revolution."

I humbly gets up. I thanks him and drags myself out the room. But after that, I swore he would never put another red mark on any report he gave me to do. Of course he still did. But very, very few. And never like that again.

In Conakry, being part of the entourage, I attended meetings with the various delegations coming in. I participated in the study group of the party and took military training with the Ghanaian unit of the civil defense. One regular responsibility of mine was preparing analytic reports, ostensibly to update President Nkrumah on various aspects of the ongoing struggle in Africa. In retrospect, I think that this may have been as much for my benefit as his. I certainly learned a lot about the politics and ongoing day-to-day realities of the African struggle. But of course, I was gung ho. I really wanted to fight. For *Africa*? What's wrong with you? So did the younger group—about five or six of us—inside the entourage, which kept pushing for action.

We saw that different people kept coming to Nkrumah proposing missions inside Ghana. Some clearly were just hustlers, taking money for missions that never happened. So the group nominated me. Decided I should be the one to approach the Old Man to get a mission for us. So I said, "The youth group sent me. You know, sir, some of these people claiming to be fighters . . . We just don't know . . . They don't seem to be having much results. After all, sir, you do have us. Give us a mission and we'll show you what we can do." He looked surprised. But he didn't say no. But we kept gently bugging him. Finally, I think he figures, "All right, let me get rid of them."

So he gives us not a mission but a problem, a test. An objective with certain firm conditions, above all, no loss of life, an attack only on property . . . a particular government building to be taken down. Exactly how would you set about such a mission. Bring me a plan of operations.

So we set to work. Entry and exit routes. What would be required: matériel, personnel, contingency plans, the entire process. We went over it from every possible angle. Changing, revising. Our slogan for when we would present the plan to the Old Man was "Not one error." Finally, we were satisfied.

He takes the plan and keeps it. Says nothing to us. But he kept studying it, trying to put holes in it. But he couldn't. No way. It was thorough, Jack, thorough. While *Osageyfo* was reviewing, I got a meeting with his copresident. See, I knew the contradiction between them. Sékou Touré was indignant. He wanted to march the army in there and put him back. It was Nkrumah who vetoed that, for reasons that, incidentally, I now think were correct. But then I was definitely with Sékou Touré.

I told him, I said, "Sir, good news."

"Oh, yes, I need some good news. What is it?"

"Yes, sir, I believe it's possible the Old Man is about to give us permission to do a mission."

He laughed. "Oh, yeah? You think so, eh?"

"Yes, sir."

"You gonna do it?"

"Of course, absolutely, sir."

"Is he really going to let you?"

"Looks like it, sir, but we're gonna really need your help." He looked over the plan and smiled broadly. "So how can I help?" So I told Sékou Touré exactly what we would need: passports, access to the diplomatic pouch, certain materials, etc., etc. I'd brought a list, which I went over along with the process. The reconnaissance, how we'd get in and out, where we'd drop the matériel. How we'd get it to the target. Every last step.

He just leaned back, threw his head back, and listened with a smile growing wider all through.

"So you seem to have taken everything into account. Okay. Those items, you've got it." He told me when and how we could start getting everything we needed just as soon as the Old Man gave his permission.

I said nothing about this to Nkrumah. Not one word. We went ahead and put everything together. People who were to go, were ready to travel. Who would take in the arms. Where we would drop them. Who would pick them up. Everything. By then the Old Man had had the plan for nearly three weeks. So I went back to see him. He's sitting at his desk holding the plan in his hand. He motions me to sit and just sat holding the plan.

Finally I say, "You know, sir, you've had that plan for quite a while now."

"Well, what about it?"

"Well, sir, we're ready to go."

"Ready to go? How can you be ready to go?"

"We're ready to send people, sir. We've got the people to go."

"Really. You will need reconnaissance. What plans . . ."

"Figured we'd do what the CIA does. Send in a journalist." He wanted to know who. I explained she would be Afro-American. A sister from the party. Smart and politically experienced.

"You seem to have taken care of the details. Let's see, what about passports, explosives, equipment—where will you get those?"

"Your copresident, sir."

"What?"

"Your copresident has offered everything we'll need, sir. Everything on this list. Everything."

So now he knew we had him because Sékou Touré was on board. He said, okay, you can go.

When our sister arrived from the States, I informed him. He said to bring her right away, I want to meet her. We go over. He greets her and tells me to return in an hour. I knew he would really grill her, but I knew this sister was clear and politically mature. Our sister blew his mind.

I gets back and he couldn't believe it. How does she come to know so much about Nkrumahism? He was surprised that someone from the

States understood his thought so well. I told him we'd been studying him closely. Anyway, he said he was impressed with her preparation for the mission. In fact, sufficiently impressed that he even had a few missions of his own he wanted her to undertake for him inside Ghana. Her reconnaissance went off well. After that it was go.

As I said, he'd entrusted missions to several groups. But we were the only one that successfully completed ours. Everything according to plan. The building came down. No loss of life. It created quite a stir inside Ghana. One of the newspapers, the *Legon,* even ran stories claiming that Kwame Ture was responsible.

After we did it, Nkrumah recognized that our group was quite capable of that kind of operation. But y'know, he then completely froze all activity of that kind. He started to move me more politically. He told me that I had no diplomatic training, which was true. Consequently, he began to send me on missions of a diplomatic nature so I could get that kind of experience.

We, of course, kept looking toward the time of his return to Accra. But he definitely seemed to be putting a brake on those activities. At the time that puzzled me a bit, but I think I understand better now. I've thought about this seriously over many, many years. And, you know, a lot of my attitude toward the cancer comes from his influence. Let me reflect carefully because I've never said this publicly. . . . But when I look at all his movements, I really think that Nkrumah knew—long before we did—that the cancer he had would not allow him to return to Ghana. But he was confident that the African revolution would triumph, whether he was here or not. I told you his example of the boat approaching and me wanting to plunge in and him saying, "All impatience is selfishness and egotism"? His attitude was, look, this is a struggle. The enemy will do anything in his power to target the generals. If you are out front, you must expect to be attacked. Survival is not guaranteed, but whatever happens to you personally, the struggle will go on. I think about his attitude often.

Unfortunately, when everything was in place and we were just about ready to go in seriously, he fell ill and had to be taken to Romania, where he died. After that, there was nothing we could do. But there's no question, with Guinea's help we could have restored him. He would have walked back, in triumph. No question. The masses loved him. It was only the bourgeoisie . . .

No one knew that better than those military CIA stooges. Even in death, Jack, they were scared of him. Look at what happened. I mean, when the plane brought the body back from Romania, they refused to let it land in Accra. Either they were terrified even of his corpse or they were paranoid. They were convinced that reports of his death were a ruse. And then, once he set foot on Ghanaian soil alive, what could they do? Even if they arrested him, they were terrified that the people—even elements of the army and police—would rise up. So they denied the plane clearance to land.

Then, afterward, when it was clear that the *Osageyfo* was truly dead, the military regime asked Sékou Touré to repatriate the body for an "appropriate" funeral. President Touré said fine. But not until the plotters apologized officially to the nation for the coup against President Nkrumah. Which, of course, they couldn't do. So President Touré ordered a state funeral and ordered the body interred with full honors in Conakry. Revolutionaries and heads of state from all over the world came. The Guinean masses turned out in their hundreds of thousands. His family came from Cairo. It was a fitting final tribute to one of the moral giants of our time. A true African patriot and visionary. A committed revolutionary. Peace be unto him.

[Gamal Nkrumah, Cairo, 1999:

"I was a young boy when the coup happened. I remember only a strange tension and silence from the people in Flagstaff House that morning. Then I remember we children and my mother being driven somewhere by soldiers and my mother berating them fiercely. You should be ashamed. Look at everything my husband has done for this country. You will come to regret this. None of the soldiers said anything. Nor could they meet her gaze. That I remember. Then President Nasser sent a plane for us and we flew to Cairo.

"I was about fourteen when I went to Conakry for my father's funeral. There were a great many people and much too much ceremony and formalities for a fourteen-year-old boy to sort out. But one impression has remained clear—my utter fascination with Stokely Carmichael and Miriam Makeba. Why? I just thought they were the most strikingly attractive and intriguing-looking couple I'd ever laid eyes on. I kept looking at them. Naturally, everyone was very solicitous and very kind, but for some reason, I particularly remember them.

"A few years ago I again saw Ture at the Seventh Pan-African Congress in Uganda. He was forceful and uncompromising in his speech. Not at all diplomatic. Some present were quite offended at his tone, feeling that he was abrasive and insufficiently respectful and decorous. Perhaps. But my feeling was that he was simply concerned, deeply so, with what he saw as a betrayal of the dream he inherited from my father and Sékou Touré. So he wasn't overly concerned about protocol.

"Last year when he was here in Cairo, David Du Bois and I visited him. Knowing he was sick, I worried about how we would find him. Well, one could see that physically his health was seriously compromised. He had difficulty walking. But his spirit was just amazing. He was just so excited to be going to South Africa for the first time. His enthusiasm was contagious. There was something youthful, even boyish, in the exuberance of his anticipation. In the intensity of his feeling for Africa."]

•   •   •

Before leaving the States, I had been aware of an organized campaign of defamation to discredit me politically. It was old-fashioned character assassination—that mess about my working for the Agency. I suspected— later confirmed—that it originated with the FBI. But I figured that everyone who knew me understood how completely silly that had to be. Which was true. However, after I left the Party and made my criticisms public, the Black Panther leadership had begun to propagate those same FBI lies. Go figure.

Once I was in Guinea, I put the nonsense out of my mind. I figured I'd left that bush-league, transparent nonsense behind in America. I would discover that this wasn't true. *[Earlier we introduced the FBI report outlining the Bureau's plan involving Sékou Touré, which was intended to "discredit" Carmichael in Pan-Africanist circles. —EMT]*

In 1969–70, somewhere about then, Sékou Touré told me that Prime Minister Fidel Castro was coming to Guinea on an official visit. Naturally I was excited, remembering his warmth and kindness during the OLAS conference. It was a good visit, as I recall, of about a week or so. Treaties of friendship, trade, cultural exchanges, and mutual defense were signed. The Guinean people gave Fidel a hero's welcome, and he won them over with his honesty and his humble and direct manner.

I was, of course, delighted to see Comandante Castro again. We met several times, all at official functions, and if he seemed a little formal or distant, I thought nothing of it. He was, after all, a guest, on state business and with a very full schedule. So I gave it no thought. Of course, I would have been pleased for the kind of face-to-face discussions we'd had in Cuba. I was therefore real surprised and upset by a tense encounter with elements of his security detail on the way to the airport to see the delegation off.

[Beyond that single elliptical aside during conversation, Ture never elaborated on that "tense encounter" with Cuban security. From other accounts, it appears that some of the Cuban bodyguards cut off the brother's car, flashed their weapons, and warned him, on pain of his life, to keep his distance from the prime minister. An unfortunate but quite understandable overreaction by men conditioned by repeated CIA attempts on their leader's life and agitated by the KGB's apparent legitimizing of the FBI disinformation. —EMT]

Shortly after the visit, President Touré called me in. He said that my name had come up at a briefing for him and his security chief by the KGB man from the Soviet embassy. The KGB was now propagating the FBI smear that I was a CIA agent. Sékou Touré's reply to the Russian was a masterpiece of African irony.

"Carmichael a CIA agent, eh? Well, very good. Then he's welcome. Everyone knows that Guinea is a revolutionary country and CIA agents always find their graves in Guinea. So all CIA agents are more than welcome here." I don't know what the KGB agent made of that. But President Touré was actually telling me this to console me. He pointed out that the KGB intelligence advisories were routinely circulated to security agencies in every revolutionary country, and Cuban security would have received one also. That cleared up the behavior of the security detail. This was causing me problems in every revolutionary country except Guinea. There was no change in President Touré's treatment of me. In fact, if anything, after that, Sékou Touré went out of his way to show greater confidence in me. I could never forget that.

Hey, there was nothing funny about it at the time, Jack. But in retrospect, after the facts emerged, one sees the ironies and absurdity of the so-called Cold War. I mean, here you have the CIA (Capitalist Intelligence Apparatchiks) putting out lies against a Pan-Africanist, then the Soviet KGB, allegedly the CIA's Cold War professional enemy, picks up the capitalist lies and circulates them? Both sides a bunch of clowns.

Were the KGB spooks merely duped to do their "enemy's" dirty trick? Or were they consciously doing a favor for their fellow spooks? Who knows? Remember now, the Soviet Union has never had an easy relationship with Pan-Africanists. They denounced George Padmore, and when Kwame Nkrumah was president of Ghana, Padmore was his adviser on African affairs. You know they could not have liked that. They also were quite nervous about Sékou Touré because of his independent streak. So who really knows why the KGB were propagating the FBI lies?

Whatever the reason, the KGB carried these charges to many revolutionary circles. The Cubans began to withdraw more and more from us. I want to make it clear that the Cuban leadership themselves never attacked us or called us a CIA agent. However, they did allow Eldridge Cleaver the use of the *Tricontinental,* their revolutionary journal, to make sweeping attacks implying that I was a CIA agent. At the time, the Cuban journal was like a bible in revolutionary circles, so you can imagine the problems it created for us around the world.

But this would pass. While we never pursued them, I and the party never changed our position of respect and support for the Cuban revolution. And gradually the lies were exposed and the relationship warmed. Later, after the coup, when I served on the Central Committee of the Democratic Party of Guinea, my job was liaison to the Cuban embassy. We did some good things. So we've had solid contacts with the Cubans to this day.

[One day in June 1998, on his birthday, I entered his room as he was hanging up the phone. He was beaming. "From Cuba," he said. "They were calling on behalf of Fidel Castro and the Cuban people to inquire about my health and to invite me to Cuba again." —EMT]

• • •

Also, you know that Huey P. Newton called me and Miriam CIA agents in the Panther newspaper? Talk about irony, the Panthers *and* the KGB propagating the same lies originating with the FBI. I mean, which side are you on, Jack?

So I knew I had to do something. Couldn't do anything with the Soviets, and Eldridge was impossible. But I figured I could get to Huey. We'd always had good vibes from the time I used to visit his mother when he was in jail. A practice I'd continued, visiting his family. I figure he *had* to know that CIA agent crap wasn't true.

Next time I was in the United States I went to California. Huey refused to speak to me. So I went to his brother Melvin, who was teaching at Merritt College. Melvin took me for a nice ride round the block. Every day Huey and I supposed to meet. Every day something happens. Then I had to leave.

"Why don't you just come out and say it, Melvin. You been chumping me off, bro. Huey has no intention . . ."

"Oh, no, no, brother. He's just really busy, man."

"Busy? Here I come all the way from Africa and the brother's too busy to see me? When *he* was in trouble, was I too busy to come here? Let's talk square." But he just kept covering for Huey. I left.

Next trip I went back to California. But I didn't seek a meeting. I asked the California party to set up a little seminar on revolution at Merritt College. Two SNCC sisters working with the party, Bennie Ivey and Dessie Woods, set up that seminar. I gets there and call Melvin. He's again noncommittal. But I purposely didn't mention the seminar at his college.

So, of course, the room is filled with Panthers. I recognized a lot of Huey's people. They were there in *numbers,* Jack. With their jaws all tight and obviously heavy, some of them. We have an intense discussion for about two hours. Just before breaking up the seminar, I said, "One thing more. This is important." I see folks exchange glances and sit up.

"One of the crude strategies used to disrupt revolutionary movements is disinformation. We call it lies. What the CIA does is to get its agents to label honest revolutionaries as CIA agents, when they know full well that these people are not agents."

Long pause. The room is silent.

"For example, Huey P. Newton, who I used to think was an honest brother, has called me and my *wife* agents. That's a serious charge. Now Huey *knows* that Miriam Makeba and I are not agents. He knows that." Silence.

"Now I used to think Huey was clean. But now I'm beginning to think that clearly he must be a CIA agent. Why else would he be doing their dirty work?"

Hey, you know, I didn't even finish dismissing the crowd before Melvin was in the room.

"Now, looka here. Looka *heah*. How can you come up in here and say that."

"How could I say what, brother?"

"You can't be calling Huey an agent up in here."

"Really. I only called him that in a little seminar room. He called me and my wife agents all over the world, Jack. We gotta talk, Melvin. I want to meet him."

Of course then, that same day, the meeting is arranged. It was up in some little restaurant, I forget exactly where. I went alone with a tape recorder. But we didn't even tape the meeting. I walk in. Huey is there with his security looking all militant. He's glowering. I walk over and hug him. He's all stiff and kinda pushes off.

"Look, mah man. You can't be coming on my turf to call me no CIA agent."

"Hey, be cool, *brother. You* called me *and my wife* agents all over the world. You know what that did?"

"Well, at the time, I had wrong information."

"You think *I* don't know you had wrong—"

"But still, you can't be coming to Oakland to call me—"

"*I* can't? What *I* did to *you*? What *have* I done to you? You want me to tell you what you did to me? What you did to me in Cuba? In the Soviet Union? Can I tell you how close you came to getting me killed? I called you in one little room full of your own people. You called me an agent before the *world.*"

That's how Huey and I began to talk again.

This is now 1972, our fourth year in Conakry. Zenzi and I had spent a quiet, pleasant evening at home. Sometimes I'd ask her to sing just for us. That was nice. We were living in Villa Andree in a nice little round house on the beach. I think we'd just retired, but were not yet asleep.

Suddenly, gunfire. Loud, close-sounding gunfire. Sounds like small-arms fire. There is noise of movement across the beach outside. The lights flicker and go out.

"Oh, man. I think it must be a coup." The phones work. I begin to call. The palace says it's no coup. It's an invasion. They think the Portuguese. I'm still not convinced. This may yet be the long-awaited coup.

[The neighboring territory, then Portuguese Guinea, now Guinea-Bissau, was undergoing a fierce and protracted war of independence. The liberation forces,

PAIGC (Partido Africano de Independencia de Guiné y Capo Verde), were led by the impressive agronomist/philosopher Amilcar Cabral, for whom Carmichael developed a high respect. Sékou Touré afforded PAIGC bases in Guinea from which to liberate their homeland, as well as military and diplomatic support. This presumably was the motive for the Portuguese aggression. —EMT]

Outside I can still hear shooting. I call the palace again. Where do you want me? Stay close. It won't come to that, but prepare to defend your wife and home. Await further instructions.

Defend the home how? My assault rifle was over at the villa with the unit's weapons. All I had in the house was a little nine-millimeter that D.C. had given me. A beautiful piece, but hardly adequate now. *[D.C.: Panther Field Marshal Donald Cox, a leader widely respected among the Panther membership for maturity and integrity. —EMT]* What I really wanted was to go join my unit, retrieve my weapon, get in the trenches, and defend the revolution. I was young and eager, bro. The radio station was still up. It was a Portuguese aggression. The armed forces were defending key points. The people's militia was engaging the invaders. People should stay inside. Members of the militia should report to their units. So maybe it really wasn't a coup after all.

About 4 A.M., we decide—whatever it was, coup or invasion—I should get Miriam to the diplomatic residence of the Tanzanian embassy. She held a Tanzanian passport and I figured, whatever went down, the diplomatic immunity of the residence would be respected. After that I'd join up with my unit and hopefully find some action. The ambassador says good. Come on over. Except the residence is clear across town on the other side of the bay.

It was hair-raising because you couldn't tell exactly what was going down. The streets were deserted, but you could hear gunfire everywhere. Sometimes real close, sometimes in the distance. At one intersection we ran up on some uniformed troops.

"Oh, good," says Miriam, "those must be our boys." But I was looking at the uniforms. Brand-new. Fancy boots. Their weapons weren't ours. New, shiny. Also, they were all wearing colored armbands.

"Baby, those ain't ours." The officer signals us to stop. Peers into the car. I smile, pump my fist, and make sounds of support. The officer smiles widely, salutes, and waves us on.

At one point the road went past the PAIGC camp. Talk about a firefight, Jack. I swear I could hear bullets whizzing over the car. I shouted, "Get down. Get low." And floored the gas. I was glad then for the SNCC training in defensive driving. Thank you, George Greene.

Turns out that was the fiercest firefight. On the PAIGC forces, who were the real target. Oh, man, those brothers and sisters of PAIGC really threw down, Jack. They weren't giving up nothing. Taking no prisoners. Stopped the mercenaries cold. The mercenaries also made a strong move on Camp Boiro to free their fellow counterrevolutionaries. That was repulsed also.

The ambassador's residence was on a slight bluff overlooking the harbor. We greet the ambassador and report to the palace. Ask again for an assignment or permission to report to my unit. A minister named Portos answered the phone. I could hear him reporting, I believe to the president. Comes back and tells me everything is cool. I should go to the bluff and observe troop movements between the shore and the ships. Take careful notes and report back every hour.

I tell him I'm ready to fight to defend the revolution. Can't I get a different assignment? He says good intelligence is what they need. Essentially, shut up and do what I'm told. I say cool, but that isn't what I really want to do. But, hey, I'm a disciplined soldier.

So the ambassador and I walk down to where we could observe the ships. A few boatloads of troops are on the water. And not far either, within easy range. With my weapon I could have done some real damage. Now, I'm wishing to God I had my weapon. The ambassador says, look down. Beneath us, on the beach is a group of Guineans. I was so engrossed with the invaders that I hadn't even noticed them. I recognize some ministers and a white businessman. They're using walkie-talkies. I think great, maybe they have guns. But the only gun on the beach is a twenty-two rifle in the hands of the businessman's son. No use.

I get mad, frustrated. I explode to the ambassador. Here I want to fight, they send me to reconnoiter. And look, they already got at least six observers here. I'm mad as I can be. He said let's go back and report. Perhaps there's some kind of mix-up. So we do. But by then I'm so frustrated that I'm almost yelling at Portos on the phone. He's repeating what I say to somebody.

"Comrade Portos, what's this? I tell you I want to fight and you send me to go reconnoiter? I go where you send me and you already got four, five ministers observing and reporting on walkie-talkies." Halfway through, Portos stopped repeating. But my voice must have carried, 'cause in the background I hear a roar. *What's that?* It was Sékou Touré. He gets on the phone. We are to go back quietly and write down all their names and everything they do. The ambassador had a little super-8 movie camera and so we filmed them.

You guessed. Those suckers were all traitors working with the Portuguese. Portos himself was implicated, which is why he stopped repeating as soon as he understood what I was saying. They were all tried and convicted.

After that, the Conakry gossip grapevine said all kinds of strange things about me. That I was really Sékou Touré's secret spy. A secret intelligence agent. That I was only pretending not to speak French and the African languages, etc., etc. I didn't care to deny any of it. I just smiled and said I'm only sorry I didn't get to really fight to defend Sékou Touré and the revolution.

It was the Bay of Pigs all over again. The Portuguese apparently allowed the traitors to convince them that the people would rise up and welcome the mercenaries as liberators *[Sounds familiar? —EMT]*. But the aggression was doomed from the git. Defeated by an organized citizenry. The element of surprise was lost when a humble fisherman pulling his fish pots spotted them and rushed back to report to his unit leader. The people's resistance started almost on the beaches. In two days it was over. The invaders who were cut off from the beaches ripped off their uniforms and tried to blend in. But they had shot up some buses and murdered some civilians and the people were angry. They hunted them down. Sékou Touré said let the people try them. So the party members set up people's courts and convicted many of them. Some were hung. So much for their welcome as liberators.

Actually the people of Portugal owe a debt of gratitude to the Guinean people. How so? The officer commanding the invasion apparently learned something. He returned to Portugal and organized the overthrow of the fascist dictatorship a few years later. Check it out for yourself.

[I did. I discovered that the young officers who later overthrew the Portuguese dictator had indeed served against the liberation forces in Mozambique, Angola, and Guinea-Bissau and had been disgusted by the behavior of their government toward people fighting to be free. —EMT]

Culture is politics; politics is culture. The two are inseparable. In fact, politics proceeds out of culture, then turns around and defines culture. Which is why all conscious Americans have good reason to be particularly worried about now.

I understood this relationship theoretically. But it was in Guinea that I really saw it in action. That is one aspect of struggle that was so graphic, in Sékou Touré's time. Sékou Touré understood the importance of culture. He loved intensely, I mean personally delighted in, his people's culture. But besides that, the party clearly understood that the traditional culture was a key element from which to mold an African character to the revolution. So they took concrete steps to preserve, develop, and institutionalize nationally many, many traditional forms. So they supported dance groups and schools, musicians, artists, and the famous griots and so on. But not just the arts, also the ethics and values of traditional culture, an *African* sensibility that I called African humanism.

And of course my wife's career brought her in touch with local musicians and dancers. She learned and adopted many traditional songs of

Guinea into her repertoire. She worked with local musicians and dancers and took them on her concert tours. So, of course, I learned a lot about the culture, especially the very sophisticated instruments (the *balafon*, the *kora*) and the complex musical legacy. African music is all about history. So in that way I came to appreciate and understand the complexity and richness of the people's history, through the culture.

You don't see that cultural emphasis with this stunted, blind, deaf, and dumb military regime in Guinea today. That's a real loss. Very serious, very sad. What is worse is that this is not only in Guinea. All over the continent many traditional cultures are disappearing, being replaced by the absolutely worst values of decadent Western pop culture exports. And with them go many beautiful, important, and irreplaceable aspects of African humanism. That is one of the real tragedies of Africa in this century. Because this fundamental element of our being can never, never be replaced. The effect of this loss on our youth is particularly painful and destructive.

But y'know this isn't limited to Africa. I hear a lot of talk in this country (the United States) about the loss of habitat and the extinction of animal species in Africa. No doubt, that is serious and also irreversible. But there seems to be little awareness of the extinction of languages and all that is lost when this happens. The disappearance of entire cultures and everything that this means. The enormity of this loss, especially for us, for our children, but also for future generations of all humanity.

Let's be clear here. I'm not talking "aesthetic losses, quaint, archaic folkways" or any such condescending nonsense here. This is about values, civilization, African humanism. I mean, even the dimmest, most arrogant Eurocentric racists you meet in the villages. After first talking about "the poverty," they have to mention the order, the discipline, and of course, the dignity. The most striking example? Always, always the youth. "Why," they'd exclaim, "are African children so dignified, so well-mannered, so respectful?" Even they couldn't miss it. The mature, responsible gravity of the youth. Their exquisite courtesy among themselves, the civilized manners to elders and strangers. A disciplined character, even in quite young children, with stable value systems. One of the first things I noticed. Couldn't miss it.

How could these values survive transition into modern societies? How to preserve them for future generations? What aspects of tradition to preserve, and how best to ensure that? When I arrived in Guinea, these were the subject of an ongoing national conversation. Between the copresidents (peace be unto them) and among people in the party.

But now, forget it! What we see across Africa—especially in those extreme situations of political and cultural destabilization—is the exact opposite. The destruction of youth, rapid, grim, merciless. The exact opposite. Feral youth in a vacuum of values, exposed, unprotected, exploited. Instead of leadership, gangsterism, criminal warlordism, greed, crude capitalism putting drugs, guns, and sharp weapons in the hands of small children. Young women and girls brutalized. So rapid. None of this could ever have happened in the Africa I first went to thirty years ago. This is the development capitalism and neocolonialism promised us?

When I travel, especially in this country, I meet fat, smug, overfed Americans who take for granted that they have *earned*, by their *own* innate superiority as human beings, all the luxuries, indulgences, and extravagances they consume so excessively. They are not simply the beneficiaries of a rich, predatory society and a rigged game, but they have earned it all by their *own* industry and effort. From their own superior intelligence, discipline, and hard work. Therefore, they *deserve* the very best the world has to offer. What a crock. While Africans, on the other hand, backward, lazy, and improvident, are doomed by *their* own deficiencies. Africans have earned their suffering. I'd love to take their fat, complacent carcasses and place them down in a village or township. Take away their "support system" and let them match the tenacity, hard work, resourcefulness, skill, and endurance that these "backward" Africans deploy every single day of their lives. See how long they and their condescending attitudes will survive. Yes, I would.

My work with the PDG took me into every region of Guinea, villages, small towns, mountains, plains, every region. I saw firsthand the grace and dignity of the traditional cultures. African humanism. In one Soussou guesthouse while waiting for the village to feed us, I met a young white Texan, a missionary. He had no idea who I was, but he explained to me that he was there to teach the people "faith and democracy." I laughed. Then I walked him through everything that had happened since he had arrived in the village. Every step. His reception, the courtesies and hospitality he'd received, and what else he could expect. He agreed. So, I said, tell me what you can teach such people about either faith or democracy?

There is one village, Dalaba, in a beautiful verdant mountain valley high in the Fouta Djallon mountains. Steep mountains covered with dense forests of tall, African hardwoods rise dramatically on all sides. There is a stillness and a powerful, lovely calm to the spirit of the place that I cannot adequately describe. Miriam agreed that it was one of the most indescribably beautiful places we'd ever seen. And the people were just so gracious and principled. Then she said, "I'd like a house here. I'll build a house." And she did. It became our treasured retreat. That mountain village is Africa to me.

[One day we were working and the phone kept ringing incessantly. The brother saw my frustration. "Don't worry, Thelwell, when we go to Guinea, I'll gather up all the documents. Then I'll take you to this village. High in the

mountains." He described the unspoiled beauty of the setting and people in great and loving detail. It reminded me of the Jamaican mountains of my childhood. "Thelwell, we'll spend a month here, and when we come down, the work will be finished." I doubted his health would allow us any such interlude and it didn't, something I will always regret deeply. But as he described this paradise, his eyes glowed and a peace and tranquillity came over his countenance. I now know that Dalaba had to have been the place he was describing. —EMT]

We'd been based in Conakry and doing a lot of traveling when a problematic invitation arrived. Between my wife's concert tours and my political work, I'd managed to visit most of Africa except the southern rim. Usually our schedules didn't coincide, but whenever possible, I'd accompany her to a concert. Or she might travel with me on a political mission. On such missions, her presence was always an added pleasure. We treasured those shared journeys.

Miriam was of course banned from the country of her birth, which was under a boycott anyway by the antiapartheid movement. So Azania (South Africa) was out. As were the Portuguese settler colonies of Mozambique and Angola, and Southern Rhodesia, where African brothers and sisters were waging people's wars to liberate their homelands. But no problem: we knew we would one day visit them as liberated territories. Which happened right on schedule in most cases.

Which left one looming enigma at the very heart of the continent. The Congo. That vast, legendary, mysterious, tragic region in central Africa. Larger than Western Europe, immensely rich in natural resources, once home to powerful and complex African civilizations, all systematically ravaged by the most brutal European colonial rapacity the world had seen. The suffering Congo was a special case. Now nominally independent, the country had been systematically looted and degraded by the CIA puppet-tyrant Joseph Mobutu after the murder of the democratically elected Patrice Lumumba. A former corporal in the French colonial army, Mobutu had been put in place by his retreating colonial masters. This brutal puppet-dictator—propped up by the CIA and a cartel of French and Belgian capitalists—had enabled the foreign looting of the wealth, while overseeing the degradation of the social fabric, of this important, potentially great, country. A country that, properly governed with vision and integrity, should have been the engine driving the economic development of the region. In the process, Mobutu had managed to stash some $4 billion of his people's wealth in his Swiss bank accounts. This was scandalous and tragic. There was absolutely no reason for us to go there, except for revolution.

Then in 1974 this invitation comes. The political contradictions were huge, Jack. Muhammad Ali would be fighting George Foreman for the heavyweight championship in, of all places, Kinshasa. I mean, it was a dream come true, right? Two great black American champions meeting in Africa. But in *Kinshasa*? C'mon. And the bagman who negotiated the deal was none other than the European banker who managed the thief Mobutu's secret Swiss accounts. This respectable banker didn't know that he was enabling and profiting from the misery of the Congolese people? No way. He should be shot. Period.

Two problems: an African-American musician named Lloyd Price was also organizing a music festival of the African diaspora. It was featuring giants of black American popular music: folks like James Brown, B. B. King, Aretha Franklin, Marvin Gaye, were supposed to be there. I believe Bob Marley was invited along with a host of African superstars. This was cultural Pan-Africanism at the highest level, the diaspora coming home to the continent in musical terms. A sheer and dramatic demonstration that we are all at our core Africans. But in the *Congo* of all places. The contradiction was bitter. Naturally, Miriam was invited. She was ambivalent but we decided she had a responsibility to represent her people's culture. I said, "Honey, hold your nose and go."

Part of me wanted to come along, but the political contradictions were greater for me. Young people today have no real idea what Muhammad Ali meant to our generation of black people in the world. He was to us our warrior saint. This was the brother's most important fight. None of the "experts" gave him a *ghost* of a chance against the "invincible" giant Foreman. How could I not go support this brother? I sought Sékou Touré's counsel. He recognized the contradiction. His contempt for Mobutu, that "greedy, thieving traitor to Africa," knew no bounds. But so did his respect for Ali. "It's your call," he said. "A tough one. What did the Old Man always say? Maybe you can find a way to make a positive out of a negative." But on this one I really couldn't. Not with what that monster Mobutu was doing to that country.

Brother Ali himself made the decision for me by sending me a personal invitation and a plane ticket. Hey, if the brother wanted me present at his greatest test . . . decision, what decision? Let me remind you of who this brother really was to us.

It wasn't just that the brother was demonstrably the very best at what he did. We've produced great athletes before who were just that. What was different with Muhammad Ali was his unconquerable moral courage and principle. His obvious undying love of our people. The many, many sacrifices he *willingly* made for principle. A young black man up from the ghetto of Louisville, capable of saying to white America and meaning every word:

"Damn the money. Damn the heavyweight championship. I will die before I sell out my people for the white man's money. The wealth of America and the

friendship of people who support the [Vietnam] war would be nothing if I'm not content in my conscience."

How could you not marvel and be moved by courage, integrity, and sacrifice like that?

But there's even more. The single greatest—I mean most important—thing he said wasn't the much quoted "I ain't got no quarrel with them Vietcong." But rather, this one was back in 1964 when, as a youth the same age as most of us in SNCC, he had become the astonishing new "I done shocked the world" heavyweight champion. I will never forget the *clarity* of that young brother standing and listening to a lot of paternalistic, off-the-wall, credit-to-your-race okeydoke from the white press corps, speaking to white America and telling them simply: *"I don't have to be what you want me to be."*

Simple as that—refusing to be owned, controlled, or defined by white arrogance. *I* don't have to be what *you* want or expect. *That* was the declaration of independence of our entire generation. If this brother wanted me in Kinshasa, then Mobutu or ten thousand Mobutus, my black behind had to be on that plane. *"I don't have to be what you want me to be."*

I was glad I went. Even though I never saw the fight—at least not there. It was inspiring to be with Ali. White America had tried their best to destroy him. The media demonized him; they stole his titles and robbed him of his most productive athletic years. And now—so they gloated—the final act. The fearsome and invincible surrogate "white hope" Foreman would end the career and close that insufferable, defiant black mouth once and for all. Hey, maybe, but not quite yet. Ali was still Ali, irreverent, unfazed, still a-rhyming and a-diming, jes' a-poking and a-smoking.

> Think y'all was shocked when Nixon resigned?
> Then just wait till I whup George Foreman's behind.

You could see that being in Africa was important to him. You could actually see and feel him drawing strength from the exuberant love of his people. You could see that the brother's spirit was home, Jack. It was unbelievable. Wherever we went. I mean, even when he ran—no matter what time—it was as if the youth of the entire city ran with him. All around him, trailing behind, a joyous procession of ragged black youth, eyes shining with pride and excitement.

Ali, we love you. *Ali, boum aye* (Ali, kill him).

If I were Foreman, I'd have been flat out terrified. Ali was bringing all Africa into the ring with him, Jack. That is the one thing I remember most about Ali. The one thing you could not miss. His undying love for his people.

I'll say it again. This generation of black superstar athletes grinning and pimping for Nike, pushing $200 Asian sweatshop sneakers on our youth, could learn a lot from Muhammad Ali, only had they the consciousness to do so. As Mrs. Hamer said to the vice president, "I'm going pray for you."

Foreman was supposed to be unbeatable, a physical phenomenon. But Ali's confidence was infectious. Watching him train, I felt a whole lot better, Jack. And, there was another issue. See in 1968, after those crackers stole Ali's title, conscious young black athletes responded. They organized and called for a black boycott of the Olympics unless Ali's titles were restored and South Africa and Rhodesia excluded from the games. I was so proud of those young brothers and sisters. It was really a lot to ask. Young athletes giving up everything they had worked, trained, and dreamt of most of their lives. The racists on the U.S. Olympic Committee played some real hardball—threats, intimidation, putting young people's futures at risk. The boycott never happened.

But then, two massively heroic young sprinters, Tommie Smith and John Carlos—all praise, honor, and respect—stepped up big time.

In winning the two hundred meters, Brother Smith had almost shattered the world record and Brother John Carlos was a close third. Instant American athletic heroes, right? Yeah, until the medal ceremony. There the brothers made it clear that they were running for black people, not racist America. As the national anthem was being played, the brothers bowed their heads and raised black-gloved fists to the sky in the Black Power salute. It was a brave and dignified statement to the entire world by two conscious brothers. When I saw them, I was on my feet shouting. I mean shouting. I can still feel the pride and admiration that flooded every fiber of my being in that moment. Black people all over the world felt that way.

Of course, white America went crazy, Jack. The media attack dogs—no that's not fair to dogs, *curs* is what they are—set to howling for real. Calling for the brothers' heads. The old Hitler-hugging racist Avery Brundage *[perennial head of the International Olympic Committee]* kicked the brothers off the team. He had them expelled from the Olympic Village, banned from the games, and sent home in disgrace all within twenty-four hours. Talk about show of force. I mean, what had been their crime? I've always been ashamed that we Africans never defended those heroes like we should have. Their careers were ended and they were denied employment in their profession. It was a disgrace, and the black community did nothing.

Which is why twelve years later in 1980, when Carter decreed his boycott of the Moscow Olympics, I strongly supported sending a team to represent black America in Moscow. Not out of any great love for the Soviets, but as a dramatic act of independence. So as not to deprive our athletes of the opportunity they trained for. And of course, for Brothers Smith and Carlos. *We don't have to be what you want us to be.* It's a shame our community couldn't unite behind that initiative.

Back at the 1968 games, Brundage, having made an example of Smith and Carlos, reads the riot act to the brothers and sisters. Then they launched a search for a great white hope and found one.

I think it was the very next day. This huge, seriously countrified young brother from Texas put a down-home serious whupping on a Russian fighter while winning the heavyweight boxing gold.

Hey, it was an impressive display of power and skill by the young brother. I always take deep pleasure in all demonstrations of black excellence. But my pride quickly turned to dismay and anger when the Negro snatches this American flag and commences to cavort gleefully around the ring. It was no accident. In the context it was a clear betrayal. A deliberate repudiation of the two sacrificed brothers' stand. It was infuriating. Of course, I know that the young man—no more than eighteen or nineteen and as country as they come—had been cynically used. But, hey, he allowed himself to be. Our lack of consciousness, our enemies' greatest weapon. No question.

[There is no question that Big George's naïveté was cynically exploited by people he trusted in the Olympic bureaucracy. In Redemption Song, *his excellent book on Ali, Mike Marqusee reports that "the (Olympic) authorities persuaded George Foreman . . ." Later Marqusee reports, "An FBI report claimed that Foreman's victory over a Soviet fighter and subsequent patriotic display gave every American* (sic) *an emotional lift." Speak for your damn self, Edgar —EMT. "The FBI also noted the sharp contrast with the earlier, despicable Black Power black-gloved demonstration of Tommie Smith and John Carlos and the anti-Vietnam stand of Cassius Clay* (sic). *After the Olympics the FBI arranged for Foreman to receive an award from the Freedom Foundation, which was linked to the J. Edgar Hoover Foundation."]*

And now, six years later, the same flag-waver, the towering, immensely powerful Big George Foreman, champion of the world, media-appointed white hope, was supposed to end Ali's career in ignominious defeat? And, insult to injury, to do this in the heart of black Africa, Mobutu's personal plantation? So you know I had a sho-nuff attitude. *"No,"* an old man in the streets of Kinshasa told me, *"no, never, the ancestors can never allow that."* "Well," I thought, "the ancestors sure better tell Foreman that."

"Champ," I said, "you gotta do just one thing for me . . ."

"First thing, I'm not the champ. George is. He destroyed Smokey Joe. Give him his respect." Ali was scrupulous that way.

"Whatever you say. But you'll always be *our* champ. Anyway, you got to whup that Negro's gnarly head. Man, you don't beat him, why, I'ma have to whup you my own self."

"Ooh, now I'm really scared, boy." The champ mugged and rolled his eyes.

I met Foreman once, and I swear he used nonviolent techniques on me. I swear. We were at a hotel. I have an attitude because I'm supposed to meet him. Soon as I enter the room, I see this huge form bearing down on me. Foreman is bounding across the room, his broad face wreathed in smiles. He engulfs my entire hand in a massive fist, just booming.

"Mr. Carmichael, *Mr. Carmichael.* An honor. A *real honor.* Such a pleasure," and on and on, Jack. But the thing was, in person he radiated such waves of sincerity and goodwill that it was hard to remember how much I was supposed to dislike the brother. I actually found myself smiling with him. That's why I say George Foreman used nonviolence on me. Could have been an act, but then the brother would have to be the world's best actor and con man.

I never even saw the fight. At least not in Africa. Foreman got injured. Mobutu calls out his army. Ain't nobody even *think* about leaving, y'all. This was September and the party in the United States had my recruitment tour all set, so I had to leave. I hated abandoning Ali, but by then I was almost sure he couldn't lose in Africa.

I saw the fight in a theater in South Side Chicago. Tell the truth, when I remembered Foreman's size and strength, I did get a little nervous for Ali. Should have kept the faith, though. For when the Africans in the stadium in Kinshasa raised the chant *Ali, boum aye* and the brothers and sisters in the Chicago theater picked it up spontaneously, I felt a wave of new confidence. When Ali stopped the invincible Foreman—in what? Eight rounds?—there was absolute pandemonium in Chicago. Then, remember? The rains came. Seems like the moment they raised Ali's hand in victory. The heavens over Kinshasa simply opened up, Jack, and these African rains just poured on down. Remember that? One minute earlier and the fight would have had to be stopped.

"No, no. The ancestors will never allow it."

[As he talked about the Congo and the fight, Kwame's mood ran a veritable gamut. For Mobutu, anger and a deep contempt; sorrow and regret for the country and its people; merry, self-deprecating laughter as "George Foreman used nonviolence on me"; to a tone of vibrant brotherly respect and appreciation of Ali. So much so that Ali's language and sentiments in the following seemed worthy of inclusion:

"I'll tell you how I'd like to be remembered: As a black man who won the world heavyweight title and who was humorous and who treated everybody right. As a man who never looked down on those who looked up to him and who helped as many of his people as he could—financially and also in their

fight for freedom, justice, and equality. As a man who wouldn't hurt his people's dignity by doing anything that would embarrass them. As a man who tried hard to unite his people through the faith of Islam . . ."

The words are Ali's, but change only a couple particulars—the heavy-weight title and Islam—and it fits Kwame to an uncanny degree. It demonstrates, I think, the shared qualities that the two brothers-in-spirit recognized and respected each in the other. —EMT]

It was my neighbor Al-Hadji Tcham who gave me the metaphor of the tree. Now, Al-Hadji was a stone businessman. He did not like the revolution at all, no way. Denounced Sékou Touré *all* the time. So you know we argued bitterly, but strangely, we became strong friends. On that one, as it were, we agreed to disagree.

Most times—except when he was denouncing the government—Al-Hadji used the proverbs and metaphors of the traditional elder, making his points by indirection. Especially if the subject was sensitive, so with this tree I knew he was teaching me something. We had been talking about Nkrumah's family being away from him in Egypt, then suddenly he's talking about a tree of the open savanna. It grows under the hot sun. A spectacular tree. I forget the name, often the only tree to be seen. Its first branches start about twenty feet off the ground and extend a distance from the trunk before the leaves appear. So there is always a circle of thick shade away from the trunk. Travelers seeking protection from the relentless sun have to sit some distances from the root. The farther you are from the trunk, the more shelter and protection you find.

"It seems to me," Al-Hadji said, "that tree must be a revolutionary like you all. With you revolutionaries, the closer people are to you, the less shade they get. Those further away get all the shelter."

In my case, he was certainly right on many levels. The painful sun was not just a lack of family time but also, in my case, the enemy. When they couldn't get to me, they would attack the homefront and target my wives. Something I wish I could have prevented, but there was nothing I could do. And it never really stopped. But as anyone who has been married knows, no outside force can wreck a marriage. If the internal strength, the dynamism of the marriage, is strong enough, it will continue. But the attempts at destabilization went on—in both my marriages.

Unfortunately I was incapable of giving my energies equally to both the revolution and the family. One had to be sacrificed, and in my case, that ended up being family. I wish it could have been otherwise, but struggle demands a price. For most people, rightly so, family is the most important thing. But for revolutionaries, family often has to be sacrificed to struggle. In his book, Nelson Mandela bemoans the price his family paid. I made my choices. Anytime I chose, I could have chosen family, sought financial security, and abandoned revolution. I don't regret the choice. What I do regret is that my wives had to suffer for my political activities.

Today, Miriam Makeba and I are the best of friends. We see each other quite frequently in Africa. We understand that along the path of our lives, our interests diverged. Unfortunately she was made to suffer a lot because of the marriage. But she's always been the best possible . . . always supportive. Because of her I grew a lot during our marriage. I thank her for that. Miriam divorced me in 1979. When he heard, Sékou Touré was quite unhappy. But this was one thing even his strong fatherly interventions could not change. It was time.

In 1979, while Miriam was away on tour, I attended a Fula wedding in Conakry. At the wedding there was an idealistic physician-in-training. A vibrant young woman, she was unusually attractive even in a people famous for beautiful women. Intelligent as well as charming, she was from a respected traditional Fulani family. Long story short, Marliatou Barre and I fell deeply in love. We were married in 1980. Our first—and only child—was a son. To me, this vigorous, alert baby had the aspect of a warrior, so we named him Boabacar Biro, Bocar for short. The leader of an indomitable clan, the original Bocar Biro had for *years* led a determined, uncompromising war of resistance to French colonialism. According to tradition, Boabacar Biro's chief lieutenant was his beloved full brother, who grew tired of the fight. When he advocated submitting to the French, Boabacar killed him because the oath under which they fought, from which he would not exempt even his own brother, was "we die before we surrender." *[Bocar Biro and his mother were with his father during his illness in this country, and the young man was also at his deathbed in Conakry. The young man graduated from the University of Virginia soon after, and is now studying for an advanced degree in politics, philosophy, and economics at the London School of Economics. —EMT]*

The mighty Nile, source of Egyptian civilization, flows out of the heart of Africa and through the middle of Cairo. In fact, Zamalek, my favorite part of this ancient city, is built on an island in the middle of the river. Once, my brother Lamin and I, on a mission that turned into a very pleasant vacation, spent two memorable weeks there.

We had time to explore the city. We haunted the Pharaonic Museum, overwhelmed by the power of thousands of artifacts of that ancient civilization. Everywhere we roamed we saw history dead up against the progressive populist vision of the great Gamal Abdel Nasser (peace be unto him). "That park," an Egyptian friend said, "used to be the private hunting preserve of the king. Hah. Nasser turned it into soccer field for the city's youth." Hey, I liked that. But the Nasser story that really sent me off had to do with American taxpayers' money.

On the island of Zamalek there is this extremely tall, dramatically beautiful tower. From its observation deck, you can see the entire city on both sides of the river as far out into the desert as the pyramids of Giza. A breathtaking view. But strangely enough, that seemed to be the sole purpose of this imposing structure.

We wondered who built it. Nasser, of course. And everything, they explained, the design and all the materials used in its construction—the woods and various kinds of stone, everything—was of Egyptian origin. As were the architects, the engineers, and the workers. Completely Egyptian. Yeah, but why? Much laughter. Well, you see, Nasser came into some unexpected funds, so why not?

Apparently—so the story goes—your CIA felt it was in the interest of the American taxpayer to engineer President Nasser's premature departure. To this end, they paid one of his generals to assassinate his leader. Instead, the loyal officer took the bribe—allegedly a million dollars—straight to the president. "With this blood money," said Nasser, "let us build something spectacular, lasting, beautiful, and Egyptian." Hence the tower. When we were there, groups of teenagers and schoolchildren were enjoying the magnificent view of their vast and ancient city.

U.S. citizens visiting Cairo should make a point of visiting that tower—hands down, the most creatively benign use of U.S. taxpayers' Cold War dollars in all of Africa. You will agree that the view is well worth the price of the ticket.

[Lamin Jangha remembers:

"In those years, the brother really traveled, eh? I went with him on missions in Africa. All over the world. Sometimes we traveled with Miriam and the band, and I was even road manager sometimes. So many stories, my brother, so many. We went to Iraq, Syria, Egypt—many times, he loved Egypt—to Ethiopia, Ghana, Liberia, Sierra Leone, Gambia, Senegal, and the Caribbean. We went together to Jamaica twice, also to Guyana.

"One thing about Kwame that was just incredible. He was always perfectly at home in every black country. I've never seen him to be the slightest bit uncomfortable, or out of place, in any black country. Sometimes he'd be more at home than some Africans who lived there. He would eat anything the people put in front of him. In fact, some things even I couldn't eat. And the people really came out to him. Especially the youth. Oh, boy.

"Once in Gambia, after the government refused to admit Kwame and Miriam, the youth shut the government down. The government got real cooperative, real quick. Then we crashed the president's new Jaguar. A brand-new black Jaguar. Of course it was an accident. So many stories, my brother. So many stories!"]

713

• • •

A visit to Jamaica with Lamin, the one in 1976, was really memorable too. For a number of reasons, political and cultural.

Actually, my first visit there in 1972 was politically quite interesting. Just after the Michael Manley government came in, Zenzi was invited down for a big concert. There she met an old friend from Kenya, Dudley Thompson, a conscious Jamaican barrister who had been part of the legal team that had defended Jomo Kenyatta, whom the British had arrested during the Kenyan freedom struggles. Now Mr. Thompson was a minister in the new democratic socialist government.

After the concert, Miriam called, all excited and happy. Everything had gone magnificently. She'd be home in two days. Oh, and by the way, Mr. Thompson asked her to tell me, "To hell with the colonizer's ban. You and your husband are welcome in Jamaica anytime." I had no idea how soon that would be necessary.

Two days later, another call. This time, Miriam is obviously angry and upset. She had not been allowed to board the plane for the flight back to the United States. Suddenly, she's informed, she now needs a visa to enter the country. At the American embassy she'd been rudely treated by the ambassador, who refused to issue a visa. I was in D.C. so I called the Black Congressional Caucus and the press and caught the next plane to Kingston.

Man, that American ambassador, what a piece of work. Whoee, boy, talk about the ugly American. The payoff for large campaign contributions was this diplomatic posting to Jamaica. Hey, y'all really have to do something about this corrupt system. Unless, of course, you don't care at all about who be representing your country out in the world. I mean, the Jamaicans had tried to prepare me. "Wait till you meet *your* ambassador." They laughed, shook their heads, and rolled their eyes. "That man gives a new resonance to the word *vulgarity.*" I saw exactly.

He told us he had absolutely no intention of issuing a visa to my wife. I smiled at him.

"Well, fine, Mr. Ambassador. Fine. As long as my wife is here, I'll be here with her. I expect it'll be time well spent. There is so much work I can be doing among my people here." With that, we leave.

Couple hours later the dude calls us. The embassy is about to close for the day. But if we come right down, we'll be admitted. So I ask why. Well, on second thought, he's decided to issue the visa. However, he blusters, we are to understand that travel to the United States is not a right. It's a privilege that he's granting. To my *wife*, a privilege he's granting? I say fine.

When we get to the embassy, he says, now there's nothing keeping you here. You both are now free to leave. He wasn't at all subtle. I thanks him. Told him that my wife had business obligations so she would soon go. But me, I anticipated a longer stay and had meetings and speeches set up all over the island. The ambassador looked most unhappy, but we had a great working vacation.

[A curious phone call from my mother must date from the visit. At that time an overseas call from Jamaica meant only family crisis. So I was apprehensive when my mother called.

"Michael? This Stokely Carmichael. Is he a friend of yours?"

"What? Well, yeah, Mom. I'm afraid so. Why?"

"Aha" (triumphantly). "I should have known. People here tell me he's the very devil out of hell. Is that true?"

"Damn, Mom. I thought someone was dead. That's why you calling?"

"Well, he's here. In Kingston. This morning I was in the Crafts Market and he came in with his wife. She's beautiful. They were surrounded by all kinds of people." From her vaguely disapproving tone, I knew they had to be radicals. "Then this tall fellow came striding over, demanding to know if I was Mike Thelwell's mother."

"Yeah, what did you say?"

"Don't be silly. What could I say? Of course I admitted that I was."

"Gee, thanks, Mom."

"Shut up. Listen to this. Then that audacious boy picks me up. Quite off my feet, spins me around twice, and gives me a great kiss, saying it was from you. Can you believe that?" Here, a quite uncharacteristic girlish titter. "Actually, y'know, I don't see a thing wrong with the young man."

As June Johnson put it, "Stokely had a charm about himself with the older folk." My mother was not the kind of lady just anyone would dare snatch off her feet. —EMT]

In 1976 I was in Jamaica to dedicate a little culture center in a working-class community in the hills over East Kingston. Then, the democratic socialist government of Michael Manley had just won election to a second term. They were, for the first time in the country's history, putting in place programs to really empower the masses. That was the government's priority and you could see the "sufferahs" beginning to assert themselves as human beings and citizens. And of course the reactionary forces, with CIA direction, were beginning to mobilize to destabilize the country. You could see the signs: propaganda, violence, etc., etc. It reminded me of what we were experiencing in Guinea. Manley's socialist government had lifted the ban on me imposed by the British imperialists back in 1967.

Lamin and I were the guests of the Mystic Revelation of Rastafari, a grassroots band of serious Rasta musicians. With their groundbreaking album, *Grounation,* this extraordinary group of grassroots musicians had injected a conscious, radically African emphasis into Jamaican popular music, influencing a generation of young Rasta musicians like Bob Marley.

Their legendary leader and master drummer, Count Ossie, had recently died. With the help of a "conscious," highly placed young government scientist, the group had secured the funds to establish in the community a living memorial to their leader. This was the Count Ossie Culture Center and Primary School.

We lived up in the center, which was still under construction, with the *brederin* and their community. Each evening, the *brederin* came bringing their instruments, fired up their chalice, and proceeded to "chant down Babylon one more time" in rehearsal for the center's dedication. Those "grounation" sessions, the drums and chanting into the early mornings, took me back strongly to my Trinidad childhood. I could easily imagine myself back in a pan yard in Belmont with the Casa Blanca steel band. It was a lovely trip into the grass roots of Jamaica.

But even then there were ominous signs—or sounds—of things to come. Occasionally we could hear distant gunfire from down in the city. The opening salvos of the vicious ghetto war that the reactionaries would launch to destabilize the socialist program of the government. The dynamic of the Jamaican class warfare at that time reminded me very much of Guinea. In a few more years the society would be completely demoralized by violence. A crime against the society and the Jamaican masses from which the country has never really recovered.

The *brederin* kept telling me that I knew their manager, "Bredda" Richard, who, though a government official, was a "conscious young bredda" and a "black-hearted" man. This brother had organized their foreign tours and helped them secure the culture center. They insisted we had met "up so," meaning in America. As soon as I saw "Bredda" Richard, I recognized that we had indeed briefly met at Howard twelve years earlier. As a student at Michigan, he'd come to visit his brother, a student at Howard, who was with us in NAG.

[When Kwame told this story for possible inclusion here, neither of us could have suspected that my brother Richard Thelwell (peace be unto him) would, a year after Kwame, also succumb to cancer before the book's appearance. —EMT]

In 1984, I was leaving for the States to do some recruitment drives for the All-African People's Revolutionary Party there. When I went to inform President Touré, he urged me to make it a short visit because the Organization of African Unity meeting was to take place in Guinea that year and there was work he wanted me to do for that meeting. There was to be a week-long conference on Pan-Africanism to precede the OAS meeting. President Touré asked me to organize the diaspora representation to that conference. Then, somehow, we got into a discussion of philosophical materialism. There had been an ongoing argument on the subject between the copresidents. Sékou Touré held that Western philosophical materialism was automatically, by definition, atheistic. Nkrumah said not necessarily, and they would set to. So we discussed that for a while, and as I was leaving, he gave me some instructions and a letter for Ambassador Ba at the embassy in D.C. As I left, he said, "Go well, hurry back."

I had been in the United States about four days and had just arrived in D.C. The ambassador had business at the United Nations mission in New York and we agreed to meet there the next day. So when my phone rang about midnight, I thought it might be the ambassador calling about our meeting. It was a brother from Cameroon named Mohammed Barre, calling from Texas.

"Where is Sékou Touré?" he asked.

"Either in Conakry or possibly in Algeria," I said.

"My brother, you sure he isn't in America?"

"No way. When I left him in Conakry, he said absolutely nothing about coming here." Besides, I thought, why would he have asked me to see the ambassador if he were planning a visit?

"No way, brother," I said. "He's in Conakry. Why?"

"Listen to this," and he held the phone to the radio. Somehow he had Radio Gabon on and they were announcing the death of Sékou Touré in a Cleveland hospital. It was a heart attack.

I thanked him and we gave each other our sympathy. My mind was racing. I was suspicious. Hoping—desperately hoping—it was no more than the usual disinformation from the enemy.

I called the French press agency and asked if they had any news of the death. They were not forthcoming. Wanted to know who I was and what my interest was.

"What you mean? I'm simply calling for confirmation of a news story." Seems they did have some information that they too were still trying to confirm. So I called the embassy. By now it's well after midnight and the ambassador's wife gets on. I apologized for the late hour. "No problem," she say, "we weren't asleep."

"May I speak to His Excellency?"

"I'm sorry, he's traveling."

"Oh, has he left for our meeting in New York?" She says no.

"He's not, by any chance, going to Cleveland?"

"Yes, Cleveland."

"Oh, ma'am. I'm so sorry and to have called so late. But I give you my sympathy. *Bon courage.*"

Soon the local news began to announce the death.

I was on the first plane to Cleveland the next morning, wondering what this would mean for the country. I knew that a coup d'état with a vengeful petite bourgeoisie coming to power was a real possibility. But the party was broad-based and entrenched. So it could be a bloody struggle, with malign foreign interests fishing in troubled waters. It would all depend on the military. If they behaved professionally . . . I would check with Njol Kouyate . . .

When I walked into the hotel room in Cleveland, all the ministers were there. I was greeting them when Madame Touré ran up to me. She was in tears and threw her head on my shoulder.

"Oh, he's gone. He's gone. Who will protect us now?"

"Oh, no, Madame Touré," I assured her. "Nothing can happen to you. The people love you."

I really thought I was speaking the truth. I'd been living in Africa long enough, studying coups in neighboring countries. So I truly thought, whatever the outcome, nothing would happen to Madame Touré. But she was arrested along with her son, Mohammad Touré. Only after much pressure and much time was she released. *[The criminals dared not torture Madame Touré who was greatly loved. However, another gracious and accomplished lady was not spared this outrage. Ambassador Jean Martine Cisse, who led the mission to the U.N. and was president of the Guinean Women's Union, was reportedly tortured in prison. Mercifully Madame Cisse survived. —EMT]*

I accompanied the body back to Conakry. That was a funeral, bro. Thirty-nine heads of state were present. But it was the people that, for me, were unforgettable. I mean, the masses, the Guinean grass roots of all ethnicities, I mean in their millions. In Conakry, and in towns and villages across the country, everywhere. An outpouring of such love and grief that you could literally feel it in the air. The people knew, as I did, that a page had been turned in their country's history.

Coming back from the funeral I ran into an older man I knew. Samory was an old soldier who had been a guard at Nkrumah's villa. I hadn't seen him since Nkrumah's death. We greeted each other and exchanged sympathies.

"Your father is dead. I see you have sorrow."

"Mori, it is a sad time for all Guinea," I said. Suddenly the sorrow left his face. It was replaced with anger. And a tone of bitterness.

"Are they weeping?" he spat. "The fools and hypocrites, many of them. Yes, let them weep now. And cover their heads with ashes. It was their ingratitude and folly that killed our father. The ones that grumbled, muttered curses, and listened to the lies of his enemies. Now he is dead, they weep. Hai, Guinea has not begun to weep, you hear me? Sékou Touré told them, did he not say? The time will come when Guinea will search for Sékou Touré and call his name in vain. Did he not say? Under the bright noonday sun, they will search with flashlights in their hands" (a popular metaphor for complete madness, futility, and desperation). At the time I thought the old soldier, deranged by grief, was being unfair. Unfortunately, he was right. Poor Guinea.

The next week was filled with the wildest of rumors. Coups and rumors of coups. Strange stories of the death, fake death, or sightings of the dead leader. In all this, the Central Committee of the party and the cabinet are scrambling around for a strategy.

One figure (whom they could have rallied around) had the stature and credibility to unify the nation. That was the prime minister, Lansana Biavougi. A respected leader, he was by profession a physician, from one of the smaller ethnic groups and widely respected. But he was arrested and died in prison. Once the prime minister was removed and the only unifying, stabilizing force gone, the coup was announced. The military arrested the entire Central Committee and the top leadership of the party, many of whom would be executed. They banned the party and then arrested and tortured a thousand of the young cadres.

The chief figure in the coup was an officer, I believe a colonel, named Diarra Traoré, who was himself later killed. He was later replaced by another military man, Lansana Conté, who is still president.

French neocolonialist fingerprints were all over this coup. French military and economic advisers suddenly appeared all over the place. Sékou Touré, his character, policies, and programs were all denounced. History was rewritten in the media for real, Jack, and the economy opened up to foreign imports. They promised the people a new age of prosperity and freedom. The country is still waiting. Of course, all the traitors who'd colluded with Portuguese aggression returned from exile. If not in triumph, then certainly without shame.

This was a time of deep sadness and anxiety for all my friends. Those not in prison. I was married to Marliatou and we had a young child, and at first we were certain that they would come for me. But when it didn't happen, I suppose I gradually became a little cocky.

My old buddy Njol Kouyate, the revolutionary young officer who had given me military training, came to my house. First time in years. He spent five hours passionately trying to justify the coup. I wasn't buying any of it. Finally he left. To this day I am not sure exactly what he was trying to do. Whether he was on a mission to recruit me or if it was just personal. I thought at the time that, perhaps as a soldier, he was between a rock and a hard place with his conscience therefore troubled. I remembered how poor, loyal Boiro had been thrown from the plane by his fellow soldiers. But I don't know, because they then gave Kouyate a ministry, Postage and Telecommunications.

We had decisions to make. I was married, had a son and an extended family. I knew and loved Guinea, had ties, but was it feasible to stay? Would I even be allowed to? So I slept listening for the midnight knock on the door. Many of my close associates in the party were already in jail. However, I held no official position in the party, which may have been what saved me.

Even if forced out, there was no question. I'd live in Africa. But the revolutionary bases in Africa had been shrinking. They were all falling to neocolonialism. And even if I went to a progressive country, there was no assurance that there wouldn't be a coup there also. So if I was to stay in Africa, it was entirely likely that I'd have to learn to live under some form of neocolonialism, struggling from inside the beast all over again. A prospect I didn't particularly relish. So no matter how reactionary Guinea became, I at least knew Guinea. Working for the party, I'd visited every region, every town. I'd been in the country fourteen years. I figured I'd sit tight and see what developed.

Ironically enough it would be my neighbor Al-Hadji Tcham, the stone businessman, very reactionary, who had the greatest effect on my decision.

One day my house was full of people, all supporters of the revolution, when Al-Hadji appeared and asked me to come on outside. He was serious, very much in his bluff, tough-talking mode. No proverbs or metaphors.

"Look, you know, I'm not like those others. I'm not here to cry for Sékou Touré or his revolution. Myself, I'd have put him in prison years ago if I could. So that's enough of that. But you. I know you are in trouble, trying to decide whether you should stay in Guinea or leave. Am I right? I thought so. Well, let me tell you one thing. If you leave Guinea now, you will be making a very great mistake. That will tell people that you came here only because of Sékou Touré. That you never cared for the people or the country. You were just following Sékou Touré's power." In essence that was what he said. But he wasn't really talking about reputation, he was talking about integrity. Not what people in Guinea would think, since, after all, I'd be long gone, but what I would reveal about myself to myself. I made up my mind to stay.

That decision behind me, I threw myself into the effort to maintain myself and the party. The military regime had executed 90 percent of the Central Committee and outlawed the party. The task was to rebuild, clandestinely, while fighting to get it unbanned, which we eventually accomplished. While Sékou Touré lived, I'd sought no formal position in the party. I'd just been a regular member. Now I accepted nomination to the Central Committee and threw myself into the work.

It was tough, a complete and sudden reversal. From being the party of the government, we went back to being outlaws, hunted and repressed.

And not by white racists either, but by black reactionary puppets this time. But you can't really fool the people for long, nor extinguish their instinct for justice and self-determination.

It didn't take long for them to see how bankrupt of vision and programs this military regime really was. All they did was open the country back up to the French capitalists and to neocolonialism. French "exports," technicians, government and nongovernmental, swept in to promote "efficiency and progress." The people said, "Sékou Touré made us proud to be Africans. These hollow men are turning Guinea into a French playground once more."

Ah, the European "expert," the bane of the black world. I won't lie. There were among the influx a few competent, decent, and hardworking Europeans with some respect for Africa and Africans and a commitment to humanity. No question. But the general run of these French experts? Help us, Jesus—the jetsam of the French civil service and academics who couldn't get tenure at home. Stone mediocrities, often racist, rushing back to the "colonies" to live large—servants, villas, cars and drivers—while flaunting their self-proclaimed superior "expertise" over the "natives." The military puppets being content to preen and posture as they returned effective operational control of the country's social institutions to these impostors. The contrast couldn't have been starker. Sékou Touré had set out to consciously seek and foster Guinean competence, confidence, and control and to put his people in charge of their society.

If the new dispensation had in any way improved the life of the people, I'd have to shut up. But it didn't. Did the economy or the standard of living of the masses improve? Gimme a break, under globalism? C'mon, be serious. Perhaps a few higher-paying positions for some of the petite bourgeoisie, yes, but for the masses, things grew demonstrably worse. For national culture and identity, for the spiritual health and direction of the country? A tragedy. Remember what Sékou Touré said of independence in 1958 about the choice between freedom in poverty or slavery in comfort? Now the masses had both poverty *and* "slavery." Any objective assessment would have to reach that conclusion.

Of course, the family in America—especially May Charles—wanted me home instantly. But the only principled decision possible for me was to stay. I wasn't about to cut and run. In the U.S. media—even the black media—we hear a lot of nonsense how out of place "black Americans"— their term—feel in Africa. *Americans,* perhaps, but black people, no way. As in everything, it all depends on how you come and what you bring.

For example, the African populace have a general perception, fashioned from lies in the movies, that life in rich, powerful America is just wonderful. So, why would anyone want to leave that to come live in Africa as Africans live? That media myth actually worked in my favor.

When doing political work, a team of us would go into the villages and they would introduce me. They'd say, "Now this brother, yeah, he look like a Fula man, but he's from America. But the brother left America. He's with us now. He's lived in Guinea x number of years. His family is here. His wife a Guinean woman. He's with the party, for the people. Sékou Touré loved this brother. He's one of us." And before I'd even said a word, instant acceptance. The village would just open up to me, overwhelming welcome and hospitality for a brother who would leave fabulous America to share their struggle.

Even in Conakry, the reactionaries were pumping up a line. "He's going run back where he come from now that Sékou Touré's dead. What else can he do?" I didn't say anything. I just wanted them to think that sooner or later I would leave. But when it became apparent to them that not only was I not leaving, but was getting myself more deeply involved in the party, that's when the military decided they had to do something. (Apparently, though, they couldn't at first agree exactly how to deal with me.) But you know, outside those hard-core reactionaries and opportunists, I think the petite bourgeoisie, many of them—the ones with a conscience—developed a grudging respect. Oh, so he wasn't in it for personal gain, or, as one said to me, "to chop Sékou Touré's money."

Brother Kouyate, I keep calling him Njol. That is not his name; *njol* is Wolof slang for "tall." So I guess I never knew his real name or, for that matter, the real him. I assume he must have figured his only future was with the military. But I could not forget the youthful patriotism of the revolutionary young officer I'd first met. Anyway, he was now a minister and we kept our distance. One day we ran into each other in the street. He was wearing an elaborate ministerial *gran* boubou. The brother throws his arms around me, warm, expansive as ever: "My brother, my brother, where you been hiding? Just the man I want to see," etc., etc. I was a little suspicious. But he takes me up to his office. Very insistent, conducts me by the elbow. Then once inside, he locks the door, draws the blinds. All very mysterious and conspiratorial. I'm sho nuff confused. What *is* going down here anyway? He sits at the desk, produces a yellow pad and a CD of rap music. Then he starts reading off the pad along with the rapper. "Listen, listen. Am I saying this right?"

I cracked up. Say what? In a ministerial office in Guinea? The power of pop culture. This must be Pan-Africanism military-style. Hell's bells.

Pretty soon they promoted him to minister of the interior, who, among other things, issued passports. I was beginning to sense a vague, nonspecific pressure. Little things. I noticed that my passport had maybe six months or so before it expired. I thought it best not to let that happen. But I wasn't at all sure the regime would issue me a new one. So I needed a plan. I got the requisite documents together, twin photographs, everything. Then I casually wandered to the minister's office. I just kind of ambled in. My turn to be expansive.

"Oh, God, big office, my brother. Big man now, eh? Honorable *minister,* what? Bet he got all the prettiest women in Conakry." He beamed and didn't convincingly deny it.

"Oh, yes. They tell me. You want see pretty woman, come to this office. Oh, yes. The man handing out passport, right and left. *All* the finest women in Conakry have convention in that office every day. So they say. Is it true? In fact, I just passed one beauty on the stairs, just grinning from ear to ear. Flashing her brand-new passport. *Uh, uh, uh.*"

"Yeah, well, you know me, my brother. Do my best. Serve the people." His turn to grin.

"Your brother. Me, your *brother?* Nobody'll believe that. I must be the only one in Conakry you don't give passport. Course, now, I know I ain't a pretty woman but . . ."

"What, you need a passport?"

"Well, yeah. Must have misplaced it. But I know you. I'm not a pretty woman so . . ."

"Nonsense. Utter nonsense. Go bring me two pictures, and this, that, and the other document."

The words weren't out of his mouth before I placed the envelope on the desk. I had everything ready.

"Yeah. But I know, not being a pretty woman . . . I'll probably have to wait months before . . ."

"What? My brother, don't be crazy." He called in his chief of staff.

"Bring this passport back to me immediately if not sooner."

"Yes, sir." In less than half an hour, the man was back. The minister signed the passport and handed it over with a flourish.

I thanked him, I thanked him profusely. I said, "My brother, you only *think* you know the pretty women in Conakry. I know all the real beauties. From now on, be my pleasure to send them *all* to you. There'll be so *many* beauties in this office, you going have to look at them and wish them well."

So we laughed, embraced, and parted, but I had my new passport. The brother was still laughing as I left. I want to think that Kouyate was at heart a good brother in impossible circumstances. I don't know whether he could have prevented the '84 coup. And he did emerge from it a minister. Within a few years he would be executed as the alleged mastermind of another coup attempt. But who can know if there had really even been such a plot? And whether, sickened by the political bankruptcy of the regime around him, our brother had experienced a resurgence of revolutionary and patriotic zeal? As the Ashanti proverb says, "A log may lie in the river for ten years, but it will never become a crocodile." Or, as some said, had it been purely a naked power grab out of personal ambition and greed? I'd like to give the brother the benefit of the doubt. He once was a most impressive young warrior and he taught me a lot. Peace be unto him.

He was still laughing as I left his office that day.

A few months later, just about when my old "Sékou Touré" passport was to expire, they came for me. No dramatic pounding on doors at midnight. This was the middle of the day (but no flashlights) when a group of regularly uniformed policemen came to the house. At first they spoke with Marliatou. I thought it was some routine stuff until Marliatou came back. "It's you they want to see," she said. They asked me to accompany them downtown, but no one said why. I get there and I am arrested. No one said why. Whereupon they take me back to the house, where they conducted a search. I was never told what they were looking for, but it was a thorough search. They searched everywhere and everything. Twice. Then I was back at the prison. Still no explanation.

I would discover that they had rounded up sixteen of our chief party activists and announced the so-called coup plot. Totally false. See, by then it was clear to all and sundry that the regime was a disaster. The economy was worse, people's lives were more difficult, especially for the poor. There were popular demonstrations regularly. The market women. The housewives banging cooking pots. The youth. What was left of the labor unions. The regime was feeling the pressure. So they rounded us up and announced the coup plot. Well, hey, certainly we were trying to throw them out. And we were being effective. But certainly no military-style coup. A popular uprising, a popular coup perhaps. There was no coup plot so there could be no proof. In my case, they thought they could just arrest me and throw me out of Africa.

Of course, I must say, of all the prisons I've been in, this was the best. I wasn't even locked in a cell. I was placed in an empty office in the central police station in Conakry. There was an open yard, so *theoretically* anyway I could have run off anytime. But perhaps that is what they were hoping. I wasn't about to test it. However, there were no policemen running in screaming and threatening. In fact, it was almost as though I weren't in prison at all. And no charges were ever brought, so I guess it was a detention. (At first I didn't understand the leniency, at least not until the commandant came to interrogate me.)

In Africa when in prison, you have to feed yourself. Your extended family sees to your meals. Al-Hadji Tcham was the first to visit and bring me food. Then, to my amazement, a lot of the conservative elements came in to visit, all bringing food. Enough food, in fact, to feed the prisoners *and* the police. How do I account for this? Why good human relationships in spite of political disagreement? I think it has to do with African humanism, deep-seated, traditional values transcending ideological differences. And perhaps Al-Hadji's example. Of course, their demonstration of support also helped me politically.

[The story that follows has everything to do with the existence of this book. In 1997 our department at the University of Massachusetts–Amherst held a tribute for Ture, who had recently been diagnosed with cancer. That evening before retiring, we were sitting around chatting. I, entirely by chance, teased him about his "arrest" for trying to overthrow the military regime.

"By the way, how on earth did you ever get out of that mess, talking about overthrowing the military? You never did tell me."

He told me the story that follows.

"Damn," I shouted, "that's one hell of a story, bro. How many people besides you know it?"

"Oh, Bob Brown and a few people in the party."

"That's what I mean, man. You got to write some of this stuff down." Which is how the conversations leading to this book began. —EMT]

Then came the interrogation. I am still not charged with any crime. Then the commanding officer comes in, all curt and brisk. Well, I knew I recognized him from somewhere. And clearly he recognized me, for he seemed embarrassed. Remember when I was first in Guinea with Madame Du Bois (1968)? The U.S. embassy tried to seize my passport and Sékou Touré gave me heightened security? And all the hotel receptionists were replaced with detectives? Remember the militant, bright young officer who had night duty and with whom I had such long political talks and became friendly? Well, eighteen years later, now the commandant of the police department, it fell to him to conduct this sorry business. I could see his deep discomfort.

First, he asks for my *passport.* (The irony didn't escape him.) I produce it, and to his great surprise it's current. In fact, brand-new. He visibly has to regroup. He curtly informs me that I'm to be expelled and I should name the country to which I want to go. But I see his great discomfort. I decide to really rub it in. Mercilessly.

"Oh, thank you, my brother. Thank you. Mighty good of you to ask where I want to go. Last time you kicked me out of Africa, no one asked."

He said, "What? What last time?"

"The time you sold me into slavery."

The brother winced. He looked ashamed. He said nothing. He looked away.

"But I can promise you this. As Africa is my mother, this time won't be like the last. I be kicking and screaming to the world, Jack. This Africa belongs to me just as much as it belongs to you."

He couldn't reply. He just looked away. Whatever they tried to say, I laid that on them. "You didn't ask when you sold me. Why you ask now?" They ended the interrogation and sent me back to prison.

I was there no more than four days before they had to release me because pressure came from everywhere. I mean, everywhere, Jack. Tell the truth, even I was surprised. I knew the All-African People's Revolutionary Party would get on the case immediately. And that old SNCC network would kick in. But this came from all over the world. In Tokyo a student delegation went into the Guinean embassy demanding the details of my arrest and calling for my release. That shocked them. The PLO representative in Guinea made inquiries. The Cuban embassy did the same. Telegrams were mobilized from all over Europe.

In Atlanta, after a little friendly persuasion from Bob Brown and a party delegation, Ambassador Andrew Young made a phone call. I thank Bro Andy for that.

By happy coincidence, the same weekend I was arrested, a delegation of Afro-American executives and politicians were at a conference with the frontline states in southern Africa. Of course Guinea had a delegation at the conference. The Afro-American delegation was led by Jesse Jackson. The agenda was to discuss closer economic and political relationships between black America and Africa. Soon as the Guineans walked in, Larry Landry (peace be unto him), a very conscious, longtime activist out of Chicago, took it to them. "You must know we Afro-Americans have a high regard for Kwame Ture. Yet here we are discussing closer relationships, trying to build cooperation and understanding, while at the same time y'all arresting a brother like Kwame? This is embarrassing. Very destructive." There were other interventions, but that one really hit home. The military regime hadn't been expecting this kind of reaction, and certainly not so soon.

They just came in one day and told me I was free to go. The first thing I did, I went round and personally thanked everyone who had brought food to the prison. Apart from personal kindness, that local turnout sent a political message to the regime. I was touched by that demonstration of respect, especially from that element. I also knew that Al-Hadji Tcham's example had led the way. That's how they had to release me.

[Bob Brown (A-APRP):

"Kwame was arrested on a Friday. David Brothers got the call from Conakry and alerted the Central Committee. The word from there was that if Kwame were not out by Monday he'd likely be tortured, possibly killed. You know that got our attention. We instantly activated the party membership as well as allies like the American Indian Movement and the Irish Republicans.

"By that evening, there were picket lines at the Guinean Embassy in D.C., their U.N. mission in New York, and even in front of a few black mayors' homes.

Not Andy Young and Harold Washington, however, those brothers made phone calls immediately. Actually, Larry Landry wasn't in Africa at all, he was in Chicago. But he tracked Jesse down at the conference in Africa and it was Brother Ron Walters who made the strong intervention there.

"On Monday, we were meeting in Andy Young's office in Atlanta to plan an international 'Free Kwame' movement when the call came. Kwame had been released."

Ture, of course, remained in Guinea and continued his work. Unfortunately, I neglected to inquire about the fate of the other party leaders reportedly arrested with him at the time of that alleged coup plot. —EMT]

CHAPTER XXVIII

Cancer Brings Out
the Best in People

In 1995 we were seeing in Africa what, at long distance and with a time lag, I took to be the spin-off effects of what had happened in the Soviet Union in the late eighties. The consequences of Gorbachev's betrayal and what my old friend Bill Hansen calls "the ignominious collapse of Soviet socialism." Whatever the causes, this year as it developed would be one of my roughest, politically speaking. Seriously. Rough.

There was very little good news. The reports coming in to Conakry from cadres in the field as well as from allies across the continent were almost all grim. Month after month, report after report, there were setbacks. Neocolonialism brazenly resurfacing and running rampant. Arrogant military dictatorships puffing themselves up, pressing down the people. Examples of opportunism, naked corruption, and greed endemic in the leadership. The greatly exaggerated collapse of progressive forces. Disappointments, allies in whom we had invested confidence and hope were being hit hard, sometimes being betrayed. Except for the military counterrevolution after President Touré's death, it was the worst I'd seen. By midyear 1995, that was clear. I knew it was only temporary, a passing phase, but it was rough.

But, as you know, in political struggle this comes with the territory. There is always movement. Some currents flow in your direction, others are in your face, pushing the movement backward. A kind of pendulum effect, rise and fall, in political fortunes. When you devote your life to organizing, whether for revolution or simply for progressive social change, the movement is never always in a positive direction or at a constant pace. Realistically you have to expect that.

There are hopeful, productive periods where you see dynamic movement, growth, the promise of progressive change. Everything seems possible. Then again, periods of stagnation where everything seems to grind to a halt. And also times of great reaction and repression, which simply have to be endured, waited out, survived.

I knew that what I was looking at this time, whatever the immediate local circumstances, was in some global sense the delayed consequence of the Soviet Union's sudden disappearance. What the American media had gleefully hailed as a "New World Order," the "victory of capitalism," and in one case, even more laughable in its parochial arrogance, "the end of history" was working its effects out in Africa (and Asia too).

Because, whatever the faults of the Soviet Union—and we in the black world have had many serious criticisms and contradictions with them—the mere existence of the Soviets had counterbalanced the forces of neocolonialism and imperialism in the black world. With the "threat of communism" believed out of the way, and the world's political equilibrium upset, the forces of neocolonialism and global capitalism felt free to plunder across the globe and to brazenly exploit working people at home, as well as abroad. What we were experiencing in Africa, no question about it, was simply the African expression of that global imbalance. The latest chapter, but by no means the last, in a long, ongoing struggle. In the liberation struggles of Africans and all oppressed and exploited peoples—some unfolding over generations, even centuries—there are low points and reverses. That's all. The struggle continues. And already the inevitable backlash against the excesses and rapacity of "global" capitalism can be seen surfacing everywhere.

In September—in the midst of all this—my mother began asking me to come visit her in Miami. I am not sure but what with that mysterious mother's intuition, May Charles hadn't sensed my general situation.

I told her—which was true—that it wasn't convenient right then. But that I was attending a conference in Cuba in January after which I would certainly come see her and her new house. Also, about that same time, I'd begun experiencing a pain in my leg up around the hip. Because I'd always been very healthy, I at first ignored it. But after a while it seemed prudent to seek medical attention. The doctor wasn't entirely sure, perhaps a pinched nerve, perhaps a problem of circulation. We'd need to watch it carefully . . . certainly do more extensive testing if it persisted. I asked him to do something for the pain. The medicine he prescribed suppressed the pain so I put it out of my mind.

Then came May Charles's reply. You know the kind of letter only a mother pulling out all the stops can write. Perhaps, as I've said, she had sensed something of my mood and situation. Whatever the cause, she clearly wanted me to come see her *now*. "Why, I am old and getting *frail*. . . . My son, at my age, tomorrow is not a given . . . we can't afford to take anything for granted at my age." You know the script. The one that always works.

It was my turn to get apprehensive. What if something *were* to happen to her? There really wasn't much choice. I'd go early.

When I arrived in Miami in mid-December, I discovered that she was indeed troubled, but not for herself . . . for her only son.

"Just look at you, just look at your clothes, and you need a haircut." It was almost word for word her greeting when I'd returned from the Freedom Rides in 1961. "And not only that . . . you are now over fifty years old and you still have nothing. . . . Why are you like that, eh? I don't know what you think this world is. . . . Look at your sisters, even the unmarried ones have their own houses. They are fighting life . . . but you have nothing . . . anything you have, you give away . . . every blessed thing. . . . I don't know what you think this world is. . . . I worry about what's going happen to my son."

Of course with my mother and me this is an old reel, an ancient dance. But this time it was a little more intense. A poignancy related to the fact, as she frequently pointed out, that she was indeed getting old and feeling it. And I was certainly no longer a kid.

What could I say that her mother's heart would understand? From her perspective she was absolutely right. To her, my life was not just unconventional; it was a provocation. Her friends' sons were in many cases professionals, solid burghers, taxpayers and property owners, some of them even *doctors* and dentists, while her son was notoriously unconcerned so far as the accumulation of material possessions was concerned.

Of course, none of the people I had most admired and who'd influenced my life—Bayard, "Prof." Brown, Dr. King, Ms. Baker, Mrs. Hamer, Malcolm, Presidents Nkrumah and Sékou Touré, and so many others—had devoted the slightest concern to material acquisition either. But try that argument on a worried West Indian mother, nuh? I knew better than to point out (yet again) that my apparent economic insecurity was entirely relative and a matter of perspective. That compared to the great majority of the people I worked with and cared most about, my own situation was quite secure, even comfortable. She knew that I could never aspire to live more lavishly than the people whose struggle I had fought to represent all my life.

And besides which, the decisions about how my life would be spent and the values that would guide it were long-settled, a done deal, not negotiable. Even had I remotely wanted to, which I did not, those were by now quite irreversible and we both knew that. Just as we both knew that this was a speech she felt she just had to make.

So in response to her "I don't know what will become of you," I resorted to my time-honored standby.

"Oh, May Charles," I said loftily, "you know you don't have to worry about me. You know, my people ain't going let me starve."

"*My* people? Your people? You always talking about 'the people.' . . . I really don't know what *you* think this *world* is. . . . But you must be hungry . . . I got some nice souse for you. Ol' man, it's only your *mother* who isn't going let you starve."

Of course, she wasn't about to retreat, and we both knew that. But we both also knew that she was always glad to have me home, especially at Christmas. So suspend the discussion. Move the agenda. Call the truce. As we say in Africa, "Why is man better than the animals? Because we have kinfolk." Live for who love you. It was a pleasant visit with the family. But, before I left for Cuba after the holidays, the pain and stiffness in the hip had begun to reassert itself, giving my mother yet another thing to worry about.

The conference in Cuba that January was just excellent. It was the thirtieth anniversary of the OLAS inaugural, a world conference of progressive forces, socialist parties and activists, a fair number of allies from Africa. The general focus was on strategies to advance the struggle and defend our people in the post-Soviet world. It was good for us to be there. Many old friends and allies were present, and so I was able to renew old alliances as well as make many new contacts for the party's work.

As one might expect, the mood of the conference was serious, but it was in no way grim. The political contours of the world had indeed shifted ominously and we had to deal with it. But in fact, the general mood of determination was inspiring. And particularly so our beleaguered hosts, the Cubans, in their steadfast and unwavering determination to preserve the humanitarian accomplishments of their revolution and to advance its revolutionary principles. I was again struck by how truly admirable a people the Cubans are. Just being surrounded by all these committed revolutionaries from all over the world caused my spirits to rise.

But before the conference was over the medicine I'd brought ran out and the pain returned more seriously. I told the doctor the situation: I'd been diagnosed with bad circulation and was now out of painkillers. The doctor thought I should have some further diagnostic tests done. I was unwilling to take time away from the conference. Especially for something as inconsequential as poor circulation. Surely there was no urgency. Just contain the pain, for the time being, please.

Reluctantly, the doctor acceded. But he seriously urged me to get a thorough examination as soon as possible. Once more, the pain subsided.

By the end of January I was back in Miami en route to New York.

"I don't know about that hip, y'know, ol' man," May Charles said. "Definitely get it taken care of in New York, you hear?"

Even four-year-old Moussa, my nephew, chimed in.

"Yes, Uncle Kwame, you not walking so good, y'know." By then I knew it could no longer be ignored. Hopefully, it would be something that could be treated while I went about my work. I simply could not afford to be confined or immobilized, not even for a day. Because New York was going to be hectic. As it always was.

• • •

I had a full calendar. A lot of commitments. A load of party work, program and policy decisions, meetings late into the night. Speaking engagements, paid and unpaid, recruitment meetings. My role: largely to analyze, give direction, reassure, encourage, inspire. And I had to report on Africa, and on the Cuban conference. Also, February, being Black History Month, meant one of my annual speaking tours. Still more commitments. No day contains enough hours. Not when I'm in New York, especially in February. And that was just the dues owed to the party.

In a wider personal and political sense, New York was "home to Harlem," an old familiar psychic landscape, circles of old friends (and some foes), constant comrades, fellow travelers, shared history and struggles, those true brothers and sisters—Sister Mawina Kouyate, Bro David "Light de Fire" Brothers, Mama Gerri, Dr. Barbara, Elombe Brath, Yuri Kuchiyami, Debbie, Sekou. All demands, but these were good demands, yes? But demands nonetheless. I could and would see my doctor in New York but could spare no time for anything like a serious illness.

I would be staying on Convent Avenue in one of those large, lovely high-ceilinged, old Harlem apartments. It belonged to Mama Gerri—Dr. Geraldine Price—a retired City College professor, Pan-Africanist, and community activist who allowed me the apartment during those cold months when she retreated to Florida. A militant spirit, Dr. Price had, during the Depression and over her father's objections, joined the Communist Party at sixteen. She had been an effective organizer before the expulsion of most of the Harlem branch. Among her many fascinating organizing stories, one of my favorites was about what clearly had to have been, in cultural terms, the grandmother of all political fund-raisers: a Harlem rally for amnesty for Ben Davis with performances by Paul Robeson *and* Charlie Parker headlining the entertainment.

I liked the space, informed as it was by a lifetime of struggle, the walls lined with artifacts of African culture and struggle from the homeland and across the diaspora. My spirit was at home in that apartment, which was a good thing, because I'd soon have infinitely more reason to be indebted for her kindness in the use of the space.

Because I was hardly in the city before the pain returned, this time with a vengeance. So much so that travel became almost impossible and I was forced to meet my appointments there in the apartment. Suddenly I could walk only with great difficulty, and then only with the assistance of a cane. Which is how my first visitors found me.

I want to tell you about one of them. In the early years of the party— 1973 to be precise—I'd had a speaking engagement at Northeastern University in Boston. As I was entering—or leaving the campus, I forget which—I was approached by a small group. A tall, impressive sister, obviously their leader, had both presence and attitude. Her face was strong in a beautiful African way. It had the bronze tones and classic bone structure most often seen in certain Mandingo women. I could not help saying so. But this sister was listening to no compliments. She was there on business.

She was the director of an antipoverty community program at the Mission Hill Housing Project adjacent to the university. Recently there had been town/gown tensions with a racial aspect. The university police had taken to administering arbitrary head whuppings to young brothers from the projects. What particularly incensed my sister was that the "blind, deaf, and dumb" black student organization that was sponsoring my talk had come out in support of the campus security and by implication their gestapo tactics against the brothers.

"So, my brother, tell me please, what you doing over there with *them*, when you should be over here with *us*?

Course I hadn't known any of this and said so. Besides, my grandmother always told me that "a quiet answer turneth away wrath," so I got into my Baptist bag.

"Well, my sister, you know, don't you, that a good shepherd must first go after the sheep that are lost?" She was having none of that, but she shushed the derisive murmur starting up among the youth behind her with a small gesture.

Before I left, we managed a rapprochement between the African students and the community. The strong sister joined the party. And oh, yes, she did in fact take a Mandingo name. The Kouyates are a lineage famous, among other things, for their great historical griots. Ten years later in 1984, as Mawina Kouyate, this sister was elected to the Central Committee of the All-African Women's Revolutionary Union. Our sister has been a tower of strength. Some years ago she moved to New York, and her Harlem apartment has for years been the party's communications center. Wherever in the world I might be, Mawina has been my contact, and her apartment is my base during the warmer months when Mama Gerri repossesses Convent Avenue. During all these years, our sister has always held a job, raised a family, and taken excellent care of the party's business. Respect and thanks.

David Brothers and Mawina Kouyate, old and trusted personal friends and members of the party's national executive, were clearly taken aback by my condition. They ordered me to the doctor, and as I would later discover, Bro David had even called Dr. Justice beforehand to share with her his apprehensions—which were, as it turned out, quite accurate. In all my friends' countenances was something I'd not seen there before. Signals I could not quite read. Somehow my friends' concern got to me more than May Charles's worry had. Her alarm was constant and expected, a mother's prerogative. And God knows, May Charles had been worrying about my health from the day I was born.

But my comrades were not excitable people. True, we had come to care deeply for each other over years of shared work, friendship, and commitment, but they never attempted to "mother" me. That was not our style. But now, much as they tried to conceal it beneath a tough, cool practicality, a real and new concern lurked behind their eyes.

But I refused to read anything too ominous into their manner. I attributed their subdued countenances to their having always seen me healthy, totally focused, and energized by immersion in our work together. It was simply, I told myself, that they were not accustomed to seeing or thinking of me as in any way physically constrained.

[William Hall:

"It was a shock at first seeing Kwame that way. In pain, barely hobbling along with a cane. As long as I knew him, my image was one of take-charge energy and competence. To a remarkable degree. That was my *personal reaction. But something else troubled me even more. His present condition was counter to the spirit of unflappable confidence, strength, and virility he always projected. And I knew how much this image was a crucial part of his own sense of himself in the world. So I really worried whether my old friend could handle, psychologically speaking, being seriously physically impaired for any length of time. Now that really concerned me. Whether or not he could handle such a drastic and sudden change."]*

"Look, in all likelihood it's just a wake-up call," I had reassured them. "It's pointless to speculate now. At worst, it's just another political problem to grapple with: We investigate it thoroughly. And once properly analyzed, we take whatever steps are indicated. That's all. No point worrying beforehand about something that most likely is nothing serious." Sufficient unto the day is the evil thereof.

But I was exhausted. For the first time, this pain really sapped my energy and made sustained concentration almost impossible. My work was my life. If my ability to work was impaired . . .

And there were other considerations as well: my entire material survival was predicated on the ability to function well. As we sometimes joked, the life of a radical organizer had something in common with that of a subsistence farmer: both were sustained only by the result of their labor. In both situations, there was little margin for sickness.

Over the years, the lifestyle of the radical organizer had become as natural to me as breathing. I was not tired. In fact I relished and had even come to depend on the daily effort required to keep us moving forward. I was confident that I'd learned how to handle any contingency that might arise. But somehow, I had never contemplated physical or mental incapacity.

We were not a party with wealthy supporters or institutional donors. As a matter of principle, we avoided certain kinds of entanglements: we would not be anyone's surrogates. Consequently, over the years, we neither sought, cultivated, nor accepted state sponsorship or patronage of any kind, even from the select few regimes with whom we shared political vision and/or interests. An example? Well, as you know, our party has come to be greatly respected in Libya. A year or so before Sékou Touré passed over, the Libyans decided to explore a Pan-Africanist approach. They decided to have an exploratory conference of all the Pan-Africanist and revolutionary formations in Africa. Naturally, the All-African People's Revolutionary Party (A-APRP) was invited.

At the time, there were a few contradictions between Colonel Qaddafi and Sékou Touré, so I decided not to attend that first conference. But I briefed the delegation. I said, look, at a certain point the Libyans will thank you for coming. They will say, "Now, please, tell us how *we* can help your struggle. If there is anything we can help you with, please tell us." That's when the shopping lists will come out. You are to ask for *nothing. Take nothing.* Sure enough, all the other groups had their requests: guns, bases, training, money, etc., etc. When our time came, our delegation thanked the Libyans. We thanked them for their solidarity and hospitality. But we asked for nothing. *Nada.* "We thank you. But we came in solidarity to see if we had common objectives. Nothing else. We are satisfied. This is generous of you but it is more appropriate for *you* to tell us how *we* may be of help to you in your struggle."

We were the only group that asked for and accepted nothing. The Libyans were astonished. But that began a relationship of mutual respect. At all subsequent meetings, I wore a Sékou Touré button prominently. Some years later, the Libyans would largely fund the 7th Pan-African Conference in Uganda.

So that in financial terms the party was very much a guerrilla operation, raising our funds as we went. Hand-to-mouth, dependent on our own efforts and the confidence and support of our people. We were convinced that this was the only way to politically healthy growth. And our people, while sacrificing and generous as their means permitted, were not rich. If you supported the work, you supported, as your means permitted, the organizers.

Lo, it had worked until now, but the lifestyle did not carry health insurance or culminate in pensions. I knew comrades who, after a lifetime of hard work for the people, had come to find themselves without, outside of movement circles, a safety net of any kind. No indeed. There were no golden parachutes for revolutionaries even if they came in from the cold. Something I certainly had no intention of doing.

• • •

Some fifteen years earlier after a speech in a Brooklyn auditorium, I'd been introduced to a vibrant and articulate sister with a warm smile. It turned out we had a lot in common: a New York childhood, a Howard education, and a commitment to serve. This impressive Howard-trained physician, Dr. Barbara Justice, was a surgical oncologist with a general practice in Harlem and an abiding interest in Africa.

I joked that years earlier I'd narrowly escaped the Howard Medical School and hence her chosen profession. She laughed and retorted that a few years later, she had narrowly escaped following me into mine. I discovered that she was a constant presence in the media and at community meetings, discussing medical questions and the politics of health care delivery for our community. She was a kindred spirit, the kind of person who I felt belonged naturally in our party. Dr. Barbara Justice never formally joined the party so, she claimed, in revenge I became her patient.

Once, around 1988, Dr. Justice had successfully treated me for abdominal pains. She had diagnosed a duodenal ulcer caused by stress and a heavy schedule. (Back in the sixties, folks on the SNCC field staff, people no more than nineteen and twenty years old, had developed bleeding ulcers.) Dr. J's treatment had been effective.

Apart from that, my only other health problem was also territorial and manageable—intermittent, annual attacks of malaria, which were almost predictable in their regularity. These attacks were usually relatively mild and endurable. I considered them an occupational hazard of work in the villages and townships of Africa. Only once, in August '95, did I have a severe attack, but the doctors in Guinea took care of that.

But that was it so far as my health was concerned. Nothing unexpected or life-threatening. In Dr. Justice's office I was startled to learn that my last medical visit had been back in '89. No good, no way. My attitude had been pretty much "If it ain't broke, why fix it?" Which, beyond a certain age, is precisely the wrong attitude for anyone, especially for the brothers. That is not acceptable. Not for anyone, and especially for us Africans. I urge you all, and especially my age-set brothers and sisters, not to repeat that error, especially those of you who have health insurance. I know not all the brothers have that access. But you all should. It is not a privilege. It's a necessity and a human right, the community and its representatives must continue to fight for it.

That morning Dr. Justice was her usual self. Personally, warm and outgoing; professionally, careful, efficient, and competent. Her questions seemed (though I could have imagined this) precise and searching, almost as if she already had some conjecture as to the source of the problem.

After conducting the examination, Dr. Justice explained that three possibilities had to be investigated. In order of ascending gravity, these were severe muscle spasms, an impacted nerve, or, worst-case scenario, metastatic prostate cancer. All would have to be systematically investigated and ruled out, but, she cautioned, certain preliminary indications were worrisome.

My prostate was enlarged and a portion of the gland was indurated (rock hard). Besides which, the doctor explained, one characteristic of prostate cancer was that once it started to spread, it tended to migrate quickly into bone, which could explain the pains in the hip. But those were only preliminary indications, which could only be confirmed or ruled out by a biopsy and PSA (prostate-specific antigen) test.

So this monster, as well as the other two less grave possibilities, would have to be checked out, while the pain was addressed aggressively with muscle relaxants and pain relievers.

[MT: When you broke the news to him, you said, "Kwame, this seems fairly clear, pending confirmation, that this is prostate cancer, metastasized in the hip." What can you remember of his response?

Dr. J: Very stoic.

MT: How so?

Dr. J: Well . . . this is a traumatic moment. Even for patients you think are well prepared. Routinely there is denial. Then can be found anger, self-pity, an utter refusal to accept the diagnosis or the process. With our brother Kwame, there was none of that. He was very rational . . . you got the impression that he was beginning to plan. . . .

MT: Can you remember where it was?

Dr. J: In my office I told him that I was fairly certain that it was prostate cancer, and his countenance was extremely stoic; his words, exact quote is difficult for me, but it was something to, something like "What is the next step? What do we have to do?"

MT: Did he ever ask you, for example, "How long do I have?"

Dr. J: He asked me how long he had and I told him what would ordinarily be said in the circumstance, which would be about six months, but that each person was different and that we were going to explore both Western and alternative methodologies and that nobody could really say, nobody could really say how long he had, that that was really in the hands of God and we would just do everything we could to extend his life. He has always said he was not going to die in bed. He was going to die doing the work that he did all his life. And that was his comment on that day. And that he would continue to work while getting the treatment.

MT: Which is what he has done.

Dr. J: Which is what exactly he has done.

Interview with Dr. Barbara Justice, September 1998 —EMT]

Folks have asked me what went through my mind as I listened to this catalog of physical disaster unfold. I can't really remember. Why is that important anyway? A million flashing thoughts? An absolute blank? An incredulous "What?" The truth is I cannot remember any profound or timeless thought in that moment. Not a one, Jack. Nor any banal ones either, come to think of it. Either I'm the most unimaginative clod under creation, or instinct simply takes over. No complicated thoughts. Just pure, immediate instinct. That's what I think happened in my case.

And my instinct was to fight. To resist. By any means necessary. Something deep inside, something way beyond conscious reason, simply knew that there could be no capitulation. Nor would I allow this thing to stop me from working. Those two were clear. Immediately.

Dr. Justice immediately called in two other specialists, whom she described to me as "committed members of the medical community here." These two physicians, a neurologist, Dr. Carolyn Brittain, and Dr. Walter Dell, a urologist, both of Columbia-Presbyterian, proved to be everything she said and more. As would Dr. Gerald Hoke, who later joined the team.

I want to say a word here about my doctors, and that is what they will always be to me, "my doctors." The medical attention they so willingly and conscientiously gave me was excellent. I know that in purely medical terms I received from them the best care possible; what they were able to do was extraordinary given the advanced nature of the illness, and for that I will always be grateful.

But in that time of shock and anxiety for me, my doctors did something more. Something that did me at least as much good, possibly even more, than the purely medical treatment I received.

I'm talking now about the commitment and sensitivity of these young African physicians. (Had I seen more of this quality in Howard premed, my youthful decision to abandon that profession would have been vastly more difficult.) Not only did none of them ever send me a bill, but each one went out of his or her way, during those stressful hours, to make personal expressions that infinitely strengthened my resolve and lifted my spirits beyond measure. I think they must have known how much psychic and therapeutic strength those words added to the medical treatment they were administering. My people, mah people. There are times when they make me so very, very proud and humble.

[The general tone of what those doctors must have all separately said is fairly well captured in something I read a year later in an Essence magazine piece:

"One black doctor volunteered his services out of respect and gratitude. He said he might not have been a doctor had Stokely Carmichael not done what he did. I told him, 'Don't expect a bill from me,' said Dr. Gerald Hoke, his urologist. 'The honor of being able to render this service to him is payment enough. This is the least I can do.'"

The writer later asked Dr. Justice, perhaps with an undertone of skepticism:

"Am I correct in my information that none of these doctors ever presented him with a bill for professional services?" She replied, "As far as I'm aware *none of us have. We feel too deeply that Kwame has committed his life to our people, and I think everyone was more than honored to be able to provide serv-ice to him." —EMT]*

I'd first gone in to see the doctor on February 3. So it must have been on the fifth or sixth that we met again in her office.

The very next day I was sent to the Columbia-Presbyterian emergency room and examined by the consultants. I underwent the indicated tests and was able to get a confirmed diagnosis in forty-eight hours. By which time it came as no great surprise, as I'd been prepared for the worst. I learned then about a rating system for prostate cancer, something called the Glea-son scale, which is calibrated from one to ten, with ten being the final stages. What I had was "adenocarcinoma of the prostate at Gleason 7."

On the first Wednesday of every February I had a long-standing com-mitment. The United African Movement (UAM), a promising Pan-Africanist formation in Brooklyn, had taken over an abandoned movie house in the heart of the Brooklyn "ghetto." Every Wednesday at the Slave Market Theatre there was a community political meeting, and for the last couple of years, the first Wednesday of February had become Kwame Ture Night. I felt it important not to break that tradition. My first appointment with Dr. Brittain was for later that evening.

During the ride from Harlem, Sister Mawina, disciplined soldier though she is, was obviously torn. While she understood and supported the necessity for the Brooklyn appearance, she equally questioned its wis-dom, given my health. That good sister apologized for every bump and pothole she couldn't avoid.

Brother David Brothers and a group of young party members met me outside the theater. Because I took a long time getting out of Mawina's small car, I could sense a debate about to develop, so I cut it off.

"The people here?"

"Yeah, Brother, the place is packed. Wall-to-wall Africans."

"All right. Let's go get this done." And without further discussion, we went in. It was a full house and a good mix. A cross section of veteran Pan-Africanists, nationalists, former Panthers, Malcolm's people, com-munity activists—stalwart souls who'd kept the faith—along with a good representation of youth. It was a good, spirited meeting, excellent. But a long one. I was glad I had come, but the trip had taken its toll. By the evening's end I had neither energy nor will to resist when the brothers from the party physically carried me off the stage. "That's it, brother," Mawina declared. "Now you go to Columbia-Presbyterian." That night I met the formidable Dr. Sister Carolyn Brittain.

"Oh, Lord, brother, emergency rooms," Mawina complained. "You know I don't like them. I just know they going have you sitting there for five hours at least. You know how they do us. I just know it." But she didn't reckon on the sister called Dr. Carolyn Brittain. That lady took control. She met us, walked me in, ran tests, ordered X rays, consulted Dr. Dell, ordered more X rays, then informed me to abandon any idea I'd had of going home that evening. The next thing I knew I was tucked away in a room upstairs. I tell you . . . women have always been saving my life.

[Mawina Kouyate remembers:

"It was the weekly meeting at the Slave Theatre in Brooklyn. He always came on the first Wednesday in February as he led off African History Month. It was packed. It was always packed when he comes. And I would say that packed there was a minimum of four hundred people, and people were standing in the back and they were standing everywhere, as they always were when he comes. That's how it is over there. And when . . . the stage is like an old movie theater, and the stage is way in the front and you have to come down the aisle. We talked to him about, 'Let us wheel you in, brother,' you know what I mean, 'In the back, we can wheel you in and you can walk . . .' And he refused. He walked down with some brothers in front of him, holding on to them. But he still walked into the theater. And of course you know, as he walked in, everyone stood on their feet to greet him. They got him a big comfortable chair and they brought him in. But even the sitting down, with the pain, it was excruciating. But he talked, he came there, and he spoke for three hours, brother.

"The group which had the theater was the United African Movement (UAM). The year before he'd given them a mission: establish an African United Front in the New York area. He said he'd given them that assignment because our party was at that time in no position to do so. But, he told them, you all are Pan-Africanists. You are here and you know New York. So it's your responsibility to undertake this work. These were old activists who'd been around for years, old Pan-Africanists. They had no right not to do this work.

"But, brother, every fifteen minutes he tried to move his position and the pain was shooting out of his eyes, but as the pain came so was his voice stronger, so was his delivery more powerful. See, brother, every time he would lift himself up off his feet with his hands because the pain was so excruciating. And at the end, I tried so hard to get a van that night. I did everything. But a couple of brothers in the party had to literally carry him out on their shoulders, out of the theater. And then, brother, he had to get into this small car. I had this little gray car of mine, but it was so tiny and you know how tall this man is, and he had to double up and get in this car. And I kept on apologizing the whole time because I knew he was in pain.

"He told us to be at the hospital at six o'clock. So I went and got, brother, because you know him, he's a stickler about being on time. So I was saying to myself even, 'You're going to this emergency room. We're going to be there five hours. Because that's how they treat the people.' You know, five, six hours you're sitting in the emergency room. So we get there at six o'clock. We sat down.

"She arrived at six-fifteen, which also surprised us. Dr. Brittain, you know I think of her often, because I think this is how doctors really should be, you understand. She took us immediately. We didn't even have to fill out any papers. She took us immediately in the back, do you understand, and began doing twenty-three or thirty-two X rays. She x-rayed every part of his body. Everywhere. And whatever . . . she saw the X rays. She looked at that one and said, 'Now, I want another X ray. Every X ray she looked . . . you understand? And she did all of this, brother, which seemed like within an hour and a half. And that's when I said to her, I said, 'Doctor, he thinks you're just going to give him X rays and he's going back.' She said, 'Oh, no. He's a very sick man. I'm admitting him immediately.' You understand. So, this sister, I'm telling you, she went and found a bed in between doing the X rays. While they were doing the X rays, she was running around finding a bed for him. She found a bed for him. And then she found a wheelchair, and then she found this brother to wheel him. Me, her, this brother, and Kwame, we all took him up to the room where he was admitted. You understand. And they began the process immediately of radiation."

In February 2002, after a long bout with cancer, Sister Mawina Kouyate went to join the ancestors. Sister Mawina specifically requested to return home to Africa. She was laid to rest in Koto Cemetery, Sierra Leone. She was a self-less and tireless fighter. Peace be unto her. —EMTJ

Hence the immediate hospitalization ordered by Dr. Brittain. Here politics reared its gnarly head. New York City politics. The recent wave of Republican budget-cutting had resulted in an accelerating attrition of resources to the Harlem Hospital. The latest service to be shut down was the radiotherapy department, which meant that when the time came, I would have to be admitted to Columbia-Presbyterian.

The last thing I want to do is to appear unappreciative, for in truth, thanks to my doctors and a gracious staff, my treatment there has been excellent. No question. But surely the people of Harlem are entitled to their own community hospital? One designed, staffed, and equipped to address the range and pattern of health issues peculiar to that population? You know we do. Tell the truth and shame the devil.

There was one obvious question that I found myself resisting. For some curious combination of reasons, which I've never quite deciphered, I was trying hard not to ask for a prognosis. So I tried to keep myself from asking. You know, "Doctor, how much time . . ."

But I needed to know from Dr. Justice exactly what that all meant. Exactly what was I facing? What could I expect? What, in realistic terms, the struggle would entail. We could fight this bad boy, couldn't we? Was the condition terminal, was it even possible or usual to make that kind of judgment at this time? How much time . . .

Dr. Justice was reluctant to go there. Too much was involved. Because, as she explained, each case and each person was so different. There

741

were so many variables beyond the merely physical or pathological. Personality factors, spiritual factors. And these can play a significant role. So, if one looked only at the pathological, what was usually said in circumstances like mine was six to eight months. But none of that was graven in concrete, and in fact, it could be quite misleading.

Terminal? Sooner or later, yes. Generally speaking a Gleason 7 is a killer. But modern treatment was sophisticated. A range of treatments were available to retard the growth and spread of the cancer and to manage the pain—hormone deprivation, radiation therapy, chemo—we would try them all. And we'd also explore the full range of non-Western medical traditions for whatever weapons—no matter how unconventional—presented themselves. But immediately we'd resort to the full range of Western medical technology to try to stabilize the situation, arrest the pain, and get me actively functional again.

This was in January of 1996 and since I'm proofreading this in September of 1998, obviously she was right. But what had also become clear was that the kind of treatment she was projecting sounded prohibitively expensive. I really did not want to saddle May Charles with massive medical bills for expensive but hopeless treatment.

"About the cost . . . ," I began.

"Hey, my brother, you are seriously ill. Let's deal with the immediate crisis. First we treat you, then we worry about paying for it."

To folks who would ask how I was feeling, I'd taken to saying, "Like a soldier wounded behind enemy lines." Which is exactly how I did feel. To this thing planted inside me I was saying, "You may kill me, but, Charlie, you sure ain't stopping my work." Bravado? Perhaps some would call it that. In the movement we say, "You gotta do what the spirit say do," in order to keep on keeping on.

This was the first of what would prove to be a number of visits to Columbia-Presbyterian over the next two and a half years. It was instructive in ways I had not anticipated and could certainly never ever have expected. But going in was easy; the most difficult thing remained.

The news of the diagnosis had to be broken to my mom. Now in addition to her uneasiness about the unconventional lifestyle and financial precariousness of her son would be the added burden of his failing health. But I should have known. May Charles Carmichael is at heart a soldier. Not only did she take the news with courage, but she was on what must certainly have been the next plane to New York and at the side of my bed by the next day. She was there every day *religiously.*

[One crucial, dramatic confrontation during this first hospitalization is not specifically mentioned in Kwame's account. It involved a knock-down-drag-out between the patient and a united front of his closest associates led by his mother.

In their account, the brother's initial response to the diagnosis was an entirely predictable, complex mixture of pride, principle, and some fundamental concerns both personal and political.

Pride would not permit him to see himself becoming the object of pity or personal charity. As a matter of political principle, he refused—even though still an American citizen—to become a ward of what he considered the grudging and unfeeling medical welfare system, the capitalism of which he was so vigorous a critic. As a son, he was not about to leave his mother under a crushing debt, incurred for expensive treatment that, according to medical opinion, was almost certain to be futile. All of which was compounded by a personal distaste for the "Western bourgeois egotism" usually expressed in desperate and craven scurryings from treatment to treatment in headlong flight from and abject fear of death. "Or as if," as he told me later, "one's petty life were important above the rest of humanity's."

His immediate, strong instinct was therefore to quietly return to his house in Conakry to continue his work as long as his strength lasted. Then, when the time came, to face death with dignity. That was the decision he announced to his closest friends: his intention to return immediately to Africa.

His inner circle was having none of that. A group, including David Brothers, Mawina Kouyate, William Hall, Cleveland Sellers, and very prominently, May Charles Carmichael, having previously met, came to his bedside in the hospital and laid down the law. It was a long, dramatic meeting and from all accounts a serious battle of wills.

Okay. We've heard you. We understand you. What you say is true enough, but there are always two sides. Now you shut up and listen. Number one, Kwame Ture is a fighter. Always has been. You do not have the right to creep off somewhere, just working and waiting to die. That's not what your life has been. Your clear duty is, once more, to set another example of struggle. In this struggle with cancer, there are important lessons you can teach.

Two, what right have you to arbitrarily deprive your friends and supporters of this opportunity to mobilize their support? What happened to "If you struggle for the people," etc.? Who indeed gave you the right to decide for us?

Also, struggle is by all means available and possible. So just forget the nonsense about being indebted to capitalism. Health care is not charity; it's a human right. A right the people have had to fight for and are still fighting for. Besides, like Othello, you too have done this state some service. If anything, this society owes you.

We, all of us here, will take full responsibility for whatever needs to be done. Your only duty right now is to stay put, rest, and follow the doctors' orders. Nothing else.

After what was described as a long, spirited encounter, the collective will prevailed. The patient, according to Cleve Sellers, after "some impressive kicking and screaming, given his physical condition," accepted the program.

Upon leaving the hospital, the brother's first public appearance (April 6) was at the National Black Theatre of Harlem, where the Nation of Islam had organized an event on his behalf.

In light of the foregoing, his remarks below on that occasion are revealing of a certain holdover from that decisive meeting. After thanking Akbar Mohammad and the Nation, the brother revisited those issues. —EMT]

Good evening. I thank you all for coming. As a young man I opted to serve my people, and I've known for years that once you serve your people, you will lack nothing. Once you fight for our people, no matter what others say about them, our people will see that you lack nothing. I know that until I die, I will lack nothing, because until I die, I will fight for my people.

Now, the capitalist system is not a system that lies some of the time, it lies *all* the time. If they do happen to tell the truth, it's usually only the result of a double lie. Tonight you are witnessing the smashing of a lie. They say black organizations cannot work together. That we are jealous of each other, etc., etc. I work for the A-APRP, but when the Nation of Islam heard that we were in trouble and had no money, they came immediately to my aid. They came *immediately.* Everything you see here tonight is the work of the Nation of Islam. We thank them.

Here's another lie. The capitalists learned from Hitler that if you tell a big lie a million times, the people will come to think it is the truth. I say a revolutionary can tell a single truth and it will demolish a million lies. Despite what they say, American capitalism is weaker today than it has ever been. It's getting weaker every day. Every day. Revolution is coming to America as surely as Africa is my mother. And she *is* my mother.

Finally we want to thank everyone here. Many people are concerned about our health. Some do not understand our actions and think that we, ourselves, are not concerned about our health. This can never be, we are conscious human beings and revolutionaries. As revolutionaries we strive always to make our bodies as perfect instruments of service to the masses of our people as is possible. So we could never be reckless with the state of our health.

When I was a young man at Howard University, I got to know Washington, D.C., a little bit, thanks to struggle. Although there was Freedman's Hospital in D.C., health care for our people was not good. In Mississippi, it was nonexistent. And it was to Mississippi that I had to go to fight. I do not decide where I go. It is the struggle that decides where I go. If it were not for struggle, I'd never have seen Mississippi. The only reason I went there was because that was where our people's struggle was.

Now when you go for struggle, you have to make sacrifices. Among the sacrifices you must make is to live in the same conditions in which the people live for whom you say you are fighting. Anytime you separate yourselves from those conditions, you cannot understand the people, nor they you.

There is no way that I want any of you to think that I am careless with my health. No. But I tell everyone: My life means absolutely nothing beside the struggle of my people. Absolutely nothing. Therefore, I have been living in Africa. It is to Africa that I shall return. It is in Africa that I shall die. Therefore, it is there that we must live with the level of health services that our brothers and sisters have in Africa. If they can have cancer and live or die in Africa, then we too can have cancer and live or die in Africa. Thank you. Ready for revolution.

Also something else began to happen. Almost as soon as I went into the hospital, the bedside phone began to ring. And it never really stopped. At this point my general condition was known only to my doctors, my family, and a few close associates. Nothing had appeared in any public media. And my admission was very much an emergency . . . unscheduled.

How did people find out and locate me so quickly? And this chorus of goodwill simply grew and expanded. The first day it was from mostly local New York folk. Then there were calls from California, Chicago, Mississippi, Alabama. And it wasn't just the A-APRP network either. These were folk from different stages of my life. Folks from Howard. From the Freedom Rides. Folks from NAG and the Mississippi years. Black Panthers called. Folks from the D.C. Black United Front, and ordinary unconnected brothers and sisters. Then by the second day it went international. Calls came in from Trinidad, Cuba, Guinea, Azania, and even Europe and Australia. *Australia?* Sho nuff, Australia. How people found out and managed to locate me, and so *quickly,* remains a mystery. In folklore, a drowning person sees his entire life flash before his eyes. Well, in this case it was the magic of technology, not folklore, but my entire life seemed to be calling in.

I can't possibly name everyone because there were hundreds of calls reflecting all aspects and periods of my life, political and personal. A distinction without a difference if ever there were one. But from Azania, the beloved homeland to which she was finally able to return after years of struggle and exile, Miriam called. Her strong, supportive self as usual. Marliatou called and volunteered to come to New York to help care for me, which she soon after did. The SNCC clan: it was good to hear from Bob Moses, Charlie Cobb, Ivanhoe, Courtland, Judy, Marion, Willie Ricks, June Johnson, so many. As Judy put it, "It's a gathering of the clan." SNCC is an extended family.

One instance of the sisters' practical considerateness particularly touched me. When I left the hospital, old good-hearted Judy from SNCC came to see me. Before she left, she whispered into my ear that a few of the SNCC sisters had concluded, knowing me, that what I probably needed most right now was a little "walking 'round money." Whereupon Judy slipped an envelope into my hand. The sisters were, of course, absolutely right. It was a generous gesture and I know that my sisters are not wealthy women. My sisters, *asanti sani*.

And, talk about the visiting hours, that was a whole 'nother scene. Folks just began to appear at the door. Actually, it wasn't even just during visiting hours. See, most of the old campaigners who began to materialize kinda took pride in talking, bluffing, conning, or in some other way maneuvering their way past casual obstacles like hospital bureaucracy, whenever the mood struck them. But especially during visiting hours, it was like a miniconvention in that room.

There was one unexpected effect: in coming to see about me, folks were running into "lost" comrades. Folks they had shared struggle with, but whom they might not have seen or even thought about in years. So there was really a quality of unplanned reunion, the best kind. Y'know, the surprise and delight of a chance meeting, the sharing of long-forgotten memories, the war stories. I guess this is something one finds at all gatherings of comrades-in-arms who have shared affection and survived struggle together.

Even, or especially, in my physical condition, it was a tonic. Truly restorative. I saw then what exactly the doctors had meant by "intangible personal factors."

An early call came from a sho-nuff daughter of the old Southern gentility. In fact, a favorite niece of one of the most powerful Dixiecrat defenders of segregation in the U.S. Senate *[Senator Richard Russell, D-GA]*. That call wasn't a surprise. I'd fully expected that Ann Evans Guise would be calling, and that sooner rather than later. What had greatly surprised me though, was the arrival the day before of a magnificent floral arrangement from her parents. Because, in my mind, this elderly couple still represented the unreconstructed South, I was especially touched by that gesture.

Their daughter and I had met as students in D.C. then lost touch. In recent years she'd appeared at a speech and we'd renewed contact. Ann has become a friend of May Charles who describes her as "the blackest white woman I've ever met."

[While Carmichael was not surprised, I was astounded to hear Ann Evans' name crop up across a chasm of some thirty years. Where, I wondered, had she come from and what might the years have wrought? It turned out to be quite a story.

Sometime in 1963, a very Southern young white woman appeared at SNCC's office in the heart of the Washington ghetto.

"Why, howdy," she announced. "Ah read about y'all in the paper. Ah jes'

thought Ah'd drop on ovah to see what y'all are up to." Her accent, diction, affect, and manners suggested a character off the pages of Gone With the Wind. *At first we were taken aback. This overprotected product of Southern gentility had quite evidently never been around young blacks in any situation bordering on social equality. And certainly none with the brashness, political edge, and intelligence of the NAG kids. (When she'd been assigned a Negro roommate at the University of North Carolina, her father called the governor of the state demanding that his daughter be moved. She wasn't.)*

We, in turn, had never seen or envisioned anyone quite like her either. She now describes herself then as "oh so naïve and innocent." But this was many degrees beyond innocent. It was cultural.

With the best will in the world, the young woman did not seem able to string together more than three sentences without coming out with something unintentionally offensive. Sharply corrected as she invariably was, she would either blush, or to our great consternation, burst into tears.

"Oh, y'all are so mean. *Why, heah Ah've come all this way to visit you folks and, why, you don't even* appreciate *it." Also, as we would discover, she was simply incapable of pronouncing the word* Negro *acceptably. After repeated attempts and much vocal coaching, the word still came out as from some redneck politician. Finally, Carmichael told her, "Look. Tell you what. You ain't never going be able to pronounce that word without giving offense. Forget it. From now on, Ann, anytime you talking about us, just say black people, okay?"*

But what exactly did the Dixiecrat's niece want with SNCC? Might she not, some suggested, be an agent? "C'mon," Carmichael laughed. "I know the government's stupid, but even they can't be this stupid."

That was Ms. Ann Evans circa 1963. What process, I wondered, could have transformed the "Southern belle" to the "blackest white woman" of Mrs. Carmichael's acquaintance?

In 1994, when Ann reappeared at Ture's speech, she was teaching at the dysfunctional black inner-city elementary school in North Philly. She told Kwame that they were losing students, some, from drug-impacted families, as early as the first grade. There was an endemic behavior problem. The culture of the school was at once coercive and violent. The principal's solution to which was something he called the Loser's Club. This was reserved for the most disruptive students who in class were made to sit on the floor.

Kwame suggested an alternative which has come to be known as the Bright Lights. A Bright Light must always: have a passion for learning. Be an avid reader, at least a book a week. Share the knowledge they acquire. Use their knowledge to help others. Study the people's history and always be an example to others.

The students wrote to Kwame, who answered all of their questions individually, by letter or by tape. From Africa he sent regular messages of encouragement and inspiration. Later he sent a pledge to be given to each student: a

Bright Light undertakes always to be bold. To be strong. To be courageous. To work for positive change. To learn something new every day. And thus to be a bright light, an example for all.

More than once, in visiting her students' homes, Ann said she has found that pledge framed and prominently displayed.

The program, she explains, is very Africa-centered. Annually, she, along with parent chaperones, takes a group to visit a school in Africa. Each student selects an individual cultural ancestor—Madame Du Bois, Mrs. Hamer, Mrs. Baker, Malcolm, Dr. King—to whom they, on special occasions, offer libations. On these occasions they wear African dress and stage performances based on their study of the culture.

To what effect? Now most students at the school aspire and compete to become Bright Lights. Reading levels, once abysmal, have risen dramatically. Also, the culture of the school has been transformed. Fights, once commonplace, have become rare. At the request of parents there, the program has been expanded into a second school. Besides observable student achievement, the program has generated an unprecedented level of parent participation.

"I am no good at fund-raising," says Mrs. Guise, "But I do know how to ask people for things." Evidently so, because the program and its costs continue to grow, and thus far she has single-handedly been able to find the funds to make it continue because "it's a small part of Kwame's legacy." —EMT]

I mean, the people's response was something I could not ever have imagined and could never, *nevah*, have *expected*. I mean, you know, I never passed a single night in that hospital room alone. There were always three or four different people who simply refused to leave me alone there at night.

And I should not forget the dignitaries, notable community leaders who found time in their busy schedules to come visit. With typical SNCC irreverence someone christened one group the "ministerial alliance": the Reverends Jesse Jackson, Calvin Butts, and Al Sharpton each took time to come, while Minister Farrakhan called almost daily from Chicago. Those visits too were much appreciated.

One day Kathleen Cleaver, formerly of SNCC and the Panthers, now a law professor, walked in with her two sons by Eldridge. I'd always liked and respected Kathleen, so I was delighted to see her. Her sons were impressive, well-spoken young men and I was happy to see them, especially because their father and I had experienced some serious, public, and potentially dangerous political differences back then. It was a healing gesture on Kathleen's part and a moving visit. They had hardly left when a call that really surprised me came. Eldridge was on the phone from California. Because of our previous political differences, I thought it was really beautiful of him to call. As I said, cancer brings out the best in all of us. It was really quite a coincidence, because it did occur to me that

Kathleen or her sons might have prompted Eldridge to call. But Kathleen assures me that "at the time we didn't even know exactly how to get in touch with him." Whatever the genesis, I was glad Eldridge called. His death a year later made me even more thankful that we had that last conversation.

But, you know . . . I suspect the person who was most helped—in the sense of being reassured—by all this was my mother. Of course, it was a hard time for her, but I am sure that seeing and feeling the obvious loyalty and affection that drew so many people to that hospital room probably did more for her understanding of my "unconventional" lifestyle than all my arguments and explanations over the years had been able to. For that, I'm truly grateful.

One incident with May Charles was—at least in the timing—just fortuitous. It happened only a couple days after I was first admitted. May Charles had just come in from Florida that day and, after a long visit, had reluctantly left to get some sleep. I know—despite her valiant efforts to conceal it—that she also had to be worrying about how we were going to pay for all this. That bothered me too. Especially since I could say nothing to reassure her. *[This was before the meeting described earlier. —EMT]*

She had only just left when an elegantly dressed, stocky, light-skinned brother came in. The brother's face looked vaguely, naggingly familiar, but I simply couldn't place him. He introduced himself as Rock Newman. Said he'd been a few classes behind me at Howard.

Then it clicked. Rock Newman, this brother, is the manager of Riddick "Big Daddy" Bowe, former world heavyweight champion. I knew that Bowe had been an unusually conscious champion. The first thing he and his manager had done after winning the title had been to bring the belt home to Africa on a goodwill tour. We'd respected that. So I started to thank him for that. But he was very unassuming.

"Oh, no," he said. He didn't want to take much of my time. He'd just come, he explained, because he wanted me to know that some associates of his in D.C. had formed a group to take care of my hospital expenses. I was floored (even if not for a ten count). I mean, this was the first time I'd laid eyes on the brother. I thanked him and said, I have to ask one other large favor. I dialed the phone and handed it to him. "Please, my brother, will you repeat what you just said to this lady?"

When May Charles came in that evening, she was relieved and surprised. I admitted to being surprised myself.

"So why are you surprised, ol' man? Aren't you always talking about how the people . . ."

"Yeah, but I was talking about po' folk. These folks here are rich and I don't even know them. So I thank them all the more for that." But of course, because of its effect on May Charles, I was grateful as much for the timing and thoughtfulness of the brother's visit as for the generosity.

My sense, close as I can tell, is that the greatest measure of support over a long illness did indeed come from numbers of people of modest means. I thank them. Still, there's another group that stands out from that generalization. Noticeably enough so that I want to mention these specifically. Professional sisters of my age set, many of them apparently of some considerable attainment. Again, people whom I've never met, but who as a group have been most generous. *Bedassi,* my age-set sisters, *bedassi.*

Hey, I fully understand that this is supposed to be an uncommonly cynical and selfish age. And especially in America. Even so, I keep saying, and it has proven to be anything but the foolish sentimentality that it must seem to many, "If you sacrifice for the people, the people will sacrifice for you."

[The following dialogue was overheard by an A-APRP cadre at a Chicago rally.

Young brother: "I ain't down with any of that rap. That there be some stone (expletive) 'bout the people. Hell, the people sure ain't never done (expletive) for me."

Young sister: "Well, yeah, suckah. And what have you done for them? You ain't done squat for the people neither. You hip to that?"

Wal, let the church say ahmen. —EMT]

I know that Mr. Newman and his associates generously covered the costs of that first unplanned hospitalization. At that time (February 1996), the prognosis given me was six, at most eight, months (without possibility of parole). My impulse, on hearing that, was to simply return to Africa, keep working long as I could, then to prepare myself to join the ancestors. It is now almost exactly two and a half years later, so something had to have intervened. What? My kinsmen: the circle, family, friends, and of course, the people, that's who.

In African tradition, the worst possible calamity that can befall a human being is to die in isolation, alone, unloved, unmourned. Also, in the Caribbean countryside, the absolutely worst malediction one can pronounce on another person is "Go dead a bush," i.e., go to the bush, alone, like an animal and die, outside of society, community, kinsmen, or friends. To Africans, that is the worst human fate imaginable. That, give thanks, would not be mine.

The intervening force was a group of old friends who rallied around May Charles. They undertook to organize a small committee that would direct and coordinate efforts to gather the resources necessary for my extended treatment. They would set up a legal fund that would receive all funds and take responsibility for all medical expenses *[the Kwame Ture Medical Fund —EMT]*.

I was deeply moved and gave the idea my blessing, which at that time was just about all I had to give. It cannot have been easy, and indeed, I know it has not been. But from that moment—up to this writing, now going on three years—those financial concerns have been out of my hands and a weight off my head. I have had to do nothing with the fund. *Nothing!* And my essential expenses are still being taken care of. It is the effort of this committee of old friends that has enabled me to receive the medical care necessary to fight the cancer, to continue my life's work, and struggle on two fronts. There are not words enough . . . The driving force in this effort has been Winky Hall. With him on the committee are my mother, David Brothers from the Central Committee of our party, and two loyal sisters whose friendship dates from the Howard University, Nonviolent Action Group period of my life: Muriel Tillinghast and the indomitable Gloria Richardson, the "militant" leader of the Cambridge, Maryland, campaign. These are busy people. Winky, for example, operates his own consultancy.

My survival until now means that medical expenses have multiplied with each new crisis, unpredictable except in their unfailing regularity. I doubt that my brothers and sisters could have anticipated so extended a need for their services. Yet with Winky at the helm, the committee has never faltered. They have met every challenge and stayed the course. The group's constancy, resourcefulness, and tireless commitment have been a revelation and an inspiration.

What is humbling about all this is that these brothers and sisters and so many, many more have done all that they have done, endured all that they have endured, during an illness that must have come to seem interminable, with such amazing grace and unfailing generosity of spirit. *I am very fortunate in my people.*

I believe my doctors might be a little surprised that I'm still around. Well, they can thank themselves for that. And certainly the overwhelming, spontaneous outpouring of love and concern on all sides. That has just lifted, I mean *lifted,* my spirits. As our people sing in the gospel, "Love lifted me." Let the church say *ahmen.*

I know that, more than anything else, it is this love that has kept me alive. Not only has it kept me alive, but it is this love that tells me, convinces me, that we are going to win. I can die tomorrow, no problem. My people are going to win. I know that.

CHAPTER XXIX

A Struggle on Two Fronts

If life were a thing that money could buy,
The rich would live and the poor would die.
—Caribbean folk song

When I first heard the diagnosis, it had occurred to me that a cancer so apparently swift and virulent might be neither natural nor accidental in origin. The few official government documents we've quoted, outlining strategies calculated to "neutralize" me or set me up for assassination are just a sampling of the documentation we have, and what we have is merely the tip of the iceberg. So could this cancer not be the result of more covert "dirty tricks" by the government? A passing thought. I had other things to occupy me. It was not until March 3, 1996, after the Medical Fund's initial press conference, that this idea became more intriguing and I began to speculate publicly on the possibility that the government had given me the cancer.

The *New York Times'* report of that press conference mentioned five men of SNCC. Four of these were from our Washington Black United Front group in the late sixties. I was the fifth of that group mentioned in the story. Of these five men mentioned in the report, all of us except Charlie Cobb have endured bouts with cancer.

Courtland Cox, Marion Barry, and now myself, prostate cancer. Ivanhoe Donaldson, lymphatic cancer.

I quickly calculated that five other SNCC men had been centrally active with us in the D.C. area around this time: Frank Smith, Lawrence Guyot, Reggie Robinson, Jim Forman, and Lester McKimmie. Of this group, to my knowledge, only Guyot and McKimmie have not been stricken with some form of cancer. Jim Forman and Reggie Robinson have both had cancerous prostates, while Frank Smith, a veteran member of the D.C. City Council, successfully fought off a fierce attack of leukemia. (But ol' Frank always was tough, stubborn, and said to be very mean.)

Now I know that the beltway environment is frequently described as "toxic," but I had always understood that to be a political reference, rather than an environmental one. So how to explain this high incidence of cancer among us. Coincidence?

None of the people—even the most mainstream of the journalists—who have questioned this assertion of mine have done so from a basis of confident moral conviction. Their objection was *always* operational, never moral. It was never an "Oh, no, our government would not do something that evil." It was rather "The government couldn't do that: they haven't the *technical* capability to give someone cancer." Perhaps. One certainly hopes so. But who among us knows what all lies buried under the blanket of top-secret, national-security concealment under which certain agencies go about their clandestine business? In any case, what the skeptics' response reveals about citizen confidence in the *morality* of government is, I would say, cause for serious concern. Not that they *wouldn't,* but that they *couldn't.*

There is a little more. Now at the time I began raising this issue, I knew about the government's infamous and shameful Tuskegee experiment on black men, but very little else in this area. And of course, like everyone else, I'd heard the vague rumors of sinister, secret government experimentation in biological warfare. But I was about to become significantly better informed and from a most unexpected source.

In April of 1997 I spoke at a large university to an audience that was large, loud, enthusiastic, young, and mostly white. I spoke for a long time to the young people. I spoke about education, social justice, capitalism, revolution, individual responsibility, and human possibility. Early on I asserted my conviction about the source of the cancer. It was, all in all, a challenging and inspiring evening, so the students said. I tended to believe them because it was a long evening, and at the end the room was still tightly packed.

Afterward though, the chief faculty sponsor was highly distressed. Finally it came out.

"I just got to say, man, I really wish you hadn't said that [expletive]."

"Said what?"

"That [expletive] about the CIA and the cancer."

"Well, I told them to investigate everything for themselves."

"Yeah, but I still wish you hadn't . . . or at least not right up front. Not so early in the talk. Everything else was thoughtful, serious, valuable, even important. But you know that's all the press will highlight."

"So what's new? Later for them. That's all they do anyway."

"But the students too, you give them an excuse to dismiss all the challenges you dropped on them: see, he's a flake, paranoid, anti-American, etc., etc."

Clearly the good professor would not be comforted, so I didn't even try. In fact, I was not even prepared to argue that, if only in a strategic sense, he wasn't right. After all, he knew the audience better than I. Were they not his students?

That was my last public lecture before a much needed visit to Guinea. But I was back in New York within a month for the regular chemotherapy I was then receiving. During that visit I spoke again with the professor. He was glad to hear from me, he said, because he'd received "some material" for me. He was, I thought, deliberately vague in order to prick my curiosity. I refused to bite.

"It's from some of the students," he volunteered.

"Oh, you mean letters, that's nice of them."

"Not exactly. I'd best just send them to you. Let's just say the students followed your injunction."

What I did finally receive was a thickish envelope filled with magazine articles, Internet printouts, and so forth all documenting secret and illegal government experiments on unsuspecting American citizens.

"Well, look at this," I thought. So at least some of the students in that audience did "check it out" for themselves.

The students' documents, from various sources, were not specifically about biological warfare. At least not in the classic, cinematic, horror-story version of the term.

What seemed to be available to their search were materials on secret, government-sponsored radiation experimentation on unsuspecting American citizens. This was far more ongoing than I had known, and much of the information seems to have originated in testimony at congressional hearings in 1980.

[Ture wished a representative sampling of the students' research to be included, beginning with a recently leaked Atomic Energy Commission internal memo from a Colonel O. G. Haywood, which advised: "It is desired that no document be released which refer to experiments with humans and [which] might have an adverse effect on public opinion or result in legal suits. Documents covering such field work should be classified 'secret.'"

As these and a steady stream of similar reports confirm, for decades, the U.S. government had not only used human guinea pigs in radiation experiments, but had also followed a policy of deliberate deception and cover-up of its misuse of both civilians and military personnel in nuclear weapons development and radiation research.

Beginning in 1949, the Quaker Oats Company, the National Institutes of Health, and the AEC fed minute doses of radioactive materials to boys at the Fernald School for the mentally retarded in Waltham, Massachusetts, to determine if chemicals used in breakfast cereals prevented the body from absorbing iron and calcium. The unwitting subjects were told that they were joining a science club.

In 1963, 131 prison inmates in Oregon and Washington state were paid *about $200 each to be exposed to six hundred roentgens of radiation (one hun-dred times the allowable annual dose for nuclear workers). Doctors later per-formed vasectomies on the inmates to avoid the possibility of contaminating the general population with irradiation-induced mutants.*

From 1960 to 1971, in experiments that may have caused the most deaths and spanned the most years, Dr. Eugene Saenger, a radiologist at the Univer-sity of Cincinnati (in Defense Department–funded research), exposed eighty-eight cancer patients to whole-body radiation. Many of the guinea pigs were poor African-Americans at Cincinnati General Hospital with inoperable tumors. All but one of the eighty-eight patients have since died.

The worst experiments that were conducted, in my opinion, were those that resulted in the deaths of their participants. Those were conducted at the Uni-versity of Cincinnati between 1960 and 1971. The purpose of the experiments was defined in the first report to the funding agency, the Defense Department: "These studies are designed to obtain new information about the metabolic effects of total body and partial body irradiation, so as to have a better under-standing of the acute and subacute effects of irradiation in the human."

Now the selection of subjects is important. They were uneducated, average education to the fourth grade . . . sixty-two of eighty-eight patients were black. If this was a cancer study, it is the first one that excluded affluent white people at its inception.

Now the methods: They were studying the effects of radiation to predict them on soldiers; the effects were known: nausea and vomiting. Treatments for nausea and vomiting were specifically denied these patients. This is just inhumane. Some of these patients had stage-four severe nausea and vomiting that went on for days and longer. And treatment for vomiting was available. —EMT]

But the item from the students I remember most vividly was a picture story from a fairly recent issue of the *New York Times* Sunday magazine. What I remember is the faces of American citizens suffering from various cancers inflicted on them by their government. The creased, suffering faces, the dull, pain-filled eyes, the pervading sense of violation and betrayal in those faces. That's what I remember most.

All of these unsuspecting human guinea pigs were working people. In the *Times* pictures, most were white. For the most part, they were poor and defenseless. All were in some way vulnerable. Some were prisoners; others were retarded boys, innocent wards of the state. And some were American soldiers serving in the military. Men proudly wearing the uni-form of their country when they unwittingly became the government's expendable guinea pigs. Those pictures really hit me. Taken overall, the information was not pleasant reading. One could not help wondering what more was lurking, still undisclosed in the files of the bureaucracy. *"It's not that they would not . . . It's that they can not . . ."*

And, pardon the "paranoia," who knows what more of those files might disclose about that bureaucracy's plans and attitudes toward those of us they regarded as black revolutionaries, hence enemies of the state. Perhaps nothing. But . . . in the fullness of time . . .

That was a year ago now. But the students' information, at least a trickle of it, continues to come. Just recently (September 1998), I received an e-mail from an Arab graduate student who had been present at that lecture.

The story, from the *Jerusalem Post* for September 4, concerned covert biological dirty tricks and was the usual combination of charges and official denials. Of course, it again proves nothing, but is interesting because it alleges a technical capacity for inducing certain cancers. I want to reproduce the first paragraphs of that story.

REPORT: MOSSAD GAVE TERRORISTS CANCER

by Douglas Davis

London (September 24)—The Mossad may have been responsible for the fatal bouts of leukemia that have struck down Palestinian terrorists Wadi Haddad and Sabri Bana (Abu Nidal), according to the London-based newsletter *Foreign Report,* to be published today.

Recalling that Mossad agents used "medical weapons" in attempting to assassinate Khaled Mashaal in Amman last year, the newsletter noted that Haddad was prominent among the masterminds of the airline hijackings in the late 1960s and early 1970s.

"The Israelis tried to kill him on several occasions without success," it said. "In the mid-1970s, however, they infected him with leukemia, according to our unconfirmed report. Haddad was treated in an East German hospital, where he died."

Prime Minister Benjamin Netanyahu's spokesman Aviv Bushinsky issued a statement calling the story "irresponsible."

"No such incident ever took place and the magazine is again displaying irresponsibility when it misleads the public," the statement said.

Earlier, I'd known of something along the same lines from Azania. I'd read disclosures from the Truth and Reconciliation Commission about the apartheid government's attempts at covert biological warfare. A government physician the press had christened "Dr. Death" had now revealed the program of crude biological-warfare experiments he had undertaken under the auspices of the government, and his attempts to deploy them against the freedom fighters. According to his testimony, these attempts were not very successful. But the program existed, the techniques were devised, and attempts were indeed made.

Generally, about half of my public speaking was on campuses, and on these trips I heard a lot of complaints from progressive young faculty and graduate students in the sciences that the Reagan "revolution's" effort to heat up the Cold War had affected the direction of scientific research in the universities. Under Reagan, they claimed, most federal funds for scientific research were channeled through the Pentagon. Can this be true?

These young scientists claimed that it had become well nigh impossible to obtain government support unless the research could be shown (or claimed) to have a military application. No matter what your field or subject, these folks claimed, to be considered at all you had to write into the proposal some military application for the result. I imagine some of these must have been quite creative, but the overall effect was chilling and perverting.

It could be that these accounts were exaggerated. Actually, for the good of society and humanity in general, I hope they were. And now that they have "won" the Cold War, I hope the government no longer feels the need to cripple the pursuit of knowledge with such destructive and inhumane conditions.

Once I was out of the hospital with my condition more widely known, the pattern of public response that has made it possible to continue my public mission began to emerge. As did the daily rhythm and structure of my new life.

My only regret is that it is not possible in these pages to recognize and thank even a fraction of the many, many people who came forward to contribute in their various ways to this effort. So, although I shall have to limit myself to discussing the pattern, please understand that I thank you all individually.

The first change was that over the next three years I would be spending more time in the United States than I had over the previous twenty.

My first circle of immediate support was family, close old friends, and the party. Once the news was out that I intended to continue working, the party chapters set to work. As did a wider network of folks from different periods of my life in the movement who began to emerge and renew contact. Internationally also, individuals, allied movements, parties, and even some friendly governments began to come forward.

In retrospect I can see how this pattern of response recapitulated the phases of my life. It makes sense of course: Who else is likely to come forward at such times but the people whom your life has in some way touched? I wasn't thinking along those lines then. But now it is clear that the pattern of events of the three years since the diagnosis not only marked a new and intensified phase of the struggle with cancer, but can be read as a kind of referendum on my political life. And, to an extent, on my personal life too. But as I always say, there is not much of a distinction to be made there.

Being in the United States again for extended periods, I found myself back in touch with people with whom I had lost contact, in effect revisiting my political past and the struggles of my youth. It helped a lot that most of my old friends have activist spirits and good organizing skills. And as invitations from groups in different countries also came in, I found myself doing the same revisiting internationally.

News of my situation was carried in the national and international media. In the United States, two new organs of the black media had not existed during my old SNCC days, and they were crucial now in getting the information to our community. Charles Cobb, who, after SNCC, had worked for many years as a staff writer for the *National Geographic* magazine, now volunteered to do a cover story for a national African magazine called *Emerge*. And later, Isabel Wilkerson, a young sister with the *New York Times,* did a similar piece for *Essence*. At the interview I discovered that Ms. Wilkerson had followed us by about ten years at Howard, where she had also been an editor of the *Hilltop*. I believe both pieces were important in reintroducing this generation of Africans in America to our version of civil rights history and the political vision for which I continue to work.

Another incident concerning the media reflected this history, albeit in a somewhat peripheral way. In the summer of 1998, Mr. Brian Lamb, the founder and driving force behind the Cable Satellite Public Affairs Network (C-SPAN), came to New York and we conducted a lengthy interview with a focus on history. Mr. Lamb assured me that our conversation would be aired intact, without editorial intervention as is their wont at C-SPAN.

Mr. Lamb proved an interesting fellow, well-informed and tough-minded. His questions were sharp but fair. Not biased or hostile as is so often the case with the U.S. media. As he was leaving, Mr. Lamb handed me the *Times* Sunday magazine story about the creation of C-SPAN, which, he suggested, I would find interesting. He was right, for reasons that surprised me. Since it concerns C-SPAN, I'll let it stand without editorial intervention on my part. A matter of respect.

NO SOUND BITES HERE

"Tell you a story," Brian Lamb says. It is employee-orientation week at the Cable Satellite Public Affairs Network, and the company's silver-haired chief is holding court before a group of fresh-faced newcomers, with tales of his early days in Washington. Just out of the Navy in the late 1960s, Lamb found his way to a black Baptist church to see Stokely Carmichael, the fiery civil rights activist.

"Well, of a thirty-minute speech, probably, and maybe two minutes was incendiary," Lamb recalls. "The rest of it was thoughtful and intelligent and very well stated." Things looked different when he caught the event that night on David Brinkley. "What made it on," he remembers, "was the fire and brimstone."

The longer he stayed in the capital, he tells them, the more such experience became the norm. He pauses a moment, then adds: "It just seemed to me we were being unfairly treated as a society by the television news."

Even then, Lamb carried around a vision of a different way to broadcast information—one, he explains, "where everybody gets to see everything from start to finish."

Twenty-five years later, Lamb, who is fifty years old, presides over C-SPAN's two channels, providing 55 million cable households with a daily, unedited chronicle of the nation's public life—what one media analyst calls "the television newspaper of record." Lamb's creation is a network without a cutting-room floor, an outlet where the only way for viewers to get the full story is to stay tuned forever.

I admire Mr. Lamb's public spiritedness and resourcefulness and I think his initiative to be especially necessary given the general debasement of political discourse in the American media, as I later wrote him. It was also thoughtful of him to bring along the story, since I'd had no idea that I had played any role, however slight and unwitting, in the formulation of his useful approach to the media.

One early public appearance was particularly pleasant and heartening. Some old movement, mostly SNCC, folk around New York secured the Schomburg and held a little reception. It wasn't a fund-raiser, but, in the parlance of the sixties, something more like a "love-in." Again, it was mostly old SNCC veterans—black and white together—who had come out simply to wish me well. Walking in with my son, Bocar Biro, and his mother, Marliatou, we found a virtual gauntlet of hugs, kisses, and benedictions.

It was possible to feel—the current debasement of the political culture and the balkanization of the progressive forces notwithstanding—an unconquerable spirit in that room. It is not sentimental nostalgia to say that in that gathering of veterans—no longer youthful or infinitely hopeful, now gray, middle-aged, with faces carrying the marks of life's lessons—there resided a certain nobility. (I would see that again many times in my travels over these last couple years.)

I was moved to see the venerable Yuri Kochiyama, friend to Malcolm and to a generation of Harlem radicals, busily organizing the refreshments. Yuri, still on the case at eighty and finding ways to be practically useful. *[Ms. Kochiyama has since passed on, peace be unto her. —EMT]* Ivanhoe Donaldson came in from D.C. to start arrangements to have me treated in the alternative clinic where he'd been successfully treated for lymphoma. Mike Thelwell came with his children, Chinua and Mikiko. His boy Chinua and Bocar, being the same age, seemed greatly relieved to discover each other in that ancient company.

It was a moving occasion and I was glad to be there, although I couldn't stay long. Tributes and messages of solidarity were read. One in particular touched me deeply because it came from an African universally respected and particularly so in the black world. Early on I had learned a lot about Africa from him. His message, if perhaps too generous, was characteristic of the sender, but it was brief and eloquent, so for these reasons I'll quote it.

My Brother:
 I am not in the habit of presuming to speak for our people. And, indeed, I am usually quite suspicious of those who claim to. But on this occasion, I am confident that I speak for multitudes of progressive African people when I say that your courage, your insight, and your devotion have adorned the struggle in our time and continue to inspire. May the ancestors continue to protect and strengthen you in this your latest battle.
 Jide ka iji,
 Your brother, Chinua Achebe

When my turn came, I spoke briefly about the sixties, the struggle we'd shared and its accomplishments. I was pleased to be able to present my doctors to the gathering as a living testimonial to that collective struggle.

"I'm only glad and very grateful," I said then, "that these young Africans were able to take advantage of the space we broke open. That they had the consciousness and the motivation to enter the man's storehouse of technology, seize what they needed, and bring it back to serve our community."

That line got the warmest and most spontaneous response all evening. The old activists came to their feet and gave the young doctors a sustained and, so it seemed, a heartfelt ovation.

Mike and I arranged to meet the next morning. We'd not seen each other in three years, and he'd only recently heard of the cancer. When he came over to Convent, neither of us suspected that this was only the first of many days we'd spend together there over the next two years.

You know, a certain kind of conversation one can only have with what in Africa we call your "age set." That small group of contemporaries with whom you share not just history, but history seen from the same vantage point and at the same age and stage of consciousness.

With age set you tend to share the same memories, to have the same references, to have the same perspective on history and the present. Which is by no means to suggest that you will invariably agree, only that whatever disagreements occur will be precise and well grounded, rather than the product of poor communication. That was the kind of visit we had—a lot of laughing and talking, a lot of catching up on our marriages, children, and inevitably politics, the state of our people, Africa, the world. Four hours went by with astonishing speed, and at the end we were reluctant to part.

In Conakry, one of my party responsibilities has over the years been liaison with the Cuban embassy. This has been an ongoing duty despite the time of the FBI's efforts to discredit me internationally as some kind of agent of the CIA, which we've discussed.

So when the party in Guinea informed the Cuban embassy there of my illness, they relayed the news to Havana. I soon received an official invitation, which I was pleased to accept, to return to Cuba for further evaluation and treatment. I thought the gesture to be typical of the generosity and thoughtfulness of the government, but I also welcomed it as the political expression of our complete rapprochement, the final failure of the FBI's campaign of slander and character assassination some years earlier.

[Recently it came to my attention that two simultaneous initiatives and members of the A-APRP in this country had also played a significant role in the Cuban invitation. In D.C., Bambose Shango worked closely with companero *Felix Wilson of the Cuban Interest Section; while in New York, the tireless Mawina Kouyate and David Brothers informed the Cuban mission to the United Nations and set the process in motion. —EMT]*

Also, in medical terms it was most welcome. The revolution was justly proud of its progress in medical research and health care delivery. During the seventies and eighties the Cubans had more doctors and medical personnel deployed usefully into the third world than did the World Health Organization. Then too I greatly respected their embrace of non-Western traditions of healing—both spiritual and herbal—that derived from African culture in Cuba.

We were a party of five, including my mother, my sister Nagib the nurse, her grandson Moussa, and Dr. Barbara Justice as physician in attendance. The *companeros* received us with warmth and courtesy and a kindness that continues to this day. (On my birthday, June 27, 1998, I received official greetings from the government and an invitation to return.)

761

I was immediately admitted to the Clinica Centro Sierra Garcia and placed under the care of an impressive brother, a prominent oncologist called Dr. Antonio Permuy Vasquez. He noted, "I am a child of the revolution. Before the revolution someone like me could not have been a doctor."

We—Dr. Justice stayed in the suite—were in hospital for fourteen days while they checked everything. *Every thang.* Dr. Justice said it was an extensive and thorough workup. At the end of which they confirmed the findings at Columbia-Presbyterian and concluded that I was responding as well as could be expected to the regimen I was already on. No need to intervene there so far as Western medicine was concerned. But there was still the African tradition to explore.

During those fourteen days at the Clinica, Sister Assata Shakur came to visit every single day. Not a day did this sister miss. I'd always known her to be revolutionary and resolute. I was reminded then of how very generous and nurturing a spirit she also is. I understood exactly how it was that she could have inspired such loyalty and courage in her brothers in the Black Liberation Army. Why, after she was framed for murder, gut-shot, jailed, and brutalized, the brothers would go under arms into the penitentiary and resolutely liberate their comrade and sister. This sister has such a luminous spirit that I'm always angered when I see her so demonized in the police-generated propaganda continually broadcast against her in the American media.

Perhaps the most renowned traditional healer in Cuba is an herbal doctor. This brother is said to have his best results—in cancer treatment—with the prostate. So impressive are his results that during our visit the Cuban medical establishment was evaluating his work and deciding which of his preparations they would make available through government pharmacies. (One ironic consequence of the U.S. economic blockade has been to cause the society to better utilize its indigenous resources. Just as in revolutionary Guinea.)

We found the herbalist on a little farm in the countryside outside Havana. There on the small herb farm was a modest farmhouse with a laboratory attached. During our consultation, there were two moments when the brother made a sharp impression. The conversation was really between him and Dr. Justice, with Assata translating between them. Listening to Assata's translation, I could hear the conversation getting steadily more technical. At one point, the herbalist launched into a lengthy explanation.

"Whoa," Assata cried, "that's all unfamiliar medical terminology. I'm not sure I can translate it."

"Tell him to continue," Dr. Justice said. "I know exactly what he's talking about." And the conversation proceeded without benefit of translation.

I was impressed. I mean it was amazing, the communication in medical terms between these two African healers who did not really share a language except the idiom of healing. Assata was as deeply impressed as I. *[Ture told me that he remembered the moment because it reminded him of the communication across languages he'd sometimes shared with Sékou Touré. —EMT]*

The second impressive moment came when the healer began to describe the treatments he would prescribe for me; it seemed like an awful lot. And he did not mention the cost, which made me uneasy. Especially because of the incalculable hardship on the population that I know was being exacerbated—and in some instances caused—by the U.S. blockade, I did not want it to appear that I had come to exploit Cuban generosity.

"Assata," I whispered, "what this brother is talking about is gonna cost a lot. We don't have much money left. Ask him the price."

"All right. I will, but if necessary we'll just have to borrow some," she said.

The brother must have picked up on our concern for he immediately smiled and explained that he was a healer. He did not, he said, understand money. A healer is not ruled by the love of money, he chided us.

That's when I understood that this one was serious. I've seen a lot of traditional healers in Africa, and invariably the best ones, the authentic and most effective ones, are the ones who do not demand money. As a matter of professional ethics. I mean, you go by their place and stay with them. By Western standards they be dirt-poor. Yet they never demand a fee; indeed, as healers they cannot. You as patient must let your conscience be your guide and pay them as you can. It works.

I am just now finishing the preparations the Cuban brother prescribed. I do believe they were helpful, but I took a lot of different treatments, and you know, this thing was very advanced.

After that he took us into his laboratory, which was being expanded and improved so as to expand his research. Dr. Justice was impressed.

The third aspect of the Cuban trip was in its own way as effective, and in a way that is impossible to quantify in Western language, very, very anchoring and strengthening. This was the treatment of the spirit. For this we were taken to prominent *babaloas.* These are priests and healers in the Santeria, a Yoruba-derived religious tradition, who would evoke for us the help of the ancestors and *orishas,* the spiritual forces of ancient Africa.

One interesting variation of this approach was that both the patient and the doctor were to be treated. Once explained, it seemed so obvious.

Of course, it was necessary to strengthen both the recipient and supplier of the healing.

So a number of different ceremonies were performed both for Dr. Justice and myself. These were designed to spiritually purify and strengthen doctor and patient. It was also quite fascinating: the appropriate deference and respect that the scientifically trained Cuban doctors—my oncologist, Dr. Permuy, for example—evinced for these traditional African religious and healing practices.

In all three phases—the reading, the cleansing, and the sacrifice—the ritual was powerful and spiritually evocative. The reading established which *orisha* (a deity or primal force) governed your spiritual being. The cleansing purged one spiritually, the ceremony culminating in evoking the influence and protection of ancient and mysterious forces.

It was perhaps to a Western observer, as Dr. Justice said, a little "eerie." But we both found it powerful. I was comforted by a sense of being reunited with powerful ancient forces that I could feel but not see, sense but not understand, coming out of our people's traditional wisdom and practice. And I did in fact *feel* cleansed and strengthened.

I left Cuba comforted by a feeling that we'd touched all necessary bases. And indeed, after that trip, the cancer seemed, at least for a time, to be under control.

That June there was another Caribbean trip. A Pan-Africanist-oriented group, the Emancipation Support Committee of Trinidad and Tobago, invited me to come assist them in organizing and spreading the message. Especially since the visit would be under the auspices of the Emancipation Committee ably led by Khafra and Aisha Kambon, two dear friends and allies over many years.

You know I was going to make space in my schedule for a working visit there. It would be my first public (legal) appearance in my native land since a succession of governments, beginning with that of Sir Eric Williams some thirty years earlier, had acquiesced to the ban imposed by the "Brutish" government. Let's be clear now. The people never accepted any British ban. That is why it had been so easy for me to visit Uncle Dowling before he passed.

The sitting regime of Prime Minister Basdeo Panday was the nation's first predominantly "Indian" one. I was curious about the official reception I was to receive this time. And of course, I very much wanted to visit again with Tante Elaine and Mommy Olga, who were getting on in age. Also, in an unexpected onset of nostalgia, I hoped for a chance to walk over scenes from childhood to see for myself exactly what changes the passage of time had brought about.

We agreed with the committee on a four-day schedule that would include time on tiny Tobago (birth island of Ms. Cecilia) and devote most of the working time to the nation's youth. Even so, it was a crowded itinerary including the obligatory ceremonial moments with government dignitaries, various media events, and some cultural affairs. But most speaking appearances were with the youth, and these were as always the most satisfying.

The country seemed every bit as beautiful as in my childhood memories but there were obvious changes. For instance, one could not fail to notice the massive economic development fueled by petroleum resources. And one did not have to be a socialist to see that this was uneven, top-heavy, as is the case with all development dominated by multinational corporate capitalism in the black world.

Another evident change, this one particularly gratifying, manifested itself at the cultural events: the visible and dramatic expression of a proud African cultural identity. African names, African dress, African ritual and music, were evident in a way they had never been in my childhood. What had been undeniably present then, but in a subdued, unrecognized way, was now beautifully and proudly articulated. When I commented on this, people attributed it to developments coming out of "the Black Power movement." I only smiled.

On the first day I was courteously received by Prime Minister Panday, and the issue of my previous banning did not arise. At a later television interview, however, the subject of the ethnicity of the new government came up, and my response apparently surprised both the questioner and—so I'm told—some of the audience.

I pointed out that the prime minister and his cabinet were native-born Trinidadian citizens. That previous governments dominated by Trinidadians of African descent had never been referred to as "African" governments. They were Trinidadian governments. So why now this talk of an "Indian" government? It too was a Trinidadian government, a national one.

I'm told the government was pleased with that answer. I doubt, though, that they were as appreciative of my follow-up. I explained that the issue around which struggle needed to be organized was not crudely racial. Under "African" governments in Trinidad I had been banned, and there had been far too many poor and oppressed Africans. Under the "Indian" government there were similarly oppressed Indians. The issue in Trinidad therefore was *class*, not race, and the need was for a revolutionary organization of the poor and progressive people of all races.

On Tobago, in a rural area, I visited a middle school that seemed almost a replica of the one I'd attended some fifty years earlier—the order, the discipline, the good manners, the school building itself, and the students in their neat uniforms. The only difference being that in my school days, a speaker with a message like mine would have been inconceivable. I enjoyed the energy and curiosity of those young people a great deal.

Wherever I went, the popular reception was warm, and especially so among the students. It was a great feeling to be working openly among the youth of the land of my birth. I have no idea whether intelligence gatherers were present at these talks, but the press reports were certainly detailed. My impression was that they were much more thorough and objective than is usually the case in the United States.

[Brother Ture's detractors in this country might not share his opinion on the objectivity of the Trinidad press coverage. You can decide. The quality of the nation's six-formers—the nation's future leaders—and their reception of his talk particularly pleased Ture. The report by Nirvan Maharaj in the Guardian *captures the spirit of that occasion, the demeanor of our brother, and the impression he gave during those times.*

When I suggested its inclusion, Kwame said, "You know it's not my habit to quote my press, Thelwell. T'ain't generally a great idea." I persisted. Finally he said, "Okay, hold off for now. We can fight about it later." That later never came. So this one is on me. Nothing I've seen from this country more accurately captures the aura of the brother during these two terminal years. —EMT]

STOKELY CARMICHAEL RETURNS HOME
Kwame Ture (Stokely Carmichael) at the National Heritage Library

by Nirvan Maharaj

On Wednesday, June 12, 1996, at approximately 10:20 A.M. a tall man of African descent walked into the National Heritage Library. Welcomed amidst the pulsating sounds of African drumming, he strode, tall and confident as a man assured of his destiny and the knowledge of its fulfillment. He was dressed in loose-fitting flowing apparel, with matching headpiece. Everything a light cloudy bluish-greenish colour. On his feet, he wore white pointed slippers reminiscent of Moroccan royalty. Indeed, he was the image of noble bearing. Smiling, the man radiated a warm and sincere aura, while his physical body, lean and frail, reflected years of stress and tension, suppressed under a cover of calm and peace. One could feel the excitement as many of African descent eagerly awaited, acting as though a messiah were coming. To them he was the embodiment of black struggle against a world dominated by white power structures. Kwame Ture, known to most as Stokely Carmichael, had arrived.

Stokely has been unrelenting in his struggle to unite all peoples of African descent for the purpose of a common goal. That is black power. The power of the black man to determine his own destiny. His single mission—the total liberation and unification of Africa under the banner of socialism. Jailed on several occasions, threatened with violence, banned from entering many different countries of the world, Stokely had returned home. In the General Reference area of the National Heritage Library, over two hundred sixth-form students had gathered from various schools, many unsure of what to expect, some perhaps never having heard his name before, others not knowing what the fuss was about. Yet all waiting to hear this man speak. The programme began with a traditional African invocation to the spiritual forces by members of the Orisha faith.

As Kwame stood at the podium, he seemed a man totally at ease. With the flair of a true orator, he engulfed his audience within the web of his words. Passionately he voiced his views, the revolutionary within him bursting forth at every opportunity. He spoke of revolution and change. He stated that change comes about only through conflict, both violent and nonviolent. He stressed the need for education and the ability to think. He urged students to expand their minds, showing that to make the changes they wanted, they needed to understand how changes occur. He said that a man who cannot reason or think is no better than an animal, only fit to eat, sleep, and reproduce. He called on students to continue the struggle for truth, equality, and justice within the society. He stated that life is a continuous struggle, when everything is pulling you to do the negative, while you have to fight to give the positive dominance. In summary, Kwame urged students to study, think, reason, and to be honest. He called upon them to strive to understand each other's culture so as to have mutual respect for each other. He saw capitalism as a dying ideology and emphasized that the struggle was one of class differences, more than anything else. In all, Kwame's philosophy, though based on the same principles as advocated in the 1970s, seemed a bit more nuanced. The fire of his beliefs was there, as was the emotion, but it was tempered by practicality and reason.

His words were eagerly absorbed by the enthusiastic audience, and in the end his address seemed too short. Seeing and hearing him for the first time, there is no doubt that Kwame Ture was born to be different. I was struck most of all by the warmth and sincerity of the man. Whatever the views expressed about Kwame—racist, revolutionary, dreamer, idealistic, insane, prophet, or pirate—there is indeed something special about him. A determination, a will, a strength of belief. Even though one may hate him or be opposed to him, one cannot help respecting him. *[Let the church say ahmen. —EMT]*

Throughout, the media persisted in referring to the visit as a "homecoming," and I saw no real need to object that Africa was now my home. It would, I thought, have seemed contrary to the spirit of the occasion. But then a serious grassroots sentiment began to emerge. I first became aware of it in a long column by Ravijohn Ali, obviously a funny and combative popular journalist, who called on the government to build me a house so I could come home.

[Mr. Ali wrote that "if ever the Prime Minister deserved unreserved kudos . . . it is for his open-arms welcome of Ture." Especially, he said, because "Ture had been banned in more than twenty-five countries (more than even Marcus Garvey), especially and including his homeland of Trinidad and Tobago."

Mr. Ali continued, "But Bas must do much more than that." Then he cited precedents, including the young Stokely's childhood hero Mr. Uriah Butler, and a cricket-playing superstar.

"Remember," thundered Mr. Ali, "how a national hero like Butler suffered interminably before a conscience-stricken regime built the old man a petty house in his old days?

"I say give Ture a proper house to rest his head in this country, provide all the amenities and a solid stipend, so that this, one of our foremost intellectuals, can live in comfort and be proud once again of this his native land."

Then it must have gotten real good to him, 'cause the brother wasn't finished. He went to the cricket precedent with a burst of indignant eloquence.

"If Brian Lara, who would hit some balls with a cricket bat and get a million-dollar mansion from the government . . . then who is Kwame Ture, a hero whose eminence and luminescence ten Laras could never attain . . .

". . . If it cost a million dollars or more, no citizen would mind the government spending this money on this eminent revolutionary, intellectual, and philosopher, this proud black icon.

"There is so much I wanted to say on this matter, but space does not permit. So I shall leave the rest for another time, rest assured of that." And as a parting shot, Mr. Ali enjoined his readers to "write, phone, petition PM Panday on the Kwame Ture issue. Light fire under his behind if you must on this matter." —EMT]

Apparently the issue was percolating upward because there were other such calls in the press, though none quite so colorful as Mr. Ali's. It reached the point where it was necessary to publicly thank the people but to respectfully point out that Africa was my home, and that work there needed my attention. There would be no need for "a house for Mr. Ture" in Trinidad this time round.

I should gratefully record, however, that in response to the people's call, the Trinidad and Tobago government did vote a contribution to my medical expenses. So maybe a fire was indeed lit underneath . . . ah, prime ministerial posteriors. It was an altogether enjoyable trip.

Back in New York, we—the family and medical advisers—agreed that we would carry the fight to all fronts. That is, we would endeavor to explore any option that seemed at all promising, no matter how unconventional. But, of course, within reason.

This aspect proved at once fascinating and repellent. Instructive on three major questions: human nature, capitalism, and death. It certainly underlined in graphic terms the need for a just, humane, and rational health care system free of the profit motive across lines of class, nationality, or race. It brought back a long-forgotten jingle from my childhood. What I remembered as an ironic comment on the unthinkable now seemed to take on a chilling aspect of possibility: *If life were a thing that money could buy, the rich would live and the poor would die.*

In many cases these were just ordinary good-hearted people coming forward in good faith to volunteer some local cure or family remedy. They meant only the best. Bless them. Then in the middle there were what seemed to be a class of compulsive nuts, messianic eccentrics, who genuinely believed in the efficacy of whatever esoteric process they had formulated. Then, at the far pole, were what were clearly businesses. Profit-making enterprises run by medical entrepreneurs of varying degrees of expertise, peddling "breakthrough" therapies described in glowing scientific or pseudoscientific terms, often claiming results ranging from the merely startling to the truly miraculous.

Some of the presentations seemed legitimately promising, while others seemed patently inflated in their claims. Many of these treatments, mostly unsanctioned by federal health authorities, were only available offshore. This necessitated travel and often exorbitant fees from people not all of whom are rich, but all of whom are desperate to cling to hope. Or at least as Bro Jesse has it, trying to keep hope alive.

I was surprised both at the extent and the variety of these enterprises. It was collectively an underground mini-industry, at least some of which seemed transparently fraudulent, the contemporary equivalents of snake oil salesmen preying on frightened people at their most vulnerable. An exploitation of the drowning-man-and-the-straw syndrome, the profit motive at its absolutely most despicable.

This is made all the worse because this profusion of hustlers only serves to muddy the waters. Perhaps some patients could indeed benefit from some of these treatments. But the few that, although unorthodox, appeared to be serious scientific initiatives with some potential to benefit somebody came surrounded by a flotilla of the obviously fraudulent.

And how to distinguish between them? The task of sorting out and sifting through fell to Dr. Justice, assisted by Eric, Winky, and my sister Nagib. As our proverb says, "Hungry belly make monkey eat red pepper." Well, necessity has made me an expert on experimental cancer treatment.

In addition to the clinic in D.C. that had served Ivanhoe so well, we decided to investigate two offshore sites of alternative treatment.

The first was a clinic in Mexico run by an Australian doctor. This center proffered an innovative technique intended to strengthen the immune system, produce antigens that would attack any cancer cells that were lingering, and thus lessen the pain. I figured that whether or not it lessened the pain, strengthening the immune system couldn't hurt. So we did that, but the pain did not decrease.

The second was a holistic center in the forested mountains of Honduras. I spent two weeks there, and while I can't gauge the effects of the treatment, the location was most beneficial. And the nearest telephone was miles away. Totally incommunicado for the first time in years, I rested and read a lot. The rest certainly helped but I won't swear for all of the reading.

One book I read there sure did nothing for my spirits, or my intellect for that matter. Called something like *The Rage of a Privileged Class,* it was about the anger, frustration, alienation, and despair prevalent among Africans born in America, who although "supremely qualified" found themselves underappreciated, rarely promoted, and insufficiently rewarded in the American corporate world. I lost patience with it rather quickly. It seemed, I'm sorry to say, one extended, self-pitying whine from people who should have known better. Having made certain life choices, they now bemoan consequences that ought to have been quite predictable. None of these brothers and sisters were poor, as the world goes. They were rich in most cases and privileged beyond their parents' dreams or the hopes of the great majority of mankind.

Now, I don't for a moment doubt their claims of discrimination. Nor do I discount the frustration and disillusionment of which they complain. It is the underlying values I question. In the first place, what on earth had they imagined the corporate world to be? Fair, just, and rational? A meritocracy? "We accepted *all* their terms," they wail, "and *did everything they required* of us: the 'right' schools, the 'right' degrees, the 'right' résumés, so why now do we feel so alienated, underutilized, and isolated?"

That is an important question indeed, which requires a clarity of perspective and politics conspicuously absent in that book. But as I sat reading in the Honduran hills, it occurred to me that the soul sickness being reported was not really race specific at all.

In all likelihood, I thought, a great many of their white colleagues in offices next door who could not claim an ethnic or culturally determined "glass ceiling" were probably equally victim to the very same ennui and disaffection and for much the same reasons: the craven abandonment of their community and culture in thoughtless pursuit of the sterility of the corporate American dream, cum nightmare, and for *acceptance* and status in that predatory culture. Whatever happened to "lifting as ye climb"?

Their complaints seemed inspired by only narcissism and self-advancement. They seemed the linear descendants of those Howard students of years ago intent on imitating only the most superficial and consumerist of white American values. For both groups the greatest—indeed the only—sin of this wasteful culture was its failure to include them.

Nowhere in the book was there the slightest recognition of the wasteful and destructive consequences of multinational corporate rapacity on the poor of the world. Nowhere the slightest recognition that the opportunities they were misusing were won out of the blood their people shed in struggle. And certainly no sense of a personal obligation to that struggle.

But, of course, the world of that book is quite distorted, thank God. It is far from the whole story. I know any number of young Africans who have survived the brainwashing of elite and privileged educations and kept faith with their community and their historical duty. Our party, for example, is full of conscious young Africans no less well academically prepared, but whose values and purposes are clear. I mean, what values or reward does corporate culture hold that would inspire any thinking person—especially an African—to subjugate his or her entire personality to such complete conformity to its alleged "values"? Gimme a cotton-picking break. Reading that book was sobering and saddening.

One incident in Honduras did teach me something unexpected about myself. The incident itself was slight enough, but I found it instructive. Instructive enough to tell you about it anyway. It concerned prayer.

Now, it goes without saying that one does not spend an adult lifetime organizing black folk without paying some considerable attention to the soul, as it were, engaging the spiritual. *[Not preaching to chickens, however. —EMT]* I certainly learned that in Mississippi. In Africa, we, of necessity, organize in Christian, Muslim, and traditional communities. We respect all religions and all faiths.

But, you say, that is merely an organizing principle, a political necessity. It's not quite the same thing as being religious. Nor did I say it was. I've never been particularly sanctimonious, or what folks in the South call "plu-pious." But I am a religious man. As you've seen, I come from a family and a community of faith, a circumstance that has profoundly affected my personality and at one point my political allegiances. I strongly believe, for instance, that the strength to survive and continue working to this point comes in some significant ways from sources outside myself. A great part of which, I'm convinced, has been the constant prayers of a great number of people of different faiths.

Since my illness, people have constantly assured me that I am in their prayers. Always, I thank them. I know also that in some Islamic congregations in America, Africa, and one Central Asian republic and also some Christian congregations across the world regularly offer prayers on my behalf. I'm also told that Native American religious ceremonies, as well as ceremonies in the traditional religious idioms of Africa and the Caribbean, have been performed for me. I cannot be convinced that I have not received powerful benefits from all that psychic and spiritual energy.

At the holistic center in Honduras, group prayer appears to have been a regular feature of the treatment, and I found myself at one such meeting. I listened as the afflicted earnestly implored divine intervention for a reprieve. The standard approach was to ask the Creator for the restoration of their health and that of their fellow sufferers.

For some reason, when my turn came, I had not prepared any language of my own. The situation was a little unusual—performing in public what I think of as the most private of communications, that between a man and his God. But I got through, as I thought, pretty well. I said in essence:

"Lord, we've come a long way together and you've never abandoned me. I've always accepted your many gifts and your will. In your book, you've taught that 'whomsoever seeketh to save his life shall lose it.' So be it. As I've accepted your goodness and mercy in the past, I now accept your will, which only you can know. Anything less would be ungrateful and unworthy. Thy will be done. Thank you." I almost ended, "Ready for revolution," but I caught myself.

Afterward, though, I was quite surprised to learn that my offering had been a mite controversial to some in the gathering. Apparently it was a little different from what had been expected and so, some felt, insufficiently humble, even confrontational.

Well, I sure ain't no theologian, but I know that those few words—entirely spontaneous and unrehearsed—captured my attitude exactly, with dignity and no disrespect to the Creator intended.

I've always been prepared to lay down my life in struggle. To accept without complaining or whimpering whatever fate comes. In that, nothing has changed.

In fact, if anything, the pace of the work picked up in '97 because I was determined to answer every call. So far as humanly possible I would respond to every politically serious request and invitation (and a few largely sentimental ones). Thus in '97 my travel schedule became very crowded indeed.

From New York Sister Mawina, and from Chicago Masani Bediako, a very steadfast and hardworking sister from the Pan African Resource Council, coordinated this aspect very skillfully. So the work continued. Thanks largely to the resourcefulness and organizing skills of my two sisters, during this year, I was able to meet public engagements and party obligations across, literally, the length and breadth of the U.S. and of course, in the African world. Give praise and thanks.

During that spring (1997), I asked Masani and Mawina to schedule as many public lectures as possible.

If, as I was being told, this cancer was supposed to kill me, then it would have to take me working. We, all of us, have to go, but as I told an interviewer from CBS, "Ain't no cancer going kill me. Hard work for my people is what will kill me."

Wherever I spoke—on campus or in the community—people, at least those who turned out to hear me, were desperately seeking for alternatives. People and not only the youth were looking for ways to come to grips with, to influence or change radically, the direction of the society.

Everywhere people expressed a palpable, pervasive sense of their own powerlessness and marginalization. And always a will to change that: a search for ways to engage the system militantly, to no longer feel ignored, discounted, and expendable.

My message: never give up. Question everything. Challenge every authority. Always seek information and organize, organize, organize. And never, ever despair. Trust yourself. Trust the people. Never settle for less. Never give up, organize, organize, organize. History is full of surprises. Especially for exploiters. Organize, organize, organize. Stand ready for revolution.

Later that year, working always with progressive and pan-Africanist forces in Africa and the Caribbean, I traveled outside the U.S. I managed to work in visits to Cuba, the Bahamas, Honduras, Ghana, Egypt, Libya, Azania (South Africa), and two exceedingly welcome and restorative intervals at home in Conakry.

The intensive regimen of chemotherapy I was receiving required that I return to New York regularly. But even that inconvenience was somewhat ameliorated because I was able to get equally effective treatment in Senegal and South Africa.

One invitation for September 1997 was of particular importance to me. The Biko Day celebration is held annually in South Africa. It commemorates the life and work of Bantu Steve Biko (peace be unto him), the great visionary and frontline leader in the struggle against apartheid, who had been murdered while in police custody.

Steve Biko and I had been allies intellectually, spiritually, ideologically. He was a leader of great clarity and principle. Of the many admirable leaders of the South African struggle, I regarded Steve as one of my closest brothers in spirit. He was totally committed and fought for the best cultural traditions of his people. So I would do whatever lay in my power to help carry forward his work in this important new stage of the struggle there. Also the invitation came from our old allies in PAC and from AZAPO (Azanian People's Organization), the organization founded by Biko.

There were other reasons also. South Africa was one of the few African countries I had not visited. Miriam had returned home after over thirty years in exile and we had always dreamed of returning together to visit a liberated South Africa.

For this trip I asked Mawina and Masani to schedule particular countries: Guinea, Ghana, Egypt, and ultimately South Africa. So that when I left New York in mid-August I was really looking forward to this trip. Every stop held particular significance for me. I had been too long from my home in Conakry. I needed to touch my extended family there again and to attend to my duties in the party (the Democratic Party of Guinea), for elections were on the horizon and there were many strategic decisions to be made.

In Ghana—land of the *Osegeyfo*—I had a personal mission. I wanted to study the program and organization of the W. E. B. Du Bois Memorial Center for Pan-African Culture in Accra. Its mission—in the tradition of the doctor—of reaching out programmatically to all Africans in the diaspora and on the continent deserves to be more widely appreciated and supported by our people.

Egypt has always held an important place in the Pan-African movement. The great Egyptian patriot, Gamal Abdel Nasser (peace unto his name) had been a powerful force in establishing the Organization of African Unity. While Mrs. Du Bois lived in Cairo, I would seize every excuse to visit that venerable city on the Nile.

So it was very good to stop again in Cairo en route to South Africa. There I was well taken care of at the home of Bro Akbar Muhammad, the Nation's representative in Africa. It was a short visit but a number of brothers and sisters reached out, among them two old friends.

I'd first met Gamal Nkrumah when, as a young teenager, he had come to Conakry for the funeral observances for his father. Gamal came in to see me with David Graham Du Bois, whose mother, Shirley, had played so influential a role in my younger life. It was, as usual, a pleasant visit in Cairo, and it was good to touch base with David and Gamal.

Then it was on to "liberated" South Africa.

South Africa, that bloodied, beautiful land, at the southernmost tip of the continent. That last stubborn outpost of overt white racism which had occupied the political attention of my entire generation, which had been the focus of so much effort across the black world, and which I had never been able to visit. I was eager to go and especially to see and visit with Zenzi. We had a very pleasant and necessary reunion. She had not changed.

Well, South Africa may be democratic, but it sure ain't liberated. Not yet. The struggle continues and is entering a crucially interesting phase.

Who can forget how the entire world breathed a sigh of relief when in 1991 South Africa appeared to have averted the racial Armageddon that had seemed inevitable? All across Africa, Nelson Mandela's emergence from jail was met with public celebrations, dancing, singing in the streets, official speechmaking, and rejoicing.

But we all understood properly that it was not DeKlerk and the racist government that had "freed" Mandela. It was his people's struggle and sacrifice. That is clear. Many gave their lives but it was the courage of the brothers and sisters, students, workers, a *united front* of many, many organizations that brought down apartheid. That's very clear. And we also understand properly that without economic justice and the restitution of *all* African rights, that violent confrontation is not really averted, it is only *postponed*. That's clear.

It is obvious that as long as those African masses, whose courage and sacrifice the world has seen, continue to be marginalized and excluded from meaningful participation in the economic life—from the fruits of their victory—the struggle will continue. This would be the classic neo-colonial situation where the government changes hands but the revolution is not implemented. The incoming "nationalist" government dare not content itself yet again with merely occupying the unchanged institutions of colonial privilege and exploitation. Every African government that has done this has inevitably degenerated into corruption and dictatorship. That must not happen in Azania. It would be a mockery of the people's struggle.

Whomever I reasoned with, the message was the same: the struggle is not over, it's just moved to a different, in some ways more difficult, stage.

People loved and respected *Madiba*, as they call President Mandela. (That is the name of his Xhosa clan.) They respected his courage, his constancy, his devotion over his many years in apartheid's jails. They recognized that his intervention from his cell saved the country incalculable destruction and loss of life. Even so, many feel that in so doing he may have conceded too much to the white minority, who seem to feel entitled to the privileges and luxuries accumulated under apartheid. While the new government is left with a near-impossible task: redressing and correcting the massive poverty, deprivation, and neglect of forty years of apartheid *without radically dismantling the social apparatus*. More power to them if they can do that, but I have my doubts.

Also, while I was there the Truth and Reconciliation Commission was constantly in the news. Which means, among other things, that the details of the criminality and brutality that the Boer dictatorship had used *as a matter of policy* to maintain its power was being revealed in all its ugliness. That by itself was a source of bitterness, especially to those who had been tortured or had lost loved ones and comrades. But what was even more rankling was the attempt to equate the people's war of resistance with the ruthless brutality of their oppressors. Come on. What kind of equivalence is this? Since when does a grievously oppressed people not have the right—indeed the duty—to resist their oppression, by as Malcolm (peace be unto him) used to say, "any means necessary"? Gimme an everloving break. *Gimme an everloving break*. It shows that a significant number of South African whites in their racial arrogance have learned nothing. The struggle continues.

There was another thing I already knew that became very clear in South Africa: the utter and complete hypocrisy of the capitalist West. Remember how as the struggle gathered force, the most barefaced international defenders and apologists for South African racism were the conservative running dogs of global capitalism? Margaret Thatcher's Britain, Ronald Reagan's America, and Helmut Kohl's Germany? Even as they trumpeted their devotion to democracy and human rights, they ran interference for apartheid.

Now South Africa is a democracy. Over 90 percent of its people vote in national elections. It has the world's most progressive and liberal constitution. So where is British, American, and German support for democracy now? A democratic African government is struggling to repair the damage and injustice of apartheid. To house millions of homeless, to create jobs, education, social services, and some degree of social justice. Where are these rich Western governments with the investments, foreign aid, the trade agreements, the interest-free loans, the varieties of technical and educational assistance that the South African government needs and the people deserve? South Africa now has the kind of "responsible democratic" government they say they wish to see in Africa. So where are they now?

These three are condemned by their own hypocrisy and racism. They were the willing financial partners of apartheid in exploiting the people of South Africa. They profess to want democracy to succeed in South Africa. Had they any commitment to their own rhetoric, they would seize this opportunity. They would mobilize massive assistance to the South African government in its effort to bring about social justice there. Instead they have abandoned South Africa to the ravages of global capitalism. This is so bare-faced and vulgar. There is a name for it and we all know it: racist hypocrisy/capitalist greed.

So there was much that I had wanted to do and see in South Africa. With the help and hospitality of my people I was able to do just about everything I'd hoped.

One of those things was to get an authentic Ndebele fertility doll. One that had been properly consecrated by a powerful *isangoma*. Not a tourist memento, but an authentic Ndebele doll. I am not a collector of African artifacts and this was hardly the time to start. But I really wanted that doll.

I had met a remarkable woman at the clinic where I received chemotherapy in New York. I first noticed this lady because of the warmth and graciousness with which she treated the patients. She seemed to radiate an instinctive kindness and a genuinely cheerful spirit for everyone.

Ms. Ellen Flowman was a bright presence in a very grim place. Sometimes we would talk and I discovered that this good woman who showed such sympathy to others had her own cross to bear. She and her husband wanted a family but thus far it had not happened. I assumed there was difficulty with conception. I knew from Zenzi whose mother was herself an *isangoma* that the Ndebele *isangomas* working with ritual dolls were very effective in matters of fertility. She had said that among traditional people in South Africa, the Ndebele were the most respected in this field.

In October when I went again for treatment I was able to give Ms. Flowman her doll. I don't know whether she was fully convinced, but she seemed touched by the gesture. On a subsequent visit, Ms. Flowman seemed even more quietly radiant than I remembered. She confided that, sure enough, she was with child.

[When Ms. Ellen Flowman heard Ture's name: "He was such a wonderful man. So courageous and so kind. And what a smile he had. He was my buddy." She confirmed the story with one caveat. "It wasn't so much that I couldn't conceive," she said. "I was more that I was ambivalent about the whole thing." Her daughter is an absolute delight and, she said, she was ambivalent no longer. —EMT]

I am now back in New York at Mama Gerri's. In a few days we shall return to my home in Conakry for the last time. I look forward to that. I am ready.

A few days ago there was a gathering—a big affair—in D.C. The organizers called it a tribute, but we all knew it was a good-bye. It was a remarkable evening. As usual, just being with my people will lift my spirits and it did again. I'm an African; when the drums start to beat, I'm gonna dance. So I did one more time. But, truthfully, I'm very tired now. It was good-bye, an appropriate leave-taking, but good-bye nonetheless. And we all knew it.

The D.C. tribute was organized by Karen Spellman, an old Howard friend from the NAG days. Karen is a truly remarkable human being. I mean, despite a severe physical disability, this woman continues to run a business. She functions very effectively as an organizer of events in D.C. At the request of the medical committee, she took on and brought off this massive, complex tribute in something less than four weeks. Now *that* was inspiring. Karen, my sister, you something else. I thank you. See, my people can really organize when they want to. We need to be doing that *all* the time.

What can I say about that evening? I certainly can't hope to name everyone present. It seems my whole life was there. See, because I was aware of the time and financial constraints under which Karen and her staff (not to mention the many, many people who volunteered their time and talents) were working, I wasn't even sure it could be done.

So I was simply amazed when I was wheeled into that ballroom. I am told there were nearly fifteen hundred guests. And, almost every face I recognized from somewhere. Folks from every period and aspect of my life: my immediate family, from Bronx Science, from Howard, NAG, SNCC, Summer Project volunteers, the Panthers, SDS, the Native American movement, the All-African People's Revolutionary Party, and new friends, my doctors and the publisher with whom I'd recently signed a contract for this book. Folks from all parts of this country and the world whom I hadn't seen in years. Lamin Jangha, our young brother from the Nkrumah years, appeared. I asked him to wheel me into the ballroom. Mutabaruka, the Jamaican roots poet, showed up from Jamaica. Representatives from the diplomatic corps of African and Caribbean nations. And so it went.

The five other SNCC chairmen sat with me on the platform, along with Minister Farrakhan from the Nation. I was glad to see Jamil al-Amin, formerly H. Rap Brown, himself now an imam. People tell me it was the most ecumenical gathering of radicals to gather under one roof in recent D.C. memory. As I say, beat the drums and you know I'm gonna dance. I took the opportunity to call, one more time, for unity, organization, and vigilance. After that I was real ready to go home. Very ready.

It is quite clear that this illness has now just about run its course. It cannot be too long before it has its way. But, hey, with the help of my people, we've fought this sucker to a standstill for two extraordinary and useful years. My Lord, didn't we though? Yes, we did. Thanks to the years we stole from the disease, we did some work, touched some bases, and paid some dues. Give praise and thanks. My soul looks back in wonder.

The most evident and concrete change the illness brought into my life was the need for constant assistance. It was a drastic change, being suddenly reduced to the status of invalid. That to a person of even minimal sensitivity can be the most onerous of afflictions, a constant dread of becoming a burden on anyone, and what is usually the case, the people you most care about. But in all this time I can honestly say that I never once had even the slightest intimation of impatience or imposition from the many people—the extended family—who have freely and lovingly given me the care that I could never have afforded to pay for. Mah people, oh mah people. Undying love, undying love. Undying love.

Of those people, three will, in a couple of days, make the return trip with me. So I do not go defenseless. And in Guinea, my extended family awaits. And in a few weeks, May Charles will join us. Very shortly, the four of us will be going.

First is my youngest sister, Nagib Malik, who is a registered nurse. She rearranged her life so as to be able to tour and travel with me. She accompanied me to Cuba on speaking engagements and will accompany me home. Brother Amadou Lee, who has been with the party from his student days in Conakry, left everything in Guinea—family, job, everything—and came to New York in the summer. He will come with us.

And then there is my brother Eric Muhammad of the Nation of Islam, who for three years has been my constant companion. He has lived and traveled with me—adviser, secretary, nurse, traveling companion, security, friend, and brother. Bro Eric stands out in another respect. While our paths had crossed over many years, I first met him up close only three years ago, so Eric and I do not share the history I do with many of the other comrades. Yet his unfailing good spirits, constancy of devotion, his thoughtfulness, spontaneous kindness, and uncommon moral and spiritual strength have been both comfort and inspiration. Bro Eric is one person I shall never be able to come close to thanking adequately.

I am going home, and so adieu. But you know me. Not quite so fast. A word or two before I go.

This being 1998, it is exactly thirty years since Zenzi and I first went to live, study, and work in Guinea. At that time, there was no shortage of people only too willing to instruct me on why this was such a bad idea. But there is one I particularly remember. Truth be told, I'd actually forgotten him until, because of my illness, I came to spend so much time in the United States.

This came from an older white man, unfortunately now dead. A radical of sorts, a writer and an "Africa hand," this man meant well, I think. At least he was painfully earnest with his arguments why, "believe me, a person like you will never be able to adjust to Africa and will inevitably be in for real future shock."

Any why so? Well, his list of reasons, once you boil them down to gravy, really amounted to the great revelation that Africa was not America. Now his was quite a list so I can't possibly remember all the reasons thirty years later. But the ones I do remember come back with great clarity.

In Africa generally, he said, there is no social contract:

- Democracy. In Africa, democracy does not exist. Elections, if they happen, are so manipulated, rigged, or outright stolen that the will of the people is a hollow mockery.
- Leadership. There is no leadership worthy of the name. The so-called

leadership is criminally irresponsible. National resources are ripped off for the benefit of foreign capitalists and the enrichment of the leaders and their cronies. With no sense of the *public interest,* these leaders pile up debt to the impoverishment of unborn generations and the nation's future. They purchase weapons and luxuries while schools, hospitals, and public services fall apart. While capitalists, foreign and domestic, pay no taxes.

- Labor. There are no real unions. So the workers are powerless against the economic depredation of the greedy and powerful. The workers exist in a state of continual economic anxiety and insecurity and must endure ever deteriorating working conditions and decreasing wages.

- Press. Forget about a free press. Such media as exists is rigidly controlled either by the government or by small coteries of the elite. A distinction without a difference, while the people are kept in darkness or shamelessly manipulated.

There was more, but those are the ones I remember. At the time, the only thing that kept me from denouncing him as a dirty racist was his all-fired sincerity. He just *knew* that I, being *American,* was in for the shock of my young life. *Why, Stokely, these are things we Americans expect, assume, and simply take for granted.*

How I wish we could pick up this conversation today. Because, y'know, thirty years later there has been some—not much, not nearly enough—small progress in parts of Africa. Were he around, though, I'd ask him to apply his list, category by category, to his model, America.

Be clear now. I don't say this with any satisfaction at all. None. In fact, it deeply saddens me to see the erosion and rollback of rights and entitlements of the American people for which we all have struggled so hard. What has happened, is happening, to America's social contract? This nation does not have the scourge—or excuse—of underdevelopment, scarcity of resources, or lack of technical capacity, as does Africa. So why in human terms is its society so cruel, unfeeling, and unjust to its poor? In effect: the third-worldization of American society.

Why, for example, does a society, by far the wealthiest and most capable in human history, need to have so many homeless people wandering its streets? Why do so many millions of its citizens not have health care? Why, of all industrial societies, does it have the greatest percentage of its citizens in jail? Why can it not have a minimum wage on which its workers can survive with some dignity? Why are so many of the nation's youth so depressed, alienated, hopeless, and prone to violence?

Should it not have, as a fundamental human right for the advancement of all humanity, the best public education system the human mind can devise? This is the one that really bothers me. In the world's richest country, is it really necessary that students leave college under a life-crippling burden of debt? That they be taught that education is something packaged, to be purchased, only to be resold to the highest bidder for personal profit? Is education not a right, knowledge not a blessing to be shared freely to the benefit and uplift of humanity? Nor merely a scarce commodity to be exploited: bought, hoarded, and resold for personal profit in the capitalist marketplace.

Why, in short, is the United States of America *not* the great and humane country it so easily could and ought to be?

Perhaps it is only spending time away that makes it easier for me to see these ominous changes so clearly. But I think you all had better start paying serious attention. For what I'm afraid I'm seeing is a society in deep moral crisis. Not democracy. Not even plutocracy, but outright kleptocracy*, as vulgar as that of Mobutu's Congo. Where both so-called political parties are totally owned subsidiaries of an increasingly predatory, cynical, irresponsible, and immoral corporate sector, who then defends the public interest? The citizens, the common people?

Friends, no matter what lies they tell you, the private greed of cartels of self-interested individuals can never result in a humane, rational, functional, just, decent, and civilized society. It never has and it never will.

That is why I say, despite its apparent power, and precisely because of its excesses, American capitalism is weaker today than it has ever been. As sure as Africa is my mother, and she is my mother, revolution will come to America. A brother in Mississippi used to tell the youth, *stay ready,* so you don't have to *git ready.*

READY FOR REVOLUTION.

Kwame Ture
August 1998, Harlem, New York

---

*Government of thieves. —EMT

POSTSCRIPT

Accompanied by his sister Nagib and Amadou Lee, a Guinean friend, Kwame Ture left New York for the last time on Friday, July 5, 1998. The party arrived in Guinea on Sunday, July 7. They were joined there a week later by Eric Muhammad and a week after that by Mrs. May Charles Carmichael.

For the next four months, attended by that group and between frequent medical crises requiring hospitalization, the brother would continue to work while receiving a stream of visitors—humble folk and dignitaries alike—from different parts of Africa and the diaspora.

The varied events, interests, and actors around the brother during this time, although dramatic, interesting, and considerably ironic when they involved overtures from the military regime or the U.S. Embassy, are beyond the scope of this work.

However, I cannot resist mentioning one, a group of visitors from war-torn Mozambique. This delegation, consisting of amputees, made their way from that country to Conakry to greet and salute the brother. What motive, I wondered, could have brought simple farmers and old soldiers so great a distance? As it turned out, gratitude. Upon learning of their plight—the consequence of land mines and war—Brother Ture had earlier brought the matter to the attention of the Cuban embassy, whose government undertook to supply the men with prostheses. The group had come all that way merely to say thanks and offer prayers and libations for the brother.

On November 15, 1998, an exhausted Kwame Ture, weighing less than a hundred pounds, danced and went to join the ancestors.

People from thirty-nine countries came to join his family, friends, and a great multitude of Guinean people for the funeral. But the last words should be his. Before leaving, our brother (peace be unto him) composed and entrusted to Brother Eric

Muhammad his obituary. In red ink on a yellow pad, he had written:

> Kwame Ture died in his beloved Africa, affirming that if Africa's children cannot alleviate her suffering, we can at least share them fully.

One United Socialist Africa,
Kwame Ture

EMT
July 25, 2003

AFTERWORD

In the Tradition
Kwame Ture: Ready for Revolution

Everyone knew that when Kwame Ture, whom most of us first met as Stokely Carmichael, flew home the following day, he would soon dance and join the ancestors. Yet there was no sadness among the friends, relatives, and comrades who had gathered to bid him farewell in the lovely Convent Avenue apartment of a Harlem comrade. For the religious among us, any possible pathos was salved by the conviction that they would meet again in some better place, "when we will be done with the troubles of this world."

Yet the ambience of celebration was set by Kwame himself, propped up on pillows on top of the covers, laughing, joking, and swapping war stories. As we talked, that devilish charming smile for which he is world famous spread across his still-handsome face. We sipped wine in a libation, marking the occasion of our last communion.

From his demeanor, he might have been recuperating from the flu . . . had his frail body not reminded us that he was dying of cancer. Even so, the feeling was that here was a life well lived, worthy of celebration. There were no tears. The evidence of that life's meaning was everywhere in evidence all around us: His condition was monitored by a posse of young black doctors under the instruction of Dr. Barbara Justice, his chief medical advisor. Also in attendance were a group of beautiful women of various ages from all corners of the black world—some of whom were also doctors.

Throughout the evening, conversation was interrupted as comrades and admirers from all over the African world, in whose interest Kwame had labored, came to pay homage to this Pan-African warrior and theoretician whose thought and struggles had so shaped their own lives and work. Witnessing this display of love and respect—received with all the gravitas and grace of an honored elder who knows that for four decades, two-thirds of his time on earth, he had kept the faith—was inspiring. It was clear that this was the reward of a selfless and consequential life. The fulfillment of an axiom by which Kwame had lived: Serve the people and the people will always take care of you.

Ready for Revolution, Kwame Ture's autobiography in collaboration with his longtime comrade-at-arms Ekwueme Michael Thelwell, essays the story of this extraordinary life to the next generation of freedom fighters of all nations. But most of all, it is a blueprint for how to live a committed life in service to the oppressed. Had I but one book to give my children explaining the meaning and methods of the world black liberation movement in our time, it would be *Ready for Revolution.*

The telling of this story has been marvelously achieved. By virtue of his scrupulous regard for the integrity of Kwame's voice and memories, Thelwell, a writer versed in the oral traditions of black folk, has rendered a narrative that brings his subject to life. And his prodigious literary skills are such that, like W. E. B. Du Bois, he even manages to give poetic resonance to discussions of the most mundane details of the socioeconomic environment and political culture against which Kwame, as organizer of the masses, would struggle.

What we have in this text, finally, is not only a quintessentially American saga about the rise of an immigrant family, but also a compelling account of the life and work of a great twentieth-century humanist and freedom fighter whose daring actions helped to change the most powerful nation in the world for the better—working to rid American society of color caste oppression and empower the black Southern masses with the right to vote. As a primary historical document it will be invaluable to future historians charting the Pan-African liberation struggle of the second half of the twentieth century.

THE LITERARY TRADITION

Ready for Revolution is the latest installment in a grand tradition of the autobiographical, black male narrative, beginning in 1775 with *The Incredible Adventures of Olaudah Equiano, The African, Written by Himself.* When this text was published in England, the year before the American Revolution began, it astonished and seduced British readers. In 1851, the *Narrative of the Life of Henry Box Brown,* which tells the story of Brown's fantastic 1849 escape from slavery by having himself mailed in a box from Richmond, Virginia, to Philadelphia, was published and gained a wide readership on both sides of the Atlantic. During the following decades, many others followed in writing their thrilling stories: Josiah Henson, William Wells Brown, Solomon Northup, J. W. C. Pennington, et al.

One could argue, however, that this genre—popularly known as the slave narrative—reached its apotheosis with the publication of the 1845 text *The Life and Times of Frederick Douglass,* written by the brilliant editor, writer/polemicist, and orator who had made a daring escape from slavery as a young man. In *The Afro-American Novel and Its Tradition,* Professor Bernard Bell tells us, "Most of the autobiographies are characterized by moral purpose, Christian values, and emotional fervor. Many read like moral and political allegories." He then reminds us of their origin in oral forms, which often gives their prose a powerful sermonic style. "Their style is largely derived from the pulpit, the lectern, and the soapbox, from scripture and antislavery materials." A measure of the effect of these highly dramatic and moralistic narratives on the intelligent reading public was clearly stated by the powerful nineteenth-century senator from Massachusetts, Charles Sumner. "They are among the heroes of our age," he said of the authors of these narratives. "Romance has no stories of more thrilling interest than theirs. Classical antiquity has preserved no examples of adventurous trial more worthy of renown."

Of course, while falling firmly within this larger tradition, *Ready for Revolution* more properly belongs to the postbellum autobiographical tradition that flowers in the twentieth century, which includes such works as Booker T. Washington's *Up from Slavery*; James Weldon Johnson's *Along This Way*; the three autobiographies of W. E. B. Du Bois; Conrad Lynn's *There Is a Fountain*; Harry Haywood's *Black Bolshevik*; *The Autobiography of Malcolm X*; James Foreman's *The Making of a Black Revolutionary*; *The Autobiography of Leroi Jones*; et al.

It is no easy feat for a writer born in freedom to match the high adventure of the runaway slave, but, as you will have seen, *Ready for Revolution* is every bit as gripping, with its tales of military coups and foreign invasions in Africa, racist white mobs in America, the struggle for voting rights in Alabama and Mississippi, and Kwame's participation in the highest councils of a revolutionary African government.

THE LEADERSHIP TRADITION

The nationalist leadership tradition to which Kwame Ture belongs is a dual tradition that includes both the revolutionary Pan-Africanism of the Martinican psychiatrist and theoretician of the Algerian revolution, Frantz Fanon, and Ture's fellow Trinidadians George Padmore and C. L. R. James, socialists trained in Marxian analysis; and such nineteenth-century racial nationalists as Alexander Crummell, Edward Wilmont

Blyden, and Dr. Martin Delaney, who advocated emigration to Africa. Having begun his life of struggle in the great civil rights movement of the 1960s, Kwame also belongs to the long tradition of reformist activism personified by Frederick Douglass, Henry Highland Garnett, and J.W.C. Pennington in the abolitionist movement of the nineteenth century, and W. E. B. Du Bois, A. Philip Randolph, Bayard Rustin, Medgar Evers, Martin Luther King Jr. in the civil rights movement that spanned the entire twentieth century. It was only after the methods employed by the nonviolent movements for reform were met by organized white violence and failed to bring about fundamental change in the condition of the black masses that Kwame turned to revolutionary nationalist activities for redress. It was the same process that Nelson Mandela describes so poignantly in *A Long Walk to Freedom.*

But whether he was a nonviolent reformist or a revolutionary nationalist, Kwame was motivated by communitarian values that mandated that those who had succeeded must struggle to uplift the rest of the race. Wilson Jeremiah Moses argues in his essay "Assimilationist Black Nationalism" that these values were rooted in "a genuine feeling of sympathy on the part of the petite bourgeoisie for the struggling masses of black people." And he correctly observes that this feeling "was clearly conveyed in the writings of Paul Laurence Dunbar, which celebrated the homely joys of courtship, family life, honest labor, and simple faith. In *The Souls of Black Folk,* W. E. B. Du Bois wrote of the struggles of the common people with a love and sympathy that went beyond mere sociological description. Like Booker T. Washington, he spoke of the obligation of the educated black people to aid in the uplifting of the masses.

And anyone reading *Ready for Revolution* can see it too, both in the artistry of Thelwell's rendering of the text and the poetry of struggle it describes. While Kwame—who was educated at New York's elite Bronx High School of Science and Howard University and is thus a splendid example of Dr. Du Bois's "Talented Tenth"—shares some of the ideas and values of all these earlier leaders, his fully formed political vision remains unique. For instance, although Kwame emigrated to Africa, the ideas that motivated him to do so were very different from those of the nationalists of the nineteenth century. The nineteenth-century nationalists who emigrated to Africa were Afro-Saxon Anglophiles who wanted to remake Africa into the image of Britain, while Kwame rejected many of the values of modern Western capitalist societies, favoring an "African socialism" based on traditional African communal values. As highly educated men—Blyden was a Presbyterian minister; Crummell, an Anglican priest with a degree in philosophy from Cambridge University; Delaney, a medical doctor who attended Harvard; and Robert Cambell, a Jamaican chemist who explored the west coast of Africa with Delaney under the sponsorship of The African

Civilization Society in 1859—these men of the Western diaspora saw themselves as much on a mission of civilization bringing Christianity and commerce to backward Africans as the French and British imperialists claimed to. (This was also true of Marcus Garvey, who built the largest mass black nationalist organization in U.S. history—Afro-Americans, West Indians, and Afro-Latinos—in the early twentieth century.)

Indeed, historian Wilson Jeremiah Moses, the biographer of Alexander Crummell and the reigning authority on black nationalism in the U.S., tells us in his essay on Crummell, "Cambridge Platonism in the Republic of Liberia," "It was inconceivable to Crummell that the hoped-for African civilization could be built on indigenous West African institutions; he conceived of civilization as a process that must be duplicated in its results by any race or nation on its way to becoming civilized. There was only one road to progress, and that road has been successfully traveled by the English-speaking peoples."

This was pretty much the same view held by Blyden and Delaney. Blyden expressed his views on the subject in his revealing book *Christianity, Islam and the Negro Race,* in which he argues that Christianity or Islam would be preferable to indigenous African polytheistic religions. And Delaney, who named his newspaper *The Anglo-African,* also expressed his belief that African development depended on their adoption of Christianity and the English language.

Kwame Ture, however, held a very different view of Africa and Europe. Part of his attitude—which is quite irreverent regarding the claims made for European civilization—was due to the times in which he lived, and part was due to his having read and been influenced by the Marxist critique of the modern capitalist society which so impressed the nineteenth-century nationalists. Unlike the emigrants of the previous century, who all assumed that there was nothing they could learn from the Africans, Kwame Ture knew that there was much he could learn from African revolutionaries and anxiously sought a chance to work with them in the struggle.

The nineteenth-century leaders began their careers as activists when Africans were held as chattel slaves by Europeans all over the New World, and as such, were regarded as livestock under the law. They could be bought, sold, and bred as beasts of the field, where the children of African slaves were legally the property of the white master. Confronted with this horror, the desire for an independent African nation that could field an army and excel at manufacturing and commerce was a natural aspiration. In fact, they were obsessed with the idea that such a modern civilization built on African soil would exonerate the humanity of the race. And this meant, in their view, getting rid of the inferior African culture that was responsible for African impotence in the face of the devastating aggression from predatory European societies.

But the world in which Kwame Ture came of age was rife with revolutionary activity in Africa, Asia, and Latin America, the so-called Bandung World—a name taken from the first conference of nonwhite peoples held in Bandung, Indonesia, in 1955. This revolutionary spirit that emboldened powerless people to confront white power and demand their freedom would also sweep black America in the 1960s. It was from this experience that Kwame developed his radical critique of Western capitalist civilization.

Hence when Kwame arrived on African shore, he was coming to settle in an independent African nation state of which the earlier generations of black nationalists could only dream, and he saw himself as fleeing an advanced Western Christian civilization both decadent and dangerous. Thus he could say, "I went to Guinea because there was a lot I needed to learn from President Nkrumah. So of course I intended to study."

Here Kwame is speaking about the time he spent as an aide-de-camp to Kwame Nkrumah during his exile in Guinea after his presidency was overthrown in a coup by the Ghanaian army. In an act of extraordinary Pan-African fraternity, Sékou Touré made Nkrumah the copresident of Guinea, an act that convinced the young Stokely Carmichael that Guinea was the model for a revolutionary Pan-African society. A man who always acted on his convictions, he took the names of these men, the men he believed to be leading Africa on the path to liberation and progressive development, and became a member of their ruling party. In a unique episode in the relations between Africans in the motherland and African descendents of the diaspora, Kwame enters the inner circle of power in revolutionary Guinea and provides us a firsthand view of the inner workings of the African revolution. "In Conakry," he recalls, "being part of the entourage, I attended meetings with the various delegations coming in. I participated in the study group of the party and took military training with the Ghanaian unit . . . I certainly learned a lot about the politics and ongoing realities of the African struggle. But of course, I was gung-ho. I really wanted to fight."

In this sense, Kwame was just like Frantz Fanon, who had actual combat experience in the Second World War, but like Fanon in Algeria, he proved most valuable in a political/diplomatic role. So he graciously accepted and became perhaps the most effective and popular ambassador of the Pan-African revolution centered in Guinea. The depth of Kwame's commitment to the Guinean experiment was inspired by the fact that, having witnessed the overthrow of other progressive regimes, he believed Guinea to be the last revolutionary outpost in Africa.

Kwame's life is unique in the history of major Pan-African leaders from the diaspora in another important regard. The three major Pan-African revolutionaries who preceded Kwame from the Caribbean—George

Padmore, C. L. R. James, and Frantz Fanon—were all married to white women. However, Kwame's remembrances include many glowing poetic references to the beauty and charms of African women, two of whom he married. Both were extraordinary women by any measure. His first wife, Miriam Makeba, is an internationally renowned singer from South Africa, and his second wife, Marliatou, is a doctor.

Neither can one find the glowing references to the importance of the indigenous African culture in previous generations of black nationalists or Marxist-oriented Pan-African revolutionaries. "Culture is politics and politics is culture," he tells us. "Sékou Touré understood the importance of culture. He loved intensely, I mean personally delighted, in his people's culture. But besides that, the party clearly understood that the traditional culture was a key element from which to mold an African character to the evolution . . . But not just the arts, also the ethics and values of traditional culture, what I call African humanism." This is a far cry from the attitudes of the first wave of pilgrims from the new world diaspora.

In the grand sweep of this book's narrative, we see how Stokely Carmichael, the upwardly mobile son of immigrant West Indian strivers who became an activist in the U.S. civil rights movement, metamorphosed into Kwame Ture, Pan-African revolutionary, who successfully made the transition and became an African. No one to my knowledge has made this transition so well. And we, the readers, are especially fortunate to be able to follow this fascinating process from the inside. This alone is worth the price of the text and the investment of time to afford it a proper reading.

But there is more too. We also get a rare glimpse of that all-too-brief moment in American history when blacks and whites in the Student Nonviolent Coordinating Committee faced down Southern mobs and redneck sheriffs with snarling dogs. Added to this is abundant and learned analysis from a frontline witness of the machinations by the U.S. government and her allies to subvert and destroy the black liberation movement at home and abroad. And finally we are provided a magnificent portrait of courage in the face of terminal disease.

Yet as we gathered around the bedside of Kwame Ture, while he prepared to return to the motherland and take his place in the pantheon of Pan-African heroes, his eyes still nurtured that sacred fire that flares when he speaks of serving the people. It was as if the question of liberating and uplifting the African masses was the pressing matter, and death a trifling fait accompli. All who witnessed it could see that here was a brother who was steeled in the fires of struggle, trained for trouble, and *Ready for Revolution!*

—Playthell Benjamin
New York, August 2003

ACKNOWLEDGMENTS

A Clearing of the Ledger

Any undertaking of the scope and duration of this book cannot fail, over its different stages, to inevitably incur an avalanche of debts, large and small. This one all the more so because I have never been associated with any project attended by so many expressions of goodwill, encouragement, and offers of assistance and cooperation. So the debts are many.

The idea for the book emerged quite by chance from a conversation between Kwame and me after a tribute to him at the University of Massachusetts–Amherst in April 1997. That event had come within hours of being cancelled and was saved only by the timely intervention of several administrators: President Ruth Simmons, then of Smith College. And, at the University: Provost Charlena Seymour, our department chair Esther Terry, and Lee Edwards, dean of Humanities and Fine Arts. Even so, without the dedication of Maasani Bediako of the Pan African Center of Chicago, the enthusiastic help of faculty in the W. E. B. Du Bois Department, and the feverish work of my graduate assistants Susan Van Pelt and Hussein Ibish, this initial event and that conversation would not have happened.

After which, the debts only multiplied and compounded. That summer, against all odds, Ms. Goldin of the Frances Goldin Literary Agency secured us the publishing contract that permitted the work to begin in earnest. We are grateful.

Among all writers, but particularly black ones, horror stories abound bemoaning the blinkered narrowness and cultural insensitivity of corporate publishing. Our experience at Scribner has been exactly the opposite. Under the leadership of Ms. Susan Moldow, their handling of this project has been, in Kwame's words, impeccable, professional, and enlightened. Over six years, that never changed. For me, this has been a revelation and a pleasure. I trust and hope the book's performance will reward their judgment and patience.

Once work began, the outpouring of support from a variety of quarters has been an unexpected benefaction, at once humbling and inspiring.

The family: in particular cousin Austin Letrin, sister Najib Malik, and the constant and unwavering Mrs. Mabel Carmichael.

The circle of trust: a host of SNCC comrades came forward in a way that regenerated in me a powerful sense of the old movement family. A great feeling. One love, y'all.

Most of these folks' interventions are identified in the text so there is no need to list their names again here. But some were above and beyond.

On almost the very first day, packages of valuable materials from Judy Richardson and Cleve Sellers arrived unbidden. And Cleve has been just stalwart throughout, a dependable source of insight and political support, virtually a third collaborator. Others followed suit: Charlie, Mary, Guyot, Betita, Faye, Ed, Kathleen, Bob, Julian, Mukassa, Courtland, Ivanhoe, Karen, and Stokely's "little sister" June J. One love, y'all.

Kwame's associates in the Party: the late Mawina Kouyate, David Brothers, Dr. Barbara Justice, Dr. Gerri Price, Bob Brown, and Sister Maasani Bediako, who began it all. With his passing, two of Kwame's loyalists, Eric Ture Mohammed and Lamin Jongha, transferred their loyalties to the project for which I am indeed grateful. These contributions have been invaluable.

All of which is greatly appreciated if not totally unexpected.

The kindness of strangers: an astonishing variety of other folk, activists, scholars, citizens, and total strangers from around the country and the world have volunteered assistance and good wishes.

Among media professionals, a hard-edged, sharp-elbowed competitiveness is a way of life; unconditional generosity is almost unknown, especially when it runs up against self-interest. Yet I would encounter professional generosity twice. Mama Nzinga [Lynn Collins] of Cy-Fax Media of Washington, D.C., has never once refused a request. Also, Ms. Mary Ann French, a truly gifted and accomplished writer, in an act of uncommon principle and decency, graciously shared her hard-won research, even though we represented real competition. My Nubian Sistahs, I have no words. . . . At a late critical juncture, three ladies on whom I have never set eyes, Ms. Rona Tuccillo of Time/Life Pictures; Ms. Christina Lumwai of *Newsday,* and Michelle Borde of the *Trinidad Guardian,* provided the kindness of strangers.

I am indebted to Professor C. E. "Bud" Schultz of Trinity College, Hartford, Connecticut, for graciously and spontaneously sharing his COINTELPRO files.

Closer to home, on my own account, the debts are enormous.

Without the encouragement and support of my department and dean, this work simply could not have been done. My colleagues of many years—Esther, John, Bill, Ernie, and Manisha—ran interference, cleared time, excused absences, read pages, unearthed obscure material, and offered a thousand other fraternal kindnesses.

My friend and brother John contributed five years of close reading; sharp, judicious yet tactful criticism; and the magnificent introduction that opens the book. My bredrin, one heart and love.

Similarly, Brother Playthell Benjamin closes a book with necessary historical perspectives. Jah Guidance.

The committed and indefatigable Barbara McGlynn, assistant and Internet researcher and archivist, came early and stayed late. She was present at the conception and hung on for the delivery. She put every word, from the first letter to Brother Ture in 1997 to the final pages a few days ago, into the computer at least twice. The magnitude of that contribution speaks for itself.

And finally, but hardly least, the community readers. Mah peoples, oh, mah peoples! The formidable Mother Bumpus and Lady Thee, Kwame, the African trader, the post office lady, the meter-reading brother in Amherst, Brother Schifman, and Sister Iris, each demanding, reading, and commenting on every new chapter.

Quite obviously, this has been a communal journey. I pray fervently yet timorously that—to change the vocabulary—our shareholders and investors are satisfied with the return.

—Ekwueme Michael Thelwell
Amherst, 2003

INDEX

Index

Index

Bevel, Diane, 445
Bevel, James, 196, 206–7, 291, 445, 447
Biavougi, Lansana, 719
Big Black River, 243, 280
Bigelow, Albert, 182–83
Bikini atoll, 182
Biko, Steven, 638, 773
Biko Day, 773
Billy (childhood friend), 62
Biloxi, Miss., 287
Bimini, 521
Birmingham, 324, 328, 330–31, 344, 442, 450, 491, 496, 533, 534, 537
  and Freedom Rides in, 183–85, 189–91, 193
  racism in, 442–43
Biro, Boabacar, 712
birth poem, 11
bizi, 34
Black Arts movement, 528–29
Blackboard Jungle (film), 70
Black Bolshevik (Haywood), 787
Black Bourgeoisie, The (Frazier), 128, 130
Black Congressional Caucus, 714
Black Consciousness movement, 638
Black History Month, 732, 740
Black Jacob (Mahoney), 144
Black Jacobins (James), 105
Black Liberation Army, 762
Black Muslims, 74
black nationalism, 535
Black Panther Party, 459, 463–64, 471, 473, 549, 606, 638, 641, 673, 676–77, 696, 698, 739, 745, 748, 778
  armed patrols of, 661–62
  chain of command, 670–71
  COINTELPRO and, 664–65
  FBI informants in, 667–68
  Forman threatened by, 671–72
  government action against, 665–66, 667–68
  growth of, 475–77, 661, 666–67
  leadership of, 666–70
  media and, 664
  police and, 664

  rank and file members of, 669–70
  SC and, 669
  SNCC and, 659–72
Black Power, 332, 507–11, 513–14, 520–30, 532–42, 550, 551–52, 567, 569, 579–80, 583, 590, 626, 634, 638, 640, 651, 660, 708
  in Britain, 576–77
  C. L. R. James on, 580–81
  cultural expression of, 528–29
  as hot media topic, 542
  liberal outrage over, 525–26
  media and, 263–64, 524–25
  1968 Olympics and, 708
  SNCC's first position paper on, 528
Black Power (Carmichael and Hamilton), 130, 473, 544, 547, 548
black pride, 546
Black Scholar, 229
black scholars, 127
Blacks in Antiquity (Snowden), 128
Black United Front, 217, 599, 640, 642–43, 648–50, 745, 752
Blair, Ezell, Jr., 139–40
Blake, Elias, 129
Blankenheim, Ed, 182
blaxploitation films, 267
Block, Sam, 32, 310
Bloody Sunday, 448, 452
Bloom, Harold, 413
Blyden, Edward Wilmont, 787, 789
Boers, 333–34, 559, 775
Bogalusa, La., 493
Bogue Chitto Swamp, 372, 404
Boiro, 688, 719
Bolivar County, 389
Bond, Julian, 142, 224, 298, 313, 363, 372, 482–83, 488, 555, 569, 650–51, 660
Bongi, 653
Bonus Marches, 647
Bork, Judge, 331
Boston, Mass., 138, 282, 358, 534, 572, 732–33
Botanical Gardens, 12, 34–35
Botha, P. W., 442
Bourgeois Blues (song), 133
Bowe, Riddick, 749
Boynton, Amelia, 444, 446

800

Index

Index

Index

Index

culture wars, 261
curfews, 147
Currier, Stephen, 436–37
Custer, George, 459

Dalaba, 704, 705
Daley, Richard, 538
Dallas, Tex., 331
Dallas County, 443, 447
Dallas County Voters League, 444, 446
Daniels, Jonathan, 466–71, 472
Dan River, 324
Danville, 247, 328, 350
  demonstrations in, 323–25
Danville Christian Progressive Association, 324
Dar es Salaam, 632, 635
Davies, Porkchop, 100
Davis, Arthur P., 129
Davis, Ben, 732
Davis, Ossie, 111, 256, 261–62
  at Howard University literature symposium, 261–62
Davison, Miss., 327
Dawson, Miss., 327
Deacons for Defense, 474, 493, 497, 501, 504–5, 509, 512
  and Meredith March, 502, 505, 512
debates, staged at Howard University, 250–53
"De Crone Pone's Hot" (Moses), 788
Dee, Henry, 380
Dee, Ruby, 111
DeFrietas, Michael, 576
de Gaulle, Charles, 609
  visit to Guinea of, 611–12
DeKlerk, F. W., 775
Delaney, Martin, 788, 789
Delappio, Cookie, 65
Dell, Walter, 738
Delta Health Center, 322
DeLucier, Vinnie, 105–6
Democratic National Convention, 287, 357, 364, 382, 392, 398, 400–411, 421
Democratic Party, 177, 382, 392, 400–403, 410, 421, 471, 561
  in Alabama, 462
  Credentials Committee of, 404–5

hybrid nature of, 185
  in Mississippi, 415
Democratic Party of Guinea for the African Democratic Revolution, 611, 697, 774
Denmark, S.C., 157, 519
Dennis, Eugene, Sr., 91
Dennis, Gene, 87–92, 95, 106–7
dependency, 251
"Destabilization and Psychological Warfare," 454
destabilization movement, 625
Destruction of Black Civilization, The (Williams), 128
Detroit, Mich., 115, 426, 474, 542, 667
Devine, Annie, 283, 409, 414, 508
  as MFDP challenger, 414, 417
DeVries, Charlotte, 182
DeWitt Clinton High School, 105–7
"Dialectics of Liberation, The," 572–82
Diamond, Dion, 118, 145, 157, 187, 196, 217, 241, 554
  in Nashville jail, 235–38
diaspora, African, 14, 16–17, 79, 613, 623
Dickerson, Eddie, 172–73
Dien Bien Phu, 596–98
Dietrich, Paul, 137, 157–58, 182, 187, 190, 225–26, 234, 478
Dimanche Gras (Big Sunday), 42
DiMilio, John, 63–65, 67, 69
discipline, 166
Dittmer, John, 283
Dixiecrats, 115, 158, 220
  racism of, 357
Dixon, Ivan, 267
Doar, John, 369–71
Dodson, Owen, 128
Dogon people, 11
Domino, Fats, 97
Donaldson, Ivanhoe, 242, 323, 372, 377–78, 383–84, 410, 480, 548, 561, 745, 752, 760, 769
Dorchester County, 342
Doris, Ruby, 480–81, 486, 490, 540
Dorsey, Emmett, 252–53
Dorsey, L. C., 322
Douglass, Frederick, 156, 204, 439, 788

Index

Index

Index

Index